CRIMINAL PROCEDURE: ADJUDICATION AND RIGHT TO COUNSEL

How to use your Connected Casebook

Step 1: Go to **www.CasebookConnect.com** and redeem your access code to get started.

Access Code:

Step 2: Go to your **BOOKSHELF** and select your Connected Casebook to start reading, highlighting, and taking notes in the margins of your e-book.

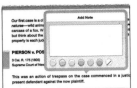

Step 3: Select the **STUDY** tab in your toolbar to access a variety of practice materials designed to help you master the course material. These materials may include explanations, videos, multiple-choice questions, flashcards, short answer, essays, and issue spotting.

Step 4: Select the **OUTLINE** tab in your toolbar to access chapter outlines that automatically incorporate your highlights and annotations from the e-book. Use the My Notes area for copying, pasting, and editing your book notes or creating new notes.

Step 5: If your professor has enrolled your class, you can select the **CLASS INSIGHTS** tab and compare your own study center results against the average of your classmates.

PIN: 9111149520   19829

D1082281

ASPEN CASEBOOK SERIES

CRIMINAL PROCEDURE: ADJUDICATION AND RIGHT TO COUNSEL

Second Edition

Ronald Jay Allen

John Henry Wigmore Professor of Law
Northwestern University

William J. Stuntz

Henry J. Friendly Professor of Law
Harvard University

Joseph L. Hoffmann

Harry Pratter Professor of Law
Indiana University Maurer School of Law

Debra A. Livingston

United States Circuit Judge, Second Circuit
Paul J. Kellner Professor of Law
Columbia University

Andrew D. Leipold

Edwin M. Adams Professor and Director,
Program in Criminal Law & Procedure
University of Illinois

Tracey L. Meares

Walton Hale Hamilton Professor of Law
Yale Law School

 Wolters Kluwer

ISBN 978-1-4548-6828-6

Library of Congress Cataloging-in-Publication Data

Names: Allen, Ronald J. (Ronald Jay), 1948- author.
Title: Criminal procedure: adjudication and right to counsel / Ronald Jay
  Allen, John Henry Wigmore Professor of Law Northwestern University,
  William J. Stuntz, Henry J. Friendly Professor of Law Harvard University,
  Joseph L. Hoffmann, Harry Pratter Professor of Law Indiana University
  Maurer School of Law, Debra A. Livingston, United States Circuit Judge,
  Second Circuit Paul J. Kellner Professor of Law Columbia University Andrew
  D. Leipold, Edwin M. Adams Professor and Director, Program in Criminal Law
  & Procedure University of Illinois, Tracey L. Meares, Walton Hale Hamilton
  Professor of Law Yale Law School.
Description: Second edition. | New York: Wolters Kluwer, 2016.
Identifiers: LCCN 2016002834 | ISBN 9781454868286
Subjects: LCSH: Criminal procedure—United States. | Criminal
  procedure—United States. | Criminal justice, Administration of—United
  States. | Criminal investigation—United States. | Right to
  counsel—United States. | LCGFT: Casebooks.
Classification: LCC KF9619.C745 2016 | DDC 345.73/056—dc23
LC record available at http://lccn.loc.gov/2016002834

About Wolters Kluwer Legal & Regulatory Solutions U.S.

Wolters Kluwer Legal & Regulatory Solutions U.S. delivers expert content and solutions in the areas of law, corporate compliance, health compliance, reimbursement, and legal education. Its practical solutions help customers successfully navigate the demands of a changing environment to drive their daily activities, enhance decision quality and inspire confident outcomes.

Serving customers worldwide, its legal and regulatory solutions portfolio includes products under the Aspen Publishers, CCH Incorporated, Kluwer Law International, ftwilliam.com and MediRegs names. They are regarded as exceptional and trusted resources for general legal and practice-specific knowledge, compliance and risk management, dynamic workflow solutions, and expert commentary.

Summary of Contents

Contents

Chapter 2
The Idea of Due Process   63

PART TWO
THE RIGHT TO COUNSEL—THE LINCHPIN OF
CONSTITUTIONAL PROTECTION   113

Chapter 3
The Right to Counsel and Other Assistance   115

PART FOUR
THE ADJUDICATION PROCESS   995

Chapter 8
Bail and Pretrial Detention   997

Chapter 9
The Charging Decision   1019

Chapter 10
Pretrial Screening and the Grand Jury   1049

Chapter 11
The Scope of the Prosecution   1117

Chapter 12
Discovery and Disclosure   1185

Chapter 13
Guilty Pleas and Plea Bargaining   1231

Chapter 14
The Jury and the Criminal Trial 1315

PART FIVE
POSTTRIAL PROCEEDINGS   1461

Chapter 15
Sentencing   1463

Chapter 16
Double Jeopardy   1549

Chapter 17
Appellate and Collateral Review

Preface to the Fourth Edition of Comprehensive Criminal Procedure

Comprehensive Criminal Procedure is a casebook for all introductory courses in criminal procedure law, including both investigation and adjudication courses as well as comprehensive and survey courses. The casebook focuses primarily on constitutional criminal procedure law, but also covers relevant statutes and court rules. The casebook is deliberately challenging—it is designed for those who wish to explore deeply not only the contemporary state of the law, but also its historical roots and theoretical foundations. The casebook incorporates a particular emphasis on empirical knowledge about the real-world impacts of law-in-action; the significance of race and class; the close relationship between criminal procedure law and substantive criminal law; the cold reality that hard choices sometimes must be made in a world of limited criminal justice resources; and, finally, the recognition that criminal procedure law always should strive to achieve both fairness to the accused and justice for society as a whole.

The casebook opens with a wide-ranging set of readings about the criminal justice system, combining hard data with expert commentary. The nature of due process adjudication is then introduced, because so much of criminal procedure law either has been constitutionalized or operates within the shadow of the Constitution. With one major exception, the casebook then follows the processing of a criminal case more or less chronologically, from initial investigation through appeal and habeas corpus. The major exception is Chapter 3, which contains a thorough examination of the right to counsel. Counsel is the linchpin of criminal procedure, obviously so with respect to its constitutional aspects but even more critically so with respect to its statutory and common law aspects. Without adequate counsel, a suspect or defendant is, with rare exceptions, lost. The most elaborate procedural protections are of little value to one who knows neither what those protections are nor how they can be used to best advantage.

Following the right to counsel chapter is a chapter chronicling the history of Boyd v. United States. We think it fair to say that the U.S. Supreme Court has been reacting to the *Boyd* case for more than a century, and that the present law of search and seizure (as regulated by the Fourth Amendment) and the right to be free from compelled self-incrimination (pursuant to the Fifth Amendment) simply cannot be understood without a grounding in *Boyd* and its aftermath. Moreover, within the past three years, the Court has explicitly revived at least some aspects of *Boyd*, and it is also becoming increasingly clear that *Boyd* has great relevance for contemporary controversies over government searches of cell phones, computer files (encrypted or otherwise), DNA and other databases, and many other kinds of digital data. This casebook encourages thoughtful reflection upon *Boyd* and an awareness of its significance to the thoroughly modern dilemma of privacy versus security.

In this fourth edition of the casebook, we welcome to our author team Tracey L. Meares of Yale University, whose nationally recognized expertise in the law and policy of police investigations has enriched the casebook tremendously. This new edition reflects our continuing commitment to keeping the casebook fresh and up-to-date, with an emphasis on the criminal procedure issues that are important in contemporary American law and society. Specific revisions in the fourth edition include: the Introduction chapter has been updated with new scholarly writings that provide an overview of important aspects of criminal procedure; the Right to Counsel chapter incorporates the new wave of structural reform litigation over the often-crushing caseloads and frequently inadequate resources of public defender offices; the Fourth and Fifth Amendment chapters have been completely rewritten to reflect the latest legal, social, and empirical developments in such areas as police discretion (including stop-and-frisk and police use of force) and data searches; the chapter on the Jury and the Criminal Trial has been revised to include the latest twists and turns of *Crawford* doctrine; the Sentencing chapter has been updated to include the most recent evolution of *Apprendi* doctrine; and all chapters have been updated, re-edited, and streamlined to improve their clarity and teachability.

As usual, we have endeavored to keep editing of cases at a minimum, opting at times for textual description over a series of edited excerpts. Editing is unavoidable, however. In all cases and materials reproduced here, we have kept the original foot-noting sequence. Wherever our own footnotes might be confused with those of the primary material, our own footnotes are identified by the legend "—Eds." There are three printed versions of this casebook: the hardcover volume (which includes everything) and two paperback volumes, one for use in Criminal Investigation courses and the other for use in Criminal Adjudication courses. As with prior editions, both of the paperback volumes include the Introduction, Due Process, and Right to Counsel chapters, plus a part of the Grand Jury chapter. The pagination of both paperback volumes remains identical to the pagination in the hardcover volume. This fourth edition contains U.S. Supreme Court and lower court cases and legislative materials current through December 2015.

Ronald J. Allen
Joseph L. Hoffmann
Debra A. Livingston
Andrew D. Leipold
Tracey L. Meares

February 2016

Acknowledgments

The authors would like to thank Northwestern Law School, Indiana University Maurer School of Law, Columbia Law School, the University of Illinois College of Law, and Yale Law School for their generous support during the writing of this edition of the casebook.

We are grateful to the following sources for permission to reprint excerpts of their work:

Ronald, J. Allen, "The Misguided Defenses of Miranda v. Arizona," Ohio State Journal of Criminal Law, 5, 2007.

Akhil Reed Amar, The Future of Constitutional Criminal Procedure, 33 Am. Crim. L. Rev. 1123, 1123-1125, 1128-1129, 1132-1134 (1996). Reprinted with permission of the publisher, American Criminal Law Review © 1996.

Anthony G. Amsterdam, The Supreme Court and the Rights of Suspects in Criminal Cases, 45 N.Y.U. L. Rev. 785, 785-794 (1970). Reprinted with permission of the New York University Law Review.

Reprinted with permission of the Saint Louis University Public Law Review © 2011 Stephanos Bibas, The Myth of the Fully Informed Rational Actor, 31 St. Louis U. Pub. L. Rev. 79 (2011).

Republished with permission of John Wiley & Sons, Inc., from The Practice of Law as Confidence Game: Organizational Cooptation of a Profession, Abraham Blumberg, 1(2) © 1967; permission conveyed through Copyright Clearance Center, Inc.

Steven J. Burton, Comment on "Empty Ideas": Logical Positivist Analyses of Equality and Rules, 91 Yale L.J. 1136-1141, 1144-1147 (1982). Used with permission of The Yale Law Journal Company from Burton, Comment on "Empty Ideas": Logical Positivist Analyses of Equality and Rules, 91 Yale Law Journal, 1983; permission conveyed through Copyright Clearance Center, Inc.

David Garland, The Culture of Control: Crime and Social Order in Contemporary Society, University of Chicago Press, 2001. Copyright © David Garland 2001. Reprinted with permission.

Joseph D. Grano, Ascertaining the Truth, 77 Cornell L. Rev., 1061, 1062-1064. Copyright © 1992. Reprinted with permission.

Randall Kennedy, Race, Crime, and the Law, pp. 158-161 (1997) Vintage Books. From Race, Crime, and the Law, by Randall Kennedy. Copyright © 1977 by Randall Kenney. Reprinted by permission of Pantheon Books, a division of Random House, Inc.

Stanton D. Krauss, The Life and Times of Boyd v. United States (1886-1976), 76 Mich. L. Rev., 184, 188-189, 190, 191-195, 211-212 (1977). Krauss, The Life and Times of Boyd v. United States (1886-1976), 76 Mich. L. Rev. 184, 212 (1977).

Reprinted from Michigan Law Review, 1977. Copyright 1977 by The Michigan Law Review Association. Reprinted with permission.

John H. Langbein, "Torture and Plea Bargaining," The University of Chicago Law Review, 46(1), 1978.

Debra Livingston, Police Discretion and the Quality of Life in Public Places: Courts, Communities, and the New Policing, 97 Colum. L. Rev., 551, 557, 558-561, 670-671 (1997). Used with permission of Columbia Law Review, from Debra Livingston, Police Discretion and the Quality of Life in Public Places: Courts, Communities, and the New Policing, 97 Columbia Law Review, 551, 1997; permission conveyed through Copyright Clearance Center, Inc.

Gary T. Marx, Undercover: Police Surveillance in America, pp. 23, 33-35, 47. Copyright © 1988, Twentieth Century Fund. Permission granted by the Regents of the University of California and the University of California Press.

Khalil Gibran Muhammad, The Condemnation of Blackness: Race, Crime, and the Making of Modern Urban America, Harvard University Press, 2011.

Carol S. Steiker, Counter-Revolution in Constitutional Criminal Procedure? Two Audiences, Two Answers, Mich. L. Rev., 2466, 2466-2470, 2536, 2543 (1996). Reprinted from Michigan Law Review, August 1996, Vol. 94, No. 8. Copyright 1996 by The Michigan Law Review Association. Reprinted with permission of the author.

William J. Stuntz, Substance, Process, and the Civil-Criminal Procedure Line, 7 J. Contemp. Legal Issues I, 14-15 (1996). Reprinted with permission of the author.

William J. Stuntz, The Uneasy Relationship Between Criminal Procedure and Criminal Justice, 107 Yale L.J. 1, 1-6 (1997). Used with permission of The Yale Law Journal Company from William J. Stuntz, The Uneasy Relationship Between Criminal Procedure and Criminal Justice, 107 Yale Law Journal, 1997; permission conveyed through Copyright Clearance Center, Inc.

Republished with permission of Princeton University Press, from Why People Obey the Law, Tom R. Tyler, 2006; permission conveyed through Copyright Clearance Center, Inc.

Republished with permission of ABC-CLIO, from Chaos in the Courthouse: The Inner Workings of the Urban Criminal Courts, by Paul Wice, © 1985; permission conveyed through Copyright Clearance Center, Inc.

CRIMINAL PROCEDURE:
ADJUDICATION AND RIGHT TO COUNSEL

PART ONE

THE CRIMINAL PROCESS

Chapter 1

Introduction to the Criminal Justice "System"

A. Introduction

The system of criminal justice America uses to deal with those crimes it cannot prevent and those criminals it cannot deter is not a monolithic, or even a consistent, system. It was not designed or built in one piece at one time. Its philosophic core is that a person may be punished by the Government if, and only if, it has been proved by an impartial and deliberate process that he has violated a specific law. Around that core layer upon layer of institutions and procedures, some carefully constructed and some improvised, some inspired by principle and some by expediency, have accumulated. Parts of the system—magistrates' courts, trial by jury, bail—are of great antiquity. Other parts—juvenile courts, probation and parole, professional policemen—are relatively new. The entire system represents an adaption of the English common law to America's peculiar structure of government, which allows each local community to construct institutions that fill its special needs. Every village, town, county, city and State has its own criminal justice system, and there is a Federal one as well. All of them operate somewhat alike. No two of them operate precisely alike.

> *President's Commission on Law Enforcement and Administration of Justice,*
> *The Challenge of Crime in a Free Society 7 (1967)*

Some of the differences in operation are a result of different formal mechanisms. For example, in the federal system and in approximately two-fifths of the state systems, a defendant cannot be prosecuted for a serious crime unless a grand jury—a group usually composed of 17 to 23 citizens selected from the voter registration lists—has reviewed the evidence and decided to return an indictment or the defendant has waived the right to a grand jury indictment; in other jurisdictions, no right to a grand jury indictment exists.[1] In some jurisdictions, the authority to decide whether to proceed with a criminal prosecution rests with the local prosecutor; in others the ultimate authority, although rarely exercised, rests with the attorney general. In some jurisdictions, the prosecutor's consent is usually required for the issuance of an arrest warrant; in others it is not. However, the Supreme Court has held that a prosecutor's judgment that an arrest warrant should be issued does not satisfy the "independent judicial officer" standard under the Constitution.

---

1. The Bill of Rights—the first ten amendments to the federal Constitution—protects citizens against certain actions by the *federal* government. Among these protections are a number of rights applicable to criminal defendants, including the Fifth Amendment right not to be prosecuted for a serious crime in the absence of a grand jury indictment. Over the years, the Supreme Court has "incorporated" most of these rights into the Due Process Clause of the Fourteenth Amendment, which restricts the actions of state governments. See Chapter 2, at page 79. The federal right to a grand jury indictment is one of the few rights that has not been so incorporated. Thus, states are free to adopt or reject the use of grand juries to screen criminal charges.

Generally, judicial approval is required for the dismissal of a serious charge; in some jurisdictions, however, the prosecutor has unilateral discretion to dismiss.

Other, less formal differences contribute even more to variations in the operation of the criminal justice process. For example, the institutional components that constitute the criminal justice system—the police agencies, the public prosecutors, the courts, the correctional departments—each has independent functions, but the operation of each is in part dependent on the operation of the others. They interrelate differently from community to community,[2] and how they interrelate will have an impact on how the entire system operates. Thus, for the most part the prosecutors, the courts, and the correctional officials can deal only with those individuals whom the police arrest. A police officer's decision whether to arrest may in turn be influenced by how the officer believes the other institutional components of the system will respond to a situation. If an officer believes that an individual will be dealt with too leniently, the officer may arrest the individual and not press charges or perhaps not even make the arrest. Samuel Walker, Taming the System 23-24, 39-41 (1993).

Allocation of resources also affects the manner in which the system operates. Limited prosecutorial or judicial resources, for example, will force prosecutors to be more selective in choosing cases with which to proceed. Even allocation of resources within a single component of the criminal justice system has an impact on its operation. For example, at some point fairly early in the process, a member of the prosecutor's staff will review a case to determine whether it is appropriate to proceed with prosecution and, if so, on what charges. Usually, the first opportunity to make this decision will be soon after an arrest, and the decision will be based on information contained in a police report. On the one hand, if the information in the report is complete enough to permit an informed decision about prosecution, and if the prosecutor is willing to assign experienced assistants to perform this screening function, cases inappropriate for prosecution can be eliminated from the system early without incurring the cost of proceeding with preliminary hearings or presentation of evidence to the grand jury. On the other hand, if experienced prosecutors are not used for this task or if the quality of initial information from the police is not high, there may be little serious screening of cases by the prosecutor until some later stage in the proceeding.

Even within a single jurisdiction, the order in which the various steps of the criminal justice process occur will depend on how the potential defendant first becomes involved in the system. Typically, for a serious crime there will be an arrest followed by a decision to prosecute. In some situations, however, the decision to prosecute may have been made secretly by the grand jury and prosecutor prior to any attempt to arrest the defendant.[3]

Despite the variations in the operation of the criminal justice process, there are substantial similarities among the federal and various state criminal justice systems

2. And there are many communities. There are somewhere on the order of 17,000 police agencies in the United States, and more than 2,000 prosecutorial offices, all with varying resources, concerns, and objectives, and largely subject to no unifying supervision.

3. The grand jury, in addition to performing a screening function, may also act as an investigatory body. Information about an individual's criminal activity may come to light from such an investigation rather than from a citizen complaint or police investigation. On the basis of such information, the grand jury may return an indictment prior to the defendant's arrest. Indeed, the arrest may be intentionally delayed for some period of time after the indictment is returned so that the grand jury can complete its investigation without alerting a defendant's confederates.

with respect to prosecutions for serious criminal violations. Variations both in the formal judicial structure and in the degree of informality with which cases are resolved increase when one focuses on relatively minor crimes. The prosecution of serious criminality in most jurisdictions shares the following characteristics:

1. The initial enforcement responsibility rests with police agencies that have vast discretion in deciding whether to involve individuals in the criminal justice process.
2. The decision whether formally to charge an individual with a crime is the responsibility of a public prosecutor, who also possesses vast discretion.
3. There is some mechanism for screening serious criminal charges to determine whether there is a factual basis for the charge.
4. A criminal defendant is entitled to the assistance of counsel and, if indigent, to have one appointed at public expense if incarceration will result from conviction.
5. The vast majority of defendants participate with prosecutors in negotiating a guilty plea before trial. Most criminal cases are disposed of by negotiated guilty pleas through mechanisms that facilitate negotiation between defendants and prosecutors.
6. A defendant may make various pretrial motions challenging the prosecutor's evidence and the fairness of the criminal process.
7. Successful challenges by a defendant to the prosecution's evidence are often remedied by excluding evidence at trial, particularly in the prosecution's case-in-chief. Exclusion of this evidence does not necessarily mean that the evidence may not be used at other stages of the process, such as in rebuttal or sentencing.
8. Prosecution and defense are occasionally required to share discovery of certain information prior to trial, but nowhere near to the extent found in civil cases.
9. A defendant is entitled to a trial before an impartial judge, to confront and cross-examine opposing witnesses, to present witnesses, to a trial by jury unless the charge is only a "petty offense,"[4] and to an acquittal unless the prosecutor proves each element of the offense beyond a reasonable doubt. All these rights, and others, are waived by guilty pleas.
10. A guilty defendant has the right to address the court prior to sentencing. At sentencing, judges usually have substantial discretion in setting the penalty.
11. A convicted defendant usually has the right to some form of appellate review.[5]

---

4. See Duncan v. Louisiana, at page 79, infra.

5. In many, but not all, jurisdictions, the decision to plead guilty is viewed as a waiver of most of the contentions that a defendant might have raised at trial. For example, if a defendant prior to trial moved to exclude a confession on the ground that it was involuntary and if the confession were admitted at the trial, the defendant on appeal could challenge the admissibility of the confession. If the defendant decided to plead guilty after receiving an unfavorable ruling on the pretrial motion to suppress, however, the defendant would not be permitted in many jurisdictions to raise the involuntariness issue on appeal. The defendant, of course, could attack the guilty plea itself as involuntary or claim ineffective assistance of counsel. See generally Lefkowitz v. Newsome, 420 U.S. 283 (1975) (describing New York procedure that permits defendant to raise constitutional claims following guilty plea and holding that existence of such procedure precludes state from relying on guilty plea to foreclose consideration of same constitutional issues in federal habeas corpus proceedings).

The criminal justice system is, in a word, complicated. Individual systems themselves are complicated, as Figure 1.1 indicates, and in addition, there is no "criminal justice system" in the United States. Rather, there are many overlapping, competing, and conflicting, "criminal justice systems" throughout the country. Even within any particular "system," various components may be more in tension with each other than working smoothly toward uniform goals. A substantial part of the subject matter of this course is the commands of the United States Supreme Court that supposedly apply uniformly to these diverse systems, but the effect of any particular command—whether it concerns requirements of warrants, rules about presenting arrested individuals to magistrates, limits on police interrogation, or whatever—obviously will be partly contingent upon the precise contours of the particular system implementing that command. Requiring warrants, for example, will have certain implications in a low-crime, high-resource system, such as the federal system, and quite different implications in a high-crime, low-resource system, such as in many major cities. As you appraise the various opinions of the Court that you will study throughout this semester, and all the other material that is presented, keep this point well in mind.

There are additional points to keep in mind that are especially pertinent to appraising the numerous cases that you will study but that again apply much more generally. There is often a sense in which legal studies tend to focus attention on texts, whether they be cases, statutes, or regulations, and to bring to bear on those texts interpretive methodologies. You will read numerous cases, for example, and one obviously pertinent question will be the fidelity of those cases to the constitutional text. Another will be the logical implications of the various decisions, and so on. These are, to be sure, important questions, but do not neglect that the material you are about to study deals both with real-life human dramas and with the exercise of some of the more extreme forms of power that the state employs. The criminal justice process exists because of crime—people behaving in unlawful and often barbarous ways toward each other. In response to crime, the state is authorized to seize and confine people, strip them of their property and liberty, and even put them to death. And thus another important question, perhaps the single most important question for you to contemplate, is how the texts that you will read relate to these human dramas—whether their commands will be implemented in ways that appropriately respond to both the costs of crime and the costs of law enforcement.

To ask such questions is to begin to get at the heart of the "criminal justice process." The formal commands of the law emanate from social conditions, affect them, and are in turn affected by them. These interactions are much less governed by the intentions or aspirations of any court, legislature, or chief executive, or for that matter by the explicit terms of the formal commands themselves, than by the realities of human affairs. Thus, in addition to focusing on the explicit terms of the materials you will read and their logical implications, we encourage you to reflect on at least five other matters:

1. How will the formal commands of the law, whether judicial or legislative, be implemented in the real world? What will their real-life consequences be? What options are available to those affected by the formal commands to dilute or strengthen their implications through strategic choices of their own? One of the crucial questions of criminal procedure at the street level is

Figure 1.1. Compendium of Federal Criminal Justice Statistics (2004).[6]

System overview

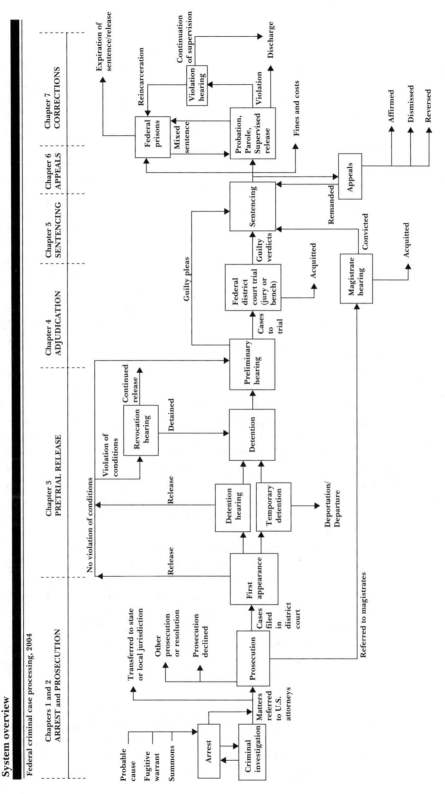

6. This graphic is from the 2004 Compendium of Federal Criminal Justice Statistics, published by the Department of Justice, Bureau of Justice Statistics. Because the publication is now produced in a different format, this graphical representation is not available for the most recent year. — Eds.

how different policies affect the exercise of discretion by the various actors in the drama, and how systems can adjust to the attempt to regulate discretion from external sources, such as federal courts attempting to impose rules of conduct on state actors through constitutional adjudication.

2. How do procedural requirements interact with the substantive law? For example, a rigorously enforced right to privacy may mean one thing if the primary social concern is the use of drugs, and quite another if it is the physical safety of the citizenry. Not surprisingly, as you will see, courts seem considerably less reluctant to suppress evidence (and thus increase the chance of an erroneous acquittal) in morals and drug crimes than in crimes of violence. You will also see that many procedural decisions are at the mercy of the scope of the substantive law, and thus for all the grand rhetoric about constitutional decisions, many of them are hostage to legislative choices. For example, decisions about the privacy of papers become largely irrelevant if the state can require the keeping of the records that form the content of those papers, and further require that government inspectors have access to those records (as you will see is sometimes the case). Constitutional rhetoric about the necessity of warrants and the sanctity of homes is substantially compromised if cities can insist on regular safety inspections without individualized suspicion (as again you will see can be done). Indeed, in some instances, you will see that procedural mandates are only required in the absence of equally effective alternatives—alternatives that the legislative or executive branches of government could provide.

3. Another important variable is the implication of discrimination based on race and ethnicity. A substantial portion of the law of criminal procedure arose to combat the effects of racial discrimination and can only be understood in that context, but the implications of discrimination are often not clear. For example, street harassment of African Americans and Latinos by the police is a serious modern problem, as Floyd v. City of New York 959 F. Supp. 540 (S.D.N.Y. 2013), and related litigation concerning the New York Police Department's "Stop Question and Frisk" order maintenance strategy indicates. However, one response to street harassment—heavier regulation of the selection of suspects—plausibly may be to withdraw police resources from poor minority neighborhoods, just those places where a heavy police presence may be most needed. The implications of racial discrimination often make questions harder rather than easier.

4. What exists today has a long history, and often can be understood only in historical context. As you will see, for example, for close to 100 years the Supreme Court's Fifth Amendment jurisprudence has been reacting to the decision of Boyd v. United States, 116 U.S. 616 (1886), and can only be understood in that light. Moreover, stability and predictability are important variables in all aspects of the law, and criminal procedure is no exception. Consequently, the forms of government and law have an inertial force that staves off change.

5. There are no free lunches. The criminal justice process competes for scarce and limited resources with all other governmental objectives. You may come across situations in your studies that you conclude demand greater resources. A good example may be the overall level of competency of counsel, which may be too low and probably could be raised by the infusion of substantial

resources. Another is that both police and prosecutorial discretion exist in substantial part because there is too much crime to handle, given the resources, and therefore both police and prosecutors can pick and choose how to spend their time. But, a dollar spent on providing better counsel or more police and prosecutors is a dollar that cannot be spent somewhere else, either within the criminal justice system, such as on providing speedier or more efficient trials, or outside the criminal justice system, such as on programs to ease the burden of poverty, or the national infrastructure, or student loans, or whatever. Governing involves an endless series of tragic choices in which competing demands must be traded off.

6. To summarize in part the previous five variables: Always keep in mind that the criminal justice process does not exist as an end in itself. Courses tend to be taught in law schools from an internal perspective. What, for example, are the fundamental principles of torts, contracts, or criminal law and procedure, and how do the various doctrines within a subject matter interrelate? These are important considerations, but the law generally and the criminal law most decidedly exists to further overall social welfare. Just as there can be too little law enforcement that leads to chaos, there can be too much that stifles a free society. A purely internal perspective may see inconsistency in doctrines and cases whereas an external perspective may suggest the criminal process is responding to felt social needs and demands. A good example of this is the pressure put upon notions of privacy by the struggle with mass terrorism.

B. Readings on the Criminal Justice Process

Perceptions of the criminal justice system are as varied as the system itself. Commentators, by virtue of their individual training and experience with the system, inevitably make their observations and evaluations from different perspectives. Moreover, commentators will have, if not different values, at least different priorities that they would like to see reflected in the criminal justice system. The materials in this chapter, without attempting to be comprehensive, offer some important perceptions and insights about the criminal justice system. You, of course, should approach these materials with the same questioning mind and skepticism that you bring to bear on the study of cases.

1. Perspectives on the System as a Whole

HERBERT PACKER, THE COURTS, THE POLICE, AND THE REST OF US

57 J. Crim. L., Criminology & Police Sci. 238, 239 (1966)

[T]he kind of criminal process that we have is profoundly affected by a series of competing value choices which, consciously or unconsciously, serve to resolve tensions that arise in the system. These values represent polar extremes which, in real life, are subject to almost infinite modulation and compromise. But the extremes can be identified. The choice, basically, is between what I have termed the Crime Control and the Due Process models. The Crime Control model sees the efficient, expeditious and reliable screening and disposition of persons suspected of crime as the central value to be served by the criminal process. The Due Process model sees that function as limited by and subordinate to the maintenance of the dignity and autonomy of the individual. The Crime Control model is administrative and managerial; the Due Process model is adversary and judicial. The Crime Control model may be analogized to an assembly line, the Due Process model to an obstacle course.[7]

What we have at work today is a situation in which the criminal process as it actually operates in the large majority of cases probably approximates fairly closely the dictates of the Crime Control model. The real-world criminal process tends to be far more administrative and managerial than it does adversary and judicial. Yet, the officially prescribed norms for the criminal process, as laid down primarily by the Supreme Court, are rapidly providing a view that looks more and more like the Due Process model. This development . . . has been in the direction of "judicializing" each stage of the criminal process, of enhancing the capacity of the accused to challenge the operation of the process, and of equalizing the capacity of all persons to avail themselves of the opportunity for challenge so created. . . .

JAMES Q. WHITMAN, PRESUMPTION OF INNOCENCE OR PRESUMPTION OF MERCY?: WEIGHING TWO WESTERN MODES OF JUSTICE

94 Tex. L. Rev. ___ (2016)

Imagine two contrasting ideas of how to build a just system of criminal justice. The first is oriented toward the presumption of innocence. It starts from the belief that the gravest danger we face in criminal justice is the danger that innocent persons will be arrested, prosecuted and convicted. Accordingly, it focuses on the threat of abusive investigations and prejudicial trials—on the dangers posed by rogue cops, unprincipled prosecutors, and biased judges and juries, all of whom threaten to undermine the liberties and the privacy of citizens. Committed to combatting those dangers, this mode of justice invests in what Herbert Packer famously called the "obstacle course" conception of due process: It protects the interests of justice by making it maximally difficult for the state to prove the case against defendants. To that end, it makes it hard for investigators to assemble evidence, and hard for prosecutors to manipulate the jury. It offers far-reaching protections to those persons who are suspected or accused. Once defendants have been duly convicted, however, it does little to protect them. Its rights are rights for the innocent, not the guilty.

The second, contrasting, idea of how to build a just criminal justice system is oriented instead toward a different presumption, a presumption of mercy. This mode

---

7. The *Crime Control* and *Due Process* concepts admittedly reflect different value choices, and the concepts provide a helpful way to articulate and focus on these value choices. But do they represent two different "models" of the criminal justice system? For a negative answer to this question, see Griffiths, Ideology in Criminal Procedure, or a Third "Model" of the Criminal Process, 79 Yale L.J. 359 (1970).—EDS.

of justice does not treat the danger that innocent persons will be convicted as the most pressing danger posed by the state. On the contrary, it tends to operate on the workaday assumption that investigators and judicial personnel are trustworthy professionals, and that virtually all accused persons are guilty as charged. In consequence, it puts lesser weight on due process protections for the accused. But that does not mean that it lacks rights: While this alternative mode of justice puts lesser weight on protections for the innocent, it puts greater weight on protections for the guilty. The most dangerous threat to justice, on this second view, is not the state that engages in rogue investigations or unfair trials, but the state that inflicts excessive punishment. The greatest fear is not that the innocent will be convicted, but that the guilty will be treated in inhumane ways. By erecting a presumption of mercy, this approach aims to force the justice system to think carefully and work hard before it carries out a criminal penalty.

These two modes of justice exist in the contemporary West. . . . The first, the mode of justice oriented toward the presumption of innocence, dominates in the criminal justice of the United States. The second mode, oriented toward the presumption of mercy, is much more powerfully present in the inquisitorial traditions of continental Europe.

And of these two Western modes of justice, the first, our familiar American mode, oriented toward the presumption of innocence, is troubled and increasingly fragile. The deep American attachment to what Packer called "the ideology of a presumption of innocence" has failed to create a humane criminal justice system. On the contrary, our tendency to think of the interests of justice as interests in protecting the innocent, not the guilty, has contributed to the making of an extraordinarily harsh culture of criminal punishment—one that threatens all of us, black and white, rich and poor. Meanwhile the rise of modern scientific evidence is making our conception of due process more and more difficult to sustain. The continental mode of justice, oriented more toward the presumption of mercy, certainly has its dangers and shortcomings; but on balance it is better suited to creating a just criminal justice order for the modern world. Americans of good will should feel uneasy about our culture of the presumption of innocence, and they should be prepared to ponder the inquisitorial presumption of mercy with an open mind. . . .

The great contrast between the United States and continental Europe is not the contrast between an adversarial tradition respectful of defendant's rights and an inquisitorial one committed only to ruthlessly hunting down the truth. Both traditions are respectful of defendant's rights. The real contrast is between one tradition driven by a more or less libertarian fear that rogue government officers will target innocent persons, and another generally respectful of the authority of professional law-enforcement personnel, but determined to keep the practice of punishment within decent, civilized limits. The contrast is between one tradition that puts all the weight on safeguards for the innocent, and another that reserves much of its compassion for the guilty. . . .

Certainly when we look at the bottom line—the basic measures of cruelty and harshness that ought to be the test of any civilized criminal justice system—America does not come off well. We trumpet our presumption of innocence to the world; but at the same time our own system of criminal punishment is out of hand. Mass incarceration and other aspects of penal harshness are among the most depressing and frightening features of contemporary American life, a great stain on the record of our national experiment. It is no justification for the harshness of our system to declare that we are committed only to punishing the guilty. Even if there were not a single wrongly convicted person in our country, something would be fearfully amiss. Our national commitment to the presumption of innocence, dearly held though it is, has done nothing to tame the worst evils of the contemporary American punishment system. For that reason alone decent Americans should be eager to reflect on the practices of neighbors who show a deeper concern for the presumption of mercy.

DAVID GARLAND, THE CULTURE OF CONTROL

8, 9, 10, 11, 12, 18, 20 (2001)

If asked to describe the major changes in penal policy in the last thirty years, most insiders would undoubtedly mention "the decline of the rehabilitative ideal". . . . "[R]ehabilitative" programmes do continue to operate in prisons and elsewhere, with treatment particularly targeted towards "high risk individuals" such as sex offenders, drug addicts, and violent offenders. . . . But today, rehabilitation programmes no longer claim to express the overarching ideology of the system, nor even to be the leading purpose of any penal measure. Sentencing law is no longer shaped by correctional concerns such as indeterminacy and early release. And the rehabilitative possibilities of criminal justice measures are routinely subordinated to other penal goals, particularly retribution, incapacitation, and the management of risk. . . .

For most of the twentieth century, penalties that appeared explicitly retributive or deliberately harsh were widely criticized as anachronisms that had no place within a "modern" penal system. In the last twenty years, however, we have seen the reappearance of "just deserts" retribution as a generalized policy goal in the US. . . . For most of the twentieth century the openly avowed expression of vengeful sentiment was virtually taboo, at least on the part of state officials. In recent years explicit attempts to express public anger and resentment have become a recurring theme of the rhetoric that accompanies penal legislation and decision-making. . . .

Fear of crime has come to have new salience. What was once regarded as a localized, situational anxiety, afflicting the worst-off individuals and neighborhoods, has come to be regarded as a major social problem and a characteristic of contemporary culture. Fear of crime has come to be regarded as a problem in and of itself, quite distinct from actual crime and victimization. . . .

The new political imperative is that victims must be protected, their voices must be heard, their memory honored, their anger expressed, their fears addressed. . . . Any untoward attention to the rights or welfare of the offender is taken to detract from the appropriate measure of respect for victims. A zero-sum policy game is assumed wherein the offender's gain is the victim's loss, and being "for" victims automatically means being tough on offenders. . . .

In the last few decades, the prison has been reinvented as a means of incapacitative restraint, supposedly targeted upon violent offenders and dangerous recidivists, but also affecting masses of more minor offenders. . . . There is a relaxation of concern about the civil liberties of suspects . . . and a new emphasis upon effective enforcement and control. . . . Procedural safeguards (such as the exclusionary rule in the USA and the defendant's right of silence in the UK) have been part-repealed, surveillance cameras have come to be a routine presence on city streets, and decisions about bail, parole or release from custody now come under intense scrutiny. . . . The risk of unrestrained state authorities, of arbitrary power and the violation of civil liberties seem no longer to figure so prominently in public concern. . . .

Until very recently, the settled assumption was that crime control and corrections were the state's responsibility, to be carried out by government employees in the public interest. These clear lines between the public and the private have now become blurred. Public sector agencies (prisons, probation, parole, the court system, etc.) are now being remodeled in ways that emulate the values and working practices of private industry. Commercial interests have come to play a role in the development and delivery of penal policy that would have been unthinkable twenty years ago. What we are witnessing is the redrawing of the established boundaries between the public and the private spheres, between the criminal justice state and the operative controls of civil society. . . .

There is now a growing sense that the "modern" arrangements for crime control . . . may no longer be adequate to the problem of crime. . . . The system's failings are now less easily viewed as a temporary problem, having to do with lack of resources or the under-implementation of correctionalist or deterrent programmes. Instead there is a developing realization that the modern strategy of crime-control-through-criminal justice has been tried and found wanting. Where high crime or recidivism rates would once have been attributed to implementation-failure, and prompted a demand to reinforce the existing system with more resources and greater professional powers, they are now interpreted as evidence of theory-failure: as signs that crime control is based upon an institutional model that is singularly inappropriate for its task.

KHALIL GIBRAN MUHAMMAD, CONDEMNATION OF BLACKNESS: RACE, CRIME AND THE MAKING OF MODERN URBAN AMERICA

1, 4-5, 272-273, 277 (2011)

Violent crime rates in the nation's biggest cities are generally understood as a reflection of the presence and behavior of black men, women, and children who live there. The U.S. prison population is larger than at any time in the history of the penitentiary anywhere in the world. Nearly half of the more than two million Americans behind bars are African Americans. . . . In all manner of conversations about race—from debates about parenting to education to urban life—black crime statistics are ubiquitous. By the same token, white crime statistics are virtually invisible, except when used to dramatize the excessive criminality of African Americans. . . . How was the statistical link between blackness and criminality forged? . . .

Tracing the emergence and evolution of the statistical discourse on black criminality sheds new light on the urban North as a crucial site for the production of modern ideas about race, crime and punishment. On the one hand dominant historical narratives about black criminality before the 1960s have been told through southern criminal justice practices and framed as premodern. Racist southern politicians, vigilante criminal justice officials, and body-parts collecting lynch mobs during the long Jim Crow era have formed the core subject matter of these backward-looking studies. On the other hand, the prevailing history of the northern criminal justice system . . . has been a modernizing narrative, one in which the development of . . . prisons . . . policing . . . juvenile justice . . . and parole has turned almost exclusively on the experiences of native-born whites and Europeans. . . .

By examining both immigrant and black crime discourses in the urban north as they were mutually constituted by new statistical data and made meaningful to a Jim Crow nations, we can more easily discern distinct (and novel) patterns of talking about race and crime. . . . The idea of black criminality was crucial to the making of modern America. In nearly every sphere it impacted how people defined fundamental differences between native whites, immigrants, and blacks. It also impacted, by comparison, how people evaluated black people's presence—the Negro Problem, as it had once been called—in the urban North. . . . Thoughtful, well-funded crime prevention and politically accountable crime fighting secured immigrants' whiteness, in contrast to the experiences of blacks, who were brutalized or left unprotected and were repeatedly told to conquer their own crime before others would help them. . . .

By illuminating the idea of black criminality in the making of modern urban America, it becomes clear that there are options in how we choose to use and interpret crime statistics. They may tell us something about the world we live in and about the people we label "criminals." But they cannot speak for themselves. They never have. . . . The falsity of past claims of race-neutral crime statistics and color-blind justice should caution us against the ubiquitous referencing of black criminality today. . . . Progressives rewrote white and immigrant criminality just as early civil rights activists rewrote, for a time, black criminality. The measure of crime, in both cases, was not racial inferiority but rather compassion towards the least among them. Sympathy and faith in humanity were chosen over scorn and contempt.

JOSEPH D. GRANO, ASCERTAINING THE TRUTH

77 Cornell L. Rev. 1061, 1062-1064 (1992)

Many lawyers and judges sanctimoniously defend our criminal injustice system as essential to individual freedom. Similarly academics, searching for anything or anyone to blame except the individual offenders, often applaud approaches that give offenders second, third, fourth, and even more chances to commit crimes. While these people defend the system, law abiding citizens desert the city's activities, restaurants, and retail merchants.

What accounts for the persistence of the world view illustrated by the misguided academic and judge? To a large extent, I believe it is the attitude of "there but for the grace of God go I," referring unfortunately to the offender rather than the victim. This attitude has its roots in the civil rights movement of the 1960s and in the conventional liberal ideology of the time that equated the typical criminal defendant in one courtroom with the civil rights plaintiff in another. Do not misunderstand me. . . . My argument is not with the civil rights revolution of the 1960s but rather with the distorted vision that saw, and still sees, the criminal offender not as the responsible perpetrator of an evil deed but as an unfortunate victim of a racist and oppressive society.

The view that the blame for crime lies with society rather than with the individual offender did not have much popular appeal even in the 1960s, and it has even less appeal today as crime runs rampant in our cities. Moreover, the "no responsibility" social determinists always have had to confront the rather insurmountable obstacle that the substantive criminal law is premised on a foundation of individual free will and responsibility. The common law requirement of mens rea aptly illustrates this free will foundation.

The procedural system, however, offered an attractive end run for those determined to undermine the substantive law's commitment to individual responsibility. The primary target was the basic notion that the paramount goal (I didn't say the only goal) of sound procedure should be the ascertainment of truth. Individual responsibility and accountability are not easy to achieve in a system that denigrates the importance of discovering the truth. The academics provided the underlying theory; the academics, lawyers, and judges together provided an abundance of truth-defeating procedural rules.

I am not going to review or critique the numerous truth-defeating procedural rules that plague our system. Most of us are familiar with the search and seizure exclusionary rule, with *Miranda* and *Massiah*, with the rule against prosecutorial comment on a defendant's silence, and with the effort to adopt the minority rule on entrapment, which would make the defendant's guilt or innocence irrelevant. We also are familiar with liberalism's continuing, and largely successful, effort to retain these truth-defeating rules. The latest example being the organized drive, spearheaded by the often-wrong ABA, to defeat the Bush Administration's badly needed reforms in the area of habeas corpus.

To facilitate the denigration of the search for truth, the academics who advocated these rules attacked the very concept of truth. We were told, for example, that any emphasis on "truth" must be simplistic, given the "plural forms and multi-faceted aspects of that beguiling concept." (I often have wondered what my mother's reaction would have been had I responded to a question about whether I locked my sister in the basement by saying, "Well, the truth is multifaceted and beguiling.")

CAROL S. STEIKER, COUNTER-REVOLUTION IN CONSTITUTIONAL CRIMINAL PROCEDURE? TWO AUDIENCES, TWO ANSWERS

94 Mich. L. Rev. 2466, 2466-2470 (1996)

When Richard M. Nixon ran for president in 1968, he campaigned on a now-familiar "law and order" platform. Among other things, he pledged to appoint Justices to the Supreme Court who would combat the Warren Court's controversial constitutional decisions limiting the power of law enforcement officials to investigate and prosecute crime. When Nixon won the presidency and then almost immediately had the opportunity to replace Chief Justice Earl Warren and three Associate Justices with appointees of his own, it was widely predicted that the major innovations of the Warren Court in constitutional criminal procedure—any list would include *Mapp*, *Massiah*, and *Miranda*—would not long survive. In the almost thirty years since Nixon's victory, the Supreme Court's pulse-takers have offered periodic updates on the fate of the Warren Court's criminal procedure "revolution" in the Burger and Rehnquist Courts.

The voluminous body of literature formed by these assessments presents something of a puzzle. The unanimity of projection about the future of the Warren Court's criminal procedure soon gave way to widespread disagreement about the nature and extent of the response of the Burger and Rehnquist Courts. On the one hand, many commentators—usually admirers of the Warren Court's handiwork—have lamented over the years about what they view as a wholesale repudiation of the Warren Court's work; their comments are full of words like "retreat," "decline," and "counter-revolution." At the very same time, other commentators—many of them also defenders of the Warren Court—have maintained that these laments are "overstated," and "considerably exaggerated," and that the basic structure of the Warren Court's criminal procedure jurisprudence is firmly "entrenched." As one critic of the Warren Court recently has bemoaned, "The voice that continues to urge repentance [from the Warren Court's criminal procedure] today is truly '[t]he voice of him that crieth in the wilderness.'"

One could attempt to resolve (or repudiate) this puzzling conflict in a variety of ways. One could, for example, attempt to explain disagreement about the nature of change by distinguishing between levels of abstraction—between "doctrinal" and "ideological" change. Or one could note that the difficulties inherent in weighing and measuring any sort of jurisprudential shift are exacerbated greatly in the broad, diffuse, and fact-specific jungle that is constitutional criminal procedure. Or one could ascribe the debate to a dispute over semantics: just how much change, after all, is "revolutionary" or "counter-revolutionary"? Or one simply could write off the more extreme statements on either side of the divide as rhetorical flourishes offered in the spirit of academic "spin control."

I, however, want to resist these temptations to downplay or deny the conflict, because I believe that the debate over continuity and change in constitutional criminal procedure can best be accounted for in an entirely different way—a way that suggests a new kind of critique of the Burger and Rehnquist Courts' criminal procedure jurisprudence. I start with the contention that the Supreme Court has profoundly changed its approach to constitutional criminal procedure since the 1960s at least in the following fairly limited (but obviously important) sense: the Court has clearly become less sympathetic to claims of individual rights and more accommodating to assertions of the need for public order. In the last three decades, the Court has granted review to and found in favor of criminal defendants much less frequently than it did in the heyday of the Warren Court. Thus, at least in Holmes' positivist sense of law as a prediction of what courts will do in fact, the law has changed radically.

The way in which this change has occurred, however, may help explain the academic divide. My contention is that much of this change has occurred quite differently from what was predicted at the close of the Warren Court era. The Burger and Rehnquist Courts have not altered radically—and indeed, occasionally have bolstered—the Warren Court's constitutional norms regarding police practices. The edifice constructed by the Warren Court governing investigative techniques under the Fourth, Fifth, and Sixth Amendments remains surprisingly intact. Rather than redrawing in any drastic fashion the line between constitutional and unconstitutional police conduct, the Supreme Court has revolutionized the consequences of deeming conduct unconstitutional. This revolution has not taken the form of wholesale abolition of the Fourth Amendment's exclusionary rule, or the Fifth or Sixth Amendments' mandates of exclusion; rather, the Court has proliferated a variety of what I would term "inclusionary rules"—rules that permit the use at trial of admittedly unconstitutionally obtained evidence or that let stand criminal convictions based on such evidence. Examples of "inclusionary rules" are the doctrines regarding standing, the good-faith exception to the warrant requirement, the "fruit of the poisonous tree," impeachment, harmless error, and limitations on federal habeas review of criminal convictions.

Thus, for the purposes of my argument, I adapt Professor Meir Dan-Cohen's distinction (which he in turn borrowed from Jeremy Bentham) between "conduct" rules and "decision" rules. Bentham and Dan-Cohen make this distinction in the context of substantive criminal law; for their purposes, "conduct" rules are addressed to the general public in order to guide its behavior (for example, "Let no person steal") and "decision" rules are addressed to public officials in order to guide their decisionmaking about the consequences of violating conduct rules (for example, "Let the judge cause whoever is convicted of stealing to be hanged"). But as any teacher of both substantive and procedural criminal law knows, constitutional criminal procedure is a species of substantive criminal law for cops. Thus, for my purposes, "conduct" rules (my "constitutional norms") are addressed to law enforcement agents regarding the constitutional legitimacy of their investigative practices and "decision" rules (my "inclusionary rules") are addressed to courts regarding the consequences of unconstitutional conduct.

. . . My primary descriptive claim . . . is that the Supreme Court's shift in constitutional criminal procedure from the 1960s to the 1990s has occasioned much more dramatic changes in decision rules than in conduct rules. . . . This claim is qualitative rather than quantitative, and comparative rather than absolute. I do not mean to say that the Supreme Court has deployed decision rules more than conduct rules in any strict numerical sense, nor do I contend that constitutional norms have not shifted at all; rather, I argue that the Court's decision-rule cases have diverged far more from the Warren Court's starting point than have its conduct-rule cases. Thus, the dichotomy between decision rules and conduct rules helps to explain the existence of such a deep academic divide. The proponents and debunkers of the "counter-revolution" hypothesis turn out to both be right: the Burger and Rehnquist Courts have accepted to a significant extent the Warren Court's definitions of constitutional "rights" while waging counter-revolutionary war against the Warren Court's constitutional "remedies" of evidentiary exclusion and its federal review and reversal of convictions.

AKHIL REED AMAR, THE FUTURE OF CONSTITUTIONAL CRIMINAL PROCEDURE

33 Am. Crim. L. Rev. 1123, 1123-1125, 1128-1129, 1132-1134 (1996)

As a subfield of constitutional law, constitutional criminal procedure stands as an anomaly. In many other areas of constitutional law, major Marshall Court opinions stand out and continue to frame debate both in courts and beyond. In thinking about judicial review and executive power, we still look to Marbury v. Madison; in pondering the puzzle of jurisdiction-stripping, we go back to Martin v. Hunter's

Lessee; in reflecting on the scope of Congress' enumerated powers, and related issues of federalism, we re-examine McCulloch v. Maryland. . . . But no comparable Marshall Court landmarks dot the plain of constitutional criminal procedure.

It is often thought that the explanation for this anomaly lies in another Marshall Court landmark, Barron v. Baltimore. Most criminal law, the argument goes, is state law; murder, rape, robbery, and the like are generally not federal crimes. Under *Barron*, the constitutional criminal procedure rules of the Bill of Rights did not apply against states, and so the Marshall Court predictably heard few cases raising issues of constitutional criminal procedure. *Barron* is indeed part of the story. . . .

Then came the Warren Court, which overruled *Barron* and began applying the Fourth, Fifth, and Sixth Amendments directly against states, under the banner of selective incorporation. With many, many more state criminal cases fueling its docket, the Warren Court proceeded to build up, in short order, a remarkable doctrinal edifice of Fourth Amendment, Fifth Amendment, and Sixth Amendment rules — the foundations of modern constitutional criminal procedure.

But these foundations were none too sure. On a lawyerly level, some of the Warren Court's most important criminal procedure pronouncements lacked firm grounding in constitutional text and structure. Key rulings ran counter to early case law both in lower federal courts and in state courts construing analogous provisions of state constitutions. Precisely because so few Marshall Court cases existed, this break with Founding-era understandings was less visible. On key issues, the Warren Court seemed to contradict itself, laying down sweeping rules in some cases that it could not quite live by in other cases. On a political level, many of the Warren Court's constitutional criminal procedure pronouncements did not sit well with the American electorate. The guilty too often seemed to spring free without good reason — and by this time the guilty regularly included murderers, rapists, and robbers and not just federal income tax frauds and customs cheats. In a constitutional democracy, the People, in the long run, usually prevail. Federal judges may be, at times, "insulated" and "countermajoritarian," but majorities elect Presidents, and Presidents, with the advice and consent of Senators, pick federal judges.

And so, with Earl Warren's retirement, and Richard Nixon's election on a "law and order" platform, the Counter-Revolution began. But the foundations of this Counter-Revolution are also none too sure. Like the Warren Court, the Burger and Rehnquist Courts have at times paid little heed to constitutional text, history, and structure and have mouthed rules one day only to ignore them the next. If the Warren Court at times was too easy on the guilty, the Burger and Rehnquist Courts at times have been too hard on the innocent.

Where does all this leave us today? At a crossroads. I submit, the present is a particularly ripe moment for a fundamental rethinking of constitutional criminal procedure, and for a choice among competing visions.

WHERE SHOULD WE GO FROM HERE? CONSTITUTIONAL METHODOLOGY

To begin with, we must distinguish constitutional criminal procedure from criminal procedure generally. Not all sensible rules of criminal procedure can or should be constitutionalized. The Constitution — when read in light of its text, history, and structure, its doctrinal elaboration in precedent, the need for principled judicial standards, and so on — simply may not speak to some issues. This is, of course, one of the reasons we have legislatures — to make sensible policy where the Constitution permits choice. Legislative solutions can be adjusted in the face of new facts or changing values far more easily than can rules that have been read into the Constitution.

Textual argument is, as I have said, a proper starting point for proper constitutional analysis. Sometimes, plain-meaning textual arguments in the end must yield to the weight of other proper constitutional arguments—from history, structure, precedent, practicality, and so on. And so the astonishing thing is not that someone might find the above-catalogued textual points to be outweighed at times by other arguments. Rather, the astonishing thing is that these textual points are almost never made, or even seen. This is true even when the text, carefully read, explains most or all of the leading cases in a given area, or when the text resonates with obvious common sense. In virtually every other area of constitutional law, such a state of affairs is unimaginable. I think it cannot last much longer in the area of constitutional criminal procedure. The field may have evolved as an insular ecosystem unto itself, but global changes in constitutional law discourse must soon affect the atmosphere here, too.

The Constitution seeks to protect the innocent. The guilty, in general, receive procedural protection only as an incidental and unavoidable byproduct of protecting the innocent because of their innocence. Law breaking, as such, is entitled to no legitimate expectation of privacy, and so if a search can detect only law breaking as such, it poses little threat to Fourth Amendment values. By the same token, the exclusionary rule is wrong, as a constitutional rule, precisely because it creates huge windfalls for guilty defendants but gives no direct remedy to the innocent woman wrongly searched. The guiltier you are, the more evidence the police find, the bigger the exclusionary rule windfall; but if the police know you are innocent, and just want to hassle you (because of your race, or politics, or whatever), the exclusionary rule offers exactly zero compensation or deterrence.

Truth and accuracy are vital values. A procedural system that cannot sort the innocent from the guilty will confound any set of substantive laws, however just. And so to throw out highly reliable evidence that can indeed help us separate the innocent from the guilty—and to throw it out by pointing to the Constitution, no less—is constitutional madness. A Constitution proclaimed in the name of We the People should be rooted in enduring values that Americans can recognize as our values. Truth and the protection of innocence are such values. Virtually everything in the Fourth, Fifth, and Sixth Amendments, properly read, promotes, or at least does not betray, these values.

If anyone believes that other nice-sounding, but far less intuitive, ideas are also in the Constitution, the burden of proof should be on him. Here are two examples: (1) "The Constitution requires that government must never profit from its own wrong. Hence, illegally obtained evidence must be excluded." (2) "No man should be compelled to be an instrument of his own destruction. Hence, reliable physical fruits of immunized testimony should be excluded." These sound nice, but where does the Constitution say that? And are we truly willing to live by these as constitutional rules? The first would require that the government return stolen goods to thieves, and illegal drugs to drug-dealers. But this has never been the law. The second would prevent coerced fingerprinting and DNA sampling. This, too, is almost impossible to imagine in practice. By contrast, the innocence-protection rock on which I stand, and the specific Fourth, Fifth, and Sixth Amendment derivations therefrom, are things that we can all live by, without cheating.

WILLIAM J. STUNTZ, THE UNEASY RELATIONSHIP BETWEEN CRIMINAL PROCEDURE AND CRIMINAL JUSTICE

107 Yale L.J. 1, 1-6 (1997)

Most talk about the law of criminal procedure treats that law as a self-contained universe. The picture looks something like this: The Supreme Court says that suspects and defendants have a right to be free from certain types of police or prosecutorial behavior. Police and prosecutors, for the most part, then do as they're told. When they don't, and when the misconduct is tied to criminal convictions, the courts reverse the convictions, thereby sending a message to misbehaving officials. Within the bounds of this picture there is room for a lot of debate about the wisdom or constitutional pedigree of particular doctrines, and the literature is filled with debate of that sort. There is also room for theorizing about the optimal specificity of the rules the Supreme Court creates; the literature contains some of that, though less than it should. Finally, there is room for arguing about remedies—about whether reversing criminal convictions is an appropriate means of getting the police, prosecutors, and trial judges to do what the law says they ought to do. At least in the sphere of Fourth and Fifth Amendment law, a lively debate along those lines exists. But for all their variety, these debates take for granted the same basic picture of the process, a process whose only variables are the rules themselves and the remedies for their violation.

The picture is, of course, wrong. Criminal procedure's rules and remedies are embedded in a larger system, a system that can adjust to those rules in ways other than obeying them. And the rules can in turn respond to the system in a variety of ways, not all of them pleasant. The more one focuses on that dynamic, the more problematic the law of criminal procedure seems.

The heart of the problem is the system's structure. The criminal justice system is dominated by a trio of forces: crime rates, the definition of crime (which of course partly determines crime rates), and funding decisions—how much money to spend on police, prosecutors, defense attorneys, judges, and prisons. These forces determine the ratio of crimes to prosecutors and the ratio of prosecutions to public defenders, and those ratios in turn go far toward determining what the system does and how the system does it. But the law that defines what the criminal process looks like, the law that defines defendants' rights, is made by judges and Justices who have little information about crime rates and funding decisions, and whose incentives to take account of those factors may be perverse. High crime rates make it easy for prosecutors to substitute cases without strong procedural claims for cases with such claims. Underfunding of criminal defense counsel limits the number of procedural claims that can be pressed. Both phenomena make criminal procedure doctrines seem inexpensive to the appellate judges who define those doctrines. Unsurprisingly, given that regulating the criminal justice system has seemed cheap, the courts have done a lot of regulating—more, one suspects, than they would have done in a world where defendants could afford to litigate more often and more aggressively, or where prosecutors could not so easily substitute some cases for others. Criminal procedure is thus distorted by forces its authors probably do not understand.

The distortion runs both ways. As courts have raised the cost of criminal investigation and prosecution, legislatures have sought out devices to reduce those costs.

Severe limits on defense funding are the most obvious example, but not the only one. Expanded criminal liability makes it easier for the government to induce guilty pleas, as do high mandatory sentences that serve as useful threats against recalcitrant defendants. And guilty pleas avoid most of the potentially costly requirements that criminal procedure imposes. These strategies would no doubt be politically attractive anyway, but the law of criminal procedure makes them more so. Predictably, underfunding, overcriminalization, and oversentencing have increased as criminal procedure has expanded.

Nor are the law's perverse effects limited to courts and legislatures. Constitutional criminal procedure raises the cost of prosecuting wealthier defendants by giving those defendants more issues to litigate. The result, at the margin, is to steer prosecutors away from such defendants and toward poorer ones. By giving defendants other, cheaper claims to raise, constitutional criminal procedure also raises the cost to defense counsel of investigating and litigating factual claims, claims that bear directly on their clients' innocence or guilt. The result is to steer defense counsel, again at the margin, away from those sorts of claims and toward constitutional issues. More Fourth, Fifth, and Sixth Amendment claims probably mean fewer self-defense claims and mens rea arguments. This turns the standard conservative criticism of the law of criminal procedure on its head. Ever since the 1960s, the right has argued that criminal procedure frees too many of the guilty. The better criticism may be that it helps to imprison too many of the innocent.

It also does little about the concern that, more than anything else, prompted its creation. The post-1960 constitutionalization of criminal procedure arose, in large part, out of the sense that the system was treating black suspects and defendants much worse than white ones. Warren-era constitutional criminal procedure began as a kind of antidiscrimination law. But the criminal justice system is characterized by extraordinary discretion—over the definition of crimes (legislatures can criminalize as much as they wish), over enforcement (police and prosecutors can arrest and charge whom they wish), and over funding (legislatures can allocate resources as they wish). In a system so dominated by discretionary decisions, discrimination is easy, and constitutional law has surprisingly little to say about it.

To some degree, these problems are the product of a particular set of contingent circumstances. Vary the circumstances, and the problems would look quite different. For example, we may someday return to the very low crime-to-prosecutor ratios of the early 1960s, either because crime takes a nosedive or because criminal justice budgets go through the roof (or both). If that happens, prosecutorial discretion will seem less important, for prosecutors will be able to pursue all strong cases and a good number of weak ones. Guilty plea rates will fall as the proportion of contestable cases rises. More trials will mean that the cost of constitutional regulation in this area will become more visible to judges, which might lead the Supreme Court to alter the regulation in important ways. This is just one set of speculations about one possible scenario; other scenarios, pushing prosecutors and courts in very different directions, could easily be spun out. The lesson seems clear: Generalizing is dangerous, for the problems that afflict the system today are the consequence of today's facts and today's law, and both facts and law are certain to change.

Yet some cautious generalizing is still possible. In a legislatively funded system with state-paid prosecutors and defense attorneys, judge-made procedural rights are bound to have some perverse effects, pushing prosecutors and defense attorneys and legislators and even the judges themselves in uncomfortable directions. The effects are impossible to measure, and they will be larger or smaller depending on background circumstances. But they remain real, and inevitable.

It may be that the broad structure of constitutional regulation of criminal justice has it backward, that courts have been not too activist, but activist in the wrong places. The system might be better off today had Warren and his colleagues worried less about criminal procedure, and more about criminal justice.

TOM R. TYLER, WHY PEOPLE OBEY THE LAW

269-270, 272, 275 (rev. ed. 2006)

MAINTAINING SOCIAL ORDER

Since the purpose of creating laws and empowering legal authorities is to create and maintain social order by regulating public behavior, the issue addressed by *Why People Obey the Law* is how such compliance can best be achieved. During the past several decades the dominant approach to securing compliance has been through the threat or use of punishment—i.e. via deterrence. . . .

Deterrence strategies are one example of instrumental strategies, which are based upon the assumption that the primary factors motivating human behavior are incentives and sanctions. In the context of regulation this vision leads to a deterrence strategy, linking sanctions to rule breaking. . . . One argument in favor of using deterrence as an approach to securing compliance is that it is a strategy that works. Interestingly, as research has accumulated about the influence of risk assessments on law related behavior this general assertion has been widely qualified. Studies suggest that deterrence is often found to significantly influence law related behavior, but does not always have a significant influence. . . . Even when risk is found to have an influence, the magnitude of that influence is small. . . .

[T]he widespread use of deterrence approaches has led to serious negative side effects. One such side effect is the dramatic growth in the American prison population. . . . Further, since these policies are directed primarily at the disadvantaged, their use has undermined police-community relations in urban areas, and especially among minority groups. One of the largest and most consistent findings in public opinion polling is of lower trust and confidence in legal authorities among minority group members than among whites.

Are there alternative ways to secure compliance that do not have these negative side effects? . . . The goal of *Why People Obey the Law* was to articulate and defend empirically an alternative vision of social order maintenance linked to gaining the consent and cooperation of the public with law and legal authorities. This alternative vision was unfolded in three stages. . . . The first stage demonstrated that legitimacy shapes compliance with the law. The second stage showed that legitimacy was itself based not upon instrumental judgments but was rooted in procedural justice judgments. And, finally, the third stage explores the meaning of procedural justice, making clear that procedural justice was defined by respondents in by reference to noninstrumental issues. Taken together, these findings support the argument that people's motivation to cooperate with others, in this case legal authorities, is rooted in social relationships and ethical judgments, and does not primarily flow from the desire to avoid punishments or gain rewards. . . .

LEGITIMACY AND COMPLIANCE

The first scholarly contribution of *Why People Obey the Law* was to provide empirical support for the value of legitimacy as a motivating force in the area of law. In fact, the findings of this study suggested that legitimacy was more influential than was the risk of being caught and punished for rule breaking. . . .

THE BASIS OF LEGITIMACY: PROCEDURAL JUSTICE

The second important argument made in *Why People Obey the Law* is that the basis of legitimacy is the justice of the procedures used by which legal authorities. . . . According to an instrumental perspective, the police and courts gain legitimacy by being effective in fighting crime; political leaders are evaluated upon their success in shaping economic performance; and workers follow those managers who lead their companies to success.

Why People Obey the Law adopts a different framework within which to evaluate legitimacy. That framework is not linked to either the favorability or fairness of the decisions made or policies pursued by legal authorities. . . . People are widely found to react to the fairness by which authorities and institutions make decisions and exercise authority, and these reactions shape both their willingness to accept decisions and their everyday rule following behavior. . . .

THE MEANING OF PROCEDURAL JUSTICE

Early work on procedural justice . . . presented an instrumental or control based interpretation of procedural justice findings. . . . The goal of a fair procedure was to produce a fair outcome. . . . [Research concerning] the psychology underlying procedural justice judgments and demonstrated that people's judgments could not be explained as a simple reflection of their indirect control over outcomes via evidence presentation. Rather, people valued the opportunity to speak to authorities and state their case, even when they did not think that their presentation would influence their outcome. . . . Subsequent studies of procedural justice have broadened this conclusion . . . by showing that people place considerable importance on a variety of . . . "relational criterion" [that] include assessments of the quality of interpersonal treatment (are people treated with dignity and respect; are their rights respected?) and evaluations of the trustworthiness of authorities, as well as judgments about the neutrality of decision making and the degree to which opportunities to participate are provided.

2. The Distinction Between Criminal Procedure, Civil Procedure, and Substantive Criminal Law

WILLIAM J. STUNTZ, SUBSTANCE, PROCESS, AND THE CIVIL-CRIMINAL LINE

7 J. Contemp. Legal Issues 1 (1996)

Criminal procedure is almost completely constitutionalized; civil procedure is not. Meanwhile, the substance of the law of crimes is not very heavily constitutionalized;

neither is the substance of the law of everything else. Those substantive restraints that exist—for instance, the First Amendment and equal protection doctrine, not to mention the famous cases that go under the label "substantive due process"—apply, with a few exceptions, to everything the government does. That is, they apply to the civil and criminal spheres alike.

So constitutional law treats the criminal side of the civil-criminal line as special, but only when crafting procedures. When it comes to the rules that regulate primary conduct, constitutional law basically has no civil-criminal line. Legislatures decide what is and is not a crime, just as they decide what (mostly civil) rules apply to sales contracts or securities offerings. Legislatures also decide what procedures apply when civil disputes arise, though they may leave a good deal of that authority to courts as a practical matter. But courts alone decide what the law of criminal procedure looks like, since courts are the system's constitutional lawmakers and criminal procedure is the province of constitutional law.

So the constitution regulates substance in a few significant pockets, but otherwise leaves it alone, and the regulation basically spans the civil-criminal divide. There is no real substantive due process aimed specially at criminal law. Meanwhile, there is some gentle constitutional regulation of the civil process, but the regulation plainly occurs around the edges; the core is governed by non-constitutional law. Only in criminal procedure does constitutional law dominate the field.

There is a standard argument for constitutional criminal procedure's many protections. Arrest, prosecution, and criminal punishment impose huge costs on their targets. The danger is that those costs will be imposed for no reason (i.e., on the whim of some government official) or for a bad reason (e.g., the defendant's race or politics). A large portion of the law of criminal procedure addresses that danger. The requirement of probable cause to justify arrest; the requirement of magistrate review, a preliminary hearing, or grand jury screening to bring a case to trial; the right to counsel at trial and at some pretrial stages; the right to trial by jury; and the beyond-a-reasonable-doubt standard for criminal conviction—all these rights ensure that the government can punish only if it can satisfy a series of neutral decisionmakers of a high probability (increasingly high as one moves from arrest to trial to conviction) that the defendant committed a crime. If the rights work, the specter of punishment for no reason or for evil reasons vanishes.

This happy scenario depends on substantive criminal law doing a good job of separating people who deserve punishment from people who don't. Accuracy is not an end in itself; it matters only if there is something meaningful to be accurate about. The best procedures in the world cannot prevent punishment for the "crime" of being black, or a Rastafarian. In short, good procedural rules require good substantive rules in order to accomplish anything.

That much is no surprise; it is the usual relationship between procedure and substance. But at least in the criminal setting, the relationship is more problematic. Special rules of criminal procedure are not just worthless without substantive limits. The procedural rules may actually be perverse: The procedures themselves give the government an incentive to generate bad substantive rules, as a means of evading or exploiting the differences between the criminal and civil processes. This perversity takes two forms. The first arises from legal boundaries that separate criminal law enforcement from civil law enforcement, boundaries that are almost never litigated yet create important incentives. These boundary rules let the government do things to criminal suspects or defendants that it can't do to civil litigants, thereby creating some incentive to broaden the scope of criminal liability. The second arises from the many rights criminal procedure grants defendants. Safeguarding those rights is, naturally, costly to the government. And broader criminal liability allows the government to escape those costs, both by easing the burden of proving guilt and by easing the task of inducing guilty pleas.

There is a natural dynamic built into our system that leads to overcriminalization. In the absence of substantive limits, broad procedural protections for criminal defendants make that dynamic worse. Meanwhile, the same logic that legitimates constitutional criminal procedure also supports constitutional criminal substance. It follows that the current allocation of authority between constitutional law and legislative power is both unstable and contradictory.

How might the contradiction be resolved? There are two possibilities, both obvious. The system might deregulate criminal procedure, leaving it to the same forces that define criminal law. Or, the system might constitutionalize the borders of criminal law, just as it has done with criminal procedure. That is, constitutional law's line between criminal and civil might be either abolished or extended.

3.   Plea Bargaining and Sentencing

JOHN H. LANGBEIN, TORTURE AND PLEA BARGAINING

46 U. Chi. L. Rev. 3, 7, 8, 9, 12 (1978)

For about half a millennium, from the middle of the thirteenth century to the middle of the eighteenth, a system of judicial torture lay at the heart of Continental criminal procedure. . . . In discussions of contemporary criminal procedure we hear the word applied to describe illegal police practices or crowded prison conditions. But torture as the medieval European lawyers understood it had nothing to do with official misconduct or with criminal sanctions. Rather, the application of torture was a routine and judicially supervised feature of European criminal procedure. . . .

[S]ubstantial safeguards were devised to govern the actual application of torture. These were rules designed to enhance the reliability of the resulting confession. Torture was not supposed to be used to elicit an abject, unsubstantiated confession of guilt. Rather, torture was supposed to be employed in such a way that the accused would disclose the factual detail of the crime-information which, in the words of a celebrated German statute, "no innocent person can know." . . . [T]hese safeguards never proved adequate to overcome the basic flaw in the system. Because torture tests the capacity of the accused to endure pain rather than his veracity, the innocent might (as one sixteenth-century commentator put it) yield to "the pain and torment and confess things that they never did". . . .

The description of the European law of torture that I have just presented has been meant to stir among American readers an unpleasant sensation of the familiar. The parallels between the modern American plea bargaining system and the ancient system of judicial torture are many and chilling. . . . Plea bargaining occurs when the prosecutor induces a criminal accused to confess guilt and to waive his right to trial in exchange for a more lenient criminal sanction than would be imposed if the accused were adjudicated guilty following trial. The prosecutor offers leniency either directly, in the form of a charge reduction, or indirectly, through the connivance of the judge, in the form of a recommendation for reduced sentence that the judge will follow. In exchange for procuring this leniency for the accused, the prosecutor is relieved of the need to prove the accused's guilt, and the court is spared having to adjudicate it. . . .

If you turn to the American Constitution in search of authority for plea bargaining, you will look in vain. Instead, you will find-in no less hallowed a place than the Bill of Rights an opposite guarantee, a guarantee of trial. . . . In our day, jury trial continues to occupy its central place both in the formal law and in the mythology of the law. . . . In truth, criminal jury trial has largely disappeared in America. The criminal justice system now disposes of virtually all cases of serious crime through plea bargaining. Depending on the jurisdiction, as many as 99 percent of all felony convictions are by plea. . . .

Let me now turn to my main theme—the parallels in function and doctrine between the medieval European system of judicial torture and our plea bargaining system. [E]ach of these substitute procedural systems arose in response to the breakdown of the formal system of trial that it subverted. Both the medieval European law of proof and the modem Anglo-American law of jury trial set out to safeguard the accused by circumscribing the discretion of the trier in criminal adjudication. The medieval Europeans were trying to eliminate the discretion of the professional judge by requiring him to adhere to objective criteria of proof. The Anglo-American trial system has been caught up over the last two centuries in an effort to protect the accused against the dangers of the jury system. . . . Each system found itself unable to recant directly on the unrealistic level of safeguard to which it had committed itself, and each then concentrated on inducing the accused to tender a confession that would waive his right to the safeguards. . . .

[T]he law of torture worked an absolutely fundamental change within the system of proof: it largely eliminated the adjudicative function. Once probable cause had been determined, the accused was made to concede his guilt rather than his accusers to prove it. In twentieth-century America we have duplicated the central experience of medieval European criminal procedure: we have moved from an adjudicatory to a concessionary system. We coerce the accused against whom we find probable cause to confess his guilt. To be sure, our means are much politer; we use no rack, no thumbscrew, no Spanish boot to mash his legs. But like the Europeans of distant centuries who did employ those machines, we make it terribly costly for an accused to claim his right to the constitutional safeguard of trial.

ALBERT W. ALSCHULER, IMPLEMENTING THE CRIMINAL DEFENDANT'S RIGHT TO TRIAL: ALTERNATIVES TO THE PLEA BARGAINING SYSTEM

50 U. Chi. L. Rev. 931, 932-936, 1048-1050 (1983)

[P]lea bargaining has come to affect almost every aspect of our criminal justice system from the legislative drafting of substantive offenses through the efforts of correctional officials to rehabilitate convicted offenders.

Even a cursory listing of objections to this practice may consume several paragraphs. Plea bargaining makes a substantial part of an offender's sentence depend, not upon what he did or his personal characteristics, but upon a tactical decision irrelevant to any proper objective of criminal proceedings. In contested cases, it substitutes a regime of split-the-difference for a judicial determination of guilt or innocence and elevates a concept of partial guilt above the requirement that criminal responsibility be established beyond a reasonable doubt. This practice also deprecates the value of human liberty and the purposes of the criminal sanction by treating these things as commodities to be traded for economic savings — savings that, when measured against common social expenditures, usually seem minor.

Plea bargaining leads lawyers to view themselves as judges and administrators rather than as advocates; it subjects them to serious financial and other temptations to disregard their clients' interests; and it diminishes the confidence in attorney-client relationships that can give dignity and purpose to the legal profession and that [are] essential to the defendant's sense of fair treatment. In addition, this practice makes figureheads of court officials who typically prepare elaborate presentence reports only after the effective determination of sentence through prosecutorial negotiations. Indeed, it tends to make figureheads of judges, whose power over the administration of criminal justice has largely been transferred to people of less experience, who commonly lack the information that judges could secure, whose temperaments have been shaped by their partisan duties, and who have not been charged by the electorate with the important responsibilities that they have assumed. Moreover, plea bargaining perverts both the initial prosecutorial formulation of criminal charges and, as defendants plead guilty to crimes less serious than those that they apparently committed, the final judicial labeling of offenses.

The negotiation process encourages defendants to believe that they have "sold a commodity and that [they have], in a sense, gotten away with something." It sometimes promotes perceptions of corruption. It has led the Supreme Court to a hypocritical disregard of its usual standards of waiver in judging the most pervasive waiver that our criminal justice system permits. The practice of plea bargaining is inconsistent with the principle that a decent society should want to hear what an accused person might say in his defense — and with constitutional guarantees that embody this principle and other professed ideals for the resolution of criminal disputes. . . . However unjust plea bargaining may seem, it has become fashionable to contend that the process is inevitable. Indeed, scholars and practitioners proclaim that "to speak of a plea bargaining-free criminal justice system is to operate in a land of fantasy." They advance two arguments in support of this contention. First, they emphasize the extent of the demon's possession. In view of the overwhelming number of cases that currently are resolved by guilty pleas, they maintain that providing the economic resources necessary to implement the right to trial would be impracticable; their view apparently is that our nation cannot afford to give its criminal defendants their day in court. Second, they suggest that in view of the mutuality of advantage that prosecutors and defense attorneys are likely to perceive in the settlement of criminal cases, any attempt to prohibit this process would be countered by widespread subterfuge. In practice, they argue, the only choice is between a system of negotiated case resolution that is open, honest, and subject to effective regulation and one that has been driven underground.

. . . [O]ne obvious solution to today's excessive dependency on the guilty plea — spending the money necessary to implement our constitutional ideals without shortcuts. Focusing first on felony prosecutions, it argues that the United

States could provide three-day jury trials to all felony defendants who reach the trial stage by adding no more than an estimated $850 million to annual criminal justice expenditures. Moreover, it contends that the actual cost of implementing a plea bargaining prohibition would be less than this amount, in part because most cases now resolved through plea bargaining could be tried in less than three days and, even more importantly, because many defendants would plead guilty without bargaining.

. . . [T]he Anglo-American legal system afforded defendants an unfettered right to trial during most of its history and . . . most legal systems of the world apparently survive without plea bargaining today. Nevertheless, every legal system that has managed without plea bargaining has employed a much more expeditious trial procedure than ours.

The impediments to implementation of a plea bargaining prohibition are not worth a fraction of the paralysis that they have prompted. Americans certainly could afford full implementation of the right to jury trial in both felony and misdemeanor prosecutions. Moreover, without additional expenditures, they could allocate existing resources more effectively by simplifying the trial process and making trials more available. Finally, states could easily substitute jury waiver bargaining for plea bargaining. Observers who proclaim that implementation of the right to trial is impossible have perpetrated a remarkable myth—one whose effectiveness depends largely on the "outsider's" fear of being thought naive or utopian and one that any glance outside our own legal system destroys.

At the end of a long investigation of plea bargaining, I confess to some bafflement concerning the insistence of most lawyers and judges that plea bargaining is inevitable and desirable. Perhaps I am wrong in thinking that a few simple precepts of criminal justice should command the unqualified support of fair-minded people:

— that it is important to hear what someone may be able to say in his defense before convicting him of crime;
— that, when he denies his guilt, it is also important to try to determine on the basis of all the evidence whether he is guilty;
— that it is wrong to punish a person, not for what he did, but for asking that the evidence be heard (and wrong deliberately to turn his sentence in significant part on his strategies rather than on his crime);
— and, finally, that it is wrong to alibi departures from these precepts by saying that we do not have the time and money to listen, that most defendants are guilty anyway, that trials are not perfect, that it is all an inevitable product of organizational interaction among stable courtroom work groups, and that any effort to listen would merely drive our failure to listen underground.

From my viewpoint, it is difficult to understand why these precepts are controversial; what is more, I do not understand why the legal profession, far from according them special reverence, apparently values them less than the public in general does. Daniel Webster thought it a matter of definition that "law" would hear before it condemned, proceed upon inquiry, and render judgment only after trial. Apparently the legal profession has lost sight of Webster's kind of law, and, for all the pages that I have written about plea bargaining, the issue in the end may be that simple.

RONALD WRIGHT & MARC MILLER, THE SCREENING/BARGAINING TRADEOFF

55 Stan. L. Rev. 29, 30-35 (2002)

When it comes to plea bargaining, we have created a false dilemma. The dilemma grows out of the central reality of criminal adjudication in the United States. The vast majority of criminal cases are resolved through guilty pleas rather than trials. Most of those guilty pleas result from negotiations between prosecution and defense.

Scholars, judges, prosecutors, defense lawyers, and politicians have offered only two basic responses to the fact that guilt is mostly resolved through negotiated guilty pleas: They take it or they leave it.

Some take the system more or less as it is. They accept negotiated pleas in the ordinary course of events, either because such a system produces good results or because it is inevitable. They might identify some exceptional cases that create an intolerable risk of convicting innocent defendants, or unusual cases where there are special reasons to doubt the knowing and voluntary nature of the defendant's plea. But the mine run of cases, in this view, must be resolved with a heavy dose of plea bargains and a sprinkling of trials.

Then there are those who leave it, arguing that our system's reliance on nego-tiated guilty pleas is fundamentally mistaken. Some call for a complete ban. . . . Others, doubting that an outright ban is feasible, still encourage a clear shift to more short trials to resolve criminal charges. Restoring the criminal trial to its right-ful place at the center of criminal justice might require major changes in public spending, and it might take a lifetime, but these critics say the monstrosity of the current system demands such a change.

This dilemma about plea bargaining—take it or leave it—is a false one. It is based on a false dichotomy. It errs in assuming that criminal trials are the only alter-native to plea bargains. In this erroneous view, fewer plea bargains lead inexorably to more trials; indeed, the whole point in limiting plea bargains is to produce more trials.

[There is] a different choice . . . prosecutorial "screening" as the principal alter-native to plea bargains. Of course all prosecutors "screen" when they make any charging decision. By prosecutorial screening we mean a far more structured and reasoned charge selection process than is typical in most prosecutors' offices in this country. The prosecutorial screening system we describe has four interrelated features, all internal to the prosecutor's office: early assessment, reasoned selection, barriers to bargains, and enforcement.

First, the prosecutor's office must make an early and careful assessment of each case, and demand that police and investigators provide sufficient information before the initial charge is filed. Second, the prosecutor's office must file only appropri-ate charges. Which charges are "appropriate" is determined by several factors. A prosecutor should only file charges that the office would generally want to result in a criminal conviction and sanction. In addition, appropriate charges must reflect reasonably accurately what actually occurred. They are charges that the prosecutor can very likely prove in court. Third, and critically, the office must severely restrict all plea bargaining, and most especially charge bargains. Prosecutors should also recognize explicitly that the screening process is the mechanism that makes such restrictions possible. Fourth, the kind of prosecutorial screening we advocate must include sufficient training, oversight, and other internal enforcement mechanisms to ensure reasonable uniformity in charging and relatively few changes to charges after they have been filed. . . .

Intense prosecutorial screening may produce a small increase in the number of trials, but the more substantial change would likely be an increase in the number of "open" pleas—defendants pleading guilty as charged without any prior negotiated agreement with the prosecutor. . . .

Jurisdictions that implement the screening/bargaining tradeoff will be more honest and more accessible. In hard screening systems, prosecutors will be less likely to "overcharge" or "undercharge." The weakest cases exit early, while those remaining should stand up at trial. A screening-based system should also be more accessible than a system of negotiated pleas, because the public (especially the victims of alleged crimes) will receive clearer and more accurate signals about how the system adjudicates and punishes crimes. The charge is declared publicly from the outset and is easy to evaluate. . . .

We know this practice is viable because it is now operating in a few American jurisdictions, without much controversy and without attracting the attention it deserves. For instance, over the last three decades New Orleans District Attorney Harry Connick has emphasized early screening of cases and has actively discouraged any changes of criminal charges as a result of negotiations after the charges are filed. . . .

[O]ur study of the New Orleans data . . . confirms that a prosecutor can invest serious resources in early evaluation of cases and maintain this practice over the long run. This screening leads to relatively high rates of declination (that is, refusals to prosecute a case after the police recommend charges). When combined with policies discouraging reductions in charges once they are filed, the results are lower levels of negotiated pleas, slightly higher rates of trial, and notably higher rates of open guilty pleas than in typical American jurisdictions. . . .

The screening/bargaining tradeoff should . . . become part of the public, political dialogue about the justice system, especially at election time. The interesting public question should not be the "conviction rate," but rather the "as charged conviction rate." . . . [T]he higher the ratio of "as charged convictions" to "convictions," the more readily a prosecutor should be praised and reelected. A ratio near one—where most convictions are "as charged," *whether they result from guilty pleas or trials*—is the best sign of a healthy, honest, and tough system. The lower the ratio of "as charged convictions" to "convictions" (approaching zero), the more the prosecutor should be criticized for sloppiness, injustice, and obfuscation. A lower ratio might also reflect a prosecutor's undue leniency. . . .

STEPHANOS BIBAS, THE MYTH OF THE FULLY INFORMED RATIONAL ACTOR

31 St. Louis U. Pub. L. Rev. 79, 80-82 (2011)

Perhaps the biggest problem [with plea bargaining] is the assumption that defendants have enough information to rationally forecast their guilt and expected sentences and whether it makes sense to plead guilty. Most defendants do indeed know whether they are guilty of something and whether they have an obvious defense, and most guilty defendants have a reasonable idea of the witnesses and other evidence against them. But criminal cases are much more complex than binary judgments of guilt or innocence. Often, there is a range of criminal charges that can fit a criminal transaction, and prosecutors start out stacking multiple charges only to bargain some away. There also is usually a range of criminal sentences that can fit a particular charge. That is most obvious in unstructured-sentencing systems, in which a judge can give zero to twenty years for a robbery, for example. Structured sentencing systems, though narrower, still preserve a range over which the parties can bargain. In the federal system, for example, the top of the range is at least 25% higher than the bottom. Even when mandatory-minimum penalties can apply, prosecutors may agree to drop charges, let them run concurrently, or recommend reductions below the minimum in exchange for cooperation against other defendants.

Today, criminal convictions not only carry prison terms and fines, but also trigger a range of so-called collateral consequences. A violent-crime conviction may cost a convict his right to carry a gun and thus to work as a police officer or security guard. A sex-offense conviction, even for flashing or public urination, may require a convict to register as a sex offender and not live in large parts of cities near schools, parks, or playgrounds. A drug conviction may count as an aggravated felony, making a noncitizen automatically removable from the country. These consequences can matter greatly to defendants; someone who has lived in America for decades and has family here may care far more about deportation than about a sentence of probation or a few months in jail. But because these consequences are nominally civil, they are not mentioned in plea agreements or plea colloquies. Traditionally, neither judges nor defense lawyers have mentioned them to their clients, as they are imposed by civil agencies and statutes rather than criminal courts. Criminal proceedings remained formally divorced from civil ones, even though collateral consequences have in effect become predictable parts of the total punishment package. And often, especially in cases of moderate severity, that package is negotiable. Traditionally, a criminal defense lawyer might ask to have a one-year sentence bumped up from 365 to 366 days, to qualify his client for good-time credits. But where a one-year sentence is the threshold for deportation, prosecutors and judges often will agree to lower a sentence by a day, to 364 days, if a defense lawyer is knowledgeable enough to request such a favor. Savvy, experienced defense lawyers knew enough to advise their clients and try to bargain over these consequences where possible, but many others did not. . . .

The traditional model has long since become an anachronism for the 95% of defendants who plead guilty. What they need is not a litany of boilerplate warnings about the procedural trial rights they are waiving, as criminal procedure rules require, because for most, a jury trial was never a serious option and the various trial procedures were immaterial. Rather, they need clear information about the substantive outcomes they will face and how good a deal they are receiving. They need to know not only the prison and parole terms but also whether they will lose custody of their children or be deported, forbidden to live at home, or barred from working in their profession.

4.   Some Distributional Consequences of the Criminal Justice System

THE FERGUSON REPORT

U.S. Department of Justice, Civil Rights Division
4 (2015)

Ferguson's law enforcement practices overwhelmingly impact African Americans. Data collected by the Ferguson Police Department from 2012 to 2014 shows that African Americans account for 85% of vehicle stops, 90% of citations, and 93% of arrests made by FPD officers, despite comprising only 67% of Ferguson's population. African Americans are more than twice as likely as white drivers to be searched during vehicle stops even after controlling for non-race based variables such as the reason the vehicle stop was initiated, but are found in possession of contraband 26% less often than white drivers, suggesting officers are impermissibly considering race as a factor when determining whether to search. African Americans are more likely to be cited and arrested following a stop regardless of why the stop was initiated and are more likely to receive multiple citations during a single incident. From 2012 to 2014, FPD issued four or more citations to African Americans on 73 occasions, but issued four or more citations to non-African Americans only twice. FPD appears to bring certain offenses almost exclusively against African Americans. For example, from 2011 to 2013, African Americans accounted for 95% of Manner of Walking in Roadway charges, and 94% of all Failure to Comply charges. Notably, with respect to speeding charges brought by FPD, the evidence shows not only that African Americans are represented at disproportionately high rates overall, but also that the disparate impact of FPD's enforcement practices on African Americans is 48% larger when citations are issued not on the basis of radar or laser, but by some other method, such as the officer's own visual assessment.

These disparities are also present in FPD's use of force. Nearly 90% of documented force used by FPD officers was used against African Americans. In every canine bite incident for which racial information is available, the person bitten was African American.

Municipal court practices likewise cause disproportionate harm to African Americans. African Americans are 68% less likely than others to have their cases dismissed by the court, and are more likely to have their cases last longer and result in more required court encounters. African Americans are at least 50% more likely to have their cases lead to an arrest warrant, and accounted for 92% of cases in which an arrest warrant was issued by the Ferguson Municipal Court in 2013. Available data show that, of those actually arrested by FPD only because of an outstanding municipal warrant, 96% are African American.

Our investigation indicates that this disproportionate burden on African Americans cannot be explained by any difference in the rate at which people of different races violate the law. Rather, our investigation has revealed that these disparities occur, at least in part, because of unlawful bias against and stereotypes about African Americans. We have found substantial evidence of racial bias among police and court staff in Ferguson. For example, we discovered emails circulated by police supervisors and court staff that stereotype racial minorities as criminals, including one email that joked about an abortion by an African-American woman being a means of crime control.

City officials have frequently asserted that the harsh and disparate results of Ferguson's law enforcement system do not indicate problems with police or court practices, but instead reflect a pervasive lack of "personal responsibility" among "certain segments" of the community. Our investigation has found that the practices about which area residents have complained are in fact unconstitutional and unduly harsh. But the City's personal-responsibility refrain is telling: it reflects many of the same racial stereotypes found in the emails between police and court supervisors. This evidence of bias and stereotyping, together with evidence that Ferguson has long recognized but failed to correct the consistent racial disparities caused by its police and court practices, demonstrates that the discriminatory effects of Ferguson's conduct are driven at least in part by discriminatory intent in violation of the Fourteenth Amendment.

JEFFREY A. FAGAN & AMANDA GELLER, FOLLOWING THE SCRIPT: NARRATIVES OF SUSPICION IN *TERRY* STOPS AND STREET POLICING

82 U. Chi. L. Rev. 51, 61, 68, 79-80, 86-87 (2015)

Stop-and-frisk as envisioned by the *Terry* Court was largely a set of distinct "retail" transactions, characterized by individualization, material or visual indicia, and specificity. But the current "wholesale" practice is quite different from the vision of the *Terry* Court. . . . Imagine, then, how individualized suspicion is constructed when police are mandated through institutional pressures to maximize stops. The answer is that it is not. Just as stops have become an administrative regime, so too has suspicion become a de-individuated feature of the encounter. In New York City, approximately 19,000 patrol officers made nearly 5 million street stops from 2004 to 2013, rising from fewer than 100,000 in 2003 to over 685,000 in 2011, before tapering off in late 2012 through 2013. Most stops were concentrated in a relatively small number of neighborhoods with high crime rates, concentrations of non-White residents, and severe socioeconomic disadvantage. The mandate for ever-increasing stops thus created a demand for narratives of suspicion to justify those stops. . . .

The New York City stop-and-frisk data provide an opportunity to assess recurring patterns and narratives of suspicion and to discern whether these patterns show sufficient consistency to take on the characteristics of a script. Data from 4.7 million stops from 2004 to 2012 reveal what officers see in the runup to street stops. First, we can exploit these data on police officers' accounts of the reasons and bases for effecting a *Terry* stop. Second, using the same data, we can assess the extent to which, within the limits of reporting, police officers adhere to *Terry*'s individualization requirement or instead develop recurring and stylized narratives of suspicion. . . .

The scripted nature of this suspicion is demonstrated in Figure 3. To construct this figure, we analyzed the specific locations of each stop and the reported crime rates in the stop's location. We divided the city into quintiles, or 20 percent brackets, in which the lowest quintile includes the safest 20 percent of precincts, and the highest quintile includes the 20 percent with the highest crime-complaint rates. As shown in Figure 3, a stop made in the lowest-crime quintile has a nearly identical

FIGURE 3. PERCENTAGE OF STOPS FOR "HIGH CRIME AREA" AND
"FURTIVE MOVEMENT" BY PRECINCT CRIME QUINTILE

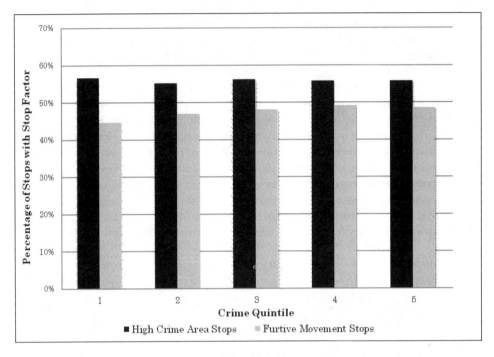

probability as a stop in the highest-crime quintile to be identified as occurring in an area with "high incidence" of crime. Similar results were found in tract-level analyses, suggesting that the propensity to identify an area as "high crime" is not driven by small hot spots in large precincts.

. . . When there is a burden on officers to develop sustainable narratives across innumerable events, social networks become important places to practice and refine plausible narratives of suspicion. The narratives, in turn, become scripts that are widely shared. They are handy cultural tools to simplify complexity. The scripts are "rules" that shape, both cognitively and perceptually, how situations are perceived, how to choose among contingent actions to proceed (or not) with a stop, what language and tone is used, and how to respond to any of several reactions from the suspect. To some extent, such formalities or patterned responses to a heavy workload and set of administrative demands are unavoidable. But when built into everyday practice, the use of scripts, memes, or stylized narratives poses critical challenges for Fourth Amendment regulation.

JENNIFER M. CHACON, OVERCRIMINALIZING IMMIGRATION

102 J. Crim. L. & Criminology 613, 614, 621-23, 631, 635-36 (2012)

Increasingly, our immigration policy provides a paradigmatic example of over-criminalization, whereby governments—both state and local—are creating "too many crimes and criminaliz[ing] things that properly should not be crimes." Like the war on drugs before it, the growing war on unauthorized migration is suddenly and dramatically being waged through the criminal justice system. The distorting effects of this use of state and federal criminal justice systems are only beginning to show. . . .

A wave of state and local immigration ordinances is sweeping across the nation. In recent years, thousands of local governments around the country have debated or enacted ordinances designed to restrict the ability of unauthorized migrants to live and work in their communities. One high-profile example comes from the town of Hazleton, Pennsylvania, where local officials enacted an ordinance that prohibited landlords from renting to noncitizens present without legal authorization and also allowed for the revocation of the business licenses of any business owner who employed an unauthorized worker. Other localities have enacted narrower provisions—such as regulations designed to deter day laborers from soliciting work in public spaces.

States have also joined the fray. . . . The Arizona legislature ignited a national firestorm when it enacted a bill—signed into law by Governor Jan Brewer on April 23, 2010—that greatly expanded the role Arizona's state and local officials play in the enforcement of immigration law. The Support Our Law Enforcement and Safe Neighborhoods Act, often referred to as S.B. 1070, effectively sought to impose criminal liability based on undocumented presence in the United States. Although proponents of the law argued that it mirrors federal immigration law, this was clearly not the case. Among other things, the law made state criminal offenses out of violations that were formally crimes only at the federal level and criminalized conduct that is neither a civil nor a criminal violation under federal law.

S.B. 1070 also "imposes new duties and creates new powers designed to increase [state and local law enforcement's] investigation of immigration status, arrests of removable individuals, reporting of undocumented immigrants to federal authorities, and assistance in removal by delivering removable noncitizens to federal authorities." Major provisions of the law were enjoined by U.S. District Court Judge Bolton, and the injunction was upheld by the Ninth Circuit Court of Appeals and largely upheld by the Supreme Court, with a significant exception. While the case was pending review in the Supreme Court, other states, including Utah, Alabama, and South Carolina, enacted provisions that looked very similar to Arizona's S.B. 1070. . . .

The growth of federal immigration enforcement efforts is manifested clearly in the rise in prosecutions of immigration crimes. In 1993, the number of suspects in matters received by U.S. Attorneys' Offices for immigration offenses was 5,934,112 of whom 5,400 were prosecuted or disposed of by a magistrate. This was only 5.4% of the total number of cases investigated in that year. In these records, immigration offenses are listed as a subcategory of "[o]ther" "[p]ublic-order" offenses. . . .

But the true explosion in criminal immigration enforcement came in the years following the September 11th attacks. Once the INS had been reorganized into three separate agencies under the auspices of the DHS and the money for immigration enforcement began pouring in, arrests and prosecutions for immigration crimes skyrocketed. This trend has continued year after year. . . .

With regard to arrests, the Bureau of Justice Statistics recently recorded that "[b]etween 2005 and 2009, immigration arrests increased at an annual average rate of 23%," and that "[i]mmigration offenses (46%) were the most common of all arrest offenses in 2009, followed by drug (17%) and supervision (13%) violations."

The government is now arresting more than twice as many people annually as it did in 1995, and the bulk of that increase is the result of increased immigration arrests originating with DHS officials.

At present, the number of immigration convictions occurring each month outstrips the annual total of immigration prosecutions in 1993. This is not a deviation, but has been the norm for several years. Between mid-2008 and September 2011, conviction rates were almost always in excess of 6,000 per month, and approached numbers as high as almost 10,000 per month.

5. The Police

HERBERT PACKER, THE LIMITS OF THE CRIMINAL SANCTION

283-284 (1968)

The aggressively interventionist character of much of our criminal law thrusts the police into the role of snoopers and harassers. There is simply no way for the police to provide so much as a semblance of enforcement of laws against prostitution, sexual deviance, gambling, narcotics, and the like without widespread and visible intrusion into what people regard as their private lives. . . .

There are three generic types of police investigatory conduct that are so at odds with values of privacy and human dignity that we should resort to them only under the most exigent circumstances. They are physical intrusion, electronic surveillance, and the use of decoys. Although there arguably are circumstances under which each of the three can justifiably be employed, it is safe to say that any use of the criminal sanction that requires consistent use to be made of any of them should be suspect.

RACHEL HARMON, THE PROBLEM OF POLICING

110 Mich. L. Rev. 761, 762-764, 790 (2012)

Police officers are granted immense authority by the state to impose harm. They walk into houses and take property. They stop and detain individuals on the street. They arrest. And they kill. They do all these things in order to reduce fear, promote civil order, and pursue criminal justice. The legal problem presented by policing is how to regulate police officers and departments to protect individual liberty and minimize the social costs the police impose while promoting these ends.

. . . While courts and commentators have written extensively on the law governing the police, they have in recent decades mostly neglected the problem of regulating them. They have largely treated the legal problem of policing as limited to preventing the violation of constitutional rights and its solution as the judicial definition and enforcement of those rights. The problem of regulating police power through law has been shoehorned into the narrow confines of constitutional criminal procedure. . . . This conventional paradigm is necessarily inadequate to regulate the police.

. . . As the Supreme Court's constitutional criminal procedure doctrine suggests, empirical and causal analysis is central to both defining and protecting constitutional rights, yet courts have limited institutional capacity to engage in that analysis.

In short, the public policy problems presented by the use of police power necessarily extend beyond constitutional law and courts. Protecting rights and balancing competing individual and social interests require a broader set of regulatory tools and institutions. . . . .

The ongoing influence of the conventional paradigm has obscured some of the conceptual preconditions for effectively regulating the police. First, the paradigm limits the regulation of the police to the problem of identifying and enforcing constitutional rights. Yet the problem of regulating the police extends beyond constitutional law to ensuring that the benefits of policing are worth the harms it imposes, including harms not prohibited by the Constitution. The law should promote policing that effectively controls crime, fear, and disorder without imposing unjustifiable and avoidable costs on individuals and communities. . . .

Second, courts have difficulty assessing the incentives affecting police officers, a task central to determining how to encourage police officers to conform their conduct to law. Scholars have studied many determinants and correlates of police conduct, but the conventional paradigm has encouraged the belief that constitutional criminal procedure is the primary legal influence on police officers and departments. In fact, nonconstitutional law plays a much greater role in influencing police officers than has previously been appreciated. . . . [F]or example, courts tailor their interpretation of § 1983 and the exclusionary rule to encourage changes in police behavior, yet civil service law, collective bargaining law, and federal and state employment discrimination law simultaneously discourage the same reforms.

Finally, courts lack the institutional capacity to undertake complex empirical analysis of policing or to constrain the police beyond identifying and enforcing constitutional rights. Because regulating the police requires such capacity, it is clear that courts cannot adequately regulate the police by themselves. Thus, regulating the police requires allocating responsibility among institutional actors to ensure a regime capable of intelligently choosing and efficiently promoting the best ends of policing. . . .

The police are already shaped by law. To be effective, however, legal regulation of the police must be grounded upon a broader conceptual foundation that the conventional paradigm has obscured. Effective governance of the police requires a normative framework for assessing whether constitutionally permissible policing practices properly balance efficacy against individual and social harms. It requires assessing means for influencing police conduct. And it requires allocating responsibility to institutional actors to ensure a regime capable of choosing and promoting the best ends.

JEROME H. SKOLNICK & DAVID H. BAYLEY, COMMUNITY POLICING: ISSUES AND PRACTICES AROUND THE WORLD

49-52 (1988)

One way of comprehending a police department is through a table of organization. Such tables do offer useful, indeed indispensable, information. . . . But however indispensable they might be, tables of organization are limited in the information they offer—they don't tell us anything about the human side of the landscape they describe. The most significant features of police departments—their attitudes, internal divisions, belief systems, traditions, values—cannot be captured by the labelled boxes of a table of organization. . . .

How police officers learn to see the world around them and their role in it has come to be acknowledged by all scholars of police as an indispensable key to understanding the behavior and attitudes of police. "It is a commonplace of the now voluminous sociological literature on police operations and discretion," writes Robert Reiner, "that the rank-and-file officer is the primary determinant of policing where it really counts—on the street."[1] Moreover, . . . there are identifiable commonalities in police culture. . . .

[There is] the perception of *danger* which, although real, is typically magnified. Police officers are sometimes shot at and killed, of course. But the first line of defense against anticipated danger is *suspicion*, the development of a cognitive map of the social world to protect against signs of trouble, offense, and potential threat.

The combination of danger and suspicion leads to a third feature of police culture, namely solidarity or *brotherhood*. Most police tend to socialize with other police. . . . There are any number of reasons for police solidarity. One is that police do not work normal hours. As emergency service workers, they often find themselves in the position of having to work nights, weekends, and other odd hours. Police work time is one of the major stresses of police work. When one's days off are Wednesday and Thursday, one becomes a deviant in the social world and is drawn to socialize with others who are similarly situated.

Another reason is that cops don't feel they fit into many worlds they might occupy. Every cop has a story about how they were stared at or otherwise adversely noted at a party or social occasion. This has been a special problem for young police in the 1970s and 1980s, when many of their peers might light up a joint and pass it around at a festive occasion. When faced with this dilemma, young police will find new friends—among police.

A third reason is the policeman's felt need for support from other police. Police are in fact in dangerous or potentially dangerous situations. When cops, looking for drug dealers, walk through a pool hall occupied by unfriendly young men, they depend on their partners for cover and assistance. But, as Mark Baker comments:

> The real reason most police officers socialize exclusively with other police officers is that they just don't trust the people they police—which is everybody who is not a cop. They know the public generally resents their authority and is fickle in its support of police policy and individual police officers. Older officers teach younger ones that it is best to avoid civilians. Civilians will try to "hurt" the cop in the end, they say.[2] . . .
>
> Students of the police have frequently noted the *machismo* qualities in the world of policing.[3]

Those who are attracted to the occupation are often very young, in chronological age and in maturity of temperament and judgment. . . . Recruits typically have athletic backgrounds, are sports minded, and are trained in self-defense. It is not uncommon for trainees to bulk the upper body—like football players, through weight lifting—so as to offer a more formidable appearance as a potential adversary

1. Robert Reiner, The Politics of the Police (Sussex, England: Wheatsheaf Books, 1985), p. 85.
2. Mark Baker, Cops: Their Lives in Their Own Words (New York: Fawcett, 1985), p. 211.
3. See Robert Reiner, The Politics of the Police, p. 99.

in street encounters. They are also trained to handle a variety of offensive weapons, including deadly weapons. They are taught how to disable and kill people with their bare hands. No matter how many warnings may be offered by superiors about limitations on the use of force, its possible use is a central feature of the police role, and of the policemen's perceptions of themselves.

The training and permission in the use of force combined with the youth of police can well inhibit the capacity of a police officer to empathize with the situation of those being policed in ethnically diverse and low-income neighborhoods. . . . Senior officers are . . . less likely to be macho. . . .

When scholars write about the culture of policing, they usually have in mind the street-wise cop who follows a blue code of solidarity with fellow officers. Street-wise officers are likely to be cynical, tough, skeptical of innovation within management. By contrast, management cops tend to project a vision of policing that is more acceptable to the general public. This concept of two contrasting cultures of policing grew out of research conducted in New York City by Ianni and Ianni (1983), who developed a distinction between "street cops" and "management cops."

The "street-wise" cop is apt to approve of cutting corners, of throwing weight around on the street, of expressing the qualities of in-group solidarity referred to above. Management cops tend to be more legalistic, rule oriented, rational. . . . [S]ome street cops are hard-boiled cynics who deride innovations in policing as needless and unworkable incursions into the true and eternal role of the cop—the one they were socialized into as recruits by a sometimes venerated field training officer. These "street-wise" police, instead of gradually developing a broader perspective, taking advanced degrees in management, law, or criminal justice and so forth, reinforce their post-recruit identity. Unfortunately, this reinforcement sometimes develops into a lifelong occupational vision rooted in an abiding, even growing, bitterness that seems impervious to any sort of hope for change or new ideas.

The cynicism typifying these officers may of course also be present at higher levels of management—after all, . . . all American police begin their career as street cops, and the learning that takes place on the street is never outgrown by many. . . . The innovative management cop employs prior street experience to overcome the resistance of the street cop. By contrast, the self-conception of the traditional street cop remains firmly rooted in his earliest training experiences.

Elizabeth Ruess-Ianni summarizes the difference between the two cultures as follows, based on her study of the New York City Police Department:

> In a sense, the management cop culture represents those police who have decided that the old way of running a police department is finished (for a variety of external reasons, such as social pressures, economic realities of the city, increased visibility, minority recruitment, and growth in size that cannot be managed easily in the informal fashion of the old days) and they are "going to get in on the ground floor of something new." They do not, like the street cops, regard community relations, for example, as "Mickey Mouse bullshit," but as something that must be done for politically expedient reasons if not for social ones.[4]

4. Elizabeth Ruess-Ianni, The Two Cultures of Policing: Street Cops and Management Cops (Brunswick, N.J.: Transaction Books, New Brunswick, 1983), p. 121.

DEBRA LIVINGSTON, POLICE DISCRETION AND THE
QUALITY OF LIFE IN PUBLIC PLACES: COURTS,
COMMUNITIES, AND THE NEW POLICING

97 Colum. L. Rev. 551, 557, 558-561, 670-671 (1997)

On the whole . . . legal scholars have paid inadequate attention to the reemergence of statutes, ordinances, and law enforcement measures aimed at public conduct and, more broadly, the quality of life in public spaces. Moreover, they have virtually ignored the implications of this new focus on quality-of-life concerns for a subject that it profoundly affects—namely, the scope of police discretion in street encounters. This inattention is surprising. After all, the aspiration to constrain police discretion on the street was in large part what prompted legal scholars over thirty years ago to mount a constitutional attack on the vagueness that characterized broadly-worded vagrancy, loitering, breach of peace, and disorderly conduct statutes and ordinances. This scholarly attack helped prompt the judicial invalidation of many such laws and left police departments with considerably less authority to intervene in street-order problems than citizens often assumed to be the case.

The ongoing transformation in the philosophy of American policing, from professional policing to community and problem-oriented policing, will likely continue to fuel interest, among these scholars, in the "order maintenance" activities of police. Such activities are aimed at preserving what might be termed the "neighborhood commons": both tangible community resources like parks, streets, playgrounds, parking lots, and libraries, and the associated intangible interactions among people, both organized and spontaneous, that take place around these resources. Proponents of these new policing strategies have increasingly asserted, as did Jane Jacobs over thirty years ago, that preservation of the neighborhood commons is essential to the vitality and well-being of American cities. . . .

For legal scholars, this new focus on addressing concerns with the quality of life in public places raises anew the tension between traditional rule of law concepts and the order maintenance activities of police. Police intervention to address neighborhood disorder is different, in kind, from the straightforward investigation, arrest, and prosecution of those who have committed serious crimes. First, problems of disorder stem not so much from isolated behaviors as from the coming together of certain conditions: the congruence of behavior, its location and circumstances, its frequency, its intent, and others' reactions. The behavior appropriate in a St. Patrick's Day parade may thus be disruptive on a quiet, residential street. And while a single person loitering on a street corner is unlikely to threaten neighborhood life, a street on which many loiter to complete drug transactions, even apart from their success, is likely to experience decline—to be seen by many as a place where children should not play, and where those with adequate resources should choose not to live. But can the police be authorized to intervene on such a street by dispersing or arresting those loiterers seemingly intent upon the narcotics trade? And can they be trusted to identify those contexts in which intervention is appropriate—that is, to distinguish the quiet residential Sunday morning from St. Patrick's Day on Main Street? Second, police intervention to address neighborhood order is often invisible to formal legal processes, since intervention often begins—and ends—with an admonition to "knock it off" or requests to "quiet down" or "move along." Should police intervene in this way? Should they intervene except by employing their resources to enforce laws against serious crime?

Contrary to the implications of some scholarship in the police literature, the police cannot perform substantial order maintenance tasks without legal authority. At the same time, the many new laws addressing problems of public disorder, even those laws that are far more specific than ones struck down in the 1960s and 1970s, raise many of the same concerns that led courts of that period to invalidate public order laws for vagueness. Courts have thus been tempted to invoke the open texture of vagueness review to facially invalidate even reasonably specific public order laws—a temptation that, when not resisted, retards positive changes in American policing. While it plays an important role in pruning the legal code of outright delegations of authority to police to maintain public order as they deem appropriate, the void-for-vagueness doctrine is itself an inadequate and even potentially destructive mechanism for constraining police discretion in the performance of order maintenance tasks. Courts cannot "solve" the problem of police discretion by invalidating reasonably specific public order laws—as some have attempted—without seriously impairing legitimate community efforts to enhance the quality of neighborhood life. Nevertheless, because the recent legislative trend does raise many of the same concerns that led courts of the 1960s and 1970s to invalidate vague laws, there is a need for renewed focus upon those political, administrative, and other "subconstitutional" controls that might assist in constraining arbitrary police enforcement. The philosophies of community and problem-oriented policing posit a new way of thinking about police and about the exercise of police discretion that themselves suggest ways in which these controls might work.

Policing, like judging, is a complex task, and the prospects and promise of the new policing reforms must at this juncture be deemed uncertain. Policing is not the simple enforcement of law, though law is important to the police role; policing that ignores the ebb and flow of community life does so only at grave peril to both police and the people for whom they work. But there are real and serious questions here. Can police departments identify those among their number "inclined toward self-directed information gathering and analysis, capable of inventive planning, and motivated to work for long-range solutions," and then use such personnel in problem solving? Can departments walk the tightrope between responsiveness to community concerns and outright deterioration in the ideal of evenhanded enforcement associated with the rule of law? "Perhaps it is better in the long run," as one scholar recently put it, "to say that the law should be equally enforced—even though equal enforcement is often unrealistic—than to say that the law should be used by the police to maintain order acceptable to local communities[.]" But if there is promise in these policing reforms, there is also peril.

Courts have little capacity—very little capacity—to constrain police and to control the discretion that they inevitably exercise on streets, in neighborhoods, in the precincts where patrol officers are given their tours of duty, and in the administrative offices in which police enforcement policies are hammered out. The reforms of the 1960s and 1970s established principles from which no thoughtful person now seeks retreat: that police cannot be delegated authority to maintain order as they see fit and that rules governing the conduct of citizens on the street must set forth intelligible limits on enforcement authority. These reforms, however, could not eliminate the significant discretion that police have in order maintenance tasks, nor could they promote the beneficial exercise of that discretion in ways that might enhance rather than imperil the public life of a community. Interpreted too broadly, the open texture of these constitutional reforms could threaten public order by invalidating the reasonable efforts of communities to regulate matters like unreasonable noise, aggressive panhandling, or loitering on a street corner to solicit customers for the sale of drugs. At the same time, the reforms could not ensure that police departments acted fairly, with restraint, and with an abiding respect for the rights of individuals and for constitutional values. The reforms could not solve the problem of police discretion.

Nor can neighborhoods and their police. But perhaps communities and police departments, prompted by the problems that beset them and the new philosophies that point in a different direction, might take up the task—an ongoing one—of better managing police discretion. . . . There is a dense complexity to the problem of public order with which communities are now grappling and to the enduring problem of controlling the police. Perhaps some views from the bottom up—views that begin with the recognition that neighborhoods and police departments will succeed or fail in their efforts to deal with local problems at the local level, in communities and in neighborhoods, where laws are passed and police policies are pursued—might be in order.

6. The Lawyers and the Trial Courts

PAUL B. WICE, CHAOS IN THE COURTHOUSE: THE INNER WORKINGS OF THE URBAN CRIMINAL COURTS

21-24, 63-65 (1985)

The first problem faced by all cities visited[8] was inadequate staffing. Although particular agencies or institutions within each city's criminal justice system may have differing levels of understaffing, all were handicapped in some degree by personnel shortages. . . . These shortages were documented by federal commission studies in 1967 and 1973.[2] . . .

. . . The judges appeared to be most understaffed at the earlier stages of the adjudicative process—initial appearance, preliminary hearing and arraignment. The arraignment court may also be responsible for deciding pretrial motions, scheduling trials, and conducting pre-sentencing hearings in addition to accepting guilty pleas. By the trial stage, the staffing shortages had generally abated to a tolerable level in most cities. . . .

Closely related to the staffing problems, is the serious backlog of cases. . . . The most common method criminal courts utilize in dealing with their caseload and delay problems is the practice of plea bargaining. Despite the negative connotations of this term, it describes a negotiating process which has been taking place within our nation's court systems . . . for many decades. A *plea bargain* is simply an agreement between the defendant (with the advice of his attorney) and the prosecutor, that in exchange for a plea of guilty, he will receive favorable consideration by the

---

8. This book is based on the study of criminal courts in 15 major jurisdictions over a 12-year period. Chaos in the Courthouse 1.—EDS.

2. President's Commission on Law Enforcement and the Administration of Justice, Task Force Report: The Courts (Washington, D.C.: Government Printing Office, 1967); National Advisory Commission on Criminal Justice Goals and Standards, Courts (Washington, D.C.: Government Printing Office, 1973).

court. This consideration usually takes the form of being charged with a less serious crime, which will usually result in a lighter sentence or receiving the minimum punishment allowable for the originally-charged offense. The rationale behind this exchange of favors is that the defendant is given the lesser sentence because of his cooperation with the court in choosing not to go to trial and thereby saving the city a great deal of time and expense. . . .

. . . Various studies have indicated that approximately 75 percent of all defendants indicted for felonies plead guilty.[5] . . .

Since nearly two thirds of all defendants accused of committing a felony are indigent, the state is constitutionally obligated to provide the overwhelming majority of defendants with assistance of counsel. In nearly every city visited, the local courts decided to establish a public defender program in order to meet this mandate. . . .

The two alternatives to the public defender plan, for indigent defendants, are either to rely entirely upon an assigned counsel system—privately-appointed members of the bar who are typically paid on a per hour basis—or a mixed system in which the courts have decided to limit the percentage of cases which the local public defender can handle, and reserve the sizable remainder for private attorneys through an assigned counsel system. Large cities rarely find the assigned counsel system cost-effective (although it is most popular in small cities and rural areas). . . .

In most cities, the defendant first notifies the judge of his indigent status and desire to have a court-appointed lawyer at his initial appearance. . . . The judge rarely inquires into the financial capabilities of the defendant. . . . Most judges seem to feel that if a defendant is willing to settle for a public defender, then he is not likely to be in possession of the funds necessary to hire a private attorney. Rarely is a representative from the public defender's office present at this initial appearance, except in an administrative capacity to commence the paperwork. . . .

Two of the major frustrations facing the indigent defendant who is being represented by a public defender are apparent very early in the process. The first, and for many defendants, the most disheartening, is the absence of choice of attorney. . . .

The second frustration, exacerbating the already noted absence of choice, is the assembly-line system of defense in which the indigent defendant may be assisted by a different attorney at nearly every stage of the proceedings up to the arraignment. This means that the indigent will briefly meet with three or four different public defenders for a few minutes before each of his pretrial proceedings. It is also likely that interviews and meetings outside of court may be with an assortment of different public defenders. . . .

For many defendants, the assembly-line style of operation is another indication that the public defender's office is simply an uncaring bureaucracy which is both financially and emotionally subservient to the criminal court judiciary. . . .

Although I am sure that their clientele would vociferously disagree, I do not believe that the quality of public defender services has suffered. After conducting national studies of both public defender programs and private criminal lawyers, I am in agreement with the findings of nearly all of the empirical research which

---

5. Pasqual DeVito. An Experiment in the Use of Court Statistics, Judicature. 56 (August/September, 1972), p. 56.

concluded that the ultimate case dispositions are not significantly affected by the type of defense.[31] I still concur with the personal conclusions reached in 1978 that

> although the middle 50 percent of public defenders and private attorneys were operating at similar levels of ability and achieving nearly identical results, there were marked differences at the extremes. Thus it was generally agreed by the criminal lawyers that the top 25 percent of private attorneys were clearly superior to the best public defenders, while the bottom 25 percent of the public defenders were believed to be significantly better than the bottom group of private attorneys. [Paul Wice, Criminal Lawyers: An Endangered Species. Beverly Hills, Sage Publications, 1978, p. 201.]

. . . [T]he public defender office may even offer some distinct advantages unavailable to certain private practitioners. Most public defenders have access to their own law libraries, as well as limited use of investigators. Additionally, the public defender is clearly a criminal law specialist. Finally, because of his continual involvement with the prosecutors and judiciary, the public defender can frequently develop a positive working relationship in which the exchange of favors, so necessary to greasing the squeaky wheel of justice, can directly benefit the indigent defendant.

ABRAHAM S. BLUMBERG, THE PRACTICE OF LAW AS CONFIDENCE GAME: ORGANIZATIONAL CO-OPTATION OF A PROFESSION

1 Law & Soc'y Rev. 15, 18-26, 29-31 (1967)

The overwhelming majority of convictions in criminal cases (usually over 90 percent) are not the product of a combative, trial-by-jury process at all, but instead merely involve the sentencing of the individual after a negotiated, bargained-for plea of guilty has been entered. . . .

Organizational goals and discipline impose a set of demands and conditions of practice on the respective professions in the criminal court, to which they respond by abandoning their ideological and professional commitments to the accused client, in the service of these higher claims of the court organization. All court personnel, including the accused's own lawyer, tend to be co-opted to become agent-mediators who help the accused redefine his situation and restructure his perceptions concomitant with a plea of guilty.

Of all the occupational roles in the court the only private individual who is officially recognized as having a special status and concomitant obligations is the lawyer. His legal status is that of "an officer of the court" and he is held to a standard of ethical performance and duty to his client as well as to the court. This obligation is thought to be far higher than that expected of ordinary individuals occupying the various occupational statuses in the court community. However, lawyers, whether privately retained or of the legal-aid, public defender variety, have close and continuing relations with the prosecuting office and the court itself through discreet relations with the judges via their law secretaries or "confidential" assistants. Indeed,

---

31. Jean Taylor et al., An Analysis of Defense Counsel in the Processing of Felony Defendants in San Diego, Denver Law Journal (1972), p. 233.

lines of communication, influence and contact with those offices, as well as with the Office of the Clerk of the court, Probation Division, and with the press, are essential to present and prospective requirements of criminal law practice. Similarly, the subtle involvement of the press and other mass media in the court's organizational network is not readily discernible to the casual observer. Accused persons come and go in the court system schema, but the structure and its occupational incumbents remain to carry on their respective career, occupational and organizational enterprises. The individual stridencies, tensions, and conflicts a given accused person's case may present to all the participants are overcome, because the formal and informal relations of all the groups in the court setting require it. The probability of continued future relations and interaction must be preserved at all costs.

This is particularly true of the "lawyer regulars," i.e., those defense lawyers, who by virtue of their continuous appearances in behalf of defendants, tend to represent the bulk of a criminal court's non-indigent case workload, and those lawyers who are not "regulars," who appear almost casually in behalf of an occasional client. Some of the "lawyer regulars" are highly visible as one moves about the major urban centers of the nation, their offices line the back streets of the courthouses, at times sharing space with bondsmen. Their political "visibility" in terms of local club house ties, reaching into the judge's chambers and prosecutor's office, are also deemed essential to successful practitioners. . . .

. . . The accused's lawyer has far greater professional, economic, intellectual and other ties to the various elements of the court system than he does to his own client. In short, the court is a closed community.

This is more than just the case of the usual "secrets" of bureaucracy which are fanatically defended from an outside view. Even all elements of the press are zealously determined to report on that which will not offend the board of judges, the prosecutor, probation, legal-aid, or other officials, in return for privileges and courtesies granted in the past and to be granted in the future. Rather than any view of the matter in terms of some variation of a "conspiracy" hypothesis, the simple explanation is one of an ongoing system handling delicate tensions, managing the trauma produced by law enforcement and administration, and requiring almost pathological distrust of "outsiders" bordering on group paranoia.

The hostile attitude toward "outsiders" is in large measure engendered by a defensiveness itself produced by the inherent deficiencies of assembly line justice, so characteristic of our major criminal courts. Intolerably large caseloads of defendants which must be disposed of in an organizational context of limited resources and personnel, potentially subject the participants in the court community to harsh scrutiny from appellate courts, and other public and private sources of condemnation. As a consequence, an almost irreconcilable conflict is posed in terms of intense pressures to process large numbers of cases on the one hand, and the stringent ideological and legal requirements of "due process of law," on the other hand. A rather tenuous resolution of the dilemma has emerged in the shape of a large variety of bureaucratically ordained and controlled "work crimes," short cuts, deviations, and outright rule violations adopted as court practice in order to meet production norms. Fearfully anticipating criticism on ethical as well as legal grounds, all the significant participants in the court's social structure are bound into an organized system of complicity. This consists of a work arrangement in which the patterned, covert, informal breaches, and evasions of "due process" are institutionalized, but are, nevertheless, denied to exist.

These institutionalized evasions will be found to occur to some degree, in all criminal courts. Their nature, scope and complexity are largely determined by the size of the court, and the character of the community in which it is located, e.g., whether it is a large, urban institution, or a relatively small rural county court. In addition, idiosyncratic, local conditions may contribute to a unique flavor in the character and quality of the criminal law's administration in a particular community. However, in most instances a variety of stratagems are employed — some subtle, some crude, in effectively disposing of what are often too large caseloads. A wide variety of coercive devices are employed against an accused-client, couched in a depersonalized, instrumental, bureaucratic version of due process of law, and which are in reality a perfunctory obeisance to the ideology of due process. These include some very explicit pressures which are exerted in some measure by all court personnel, including judges, to plead guilty and avoid trial. In many instances the sanction of a potentially harsh sentence is utilized as the visible alternative to pleading guilty, in the case of recalcitrants. Probation and psychiatric reports are "tailored" to organizational needs, or are at least responsive to the court organization's requirements for the refurbishment of a defendant's social biography, consonant with his new status. A resourceful judge can, through his subtle domination of the proceedings, impose his will on the final outcome of a trial. Stenographers and clerks, in their function as record keepers, are on occasion pressed into service in support of a judicial need to "rewrite" the record of a courtroom event. Bail practices are usually employed for purposes other than simply assuring a defendant's presence on the date of a hearing in connection with his case. Too often, the discretionary power as to bail is part of the arsenal of weapons available to collapse the resistance of an accused person. The foregoing is a most cursory examination of some of the more prominent "short cuts" available to any court organization. . . .

The real key to understanding the role of defense counsel in a criminal case is to be found in the area of the fixing of the fee to be charged and its collection. The problem of fixing and collecting the fee tends to influence to a significant degree the criminal court process itself, and not just the relationship of the lawyer and his client. In essence, a lawyer-client "confidence game" is played. . . . Legal service lends itself particularly well to confidence games. . . .

. . . [M]uch legal activity, whether it is at the lowest or highest "white shoe" law firm levels, is of the brokerage, agent, sales representative, lobbyist type of activity, in which the lawyer acts for someone else in pursuing the latter's interests and designs. The service is intangible. . . .

. . . Defense lawyers condition even the most obtuse clients to recognize that there is a firm interconnection between fee payment and the zealous exercise of professional expertise, secret knowledge, and organizational "connections" in their behalf. Lawyers, therefore, seek to keep their clients in a proper state of tension, and to arouse in them the precise edge of anxiety which is calculated to encourage prompt fee payment. Consequently, the client attitude in the relationship between defense counsel and an accused is in many instances a precarious admixture of hostility, mistrust, dependence, and sycophancy. By keeping his client's anxieties aroused to the proper pitch, and establishing a seemingly causal relationship between a requested fee and the accused's ultimate extrication from his onerous difficulties, the lawyer will have established the necessary preliminary groundwork to assure a minimum of haggling over the fee and its eventual payment.

In varying degrees, as a consequence, all law practice involves a manipulation of the client and a stage management of the lawyer-client relationship so that at least an *appearance* of help and service will be forthcoming. This is accomplished in a variety of ways, often exercised in combination with each other. At the outset, the lawyer-professional employs with suitable variation a measure of sales-puff which may range from an air of unbounding self-confidence, adequacy, and dominion over events, to that of complete arrogance. This will be supplemented by the affectation of a studied, faultless mode of personal attire. In the larger firms, furnishings and office trappings will serve as the backdrop to help in impression management and client intimidation. In all firms, solo or large scale, an access to secret knowledge, and to the seats of power and influence is inferred, or presumed to a varying degree as the basic vendible commodity of the practitioners. . . .

The fee is often collected in stages, each installment usually payable prior to a necessary court appearance required during the course of an accused's career journey. At each stage, in his interviews and communications with the accused, or in addition, with members of his family, if they are helping with the fee payment, the lawyer employs an air of professional confidence and "inside-dopesterism" in order to assuage anxieties on all sides. He makes the necessary bland assurances, and in effect manipulates his client, who is usually willing to do and say the things, true or not, which will help his attorney extricate him. Since the dimensions of what he is essentially selling, organizational influence and expertise, are not technically and precisely measurable, the lawyer can make extravagant claims of influence and secret knowledge with impunity. Thus, lawyers frequently claim to have inside knowledge in connection with information in the hands of the D.A., police, probation officials or to have access to these functionaries. Factually, they often do, and need only to exaggerate the nature of their relationships with them to obtain the desired effective impression upon the client. But, as in the genuine confidence game, the victim who has participated is loathe to do anything which will upset the lesser plea which his lawyer has "conned" him into accepting.

In effect, in his role as double agent, the criminal lawyer performs an extremely vital and delicate mission for the court organization and the accused. Both principals are anxious to terminate the litigation with a minimum of expense and damage to each other. There is no other personage or role incumbent in the total court structure more strategically located, who by training and in terms of his own requirements, is more ideally suited to do so than the lawyer. In recognition of this, judges will cooperate with attorneys in many important ways. For example, they will adjourn the case of an accused in jail awaiting plea or sentence if the attorney requests such action. While explicitly this may be done for some innocuous and seemingly valid reason, the tacit purpose is that pressure is being applied by the attorney for the collection of his fee, which he knows will probably not be forthcoming if the case is concluded. Judges are aware of this tactic on the part of lawyers, who, by requesting an adjournment, keep an accused incarcerated a while longer as a not too subtle method of dunning a client for payment. However, the judges will go along with this, on the ground that important ends are being served. Often, the only end served is to protect a lawyer's fee.

The judge will help an accused's lawyer in still another way. He will lend the official aura of his office and courtroom so that a lawyer can stage manage an impression of an "all out" performance for the accused in justification of his fee. The judge and other court personnel will serve as a backdrop for a scene charged with dramatic fire, in which the accused's lawyer makes a stirring appeal in his behalf. With a show of restrained passion, the lawyer will intone the virtues of the accused and recite the social deprivations which have reduced him to his present state. The speech varies somewhat, depending on whether the accused has been convicted after trial or has pleaded guilty. In the main, however, the incongruity, superficiality, and ritualistic character of the total performance is underscored by a visibly impassive, almost bored reaction on the part of the judge and other members of the court retinue.

Afterward, there is a hearty exchange of pleasantries between the lawyer and district attorney, wholly out of context in terms of the supposed adversary nature of the preceding events. The fiery passion in defense of his client is gone, and the lawyers for both sides resume their offstage relations, chatting amiably and perhaps including the judge in their restrained banter. No other aspect of their visible conduct so effectively serves to put even a casual observer on notice, that these individuals have claims upon each other. These seemingly innocuous actions are indicative of continuing organizational and informal relations, which, in their intricacy and depth, range far beyond any priorities or claims a particular defendant may have. . . .

RODNEY J. UPHOFF, THE CRIMINAL DEFENSE LAWYER AS EFFECTIVE NEGOTIATOR: A SYSTEMIC APPROACH

2 Clinical L. Rev. 73-94 (1995)

I.   UNDERSTANDING THE CONTEXT: THE PRESSURE TO PLEA BARGAIN

A. SYSTEMIC PRESSURES TO PLEAD GUILTY . . .

Blumberg undoubtedly is correct that there are criminal defense lawyers of limited ability, zeal or professional commitment who do manipulate their clients into ill-advised plea bargains. Some lawyers do promote their own interests at the expense of their client's best interest. Moreover, Blumberg's analysis highlights the substantial systemic pressures on criminal defense lawyers to behave in a cooperative, non-adversarial manner. And yet, Blumberg's condemnation of criminal defense lawyers as double agents sweeps too broadly. There are simply too many dedicated defense lawyers, too much litigation and too many other variables affecting client decision-making to conclude that manipulative, complicitous criminal defense lawyers are the cause of most plea bargaining. . . .

2. The Pressures on Defendants to Plead Guilty

The decision of many defendants to plead guilty is the product of a number of individual forces and systemic factors which have little to do with the behavior of criminal defense lawyers. Indeed, the zeal or even the availability of counsel may have little [effect] on the defendant's decision. Simply put, a significant number of defendants just want to plead guilty. Few criminal defendants, even those who are innocent, actually want to go to trial. Many who are accused of a crime do not even consider going to trial a viable option.

Criminal defendants offer a variety of reasons to explain their reluctance to go to trial and their interest in a plea bargain. Internal as well as external pressures may shape the defendant's attitude. For many defendants, the prospect of actually going through a trial and having to take the witness stand is very intimidating. Fear, embarrassment, or the risk of adverse publicity drives some defendants to negotiate and to avoid trial. Unquestionably, the risk of a jail sentence or the prospects of a harsher sentence also deters many defendants from viewing a trial as a desirable alternative to pleading guilty. For some, a pessimistic or fatalistic mind-set dampens any enthusiasm for going to trial. Standing up to the state by taking a case to trial is similar to taking on city hall, a Sisyphean task few are willing to readily embrace.

Some defendants, of course, have been through the system before and these prior experiences significantly influence their attitude toward plea bargaining. For some, especially defendants of color, their perception that the system is heavily stacked against them adversely affects their view of a trial as a viable option. For other defendants, many criminal cases just do not seem to be "that big a deal" or are "nothing really to worry about." For these defendants, the time and trouble it would take to fight a particular charge is outweighed by the inconvenience the defendant feels. It is easier and quicker simply to plead guilty and to get the matter resolved rather than spend time going to trial even if the charge is baseless or the prosecution's evidence is very weak. Thus, the defendant's attitude about the charge, his or her other responsibilities and time commitments, financial resources, past experiences and perceptions about the criminal justice system all affect the defendant's ability to resist the pressure to enter a negotiated plea.

Some defendants readily admit their guilt and are reluctant to do anything other than acknowledge responsibility for the crime or crimes committed. Sometimes this reaction is fed by the defendant's religious or moral feelings. In other instances, the defendant's "get it over with" attitude is spurred on by concerns that contesting a charge will have a negative effect on the defendant's family, financial situation or employment status. Such defendants may be unaware of or fail to consider the long-term consequences of a hasty decision to plead guilty. . . .

Many defendants, especially those who have already been through the system, recognize that the criminal justice system encourages the resolution of cases through plea bargaining. The prospect of securing a more lenient sentence, in fact, drives many defendants to want to plead guilty. The defendant who received a significant break in an earlier case may be particularly anxious to enter into a plea bargain. Or the defendant may be savvy enough to know that it is advantageous to deal quickly with the police or prosecutor before other potential defendants or coconspirators do. Indeed, a lawyer bent on finding the facts in an initial interview may be brusquely instructed or directed by a seasoned defendant just to "cut a deal." . . .

Notwithstanding counsel's advice, it is often the defendant, not the so-called "double agent" defense lawyer, who is insistent on working out a plea bargain. In many cases defendants simply recognize that our overburdened criminal justice system has been structured to discourage them from going to trial. Too few criminal defendants can really afford to pay the cost of mounting an effective defense. In some jurisdictions, access to appointed counsel, the quality of indigent defenders and the resources provided to support the defense of the indigent affect the extent to which defendants have a meaningful right to go to trial. The unrepresented defendant or the accused able to scrape up only a minimal retainer faces substantial pressure to plead guilty. Take, for example, the defendant who has used his last $500 to bail himself out and to retain counsel. His lawyer threatens to withdraw unless the defendant pays an additional $2,000 for a trial. Rather than fight the charge, the defendant pleads guilty to save the $2,000 fee. Or he accepts the proffered plea bargain because he simply cannot raise any more money. Thus, economic pressures often eliminate the criminal defendant's right to trial as a viable option.

Those pressures intensify for the defendant who is held in jail unable to make bail. Many defendants, especially first offenders, will agree to almost anything to get out of jail. It is all too common for defendants to enter a guilty plea merely as the quickest means to secure their release from jail. Accordingly, defense counsel's ability to secure her client's release on bond is likely to minimize pressure on the defendant to agree to a poor plea bargain, thereby significantly improving counsel's negotiating position.

3. Judicial and Prosecutorial Pressures

Both trial judges and appellate courts contribute to the systemic pressure on defendants to plea bargain. Judges are increasingly under fire by the public and state legislators who clamor for tougher sentences and an end to the "coddling" of criminals. Trial judges, many of whom are elected, cannot grant defendants too many sentencing concessions without being labeled "soft on crime." Yet, overflowing court dockets and prison overcrowding create conflicting pressure on judges to move cases efficiently while still imposing tough sentences. Plea bargaining enables trial judges to resolve large numbers of cases in an orderly, timely fashion that would not be possible if more cases actually went to trial.

Criminal defendants also are discouraged from challenging questionable rulings on suppression issues or taking marginal cases to trial because appellate review often is a lengthy process in which defendants enjoy only limited success. In addition, the expanded application of the harmless error doctrine, the diminution of the exclusionary rule, the narrowing of the scope of federal habeas corpus relief and the difficulty of showing ineffective assistance of counsel also encourage defendants to settle their cases. The message sent to defendants and defense lawyers, whether intended or not, is to cooperate and not litigate.

Trial judges send a similar message to defendants contemplating a trial: go to trial and if you lose, you will get a stiffer sentence. Even if the defendant is initially unaware of this reality, defense counsel when discussing the defendant's options usually will raise this consideration. The uncertainty of success at trial, combined with the real prospect of a harsher penalty should the defendant lose, makes the trial option for many defendants a risky gamble. Thus, the defendant's fear of jail not only may seriously undercut counsel's ability to project a credible threat to go to trial, but also cripple the client's will to hold out for a better bargain.

Like their indigent defender counterparts, most prosecutors' offices lack sufficient resources to adequately investigate, prepare and try many cases. Prosecutors, therefore, also are subject to considerable pressure to settle the vast majority of cases. Unlike defense lawyers, however, prosecutors retain considerable power and discretion in determining when cases are brought, which cases are dismissed or pushed and how cases are ultimately settled. Courts have given prosecutors broad latitude both in the charging decision and in the bargaining process. The prosecutor often can select from a wide range of potential charges growing out of any criminal episode, which permits the prosecutor to charge one or multiple counts.

In addition, prosecutors generally are free to offer concessions or to threaten additional punishment to force defendants to accept some negotiated deal. Prosecutors are well aware of the allure of a "no jail" recommendation and use it frequently to entice a defendant into a guilty plea in a marginal case, especially if the offer includes a reduction to a misdemeanor charge. Because a prosecutor's sentencing recommendations are readily accepted by most judges and the prosecutor is vested with virtually unfettered charging discretion, it is the prosecutor who really is in the position to dictate the level of punishment meted out to most defendants. . . .

B. RESISTING THE PRESSURE TO CONFORM

The culture in any particular criminal justice system ultimately influences how plea bargaining is conducted in that jurisdiction and how many cases actually go to trial. If in a particular jurisdiction few defense lawyers file motions or take cases to trial, the pressure on other defense lawyers and defendants to follow suit is much greater than in a jurisdiction in which defendants regularly exercise their right to go to trial. A defense lawyer in a jurisdiction in which prosecutors rarely have to make any concessions because few cases are tried may find it more difficult to extract reasonable concessions from the prosecutor, even though the state's case is weak, than defense counsel in a county with a vigorous defense bar. The prosecutor in a county with a timid defense bar may single out the more zealous defense lawyer and refuse to provide her clients the kind of concessions generally provided the more pliant defense lawyers. Defense counsel who stands up to fight in one case may be concerned that the prosecutor will take it out on her other clients. . . .

Thus, the conscientious defense lawyer is often in a precarious position. Defense counsel must attempt to provide zealous representation in a system geared to the efficient resolution of cases which, for the most part, means entering into negotiated settlements. It is the criminal defense lawyer who vigorously investigates the facts, researches the law, raises appropriate and creative motions, demonstrates a willingness to go to trial and competently handles the trial who is providing the representation demanded by the ethical rules and ABA Standards. Yet, counsel who seeks to gain an advantage for her client in the plea bargaining process by engaging in legitimate tactics—such as filing and aggressively litigating discovery motions, suppression motions, requests for jury instructions, and the like—runs the risk of alienating judges and prosecutors primarily concerned about efficiently disposing of the mass of cases on their crowded dockets. Similarly, a good defense lawyer may want to respond to a prosecutor's inappropriate or unjustified threats in the plea bargaining process by refusing to continue to negotiate and going to trial. She may want to do so not only to secure justice for her individual client but also to demonstrate her willingness to go to trial rather than accept a poor plea bargain. Defense counsel may find herself, however, forced to agree to a poor plea bargain despite her efforts, recommendations and desires because ultimately the choice of accepting a proffered settlement is the client's.

It is important to recognize, then, that it is the defendant's interests, attitude and desires, together with various systemic pressures, that frequently put criminal defense lawyers in a difficult and frustrating position. Defense lawyers all too often find themselves representing an unsympathetic defendant with a lengthy criminal record in a case without any apparent defense. The zealous advocate with a case in which the defendant has little or no leverage confronts a daunting challenge. Many defense lawyers have endured the unpleasant task of going to negotiate on behalf of an unemployed recidivist who simply wants to plead guilty and "bargaining" with a particularly hard-headed prosecutor who is perfectly aware that the state's case is virtually unassailable. In such a case, defense counsel may feel more like a beggar than a bargainer, left with little more than the unenviable chore of imploring a mean-spirited prosecutor to be fair or reasonable. . . .

ALEXANDRA NATAPOFF, *GIDEON* SKEPTICISM

70 Wash. & Lee L. Rev. 1049, 1050-1055 (2013)

Ever since Gideon v. Wainwright proclaimed that "any person haled into court, who is too poor to hire a lawyer, cannot be assured a fair trial unless counsel is provided for him," the Supreme Court has quietly established the inverse proposition: if a person had competent counsel, his conviction was probably fair. As the right that ensures that "all other rights of the accused are protected," the right to counsel has become a central lens through which to evaluate the criminal process, and it is often seen not only as a necessary but increasingly sufficient guarantor of core defendant entitlements. The Supreme Court treats counsel as a cure for coercion and inaccuracy; a competently counseled plea is all but unassailable. A convicted defendant who had a lawyer by his side will have a tough time overturning his conviction unless he can show counsel to have been ineffective. In various ways, having a competent lawyer has become a kind of proxy for the conclusion that a defendant was treated fairly by the criminal system.

This conflation of counsel with fair treatment is highly problematic. A person can be convicted in myriad unfair ways unrelated to the presence or absence of counsel. Defendants may have been selected in racially tainted processes, or overcharged by overzealous prosecutors under overbroad laws. Innocent defendants may plead guilty because they cannot afford bail pending trial and will lose jobs, homes, or children by remaining incarcerated, or they may plead because the trial penalty is too great relative to the plea offer. If they do not plead, defendants may be convicted by jurors hostile to their appearance, race, or prior criminal record. Once convicted, they may be sentenced in ways that bear little relation to their personal culpability under mandatory minimum sentencing laws or overly harsh guidelines, or by judges who exercise their discretion subtly affected by racial or other biases. In other words, the treatment, conviction and punishment of individuals may be unfair in ways that their attorney, no matter how skilled, cannot meaningfully address.

Such limitations on the role of counsel are at their height in the misdemeanor context. The petty offense system generates cases and convictions by the millions in a speedy, low-scrutiny process in which outcomes are largely predetermined. Some of the dysfunctions of the misdemeanor process are themselves counsel-related, flowing from staggering caseloads and lack of time that defense counsel have to consult with clients, investigate, or litigate cases. But many other flaws are structural and insensitive to counsel's performance. Police arrest large numbers of young African American men for disorder crimes as a way of managing urban spaces. Prosecutors often convert urban arrests into formal charges with little or no scrutiny, thereby ensuring that urban populations will face the criminal adjudicatory process one way or another. Because poor defendants often cannot make bail, they may have to sacrifice work or child care in order to contest their cases, and therefore plead guilty in large numbers. Punishments for petty offenses are also standardized, expected, and accepted by prosecutors and courts alike so that defendants face strong barriers to individualized consideration. Most of these factors are beyond the control of defense counsel, and even lawyers with time and resources to contest such cases can do little to alleviate the hydraulic pressures on defendants—even innocent ones—to plead.

The classic model of counsel as the guarantor of defendant rights and dignity turns out to be a partial picture. There are some things that defense lawyers are well-situated to handle, and they mostly have to do with litigating evidence and law—in other words, the adversarial process. If the evidence is weak, counsel have litigation weapons to attack the government's case. If police violate the Fourth or Fifth Amendment during an investigation, counsel have constitutional tools to eliminate the evidence obtained. Good defense counsel are well-situated to uncover government errors with respect to law, evidentiary admissibility, guidelines calculations, and the like. Even in petty cases in which there may not be much evidence in the first place, defense counsel can theoretically challenge police accounts or produce witnesses of their own. But these opportunities are by their nature limited. When unfairness flows not from lack of evidence or a government mistake, but from institutional features of the criminal process, defense lawyers have fewer tools to protect their clients. When the process has become more bureaucratic and less adversarial, as it has in the petty offense context, classic adversarial defense weaponry matters less.

To put it another way, when case outcomes actually depend on the law and the evidence, defense counsel can be very powerful. But at the bottom of the penal pyramid where offenses are petty, caseloads immense, and litigation rare, law and evidence exert weak influences. Instead, prosecutorial discretion and institutional habits dominate cases, and defense lawyers are at a structural disadvantage. William Stuntz made this point indirectly when he noted that as law recedes, prosecutors have more power over case outcomes than defense counsel.

7. The Supreme Court

ANTHONY AMSTERDAM, THE SUPREME COURT AND THE RIGHTS OF SUSPECTS IN CRIMINAL CASES

45 N.Y.U. L. Rev. 785, 785-794 (1970)

The impression is widespread that decisions of the Supreme Court of the United States during the past decade have vastly enlarged the rights of criminal suspects and defendants. That impression is not wholly unfounded, but the broad form in which it is generally entertained ignores very significant limitations upon what the Supreme Court can do, and what it has in fact done, to create and enforce such rights. . . .

According to Par Lagerkvist,[1] the role of the Pythia or priestess of the Oracle at Delphi was of incomparable grandeur and futility. This young maiden was periodically lashed to a tripod above a noisome abyss, where her god dwelt and from which

---

1. P. Lagerkvist, The Sibyl (N. Walford transl., 1958).

nauseating odors rose and assaulted her. There, the god entered her body and soul, so that she thrashed madly and uttered inspired, incomprehensible cries. The cries were interpreted by the corps of professional priests of the Oracle, and their interpretations were, of course, for mere mortals the words of the god. The Pythia experienced incalculable ecstasy and degradation; she was viewed with utmost reverence and abhorrence; to her every utterance, enormous importance attached; but, from the practical point of view, what she said did not matter much.

On its tripod atop the system of American criminal justice, the Supreme Court of the United States performs in remarkably Pythian fashion. Occasional ill-smelling cases are wafted up to it by the fortuities of litigation, evoking its inspired and spasmodic reaction. Neither the records nor the issues presented by these cases give the Court a comprehensive view—or even a reliably representative view—of the doings in the dark pit in which criminal suspects, police and the functionaries of the criminal courts wrestle with each other in the sightless ooze. It is not surprising, then, that in these cases the Court should be incapable of announcing judgments which respond coherently to the real problems of the pit. No matter. The significance of the Court's pronouncements—their power to shake the assembled faithful with awful tremors of exultation and loathing—does not depend upon their correspondence with reality. Once uttered, these pronouncements will be interpreted by arrays of lower appellate courts, trial judges, magistrates, commissioners and police officials. *Their* interpretation of the Pythia, for all practical purposes, will become the word of god.

To some extent this Pythian metaphor describes the Supreme Court's functioning in all the fields of law with which the Court deals. But the metaphor has special cogency with regard to the field of criminal procedure and particularly procedure that regulates the rights of suspects in their dealings with police prior to the time of the suspect's first court appearance. Let me explain why this is so and some of the implications of that fact.

First, the Supreme Court, like any other court, lacks the sort of supervisory power over the practices of the police that is possessed by the chief of police or the district attorney. The Court can only review those practices, and thus can only define the rights of suspects subject to those practices, when the practices become an issue in a lawsuit. There are several ways in which police practices may become the subject of a lawsuit. An individual who thinks that he has been mistreated by the police may file a civil action for damages or, in limited circumstances, for an injunction, complaining of false arrest or false imprisonment or assault or the violation of his constitutional rights. But such lawsuits are very rare, and until recently were so rare as to be insignificant, because the obstacles to their maintenance are formidable. Most persons mistreated by the police are marginal types who are quite happy, once out of police clutches, to let well enough alone. Few have the knowledge or resources to obtain the services of a lawyer. Many lawyers who might otherwise be available to them cannot afford to tangle with the police because these lawyers depend upon the good will of the police in other cases (e.g., to protect a divorce client who is being badgered by her estranged husband or to reduce charges against a criminal client) or upon police testimony in other cases (e.g., motor vehicle accident cases) or upon more dubious police services (e.g., referrals).

Juries are not sympathetic to suits against the police; policemen are seldom sufficiently solvent to make verdicts against them worth the trouble to obtain; even fairly solid citizens who sue policemen may have to fear reprisals in the form of traffic tickets, refusals to give needed aid and similar harassments. As a result, civil suits seldom bring police practices under judicial scrutiny. And for reasons too obvious to detail, criminal charges against policemen for mistreatment of citizens are even rarer than civil suits.

So, to date the Supreme Court has had occasion to review the conduct of police almost exclusively in criminal cases where the defendant is the asserted victim of police misconduct. The way in which the issue of police misconduct is presented in such cases almost invariably involves the application of the "exclusionary rule"—that is, an evidentiary rule which disallows the admission against a criminal defendant, at his trial, of certain kinds of evidence obtained in violation of his rights. This exclusionary rule, whose scope and utility in enforcing various constitutional guarantees has been considerably expanded by the Supreme Court in the past decade, is today the principal instrument of judicial control of the police and the principal vehicle for announcement by the courts of the rights of suspects in their dealings with the police.

This last point, in itself, has important implications. Certain police practices (for example, the "booking" and "mugging" of suspects and the assorted minor or major indignities that attend station-house detention of suspects, ranging from the taking of a suspect's belt and shoelaces to vicious beatings) will virtually never become the subjects of judicial scrutiny because they virtually never produce evidence against the suspect. Since there can arise no exclusionary rule challenges to these practices, there have been no significant judicial decisions concerning them; and since (as I shall develop shortly) judicial decisions are almost the only source of legal rights of suspects, suspects do not now have legal rights against or in connection with such practices.

Other police practices (for example, refusing arrested suspects the right to use the telephone or detaining them in pig-sty cells) may or may not come under judicial consideration, depending upon whether they do or do not produce evidentiary consequences such as confessions. For several reasons, judicial control of the latter practices and judicial definition of a suspect's rights in connection with those practices must remain an imprecise, haphazard business. Under the exclusionary rule, judicial attention is focused upon an evidentiary product of the practices rather than upon the practices themselves. For example, a confession will ordinarily be the product of several such practices and of other adventitious circumstances such as the suspect's age and psychological makeup, the nature of police interrogation, etc. Consequently, a judicial ruling admitting or excluding it will seldom give occasion for a clear-cut pronouncement concerning the legality of any one of the underlying practices. Moreover, because these practices themselves are not the focus of the litigation, they will usually be imperfectly explained and explored in the record made before the courts. Courts which pass judgment on them may do so half-sightedly; or, realizing this danger, the courts may strive to avoid passing judgment upon practices that they know they do not understand. The result, once again, is that courts are unable to speak clearly concerning any particular or specific rights of a criminal suspect. Still less are they able to develop systematically any comprehensive canon or register of suspects' rights in the context of the entire range of police practices that affect the suspect.

Second, the Supreme Court of the United States is uniquely unable to take a comprehensive view of the subject of suspects' rights. In part its inability is simply a function of the Court's workload. Saddled with a back-breaking docket and properly occupied with other matters of grave national importance, the Court can only hear three or four cases a year involving the treatment of criminal suspects by the police.

Workload is not the Court's only problem. I have said earlier that fortuities determine which criminal cases reach the Supreme Court. Because police practices are ordinarily challengeable only through the exclusionary rule and because the exclusionary rule ordinarily comes into play only at trial following a plea of not guilty, police treatment of a suspect is effectively insulated against Supreme Court review in that large percentage of criminal convictions (as many as 90 percent in some jurisdictions) that rest upon a guilty plea.

Guilty pleas may be entered for many reasons in cases that involve serious questions of violations of a suspect's rights in the precourt phases. The arguable violations may have had no evidentiary consequences. The prosecution may have sufficient evidence for conviction apart from that obtained through the arguable violations. The defendant may be detained pending trial in default of bail on a charge for which a probationary or "time-served" sentence is likely, so that he will be imprisoned longer awaiting trial on a plea of not guilty than he would as a result of a quick guilty plea. The prosecutor may offer an attractive plea bargain, or the known sentencing practices of the trial judge may promise similar consideration for a guilty plea. Obviously, these factors that determine the entry of a guilty plea do not systematically send to trial a selection of cases which present the courts with any comprehensive set of issues relative to suspects' rights.

Additional selective factors prevent many of the cases that are tried from being appealed or from being carried all the way to the Supreme Court. Factual findings by the trial judge concerning contested police conduct frequently obscure or entirely obstruct the presentation to appellate courts of issues relating to that conduct. A convicted defendant cannot challenge on appeal any treatment by the police that the trial court, crediting incredible police denials, finds did not occur. (For example, suspects invariably "trip" and strike their heads while entering their cells; they are never shoved against the bars by police.) Also, the trial court may admit the police conduct but credit incredible explanations of it. (For example, the humiliating anal examinations to which some suspects are subjected in police stations are justified as "weapons searches" on police testimony that such suspects are known to conceal razor blades between their buttocks.) Finally, the trial court may admit and resolve against the defendant an issue relating to the legality of police conduct, then sentence him so lightly that an appeal is not worthwhile. (Some trial judges will impose light sentences in cases in which they have made dubious evidentiary rulings, thereby "buying off" appeals.) In any event the presentation of a convicted defendant's appeal—still more, the taking of his case to the Supreme Court—depends upon the energy, dedication and painstaking care of his lawyer, commodities understandably scarce on the part of overworked public defenders or private lawyers conscripted without compensation to represent the indigents who constitute the bulk of convicted persons.

For these reasons, the Supreme Court simply never gets to see many of the police practices that raise the most pervasive and significant issues of suspects' rights. The cases which do come to the Court are selected by a process that can only be described as capricious insofar as it may be relied upon to present the Court any opportunity for systematic development of a body of legal rights of individuals in the police, or precourt, phases of criminal proceedings. Therefore, the Court's ability to serve as architect of such a body of rights is woefully slight.

Third, the Court is further disabled by the fact that almost the only law relating to police practices or to suspects' rights is the law that the Court itself makes by its judicial decisions. Statutes and administrative regulations governing these matters are virtually nonexistent. The ubiquitous lack of legislative and executive attention to the problems of police treatment of suspects both forces the Court into the role of lawmaker in this area and makes it virtually impossible for the Court effectively to play that role.

This point has been largely ignored by the Court's conservative critics. The judicial "activism" that they deplore, usually citing the Court's "handcuffing" of the police, has been the almost inevitable consequence of the failure of other agencies of law to assume responsibility for regulating police practices. In most areas of constitutional law the Supreme Court of the United States plays a back-stopping role, reviewing the ultimate permissibility of dispositions and policies guided in the first instance by legislative enactments, administrative rules or local common-law traditions. In the area of controls upon the police, a vast abnegation of responsibility at the level of each of these ordinary sources of legal rulemaking has forced the Court to construct *all* the law regulating the everyday functioning of the police. Of course, the Court has responded by being "activist"; it has had to. Its decisions have seemed wildly "liberal" because the only other body of principles operating in the field, against which the Court's principles may be measured, are the principles under which individual policemen act in the absence of any legal restraint.

This same subconstitutional lawlessness which forces the Court to act also prevents it from acting informedly. When the Court reviews the operation of legislation or of administrative regulations or of common-law rules governing, for example, criminal trial procedure, its consideration of the constitutional issues raised is informed and greatly assisted by the very fact that it *is* legislation or a regulation or a rule of some sort that is in question. Because the rule is articulated in more or less general terms, its contour is more or less visible; its relations and interactions with the rules are more or less perceptible, and some of the judgments and policies that underlie or oppose its acceptance are more or less intelligible. However, when the Court reviews conduct, such as police conduct, that is essentially rule-less, it is seriously impeded in understanding the nature, purposes and effects of what it is reviewing. Its view of the questioned conduct is limited to the appearance of the conduct on a particular trial record or records—records which may not even isolate or focus precisely upon that conduct. The Court cannot know whether the conduct before it is typical or atypical, unconnected or connected with a set of other practices or—if there is some connection—what is the comprehensive shape of the set of practices involved, what are their relations, their justifications, their consequences.

Operating thus darkly, the Court is obviously deprived of the ability to make any coherent response to, or to develop any organized regulation of, police conduct. Nor can the Court predict or understand the implications of any rule of constitutional law that it may itself project into this well of shadows. If the Court announces a decision striking down or modifying, for example, some rule of criminal trial practice, it can reasonably foresee how a trial will be conducted following its decision since the decision will operate within a system governed by other visible and predictable rules. But if the Court strikes down a police practice, announces a "right" of a criminal suspect in his dealings with the police, God only knows what the result will be.[9] Out there in the formless void, some adjustment will undoubtedly be made to accommodate the new "right," but what the product of this whole exercise will be remains unfathomable. So, again, the Court is effectively disarmed.

Fourth, when and if the Supreme Court ventures to announce some constitutional right of a suspect, that "right" filters down to the level of flesh and blood suspects only through the refracting layers of lower courts, trial judges, magistrates and police officials. All pronouncements of the Supreme Court undergo this filtering process, but in few other areas of law are the filters as opaque as in the area of suspects' rights.

Let there be no mistake about it. To a mind-staggering extent—to an extent that conservatives and liberals alike who are not criminal trial lawyers simply cannot conceive—the entire system of criminal justice below the level of the Supreme Court of the United States is solidly massed against the criminal suspect. Only a few appellate judges can throw off the fetters of their middle-class backgrounds—the dimly remembered, friendly face of the school crossing guard, their fear of a crowd of "toughs," their attitudes engendered as lawyers before their elevation to the bench by years of service as prosecutors or as private lawyers for honest, respectable business clients—and identify with the criminal suspect instead of with the policeman or with the putative victim of the suspect's theft, mugging, rape or murder. Trial judges still more, and magistrates beyond belief, are functionally and psychologically allied with the police, their co-workers in the unending and scarifying work of bringing criminals to book.

These trial judges and magistrates are the human beings that must find the "facts" when cases involving suspects' rights go into court (that is, when police treatment of a suspect is not conclusively masked behind a guilty plea or ignored by a defense lawyer too overworked or undercompensated to develop the issues adequately). Their factual findings resolve the inevitable conflict between the testimony of the police and the testimony of the suspect—usually a down-and-outer or a bad type, and often a man with a record. The result is about what one would expect. Even when the cases go to court, a suspect's rights as announced by the Supreme Court are something he has, not something he gets.

But, of course, for the reasons mentioned previously, most cases do not go to court. In these cases, the "rights" of the suspect are defined by how the police are willing to treat him. With regard to matters of treatment that have no evidentiary consequences and hence will not be judicially reviewable in exclusionary rule proceedings, the police have no particular reason to obey the law, even if the Supreme Court has had occasion to announce it. With regard to police practices that may have evidentiary consequences, the police are motivated to obey the law only to the extent that (1) they are more concerned with securing a conviction than with some other police purpose which is served by disobeying the law (in this connection, it is worth noting that police departments almost invariably measure their own efficiency in terms of "clearances by arrest," not by conviction), and (2) they think that they can secure the evidence necessary for conviction within the law.

---

9. One possible result is that prosecutors may offer greater concessions to defendants during plea bargaining. If a bargain is too good to refuse, the defendant may forgo the opportunity to challenge a police practice or assert a constitutional right. To the extent that this occurs, "what the due process revolution will have gained is simply shorter sentences." D. Oaks & W. Lehman, A Criminal Justice System and the Indigent 80 (1968).—EDS.

Police work is hard work; it is righteous work; it is combative work, and competitive. Policemen are undereducated, they are scandalously underpaid, and their personal advancement lies in producing results according to the standards of the police ethic. When they go to the commander's office or to court, their conformity to this ethic is almost always vindicated. Neither their superiors nor the judges whom they know nor the public find it necessary to impede the performance of their duties with fettering rules respecting rights of suspects. If the Supreme Court finds this necessary, it must be that the Court is out of step. So its decisions—which are difficult to understand anyway—cannot really be taken seriously.

This concludes my observations concerning the Supreme Court's power to guarantee rights of criminal suspects in any other than an unworldly sense. The idealist would conclude from what I have said that the priests surrounding the Pythia are unfaithful to their priesthood. The cynic would conclude that the whole damned system is corrupt. I forgo such judgments and conclude only that Supreme Court power to enlarge the rights of suspects is very, very limited. . . .

. . . I do not mean to suggest that Supreme Court decisions respecting suspects' and defendants' rights are unimportant. Like the Pythia's cries, they have vast mystical significance. They state our aspirations. They give a few good priests something to work with. They give some of the faithful the courage to carry on and reason to improve the priesthood instead of tearing down the temple.

Also, they have *some* practical significance. With the Pythia shrieking underground, the priests may pervert the word of god, but they cannot ignore it entirely, nor entirely silence those who offer interpretations of it different from their own. Indeed, fear lest these alternative explanations gain popular support may cause the priests to bend a little in their direction.

So it is worth the effort to examine what the Supreme Court has pronounced concerning suspects' and defendants' rights. . . .[10]

8.   The Role of State Constitutions and State Constitutional Law

WILLIAM J. BRENNAN, JR., STATE CONSTITUTIONS AND THE PROTECTION OF INDIVIDUAL RIGHTS

90 Harv. L. Rev. 489, 489-497 (1977)

Reaching the biblical summit of three score and ten seems the occasion—or the excuse—for looking back. Forty-eight years ago I entered law school and forty-four years ago was admitted to the New Jersey Bar. In those days of innocence, the preoccupation of the profession, bench and bar, was with questions usually answered by *application* of state common law principles or state statutes. Any necessity to consult federal law was at best episodic. But those were also the grim days of the Depression, and its cure was dramatically to change the face of American law. The year 1933 witnessed the birth of a plethora of new federal laws and new federal agencies

---

10. For more on the relationship between Supreme Court decisionmaking and the operation of the criminal justice system, see Weisberg, Foreword: Criminal Procedure Doctrine: Some Versions of the Skeptical, 76 J. Crim. L. & Criminology 832 (1985).—EDS.

developing and enforcing those laws; ones that were to affect profoundly the daily lives of every person in the nation.

In recent years, however, another variety of federal law—that fundamental law protecting all of us from the use of governmental powers in ways inconsistent with American conceptions of human liberty—has dramatically altered the grist of the state courts. Over the past two decades, decisions of the Supreme Court of the United States have returned to the fundamental promises wrought by the blood of those who fought our War between the States, promises which were thereafter embodied in our fourteenth amendment—that the citizens of all our states are also and no less citizens of our United States, that this birthright guarantees our federal constitutional liberties against encroachment by governmental action at any level of our federal system, and that each of us is entitled to due process of law and the equal protection of the laws from our state governments no less than from our national one. Although courts do not today substitute their personal economic beliefs for the judgments of our democratically elected legislatures, Supreme Court decisions under the fourteenth amendment have significantly affected virtually every other area, civil and criminal, of state action. And while these decisions have been accompanied by the enforcement of federal rights by federal courts, they have significantly altered the work of state court judges as well. This is both necessary and desirable under our federal system—state courts no less than federal are and ought to be the guardians of our liberties.

But the point I want to stress here is that state courts cannot rest when they have afforded their citizens the full protections of the federal Constitution. State constitutions, too, are a font of individual liberties, their protections often extending beyond those required by the Supreme Court's interpretation of federal law. The legal revolution which has brought federal law to the fore must not be allowed to inhibit the independent protective force of state law—for without it, the full realization of our liberties cannot be guaranteed.

Of late, however, more and more state courts are construing state constitutional counterparts of provisions of the Bill of Rights as guaranteeing citizens of their states even more protection than the federal provisions, even those identically phrased. This is surely an important and highly significant development for our constitutional jurisprudence and for our concept of federalism. I suppose it was only natural that when during the 1960s our rights and liberties were in the process of becoming increasingly federalized, state courts saw no reason to consider what protections, if any, were secured by state constitutions. It is not easy to pinpoint why state courts are now beginning to emphasize the protections of their states' own bills of rights. It may not be wide of the mark, however, to suppose that these state courts discern, and disagree with, a trend in recent opinions of the United States Supreme Court to pull back from, or at least suspend for the time being, the enforcement of the *Boyd* principle with respect to application of the federal Bill of Rights and the restraints of the due process and equal protection clauses of the fourteenth amendment.

The essential point I am making, of course, is not that the United States Supreme Court is necessarily wrong in its interpretation of the federal Constitution, or that ultimate constitutional truths invariably come prepackaged in the dissents, including my own, from decisions of the Court. It is simply that the decisions of the Court are not, and should not be, dispositive of questions regarding rights guaranteed by counterpart provisions of state law. Accordingly, such decisions are not mechanically applicable to state law issues, and state court judges and the members of the bar seriously err if they so treat them. Rather, state court judges, and also practitioners, do well to scrutinize constitutional decisions by federal courts, for only if they are found to be logically persuasive and well-reasoned, paying due regard to precedent and the policies underlying specific constitutional guarantees, may they properly claim persuasive weight as guide-posts when interpreting counterpart state guarantees. I suggest to the bar that, although in the past it might have been safe for counsel to raise only federal constitutional issues in state courts, plainly it would be most unwise these days not also to raise the state constitutional questions.

BARRY LATZER, TOWARD THE DECENTRALIZATION OF CRIMINAL PROCEDURE: STATE CONSTITUTIONAL LAW AND SELECTIVE INCORPORATION

87 J. Crim. L. & Criminology 63, 63-66, 68 (1996)

When one surveys the growing body of criminal procedure cases in which the decision is grounded in a state constitutional provision, a rather startling trend becomes manifest. It is increasingly evident that at some time during the early years of the next century virtually every significant federal constitutional criminal procedure right will have been duplicated or expanded as a matter of state law by the appellate courts of most of the states. That is, the *same* rights that *defendants* now enjoy as a *result of* United States Supreme Court cases construing the federal Bill of Rights, or an even broader state-law-based version of those rights, will be established in most of the states by cases construing state bills of rights. Little if any thought has been given to the implications of this development for constitutional law in the United States, or on the relations between state courts and the United States Supreme Court.

For openers, consider this question: if defendants' rights are protected by state law, why is there a need for redundant federal law? Why provide federal protections where state rights exist, especially in light of the fact that the state rights are as broad or broader? This is in part, of course, a question about the Supreme Court's incorporation policy by which federal rights have been applied to the states through the Fourteenth Amendment Due Process Clause. The stock answer is that together, the federal rights established through incorporation and the rights established through interpretation of state constitutions afford a double-barreled protection for individual rights in America, and we all benefit from such dual assurances. Upon close examination, however, rights-redundancy has distinct disadvantages.

There can be little question that incorporation forced the states to adopt uniform procedures without regard to local needs. In the decades since the 1960s, when the Supreme Court "selectively" incorporated nearly all of the criminal procedure rights in the Bill of Rights, the state courts have had little choice but to give force to these federal procedures (absent broader state rights). No matter how costly, no matter how inefficient, no matter how difficult to implement, no matter how much injustice they might cause, and no matter how inappropriate to local circumstances they might be, the state courts have had to give effect to these federal procedural rights. These disadvantages of incorporation were acknowledged even in the 1960s, but they were believed to be outweighed by one important value: equality. Whatever the disadvantages in stifling state uniqueness, independence, and freedom to experiment, the advantage of uniform treatment of defendants throughout the United States, at least with respect to the fundamental rights of the Bill of Rights, seemed to justify incorporation.

But let us be candid. Incorporation was also predicated upon an assumption—a very negative assumption—about the states, and especially about state courts. The assumption was that some state courts were chronically, and virtually all state courts were occasionally, backward. Without the Supreme Court to stand over them, ready to review and reverse, the state *courts* would fail to provide the minimal rights that all defendants were entitled to at all times. In short, incorporation was motivated by the Mississippi Problem: the assumption that the state bench was, at its worst racist and incompetent, and merely competent most of the time. . . .

[T]he Mississippi Problem is history. . . . [T]he state courts are no longer rights-antediluvians, and . . . therefore an entire set of assumptions underlying incorporation has eroded. The proof of the change in the state courts lies in their eagerness to protect federal constitutional rights, but even more, in the development of state constitutional law. State constitutionalism has not only created rights-redundancy, it has undermined the very reasons for that redundancy. It gives the lie to the assumption that the state bench is rights-backward. Unlike federal constitutional law, which is imposed upon the state courts, state constitutional law is a matter of choice. Whereas state courts must enforce federal procedural rights incorporated into due process, they need not provide equivalent state constitutional rights. State constitutional rights need not be as protective as comparable federal rights, and they certainly do not have to be more protective, as they so often are. State constitutional law epitomizes the change in the attitude and orientation of state judges. It shows that state courts are now every bit as rights-sensitive as the United States Supreme Court, if not more so.

. . . [O]nly those procedures that are both fundamental and required by the Bill of Rights, or are at least demonstrably essential to the implementation of a fundamental right in the Bill of Rights, may be imposed upon the states. Where a procedure is none of the above it is not a proper part of due process and the Supreme Court has no authority to compel the state courts to adopt it. Where a previously incorporated procedure is challenged and it cannot be proven essential to a fundamental right, it should be disincorporated, by which I mean that the incorporation decision should be reversed and the procedure should no longer be required by the Fourteenth Amendment Due Process Clause.

Chapter 2

The Idea of Due Process

One of the defining characteristics of the modern state is its monopoly on criminal law enforcement. Government officials, not private individuals, investigate, apprehend, try, and punish criminals. Much of this business is routine and bureaucratic, but some of it is terrifying, and it can be brutal. Suspects' homes and cars must be searched (and the searches can be rough); arrests must be made, sometimes by force; defendants must be incarcerated. Giving the government a monopoly on that kind of power may be necessary, but it is also very dangerous—consider the use of the phrase "police state" to describe less-than-free societies. Police, prosecutors, and the courts can do enormous good: They are the difference between a decent society and an unlivable one. But they can also do enormous harm.

The basic goal of the law of criminal procedure is to limit the harm without too severely limiting the good. In our system, the entity that does most of the limiting is courts. Most of the law of criminal procedure is constitutional, and American constitutional law is largely judge-defined. Which means that judges—and, especially, Supreme Court Justices—are the primary generators of rules for regulating the behavior of police, prosecutors, defense attorneys, and the other actors who administer the criminal process. That explains why books like this one devote so much space to Supreme Court opinions: Those opinions define what Henry Friendly properly labeled our constitutional code of criminal procedure.[1]

All this constitutional regulation begins with the idea of due process: When the state uses its coercive machinery to catch and punish criminals, it must treat people fairly, even the people it wishes to punish. That idea probably underlies the law of criminal procedure in all free societies. In ours, the connection is particularly clear, since the law of criminal procedure begins not only with the idea but with the phrase, "due process of law." The Fifth Amendment bars the federal government from depriving anyone of "life, liberty, or property" without it; the Fourteenth Amendment applies that same prohibition to the states. Since the criminal justice system is in the business of depriving people of liberty and property (and occasionally deprives them of life itself), those constitutional bans naturally have their most frequent application to criminal procedure.

That last point deserves emphasis. An enormous amount of ink has been spilled debating the proper meaning of the Due Process Clauses of the Fifth and Fourteenth Amendments—the subject is central to most constitutional law courses. Those debates usually focus on things like economic regulation (see Lochner v. New York, 198 U.S. 45 (1905)) and administrative law (see Mathews v. Eldridge, 424 U.S. 319 (1976)), birth control (see Griswold v. Connecticut, 381 U.S. 479 (1965)), abortion

---

1. See Henry J. Friendly, The Bill of Rights as a Code of Criminal Procedure, 53 Cal. L. Rev. 929 (1965). It should be noted that Friendly thought this constitutional code was a bad development—that it risked stifling reform efforts by other, nonjudicial actors.

(see Roe v. Wade, 410 U.S. 113 (1973)), and gay rights (see Lawrence v. Texas, 539 U.S. 558 (2003)). But the Due Process Clauses have had their greatest impact not in these places, but in criminal procedure. At the end of 2013, almost 2.1 million men, and about 210,000 women, were incarcerated in the United States; counting probationers and parolees as well, nearly 7 million persons were under the direct supervision of the criminal justice system.[2] The legal system that put them there is filled with rules that have their origins in the Fourteenth Amendment's Due Process Clause. And the question whether those rules ensure fair punishment begins with the idea of due process.

A Brief History

The relationship between that idea and the American criminal justice system has a long and strange history. Broadly speaking, the history has three phases. The first phase lasts from independence to the passage of the Fourteenth Amendment; the second extends to the 1960s; the third runs to the present.

The first phase is when the criminal justice system as we know it came into being. In 1776 (or 1787 or 1791—the choice of starting date does not matter here),[3] career public prosecutors basically didn't exist; prosecution was either the crime victim's job, the constable's job, or the job of some private lawyer serving as a temporary public advocate. Police forces didn't exist either; constables and sheriffs performed their law enforcement task largely through the aid of private parties.[4] There seems to have been no plea bargaining—the best history of that topic to date puts its origins in the early nineteenth century.[5] Criminal law, the body of rules that define the elements of crimes, had little meaning, since juries could decide what the law was on an ad hoc basis.[6] And imprisonment for crime was rare; penitentiaries were still a half-century in the future.[7] Many of the most basic, taken-for-granted features of contemporary criminal justice were absent at the time of the Founding—indeed, they were unimaginable.

By 1868, the year the Fourteenth Amendment was ratified, all that had changed, and changed dramatically. Public prosecutors, police forces, plea bargains, and prisons were all common. Criminal law was defined by a mix of courts and legislatures, just as it is today. The criminal justice system of 1868—an interlocking set of public institutions that managed large numbers of cases and administered punishment to large numbers of people—would be quite recognizable to us today, for the system then and the system now share most basic features.

2. Bureau of Justice Statistics, U.S. Department of Justice, Correctional Populations in the United States, 2013, available online at http://www.bjs.gov/content/pub/pdf/cpus13.pdf.

3. Independence was declared in 1776, the convention that produced our Constitution was held in 1787, and the Bill of Rights was ratified in 1791. Whichever of these is the relevant date, the statements in the text hold true.

4. See generally Peter Charles Hoffer, Law and People in Colonial America 80-89 (1992).

5. See George Fisher, Plea Bargaining's Triumph, 109 Yale L.J. 857 (2000).

6. See, e.g., William E. Nelson, The Eighteenth-Century Background of John Marshall's Constitutional Jurisprudence, 76 Mich. L. Rev. 904 (1978).

7. At the time of the Founding, penitentiaries were first being used in England. See George Fisher, The Birth of the Prison Retold, 104 Yale L.J. 1235 (1994). The widespread use of incarceration in America began only in the 1820s and 1830s. See David J. Rothman, Perfecting the Prison: United States, 1789-1865, in The Oxford History of the Prison 100 (Norval Morris & David J. Rothman eds., 1998).

In other words, when the Constitution (including the Bill of Rights) was written, no criminal justice system in the modern sense existed. Constitutional norms came first; the system came later. Given that timing, it would hardly be surprising if there was some tension between the norms and the system.

All the more so, since the criminal justice system evolved in the nineteenth century with basically no input from constitutional law. The Bill of Rights included a number of rules that were specifically about criminal procedure—the Fifth Amendment's ban on double jeopardy, requirement of indictment by grand jury, and privilege against self-incrimination, the Sixth Amendment's rights to counsel and trial by jury, the Eighth Amendment's ban on cruel and unusual punishments. But like the rest of the Bill of Rights, those criminal procedure rules applied only to the federal government. See Barron v. Baltimore, 32 U.S. 243 (1833). And the federal government did very, very little in the way of criminal law enforcement—as late as 1904, the federal government incarcerated only 1,641 people, a mere 3 percent of the number of state prisoners. See Margaret Werner Cahalan, Historical Corrections Statistics in the United States, 1850-1984, at 29 tbl. 3-2 (1986). State constitutions seem not to have played any particular role either, perhaps because criminal appeals were still so unusual. The criminal justice system that emerged in the nineteenth century was generated from the bottom up, not from the top down; institutions like public prosecutors and police forces sprang up locally without any overall design and without any constitutional regulation. The same was true of practices like plea bargaining.

Enter the Fourteenth Amendment. The Fourteenth Amendment's ban on deprivations of life, liberty, or property without due process of law, unlike the similar ban in the Fifth Amendment, applied to the *states*. Then as now, the states are the locus of the huge majority of criminal law enforcement. Thus, though there is no reason to believe its authors viewed it this way, the Fourteenth Amendment's Due Process Clause amounted to a textual invitation to courts to define some limits on the newly emerged criminal justice system, by defining what a fair criminal process must entail.

Beginning with Hurtado v. California, 110 U.S. 516 (1884), reprinted at page 66, infra, the Supreme Court began accepting that invitation; for the next 75 years, the Court engaged in the business of placing constitutional limits on the criminal process, with the limits anchored in due process. The results are described in the notes following *Hurtado*. For now, it is enough to note that the limits were both few and vague. By 1960, there were at most a handful of things state criminal justice systems were clearly not allowed to do—they could not run mob-dominated trials;[8] they could not pay judges by the conviction;[9] they could not beat confessions out of suspects[10]—but otherwise, they were subject only to the amorphous notion that whatever they did had to comply with "fundamental fairness," which seemed to permit anything that did not "shock the conscience" of the judiciary. What any of that meant was a mystery, apparently even to the Justices, but what it did *not* mean was a substantial body of law regulating the criminal process. There was a law of due process in 1960, but it barely deserved the label "law," and it hardly ensured a fair process.

---

8. Moore v. Dempsey, 261 U.S. 86 (1923).
9. Tumey v. Ohio, 273 U.S. 510 (1927).
10. Brown v. Mississippi, 297 U.S. 278 (1936).

The 1960s at least remedied the first of those two deficiencies: At the end of that decade, we had, for the first time, a large law of constitutional criminal procedure. The 1960s saw a series of major reforms in the criminal justice system, and the reforms were both based on federal constitutional law and driven by the Supreme Court. But these reforms had a different constitutional basis than the sporadic limits the Court had imposed between 1884 and 1960. For the most part, as it sought to rein in what it saw as an abusive criminal justice system, Earl Warren's Supreme Court relied not on due process but on the Bill of Rights. Limits on search and seizure and police interrogation, the right to counsel, the privilege against self-incrimination, the ban on double jeopardy, the right to jury trial—these became the foundations of American criminal procedure, and each has spawned its own elaborate body of law. These bodies of law will occupy the bulk of this large book. But the words "due process" rarely appear in the cases that define these constitutional rules; instead, the relevant piece of constitutional text comes from the Fourth, Fifth, or Sixth Amendments. In effect, the Supreme Court decided that defining due process was impossible, so it turned to the enterprise of defining the more specific guarantees of the Bill of Rights. But the point of those guarantees is itself due process; the goal remains to define criminal procedure in a way that ensures fair treatment for the millions of people who pass through the criminal justice system's large net. The basic question that so bothered the Court from 1884 to 1960—what are the conditions of a fair criminal process?—has not so much been answered as recast, and perhaps avoided.

In short, for roughly its first century, our nation had no law of constitutional criminal procedure. For roughly the next 80 years, the Supreme Court tried, and largely failed, to define a law of criminal procedure built on the phrase "due process of law." For the 40 years after that, down to the present, the phrase "due process of law" has faded in importance; a huge, nearly comprehensive law of criminal procedure has been built on the various provisions of the Bill of Rights. But the idea of due process still lurks in the background, posing the basic question any criminal process must face: Is this fair?

A. Defining Due Process

HURTADO v. CALIFORNIA

Writ of Error to the Supreme Court of California
110 U.S. 516 (1884)

MR. JUSTICE MATTHEWS delivered the opinion of the Court.

[Hurtado was charged and convicted of first-degree murder. He was charged by information, not indictment; that is, no grand jury ever considered his case. He argued that the absence of grand jury indictment for a serious crime violated the Fourteenth Amendment's guarantee of due process. —EDS.]

. . . The proposition of law we are asked to affirm is that an indictment or presentment by a grand jury, as known to the common law of England, is essential to that "due process of law," when applied to prosecutions for felonies, which is secured and guaranteed by [the Fourteenth Amendment to] the Constitution of the United States, and which accordingly it is forbidden to the States respectively to dispense with in the administration of criminal law. . . .

. . . [I]t is maintained on behalf of the plaintiff in error that the phrase "due process of law" is equivalent to "law of the land," as found in the 29th chapter of Magna Charta; that by immemorial usage it has acquired a fixed, definite, and technical meaning; that it refers to and includes, not only the general principles of public liberty and private right, which lie at the foundation of all free government, but the very institutions which, venerable by time and custom, have been tried by experience and found fit and necessary for the preservation of those principles. . . .

This, it is argued, furnishes an indispensable test of what constitutes "due process of law"; that any proceeding otherwise authorized by law, which is not thus sanctioned by usage, or which supersedes and displaces one that is, cannot be regarded as due process of law.

But this inference is unwarranted. The real [principle] is, that a process of law, which is not otherwise forbidden, must be taken to be due process of law, if it can show the sanction of settled usage both in England and in this country; but it by no means follows that nothing else can be due process of law. . . . [T]o hold that such a characteristic is essential to due process of law, would be to deny every quality of the law but its age, and to render it incapable of progress or improvement. It would be to stamp upon our jurisprudence the unchangeableness attributed to the laws of the Medes and Persians. . . .

The Constitution of the United States was ordained, it is true, by descendants of Englishmen, who inherited the traditions of English law and history; but it was made for an undefined and expanding future, and for a people gathered and to be gathered from many nations and of many tongues. . . . There is nothing in Magna Charta, rightly construed as a broad charter of public right and law, which ought to exclude the best ideas of all systems and of every age; and as it was the characteristic principle of the common law to draw its inspiration from every fountain of justice, we are not to assume that the sources of its supply have been exhausted. On the contrary, we should expect that the new and various experiences of our own situation and system will mould and shape it into new and not less useful forms. . . .

We are to construe this phrase in the Fourteenth Amendment by the [usage] of the Constitution itself. The same words are contained in the Fifth Amendment. That article makes specific and express provision for perpetuating the institution of the grand jury, so far as relates to prosecutions for the more aggravated crimes under the laws of the United States. It declares that:

> No person shall be held to answer for a capital or otherwise infamous crime, unless on a presentment or indictment of a grand jury, except in cases arising in the land or naval forces, or in the militia when in actual service in time of war or public danger; nor shall any person be subject for the same offence to be twice put in jeopardy of life or limb; nor shall he be compelled in any criminal case to be a witness against himself. [It then immediately adds]: Nor be deprived of life, liberty, or property, without due process of law.

According to a recognized canon of interpretation, especially applicable to formal and solemn instruments of constitutional law, we are forbidden to assume, without clear reason to the contrary, that any part of this most important amendment is superfluous. The natural and obvious inference is, that in the sense of the Constitution, "due process of law" was not meant or intended to include . . . the institution and procedure of a grand jury in any case. The conclusion is equally irresistible, that when the same phrase was employed in the Fourteenth Amendment to restrain the action of the States, it was used in the same sense and with no greater extent; and that if in the adoption of that amendment it had been part of its purpose to perpetuate the institution of the grand jury in all the States, it would have embodied, as did the Fifth Amendment, express declarations to that effect. Due process of law in the latter refers to that law of the land which derives its authority from the legislative powers conferred upon Congress by the Constitution of the United States, exercised within the limits therein prescribed, and interpreted according to the principles of the common law. In the Fourteenth Amendment, by parity of reason, it refers to that law of the land in each State, which derives its authority from the inherent and reserved powers of the State, exerted within the limits of those fundamental principles of liberty and justice which lie at the base of all our civil and political institutions, and the greatest security for which resides in the right of the people to make their own laws, and alter them at their pleasure. . . .

But it is not to be supposed that these legislative powers are absolute and despotic, and that the amendment prescribing due process of law is too vague and indefinite to operate as a practical restraint. It is not every act, legislative in form, that is law. Law is something more than mere will exerted as an act of power. It must be not a special rule for a particular person or a particular case, but, in the language of Mr. Webster, in his familiar definition, "the general law, a law which hears before it condemns, which proceeds upon inquiry, and renders judgment only after trial," so "that every citizen shall hold his life, liberty, property and immunities under the protection of the general rules which govern society," and thus excluding, as not due process of law, acts of attainder, bills of pains and penalties, acts of confiscation, acts reversing judgments, and acts directly transferring one man's estate to another, legislative judgments and decrees, and other similar special, partial and arbitrary exertions of power under the forms of legislation. Arbitrary power, enforcing its edicts to the injury of the persons and property of its subjects, is not law, whether manifested as the decree of a personal monarch or of an impersonal multitude. . . . The enforcement of these limitations by judicial process is the device of self-governing communities to protect the rights of individuals and minorities, as well against the power of numbers, as against the violence of public agents transcending the limits of lawful authority, even when acting in the name and wielding the force of the government. . . .

It follows that any legal proceeding enforced by public authority, whether sanctioned by age and custom, or newly devised in the discretion of the legislative power, in furtherance of the general public good, which regards and preserves these principles of liberty and justice, must be held to be due process of law. . . .

Tried by these principles, we are unable to say that the substitution for a presentment or indictment by a grand jury of the proceeding by information, after examination and commitment by a magistrate, certifying to the probable guilt of the defendant, with the right on his part to the aid of counsel, and to the cross-examination of the witnesses produced for the prosecution, is not due process of law. . . .

MR. JUSTICE HARLAN, dissenting.

. . . [I]t is said that the framers of the Constitution did not suppose that due process of law necessarily required for a capital offence the institution and procedure of a grand jury, else they would not in the same amendment prohibiting the deprivation of life, liberty, or property, without due process of law, have made specific and express provision for a grand jury where the crime is capital or otherwise infamous. . . .

This line of argument, it seems to me, would lead to results which are inconsistent with the vital principles of republican government. If the presence in the Fifth Amendment of a specific provision for grand juries in capital cases, alongside the provision for due process of law . . . is held to prove that "due process of law" did not . . . require a grand jury in capital cases, inexorable logic would require it to be, likewise, held that the right not to be put twice in jeopardy of life and limb for the same offence, nor compelled in a criminal case to testify against one's self—rights and immunities also specifically recognized in the Fifth Amendment—were not protected by that [same] due process of law. . . . More than that, other amendments of the Constitution proposed at the same time, expressly recognize the right of persons to just compensation for private property taken for public use; their right, when accused of crime, to be informed of the nature and cause of the accusation against them, and to a speedy and public trial, by an impartial jury of the State and district wherein the crime was committed; to be confronted by the witnesses against them; and to have compulsory process for obtaining witnesses in their favor. Will it be claimed that these rights were not secured by the "law of the land" or by "due process of law," as declared and established at the foundation of our government? Are they to be excluded from the enumeration of the fundamental principles of liberty and justice, and, therefore, not embraced by "due process of law"? If the argument of my brethren be sound, those rights—although universally recognized at the establishment of our institutions as secured by that due process of law which for centuries had been the foundation of Anglo-Saxon liberty—were not deemed by our fathers as essential in the due process of law prescribed by our Constitution; because—such seems to be the argument—had they been regarded as involved in due process of law they would not have been specifically and expressly provided for. . . .

Still further, it results from the doctrines of the opinion—if I do not misapprehend its scope—that the clause of the Fourteenth Amendment forbidding the deprivation of life or liberty without due process of law, would not be violated by a State regulation, dispensing with petit juries in criminal cases, and permitting a person charged with a crime involving life to be tried before a single judge, or even a justice of the peace, upon a rule to show cause why he should not be hanged. . . .

. . . My sense of duty constrains me to dissent from this interpretation of the supreme law of the land.

MR. JUSTICE FIELD did not take part in the decision of this case.

NOTES ON THE MEANING OF "DUE PROCESS OF LAW" IN CRIMINAL CASES

1. *Hurtado* was the Supreme Court's first extended discussion of what "due process of law" means for criminal procedure. How well did the Court do? Do the majority and dissenting opinions reflect the kinds of concerns you would expect to see? Do the opinions make you think better or worse of the idea of giving the Supreme Court the power to define the rules that govern the criminal process?

In answering these questions, it helps to have some more information about the issue in *Hurtado*. The question before the Court was whether California was required to proceed by indictment in capital cases. To translate, the question was whether murder defendants like Hurtado (and perhaps defendants in other felony cases) were constitutionally entitled to a judgment by a grand jury that they should be charged, as a prerequisite to going to trial. How one answers that question, in turn, might plausibly depend on one's sense of what grand juries do, how they function. Consider the following description of contemporary grand jury practice in federal cases:[11]

> The operation of a typical federal grand jury is straightforward. A pool of citizens is summoned at random from the judicial district where the jury will sit. From the group of qualified people who appear, twenty-three are chosen to serve on the jury. The jurors sit for an indefinite period not to exceed eighteen months; the number of days per month when they must actually appear depends on the prosecutor's case load. A district court judge administers the oath and gives the jurors general instructions about their duties. This marks the end of the judge's formal involvement in the process. From that point forward, the prosecutor dictates the course of the proceedings.
>
> The most striking feature of grand jury hearings is their secrecy. The press and public are barred from the proceedings, as are suspects and their counsel. Even judges are not allowed in the grand jury room; attendance is limited to the prosecutor, the jurors, the court reporter, and the single witness being questioned. Those who participate in the hearing are sworn to secrecy, and the court may use its contempt powers to ensure that this silence is maintained even after the case is resolved.
>
> Once in session, the grand jury's primary task is to review the cases presented to it by the government. The prosecutor calls and questions witnesses, and presents documentary evidence related to the crime in question. Unlike trial jurors, grand jurors may ask questions of the witness and may discuss the case with the prosecutor as evidence is submitted. After the case is presented, the prosecutor asks the jurors to vote to return an indictment accusing the defendant of a specific crime that the prosecutor believes is supported by the evidence. The jurors then deliberate in private. If at least twelve agree that there is probable cause to believe that the suspect committed the crime, the grand jury returns a "true bill" that, when signed by the prosecutor, becomes the indictment. If the grand jury concludes that the evidence is insufficient, it returns a "no bill" (or "no true bill"), and any preliminary charges filed against the suspect are dismissed.
>
> By traditional trial standards, a grand jury is allowed to consider a surprising, even shocking, mix of evidence. . . . The Rules of Evidence do not apply, so the prosecutor can ask leading questions and pursue matters that would be considered irrelevant if presented at trial. The decision of which evidence to present is also in the prosecutor's hands: the suspect has no right to testify in his own defense, and if he does testify, is not allowed to bring counsel with him into the grand jury room. The suspect may not put on contrary evidence, is not given access to the testimony of his accusers until the trial begins, and indeed, may not even be told he is being investigated. The result . . . is that grand jurors hear only what the prosecution wants them to hear. . . .

Andrew Leipold, Why Grand Juries Do Not (and Cannot) Protect the Accused, 80 Cornell L. Rev. 260, 265-267 (1995) (footnotes omitted). As the title of Leipold's article suggests, it is not clear how this process protects criminal defendants. On the contrary, its chief use today seems to be as a device the government uses to

---

11. This description is reprinted at page 1051, infra, as part of the consideration of grand juries as screening devices.

obtain information—hence the widespread use of grand jury subpoenas in white-collar criminal investigations.

Of course, white-collar criminal practice was well in the future when *Hurtado* was decided, and grand jury practice was no doubt different in some respects in 1884 than it is today. But the essential point—prosecutorial control over the information grand jurors receive—would have been true then as now. Given that point, is there any serious argument for constitutionally requiring grand juries? What could Justice Harlan have been worrying about?

2. Both Justice Matthews and Justice Harlan offered coherent, fairly well-developed interpretations of due process. Justice Matthews construes "due process of law" with special emphasis on the words "of law"; the result is a constitutional requirement of legality and nonarbitrariness. Justice Harlan sees due process as incorporating the list of protections that appear in the Bill of Rights; the result of this view is to transfer interpretive questions from the Fourteenth Amendment to the more particular guarantees of the Fourth, Fifth, and Sixth Amendments. Though these positions competed with each other in *Hurtado*, each has prevailed in its own sphere over the years. (Harlan's argument has won the greater victory, as the next main case shows.) In addition to these two interpretations, two other views of due process in criminal cases have won judicial favor from time to time. Some cases treat due process as a guarantee of accurate procedures, meaning procedures that minimize the risk that innocent defendants will be convicted of crime. And some cases define "due process" as "fundamental fairness," which turns out to be a term defined more by judicial intuition than by any analytic structure.

Each of these four strands—due process as the rule of law, due process as the Bill of Rights, due process as accuracy, and due process as "fundamental fairness"—survives in the law of due process today. Oddly, none of the four views seems to have much to do with any of the others. That strange fact has its origins in cases from early in the twentieth century. In the decades following *Hurtado*, the Supreme Court saw a wide range of cases challenging one or another aspect of state criminal procedure, but as it decided those cases the Court did not follow a consistent path. Rather, the Court seized on whichever of the four approaches mentioned in the preceding paragraph seemed most applicable to the issue at hand (and whichever was able to attract a majority of the Court). Cases taking one approach usually made no mention of cases taking another, and at some times the Court seemed unaware that some of the approaches even existed. The upshot is that today, there are (at least) four meanings of due process in criminal cases, and there is no obvious answer to the question why one meaning prevails in one kind of case and another in a different kind of case.

The material that follows briefly traces the development of each of those four meanings. As you read, ask yourself whether one or another of these approaches seems clearly superior to the others, or (alternatively) whether the law is better off with strands of each.

The Rule of Law.   The following passage in Justice Matthews's opinion in *Hurtado* offers a good summary of what is meant by the "rule of law":

> It is not every act, legislative in form, that is law. Law is something more than mere will exerted as an act of power. It must be not a special rule for a particular person or a particular case, but, in the language of Mr. Webster, in his familiar definition,

"the general law, a law which hears before it condemns, which proceeds upon inquiry, and renders judgment only after trial," . . . and thus excluding, as not due process of law, acts of attainder, bills of pains and penalties, acts of confiscation, acts reversing judgments, and acts directly transferring one man's estate to another, legislative judgments and decrees, and other similar special, partial and arbitrary exertions of power under the forms of legislation. Arbitrary power, enforcing its edicts to the injury of the persons and property of its subjects, is not law, whether manifested as the decree of a personal monarch or of an impersonal multitude. . . .

For a good contemporary statement of the same principle, see John C. Jeffries, Jr., Legality, Vagueness, and the Construction of Penal Statutes, 71 Va. L. Rev. 189, 212 (1985):

The rule of law signifies the constraint of arbitrariness in the exercise of government power. In the context of the penal law, it means that the agencies of official coercion should, to the extent feasible, be guided by rules—that is, by openly acknowledged, relatively stable, and generally applicable statements of proscribed conduct. The evils to be retarded are caprice and whim, the misuse of government power for private ends, and the unacknowledged reliance on illegitimate criteria of selection. The goals to be advanced are regularity and evenhandedness in the administration of justice and accountability in the use of government power.

This idea of ensuring that criminal punishment is according to law and not "mere will" requires, at the least, that crimes be defined generally rather than (as Matthews put it) as a "special rule for a particular person or a particular case." That much is easy. Legislatures cannot make it a crime to *be* Hurtado, nor can they wait until Hurtado acts and then criminalize whatever he has done.

More importantly as a practical matter, the rule-of-law idea might be thought to require that legislatures define crimes with some specificity, that vague criminal statutes be deemed unconstitutional. Jeffries states the basic argument well:

The power to define a vague law is effectively left to those who enforce it, and those who enforce the penal law characteristically operate in settings of secrecy and informality, often punctuated by a sense of emergency, and rarely constrained by self-conscious generalization of standards. In such circumstances, the wholesale delegation of discretion naturally invites its abuse, and an important first step in constraining that discretion is the invalidation of indefinite laws.

Id., at 215.

For a long period following *Hurtado*, this idea lay mostly dormant. Vagueness doctrine existed, but it was mostly used as an adjunct to First Amendment law, a way to invalidate laws that might chill protected speech. See Note, The Void-for-Vagueness Doctrine in the Supreme Court, 109 U. Pa. L. Rev. 67 (1960). Beginning in the early 1970s, though, the Supreme Court began to apply vagueness doctrine to strike down statutes that seemed to criminalize ordinary street behavior. Thus, in Coates v. Cincinnati, 402 U.S. 611 (1971), the Court invalidated an ordinance that forbade conduct "annoying to persons passing by." In Papachristou v. Jacksonville, 405 U.S. 156 (1972), the Court struck down a vagrancy law that criminalized, inter alia, "rogues and vagabonds," "habitual loafers," and "persons wandering or strolling around from place to place without any lawful purpose or object." More recently, in Chicago v. Morales, 527 U.S. 41 (1999), the Court invalidated a local ordinance that prohibited loitering by two or more people, at least one of whom was a "street gang member." *Morales* is excerpted at page 593, infra.

Cases like *Coates, Papachristou,* and *Morales* are all applications of Justice Matthews's rule-of-law view of due process. Are the applications sound? Does the rule-of-law idea go farther? Suppose a given jurisdiction forbids knowing possession of marijuana. Suppose further that there have been no prosecutions for this offense for several years and that marijuana possession is fairly common in some communities. Under these circumstances, would an arrest or prosecution for marijuana possession violate the rule of law? Does the answer depend on why the defendant was selected for arrest and prosecution? Is that something courts will be able to uncover?

More generally, is the rule-of-law ideal a good basis for constitutional regulation of the criminal justice system generally? Consider how one might apply the ideal to, say, police brutality. Is the problem with excessive police violence that the violence is lawless? Or is it something else?

The Bill of Rights.   The Fourth Amendment forbids unreasonable searches and seizures. The Fifth Amendment requires indictment by grand jury for "capital, or otherwise infamous crime[s]," and bans double jeopardy and compelled self-incrimination. The Sixth Amendment grants defendants "the right to a speedy and public trial, by an impartial jury," as well as the right to be informed of the charges, to be confronted with opposing witnesses, to have "compulsory process for obtaining witnesses in his favor," and to have "the Assistance of Counsel for his defence."

As Justice Harlan's dissent in *Hurtado* shows, one longstanding reading of due process in criminal cases is that it incorporates all these rights. That position was rejected in *Hurtado* and for a long time afterward: In 1908, the Court declined to incorporate the privilege against self-incrimination into due process, see Twining v. New Jersey, 211 U.S. 78 (1908); three decades later, the Court similarly declined to incorporate the prohibition against double jeopardy into due process. See Palko v. Connecticut, 302 U.S. 319 (1937). But beginning in the middle of the twentieth century, the Court reversed course. In Wolf v. Colorado, 338 U.S. 25 (1949), the Court concluded that the Fourth Amendment's ban on unreasonable searches and seizures applied to the states through the Due Process Clause. (The Court waited until 1961, however, to apply the exclusionary rule to the states. See Mapp v. Ohio, 367 U.S. 643 (1961), reprinted at page 324.) And in the 1960s, a series of decisions incorporated every one of the rights listed in the preceding paragraph except for the right to a grand jury. *Hurtado* still stands, but today it stands alone—everywhere else, the argument of the first Justice Harlan has prevailed. Duncan v. Louisiana, the next main case, discusses this development.

There is a lively debate about the historical accuracy of incorporation—about the question whether the authors and ratifiers of the Fourteenth Amendment intended to apply the Bill of Rights to state and local governments. For the classic arguments on each side, see Charles Fairman, Does the Fourteenth Amendment Incorporate the Bill of Rights? The Original Understanding, 2 Stan. L. Rev. 5 (1949) (against incorporation); William Winslow Crosskey, Charles Fairman, "Legislative History," and the Constitutional Limitations on State Authority, 22 U. Chi. L. Rev. 1 (1954) (for incorporation). That debate is, to say the least, not easily summarized. The tide seems to be shifting among the historians toward the conclusion that there is substantial evidence indicating that the Due Process Clause was designed in part to make the Bill of Rights enforceable against the states, although more through action of Congress than the judiciary. For a thorough airing, see the symposium, The Fourteenth Amendment and the Bill of Rights, 18 J. Contemp. Legal Issues 1-533 (2009). In the most recent case to reach the issue, the Supreme Court, relying almost entirely on an historical analysis, concluded that the Second Amendment is incorporated into the Due Process Clause. McDonald v. City of Chicago, IL, 561 U.S. 742 (2010). For more on *McDonald*, see note 5, at page 86, infra.

Putting historical questions aside, what is the case, either principled or pragmatic, for reading "due process" as meaning, roughly, "that process which complies with the Bill of Rights"? One possible answer is that compliance with the Bill of Rights will generate a fair criminal process. But it would be surprising if that were true. Recall that the Bill of Rights arose out of a legal system that had none of the basic institutions of contemporary American criminal justice. For the Framers to have accurately anticipated the conditions of a fair criminal process today, they would have to have accurately anticipated district attorneys' offices and police forces, plea bargaining and prison systems. That kind of foresight seems, literally, incredible. It seems more likely that some Bill of Rights protections improve the criminal process, others make that process worse, and still others make no real difference. That hardly sounds like a recipe for sound constitutional regulation.

And there is another difficulty. One might imagine that due process of law flows out of some principle, that constitutional regulation of the criminal process is in pursuit of some definable goal. The rule of law is a plausible candidate for such a goal or principle, as is accuracy. But the Bill of Rights is not. There is no obvious unifying principle to the disparate set of protections in the Fourth, Fifth, and Sixth Amendments. That makes it hard to see how the phrase "due process of law" has room to hold all those protections.

Accuracy (and Race).   In a series of decisions in the 1920s and 1930s, the Supreme Court overturned convictions of black defendants in Southern state courts in circumstances where there was good reason to believe the defendants were innocent. Michael Klarman describes four such cases:

> . . . [All of the cases] involved southern black criminal defendants convicted and sentenced to death after egregiously unfair trials. In Moore v. Dempsey,[5] the Supreme Court interpreted the Due Process Clause of the Fourteenth Amendment to forbid criminal convictions obtained through mob-dominated trials. In Powell v. Alabama,[6] the Court ruled that the Due Process Clause requires state appointment of counsel in capital cases and overturned convictions where defense counsel had been appointed the morning of trial. In Norris v. Alabama,[7] the Court reversed a conviction under the Equal Protection Clause where blacks had been intentionally excluded from juries. To reach that result, the Court had to revise the critical "subconstitutional"[8] rules that previously had made such claims nearly impossible to prove. In Brown v. Mississippi,[9] the Court construed the Due Process Clause to forbid criminal convictions based on confessions extracted through torture.

5. 261 U.S. 86 (1923).
6. 287 U.S. 45 (1932).
7. 294 U.S. 587 (1935).
8. By "subconstitutional" rules, I mean not the substantive liability standards, but rather the all-important rules bearing on standards of proof, standards of appellate review, and access to federal court. For a fuller discussion, see Michael J. Klarman, The *Plessy* Era, 1998 Sup. Ct. Rev. 303, 376-378.
9. 297 U.S. 278 (1936).

These four decisions arose from three distinct episodes. In Moore, six black defendants appealed death sentences imposed for a murder allegedly committed in connection with the infamous race riot in Phillips County, Arkansas in the fall of 1919.[10] Phillips was a typical deep South cotton county with a black majority of approximately three-to-one. According to the local black community, the cause of the racial altercation that culminated in the Moore litigation was the brutal suppression by whites of an effort by black sharecroppers after World War I to form a tenant farmers' union and to seek legal redress for their landlords' peonage practices. The white community, on the contrary, charged that the cause of the conflagration was a black conspiracy to murder white planters throughout the county. An initial altercation in which whites shot into a black union meeting at a church and blacks returned the gunfire, killing a white man, quickly escalated into mayhem. Marauding whites, some of whom flocked to Phillips County from adjoining states and enjoyed the assistance of federal troops ostensibly employed to quell the disturbance, went on a rampage against blacks, tracking them down through the rural county, and killing (on one estimate) as many as 250 of them. Seventy-nine blacks (and no whites) were prosecuted as a result of the riot; twelve received the death penalty for murder; and six were involved in the appeal to the United States Supreme Court in Moore v. Dempsey. The Court reversed their convictions on the ground that mob-dominated trial proceedings violated the Due Process Clause.

The second and third race-based criminal procedure cases of the interwar period, Powell v. Alabama and Norris v. Alabama, both arose out of the famous Scottsboro Boys episode.[11] Nine black youths, ranging in age from thirteen to twenty, impoverished, illiterate, and transient, were charged with raping two young white women, alleged to be prostitutes, on a freight train in northern Alabama in the spring of 1931. They were tried in a mob-dominated atmosphere, and eight of the defendants received the death penalty. The state supreme court reversed one of these death sentences on the ground that the defendant was too young to be executed under state law and affirmed the other seven. The United States Supreme Court twice reversed the Scottsboro Boys' convictions—the first time on the ground that they had been denied the right to counsel, and the second time on the ground that blacks had been intentionally excluded from the grand jury that indicted them and the trial jury that convicted them.

Fourth and finally, in Brown v. Mississippi the Supreme Court reversed the death sentences of three black sharecroppers convicted of murdering their white landlord.[12] The principal evidence against the defendants was their own confessions, extracted through torture. The Supreme Court ruled that convictions so obtained violated the Due Process Clause of the Fourteenth Amendment.

These four cases arose out of three quite similar episodes. Southern black defendants were charged with serious crimes against whites—either rape or murder. All three sets of defendants nearly were lynched before their cases could be brought to trial. In all three episodes, mobs comprised of hundreds or even thousands of whites surrounded the courthouse during the trial, demanding that the defendants be turned over for a swift execution. No change of venue was granted in these cases (except in the retrial of the Scottsboro Boys). Lynchings were avoided only through

10. The most detailed treatment of *Moore* is Richard C. Cortner, A Mob Intent on Death: The NAACP and the Arkansas Riot Cases (1988). A briefer description appears in O. A. Rogers, Jr., The Elaine Race Riots of 1919, 19 Ark. Hist. Q. 142 (1960).

11. For extensive treatment of the Scottsboro Boys episode, see Dan T. Carter, Scottsboro: A Tragedy of the American South (rev. ed. 1979) and James Goodman, Stories of Scottsboro (1994).

12. The most complete treatment is Richard C. Cortner, A "Scottsboro" Case in Mississippi: The Supreme Court and Brown v. Mississippi (1986).

the presence of state militiamen armed with machine guns surrounding the court-house. There was a serious doubt—not just with the aid of historical hindsight, but at the time of the trial—as to whether any of the defendants was in fact guilty of the crime charged. The defendants in Moore and Brown were tortured into confessing. In all three cases, defense lawyers were appointed either the day of or the day preceding trial, with no adequate opportunity to consult with their clients, to interview witnesses, or to prepare a defense strategy. Trials took place quickly after the alleged crimes in order to avoid a lynching—less than a week afterwards in Brown, twelve days in Powell, and a month in Moore. The trials were completed within a matter of hours (forty-five minutes in Moore), and the juries, from which blacks were intentionally excluded in all three cases, deliberated for only a matter of minutes before imposing death sentences.[13]

Michael J. Klarman, The Racial Origins of Modern Criminal Procedure, 99 Mich. L. Rev. 48, 50-52 (2000). For a more general treatment of the role of race in Supreme Court adjudication, see Michael J. Klarman, From Jim Crow to Civil Rights: The Supreme Court and the Struggle for Racial Equality (2004).

As Klarman argues in his article, these cases are as much about race as about criminal procedure. But they gave rise to an idea that goes beyond race—the idea that due process should ensure accurate procedures, procedures that would prevent conviction of innocent defendants. Thus, the problem with the mob-dominated trial in *Moore*, with the absence of any real defense counsel in *Powell*, and with the beating-induced confession in *Brown* was the same: All tended to lead to conviction and punishment without regard to whether the defendants were guilty.

From roughly 1940 to 1960, this strand of due process produced two major lines of cases. First, indigent criminal defendants were entitled to appointed counsel if there were "special circumstances" that made it impossible for them to represent themselves. See Betts v. Brady, 316 U.S. 455 (1942). Obviously, this standard required a good deal of ad hoc evaluation of the nature of the case in order to decide whether appointed counsel was really necessary. The second line of cases held, following Brown v. Mississippi, that involuntary confessions were inadmissible. That standard prompted a good deal of litigation in the 1940s and 1950s; one of the themes running through those cases was the need to ensure that confessions were truthful. See, e.g., Stein v. New York, 346 U.S. 156, 182 (1953) ("The tendency of the innocent . . . to risk remote results of a false confession rather than suffer immediate pain is so strong that judges long ago found it necessary to . . . treat[ ] any confession made concurrently with torture or threat of brutality as too untrustworthy to be received as evidence of guilt.").

13. On Scottsboro, see Carter, supra note 11, chs. 1-2; Goodman, supra note 11, chs. 1-2. On *Moore*, see Cortner, *Mob*, supra note 10, ch. 1. On *Brown*, see Cortner, *Brown*, supra note 12, chs. 1-2. The Scottsboro Boys certainly were innocent of the crimes charged, as revealed in a subsequent recantation by one of the alleged victims. Their innocence should have been reasonably clear at the trial both from the medical evidence and from the conflicting testimony of the prosecution's witnesses. See Brief for Petitioners at 28-30, Powell v. Alabama, 287 U.S. 45 (1932) (Nos. 98-100), reprinted in 27 Landmark Briefs and Arguments of the Supreme Court of the United States: Constitutional Law 291, 324-326 (Philip B. Kurland & Gerhard Casper eds., 1975); Carter, supra, at 27-30, 227-228, 232. The *Brown* defendants possibly were innocent, and the State surely lacked sufficient evidence to convict them apart from their tortured [confessions]. See Brown v. State, 161 So. 465, 471 (Miss. 1935) (Griffith, J., dissenting). The *Moore* defendants at most were guilty of being present when the lethal shots were fired, and not even clearly of this. See Cortner, *Mob*, supra note 10, 124-125.

Since 1960, due-process-as-accuracy has produced a variety of doctrines. Under Brady v. Maryland, 373 U.S. 83 (1963), and its progeny, the prosecution must turn over exculpatory evidence to the defense. (This requirement is discussed in Chapter 12.) Under Drope v. Missouri, 420 U.S. 162 (1975), defendants cannot be made to stand trial unless they are competent to assist in their own defense. (This line of cases is discussed in Medina v. California, at page 86, infra.) Ake v. Oklahoma, 470 U.S. 168 (1985), holds that in some cases the court must appoint a mental health expert to assist in the preparation of a defendant's insanity claim.

Are these rules adequate to ensure a fair process? Is there anything beyond accuracy that needs constitutional protection?

"Fundamental Fairness."   The last of the four strands is the hardest to describe, because it boils down to little more than judicial intuition. In a series of cases going back to the first decade of the twentieth century, the Supreme Court has decided whether due process requires a given practice by asking whether the practice is somehow basic to a decent criminal justice system—whether it is the sort of protection any free society ought to provide. The Court has used different phrases to capture this approach at different times; today the phrase of choice is "fundamental fairness." What is meant by that phrase (or by its earlier substitutes) is not clear; it seems to be a stand-in for a generalized sense that some kinds of government conduct are outrageous (never mind why) or that some procedures are essential (never mind for what).

An early example of this approach is Twining v. New Jersey, 211 U.S. 78 (1908). Twining's jury was told it could draw adverse inferences from his failure to take the witness stand; Twining's claim was that this violated the privilege against self-incrimination, which, he argued, applied to New Jersey through the Fourteenth Amendment's Due Process Clause. The Court's analysis is captured by the following strange sentence: "We have to consider whether the right is so fundamental in due process that a refusal of the right is a denial of due process." Id., at 107. The Court's answer was no.

In Palko v. Connecticut, 302 U.S. 319 (1937), the Court gave the same answer when asked whether the prohibition against double jeopardy was sufficiently "fundamental." (Palko was tried and convicted of second-degree murder; he successfully appealed the conviction; the state then retried him and this time convicted him of capital murder and sentenced him to death.) Justice Cardozo, speaking for the majority, explained the line between those procedures required by due process and those not:

> There emerges the perception of a rationalizing principle which gives . . . a proper order and coherence. The right to trial by jury and the immunity from prosecution except as the result of an indictment may have value and importance. Even so, they are not of the very essence of a scheme of ordered liberty. To abolish them is not to violate a "principle of justice so rooted in the traditions and conscience of our people as to be ranked as fundamental." Snyder v. Massachusetts, [291 U.S. 97,] 105. Few would be so narrow or provincial as to maintain that a fair and enlightened system of justice would be impossible without them. What is true of jury trials and indictments is true also, as the cases show, of the immunity from compulsory self-incrimination. Twining v. New Jersey, supra. This too might be lost, and justice still be done. . . . Justice . . . would not perish if the accused were subject to a duty to respond to orderly inquiry. . . .

. . . Is that kind of double jeopardy to which the statute has subjected [the defendant] a hardship so acute and shocking that our polity will not endure it? Does it violate those "fundamental principles of liberty and justice which lie at the base of all our civil and political institutions"? Hebert v. Louisiana, [272 U.S. 312]. The answer surely must be "no."

One is tempted to ask, "Why not?"

This sort of analysis reached its nadir in Rochin v. California, 342 U.S. 165 (1952). The Court recounted the facts in *Rochin* as follows:

Having "some information that [the petitioner here] was selling narcotics," three deputy sheriffs of the County of Los Angeles, on the morning of July 1, 1949, made for the two-story dwelling house in which Rochin lived with his mother, common-law wife, brothers and sisters. Finding the outside door open, they entered and then forced open the door to Rochin's room on the second floor. Inside they found petitioner sitting partly dressed on the side of the bed, upon which his wife was lying. On a "night stand" beside the bed the deputies spied two capsules. When asked "Whose stuff is this?" Rochin seized the capsules and put them in his mouth. A struggle ensued, in the course of which the three officers "jumped upon him" and attempted to extract the capsules. The force they applied proved unavailing against Rochin's resistance. He was handcuffed and taken to a hospital. At the direction of one of the officers a doctor forced an emetic solution through a tube into Rochin's stomach against his will. This "stomach pumping" produced vomiting. In the vomited matter were found two capsules which proved to contain morphine.

In a stunningly uninformative opinion by Justice Frankfurter, the Court concluded that the stomach pumping violated due process:

The vague contours of the Due Process Clause do not leave judges at large. We may not draw on our merely personal and private notions and disregard the limits that bind judges in their judicial function. Even though the concept of due process of law is not final and fixed, these limits are derived from considerations that are fused in the whole nature of our judicial process. These are considerations deeply rooted in reason and in the compelling traditions of the legal profession. The Due Process Clause places upon this Court the duty of exercising a judgment, within the narrow confines of judicial power in reviewing State convictions, upon interests of society pushing in opposite directions. . . .

. . . [T]hat does not make due process of law a matter of judicial caprice. The faculties of the Due Process Clause may be indefinite and vague, but the mode of their ascertainment is not self-willed. In each case "due process of law" requires an evaluation based on a disinterested inquiry pursued in the spirit of science, on a balanced order of facts exactly and fairly stated, on the detached consideration of conflicting claims, on a judgment not ad hoc and episodic but duly mindful of reconciling the needs both of continuity and of change in a progressive society.

Applying these general considerations to the circumstances of the present case, we are compelled to conclude that the proceedings by which this conviction was obtained do more than offend some fastidious squeamishness or private sentimentalism about combatting crime too energetically. This is conduct that shocks the conscience. Illegally breaking into the privacy of the petitioner, the struggle to open his mouth and remove what was there, the forcible extraction of his stomach's contents—this course of proceeding by agents of government to obtain evidence is bound to offend even hardened sensibilities. They are methods too close to the rack and the screw to permit of constitutional differentiation.

342 U.S. at 170-172. Is Justice Frankfurter saying anything more than that he thinks the police behaved very badly? Does he say why?

Rochin-style due process analysis survives today, at least in a few outposts. A good modern example is Darden v. Wainwright, 477 U.S. 168 (1986). *Darden* was a capital murder case; in his closing argument, the prosecutor called the defendant an "animal," said "he shouldn't be out of his cell unless he has a leash on him," and expressed the wish that someone could have "blown his head off" before he had committed the crime. The Court held that the argument was improper, but not improper enough to amount to a violation of due process:

> . . . The relevant question is whether the prosecutors' comments "so infected the trial with unfairness as to make the resulting conviction a denial of due process." Donnelly v. DeChristoforo, 416 U.S. 637 (1974). . . .
>
> Under this standard of review, we agree with the reasoning of every court to consider these comments that they did not deprive petitioner of a fair trial. The prosecutors' argument did not manipulate or misstate the evidence, nor did it implicate other specific rights of the accused such as the right to counsel or the right to remain silent. . . . The trial court instructed the jurors several times that their decision was to be made on the basis of the evidence alone, and that the arguments of counsel were not evidence. The weight of the evidence against petitioner was heavy . . . [reducing] the likelihood that the jury's decision was influenced by argument. . . . For these reasons, we agree with the District Court below that "Darden's trial was not perfect—few are—but neither was it fundamentally unfair."

477 U.S., at 181-183. So the search in *Rochin* was shocking, while the prosecutor's argument in *Darden* was not (though it was close). Why are some things shocking and others not? Is there any content to these cases? Does the idea of fundamental fairness seem empty?

B. Incorporation

DUNCAN v. LOUISIANA

Appeal from the Supreme Court of Louisiana
391 U.S. 145 (1968)

MR. JUSTICE WHITE delivered the opinion of the Court.

Appellant, Gary Duncan, was convicted of simple battery. . . . Under Louisiana law simple battery is a misdemeanor, punishable by a maximum of two years' imprisonment and a $300 fine. Appellant sought trial by jury, but because the Louisiana Constitution grants jury trials only in cases in which capital punishment or imprisonment at hard labor may be imposed, the trial judge denied the request. Appellant was convicted and sentenced to serve 60 days in the parish prison and pay a fine of $150. [The conviction was affirmed on appeal.] . . .

Appellant was 19 years of age when tried. While driving on Highway 23 in Plaquemines Parish on October 18, 1966, he saw two younger cousins engaged in a conversation by the side of the road with four white boys. Knowing his cousins, Negroes who had recently transferred to a formerly all-white high school, had reported the occurrence of racial incidents at the school, Duncan stopped the car, got out, and approached the six boys. At trial the white boys and a white onlooker testified, as did appellant and his cousins. The testimony was in dispute on many points, but the witnesses agreed that appellant and the white boys spoke to each other, that appellant encouraged his cousins to break off the encounter and enter his car, and that appellant was about to enter the car himself for the purpose of driving away with his cousins. The whites testified that just before getting in the car appellant slapped Herman Landry, one of the white boys, on the elbow. The Negroes testified that appellant had not slapped Landry, but had merely touched him. The trial judge concluded that the State had proved beyond a reasonable doubt that Duncan had committed simple battery, and found him guilty.

The Fourteenth Amendment denies the States the power to "deprive any person of life, liberty, or property, without due process of law." In resolving conflicting claims concerning the meaning of this spacious language, the Court has looked increasingly to the Bill of Rights for guidance; many of the rights guaranteed by the first eight Amendments to the Constitution have been held to be protected against state action by the Due Process Clause of the Fourteenth Amendment. That clause now protects the right to compensation for property taken by the State;[4] the rights of speech, press, and religion covered by the First Amendment;[5] the Fourth Amendment rights to be free from unreasonable searches and seizures and to have excluded from criminal trials any evidence illegally seized;[6] the right guaranteed by the Fifth Amendment to be free of compelled self-incrimination;[7] and the Sixth Amendment rights to counsel,[8] to a speedy[9] and public[10] trial, to confrontation of opposing witnesses,[11] and to compulsory process for obtaining witnesses.[12]

The test for determining whether a right extended by the Fifth and Sixth Amendments with respect to federal criminal proceedings is also protected against state action by the Fourteenth Amendment has been phrased in a variety of ways in the opinions of this Court. The question has been asked whether a right is among those "fundamental principles of liberty and justice which lie at the base of all our civil and political institutions," Powell v. Alabama, 287 U.S. 45, 67 (1932); whether it is "basic in our system of jurisprudence," In re Oliver, 333 U.S. 257, 273 (1948); and whether it is "a fundamental right, essential to a fair trial," Gideon v. Wainwright, 372 U.S. 335, 343-344 (1963). The claim before us is that the right to trial by jury guaranteed by the Sixth Amendment meets these tests. The position of Louisiana, on the other hand, is that the Constitution imposes upon the States no duty to give a jury trial in any criminal case, regardless of the seriousness of the crime or the size of the punishment which may be imposed. Because we believe that trial by jury in criminal cases is fundamental to the American scheme of justice, we hold that the Fourteenth Amendment guarantees a right of jury trial in all criminal cases which—were they to be tried in a federal court—would come within the Sixth

[handwritten note in margin: Incorporation of BOR]

---

4. Chicago, B. & Q. R. Co. v. Chicago, 166 U.S. 226 (1897).
5. See, e.g., Fiske v. Kansas, 274 U.S. 380 (1927).
6. See Mapp v. Ohio, 367 U.S. 643 (1961).
7. Malloy v. Hogan, 378 U.S. 1 (1964).
8. Gideon v. Wainwright, 372 U.S. 335 (1963).
9. Klopfer v. North Carolina, 386 U.S. 213 (1967).
10. In re Oliver, 333 U.S. 257 (1948).
11. Pointer v. Texas, 380 U.S. 400 (1965).
12. Washington v. Texas, 388 U.S. 14 (1967).

Amendment's guarantee.[14] Since we consider the appeal before us to be such a case, we hold that the Constitution was violated when appellant's demand for jury trial was refused.

The history of trial by jury in criminal cases has been frequently told. It is sufficient for present purposes to say that by the time our Constitution was written, jury trial in criminal cases had been in existence in England for several centuries and carried impressive credentials traced by many to Magna Carta. Its preservation and proper operation as a protection against arbitrary rule were among the major objectives of the revolutionary settlement which was expressed in the Declaration and Bill of Rights of 1689. . . . Jury trial came to America with English colonists, and received strong support from them. Royal interference with the jury trial was deeply resented. . . . The Declaration of Independence stated solemn objections to the King's . . . "depriving us in many cases, of the benefits of Trial by Jury." . . . The Constitution itself, in Art. III, §2, commanded: "The Trial of all Crimes, except in Cases of Impeachment, shall be by Jury; and such Trial shall be held in the State where the said Crimes shall have been committed." . . .

The constitutions adopted by the original States guaranteed jury trial. Also, the constitution of every State entering the Union thereafter in one form or another protected the right to jury trial in criminal cases. Even such skeletal history is impressive support for considering the right to jury trial in criminal cases to be fundamental to our system of justice. . . .

Jury trial continues to receive strong support. The laws of every State guarantee a right to jury trial in serious criminal cases; no State has dispensed with it; nor are there significant movements under way to do so. . . .

14. In one sense recent cases applying provisions of the first eight Amendments to the States represent a new approach to the "incorporation" debate. Earlier the Court can be seen as having asked, when inquiring into whether some particular procedural safeguard was required of a State, if a civilized system could be imagined that would not accord the particular protection. For example, Palko v. Connecticut, 302 U.S. 319, 325 (1937), stated: "The right to trial by jury and the immunity from prosecution except as the result of an indictment may have value and importance. Even so, they are not of the very essence of a scheme of ordered liberty. . . . Few would be so narrow or provincial as to maintain that a fair and enlightened system of justice would be impossible without them." The recent cases, on the other hand, have proceeded upon the valid assumption that state criminal processes are not imaginary and theoretical schemes but actual systems bearing virtually every characteristic of the common-law system that has been developing contemporaneously in England and in this country. The question thus is whether given this kind of system a particular procedure is fundamental—whether, that is, a procedure is necessary to an Anglo-American regime of ordered liberty. It is this sort of inquiry that can justify the conclusions that state courts must exclude evidence seized in violation of the Fourth Amendment, Mapp v. Ohio, 367 U.S. 643 (1961); that state prosecutors may not comment on a defendant's failure to testify, Griffin v. California, 380 U.S. 609 (1965); and that criminal punishment may not be imposed for the status of narcotics addiction, Robinson v. California, 370 U.S. 660 (1962). Of immediate relevance for this case are the Court's holdings that the States must comply with certain provisions of the Sixth Amendment, specifically that the States may not refuse a speedy trial, confrontation of witnesses, and the assistance, at state expense if necessary, of counsel. See cases cited in nn. 8-12, supra. Of each of these determinations that a constitutional provision originally written to bind the Federal Government should bind the States as well it might be said that the limitation in question is not necessarily fundamental to fairness in every criminal system that might be imagined but is fundamental in the context of the criminal processes maintained by the American States.

. . . A criminal process which was fair and equitable but used no juries is easy to imagine. It would make use of alternative guarantees and protections which would serve the purposes that the jury serves in the English and American systems. Yet no American State has undertaken to construct such a system. Instead, every American State, including Louisiana, uses the jury extensively, and imposes very serious punishments only after a trial at which the defendant has a right to a jury's verdict. In every State, including Louisiana, the structure and style of the criminal process—the supporting framework and the subsidiary procedures—are of the sort that naturally complement jury trial, and have developed in connection with and in reliance upon jury trial.

. . . The guarantees of jury trial in the Federal and State Constitutions reflect a profound judgment about the way in which law should be enforced and justice administered. A right to jury trial is granted to criminal defendants in order to prevent oppression by the Government. Those who wrote our constitutions knew from history and experience that it was necessary to protect against unfounded criminal charges brought to eliminate enemies and against judges too responsive to the voice of higher authority. . . . Providing an accused with the right to be tried by a jury of his peers gave him an inestimable safeguard against the corrupt or overzealous prosecutor and against the compliant, biased, or eccentric judge. If the defendant preferred the common-sense judgment of a jury to the more tutored but perhaps less sympathetic reaction of the single judge, he was to have it. Beyond this, the jury trial provisions in the Federal and State Constitutions reflect a fundamental decision about the exercise of official power—a reluctance to entrust plenary powers over the life and liberty of the citizen to one judge or to a group of judges. . . . The deep commitment of the Nation to the right of jury trial in serious criminal cases as a defense against arbitrary law enforcement qualifies for protection under the Due Process Clause of the Fourteenth Amendment, and must therefore be respected by the States.

. . . We are aware of the long debate, especially in this century, among those who write about the administration of justice, as to the wisdom of permitting untrained laymen to determine the facts in civil and criminal proceedings. . . . [A]t the heart of the dispute have been express or implicit assertions that juries are incapable of adequately understanding evidence or determining issues of fact, and that they are unpredictable, quixotic, and little better than a roll of dice. Yet, the most recent and exhaustive study of the jury in criminal cases concluded that juries do understand the evidence and come to sound conclusions in most of the cases presented to them and that when juries differ with the result at which the judge would have arrived, it is usually because they are serving some of the very purposes for which they were created and for which they are now employed.[26]

The State of Louisiana urges that holding that the Fourteenth Amendment assures a right to jury trial will cast doubt on the integrity of every trial conducted without a jury. Plainly, this is not the import of our holding. . . . We would not assert . . . that every criminal trial—or any particular trial—held before a judge alone is unfair or that a defendant may never be as fairly treated by a judge as he would be by a jury. Thus we hold no constitutional doubts about the practices, common in both federal and state courts, of accepting waivers of jury trial and prosecuting petty crimes without extending a right to jury trial. However, the fact is that in most places more trials for serious crimes are to juries than to a court alone; a great many defendants prefer the judgment of a jury to that of a court. Even where defendants are satisfied with bench trials, the right to a jury trial very likely serves its intended purpose of making judicial or prosecutorial unfairness less likely.

Louisiana's final contention is that even if it must grant jury trials in serious criminal cases, the conviction before us is valid and constitutional because here the petitioner was tried for simple battery and was sentenced to only 60 days in the parish prison. . . . It is doubtless true that there is a category of petty crimes or offenses which is not subject to the Sixth Amendment jury trial provision and should not be

---

26. [Citing Harry Kalven, Jr. & Hans Zeisel, The American Jury (1966).]

subject to the Fourteenth Amendment jury trial requirement here applied to the States. . . . In the case before us the Legislature of Louisiana has made simple battery a criminal offense punishable by imprisonment for up to two years and a fine. The question, then, is whether a crime carrying such a penalty is an offense which Louisiana may insist on trying without a jury. . . .

. . . In the federal system, petty offenses are defined as those punishable by no more than six months in prison and a $500 fine. In 49 of the 50 States crimes subject to trial without a jury, which occasionally include simple battery, are punishable by no more than one year in jail. Moreover, in the late 18th century in America crimes triable without a jury were for the most part punishable by no more than a six-month prison term, although there appear to have been exceptions to this rule. We need not, however, settle in this case the exact location of the line between petty offenses and serious crimes. It is sufficient for our purposes to hold that a crime punishable by two years in prison is, based on past and contemporary standards in this country, a serious crime and not a petty offense. Consequently, appellant was entitled to a jury trial and it was error to deny it. . . .

[The concurring opinion of Justice Black, joined by Justice Douglas, and the dissenting opinion of Justice Harlan, joined by Justice Stewart, are omitted.]

NOTES ON *DUNCAN* AND THE INCORPORATION OF THE BILL OF RIGHTS

1. *Duncan*'s facts, at least as the Court recounts them, suggest a racially rigged proceeding, do they not? In this respect, *Duncan* looks like Moore v. Dempsey, 261 U.S. 86 (1923), Powell v. Alabama, 287 U.S. 45 (1932), and Brown v. Mississippi, 297 U.S. 278 (1936)—earlier cases in which the Court overturned convictions of black defendants in proceedings that seemed racially rigged. (*Moore*, *Powell*, and *Brown* are discussed at pages 74-76, supra.)

In none of these cases did the Court treat the legal issue as one of race discrimination. Instead, the Court's rulings were general, mandating or prohibiting certain procedures across the board—no mob-dominated trials in *Moore*, no uncounseled convictions in capital cases in *Powell*, no involuntary confessions in *Brown*, no denial of jury trial in *Duncan*. This has been a longstanding pattern in the law of constitutional criminal procedure. A great deal of the law covered in books like this one arises out of cases like *Duncan*—cases in which the real concern seems to be race-based injustice. Yet the law almost always deals with that concern indirectly, by regulating procedures that have little to do with race.

Why the indirection? Why not say Duncan's conviction was discriminatory, and leave it at that? One answer is that regulating discrimination directly would have led the Court, and the judiciary, into some very large and complex thickets. Suppose in a given jurisdiction, black Americans constitute 10 percent of the population but 25 percent of those arrested and convicted of crimes. Does that suggest discrimination? It might. But it might mean instead that the black population of that jurisdiction is disproportionately poor, and hence disproportionately involved in (and victimized by) crime. Indeed, the *absence* of a racial disproportion might be a sign of discrimination. Consider: In South Carolina in 1950—the Deep South, during the heyday of Jim Crow—the imprisoned felon population was slightly *whiter* than the population as a whole. Compare Federal Bureau of Prisons, National Prisoner Statistics: Prisoners in State and Federal Institutions—1950, at 55 tbl. 21 (1954) (prison population nearly two-thirds white) with U.S. Department of Commerce, Statistical Abstract of the United States—1953, at 36 tbl. 25 (overall population 61 percent white). South Carolina in 1950 was not running a color-blind criminal justice system. The more plausible possibility is that local police forces and local prosecutors were neglecting to investigate and prosecute crimes *against* blacks. Since most crime is intraracial, that tendency would naturally lead to fewer black prisoners. For a good discussion of this two-sided nature of discrimination in the criminal justice system, see Randall Kennedy, Race, Crime, and the Law (1997). All of which means that it is much harder than one might think to draw the line between racist law enforcement and law enforcement that is trying as best it can to advance the interests of the communities it serves.

Spotting clear cases of discrimination, like *Duncan*, may be easy. But once the easy cases are put aside, discrimination becomes much more subtle—which is not to say it is less real or less substantial—and much harder for courts to identify. Should the focus be on discrimination against black suspects? Black crime victims? Should courts be in the business of allocating police and prosecutorial resources across different racial communities? These questions, and others equally hard, would have to be faced if the Court sought to attack the criminal justice system's race problems directly.

None of this is to say that the Court's approach in *Duncan*, or in earlier cases like *Moore*, *Powell*, and *Brown*, was right. Perhaps we would be better off if race were addressed more directly in the law of criminal procedure. Whatever the right answer to that question is, the Supreme Court's usual strategy has been to sidestep—and to regulate procedures aggressively on *non*-racial grounds.

2. Notice one key difference between *Duncan* and most of the pre-incorporation due process cases. In the older due process cases, the Court almost always responded to apparent injustices with standards that required case-by-case development and application. Brown v. Mississippi, 297 U.S. 278 (1936), barred the use of involuntary confessions, but left open what voluntariness meant. Betts v. Brady, 316 U.S. 455 (1942), required use of appointed counsel where special circumstances suggested a particular need, but left undefined what those circumstances were. In *Duncan*, by contrast, the Court established a hard-and-fast rule. At the least, the Court said, any crime punishable by two years in prison triggers the right to a jury; the Court hinted that any crime punishable by more than six months would do so as well. (The hint was soon confirmed by Baldwin v. New York, 399 U.S. 66 (1970).) Why the shift from standards to rules? What would a standard (as opposed to a rule) look like in *Duncan*?

3. The move from standards to rules is one of the most important effects of incorporation; in one area after another, the Court of the 1960s and 1970s created a large body of detailed legal rules where previously constitutional law had said little more than "be fair." Examples include the right to jury trial in *Duncan*, covered in more detail in Chapter 14; the detailed rules governing the Fourth Amendment's warrant requirement (and exceptions thereto) covered in Chapter 5; the rules governing application of the Fifth Amendment's privilege against self-incrimination to police interrogation, covered in Chapter 7; or the rules defining the ban on double jeopardy, the subject of Chapter 16. In each of these areas, pre-incorporation constitutional law either said nothing at all or offered only a vague prohibition of extreme misconduct. Constitutional law today says a great deal, and a great deal of it is in the form of rules.

As that description suggests, there are two other changes that went alongside the move from standards to rules. Before incorporation, constitutional law regulated the criminal process very lightly. After incorporation, it regulates much more extensively. Constitutional law today goes far toward defining the criminal process—it is not a marginal presence in criminal procedure; on the contrary, it *dominates* criminal procedure. So constitutional regulation has become much more intrusive—much larger—as it has become much more rulelike. The last of these three changes is the most obvious. Incorporation shifts the constitutional focus from the Due Process Clause to the various criminal procedure provisions of the Bill of Rights. Instead of construing the phrase "due process of law," courts today are more likely to be interpreting phrases like "the assistance of counsel," or "compelled to be a witness against himself," or "unreasonable searches and seizures."

These three changes—from standards to rules, from light regulation to heavy regulation, from due process to the Bill of Rights—happened together. Is that anything more than an accident? Couldn't the Supreme Court have crafted a law of due process that was more rule-like? That regulated criminal procedure more extensively? As you study subsequent chapters in this book, consider this question: How might the law differ if it were based on due process and not on some provision of the Fourth, Fifth, or Sixth Amendment?

4. One common complaint about pre-incorporation due process cases is the absence of any clear, agreed-upon value being advanced. In some cases, the Court seemed concerned with ensuring accurate trials; in other cases, it was more concerned with preserving the rule of law; in still others, it was concerned with something the Justices found impossible to articulate, capturing it in labels like "fundamental fairness" or "shocks the conscience." Incorporation seems, at first blush, to solve that problem, by anchoring the Court's criminal procedure decisions in more definite pieces of constitutional text. The right to a jury, the right to counsel, the privilege against self-incrimination—all these things seem clearer than "due process of law."

But that clarity may be an illusion. Think about *Duncan* and the right to jury trial. What is the point of that right? There are several possible answers. Juries could be designed to ensure accuracy—the idea here would be that a single judge is more likely to convict an innocent defendant than are 12 citizens. Or juries could be designed as a democratic check on the judiciary. Here, the image is of juries as mini-legislatures, supervising the behavior of police, prosecutors, and judges. Yet a third possibility is suggested by the facts in *Duncan*: Juries could be a way to ensure that racial or ethnic minorities are punished with the consent of their peers. That might translate into juries that always have black or Latino members when judging black or Latino defendants.

These possibilities lead to very different visions of the right. If accuracy is the point, the right to a jury ought to be available, at the least, for all serious crimes—as *Duncan* holds. If preserving a democratic check on the courts is the point, perhaps juries ought to be required in *all* criminal trials (and perhaps *trials* should be required, since plea bargains are hidden from the public). If ensuring minority representation is the point, maybe the right to a jury ought to be available to black defendants like Duncan, but not to the white teenagers with whom Duncan was allegedly fighting.

In short, the Court must, at least tacitly, decide what the right to a jury is *about* in order to decide what that right entails. Answering that question may be no easier than answering the question of what due process is about. And with incorporation, the question is repeated for every Bill of Rights provision. What is the point of banning "unreasonable searches and seizures"? Privacy protection? Protecting against police coercion? Something else? What about the privilege against self-incrimination—is it a protection for the guilty, or for the innocent? Does it protect freedom of thought, or does it only limit the government's ability to twist people's arms? Is the right to counsel a means of ensuring equality between rich and poor defendants, or a tool for generating accurate results? Because of incorporation, the law of criminal procedure must answer all these questions. And the questions are just as difficult as the question the Due Process Clause poses: What does it mean to treat people fairly?

5. As mentioned above, McDonald v. City of Chicago, IL, 561 U.S. 742 (2010), is the most recent incorporationist case concluding that the Second Amendment is implicit in the Due Process Clause of the Fourteenth Amendment. In a somewhat stunning development, the positions of the various justices were completely reversed from that of their intellectual precursors on the Court. Incorporationist theory was employed by the "liberal" wing of the Court throughout the Warren era, and steadfastly resisted by "conservative" wing. In *McDonald*, by contrast, Justice Alito wrote for a plurality that included Chief Justice Roberts and Justices Kennedy and Scalia. Justice Thomas concurred with the result on the ground that the Privileges and Immunities Clause, not the Due Process Clause, does the work here, and the last 60 years or so of constitutional development should be rethought. Justices Stevens, Breyer, Ginsburg, and Sotomayor dissented. After *McDonald*, only four of the specific provisions of the Bill of Rights are not incorporated into Due Process: the Third Amendment's protection against the quartering of soldiers; the grand jury provision dealt with in *Hurtado*; the right to a civil jury in the Seventh Amendment; and the excessive fines provision in the Eighth Amendment. We leave it to you to determine what you think the implications of this development might be.

C.   The Residual Due Process Clause

What is left of due process in criminal cases apart from the Bill of Rights? Consider the following case.

MEDINA v. CALIFORNIA

Certiorari to the Supreme Court of California
505 U.S. 437 (1992)

JUSTICE KENNEDY delivered the opinion of the Court.

It is well established that the Due Process Clause of the Fourteenth Amendment prohibits the criminal prosecution of a defendant who is not competent to stand trial. Drope v. Missouri, 420 U.S. 162 (1975); Pate v. Robinson, 383 U.S. 375 (1966). The issue in this case is whether the Due Process Clause permits a State to require a defendant who alleges incompetence to stand trial to bear the burden of proving so by a preponderance of the evidence.

In 1984, petitioner Teofilo Medina, Jr., stole a gun from a pawnshop in Santa Ana, California. In the weeks that followed, he held up two gas stations, a drive-in dairy, and a market, murdered three employees of those establishments, attempted to rob a fourth employee, and shot at two passers-by who attempted to follow his get-away car. Petitioner was . . . charged with a number of criminal offenses, including three counts of first-degree murder. Before trial, petitioner's counsel moved for a competency hearing . . . on the ground that he was unsure whether petitioner had the ability to participate in the criminal proceedings against him.

Under California law, "[a] person cannot be tried or adjudged to punishment while such person is mentally incompetent." Cal. Penal Code Ann. §1367 (West 1982). A defendant is mentally incompetent "if, as a result of mental disorder or developmental disability, the defendant is unable to understand the nature of the criminal proceedings or to assist counsel in the conduct of a defense in a rational manner." Ibid. The statute establishes a presumption that the defendant is competent, and the party claiming incompetence bears the burden of proving that the defendant is incompetent by a preponderance of the evidence. . . .

The trial court granted the motion for a hearing and the preliminary issue of petitioner's competence to stand trial was tried to a jury. Over the course of the 6-day hearing, in addition to lay testimony, the jury heard conflicting expert testimony about petitioner's mental condition. The Supreme Court of California gives this summary:

> Dr. Gold, a psychiatrist who knew defendant while he was in the Arizona prison system, testified that defendant was a paranoid schizophrenic and was incompetent to assist his attorney at trial. Dr. Echeandia, a clinical psychologist at the Orange County jail, doubted the accuracy of the schizophrenia diagnosis, and could not express an opinion on defendant's competence to stand trial. Dr. Sharma, a psychiatrist, likewise expressed doubts regarding the schizophrenia diagnosis and leaned toward a finding of competence. Dr. Pierce, a psychologist, believed defendant was schizophrenic, with impaired memory and hallucinations, but nevertheless was competent to stand trial. Dr. Sakurai, a jail psychiatrist, opined that although defendant suffered from depression, he was competent, and that he may have been malingering. Dr. Sheffield, who treated defendant for knife wounds he incurred in jail, could give no opinion on the competency issue.

51 Cal. 3d 870, 880, 799 P.2d 1282, 1288 (1990).

During the competency hearing, petitioner engaged in several verbal and physical outbursts. On one of these occasions, he overturned the counsel table.

. . . The jury found petitioner competent to stand trial. A new jury was empaneled for the criminal trial, and . . . found [petitioner] guilty of all three counts of first-degree murder and a number of lesser offenses. . . . A sanity hearing was held, and the jury found that petitioner was sane at the time of the offenses. At the penalty phase, the jury found that the murders were premeditated and deliberate and returned a verdict of death. The trial court imposed the death penalty for the murder convictions and sentenced petitioner to a prison term for the remaining offenses. . . . [The California Supreme Court affirmed.]

Petitioner argues that our decision in Mathews v. Eldridge, 424 U.S. 319 (1976), provides the proper analytical framework for determining whether California's allocation of the burden of proof in competency hearings comports with due process. We disagree. In *Mathews*, we articulated a three-factor test for evaluating procedural due process claims which requires a court to consider first, the private interest that will be affected by the official action; second, the risk of an erroneous deprivation of such interest through the procedures used, and the probable value, if any, of additional or substitute procedural safeguards; and finally, the Government's interest, including the function involved and the fiscal and administrative burdens that the additional or substitute procedural requirement would entail.

Id., at 335.

In our view, the *Mathews* balancing test does not provide the appropriate framework for assessing the validity of state procedural rules which, like the one at bar, are part of the criminal process. . . .

In the field of criminal law, we "have defined the category of infractions that violate 'fundamental fairness' very narrowly" based on the recognition that, "beyond the specific guarantees enumerated in the Bill of Rights, the Due Process Clause has limited operation." Dowling v. United States, 493 U.S. 342, 352 (1990). The Bill of Rights speaks in explicit terms to many aspects of criminal procedure, and the expansion of those constitutional guarantees under the open-ended rubric of the Due Process Clause invites undue interference with both considered legislative judgments and the careful balance that the Constitution strikes between liberty and order. As we said in Spencer v. Texas, 385 U.S. 554, 564 (1967), "it has never been thought that [decisions under the Due Process Clause] establish this Court as a rule-making organ for the promulgation of state rules of criminal procedure."

Mathews itself involved a due process challenge to the adequacy of administrative procedures established for the purpose of terminating Social Security disability benefits, and the *Mathews* balancing test was first conceived to address due process claims arising in the context of administrative law. . . .

The proper analytical approach, and the one that we adopt here, is that set forth in Patterson v. New York, 432 U.S. 197 (1977), which was decided one year after *Mathews*. In *Patterson*, we rejected a due process challenge to a New York law which placed on a criminal defendant the burden of proving the affirmative defense of extreme emotional disturbance. Rather than relying upon the *Mathews* balancing test, however, we reasoned that a narrower inquiry was more appropriate:

> It goes without saying that preventing and dealing with crime is much more the business of the States than it is of the Federal Government, and that we should not lightly construe the Constitution so as to intrude upon the administration of justice by the individual States. Among other things, it is normally "within the power of the State to regulate procedures under which its laws are carried out, including the burden of producing evidence and the burden of persuasion," and its decision in this regard is not subject to proscription under the Due Process Clause unless "it offends some principle of justice so rooted in the traditions and conscience of our people as to be ranked as fundamental." Speiser v. Randall, 357 U.S. 513, 523 (1958).

Patterson v. New York, 432 U.S., at 201-202.

As *Patterson* suggests, because the States have considerable expertise in matters of criminal procedure and the criminal process is grounded in centuries of common-law tradition, it is appropriate to exercise substantial deference to legislative judgments in this area. The analytical approach endorsed in *Patterson* is thus far less intrusive than that approved in *Mathews*.

Based on our review of the historical treatment of the burden of proof in competency proceedings, the operation of the challenged rule, and our precedents, we cannot say that the allocation of the burden of proof to a criminal defendant to prove incompetence "offends some principle of justice so rooted in the traditions and conscience of our people as to be ranked as fundamental." Patterson v. New York, 432 U.S., at 202 (internal quotation marks omitted). Historical practice is probative of whether a procedural rule can be characterized as fundamental. See In re Winship, 397 U.S. 358, 361 (1970). The rule that a criminal defendant who is incompetent should not be required to stand trial has deep roots in our common-law heritage. Blackstone acknowledged that a defendant "who became 'mad' after the commission of an offense should not be arraigned for it 'because he is not able to plead to it with that advice and caution that he ought,'" and "if he became 'mad' after pleading, he should not be tried, 'for how can he make his defense?'" Drope v. Missouri, 420 U.S., at 171 (quoting 4 W. Blackstone, Commentaries *24); accord, 1 M. Hale, Pleas of the Crown *34-*35.

By contrast, there is no settled tradition on the proper allocation of the burden of proof in a proceeding to determine competence. . . . Contemporary practice, while of limited relevance to the due process inquiry, demonstrates that there remains no settled view of where the burden of proof should lie. . . . Some States have enacted statutes that, like §1369(f), place the burden of proof on the party raising the issue. E.g., Conn. Gen. Stat. §54-56d(b) (1991); Pa. Stat. Ann., Tit. 50, §7403(a) (Purdon Supp. 1991). A number of state courts have said that the burden of proof may be placed on the defendant to prove incompetence. E.g., Wallace v. State, 248 Ga. 255, 258-259, 282 S.E.2d 325, 330 (1981); State v. Aumann, 265 N.W.2d 316, 319-320 (Iowa 1978); State v. Chapman, 104 N.M. 324, 327-328, 721 P.2d 392, 395-396 (1986); Barber v. State, 757 S.W.2d 359, 362-363 (Tex. Crim. App. 1988) (en banc). Still other state courts have said that the burden rests with the prosecution. E.g., Diaz v. State, 508 A.2d 861, 863-864 (Del. 1986); Commonwealth v. Crowley, 393 Mass. 393, 400-401, 471 N.E.2d 353, 357-358 (1984); State v. Bertrand, 123 N.H. 719, 727-728, 465 A.2d 912, 916 (1983); State v. Jones, 406 N.W.2d 366, 369-370 (S.D. 1987).

Discerning no historical basis for concluding that the allocation of the burden of proving incompetence to the defendant violates due process, we turn to consider whether the rule transgresses any recognized principle of "fundamental fairness" in operation. . . .

Under California law, the allocation of the burden of proof to the defendant will affect competency determinations only in a narrow class of cases where the evidence is in equipoise; that is, where the evidence that a defendant is competent is just as strong as the evidence that he is incompetent. Our cases recognize that a defendant has a constitutional right "not to be tried while legally incompetent," and that a State's "failure to observe procedures adequate to protect a defendant's right not to be tried or convicted while incompetent to stand trial deprives him of his due process right to a fair trial." Drope v. Missouri, 420 U.S., at 172, 173. Once a State provides a defendant access to procedures for making a competency evaluation, however, we perceive no basis for holding that due process further requires the State to assume the burden of vindicating the defendant's constitutional right by persuading the trier of fact that the defendant is competent to stand trial.

Petitioner relies upon federal—and state—court decisions which have said that the allocation of the burden of proof to the defendant in these circumstances is inconsistent with the rule of Pate v. Robinson, 383 U.S., at 384, where we held that a defendant whose competence is in doubt cannot be deemed to have waived his right to a competency hearing. . . . In our view, the question whether a defendant whose competence is in doubt may waive his right to a competency hearing is quite different from the question whether the burden of proof may be placed on the defendant once a hearing is held. The rule announced in *Pate* was driven by our concern that it is impossible to say whether a defendant whose competence is in doubt has made a knowing and intelligent waiver of his right to a competency hearing. Once a competency hearing is held, however, the defendant is entitled to the assistance of counsel, and psychiatric evidence is brought to bear on the question of the defendant's mental condition. Although an impaired defendant might be limited in his ability to assist counsel in demonstrating incompetence, the defendant's inability to assist counsel can, in and of itself, constitute probative evidence of incompetence, and defense counsel will often have the best-informed view of the defendant's ability to participate in his defense. While reasonable minds may differ as to the wisdom of placing the burden of proof on the defendant in these circumstances, we believe that a State may take such factors into account in making judgments as to the allocation of the burden of proof. . . .

Petitioner argues that psychiatry is an inexact science, and that placing the burden of proof on the defendant violates due process because it requires the defendant to "bear the risk of being forced to stand trial as a result of an erroneous finding of competency." Brief for Petitioner 8. . . . The Due Process Clause does not, however, require a State to adopt one procedure over another on the basis that it may produce results more favorable to the accused. See, e.g., Patterson v. New York, 432 U.S., at 208 ("Due process does not require that every conceivable step be taken, at whatever cost, to eliminate the possibility of convicting an innocent person"). Consistent with our precedents, it is enough that the State affords the criminal defendant on whose behalf a plea of incompetence is asserted a reasonable opportunity to demonstrate that he is not competent to stand trial.

Petitioner further contends that the burden of proof should be placed on the State because we have allocated the burden to the State on a variety of other issues that implicate a criminal defendant's constitutional rights. E.g., Colorado v. Connelly, 479 U.S. 157, 168-169 (1986) (waiver of *Miranda* rights); Nix v. Williams, 467 U.S. 431, 444-445, n. 5 (1984) (inevitable discovery of evidence obtained by unlawful means); United States v. Matlock, 415 U.S. 164, 177-178, n. 14 (1974) (voluntariness of consent to search); Lego v. Twomey, 404 U.S. 477, 489 (1972) (voluntariness of confession). The decisions upon which petitioner relies, however, do not control the result here, because they involved situations where the government sought to introduce inculpatory evidence obtained by virtue of a waiver of, or in violation of, a defendant's constitutional rights. In such circumstances, allocating the burden of proof to the government furthers the objective of "deterring lawless conduct by police and prosecution." Ibid. No such purpose is served by allocating the burden of proof to the government in a competency hearing.

In light of our determination that the allocation of the burden of proof to the defendant does not offend due process, it is not difficult to dispose of petitioner's challenge to the presumption of competence imposed by §1369(f). . . . [I]n essence, the challenged presumption is a restatement of the burden of proof, and it follows from what we have said that the presumption does not violate the Due Process Clause.

Nothing in today's decision is inconsistent with our long-standing recognition that the criminal trial of an incompetent defendant violates due process. Rather, our rejection of petitioner's challenge to §1369(f) is based on a determination that the California procedure is "constitutionally adequate" to guard against such results, Drope v. Missouri, 420 U.S., at 172, and reflects our considered view that "traditionally, due process has required that only the most basic procedural safeguards be observed; more subtle balancing of society's interests against those of the accused has been left to the legislative branch," Patterson v. New York, 432 U.S., at 210. . . .

JUSTICE O'CONNOR, with whom JUSTICE SOUTER joins, concurring in the judgment.

I concur in the judgment of the Court, but I reject its intimation that the balancing of equities is inappropriate in evaluating whether state criminal procedures amount to due process. . . . The balancing of equities that Mathews v. Eldridge[, 424 U.S. 319 (1976),] outlines remains a useful guide in due process cases.

In *Mathews*, however, we did not have to address the question of how much weight to give historical practice; in the context of modern administrative procedures, there was no historical practice to consider. . . . While I agree with the Court that historical pedigree can give a procedural practice a presumption of constitutionality, the presumption must surely be rebuttable.

. . . Against the historical status quo, I read the Court's opinion to allow some weight to be given countervailing considerations of fairness in operation, considerations much like those we evaluated in *Mathews*. Any less charitable reading of the Court's opinion would put it at odds with many of our criminal due process cases, in which we have required States to institute procedures that were neither required at common law nor explicitly commanded by the text of the Constitution. See, e.g., Griffin v. Illinois[, 351 U.S. 12 (1956)] (due process right to trial transcript on appeal); Brady v. Maryland, 373 U.S. 83 (1963) (due process right to discovery of exculpatory evidence); Sheppard v. Maxwell, 384 U.S. 333 (1966) (due process right to protection from prejudicial publicity and courtroom disruptions); Chambers v. Mississippi, 410 U.S. 284 (1973) (due process right to introduce certain evidence); Gagnon v. Scarpelli, 411 U.S. 778 (1973) (due process right to hearing and counsel before probation revoked); Ake v. Oklahoma[, 470 U.S. 68 (1985)] (due process right to psychiatric examination when sanity is significantly in question).

In determining whether the placement of the burden of proof is fundamentally unfair, relevant considerations include: whether the government has superior access to evidence; whether the defendant is capable of aiding in the garnering and evaluation of evidence on the matter to be proved; and whether placing the burden of proof on the government is necessary to help enforce a further right, such as the right to be presumed innocent, the right to be free from self-incrimination, or the right to be tried while competent.

After balancing the equities in this case, I agree with the Court that the burden of proof may constitutionally rest on the defendant. . . . [T]he competency determination is based largely on the testimony of psychiatrists. The main concern of the prosecution, of course, is that a defendant will feign incompetence in order to avoid trial. If the burden of proving competence rests on the government, a defendant will have less incentive to cooperate in psychiatric investigations, because an inconclusive examination will benefit the defense, not the prosecution. A defendant may also be less cooperative in making available friends or family who might have information about the defendant's mental state. States may therefore decide that a more complete picture of a defendant's competence will be obtained if the defense has the incentive to produce all the evidence in its possession. The potentially greater overall access to information provided by placing the burden of proof on the defense may outweigh the danger that, in close cases, a marginally incompetent defendant is brought to trial. Unlike the requirement of a hearing or a psychiatric examination, placing the burden of proof on the government will not necessarily increase the reliability of the proceedings. The equities here, then, do not weigh so much in petitioner's favor as to rebut the presumption of constitutionality that the historical toleration of procedural variation creates. . . .

[The dissenting opinion of Justice Blackmun, joined by Justice Stevens, is omitted.]

NOTES AND QUESTIONS

1. The Supreme Court first held, squarely, that due process requires a hearing on the defendant's competence to stand trial in cases where competence is plausibly at issue in Pate v. Robinson, 383 U.S. 375 (1966). In that case, the state conceded the existence of the legal right but argued that the defendant had waived it. The Court rejected the argument out of hand, saying only that "it is contradictory to argue that a defendant may be incompetent, and yet knowingly or intelligently 'waive' his right to have the court determine his capacity to stand trial." Id., at 384. Is that right? Does the presence of competent defense counsel affect the waiver issue?

Pate left the law of competence to stand trial in an uncertain state. Drope v. Missouri, 420 U.S. 162 (1975), resolved some of the uncertainty. The defendant in *Drope* had a history of mental illness. During his rape trial, he tried unsuccessfully to kill himself; the trial court ruled that the trial could continue in the defendant's absence, and he was convicted. No inquiry into the defendant's competence to stand trial was conducted. A unanimous Court concluded that due process was violated:

> It has long been accepted that a person whose mental condition is such that he lacks the capacity to understand the nature and object of the proceedings against him, to consult with counsel, and to assist in preparing his defense may not be subjected to a trial. Thus, Blackstone wrote that one who became "mad" after the commission of an offense should not be arraigned for it "because he is not able to plead to it with that advice and caution that he ought." Similarly, if he became "mad" after pleading, he should not be tried, "for how can he make his defense?" 4 W. Blackstone, Commentaries *24. . . . Accordingly, as to federal cases, we have approved a test of incompetence which seeks to ascertain whether a criminal defendant "has sufficient present ability to consult with his lawyer with a reasonable degree of rational understanding—and whether he has a rational as well as factual understanding of the proceedings against him." Dusky v. United States, 362 U.S., at 402.
>
> In Pate v. Robinson, 383 U.S. 375 (1966), we held that the failure to observe procedures adequate to protect a defendant's right not to be tried or convicted while incompetent to stand trial deprives him of his due process right to a fair trial. . . . [T]he Court did not prescribe a general standard with respect to the nature or quantum of evidence necessary to require resort to an adequate procedure. Rather, it noted that under the Illinois statute a hearing was required where the evidence raised a "bona fide doubt" as to a defendant's competence, and the Court concluded "that the evidence introduced on Robinson's behalf entitled him to a hearing on this issue." 383 U.S., at 385. . . .
>
> In the present case . . . , [the question is] whether, in light of what was then known, the failure to make further inquiry into petitioner's competence to stand trial, denied him a fair trial. . . .

Notwithstanding the difficulty of making evaluations of the kind required in these circumstances, we conclude that the record reveals a failure to give proper weight to the information suggesting incompetence which came to light during trial. . . .

The import of our decision in Pate v. Robinson is that evidence of a defendant's irrational behavior, his demeanor at trial, and any prior medical opinion on competence to stand trial are all relevant in determining whether further inquiry is required, but that even one of these factors standing alone may, in some circumstances, be sufficient. There are, of course, no fixed or immutable signs which invariably indicate the need for further inquiry to determine fitness to proceed; the question is often a difficult one in which a wide range of manifestations and subtle nuances are implicated. That they are difficult to evaluate is suggested by the varying opinions trained psychiatrists can entertain on the same facts.

. . . Petitioner's absence [from much of his trial] bears on the analysis in two ways: first, it was due to an act which suggests a rather substantial degree of mental instability contemporaneous with the trial; second, as a result of petitioner's absence the trial judge and defense counsel were no longer able to observe him in the context of the trial and to gauge from his demeanor whether he was able to cooperate with his attorney and to understand the nature and object of the proceedings against him.

Even when a defendant is competent at the commencement of his trial, a trial court must always be alert to circumstances suggesting a change that would render the accused unable to meet the standards of competence to stand trial. Whatever the relationship between mental illness and incompetence to stand trial, in this case the bearing of the former on the latter was sufficiently likely that, in light of the evidence of petitioner's behavior including his suicide attempt, and there being no opportunity without his presence to evaluate that bearing in fact, the correct course was to suspend the trial until such an evaluation could be made. . . .

420 U.S., at 172-175, 179-181. *Drope* was an easy case: Defense counsel had moved for a hearing on competence prior to trial, and moved for a continuance when his client attempted suicide. What if no such motion is made?

The question is not merely hypothetical. The usual consequence of a finding of incompetence to stand trial is not that the defendant goes free—rather, the state is likely to initiate some form of civil commitment proceeding. Civil commitment statutes generally authorize holding defendants in custody as long as they are a danger to themselves or to others. For some defendants, that may mean a de facto life sentence, which may be considerably worse than the prison term the defendant faces if he is convicted of a crime. Notice what this means: Competence to stand trial is unlike most criminal procedure issues. Ordinarily, defendants have a strong incentive to raise valid procedural claims. In the case of competence, a rational defendant may wish to ignore the issue. Of course, if the defendant is arguably incompetent, he is not likely to *be* rational. But his lawyer is. What should defense counsel do if her client (i) may well be incompetent to stand trial, (ii) faces a brief prison term if convicted, and (iii) faces a long stay in a state-run mental institution if civilly committed? How does your answer to this question bear on the burden-of-proof issue in *Medina?*

2. During the same Term as *Medina*, the Court decided Riggins v. Nevada, 504 U.S. 127 (1992). In *Riggins*, following a sparse evidentiary hearing, the trial court permitted the forced medication of the defendant with an antipsychotic drug. The trial court's order "gave no indication of the court's rationale." In reversing, the Court, per Justice O'Connor, opined:

Although we have not had occasion to develop substantive standards for judging forced administration of such drugs in the trial or pretrial settings, Nevada certainly would have satisfied due process if the prosecution had demonstrated and the District Court had found that treatment with antipsychotic medication was medically appropriate and, considering less intrusive alternatives, essential for the sake of Riggins' own safety or the safety of others. Similarly, the State might have been able to justify medically appropriate, involuntary treatment with the drug by establishing that it could not obtain an adjudication of Riggins' guilt or innocence by using less intrusive means.

. . . We have no occasion to finally prescribe such substantive standards . . . , since the District Court allowed the administration of Mellaril to continue without making any determination of the need for this course or any findings about reasonable alternatives. The court's laconic order denying Riggins' motion did not adopt the State's view, which was that continued administration of Mellaril was required to ensure that the defendant could be tried; in fact, the hearing testimony casts considerable doubt on that argument. Nor did the order indicate a finding that safety considerations or other compelling concerns outweighed Riggins' interest in freedom from unwanted antipsychotic drugs.

504 U.S., at 135-136. Is *Riggins* consistent with *Medina*?

3. In Cooper v. Oklahoma, 517 U.S. 348 (1996), the Court confronted a state statute that required defendants to prove incompetence by clear and convincing evidence. The Court found that rule, unlike the burden-of-proof rule in *Medina*, violated due process:

> The question we address today is quite different from the question posed in *Medina*. Petitioner's claim requires us to consider whether a State may proceed with a criminal trial after the defendant has demonstrated that he is more likely than not incompetent. Oklahoma does not contend that it may require the defendant to prove incompetence beyond a reasonable doubt. The State maintains, however, that the clear and convincing standard provides a reasonable accommodation of the opposing interests of the State and the defendant. We are persuaded, by both traditional and modern practice and the importance of the constitutional interest at stake, that the State's argument must be rejected.
>
> "Historical practice is probative of whether a procedural rule can be characterized as fundamental," *Medina*, 505 U.S., at 446. In this case, unlike in *Medina*, there is no indication that the rule Oklahoma seeks to defend has any roots in prior practice. Indeed, it appears that a rule significantly more favorable to the defendant has had a long and consistent application. . . .
>
> [The Court then discussed a series of cases suggesting that the traditional common law rule required only proof of incompetence by a preponderance of the evidence.]
>
> Contemporary practice demonstrates that the vast majority of jurisdictions remain persuaded that the heightened standard of proof imposed on the accused in Oklahoma is not necessary to vindicate the State's interest in prompt and orderly disposition of criminal cases. Only 4 of the 50 States presently require the criminal defendant to prove his incompetence by clear and convincing evidence. None of the remaining 46 jurisdictions imposes such a heavy burden on the defendant. Indeed, a number of States place no burden on the defendant at all, but rather require the prosecutor to prove the defendant's competence to stand trial once a question about competency has been credibly raised. The situation is no different in federal court. Congress has directed that the accused in a federal prosecution must prove incompetence by a preponderance of the evidence. 18 U.S.C. §4241. . . .
>
> The near-uniform application of a standard that is more protective of the defendant's rights than Oklahoma's clear and convincing evidence rule supports our conclusion that the heightened standard offends a principle of justice that is deeply

"rooted in the traditions and conscience of our people." *Medina*, 505 U.S., at 445 (internal quotation marks omitted).

517 U.S., at 355-356, 360-362. After *Cooper*, states may force defendants to prove incompetence, but not by more than a preponderance. Does this seem like a sensible splitting of the difference, or like an arbitrary splitting of constitutional hairs?

Perhaps *Medina* and *Cooper*, taken together, represent a sound pragmatic judgment—that defendants are better able to gather evidence of incompetence than the government is to prove competence, *but* that a "clear and convincing" burden would risk too many incompetent defendants going to trial. But is there any principled basis for drawing the line where *Medina* and *Cooper* draw it?

This is a persistent problem in criminal procedure. Protections for defendants' rights constantly involve questions of degree—infinite protection is impossible, so protection must be rationed, graded. And there is rarely any obvious reason to choose this degree of protection rather than something a little more, or a little less. More than most areas of law, criminal procedure may be in the business of splitting differences, and splitting differences rarely seems principled.

4. Notice the *Medina* Court's statement that the Mathews v. Eldridge test for due process, the test used in civil cases, is not to be used in criminal procedure. Instead, the Court says in *Medina*, "because the States have considerable expertise in matters of criminal procedure and the criminal process is grounded in centuries of common-law tradition, it is appropriate to exercise substantial deference to legislative judgments in this area."

Does this statement seem strange? One would ordinarily think of criminal procedure as deserving greater constitutional regulation than the civil process. Yet the *Medina* Court seems to flip the two categories. Why?

The reason, the Court says, is the Bill of Rights: "The Bill of Rights speaks in explicit terms to many aspects of criminal procedure, and the expansion of those constitutional guarantees under the open-ended rubric of the Due Process Clause invites undue interference with both considered legislative judgments and the careful balance that the Constitution strikes between liberty and order." The idea resembles a kind of constitutional displacement, with the Bill of Rights occupying the relevant constitutional space, leaving very little space left over for an expansive reading of due process.

What do you think of that idea? Does it affect your view of incorporation? Decisions like *Duncan* plainly offered greater protection to criminal defendants in some respects; the reasoning in *Medina* suggests those decisions may have led to reduced protection in other areas.

5. The Court reentered the thicket of freestanding Due Process analysis in the context of the "war on terror." Consider the following case.

HAMDI v. RUMSFELD

Certiorari to the United States Court of Appeals for the Fourth Circuit
542 U.S. 507 (2004)

JUSTICE O'CONNOR announced the judgment of the Court and delivered an opinion, in which CHIEF JUSTICE REHNQUIST, JUSTICE KENNEDY, and JUSTICE BREYER join.

At this difficult time in our Nation's history, we are called upon to consider the legality of the Government's detention of a United States citizen on United States soil as an "enemy combatant" and to address the process that is constitutionally owed to one who seeks to challenge his classification as such. . . .

I

On September 11, 2001, the al Qaeda terrorist network used hijacked commercial airliners to attack prominent targets in the United States. Approximately 3,000 people were killed in those attacks. One week later, in response to these "acts of treacherous violence," Congress passed a resolution authorizing the President to "use all necessary and appropriate force against those nations, organizations, or persons he determines planned, authorized, committed, or aided the terrorist attacks" or "harbored such organizations or persons, in order to prevent any future acts of international terrorism against the United States by such nations, organizations, or persons." Authorization for Use of Military Force ("the AUMF"), 115 Stat. 224. Soon thereafter, the President ordered United States Armed Forces to Afghanistan, with a mission to subdue al Qaeda and quell the Taliban regime that was known to support it.

This case arises out of the detention of a man whom the Government alleges took up arms with the Taliban during this conflict. His name is Yaser Esam Hamdi. Born an American citizen in Louisiana in 1980, Hamdi moved with his family to Saudi Arabia as a child. By 2001, the parties agree, he resided in Afghanistan. At some point that year, he was seized by members of the Northern Alliance, a coalition of military groups opposed to the Taliban government, and eventually was turned over to the United States military. The Government asserts that it initially detained and interrogated Hamdi in Afghanistan before transferring him to the United States Naval Base in Guantanamo Bay in January 2002. In April 2002, upon learning that Hamdi is an American citizen, authorities transferred him to a naval brig in Norfolk, Virginia, where he remained until a recent transfer to a brig in Charleston, South Carolina. The Government contends that Hamdi is an "enemy combatant," and that this status justifies holding him in the United States indefinitely—without formal charges or proceedings—unless and until it makes the determination that access to counsel or further process is warranted.

In June 2002, Hamdi's father, Esam Fouad Hamdi, filed the present petition for a writ of habeas corpus under 28 U.S.C. §2241 in the Eastern District of Virginia, naming as petitioners his son and himself as next friend. The elder Hamdi alleges in the petition that he has had no contact with his son since the Government took custody of him in 2001, and that the Government has held his son "without access to legal counsel or notice of any charges pending against him." . . . The habeas petition asks that the court, among other things, (1) appoint counsel for Hamdi; (2) order respondents to cease interrogating him; (3) declare that he is being held in violation of the Fifth and Fourteenth Amendments; (4) "[t]o the extent Respondents contest any material factual allegations in this Petition, schedule an evidentiary hearing, at which Petitioners may adduce proof in support of their allegations"; and (5) order that Hamdi be released from his "unlawful custody." Although his habeas petition provides no details with regard to the factual circumstances surrounding his son's capture and detention, Hamdi's father has asserted in documents found elsewhere in the record that his son went to Afghanistan to do "relief work," and that he had been in that country less than two months before September 11, 2001, and could not have received military training. The 20-year-old was traveling on his own for the first time, his father says, and "[b]ecause of his lack of experience, he was trapped in Afghanistan once that military campaign began."

The District Court . . . appointed the federal public defender as counsel for the petitioners, and ordered that counsel be given access to Hamdi. The United States Court of Appeals for the Fourth Circuit reversed that order, holding that the District Court had failed to extend appropriate deference to the Government's security and intelligence interests. 296 F.3d 278, 279, 283 (2002). It directed the District Court to consider "the most cautious procedures first," id., at 284, and to conduct a deferential inquiry into Hamdi's status, id., at 283. It opined that "if Hamdi is indeed an 'enemy combatant' who was captured during hostilities in Afghanistan, the government's present detention of him is a lawful one." Ibid.

On remand, the Government filed a response and a motion to dismiss the petition. It attached to its response a declaration from one Michael Mobbs (hereinafter "Mobbs Declaration"), who identified himself as Special Advisor to the Under Secretary of Defense for Policy. Mobbs indicated that in this position, he has been "substantially involved with matters related to the detention of enemy combatants in the current war against the al Qaeda terrorists and those who support and harbor them (including the Taliban)." . . . Mobbs . . . set forth what remains the sole evidentiary support that the Government has provided to the courts for Hamdi's detention. The declaration states that Hamdi "traveled to Afghanistan" in July or August 2001, and that he thereafter "affiliated with a Taliban military unit and received weapons training." It asserts that Hamdi "remained with his Taliban unit following the attacks of September 11" and that, during the time when Northern Alliance forces were "engaged in battle with the Taliban," "Hamdi's Taliban unit surrendered" to those forces, after which he "surrender[ed] his Kalishnikov assault rifle" to them. The Mobbs Declaration also states that, because al Qaeda and the Taliban "were and are hostile forces engaged in armed conflict with the armed forces of the United States," "individuals associated with" those groups "were and continue to be enemy combatants." Mobbs states that Hamdi was labeled an enemy combatant "[b]ased upon his interviews and in light of his association with the Taliban." According to the declaration, a series of "U.S. military screening team[s]" determined that Hamdi met "the criteria for enemy combatants," and "a subsequent interview of Hamdi has confirmed that he surrendered and gave his firearm to Northern Alliance forces, which supports his classification as an enemy combatant."

After the Government submitted this declaration, the Fourth Circuit directed the District Court to proceed in accordance with its earlier ruling and, specifically, to "consider the sufficiency of the Mobbs Declaration as an independent matter before proceeding further." 316 F.3d 450, 462 (2003). The District Court found that the Mobbs Declaration fell "far short" of supporting Hamdi's detention. . . . It ordered the Government to turn over numerous materials for *in camera* review, including copies of all of Hamdi's statements and the notes taken from interviews with him that related to his reasons for going to Afghanistan and his activities therein; a list of all interrogators who had questioned Hamdi and their names and addresses; statements by members of the Northern Alliance regarding Hamdi's surrender and capture; a list of the dates and locations of his capture and subsequent detentions; and the names and titles of the United States Government officials who made the determinations that Hamdi was an enemy combatant and that he should be moved to a naval brig. . . .

The Government sought to appeal the production order, and the District Court certified the question of whether the Mobbs Declaration, "standing alone, is sufficient as a matter of law to allow meaningful judicial review of [Hamdi's] classification as an enemy combatant." 316 F.3d, at 462. The Fourth Circuit reversed, but did not squarely answer the certified question. It instead stressed that, because it was "undisputed that Hamdi was captured in a zone of active combat in a foreign theater of conflict," no factual inquiry or evidentiary hearing allowing Hamdi to be heard or to rebut the Government's assertions was necessary or proper. Id., at 459. Concluding that the factual averments in the Mobbs Declaration, "if accurate," provided a sufficient basis upon which to conclude that the President had constitutionally detained Hamdi pursuant to the President's war powers, it ordered the habeas petition dismissed. Id., at 473. . . .

II

The threshold question before us is whether the Executive has the authority to detain citizens who qualify as "enemy combatants." There is some debate as to the proper scope of this term, and the Government has never provided any court with the full criteria that it uses in classifying individuals as such. It has made clear, however, that, for purposes of this case, the "enemy combatant" that it is seeking to detain is an individual who, it alleges, was "part of or supporting forces hostile to the United States or coalition partners" in Afghanistan and who "engaged in an armed conflict against the United States" there. Brief for Respondents 3. We therefore answer only the narrow question before us: whether the detention of citizens falling within that definition is authorized. . . .

The Government . . . maintains that [18 U.S.C.] §4001(a)[12] is satisfied, because Hamdi is being detained "pursuant to an Act of Congress"—the AUMF. Id., at 21-22. . . . [W]e conclude that the AUMF is explicit congressional authorization for the detention of individuals in the narrow category we describe (assuming, without deciding, that such authorization is required), and that the AUMF satisfied §4001(a)'s requirement that a detention be "pursuant to an Act of Congress" (assuming, without deciding, that §4001(a) applies to military detentions). . . .

There is no bar to this Nation's holding one of its own citizens as an enemy combatant. In [Ex parte Quirin, 317 U.S. 1 (1942)], one of the detainees, Haupt, alleged that he was a naturalized United States citizen. 317 U.S., at 20. We held that "[c]itizens who associate themselves with the military arm of the enemy government, and with its aid, guidance and direction enter this country bent on hostile acts, are enemy belligerents within the meaning of . . . the law of war." Id., at 37-38. While Haupt was tried for violations of the law of war, nothing in *Quirin* suggests that his citizenship would have precluded his mere detention for the duration of the relevant hostilities. See id., at 30-31. . . . A citizen, no less than an alien, can be "part of or supporting forces hostile to the United States or coalition partners" and "engaged in an armed conflict against the United States," Brief for Respondents 3;

---

12. "No citizen shall be imprisoned or otherwise detained by the United States except pursuant to an Act of Congress."—EDS.

such a citizen, if released, would pose the same threat of returning to the front during the ongoing conflict. . . .

Hamdi objects, nevertheless, that Congress has not authorized the *indefinite* detention to which he is now subject. . . . We take Hamdi's objection to be not to the lack of certainty regarding the date on which the conflict will end, but to the substantial prospect of perpetual detention. We recognize that the national security underpinnings of the "war on terror," although crucially important, are broad and malleable. As the Government concedes, given its unconventional nature, the current conflict is unlikely to end with a formal cease-fire agreement. The prospect Hamdi raises is therefore not far-fetched. If the Government does not consider this unconventional war won for two generations, and if it maintains during that time that Hamdi might, if released, rejoin forces fighting against the United States, then the position it has taken throughout the litigation of this case suggests that Hamdi's detention could last for the rest of his life. . . .

. . . Certainly, we agree that indefinite detention for the purpose of interrogation is not authorized. Further, we understand Congress' grant of authority for the use of "necessary and appropriate force" to include the authority to detain for the duration of the relevant conflict, and our understanding is based on longstanding law-of-war principles. If the practical circumstances of a given conflict are entirely unlike those of the conflicts that informed the development of the law of war, that understanding may unravel. But that is not the situation we face as of this date. Active combat operations against Taliban fighters apparently are ongoing in Afghanistan. . . . The United States may detain, for the duration of these hostilities, individuals legitimately determined to be Taliban combatants who "engaged in an armed conflict against the United States." If the record establishes that United States troops are still involved in active combat in Afghanistan, those detentions are part of the exercise of "necessary and appropriate force," and therefore are authorized by the AUMF. . . .

III

Even in cases in which the detention of enemy combatants is legally authorized, there remains the question of what process is constitutionally due to a citizen who disputes his enemy-combatant status. Hamdi argues that he is owed a meaningful and timely hearing and that "extra-judicial detention [that] begins and ends with the submission of an affidavit based on third-hand hearsay" does not comport with the Fifth and Fourteenth Amendments. Brief for Petitioners 16. The Government counters that any more process than was provided below would be both unworkable and "constitutionally intolerable." Brief for Respondents 46. Our resolution of this dispute requires a careful examination both of the writ of habeas corpus, which Hamdi now seeks to employ as a mechanism of judicial review, and of the Due Process Clause, which informs the procedural contours of that mechanism in this instance. . . .

The Government [argues] that further factual exploration is unwarranted and inappropriate in light of the extraordinary constitutional interests at stake. Under the Government's most extreme rendition of this argument, "[r]espect for separation of powers and the limited institutional capabilities of courts in matters of military decision-making in connection with an ongoing conflict" ought to eliminate entirely any individual process, restricting the courts to investigating only whether legal authorization exists for the broader detention scheme. Brief for Respondents

26. At most, the Government argues, courts should review its determination that a citizen is an enemy combatant under a very deferential "some evidence" standard. Id., at 34. Under this review, a court would assume the accuracy of the Government's articulated basis for Hamdi's detention, as set forth in the Mobbs Declaration, and assess only whether that articulated basis was a legitimate one. Brief for Respondents 36. . . .

In response, Hamdi emphasizes that this Court consistently has recognized that an individual challenging his detention may not be held at the will of the Executive without recourse to some proceeding before a neutral tribunal to determine whether the Executive's asserted justifications for that detention have basis in fact and warrant in law. See, e.g., Zadvydas v. Davis, 533 U.S. 678, 690 (2001); Addington v. Texas, 441 U.S. 418, 425-427 (1979). He argues that the Fourth Circuit inappropriately "ceded power to the Executive during wartime to define the conduct for which a citizen may be detained, judge whether that citizen has engaged in the proscribed conduct, and imprison that citizen indefinitely," Brief for Petitioners 21, and that due process demands that he receive a hearing in which he may challenge the Mobbs Declaration and adduce his own counter evidence. The District Court, agreeing with Hamdi, apparently believed that the appropriate process would approach the process that accompanies a criminal trial. It therefore disapproved of the hearsay nature of the Mobbs Declaration and anticipated quite extensive discovery of various military affairs. Anything less, it concluded, would not be "meaningful judicial review."

Both of these positions highlight legitimate concerns. And both emphasize the tension that often exists between the autonomy that the Government asserts is necessary in order to pursue effectively a particular goal and the process that a citizen contends he is due before he is deprived of a constitutional right. The ordinary mechanism that we use for balancing such serious competing interests, and for determining the procedures that are necessary to ensure that a citizen is not "deprived of life, liberty, or property, without due process of law," U.S. Const., Amdt. 5, is the test that we articulated in Mathews v. Eldridge, 424 U.S. 319 (1976). *Mathews* dictates that the process due in any given instance is determined by weighing "the private interest that will be affected by the official action" against the Government's asserted interest, "including the function involved" and the burdens the Government would face in providing greater process. 424 U.S., at 335. The *Mathews* calculus then contemplates a judicious balancing of these concerns, through an analysis of "the risk of an erroneous deprivation" of the private interest if the process were reduced and the "probable value, if any, of additional or substitute safeguards." Ibid. . . .

It is beyond question that substantial interests lie on both sides of the scale in this case. Hamdi's "private interest . . . affected by the official action," ibid., is the most elemental of liberty interests—the interest in being free from physical detention by one's own government. . . .

On the other side of the scale are the weighty and sensitive governmental interests in ensuring that those who have in fact fought with the enemy during a war do not return to battle against the United States. . . .

The Government also argues at some length that its interests in reducing the process available to alleged enemy combatants are heightened by the practical difficulties that would accompany a system of trial-like process. In its view, military officers who are engaged in the serious work of waging battle would be unnecessarily and dangerously distracted by litigation half a world away, and discovery into military operations would both intrude on the sensitive secrets of national defense and result in a futile search for evidence buried under the rubble of war. Brief for Respondents 46-49. To the extent that these burdens are triggered by heightened procedures, they are properly taken into account in our due process analysis.

Striking the proper constitutional balance here is of great importance to the Nation during this period of ongoing combat. But it is equally vital that our calculus not give short shrift to the values that this country holds dear or to the privilege that is American citizenship. It is during our most challenging and uncertain moments that our Nation's commitment to due process is most severely tested; and it is in those times that we must preserve our commitment at home to the principles for which we fight abroad. . . .

With due recognition of these competing concerns, we believe that neither the process proposed by the Government nor the process apparently envisioned by the District Court below strikes the proper constitutional balance when a United States citizen is detained in the United States as an enemy combatant. That is, "the risk of erroneous deprivation" of a detainee's liberty interest is unacceptably high under the Government's proposed rule, while some of the "additional or substitute procedural safeguards" suggested by the District Court are unwarranted in light of their limited "probable value" and the burdens they may impose on the military in such cases. *Mathews*, 424 U.S., at 335.

We therefore hold that a citizen-detainee seeking to challenge his classification as an enemy combatant must receive notice of the factual basis for his classification, and a fair opportunity to rebut the Government's factual assertions before a neutral decisionmaker. . . . These essential constitutional promises may not be eroded.

At the same time, the exigencies of the circumstances may demand that, aside from these core elements, enemy combatant proceedings may be tailored to alleviate their uncommon potential to burden the Executive at a time of ongoing military conflict. Hearsay, for example, may need to be accepted as the most reliable available evidence from the Government in such a proceeding. Likewise, the Constitution would not be offended by a presumption in favor of the Government's evidence, so long as that presumption remained a rebuttable one and fair opportunity for rebuttal were provided. Thus, once the Government puts forth credible evidence that the habeas petitioner meets the enemy-combatant criteria, the onus could shift to the petitioner to rebut that evidence with more persuasive evidence that he falls outside the criteria. A burden-shifting scheme of this sort would meet the goal of ensuring that the errant tourist, embedded journalist, or local aid worker has a chance to prove military error while giving due regard to the Executive once it has put forth meaningful support for its conclusion that the detainee is in fact an enemy combatant. In the words of *Mathews*, process of this sort would sufficiently address the "risk of erroneous deprivation" of a detainee's liberty interest while eliminating certain procedures that have questionable additional value in light of the burden on the Government. 424 U.S., at 335. . . .

In sum, while the full protections that accompany challenges to detentions in other settings may prove unworkable and inappropriate in the enemy-combatant setting, the threats to military operations posed by a basic system of independent review are not so weighty as to trump a citizen's core rights to challenge meaningfully the Government's case and to be heard by an impartial adjudicator.

In so holding, we necessarily reject the Government's assertion that separation of powers principles mandate a heavily circumscribed role for the courts in such circumstances. Indeed, the position that the courts must forgo any examination of the individual case and focus exclusively on the legality of the broader detention scheme cannot be mandated by any reasonable view of separation of powers, as this approach serves only to *condense* power into a single branch of government. . . . Thus, while we do not question that our due process assessment must pay keen attention to the particular burdens faced by the Executive in the context of military action, it would turn our system of checks and balances on its head to suggest that a citizen could not make his way to court with a challenge to the factual basis for his detention by his government, simply because the Executive opposes making available such a challenge. Absent suspension of the writ [of habeas corpus] by Congress, a citizen detained as an enemy combatant is entitled to this process. . . .

There remains the possibility that the standards we have articulated could be met by an appropriately authorized and properly constituted military tribunal. . . . In the absence of such process, however, a court that receives a petition for a writ of habeas corpus from an alleged enemy combatant must itself ensure that the minimum requirements of due process are achieved. . . . We have no reason to doubt that courts faced with these sensitive matters will pay proper heed both to the matters of national security that might arise in an individual case and to the constitutional limitations safeguarding essential liberties that remain vibrant even in times of security concerns.

IV

Hamdi asks us to hold that the Fourth Circuit also erred by denying him immediate access to counsel upon his detention and by disposing of the case without permitting him to meet with an attorney. Brief for Petitioners 19. Since our grant of certiorari in this case, Hamdi has been appointed counsel, with whom he has met for consultation purposes on several occasions, and with whom he is now being granted unmonitored meetings. He unquestionably has the right to access to counsel in connection with the proceedings on remand. No further consideration of this issue is necessary at this stage of the case.

The judgment of the United States Court of Appeals for the Fourth Circuit is vacated, and the case is remanded for further proceedings. . . .

JUSTICE SOUTER, with whom JUSTICE GINSBURG joins, concurring in part, dissenting in part, and concurring in the judgment.

. . . The Government [argues] that Hamdi's incommunicado imprisonment as an enemy combatant seized on the field of battle falls within the President's power as Commander in Chief under the laws and usages of war, and is in any event authorized by two statutes. Accordingly, the Government contends that Hamdi has no basis for any challenge by petition for habeas except to his own status as an enemy combatant; and even that challenge may go no further than to enquire whether "some evidence" supports Hamdi's designation, see Brief for Respondents 34-36; if there is "some evidence," Hamdi should remain locked up at the discretion of the Executive. . . .

The plurality rejects any such limit on the exercise of habeas jurisdiction and so far I agree with its opinion. The plurality does, however, accept the Government's position that if Hamdi's designation as an enemy combatant is correct, his detention (at least as to some period) is authorized by an Act of Congress as required by

§4001(a). . . . Here, I disagree and respectfully dissent. The Government has failed to demonstrate that the Force Resolution authorizes the detention complained of here even on the facts the Government claims. If the Government raises nothing further than the record now shows, . . . Hamdi [should] be released. . . .

Because I find Hamdi's detention forbidden by §4001(a) and unauthorized by the Force Resolution, I would not reach any questions of what process he may be due in litigating disputed issues in a proceeding under the habeas statute or prior to the habeas enquiry itself. For me, it suffices that the Government has failed to justify holding him in the absence of a further Act of Congress, criminal charges, a showing that the detention conforms to the laws of war, or a demonstration that §4001(a) is unconstitutional. I would therefore vacate the judgment of the Court of Appeals and remand for proceedings consistent with this view.

Since this disposition does not command a majority of the Court, however, the need to give practical effect to the conclusions of eight members of the Court rejecting the Government's position calls for me to join with the plurality in ordering remand on terms closest to those I would impose. Although I think litigation of Hamdi's status as an enemy combatant is unnecessary, the terms of the plurality's remand will allow Hamdi to offer evidence that he is not an enemy combatant, and he should at the least have the benefit of that opportunity.

It should go without saying that in joining with the plurality to produce a judgment, I do not adopt the plurality's resolution of constitutional issues that I would not reach. It is not that I could disagree with the plurality's determinations (given the plurality's view of the Force Resolution) that someone in Hamdi's position is entitled at a minimum to notice of the Government's claimed factual basis for holding him, and to a fair chance to rebut it before a neutral decision maker; nor, of course, could I disagree with the plurality's affirmation of Hamdi's right to counsel. On the other hand, I do not mean to imply agreement that the Government could claim an evidentiary presumption casting the burden of rebuttal on Hamdi, or that an opportunity to litigate before a military tribunal might obviate or truncate enquiry by a court on habeas.

Subject to these qualifications, I join with the plurality in a judgment of the Court vacating the Fourth Circuit's judgment and remanding the case.

JUSTICE SCALIA, with whom JUSTICE STEVENS joins, dissenting.
. . . Where the Government accuses a citizen of waging war against it, our constitutional tradition has been to prosecute him in federal court for treason or some other crime. Where the exigencies of war prevent that, the Constitution's Suspension Clause, Art. I, §9, cl. 2, allows Congress to relax the usual protections temporarily. Absent suspension, however, the Executive's assertion of military exigency has not been thought sufficient to permit detention without charge. No one contends that the congressional Authorization for Use of Military Force, on which the Government relies to justify its actions here, is an implementation of the Suspension Clause. Accordingly, I would reverse the decision below.

I

. . . The gist of the Due Process Clause, as understood at the founding and since, was to force the Government to follow those common-law procedures traditionally deemed necessary before depriving a person of life, liberty, or property. When a citizen was deprived of liberty because of alleged criminal conduct, those procedures typically required committal by a magistrate followed by indictment and trial. 3 J. Story, Commentaries on the Constitution of the United States §1783, p. 661 (1833) (hereinafter Story) (equating "due process of law" with "due presentment or indictment, and being brought in to answer thereto by due process of the common law"). The Due Process Clause "in effect affirms the right of trial according to the process and proceedings of the common law." Ibid. See also T. Cooley, General Principles of Constitutional Law 224 (1880) ("When life and liberty are in question, there must in every instance be judicial proceedings; and that requirement implies an accusation, a hearing before an impartial tribunal, with proper jurisdiction, and a conviction and judgment before the punishment can be inflicted" (internal quotation marks omitted)). . . .

These due process rights have historically been vindicated by the writ of habeas corpus. . . . The writ of habeas corpus was preserved in the Constitution — the only common-law writ to be explicitly mentioned. See Art. I, §9, cl. 2. Hamilton lauded "the establishment of the writ of habeas corpus" in his Federalist defense as a means to protect against "the practice of arbitrary imprisonments . . . in all ages, [one of] the favourite and most formidable instruments of tyranny." The Federalist No. 84. . . .

II

The allegations here, of course, are no ordinary accusations of criminal activity. Yaser Esam Hamdi has been imprisoned because the Government believes he participated in the waging of war against the United States. The relevant question, then, is whether there is a different, special procedure for imprisonment of a citizen accused of wrongdoing *by aiding the enemy in wartime.*

Justice O'Connor, writing for a plurality of this Court, asserts that captured enemy combatants (other than those suspected of war crimes) have traditionally been detained until the cessation of hostilities and then released. That is probably an accurate description of wartime practice with respect to enemy *aliens.* The tradition with respect to American citizens, however, has been quite different. Citizens aiding the enemy have been treated as traitors subject to the criminal process. . . .

The modern treason statute is 18 U.S.C. §2381; it basically tracks the language of the constitutional provision. Other provisions of Title 18 criminalize various acts of warmaking and adherence to the enemy. See, e.g., §32 (destruction of aircraft or aircraft facilities), §2332a (use of weapons of mass destruction), §2332b (acts of terrorism transcending national boundaries), §2339A (providing material support to terrorists), §2339B (providing material support to certain terrorist organizations), §2382 (misprision of treason), §2383 (rebellion or insurrection), §2384 (seditious conspiracy), §2390 (enlistment to serve in armed hostility against the United States). See also 31 CFR §595.204 (2003) (prohibiting the "making or receiving of any contribution of funds, goods, or services" to terrorists); 50 U.S.C. §1705(b) (criminalizing violations of 31 CFR §595.204). The only citizen other than Hamdi known to be imprisoned in connection with military hostilities in Afghanistan against the United States *was* subjected to criminal process and convicted upon a guilty plea. See United States v. Lindh, 212 F. Supp. 2d 541 (E.D. Va. 2002) (denying motions for dismissal); Seelye, N.Y. Times, Oct. 5, 2002, p. A1, col. 5.

There are times when military exigency renders resort to the traditional criminal process impracticable. English law accommodated such exigencies by allowing legislative suspension of the writ of habeas corpus for brief periods. Blackstone explained:

> And yet sometimes, when the state is in real danger, even this [i.e., executive detention] may be a necessary measure. But the happiness of our constitution is, that it is not left to the executive power to determine when the danger of the state is so great, as to render this measure expedient. For the parliament only, or legislative power, whenever it sees proper, can authorize the crown, by suspending the habeas corpus act for a short and limited time, to imprison suspected persons without giving any reason for so doing. . . . In like manner this experiment ought only to be tried in case of extreme emergency; and in these the nation parts with it[s] liberty for a while, in order to preserve it for ever.

1 Blackstone 132.

Where the Executive has not pursued the usual course of charge, committal, and conviction, it has historically secured the Legislature's explicit approval of a suspension. In England, Parliament on numerous occasions passed temporary suspensions in times of threatened invasion or rebellion. . . .

Our Federal Constitution contains a provision explicitly permitting suspension, but limiting the situations in which it may be invoked: "The privilege of the Writ of Habeas Corpus shall not be suspended, unless when in Cases of Rebellion or Invasion the public Safety may require it." Art. I, §9, cl. 2. Although this provision does not state that suspension must be effected by, or authorized by, a legislative act, it has been so understood, consistent with English practice and the Clause's placement in Article I. See Ex parte Merryman, 17 F. Cas. 144, 151-152 (CD Md. 1861) (Taney, C. J., rejecting Lincoln's unauthorized suspension); 3 Story §1336, at 208-209.

The Suspension Clause was by design a safety valve, the Constitution's only "express provision for exercise of extraordinary authority because of a crisis," Youngstown Sheet & Tube Co. v. Sawyer, 343 U.S. 579, 650 (1952) (Jackson, J., concurring). . . .

III

. . . President Lincoln, when he purported to suspend habeas corpus without congressional authorization during the Civil War, apparently did not doubt that suspension was required if the prisoner was to be held without criminal trial. In his famous message to Congress on July 4, 1861, he argued only that he could suspend the writ, not that even without suspension, his imprisonment of citizens without criminal trial was permitted. . . .

The proposition that the Executive lacks indefinite wartime detention authority over citizens is consistent with the Founders' general mistrust of military power permanently at the Executive's disposal. In the Founders' view, the "blessings of liberty" were threatened by "those military establishments which must gradually poison its very fountain." The Federalist No. 45, p. 238 (J. Madison). No fewer than 10 issues of the Federalist were devoted in whole or part to allaying fears of oppression from the proposed Constitution's authorization of standing armies in peacetime. Many safeguards in the Constitution reflect these concerns. Congress's authority "[t]o raise and support Armies" was hedged with the proviso that "no Appropriation of Money to that Use shall be for a longer Term than two Years." U.S. Const., Art. 1, §8, cl. 12. Except for the actual command of military forces, all authorization for their maintenance and all explicit authorization for their use is placed in the control of Congress under Article I, rather than the President under Article II. . . . A view of the Constitution that gives the Executive authority to use military force rather than the force of law against citizens on American soil flies in the face of the mistrust that engendered these provisions. . . .

V

It follows from what I have said that Hamdi is entitled to a habeas decree requiring his release unless (1) criminal proceedings are promptly brought, or (2) Congress has suspended the writ of habeas corpus. A suspension of the writ could, of course, lay down conditions for continued detention, similar to those that today's opinion prescribes under the Due Process Clause. Cf. Act of Mar. 3, 1863, 12 Stat. 755. But there is a world of difference between the people's representatives' determining the need for that suspension (and prescribing the conditions for it) and this Court's doing so.

The plurality finds justification for Hamdi's imprisonment in the Authorization for Use of Military Force, 115 Stat. 224, which provides:

> That the President is authorized to use all necessary and appropriate force against those nations, organizations, or persons he determines planned, authorized, committed, or aided the terrorist attacks that occurred on September 11, 2001, or harbored such organizations or persons, in order to prevent any future acts of international terrorism against the United States by such nations, organizations or persons.

§2(a).

This is not remotely a congressional suspension of the writ, and no one claims that it is. Contrary to the plurality's view, I do not think this statute even authorizes detention of a citizen with the clarity necessary to satisfy the interpretive canon that statutes should be construed so as to avoid grave constitutional concerns, . . . or with the clarity necessary to overcome the statutory prescription that "[n]o citizen shall be imprisoned or otherwise detained by the United States except pursuant to an Act of Congress." 18 U.S.C. §4001(a). But even if it did, I would not permit it to overcome Hamdi's entitlement to habeas corpus relief. The Suspension Clause of the Constitution, which carefully circumscribes the conditions under which the writ can be withheld, would be a sham if it could be evaded by congressional prescription of requirements *other than the common-law requirement of committal for criminal prosecution* that render the writ, though available, unavailing. If the Suspension Clause does not guarantee the citizen that he will either be tried or released, unless the conditions for suspending the writ exist and the grave action of suspending the writ has been taken; if it merely guarantees the citizen that he will not be detained unless Congress by ordinary legislation says he can be detained; it guarantees him very little indeed.

It should not be thought, however, that the plurality's evisceration of the Suspension Clause augments, principally, the power of Congress. As usual, the major effect of its constitutional improvisation is to increase the power of the Court.

Having found a congressional authorization for detention of citizens where none clearly exists; and having discarded the categorical procedural protection of the Suspension Clause; the plurality then proceeds, under the guise of the Due Process Clause, to prescribe what procedural protections it thinks appropriate. It "weigh[s] the private interest . . . against the Government's asserted interest," and—just as though writing a new Constitution—comes up with an unheard-of system in which the citizen rather than the Government bears the burden of proof, testimony is by hearsay rather than live witnesses, and the presiding officer may well be a "neutral" military officer rather than judge and jury. It claims authority to engage in this sort of "judicious balancing" from Mathews v. Eldridge, 424 U.S. 319 (1976), a case involving . . . *the withdrawal of disability benefits!* Whatever the merits of this technique when newly recognized property rights are at issue (and even there they are questionable), it has no place where the Constitution and the common law already supply an answer. . . .

There is a certain harmony of approach in the plurality's making up for Congress's failure to invoke the Suspension Clause and its making up for the Executive's failure to apply what it says are needed procedures—an approach that reflects what might be called a Mr. Fix-it Mentality. The plurality seems to view it as its mission to Make Everything Come Out Right, rather than merely to decree the consequences, as far as individual rights are concerned, of the other two branches' actions and omissions. Has the Legislature failed to suspend the writ in the current dire emergency? Well, we will remedy that failure by prescribing the reasonable conditions that a suspension should have included. And has the Executive failed to live up to those reasonable conditions? Well, we will ourselves make that failure good, so that this dangerous fellow (if he is dangerous) need not be set free. The problem with this approach is not only that it steps out of the courts' modest and limited role in a democratic society; but that by repeatedly doing what it thinks the political branches ought to do it encourages their lassitude and saps the vitality of government by the people. . . .

VI

Several limitations give my views in this matter a relatively narrow compass. They apply only to citizens, accused of being enemy combatants, who are detained within the territorial jurisdiction of a federal court. This is not likely to be a numerous group; currently we know of only two, Hamdi and Jose Padilla. Where the citizen is captured outside and held outside the United States, the constitutional requirements may be different. Moreover, even within the United States, the accused citizen-enemy combatant may lawfully be detained once prosecution is in progress or in contemplation. See, e.g., County of Riverside v. McLaughlin, 500 U.S. 44 (1991) (brief detention pending judicial determination after warrantless arrest); United States v. Salerno, 481 U.S. 739 (1987) (pretrial detention under the Bail Reform Act). The Government has been notably successful in securing conviction, and hence long-term custody or execution, of those who have waged war against the state.

I frankly do not know whether these tools are sufficient to meet the Government's security needs, including the need to obtain intelligence through interrogation. It is far beyond my competence, or the Court's competence, to determine that. But it is not beyond Congress's. If the situation demands it, the Executive can ask Congress to authorize suspension of the writ—which can be made subject to whatever conditions Congress deems appropriate, including even the procedural novelties invented by the plurality today. To be sure, suspension is limited by the Constitution to cases of rebellion or invasion. But whether the attacks of September 11, 2001, constitute an "invasion," and whether those attacks still justify suspension several years later, are questions for Congress rather than this Court. If civil rights are to be curtailed during wartime, it must be done openly and democratically, as the Constitution requires, rather than by silent erosion through an opinion of this Court. . . .

JUSTICE THOMAS, dissenting.

The Executive Branch, acting pursuant to the powers vested in the President by the Constitution and with explicit congressional approval, has determined that Yaser Hamdi is an enemy combatant and should be detained. This detention falls squarely within the Federal Government's war powers, and we lack the expertise and capacity to second-guess that decision. As such, petitioners' habeas challenge should fail, and there is no reason to remand the case. . . .

Although the President very well may have inherent authority to detain those arrayed against our troops, I agree with the plurality that we need not decide that question because Congress has authorized the President to do so. The Authorization for Use of Military Force (AUMF), 115 Stat. 224, authorizes the President to "use all necessary and appropriate force against those nations, organizations, or persons he determines planned, authorized, committed, or aided the terrorist attacks" of September 11, 2001. Indeed, the Court has previously concluded that language materially identical to the AUMF authorizes the Executive to "make the ordinary use of the soldiers . . . ; that he may kill persons who resist and, of course, that he may use the milder measure of seizing [and detaining] the bodies of those whom he considers to stand in the way of restoring peace." Moyer v. Peabody, 212 U.S. 78, 84 (1909). . . .

I agree with the plurality that the Federal Government has power to detain those that the Executive Branch determines to be enemy combatants. But I do not think that the plurality has adequately explained the breadth of the President's authority to detain enemy combatants, an authority that includes making virtually conclusive factual findings. . . . In my view, . . . we lack the capacity and responsibility to second-guess this determination. . . .

The Government's asserted authority to detain an individual that the President has determined to be an enemy combatant, at least while hostilities continue, comports with the Due Process Clause. . . . [T]he Executive's decision that a detention is necessary to protect the public need not and should not be subjected to judicial second-guessing. Indeed, at least in the context of enemy-combatant determinations, this would defeat the unity, secrecy, and dispatch that the Founders believed to be so important to the warmaking function. . . .

Accordingly, I conclude that the Government's detention of Hamdi as an enemy combatant does not violate the Constitution. By detaining Hamdi, the President, in the prosecution of a war and authorized by Congress, has acted well within his authority. Hamdi thereby received all the process to which he was due under the circumstances. I therefore believe that this is no occasion to balance the competing interests, as the plurality unconvincingly attempts to do. . . .

Although I do not agree with the plurality that the balancing approach of Mathews v. Eldridge, 424 U.S. 319 (1976), is the appropriate analytical tool with which to analyze this case,[5] I cannot help but explain that the plurality misapplies its chosen framework, one that if applied correctly would probably lead to the result I have reached. . . . In *Moyer*, the Court recognized the paramount importance of the Governor's interest in the tranquility of a Colorado town. At issue here is the far more significant interest of the security of the Nation. The Government seeks to further that interest by detaining an enemy soldier not only to prevent him from rejoining the ongoing fight. Rather, as the Government explains, detention can serve to gather critical intelligence regarding the intentions and capabilities of our adversaries, a function that the Government avers has become all the more important in the war on terrorism.

Additional process, the Government explains, will destroy the intelligence gathering function. Brief for Respondents 43-45. It also does seem quite likely that, under the process envisioned by the plurality, various military officials will have to take time to litigate this matter. And though the plurality does not say so, a meaningful ability to challenge the Government's factual allegations will probably require the Government to divulge highly classified information to the purported enemy combatant, who might then upon release return to the fight armed with our most closely held secrets. . . .

Undeniably, Hamdi has been deprived of a serious interest, one actually protected by the Due Process Clause. Against this, however, is the Government's overriding interest in protecting the Nation. If a deprivation of liberty can be justified by the need to protect a town, the protection of the Nation, *a fortiori*, justifies it. . . .

NOTES AND QUESTIONS

1. As Justice Scalia's opinion emphasizes, *Hamdi* isn't a criminal case. But the various opinions in *Hamdi* sound a number of themes that run through much of the law of criminal procedure: the role of the Founders' understandings in interpreting the Constitution, the role of open-ended interest balancing in deciding on the scope of proper procedures, the boundaries (if any) of enforcement discretion by the executive branch, the relevance of public safety needs to a sound interpretation of constitutional restrictions on government power, the relevance of the government's need to gather information—and its need to avoid *disclosing* information—to a sound interpretation of those restrictions, and the list could go on. Though not itself a part of the law of criminal procedure, *Hamdi* is a window on that law, a way of looking at the most fundamental debates in the field in a different context than the ones that dominate this book.

One of those debates, one that is central to the decision in *Hamdi*, concerns the nature and meaning of due process. Notice the different approaches Justices O'Connor, Scalia, and Thomas take to that basic question. Justice O'Connor seems to see due process as a question for the courts, to be decided by a common-law process, with interest balancing as the appropriate method of decision. Justice Scalia uses a different interpretive method—a mix of textualism and originalism—to reach a very different conclusion: In his preferred world, the key player in defining the process for prisoners like Hamdi is the legislative branch, not the judiciary.

5. Evidently, neither do the parties, who do not cite *Mathews* even once.

Justice Thomas deploys the same interpretive method as Justice Scalia, but comes to yet another conclusion: It is the executive branch that should decide what process Hamdi should receive. Which branch is best suited to defining due process? The executive? The legislature? The courts? How much should courts defer to the definitions the political branches use?

2. The *Hamdi* plurality approves a set of procedures that is significantly less protective than those used in criminal trials. It follows that it is a good deal easier for the government to detain suspected terrorists—even when they are American citizens—than it is to detain other suspected criminals. One might reasonably wonder about the incentives that procedural gap creates. If the government finds it more procedurally convenient to fight the war on terrorism with military and intelligence agencies than with criminal law enforcement agencies, what effect will that have on civil liberties? What effect will it have on the progress of the fight against terrorism?

Perhaps the answer is "not much." After all, Hamdi belongs to a very small class of people: American citizens (allegedly) fighting American armed forces in a foreign country. On the other hand, the logic of the Court's position—is it even possible to say what that is, given the fractured decision in *Hamdi*?—might apply to suspected terrorists found *within* the United States. Does it?

3. *Hamdi* is part of a substantial legal tradition, one you will encounter a number of times in this book. The essence of the tradition is this: Often, the government wishes to justify detention that looks a lot like criminal punishment without using the procedures that generally attend criminal punishment. In general, the Supreme Court has been quite receptive to government claims of this sort. The usual legal justification is that, for one or another reason, the relevant detention is something other than "punishment." Thus pretrial detention of criminal defendants is authorized based on much less protective procedures than those used in criminal trials because the detention is "regulatory" rather than punitive. See United States v. Salerno, 481 U.S. 739 (1987). (*Salerno* is excerpted in Chapter 8, at page 1005.) The long-term incarceration of sex offenders can be authorized with less than the usual processes in criminal cases, as long as the incarceration can be seen as a response to the offenders' mental abnormality rather than punishment for their wrongful conduct. See Kansas v. Hendricks, 521 U.S. 346 (1997). (*Hendricks* is noted in Chapter 16, at page 1612.) There are other examples.

Cases like *Salerno*, *Hendricks*, and *Hamdi* raise the following question: What does, and doesn't, count as criminal punishment for purposes of defining appropriate procedures? How is the question to be answered? One approach would be to look at the nature of the harm to the claimant. Under that approach, whenever a prisoner is detained in circumstances that seem similar to the detention of prison or jail inmates, criminal procedure protections would be triggered. Another approach would be to allow legislatures to classify detention as punitive or not, and defer to their classification. Under that approach, legislative labels would decide such cases. Yet another approach would be to decide whether a given detention is or isn't "punishment" based on the strength of the government's interest in more flexible procedures than those used in criminal litigation. (Arguably, the last is the approach taken by the *Hamdi* plurality.) Each of these approaches has support in the case law. Which is best?

4. The government claims that its interest in detaining Hamdi justifies special—and, from the government's point of view, specially favorable—procedures. Assume for the moment that the government's claim has substantial merit. (A majority of the

Justices so assumed.) Should the government get especially favorable procedures when it prosecutes serial killers? After all, there is a very strong social interest in catching and punishing murderers, especially those who keep killing until they are caught. Should that interest be weighed in the balance when deciding what murder defendants' procedural rights should include? If not, why not?

Speaking of interest balancing, Justice O'Connor's plurality opinion relied on Mathews v. Eldridge, 424 U.S. 319 (1976), to determine how much process to grant Hamdi; *Mathews* requires weighing both sides' interests as the means by which courts decide what process is due in particular cases. It would seem to follow that whatever process the Court deems necessary represents, at least in the Justices' view, the optimal accommodation of the competing interests. That is not the usual method by which criminal procedure rights are defined. Should it be? Presumably, everyone wants optimal procedures. Why not perform a *Mathews*-style balance throughout the criminal process? Do the opinions in *Hamdi* suggest an answer?

5. Much of the debate in *Hamdi* concerns the proper balance between legislative and executive power. In the criminal justice system, those two sources of government power are usually allies, not competitors. Legislatures draft broad criminal statutes and allow police and prosecutors nearly total discretion in deciding when, how, and against whom to enforce those statutes. As a general matter, legislative power has not been a check on executive-branch agencies—more like a blank check, authorizing the executive to do pretty much what it pleases. Courts, not legislatures, are the source of most restrictions on executive power to enforce the criminal law. How does that affect your view of the arguments in Justice Scalia's dissent? How do you suppose he would respond?

6. The Supreme Court reentered the fray of the rights of enemy combatants in Boumediene v. Bush, 553 U.S. 723 (2008), holding that they had the right to file a habeas corpus petition in federal court challenging their continued detention, which in turn could result in further Due Process rulings of their rights. *Boumediene* is considered further in Chapter 17, at page 1652.

7. Return to the interpretive question that lies at the heart of *Hamdi, Medina, Duncan, Hurtado,* and a host of other due process cases: What values does due process protect? In criminal cases, one's answer probably begins with accuracy: Above all else, the criminal process should be designed to ensure that innocent defendants are not convicted and punished. How well does American criminal procedure protect against punishment of innocent defendants? Perhaps not very well:

> . . . As the scope of various constitutional protections has continued to expand [in the years since incorporation], judicial review targeted at potential errors on the merits—at cases where the wrong person was convicted—has been surprisingly muted. When, for example, the Supreme Court established constitutional sufficiency-of-the-evidence review in 1979, Justice Stevens predicted that federal judges would be swamped by the resulting additional work. The flood of new work never materialized, in part because appellate treatment of the relevant claims has been so perfunctory. Ineffective assistance doctrine, created in the 1970s and 1980s, has regulated conflicts of interest much more rigorously than it has regulated attorney decisions not to make plausible factual arguments. The Court's 1985 decision in Ake v. Oklahoma, requiring appointment of mental health experts to assist in preparing a criminal defense, has had few ripple effects, remaining basically restricted to the very small pool of insanity defense claims that go to trial.

Most strikingly, as the Supreme Court and lower appellate courts have developed standards of review for different kinds of constitutional claims, the courts consistently have adopted more favorable standards of review for *non*-guilt-related claims than for those claims most likely to be tied to guilt and innocence. The erroneous denial of Fourth Amendment and *Miranda* claims must be harmless beyond a reasonable doubt for the government to escape reversal on appeal. But a defendant making an ineffective-assistance-of-counsel claim (again, outside of conflicts of interest, which may be least tied to guilt or innocence and which require no showing of prejudice at all) must show a reasonable probability—substantially more than a reasonable doubt—that counsel's error or errors caused the defendant's conviction. The same tougher standard applies to claims that the government wrongfully withheld material exculpatory evidence. Nonconstitutional claims of newly discovered evidence . . . must meet an even tougher standard: The new evidence must not only have been unavailable at the time of trial but must also prove that the result reached at trial was probably wrong.

William J. Stuntz, The Uneasy Relationship Between Criminal Procedure and Criminal Justice, 107 Yale L.J. 1, 61-62 (1997). Perhaps incorporation of the Bill of Rights has yielded not so much *expansion* of defendants' rights as the *displacement* of some rights by others. Is the trade worth it? Has the Bill of Rights distracted attention from the system's central job: separation of the guilty from the innocent? Or is that not the system's central job?

PART TWO

THE RIGHT TO COUNSEL—THE LINCHPIN OF CONSTITUTIONAL PROTECTION

Chapter 3

The Right to Counsel and Other Assistance

A. The Constitutional Requirements

1. The Right to the Assistance of Counsel at Trial

In all criminal prosecutions, the accused shall enjoy the right . . . to have the Assistance of Counsel for his defence.

U.S. Const. amend. VI

It never has been doubted by this court, or any other so far as we know, that notice and hearing are preliminary steps essential to the passing of an enforceable judgment, and that they, together with a legally competent tribunal having jurisdiction of the case, constitute basic elements of the constitutional requirement of due process of law. . . .

What, then, does a hearing include? Historically and in practice, in our own country at least, it has always included the right to the aid of counsel when desired and provided by the party asserting the right. The right to be heard would be, in many cases, of little avail if it did not comprehend the right to be heard by counsel. Even the intelligent and educated layman has small and sometimes no skill in the science of law. If charged with crime, he is incapable, generally, of determining for himself whether the indictment is good or bad. He is unfamiliar with the rules of evidence. Left without the aid of counsel he may be put on trial without a proper charge, and convicted upon incompetent evidence, or evidence irrelevant to the issue or otherwise inadmissible. He lacks both the skill and knowledge adequately to prepare his defense, even though he have a perfect one. He requires the guiding hand of counsel at every step in the proceedings against him. Without it, though he be not guilty, he faces the danger of conviction because he does not know how to establish his innocence. If that be true of men of intelligence, how much more true is it of the ignorant and illiterate, or those of feeble intellect. If in any case, civil or criminal, a state or federal court were arbitrarily to refuse to hear a party by counsel, employed by and appearing for him, it reasonably may not be doubted that such a refusal would be a denial of a hearing, and, therefore, of due process in the constitutional sense.

Justice Sutherland, for the Court, in Powell v. Alabama,
287 U.S. 45, 68-69 (1932)

The meaning and scope of the Sixth Amendment right to counsel in criminal proceedings have been contested, for the most part, in the context of the right of an indigent to have counsel appointed and financed by the state.[1] As the preceding quotation from *Powell* indicates, the right to be heard by retained counsel has never been seriously questioned in the United States. Quite early in our history, we rejected the English common law that denied accused felons the right to the assistance of retained counsel. For a discussion of the history of the right to counsel, see Note, An Historical Argument for the Right to Counsel during Police Interrogation, 73 Yale L.J. 1000, 1018-1034 (1964).

However, we proved to be much less solicitous of the plight of the indigent. In capital cases, federal law has always required the appointment of counsel, 1 Stat. 118 (1790), and a number of states followed a similar path. Nonetheless, it was not until *Powell* that the Supreme Court held that in capital cases Fourteenth Amendment due process is violated by state action that in effect denied a defendant access to effective assistance of counsel. Moreover, *Powell* appeared to be limited to those cases in which the defendant is "incapable adequately of making his own defense because of ignorance, feeble-mindedness, illiteracy, or the like." *Powell*, 287 U.S., at 71. The Court did hold, however, that the state's "duty is not discharged by an assignment [of counsel] at such a time or under such circumstances as to preclude the giving of effective aid in the preparation and trial of the case." Ibid.

Powell, in essence, created a *special circumstances rule*—effective assistance, or an adequate opportunity to obtain it, must be provided in capital cases if defendants are unable to represent themselves adequately. By 1961, this special circumstances rule had been transmuted into a "flat" constitutional requirement of counsel in capital cases, Hamilton v. Alabama, 368 U.S. 52 (1961), in large measure due to the awesome finality of capital punishment. See Yale Kamisar, Betts v. Brady Twenty Years Later: The Right to Counsel and Due Process Values, 61 Mich. L. Rev. 219, 255 (1962). But see id., at 255-260 (arguing that sentence should be immaterial to need for counsel).

In noncapital cases, a special circumstances rule also developed that constitutionally required the appointment of counsel only when the absence of counsel would result in a "trial . . . offensive to the common and fundamental ideas of fairness and right." Betts v. Brady, 316 U.S. 455, 473 (1942). In *Betts*, the Court, over a sharp and prescient dissent by Justice Black, held that due process does not demand the appointment of counsel for indigent defendants in every state criminal case because "the furnishing of counsel in all cases whatever" is *not* "dictated by natural, inherent and fundamental principles of justice." Id., at 464.[2]

Four years prior to *Betts*, however, the Supreme Court had held that the Sixth Amendment required the appointment of counsel in all *federal* noncapital criminal prosecutions. In doing so, the Court commented:

---

1. Today, best estimates are that more than 80 percent of all criminal defendants qualify as "indigent," meaning that they cannot afford to hire their own lawyer. See Mary Sue Backus & Paul Marcus, The Right to Counsel in Criminal Cases: A National Crisis, 57 Hastings L.J. 1031, 1034 (2006).

2. Some states *did* provide a right to appointed counsel, by either statute or state constitutional interpretation, long before Betts v. Brady. See, e.g., Webb v. Baird, 6 Ind. 13 (1854), where the Indiana Supreme Court recognized the right as deriving from the state's constitution: "It is not to be thought of in a civilized community for a moment that any citizen put in jeopardy of life or liberty should be debarred of counsel because he is too poor to employ such aid. No court could be expected to respect itself to sit and hear such a trial. The defense of the poor in such cases is a duty which will at once be conceded as essential to the accused, to the court and to the public. . . . [T]he only question is, who shall pay? . . . It seems eminently proper and just that the treasury of the county should be chargeable with his defense."

> The Sixth Amendment stands as a constant admonition that if the constitutional safe-
> guards it provides be lost, justice will not "still be done." It embodies a realistic recog-
> nition of the obvious truth that the average defendant does not have the professional
> legal skill to protect himself when brought before a tribunal with power to take his life
> or liberty, wherein the prosecution is presented by experienced and learned counsel.
> That which is simple, orderly and necessary to the lawyer, to the untrained layman
> may appear intricate, complex and mysterious.

Johnson v. Zerbst, 304 U.S. 458, 462-463 (1938).

But if "justice cannot be done" in all federal prosecutions and in state capital cases
without the assistance of counsel, and if, in state noncapital cases, the right to counsel
"when desired and provided by the party asserting the right" is something that the
party "requires . . . at every step," in order to minimize the chance of an erroneous
conviction,[3] how could the *Betts* "special circumstances rule" be maintained? How
could it be possible that justice *could* be done in a state prosecution, but not in a federal one, when an indigent is tried without counsel? And why would the absence of
wealth minimize the need for counsel's guiding hand, whether in a capital or a noncapital case? Prior to *Gideon*, in short, had not the Court *already concluded*, even if it had
still to be articulated, that the absence of counsel was itself a "special circumstance"?[4]

GIDEON v. WAINWRIGHT

Certiorari to the Supreme Court of Florida
372 U.S. 335 (1963)

MR. JUSTICE BLACK delivered the opinion of the Court.

Petitioner was charged in a Florida state court with having broken and entered
a poolroom with intent to commit a misdemeanor. This offense is a felony under
Florida law. Appearing in court without funds and without a lawyer, petitioner asked
the court to appoint counsel for him, whereupon the following colloquy took place:

> *The Court:*   Mr. Gideon, I am sorry, but I cannot appoint Counsel to represent
> you in this case. Under the laws of the State of Florida, the only time the
> Court can appoint Counsel to represent a Defendant is when that person
> is charged with a capital offense. I am sorry, but I will have to deny your
> request to appoint Counsel to defend you in this case.
>
> *The Defendant:*   The United States Supreme Court says I am entitled to be
> represented by Counsel.

Put to trial before a jury, Gideon conducted his defense about as well as could be
expected from a layman. He made an opening statement to the jury, cross-examined

3. Indeed, the Supreme Court had gone so far as to say that a defendant's right to be heard by
retained counsel was "unqualified." Chandler v. Fretag, 348 U.S. 3, 9 (1954). The reason for this conclusion surely was the Court's recognition of the significance of counsel. Id., at 9-10. But the very same
"significance" that results in a conclusion of an unqualified right to be heard by retained counsel obviously highlights the untenable plight of the indigent unable to obtain counsel. This, too, appears to have
contributed to the Court's willingness to reconsider *Betts.*

4. From 1950 until *Gideon,* the Supreme Court found a "special circumstance" requiring the appointment of counsel in every case it heard that raised the issue. By 1962, the standard had apparently become
"potential prejudice," a standard that will virtually always be met. Chewning v. Cunningham, 368 U.S.
443 (1962).

the State's witnesses, presented witnesses in his own defense, declined to testify himself, and made a short argument "emphasizing his innocence to the charge contained in the Information filed in this case." The jury returned a verdict of guilty, and petitioner was sentenced to serve five years in the state prison. . . . Since 1942, when Betts v. Brady, 316 U.S. 455, was decided by a divided Court, the problem of a defendant's federal constitutional right to counsel in a state court has been a continuing source of controversy and litigation in both state and federal courts. To give this problem another review here, we granted certiorari. Since Gideon was proceeding in forma pauperis, we appointed counsel to represent him and requested both sides to discuss in their briefs and oral arguments the following: "Should this Court's holding in Betts v. Brady . . . be reconsidered?" . . .

I

The facts upon which Betts claimed that he had been unconstitutionally denied the right to have counsel appointed to assist him are strikingly like the facts upon which Gideon here bases his federal constitutional claim. Betts was indicted for robbery in a Maryland state court. On arraignment, he told the trial judge of his lack of funds to hire a lawyer and asked the court to appoint one for him. Betts was advised that it was not the practice in that county to appoint counsel for indigent defendants except in murder and rape cases. He then pleaded not guilty, had witnesses summoned, cross-examined the State's witnesses, examined his own, and chose not to testify himself. He was found guilty by the judge, sitting without a jury, and sentenced to eight years in prison. Like Gideon, Betts sought release by habeas corpus, alleging that he had been denied the right to assistance of counsel in violation of the Fourteenth Amendment. Betts was denied any relief, and on review this Court affirmed. It was held that a refusal to appoint counsel for an indigent defendant charged with a felony did not necessarily violate the Due Process Clause of the Fourteenth Amendment, which for reasons given the Court deemed to be the only applicable federal constitutional provision. The Court said:

> Asserted denial [of due process] is to be tested by an appraisal of the totality of facts in a given case. That which may, in one setting, constitute a denial of fundamental fairness, shocking to the universal sense of justice, may, in other circumstances, and in the light of other considerations, fall short of such denial. [316 U.S., at 462.]

Treating due process as "a concept less rigid and more fluid than those envisaged in other specific and particular provisions of the Bill of Rights," the Court held that refusal to appoint counsel under the particular facts and circumstances in the Betts case was not so "offensive to the common and fundamental ideas of fairness" as to amount to a denial of due process. Since the facts and circumstances of the two cases are so nearly indistinguishable, we think the Betts v. Brady holding if left standing would require us to reject Gideon's claim that the Constitution guarantees him the assistance of counsel. Upon full reconsideration we conclude that Betts v. Brady should be overruled.

II

The Sixth Amendment provides, "In all criminal prosecutions, the accused shall enjoy the right . . . to have the Assistance of Counsel for his defence." We have construed this to mean that in federal courts counsel must be provided for defendants unable to employ counsel unless the right is competently and intelligently waived.[3] Betts argued that this right is extended to indigent defendants in state courts by the Fourteenth Amendment. In response the Court stated that, while the Sixth Amendment laid down "no rule for the conduct of the States, the question recurs whether the constraint laid by the Amendment upon the national courts expresses a rule so fundamental and essential to a fair trial, and so, to due process of law, that it is made obligatory upon the States by the Fourteenth Amendment." 316 U.S., at 465. In order to decide whether the Sixth Amendment's guarantee of counsel is of this fundamental nature, the court in *Betts* set out and considered "[r]elevant data on the subject . . . afforded by constitutional and statutory provisions subsisting in the colonies and the States prior to the inclusion of the Bill of Rights in the national Constitution, and in the constitutional, legislative, and judicial history of the States to the present date." 316 U.S., at 465. On the basis of this historical data the Court concluded that "appointment of counsel is not a fundamental right, essential to a fair trial." 316 U.S., at 471. It was for this reason the *Betts* Court refused to accept the contention that the Sixth Amendment's guarantee of counsel for indigent federal defendants was extended to or, in the words of that Court, "made obligatory upon the States by the Fourteenth Amendment." Plainly, had the Court concluded that appointment of counsel for an indigent criminal defendant was "a fundamental right, essential to a fair trial," it would have held that the Fourteenth Amendment requires appointment of counsel in a state court, just as the Sixth Amendment requires in a federal court.

We think the Court in *Betts* had ample precedent for acknowledging that those guarantees of the Bill of Rights which are fundamental safeguards of liberty immune from federal abridgment are equally protected against state invasion by the Due Process Clause of the Fourteenth Amendment. This same principle was recognized, explained, and applied in Powell v. Alabama, 287 U.S. 45 (1932), a case upholding the right of counsel, where the Court held that despite sweeping language to the contrary in Hurtado v. California, 110 U.S. 516 (1884), the Fourteenth Amendment "embraced" those "fundamental principles of liberty and justice which lie at the base of all our civil and political institutions," even though they had been "specifically dealt with in another part of the federal Constitution." 287 U.S., at 67. In many cases other than *Powell* and *Betts*, this Court has looked to the fundamental nature of original Bill of Rights guarantees to decide whether the Fourteenth Amendment makes them obligatory on the States. Explicitly recognized to be of this "fundamental nature" and therefore made immune from state invasion by the Fourteenth, or some part of it, are the First Amendment's freedoms of speech, press, religion, assembly, association, and petition for redress of grievances. For the same reason, though not always in precisely the same terminology, the Court has made obligatory on the States the Fifth Amendment's command that private property shall not be taken for public use without just compensation, the Fourth Amendment's prohibition of unreasonable searches and seizures, and the Eighth's ban on cruel and unusual punishment. On the other hand, this Court in Palko v. Connecticut, 302 U.S. 319 (1937), refused to hold that the Fourteenth Amendment made the double

---

3. Johnson v. Zerbst, 304 U.S. 458 (1938).

jeopardy provision of the Fifth Amendment obligatory on the States. In so refusing, however, the Court, speaking through Mr. Justice Cardozo, was careful to emphasize that "immunities that are valid as against the federal government by force of the specific pledges of particular amendments have been found to be implicit in the concept of ordered liberty, and thus, through the Fourteenth Amendment, become valid as against the states" and that guarantees "in their origin . . . effective against the federal government alone" had by prior cases "been taken over from the earlier articles of the federal bill of rights and brought within the Fourteenth Amendment by a process of absorption." 302 U.S., at 324-325, 326.

We accept Betts v. Brady's assumption, based as it was on our prior cases, that a provision of the Bill of Rights which is "fundamental and essential to a fair trial" is made obligatory upon the States by the Fourteenth Amendment. We think the Court in Betts was wrong, however, in concluding that the Sixth Amendment's guarantee of counsel is not one of these fundamental rights. Ten years before Betts v. Brady, this Court, after full consideration of all the historical data examined in Betts, had unequivocally declared that "the right to the aid of counsel is of this fundamental character." Powell v. Alabama, 287 U.S. 25, 68 (1932). . . . And again in 1938 this Court said:

> [The assistance of counsel] is one of the safeguards of the Sixth Amendment deemed necessary to insure fundamental human rights of life and liberty. . . . The Sixth Amendment stands as a constant admonition that if the constitutional safeguards it provides be lost, justice will not "still be done." [Johnson v. Zerbst, 304 U.S. 458, 462 (1938).] . . .

In light of these and many other prior decisions of this Court, it is not surprising that the Betts Court, when faced with the contention that "one charged with crime, who is unable to obtain counsel, must be furnished counsel by the State," conceded that "[e]xpressions in the opinions of this court lend color to the argument. . . ." 316 U.S., at 462-463. The fact is that in deciding as it did—that "appointment of counsel is not a fundamental right, essential to a fair trial"—the Court in Betts v. Brady made an abrupt break with its own well-considered precedents. In returning to these old precedents, sounder we believe than the new, we but restore constitutional principles established to achieve a fair system of justice. Not only these precedents but also reason and reflection require us to recognize that in our adversary system of criminal justice, any person haled into court, who is too poor to hire a lawyer, cannot be assured a fair trial unless counsel is provided for him. This seems to us to be an obvious truth. Governments, both state and federal, quite properly spend vast sums of money to establish machinery to try defendants accused of crime. Lawyers to prosecute are everywhere deemed essential to protect the public's interest in an orderly society. Similarly, there are few defendants charged with crime, few indeed, who fail to hire the best lawyers they can get to prepare and present their defenses. That government hires lawyers to prosecute and defendants who have the money hire lawyers to defend are the strongest indications of the widespread belief that lawyers in criminal courts are necessities, not luxuries. The right of one charged with crime to counsel may not be deemed fundamental and essential to fair trials in some countries, but it is in ours. From the very beginning, our state and national constitutions and laws have laid great emphasis on procedural and substantive safeguards designed to assure fair trials before impartial tribunals in which every defendant stands equal before the law. This noble idea cannot be realized if the poor man charged with crime has to face his accusers without a lawyer to assist him . . . . The Court in Betts v. Brady departed from the sound wisdom upon which the Court's holding in Powell v. Alabama rested. Florida, supported by two other States, has asked that Betts v. Brady be left intact. Twenty-two states, as friends of the Court, argue that *Betts* was "an anachronism when handed down" and that it should now be overruled. We agree.

Reversed.

MR. JUSTICE DOUGLAS, concurring.

While I join the opinion of the Court, a brief historical resume of the relation between the Bill of Rights and the first section of the Fourteenth Amendment seems pertinent. Since the adoption of that Amendment, ten Justices have felt that it protects from infringement by the States the privileges, protections, and safeguards granted by the Bill of Rights. . . . Unfortunately it has never commanded a Court. Yet, happily, all constitutional questions are always open. And what we do today does not foreclose the matter.

My Brother Harlan is of the view that a guarantee of the Bill of Rights that is made applicable to the States by reason of the Fourteenth Amendment is a lesser version of that same guarantee as applied to the Federal Government. Mr. Justice Jackson shared that view. But that view has not prevailed and rights protected against state invasion by the Due Process Clause of the Fourteenth Amendment are not watered-down versions of what the Bill of Rights guarantees.

MR. JUSTICE CLARK, concurring in the result.

That the Sixth Amendment requires appointment of counsel in "all criminal prosecutions" is clear, both from the language of the Amendment and from this Court's interpretation. . . . It is equally clear . . . that the Fourteenth Amendment requires such appointment in all prosecutions for capital crimes. The Court's decision today, then, does no more than erase a distinction which has no basis in logic and an increasingly eroded basis in authority. . . .

. . . [T]he Constitution makes no distinction between capital and noncapital cases. The Fourteenth Amendment requires due process of law for the deprival of "liberty" just as for deprival of "life," and there cannot constitutionally be a difference in the quality of the process based merely upon a supposed difference in the sanction involved. How can the Fourteenth Amendment tolerate a procedure which it condemns in capital cases on the ground that deprival of liberty may be less onerous than deprival of life—a value judgment not universally accepted—or that only the latter deprival is irrevocable? I can find no acceptable rationalization for such a result, and I therefore concur in the judgment of the Court.

MR. JUSTICE HARLAN, concurring.

I agree that Betts v. Brady should be overruled, but consider it entitled to a more respectful burial than has been accorded, at least on the part of those of us who were not on the Court when that case was decided.

I cannot subscribe to the view that Betts v. Brady represented "an abrupt break with its own well-considered precedents." . . . In 1932, in Powell v. Alabama, . . . a capital case, this Court declared that under the particular facts there presented—"the ignorance and illiteracy of the defendants, their youth, the circumstances of public hostility . . . and above all that they stood in deadly peril of their lives" (287 U.S., at

71)—the state court had a duty to assign counsel for the trial as a necessary requisite of due process of law. It is evident that these limiting facts were not added to the opinion as an afterthought; they were repeatedly emphasized, see 287 U.S., at 52, 57-58, 71, and were clearly regarded as important to the result.

Thus when this Court, a decade later, decided Betts v. Brady, it did no more than to admit of the possible existence of special circumstances in noncapital as well as capital trials, while at the same time insisting that such circumstances be shown in order to establish a denial of due process. The right to appointed counsel had been recognized as being considerably broader in federal prosecutions, see Johnson v. Zerbst, 304 U.S. 458, but to have imposed these requirements on the States would indeed have been "an abrupt break" with the almost immediate past. The declaration that the right to appointed counsel in state prosecutions, as established in Powell v. Alabama, was not limited to capital cases was in truth not a departure from, but an extension of, existing precedent. The principles declared in *Powell* and in *Betts*, however, have had a troubled journey throughout the years that have followed first the one case and then the other. Even by the time of the *Betts* decision, dictum in at least one of the Court's opinions had indicated that there was an absolute right to the services of counsel in the trial of state capital cases.[1] Such dicta continued to appear in subsequent decisions,[2] and any lingering doubts were finally eliminated by the holding of Hamilton v. Alabama, 368 U.S. 52.

In noncapital cases, the "special circumstances" rule has continued to exist in form while its substance has been substantially and steadily eroded. In the first decade after *Betts*, there were cases in which the Court found special circumstances to be lacking, but usually by a sharply divided vote. However, no such decision has been cited to us, and I have found none, [since] 1950. At the same time, there have been not a few cases in which special circumstances were found in little or nothing more than the "complexity" of the legal questions presented, although those questions were often of only routine difficulty. The Court has come to recognize, in other words, that the mere existence of a serious criminal charge constituted in itself special circumstances requiring the services of counsel at trial. In truth the Betts v. Brady rule is no longer a reality.

This evolution, however, appears not to have been fully recognized by many state courts, in this instance charged with the front-line responsibility for the enforcement of constitutional rights. To continue a rule which is honored by this Court only with lip service is not a healthy thing and in the long run will do disservice to the federal system. . . .

In agreeing with the Court that the right to counsel in a case such as this should now be expressly recognized as a fundamental right embraced in the Fourteenth Amendment, I wish to make a further observation. When we hold a right or immunity, valid against the Federal Government, to be "implicit in the concept of ordered liberty" and thus valid against the States, I do not read our past decisions to suggest that by so holding, we automatically carry over an entire body of federal law and apply it in full sweep to the States. Any such concept would disregard the frequently wide disparity between the legitimate interests of the States and of the Federal Government, the divergent problems that they face, and the significantly different consequences of their actions. . . .

1. Avery v. Alabama, 308 U.S. 444, 445.
2. E.g., Bute v. Illinois, 333 U.S. 640, 674; Uveges v. Pennsylvania, 335 U.S. 437, 441.

NOTES AND QUESTIONS

1. In one sense, the result in *Gideon* appears to have been inevitable. Even if there are cases that could be tried fairly without defense counsel, one cannot determine from the record in uncounseled cases which ones would have benefited from counsel. Records that look good on appeal might have looked quite different had counsel been present. Indeed, *Betts* is such a case. Each court that reviewed the record in *Betts* concluded that Betts had not been prejudiced by the absence of counsel. In an insightful analysis of the factual setting of *Betts*, Professor Kamisar demonstrated quite forcefully that a competent lawyer may very well have had an impact on the outcome of the trial. Yale Kamisar, The Right to Counsel and the Fourteenth Amendment: A Dialogue on "The Most Pervasive Right" of an Accused, 30 U. Chi. L. Rev. 1, 42-56 (1962). For example, one of the trial witnesses, Bollinger, identified Betts at the jailhouse, as well as a coat, dark glasses, and a handkerchief allegedly worn by Betts during the robbery. *But*:

> *What* coat? *Whose* dark glasses and handkerchief? . . .
>
> Is it possible that the coat Bollinger "identified" at the jail was simply one the police procured from somebody other than Betts—pursuant to Bollinger's own description of the dark gray, bagged-pocketed coat the man wore who robbed him?
>
> Even if a coat were offered in evidence, "objects or things offered in evidence do not generally identify themselves." The object must be shown to have some connection with Betts. Not only was this not done; no coat was ever offered in evidence. . . .
>
> As for the other items, there was testimony by the state that "smoked glasses were put on Betts' eyes and a handkerchief around his neck like the man was supposed to have had that did the holding up." But once again, no handkerchief or glasses were offered in evidence. Presumably, Betts owned a handkerchief or two, but once again, the state failed to establish that he even owned a pair of dark glasses. One alibi witness who was asked about this on cross simply did "not know," and the matter was dropped.

Why did the state fail to offer any of these items in evidence? Why was one of Betts' own witnesses cross-examined, albeit casually, about the defendant's ownership of a dark gray overcoat and smoked glasses? If the state had possessed these items, why would it have asked such questions? Although the matter is not free from doubt—because neither trial judge nor prosecutor seemed to care much, and Betts evidently failed to realize how this would weaken the state's case—it is difficult to avoid the conclusion that the following "bootstraps" operation occurred: Bollinger described to the police the various items the robber was supposed to have worn; the police simply went out, begged or borrowed the requisite coat, glasses, and handkerchief, and slapped them on Betts; Bollinger then made his identification, based largely on the coat, glasses, and handkerchief the police had put on Betts.

2. Even if it is true that defense counsel normally is of value, does it follow that the result in *Gideon* is constitutionally mandated? There is no requirement that the state provide everything that is useful or of value to defendants. Thus, there must be some other criteria that determine what the state must provide. To what extent, for example, should constitutional analysis be informed by general practice in the states? By the "intent of the Framers" of the relevant constitutional provisions? By the cost to government of a decision one way or the other? By what is "fair" or "just"? If notions of fairness or justice are to play a role, how does one determine what those words mean?

3. Regardless of the scope of words such as "fairness" or "justice," there probably would be general agreement that any practice that generated a relatively high risk of erroneous convictions is "unfair," as the absence of counsel most likely does. Why was that not emphasized more in *Gideon?* Justice Black's opinion for the Court in *Gideon* primarily asserted that *Betts* was an abrupt change from its precedents and thus was wrong, although the excerpt from *Powell* at the beginning of this section was quoted but not developed. Is that adequate? If a court decides to overrule a case, how can it go about it? How *should* it go about it, or does it matter? See Jerold Israel, Gideon v. Wainwright: The "Art" of Overruling, [1963] Sup. Ct. Rev. 211. Does the method employed in the majority opinion explain, at least in part, why the concurrences were written to what was a unanimous judgment?

4. What are *Gideon*'s consequences? At one level, the answer seems easy: Presumably, the system functions better and more accurately when defendants have lawyers than when they must fend for themselves. But the answer may be more complicated than first appears. Defense lawyers make criminal trials more elaborate and hence more expensive. The state presumably must bear that cost. Yet the state need not hold a trial in order to obtain a conviction: Most convictions — in the neighborhood of 90 percent by most estimates — are the result of guilty pleas, not criminal trials. And the more costly trials are to the state, the more the state may be willing to pay, in the form of reduced charges or sentences, in order to get the defendant to plead guilty. These "payments" are, of course, the centerpiece of plea bargaining. The point is that *Gideon*, like other defense rights that raise the expense of criminal prosecution, may significantly improve the criminal trial process, but it may also lead to a system in which fewer defendants actually use that process. Which is better — a careful and expensive trial process coupled with lots of guilty pleas, or a more casual trial process that is used by more defendants?

NOTES ON THE *GIDEON* RIGHT TO COUNSEL AS APPLIED TO MISDEMEANORS

1. What was the judgment in *Gideon*, apart from the overruling of *Betts?* What, in other words, is the scope of the right to counsel imposed on the states by *Gideon?* Must counsel be appointed in every criminal case? Every felony? What about trials of misdemeanors with a jury, or when a somewhat complicated issue may be contested? The Supreme Court first faced that question in Argersinger v. Hamlin, 407 U.S. 25 (1972). Justice Brennan wrote the majority opinion:

> Petitioner, an indigent, was charged in Florida with carrying a concealed weapon, an offense punishable by imprisonment up to six months, a $1,000 fine, or both. The trial was to a judge, and petitioner was unrepresented by counsel. He was sentenced to serve 90 days in jail, and brought this habeas corpus action in the Florida Supreme Court, alleging that, being deprived of his right to counsel, he was unable as an indigent layman properly to raise and present to the trial court good and sufficient defenses to the charge for which he stands convicted. The Florida Supreme Court by a four-to-three decision, in ruling on the right to counsel, followed the line we marked out in Duncan v. Louisiana, 391 U.S. 145, 159, as respects the right to trial by jury and held that the right to court-appointed counsel extends only to trials "for non-petty offenses punishable by more than six months imprisonment." . . . We reverse.

In rejecting the analogy to trial by jury, the Court noted:

The right to trial by jury, also guaranteed by the Sixth Amendment by reason of the Fourteenth, was limited by Duncan v. Louisiana to trials where the potential punishment was imprisonment for six months or more. But . . . the right to trial by jury has a different genealogy and is brigaded with a system of trial to a judge alone. . . .

While there is historical support for limiting the "deep commitment" to trial by jury to "serious criminal cases," there is no such support for a similar limitation on the right to assistance of counsel:

> Originally, in England, a person charged with treason or felony was denied the aid of counsel, except in respect of legal questions which the accused himself might suggest. At the same time parties in civil cases and persons accused of misdemeanors were entitled to the full assistance of counsel. . . .[It] appears that in at least twelve of the thirteen colonies the rule of the English common law, in the respect now under consideration, had been definitively rejected and the right to counsel fully recognized in all criminal prosecutions, save that in one or two instances the right was limited to capital offenses or to the more serious crimes. . . . [Powell v. Alabama, 287 U.S. 45, 60 and 64-65.]

The Sixth Amendment thus extended the right to counsel beyond its common-law dimensions. But there is nothing in the language of the Amendment, its history, or in the decisions of this Court, to indicate that it was intended to embody a retraction of the right in petty offenses wherein the common law previously did require that counsel be provided. . . .

We reject, therefore, the premise that since prosecutions for crimes punishable by imprisonment for less than six months may be tried without a jury, they may also be tried without a lawyer. . . .

The requirement of counsel may well be necessary for a fair trial even in a petty-offense prosecution. We are by no means convinced that legal and constitutional questions involved in a case that actually leads to imprisonment even for a brief period are any less complex than when a person can be sent off for six months or more. . . .

We hold, therefore, that absent a knowing and intelligent waiver, no person may be imprisoned for any offense, whether classified as petty, misdemeanor, or felony, unless he was represented by counsel at his trial. . . .

Justice Powell concurred in the result, but expressed doubts about the breadth of the decision:

> . . . Due process, perhaps the most fundamental concept in our law, embodies principles of fairness rather than immutable line drawing as to every aspect of a criminal trial. While counsel is often essential to a fair trial, this is by no means a universal fact. Some petty offense cases are complex; others are exceedingly simple. As a justification for furnishing counsel to indigents accused of felonies, the Court noted, "That government hires lawyers to prosecute and defendants who have the money hire lawyers to defend are the strongest indications of the widespread belief that lawyers in criminal courts are necessities, not luxuries." Yet government often does not hire lawyers to prosecute petty offenses; instead the arresting police officer presents the case. Nor does every defendant who can afford to do so hire lawyers to defend petty charges. Where the possibility of a jail sentence is remote and the probable fine seems small, or where the evidence of guilt is overwhelming, the costs of assistance of counsel may exceed the benefits. It is anomalous that the Court's opinion today will extend the right of appointed counsel to indigent defendants in cases where the right to counsel would rarely be exercised by nonindigent defendants. . . .
>
> There are thousands of statutes and ordinances which authorize imprisonment for six months or less, usually as an alternative to a fine. These offenses include some of the most trivial of misdemeanors, ranging from spitting on the sidewalk to certain traffic offenses. They also include a variety of more serious misdemeanors. This broad

spectrum of petty-offense cases daily floods the lower criminal courts. The rule laid down today will confront the judges of each of these courts with an awkward dilemma. If counsel is not appointed or knowingly waived, no sentence of imprisonment for any duration may be imposed. The judge will therefore be forced to decide in advance of trial—and without hearing the evidence—whether he will forgo entirely his judicial discretion to impose some sentence of imprisonment and abandon his responsibility to consider the full range of punishments established by the legislature. His alternatives, assuming the availability of counsel, will be to appoint counsel and retain the discretion vested in him by law, or to abandon this discretion in advance and proceed without counsel. . . .

I would hold that the right to counsel in petty-offense cases is not absolute but is one to be determined by the trial courts exercising a judicial discretion on a case-by-case basis. The determination should be made before the accused formally pleads; many petty cases are resolved by guilty pleas in which the assistance of counsel may be required.

Why does Justice Powell wish to resurrect the *Betts* special circumstances rule? Are you convinced or unpersuaded? Note his assertion that "Due Process . . . embodies principles of fairness rather than immutable line drawing." How helpful is that? How do you determine what is "fair" without "drawing a line" between that and what is "unfair"?

2. What is the holding in *Argersinger*? Does *Argersinger* supplement, or does it modify, *Gideon*? Does counsel need to be appointed in a felony case in which the judge determines before trial not to sentence the defendant to a term of imprisonment? If so, why? What is the significance of labeling one offense a felony and another a misdemeanor? How do aggravated misdemeanors fit into the taxonomy? See, e.g., Iowa Crim. Code §903.1 (aggravated misdemeanor punishable by two-year imprisonment).

The Court in Scott v. Illinois, 440 U.S. 367 (1979), addressed some of these issues, in a majority opinion written by Justice Rehnquist:

> We granted certiorari in this case to resolve a conflict among state and lower federal courts regarding the proper application of our decision in Argersinger v. Hamlin. . . . Scott was convicted of theft and fined $50 after a bench trial in the Circuit Court of Cook County, Ill. . . . The applicable Illinois statute set the maximum penalty for such an offense at a $500 fine or one year in jail, or both. The petitioner argues that a line of this Court's cases culminating in Argersinger v. Hamlin, . . . requires state provision of counsel whenever imprisonment is an authorized penalty. . . .
>
> Although the intentions of the *Argersinger* Court are not unmistakably clear from its opinion, we conclude today that *Argersinger* did indeed delimit the constitutional right to appointed counsel in state criminal proceedings. Even were the matter res nova, we believe that the central premise of *Argersinger*—that actual imprisonment is a penalty different in kind from fines or the mere threat of imprisonment—is eminently sound and warrants adoption of actual imprisonment as the line defining the constitutional right to appointment of counsel. *Argersinger* has proved workable, whereas any extension would create confusion and impose unpredictable, but necessarily substantial, costs on 50 quite diverse States. We therefore hold that the Sixth and Fourteenth Amendments to the United States Constitution require only that no indigent criminal defendant be sentenced to a term of imprisonment unless the State has afforded him the right to assistance of appointed counsel in his defense. The judgement of the Supreme Court of Illinois is accordingly affirmed.

Justice Brennan (the author of *Argersinger*) dissented:

In my view petitioner could prevail in this case without extending the right to counsel beyond what was assumed to exist in *Argersinger*. Neither party in that case questioned the existence of the right to counsel in trials involving "non-petty" offenses punishable by more than six months in jail. The question the Court addressed was whether the right applied to some "petty" offenses to which the right to jury trial did not extend. The Court's reasoning in applying the right to counsel in the case before it—that the right to counsel is more fundamental to a fair proceeding than the right to jury trial and that the historical limitations on the jury trial right are irrelevant to the right to counsel—certainly cannot support a standard for the right to counsel that is more restrictive than the standard for granting a right to jury trial. . . . *Argersinger* thus established a "two dimensional" test for the right to counsel: the right attaches to any "nonpetty" offense punishable by more than six months in jail and in addition to any offense where actual incarceration is likely regardless of the maximum authorized penalty. See Duke, The Right to Appointed Counsel: *Argersinger* and Beyond, 12 Am. Crim. L. Rev. 601 (1975).

   . . . Not only is the "actual imprisonment" standard unprecedented as the exclusive test, but also the problems inherent in its application demonstrate the superiority of an "authorized imprisonment" standard that would require the appointment of counsel for indigents accused of any offense for which imprisonment for any time is authorized.

   First, the "authorized imprisonment" standard more faithfully implements the principles of the Sixth Amendment identified in *Gideon*. The procedural rules established by state statutes are geared to the nature of the potential penalty for an offense, not to the actual penalty imposed in particular cases. The authorized penalty is also a better predictor of the stigma and other collateral consequences that attach to conviction of an offense. . . .

   Second, the "authorized imprisonment" test presents no problems of administration. It avoids the necessity for time-consuming consideration of the likely sentence in each individual case before trial and the attendant problems of inaccurate predictions, unequal treatment, and apparent and actual bias. . . .

   Finally, the "authorized imprisonment" test ensures that courts will not abrogate legislative judgments concerning the appropriate range of penalties to be considered for each offense. . . .

   The apparent reason for the Court's adoption of the "actual imprisonment" standard for all misdemeanors is concern for the economic burden that an "authorized imprisonment" standard might place on the States. But, with all respect, that concern is both irrelevant and speculative.

   This Court's role in enforcing constitutional guarantees for criminal defendants cannot be made dependent on the budgetary decisions of state governments. . . .

3. *Argersinger* referred explicitly to "the trial of a misdemeanor," thus apparently leaving intact the general contemporary understanding that *Gideon* required the appointment of counsel for indigents in all felony cases. Is that understanding consistent with *Scott*? If the only constitutional criterion is actual imprisonment, then presumably it should apply to misdemeanors and felonies alike. Nevertheless, lower courts have mostly assumed, even after *Scott*, that felonies are governed by *Gideon*'s across-the-board requirement of appointment of counsel. In an offhand statement in a footnote, the Supreme Court seems to have approved that view. Nichols v. United States, 511 U.S. 738, 743 n. 9 (1994) ("In felony cases, in contrast to misdemeanor charges, the Constitution requires that an indigent defendant

be offered appointed counsel unless that right is intelligently and competently waived.") (citing *Gideon*).

4. If you read *Scott* broadly, it fundamentally reworks the meaning of the Sixth Amendment right to counsel, but can it also be read more narrowly, as essentially refining *Argersinger*'s treatment of less serious criminal cases? Read more narrowly, would the aftermath of *Scott* contain a series of principles, any one of which would be adequate to require counsel in any particular case? What are those principles?

Compare the Sixth Amendment right to a jury trial, and consider the implications of United States v. Nachtigal, 507 U.S. 1 (1993), in which the court of appeals held that a jury trial was constitutionally required even though the maximum punishment did not exceed six months. The Court summarily reversed but in doing so emphasized the importance of Blanton v. North Las Vegas, 489 U.S. 538 (1989), which implies that factors other than length of sentence may be relevant to a crime's "seriousness" and therefore the Sixth Amendment right to a jury trial. What factors? Perhaps the stigmatizing effect of a conviction? Or more tangible collateral consequences, such as the loss of various kinds of licenses or of the right to vote?

In Lewis v. United States, 518 U.S. 322 (1996), the Court concluded that a defendant does not have a constitutional right to trial by jury when prosecuted in a single proceeding for multiple petty offenses, even if the possible aggregate prison term exceeds six months. But the Court reiterated (citing *Blanton*) that other factors may be relevant to determining whether an offense is "serious" or "petty" for purposes of the Sixth Amendment: "An offense carrying a maximum prison term of six months or less is presumed petty, unless the legislature has authorized additional statutory penalties so severe as to indicate that the legislature considered the offense serious." For a critical analysis of *Lewis*, see Colleen P. Murphy, The Narrowing of the Entitlement to Criminal Jury Trial, [1997] Wis. L. Rev. 133.

And in Southern Union Co. v. United States, 132 S. Ct. 2344 (2012), the Court reaffirmed the view set forth in its earlier decision in International Union, United Mine Workers v. Bagwell, 512 U.S. 821 (1993), that a fine can be a sufficiently serious criminal sanction to trigger the constitutional right to a jury trial. Presumably, the same thing can be said with respect to the constitutional right to counsel. *Southern Union Co.* is discussed further in Chapter 15, at page 1546, in connection with the application of Apprendi v. New Jersey, 530 U.S. 466 (2000), to criminal fines.

5. The most serious collateral consequence that can flow from a criminal conviction is a dramatically increased sentence for a subsequent criminal conviction. In Baldasar v. Illinois, 446 U.S. 222 (1980), the Court reviewed the constitutionality of a statute that converted a second conviction for misdemeanor theft (property worth less than $150) into a felony with enhanced punishment. Baldasar was convicted of the first offense without counsel, and the question before the Court was whether the uncounseled conviction could trigger the enhancement provisions after the second, counseled conviction. By a 5-4 vote, the Court said "no," though no single opinion commanded a majority.

In Nichols v. United States, 511 U.S. 738 (1994), the defendant was convicted of driving under the influence, a misdemeanor, for which he was fined but not jailed. He was not represented in the DUI proceeding. Seven years later, he was convicted on federal drug charges, and under the federal sentencing guidelines, the earlier, uncounseled DUI conviction led to an addition of roughly two years to his federal prison sentence. The Court upheld the sentence. In an opinion by Chief Justice Rehnquist, one of the dissenters in *Baldasar*, the Court concluded that *Baldasar* should be overruled, and that uncounseled convictions can be used to enhance sentences for subsequent crimes. The Court reasoned that this was the only position "consistent with the traditional understanding of the sentencing process, which we have often recognized as less exacting than the process of establishing guilt":

> As a general proposition, a sentencing judge "may appropriately conduct an inquiry broad in scope, largely unlimited either as to the kind of information he may consider, or the source from which it may come." (U.S. v. Tucker, 404 U.S. 443, 448.) . . . "Traditionally, sentencing judges have considered a wide variety of factors in addition to evidence of guilt in determining what sentence to impose on a convicted defendant." (Wisconsin v. Mitchell, 508 U.S. 476, 485.) . . . One such important factor . . . is a defendant's prior convictions. Sentencing courts have not only taken into consideration a defendant's prior convictions, but have also considered a defendant's past criminal behavior, even if no conviction resulted from that behavior. We have upheld the constitutionality of considering such previous conduct in Williams v. New York, 337 U.S. 241 (1949). . . . [And] in McMillan v. Pennsylvania, 477 U.S. 79 (1986) . . . we held that the state could consider, as a sentence enhancement factor, visible possession of a firearm during the felonies of which defendant was found guilty.
>
> Thus, consistently with due process, petitioner in the present case could have been sentenced more severely based simply on evidence of the underlying conduct which gave rise to the previous DUI offense. And the state need prove such conduct only by a preponderance of the evidence. Surely, then, it must be constitutionally permissible to consider a prior uncounseled misdemeanor conviction based on the same conduct where that conduct must be proven beyond a reasonable doubt.

511 U.S., at 747-748. Justice Blackmun, joined by Justices Stevens and Ginsburg, dissented, arguing that *Scott* stands for the proposition that Nichols's uncounseled DUI conviction may not be "used as the basis for any incarceration, not even a 1-day jail sentence," id., at 754, much less the two years of additional time Nichols had to serve.

Which position in *Nichols* is more faithful to *Scott*? Which position is more faithful to *Gideon*? What you are beginning to see is that such questions are often quite difficult to answer. Constitutional principles can arise in cases in virtually limitless ways. Any single case applies those principles to the facts of that case, but their applicability to some other case with different facts can be unpredictable. The right to counsel area is a good example of this because of the enormous complexity involved in the various ways that states can sanction offenders, and the numerous variables that can affect the decision to sanction. One sees in the path forward from *Gideon* the implications of this dynamic. Rather than laying down immutable principles to then be faithfully applied in a straightforward fashion, the Court is engaged in a common law process of building up a system of precedent sensitive to the factual nuances of the cases that arise. This may be generally true with respect to the Court's constitutional criminal procedure jurisprudence. See, e.g., Ronald J. Allen & Ross M. Rosenberg, The Fourth Amendment and the Limits of Theory: Local Versus General Theoretical Knowledge, 72 St. John's L. Rev. 1149 (1998); Ronald J. Allen & M. Kristin Mace, The Self-Incrimination Clause Explained and Its Future Predicted, 94 J. Crim. L. & Criminology 243 (2004); Craig M. Bradley, The Uncertainty Principle in the Supreme Court, 1986 Duke L.J. 1.

ALABAMA v. SHELTON

Certiorari to the Alabama Supreme Court
535 U.S. 654 (2002)

JUSTICE GINSBURG delivered the opinion of the Court.

. . . Defendant-respondent LeReed Shelton, convicted of third-degree assault, was sentenced to a jail term of 30 days, which the trial court immediately suspended, placing Shelton on probation for two years. The question presented is whether the Sixth Amendment right to appointed counsel, as delineated in *Argersinger* and *Scott*, applies to a defendant in Shelton's situation. We hold that a suspended sentence that may "end up in the actual deprivation of a person's liberty" may not be imposed unless the defendant was accorded "the guiding hand of counsel" in the prosecution for the crime charged. *Argersinger*, 407 U.S., at 40.

I

After representing himself at a bench trial in the District Court of Etowah County, Alabama, Shelton was convicted of third-degree assault, a class A misdemeanor carrying a maximum punishment of one year imprisonment and a $2000 fine. He invoked his right to a new trial before a jury in Circuit Court, where he again appeared without a lawyer and was again convicted. The court repeatedly warned Shelton about the problems self-representation entailed, but at no time offered him assistance of counsel at state expense.

The Circuit Court sentenced Shelton to serve 30 days in the county prison. As authorized by Alabama law, however, the court suspended that sentence and placed Shelton on two years' unsupervised probation, conditioned on his payment of court costs, a $500 fine, reparations of $25, and restitution in the amount of $516.69.

Shelton appealed his conviction and sentence on Sixth Amendment grounds. . . . A suspended sentence, the [Alabama Court of Criminal Appeals] concluded, does not trigger the Sixth Amendment right to appointed counsel unless there is "evidence in the record that the [defendant] has actually been deprived of liberty." Because Shelton remained on probation, the court held that he had not been denied any Sixth Amendment right at trial.

The Supreme Court of Alabama reversed the Court of Criminal Appeals in relevant part. . . . In the Alabama high court's view, a suspended sentence constitutes a "term of imprisonment" within the meaning of *Argersinger* and *Scott* even though incarceration is not immediate or inevitable. And because the State is constitutionally barred from activating the conditional sentence, the Alabama court concluded, "the threat itself is hollow and should be considered a nullity." Accordingly, the court affirmed Shelton's conviction and the monetary portion of his punishment, but invalidated "that aspect of his sentence imposing 30 days of suspended jail time." By reversing Shelton's suspended sentence, the State informs us, the court also vacated the two-year term of probation.

Courts have divided on the Sixth Amendment question presented in this case. Some have agreed with the decision below that appointment of counsel is a constitutional prerequisite to imposition of a conditional or suspended prison sentence. . . . Others have rejected that proposition. . . . We granted certiorari to resolve the conflict.

II

. . . Applying the "actual imprisonment" rule to the case before us, we take up first the [following] question . . . : Where the State provides no counsel to an indigent defendant, does the Sixth Amendment permit activation of a suspended sentence upon the defendant's violation of the terms of probation? We conclude that it does not. A suspended sentence is a prison term imposed for the offense of conviction. Once the prison term is triggered, the defendant is incarcerated not for the probation violation, but for the underlying offense. The uncounseled conviction at that point "results in imprisonment," Nichols [v. United States, 511 U.S. 738, 746 (1994)]; it "ends up in the actual deprivation of a person's liberty," *Argersinger*, 407 U.S., at 40. This is precisely what the Sixth Amendment, as interpreted in *Argersinger* and *Scott*, does not allow.

Amicus[5] resists this reasoning primarily on two grounds. First, he attempts to align this case with our decisions in *Nichols* and Gagnon v. Scarpelli, 411 U.S. 778 (1973). . . .

Nichols presented the question whether the Sixth Amendment barred consideration of a defendant's prior uncounseled misdemeanor conviction in determining his sentence for a subsequent felony offense. 511 U.S., at 740. [We concluded that] "an uncounseled misdemeanor conviction, valid under *Scott* because no prison term was imposed, is also valid when used to enhance punishment at a subsequent conviction." Id., at 749. In *Gagnon*, the question was whether the defendant, who was placed on probation pursuant to a suspended sentence for armed robbery, had a due process right to representation by appointed counsel at a probation revocation hearing. 411 U.S., at 783. We held that counsel was not invariably required in parole or probation revocation proceedings; we directed, instead, a "case-by-case approach" turning on the character of the issues involved. Id., at 788-791.

Considered together, amicus contends, *Nichols* and *Gagnon* establish this principle: Sequential proceedings must be analyzed separately for Sixth Amendment purposes, and only those proceedings "resulting in *immediate* actual imprisonment" trigger the right to state-appointed counsel, id., at 13 (emphasis added). Thus, the defendant in *Nichols* had no right to appointed counsel in the DUI proceeding because he was not immediately imprisoned at the conclusion of that proceeding. The uncounseled DUI, valid when imposed, did not later become invalid because it was used to enhance the length of imprisonment that followed a separate and subsequent felony proceeding. Just so here, amicus contends: Shelton had no right to appointed counsel in the Circuit Court because he was not incarcerated immediately after trial; his conviction and suspended sentence were thus valid and could serve as proper predicates for actual imprisonment at a later hearing to revoke his probation.

Gagnon and *Nichols* do not stand for the broad proposition amicus would extract from them. The dispositive factor in those cases was not whether incarceration occurred immediately or only after some delay. Rather, the critical point was that the defendant had a recognized right to counsel when adjudicated guilty of the felony offense for which he was imprisoned. . . . Unlike this case, in which revocation of probation would trigger a prison term imposed for a misdemeanor of

---

5. Oddly, when this case got to the Supreme Court, Alabama refused to defend its own statute, so the Court appointed Professor Charles Fried as amicus to defend that position. — EDS.

which Shelton was found guilty without the aid of counsel, the sentences imposed in *Nichols* and *Gagnon* were for felony convictions—a federal drug conviction in *Nichols*, and a state armed robbery conviction in *Gagnon*—for which the right to counsel is unquestioned. . . .

Thus, neither *Nichols* nor *Gagnon* altered or diminished *Argersinger*'s command that "no person may be imprisoned *for any offense* . . . unless he was represented by counsel at his trial," 407 U.S., at 37 (emphasis added). Far from supporting amicus' position, *Gagnon* and *Nichols* simply highlight that the Sixth Amendment inquiry trains on the stage of the proceedings corresponding to Shelton's Circuit Court trial, where his guilt was adjudicated, eligibility for imprisonment established, and prison sentence determined. . . .

Amicus also contends that "practical considerations clearly weigh against" the extension of the Sixth Amendment appointed-counsel right to a defendant in Shelton's situation. He cites figures suggesting that although conditional sentences are commonly imposed, they are rarely activated. Tr. of Oral Arg. 20-21 (speculating that "hundreds of thousands" of uncounseled defendants receive suspended sentences, but only "thousands" of that large number are incarcerated upon violating the terms of their probation). Based on these estimations, amicus argues that a rule requiring appointed counsel in every case involving a suspended sentence would unduly hamper the States' attempts to impose effective probationary punishment. A more "workable solution," he contends, would permit imposition of a suspended sentence on an uncounseled defendant and require appointment of counsel, if at all, only at the probation revocation stage, when incarceration is imminent.

. . . [But] the sole issue at the [probation revocation] hearing . . . is whether the defendant breached the terms of probation. . . . The validity or reliability of the underlying conviction is beyond attack. . . .

We think it plain that a hearing so timed and structured cannot compensate for the absence of trial counsel, for it does not even address the key Sixth Amendment inquiry: whether the adjudication of guilt corresponding to the prison sentence is sufficiently reliable to permit incarceration. Deprived of counsel when tried, convicted, and sentenced, and unable to challenge the original judgment at a subsequent probation revocation hearing, a defendant in Shelton's circumstances faces incarceration on a conviction that has never been subjected to "the crucible of meaningful adversarial testing," United States v. Cronic, 466 U.S. 648, 656 (1984). The Sixth Amendment does not countenance this result.

In a variation on amicus' position, the dissent would limit review in this case to the question whether the *imposition* of Shelton's suspended sentence required appointment of counsel, answering that question "plainly no" because such a step "does not deprive a defendant of his personal liberty." Only if the sentence is later activated, the dissent contends, need the Court "ask whether the procedural safeguards attending the imposition of [Shelton's] sentence comply with the Constitution."

Severing the analysis in this manner makes little sense. One cannot assess the constitutionality of imposing a suspended sentence while simultaneously walling off the procedures that will precede its activation. The dissent imagines a set of safeguards Alabama might provide at the probation revocation stage sufficient to cure its failure to appoint counsel prior to sentencing, including, perhaps, "complete retrial of the misdemeanor violation with assistance of counsel." But there is no cause for speculation about Alabama's procedures; they are established by Alabama statute and decisional law, and they bear no resemblance to those the dissent invents in its effort to sanction the prospect of Shelton's imprisonment on an uncounseled conviction. Assessing the issue before us in light of actual circumstances, we do not comprehend how the procedures Alabama in fact provides at the probation revocation hearing could bring Shelton's sentence within constitutional bounds.

. . . Most jurisdictions already provide a state-law right to appointed counsel more generous than that afforded by the Federal Constitution. All but 16 States, for example, would provide counsel to a defendant in Shelton's circumstances, either because he received a substantial fine or because state law authorized incarceration for the charged offense or provided for a maximum prison term of one year. There is thus scant reason to believe that a rule conditioning imposition of a suspended sentence on provision of appointed counsel would affect existing practice in the large majority of the States. And given the current commitment of most jurisdictions to affording court-appointed counsel to indigent misdemeanants while simultaneously preserving the option of probationary punishment, we do not share amicus' concern that other States may lack the capacity and resources to do the same.

Moreover, even if amicus is correct that "some courts and jurisdictions at least cannot bear" the costs of the rule we confirm today, those States need not abandon probation or equivalent measures as viable forms of punishment. Although they may not attach probation to an imposed and suspended prison sentence, States unable or unwilling routinely to provide appointed counsel to misdemeanants in Shelton's situation are not without recourse to another option capable of yielding a similar result.

That option is pretrial probation, employed in some form by at least 23 States. . . . Under such an arrangement, the prosecutor and defendant agree to the defendant's participation in a pretrial rehabilitation program, which includes conditions typical of post-trial probation. The adjudication of guilt and imposition of sentence for the underlying offense then occur only if and when the defendant breaches those conditions. . . .

Like the regime urged by amicus, this system reserves the appointed-counsel requirement for the "small percentage" of cases in which incarceration proves necessary, thus allowing a State to "supervise a course of rehabilitation" without providing a lawyer every time it wishes to pursue such a course, *Gagnon*, 411 U.S., at 784. Unlike amicus' position, however, pretrial probation also respects the constitutional imperative that "no person may be imprisoned for any offense . . . unless he was represented by counsel at his trial," *Argersinger*, 407 U.S., at 37. . . .

Satisfied that Shelton is entitled to appointed counsel at the critical stage when his guilt or innocence of the charged crime is decided and his vulnerability to imprisonment is determined, we affirm the judgment of the Supreme Court of Alabama.

It is so ordered.

JUSTICE SCALIA, with whom CHIEF JUSTICE REHNQUIST, JUSTICE KENNEDY, and JUSTICE THOMAS join, dissenting.

. . . Respondent's 30-day suspended sentence, and the accompanying 2-year term of probation, are invalidated for lack of appointed counsel even though respondent has not suffered, and may never suffer, a deprivation of liberty. The Court holds that the suspended sentence violates respondent's Sixth Amendment right to counsel because it "*may* 'end up in the actual deprivation of [respondent's] liberty,'" ante (emphasis added), *if* he someday violates the terms of probation, *if* a court determines that the violation merits revocation of probation, and *if* the court determines that no other punishment will "adequately protect the community from further criminal activity" or "avoid depreciating the seriousness of the violation," Ala. Code §15-22-54(d)(4). And to all of these contingencies there must yet be added, before the Court's decision makes sense, an element of rank speculation. Should all these contingencies occur, the Court speculates, the Alabama Supreme Court would mechanically apply its decisional law applicable to routine probation revocation (which establishes procedures that the Court finds inadequate) rather than adopt special procedures for situations that raise constitutional questions in light of *Argersinger* and *Scott.* . . .

But that question is not the one before us, and the Court has no business offering an advisory opinion on its answer. We are asked to decide whether "imposition of a suspended or conditional sentence in a misdemeanor case invoke[s] a defendant's Sixth Amendment right to counsel." Pet. for Cert. i. Since *imposition of a suspended sentence does not deprive a defendant of his personal liberty,* the answer to that question is plainly no. In the future, *if and when* the State of Alabama seeks to imprison respondent on the previously suspended sentence, we can ask whether the procedural safeguards attending the imposition of that sentence comply with the Constitution. But that question is *not* before us now. . . .

. . . Surely the procedures attending reimposition of a suspended sentence would be adequate if they required, upon the defendant's request, complete retrial of the misdemeanor violation with assistance of counsel. By what right does the Court deprive the State of that option? It may well be a sensible option, since most defendants will be induced to comply with the terms of their probation by the mere threat of a retrial that could send them to jail, and since the expense of those rare, counseled retrials may be much less than the expense of providing counsel initially in all misdemeanor cases that bear a possible sentence of imprisonment. And it may well be that, in some cases, even procedures short of complete retrial will suffice.

. . . [The Court's] observation that "[a]ll but 16 States" already appoint counsel for *defendants like respondent,* is interesting but quite irrelevant, since today's holding is not confined to defendants like respondent. Appointed counsel must henceforth be offered before *any* defendant can be awarded a suspended sentence, no matter how short. Only 24 States have announced a rule of this scope.[4] Thus, the Court's decision imposes a large, new burden on a majority of the States, including some of the poorest. . . . That burden consists not only of the cost of providing state-paid counsel in cases of such insignificance that even financially prosperous defendants sometimes forgo the expense of hired counsel, but also the cost of enabling courts and prosecutors to respond to the "over-lawyering" of minor cases. Nor should we discount the burden placed on the minority 24 States that currently provide counsel: that they keep their current disposition forever in place, however imprudent experience proves it to be.

Today's imposition upon the States finds justification neither in the text of the Constitution, nor in the settled practices of our people, nor in the prior jurisprudence of this Court. I respectfully dissent.

---

4. Ten of the thirty-four States cited by the Court do not offer appointed counsel in all cases where a misdemeanor defendant might suffer a suspended sentence. Six States guarantee counsel only when the authorized penalty is at least three or six months' imprisonment. [Justice Scalia then explained in detail the exceptions that apply in the other four states. — EDS.] . . .

NOTES AND QUESTIONS

1. The subject of *Shelton* is the scope of the *Gideon* right to state-paid counsel for indigent defendants. The Court decided that the scope of that right is broad — broader, by some measures, than most states previously provided. Why? Is there a rationale for the *Gideon* right that explains *Shelton*, but that also explains why the right does not extend to misdemeanor cases where neither incarceration nor the threat of it is part of the defendant's sentence?

2. Why isn't it good enough, as the dissenters suggest, to give Shelton an elaborate process, *with* counsel, if and when his probation is revoked? What do you think about the majority's asserted justification for precluding Alabama from trying to develop such a process, if and when it is needed?

3. In the Supreme Court, Alabama also argued for an alternative, creative way around the Sixth Amendment problem: Enforce the conditions of probation through contempt proceedings for failure to abide by those conditions, which could in turn lead to jail or prison as long as defense counsel is provided at the time of the contempt proceeding. The Court did not address this argument, as it had not been presented below.

If the state's contempt argument loses, *Shelton* has potentially huge effects on the prosecution of low-grade misdemeanors. At least in a few states, it is common to prosecute such cases, and impose probation or a suspended sentence, without offering counsel to defendants. This amounts to an order to the defendant to keep his nose clean — if he fails to do so, he can go to jail; otherwise, his conviction will carry no significant penalty. Most defendants faced with that threat do keep their noses clean; only a very small minority of suspended sentences are ever imposed, and a similarly small minority of probations are revoked. After *Shelton*, though, trial judges must provide counsel in all these cases, even where (as in the great majority) the defendant is never incarcerated, or else abandon even the threat of jail time (and run the risk of being labeled "soft on crime"). Perhaps the judges will do just that. But abandoning the threat might make the misdemeanor proceeding pointless: Remember that we're talking about indigent defendants (nonindigents can, of course, hire counsel for themselves), so significant fines are not available as a deterrent to further crimes. The obvious alternative is to see that many more misdemeanor defendants get lawyers — but also that many more misdemeanor defendants go directly to jail.

2. The Right to the Assistance of Counsel Before and After Trial

The cases in the preceding section all deal with one particular aspect of the scope of the Sixth Amendment right to counsel: To what criminal cases does that right apply? All criminal cases, or only some kinds of criminal cases? The Court's focus in *Gideon, Argersinger, Scott,* and *Shelton* is on the application of the right to counsel to the "main event" in each case: the trial (or its functional equivalent, the plea hearing).

In this section, we take up a different aspect: In any particular criminal case to which the Sixth Amendment right to counsel *does* apply, exactly *when* in the case does that right "attach," or begin? When does it end? And, along the way, to what particular legal proceedings, or stages of the case, does the right apply?

a.   *When Does the Right to Counsel Begin?*

The Supreme Court has held that the Sixth Amendment right to counsel "attaches" when a defendant becomes the subject of "adversary judicial criminal proceedings—whether by way of formal charge, preliminary hearing, indictment, information, or arraignment." United States v. Gouveia, 467 U.S. 180, 188 (1984). This means that suspects who are under investigation, but not yet charged with a crime, have no Sixth Amendment right to counsel (although, upon the moment of their arrest, they acquire a limited Fifth Amendment right to counsel pursuant to Miranda v. Arizona, 384 U.S. 436 (1966)[6]). But once the defendant is formally charged, and brought to court to begin "formal legal proceedings," see Michigan v. Jackson, 475 U.S. 625, 629 n. 3 (1986), the Sixth Amendment right officially attaches.

Even after the Sixth Amendment right *attaches*, that does not necessarily mean the defendant has a right to counsel in connection with every single event thereafter; *that* question is determined by whether or not the particular event is a "critical stage" in the proceedings. A critical stage, simply put, is one where the presence of counsel is required to protect the legal rights of the defendant. When a jailed defendant gets a visit from his family, that is not a "critical stage." But when the defendant enters a plea, or when a court hearing is held about the admissibility of evidence, that *is* a critical stage at which the defendant is entitled to representation. The Court has held that preliminary hearings, Coleman v. Alabama, 399 U.S. 1 (1970); initial appearances, Brewer v. Williams, 430 U.S. 387 (1977); and arraignments, Hamilton v. Alabama, 368 U.S. 52 (1961), are all critical stages. The concept has also been extended to any *informal* meeting between the defendant and a representative of the state that is designed or is likely to elicit incriminating information from the defendant (see Massiah v. United States, 377 U.S. 201 (1964), discussed in Chapter 7, at page 870).

Even experienced attorneys (and judges) easily can get confused about the difference between "attachment" and "critical stage" analysis, as demonstrated in the following case:

ROTHGERY v. GILLESPIE COUNTY, TEXAS, 554 U.S. 191 (2008):   [Rothgery was arrested for being a felon in possession of a weapon, based on a criminal background check that erroneously indicated he had been convicted of a felony crime. Before the police brought him to his so-called "article 15.17 hearing"—at which a Texas criminal defendant first appears before a magistrate for a judicial determination of probable cause to arrest under the Fourth Amendment, notification of the charges, and the initial setting of bail—Rothgery, an indigent, several times requested the appointment of counsel. His requests were refused, and Rothgery was released on bail. Six months later, Rothgery finally was indicted for the felon-in-possession crime, and he was rearrested. Because he could not make bail this time, he spent three weeks in jail. At that point, Rothgery finally was appointed counsel, who obtained a reduction of bail (so that Rothgery could get out of jail) and then filed the necessary paperwork proving that Rothgery had never been convicted of a felony crime. The indictment was swiftly dismissed. Rothgery sued in federal court under 42 U.S.C. §1983, claiming that the county's policy of denying appointed

---

6. The *Miranda* right to counsel is limited in the sense that it applies only to the context of custodial police interrogation; police cannot question a suspect in custody unless the suspect has waived his *Miranda* rights. *Miranda* is discussed at length in Chapter 7.

counsel for article 15.17 hearings violated his Sixth Amendment right to counsel. The district court granted summary judgment for the county on the ground that Rothgery's right to counsel had not attached at the time of the article 15.17 hearing; the court noted that (per the usual local practice) the prosecutor also did not appear at the article 15.17 hearing. The Fifth Circuit affirmed, and the Supreme Court granted certiorari. — EDS.]

. . . If, indeed, the County had simply taken [our prior] cases at face value, it would have avoided the mistake of merging the attachment question (whether formal judicial proceedings have begun) with the distinct "critical stage" question (whether counsel must be present at a postattachment proceeding unless the right to assistance is validly waived). Attachment occurs when the government has used the judicial machinery to signal a commitment to prosecute. . . . Once attachment occurs, the accused at least[15] is entitled to the presence of appointed counsel during any "critical stage" of the postattachment proceedings; what makes a stage critical is what shows the need for counsel's presence. Thus, counsel must be appointed within a reasonable time after attachment to allow for adequate representation at any critical stage before trial, as well as at trial itself.

The County thus makes an analytical mistake in its assumption that attachment necessarily requires the occurrence or imminence of a critical stage. . . . On the contrary, it is irrelevant to attachment that the presence of counsel at an article 15.17 hearing, say, may not be critical, just as it is irrelevant that counsel's presence may not be critical when a prosecutor walks over to the trial court to file an information. As we said in [Michigan v.] Jackson, "[t]he question whether arraignment signals the initiation of adversary judicial proceedings . . . is distinct from the question whether the arraignment itself is a critical stage requiring the presence of counsel." 475 U.S., at 60. Texas's article 15.17 hearing plainly signals attachment, even if it is not itself a critical stage.

Our holding is narrow. . . . We merely reaffirm what we have held before and what an overwhelming majority of American jurisdictions understand in practice: a criminal defendant's initial appearance before a judicial officer, where he learns the charge against him and his liberty is subject to restriction, marks the start of adversary judicial proceedings that trigger attachment of the Sixth Amendment right to counsel. Because the Fifth Circuit came to a different conclusion on this threshold issue, its judgment is vacated, and the case is remanded for further proceedings consistent with this opinion.

JUSTICE ALITO, joined by CHIEF JUSTICE ROBERTS and JUSTICE SCALIA, concurring.

I join the Court's opinion because I do not understand it to hold that a defendant is entitled to the assistance of appointed counsel as soon as his Sixth Amendment right attaches. As I interpret our precedents, the term "attachment" signifies nothing more than the beginning of the defendant's prosecution. It does not mark the beginning of a substantive entitlement to the assistance of counsel. . . .

As the Court notes, . . . we have previously held that "arraignments" that were functionally indistinguishable from the Texas magistration marked the point at which the Sixth Amendment right to counsel "attached."

___

15. We do not here purport to set out the scope of an individual's postattachment right to the presence of counsel. It is enough for present purposes to highlight that the enquiry into that right is a different one from the attachment analysis.

It does not follow, however, and I do not understand the Court to hold, that the county had an obligation to appoint an attorney to represent petitioner within some specified period after his [appearance]. To so hold, the Court would need to do more than conclude that petitioner's criminal prosecution had begun. It would also need to conclude that the assistance of counsel in the wake of the Texas magistration is part of the substantive guarantee of the Sixth Amendment. That question lies beyond our reach, petitioner having never sought our review of it. . . . [W]e have been asked to address only the *when* question, not the *what* question. Whereas the temporal scope of the right is defined by the words "[i]n all criminal prosecutions," the right's substantive guarantee flows from a different textual font: the words "Assistance of Counsel for his defence."

In interpreting this latter phrase, we have held that "defence" means defense at trial, not defense in relation to other objectives that may be important to the accused. . . . We have thus rejected the argument that the Sixth Amendment entitles the criminal defendant to the assistance of appointed counsel at a probable cause hearing. See Gerstein v. Pugh, 420 U.S. 103, 122-123 (1975) (observing that the Fourth Amendment hearing "is addressed only to pretrial custody" and has an insubstantial effect on the defendant's trial rights). . . .

. . . I interpret the Sixth Amendment to require the appointment of counsel only after the defendant's prosecution has begun, and then only as necessary to guarantee the defendant effective assistance at trial. . . . Texas counties need only appoint counsel as far in advance of trial, and as far in advance of any pretrial "critical stage," as necessary to guarantee effective assistance at trial. . . .

[The dissenting opinion of Justice Thomas is omitted.]

NOTES AND QUESTIONS

1. The *Rothgery* majority finds the "narrow" issue of attachment to be "simpl[e]" and "plain[]." The concurring justices seem to agree, but Justice Alito writes separately to emphasize their view that "critical stages" include *only* those stages that substantially affect the fairness of the defendant's *trial.* Does that mean that bail hearings (which do not directly implicate a defendant's trial rights, but instead focus on whether or not the defendant can go home pending trial) are *not* "critical stages"? Perhaps surprisingly, the Court has never clearly held that bail hearings *are* "critical stages" at which a defendant must be represented by counsel. See also Chapter 8, at page 1002.

2. *Rothgery* involved an adjudication (the context where the assistance of counsel would seem to be the most "critical"). But many of the Court's leading "critical stage" decisions have involved the very different context of eyewitness identification procedures conducted at the police station. Should this difference matter?

NOTES ON THE RIGHT TO COUNSEL AT LINEUPS, SHOW-UPS, AND PHOTO ARRAYS

1. In 1967, the Supreme Court decided three companion cases involving constitutional challenges to pretrial eyewitness identification procedures. The lead case, United States v. Wade, 388 U.S. 218 (1967), as well as one companion case, Gilbert v. California, 388 U.S. 263 (1967), involved postindictment lineups conducted in the

absence of defense counsel at which eyewitnesses identified the respective defendants as the perpetrators of the crimes. In both cases, the same eyewitnesses later identified the defendant, at trial, as the perpetrator of the crime; in *Gilbert*, the eyewitnesses also testified that they had previously identified the defendant at the pretrial lineup. The other companion case, Stovall v. Denno, 388 U.S. 293 (1967), involved a "show-up," in which the defendant alone was shown to the eyewitness, who identified him as the perpetrator, again in the absence of defense counsel; the same eyewitness later identified the defendant in court, and also testified about the prior "show-up" identification.

In *Wade*, the Court held that postindictment lineups and show-ups are critical stages of the case at which the defendant's Sixth Amendment right to counsel applies:

> [T]he confrontation compelled by the State between the accused and the victim or witnesses to a crime to elicit identification evidence is peculiarly riddled with innumerable dangers and variable factors which might seriously, even crucially, derogate from a fair trial. The vagaries of eyewitness identification are well-known; the annals of criminal law are rife with instances of mistaken identification. . . . A major factor contributing to the high incidence of miscarriage of justice from mistaken identification has been the degree of suggestion inherent in the manner in which the prosecution presents the suspect to witnesses for pretrial identification. A commentator has observed that "[t]he influence of improper suggestion upon identifying witnesses probably accounts for more miscarriages of justice than any other single factor—perhaps it is responsible for more such errors than all other factors combined." Patrick M. Wall, Eye-Witness Identification in Criminal Cases 26. Suggestion can be created intentionally or unintentionally in many subtle ways. And the dangers for the suspect are particularly grave when the witness' opportunity for observation was insubstantial, and thus his susceptibility to suggestion the greatest.
>
> Moreover, "[i]t is a matter of common experience that, once a witness has picked out the accused at the line-up, he is not likely to go back on his word later on, so that in practice the issue of identity may (in the absence of other relevant evidence) for all practical purposes be determined there and then, before the trial."[8]
>
> The pretrial confrontation for purpose of identification may take the form of a lineup, . . . as in the present case, or presentation of the suspect alone to the witness, as in Stovall v. Denno. It is obvious that risks of suggestion attend either form of confrontation and increase the dangers inhering in eyewitness identification. But as is the case with secret interrogations, there is serious difficulty in depicting what transpires at lineups and other forms of identification confrontations. . . . [T]he defense can seldom reconstruct the manner and mode of lineup identification for judge or jury at trial. Those participating in a lineup with the accused may often be police officers; in any event, the participants' names are rarely recorded or divulged at trial. The impediments to an objective observation are increased when the victim is the witness. Lineups are prevalent in rape and robbery prosecutions and present a particular hazard that a victim's understandable outrage may excite vengeful or spiteful motives. In any event, neither witnesses nor lineup participants are apt to be alert for conditions prejudicial to the suspect. And if they were, it would likely be of scant benefit to the suspect since neither witnesses nor lineup participants are likely to be schooled in

---

8. Glanville Williams & H.A. Hammelmann, Identification Parades, Part I, [1963] Crim. L. Rev. 479, 482.

the detection of suggestive influences.[13] Improper influences may go undetected by a suspect, guilty or not, who experiences the emotional tension which we might expect in one being confronted with potential accusers. Even when he does observe abuse, if he has a criminal record he may be reluctant to take the stand and open up the admission of prior convictions. Moreover, any protestations by the suspect of the fairness of the lineup made at trial are likely to be in vain; the jury's choice is between the accused's unsupported version and that of the police officers present. In short, the accused's inability to reconstruct at trial any unfairness that occurred at the lineup may deprive him of his only opportunity meaningfully to attack the credibility of the witness' courtroom identification. . . .

The Court held that Wade's right to counsel was violated because he neither was represented by nor had waived counsel for purposes of the lineup. However, the Court remanded the case to give the prosecution a chance to try to prove (by "clear and convincing evidence") that the in-court eyewitness identifications were "based upon observations of the suspect other than the lineup identification," in which instance the in-court IDs would be independent of the constitutional violation and the conviction could therefore be upheld. In *Gilbert*, the Court went a step further, imposing a per se exclusionary rule with respect to the in-court testimony of the eyewitnesses specifically mentioning the unconstitutional lineup. And in *Stovall*, the Court held that *Wade* and *Gilbert* applied only to lineups or show-ups occurring *after* those Court decisions, but that *prior* lineups could still be evaluated as to whether they were "so unnecessarily suggestive and conducive to irreparable mistaken identification" as to violate due process. On the specific facts of *Stovall*, which involved an "imperative" need to show the defendant to an eyewitness who was seriously injured during the crime and about to undergo major surgery, the Court found no due process violation.

2. What about preindictment lineups and show-ups? One might think that they should be governed by the same rules announced in *Wade* and *Gilbert*; after all, the existence of an indictment would seem irrelevant to the particular dangers identified in *Wade*. The Court first addressed such issues just five years after *Wade* in Kirby v. Illinois, 406 U.S. 682 (1972),[7] which involved a preindictment show-up:

> In a line of constitutional cases in this Court stemming back to the Court's landmark opinion in Powell v. Alabama, it has been firmly established that a person's Sixth and Fourteenth Amendment right to counsel attaches only at or after the time that adversary judicial proceedings have been initiated against him. . . .
>
> The initiation of judicial criminal proceedings is far from a mere formalism. It is the starting point of our whole system of adversary criminal justice. For it is only then that the government has committed itself to prosecute, and only then that the adverse positions of government and defendant have solidified. It is then that a defendant finds himself faced with the prosecutorial forces of organized society, and immersed in the intricacies of substantive and procedural criminal law. It is this point, therefore,

---

13. An additional impediment to the detection of such influences by participants, including the suspect, is the physical conditions often surrounding the conduct of the lineup. In many, lights shine on the stage in such a way that the suspect cannot see the witness. See Gilbert v. United States, 366 F.2d 923 (C.A. 9th Cir. 1966). In some a one-way mirror is used and what is said on the witness' side cannot be heard. . . .

7. Although *Kirby* was technically a plurality opinion (Justice Powell concurred only in the result), a majority of the Court subsequently has cited and relied upon it. See, e.g., Brewer v. Williams, 430 U.S. 387, 398 (1997).

that marks the commencement of the "criminal prosecutions" to which alone the explicit guarantees of the Sixth Amendment are applicable. . . .

In this case we are asked to import into a routine police investigation an absolute constitutional guarantee historically and rationally applicable only after the onset of formal prosecutorial proceedings. We decline to do so. Less than a year after *Wade* and *Gilbert* were decided, the Court explained the rule of those decisions as follows: "The rationale of those cases was that an accused is entitled to counsel at any 'critical stage of the *prosecution*,' and that a post-indictment lineup is such a 'critical stage.'" (Emphasis supplied.) We decline to depart from that rationale today by imposing a per se exclusionary rule upon testimony concerning an identification that took place long before the commencement of any prosecution whatever.

. . . What has been said is not to suggest that there may not be occasions during the course of a criminal investigation when the police do abuse identification procedures. Such abuses are not beyond the reach of the Constitution. As the Court pointed out in *Wade* itself, it is always necessary to "scrutinize *any* pretrial confrontation. . . ." The Due Process Clause of the Fifth and Fourteenth Amendments forbids a lineup that is unnecessarily suggestive and conducive to irreparable mistaken identification. When a person has not been formally charged with a criminal offense, *Stovall* strikes the appropriate constitutional balance between the right of a suspect to be protected from prejudicial procedures and the interest of society in the prompt and purposeful investigation of an unsolved crime.

The *Kirby* dissenters made the obvious point that *Wade* and *Kirby* are impossible to reconcile on *Wade*'s rationale. Of course, the cases are easy to reconcile on *Kirby*'s rationale. Which strikes you as more persuasive? As more rational? As more appropriate?

3. What if the criminal case against the defendant does not originate with an indictment? Does that render *Wade* inapplicable? In Moore v. Illinois, 434 U.S. 220 (1977), the defendant was identified by the complaining witness at a preliminary hearing at which he was not represented by counsel. The defendant was convicted and appealed on the grounds that the preliminary-hearing identification violated *Wade*. The Court of Appeals was unpersuaded, but the Supreme Court reversed:

. . . The prosecution in this case was commenced under Illinois law when the victim's complaint was filed in court. The purpose of the preliminary hearing was to determine whether there was probable cause to bind petitioner over to the grand jury and to set bail. Petitioner had the right to oppose the prosecution at that hearing by moving to dismiss the charges and to suppress the evidence against him. He faced counsel for the State, who elicited the victim's identification, summarized the State's other evidence against petitioner, and urged that the State be given more time to marshal its evidence. It is plain that "the government ha[d] committed itself to prosecute," and that petitioner found "himself faced with the prosecutorial forces of organized society, and immersed in the intricacies of substantive and procedural criminal law." *Kirby*. The State candidly concedes that this preliminary hearing marked the "initiation of adversary judicial criminal proceedings" against petitioner, . . . and it hardly could contend otherwise. The Court of Appeals therefore erred in holding that petitioner's rights under *Wade* and *Gilbert* had not yet attached at the time of the preliminary hearing. . . .

If the court believed that petitioner did not have a right to counsel at this identification procedure because it was conducted in the course of a judicial proceeding, we do not agree. The reasons supporting *Wade*'s holding that a corporeal identification is a critical stage of a criminal prosecution for Sixth Amendment purposes apply with equal force to this identification. It is difficult to imagine a more suggestive manner in which to present a suspect to a witness for their critical first confrontation than was employed in this case. The victim, who had seen her assailant for only 10 to 15 seconds, was asked to make her identification after she was told that she was going to view a suspect, after she was told his name and heard it called as he was led before the bench, and after she heard the prosecutor recite the evidence believed to implicate petitioner. Had petitioner been represented by counsel, some or all of this suggestiveness could have been avoided.[5] . . .

Id., at 228-230.

4. How do the principles of *Wade* and *Kirby* apply to photo arrays (where the witness is presented with a set of photos of possible suspects and asked to identify the photo of the perpetrator)? That question was addressed in United States v. Ash, 413 U.S. 300 (1973):

. . . [T]he test utilized by the Court [to determine whether a particular event is a "critical stage" for purposes of the Sixth Amendment] has called for examination of the event in order to determine whether the accused required aid in coping with legal problems or assistance in meeting his adversary. . . .

A substantial departure from the historical test would be necessary if the Sixth Amendment were interpreted to give Ash a right to counsel at the photographic identification in this case. Since the accused himself is not present at the time of the photographic display, and asserts no right to be present, no possibility arises that the accused might be misled by his lack of familiarity with the law or overpowered by his professional adversary. Similarly, the counsel guarantee would not be used to produce equality in a trial-like adversary confrontation. . . .

Even if we were willing to view the counsel guarantee in broad terms as a generalized protection of the adversary process, we would be unwilling to go so far as to extend the right to a portion of the prosecutor's trial-preparation interviews with witnesses. Although photography is relatively new, the interviewing of witnesses before trial is a procedure that predates the Sixth Amendment. In England in the 16th and 17th centuries counsel regularly interviewed witnesses before trial. 9 W. Holdsworth, History of English Law 226-228 (1926). The traditional counterbalance in the American adversary system for these interviews arises from the equal ability of defense counsel to seek and interview witnesses himself.

That adversary mechanism remains as effective for a photographic display as for other parts of pretrial interviews. No greater limitations are placed on defense counsel in constructing displays, seeking witnesses, and conducting photographic identifications than those applicable to the prosecution. Selection of the picture of a person other than the accused, or the inability of a witness to make any selection, will be useful to the defense in precisely the same manner that the selection of a picture of the defendant would be useful to the prosecution. In this very case, for example, the initial tender of the photographic display was by [defense] counsel, who sought

---

5. For example, counsel could have requested that the hearing be postponed until a lineup could be arranged at which the victim would view petitioner in a less suggestive setting. Short of that, counsel could have asked that the victim be excused from the courtroom while the charges were read and the evidence against petitioner was recited, and that petitioner be seated with other people in the audience when the victim attempted an identification. Counsel might have sought to cross-examine the victim to test her identification before it hardened. Because it is in the prosecution's interest as well as the accused's that witnesses' identifications remain untainted, we cannot assume that such requests would have been in vain. Such requests ordinarily are addressed to the sound discretion of the court; we express no opinion as to whether the preliminary hearing court would have been required to grant any such requests.

to demonstrate that the witness had failed to make a photographic identification. Although we do not suggest that equality of access to photographs removes all potential for abuse, it does remove any inequality in the adversary process itself and thereby fully satisfies the historical spirit of the Sixth Amendment's counsel guarantee.

Pretrial photographic identifications . . . are hardly unique in offering possibilities for the actions of the prosecutor unfairly to prejudice the accused. Evidence favorable to the accused may be withheld; testimony of witnesses may be manipulated; the results of laboratory tests may be contrived. In many ways the prosecutor, by accident or by design, may improperly subvert the trial. The primary safeguard against abuses of this kind is the ethical responsibility of the prosecutor, who, as so often has been said, may "strike hard blows" but not "foul ones." If that safeguard fails, review remains available under due process standards. . . .

Id., at 313-321. Justices Brennan, Marshall, and Douglas dissented:

. . . [W]e have expressly recognized that "a corporeal identification . . . is normally more accurate" than a photographic identification. Simmons v. United States[, 390 U.S. 377 (1968)]. Thus, in this sense at least, the dangers of misidentification are even greater at a photographic display than at a lineup.

Moreover, as in the lineup situation, the possibilities for impermissible suggestion in the context of a photographic display are manifold. Such suggestion, intentional, or unintentional, may derive from three possible sources. First, the photographs themselves might tend to suggest which of the pictures is that of the suspect. For example, differences in age, pose, or other physical characteristics of the persons represented, and variations in the mounting, background, lighting, or markings of the photographs all might have the effect of singling out the accused.

Second, impermissible suggestion may inhere in the manner in which the photographs are displayed to the witness. . . .

Third, gestures or comments of the prosecutor at the time of the display may lead an otherwise uncertain witness to select the "correct" photograph. For example, the prosecutor might "indicate to the witness that [he has] other evidence that one of the persons pictured committed the crime,"[11] and might even point to a particular photograph and ask whether the person pictured "looks familiar." More subtly, the prosecutor's inflection, facial expressions, physical motions, and myriad other almost imperceptible means of communication might tend, intentionally or unintentionally, to compromise the witness' objectivity. . . .

Finally, and *unlike* the lineup situation, the accused himself is not even present at the photographic identification, thereby reducing the likelihood that irregularities in the procedures will ever come to light. . . . [T]he difficulties of reconstructing at trial an uncounseled photographic display are at least equal to, and possibly greater than, those involved in reconstructing an uncounseled lineup.[15] . . . As a result, both

11. Simmons v. United States, supra, at 383.

15. The Court's assertion, . . . that these difficulties of reconstruction are somehow minimized because the defense can "duplicate" a photographic identification reflects a complete misunderstanding of the issues in this case. . . . Due to the "freezing effect" recognized in *Wade*, once suggestion has tainted the identification, its mark is virtually indelible. For once a witness has made a mistaken identification, "he is not likely to go back on his word later on." United States v. Wade. As a result, any effort of the accused to "duplicate" the initial photographic display will almost necessarily lead to a reaffirmation of the initial misidentification.

The Court's related assertion, that "equality of access" to the results of a Government conducted photographic display "remove[s] any inequality in the adversary process," . . . is similarly flawed. For due to the possibilities for suggestion, intentional or unintentional, the so-called "equality of access" is, in reality, skewed sharply in favor of the prosecution.

photographic and corporeal identifications create grave dangers that an innocent defendant might be convicted simply because of his inability to expose a tainted identification. This being so, considerations of logic, consistency, and, indeed, fairness compel the conclusion that a pretrial photographic identification, like a pretrial corporeal identification, is a "critical stage of the prosecution. . . ."

Id., at 332-338.

5. *Ash* holds that the Sixth Amendment right to counsel does not apply to photo arrays; as in *Stovall* and *Kirby*, however, this does not preclude finding a due process violation. In Manson v. Brathwaite, 432 U.S. 98 (1977), the defendant's photo was shown to an undercover police officer who identified him as the perpetrator. When the case reached the Supreme Court, the prosecution argued for a "totality of the circumstances" approach to the due process question, focusing on the reliability of the challenged evidence, as in *Stovall* and Neil v. Biggers, 409 U.S. 183 (1972). The defendant, however, advocated a per se rule requiring "exclusion of the out-of-court identification evidence, without regard to reliability, whenever it has been obtained through unnecessarily [suggestive] confrontation procedures." According to the Court:

> . . . *Wade* and its companion cases reflect the concern that the jury not hear eyewitness testimony unless that evidence has aspects of reliability. It must be observed that both approaches before us are responsive to this concern. The per se rule, however, goes too far since its application automatically and peremptorily, and without consideration of alleviating factors, keeps evidence from the jury that is reliable and relevant.
>
> The second factor is deterrence. Although the per se approach has the more significant deterrent effect, the totality approach also has an influence on police behavior. The police will guard against unnecessarily suggestive procedures under the totality rule, as well as the per se one, for fear that their actions will lead to the exclusion of identifications as unreliable.
>
> The third factor is the effect on the administration of justice. Here the per se approach suffers serious drawbacks. Since it denies the trier reliable evidence, it may result, on occasion, in the guilty going free. Also, because of its rigidity, the per se approach may make error by the trial judge more likely than the totality approach. And in those cases in which the admission of identification evidence is error under the per se approach but not under the totality approach—cases in which the identification is reliable despite an unnecessarily suggestive identification procedure—reversal is a Draconian sanction. Certainly, inflexible rules of exclusion that may frustrate rather than promote justice have not been viewed recently by this Court with unlimited enthusiasm. . . .
>
> The standard, after all, is that of fairness as required by the Due Process Clause of the Fourteenth Amendment. . . .
>
> We therefore conclude that reliability is the linchpin in determining the admissibility of identification testimony. . . . The factors to be considered . . . include the opportunity of the witness to view the criminal at the time of the crime, the witness' degree of attention, the accuracy of his prior description of the criminal, the level of certainty demonstrated at the confrontation, and the time between the crime and the confrontation. Against these factors is to be weighed the corrupting effect of the suggestive identification itself.

Id., at 111-114.

6. In today's world, police departments are increasingly likely to conduct identifications by means of digital photos displayed for the eyewitness on a computer

screen, instead of the more traditional photographic array. Do computer-based identifications present any special issues or concerns? Or do they instead create opportunities? For example, digital photos can easily be modified to make them more, or less, comparable to each other. Does this make you feel more, or less, comfortable about the reliability of eyewitness identifications?

7. In Perry v. New Hampshire, 132 S. Ct. 716 (2012), the police responded to a report of a car break-in in an apartment parking lot. A suspect was found at the scene, and while one officer stayed with the suspect, a second officer went up into the apartments to speak to a witness. When the officer in the apartment asked the witness for a description of the perpetrator, the witness pointed out the window and said the suspect was the person standing next to the police officer in the parking lot. The suspect moved to suppress the witness's identification as being too suggestive. The Supreme Court held, per Justice Ginsburg, that there was no due process violation because there was no "state action"; any possible suggestiveness was not caused by the behavior of the police.

8. The *Wade* Court, in a separate passage not reproduced above, stated that "[l]egislative or other regulations . . . which eliminate the risks of abuse and unintentional suggestion at lineup proceedings and the impediments to meaningful confrontation at trial may also remove the basis for regarding the stage as 'critical.'" 388 U.S., at 239. In response, Professor Frank Read proposed the following Model Regulation:

Proposed Regulation of Eyewitness Identification Proceduresc

(1) *Restrictions on Identification*

(a) Restrictions on Police. No law enforcement officer shall conduct a lineup or otherwise attempt, by having a witness view or hear the voice of an arrested person, to secure the identification of an arrested person as a person involved in a crime unless such identification procedure is authorized by this regulation. . . .

(b) Restrictions on Witnesses. No witness at trial shall hereafter be permitted to identify a criminal defendant as the person involved in a crime unless the prosecution has first shown, to the Court's satisfaction, and in the absence of the jury:

(1) That the witness was sufficiently acquainted with the defendant before the alleged offense to make recognition then likely; or

(2) That the witness' recognition of the defendant arose from an independent origin or source under circumstances other than that the police or other authorities were attempting to elicit identification; or

(3) That all pertinent provisions of this regulation were followed by police in conducting eyewitness confrontation or lineup identification procedures. . . .

(2) *Required Procedures*

A lineup or identification procedure is authorized only if there has been compliance with the following rules:

(a) No person participating in any police lineup or other identification procedure and no person present at such lineup or identification procedure shall do any act or say any thing which shall directly, indirectly, or impliedly suggest to or influence any identifying witness to make or not to make a particular identification, or which suggests to or influences any identifying witness to believe or suspect that any member or members of the group standing [in] the lineup has been arrested for the offense in question or for any offense.

(b) The officer conducting any police lineup or identification proceeding shall take all steps necessary to guarantee that any identification or failure to identify shall be the product of the free choice of the identifying witness based on the independent recollection or recognition of such witness. . . .

(c) All police lineups or identification proceedings shall be composed of a minimum of five persons, in addition to the suspect, and these additional five or more persons shall be of the same general age, sex, race and general physical characteristics as the suspect and be required to wear clothing similar to that worn by the suspect. . . .

(d) All body movements, gestures or verbal statements that may be necessary shall be done one time only by each person participating in the lineup and shall be repeated only at the express request of the identifying witness. . . .

(e) The suspect may select his own position in any police lineup or identification procedure and may change his position after each identifying witness has completed his viewing. . . .

(f) Under no circumstances shall any identifying witness be allowed to see a suspect or any member of the lineup in custody or otherwise prior to the lineup or identification procedure and no interrogation of the suspect or any member of the lineup group shall occur in the presence of an identifying witness. . . .

(g) Two (2) or more identifying witnesses shall not view the same lineup or identification procedure in each other's presence nor shall they be permitted to communicate with each other before completion of all attempted identifications by all witnesses. . . .

(h) Prior to viewing the lineup, an identifying witness shall be required to give a description of the person or persons responsible for the crime in question and such description shall be written and signed or otherwise verified and a copy of such description and all other descriptions that may have been given to the police prior to the lineup shall be made available to defense counsel. . . .

(i) Any identifying witness may remain unseen or masked when viewing the lineup or identification procedure. . . .

(j) The officer conducting any police lineup or identification proceeding shall record the names and addresses of persons participating in the lineup or identification, including the suspect or defendant, the others standing in the lineup group with the suspect or defendant, the police officers present, any person representing the suspect, and any independent observers; provided however, that names of identifying witnesses shall not be required to be disclosed; a copy of said list of names and addresses so recorded shall be furnished to defense counsel.

(k) A full record of all statements made by the identifying witness regarding the identification shall be made by voice recording, or, if no such recording equipment is available, a complete transcript of all statements made by the identifying witness regarding the identification shall be made; a copy of such voice recording or transcript shall be made available to defense counsel.

(l) A visual recording of the conduct of the lineup or identification procedure shall be made by videotape or other appropriate moving picture-type process, or, if no such videotape or moving picture type equipment is available, a minimum of one good quality color photograph of the entire group included in the lineup which was viewed by the identifying witness shall be taken and a copy of such photograph shall be made available to defense counsel. . . .

(3) *Urgent Necessity*

In cases of urgent necessity, as where a witness is dying at the scene of the crime, an identification confrontation shall be lawful with only such compliance with subsections a, b, j, k, and l of section 2, above, as may be reasonable under the circumstances. . . .

Frank T. Read, Lawyers at Lineups: Constitutional Necessity or Avoidable Extravagance?, 17 UCLA L. Rev. 339, 388-393 (1969). Prof. Read's proposal anticipated work that would be done by research psychologists decades later.

In the 1980s, some defense lawyers proposed to assist the jury by employing experts—usually psychologists—to testify to the limits of human perception, memory, etc., as well as to the potential for suggestiveness that lineups and similar procedures possess. The courts were not very receptive to such evidence, although a few courts admitted it, and a few appellate cases held that exclusion of such expert testimony was an abuse of discretion. See, e.g., People v. McDonald, 37 Cal. 3d 351 (1984). By the 1990s, it could be said that "the admission of expert psychological testimony on eyewitness memory appears to be the exception rather than the rule." Steven Penrod, Solomon M. Fulero & Brian L. Cutler, Expert Psychological Testimony on Eyewitness Reliability before and after *Daubert*: The State of the Law and the Science 229, 230 (1995). This judicial reluctance was largely for two reasons. First, science had not produced the kind of clear-cut answers most amenable to judicial use. See Rogers Elliott, Expert Testimony about Eyewitness Identification, 17 L. & Hum. Behav. 423 (1993). Second, the critical empirical question is not the extent of human foibles in eyewitness identification but whether expert testimony will positively contribute to accurate verdicts, a proposition not easy to establish. See Michael McCloskey & Howard E. Egeth, Eyewitness Identification: What Can a Psychologist Tell a Jury?, 38 Am. Psychol. 550 (1983).

In the late 1990s, growing national concern over false confessions—prompted by highly publicized DNA exonerations—generated a new round of psychology research on the operation of memory and the ability of individuals to make reliable identifications. See Jim Dwyer, Peter Neufeld & F. Barry Scheck, Actual Innocence: Five Days to Execution and Other Dispatches from the Wrongly Convicted (2000) (false identifications often play a role in erroneous convictions). One study found that eyewitness identifications made during events "personally relevant, highly stressful, and realistic in nature" are prone to "substantial error"—even when the eyewitness views the target for more than 30 minutes. Charles A. Morgan III, Gary Hazlett, Anthony Doran, Stephan Garrett, Gary Hoyt, Paul Thomas, Madelon Baranoski & Steven Southwicket, Accuracy of Eyewitness Memory for Persons Encountered During Exposure to Highly Intense Stress, 27 Intl. J.L. & Psychiatry 265 (2004). Cross-racial identifications, which are systematically harder to make than own-race identifications, pose a special problem. Christian A. Meissner & John C. Brigham, Eyewitness Identification: Thirty Years of Investigating the Own-Race Bias in Memory for Faces: A Meta-Analytic Review, 7 Psychol. Pub. Pol'y & L. 3 (2001). And identifications by children are often influenced by their susceptibility to suggestiveness. M. Bruck & J. Ceci, The Description of Children's Suggestibility, in Nancy L. Stein et al. (eds.), Memory for Everyday and Emotional Events (1997).

Can eyewitness identifications be improved? A group of researchers led by Gary Wells proposed the following:

1.   The person conducting a lineup should not know who is accused;
2.   The person making an identification should be told that perhaps the suspect is not in the lineup;
3.   The suspect should look like everyone else in the lineup; and
4.   Statements of confidence from those identifying should be obtained.

Gary L. Wells, Mark Small, Steven Penrod, Roy S. Malpass, Solomon M. Fulero & C. A. E. Brimacombe, Eyewitness Identification Procedures: Recommendations for Lineups and Photospreads, 22 Law & Hum. Behav. 603 (1998). Professor Wells also suggested that lineups (and photo arrays, which are more common today) should be conducted sequentially rather than simultaneously; in other words, the eyewitness should view the possible matches one at a time, and should answer "yes" or "no" for each possible match before moving on to the next one.

Based largely on Professor Wells's research, and similar work done by the National Institute of Justice (see "Eyewitness Evidence: A Guide for Law Enforcement," NIJ, U.S. Department of Justice, October 1999), a strong push was made in some jurisdictions to replace traditional simultaneous lineups (where the suspect appears together with other persons) with double-blind sequential lineups (where neither the eyewitness nor the person administering the lineup knows in advance the suspect's position in the lineup). These new procedures were implemented in New Jersey, Boston, Hennepin County, Minnesota, and elsewhere. See Kate Zernike, Questions Raised over New Trend in Police Lineups, N.Y. Times, Apr. 19, 2006, at A1.

In Illinois, similar new lineup procedures were proposed for all homicide cases by Governor George Ryan's Commission on Capital Punishment[8] in 2002, and thereafter became the subject of a controversial pilot study by police departments that purported to show an overall *decrease* in accuracy under the new procedures. See Zack L. Winzeler, Whoa, Whoa, Whoa . . . One at a Time: Examining the Responses to the Illinois Study on Double-Blind Sequential Lineup Procedures, 2008 Utah L. Rev. 1595; Jack King, NACDL News: NACDL Files Suit over Illinois "Lineup" Report, 31 Champion 6 (2007) (detailing efforts by the National Association of Criminal Defense Lawyers to challenge the validity of the Illinois pilot study).

Legal reforms based on social science, like those proposed for eyewitness identification procedures, often end up being controversial. For one thing, the ongoing march of science pretty much guarantees that there will be discomforting fits and starts in any such science-based reform effort. In late 2014, the National Academy of Sciences issued a comprehensive report based on all of the available research to date about eyewitness identifications[9]; the report recommended double-blind procedures, standardized instructions for participants, videotaping of identifications, and recording of the participants' expressed confidence levels at the time of the identification. Notably, however, the report made no recommendation about sequential versus simultaneous identifications. The reason: Credible new scientific research has emerged that questions the superiority of the sequential approach. What previously seemed like a definitive answer ("sequential is better than simultaneous") is no longer so clear, and more research will be needed to resolve the issue. In science, that is no problem. In law, however, scientific progress can undermine legal stability and generate skepticism.

Moreover, even when social science produces clear answers, they are the answers to *empirical* questions—not the *normative* ones with which the law is usually most concerned. In the particular context of eyewitness identifications, it's not only false-positive identifications (those that erroneously identify an innocent person) that we

8. The Commission did not propose to make the new procedures mandatory, due to concerns about the practicalities of implementation. The Committee's Report is available online at http://www.idoc. state.il.us/ccp/ccp/reports/commission_report/complete_report.pdf.

9. The 2014 NAS Report, entitled "Identifying the Culprit: Assessing Eyewitness Identification," can be found online here: http://www.nap.edu/catalog/18891/identifying-the-culprit-assessing-eyewitness-identification?utm_expid=4418042-5.krRTDpXJQISoXLpdo-1Ynw.0&utm_referrer=http%3A%2F%2Fnap. edu%2F.

care about; we also care about false-negative ones (those that fail to identify a guilty person). False negatives, after all, put criminals back on the street where they can commit more crimes against more innocent victims. (In one well-known instance, serial killer Ted Bundy was able to continue his murder spree because an eyewitness was unable to pick out his photo from a photo array in connection with a 1974 abduction.) And some of the proposed identification reforms might decrease false positives at the cost of substantially increasing false negatives. That presents the law with a tough normative choice: Which approach, the one that catches more criminals or the one that protects more innocent suspects, is better? Social science can inform the choice, but it cannot make the choice. See Steven E. Clark & Ryan D. Godfrey, Eyewitness Identification Evidence and Innocence Risk, 16 Psychonomic Bull. & Rev. 22, 38 (2009).

9. In this area, as in others, some state courts of last resort have extended procedural protections to defendants as a matter of state law that exceed the federal constitutional requirements. See, e.g., State v. Dubose, 699 N.W.2d 582 (Wis. 2005) (per se exclusion of all out-of-court show-up identifications unless necessary); Commonwealth v. Johnson, 650 N.E.2d 1257 (Mass. 1995) (per se exclusion of identification evidence resulting from unnecessarily suggestive show-ups); State v. Ramirez, 817 P.2d 774 (Utah 1991) (expanding *Biggers* criteria for evaluating reliability, and thus admissibility, of identification evidence); People v. Adams, 440 N.Y.S.2d 902 (N.Y. 1981) (forbidding the admission of testimony concerning an unnecessarily suggestive identification, but also applying harmless-error analysis); People v. Bustamonte, 634 P.2d 927, 177 Cal. Rptr. 576 (1981) (extending right to counsel to preindictment lineups).

b. When Does the Right to Counsel End?

Once the Sixth Amendment right to counsel "attaches," the right continues to apply to all "critical stages" until the final determination by the trial judge of the sentence to be imposed. Mempa v. Rhay, 389 U.S. 128 (1967) (right to counsel applicable at probation revocation hearing at which judge imposed sentence). But the Sixth Amendment right to counsel does not apply past the point of sentencing. In Morrissey v. Brewer, 408 U.S. 471 (1972), the Court held that parole revocation is not a part of a criminal prosecution, although due process nonetheless mandates certain procedural protections. In Gagnon v. Scarpelli, 411 U.S. 778 (1973), the Court held that one of those protections is a right to counsel at parole or probation revocation proceedings where, unlike in *Mempa*, sentence was not imposed at the hearing and where there are "special circumstances." The special circumstances calling for counsel exist whenever the probationer or parolee makes a request for counsel, based on a timely and colorable claim (i) that he has not committed the alleged violation of the conditions upon which he is at liberty; or (ii) that, even if the violation is a matter of public record and is uncontested, there are substantial reasons that justified or mitigated the violation and make revocation inappropriate, and that the reasons are complex or otherwise difficult to develop or present. Id., at 790. The Court has also determined that a prisoner has a right to be heard in prison disciplinary hearings that could adversely affect his liberty interests, but not necessarily with the assistance of counsel. Wolff v. McDonnell, 418 U.S. 539 (1974). For a discussion, see David A. Harris, The Constitution and Truth Seeking: A New

Theory on Expert Services for Indigent Defendants, 83 J. Crim. L. & Criminology 469 (1992). Curiously enough, the Court in *Gagnon* made a point of emphasizing that it was *not* deciding anything about the scope of the right to be heard by *retained* counsel in revocation proceedings. 411 U.S., at 783 n. 6. Counsel need not be appointed for inmates placed in administrative segregation as a result of crimes committed while incarcerated, unless adversary judicial proceedings are initiated against the inmates. United States v. Gouveia, 467 U.S. 180 (1984).

What about the appeal of a criminal conviction? Perhaps surprisingly, the Court regularly declares—as it has for well over a century—that there is no constitutional due process right to an appeal at all. See McKane v. Durston, 153 U.S. 684, 687 (1894). The fact remains that all 50 states do, in fact, provide opportunity for appellate review of criminal convictions, and have long done so. Why would the Court insist that they need not do so? *McKane* is a strange case to cite for that strange proposition, since the petitioner in that case—John Y. McKane, a New York politician—*did* appeal his conviction, and a court heard his appeal. McKane complained not of the absence of appellate review and certainly not of the denial of counsel (he could afford the best lawyers); rather, he claimed that the Constitution entitled him to be free on bail while his appeal was pending. New York law said otherwise. In *McKane*, Justice Harlan (the first Justice Harlan) found the relevant state law constitutional.

The story behind *McKane* is interesting. John McKane was the late-nineteenth-century political boss of Coney Island. He made his living by requiring local businesses to pay protection money in order to receive police services and through kickbacks from friends to whom he sold valuable public land for below-market prices. The kickbacks and extortion not only lined McKane's pockets but also paid for the local police force. A court order mandated the monitoring of an 1893 election in McKane's town; when the monitors showed up with the order in hand, McKane said, "Injunctions don't go here"—and then ordered the monitors beaten and jailed. One of them escaped and told his story to a Brooklyn newspaper. McKane's dismissive words made national headlines. He was tried and convicted of state election law violations and sentenced to six years at Sing Sing—a remarkably severe sentence for that time. By the time he got out of prison, Coney Island and its environs had been annexed by Brooklyn, then the second-largest city in the United States, and McKane was not on good terms with Brooklyn's leading politicians. His power base was gone; he never returned to public office.

In criminal procedure as elsewhere, it is exceedingly rare for the Supreme Court to rest some important legal proposition on the authority of a more-than-century-old decision. Yet *McKane* continues to be cited with approval. Why? Perhaps the answer is that the legal proposition for which *McKane* now stands is actually less well-settled than first appears. All 50 states *do* provide some kind of appellate review—so no one really knows how the Justices would respond if a state suddenly chose to stop doing so. If that ever happens, *McKane*'s authority may prove less substantial than first appears, which is pretty much what happened to John McKane.

In any event, it is clear that the Sixth Amendment right to counsel does not apply to whatever criminal appeals a state may choose to provide. But in Douglas v. California, 372 U.S. 353 (1963), the Court identified a different constitutional source for a right to appointed counsel on appeal. *Douglas* was premised upon the Court's earlier decision in Griffin v. Illinois, 351 U.S. 12 (1956), where the Court held that whenever a state conditions a criminal appeal on the defendant's provision of a trial transcript to the appellate court, the state must furnish free transcripts to indigent defendants who wish to appeal. Justice Frankfurter's plurality opinion in *Griffin* famously stated:

> There can be no equal justice when the kind of trial a man gets depends on the amount of money he has.

Id., at 24. Despite this language, however, *Griffin* never quite explained whether the right in question derived from equal protection considerations, from the due process right to "fundamental fairness," or from some combination of both.

In *Douglas*, petitioners were convicted and appealed as of right to the California Court of Appeal. They requested, and were denied, the assistance of appointed counsel. However, the denial came only after the court of appeal, following the applicable California rule of criminal procedure, made an independent investigation of the record to determine whether the assistance of appellate counsel would be helpful to the petitioner or the court. Thus, unlike in *Griffin*, petitioners in *Douglas* were not denied *access* to the appellate process; they were only denied state-financed *assistance* after a determination was made that such assistance would be futile. Nonetheless, the Court found the California procedure unconstitutional, in large part on the basis of *Griffin*. *Douglas* thereby gave the appearance of beginning to take literally the famous dicta of *Griffin*.

Read broadly, *Griffin* and *Douglas* might seem to require the extirpation of all differences resulting from the financial condition of defendants. However, it was difficult to tell from the opinions in *Douglas* just how broadly to read that decision, because the underlying rationale was never adequately specified. As in *Griffin*, the decision could have been based either upon some notion of fairness that was now seen to extend beyond mere questions of access or, by contrast, upon the requirement of equal treatment. The greater the reliance on equal treatment as the operative principle, however, the more difficult it would become to draw *any* limits on the reach of *Douglas*. And, indeed, as time went by, the Court appeared to interpret *Douglas* as establishing an equality principle that was then extended in a series of cases, with each succeeding case heightening the perceived tension between the equality principle and the other possible explanation for *Douglas*—fundamental fairness. See, e.g., Mayer v. City of Chicago, 404 U.S. 189 (1971) (state must provide indigent defendant, free of charge, with record of sufficient completeness to permit proper consideration of his claims on appeal, even though such a record is *not* a condition precedent for an appeal).

By the mid-1970s, the worm turned. In several cases involving discretionary review of criminal convictions, the Court—led mostly by Justice Rehnquist—distinguished *Douglas* and reached a contrary result, rejecting the claim of a *Griffin*-based equal protection/due process right to counsel. These cases included Ross v. Moffitt, 417 U.S. 600 (1974) (no right to appointed counsel in state discretionary appeals, or for U.S. Supreme Court certiorari petitions), and Murray v. Giarratano, 492 U.S. 1 (1989) (no right to appointed counsel for federal habeas corpus cases). The distinction was based largely on the different main function of discretionary review: namely, to address legal issues of significance, rather than to correct trial errors.

These two lines of cases—one based on *Griffin/Douglas*, and the other starting with Ross v. Moffitt—eventually culminated in Halbert v. Michigan, 545 U.S. 605 (2005). Under Michigan law, defendants who plead guilty (or nolo contendere) do not get to file an appeal "as of right"; instead, they must first petition the Michigan Court of Appeals for permission to appeal, and the appellate court has discretion to accept or deny the petition. Michigan argued that this system of discretionary appeals was not governed by *Douglas*, since that decision was limited by its own terms to the "first appeal as of right." In a 6-3 decision, the Court held (per Justice Ginsburg) that the proper emphasis in *Douglas* should be on the word "first," rather than on the words "as of right":

> Petitioner Halbert's case is framed by two prior decisions of this Court concerning state-funded appellate counsel, *Douglas* and *Ross*. The question before us is essentially one of classification: With which of those decisions should the instant case be aligned? We hold that *Douglas* provides the controlling instruction. Two aspects of the Michigan Court of Appeals' process following plea-based convictions lead us to that conclusion. First, in determining how to dispose of an application for leave to appeal, Michigan's intermediate appellate court looks to the merits of the claims made in the application. Second, indigent defendants pursuing first-tier review in the Court of Appeals are generally ill equipped to represent themselves.

545 U.S., at 616-617. Justice Thomas, in dissent, took issue with the majority's view of what would be best for indigent appellants:

> Today's decision will . . . do no favors for indigent defendants in Michigan—at least, indigent defendants with nonfrivolous claims. While defendants who admit their guilt will receive more attention, defendants who maintain their innocence will receive less. . . . Holding Michigan's resources constant (since we have no control over the State's bar or budget), the majority's policy choice to redistribute the State's limited resources only harms those most likely to have worthwhile claims. . . . Then, too, Michigan is under no constitutional obligation to provide appeals for plea-convicted defendants. Ante, at 610 (citing McKane v. Durston, 153 U.S. 684 (1894)). Michigan may decline to provide an appellate process altogether (since the Court's ruling increases the cost of having a system of appellate review). Surely plea-convicted defendants would prefer appeals with limited access to counsel than no appeals at all. . . .

545 U.S., at 630-631. Notwithstanding Justice Thomas's concerns, the rule after *Halbert* is now clear: All first-level criminal appeals, whether discretionary or "as of right," must be accompanied by the *Douglas* right to appointed counsel for indigents.

Even where neither the Sixth Amendment nor *Douglas* provide a right to appointed counsel, there may be still other possible sources of law that might do so. For example, statutes in various jurisdictions provide for the furnishing of various kinds of aid to indigents, including both appointed counsel and other forms of assistance in the preparation for and/or conduct of the trial (e.g., investigative aids or expert evaluation and testimony). Indigents who are charged with federal capital crimes or who file federal habeas petitions to challenge their state death sentences have a statutory right to appointed counsel (one or more) in federal habeas, as well as "investigative, expert, or other reasonably necessary services," under 18

U.S.C. §3599(a)(2); in noncapital federal habeas cases, 18 U.S.C. §3006A requires the appointment of counsel whenever it is "in the interests of justice."

And in Ake v. Oklahoma, 470 U.S. 68 (1985), the Court held that whenever an indigent defendant "demonstrates to the trial judge that his sanity at the time of the offense is to be a significant factor at trial, the State must, at a minimum, assure the defendant access to a competent psychiatrist who will conduct an appropriate examination and assist in evaluation, preparation, and presentation of the defense." 470 U.S., at 83. In emphasizing that a defendant must have access to the "basic tools of an adequate defense," id., at 77, the Court further held that a defendant must have access to psychiatric expertise if his future dangerousness is relevant as an aggravating factor in a capital sentencing proceeding. The Court's decision in *Ake* was based on the Mathews v. Eldridge balancing test for due process, see Chapter 2, at pages 87-88.

B. *Effective Assistance of Counsel*

The right "to have the assistance of counsel," guaranteed by the Sixth Amendment and extended to the states through the Fourteenth Amendment, is perhaps the most important of all of the many procedural rights that our American criminal justice system provides to criminal defendants. And for the roughly 80 percent of all criminal defendants who are too poor to hire their own defense lawyers, the decision in Gideon v. Wainwright, 372 U.S. 335 (1963)—one of the most famous cases in history—represented a landmark step toward the ideal of "equal justice under law," the ideal engraved on the front of the United States Supreme Court building in Washington, D.C.

But almost everybody who is familiar with the day-to-day workings of the American criminal justice system would agree that, more than 50 years after *Gideon*, the system remains riddled with problems resulting in large measure from pervasive disparities in the public resources that are allocated to prosecutors and to those who are called upon to represent the indigent. Whether by means of public defender agencies (as in most large urban areas) or through the appointment of private defense counsel compensated by the government, indigent defense representation is almost universally underfunded, sometimes severely, by comparison to the funding of prosecutor's offices.[10] (Moreover, prosecutors often can rely on the police to perform much of the investigation required in a criminal case—a resource advantage generally unavailable to defense lawyers.) The inadequacy of funding for defense services has a direct impact on the quality of representation that indigent defendants receive. Public defenders are underpaid, and also are assigned caseloads beyond their ability to handle adequately; and in jurisdictions that still rely on the appointment of private defense lawyers, judges have to dig deeper and deeper to obtain indigent

---

10. The extent of the disparity varies, but recently was estimated as about 40 percent in California, and more than 50 percent in many other jurisdictions. This is by sharp contrast to England, which devotes roughly twice as much funding to criminal defense services as to prosecution services. See ABA Report, *Gideon*'s Broken Promise: America's Continuing Quest for Equal Justice (2004), at p. 13.

representation, often to the point where reliance on inexperienced and/or less-than-stellar lawyers becomes the norm.[11]

Recall the lofty language of Griffin v. Illinois, 351 U.S. 12, 24 (1956): "There can be no equal justice when the kind of trial a man gets depends on the amount of money he has." Measured in those terms, America today does not provide "equal justice."

But is that really the right goal in the first place? Should the American criminal justice system be focused primarily on trying to equalize the resources available to the prosecution and the defense? Or the resources available to rich and poor defendants? Might it be more important instead to focus on ways to ensure that all criminal defendants, rich *and* poor, receive a fundamentally fair adjudication — whether by trial or, as in the overwhelming majority of criminal cases today, through plea negotiations? Are courts capable of providing such assurance through the promulgation and enforcement of legal standards for effective defense representation (or otherwise)? In the end, what is the best way to try to achieve the unfulfilled promise of *Gideon*? Keep these fundamental questions in mind as you work your way through the following materials.

1. The Meaning of Effective Assistance

The mere appointment of counsel does not satisfy the constitutional guarantee of right to counsel. Indeed, the trial court in Powell v. Alabama appointed counsel but in such a way as to preclude the giving of effective aid in the preparation and trial of the case. The concern for effectiveness has been a consistent thread running through the Supreme Court's cases, as evidenced by the rhetoric in McMann

---

11. Former U.S. Attorney General Eric Holder, in a speech at the Annual Meeting of the National Association of Criminal Defense Lawyers (NACDL) on August 1, 2014, stated:

> "[M]ore than five decades after *Gideon*, and 50 years after the Criminal Justice Act established a framework for compensating attorneys who serve indigent federal defendants, millions of Americans remain unable to access or afford the legal assistance they need. Far too many hard-working public defenders are overwhelmed by crushing caseloads or undermined by a shameful lack of resources. And it's clear that, despite the progress we've seen over the years, a persistent and unacceptable 'justice gap' remains all too real. It poses a significant threat to the integrity of our criminal justice system."

For more information about the problem of indigent defense, see ABA Report, Gideon's Broken Promise, supra note 10; see also David Carroll, Commentary: Gideon's Despair, The Marshall Project, January 2, 2015 (available online at https://www.themarshallproject.org/2015/01/02/four-things-the-next-attorney-general-needs-to-know-about-america-s-indigent-defense-crisis); Thomas Giovanni & Roopal Patel, Gideon at 50: Three Reforms to Revive the Right to Counsel (Brennan Center for Justice, 2013); Laurel Bellows, The "Obvious Truth": Gideon Asserts Only a Lawyer's Advocacy Can Ensure a Defendant a Fair Trial, ABA Journal, March 1, 2013 (available online at: http://www.abajournal.com/magazine/article/the_obvious_truth_Gideon); Norman Lefstein & Robert L. Spangenberg, Justice Denied: America's Continuing Neglect of Our Constitutional Right to Counsel (2009); Note, Effectively Ineffective: The Failure of Courts to Address Underfunded Indigent Defense Systems, 118 Harv. L. Rev. 1731 (2005); The Spangenberg Group, Rates of Compensation Paid to Court-Appointed Counsel in Non-Capital Felony Cases at Trial: A State-by-State Overview (August 2003) (available at http://www.abanet.org/legalservices/downloads/sclaid/indigentdefense/compensationratesnoncapital2003.pdf); Jonathan Ross, Ten Principles of Public Defense Delivery System (ABA, 2002).

v. Richardson, 397 U.S. 759 (1970) ("if the right to counsel guaranteed by the Constitution is to serve its purpose, defendants cannot be left to the mercies of incompetent counsel," id., at 771).

To ensure the basic conditions under which effective assistance is likely to be obtained, the Supreme Court has rendered a series of decisions prohibiting certain forms of interference with the attorney-client relationship. An attorney may not be prohibited from conferring with the client during an overnight recess that falls between direct examination and cross-examination, Geders v. United States, 425 U.S. 80 (1976). A lawyer may not be denied the right to give a closing summation in a nonjury trial, Herring v. New York, 422 U.S. 853 (1975). The state may not prohibit the attorney from eliciting the client's testimony on direct examination, Ferguson v. Georgia, 365 U.S. 570 (1961), nor may the state restrict the attorney's choice as to when to put the defendant on the stand, Brooks v. Tennessee, 406 U.S. 605 (1972). There are limits on the Court's solicitude for criminal defendants, however. In Perry v. Leeke, 488 U.S. 272 (1989), the Court held that the trial court did not err by ordering the defendant not to consult with his lawyer during a 15-minute recess that immediately followed his direct examination and preceded cross-examination.

Outside of these, and similar, relatively narrow areas, during much of the nation's history the lower courts almost uniformly adopted the "mockery of justice" standard to test claims of ineffectiveness under which ineffectiveness was found only in such shocking circumstances as to reduce the trial to a farce or charade. Even inebriated counsel often was insufficient cause to find lack of effectiveness.

The mockery of justice standard seems inordinately low, but there are some justifications for it. The higher the level of scrutiny, the greater is the impetus on the part of the trial judge to intervene in derogation of basic premises of the adversary system. Moreover, intervention may occur at a point of what appears to be problematic action by counsel but in fact is an integral part of a trial strategy known only to counsel. Also, the more active trial judges become, the more they are implicitly or explicitly critical of the bar that practices before them; and the more active appellate courts become, the more critical they become of the trial judges.

Beginning around 1970, a large proportion of the states, and most of the federal circuits, replaced the mockery of justice standard with one that requires counsel to possess and exercise the legal competence customarily found in the jurisdiction. For an early and influential example, see Moore v. United States, 432 F.2d 730 (3d Cir. 1970). Two developments stimulated this change. The first was the Supreme Court's legitimation of plea bargaining in 1970. See Chapter 13. If pleas were now to receive greater protection against challenge, then the legal advice received by an accused becomes of greater importance. Moreover, one of the challenges to a guilty plea that could not be deemed waived by it is the very advice that led to the plea in the first instance, which has the effect of focusing greater attention on the competency of counsel throughout the plea negotiations. The second development that stimulated a greater concern for the competency of counsel was the Supreme Court's tightening of the rules of habeas corpus (recently furthered by Congress). See Chapter 17. As most avenues to relief for habeas petitioners have narrowed, the incentive to relitigate those closed avenues under the alternative rubric of the effective assistance of counsel has grown.

The Supreme Court finally turned to these issues in:

STRICKLAND v. WASHINGTON

Certiorari to the United States Court of Appeals for the Eleventh Circuit
466 U.S. 668 (1984)

JUSTICE O'CONNOR delivered the opinion of the Court.

This case requires us to consider the proper standards for judging a criminal defendant's contention that the Constitution requires a conviction or death sentence to be set aside because counsel's assistance at the trial or sentencing was ineffective.

I

A

During a ten-day period in September 1976, respondent planned and committed three groups of crimes, which included three brutal stabbing murders, torture, kidnapping, severe assaults, attempted murders, attempted extortion, and theft. After his two accomplices were arrested, respondent surrendered to police and voluntarily gave a lengthy statement confessing to the third of the criminal episodes. The State of Florida indicted respondent for kidnapping and murder and appointed an experienced criminal lawyer to represent him.

Counsel actively pursued pretrial motions and discovery. He cut his efforts short, however, and he experienced a sense of hopelessness about the case, when he learned that, against his specific advice, respondent had also confessed to the first two murders. By the date set for trial, respondent was subject to indictment for three counts of first degree murder and multiple counts of robbery, kidnapping for ransom, breaking and entering and assault, attempted murder, and conspiracy to commit robbery. Respondent waived his right to a jury trial, again acting against counsel's advice, and pleaded guilty to all charges, including the three capital murder charges.

In the plea colloquy, respondent told the trial judge that, although he had committed a string of burglaries, he had no significant prior criminal record and that at the time of his criminal spree he was under extreme stress caused by his inability to support his family. . . . He also stated, however, that he accepted responsibility for the crimes. . . . The trial judge told respondent that he had "a great deal of respect for people who are willing to step forward and admit their responsibility" but that he was making no statement at all about his likely sentencing decision. . . .

Counsel advised respondent to invoke his right under Florida law to an advisory jury at his capital sentencing hearing. Respondent rejected the advice and waived the right. He chose instead to be sentenced by the trial judge without a jury recommendation.

In preparing for the sentencing hearing, counsel spoke with respondent about his background. He also spoke on the telephone with respondent's wife and mother, though he did not follow up on the one unsuccessful effort to meet with them. He did not otherwise seek out character witnesses for respondent. . . . Nor did he request a psychiatric examination, since his conversations with his client gave no indication that respondent had psychological problems. . . .

Counsel decided not to present and hence not to look further for evidence concerning respondent's character and emotional state. That decision reflected trial counsel's sense of hopelessness about overcoming the evidentiary effect of respondent's confessions to the gruesome crimes. . . . It also reflected the judgment that it was advisable to rely on the plea colloquy for evidence about respondent's background and about his claim of emotional stress: The plea colloquy communicated sufficient information about these subjects, and by [forgoing] the opportunity to present new evidence on these subjects, counsel prevented the State from cross-examining respondent on his claim and from putting on psychiatric evidence of its own. . . .

Counsel also excluded from the sentencing hearing other evidence he thought was potentially damaging. He successfully moved to exclude respondent's "rap sheet." . . . Because he judged that a presentence report might prove more detrimental than helpful, as it would have included respondent's criminal history and thereby undermined the claim of no significant history of criminal activity, he did not request that one be prepared. . . .

At the sentencing hearing, counsel's strategy was based primarily on the trial judge's remarks at the plea colloquy as well as on his reputation as a sentencing judge who thought it important for a convicted defendant to own up to his crime. Counsel argued that respondent's remorse and acceptance of responsibility justified sparing him from the death penalty. . . . Counsel also argued that respondent had no history of criminal activity and that respondent committed the crimes under extreme mental or emotional disturbance, thus coming within the statutory list of mitigating circumstances. He further argued that respondent should be spared death because he had surrendered, confessed, and offered to testify against a co-defendant and because respondent was fundamentally a good person who had briefly gone badly wrong in extremely stressful circumstances. The State put on evidence and witnesses largely for the purpose of describing the details of the crimes. Counsel did not cross-examine the medical experts who testified about the manner of death of respondent's victims. . . .

. . . The trial judge found numerous aggravating circumstances and no (or a single comparatively insignificant) mitigating circumstance. With respect to each of the three convictions for capital murder, the trial judge concluded: "A careful consideration of all matters presented to the court impels the conclusion that there are insufficient mitigating circumstances . . . to outweigh the aggravating circumstances." He therefore sentenced respondent to death on each of the three counts of murder and to prison terms for the other crimes. The Florida Supreme Court upheld the convictions and sentences on direct appeal. . . .

C

Respondent next filed a petition for a writ of habeas corpus in the United States District Court for the Southern District of Florida.

The District Court held an evidentiary hearing to inquire into trial counsel's efforts to investigate and to present mitigating circumstances. Respondent offered the affidavits and reports he had submitted in the state collateral proceedings; he also called his trial counsel to testify. The State of Florida, over respondent's objection, called the trial judge to testify. [The court denied the petition for a writ of habeas corpus.]

On appeal, . . . the Court of Appeals stated that the Sixth Amendment right to assistance of counsel accorded criminal defendants a right to "counsel reasonably likely to render and rendering reasonably effective assistance given the totality of the circumstances." . . . Summarily rejecting respondent's claims other than ineffectiveness of counsel, the court . . . reversed the judgment of the District Court and remanded the case. . . .

D

Petitioners, who are officials of the State of Florida, filed a petition for a writ of certiorari seeking review of the decision of the Court of Appeals. The petition presents a type of Sixth Amendment claim that this Court has not previously considered in any generality. . . . With the exception of Cuyler v. Sullivan [see page 188, infra—EDS.] which involved a claim that counsel's assistance was rendered ineffective by a conflict of interest, the Court has never directly and fully addressed a claim of "actual ineffectiveness" of counsel's assistance in a case going to trial. . . .

II

. . . In giving meaning to the requirement [of effective assistance of counsel,] we must take its purpose—to ensure a fair trial—as the guide. The benchmark for judging any claim of ineffectiveness must be whether counsel's conduct so undermined the proper functioning of the adversarial process that the trial cannot be relied on as having produced a just result.

The same principle applies to a capital sentencing proceeding such as that provided by Florida law. We need not consider the role of counsel in an ordinary sentencing, which may involve informal proceedings and standardless discretion in the sentencer, and hence may require a different approach to the definition of constitutionally effective assistance. . . .

III

A convicted defendant's claim that counsel's assistance was so defective as to require reversal of a conviction or death sentence has two components. First, the defendant must show that counsel's performance was deficient. This requires showing that counsel made errors so serious that counsel was not functioning as the "counsel" guaranteed the defendant by the Sixth Amendment. Second, the defendant must show that the deficient performance prejudiced the defense. This requires showing that counsel's errors were so serious as to deprive the defendant of a fair trial, a trial whose result is reliable. Unless a defendant makes both showings, it cannot be said that the conviction or death sentence resulted from a breakdown in the adversary process that renders the result unreliable.

A

As all the Federal Courts of Appeals have now held, the proper standard for attorney performance is that of reasonably effective assistance. . . . When a convicted defendant complains of the ineffectiveness of counsel's assistance, the defendant must show that counsel's representation fell below an objective standard of reasonableness.

More specific guidelines are not appropriate. The Sixth Amendment refers simply to "counsel," not specifying particular requirements of effective assistance. It relies instead on the legal profession's maintenance of standards sufficient to justify the law's presumption that counsel will fulfill the role in the adversary process that the Amendment envisions. . . . The proper measure of attorney performance remains simply reasonableness under prevailing professional norms.

Representation of a criminal defendant entails certain basic duties. Counsel's function is to assist the defendant, and hence counsel owes the client a duty of loyalty, a duty to avoid conflicts of interest. . . . From counsel's function as assistant to the defendant derive the overarching duty to advocate the defendant's cause and the more particular duties to consult with the defendant on important decisions and to keep the defendant informed of important developments in the course of the prosecution. Counsel also has a duty to bring to bear such skill and knowledge as will render the trial a reliable adversarial testing process. . . .

These basic duties neither exhaustively define the obligations of counsel nor form a checklist for judicial evaluation of attorney performance. In any case presenting an ineffectiveness claim, the performance inquiry must be whether counsel's assistance was reasonable considering all the circumstances. Prevailing norms of practice as reflected in American Bar Association standards and the like, e.g., ABA Standards for Criminal Justice 4-1.1 to 4-8.6 (2d ed. 1980) ("The Defense Function"), are guides to determining what is reasonable, but they are only guides. No particular set of detailed rules for counsel's conduct can satisfactorily take account of the variety of circumstances faced by defense counsel or the range of legitimate decisions regarding how best to represent a criminal defendant. Any such set of rules would interfere with the constitutionally protected independence of counsel and restrict the wide latitude counsel must have in making tactical decisions. . . . Indeed, the existence of detailed guidelines for representation could distract counsel from the overriding mission of vigorous advocacy of the defendant's cause. Moreover, the purpose of the effective assistance guarantee of the Sixth Amendment is not to improve the quality of legal representation, although that is a goal of considerable importance to the legal system. The purpose is simply to ensure that criminal defendants receive a fair trial.

Judicial scrutiny of counsel's performance must be highly deferential. It is all too tempting for a defendant to second-guess counsel's assistance after conviction or adverse sentence, and it is all too easy for a court, examining counsel's defense after it has proved unsuccessful, to conclude that a particular act or omission of counsel was unreasonable. . . . A fair assessment of attorney performance requires that every effort be made to eliminate the distorting effects of hindsight, to reconstruct the circumstances of counsel's challenged conduct, and to evaluate the conduct from counsel's perspective at the time. Because of the difficulties inherent in making the evaluation, a court must indulge a strong presumption that counsel's conduct falls within the wide range of reasonable professional assistance. . . . There are countless ways to provide effective assistance in any given case. Even the best criminal defense attorneys would not defend a particular client in the same way. See Gary Goodpaster, The Trial for Life: Effective Assistance of Counsel in Death Penalty Cases, 58 N.Y.U. L. Rev. 299, 343 (1983).

The availability of intrusive post-trial inquiry into attorney performance or of detailed guidelines for its evaluation would encourage the proliferation of ineffectiveness challenges. Criminal trials resolved unfavorably to the defendant would increasingly come to be followed by a second trial, this one of counsel's unsuccessful defense. Counsel's performance and even willingness to serve could be adversely affected. Intensive scrutiny of counsel and rigid requirements for acceptable assistance could dampen the ardor and impair the independence of defense counsel, discourage the acceptance of assigned cases, and undermine the trust between attorney and client.

Thus, a court deciding an actual ineffectiveness claim must judge the reasonableness of counsel's challenged conduct on the facts of the particular case, viewed as of the time of counsel's conduct. A convicted defendant making a claim of ineffective assistance must identify the acts or omissions of counsel that are alleged not to have been the result of reasonable professional judgment. The court must then determine whether, in light of all the circumstances, the identified acts or omissions were outside the wide range of professionally competent assistance. In making that determination, the court should keep in mind that counsel's function, as elaborated in prevailing professional norms, is to make the adversarial testing process work in the particular case. At the same time, the court should recognize that counsel is strongly presumed to have rendered adequate assistance and made all significant decisions in the exercise of reasonable professional judgment.

These standards require no special amplification in order to define counsel's duty to investigate, the duty at issue in this case. As the Court of Appeals concluded, strategic choices made after thorough investigation of law and facts relevant to plausible options are virtually unchallengeable; and strategic choices made after less than complete investigation are reasonable precisely to the extent that reasonable professional judgments support the limitations on investigation. In other words, counsel has a duty to make reasonable investigations or to make a reasonable decision that makes particular investigations unnecessary. In any ineffectiveness case, a particular decision not to investigate must be directly assessed for reasonableness in all the circumstances, applying a heavy measure of deference to counsel's judgments.

The reasonableness of counsel's actions may be determined or substantially influenced by the defendant's own statements or actions. Counsel's actions are usually based, quite properly, on informed strategic choices made by the defendant and on information supplied by the defendant. In particular, what investigation decisions are reasonable depends critically on such information. For example, when the facts that support a certain potential line of defense are generally known to counsel because of what the defendant has said, the need for further investigation may be considerably diminished or eliminated altogether. And when a defendant has given counsel reason to believe that pursuing certain investigations would be fruitless or even harmful, counsel's failure to pursue those investigations may not later be challenged as unreasonable. In short, inquiry into counsel's conversations with the defendant may be critical to a proper assessment of counsel's investigation decisions, just as it may be critical to a proper assessment of counsel's other litigation decisions. . . .

B

An error by counsel, even if professionally unreasonable, does not warrant setting aside the judgment of a criminal proceeding if the error had no effect on the judgment. . . . The purpose of the Sixth Amendment guarantee of counsel is to ensure that a defendant has the assistance necessary to justify reliance on the outcome of the proceeding. Accordingly, any deficiencies in counsel's performance must be prejudicial to the defense in order to constitute ineffective assistance under the Constitution.

In certain Sixth Amendment contexts, prejudice is presumed. Actual or constructive denial of the assistance of counsel altogether is legally presumed to result in prejudice. So are various kinds of state interference with counsel's assistance. . . . Prejudice in these circumstances is so likely that case by case inquiry into prejudice is not worth the cost. Moreover, such circumstances involve impairments of the Sixth Amendment right that are easy to identify and, for that reason and because the prosecution is directly responsible, easy for the government to prevent.

One type of actual ineffectiveness claim warrants a similar, though more limited, presumption of prejudice. In Cuyler v. Sullivan, 446 U.S., at 345-350, the Court held that prejudice is presumed when counsel is burdened by an actual conflict of interest. In those circumstances, counsel breaches the duty of loyalty, perhaps the most basic of counsel's duties. . . .

Conflict of interest claims aside, actual ineffectiveness claims alleging a deficiency in attorney performance are subject to a general requirement that the defendant affirmatively prove prejudice. The government is not responsible for, and hence not able to prevent, attorney errors that will result in reversal of a conviction or sentence. Attorney errors come in an infinite variety and are as likely to be utterly harmless in a particular case as they are to be prejudicial. They cannot be classified according to likelihood of causing prejudice. Nor can they be defined with sufficient precision to inform defense attorneys correctly just what conduct to avoid. Representation is an art, and an act or omission that is unprofessional in one case may be sound or even brilliant in another. Even if a defendant shows that particular errors of counsel were unreasonable, therefore, the defendant must show that they actually had an adverse effect on the defense.

It is not enough for the defendant to show that the errors had some conceivable effect on the outcome of the proceeding. Virtually every act or omission of counsel would meet that test, . . . and not every error that conceivably could have influenced the outcome undermines the reliability of the result of the proceeding. Respondent suggests requiring a showing that the errors "impaired the presentation of the defense." That standard, however, provides no workable principle. Since any error, if it is indeed an error, "impairs" the presentation of the defense, the proposed standard is inadequate because it provides no way of deciding what impairments are sufficiently serious to warrant setting aside the outcome of the proceeding.

On the other hand, we believe that a defendant need not show that counsel's deficient conduct more likely than not altered the outcome in the case. This outcome-determinative standard has several strengths. It defines the relevant inquiry in a way familiar to courts, though the inquiry, as is inevitable, is anything but precise. The standard also reflects the profound importance of finality in criminal proceedings. Moreover, it comports with the widely used standard for assessing motions for new trial based on newly discovered evidence. . . . Nevertheless, the standard is not quite appropriate.

Even when the specified attorney error results in the omission of certain evidence, the newly discovered evidence standard is not an apt source from which to draw a prejudice standard for ineffectiveness claims. The high standard for newly discovered evidence claims presupposes that all the essential elements of a presumptively accurate and fair proceeding were present in the proceeding whose result is challenged. . . . An ineffective assistance claim asserts the absence of one of the crucial assurances that the result of the proceeding is reliable, so finality concerns are somewhat weaker and the appropriate standard of prejudice should be somewhat lower. The result of a proceeding can be rendered unreliable, and hence the proceeding itself unfair, even if the errors of counsel cannot be shown by a preponderance of the evidence to have determined the outcome.

Accordingly, the appropriate test for prejudice finds its roots in the test for materiality of exculpatory information not disclosed to the defense by the prosecution, United States v. Agurs, 427 U.S., at 104, 112-113, and in the test for materiality of testimony made unavailable to the defense by Government deportation of a witness, United States v. Valenzuela-Bernal, 458 U.S., at 872-874. The defendant must show that there is a reasonable probability that, but for counsel's unprofessional errors, the result of the proceeding would have been different. A reasonable probability is a probability sufficient to undermine confidence in the outcome.

In making the determination whether the specified errors resulted in the required prejudice, a court should presume, absent challenge to the judgment on grounds of evidentiary insufficiency, that the judge or jury acted according to law. An assessment of the likelihood of a result more favorable to the defendant must exclude the possibility of arbitrariness, whimsy, caprice, "nullification," and the like. A defendant has no entitlement to the luck of a lawless decisionmaker, even if a lawless decision cannot be reviewed. The assessment of prejudice should proceed on the assumption that the decisionmaker is reasonably, conscientiously, and impartially applying the standards that govern the decision. It should not depend on the idiosyncrasies of the particular decisionmaker, such as unusual propensities toward harshness or leniency. Although these factors may actually have entered into counsel's selection of strategies and, to that limited extent, may thus affect the performance inquiry, they are irrelevant to the prejudice inquiry. Thus, evidence about the actual process of decision, if not part of the record of the proceeding under review, and evidence about, for example, a particular judge's sentencing practices, should not be considered in the prejudice determination.

The governing legal standard plays a critical role in defining the question to be asked in assessing the prejudice from counsel's errors. When a defendant challenges a conviction, the question is whether there is a reasonable probability that, absent the errors, the fact-finder would have had a reasonable doubt respecting guilt. When a defendant challenges a death sentence such as the one at issue in this case, the question is whether there is a reasonable probability that, absent the errors, the sentencer—including an appellate court, to the extent it independently reweighs the evidence—would have concluded that the balance of aggravating and mitigating circumstances did not warrant death.

In making this determination, a court hearing an ineffectiveness claim must consider the totality of the evidence before the judge or jury. Some of the factual findings will have been unaffected by the errors, and factual findings that were affected will have been affected in different ways. Some errors will have had a pervasive effect on the inferences to be drawn from the evidence, altering the entire evidentiary picture, and some will have had an isolated, trivial effect. Moreover, a verdict or conclusion only weakly supported by the record is more likely to have been affected by the errors than one with overwhelming record support. Taking the unaffected findings as a given, and taking due account of the effect of the errors on the remaining findings, a court making the prejudice inquiry must ask if the defendant has met the burden of showing that the decision reached would reasonably likely have been different absent the errors.

IV

A number of practical considerations are important for the application of the standards we have outlined. Most important, in adjudicating a claim of actual ineffectiveness of counsel, a court should keep in mind that the principles we have stated do not establish mechanical rules. Although those principles should guide the process of decision, the ultimate focus of inquiry must be on the fundamental fairness of the proceeding whose result is being challenged. In every case the court should be concerned with whether, despite the strong presumption of reliability, the result of the particular proceeding is unreliable because of a breakdown in the adversarial process that our system counts on to produce just results. . . .

Although we have discussed the performance component of an ineffectiveness claim prior to the prejudice component, there is no reason for a court deciding an ineffective assistance claim to approach the inquiry in the same order or even to address both components of the inquiry if the defendant makes an insufficient showing on one. In particular, a court need not determine whether counsel's performance was deficient before examining the prejudice suffered by the defendant as a result of the alleged deficiencies. The object of an ineffectiveness claim is not to grade counsel's performance. If it is easier to dispose of an ineffectiveness claim on the ground of lack of sufficient prejudice, which we expect will often be so, that course should be followed. Courts should strive to ensure that ineffectiveness claims not become so burdensome to defense counsel that the entire criminal justice system suffers as a result.

The principles governing ineffectiveness claims should apply in federal collateral proceedings as they do on direct appeal or in motions for a new trial. As indicated by the "cause and prejudice" test for overcoming procedural waivers of claims of error, the presumption that a criminal judgment is final is at its strongest in collateral attacks on that judgment. . . . An ineffectiveness claim, however, as our articulation of the standards that govern decision of such claims makes clear, is an attack on the fundamental fairness of the proceeding whose result is challenged. Since fundamental fairness is the central concern of the writ of habeas corpus, . . . no special standards ought to apply to ineffectiveness claims made in habeas proceedings.

Finally, in a federal habeas challenge to a state criminal judgment, a state court conclusion that counsel rendered effective assistance is not a finding of fact binding on the federal court to the extent stated by 28 U.S.C. §2254(d). Ineffectiveness is not a question of "basic, primary, or historical fac[t]." Rather, like the question whether multiple representation in a particular case gave rise to a conflict of interest, it is a mixed question of law and fact. . . . Although state court findings of fact made in the course of deciding an ineffectiveness claim are subject to the deference requirement of §2254(d), and although District Court findings are subject to the clearly erroneous standard of Fed. R. Civ. Proc. 52(a), both the performance and prejudice components of the ineffectiveness inquiry are mixed questions of law and fact.

V

. . . Application of the governing principles is not difficult in this case. The facts as described above, . . . make clear that the conduct of respondent's counsel at and before respondent's sentencing proceeding cannot be found unreasonable.

They also make clear that, even assuming the challenged conduct of counsel was unreasonable, respondent suffered insufficient prejudice to warrant setting aside his death sentence.

With respect to the performance component, the record shows that respondent's counsel made a strategic choice to argue for the extreme emotional distress mitigating circumstance and to rely as fully as possible on respondent's acceptance of responsibility for his crimes. Although counsel understandably felt hopeless about respondent's prospects, . . . nothing in the record indicates, as one possible reading of the District Court's opinion suggests . . . that counsel's sense of hopelessness distorted his professional judgment. Counsel's strategy choice was well within the range of professionally reasonable judgments, and the decision not to seek more character or psychological evidence than was already in hand was likewise reasonable.

The trial judge's views on the importance of owning up to one's crimes were well known to counsel. The aggravating circumstances were utterly overwhelming. Trial counsel could reasonably surmise from his conversations with respondent that character and psychological evidence would be of little help. Respondent had already been able to mention at the plea colloquy the substance of what there was to know about his financial and emotional troubles. Restricting testimony on respondent's character to what had come in at the plea colloquy ensured that contrary character and psychological evidence and respondent's criminal history, which counsel had successfully moved to exclude, would not come in. On these facts, there can be little question, even without application of the presumption of adequate performance, that trial counsel's defense, though unsuccessful, was the result of reasonable professional judgment.

With respect to the prejudice component, the lack of merit of respondent's claim is even more stark. The evidence that respondent says his trial counsel should have offered at the sentencing hearing would barely have altered the sentencing profile presented to the sentencing judge. As the state courts and District Court found, at most this evidence shows that numerous people who knew respondent thought he was generally a good person and that a psychiatrist and a psychologist believed he was under considerable emotional stress that did not rise to the level of extreme disturbance. Given the overwhelming aggravating factors, there is no reasonable probability that the omitted evidence would have changed the conclusion that the aggravating circumstances outweighed the mitigating circumstances and, hence, the sentence imposed. Indeed, admission of the evidence respondent now offers might even have been harmful to his case: his "rap sheet" would probably have been admitted into evidence, and the psychological reports would have directly contradicted respondent's claim that the mitigating circumstance of extreme emotional disturbance applied to his case.

Our conclusions on both the prejudice and performance components of the ineffectiveness inquiry do not depend on the trial judge's testimony at the District Court hearing. We therefore need not consider the general admissibility of that testimony, although, as noted . . . , that testimony is irrelevant to the prejudice inquiry. Moreover, the prejudice question is resolvable, and hence the ineffectiveness claim can be rejected, without regard to the evidence presented at the District Court hearing. The state courts properly concluded that the ineffectiveness claim was meritless without holding an evidentiary hearing.

Failure to make the required showing of either deficient performance or sufficient prejudice defeats the ineffectiveness claim. Here there is a double failure.

More generally, respondent has made no showing that the justice of his sentence was rendered unreliable by a breakdown in the adversary process caused by deficiencies in counsel's assistance. Respondent's sentencing proceeding was not fundamentally unfair.

We conclude, therefore, that the District Court properly declined to issue a writ of habeas corpus. The judgment of the Court of Appeals is accordingly reversed.

JUSTICE MARSHALL, dissenting. . . .

I

The opinion of the Court revolves around two holdings. First, the majority ties the constitutional minima of attorney performance to a simple "standard of reasonableness." . . . Second, the majority holds that only an error of counsel that has sufficient impact on a trial to "undermine confidence in the outcome" is grounds for overturning a conviction. . . . I disagree with both of these rulings.

A

My objection to the performance standard adopted by the Court is that it is so malleable that, in practice, it will either have no grip at all or will yield excessive variation in the manner in which the Sixth Amendment is interpreted and applied by different courts. To tell lawyers and the lower courts that counsel for a criminal defendant must behave "reasonably" and must act like "a reasonably competent attorney," . . . is to tell them almost nothing. In essence, the majority has instructed judges called upon to assess claims of ineffective assistance of counsel to advert to their own intuitions regarding what constitutes "professional" representation, and has discouraged them from trying to develop more detailed standards governing the performance of defense counsel. In my view, the Court has thereby not only abdicated its own responsibility to interpret the Constitution, but also impaired the ability of the lower courts to exercise theirs.

The debilitating ambiguity of an "objective standard of reasonableness" in this context is illustrated by the majority's failure to address important issues concerning the quality of representation mandated by the Constitution. It is an unfortunate but undeniable fact that a person of means, by selecting a lawyer and paying him enough to ensure he prepares thoroughly, usually can obtain better representation than that available to an indigent defendant, who must rely on appointed counsel, who, in turn, has limited time and resources to devote to a given case. Is a "reasonably competent attorney" a reasonably competent adequately paid retained lawyer or a reasonably competent appointed attorney? It is also a fact that the quality of representation available to ordinary defendants in different parts of the country varies significantly. Should the standard of performance mandated by the Sixth Amendment vary by locale? The majority offers no clues as to the proper responses to these questions. . . .

The opinion of the Court of Appeals in this case represents one sound attempt to develop particularized standards designed to ensure that all defendants receive effective legal assistance. . . . By refusing to address the merits of these proposals, and indeed suggesting that no such effort is worthwhile, the opinion of the Court, I fear, will stunt the development of constitutional doctrine in this area.

B

I object to the prejudice standard adopted by the Court for two independent reasons. *First,* it is often very difficult to tell whether a defendant convicted after a trial in which he was ineffectively represented would have fared better if his lawyer had been competent. Seemingly impregnable cases can sometimes be dismantled by good defense counsel. On the basis of a cold record, it may be impossible for a reviewing court confidently to ascertain how the government's evidence and arguments would have stood up against rebuttal and cross-examination by a shrewd, well prepared lawyer. The difficulties of estimating prejudice after the fact are exacerbated by the possibility that evidence of injury to the defendant may be missing from the record precisely because of the incompetence of defense counsel. In view of all these impediments to a fair evaluation of the probability that the outcome of a trial was affected by ineffectiveness of counsel, it seems to me senseless to impose on a defendant whose lawyer has been shown to have been incompetent the burden of demonstrating prejudice.

Second and more fundamentally, the assumption on which the Court's holding rests is that the only purpose of the constitutional guarantee of effective assistance of counsel is to reduce the chance that innocent persons will be convicted. In my view, the guarantee also functions to ensure that convictions are obtained only through fundamentally fair procedures. The majority contends that the Sixth Amendment is not violated when a manifestly guilty defendant is convicted after a trial in which he was represented by a manifestly ineffective attorney. I cannot agree. Every defendant is entitled to a trial in which his interests are vigorously and conscientiously advocated by an able lawyer. A proceeding in which the defendant does not receive meaningful assistance in meeting the forces of the state does not, in my opinion, constitute due process. . . .

III

The majority suggests that, "[f]or purposes of describing counsel's duties," a capital sentencing proceeding "need not be distinguished from an ordinary trial." I cannot agree. . . . In my view, a person on death row, whose counsel's performance fell below constitutionally acceptable levels, should not be compelled to demonstrate a "reasonable probability" that he would have been given a life sentence if his lawyer had been competent . . . ; if the defendant can establish a significant chance that the outcome would have been different, he surely should be entitled to a redetermination of his fate. . . .

IV

The views expressed in the preceding section oblige me to dissent from the majority's disposition of the case before us. It is undisputed that respondent's trial counsel made virtually no investigation of the possibility of obtaining testimony from respondent's relatives, friends, or former employers pertaining to respondent's character or background. Had counsel done so, he would have found several persons willing and able to testify that, in their experience, respondent was a responsible, nonviolent man, devoted to his family, and active in the affairs of his church. . . . Respondent contends that his lawyer could have and should have used that testimony to "humanize" respondent, to counteract the impression conveyed by the trial that he was little more than a cold-blooded killer. Had this evidence been admitted, respondent argues, his chances of obtaining a life sentence would have been significantly better.

. . . The State makes a colorable — though in my view not compelling — argument that defense counsel in this case might have made a reasonable "strategic" decision not to present such evidence at the sentencing hearing on the assumption that an unadorned acknowledgement of respondent's responsibility for his crimes would be more likely to appeal to the trial judge, who was reputed to respect persons who accepted responsibility for their actions. But however justifiable such a choice might have been after counsel had fairly assessed the potential strength of the mitigating evidence available to him, counsel's failure to make any significant effort to find out what evidence might be garnered from respondent's relatives and acquaintances surely cannot be described as "reasonable." . . .

That the aggravating circumstances implicated by respondent's criminal conduct were substantial . . . does not vitiate respondent's constitutional claim; judges and juries in cases involving behavior at least as egregious have shown mercy, particularly when afforded an opportunity to see other facets of the defendant's personality and life. . . .

If counsel had investigated the availability of mitigating evidence, he might well have decided to present some such material at the hearing. If he had done so, there is a significant chance that respondent would have been given a life sentence. In my view, those possibilities, conjoined with the unreasonableness of counsel's failure to investigate, are more than sufficient to establish a violation of the Sixth Amendment and to entitle respondent to a new sentencing proceeding.

I respectfully dissent.

NOTES AND QUESTIONS

1. On the same day as *Strickland*, the Court also decided the companion case of United States v. Cronic, 466 U.S. 648 (1984), in which the defendant was convicted of mail fraud in connection with a "check kiting" scheme.[12] Shortly before trial, Cronic's defense counsel withdrew; the trial judge "appointed a young lawyer with a real estate practice to represent [Cronic], but allowed him only 25 days for pretrial preparation, even though it had taken the Government over four and one-half years to investigate the case and it had reviewed thousands of documents during that investigation." Id., at 652. At trial, the prosecution introduced extensive testimony from two co-conspirators who had entered into plea bargains; Cronic declined to take the stand due to concerns about his prior convictions being introduced against him. Cronic's lawyer presented no defense, but did cross-examine the prosecution's witnesses with some success. Cronic was convicted on 11 out of 13 counts, and received a 25-year sentence; he appealed on the grounds, inter alia, that his trial counsel was constitutionally ineffective. The Tenth Circuit did not find specific flaws in defense counsel's performance, but reversed the convictions nevertheless, holding that the Sixth Amendment was violated because the circumstances of the

---

12. "Check kiting" involves writing a series of checks from different bank accounts in order to take advantage of the "float," or delay in cashing the checks, in order to hide a lack of sufficient funds to cover the checks.

case created an "inference" that defense counsel could not perform effectively; this inference was based on: "(1) [T]he time afforded for investigation and preparation; (2) the experience of counsel; (3) the gravity of the charge; (4) the complexity of possible defenses; and (5) the accessibility of witnesses to counsel." 675 F.2d 1126, 1129 (10th Cir. 1982).

The Supreme Court, in an opinion by Justice Stevens, held unanimously (Justice Marshall concurred in the judgment) that no such "inference" of constitutional ineffectiveness arose from the facts of the *Cronic* case:

> [T]he adversarial process protected by the Sixth Amendment requires that the accused have "counsel acting in the role of an advocate." Anders v. California, 386 U.S. 738, 743 (1967). The right to the effective assistance of counsel is thus the right of the accused to require the prosecution's case to survive the crucible of meaningful adversarial testing. When a true adversarial criminal trial has been conducted—even if defense counsel may have made demonstrable errors—the kind of testing envisioned by the Sixth Amendment has occurred. But if the process loses its character as a confrontation between adversaries, the constitutional guarantee is violated. . . .
>
> . . . [T]he right to the effective assistance of counsel is recognized not for its own sake, but because of the effect it has on the ability of the accused to receive a fair trial. Absent some effect of challenged conduct on the reliability of the trial process, the Sixth Amendment guarantee is generally not implicated. Moreover, because we presume that the lawyer is competent to provide the guiding hand that the defendant needs, . . . the burden rests on the accused to demonstrate a constitutional violation. There are, however, circumstances that are so likely to prejudice the accused that the cost of litigating their effect in a particular case is unjustified.
>
> Most obvious, of course, is the complete denial of counsel. The presumption that counsel's assistance is essential requires us to conclude that a trial is unfair if the accused is denied counsel at a critical stage of his trial. Similarly, if counsel entirely fails to subject the prosecution's case to meaningful adversarial testing, then there has been a denial of Sixth Amendment rights that makes the adversary process itself presumptively unreliable. No specific showing of prejudice was required in Davis v. Alaska, 415 U.S. 308 (1974), because the petitioner had been "denied the right of effective cross-examination" which "would be constitutional error of the first magnitude, and no amount of showing of want of prejudice would cure it." Id., at 318.
>
> Circumstances of that magnitude may be present on some occasions when, although counsel is available to assist the accused during trial, the likelihood that any lawyer, even a fully competent one, could provide effective assistance is so small that a presumption of prejudice is appropriate without inquiry into the actual conduct of the trial. Powell v. Alabama, 287 U.S. 45 (1932), was such a case.
>
> The defendants had been indicted for a highly publicized capital offense. Six days before trial, the trial judge appointed "all the members of the bar" for purposes of arraignment. . . . On the day of trial, a lawyer from Tennessee appeared on behalf of persons "interested" in the defendants, but stated that he had not had an opportunity to prepare the case or to familiarize himself with local procedure, and therefore was unwilling to represent the defendants on such short notice. The problem was resolved when the court decided that the Tennessee lawyer would represent the defendants, with whatever help the local bar could provide.
>
>> "The defendants, young, ignorant, illiterate, surrounded by hostile sentiment, haled back and forth under guard of soldiers, charged with an atrocious crime regarded with especial horror in the community where they were to be tried, were thus put in peril of their lives within a few moments after counsel for the first time charged with any degree of responsibility began to represent them." Id., at 57-58.

This Court held that "such designation of counsel as was attempted was either so indefinite or so close upon the trial as to amount to a denial of effective and substantial aid in that regard." Id., at 53. . . . *Powell* was thus a case in which the surrounding circumstances made it so unlikely that any lawyer could provide effective assistance that ineffectiveness was properly presumed without inquiry into actual performance at trial.

But every refusal to postpone a criminal trial will not give rise to such a presumption. In Avery v. Alabama, 308 U.S. 444 (1940), counsel was appointed in a capital case only three days before trial, and the trial court denied counsel's request for additional time to prepare. Nevertheless, the Court held that, since evidence and witnesses were easily accessible to defense counsel, the circumstances did not make it unreasonable to expect that counsel could adequately prepare for trial during that period of time, id., at 450-453. Thus, only when surrounding circumstances justify a presumption of ineffectiveness can a Sixth Amendment claim be sufficient without inquiry into counsel's actual performance at trial. . . .

The five factors listed in the Court of Appeals' opinion are relevant to an evaluation of a lawyer's effectiveness in a particular case, but neither separately nor in combination do they provide a basis for concluding that competent counsel was not able to provide this respondent with the guiding hand that the Constitution guarantees. . . .

This case is not one in which the surrounding circumstances make it unlikely that the defendant could have received the effective assistance of counsel. The criteria used by the Court of Appeals do not demonstrate that counsel failed to function in any meaningful sense as the Government's adversary. Respondent can therefore make out a claim of ineffective assistance only by pointing to specific errors made by trial counsel. . . .

466 U.S., at 656-666.

2. In *Strickland*, the Court exempted several categories of cases from the requirement that the defendant, in order to win on an ineffective-assistance-of-counsel claim, must show prejudice as a result of counsel's specific errors of performance:[13] (1) actual or constructive denial of counsel (as in *Gideon* or *Powell*); (2) certain kinds of state interference with counsel (e.g., refusing to allow counsel to meet with the defendant during an overnight recess, see Geders v. United States, 425 U.S. 80 (1976)); and (3) some situations involving attorney conflicts of interest, see Cuyler v. Sullivan, 446 U.S. 335 (1980), discussed infra, at page 188. *Cronic* adds a fourth category of "presumed prejudice": where "counsel failed to function in any meaningful sense as the government's adversary."

The *Cronic* category potentially could have become very significant, at least in terms of opening up floodgates of litigation, but in actuality its scope has turned out to be quite limited. In Bell v. Cone, 535 U.S. 685 (2002), the defendant was convicted of robbery and capital murder and sentenced to death. At the sentencing proceeding, the defense counsel cross-examined government witnesses but called no defense witnesses, referring instead to the evidence introduced at trial in support of the defendant's insanity claim. The defense counsel also waived the closing

---

13. A few brief terminological notes about *Strickland*: Ineffective assistance of counsel claims are often referred to as "IAC" claims. The two requirements to establish a *Strickland* violation are usually called the "performance prong" and the "prejudice prong." Finally, notice that the case probably should be called *Washington*, not *Strickland*—after all, the defendant was Washington. Universal custom, however—including within the Supreme Court itself—long ago decided that the case would be called *Strickland*, and we must abide.—EDS.

argument, ostensibly to avoid giving the prosecutor a chance to argue in rebuttal. The defendant argued that this amounted to a "fail[ure] to subject the prosecution's case to meaningful adversarial testing," and so amounted to ineffective assistance of counsel without regard to whether there was any prejudice. With only Justice Stevens dissenting, the Court disagreed:

> . . . When we spoke in *Cronic* of the possibility of presuming prejudice based on an attorney's failure to test the prosecutor's case, we indicated that the attorney's failure must be complete. . . . Here, respondent's argument is not that his counsel failed to oppose the prosecution throughout the sentencing proceeding as a whole, but that his counsel failed to do so at specific points. For purposes of distinguishing between the rule of *Strickland* and that of *Cronic*, this difference is not of degree but of kind. . . .
>
> We hold, therefore, that the state correctly identified the principles announced in *Strickland* as those governing the analysis of respondent's claim.

Id., at 697. Given the analysis in *Bell*, one suspects that successful *Cronic* claims will be rare. Lower-court cases generally confirm this observation: The number of reported *Strickland* claims is enormous—*Strickland* claims comprise probably the single largest category of criminal procedure claims in post-trial litigation—while the number of *Cronic* claims is very small.

3. The majority and dissent in *Strickland* disagree on the role of the defendant's probable guilt and whether the purported error likely would have affected the outcome. What do you think of the dissenters' argument that these factors should be largely irrelevant? What is the significance of these two points? Is all well that ends well, or not? Does the majority's position overestimate the value of stability and finality, or does the minority's underestimate it?

4. Note that the *Strickland* majority has a complicated view of the question whether hindsight is appropriate in these cases. The Court states explicitly that attorney performance must *not* be judged in hindsight; lawyers' judgments are to be assessed according to how those judgments appeared at the time they were made. But the prejudice standard is applied with hindsight: The defendant cannot obtain relief unless he shows it is reasonably likely that his attorney's errors altered the outcome. This two-pronged approach rules out two kinds of claims. The first was mentioned in the preceding note: a claim by a defendant whose lawyer behaved incompetently but who would have been convicted (or, as in *Strickland*, sentenced to death) regardless. The second is a claim by a defendant whose lawyer made a reasonable (or perhaps only marginally negligent) mistake that cost her client the case. Justice Marshall's dissent in *Strickland* essentially argues that the defendant in the first case should get relief. Doesn't the second case deserve relief even more? What does that say about the relationship between attorney incompetence and prejudice, and about the role of the ineffective-assistance doctrine?

5. There are two key practical observations to be made about *Strickland*. First, *Strickland* emphasizes that, with respect to defense attorney performance, "strategic choices made after thorough investigation of law and facts relevant to plausible options are virtually unchallengeable; and strategic choices made after less than complete investigation are reasonable precisely to the extent that reasonable professional judgments support the limitations on investigation." In other words, as soon as a reviewing court decides that defense counsel acted "strategically," it's pretty much game over for the defendant's claim of ineffective assistance of counsel.

Second, *Strickland* explains that "a court need not determine whether counsel's performance was deficient before examining the prejudice suffered by the defendant as a result of the alleged deficiencies. . . . If it is easier to dispose of an ineffectiveness claim on the ground of lack of sufficient prejudice, which we expect will often be so, that course should be followed." In other words, reviewing courts can quickly and easily dispose of most ineffective-assistance claims simply by determining that, given the totality of the evidence of guilt, the defendant most likely would have been convicted no matter what the defense attorney did — and courts generally do so, because it is an approach that avoids unnecessarily critiquing defense attorneys.

6. Why didn't *Strickland* choose instead the simpler approach of articulating a checklist of basic obligations for defense counsel and then requiring courts to enforce those obligations in an appropriate manner? Is anything wrong with the "checklist" approach — which, by the way, is exactly the same approach used by the professional airline pilots to whom we entrust our lives whenever we fly? The first such proposal for defense lawyers was made by Professor Joseph D. Grano, The Right to Counsel: Collateral Issues Affecting Due Process, 54 Minn. L. Rev. 1175, 1248 (1970). Judge David L. Bazelon later developed Grano's suggestion in his article, The Realities of *Gideon* and *Argersinger*, 64 Geo. L.J. 811 (1976). Consider one part of his proposed checklist, id., at 837-838:

PRELIMINARY HEARING

Date _____

Comments _____

_____

_____

_____

_____

_____

	Official Records	*Obtained**
1.	Complaint	_____
2.	Bail Agency form	_____
3.	Narcotics Treatment Ad. Report	_____
4.	Arrest warrant (affidavit)	_____
5.	Search warrant (affidavit)	_____
6.	Defendant's record	_____
7.	PD 251	_____
8.	PD 252, 253, 254	_____
9.	PD 163	_____
10.	Other _____	_____

	Statements	*Obtained**
1.	Written	_____
2.	Oral	_____
3.	Co-defendant	_____

Scientific Exams	AUSA Requested	Obtained*
1. Mental	_____	_____
2. Fingerprints	_____	_____
3. Blood	_____	_____
4. Semen	_____	_____
5. Hair	_____	_____
6. Fiber	_____	_____
7. Pathologist	_____	_____
8. Ballistics	_____	_____
9. Chemist report	_____	_____
10. Handwriting	_____	_____
11. Other	_____	_____

Police Officer Witnesses	Name & Precinct	Interview Obtained*
1. Arresting Officer	_____	_____
2. Mobile Crime Lab	_____	_____
3. Invest. Officer	_____	_____
4. Line-Up Officer	_____	_____
5. Search Officer	_____	_____
6. Confession Officer	_____	_____

Other Witnesses	Name & Address	Interview Obtained*
1. Victim	_____	_____
2. Eyewitnesses	_____	_____
3. Other	_____	_____

Motions to Be Filed (check)   *Comments*

_____1. Suppression of Tangible Object _____

_____

_____2. Suppression of Statements _____

_____

_____3. Identification _____

_____

_____4. Severance _____

_____

_____5. Notice of Alibi _____

_____

_____ 6. Notice of Insanity Defense _____

_____

_____ 7. Mental Competency Exam _____

      _____

_____ 8. Bond Review _____

      _____

_____ 9. Other _____

      _____

Defendant's Version of Events _____

_____

_____

_____

_____

I hereby certify that the case referred to in the above work-sheet has been completely investigated and information contained therein and attached thereto is accurate to the best of my knowledge.

*Date*_____*Attorney's Signature*_____

* Attached is a copy of all statements, oral or written, obtained by counsel, all documents, reports, interviews, and other materials received in the preparation of this case. A completed time sheet is also to be maintained for purposes of administrative records.

Do you see any problems with the so-called "checklist" approach to defense lawyering? Would defendants universally benefit from such an approach? Why or why not? What about unintended collateral consequences? Might the checklist approach indirectly undermine the goals of *Strickland*, by discouraging bright young lawyers from pursuing a career in defense representation?

The Court in *Strickland* specifically rejected the idea of adopting a checklist like the one above. Instead, the Court adopted a more general reasonableness standard. But "reasonableness" in this context seems to mean something other than ordinary negligence: The Court's discussion in *Strickland* suggests something more like a gross negligence standard. Why such a deferential approach? Why not hold defense counsel to a tougher standard? What would be the consequences of doing so for the independence of defense counsel, the attorney-client relationship, and the functions of the adversary system?

7. In Cuyler v. Sullivan, 446 U.S. 335 (1980), the aforementioned leading case on attorney conflicts of interest (discussed further at page 188, infra), the Court also held that ineffective assistance by *retained* counsel can violate the Sixth Amendment right to counsel, thus disposing of the issue whether there is "state action" in such circumstances. Nonetheless, whatever the "state action" may be in criminal cases generally, it is insufficient to permit an indigent to sue, under 42 U.S.C. §1983, the public defender who represented him for damages resulting from allegedly ineffective assistance in derogation of the indigent's right to counsel. In Polk County v. Dodson, 454 U.S. 312 (1981), the Court held that a public defender appointed

to represent an indigent client does not act "under color of state law." Therefore, §1983 is not applicable.

8. Recall that *Douglas* held that a criminal defendant has the right to counsel—under the Fourteenth Amendment, not the Sixth Amendment—on his first appeal as of right (later clarified by *Halbert* to include all first-level appeals). Evitts v. Lucey, 469 U.S. 387 (1985), addressed the related question "whether the Due Process Clause of the Fourteenth Amendment guarantees the criminal defendant the effective assistance of counsel on such an appeal." In other words, does the right to counsel on appeal carry with it the corresponding right to have that appellate counsel perform to a minimally acceptable level? In *Evitts*, the Court, in an opinion by Justice Brennan, held that the answer to this question is "yes":

> Almost a century ago, the Court held that the Constitution does not require States to grant appeals as of right to criminal defendants seeking to review alleged trial court errors. McKane v. Durston, 153 U.S. 684 (1894). Nonetheless, if a State has created appellate courts as "an integral part of the . . . system for finally adjudicating the guilt or innocence of a defendant," Griffin v. Illinois, 351 U.S., at 18, the procedures used in deciding appeals must comport with the demands of the Due Process and Equal Protection Clauses of the Constitution. . . .
>
> The two lines of cases . . . recognizing the right to counsel on a first appeal as of right and . . . recognizing that the right to counsel at trial includes a right to effective assistance of counsel . . . are dispositive of respondent's claim. In bringing an appeal as of right from his conviction, a criminal defendant is attempting to demonstrate that the conviction, and the consequent drastic loss of liberty, is unlawful. To prosecute the appeal, a criminal appellant must face an adversary proceeding that—like a trial—is governed by intricate rules that to a layperson would be hopelessly forbidding. An unrepresented appellant—like an unrepresented defendant at trial—is unable to protect the vital interests at stake. . . .
>
> A first appeal as of right therefore is not adjudicated in accord with due process of law if the appellant does not have the effective assistance of an attorney.[7] . . .
>
> The right to an appeal would be unique among state actions if it could be withdrawn without consideration of applicable due process norms. For instance, although a State may choose whether it will institute any given welfare program, it must operate whatever programs it does establish subject to the protections of the Due Process Clause. See Goldberg v. Kelly, 397 U.S. 254, 262 (1970). . . . In short, when a State opts to act in a field where its action has significant discretionary elements, it must nonetheless act in accord with the dictates of the Constitution—and, in particular, in accord with the Due Process Clause. . . .
>
> According to the petitioners, the constitutional requirements recognized in *Griffin*, *Douglas*, and the cases that followed had their source in the Equal Protection Clause, and not the Due Process Clause, of the Fourteenth Amendment. In support of this contention, petitioners point out that all of the cases in the *Griffin* line have involved claims by indigent defendants that they have the same right to a decision on the merits of their appeal as do wealthier defendants who are able to afford lawyers, transcripts, or the other prerequisites of a fair adjudication on the merits. As such, petitioners claim, the cases all should be understood as equal protection cases challenging the constitutional validity of the distinction made between rich and poor criminal defendants. Petitioners conclude that if the Due Process Clause permits criminal appeals as of right to be forfeited because the appellant has no transcript or

---

7. As Ross v. Moffitt, 417 U.S. 600 (1974), held, the considerations governing a discretionary appeal are somewhat different. Of course, the right to effective assistance of counsel is dependent on the right to counsel itself. . . .

no attorney, it surely permits such appeals to be forfeited when the appellant has an attorney who is unable to assist in prosecuting the appeal.

Petitioners' argument rests on a misunderstanding of the diverse sources of our holdings in this area. In *Ross v. Moffitt*, we held that "[t]he precise rationale for the *Griffin* and *Douglas* lines of cases has never been explicitly stated, some support being derived from the Equal Protection Clause of the Fourteenth Amendment, and some from the Due Process Clause of that Amendment." This rather clear statement in *Ross* that the Due Process Clause played a significant role in prior decisions is well supported by the cases themselves. . . .

Id., at 393, 396, 400-401, and 403.

Justice Rehnquist, in dissent, responded:

There is no constitutional requirement that a State provide an appeal at all. . . . McKane v. Durston, 153 U.S. 684, 687 (1894). If a State decides to confer a right of appeal, it is free to do so "upon such terms as in its wisdom may be deemed proper." Id., at 687-688. . . . Proper analysis of our precedents would indicate that apart from the Equal Protection Clause, which respondent has not invoked in this case, there cannot be a constitutional right to *counsel* on appeal, and that, therefore, even under the logic of the Court there cannot be derived a constitutional right to *effective assistance of counsel* on appeal.

Id., at 409-410.

According to Justice Rehnquist, in other words, the defendant must "take the bitter with the sweet"—having no constitutional right to an appeal at all, due process cannot be violated when the state chooses to give him an appeal but then precludes him from complaining about his appellate lawyer's alleged ineffectiveness. Nor, in Rehnquist's view, can this possibly be an equal protection violation, because the state's rule applies to all appellate lawyers—whether retained or appointed—exactly the same way. In essence, the state has adopted a rule that harms all defendants equally.

9. Compare *Evitts* with the earlier per curiam decision in Wainwright v. Torna, 455 U.S. 586 (1982), refusing to extend the right to the effective assistance of counsel to petitions for discretionary review. Justice Rehnquist wrote for the majority in *Torna*:

Respondent is in custody pursuant to several felony convictions. The Florida Supreme Court dismissed an application for a writ of certiorari, on the ground that the application was not filed timely. . . . A petition for rehearing and clarification was later denied. . . .

In Ross v. Moffitt, . . . this Court held that a criminal defendant does not have a constitutional right to counsel to pursue discretionary state appeals or applications for review in this Court. Respondent does not contest the finding of the District Court that he had no absolute right to appeal his convictions to the Florida Supreme Court. Since respondent had no constitutional right to counsel, he could not be deprived of the effective assistance of counsel by his retained counsel's failure to file the application timely.[4] The District Court was correct in dismissing the petition.

Id., at 586-587.

---

4. Respondent was not denied due process of law by the fact that counsel deprived him of his right to petition the Florida Supreme Court for review. Such deprivation—even if implicating a due process interest—was caused by his counsel, and not by the State. Certainly, the actions of the Florida Supreme Court in dismissing an application for review that was not filed timely did not deprive respondent of due process of law.

NOTES AND QUESTIONS ON THE APPLICATION OF *STRICKLAND*

1. What is a defense lawyer's responsibility when dealing with possibly perjurious testimony? In Nix v. Whiteside, 475 U.S. 157 (1986), the defendant (Whiteside) was charged with murder. Initially, he told his court-appointed lawyer (Robinson) that he stabbed the victim while the victim was reaching for a gun. Upon further questioning, however, he admitted that he had not actually seen a gun. No gun was found at the crime scene, and none of the other witnesses reported seeing a gun. About one week before the trial, Whiteside told Robinson that he had seen something "metallic" in the victim's hand. He added, "If I don't say I saw a gun I'm dead." Robinson informed Whiteside that this would be perjury, and that he would not assist in it. Robinson told Whiteside that if he insisted on perjuring himself, Robinson would advise the trial court about the perjury, impeach Whiteside's testimony, and withdraw from Whiteside's representation.

The Court split 5-4 on the application of *Strickland*'s performance prong to Robinson's conduct, with the dissent critical of Robinson for essentially "judging" his own client, but the majority found Robinson's conduct acceptable under prevailing professional norms:

> . . . Considering Robinson's representation of respondent in light of the accepted norms of professional conduct, we discern no failure to adhere to reasonable professional standards that would in any sense make out a deprivation of the Sixth Amendment right to counsel. Whether Robinson's conduct is seen as a successful attempt to dissuade his client from committing the crime of perjury, or whether seen as a "threat" to withdraw from representation and disclose the illegal scheme, Robinson's representation of Whiteside falls well within accepted standards of professional conduct and the range of reasonable professional conduct acceptable under *Strickland*. . . .
>
> Whatever the scope of a constitutional right to testify, it is elementary that such a right does not extend to testifying *falsely*. In Harris v. New York, we assumed the right of an accused to testify "in his own defense, or to refuse to do so" and went on to hold that "that privilege cannot be construed to include the right to commit perjury. Having voluntarily taken the stand, petitioner was under an obligation to speak truthfully. . . ." 401 U.S., at 225. In *Harris* we held the defendant could be impeached by prior contrary statements which had been ruled inadmissible under Miranda v. Arizona. *Harris* and other cases make it crystal clear that there is no right whatever—constitutional or otherwise—for a defendant to use false evidence. . . .
>
> Robinson's admonitions to his client can in no sense be said to have forced respondent into an *impermissible* choice between his right to counsel and his right to testify as he proposed for there was no *permissible* choice to testify falsely. For defense counsel to take steps to persuade a criminal defendant to testify truthfully, or to withdraw, deprives the defendant of neither his right to counsel nor the right to testify truthfully. In United States v. Havens we made clear that "when defendants testify, they must testify truthfully or suffer the consequences." When an accused proposes to resort to perjury or to produce false evidence, one consequence is the risk of withdrawal of counsel.

All nine Justices agreed, however, that whether or not Robinson's performance was adequate, Whiteside could not have suffered "prejudice," within the meaning of *Strickland*. According to the majority:

We hold that, as a matter of law, counsel's conduct complained of here cannot establish the prejudice required for relief under the second strand of the *Strickland* inquiry. . . . The *Strickland* Court noted that the "benchmark" of an ineffective assistance claim is the fairness of the adversary proceeding, and that in judging prejudice and the likelihood of a different outcome, "[a] defendant has no entitlement to the luck of a lawless decisionmaker." . . .

In his attempt to evade the prejudice requirement of *Strickland*, Whiteside relies on cases involving conflicting loyalties of counsel. [See, e.g.,] Cuyler v. Sullivan, 446 U.S. 335 (1980). . . . Here, there was indeed a "conflict," but of a quite different kind; it was one imposed on the attorney by the client's proposal to commit the crime of fabricating testimony without which, as he put it, "I'm dead." . . . If a "conflict" between a client's proposal and counsel's ethical obligation gives rise to a presumption that counsel's assistance was prejudicially ineffective, every guilty criminal's conviction would be suspect if the defendant had sought to obtain an acquittal by illegal means. Can anyone doubt what practices and problems would be spawned by such a rule and what volumes of litigation it would generate?

Whether he was persuaded or compelled to desist from perjury, Whiteside has no valid claim that confidence in the result of his trial has been diminished by his desisting from the contemplated perjury. Even if we were to assume that the jury might have believed his perjury, it does not follow that Whiteside was prejudiced. . . .

Whiteside's attorney treated Whiteside's proposed perjury in accord with professional standards, and since Whiteside's truthful testimony could not have prejudiced the result of his trial, the Court of Appeals was in error to direct the issuance of a writ of habeas corpus and must be reversed.

Id., at 171-176.

What effect does *Whiteside* have on the meaning of *Strickland*'s "prejudice" requirement? The one proposition that all nine Justices agreed upon in *Whiteside* was that the failure to use perjured testimony cannot satisfy that requirement. Why not? Preventing client perjury can of course affect the outcome of a case—indeed, affecting the outcome is presumably the entire point of the perjury. Yet all the Justices were prepared to hold that even if attorney Robinson's performance violated constitutional standards, and apparently even if his performance led to Whiteside's conviction, Whiteside suffered no Sixth Amendment prejudice. This position suggests that *Strickland* prejudice requires more than that attorney ineffectiveness have an effect on the outcome of the case; it requires the *right kind* of outcome effect. What kind of outcome effect counts? The idea seems to be that preventing perjured testimony by the defendant is not the sort of thing that leads to an unjust result, regardless of what one thinks of defense counsel's conduct. But what does "unjust" mean in this context? Must a defendant show a reasonable probability that he is innocent?

2. Lockhart v. Fretwell, 506 U.S. 364 (1993), was a capital case in which Fretwell's defense counsel failed to object to one of the aggravating circumstances that was used to authorize the death penalty. Under binding Eighth Circuit precedent, the objection surely would have succeeded, and the defendant almost surely would have avoided the death sentence. By the time the issue was raised in Fretwell's federal habeas corpus petition, however, an intervening Supreme Court decision had reversed the Eighth Circuit's prior precedent. Reviewing Fretwell's ineffective-assistance claim, the Court held that he suffered no "prejudice" under *Strickland*, because the outcome in his case was "neither unfair nor unreliable"; avoiding the death sentence based on erroneous precedent would have been a "windfall to which the law does not entitle" Fretwell. Id., at 366.

3. In Williams v. Taylor, 529 U.S. 362 (2000), the Court tried to explain the relationship among *Strickland*, *Fretwell*, and *Whiteside*:

> The Virginia Supreme Court erred in holding that our decision in Lockhart v. Fretwell modified or in some way supplanted the rule set down in *Strickland*. It is true that while the *Strickland* test provides sufficient guidance for resolving virtually all ineffective-assistance-of-counsel claims, there are situations in which the overriding focus on fundamental fairness may affect the analysis. Thus, on the one hand, as *Strickland* itself explained, there are a few situations in which prejudice may be presumed. And, on the other hand, there are also situations in which it would be unjust to characterize the likelihood of a different outcome as legitimate "prejudice." Even if a defendant's false testimony might have persuaded the jury to acquit him, it is not fundamentally unfair to conclude that he was not prejudiced by counsel's interference with his intended perjury. Nix v. Whiteside.
>
> Similarly, in [*Fretwell*,] we concluded that, given the overriding interest in fundamental fairness, the likelihood of a different outcome attributable to an incorrect interpretation of the law should be regarded as a potential "windfall" to the defendant rather than the legitimate "prejudice" contemplated by our opinion in *Strickland*. . . . Because the ineffectiveness of Fretwell's counsel had not deprived him of any substantive or procedural right to which the law entitled him, we held that his claim did not satisfy the "prejudice" component of the *Strickland* test.
>
> Cases such as Nix v. Whiteside and Lockhart v. Fretwell do not justify a departure from a straightforward application of *Strickland* when the ineffectiveness of counsel does deprive the defendant of a substantive or procedural right to which the law entitles him. In the instant case, it is undisputed that Williams had a right—indeed, a constitutionally protected right—to provide the jury with the mitigating evidence that his trial counsel either failed to discover or failed to offer.

Id., at 391-393. Are *Whiteside* and *Fretwell* now limited to their facts?

4. In Glover v. United States, 531 U.S. 198 (2001), the Court considered the kinds of errors in sentencing proceedings that might be deemed prejudicial enough to support an ineffective-assistance claim. Justice Kennedy wrote for a unanimous Court:

> The issue presented rests upon the initial assumption, which we accept for analytic purposes, that the trial court erred in a Sentencing Guidelines determination after petitioner's conviction of a federal offense. [The petitioner was sentenced by the trial court to 84 months in prison.—Eds.] The legal error, petitioner alleges, increased his prison sentence by at least 6 months and perhaps by 21 months. We must decide whether this would be "prejudice" under Strickland v. Washington, 466 U.S. 668 (1984). . . .
>
> It appears the Seventh Circuit drew the substance of its no-prejudice rule from our opinion in Lockhart v. Fretwell[, 506 U.S. 364 (1993)]. *Fretwell* holds that in some circumstances a mere difference in outcome will not suffice to establish prejudice. The Seventh Circuit extracted from this holding the rule at issue here, which denies relief when the increase in sentence is said to be not so significant as to render the outcome of sentencing unreliable or fundamentally unfair. . . . The Seventh Circuit was incorrect to rely on *Fretwell* to deny relief to persons attacking their sentence who might show deficient performance in counsel's failure to object to an error of law affecting the calculation of a sentence because the sentence increase does not meet some baseline standard of prejudice. Authority does not suggest that a minimal amount of additional time in prison cannot constitute prejudice. Quite to the contrary, our

jurisprudence suggests that any amount of actual jail time has Sixth Amendment significance. Compare Argersinger v. Hamlin, 407 U.S. 25 (1972) (holding that the assistance of counsel must be provided when a defendant is tried for a crime that results in a sentence of imprisonment), with Scott v. Illinois, 440 U.S. 367 (1979) (holding that a criminal defendant has no Sixth Amendment right to counsel when his trial does not result in a sentence of imprisonment). . . .

. . . We hold that the Seventh Circuit erred in engrafting this additional requirement onto the prejudice branch of the *Strickland* test. This is not a case where trial strategies, in retrospect, might be criticized for leading to a harsher sentence. Here we consider the sentencing calculation itself, a calculation resulting from a ruling which, if it had been error, would have been correctable on appeal. We express no opinion on the ultimate merits of Glover's claim because the question of deficient performance is not before us, but it is clear that prejudice flowed from the asserted error in sentencing. . . .

Id., at 199-204.

How does the result in *Glover* square with the way trial errors are analyzed? Suppose defense counsel in *Glover* had made a mistake at Glover's trial; suppose further that the mistake had raised the odds of Glover's conviction by, say, 1 percent. Glover was then convicted. Presumably, counsel's error would not satisfy *Strickland*'s prejudice prong, because it did not raise a "reasonable probability" that, but for the error, the outcome would have been different.

Now suppose Glover's counsel's error cost Glover one extra month in prison—i.e., but for the error, Glover would have been sentenced to 83 months, instead of the 84-month sentence he actually received. Why does that extra month amount to prejudice, when adding 1 percent to the odds of a conviction doesn't? And if the latter premise is wrong—if even a small increase in the odds of a conviction *does* amount to prejudice—then what is left of the "reasonable probability" standard?

Perhaps these questions misconceive what is really at stake in these cases. Perhaps the right question to ask is whether a change in the probability of guilt plausibly could affect the conclusion of guilt beyond a reasonable doubt. If so, the error would be prejudicial; if not, it would not be. This harmonizes *Glover* with *Strickland*, although it is by no means clear that this is what the Court had in mind.

Note, incidentally, that *Glover*-type ineffectiveness claims would seem to be plausible only where the defendant is deprived, as a result of his lawyer's mistake, of a particular sentence (or sentencing range) to which he is legally entitled. This, in turn, is likely to be true only where the sentence is determinate, as opposed to broadly discretionary. Otherwise, it would be very difficult for the reviewing court to say that the lawyer's mistake made a "reasonable probability" of a difference in the sentencing outcome. For more on determinate sentencing and its consequences, see Chapter 15.

NOTES ON INEFFECTIVE ASSISTANCE, HABEAS CORPUS, AND THE DEATH PENALTY

Most of the Supreme Court's key ineffective assistance cases—including Strickland v. Washington, 466 U.S. 668 (1984), Nix v. Whiteside, 475 U.S. 157 (1986), Williams v. Taylor, 529 U.S. 362 (2000), and Bell v. Cone, 535 U.S. 685 (2002)—are federal habeas corpus cases. That is no accident. Ineffective assistance claims are usually first raised after the defendant has lost both at trial *and* on direct appeal. This is for two separate reasons: (1) defendant's trial counsel, who usually handles the direct appeal as well, is unlikely to raise his own ineffectiveness as an appellate issue; and (2) most appellate courts lack the authority (and the capacity) to hold evidentiary hearings, which are usually required to flesh out the details of an IAC claim. (Appeals generally are based entirely upon the written record of the proceedings at the trial court; ineffective-assistance claims, on the other hand, require knowing more—such as *why* the defense attorney did or did not do whatever the defendant now complains about, and *whether* anything else the defense attorney could have done would have made any difference.) For these reasons, most defendants first raise their IAC claims pro se in a separate proceeding in the state trial court, after losing on appeal. That separate proceeding, which all state court systems provide (with some variations as to procedural details), is usually referred to as "state post-conviction" or "state habeas corpus."[14] In all of the cases cited at the beginning of this paragraph, the defendant's IAC claim was first rejected in *state* habeas, after which the defendant then filed the same claim in federal district court under the *federal* habeas statute.

In the Anti-Terrorism and Effective Death Penalty Act of 1996 (AEDPA), Congress established a deferential standard of review for federal habeas decisions. Federal courts are authorized to grant relief and overturn state-court decisions only when they are "contrary to, or involved an unreasonable application of, clearly established Federal law, as determined by the Supreme Court of the United States." 28 U.S.C. §2254(d)(1). The Court has stressed that "an *unreasonable* application of federal law is different from an *incorrect* application of federal law." Williams v. Taylor, 529 U.S. 362, 410-411 (2000) (emphasis in original).

Recall that in *Strickland*, the Court emphasized that, when judging ineffective assistance claims, courts should defer to the decision making of defense counsel. AEDPA requires similar deference to state court judges who deny IAC claims. The result, when deference is piled upon deference, is a tall mountain for defendants to climb. To prevail in federal court, the defendant (now called a "habeas petitioner") must show that trial counsel behaved so unreasonably that it was unreasonable—and not merely incorrect—for the state habeas court to deny relief. (Got that?) If AEDPA means what it says, then federal habeas is an exceedingly unfriendly environment for ineffective assistance claims.

That is the harsh reality for most ineffective assistance litigation. A recent study of more than 2,300 federal habeas corpus petitions filed after AEDPA showed that the overall success rate in noncapital cases was less than one-third of 1 percent; the study also found that, although about half of the petitions studied contained an IAC claim, *not one* of those claims ultimately led to a grant of relief. See Nancy J. King, Fred L. Cheesman II & Brian J. Ostrom, Final Technical Report: Habeas Litigation in U.S. District Courts, 52, 58 (2007), available at http://www.ncjrs.gov/pdffiles1/nij/grants/219559.pdf.

But the story is quite different in capital cases. In Williams v. Taylor, 529 U.S. 362 (2000), for example, a capital defendant claimed that his counsel was ineffective for failing to raise various mitigating arguments; on state habeas, the Virginia Supreme

---

14. One important variation, seen today in numerous states, is the "consolidated appeal," in which the direct appeal and the state postconviction proceeding are combined into a single procedural stage.

Court rejected the claim. Notwithstanding the AEDPA language quoted above, the Supreme Court *granted* relief. Another example is Wiggins v. Smith, 539 U.S. 510 (2003). Again, a capital defendant claimed that his counsel failed to raise appropriate mitigating arguments; again, the state habeas courts rejected the claim. And once again, the Supreme Court *granted* relief, notwithstanding AEDPA.

The next case, decided by a 5-4 Court, represents perhaps the best example of how ineffective assistance of counsel seems to work differently in capital cases:

ROMPILLA v. BEARD, 545 U.S. 374 (2005): This case calls for specific application of the standard of reasonable competence required on the part of defense counsel by the Sixth Amendment. We hold that even when a capital defendant's family members and the defendant himself have suggested that no mitigating evidence is available, his lawyer is bound to make reasonable efforts to obtain and review material that counsel knows the prosecution will probably rely on as evidence of aggravation at the sentencing phase of trial.

On the morning of January 14, 1988, James Scanlon was discovered dead in a bar he ran in Allentown, Pennsylvania, his body having been stabbed repeatedly and set on fire. Rompilla was indicted for the murder . . . and the Commonwealth gave notice of intent to ask for the death penalty. Two public defenders were assigned to the case.

The jury at the guilt phase of trial found Rompilla guilty on all counts, and during the ensuing penalty phase, the prosecutor sought to prove three aggravating factors to justify a death sentence: that the murder was committed in the course of another felony; that the murder was committed by torture; and that Rompilla had a significant history of felony convictions indicating the use or threat of violence. See 42 Pa. Cons. Stat. §§9711(d)(6), (8), (9) (2002). The Commonwealth presented evidence on all three aggravators, and the jury found all proven. Rompilla's evidence in mitigation consisted of relatively brief testimony: five of his family members argued in effect for residual doubt, and beseeched the jury for mercy, saying that they believed Rompilla was innocent and a good man. Rompilla's 14-year-old son testified that he loved his father and would visit him in prison. The jury acknowledged this evidence to the point of finding, as two factors in mitigation, that Rompilla's son had testified on his behalf and that rehabilitation was possible. But the jurors assigned the greater weight to the aggravating factors, and sentenced Rompilla to death. The Supreme Court of Pennsylvania affirmed both conviction and sentence.

[In December 1995, Rompilla filed a state habeas petition alleging] ineffective assistance by trial counsel in failing to present significant mitigating evidence about Rompilla's childhood, mental capacity and health, and alcoholism. The [state habeas] court found that trial counsel had done enough to investigate the possibilities of a mitigation case, and the Supreme Court of Pennsylvania affirmed the denial of relief.

Rompilla then petitioned for a writ of habeas corpus under 28 U.S.C. §2254 in Federal District Court. . . . The District Court found that the State Supreme Court had unreasonably applied Strickland v. Washington, 466 U.S. 668 (1984), as to the penalty phase of the trial, and granted relief for ineffective assistance of counsel. . . . A divided Third Circuit panel reversed. Rompilla v. Horn, 355 F.3d 233 (2004). . . .

. . . This is not a case in which defense counsel simply ignored their obligation to find mitigating evidence, and their workload as busy public defenders did not keep them from making a number of efforts, including interviews with Rompilla and some members of his family, and examinations of reports by three mental health experts who gave opinions at the guilt phase. None of the sources proved particularly helpful.

Rompilla's own contributions to any mitigation case were minimal. Counsel found him uninterested in helping, as on their visit to his prison to go over a proposed mitigation strategy, when Rompilla told them he was "bored being here listening" and returned to his cell. App. 668. To questions about childhood and schooling, his answers indicated they had been normal, save for quitting school in the ninth grade. There were times when Rompilla was even actively obstructive by sending counsel off on false leads.

The lawyers also spoke with five members of Rompilla's family (his former wife, two brothers, a sister-in-law, and his son), and counsel testified that they developed a good relationship with the family in the course of their representation. The state postconviction court found that counsel spoke to the relatives in a "detailed manner," attempting to unearth mitigating information, although the weight of this finding is qualified by the lawyers' concession that "the overwhelming response from the family was that they didn't really feel as though they knew him all that well since he had spent the majority of his adult years and some of his childhood years in custody," App. 495. Defense counsel also said that because the family was "coming from the position that [Rompilla] was innocent . . . they weren't looking for reasons for why he might have done this." Id., at 494.

The third and final source tapped for mitigating material was the cadre of three mental health witnesses who were asked to look into Rompilla's mental state as of the time of the offense and his competency to stand trial, but their reports revealed "nothing useful" to Rompilla's case, App. 1358, and the lawyers consequently did not go to any other historical source that might have cast light on Rompilla's mental condition.

When new counsel entered the case to raise Rompilla's postconviction claims, however, they identified a number of likely avenues the trial lawyers could fruitfully have followed in building a mitigation case[, including school records and] records of Rompilla's juvenile and adult incarcerations. . . . And while counsel knew from police reports provided in pretrial discovery that Rompilla had been drinking heavily at the time of his offense, . . . and although one of the mental health experts reported that Rompilla's troubles with alcohol merited further investigation, counsel did not look for evidence of a history of dependence on alcohol that might have extenuating significance.

. . . The Commonwealth argues that the information trial counsel gathered from Rompilla and the other sources gave them sound reason to think it would have been pointless to spend time and money on . . . additional investigation . . . , and we can say that there is room for debate about trial counsel's obligation to follow at least some of those potential lines of enquiry. There is no need to say more, however, for a further point is clear and dispositive: the lawyers were deficient in failing to examine the court file on Rompilla's prior conviction.

There is an obvious reason that the failure to examine Rompilla's prior conviction file fell below the level of reasonable performance. Counsel knew that the Commonwealth intended to seek the death penalty by proving Rompilla had a significant history of felony convictions indicating the use or threat of violence, an aggravator under state law. Counsel further knew that the Commonwealth would attempt to establish this history by proving Rompilla's prior conviction for rape and assault, and would emphasize his violent character by introducing a transcript of the rape victim's testimony given in that earlier trial. . . . It is also undisputed that the prior conviction file was a public document, readily available for the asking at the very courthouse where Rompilla was to be tried.

It is clear, however, that defense counsel did not look at any part of that file, including the transcript, until warned by the prosecution [twice]. . . . [C]rucially, even after obtaining the transcript of the victim's testimony on the eve of the sentencing hearing, counsel apparently examined none of the other material in the file.

. . . The dissent thinks this analysis creates a "rigid, *per se*" rule that requires defense counsel to do a complete review of the file on any prior conviction introduced, but that is a mistake. Counsel fell short here because they failed to make reasonable efforts to review the prior conviction file, despite knowing that the prosecution intended to introduce Rompilla's prior conviction not merely by entering a notice of conviction into evidence but by quoting damaging testimony of the rape victim in that case. The unreasonableness of attempting no more than they did was heightened by the easy availability of the file at the trial courthouse, and the great risk that testimony about a similar violent crime would hamstring counsel's chosen defense of residual doubt. . . . Other situations, where a defense lawyer is not charged with knowledge that the prosecutor intends to use a prior conviction in this way, might well warrant a different assessment.

Since counsel's failure to look at the file fell below the line of reasonable practice, there is a further question about prejudice, that is, whether "there is a reasonable probability that, but for counsel's unprofessional errors, the result of the proceeding would have been different." *Strickland*, 466 U.S., at 694. . . . We think Rompilla has shown beyond any doubt that counsel's lapse was prejudicial. . . .

. . . [A]lthough we suppose it is possible that a jury could have heard [all this evidence] and still have decided on the death penalty, that is not the test. It goes without saying that the undiscovered "mitigating evidence, taken as a whole, 'might well have influenced the jury's appraisal' of [Rompilla's] culpability," [Wiggins v. Smith,] 539 U.S. [510], 538 [(2003)], quoting Williams v. Taylor, 529 U.S. [362], 398 [(2000)]), and the likelihood of a different result if the evidence had gone in is "sufficient to undermine confidence in the outcome" actually reached at sentencing, *Strickland*, 466 U.S., at 694.

NOTES AND QUESTIONS

1. Compare *Rompilla* to *Strickland*. Both are capital cases; in both, the government had strong evidence of aggravating factors that would make the defendant eligible for the death penalty. And both defendants claimed that their defense counsel failed to do enough to uncover mitigating evidence to avoid the death penalty. There are differences, of course — but some of those differences make Washington's claim actually look much stronger than Rompilla's. For example: Washington's lawyer basically did nothing to come up with an argument in mitigation. Rompilla's lawyers did quite a lot. It is hard to explain why Washington's lawyer passed *Strickland*'s performance standard, while Rompilla's lawyers flunked that same standard.

Was the standard really the same? Is the majority opinion in *Rompilla* consistent with Justice O'Connor's majority opinion in *Strickland?* Judging from the fact that she concurred in *Rompilla*, Justice O'Connor seems to think so. Is she right?

2. Consider another potentially relevant factual difference between *Rompilla* and *Strickland.* Even the most comprehensive investigation would have turned up little in *Strickland,* because there wasn't much of a mitigating case to be made. Washington had killed three people (a fourth died later)—a college student, a minister, and an elderly woman—because he was upset that he had lost his job. (In the words of one psychiatric report, he was "chronically frustrated and depressed because of his economic dilemma." *Strickland,* 466 U.S., at 676.) Even in the hands of the most skillful defense lawyer, that is not a winning argument. Rompilla's lawyers, by contrast, had a much stronger case on sentencing to begin with: Rompilla was charged with one murder rather than three, and his key prior conviction was decades old. If they managed to find it, they also had a mother lode of mitigating evidence. Where Washington was "chronically frustrated and depressed," Rompilla may have been schizophrenic. Add to that the hellish childhood described by Judge Sloviter in the passage quoted by the majority opinion, and you have a substantial case for mitigation. One can easily imagine that a jury confronted with that evidence and argument would decide that Rompilla should be incarcerated, not executed.

3. The preceding two notes suggest that the main difference between *Rompilla* and *Strickland* might be the following: In *Strickland,* on the one hand, the Court evaluated the defense attorney's performance from the perspective of the lawyer *at the time he made his decisions* about what to do or what not to do. In *Rompilla,* on the other hand, the Court seems to have evaluated the defense attorney's performance with the benefit of hindsight. In other words, the *Rompilla* Court seems to have judged performance based on what eventually came to light (i.e., the fact that there actually existed helpful mitigating evidence that never was presented to the jury). To put it another way, *Strickland*'s performance analysis was ex ante, whereas *Rompilla*'s was ex post.

Is this a good idea? An ex post approach to evaluating defense attorney performance results in something like strict liability—no matter how reasonable the attorney's decisions may have been at the time, those decisions will be found constitutionally ineffective if it turns out that something truly helpful was missed. This essentially conflates the "prejudice" and "performance" prongs of *Strickland.* Such a conflated analysis means that a very small number of defendants will obtain judicial relief, at great cost to society, in a manner that seems highly unlikely to produce an effective and comprehensive solution to the general problem of ineffective defense representation.

4. Why would the Court treat capital cases (with the seeming exception of *Strickland* itself) so differently from noncapital cases? Perhaps the answer is simply that the death penalty is different from all other punishments. But is it different in a way that relates specifically to ineffective assistance claims? Should defense lawyers at capital sentencing hearings be held to a higher standard than at criminal trials in general? See Stephen B. Bright, Counsel for the Poor: The Death Sentence Not for the Worst Crime but for the Worst Lawyer, 103 Yale L.J. 1835 (1994); and Welsh S. White, Effective Assistance of Counsel in Capital Cases: The Evolving Standard of Care, [1993] U. Ill. L. Rev. 323 (both answering "yes").

Maybe the real point of cases like *Williams, Wiggins,* and *Rompilla* isn't that ineffective assistance standards are different in death penalty cases. Maybe it's just that the Court *feels* differently about death penalty cases. Maybe the Court simply wants to regulate capital cases more closely than other state criminal cases—and ineffective assistance doctrine provides a useful method for doing so. Indeed, it may be one of the *only* remaining methods for doing so—precisely because AEDPA, together with many of the Court's own modern decisions restricting access to federal habeas, has largely taken away from the federal courts the power to reverse state criminal convictions and sentences on most federal constitutional grounds. Today, just about the only constitutional claims that still get relatively full federal review are ineffective assistance claims and *Brady* claims (i.e., claims that the prosecution withheld helpful evidence from the defense—see Chapter 12). Not surprisingly, IAC claims and *Brady* claims tend to dominate federal habeas litigation.

5. There are limits on the use of ineffective assistance doctrine to regulate capital cases. In Schriro v. Landrigan, 550 U.S. 465 (2007), the defendant refused to allow his defense counsel to present mitigating evidence at capital sentencing, and indeed told the trial judge that he did not want to have such evidence introduced, preferring instead to "bring on" the death penalty. The Court, by 5-4, held that the Ninth Circuit erroneously ordered a federal district court to hold an evidentiary hearing on the defendant's ineffective assistance claim, finding instead that the denial of the evidentiary hearing was within the district court's discretion in light of the defendant's own actions.

Schriro suggests that, at least in some cases, a capital defendant will be held to the negative consequences of his own decisions. In light of this, should a defense lawyer always be required to secure the defendant's prior consent before conceding guilt at trial and focusing his efforts entirely on arguing for leniency at capital sentencing? If the lawyer concedes guilt without the defendant's consent, is this the kind of "fail[ure] to subject the prosecution's case to meaningful adversarial testing," that triggers the *Cronic* presumption of prejudice? In Florida v. Nixon, 543 U.S. 175 (2004), the Supreme Court unanimously answered "no" to both questions (Chief Justice Rehnquist was ill and did not participate). According to the Court, the decision to concede guilt in a capital case is not the same as entering a guilty plea or waiving basic trial rights (both of which would have to be done with the defendant's express consent).

6. Might the Court have had second thoughts about its decision in *Rompilla?* In Cullen v. Pinholster, 131 S. Ct. 1388 (2011), a narrow 5-4 majority reversed the Ninth Circuit and rejected a death-row inmate's claim of ineffective assistance of counsel based on his lawyer's alleged failure to investigate (and present) mitigating evidence. The Court reviewed in detail the evidence of defense counsel's behavior, and concluded that—especially in light of the "doubly deferential" review standard applicable to ineffective-assistance claims in habeas corpus cases under AEDPA—the defense lawyer (1) pursued reasonable investigation of mitigation evidence, (2) acted reasonably in trying to exclude the prosecution's aggravation evidence rather than relying on dubious mitigation evidence, and (3) given the overall weakness of the defendant's case, chose a reasonable strategy based primarily on trying to evoke sympathy for the defendant's mother.

7. What, if anything, does a decision like *Rompilla* mean for noncapital cases? So far, the Supreme Court seems to have limited the ex post performance analysis of *Rompilla* to the special context of capital cases. In general, noncapital defendants have had little success in making *Strickland* claims based on their lawyers' inaction. Perhaps not coincidentally, inaction by defense lawyers is the norm in most criminal cases. One study of appointed counsel in New York City in the mid-1980s found that counsel filed written motions in 26 percent of homicide cases and 11 percent of other felony cases, interviewed witnesses in 21 percent of homicides and 4 percent

of other felonies, employed experts in 17 percent of homicides and 2 percent of other felonies, and visited the crime scene in 12 percent of homicides and 4 percent of other felonies. See Michael McConville & Chester L. Mirsky, Criminal Defense of the Poor in New York City, 15 N.Y.U. Rev. L. & Soc. Change 581, 762-767 (1986-87).

8. Maybe the real problem with trying to reconcile *Rompilla* with *Strickland* is that—like virtually all ineffective-assistance cases litigated pursuant to *Strickland*—the IAC issues in each individual case are so inherently and heavily fact-bound that no meaningful comparisons are possible. In other words, a search for the kind of consistency that can be translated into a clearly articulable and applicable legal rule may be doomed from the start.

Think about the daunting task that faced the Court in *Strickland*. Even back in 1984, the Court clearly (and no doubt correctly) perceived serious problems with the quality of defense representation in the state courts—especially for indigent defendants. Such problems were well documented at the time in lower-court decisions as well as in national research reports. See, e.g., ABA, *Gideon* Undone: The Crises in Indigent Defense Funding (John Thomas Moran ed. 1982). Many of the problems were (and still remain) structural, in the sense that they resulted from chronic underfunding of defense services by financially strapped states and localities.[15]

But what to do about these serious problems? If the Court were an executive or a legislature, it might try to design a new federal program to help improve the quality of defense lawyering in the states. Indeed, a well-known proposal for such a federal program has been kicking around for many years; the American Bar Association first rolled out the proposal back in 1979, and it was introduced into Congress later that same year.[16] The ABA proposal—which would have included federal matching funds to help the states accomplish necessary reforms—remains viable today,[17] and continues to attract scholarly attention. See, e.g., Joseph L. Hoffmann & Nancy J. King, Rethinking the Federal Role in State Criminal Justice, 84 N.Y.U. L. Rev. 791 (2009) (advocating cutbacks in federal habeas corpus review of state criminal cases combined with adoption and funding of a new Federal Center for Defense Services, modeled on the ABA proposal).

As a judicial institution, however, the Court in *Strickland* had fewer good options. It could try to create, by judicial fiat, a new and comprehensive set of *ex ante* prophylactic federal rules, enforceable by courts, to try to prevent or reduce the prevalence of defense attorney errors. But that undoubtedly would have enmeshed the state and lower federal courts in highly controversial administrative and supervisory roles. And it would have opened up the Court itself to serious criticism for overreaching the scope of its legitimate judicial powers.

---

15. A 1982 study by the ABA found, among other things, that "The financing of criminal defense services for indigents is generally inadequate, constituting only 1.5 percent of total expenditures for criminal justice matters by state and local governments." See Norman Lefstein, In Search of *Gideon*'s Promise: Lessons from England and the Need for Federal Help, 55 Hastings L.J. 835, 838 n. 15 (2004).

16. See ABA Standing Committee on Legal Aid and Indigent Defendants, ABA Principal Indigent Defense Resolution No. 121, Report to the House of Delegates, at 3 (1979), available online at http://www.abanet.org/legalservices/downloads/sclaid/121.pdf; Center for Defense Services Act, S. 2170, 96th Cong. 4(a), 5(a) (1979) (cosponsored by Senators Dennis DeConcini (R-Ariz.) and Robert F. Kennedy (D-Mass.).

17. The ABA reconfirmed its support for the proposal in 1998, and again in 2005.

Or the Court could do instead what it actually did in *Strickland*, which was to authorize *post hoc*, fact-based, case-by-case litigation about the deficient performance of defense counsel and its prejudicial effects on the individual defendant. The Court undoubtedly recognized that such issues must be decided primarily by the trial courts that observed the proceedings in the first instance — no appellate or habeas court could ever successfully reconstruct, in sufficient detail, the factual context within which the defense attorney acted (or failed to act). So the Court's role in *Strickland* was largely limited to laying out an exhortatory standard that would at least allow appellate and habeas courts to remedy the most obvious injustices (such as drunk, drugged, or sleeping lawyers), and then leaving the matter primarily to the trial courts to enforce.

That is probably the main reason why the legal rules declared in *Strickland* have not changed one iota for more than 30 years. The Court occasionally returns to the subject of ineffective assistance, to address a novel fact pattern or to send signals that the lower courts should become either more or less aggressive in policing defense attorney performance. But the *post hoc* regulatory system created by *Strickland* remains completely intact — for better or for worse.

Do you find this account of *Strickland* disturbing, or just depressing? If so, can you think of a better approach for solving the problem of inadequate defense representation? Might systemic reform litigation to improve the funding of state indigent defense representation systems, based on the Sixth Amendment, be a better approach? We will return to these questions shortly, in Section B.4., infra, at page 226.

2. Multiple Representation

A special problem of effective assistance arises in cases in which a lawyer represents more than one client in either joint or separate proceedings. The difficulty results from the potential conflict of interest among the defendants. In separate trials of accomplices, for example, a lawyer will have to choose whether to call certain potentially exculpating witnesses at the first trial. On the one hand, if the lawyer chooses not to call the witnesses, the defense in the present case will be impaired in order to protect the defense in the later trial. On the other hand, if the witnesses are called, the defense at the first trial will be bolstered at the cost to the defense at the second trial of exposing to the prosecution the contents of the defendant's case. Moreover, it is the lawyer, who owes the duty of essentially undivided allegiance to the client, who will have to make the choices. Obviously, the necessity of making such choices compromises the faithful discharge of the duty and may impact adversely on the client's interests.

The problems are exacerbated in joint proceedings. Consider the following true story, recounted in Gary T. Lowenthal, Joint Representation in Criminal Cases: A Critical Appraisal, 64 Va. L. Rev. 939, 941-942 (1978):

> An attorney appeared in a municipal court for the purpose of requesting a reduction of bail for four defendants jointly charged with possession of a large cache of drugs seized from a communal house. Referring to the first of his clients, the lawyer stated: "This defendant should be released on his own recognizance, Your Honor, because he has no rap sheet. Obviously he is not a hardened criminal and should not be locked up with others who are." When the second defendant's case was called, counsel argued: "No drugs were found in this defendant's bedroom, Your Honor. His

chance for an acquittal is great and consequently it is highly likely that he will show up for trial." On behalf of the third defendant, the lawyer began to argue that his client had lived in the area all of his life. The judge interrupted the lawyer, asking him if any drugs had been seized from the bedroom of defendant number three. The lawyer responded. "No comment, Your Honor." The judge countered with the remark: "I suppose that this client also has a prior record, making him a hardened criminal," evoking the response that although the defendant had a prior record, he certainly was not a hardened criminal. The fourth defendant then interrupted the proceedings by eagerly requesting to be represented by the public defender.[11] . . .

The episode related above illustrates a circumstance of the criminal process that is essential to an understanding of joint representation in practice. Decisionmakers exercise considerable discretion in evaluating and comparing defendants at every stage of a criminal case. The government, for example, has substantial leeway in determining which charges, if any, to file against an accused; a judge or magistrate may consider a broad range of factors when predicting whether a defendant will appear in court if released on bail; the prosecutor's discretion in plea bargaining is almost unlimited in most jurisdictions; a trier of fact is free to ignore the evidence in acquitting the defendant; and a judge or jury is expected to differentiate among convicted offenders to arrive at an appropriate sentence for each. At each step in the process, a defendant's appearance, attitude, and background, as well as the extent of his culpability, will influence decisionmakers. As a result, a lawyer's effectiveness in representing a client will depend in virtually every case on how well he can manipulate these factors to the advantage of the client. Thus the lawyer must differentiate his client from others charged with the same or similar conduct and emphasize those attributes of his client that will have a favorable effect on the prosecutor, judge, or jury.

As Professor Lowenthal explains, the ability of a lawyer to distinguish one client from another is greatly compromised in cases of joint representation. Yet joint representation may offer some advantages, including efficiency as well as the possibility of discouraging codefendants from turning on each other. The question thus arises whether there are circumstances that render joint representation—either at the request, or over the objection, of the codefendants—so defective as to violate the right to counsel.

CUYLER v. SULLIVAN

Certiorari to the United States Court of Appeals for the Third Circuit
446 U.S. 335 (1980)

Mr. Justice Powell delivered the opinion of the Court.

I

Respondent John Sullivan was indicted with Gregory Carchidi and Anthony DiPasquale for the first-degree murders of John Gorey and Rita Janda. The victims,

11. This incident occurred in March 1972, before Judge Jacqueline Taber in Department Six of the Oakland-Piedmont Municipal Court, Oakland, California, when I was an Assistant Public Defender for Alameda County, California. See Letter from Judge Jacqueline Taber to Gary T. Lowenthal (Oct. 23, 1978) (copy on file with the Virginia Law Review Association). It is the most vivid of many such incidents that prompted me to write this article.

a labor official and his companion, were shot to death in Gorey's second-story office at the Philadelphia headquarters of Teamsters' Local 107. Francis McGrath, a janitor, saw the three defendants in the building just before the shooting. They appeared to be awaiting someone, and they encouraged McGrath to do his work on another day. McGrath ignored their suggestions. Shortly afterward, Gorey arrived and went to his office. McGrath then heard what sounded like firecrackers exploding in rapid succession. Carchidi, who was in the room where McGrath was working, abruptly directed McGrath to leave the building and to say nothing. McGrath hastily complied. When he returned to the building about 15 minutes later, the defendants were gone. The victims' bodies were discovered the next morning.

Two privately retained lawyers, G. Fred DiBona and A. Charles Peruto, represented all three defendants throughout the state proceedings that followed the indictment. Sullivan had different counsel at the medical examiner's inquest, but he thereafter accepted representation from the two lawyers retained by his codefendants because he could not afford to pay his own lawyer.[1] At no time did Sullivan or his lawyers object to the multiple representation. Sullivan was the first defendant to come to trial. The evidence against him was entirely circumstantial, consisting primarily of McGrath's testimony. At the close of the Commonwealth's case, the defense rested without presenting any evidence. The jury found Sullivan guilty and fixed his penalty at life imprisonment. . . . Sullivan's codefendants, Carchidi and DiPasquale, were acquitted at separate trials.

Sullivan then petitioned for collateral relief. . . . He alleged, among other claims, that he had been denied effective assistance of counsel because his defense lawyers represented conflicting interests. In five days of hearings, the Court of Common Pleas heard evidence from Sullivan, Carchidi, Sullivan's lawyers, and the judge who presided at Sullivan's trial.

DiBona and Peruto had different recollections of their roles at the trials of the three defendants. DiBona testified that he and Peruto had been "associate counsel" at each trial. . . . Peruto recalled that he had been chief counsel for Carchidi and DiPasquale, but that he merely had assisted DiBona in Sullivan's trial. DiBona and Peruto also gave conflicting accounts of the decision to rest Sullivan's defense. DiBona said he had encouraged Sullivan to testify even though the Commonwealth had presented a very weak case. Peruto remembered that he had not "want[ed] the defense to go on because I thought we would only be exposing the [defense] witnesses for the other two trials that were coming up." . . . Sullivan testified that he had deferred to his lawyers' decision not to present evidence for the defense. But other testimony suggested that Sullivan preferred not to take the stand because cross-examination might have disclosed an extramarital affair. Finally, Carchidi claimed he would have appeared at Sullivan's trial to rebut McGrath's testimony about Carchidi's statement at the time of the murders.

The Court of Common Pleas . . . did not pass directly on the claim that defense counsel had a conflict of interest, but it found that counsel fully advised Sullivan about his decision not to testify. . . . All other claims for collateral relief were rejected or reserved for consideration in the new appeal.

---

1. DiBona and Peruto were paid in part with funds raised by friends of the three defendants. The record does not disclose the source of the balance of their fee, but no part of the money came from either Sullivan or his family.

The Pennsylvania Supreme Court affirmed both Sullivan's original conviction and the denial of collateral relief. . . .

Having exhausted his state remedies, Sullivan sought habeas corpus relief in the United States District Court for the Eastern District of Pennsylvania. The petition was referred to a Magistrate, who found that Sullivan's defense counsel had represented conflicting interests. The District Court, however, accepted the Pennsylvania Supreme Court's conclusion that there had been no multiple representation. The court also found that, assuming there had been multiple representation, the evidence adduced in the state postconviction proceeding revealed no conflict of interest. . . .

The Court of Appeals for the Third Circuit reversed. . . . We granted certiorari to consider recurring issues left unresolved by Holloway v. Arkansas, 435 U.S. 475 (1978). We now vacate and remand. . . .

IV

We come . . . to Sullivan's claim that he was denied the effective assistance of counsel guaranteed by the Sixth Amendment because his lawyers had a conflict of interest. The claim raises two issues expressly reserved in Holloway v. Arkansas, [id.] at 483-484. The first is whether a state trial judge must inquire into the propriety of multiple representation even though no party lodges an objection. The second is whether the mere possibility of a conflict of interest warrants the conclusion that the defendant was deprived of his right to counsel.

A

In *Holloway*, a single public defender represented three defendants at the same trial. The trial court refused to consider the appointment of separate counsel despite the defense lawyer's timely and repeated assertions that the interests of his clients conflicted. This Court recognized that a lawyer forced to represent codefendants whose interests conflict cannot provide the adequate legal assistance required by the Sixth Amendment. Given the trial court's failure to respond to timely objections, however, the Court did not consider whether the alleged conflict actually existed. It simply held that the trial court's error unconstitutionally endangered the right to counsel.

Holloway requires state trial courts to investigate timely objections to multiple representation. But nothing in our precedents suggests that the Sixth Amendment requires state courts themselves to initiate inquiries into the propriety of multiple representation in every case.[10] Defense counsel have an ethical obligation to avoid conflicting representations and to advise the court promptly when a conflict of

---

10. In certain cases, proposed Federal Rule of Criminal Procedure 44(c) provides that the federal district courts "shall promptly inquire with respect to . . . joint representation and shall personally advise each defendant of his right to the effective assistance of counsel, including separate representation." See also ABA Project on Standards for Criminal Justice, Function of the Trial Judge §3.4(b) (App. Draft 1972).

Several Courts of Appeals already invoke their supervisory power to require similar inquiries. As our promulgation of Rule 44(c) suggests, we view such an exercise of the supervisory power as a desirable practice. See generally William W. Schwarzer, Dealing with Incompetent Counsel—The Trial Judge's Role, 93 Harv. L. Rev. 633, 653-654 (1980). . . .

interest arises during the course of trial. Absent special circumstances, therefore, trial courts may assume either that multiple representation entails no conflict or that the lawyer and his clients knowingly accept such risk of conflict as may exist. Indeed, as the Court noted in *Holloway*, trial courts necessarily rely in large measure upon the good faith and good judgment of defense counsel. "An 'attorney representing two defendants in a criminal matter is in the best position professionally and ethically to determine when a conflict of interest exists or will probably develop in the course of a trial.'" Unless the trial court knows or should have known that a particular conflict exists, the court need not initiate an inquiry.

Nothing in the circumstances of this case indicates that the trial court had a duty to inquire whether there was a conflict of interest. The provision of separate trials for Sullivan and his codefendants significantly reduced the potential for a divergence in their interests. No participant in Sullivan's trial ever objected to the multiple representation. DiBona's opening argument for Sullivan outlined a defense compatible with the view that none of the defendants was connected with the murders. . . . The opening argument also suggested that counsel was not afraid to call witnesses whose testimony might be needed at the trials of Sullivan's codefendants. . . . Finally, as the Court of Appeals noted, counsel's critical decision to rest Sullivan's defense was on its face a reasonable tactical response to the weakness of the circumstantial evidence presented by the prosecutor. On these facts, we conclude that the Sixth Amendment imposed upon the trial court no affirmative duty to inquire into the propriety of multiple representation.

B

Holloway reaffirmed that multiple representation does not violate the Sixth Amendment unless it gives rise to a conflict of interest. Since a possible conflict inheres in almost every instance of multiple representation, a defendant who objects to multiple representation must have the opportunity to show that potential conflicts impermissibly imperil his right to a fair trial. But unless the trial court fails to afford such an opportunity, a reviewing court cannot presume that the possibility for conflict has resulted in ineffective assistance of counsel. Such a presumption would preclude multiple representation even in cases where "[a] common defense . . . gives strength against a common attack." Id., at 482-483, quoting Glasser v. United States, 315 U.S. 60, 92 (Frankfurter, J., dissenting).

In order to establish a violation of the Sixth Amendment, a defendant who raised no objection at trial must demonstrate that an actual conflict of interest adversely affected his lawyer's performance. In Glasser v. United States, for example, the record showed that defense counsel failed to cross-examine a prosecution witness whose testimony linked Glasser with the crime, and failed to resist the presentation of arguably inadmissible evidence. The Court found that both omissions resulted from counsel's desire to diminish the jury's perception of a codefendant's guilt. Indeed, the evidence of counsel's "struggle to serve two masters [could not] seriously be doubted." Since this actual conflict of interest impaired Glasser's defense, the Court reversed his conviction.

Dukes v. Warden, 406 U.S. 250 (1972), presented a contrasting situation. Dukes pleaded guilty on the advice of two lawyers, one of whom also represented Dukes' codefendants on an unrelated charge. Dukes later learned that this lawyer had sought leniency for the codefendants by arguing that their cooperation with the police induced Dukes to plead guilty. Dukes argued in this Court that his lawyer's conflict of interest had infected his plea. We found "nothing in the record . . . which would indicate that the alleged conflict resulted in ineffective assistance of counsel and did in fact render the plea in question involuntary and unintelligent." Since Dukes did not identify an actual lapse in representation, we affirmed the denial of habeas corpus relief.

Glasser established that unconstitutional multiple representation is never harmless error. Once the Court concluded that Glasser's lawyer had an actual conflict of interest, it refused "to indulge in nice calculations as to the amount of prejudice" attributable to the conflict. The conflict itself demonstrated a denial of the "right to have the effective assistance of counsel." 315 U.S., at 76. Thus, a defendant who shows that a conflict of interest actually affected the adequacy of his representation need not demonstrate prejudice in order to obtain relief. But until a defendant shows that his counsel actively represented conflicting interests, he has not established the constitutional predicate for his claim of ineffective assistance. . . .

C

The Court of Appeals granted Sullivan relief because he had shown that the multiple representation in this case involved a possible conflict of interest. We hold that the possibility of conflict is insufficient to impugn a criminal conviction. In order to demonstrate a violation of his Sixth Amendment rights, a defendant must establish that an actual conflict of interest adversely affected his lawyer's performance. Sullivan believes he should prevail even under this standard. He emphasizes Peruto's admission that the decision to rest Sullivan's defense reflected a reluctance to expose witnesses who later might have testified for the other defendants. The petitioner, on the other hand, points to DiBona's contrary testimony and to evidence that Sullivan himself wished to avoid taking the stand. Since the Court of Appeals did not weigh these conflicting contentions under the proper legal standard, its judgment is vacated and the case is remanded for further proceedings consistent with this opinion.

So ordered.

MR. JUSTICE MARSHALL, concurring in part and dissenting in part. . . .

I believe . . . that the potential for conflict of interest in representing multiple defendants is "so grave," see ABA Project on Standards for Criminal Justice, Defense Function, Standard 4-3.5(b) (App. Draft, 2d ed. 1979), that whenever two or more defendants are represented by the same attorney the trial judge must make a preliminary determination that the joint representation is the product of the defendants' informed choice. I therefore [think] . . . that the trial court has a duty to inquire whether there is multiple representation, to warn defendants of the possible risks of such representation, and to ascertain that the representation is the result of the defendants' informed choice.

I dissent from the Court's formulation of the proper standard for determining whether multiple representation has violated the defendant's right to the effective assistance of counsel. The Court holds that in the absence of an objection at trial, the defendant must show "that an actual conflict of interest adversely affected his lawyer's performance." . . . If the Court's holding would require a defendant to demonstrate that his attorney's trial performance differed from what it would have been if the defendant had been the attorney's only client, I believe it is inconsistent with our previous cases. Such a test is not only unduly harsh, but incurably speculative as well. The appropriate question under the Sixth Amendment is whether an actual, relevant conflict of interests existed during the proceedings. If it did, the conviction must be reversed. Since such a conflict was present in this case, I would affirm the judgment of the Court of Appeals.

Our cases make clear that every defendant has a constitutional right to "the assistance of an attorney unhindered by a conflict of interests." Holloway v. Arkansas, 435 U.S. 475, 483, n. 5 (1978). "[T]he 'assistance of counsel' guaranteed by the Sixth Amendment contemplates that such assistance be untrammeled and unimpaired by a court order requiring that one lawyer shall simultaneously represent conflicting interests." Glasser v. United States, 315 U.S. 60, 70 (1942). If "[t]he possibility of the inconsistent interests of [the clients] was brought home to the court" by means of an objection at trial, id., at 71, the court may not require joint representation. But if no objection was made at trial, the appropriate inquiry is whether a conflict actually existed during the course of the representation.

Because it is the simultaneous representation of conflicting interests against which the Sixth Amendment protects a defendant, he need go no further than to show the existence of an actual conflict. An actual conflict of interests negates the unimpaired loyalty a defendant is constitutionally entitled to expect and receive from his attorney.

Moreover, a showing that an actual conflict adversely affected counsel's performance is not only unnecessary, it is often an impossible task. As the Court emphasized in *Holloway*:

> [I]n a case of joint representation of conflicting interests the evil—it bears repeating—is in what the advocate finds himself compelled to *refrain* from doing. . . . It may be possible in some cases to identify from the record the prejudice resulting from an attorney's failure to undertake certain trial tasks, but even with a record of the sentencing hearing available it would be difficult to judge intelligently the impact of a conflict on the attorney's representation of a client. And to assess the impact of a conflict of interests on the attorney's options, tactics, and decisions in plea negotiations would be virtually impossible. 435 U.S., at 490-491.

Accordingly, in *Holloway* we emphatically rejected the suggestion that a defendant must show prejudice in order to be entitled to relief. For the same reasons, it would usually be futile to attempt to determine how counsel's conduct would have been different if he had not been under conflicting duties. . . .

NOTES AND QUESTIONS

1. What does it mean to say that "a defendant who shows that a conflict of interest actually affected the adequacy of his representation need not demonstrate prejudice in order to obtain relief"?

2. In Burger v. Kemp, 483 U.S. 776 (1987), the Court held that an actual conflict of interest was not present in the following circumstances: Two law partners represented two codefendants in a capital murder case. One of the partners wrote the appellate briefs for both defendants. The brief filed on Burger's behalf did not make a "lesser culpability" argument (i.e., argue that Burger was the less culpable

of the killers); Burger argued that that omission showed an actual conflict that adversely affected counsel's representation. The Court concluded that the "decision to forgo this [argument] had a sound strategic basis," and found that if there were any conflict, it had not affected the representation Burger received.

3. The *Holloway* case, cited and discussed in *Sullivan*, is a prime example of what can go wrong when a trial judge is insensitive to the potential problems of joint representation. Public defender Harold Hall, appointed to represent three codefendants charged with robbery and rape, moved twice before trial for separate counsel based on conflict of interest, but the trial judge denied both motions. Here is what happened next:

On the second day of trial, after the prosecution had rested its case, Hall advised the court that, against his recommendation, all three defendants had decided to testify. He then stated:

> *Mr. Hall:* Now, since I have been appointed, I had previously filed a motion asking the Court to appoint a separate attorney for each defendant because of a possible conflict of interest. This conflict will probably be now coming up since each one of them wants to testify.
>
> *The Court:* That's all right; let them testify. There is no conflict of interest. Every time I try more than one person in this court each one blames it on the other one.
>
> *Mr. Hall:* I have talked to each one of these defendants, and I have talked to them individually, not collectively.
>
> *The Court:* Now talk to them collectively.

The court then indicated satisfaction that each petitioner understood the nature and consequences of his right to testify on his own behalf, whereupon Hall observed:

> *Mr. Hall:* I am in a position now where I am more or less muzzled as to any cross-examination.
>
> *The Court:* You have no right to cross-examine your own witness.
>
> *Mr. Hall:* Or to examine them.
>
> *The Court:* You have a right to examine them, but have no right to cross-examine them. The prosecuting attorney does that.
>
> *Mr. Hall:* If one [defendant] takes the stand, somebody needs to protect the other two's interest while that one is testifying, and I can't do that since I have talked to each one individually.
>
> *The Court:* Well, you have talked to them, I assume, individually and collectively, too. They all say they want to testify. I think it's perfectly alright [*sic*] for them to testify if they want to, or not. It's their business. . . . Each defendant said he wants to testify, and there will be no cross-examination of these witnesses, just a direct examination by you.
>
> *Mr. Hall:* Your Honor, I can't even put them on direct examination because if I ask them—
>
> *The Court:* (Interposing) You can just put them on the stand and tell the Court that you have advised them of their rights and they want to testify; then you tell the man to go ahead and relate what he wants to. That's all you need to do.

Holloway took the stand on his own behalf, testifying that during the time described as the time of the robbery, he was at his brother's home. His brother had previously given similar testimony. When Welch, a codefendant, took the witness stand, the record shows Hall advised him, as he had Holloway, that "I cannot ask you any questions that might tend to incriminate any one of the three of you. . . . Now, the only thing I can say is tell these ladies and gentlemen of the jury what you know about this case." Welch responded that he did not "have any kind of speech ready for the jury or anything. I thought I was going to be questioned." When Welch denied, from the witness stand, that he was at the restaurant the night of the robbery, Hall interrupted, asking:

> *Mr. Hall:*   Your Honor, are we allowed to make an objection?
> *The Court:*   No, sir. Your counsel will take care of any objections.
> *Mr. Hall:* Your Honor, that is what I am trying to say. I can't cross-examine them.
> *The Court:*   You proceed like I tell you to, Mr. Hall. You have no right to cross-examine your own witness anyhow.

Id., at 478-480. The Court reversed Holloway's convictions:

> Here trial counsel, by the pretrial motions . . . and by his accompanying representations, made as an officer of the court, focused explicitly on the probable risk of a conflict of interests. The judge then failed either to appoint separate counsel or to take adequate steps to ascertain whether the risk was too remote to warrant separate counsel. We hold that the failure, in the face of the representations made by counsel weeks before trial and again before the jury was empaneled, deprived petitioners of the guarantee of "assistance of counsel."

Id. at 484. The Court also concluded that "whenever a trial court improperly requires joint representation over timely objection reversal is automatic." Id., at 488.

After *Sullivan*, and taking *Holloway* into account, what are the consequences of making, as compared to not making, a pretrial objection to joint representation?

4. In *Sullivan*, the trial judge had no good reason to suspect the potential conflict. What should the standard of effective assistance be if the trial judge was, or should have been, aware of a potential conflict? Should there be a duty to inquire, even if nobody objects? In the absence of judicial inquiry, should prejudice be presumed if counsel has any conflict whatsoever? Does *Sullivan* apply to every conflict of interest or only to those involving multiple representations? Ought there be different standards for "active" representation of conflicted interests as compared to the kind of conflict that may emerge from the prior representation of a different person?

MICKENS v. TAYLOR, 535 U.S. 162 (2002):   In 1993, a Virginia jury convicted petitioner Mickens of the premeditated murder of Timothy Hall during or following the commission of an attempted forcible sodomy. Finding the murder outrageously and wantonly vile, it sentenced petitioner to death. In June 1998, Mickens filed a petition for writ of habeas corpus . . . in the United States District Court for the Eastern District of Virginia, alleging, inter alia, that he was denied effective assistance of counsel because one of his court-appointed attorneys had a conflict of interest at trial. Federal habeas counsel had discovered that petitioner's lead trial attorney, Bryan Saunders, was representing Hall (the victim) on assault and concealed-weapons charges at the time of the murder. Saunders had been appointed to represent Hall, a juvenile, on March 20, 1992, and had met with him once for 15 to 30 minutes some time the following week. Hall's body was discovered on March 30, 1992, and four days later a juvenile court judge dismissed the charges against him, noting on the docket sheet that Hall was deceased. The one-page docket sheet also listed Saunders as Hall's counsel. On April 6, 1992, the same judge appointed Saunders to represent petitioner. Saunders did not disclose to the court, his co-counsel, or petitioner that he had previously represented Hall. Under Virginia law, juvenile case files are confidential and may not generally be disclosed without a court order, but petitioner learned about Saunders' prior representation when a clerk mistakenly produced Hall's file to federal habeas counsel. . . .

The District Court held an evidentiary hearing and denied petitioner's habeas petition. . . . [The en banc Fourth Circuit] assumed that the juvenile court judge had neglected a duty to inquire into a potential conflict, but rejected petitioner's argument that this failure either mandated automatic reversal of his conviction or relieved him of the burden of showing that a conflict of interest adversely affected his representation. . . . Concluding that petitioner had not demonstrated adverse effect, it affirmed. . . .

Petitioner's proposed rule of automatic reversal when there existed a conflict that did not affect counsel's performance, but the trial judge failed to make the *Sullivan*-mandated inquiry, makes little policy sense. . . . [T]he rule applied when the trial judge is not aware of the conflict (and thus not obligated to inquire) is that prejudice will be presumed only if the conflict has significantly affected counsel's performance—thereby rendering the verdict unreliable, even though *Strickland* prejudice cannot be shown. The trial court's awareness of a potential conflict neither renders it more likely that counsel's performance was significantly affected nor in any other way renders the verdict unreliable. Nor does the trial judge's failure to make the *Sullivan*-mandated inquiry often make it harder for reviewing courts to determine conflict and effect, particularly since those courts may rely on evidence and testimony whose importance only becomes established at the trial.

Nor, finally, is automatic reversal simply an appropriate means of enforcing *Sullivan*'s mandate of inquiry. Despite [the dissent's] belief that there must be a threat of sanction (to-wit, the risk of conferring a windfall upon the defendant) in order to induce "resolutely obdurate" trial judges to follow the law, we do not presume that judges are as careless or as partial as those police officers who need the incentive of the exclusionary rule. And in any event, the *Sullivan* standard, which requires proof of effect upon representation but (once such effect is shown) presumes prejudice, already creates an "incentive" to inquire into a potential conflict. In those cases where the potential conflict is in fact an actual one, only inquiry will enable the judge to avoid all possibility of reversal by either seeking waiver or replacing a conflicted attorney. We doubt that the deterrence of "judicial dereliction" that would be achieved by an automatic reversal rule is significantly greater.

Since this was not a case in which (as in *Holloway*) counsel protested his inability simultaneously to represent multiple defendants; and since the trial court's failure to make the *Sullivan*-mandated inquiry does not reduce the petitioner's burden of proof; it was at least necessary, to void the conviction, for petitioner to establish that the conflict of interest adversely affected his counsel's performance. The

Court of Appeals having found no such effect, the denial of habeas relief must be affirmed. . . .

Lest today's holding be misconstrued, we note that the only question presented was the effect of a trial court's failure to inquire into a potential conflict upon the *Sullivan* rule that deficient performance of counsel must be shown. The case was presented and argued on the assumption that (absent some exception for failure to inquire) *Sullivan* would be applicable. . . . That assumption was not unreasonable in light of the holdings of Courts of Appeals, which . . . have invoked the Sullivan standard not only when (as here) there is a conflict rooted in counsel's obligations to *former* clients, but even when representation of the defendant somehow implicates counsel's personal or financial interests, including a book deal, a job with the prosecutor's office, the teaching of classes to Internal Revenue Service agents, a romantic "entanglement" with the prosecutor, or fear of antagonizing the trial judge.

It must be said, however, that the language of *Sullivan* itself does not clearly establish, or indeed even support, such expansive application. "[U]ntil," it said, "a defendant shows that his counsel *actively represented* conflicting interests, he has not established the constitutional predicate for his claim of ineffective assistance." 446 U.S., at 350 (emphasis added). Both *Sullivan* itself, and *Holloway*, stressed the high probability of prejudice arising from multiple concurrent representation, and the difficulty of proving that prejudice. . . . Not all attorney conflicts present comparable difficulties. Thus, the Federal Rules of Criminal Procedure treat concurrent representation and prior representation differently, requiring a trial court to inquire into the likelihood of conflict whenever jointly charged defendants are represented by a single attorney (Rule 44(c)), but not when counsel previously represented another defendant in a substantially related matter, even where the trial court is aware of the prior representation.

JUSTICE KENNEDY, joined by JUSTICE O'CONNOR, concurring:
. . . The constitutional question must turn on whether trial counsel had a conflict of interest that hampered the representation, not on whether the trial judge should have been more assiduous in taking prophylactic measures. If it were otherwise, the judge's duty would not be limited to cases where the attorney is suspected of harboring a conflict of interest. The Sixth Amendment protects the defendant against an ineffective attorney, as well as a conflicted one. . . . It would be a major departure to say that the trial judge must step in every time defense counsel appears to be providing ineffective assistance, and indeed, there is no precedent to support this proposition. As the Sixth Amendment guarantees the defendant the assistance of counsel, the infringement of that right must depend on a deficiency of the lawyer, not of the trial judge. . . .

[Justice Stevens and Justice Breyer, joined by Justice Ginsburg, dissented based on (1) the risk of prejudice arising from the conflict present in this case, and (2) the perception that—especially in a capital case—the "appearance of justice" was not satisfied.—EDS.]

JUSTICE SOUTER, dissenting:
. . . The different burdens on the *Holloway* and *Sullivan* defendants are consistent features of a coherent scheme for dealing with the problem of conflicted defense counsel; a prospective risk of conflict subject to judicial notice is treated differently from a retrospective claim that a completed proceeding was tainted by conflict,

although the trial judge had not been derelict in any duty to guard against it. When the problem comes to the trial court's attention before any potential conflict has become actual, the court has a duty to act prospectively to assess the risk and, if the risk is not too remote, to eliminate it or to render it acceptable through a defendant's knowing and intelligent waiver. This duty is something more than the general responsibility to rule without committing legal error; it is an affirmative obligation to investigate a disclosed possibility that defense counsel will be unable to act with uncompromised loyalty to his client. It was the judge's failure to fulfill that duty of care to enquire further and do what might be necessary that the *Holloway* Court remedied by vacating the defendant's subsequent conviction. The error occurred when the judge failed to act, and the remedy restored the defendant to the position he would have occupied if the judge had taken reasonable steps to fulfill his obligation. But when the problem of conflict comes to judicial attention not prospectively, but only after the fact, the defendant must show an actual conflict with adverse consequence to him in order to get relief. Fairness requires nothing more, for no judge was at fault in allowing a trial to proceed even though fraught with hidden risk.

In light of what the majority holds today, it bears repeating that, in this coherent scheme established by *Holloway* and *Sullivan*, there is nothing legally crucial about an objection by defense counsel to tell a trial judge that conflicting interests may impair the adequacy of counsel's representation. Counsel's objection in *Holloway* was important as a fact sufficient to put the judge on notice that he should enquire. In most multiple-representation cases, it will take just such an objection to alert a trial judge to prospective conflict, and the *Sullivan* Court reaffirmed that the judge is obliged to take reasonable prospective action whenever a timely objection is made. But the Court also indicated that an objection is not required as a matter of law: "Unless the trial court knows or reasonably should know that a particular conflict exists, the court need not initiate an enquiry." The Court made this clear beyond cavil 10 months later when Justice Powell, the same Justice who wrote the *Sullivan* opinion, explained in Wood v. Georgia[, 450 U.S. 261 (1981),] that *Sullivan* "*mandates* a reversal when the trial court has failed to make an inquiry even though it 'knows or reasonably should know that a particular conflict exists.'" [Id.] at 272, n. 18 (emphasis in original).

Since the District Court in this case found that the state judge was on notice of a prospective potential conflict, this case calls for nothing more than the application of the prospective notice rule announced and exemplified by *Holloway* and confirmed in *Sullivan* and *Wood*. The remedy for the judge's dereliction of duty should be an order vacating the conviction and affording a new trial.

NOTES AND QUESTIONS

1. Justice Souter's reliance on Wood v. Georgia is a bit peculiar, as the actual holding in *Wood* sent the case back to the district court to make the *Sullivan* "adverse effect" inquiry. In a passage unremarked by Justice Souter, the *Wood* Court stated: "On the record before us, we cannot be sure whether counsel was influenced in his basic strategic decisions by the interests of his employer who hired him. If this was the case, the due process rights of petitioners were not respected." 450 U.S. at 272.

Regardless who wins the game of parsing prior opinions, what should the respective burdens be in cases like this? If a defendant makes no objection to his representation, why should there be any after-the-fact review that does not, at a minimum, focus on whether the defendant was actually harmed? For that matter, why shouldn't the defendant meet the *Strickland* burden of showing a reasonable probability that the conflicted representation might have affected the outcome in the case? Why is it the trial court's, or the prosecutor's, responsibility to police the relationship between defense counsel and client?

Reversals of reliable convictions impose substantial costs. A plausibly erroneous, or just different, outcome may justify such costs, but do you think the "appearance of justice" does? And what, exactly, is the "appearance of justice"? Wouldn't Justice Souter's proposed approach create perverse incentives for a defendant to proceed with conflicted representation? If he gets acquitted, the case is over; if he gets convicted, he may well obtain a reversal and a second bite at the apple. Bear in mind that there are other possible means of regulating cases like this, including sanctions against the lawyer. After all, it is the lawyer and the client who create these problems; shouldn't they have some incentive to correct them, rather than to benefit from them?

2. What result under *Sullivan* if a defendant, in full knowledge of a potential conflict, waives the right not to have separate counsel, and subsequently the potential conflict is actualized? In this regard, consider Rule 44(c) of the Federal Rules of Criminal Procedure, which was cited in footnote 10 of *Sullivan*, and which has (with some stylistic changes) since gone into effect:

> **Rule 44. Right to and Appointment of Counsel**
> (c) Inquiry Into Joint Representation.
>> (1) Joint Representation. Joint representation occurs when:
>>> (A) two or more defendants have been charged jointly under Rule 8(b) or have been joined for trial under Rule 13; and
>>> (B) the defendants are represented by the same counsel or counsel who are associated in law practice.
>> (2) Court's Responsibilities in Cases of Joint Representation. The court must promptly inquire about the propriety of joint representation and must personally advise each defendant of the right to the effective assistance of counsel, including separate representation. Unless there is good cause to believe that no conflict of interest is likely to arise, the court must take appropriate measures to protect each defendant's right to counsel.

In an insightful analysis of Rule 44(c) prior to its effective date, Professor Tague commented:

> If the rule values the assistance of conflict-free representation above the right to choose one's attorney, it has three distressing omissions. First, the rule orders the "court" to make an inquiry about possible conflicts whenever defendants "are charged pursuant to Rule 8(b) or have been joined for trial pursuant to Rule 13." Does the rule apply only after the defendants have been indicted or an information has been filed in district court? Is there then no obligation to inquire at any earlier stage, such as at the presentment or the preliminary hearing? The rule's reference to the "court" [and not the "magistrate"] as the inquiring entity supports this apparent restriction. . . . Indeed, the Advisory Committee implies that separate counsel need not be initially appointed for each defendant. This limitation is unfortunate. . . . Many defendants seek to plead guilty before they are indicted, because the defendants frequently obtain a more favorable plea bargain if they plead early in the process. A guilty plea might bury a glaring conflict that infected the plea bargaining for the codefendants.

Second, the rule does not appear to cover cases like Dukes v. Warden, in which a defendant, charged alone in one proceeding, is a codefendant in a second proceeding and one attorney represents defendants in both proceedings. The rule's reference to Rules 8(b) and 13 suggests that the court is not under any obligation even if it knows of the separate indictments. The rule also would appear to apply if the codefendants are severed under Rule 14.

Third, the rule fails to provide adequate guidelines for review of a postconviction attack based on conflict. The Committee indicates that although a trial court's failure to make a Rule 44(c) inquiry will not necessarily result in reversal, an appellate court is more likely to find that a conflict existed in this instance. Further, because conflicts that were not apparent initially may surface later in the proceeding, even an adequate initial inquiry does not preclude reversal on conflict grounds. If the trial court makes an inadequate inquiry or none at all, the appellate court would still face the problem of defining and allocating the burden of proving the existence of a conflict. The proposed rule thus fails to solve one of the major problems of multiple representation.

Peter Tague, Multiple Representation and Conflicts of Interest in Criminal Cases, 67 Geo. L.J. 1075, 1094-1095 (1979). Professor Tague concluded that the Rule should require (1) the appointment of separate counsel for all indigents; (2) that nonindigents must at least discuss the matter with separate counsel; and (3) that if defendants insist on joint representation, they should have to establish an intelligent waiver. Would it be better simply to have a flat prohibition against joint representation?

3. The general view seems to be that a client may waive the right to conflict-free representation. See, e.g., United States v. Curcio, 680 F.2d 881 (2d Cir. 1982). However, in Wheat v. United States, 486 U.S. 153 (1988), the Court held that trial courts are not required to accept defendants' waivers of conflict-free representation, notwithstanding the presumption in favor of counsel of choice. In part, the Court was motivated by the fact that the courts of appeals have been willing to entertain ineffective-assistance-of-counsel claims even from defendants who have specifically waived the right to conflict-free representation.

4. What about the *government's* interest in separate counsel? Consider the following:

> In *Wheat*, there are two reasons why the coconspirators might have wished to use Iredale [the defendants' attorney] as common counsel. The first, offered by the defendants, is unobjectionable: The defendants believed Iredale to be a very good attorney, better than the likely alternatives. But the second is troubling. If the three defendants in question were guilty, they may well have faced a classic prisoners' dilemma: It may have been in each individual's interest to "sell out" to the government and implicate his colleagues, but may have been far better for all if all either lied or remained silent. Common counsel may have removed the dilemma by facilitating the enforcement of an agreement not to finger each other. Obtaining the testimony of one conspirator against others may require careful negotiation with the would-be witness. If all the conspirators have the same lawyer, the government is, in effect, able to deal with one defendant only by dealing with all.

William J. Stuntz, Waiving Rights in Criminal Procedure, 75 Va. L. Rev. 761, 798-799 (1989). But if the government's interests do count, what is to prevent the government from objecting to common counsel solely in order to get an unusually strong defense lawyer out of the case, at least with respect to some of the defendants?

There is some reason to believe that that is exactly what happened in *Wheat*. See Pamela S. Karlan, Discrete and Relational Criminal Representation: The Changing Vision of the Right to Counsel, 105 Harv. L. Rev. 670, 687 n. 79 (1992) (noting that Iredale was reportedly an exceptionally good lawyer). See also Bruce A. Green, "Through a Glass, Darkly": How the Court Sees Motions to Disqualify Criminal Defense Lawyers, 89 Colum. L. Rev. 1201 (1989) (criticizing *Wheat*).

Are there any situations in which defendants should simply be barred from proceeding with conflicted counsel? Some courts have said "yes." For example, in United States v. Fulton, 5 F.3d 605 (2d Cir. 1993), during trial the government disclosed that a government witness presently on the stand had alleged that he had illegally imported heroin for Fulton's defense counsel. The court informed the defendant that this injected the defense counsel's interests into the trial, and further that counsel would not be able to cross-examine the witness on these matters, because to do so would reveal confidences of a former client. The client nonetheless wished to proceed with counsel and to waive the conflict. The court of appeals reversed the ensuing conviction on the ground that "no rational defendant would knowingly and intelligently be represented by a lawyer whose conduct was guided largely by a desire for self-preservation."

The Second Circuit extended the *Fulton* holding in the infamous case of United States v. Schwarz, 283 F.3d 76 (2d Cir. 2002), which dealt with two police officers, Schwarz and Bruder, who were charged with crimes in connection with a brutal assault on Abner Louima at a police station in Brooklyn. Following two jury trials, the defendants were convicted, and Schwarz appealed on the ground that his defense counsel had unwaivable conflicts. Schwarz's defense counsel, Stephen Worth, worked for the same law firm as Stuart London, who represented Bruder. In addition, the same law firm had been paid a $10 million retainer as counsel for the Policeman's Benevolent Association; the police union was a codefendant in a civil suit filed by Louima for conspiracy, and negligent failure to supervise and monitor, in connection with the assault. The government strenuously raised these potential conflicts with the judge before trial, arguing that they "cannot be waived," but both Worth and London, as well as defendants Schwarz and Bruder themselves, told the judge that they did not want any substitutions of counsel. The judge then held a pretrial hearing at which he personally informed Schwartz and Bruder about some of the possible conflicts that could arise. After the hearing, the judge appointed independent counsel to further advise each of the codefendants about the risks of joint representation, and also barred Worth's and London's law firm from representing the PBA in the civil suit. At the next court hearing on the matter, the following colloquy ensued:

> *The Court:*   Mr. Schwarz, tell me what you see here as inconsistencies between your case and Mr. Bruder's case.
>
> *Defendant Schwarz:*   I understand that with this case, there may be some potential conflicts of interest, one being that my attorney and Mr. Bruder's attorney are now with the same firm. This is a conflict in that one defendant may receive a better defense at the expense of the other defendant.
>
>   I'm also aware of the contract that my attorney has with the PBA. I know that there's another conflict with that, in that the government may call other police officers who are a member of the PBA or even PBA officials.

There's a concern that possibly my attorney may have another agenda and may not be vigorous in his cross-examination of these witnesses.

I'm also aware of in the calling of witnesses with this potential conflict, with the two lawyers in the same firm. If they call a witness who — my lawyer may be reluctant to call a witness who may be able to help me but who in his testimony may be harmful to the other defendant. I understand that there could be a conflict in that.

Other conflict issues were if the government were to offer some type of plea to one defendant, that would probably be harmful to the other defendant. Also, if there were a guilty conviction, another conflict may be that my attorney may be reluctant, if he was trying to plead for some type of leniency, he may be reluctant to try to shift blame on to the other defendant in this case. . . .

The Court: Do you want to keep your lawyer?
Defendant Schwarz: Yes, sir.

After the independent counsel for Schwarz told the court that he had also advised Schwarz of all of these conflicts and believed Schwarz understood them, the court accepted Schwarz's waiver of the right to conflict-free counsel and permitted Worth to continue representing Schwarz; Worth's partner, London, was permitted to continue representing Bruder.

In a peculiar opinion on the issue of waiver of conflict, the Second Circuit said:

> The waiver given by Schwarz . . . would defeat his claim of ineffective assistance of counsel unless it is determined that (1) the conflict with respect to the PBA retainer was so severe as to be unwaivable, or (2) the . . . waiver by Schwarz was not knowing and intelligent with respect to the specific conflict that led to the lapse in Worth's representation. We need not decide whether Schwarz's waiver was knowing and intelligent because we conclude that the actual conflict that Schwarz's attorney faced was unwaivable. . . .
>
> . . . *Fulton*'s rationale with respect to when an attorney's self-interest renders a conflict unwaivable is equally applicable to the unusual facts of this case. As noted above, Worth's representation of Schwarz was in conflict not only with his ethical obligation to the PBA as his client, but also with his own substantial self-interest in the two-year, $10 million retainer agreement his newly formed firm had entered into with the PBA. Like the conflict in *Fulton*, Worth's conflict "so permeate[d] the defense that no meaningful waiver could be obtained." *Fulton*, 5 F.3d at 613. We must assume that, under such circumstances, the distinct possibility existed that, at each point the conflict was felt, Worth would sacrifice Schwarz's interests for those of the PBA. Indeed, we think it likely that these very concerns motivated the government to argue to the district court . . . that the conflict created by the PBA retainer could not be waived. Thus, we conclude that the conflict between Worth's representation of Schwarz, on the one hand, and his ethical obligation to the PBA as his client and his self interest in the PBA retainer, on the other, was so severe that no rational defendant in Schwarz's position would have knowingly and intelligently desired Worth's representation. . . .
>
> In sum, we hold that Schwarz's counsel suffered an actual conflict, that the conflict adversely affected his counsel's representation, and that the conflict was unwaivable. Accordingly, we are required to vacate Schwarz's conviction in the first trial and remand for a new trial.

Id. at 95-98.

"In sum," hasn't the court essentially held that it needn't decide if the waiver in this case was knowing and intelligent because under these facts, it could never be knowing and intelligent? Review the colloquy with the defendant reproduced above. Did the Second Circuit take this peculiar tack because plainly this *was* a knowing and intelligent waiver? Why sacrifice the interests in effective law enforcement through a reversal of a conviction in a case like this rather than sanction the lawyers—if indeed there is any problem at all?

3. Effective Assistance of Counsel and Plea Bargaining

Does the Sixth Amendment requirement of effective assistance of counsel, as articulated in Strickland v. Washington, apply beyond the context of preparation for, and advocacy during, a criminal trial? Does the requirement also apply to plea bargaining? If so, exactly *how* does the *Strickland* standard apply to plea bargaining? These are very important questions, especially given that well over 90 percent of all criminal cases are resolved through plea bargaining, but the Supreme Court has only recently begun to address these questions.

In Hill v. Lockhart, 477 U.S. 52 (1985), the defendant pled guilty to first degree murder in state court, then two years later sought habeas relief on the ground that his guilty plea was involuntary as a result of ineffective assistance of counsel because he received erroneous information about his parole eligibility from his counsel. Counsel advised the defendant that he would have to serve one-third of his time before he would be eligible for parole, whereas in fact he had to serve one-half of his time as a result of a previous conviction, of which counsel was apparently not informed by the defendant.

The Supreme Court, per Justice Rehnquist, disagreed. The Court first concluded that the *Strickland* test for ineffective assistance of counsel—that the lawyer performed deficiently, and that but for his deficient performance, there is a reasonable probability that the outcome of the case would have been different—applied in the plea bargain context, with qualification. The "performance" prong is the same in the plea context as it is in a challenge to a defense lawyer's performance at trial: Did the lawyer's representation fall below an objective standard of reasonableness? But the "prejudice" prong, said the Court, needs to be stated somewhat differently: "[I]n order to satisfy the 'prejudice' requirement, the defendant must show that there is a reasonable probability that, but for counsel's errors, he would not have pleaded guilty and would have insisted on going to trial."

The Court then elaborated on the prejudice prong, explaining what it meant to say that the defendant "would not have pleaded guilty and would have insisted on going to trial":

> In many guilty plea cases, the "prejudice" inquiry will closely resemble the inquiry engaged in by courts reviewing ineffective-assistance challenges to convictions obtained through a trial. For example, where the alleged error of counsel is a failure to investigate or discover potentially exculpatory evidence, the determination whether the error "prejudiced" the defendant by causing him to plead guilty rather than go to trial will depend on the likelihood that discovery of the evidence would have led counsel to change his recommendation as to the plea. This assessment, in turn, will depend in large part on a prediction whether the evidence likely would have

changed the outcome of a trial. Similarly, where the alleged error of counsel is a failure to advise the defendant of a potential affirmative defense to the crime charged, the resolution of the "prejudice" inquiry will depend largely on whether the affirmative defense likely would have succeeded at trial. . . .

474 U.S. at 370-371.

Hill addressed the application of the *prejudice* prong of *Strickland* to guilty pleas. In Padilla v. Kentucky, 559 U.S. 356 (2010), by contrast, the Court concluded that a defense attorney's failure to fully advise the defendant concerning one special consequence of pleading guilty was ineffective *performance*. Counsel did not inform Padilla, a noncitizen who had resided lawfully in the United States for 40 years and had served with honor in Vietnam, that his plea of guilty to a drug charge would render him automatically removable and further told him that he need not worry about the immigration consequences of the plea. The prior law had been reasonably clear that, at most, the right to effective assistance extended to advice concerning the direct consequences of a plea, and not to collateral consequences. The effect of a conviction on immigration status had largely been viewed as collateral. However, the Court concluded that the effect on Padilla was so dramatic — automatic deportation after having spent 40 years in the United States — that the direct/collateral distinction was blurred, and that, in any event, a reasonably competent lawyer would have advised of such a clear and dramatic consequence. The Court remanded for a determination of whether or not Padilla suffered *Strickland* prejudice as a result of his attorney's mistaken advice. (On remand, the Kentucky Court of Appeals found that Mr. Padilla had indeed been prejudiced, and vacated his conviction. 381 S.W.3d 322 (2012).) Justice Scalia dissented on the ground that the Court's opinion impermissibly breached the direct/collateral divide, leaving a highly ambiguous admonition in its place that would lead to further instability in pleas and to substantial litigation.

Note that the potential importance of the immigration consequences upon a defendant's decision to plead guilty — the specific issue on which defense counsel performed deficiently in *Padilla* — is so great that the Federal Rules of Criminal Procedure were amended in 2013 to require district judges to inform a defendant that if he is not a U.S. citizen, a guilty plea could result in removal, denial of citizenship, and exclusion from the U.S. in the future. See Rule 11(b)(1)(O).

What about the flip side of *Hill* and *Padilla*? What about a case in which the defendant, due to allegedly poor advice from his defense lawyer, *rejects* a favorable plea bargain offered by the prosecution and then later gets convicted, either after a trial or pursuant to a subsequent (but less favorable) plea bargain? Can this be a basis for a successful *Strickland* claim of ineffective assistance of counsel?

Lower courts split on this issue for many years. In 2012, the Supreme Court finally weighed in on the issue when it decided the companion cases of Missouri v. Frye and Lafler v. Cooper. Unfortunately, these two decisions raised at least as many new and difficult questions as they answered, and the Court explicitly acknowledged as much. Once again, as with Crawford v. Washington (which dramatically altered the application of the Confrontation Clause to hearsay evidence, see Chapter 14) and Apprendi v. New Jersey (which dramatically changed the constitutional rules applicable to criminal sentencing, see Chapter 15), we face an extended period of uncertainty and instability in constitutional criminal procedure law, as lower courts struggle to respond and adapt to *Frye* and *Cooper*.

In reading these two companion cases, it is important to understand that—notwithstanding the pagination of the two cases—the Court majority treated *Frye* as the lead case, and then treated *Cooper* as a further iteration of the ruling in *Frye*. However, Justice Scalia—author of the lead dissents in both cases—treated them in the opposite order. Thus, Justice Scalia's principal dissent appears in the *Cooper* case, and his *Frye* dissent incorporates and builds upon his *Cooper* dissent. Given this anomaly, we strongly suggest reading the opinions in the following order: (1) the *Frye* majority opinion; (2) the *Cooper* majority opinion; (3) Justice Scalia's *Cooper* dissent; (4) Justice Alito's *Cooper* dissent; and, finally, (5) Justice Scalia's *Frye* dissent.

MISSOURI v. FRYE

Certiorari to the Court of Appeals of Missouri, Western District
132 S. Ct. 1399 (2012)

JUSTICE KENNEDY delivered the opinion of the Court.

The Sixth Amendment, applicable to the States by the terms of the Fourteenth Amendment, provides that the accused shall have the assistance of counsel in all criminal prosecutions. The right to counsel is the right to effective assistance of counsel. See Strickland v. Washington, 466 U.S. 668, 686 (1984). This case arises in the context of claimed ineffective assistance that led to the lapse of a prosecution offer of a plea bargain, a proposal that offered terms more lenient than the terms of the guilty plea entered later. The initial question is whether the constitutional right to counsel extends to the negotiation and consideration of plea offers that lapse or are rejected. If there is a right to effective assistance with respect to those offers, a further question is what a defendant must demonstrate in order to show that prejudice resulted from counsel's deficient performance. Other questions relating to ineffective assistance with respect to plea offers, including the question of proper remedies, are considered in a second case decided today. See Lafler v. Cooper, post.

I

[Here Justice Kennedy described the facts of the *Frye* case: Frye was charged with driving on a revoked license. Because he had three prior convictions for the same offense, he was subject to a felony charge with a possible maximum sentence of four years in prison. The prosecution sent a letter to Frye's defense lawyer, offering two possible plea bargains. One of those offers would have substituted a misdemeanor charge, with a recommendation of a 90-day sentence, for the felony charge. The defense lawyer never told Frye about the plea offers, and the offers expired. A few days before Frye's preliminary hearing, he was once again arrested for driving on a revoked license. Frye then pleaded guilty, with no plea bargain, to the original felony charge and was sentenced to three years in prison. In a state post-conviction motion, Frye alleged that his defense lawyer rendered him constitutionally ineffective assistance of counsel. Frye testified that he would have accepted the plea bargain to the misdemeanor charge if he had been told about it. The post-conviction court denied Frye's motion, but the Missouri Court of Appeals reversed, finding that Frye satisfied both the performance and prejudice prongs of *Strickland*.—EDS.]

II

A

It is well settled that the right to the effective assistance of counsel applies to certain steps before trial. . . .

With respect to the right to effective counsel in plea negotiations, a proper beginning point is to discuss two cases from this Court considering the role of counsel in advising a client about a plea offer and an ensuing guilty plea: Hill v. Lockhart, 474 U.S. 52 (1985); and Padilla v. Kentucky, 559 U.S. 356 (2010).

Hill established that claims of ineffective assistance of counsel in the plea bargain context are governed by the two-part test set forth in *Strickland.* See *Hill,* supra, at 57. As noted above, in Frye's case, the Missouri Court of Appeals, applying the two part test of *Strickland,* determined first that defense counsel had been ineffective and second that there was resulting prejudice.

. . . In *Padilla,* the Court . . . made clear that "the negotiation of a plea bargain is a critical phase of litigation for purposes of the Sixth Amendment right to effective assistance of counsel." 559 U.S., at ___. It also rejected the argument made by petitioner in this case that a knowing and voluntary plea supersedes errors by defense counsel. . . .

In the case now before the Court the State, as petitioner, points out that the legal question presented is different from that in *Hill* and *Padilla.* In those cases the claim was that the prisoner's plea of guilty was invalid because counsel had provided incorrect advice pertinent to the plea. In the instant case, by contrast, the guilty plea that was accepted, and the plea proceedings concerning it in court, were all based on accurate advice and information from counsel. The challenge is not to the advice pertaining to the plea that was accepted but rather to the course of legal representation that preceded it with respect to other potential pleas and plea offers.

To give further support to its contention that the instant case is in a category different from what the Court considered in *Hill* and *Padilla,* the State urges that there is no right to a plea offer or a plea bargain in any event. See Weatherford v. Bursey, 429 U.S. 545, 561 (1977). It claims Frye therefore was not deprived of any legal benefit to which he was entitled. Under this view, any wrongful or mistaken action of counsel with respect to earlier plea offers is beside the point.

The State is correct to point out that *Hill* and *Padilla* concerned whether there was ineffective assistance leading to acceptance of a plea offer, a process involving a formal court appearance with the defendant and all counsel present. Before a guilty plea is entered the defendant's understanding of the plea and its consequences can be established on the record. This affords the State substantial protection against later claims that the plea was the result of inadequate advice. At the plea entry proceedings the trial court and all counsel have the opportunity to establish on the record that the defendant understands the process that led to any offer, the advantages and disadvantages of accepting it, and the sentencing consequences or possibilities that will ensue once a conviction is entered based upon the plea. See, e.g., Fed. Rule Crim. Proc. 11; Mo. Sup. Ct. Rule 24.02 (2004). *Hill* and *Padilla* both illustrate that, nevertheless, there may be instances when claims of ineffective assistance can arise after the conviction is entered. Still, the State, and the trial court itself, have had a substantial opportunity to guard against this contingency by establishing at the plea entry proceeding that the defendant has been given proper advice or, if the advice received appears to have been inadequate, to remedy that deficiency before the plea is accepted and the conviction entered.

When a plea offer has lapsed or been rejected, however, no formal court proceedings are involved. This underscores that the plea-bargaining process is often in flux, with no clear standards or timelines and with no judicial supervision of the discussions between prosecution and defense. Indeed, discussions between client and defense counsel are privileged. So the prosecution has little or no notice if something may be amiss and perhaps no capacity to intervene in any event. And, as noted, the State insists there is no right to receive a plea offer. For all these reasons, the State contends, it is unfair to subject it to the consequences of defense counsel's inadequacies, especially when the opportunities for a full and fair trial, or, as here, for a later guilty plea albeit on less favorable terms, are preserved.

The State's contentions are neither illogical nor without some persuasive force, yet they do not suffice to overcome a simple reality. Ninety-seven percent of federal convictions and ninety-four percent of state convictions are the result of guilty pleas. See Dept. of Justice, Bureau of Justice Statistics, Sourcebook of Criminal Justice Statistics Online, Table 5.22.2009, http://www.albany.edu/sourcebook/pdf/t5222009.pdf (all Internet materials as visited Mar. 1, 2012, and available in Clerk of Court's case file); Dept. of Justice, Bureau of Justice Statistics, S. Rosenmerkel, M. Durose, & D. Farole, Felony Sentences in State Courts, 2006-Statistical Tables, p. 1 (NCJ226846, rev. Nov. 2010), http://bjs.ojp.usdoj.gov/content/pub/pdf/fssc06st.pdf; *Padilla*, supra, at ___, (recognizing pleas account for nearly 95% of all criminal convictions). The reality is that plea bargains have become so central to the administration of the criminal justice system that defense counsel have responsibilities in the plea bargain process, responsibilities that must be met to render the adequate assistance of counsel that the Sixth Amendment requires in the criminal process at critical stages. Because ours "is for the most part a system of pleas, not a system of trials," *Lafler*, post, at 11, it is insufficient simply to point to the guarantee of a fair trial as a backstop that inoculates any errors in the pretrial process. "To a large extent . . . horse trading [between prosecutor and defense counsel] determines who goes to jail and for how long. That is what plea bargaining is. It is not some adjunct to the criminal justice system; it *is* the criminal justice system." Scott & Stuntz, Plea Bargaining as Contract, 101 Yale L. J. 1909, 1912 (1992). See also Barkow, Separation of Powers and the Criminal Law, 58 Stan. L. Rev. 989, 1034 (2006) ("[Defendants] who do take their case to trial and lose receive longer sentences than even Congress or the prosecutor might think appropriate, because the longer sentences exist on the books largely for bargaining purposes. This often results in individuals who accept a plea bargain receiving shorter sentences than other individuals who are less morally culpable but take a chance and go to trial" (footnote omitted)). In today's criminal justice system, therefore, the negotiation of a plea bargain, rather than the unfolding of a trial, is almost always the critical point for a defendant.

To note the prevalence of plea bargaining is not to criticize it. The potential to conserve valuable prosecutorial resources and for defendants to admit their crimes and receive more favorable terms at sentencing means that a plea agreement can benefit both parties. In order that these benefits can be realized, however, criminal defendants require effective counsel during plea negotiations. "Anything less . . . might deny a defendant 'effective representation by counsel at the only stage when legal aid and advice would help him.' " *Massiah*, 377 U.S., at 204 (quoting Spano v. New York, 360 U.S. 315, 326 (1959) (Douglas, J., concurring)).

B

The inquiry then becomes how to define the duty and responsibilities of defense counsel in the plea bargain process. This is a difficult question. "The art of negotiation is at least as nuanced as the art of trial advocacy and it presents questions farther removed from immediate judicial supervision." Premo v. Moore, 562 U.S. ___, ___ (2011). Bargaining is, by its nature, defined to a substantial degree by personal style. The alternative courses and tactics in negotiation are so individual that it may be neither prudent nor practicable to try to elaborate or define detailed standards for the proper discharge of defense counsel's participation in the process. Cf. ibid.

This case presents neither the necessity nor the occasion to define the duties of defense counsel in those respects, however. Here the question is whether defense counsel has the duty to communicate the terms of a formal offer to accept a plea on terms and conditions that may result in a lesser sentence, a conviction on lesser charges, or both.

This Court now holds that, as a general rule, defense counsel has the duty to communicate formal offers from the prosecution to accept a plea on terms and conditions that may be favorable to the accused. Any exceptions to that rule need not be explored here, for the offer was a formal one with a fixed expiration date. When defense counsel allowed the offer to expire without advising the defendant or allowing him to consider it, defense counsel did not render the effective assistance the Constitution requires.

Though the standard for counsel's performance is not determined solely by reference to codified standards of professional practice, these standards can be important guides. The American Bar Association recommends defense counsel "promptly communicate and explain to the defendant all plea offers made by the prosecuting attorney," ABA Standards for Criminal Justice, Pleas of Guilty 14-3.2(a) (3d ed. 1999), and this standard has been adopted by numerous state and federal courts over the last 30 years. . . . The standard for prompt communication and consultation is also set out in state bar professional standards for attorneys. See, e.g., Fla. Rule Regulating Bar 4-1.4 (2008); Ill. Rule Prof. Conduct 1.4 (2011); Kan. Rule Prof. Conduct 1.4 (2010); Ky. Sup. Ct. Rule 3.130, Rule Prof. Conduct 1.4 (2011); Mass. Rule Prof. Conduct 1.4 (2011-2012); Mich. Rule Prof. Conduct 1.4 (2011).

The prosecution and the trial courts may adopt some measures to help ensure against late, frivolous, or fabricated claims after a later, less advantageous plea offer has been accepted or after a trial leading to conviction with resulting harsh consequences. First, the fact of a formal offer means that its terms and its processing can be documented so that what took place in the negotiation process becomes more clear if some later inquiry turns on the conduct of earlier pretrial negotiations. Second, States may elect to follow rules that all offers must be in writing, again to ensure against later misunderstandings or fabricated charges. See N.J. Ct. Rule 3:9-1(b) (2012) ("Any plea offer to be made by the prosecutor shall be in writing and forwarded to the defendant's attorney"). Third, formal offers can be made part of the record at any subsequent plea proceeding or before a trial on the merits, all to ensure that a defendant has been fully advised before those further proceedings commence. At least one State often follows a similar procedure before trial. See Brief for National Association of Criminal Defense Lawyers et al. as Amici Curiae 20 (discussing hearings in Arizona conducted pursuant to State v. Donald, 198 Ariz. 406, 10 P.3d 1193 (App. 2000)). . . .

Here defense counsel did not communicate the formal offers to the defendant. As a result of that deficient performance, the offers lapsed. Under *Strickland*, the question then becomes what, if any, prejudice resulted from the breach of duty.

C

To show prejudice from ineffective assistance of counsel where a plea offer has lapsed or been rejected because of counsel's deficient performance, defendants must demonstrate a reasonable probability they would have accepted the earlier plea offer had they been afforded effective assistance of counsel. Defendants must also demonstrate a reasonable probability the plea would have been entered without the prosecution canceling it or the trial court refusing to accept it, if they had the authority to exercise that discretion under state law. To establish prejudice in this instance, it is necessary to show a reasonable probability that the end result of the criminal process would have been more favorable by reason of a plea to a lesser charge or a sentence of less prison time. Cf. Glover v. United States, 531 U.S. 198, 203 (2001) ("[A]ny amount of [additional] jail time has Sixth Amendment significance").

This application of *Strickland* to the instances of an uncommunicated, lapsed plea does nothing to alter the standard laid out in *Hill*. In cases where a defendant complains that ineffective assistance led him to accept a plea offer as opposed to proceeding to trial, the defendant will have to show "a reasonable probability that, but for counsel's errors, he would not have pleaded guilty and would have insisted on going to trial." *Hill*, 474 U.S., at 59. *Hill* was correctly decided and applies in the context in which it arose. *Hill* does not, however, provide the sole means for demonstrating prejudice arising from the deficient performance of counsel during plea negotiations. Unlike the defendant in *Hill*, Frye argues that with effective assistance he would have accepted an earlier plea offer (limiting his sentence to one year in prison) as opposed to entering an open plea (exposing him to a maximum sentence of four years' imprisonment). In a case, such as this, where a defendant pleads guilty to less favorable terms and claims that ineffective assistance of counsel caused him to miss out on a more favorable earlier plea offer, *Strickland*'s inquiry into whether "the result of the proceeding would have been different," 466 U.S., at 694, requires looking not at whether the defendant would have proceeded to trial absent ineffective assistance but whether he would have accepted the offer to plead pursuant to the terms earlier proposed.

In order to complete a showing of *Strickland* prejudice, defendants who have shown a reasonable probability they would have accepted the earlier plea offer must also show that, if the prosecution had the discretion to cancel it or if the trial court had the discretion to refuse to accept it, there is a reasonable probability neither the prosecution nor the trial court would have prevented the offer from being accepted or implemented. This further showing is of particular importance because a defendant has no right to be offered a plea, see *Weatherford*, 429 U.S., at 561, nor a federal right that the judge accept it, Santobello v. New York, 404 U.S. 257, 262 (1971). In at least some States, including Missouri, it appears the prosecution has some discretion to cancel a plea agreement to which the defendant has agreed, see, e.g., 311 S.W.3d, at 359 (case below); Ariz. Rule Crim. Proc. 17.4(b) (Supp. 2011). The Federal Rules, some state rules including in Missouri, and this Court's precedents give trial courts some leeway to accept or reject plea agreements, see Fed. Rule Crim.

Proc. 11(c)(3); see Mo. Sup. Ct. Rule 24.02(d)(4); Boykin v. Alabama, 395 U.S. 238, 243-244 (1969). It can be assumed that in most jurisdictions prosecutors and judges are familiar with the boundaries of acceptable plea bargains and sentences. So in most instances it should not be difficult to make an objective assessment as to whether or not a particular fact or intervening circumstance would suffice, in the normal course, to cause prosecutorial withdrawal or judicial nonapproval of a plea bargain. The determination that there is or is not a reasonable probability that the outcome of the proceeding would have been different absent counsel's errors can be conducted within that framework.

III

These standards must be applied to the instant case. As regards the deficient performance prong of *Strickland*, the Court of Appeals found the "record is void of *any* evidence of any effort by trial counsel to communicate the [formal] Offer to Frye during the Offer window, let alone any evidence that Frye's conduct interfered with trial counsel's ability to do so." 311 S.W.3d, at 356. On this record, it is evident that Frye's attorney did not make a meaningful attempt to inform the defendant of a written plea offer before the offer expired. See supra, at 2. The Missouri Court of Appeals was correct that "counsel's representation fell below an objective standard of reasonableness." *Strickland*, supra, at 688.

The Court of Appeals erred, however, in articulating the precise standard for prejudice in this context. As noted, a defendant in Frye's position must show not only a reasonable probability that he would have accepted the lapsed plea but also a reasonable probability that the prosecution would have adhered to the agreement and that it would have been accepted by the trial court. Frye can show he would have accepted the offer, but there is strong reason to doubt the prosecution and the trial court would have permitted the plea bargain to become final.

There appears to be a reasonable probability Frye would have accepted the prosecutor's original offer of a plea bargain if the offer had been communicated to him, because he pleaded guilty to a more serious charge, with no promise of a sentencing recommendation from the prosecutor. It may be that in some cases defendants must show more than just a guilty plea to a charge or sentence harsher than the original offer. For example, revelations between plea offers about the strength of the prosecution's case may make a late decision to plead guilty insufficient to demonstrate, without further evidence, that the defendant would have pleaded guilty to an earlier, more generous plea offer if his counsel had reported it to him. Here, however, that is not the case. The Court of Appeals did not err in finding Frye's acceptance of the less favorable plea offer indicated that he would have accepted the earlier (and more favorable) offer had he been apprised of it; and there is no need to address here the showings that might be required in other cases.

The Court of Appeals failed, however, to require Frye to show that the first plea offer, if accepted by Frye, would have been adhered to by the prosecution and accepted by the trial court. Whether the prosecution and trial court are required to do so is a matter of state law, and it is not the place of this Court to settle those matters. The Court has established the minimum requirements of the Sixth Amendment as interpreted in *Strickland*, and States have the discretion to add procedural protections under state law if they choose. A State may choose to preclude the prosecution from withdrawing a plea offer once it has been accepted or perhaps to preclude a trial court from rejecting a plea bargain. In Missouri, it appears "a plea offer once accepted by the defendant can be withdrawn without recourse" by the prosecution. 311 S.W.3d, at 359. The extent of the trial court's discretion in Missouri to reject a plea agreement appears to be in some doubt. Compare id., at 360, with Mo. Sup. Ct. Rule 24.02(d)(4).

We remand for the Missouri Court of Appeals to consider these state-law questions, because they bear on the federal question of *Strickland* prejudice. If, as the Missouri court stated here, the prosecutor could have canceled the plea agreement, and if Frye fails to show a reasonable probability the prosecutor would have adhered to the agreement, there is no *Strickland* prejudice. Likewise, if the trial court could have refused to accept the plea agreement, and if Frye fails to show a reasonable probability the trial court would have accepted the plea, there is no *Strickland* prejudice. In this case, given Frye's new offense for driving without a license on December 30, 2007, there is reason to doubt that the prosecution would have adhered to the agreement or that the trial court would have accepted it at the January 4, 2008, hearing, unless they were required by state law to do so.

It is appropriate to allow the Missouri Court of Appeals to address this question in the first instance. The judgment of the Missouri Court of Appeals is vacated, and the case is remanded for further proceedings not inconsistent with this opinion.

JUSTICE SCALIA, with whom CHIEF JUSTICE ROBERTS, JUSTICE THOMAS, and JUSTICE ALITO join, dissenting.

This is a companion case to Lafler v. Cooper. The principal difference between the cases is that the fairness of the defendant's conviction in *Lafler* was established by a full trial and jury verdict, whereas Frye's conviction here was established by his own admission of guilt, received by the court after the usual colloquy that assured it was voluntary and truthful. In *Lafler* all that could be said (and as I discuss there it was quite enough) is that the fairness of the conviction was clear, though a unanimous jury finding beyond a reasonable doubt can sometimes be wrong. Here it can be said not only that the process was fair, but that the defendant acknowledged the correctness of his conviction. Thus, as far as the reasons for my dissent are concerned, this is an a fortiori case. I will not repeat here the constitutional points that I discuss at length in *Lafler*, but I will briefly apply those points to the facts here and comment upon a few statements in the Court's analysis.

Galin Frye's attorney failed to inform him about a plea offer, and Frye ultimately pleaded guilty without the benefit of a deal. Counsel's mistake did not deprive Frye of any substantive or procedural right; only of the opportunity to accept a plea bargain to which he had no entitlement in the first place. So little entitlement that, had he known of and accepted the bargain, the prosecution would have been able to withdraw it right up to the point that his guilty plea pursuant to the bargain was accepted. See 311 S.W.3d 350, 359, and n. 4 (Mo. App. 2010).

The Court acknowledges, moreover, that Frye's conviction was untainted by attorney error: "[T]he guilty plea that was accepted, and the plea proceedings concerning it in court, were all based on accurate advice and information from counsel." Given the "ultimate focus" of our ineffective-assistance cases on "the fundamental fairness of the proceeding whose result is being challenged," Strickland v. Washington, 466 U.S. 668, 696 (1984), that should be the end of the matter. Instead, here, as in *Lafler*, the Court mechanically applies an outcome-based test for prejudice, and mistakes the possibility of a different result for constitutional injustice. As

I explain in *Lafler* (dissenting opinion), that approach is contrary to our precedents on the right to effective counsel, and for good reason.

The Court announces its holding that "as a general rule, defense counsel has the duty to communicate formal offers from the prosecution" as though that resolves a disputed point; in reality, however, neither the State nor the Solicitor General argued that counsel's performance here was adequate. The only issue was whether the inadequacy deprived Frye of his constitutional right to a fair trial. In other cases, however, it will not be so clear that counsel's plea-bargaining skills, which must now meet a constitutional minimum, are adequate. "[H]ow to define the duty and responsibilities of defense counsel in the plea bargain process," the Court acknowledges, "is a difficult question," since "[b]argaining is, by its nature, defined to a substantial degree by personal style." Indeed. What if an attorney's "personal style" is to establish a reputation as a hard bargainer by, for example, advising clients to proceed to trial rather than accept anything but the most favorable plea offers? It seems inconceivable that a lawyer could compromise his client's *constitutional rights* so that he can secure better deals for other clients in the future; does a hard-bargaining "personal style" now violate the Sixth Amendment? The Court ignores such difficulties, however, since "[t]his case presents neither the necessity nor the occasion to define the duties of defense counsel in those respects." Perhaps not. But it does present the necessity of confronting the serious difficulties that will be created by constitutionalization of the plea-bargaining process. It will not do simply to announce that they will be solved in the sweet by-and-by.

While the inadequacy of counsel's performance in this case is clear enough, whether it was prejudicial (in the sense that the Court's new version of *Strickland* requires) is not. The Court's description of how that question is to be answered on remand is alone enough to show how unwise it is to constitutionalize the plea-bargaining process. Prejudice is to be determined, the Court tells us, by a process of retrospective crystal-ball gazing posing as legal analysis. First of all, of course, we must estimate whether the defendant *would have accepted* the earlier plea bargain. Here that seems an easy question, but as the Court acknowledges, ante, at 14, it will not always be. Next, since Missouri, like other States, permits accepted plea offers to be withdrawn by the prosecution (a reality which alone should suffice, one would think, to demonstrate that Frye had no entitlement to the plea bargain), we must estimate whether the prosecution *would have withdrawn* the plea offer. And finally, we must estimate whether the trial court *would have approved* the plea agreement. These last two estimations may seem easy in the present case, since Frye committed a new infraction before the hearing at which the agreement would have been presented; but they assuredly will not be easy in the mine run of cases.

The Court says "[i]t can be assumed that in most jurisdictions prosecutors and judges are familiar with the boundaries of acceptable plea bargains and sentences." Assuredly it can, just as it can be assumed that the sun rises in the west; but I know of no basis for the assumption. Virtually no cases deal with the standards for a prosecutor's withdrawal from a plea agreement beyond stating the general rule that a prosecutor may withdraw any time prior to, but not after, the entry of a guilty plea or other action constituting detrimental reliance on the defendant's part. See, e.g., United States v. Kuchinski, 469 F.3d 853, 857-858 (CA9 2006). And cases addressing trial courts' authority to accept or reject plea agreements almost universally observe that a trial court enjoys broad discretion in this regard. See, e.g., Missouri v. Banks, 135 S.W.3d 497, 500 (Mo. App. 2004) (trial court abuses its discretion in rejecting a plea only if the decision "is so arbitrary and unreasonable that it shocks the sense of justice and indicates a lack of careful consideration" (internal quotation marks omitted)). Of course after today's opinions there will be cases galore, so the Court's *assumption* would better be cast as an optimistic *prediction* of the certainty that will emerge, many years hence, from our newly created constitutional field of plea-bargaining law. Whatever the "boundaries" ultimately devised (if that were possible), a vast amount of discretion will still remain, and it is extraordinary to make a defendant's constitutional rights depend upon a series of retrospective mind-readings as to how that discretion, in prosecutors and trial judges, *would have been* exercised.

The plea-bargaining process is a subject worthy of regulation, since it is the means by which most criminal convictions are obtained. It happens not to be, however, a subject covered by the Sixth Amendment, which is concerned not with the fairness of bargaining but with the fairness of conviction. "The Constitution . . . is not an all-purpose tool for judicial construction of a perfect world; and when we ignore its text in order to make it that, we often find ourselves swinging a sledge where a tack hammer is needed." Padilla v. Kentucky, 559 U.S. 356, ___ (2010) (Scalia, J., dissenting). In this case and its companion, the Court's sledge may require the reversal of perfectly valid, eminently just, convictions. A legislature could solve the problems presented by these cases in a much more precise and efficient manner. It might begin, for example, by penalizing the attorneys who made such grievous errors. That type of sub-constitutional remedy is not available to the Court, which is limited to penalizing (almost) everyone else by reversing valid convictions or sentences. Because that result is inconsistent with the Sixth Amendment and decades of our precedent, I respectfully dissent.

LAFLER v. COOPER

Certiorari to the United States Court of Appeals for the Sixth Circuit
132 S. Ct. 1376 (2012)

JUSTICE KENNEDY delivered the opinion of the Court.

In this case, as in Missouri v. Frye, also decided today, a criminal defendant seeks a remedy when inadequate assistance of counsel caused nonacceptance of a plea offer and further proceedings led to a less favorable outcome. In *Frye*, defense counsel did not inform the defendant of the plea offer; and after the offer lapsed the defendant still pleaded guilty, but on more severe terms. Here, the favorable plea offer was reported to the client but, on advice of counsel, was rejected. In *Frye* there was a later guilty plea. Here, after the plea offer had been rejected, there was a full and fair trial before a jury. After a guilty verdict, the defendant received a sentence harsher than that offered in the rejected plea bargain. The instant case comes to the Court with the concession that counsel's advice with respect to the plea offer fell below the standard of adequate assistance of counsel guaranteed by the Sixth Amendment, applicable to the States through the Fourteenth Amendment.

I

[Here Justice Kennedy described the facts of the *Cooper* case: Cooper was charged with assault with intent to murder, along with three other offenses. The prosecution offered to dismiss two of the charges, and to recommend a sentence of 51 to 85 months in prison on the remaining two charges, in exchange for a guilty plea. Cooper communicated to the trial judge his willingness to accept the plea offer and admit his guilt. But he ultimately rejected the plea offer, allegedly because his defense counsel advised him that the prosecution would not be able to prove his intent to kill because the victim had been shot below the waist. At trial, Cooper was convicted on all counts and received a mandatory minimum sentence of 185 to 360 months in prison. In a post-conviction motion, Cooper alleged ineffective assistance of counsel in connection with his attorney's advice to reject the plea offer. The post-conviction court rejected the claim, and the Michigan Court of Appeals affirmed. Cooper then filed a federal habeas corpus petition raising the same claim of ineffective assistance. The federal district court found ineffective assistance, conditionally granted the writ of habeas corpus, and ordered specific performance of the original plea offer. The Sixth Circuit affirmed. — EDS.]

II

A

Defendants have a Sixth Amendment right to counsel, a right that extends to the plea-bargaining process. *Frye,* ante, at 8; see also Padilla v. Kentucky, 559 U.S. 356, ___ (2010); *Hill,* supra, at 57. During plea negotiations defendants are "entitled to the effective assistance of competent counsel." McMann v. Richardson, 397 U.S. 759, 771 (1970). In *Hill,* the Court held "the two part Strickland v. Washington test applies to challenges to guilty pleas based on ineffective assistance of counsel." 474 U.S., at 58. The performance prong of *Strickland* requires a defendant to show " 'that counsel's representation fell below an objective standard of reasonableness.' " 474 U.S., at 57 (quoting *Strickland,* 466 U.S., at 688). In this case all parties agree the performance of respondent's counsel was deficient when he advised respondent to reject the plea offer on the grounds he could not be convicted at trial. In light of this concession, it is unnecessary for this Court to explore the issue.

The question for this Court is how to apply *Strickland*'s prejudice test where ineffective assistance results in a rejection of the plea offer and the defendant is convicted at the ensuing trial.

B

To establish *Strickland* prejudice a defendant must "show that there is a reasonable probability that, but for counsel's unprofessional errors, the result of the proceeding would have been different." Id., at 694. In the context of pleas a defendant must show the outcome of the plea process would have been different with competent advice. See *Frye,* ante (noting that *Strickland*'s inquiry, as applied to advice with respect to plea bargains, turns on "whether 'the result of the proceeding would have been different' " (quoting *Strickland,* supra, at 694)); see also *Hill,* 474 U.S., at 59 ("The . . . 'prejudice,' requirement . . . focuses on whether counsel's constitutionally ineffective performance affected the outcome of the plea process"). In *Hill,* when evaluating the petitioner's claim that ineffective assistance led to the improvident acceptance of a guilty plea, the Court required the petitioner to show "that there is a reasonable probability that, but for counsel's errors, [the defendant] would not have pleaded guilty and would have insisted on going to trial." Ibid.

In contrast to *Hill*, here the ineffective advice led not to an offer's acceptance but to its rejection. Having to stand trial, not choosing to waive it, is the prejudice alleged. In these circumstances a defendant must show that but for the ineffective advice of counsel there is a reasonable probability that the plea offer would have been presented to the court (i.e., that the defendant would have accepted the plea and the prosecution would not have withdrawn it in light of intervening circumstances), that the court would have accepted its terms, and that the conviction or sentence, or both, under the offer's terms would have been less severe than under the judgment and sentence that in fact were imposed. Here, the Court of Appeals for the Sixth Circuit agreed with that test for *Strickland* prejudice in the context of a rejected plea bargain. This is consistent with the test adopted and applied by other appellate courts without demonstrated difficulties or systemic disruptions. . . .

Petitioner and the Solicitor General propose a different, far more narrow, view of the Sixth Amendment. They contend there can be no finding of *Strickland* prejudice arising from plea bargaining if the defendant is later convicted at a fair trial. The three reasons petitioner and the Solicitor General offer for their approach are unpersuasive.

First, petitioner and the Solicitor General claim that the sole purpose of the Sixth Amendment is to protect the right to a fair trial. Errors before trial, they argue, are not cognizable under the Sixth Amendment unless they affect the fairness of the trial itself. See Brief for Petitioner 12-21; Brief for United States as Amicus Curiae 10-12. The Sixth Amendment, however, is not so narrow in its reach. Cf. *Frye*, ante (holding that a defendant can show prejudice under *Strickland* even absent a showing that the deficient performance precluded him from going to trial). The Sixth Amendment requires effective assistance of counsel at critical stages of a criminal proceeding. . . . The constitutional guarantee applies to pretrial critical stages that are part of the whole course of a criminal proceeding, a proceeding in which defendants cannot be presumed to make critical decisions without counsel's advice. This is consistent, too, with the rule that defendants have a right to effective assistance of counsel on appeal, even though that cannot in any way be characterized as part of the trial. . . . The precedents also establish that there exists a right to counsel during sentencing in both noncapital . . . and capital cases. . . . Even though sentencing does not concern the defendant's guilt or innocence, ineffective assistance of counsel during a sentencing hearing can result in *Strickland* prejudice because "any amount of [additional] jail time has Sixth Amendment significance." *Glover*, supra, at 203.

The Court, moreover, has not followed a rigid rule that an otherwise fair trial remedies errors not occurring at the trial itself. It has inquired instead whether the trial cured the particular error at issue. Thus, in Vasquez v. Hillery, 474 U.S. 254 (1986), the deliberate exclusion of all African-Americans from a grand jury was prejudicial because a defendant may have been tried on charges that would not have been brought at all by a properly constituted grand jury. Id., at 263. . . . By contrast, in United States v. Mechanik, 475 U.S. 66 (1986), the complained-of error was a violation of a grand jury rule meant to ensure probable cause existed to believe a defendant was guilty. A subsequent trial, resulting in a verdict of guilt, cured this error. See id., at 72-73.

In the instant case respondent went to trial rather than accept a plea deal, and it is conceded this was the result of ineffective assistance during the plea negotiation process. Respondent received a more severe sentence at trial, one 3½ times more severe than he likely would have received by pleading guilty. Far from curing the error, the trial caused the injury from the error. Even if the trial itself is free from constitutional flaw, the defendant who goes to trial instead of taking a more favorable plea may be prejudiced from either a conviction on more serious counts or the imposition of a more severe sentence.

Second, petitioner claims this Court refined *Strickland*'s prejudice analysis in *Fretwell* to add an additional requirement that the defendant show that ineffective assistance of counsel led to his being denied a substantive or procedural right. The Court has rejected the argument that *Fretwell* modified *Strickland* before and does so again now. See Williams v. Taylor, 529 U.S. 362, 391 (2000) ("The Virginia Supreme Court erred in holding that our decision in Lockhart v. Fretwell, 506 U.S. 364 (1993), modified or in some way supplanted the rule set down in *Strickland*"). . . .

. . . Because the objection upon which his ineffective-assistance-of-counsel claim was premised was meritless, Fretwell could not demonstrate an error entitling him to relief. The case presented the "unusual circumstance where the defendant attempts to demonstrate prejudice based on considerations that, as a matter of law, ought not inform the inquiry." Ibid. (O'Connor, J., concurring). . . .

. . . Here, however, the injured client seeks relief from counsel's failure to meet a valid legal standard, not from counsel's refusal to violate it. He maintains that, absent ineffective counsel, he would have accepted a plea offer for a sentence the prosecution evidently deemed consistent with the sound administration of criminal justice. The favorable sentence that eluded the defendant in the criminal proceeding appears to be the sentence he or others in his position would have received in the ordinary course, absent the failings of counsel. See Bibas, Regulating the Plea-Bargaining Market: From Caveat Emptor to Consumer Protection, 99 Cal. L. Rev. 1117, 1138 (2011) ("The expected posttrial sentence is imposed in only a few percent of cases. It is like the sticker price for cars: only an ignorant, ill-advised consumer would view full price as the norm and anything less a bargain"); see also *Frye*, ante, at 7-8. If a plea bargain has been offered, a defendant has the right to effective assistance of counsel in considering whether to accept it. If that right is denied, prejudice can be shown if loss of the plea opportunity led to a trial resulting in a conviction on more serious charges or the imposition of a more severe sentence.

It is, of course, true that defendants have "no right to be offered a plea . . . nor a federal right that the judge accept it." *Frye*, ante. In the circumstances here, that is beside the point. If no plea offer is made, or a plea deal is accepted by the defendant but rejected by the judge, the issue raised here simply does not arise. Much the same reasoning guides cases that find criminal defendants have a right to effective assistance of counsel in direct appeals even though the Constitution does not require States to provide a system of appellate review at all. See *Evitts*, 469 U.S. 387; see also Douglas v. California, 372 U.S. 353 (1963). As in those cases, "[w]hen a State opts to act in a field where its action has significant discretionary elements, it must nonetheless act in accord with the dictates of the Constitution." *Evitts*, supra, at 401.

Third, petitioner seeks to preserve the conviction obtained by the State by arguing that the purpose of the Sixth Amendment is to ensure "the reliability of [a] conviction following trial." Brief for Petitioner 13. This argument, too, fails to comprehend the full scope of the Sixth Amendment's protections; and it is refuted by precedent. *Strickland* recognized "[t]he benchmark for judging any claim of ineffectiveness must be whether counsel's conduct so undermined the proper functioning of the adversarial process that the trial cannot be relied on as having produced a just result." 466 U.S., at 686. The goal of a just result is not divorced from the reliability of a conviction, see United States v. Cronic, 466 U.S. 648, 658 (1984); but here the question is not the fairness or reliability of the trial but the fairness and regularity of the processes that preceded it, which caused the defendant to lose benefits he would have received in the ordinary course but for counsel's ineffective assistance.

There are instances, furthermore, where a reliable trial does not foreclose relief when counsel has failed to assert rights that may have altered the outcome. In Kimmelman v. Morrison, 477 U.S. 365 (1986), the Court held that an attorney's failure to timely move to suppress evidence during trial could be grounds for federal habeas relief. The Court rejected the suggestion that the "failure to make a timely request for the exclusion of illegally seized evidence" could not be the basis for a Sixth Amendment violation because the evidence "is 'typically reliable and often the most probative information bearing on the guilt or innocence of the defendant.'" Id., at 379 (quoting Stone v. Powell, 428 U.S. 465, 490 (1976)). "The constitutional rights of criminal defendants," the Court observed, "are granted to the innocent and the guilty alike. Consequently, we decline to hold either that the guarantee of effective assistance of counsel belongs solely to the innocent or that it attaches only to matters affecting the determination of actual guilt." 477 U.S., at 380. The same logic applies here. The fact that respondent is guilty does not mean he was not entitled by the Sixth Amendment to effective assistance or that he suffered no prejudice from his attorney's deficient performance during plea bargaining.

In the end, petitioner's three arguments amount to one general contention: A fair trial wipes clean any deficient performance by defense counsel during plea bargaining. That position ignores the reality that criminal justice today is for the most part a system of pleas, not a system of trials. Ninety-seven percent of federal convictions and ninety-four percent of state convictions are the result of guilty pleas. See *Frye*, ante. As explained in *Frye*, the right to adequate assistance of counsel cannot be defined or enforced without taking account of the central role plea bargaining plays in securing convictions and determining sentences. Ibid. ("[I]t is insufficient simply to point to the guarantee of a fair trial as a backstop that inoculates any errors in the pretrial process").

C

Even if a defendant shows ineffective assistance of counsel has caused the rejection of a plea leading to a trial and a more severe sentence, there is the question of what constitutes an appropriate remedy. That question must now be addressed.

Sixth Amendment remedies should be "tailored to the injury suffered from the constitutional violation and should not unnecessarily infringe on competing interests." United States v. Morrison, 449 U.S. 361, 364 (1981). Thus, a remedy must "neutralize the taint" of a constitutional violation, id., at 365, while at the same time not grant a windfall to the defendant or needlessly squander the considerable resources the State properly invested in the criminal prosecution. See *Mechanik*, 475 U.S., at 72 ("The reversal of a conviction entails substantial social costs: it forces jurors, witnesses, courts, the prosecution, and the defendants to expend further time, energy, and other resources to repeat a trial that has already once taken place; victims may be asked to relive their disturbing experiences").

The specific injury suffered by defendants who decline a plea offer as a result of ineffective assistance of counsel and then receive a greater sentence as a result of trial can come in at least one of two forms. In some cases, the sole advantage a defendant would have received under the plea is a lesser sentence. This is typically the case when the charges that would have been admitted as part of the plea bargain are the same as the charges the defendant was convicted of after trial. In this situation the court may conduct an evidentiary hearing to determine whether the defendant has shown a reasonable probability that but for counsel's errors he would have accepted the plea. If the showing is made, the court may exercise discretion in determining whether the defendant should receive the term of imprisonment the government offered in the plea, the sentence he received at trial, or something in between.

In some situations it may be that resentencing alone will not be full redress for the constitutional injury. If, for example, an offer was for a guilty plea to a count or counts less serious than the ones for which a defendant was convicted after trial, or if a mandatory sentence confines a judge's sentencing discretion after trial, a resentencing based on the conviction at trial may not suffice. See, e.g., *Williams*, 571 F.3d, at 1088; Riggs v. Fairman, 399 F.3d 1179, 1181 (CA9 2005). In these circumstances, the proper exercise of discretion to remedy the constitutional injury may be to require the prosecution to reoffer the plea proposal. Once this has occurred, the judge can then exercise discretion in deciding whether to vacate the conviction from trial and accept the plea or leave the conviction undisturbed.

In implementing a remedy in both of these situations, the trial court must weigh various factors; and the boundaries of proper discretion need not be defined here. Principles elaborated over time in decisions of state and federal courts, and in statutes and rules, will serve to give more complete guidance as to the factors that should bear upon the exercise of the judge's discretion. At this point, however, it suffices to note two considerations that are of relevance.

First, a court may take account of a defendant's earlier expressed willingness, or unwillingness, to accept responsibility for his or her actions. Second, it is not necessary here to decide as a constitutional rule that a judge is required to prescind (that is to say disregard) any information concerning the crime that was discovered after the plea offer was made. The time continuum makes it difficult to restore the defendant and the prosecution to the precise positions they occupied prior to the rejection of the plea offer, but that baseline can be consulted in finding a remedy that does not require the prosecution to incur the expense of conducting a new trial.

Petitioner argues that implementing a remedy here will open the floodgates to litigation by defendants seeking to unsettle their convictions. Petitioner's concern is misplaced. Courts have recognized claims of this sort for over 30 years, and yet there is no indication that the system is overwhelmed by these types of suits or that defendants are receiving windfalls as a result of strategically timed *Strickland* claims. . . . In addition, the "prosecution and the trial courts may adopt some measures to help ensure against late, frivolous, or fabricated claims after a later, less advantageous plea offer has been accepted or after a trial leading to conviction." *Frye,* ante. This, too, will help ensure against meritless claims.

III

The standards for ineffective assistance of counsel when a defendant rejects a plea offer and goes to trial must now be applied to this case. [Here Justice Kennedy concluded that the instant case was governed by the established legal rule set forth in

Strickland v. Washington, and that the state court did not properly apply *Strickland* to the case, thus permitting a federal habeas court to review the state court's decision and provide appropriate relief. — EDS.]

Respondent has satisfied *Strickland*'s two-part test. Regarding performance, perhaps it could be accepted that it is unclear whether respondent's counsel believed respondent could not be convicted for assault with intent to murder as a matter of law because the shots hit [the victim] below the waist, or whether he simply thought this would be a persuasive argument to make to the jury to show lack of specific intent. And, as the Court of Appeals for the Sixth Circuit suggested, an erroneous strategic prediction about the outcome of a trial is not necessarily deficient performance. Here, however, the fact of deficient performance has been conceded by all parties. The case comes to us on that assumption, so there is no need to address this question.

As to prejudice, respondent has shown that but for counsel's deficient performance there is a reasonable probability he and the trial court would have accepted the guilty plea. See 376 Fed. Appx., at 571-572. In addition, as a result of not accepting the plea and being convicted at trial, respondent received a minimum sentence 3½ times greater than he would have received under the plea. The standard for ineffective assistance under *Strickland* has thus been satisfied.

As a remedy, the District Court ordered specific performance of the original plea agreement. The correct remedy in these circumstances, however, is to order the State to reoffer the plea agreement. Presuming respondent accepts the offer, the state trial court can then exercise its discretion in determining whether to vacate the convictions and resentence respondent pursuant to the plea agreement, to vacate only some of the convictions and resentence respondent accordingly, or to leave the convictions and sentence from trial undisturbed. See Mich. Ct. Rule 6.302(C) (3) (2011) ("If there is a plea agreement and its terms provide for the defendant's plea to be made in exchange for a specific sentence disposition or a prosecutorial sentence recommendation, the court may . . . reject the agreement"). Today's decision leaves open to the trial court how best to exercise that discretion in all the circumstances of the case.

The judgment of the Court of Appeals for the Sixth Circuit is vacated, and the case is remanded for further proceedings consistent with this opinion.

JUSTICE SCALIA, with whom JUSTICE THOMAS joins, and with whom CHIEF JUSTICE ROBERTS joins as to all but Part IV, dissenting.

> "If a plea bargain has been offered, a defendant has the right to effective assistance of counsel in considering whether to accept it. If that right is denied, prejudice can be shown if loss of the plea opportunity led to a trial resulting in a conviction on more serious charges or the imposition of a more severe sentence." Ante.

> "The inquiry then becomes how to define the duty and responsibilities of defense counsel in the plea bargain process. This is a difficult question. . . . Bargaining is, by its nature, defined to a substantial degree by personal style. . . . This case presents neither the necessity nor the occasion to define the duties of defense counsel in those respects. . . ." Missouri v. Frye, ante.

With those words from this and the companion case, the Court today opens a whole new field of constitutionalized criminal procedure: plea-bargaining law. The ordinary criminal process has become too long, too expensive, and unpredictable, in no small part as a consequence of an intricate federal Code of Criminal Procedure imposed on the States by this Court in pursuit of perfect justice. See Friendly, The Bill of Rights as a Code of Criminal Procedure, 53 Cal. L. Rev. 929 (1965). The Court now moves to bring perfection to the alternative in which prosecutors and defendants have sought relief. Today's opinions deal with only two aspects of counsel's plea-bargaining inadequacy, and leave other aspects (who knows what they might be?) to be worked out in further constitutional litigation that will burden the criminal process. And it would be foolish to think that "constitutional" rules governing *counsel's* behavior will not be followed by rules governing the *prosecution's* behavior in the plea-bargaining process that the Court today announces "'*is* the criminal justice system,'" *Frye*, ante (quoting approvingly from Scott & Stuntz, Plea Bargaining as Contract, 101 Yale L.J. 1909, 1912 (1992) (hereinafter Scott)). Is it constitutional, for example, for the prosecution to withdraw a plea offer that has already been accepted? Or to withdraw an offer before the defense has had adequate time to consider and accept it? Or to make no plea offer at all, even though its case is weak — thereby excluding the defendant from "the criminal justice system"?

Anthony Cooper received a full and fair trial, was found guilty of all charges by a unanimous jury, and was given the sentence that the law prescribed. The Court nonetheless concludes that Cooper is entitled to some sort of habeas corpus relief (perhaps) because his attorney's allegedly incompetent advice regarding a plea offer *caused* him to receive a full and fair trial. That conclusion is foreclosed by our precedents. Even if it were not foreclosed, the constitutional right to effective plea-bargainers that it establishes is at least a new rule of law, which does not undermine the Michigan Court of Appeals' decision and therefore cannot serve as the basis for habeas relief. And the remedy the Court announces — namely, whatever the state trial court in its discretion prescribes, down to and including no remedy at all — is unheard-of and quite absurd for violation of a constitutional right. I respectfully dissent.

I

This case and its companion, Missouri v. Frye, raise relatively straightforward questions about the scope of the right to effective assistance of counsel. Our case law originally derived that right from the Due Process Clause, and its guarantee of a fair trial, see United States v. Gonzalez-Lopez, 548 U.S. 140, 147 (2006), but the seminal case of Strickland v. Washington, 466 U.S. 668 (1984), located the right within the Sixth Amendment. As the Court notes, the right to counsel does not begin at trial. It extends to "any stage of the prosecution, formal or informal, in court or out, where counsel's absence might derogate from the accused's right to a fair trial." United States v. Wade, 388 U.S. 218, 226 (1967). Applying that principle, we held that the "entry of a guilty plea, whether to a misdemeanor or a felony charge, ranks as a 'critical stage' at which the right to counsel adheres." Iowa v. Tovar, 541 U.S. 77, 81 (2004); see also Hill v. Lockhart, 474 U.S. 52, 58 (1985). And it follows from this that acceptance of a plea offer is a critical stage. That, and nothing more, is the point of the Court's observation in Padilla v. Kentucky, 559 U.S. 356, ___ (2010), that "the negotiation of a plea bargain is a critical phase of litigation for purposes of the Sixth Amendment right to effective assistance of counsel." The defendant in *Padilla* had accepted the plea bargain and pleaded guilty, abandoning his right to a fair trial; he was entitled to advice of competent counsel before he did so. The Court has never held that the rule articulated in *Padilla, Tovar,* and *Hill* extends to all aspects of plea negotiations, requiring not just advice of competent counsel before the defendant accepts a plea bargain and pleads guilty, but also the advice of competent counsel before the defendant rejects a plea bargain and stands on his constitutional right to a fair trial. The latter is a vast departure from our past cases, protecting not just the constitutionally prescribed right to a fair adjudication of guilt and punishment, but a judicially invented right to effective plea bargaining.

It is also apparent from *Strickland* that bad plea bargaining has nothing to do with ineffective assistance of counsel in the constitutional sense. *Strickland* explained that "[i]n giving meaning to the requirement [of effective assistance], . . . we must take its purpose—to ensure a fair trial—as the guide." 466 U.S., at 686. Since "the right to the effective assistance of counsel is recognized not for its own sake, but because of the effect it has on the ability of the accused to receive a fair trial," United States v. Cronic, 466 U.S. 648, 658 (1984), the "benchmark" inquiry in evaluating any claim of ineffective assistance is whether counsel's performance "so undermined the proper functioning of the adversarial process" that it failed to produce a reliably "just result." *Strickland,* 466 U.S., at 686. That is what *Strickland*'s requirement of "prejudice" consists of: Because the right to effective assistance has as its purpose the assurance of a fair trial, the right is not infringed unless counsel's mistakes call into question the basic justice of a defendant's conviction or sentence. That has been, until today, entirely clear. A defendant must show "that counsel's errors were so serious as to deprive the defendant of a fair trial, a trial whose result is reliable." Id., at 687. See also *Gonzalez-Lopez,* supra, at 147. Impairment of fair trial is how we distinguish between unfortunate attorney error and error of constitutional significance.[1]

To be sure, *Strickland* stated a rule of thumb for measuring prejudice which, applied blindly and out of context, could support the Court's holding today. . . . *Strickland* itself cautioned, however, that its test was not to be applied in a mechanical fashion, and that courts were not to divert their "ultimate focus" from "the fundamental fairness of the proceeding whose result is being challenged." Id., at 696. And until today we have followed that course. . . .

Those precedents leave no doubt about the answer to the question presented here. As the Court itself observes, a criminal defendant has no right to a plea bargain. "[T]here is no constitutional right to plea bargain; the prosecutor need not do so if he prefers to go to trial." Weatherford v. Bursey, 429 U.S. 545, 561 (1977). Counsel's mistakes in this case thus did not "deprive the defendant of a substantive or procedural right to which the law entitles him," Williams [v. Taylor, 529 U.S. 362,] 393 [(2000)]. Far from being "beside the point," ante, at 9, that is critical to correct application of our precedents. Like [Lockhart v.] Fretwell, [506 U.S. 364 (1993),] this case "concerns the unusual circumstance where the defendant attempts to demonstrate prejudice based on considerations that, as a matter of law, ought not

---

1. Rather than addressing the constitutional origins of the right to effective counsel, the Court responds to the broader claim (raised by no one) that "the sole purpose of the Sixth Amendment is to protect the right to a fair trial." . . . To destroy that straw man, the Court cites cases in which violations of rights other than the right to effective counsel—and, perplexingly, even rights found outside the Sixth Amendment and the Constitution entirely—were not cured by a subsequent trial. . . . Unlike the right to effective counsel, no showing of prejudice is required to make violations of the rights at issue in [such cases] complete. . . . Those cases are thus irrelevant to the question presented here, which is whether a defendant can establish prejudice under Strickland v. Washington, 466 U.S. 668 (1984), while conceding the fairness of his conviction, sentence, and appeal.

inform the inquiry," 506 U.S., at 373 (O'Connor, J., concurring); he claims "that he might have been denied 'a right the law simply does not recognize,'" id., at 375 (same). *Strickland, Fretwell,* and *Williams* all instruct that the pure outcome-based test on which the Court relies is an erroneous measure of cognizable prejudice. In ignoring *Strickland's* "ultimate focus . . . on the fundamental fairness of the proceeding whose result is being challenged," 466 U.S., at 696, the Court has lost the forest for the trees, leading it to accept what we have previously rejected, the "novel argument that constitutional rights are infringed by trying the defendant rather than accepting his plea of guilty." *Weatherford,* supra, at 561.

II

[Here, Justice Scalia argued that—even if the decision of the Michigan Court of Appeals was incorrect—that decision should not be subject to reversal by a federal court sitting in habeas, because the federal habeas corpus statute permits such a reversal only if the relevant state court decision was "contrary to, or involved an unreasonable application of, clearly established Federal law, as determined by the Supreme Court of the United States." 28 U.S.C. § 2254(d)(1). In Justice Scalia's view, the Michigan Court of Appeals faithfully interpreted and applied *Strickland's* performance and prejudice prongs, and thus its decision should have been insulated from federal habeas reversal.—EDS.]

III

It is impossible to conclude discussion of today's extraordinary opinion without commenting upon the remedy it provides for the unconstitutional conviction. It is a remedy unheard-of in American jurisprudence—and, I would be willing to bet, in the jurisprudence of any other country.

The Court requires Michigan to "reoffer the plea agreement" that was rejected because of bad advice from counsel. Ante, at 16. That would indeed be a powerful remedy—but for the fact that Cooper's acceptance of that reoffered agreement is not conclusive. Astoundingly, "the state trial court can then *exercise its discretion* in determining whether to vacate the convictions and resentence respondent pursuant to the plea agreement, to vacate only some of the convictions and resentence respondent accordingly, *or to leave the convictions and sentence from trial undisturbed."* Ibid. (emphasis added).

Why, one might ask, require a "reoffer" of the plea agreement, and its acceptance by the defendant? If the district court finds (as a necessary element, supposedly, of *Strickland* prejudice) that Cooper *would have accepted* the original offer, and would thereby have avoided trial and conviction, why not skip the reoffer-and-reacceptance minuet and simply leave it to the discretion of the state trial court what the remedy shall be? The answer, of course, is camouflage. Trial courts, after all, *regularly* accept or reject plea agreements, so there seems to be nothing extraordinary about their accepting or rejecting the new one mandated by today's decision. But the acceptance or rejection of a plea agreement that has no status whatever under the United States Constitution is worlds apart from what this is: "discretionary" specification of a remedy for an unconstitutional criminal conviction.

To be sure, the Court asserts that there are "factors" which bear upon (and presumably limit) exercise of this discretion—factors that it is not prepared to specify in full, much less assign some determinative weight. "Principles elaborated over time in decisions of state and federal courts, and in statutes and rules" will (in the Court's rosy view) sort all that out. Ante, at 13. I find it extraordinary that "statutes and rules" can specify the remedy for a criminal defendant's unconstitutional conviction. Or that the remedy for an unconstitutional conviction should *ever* be subject *at all* to a trial judge's discretion. Or, finally, that the remedy could *ever* include no remedy at all.

I suspect that the Court's squeamishness in fashioning a remedy, and the incoherence of what it comes up with, is attributable to its realization, deep down, that there is no real constitutional violation here anyway. The defendant has been fairly tried, lawfully convicted, and properly sentenced, and *any* "remedy" provided for this will do nothing but undo the just results of a fair adversarial process.

IV

In many—perhaps most—countries of the world, American-style plea bargaining is forbidden in cases as serious as this one, even for the purpose of obtaining testimony that enables conviction of a greater malefactor, much less for the purpose of sparing the expense of trial. See, e.g., World Plea Bargaining 344, 363-366 (S. Thaman ed. 2010). In Europe, many countries adhere to what they aptly call the "legality principle" by requiring prosecutors to charge all prosecutable offenses, which is typically incompatible with the practice of charge-bargaining. See, e.g., id., at xxii; Langbein, Land Without Plea Bargaining: How the Germans Do It, 78 Mich. L. Rev. 204, 210-211 (1979) (describing the "Legalitätsprinzip," or rule of compulsory prosecution, in Germany). Such a system reflects an admirable belief that the law is the law, and those who break it should pay the penalty provided.

In the United States, we have plea bargaining aplenty, but until today it has been regarded as a necessary evil. It presents grave risks of prosecutorial overcharging that effectively compels an innocent defendant to avoid massive risk by pleading guilty to a lesser offense; and for guilty defendants it often—perhaps usually —results in a sentence well below what the law prescribes for the actual crime. But even so, we accept plea bargaining because many believe that without it our long and expensive process of criminal trial could not sustain the burden imposed on it, and our system of criminal justice would grind to a halt. See, e.g., Alschuler, Plea Bargaining and Its History, 79 Colum. L. Rev. 1, 38 (1979).

Today, however, the Supreme Court of the United States elevates plea bargaining from a necessary evil to a constitutional entitlement. It is no longer a somewhat embarrassing adjunct to our criminal justice system; rather, as the Court announces in the companion case to this one, " 'it *is* the criminal justice system.' " *Frye*, ante (quoting approvingly from Scott 1912). Thus, even though there is no doubt that the respondent here is guilty of the offense with which he was charged; even though he has received the exorbitant gold standard of American justice—a full-dress criminal trial with its innumerable constitutional and statutory limitations upon the evidence that the prosecution can bring forward, and (in Michigan as in most States) the requirement of a unanimous guilty verdict by impartial jurors; the Court says that his conviction is invalid because he was deprived of his *constitutional entitlement* to plea-bargain.

I am less saddened by the outcome of this case than I am by what it says about this Court's attitude toward criminal justice. The Court today embraces the sporting chance theory of criminal law, in which the State functions like a conscientious casino-operator, giving each player a fair chance to beat the house, that is, to serve less time than the law says he deserves. And when a player is excluded from the tables, his *constitutional rights* have been violated. I do not subscribe to that theory. No one should, least of all the Justices of the Supreme Court.

* * *

Today's decision upends decades of our cases, violates a federal statute, and opens a whole new boutique of constitutional jurisprudence ("plea-bargaining law") without even specifying the remedies the boutique offers. The result in the present case is the undoing of an adjudicatory process that worked *exactly* as it is supposed to. Released felon Anthony Cooper, who shot repeatedly and gravely injured a woman named Kali Mundy, was tried and convicted for his crimes by a jury of his peers, and given a punishment that Michigan's elected representatives have deemed appropriate. Nothing about that result is unfair or unconstitutional. To the contrary, it is wonderfully just, and infinitely superior to the trial-by-bargain that today's opinion affords constitutional status. I respectfully dissent.

JUSTICE ALITO, dissenting
. . . The weakness in the Court's analysis is highlighted by its opaque discussion of the remedy that is appropriate when a plea offer is rejected due to defective legal representation. If a defendant's Sixth Amendment rights are violated when deficient legal advice about a favorable plea offer causes the opportunity for that bargain to be lost, the only logical remedy is to give the defendant the benefit of the favorable deal. But such a remedy would cause serious injustice in many instances, as I believe the Court tacitly recognizes. The Court therefore eschews the only logical remedy and relies on the lower courts to exercise sound discretion in determining what is to be done.

Time will tell how this works out. The Court, for its part, finds it unnecessary to define "the boundaries of proper discretion" in today's opinion. Ante. In my view, requiring the prosecution to renew an old plea offer would represent an abuse of discretion in at least two circumstances: first, when important new information about a defendant's culpability comes to light after the offer is rejected, and, second, when the rejection of the plea offer results in a substantial expenditure of scarce prosecutorial or judicial resources.

The lower court judges who must implement today's holding may—and I hope, will—do so in a way that mitigates its potential to produce unjust results. But I would not depend on these judges to come to the rescue. The Court's interpretation of the Sixth Amendment right to counsel is unsound, and I therefore respectfully dissent.

NOTES AND QUESTIONS

1. Exactly how big of a deal are these two cases? The answer, as suggested by Justice Alito's *Cooper* dissent, may depend heavily on the way that lower courts give additional content to the bare-bones rule of law declared by the Court in *Frye* and *Cooper*.

For example, the Court in these two cases doesn't say very much at all about the performance prong of *Strickland*—in *Frye*, the deficiency of the defense lawyer's performance (i.e., not telling the client at all about two plea offers) was self-evident (even to Justice Scalia), whereas in *Cooper*, the Court was required to assume deficient performance because the state chose not to litigate the issue. In the future, what will constitute deficient performance in connection with plea bargaining?

The Court in *Cooper* hints that the scope of deficient performance in this context might turn out to be relatively narrow. Should it be limited to deficient advice about pure issues of law, or does it also extend to poor advice about matters that might be described as "strategic"? In *Cooper* itself (had the performance issue been litigated), would it have mattered whether Cooper's defense attorney mistakenly believed that state law would bar a finding of "intent to kill" where the victim was shot below the waist (i.e., if he made a pure error of law), or whether he simply believed that no jury would ever be likely to convict on such facts (i.e., if he made a "strategic" blunder)? Can these categories always be distinguished? Keep in mind that in the traditional *Strickland* context of errors committed by defense counsel at trial, characterizing the defense attorney's decision as "strategic" is usually the kiss of death for a *Strickland* claim. As Justice Kennedy notes in *Cooper*, "an erroneous strategic prediction about the outcome of a trial is not necessarily deficient performance."

If the scope of deficient performance, in connection with plea bargaining, is defined narrowly, then *Frye* and *Cooper* may turn out to have much less impact than Justice Scalia (for one) currently fears.

2. Turning to the prejudice prong of *Strickland*: Does it seem strange that the required finding of prejudice in this context must take into account such unknowns as (1) whether the defendant would likely have accepted the plea offer, (2) whether the prosecution would likely have withdrawn the plea offer, and (3) whether the trial judge would likely have accepted the terms of the plea offer? Doesn't this seem much more difficult than what trial judges are required to do in the usual *Strickland* prejudice inquiry (including the Hill v. Lockhart variation), i.e., decide (as they would in any bench trial) whether or not the evidence proves the defendant's guilt? Is it really possible for anyone to "unring the bell" and reconstruct what any of the relevant actors would likely have done in a counter-factual plea scenario like this? In practice, might this mean that trial judges will be likely to find *Strickland* prejudice — or not — based largely on whatever they feel would be an appropriate disposition of the defendant's case, as of the time (most commonly, after the end of the defendant's appeal, pursuant to a motion for postconviction relief) when the ineffective-assistance claim is being reviewed?

3. More generally, how should prejudice be measured in a guilty plea case? The problem with these cases is that *everything* defense counsel does or fails to do has *some* potential effect on the precise contents of the deal that is finally struck. Whenever a defendant pleads guilty pursuant to an agreement that results in a long sentence, won't he always be able to claim that there was a better deal to be made? If so, this likely puts an enormous amount of pressure on the "performance" prong of ineffective assistance analysis in guilty plea cases. Otherwise the ineffective assistance doctrine might become a general regulator of the wisdom of defense attorney behavior in all plea bargaining cases. (Note that this is the reverse of the situation for alleged *trial* ineffectiveness under *Strickland*—where, as we have seen, the "prejudice" prong usually does most of the work.)

That may explain why the Court framed the inquiry in *Hill* as whether, but for counsel's errors, Hill would have declined to plead guilty and insisted on going to trial. Notice what sort of errors tend to satisfy *that* prejudice standard: attorney errors that suggest not only that the defendant would have gone to trial, but that he would have *won* at trial.

4. Finally—and perhaps most interestingly—note the extraordinary nature of the remedial scheme created by Justice Kennedy (albeit a scheme that even he admits will have to evolve, based upon the experience of lower courts). How is a court supposed to decide whether or not a defendant is entitled to the benefit of a forgone plea bargain—especially after trial, when the remedial issue becomes even more convoluted than after a subsequent guilty plea?

What does Justice Kennedy mean when he says that, in cases involving only possible sentencing relief, "the court may exercise discretion in determining whether the defendant should receive the term of imprisonment the government offered in the plea, the sentence he received at trial, or something in between"? Or that, in cases involving possible reduction of charges, "the judge can then exercise discretion in deciding whether to vacate the conviction from trial and accept the plea or leave the conviction undisturbed"? How are judges supposed to "exercise discretion" in such situations, when a defendant has been deprived of a constitutional right?

And to make matters even worse, Justice Kennedy then adds the following: "In implementing a remedy in both of these situations, the trial court must weigh various factors; and the boundaries of proper discretion need not be defined here. Principles elaborated over time in decisions of state and federal courts, and in statutes and rules, will serve to give more complete guidance as to the factors that should bear upon the exercise of the judge's discretion." How would you explain to a lower court judge what these pronouncements mean? Judges across the land undoubtedly are shaking their heads—or pulling out their hair—over such Delphic opaqueness.

4. The Right to Effective Counsel as a Basis for Systemic Reform Litigation

The practical meaning of the right to counsel depends on how indigent defendants are given lawyers and on how those lawyers are paid. There are several different methods. Most densely populated areas use public defender offices. These offices consist of full-time attorneys who do nothing but indigent defense; the offices are usually funded by annual appropriations from local (or, less frequently, state) governments. If the appropriation is low and the number of criminal cases high, the results can be staggering: In 2004, one public defender sought an opinion from the Ethics Advisory Committee of the South Carolina Bar because he was burdened with a crushing caseload of more than 1,000 felonies.[18] Where public defender offices do not exist, indigent defendants are assigned private counsel from a list of those who are willing (however grudgingly) and able to serve. The pay scale is typically low, although there have been significant improvements in many jurisdictions over the past decade or so.

---

18. See Norman Lefstein & Georgia Vagenas, Restraining Excessive Defender Caseloads: The ABA Ethics Committee Requires Action, The Champion, at 16 (Dec. 2006) (available at http://www.abanet. org/legalservices/sclaid/defender/downloads/ABA_ethicsp10-22.pdf).

What is the proper judicial response to inadequate indigent defense services? *Gideon* was a federal mandate imposed by the federal judiciary against reluctant states. Should the federal courts now ratchet up Sixth and Fourteenth Amendment standards to try to force states and localities to provide greater resources for indigent defense, or otherwise to reform their systems of indigent defense representation? Would that work?

Consider the protracted saga of Horace Luckey III. In the late 1980's, Luckey and other plaintiffs (including both indigent individuals who had been prosecuted for crimes and civil-rights organizations) filed a class-action federal civil rights action against the Governor of Georgia and several other state officials, in the U.S. District Court for the Northern District of Georgia, under 42 U.S.C. §1983. The plaintiffs claimed that the Georgia indigent defense system violated the Sixth and Fourteenth Amendments, and sought equitable relief to force the State of Georgia to reform the system. More specifically, the plaintiffs requested:

> (1) a court order providing for an indigent defense system that:
>   (a) furnishes counsel, if requested, at probable cause determinations,
>   (b) furnishes speedy appointment of counsel for critical stages,
>   (c) furnishes adequate services and experts, and
>   (d) furnishes adequate compensation for counsel;
> (2) a court order that "uniform standards be promulgated and adopted governing the representation of indigent consistent with the judgment in this case";
> (3) monitoring of the implementation of those standards; and
> (4) an award of attorney's fees and other proper relief.

The *Luckey* case reached the U.S. Court of Appeals for the Eleventh Circuit *five times* before eventually being dismissed. In *Luckey I*, the circuit court reversed the district court's initial dismissal of the action, finding that the complaint stated a claim upon which relief could be granted and the action was not barred by the Eleventh Amendment. Luckey v. Harris, 860 F.2d 1012 (11th Cir. 1988). But five years (and one Georgia governor) later—after three intervening appellate rulings that addressed various arcane issues of appellate procedure—the circuit court ultimately concluded, in *Luckey V*, that the federal action must be dismissed under the abstention doctrine of Younger v. Harris, 401 U.S. 37 (1971) and O'Shea v. Littleton, 414 U.S. 488 (1974), which holds that "courts of equity should not act, and particularly should not act to restrain a criminal prosecution, when the moving party has an adequate remedy at law and will not suffer irreparable injury if denied equitable relief," *Younger*, 401 U.S., at 43-44. Luckey v. Miller, 976 F.2d 673 (per curiam) (11th Cir. 1992). The appellate court in *Luckey V* adopted the most recent opinion of the district judge, who had explained:

> "In the instant case, . . . a decree of the sort requested by the plaintiffs would, inevitably, interfere with every state criminal proceeding. Moreover, in the instant case, the state courts do have the authority to consider the claims raised by the plaintiffs. . . . Moreover this Court cannot concur in the Plaintiff's characterization of their claims. Although it is true that Plaintiffs do not seek to contest any single criminal conviction nor restrain any individual prosecution, it is nonetheless clear that plaintiff's intend to restrain every indigent prosecution and contest every indigent conviction until the systemic improvements they seek are in place."

The *Luckey* litigation exemplifies the reluctance of contemporary federal courts to use their equitable powers of injunction to require the states to reform their indigent defense representation systems. This reluctance may have more to do with timing than with constitutional principle. The late 1960s and 1970s saw a boom in federal class actions seeking complex injunctions against various government agencies (they became known as "structural injunctions"). Plaintiffs in a number of these cases succeeded—meaning that a number of federal courts issued injunctions that directed government officials to manage their agencies in particular ways; most of those edicts also required the expenditure of large amounts of money. But most of those cases were brought by parents of public-school children seeking the busing of students to achieve racial balance, or by inmates of state prisons or local jails seeking improvements in the conditions of their incarceration. No similar suits were brought at that time by criminal defendants seeking better funding for indigent defense counsel. By the time *those* claims began to arise, in the late 1980s and 1990s, structural injunctions had gone out of fashion; the Supreme Court had cut back on judges' authority to issue broad orders to government agencies—especially when the orders required those agencies to spend large sums of money. For the classic example of this new, more restrictive attitude, see Missouri v. Jenkins, 515 U.S. 70 (1995), where the Court overturned a broad injunctive order aimed at reforming the Kansas City school system. Given that attitude, it is not exactly surprising that Sixth Amendment funding claims have not enjoyed much success in federal court.

In other words, underfunding-of-indigent-defense claims may have simply arrived at the federal courthouse too late. If those claims had arisen in 1970 or 1975, they might have won the day: States might have been required by the federal courts to establish the kinds of institutional arrangements and budget practices that would ensure adequate provision of defense counsel to indigents. But because structural injunctions were tried elsewhere—especially in schools and prisons—and found wanting, contemporary federal courts have been loath to use them to enforce Sixth Amendment rights.

The story in the state courts is more interesting, and recently has become much more optimistic (at least for those who support systemic reform of indigent defense systems). One of the earliest examples of systemic reform litigation was the well-known case of State v. Peart, 621 So. 2d 780 (La. 1993). In *Peart*, the Louisiana Supreme Court concluded that indigent defendants in New Orleans were frequently being deprived of effective assistance of counsel due to the extremely high caseloads that public defenders were required to carry. Id., at 788-790. The court held that, henceforth, defendants in that district would enjoy a rebuttable presumption that counsel was ineffective, at least until the funding problem was rectified. Id., at 790-792. *Peart* was decided under Louisiana law, although the content of Louisiana's requirement of effective assistance was not obviously different from the content of the federal requirement.

For many years, it appeared that *Peart* might be a one-off exception to the general rule that contemporary courts (both state *and* federal) don't like to get involved in systemic reform. But in the last decade or so, such systemic reform litigation has metaphorically exploded across the United States. The next case is an example of this new and important trend.

HURRELL-HARRING v. STATE OF NEW YORK

Court of Appeals of New York
15 N.Y.3d 8; 930 N.E.2d 217 (2010)

CHIEF JUDGE LIPPMAN:

The Sixth Amendment to the United States Constitution guarantees a criminal defendant "the right to . . . have the Assistance of Counsel for his defence," and since Gideon v. Wainwright (372 U.S. 335 [1963]) it has been established that that entitlement may not be effectively denied by the State by reason of a defendant's inability to pay for a lawyer. *Gideon* is not now controversial either as an expression of what the Constitution requires or as an exercise in elemental fair play. Serious questions have, however, arisen in this and other jurisdictions as to whether *Gideon*'s mandate is being met in practice (see e.g. Lavallee v. Justices in Hampden Superior Ct.., 442 Mass. 228, 812 N.E.2d 895 [2004].)

In New York, the Legislature has left the performance of the State's obligation under *Gideon* to the counties, where it is discharged, for the most part, with county resources and according to local rules and practices (see County Law arts. 18-A, 18-B). Plaintiffs in this action, defendants in various criminal prosecutions ongoing at the time of the action's commencement in Washington, Onondaga, Ontario, Schuyler and Suffolk counties, contend that this arrangement, involving what is in essence a costly, largely unfunded and politically unpopular mandate upon local government, has functioned to deprive them and other similarly situated indigent defendants in the aforementioned counties of constitutionally and statutorily guaranteed representational rights. They seek a declaration that their rights and those of the class they seek to represent are being violated and an injunction to avert further abridgment of their right to counsel; they do not seek relief within the criminal cases out of which their claims arise.

This appeal results from dispositions of defendants' motion . . . to dismiss the action as nonjusticiable. Supreme Court denied the motion, but in the decision and order now before us (66 A.D.3d 84, 883 N.Y.S.2d 349 [2009]) the sought relief was granted by the Appellate Division. That court held that there was no cognizable claim for ineffective assistance of counsel other than one seeking postconviction relief, and, relatedly, that violation of a criminal defendant's right to counsel could not be vindicated in a collateral civil proceeding, particularly where the object of the collateral action was to compel an additional allocation of public resources, which the court found to be a properly legislative prerogative. Two Justices dissented. They were of the view that violations of the right to counsel were actionable in contexts other than claims for postconviction relief, including a civil action such as that brought by plaintiffs. While recognizing that choices between competing social priorities are ordinarily for the Legislature, this did not, in the dissenters' judgment, excuse the Judiciary from its obligation to provide a remedy for violations of constitutional rights, especially when the alleged violations were "so interwoven with, and necessarily implicate[d], the proper functioning of the court system itself" (*id.* at 96).

Plaintiffs have appealed as of right from the Appellate Division's order. . . . We now reinstate the action, albeit with some substantial qualifications upon its scope.

Defendants' claim that the action is not justiciable rests principally on two theories: first, that there is no cognizable claim for ineffective assistance of counsel apart from one seeking relief from a conviction, and second, that recognition of a claim for systemic relief of the sort plaintiffs seek will involve the courts in the performance of properly legislative functions, most notably determining how public resources are to be allocated.

The first of these theories is rooted in case law conditioning relief for constitutionally ineffective assistance upon findings that attorney performance, when viewed in its total, case specific aspect, has both fallen below the standard of objective reasonableness (see Strickland v. Washington, 466 U.S. 668, 687-688 [1984]), and resulted in prejudice, either with respect to the outcome of the proceeding or, under this Court's somewhat less outcome oriented standard of "meaningful assistance," to the defendant's right to a fair trial (People v. Benevento, 91 N.Y.2d 708, 713-714, 697 N.E.2d 584 [1998]). Defendants reason that the prescribed, deferential (see Strickland, 466 U.S. at 689; Benevento, 91 N.Y.2d at 712) and highly context sensitive inquiry into the adequacy and particular effect of counsel's performance cannot occur until a prosecution has concluded in a conviction, and that, once there is a conviction, the appropriate avenues of relief are direct appeals and the various other established means of challenging a conviction, such as . . . motions and petitions for writs of habeas corpus or coram nobis. They urge, in essence, that the present plaintiffs can, based upon their ongoing prosecutions, possess no ripe claim of ineffective assistance and that any ineffective assistance claims that might eventually be brought by them would, given the nature of the claim, have to be individually asserted and determined; they argue that a finding of constitutionally deficient performance—one necessarily rooted in the particular circumstances of an individual case—cannot serve as a predicate for systemic relief. Indeed, they remind us that the Supreme Court in Strickland has noted pointedly that "the purpose of the effective assistance guarantee of the Sixth Amendment is not to improve the quality of legal representation, although that is a goal of considerable importance to the legal system[,] . . . [but rather] to ensure that criminal defendants receive a fair trial" (466 U.S. at 689).

These arguments possess a measure of merit. A fair reading of Strickland and our relevant state precedents supports defendants' contention that effective assistance is a judicial construct designed to do no more than protect an individual defendant's right to a fair adjudication; it is not a concept capable of expansive application to remediate systemic deficiencies. The cases in which the concept has been explicated are in this connection notable for their intentional omission of any broadly applicable defining performance standards. Indeed, Strickland is clear that articulation of any standard more specific than that of objective reasonableness is neither warranted by the Sixth Amendment nor compatible with its objectives:

> "More specific guidelines are not appropriate. The Sixth Amendment refers simply to 'counsel,' not specifying particular requirements of effective assistance. It relies instead on the legal profession's maintenance of standards sufficient to justify the law's presumption that counsel will fulfill the role in the adversary process that the Amendment envisions. The proper measure of attorney performance remains simply reasonableness under prevailing professional norms. . . .
>
> "In any case presenting an ineffectiveness claim, the performance inquiry must be whether counsel's assistance was reasonable considering all the circumstances. . . . No particular set of detailed rules for counsel's conduct can satisfactorily take account of the variety of circumstances faced by defense counsel or the range of legitimate decisions regarding how best to represent a criminal defendant. Any such set of rules would interfere with the constitutionally protected independence of counsel and restrict the wide latitude counsel must have in making tactical decisions. Indeed,

the existence of detailed guidelines for representation could distract counsel from the overriding mission of vigorous advocacy of the defendant's cause" (466 U.S. at 688-689).

We too have for similar reasons eschewed the articulation of more specific, generally applicable performance standards for judging the effectiveness of counsel in the context of determining whether constitutionally mandated representation has been provided (see People v. Benevento, 91 N.Y.2d at 712; People v. Baldi, 54 N.Y.2d 137, 146-147, 429 N.E.2d 400 [1981]). This is not to say that performance standards are not highly relevant in assuring that constitutionally effective assistance is provided and in judging whether in a particular case an attorney's performance has been deficient, only that such standards do not and cannot usefully define the Sixth Amendment-based concept of effective assistance. While the imposition of such standards may be highly salutary, it is not under *Strickland* appropriate as an exercise in Sixth Amendment jurisprudence.

Having said this, however, we would add the very important caveat that *Strickland*'s approach is expressly premised on the supposition that the fundamental underlying right to representation under *Gideon* has been enabled by the State in a manner that would justify the presumption that the standard of objective reasonableness will ordinarily be satisfied (*see Strickland*, 466 U.S. at 687-689). The questions properly raised in this Sixth Amendment-grounded action, we think, go not to whether ineffectiveness has assumed systemic dimensions, but rather to whether the State has met its foundational obligation under *Gideon* to provide legal representation.

Inasmuch as general prescriptive relief is unavailable and indeed incompatible with the adjudication of claims alleging constitutionally ineffective assistance of counsel, it follows that plaintiffs' claims for prospective systemic relief cannot stand if their gravamen is only that attorneys appointed for them have not, so far, afforded them meaningful and effective representation. While it is defendants' position, and was evidently that of the Appellate Division majority, that the complaint contains only performance-based claims for ineffective assistance, our examination of the pleading leads us to a different conclusion.

According to the complaint, 10 of the 20 plaintiffs—two from Washington, two from Onondaga, two from Ontario and four from Schuyler County—were altogether without representation at the arraignments held in their underlying criminal proceedings. Eight of these unrepresented plaintiffs were jailed after bail had been set in amounts they could not afford. It is alleged that the experience of these plaintiffs is illustrative of what is a fairly common practice in the aforementioned counties of arraigning defendants without counsel and leaving them, particularly when accused of relatively low level offenses, unrepresented in subsequent proceedings where pleas are taken and other critically important legal transactions take place. One of these plaintiffs remained unrepresented for some five months and it is alleged that the absence of clear and uniform guidelines reasonably related to need has commonly resulted in denials of representation to indigent defendants based on the subjective judgments of individual jurists.

In addition to the foregoing allegations of outright nonrepresentation, the complaint contains allegations to the effect that although lawyers were eventually nominally appointed for plaintiffs, they were unavailable to their clients—that they conferred with them little, if at all, were often completely unresponsive to their urgent inquiries and requests from jail, sometimes for months on end, waived important rights without consulting them, and ultimately appeared to do little more on their behalf than act as conduits for plea offers, some of which purportedly were highly unfavorable. It is repeatedly alleged that counsel missed court appearances, and that when they did appear they were not prepared to proceed, often because they were entirely new to the case, the matters having previously been handled by other similarly unprepared counsel. There are also allegations that the counsel appointed for at least one of the plaintiffs was seriously conflicted and thus unqualified to undertake the representation.

The allegations of the complaint must at this stage of the litigation be deemed true and construed in plaintiffs' favor, affording them the benefit of every reasonable inference (Leon v. Martinez, 84 N.Y.2d 83, 87-88, 638 N.E.2d 511 [1994]), the very limited object being to ascertain whether any cognizable claim for relief is made out. If there is a discernible claim, that is where the inquiry must end; the difficulty of its proof is not the present concern. The above summarized allegations, in our view, state cognizable Sixth Amendment claims.

It is clear that a criminal defendant, regardless of wherewithal, is entitled to " 'the guiding hand of counsel at every step in the proceedings against him' " (Gideon v. Wainwright, 372 U.S. at 345, quoting Powell v. Alabama, 287 U.S. 45, 69 [1932]). The right attaches at arraignment (see Rothgery v. Gillespie County, 554 U.S. 191 [2008]) and entails the presence of counsel at each subsequent "critical" stage of the proceedings (Montejo v. Louisiana, 556 U.S. [2009]). As is here relevant, arraignment itself must under the circumstances alleged be deemed a critical stage since, even if guilty pleas were not then elicited from the presently named plaintiffs,[2] a circumstance which would undoubtedly require the "critical stage" label (see Coleman v. Alabama, 399 US 1, 9 [1970]), it is clear from the complaint that plaintiffs' pretrial liberty interests were on that occasion regularly adjudicated with most serious consequences, both direct and collateral, including the loss of employment and housing, and inability to support and care for particularly needy dependents. There is no question that "a bail hearing is a critical stage of the State's criminal process" (Higazy v. Templeton, 505 F.3d 161, 172 [2d Cir. 2007]).

Recognizing the crucial importance of arraignment and the extent to which a defendant's basic liberty and due process interests may then be affected, CPL 180.10 (3) expressly provides for the "right to the aid of counsel at the arraignment and at every subsequent stage of the action" and forbids a court from going forward with the proceeding without counsel for the defendant, unless the defendant has knowingly agreed to proceed in counsel's absence (CPL 180.10 [5]). Contrary to defendants' suggestion and that of the dissent, nothing in the statute may be read to justify the conclusion that the presence of defense counsel at arraignment is ever dispensable, except at a defendant's informed option, when matters affecting the defendant's pretrial liberty or ability subsequently to defend against the charges are to be decided. Nor is there merit to defendants' suggestion that the Sixth Amendment right to counsel is not yet fully implicated (see *Rothgery*, 554 U.S. at 209).

The cases cited by the dissent in which the allegedly consequential event at arraignment was the entry of a not guilty plea . . . do not stand for the proposition that counsel, as a general matter, is optional at arraignment. Indeed, such a proposition would

2. It is, however, alleged that in the counties at issue pleas are often elicited from unrepresented defendants at arraignment.

plainly be untenable since arraignments routinely, and in New York as a matter of statutory design, encompass matters affecting a defendant's liberty and ability to defend against the charges. The cited cases rather stand for the very limited proposition that where it happens that what occurs at arraignment does not affect a defendant's ultimate adjudication, a defendant is not on the ground of nonrepresentation entitled to a reversal of his or her conviction. Plaintiffs here do not seek that relief. Rather, they seek prospectively to assure the provision of what the Constitution undoubtedly guarantees—representation at all critical stages of the criminal proceedings. In New York, arraignment is, as a general matter, such a stage.

Also "critical" for Sixth Amendment purposes is the period between arraignment and trial when a case must be factually developed and researched, decisions respecting grand jury testimony made, plea negotiations conducted, and pretrial motions filed. Indeed, it is clear that "to deprive a person of counsel during the period prior to trial may be more damaging than denial of counsel during the trial itself" (Maine v. Moulton, 474 U.S. 159, 170 [1985]).

This complaint contains numerous plain allegations that in specific cases counsel simply was not provided at critical stages of the proceedings. The complaint additionally contains allegations sufficient to justify the inference that these deprivations may be illustrative of significantly more widespread practices; of particular note in this connection are the allegations that in numerous cases representational denials are premised on subjective and highly variable notions of indigency, raising possible due process and equal protection concerns. These allegations state a claim, not for ineffective assistance under *Strickland*, but for basic denial of the right to counsel under *Gideon*.

Similarly, while variously interpretable, the numerous allegations to the effect that counsel, although appointed, were uncommunicative, made virtually no efforts on their nominal clients' behalf during the very critical period subsequent to arraignment, and, indeed, waived important rights without authorization from their clients, may be reasonably understood to allege nonrepresentation rather than ineffective representation. Actual representation assumes a certain basic representational relationship. The allegations here, however, raise serious questions as to whether any such relationship may be really said to have existed between many of the plaintiffs and their putative attorneys and cumulatively may be understood to raise the distinct possibility that merely nominal attorney-client pairings occur in the subject counties with a fair degree of regularity, allegedly because of inadequate funding and staffing of indigent defense providers. It is very basic that

> "[i]f no actual 'Assistance' 'for' the accused's 'defence' is provided, then the constitutional guarantee has been violated. To hold otherwise 'could convert the appointment of counsel into a sham and nothing more than a formal compliance with the Constitution's requirement that an accused be given the assistance of counsel. The Constitution's guarantee of assistance of counsel cannot be satisfied by mere formal appointment.' Avery v. Alabama, 308 U.S. 444, 446 (1940)" (United States v. Cronic, 466 U.S. 648, 654-655 [1984]).

While it may turn out after further factual development that what is really at issue is whether the representation afforded was effective—a subject not properly litigated in this civil action—at this juncture, construing the allegations before us as we must, in the light most favorable to plaintiffs, the complaint states a claim for constructive denial of the right to counsel by reason of insufficient compliance with the constitutional mandate of *Gideon*. The dissent's conclusion that these allegations assert only performance based claims, and not claims for nonrepresentation, seems to us premature. The picture which emerges from a fair and procedurally appropriate reading of the complaint is that defendants are with some regularity going unrepresented at arraignment and subsequent critical stages. As noted, half the plaintiffs claim to have been without counsel at arraignment, and nearly all claim to have been left effectively without representation for lengthy periods subsequent to arraignment. If all that were involved was a "lumping together of 20 generic ineffective assistance of counsel claims" (dissenting op. at 30) we would agree with the dissent that no cognizable claim had been stated, but we do not think that this detailed, multi-tiered complaint meticulously setting forth the factual bases of the individual claims and the manner in which they are linked to and illustrative of broad systemic deficiencies is susceptible of such characterization.

Collateral preconviction claims seeking prospective relief for absolute, core denials of the right to the assistance of counsel cannot be understood to be incompatible with *Strickland*. These are not the sort of contextually sensitive claims that are typically involved when ineffectiveness is alleged. The basic, unadorned question presented by such claims where, as here, the defendant-claimants are poor, is whether the State has met its obligation to provide counsel, not whether under all the circumstances counsel's performance was inadequate or prejudicial. Indeed, in cases of outright denial of the right to counsel prejudice is presumed. *Strickland* itself, of course, recognizes the critical distinction between a claim for ineffective assistance and one alleging simply that the right to the assistance of counsel has been denied and specifically acknowledges that the latter kind of claim may be disposed of without inquiring as to prejudice:

> "In certain Sixth Amendment contexts, prejudice is presumed. Actual or constructive denial of the assistance of counsel altogether is legally presumed to result in prejudice. So are various kinds of state interference with counsel's assistance. See United States v. Cronic, [466 U.S.] at 659, and n. 25. Prejudice in these circumstances is so likely that case-by-case inquiry into prejudice is not worth the cost. Moreover, such circumstances involve impairments of the Sixth Amendment right that are easy to identify and, for that reason and because the prosecution is directly responsible, easy for the government to prevent" (466 U.S. at 692).

The allegations before us state claims falling precisely within this described category. It is true, as the dissent points out, that claims, even within this category, have been most frequently litigated postconviction, but it does not follow from this circumstance that they are not cognizable apart from the postconviction context. Given the simplicity and autonomy of a claim for nonrepresentation, as opposed to one truly involving the adequacy of an attorney's performance, there is no reason — and certainly none is identified in the dissent — why such a claim cannot or should not be brought without the context of a completed prosecution.

Although defendants contend otherwise, we perceive no real danger that allowing these claims to proceed would impede the orderly progress of plaintiffs' underlying criminal actions. Those actions have, for the most part, been concluded,[5] and we

---

5. Defendants' contention that the action is, in light of this circumstance, moot overlooks the well-established exception to the mootness doctrine for recurring claims of public importance typically evading review (see Matter of Hearst Corp. v. Clyne, 50 N.Y.2d 707, 714-715, 409 N.E.2d 876 [1980]).

have, in any event, removed from the action the issue of ineffective assistance, thus eliminating any possibility that the collateral adjudication of generalized claims of ineffective assistance might be used to obtain relief from individual judgments of conviction.[6] Here we emphasize that our recognition that plaintiffs may have claims for constructive denial of counsel should not be viewed as a back door for what would be nonjusticiable assertions of ineffective assistance seeking remedies specifically addressed to attorney performance, such as uniform hiring, training and practice standards. To the extent that a cognizable Sixth Amendment claim is stated in this collateral civil action, it is to the effect that in one or more of the five counties at issue the basic constitutional mandate for the provision of counsel to indigent defendants at all critical stages is at risk of being left unmet because of systemic conditions, not by reason of the personal failings and poor professional decisions of individual attorneys. While the defense of indigents in the five subject counties might perhaps be improved in many ways that the Legislature is free to explore, the much narrower focus of the constitutionally based judicial remedy here sought must be simply to assure that every indigent defendant is afforded actual assistance of counsel, as *Gideon* commands. Plainly, we do not, even while narrowing the scope of this action as we believe the law requires, deny plaintiffs a remedy for systemic violations of *Gideon*, as the dissent suggests. It is rather the dissent that would foreclose plaintiffs from any prospect of obtaining such relief. And, when all is said and done, the dissent's proposed denial is premised solely upon the availability of relief from a judgment of conviction. Neither law, nor logic, nor sound public policy dictates that one form of relief should be preclusive of the other.

As against the fairly minimal risks involved in sustaining the closely defined claim of nonrepresentation we have recognized must be weighed the very serious dangers that the alleged denial of counsel entails. " 'Of all [of] the rights that an accused person has, the right to be represented by counsel is by far the most pervasive for it affects his ability to assert any other rights he may have' " (United States v. Cronic, 466 U.S. at 654, quoting Schaefer, Federalism and State Criminal Procedure, 70 Harv. L. Rev. 1, 8 [1956]). The failure to honor this right, then, cannot but be presumed to impair the reliability of the adversary process through which criminal justice is under our system of government dispensed. This action properly understood, as it has been by distinguished members of the prosecution and defense bars alike, does not threaten but endeavors to preserve our means of criminal adjudication from the inevitably corrosive effects and unjust consequences of an unfair adversary process.

It is not clear that defendants actually contend that stated claims for the denial of assistance of counsel would be nonjusticiable; their appellate presentation, both written and oral, has been principally to the effect that the claims alleged are exclusively predicated on deficient performance, a characterization which we have rejected. Supposing, however, a persisting, relevant contention of nonjusticiability, it is clear that it would be without merit. This is obvious because the right that plaintiffs would

---

6. It follows that if plaintiffs' claims are found to be meritorious after trial, such a determination will not entitle them to vacatur of their criminal convictions. And, although the issue is not specifically raised, we note in the same connection that, in view of the circumstance that this action will not disturb the progress or outcomes of plaintiffs' criminal actions, and that the action seeks relief largely unavailable in the context of the underlying individual criminal actions, the rule generally applicable to bar collateral claims for equitable intervention in ongoing criminal prosecutions would not be properly relied upon by the State here.

enforce—that of a poor person accused of a crime to have counsel provided for his or her defense—is the very same right that *Gideon* has already commanded the states to honor as a matter of fundamental constitutional necessity. There is no argument that what was justiciable in *Gideon* is now beyond the power of a court to decide.

It is, of course, possible that a remedy in this action would necessitate the appropriation of funds and perhaps, particularly in a time of scarcity, some reordering of legislative priorities. But this does not amount to an argument upon which a court might be relieved of its essential obligation to provide a remedy for violation of a fundamental constitutional right (see Marbury v. Madison, 1 Cranch [5 U.S.] 137, 147, 2 L. Ed. 60 [1803] ["every right, when withheld, must have a remedy, and every injury its proper redress"]).

We have consistently held that enforcement of a clear constitutional or statutory mandate is the proper work of the courts (see Campaign for Fiscal Equity v. State of New York, 86 N.Y.2d 307, 655 N.E.2d 661 [1995]), and it would be odd if we made an exception in the case of a mandate as well-established and as essential to our institutional integrity as the one requiring the State to provide legal representation to indigent criminal defendants at all critical stages of the proceedings against them.

Assuming the allegations of the complaint to be true, there is considerable risk that indigent defendants are, with a fair degree of regularity, being denied constitutionally mandated counsel in the five subject counties. The severe imbalance in the adversary process that such a state of affairs would produce cannot be doubted. Nor can it be doubted that courts would in consequence of such imbalance become breeding grounds for unreliable judgments. Wrongful conviction, the ultimate sign of a criminal justice system's breakdown and failure, has been documented in too many cases. Wrongful convictions, however, are not the only injustices that command our present concern. . . . [T]he absence of representation at critical stages is capable of causing grave and irreparable injury to persons who will not be convicted. *Gideon*'s guarantee to the assistance of counsel does not turn upon a defendant's guilt or innocence, and neither can the availability of a remedy for its denial.

Accordingly, the order of the Appellate Division should be modified, without costs, by reinstating the complaint in accordance with this opinion, and remitting the case to that court to consider issues raised but not determined on the appeal to that court, and, as so modified, affirmed.

PIGOTT, J. (dissenting).

There is no doubt that there are inadequacies in the delivery of indigent legal services in this state, as pointed out by the New York State Commission on the Future of Indigent Defense Services, convened by former Chief Judge Kaye. I respectfully dissent, however, because, despite this, in my view, the complaint here fails to state a claim, either under the theories proffered by plaintiffs—ineffective assistance of counsel and deprivation of the right to counsel at a critical stage (arraignment)—or under the "constructive denial" theory read into the complaint by the majority.

The majority rightly rejects plaintiffs' ineffective assistance cause of action; such claims are limited to a case-by-case analysis and cannot be redressed in a civil proceeding. Rather than dismissing that claim, however, the majority replaces it with a "constructive denial" cause of action that, in my view, is nothing more than an ineffective assistance claim under another name.

The allegations in the complaint can be broken down into two categories: (1) the deprivation of "meaningful and effective assistance of counsel," and (2) the deprivation of the right to counsel at a "critical stage" of the proceedings, i.e., the arraignment. The claims under the former category are many: lack of a sufficient opportunity to discuss the charges with their attorney or participate in their defense; lack of preparation by counsel; denial of investigative services; lack of "vertical representation;"[1] refusal of assigned counsel to return phone calls or accept collect calls; inability to leave messages on assigned counsel's answering machine due to a full voicemail box, etc.

The majority rejects plaintiffs' main claim that the complaint states a cause of action for ineffective assistance of counsel under Strickland v. Washington (466 U.S. 668 [1984]), finding "a measure of merit" to defendants' arguments that such claims are premised on trial counsel's constitutionally deficient performance and do not form the basis for systemic relief. I agree, and would affirm the Appellate Division's determination in that regard, because the *Strickland* standard is limited to whether an individual has received the effective assistance of counsel and cannot be used to attack alleged systemic failures, and the allegations of the complaint support no broader reading.

Rather than stopping at its rejection of the *Strickland* standard with respect to these allegations, however, the majority advances a third theory, and reads the complaint as stating a claim for "constructive denial" of the right to counsel, i.e., that upon having counsel appointed, plaintiffs received only "nominal" representation, such that there is a question as to whether the counties were in compliance with the constitutional mandate of *Gideon*.

In support of this rationale, the majority relies on United States v. Cronic (466 U.S. 648 [1984]), which recognizes a "narrow exception" to *Strickland*'s requirement that a defendant asserting an ineffective assistance of counsel claim must demonstrate a deficient performance and prejudice. In other words, *Cronic*, too, is an ineffective assistance of counsel case—decided on the same day as *Strickland*—but one that allows the courts to find a Sixth Amendment violation " 'without inquiring into counsel's actual performance or requiring the defendant to show the effect it had on the trial,' when 'circumstances [exist] that are so likely to prejudice the accused that the cost of litigating their effect on a particular case is unjustified' " (Wright v. Van Patten, 552 U.S. 120, 124 [2008]).

Cronic's "narrow exception" applies to individual cases where: (1) there has been a "complete denial of counsel"; i.e., the defendant is denied counsel at a critical stage of the trial; (2) "counsel entirely fails to subject the prosecution's case to meaningful adversarial testing"; or (3) "the likelihood that any lawyer, even a fully competent one, could provide effective assistance is so small that a presumption of prejudice is appropriate without inquiry into the actual conduct of the trial" (466 U.S. at 659-660).

Cronic's holding is instructive, if only to point out that the Supreme Court was reaching the obvious conclusion that, in *individual cases*, the absence or inadequacy of counsel must generally fall within one of those three narrow exceptions.[3] Constructive denial of counsel is a branch from the *Strickland* tree, with *Cronic* applying only when

---

1. Presumably this refers to the fact that in some jurisdictions, a defendant may be represented by one lawyer in the local criminal court and have a different lawyer assigned in superior court.

3. Even the defendant in *Cronic* was not entitled to rely on any of the exceptions delineated in that opinion, notwithstanding the fact that his retained counsel withdrew shortly before the trial date and, just 25 days before trial, the court appointed a young lawyer with a real estate practice to represent defendant in a mail fraud case that had taken the Government 4½ years to investigate. Supreme Court held that any errors by counsel at trial were to be examined using the *Strickland* test.

the appointed attorney's representation is so egregious that it's as if defendant had no attorney at all. Therefore, whether a defendant received ineffective assistance of counsel under *Strickland* or is entitled to a presumption of prejudice under *Cronic* is a determination that can only be made *after* the criminal proceeding has ended; neither approach lends itself to a proceeding like the one at bar where plaintiffs allege prospective violations of their Sixth Amendment rights.

The majority does not explain how it can conclude, on one hand, "that effective assistance is a judicial construct designed to do no more than protect an *individual* defendant's right to fair adjudication" and "is *not* a concept capable of expansive application to remediate systemic deficiencies" (majority op. at 17 [emphasis supplied]), and on the other hand that a "constructive denial" of counsel theory could potentially apply to this class of individuals who, when they commenced the action, had not reached a resolution of their criminal cases. Courts reviewing the rare constructive denial claims have done so by looking at the particular egregious behavior of the attorney in the particular case *after* the representation has concluded (see, e.g., Burdine v. Johnson, 262 F.3d 336 [5th Cir. 2001] [defense counsel slept during capital trial]; Rickman v. Bell, 131 F.3d 1150 [6th Cir. 1997] [defense counsel acted as second prosecutor]; Tippins v. Walker, 77 F.3d 682, 686 [2d Cir. 1996] [counsel slept through trial]; Harding v. Davis, 878 F.2d 1341 [11th Cir. 1989] [constructive denial where counsel responded to defendant's displeasure of his representation by remaining silent and inactive at trial until replaced by the pro se defendant]; Jenkins v. Coombe, 821 F.2d 158, 161 [2d Cir. 1987] [1988] [filing cursory five-page brief on appeal]).

That is not to say that a claim of constructive denial could never apply to a class where the State effectively deprives indigent defendants their right to counsel, only that the various claims asserted by plaintiffs here do not rise to that level. Here, plaintiffs' complaint raises basic ineffective assistance of counsel claims in the nature of *Strickland* (i.e., counsel was unresponsive, waived important rights, failed to appear at hearings, and was unprepared at court proceedings) and not the egregious type of conduct found in *Cronic*. Plaintiffs' mere lumping together of 20 generic ineffective assistance of counsel claims into one civil pleading does not ipso facto transform it into one alleging a systemic denial of the right to counsel.

Addressing plaintiffs' second theory—deprivation of the right to counsel at the arraignment—the majority posits that plaintiffs have stated a cognizable claim because 10 of them were arraigned without counsel, and eight of those remained in custody because they could not meet the bail that was set.

It is undisputed that a criminal defendant "'requires the guiding hand of counsel at every step in the proceedings against him'" (Gideon v. Wainwright, 372 U.S. 335, 345 [1963], quoting Powell v. Alabama, 287 U.S. 45, 69 [1932]). But the majority's bare conclusion that any arraignment conducted without the presence of counsel renders the proceedings a violation of the Sixth Amendment flies in the face of reality.

The framework of CPL article 180 illustrates this point. That provision presupposes that a criminal defendant, upon arraignment, may not have yet retained counsel or, due to indigency, requires the appointment of one. CPL 180.10 mandates that, in addition to apprising him of, and furnishing him with, a copy of the charges against him (see CPL 180.10[1]), the court must also inform an unrepresented defendant that he is entitled to, among other things, "an adjournment for the purpose of obtaining counsel" (CPL 180.10[3][a]) and the appointment of counsel by the court if "he is financially unable to obtain the same" (CPL 180.10 [3][c]).[6] The court must also give the defendant the opportunity to avail himself of those rights and "must itself take such affirmative action as is necessary to effectuate them" (CPL 180.10[4]). This statute is a prophylactic one whose purpose is to protect a defendant's Sixth Amendment rights because, even in a situation where a defendant chooses to go forward without counsel, "the court must permit him to do so if it is satisfied that he made such decision with the knowledge and significance thereof" and, in a situation where it is not so satisfied, may decide not to proceed until defendant obtains or is appointed counsel (CPL 180.10[5]).

Giving plaintiffs the benefit of every favorable inference (see Leon v. Martinez, 84 N.Y.2d 83, 87-88, 638 N.E.2d 511 [1994]), the complaint nevertheless fails to state a cause of action for the deprivation of the right to counsel at arraignment. One reason is that there is no allegation that the failure to have counsel at one's first court appearance had an adverse effect on the criminal proceedings. The Second Circuit has rejected the assertion "that the absence of counsel upon arraignment is an inflexible, per se violation of the Sixth Amendment" (United States ex rel. Caccio v. Fay, 350 F.2d 214, 215 [2d Cir. 1965]). Where a criminal defendant is arraigned without the presence of counsel and pleads not guilty—or the court enters a not guilty plea on his behalf—there is no Sixth Amendment violation (see United States ex rel. Combs v. Denno, 357 F.2d 809, 812 [2d Cir. 1966]; United States ex rel. Hussey v. Fay, 220 F. Supp. 562 [S.D.N.Y. 1963]). The explanation as to why this is so is simple:

> "Under New York law, a defendant suffers no . . . prejudice [by the imposition of a not guilty plea on arraignment without benefit of counsel], for whatever counsel could have done upon arraignment on defendant's behalf, counsel were free to do thereafter. There is nothing in New York law which in any way prevents counsel's later taking advantage of every opportunity or defense which was originally available to a defendant upon his initial arraignment" (*Hussey*, 220 F. Supp. at 563, citing People v. Combs, 19 A.D.2d 639, 640 [2d Dept. 1963]).

As pleaded, none of the 10 plaintiffs arraigned without counsel entered guilty pleas and, indeed, in compliance with the strictures of CPL 180.10, all met with counsel shortly after the arraignment. Nor is there any claim that the absence of counsel prejudiced these plaintiffs. . . .

The majority implies that the complaint pleads a *Gideon* violation because certain of the plaintiffs were not represented when the court arranged for the imposition of bail at the arraignment (see CPL 170.10[7]; 180.10[6]; 210.15[6]).[7] Quite often this initial appearance inures to the benefit of defendant who may be released on his own recognizance or on manageable bail within hours of arrest. The only substantive allegations plaintiffs make relative to bail is that assigned counsel failed to advocate for lower bail at the arraignment or move for a bail reduction post-arraignment. If

---

6. Indeed, the Supreme Court of the United States has favorably cited to CPL 180.10 in support of its observation that New York is one of the 43 states that "takes the first step toward appointing counsel 'before, at or just after initial appearance'" (Rothgery v. Gillespie County, 554 U.S. 191, 204 and n14 [2008]).

7. The majority observes that a bail hearing is a critical stage of the criminal process. While that may be a correct statement of the law, it has little application to these facts, as none of these plaintiffs asserts that they were forced to participate in a bail hearing without the aid of counsel.

anything, the complaint alleges a claim for ineffective assistance of counsel under the federal or state standard, but the majority has rejected such a claim in this litigation.

Finally, the majority notes that plaintiffs do not seek relief within the context of their own criminal cases, and therefore allowing plaintiffs to proceed on their claims "would [not] impede the orderly progress of [the] underlying criminal actions," asserting that even if plaintiffs' claims are found to be meritorious after trial they would not be entitled to a vacatur of their criminal convictions. In my view, if plaintiffs are able to establish a violation of *Gideon*, they should not be foreclosed from seeking a remedy; if plaintiffs are willing to waive any remedy to which they may be entitled, as they are doing here, then I see no reason why the courts have any business adjudicating this matter.

While the perfect system of justice is beyond human attainment, plaintiff's frustration with the deficiencies in the present indigent defense system is understandable. Legal services for the indigent have routinely been underfunded, and appointed counsel are all too often overworked and confronted with excessive caseloads, which affects the amount of time counsel may spend with any given client. Many, if not all, of plaintiffs' grievances have been acknowledged in the Kaye Commission Report, which is implicitly addressed — as it should be — to the Legislature, the proper forum for weighing proposals to enhance indigent defense services in New York. This complaint is, at heart, an attempt to convert what are properly policy questions for the Legislature into constitutional claims for the courts.

Accordingly, I would affirm the order of the Appellate Division.

JUDGES CIPARICK, GRAFFEO and JONES concur with CHIEF JUDGE LIPPMAN; JUDGE PIGOTT dissents and votes to affirm in a separate opinion in which JUDGES READ and SMITH concur.

NOTES AND QUESTIONS

1. Who's got the better of the argument here? Judge Pigott, in dissent, claims that the plaintiffs have a fully effective (no pun intended) remedy for any deficiencies in counsel's representation: namely, they can pursue an ineffective-assistance claim after conviction. By what legitimate authority does a court intervene before the fact, to prevent a hypothetical Sixth Amendment violation that has not yet occurred? Doesn't that seem like a highly unusual action for a court to take? On the other hand, isn't the majority right to think that after more than 50 years, it's about high time that *somebody* did *something* to try to make sure that the *Gideon* right to counsel gets adequately respected and enforced? Isn't case-by-case ineffective-assistance litigation a little bit like playing judicial "whack-a-mole"?[19] And doesn't it seem like the state's highest court is a particularly appropriate institution to insist on the proper enforcement of *Gideon*—because the courts are the ones who see the problem, and must deal with the consequences, every single day?

___

19. The reference here is to a common carnival game, in which the participant uses a mallet to try to hit a plastic mole whenever it pops out of a hole. The frustrating part of the game is that every time the participant tries to hit the mole, the mole suddenly disappears and another mole appears out of a different hole.

2. What, exactly, is the Sixth Amendment right that the majority believes the plaintiffs have properly asserted here? Isn't there a fair amount of confusion over the nature of that right? The *Hurrell-Harring* majority concedes that a standard Sixth Amendment claim of ineffective assistance of counsel, pursuant to *Strickland,* must await the adjudication of the individual case and must be analyzed in retrospect. The majority then proceeds to re-characterize the plaintiffs' claim as one of *non*-representation, under some variant of *Cronic,* rather than ineffective representation. What's the difference? If (as in one of the instances mentioned in *Hurrell-Harring*) a public defender fails to return a defendant's call in a timely manner due to an overload of cases, is that "ineffective representation" or "non-representation"? It seems like a pretty fine line, doesn't it?

3. The *Hurrell-Harring* decision decides only that the plaintiffs have stated a Sixth Amendment claim upon which relief can be granted. What would the proper remedy be, if the plaintiffs eventually succeed at trial? This is an exceedingly difficult question, but fortunately for the New York courts, they will not have to decide it. On October 21, 2014, the parties reached a settlement in the *Hurrell-Harring* litigation; the settlement was approved by the trial judge on March 18, 2015.

The 34-page settlement, which covers only the five specific New York counties that were the subject of the class-action litigation, includes the following: The State Office of Indigent Legal Services will monitor compliance with the agreed-upon reforms by the 11 legal-services providers in the five relevant counties; the Office will guarantee that defendants have counsel at arraignment, institute quality standards for defense counsel, and insure that public defenders have manageable caseloads for the next 7-½ years. A "chief implementation attorney," to be assisted by four attorneys and three staff members, will be hired to oversee compliance. The state will spend $4 million in the next fiscal year, and more in future years, to fund these improvements.

The state did not admit fault, and the settlement cannot be used as precedent in other court cases involving other counties—which pretty much ensures more litigation. The State Office of Indigent Legal Services estimates that it would cost $105 million per year to extend the same reforms to all 57 counties in New York.

4. The Civil Rights Division of the U.S. Department of Justice filed a "statement of interest" in support of the plaintiffs in the *Hurrell-Harring* litigation. The Justice Department has filed similar statements in a number of other states where similar litigation has occurred or is currently ongoing (including in Alabama, Georgia, Idaho, and Washington). What exactly is the interest of the Justice Department in these state cases? If the federal courts are so reluctant to intervene and impose systemic reforms on the states, largely out of concern for federalism and comity, why should the federal executive feel less reluctant to do so?

5. One state court recently *did* address, at least preliminarily, the appropriate remedy for a state's failure to fund adequately indigent defense representation. In Public Defender, Eleventh Judicial Circuit v. State of Florida, 115 So. 3d 261 (2013), the Florida Supreme Court ruled that the public defender's office for the Eleventh Judicial Circuit (the judicial circuit that includes Miami) was legally entitled to withdraw from representing indigent noncapital felony defendants, based on a "conflict of interest" because "excessive caseloads caused by underfunding meant the office could not carry out its legal and ethical obligations to the defendants." One interesting aspect of the case is that Florida's legislature had enacted a statute, section 27.5303(1)(d), specifically prohibiting Florida trial courts from allowing such

attorney withdrawal based on "conflicts arising from underfunding, excessive casel-oad or the prospective inability to adequately represent a client." The constitution-ality of the statute was challenged in the litigation.

The Florida Supreme Court began by reviewing extensively the problem of inad-equate funding of indigent defense services in Florida, and the negative conse-quences for the quality of representation:

> "While we cannot succinctly recount the lengthy records in these two cases, we are struck by the breadth and depth of the evidence of how the excessive caseload has impacted the Public Defender's representation of indigent defendants. For example, the number of criminal cases assigned to the Public Defender has increased by 29% since 2004, while his trial budget was reduced by 12.6% through budget cuts and holdbacks over the fiscal years 2007-2008 and 2008-2009. After the implementation of Article V revisions in July 2004, the Legislature only funded 32 of the 82 overload attorneys that Miami-Dade County had been funding. The noncapital felony caseload has been in the range of 400 cases per attorney for a number of years. Yet, even the *highest* caseload standard recommended by professional legal organizations is 200 to 300 *less*.[7] At the time the motions were filed in these cases, there were 105 attorneys to represent clients in 45,055 new and reopened cases. . . . Third-degree felony attorneys often have as many as fifty cases set for trial in one week because of the excessive case-load. Clients who are not in custody are essentially unrepresented for long periods between arraignment and trial. Attorneys are routinely unable to interview clients, conduct investigations, take depositions, prepare mitigation, or counsel clients about pleas offered at arraignment. Instead, the office engages in "triage" with the clients who are in custody or who face the most serious charges getting priority to the detri-ment of the other clients. . . . [T]his evidence is . . . a damning indictment of the poor quality of trial representation that is being afforded indigent defendants by the Public Defender in the Eleventh Circuit."

The court next decided that it possesses the "inherent judicial authority" to "do things that are absolutely essential to the performance of their judicial functions," including "aggregate or systemic relief," because limiting itself to ruling on indi-vidual motions to withdraw would be "tantamount to applying a band aid to an open head wound."

With respect to the appropriate constitutional standard for defense attorney withdrawal, the court noted that "[t]he *Strickland* standard has been criticized as 'inappropriate' for suits seeking prospective relief," due to *Strickland*'s focus on case-by-case showings of inadequate performance and prejudice. However, the court cited *Luckey I, Peart,* and *Hurrell-Harring* for the proposition that the Sixth Amendment *can* be applied prospectively in extreme situations of inadequate fund-ing and case overloads. The court noted the similarity between the factual allega-tions in the case before it and those in *Hurrell-Harring,* pointed out that the New York court based its ruling on "non-representation" rather than "ineffective repre-sentation," and found the New York court's terminology at least partly applicable to

---

7. The American Council of Chief Defenders and the National Advisory Commission on Criminal Justice Standards and Goals recommend a caseload of 150 felonies per year. The Governor's Commission on Criminal Justice Standards and Goals set the standard at 100 cases. Even the highest standard offered by the Florida Public Defender Association is 200 cases.

the case at bar as well. The court also cited the Supreme Court's decisions in Lafler v. Cooper, 132 S. Ct. 1376 (2012), and Missouri v. Frye, 132 S. Ct. 1399 (2012), as establishing that the chance of a fair trial should not be seen as a "backstop" that "inoculates" pretrial errors. The court concluded that the required showing for defense attorney withdrawal based on the Sixth Amendment is "a substantial risk that the representation of [one] or more clients will be materially limited by the lawyer's responsibilities to another client."

Finally, the court concluded that Section 27.5303(1)(d) was not facially unconstitutional, but could become unconstitutional as applied:

> If section 27.5303(1)(d) is interpreted as prohibiting *any* motions to withdraw based on excessive caseloads or underfunding, then it would violate the courts' inherent authority to ensure adequate representation of indigent defendants. . . . [T]he statute should not be applied to preclude a public defender from filing a motion to withdraw based on excessive caseload or underfunding that would result in ineffective representation of indigent defendants nor to preclude a trial court from granting a motion to withdraw under those circumstances.

The court remanded the case back to the trial court to determine whether the Sixth Amendment standard for defense attorney withdrawal was satisfied. Two justices dissented in part, based on the fact that "there has been no proof of harm (or even proof of the likelihood of imminent harm) to individual defendants' constitutional rights due to excessive caseload."

Does the Florida Supreme Court's decision seem like the best way to address the obvious problems with inadequate funding of indigent defense services? Did the court make the right decision about the remedy? Does the answer depend upon how one feels about the "inherent judicial authority" to "do things" that spend considerable amounts of public money on items that have not been authorized or approved by the state legislature?

6. In more general terms, doesn't the debate about how much public funding should be allocated to the representation of indigent criminal defendants force one to confront the issue raised by the *Griffin* language quoted at the start of this section, see supra at page 151? Complete equality of funding between prosecutors and defendants—or between rich defendants and poor defendants—may be impossible to achieve (politically, if not economically, speaking). How "equal" does "equal justice" have to be? Is it enough if we provide sufficient equality to achieve fairness for indigent criminal defendants?

NOTES ON FAIRNESS, EQUALITY, AND THE RIGHT TO EFFECTIVE COUNSEL

Assuming that it is helpful to try to distinguish "fairness" from "equality," what does fairness mean in the context of effective representation? How much fairness does it take to be fair? Or, if you prefer, to be "fundamentally fair"? What are the parameters and, more important, how are they reached?

Maybe the real problem is not with the meaning of fairness, but instead with the meaning of equality. Does fairness really differ from equality in any meaningful or useful way? Consider the following exchange:

PETER WESTEN, THE EMPTY IDEA OF EQUALITY, 95 HARV. L. REV. 537, 539-540, 543-545, 545-550 (1982):   Equality is commonly perceived to differ from rights and liberties. . . .

I believe that this contrasting of rights and equality is fundamentally misconceived. It is based on a misunderstanding, both in law and in morals, about the role of equality in ethical discourse. To avoid possible misunderstanding, let me emphasize what I mean by equality and rights. By "equality" I mean the proposition in law and morals that "people who are alike should be treated alike" and its correlative, that "people who are unalike should be treated unalike." Equality thus includes all statements to the effect that the reason one person should be treated in a certain way is that he is "like" or "equal to" or "similar to" or "identical to" or "the same as" another who receives such treatment. "Rights," by contrast, means all claims that can justly be made by or on behalf of an individual or group of individuals to some condition or power—except claims that "people who are alike be treated alike." . . .

The proposition that "likes should be treated alike" is said to be a universal moral truth—a truth that can "be intuitively known with perfect clearness and certainty." Why? What is the connection between the fact that people are alike and the normative conclusion that they ought to be treated alike? How can one move from an "is" to an "ought"?

The answer can be found in the component parts of the equality formula. The formula "people who are alike should be treated alike" involves two components: (1) a determination that two people are alike; and (2) a moral judgment that they ought to be treated alike. The determinative component is the first. Once one determines that two people are alike for purposes of the equality principle, one knows how they ought to be treated. To understand why this is so—that is, to understand how (1) works—one must understand what kind of determination (1) is. One must know precisely what it means to say for purposes of equality that two persons are alike.

First, "people who are alike" might mean people who are alike in every respect. The trouble is that no two people are alike in every respect. The only things that are completely alike in every respect are immaterial symbols and forms, such as ideal numbers and geometric figures, which are not themselves the subject of morals.

Second, "people who are alike" may mean people, who, though not alike in every respect, are alike in some respects. Unfortunately, while the previous definition excludes every person in the world, the present definition includes every person and thing because all people and things are alike in some respect; and one is left with the morally absurd proposition that "all people and things should be treated alike."

Third, "people who are alike" may refer to people who are *morally* alike in a certain respect. The latter interpretation successfully avoids the philosophical hurdle of deriving an "ought" from an "is." It starts with a normative determination that two people are alike in a morally significant respect and moves to a normative conclusion that the two should be treated alike. Instead of deriving an "ought" from an "is," it derives an "ought" from an "ought." However, categories of morally alike objects do not exist in nature; moral alikeness is established only when people define categories. To say that people are morally alike is therefore to articulate a moral standard of treatment—a standard or rule specifying certain treatment for certain people—by reference to which they are, and thus are to be treated, alike. . . . Just as no categories of "like" people exist in nature, neither do categories of "like" treatment exist; treatments can be alike only in reference to some moral rule. Thus, to say that people who are morally alike in a certain respect "should be treated alike" means that they should be treated in accord with the moral rule by which they are determined to be alike. Hence "likes should be treated alike" means that people for whom a certain treatment is prescribed by a standard should all be given the treatment prescribed by the standard. Or, more simply, people who by a rule should be treated alike should by the rule be treated alike.

So there it is: Equality is entirely "[c]ircular." It tells us to treat like people alike; but when we ask who "like people" are, we are told they are "people who should be treated alike." Equality is an empty vessel with no substantive moral content of its own. Without moral standards, equality remains meaningless, a formula that can have nothing to say about how we should act. With such standards, equality becomes superfluous, a formula that can do nothing but repeat what we already know. As Bernard Williams observed, "when the statement of equality ceases to claim more than is warranted, it rather rapidly reaches the point where it claims less than is interesting." . . . Relationships of equality (and inequality) are derivative, secondary relationships; they are logically posterior, not anterior, to rights. To say that two persons are the same in a certain respect is to presuppose a rule—a prescribed standard for treating them—that both fully satisfy. Before such a rule is established, no standard of comparison exists. After such a rule is established, equality between them is a "logical consequence" of the established rule. They are then "equal" in respect of the rule because that is what equal means: "Equally" means "according to one and the same rule." They are also then entitled to equal treatment under the rule because that is what possessing a rule means: "To conform to a rule is (tautologically) to apply it to the cases to which it applies." To say that two people are "equal" and entitled to be treated "equally" is to say that they both fully satisfy the criteria of a governing rule of treatment. It says nothing at all about the content or wisdom of the governing rule. . . .

It might be thought that, while relationships of equality logically follow substantive definitions of right, equality may also precede definitions of right. Thus, it might be thought that a substantive right of persons to be treated with human respect is itself a product of an antecedent judgment that all persons are equal. That is not so. To see why, consider how one would go about deciding whether monstrously deformed neonates or human embryos or stroke victims in irreversible comas should be treated as "persons" for purposes of the right to respect. In trying to make the decision, one gets nowhere by intoning that all persons are equal, because the very question is whether the three candidates are indeed "persons" within the meaning of the rule. Nor does it do any good to say that likes should be treated alike, because the very question is whether the three candidates are indeed alike for purposes of human respect. Rather, one must first identify the trait that entitles anyone to be treated with respect and then ascertain empirically whether the trait appears in one or more of the three candidates.[40] If the candidates possess

---

40. The issue of the empirical basis for moral traits has caused some confusion. Some commentators, believing that relationships of equality must be grounded in some verifiable traits, tend to conclude that equality is entirely empirical. . . . Others, believing that an "ought" cannot be inferred from an "is," tend to conclude that moral notions of equality have no empirical basis. . . . In fact, both contending camps are correct. Statements of moral and legal equality do have an empirical base, because otherwise one would have no way of distinguishing those creatures who are equal from those who are not. . . . Yet at the same time, statements of moral or legal equality also presuppose a normative element. . . . In short, statements of equality presuppose the presence of empirical traits that we decide ought to carry certain moral consequences.

the relevant trait, they become "persons" within the meaning of the rule and hence entitled to respect. If they lack the relevant trait, they are not "persons," not equal to persons, and not to be treated like persons for purposes of the rule.

STEVEN BURTON, COMMENT ON "EMPTY IDEAS": LOGICAL POSITIVIST ANALYSES OF EQUALITY AND RULES, 91 YALE L.J. 1136-1141, 1144-1147 (1982): In a recent article in the Harvard Law Review, Professor Peter Westen directs his considerable capacity for logical analysis at the idea of equality. Professor Westen asserts and defends "two propositions: (1) that statements of equality logically entail (and necessarily collapse into) simpler statements of rights; and (2) that the additional step of transforming simple statements of rights into statements of equality not only involves unnecessary work but also engenders profound conceptual confusion." Therefore, he says, equality is an "empty idea" that "should be banished from moral and legal discourse as an explanatory norm."

Many, no doubt, will wish to defend equality as a concept with independent content, at least in some situations. This Comment takes a different tack. "Statements of rights" (rules) are the heroes of Professor Westen's story, though they are spared the scrutiny lavished on equality. He seems to regard rules as suitable norms for explanatory moral and legal discourse — norms that in themselves are independent of equality, imbued with content, and comparatively simple to apply without confusion.[4] Using methods of logical analysis similar to those Westen used to criticize equality, this Comment will demonstrate that rules collapse into equality and also are empty, in the sense that Westen regards equality as empty. By the logical positivist method of analysis, both equality and rules must be banished from explanatory legal and moral discourse, a move that would render such discourse impossible. The alternative is to reject that method of analysis because it proves too much, and to retain both equality and rules as instruments of thought and argument. . . .

Now the assumption seems to be that "the terms of the rule *dictate* that it be applied," and that they do so by an intellectual process that does not depend of necessity on considerations of equality, or on other norms that are vulnerable to the criticisms made of equality.[13] Though Professor Westen did not undertake to analyze the logic of rules in his paper, such an analysis is necessary to the soundness of his thesis, which appeals to the meaningfulness and analytical simplicity of rules as contrasted with equality. We would have two choices if the idea of substantive rights, determined by the language of rules, were as empty as, and collapsed

4. Professor Westen might regard substantive rights as empty ideas analytically, but useful ones nonetheless. Cf. Westen at 579 n. 147. ("Some formal concepts [such as rights] are quite handy, even indispensible [*sic*].") He argues that equality as a form of analysis is not useful, largely because "people do not realize that [equality] is derivative [from substantive rights], and not realizing it, they allow equality to distort the substance of their decisionmaking." It would seem to be at least equally so that "people" often do not realize that statements of substantive rights themselves are empty of content in the same sense, and allow the so-called plain meanings of such statements to distort their decision making. Westen offers no empirical grounds for concluding that equality causes more confusion than rules.

13. To summarize, the principal criticisms were (1) that statements of equality have no substantive content *of their own*, but depend on norms outside equality *itself;* (2) that equality is a wholly normative concept, lacking the identification of empirical traits, the presence of which would entitle a person to the treatment claimed; and (3) that application of the equality norm requires logically illicit moves between "is" and "ought." To justify banishing equality while retaining rules requires at least that rules be different from and better than equality by the same criteria.

into, the idea of equality. We could conclude that rules also should be "banished from moral and legal discourse as an explanatory norm," or that neither concept should be banished because the method of analysis yielding such an absurd result is inappropriate. . . .

It is simply wrong, however, to suggest that substantive rights can be determined in any case without reference to a person's normative relationship to other right-sholders, at least if the statement is meant to convey what is involved in legal reasoning. Let us consider the right of free speech. The general terms of the First Amendment appear on their face to be simple to apply: "Congress shall make no law . . . abridging the freedom of speech. . . ." We will apply this general proscription to two particular cases, which will serve as illustrations throughout the remainder of this Part.

Imagine that a state has made it a crime to hang the Governor in effigy, and that a state has made it a crime to hang any person, including the Governor. It will be seen that the Supreme Court could not reach conclusions as to the validity of these laws without considering the normative relationship of (1) hanging the Governor or (2) hanging the Governor in effigy to other activities that enjoy (or do not enjoy) First Amendment protection. The Court must determine whether hanging the Governor in effigy or in the flesh is in some important aspect "like" such other activities—for example, (3) making a public speech criticizing the Governor or (4) hanging one's spouse. Because "the terms of the rule" do not "dictate" which aspect of each activity is *important*, arguments based on the rule collapse into arguments by analogy, which themselves are claims to equal treatment under the law. . . .

. . . In the analysis of reasoning, analogies necessarily appeal to the principle that "like cases should be treated alike"—the equality principle—and are vulnerable to the criticisms Westen makes of equality, to the same extent. . . .

To separate rules from equality completely, one who would adopt Professor Westen's position seems forced to regard legal reasoning as fundamentally deductive, rather than purposive, inductive, or analogical in character. Only a logical positivist model of legal reasoning can purport to explain rules and rights independently of equality or other similarly vulnerable norms. Thus, in the hypothetical free speech cases, a statement of the state's general duty of behavior (the rule) would stand as the major premise of a syllogism. A statement of the state's treatment of the person (the facts) would stand as the minor premise. Whether the state acted in accord with its duty would depend on whether the rule logically entailed the facts.

That this is Professor Westen's view of all defensible legal reasoning seems a fair interpretation of his expressions in this work, despite the facial implausibility of such a mechanical model. To repeat, he says that "[t]o decide whether a person's speech rights are violated, one *juxtaposes* the state's general duty of behavior against the state's particular treatment of the person to determine whether the state treats the person in *accord* with its prescribed duty." He emphasizes that equality between two persons "is a 'logical consequence' of the established rule." Thus, "[r]elationships of equality are derivative, secondary relationships; they are logically posterior, not anterior, to rights." . . .

I suggest that the two Governor-hanging cases are clear because we engage in analogical reasoning. We posit a clear case of protected speech (a lecture criticizing the Governor's policies) and a clear case of murder (killing one's spouse). In the light of the values underlying the First Amendment, we regard hanging the

Governor in effigy as more like the first case, and hanging the Governor as more like the second. And we regard all four cases as easy ones. Of course, no two of the four cases are alike in all respects, and all four cases are alike in some respects. We make a normative judgment as to what respects are the important ones.

That judgment, however, is not a logical consequence of the terms of the First Amendment, which cannot be applied in a particular case without recourse to such analogies. For example, all four cases are "expression" in some respect, while none of the four cases is "expression" in all respects; and all are "anti-social behaviors" in some but not all respects. To apply the rule, we must make judgments about which respects are important in each case. The judgment of importance in applying a rule, like the judgment of similarity in using an analogy, depends on unspecified values outside the rule itself, and involves us in analytical problems of moving from "ought" to "is" when we apply the rule. Professor Westen therefore errs in stating that the conclusions are the "logical consequences" of the rule—not normative judgments but logically deduced from a "given." Where are the "given" rules that distinguish the Governor-hanging cases?

To test the point further, let us posit some rules (really meta-rules) that stand on a different logical plane and tell us how to apply the enacted rules: (1) The First Amendment shall not invalidate state statutes if the statutes are necessary to protect a compelling state interest; and (2) a constitutional provision shall be construed according to the intention of the Framers or according to its purpose. It should be observed that both of the meta-rules are judge-made and consequently partake of the problems of common-law rules, making the process of applying enacted rules wholly dependent on analogical reasoning in the same manner. But let us pass over that problem and inquire whether these rules can be applied without engaging in reasoning by analogy—without using the equality principle to determine substantive rights.

The logic of the so-called "compelling state interest" test is fairly transparent. To say that the First Amendment invalidates a state statute unless the statute is necessary to protect a compelling state interest is logically reducible to saying something like: Freedom of expression is more important than a state statute unless the state statute is more important than freedom of expression. Again, what do we mean by "important"? Surely nothing follows as a "logical consequence" in any real-world case from "important" as the key term in the major premise of a syllogism. Neither "compelling state interest" nor "importance" are things that exist in nature (observables), nor can they be reduced analytically to necessary and sufficient conditions that are observable without deriving an "is" from an "ought." They are normative concepts. As such, they beg the question whether application of a state murder statute to one who hung the Governor, or a state statute against hanging the Governor in effigy, should be invalidated by the First Amendment: It should if it should. One might offer another rule to tell us, as a "logical consequence," what a compelling state interest is—a meta-meta-rule—but it should be apparent that this tack leads to an infinite regress of no small significance.

The logic of construing a constitutional provision according to the intention of the Framers or according to its purpose could lead us into a similar regress. Neither "intention" nor "purpose" are observables, if we state them in the abstract. We can say that the Framers intended the First Amendment to protect "expression" or "political expression," though they said "speech" or that this was the purpose of the text. The problems of knowing such things, with the assurance necessary to exclude de novo normative judgments, are well-known. And even if we knew that the Framers had such an intention or purpose, we still do not know that hanging the Governor in effigy and in the flesh are not both "expression," or neither "expression," or one "expression" and the other not, or the other "expression" and the one not, so far as the logical consequences of the meta-rule take us. Again, we need a meta-meta-rule and are off into the darkness of a regress.

Alternatively, the purpose or intention (of "freedom of speech" or of "compelling state interest") can be stated in the particular. To do so, however, is to state a case, be it hypothetical or historical. To say merely that the evil before the minds of the Framers was, for example, suppression of the political opposition is again abstract, a negative version of the statement analyzed in the preceding paragraph. We must have a *case*, such as what happened to Zenger, or what Zenger did. As "general propositions do not decide concrete cases," however, "[c]oncrete decisions do not make law." What Zenger did can be described in narrow terms and limited to the press, or in broad terms and expanded to cover all thought and action. Another meta-meta-rule seems necessary to tell us what the rule of the Zenger case is, unless we break the regress by shifting from deduction to analogy. Then, we might say, hanging the Governor in effigy is like what Zenger did but hanging the Governor is not, and all might agree.

Of course, shifting from deduction to analogy (equality) does not solve our problems as analysts of legal reasoning. The problem identified by Professor Westen and others—identifying normative grounds for purposes of determining whether cases are alike or unalike—is no small problem. It is not solved, however, by shifting from equality to rules, which also depend on unspecified values outside the rules themselves. Thus, if rules are given the same kind of intensive logical analysis that Westen gives to equality, they too stand empty and collapse into equality. This logical analysis of rules and equality drives us back and forth between the two in a regress, as when we stand between the barber's mirrors. . . .

The debate over the nature of equality (as reflected in the dialogue between Westen and Burton) has a long philosophical history, but it also has an immediate practical significance. The notion that like cases should be treated alike has a strong rational and emotional pull; but without substantive determinations of what counts in determining "like cases," the commitment to treating like cases alike appears empty. Consider a concrete example. What does it mean to provide equal medical insurance to males and females? Does it violate equality to cover pregnancy, since that provides a benefit that only females can take advantage of? Or does it violate equality by excluding a major health issue from coverage, and where no analogous issue is excluded for males? Or consider pension benefits on the assumption that the life expectancy of males is shorter than females. Should males and females be paid the same monthly benefits or instead an amount that actuarially will result in equal payouts over the lives of both? These examples point out what is at stake in the Westen/Burton debate: Before one can analyze "equality," one needs to know what counts for the analysis. For an extended development of this idea, see Amartya Sen, Inequality Reexamined (1992).

C.　Autonomy, Choice, and the Right to Counsel

1.　The Right to Proceed Pro Se

Somewhat counterintuitively, possessing a right does not necessarily mean that one also possesses the right to dispense with that right. The right to trial by jury, for example, does not mean that a defendant has a *right* to a bench trial; the prosecution has an interest as well, and the trial judge has some discretion whether or not to proceed with a bench trial. And as we saw in Section B.2., the right to conflict-free counsel does not necessarily engender a right to proceed with conflicted counsel.

What about the right to counsel itself? Does *Gideon*, with its emphasis on the indispensable role of counsel for ensuring the fairness of trials, suggest that defendants should be *required* to proceed with counsel? That might have been a logical assumption. But in Faretta v. California, 422 U.S. 806 (1975), the Court, in an opinion by Justice Stewart, held that a defendant has a constitutional right to proceed *without* counsel:

> Although not stated in the [Sixth] Amendment in so many words, the right to self-representation—to make one's own defense personally—is thus necessarily implied by the structure of the Amendment.[15] The right to defend is given directly to the accused; for it is he who suffers the consequences if the defense fails.
>
> The counsel provision supplements this design. It speaks of the "assistance" of counsel, and an assistant, however expert, is still an assistant. The language and spirit of the Sixth Amendment contemplate that counsel, like the other defense tools guaranteed by the Amendment, shall be an aid to a willing defendant—not an organ of the State interposed between an unwilling defendant and his right to defend himself personally. To thrust counsel upon the accused, against his considered wish, thus violates the logic of the Amendment. In such a case, counsel is not an assistant, but a master; and the right to make a defense is stripped of the personal character upon which the Amendment insists. It is true that when a defendant chooses to have a lawyer manage and present his case, law and tradition may allocate to the counsel the power to make binding decisions of trial strategy in many areas. . . . This allocation can only be justified, however, by the defendant's consent, at the outset, to accept counsel as his representative. An unwanted counsel "represents" the defendant only through a tenuous and unacceptable legal fiction. Unless the accused has acquiesced in such representation, the defense presented is not the defense guaranteed him by the Constitution, for, in a very real sense, it is not *his* defense.
>
> . . . There can be no blinking the fact that the right of an accused to conduct his own defense seems to cut against the grain of this Court's decisions holding that the Constitution requires that no accused can be convicted and imprisoned unless he has been accorded the right to the assistance of counsel. . . . For it is surely true that the basic thesis of those decisions is that the help of a lawyer is essential to assure

---

15. . . . The inference of rights is not, of course, a mechanical exercise. In Singer v. United States, 380 U.S. 24, the Court held that an accused has no right to a bench trial, despite his capacity to waive his right to a jury trial. In so holding, the Court stated that "[t]he ability to waive a constitutional right does not ordinarily carry with it the right to insist upon the opposite of that right." Id., at 34-35. . . .

We follow the approach of *Singer* here. Our concern is with an independent right of self-representation. We do not suggest that this right arises mechanically from a defendant's power to waive the right to the assistance of counsel. On the contrary, the right must be independently found in the structure and history of the constitutional text.

the defendant a fair trial. And a strong argument can surely be made that the whole thrust of those decisions must inevitably lead to the conclusion that a State may constitutionally impose a lawyer upon even an unwilling defendant.

But it is one thing to hold that every defendant, rich or poor, has the right to the assistance of counsel, and quite another to say that a State may compel a defendant to accept a lawyer he does not want. The value of state-appointed counsel was not unappreciated by the Founders, yet the notion of compulsory counsel was utterly foreign to them. And whatever else may be said of those who wrote the Bill of Rights, surely there can be no doubt that they understood the inestimable worth of free choice.

It is undeniable that in most criminal prosecutions defendants could better defend with counsel's guidance than by their own unskilled efforts. But where the defendant will not voluntarily accept representation by counsel, the potential advantage of a lawyer's training and experience can be realized, if at all, only imperfectly. To force a lawyer on a defendant can only lead him to believe that the law contrives against him. Moreover, it is not inconceivable that in some rare instances, the defendant might in fact present his case more effectively by conducting his own defense. Personal liberties are not rooted in the law of averages. The right to defend is personal. The defendant, and not his lawyer or the State, will bear the personal consequences of a conviction. It is the defendant, therefore, who must be free personally to decide whether in his particular case counsel is to his advantage. And although he may conduct his own defense ultimately to his own detriment, his choice must be honored out of "that respect for the individual which is the lifeblood of the law." Illinois v. Allen, 397 U.S. 337, 350-351 (Brennan, J., concurring).[46]

Chief Justice Burger, Justice Rehnquist, and Justice Blackmun dissented, mostly out of concern that recognizing a constitutional right of self-representation might lead to the reversal of convictions when defendants proceed pro se and then botch their trials.

Pro se representation is uncommon, and thus not a large practical problem for the legal system. Moreover, those few defendants who elect to proceed pro se are systematically convicted in short order, largely because (precisely as the *Faretta* dissenters predicted) such individuals typically are incompetent to conduct their own defense. One famous case involved the so-called "twentieth hijacker," Zacarias Moussaoui, who was accused of involvement in the plot to destroy the World Trade Center on Sept. 11, 2001. He exercised his right to proceed pro se, but in a curious twist, the decision worked temporarily to his advantage. This is because he insisted on interviewing other terrorism-related prisoners held by the United States whom he asserted might provide exculpatory evidence. The U.S. government objected on national security grounds. The district court initially ordered that adequate access be provided to Moussaoui (acting as his own lawyer), but the Fourth Circuit later

---

46. We are told that many criminal defendants representing themselves may use the courtroom for deliberate disruption of their trials. But the right of self-representation has been recognized from our beginnings by federal law and by most of the States, and no such result has thereby occurred. Moreover, the trial judge may terminate self-representation by a defendant who deliberately engages in serious and obstructionist misconduct. See Illinois v. Allen, 397 U.S. 337. Of course, a State may—even over objection by the accused—appoint a "standby counsel" to aid the accused if and when the accused requests help, and to be available to represent the accused in the event that termination of the defendant's self-representation is necessary. See United States v. Dougherty, 473 F.2d 1113, 1124-1126 (D.C. Cir.).

The right of self-representation is not a license to abuse the dignity of the courtroom. Neither is it a license not to comply with relevant rules of procedural and substantive law. Thus, whatever else may or may not be open to him on appeal, a defendant who elects to represent himself cannot thereafter complain that the quality of his own defense amounted to a denial of "effective assistance of counsel."

ruled that in-person meetings were not required. See United States v. Moussaoui, 365 F.3d 292 (4th Cir. 2004); 382 F.3d 453 (4th Cir. 2004). Moussaoui eventually pleaded guilty to six counts of conspiracy, and was sentenced to six terms of life imprisonment without possibility of parole.

For a good example of the dangers (and maybe the benefits?) of self-representation, consider the case of Adam Martin, accused—along with two of his brothers—of robbing several banks along I-35 in Austin, Texas. Adam chose to represent himself. At a pretrial hearing, he subpoenaed his brother, Michael (who was already serving time after pleading guilty to one of the robberies), and asked him to state whether Adam had committed any crimes. To which Michael replied: "Yeah. You were with me on four different bank robberies, Adam, you know that."

At trial, things did not get better for Adam. His cross-examination of Michael (by now, a prosecution witness) included bizarre questions about Michael's nicknames, his religion, and the time the brothers spent together in jail. At one point, Adam asked Michael, "Do you fear me in any way?" Michael responded, "I've seen you do people bad ways," and related how Adam had attacked people with knives and was once involved with organized crime. When Adam noted that "I haven't been convicted of it," Michael replied, "That doesn't mean it's not true."

Adam was convicted on all charges. Afterward, he explained: "The right to defend yourself in this country is one of the greatest rights you have." He also said that he considered disrupting the trial, but decided not to do so because he feared it might jeopardize the rights of future pro se litigants. See Steven Kreytak, "Eldest of Three Bank-Robbing Brothers Guilty; 'I-35 Robber,' Who Acted as Own Attorney, Not Surprised at Verdict," Austin American-Statesman, August 19, 2004, p. A1.

In McCaskle v. Wiggins, 465 U.S. 168 (1984), the Court fleshed out the concept of "standby counsel" mentioned in footnote 46 of *Faretta*. The defendant, Wiggins, initially exercised his *Faretta* right of self-representation and objected to the appointment of standby counsel, but over the course of two separate trials on the same charges he repeatedly changed his mind about whether or not he truly wanted to go it alone (the Court aptly described Wiggins's position regarding appointed counsel as "volatile"). As the second trial approached, Wiggins requested appointment of not one but two standby counsel (Samples and Graham). According to the Court, here is what happened next:

> The trial began . . . and shortly thereafter Wiggins interrupted his cross-examination of a witness to consult with Graham off the record. Still later, Wiggins expressly agreed to allow Graham to conduct voir dire of another witness.
>
> Wiggins started the next day of trial . . . with a request that the trial not proceed in Samples' absence from the courtroom. Later that morning Wiggins requested that counsel not be allowed to assist or interrupt, but a short while after Wiggins interrupted his own cross-examination of a witness to confer with Samples off the record. When the trial reconvened in the afternoon, Wiggins agreed to proceed in Samples' absence. After Samples returned, however, Wiggins again interrupted his own cross-examination of a witness to confer with him. Later Wiggins insisted that counsel should not initiate private consultations with Wiggins. Before the end of the day Wiggins once again found occasion to interrupt his own examination of a witness to confer with Samples.
>
> On the following day, . . . Wiggins agreed that Graham would make Wiggins' opening statement to the jury. [The next day], Wiggins was once again willing to have the trial proceed in the absence of one of his standby counsel. Following his conviction,

Wiggins moved for a new trial. . . . Wiggins denounced the services standby counsel had provided. He insisted that they had unfairly interfered with his presentation of his defense.

Id., at 173-174. The Court held that Wiggins's *Faretta* rights were not violated:

In determining whether a defendant's *Faretta* rights have been respected, the primary focus must be on whether the defendant had a fair chance to present his case in his own way. *Faretta* itself dealt with the defendant's affirmative right to participate, not with the limits on standby counsel's additional involvement. The specific rights to make his voice heard that Wiggins was plainly accorded, form the core of a defendant's right of self-representation.

We recognize, nonetheless, that the right to speak for oneself entails more than the opportunity to add one's voice to a cacophony of others. . . . [T]he objectives underlying the right to proceed pro se may be undermined by unsolicited and excessively intrusive participation by standby counsel. In proceedings before a jury the defendant may legitimately be concerned that multiple voices "for the defense" will confuse the message the defendant wishes to convey, thus defeating *Faretta*'s objectives.[7] Accordingly, the *Faretta* right must impose some limits on the extent of standby counsel's unsolicited participation.[8]

First, the pro se defendant is entitled to preserve actual control over the case he chooses to present to the jury. This is the core of the *Faretta* right. If standby counsel's participation over the defendant's objection effectively allows counsel to make or substantially interfere with any significant tactical decisions, or to control the questioning of witnesses, or to speak *instead* of the defendant on any matter of importance, the *Faretta* right is eroded.

Second, participation by standby counsel without the defendant's consent should not be allowed to destroy the jury's perception that the defendant is representing himself. The defendant's appearance in the status of one conducting his own defense is important in a criminal trial, since the right to appear pro se exists to affirm the accused's individual dignity and autonomy. . . . From the jury's perspective, the message conveyed by the defense may depend as much on the messenger as on the message itself. From the defendant's own point of view, the right to appear pro se can lose much of its importance if only the lawyers in the courtroom know that the right is being exercised.

Participation by standby counsel outside the presence of the jury engages only the first of these two limitations. . . . *Faretta* rights are adequately vindicated in proceedings outside the presence of the jury if the pro se defendant is allowed to address the court freely on his own behalf and if disagreements between counsel and the pro se defendant are resolved in the defendant's favor whenever the matter is one that would normally be left to the discretion of counsel.

Participation by standby counsel in the presence of the jury is more problematic. It is here that the defendant may legitimately claim that excessive involvement by counsel will destroy the appearance that the defendant is acting pro se. This, in turn, may erode the dignitary values that the right to self-representation is intended to promote

---

7. A pro se defendant must generally accept any unsolicited help or hindrance that may come from the judge who chooses to call and question witnesses, from the prosecutor who faithfully exercises his duty to present evidence favorable to the defense, from the plural voices speaking "for the defense" in a trial of more than one defendant, or from an amicus counsel appointed to assist the court, see Brown v. United States, 264 F.2d 363, 369 (C.A.D.C. 1959) (Judge Burger, concurring in part).

8. Since the right of self-representation is a right that when exercised usually increases the likelihood of a trial outcome unfavorable to the defendant, its denial is not amenable to "harmless error" analysis. The right is either respected or denied; its deprivation cannot be harmless. . . .

and may undercut the defendant's presentation to the jury of his own most effective defense. . . .

The record in this case reveals that Wiggins' pro se efforts were undermined primarily by his own, frequent changes of mind regarding counsel's role. . . . In these circumstances it is very difficult to determine how much of counsel's participation was in fact contrary to Wiggins' desires of the moment.

Faretta does not require a trial judge to permit "hybrid" representation of the type Wiggins was actually allowed. But if a defendant is given the opportunity and elects to have counsel appear before the court or jury, his complaints concerning counsel's subsequent unsolicited participation lose much of their force. A defendant does not have a constitutional right to choreograph special appearances by counsel. Once a pro se defendant invites or agrees to any substantial participation by counsel, subsequent appearances by counsel must be presumed to be with the defendant's acquiescence, at least until the defendant expressly and unambiguously renews his request that standby counsel be silenced. . . .

[W]e make explicit today what is already implicit in *Faretta*: A defendant's Sixth Amendment rights are not violated when a trial judge appoints standby counsel—even over the defendant's objection—to relieve the judge of the need to explain and enforce basic rules of courtroom protocol or to assist the defendant in overcoming routine obstacles that stand in the way of the defendant's achievement of his own clearly indicated goals. Participation by counsel to steer a defendant through the basic procedures of trial is permissible even in the unlikely event that it somewhat undermines the pro se defendant's appearance of control over his own defense. . . .

Faretta affirmed the defendant's constitutional right to appear on stage at his trial. We recognize that a pro se defendant may wish to dance a solo, not a pas de deux. Standby counsel must generally respect that preference. But counsel need not be excluded altogether, especially when the participation is outside the presence of the jury or is with the defendant's express or tacit consent. The defendant in this case was allowed to make his own appearances as he saw fit. In our judgment counsel's unsolicited involvement was held within reasonable limits.

Id., at 168-188.

May counsel "waive" the honor of representing an indigent defendant? The problem arises primarily after conviction, when counsel believes that an appeal would be fruitless. In Anders v. California, 386 U.S. 738 (1967), the Court held that an attorney who wishes to withdraw from a case after conviction on the grounds that an appeal would be wholly frivolous may request permission to do so but must file a brief referring to anything in the record that might support an appeal. The court must then to decide whether to permit withdrawal. Requiring counsel to write a brief in support of what counsel believes to be a wholly frivolous appeal may seem curious, but there are cases in which such briefs have led to reversals. See Paul D. Carrington, Daniel J. Meador & Maurice Rosenberg, Justice on Appeal 77 (1976).

The Court reaffirmed *Anders* in Penson v. Ohio, 488 U.S. 75 (1988), holding that it was error to fail to appoint counsel to brief and argue any claim that a court of appeals finds to be colorable, even if problematic. The Court also held that *Strickland* does not apply in this context, for otherwise *Anders* would be effectively overruled. But the states still retain some flexibility in complying with *Anders*. In McCoy v. Court of Appeals of Wisconsin, District 1, 486 U.S. 429 (1988), the Court upheld a Wisconsin statute requiring *Anders* briefs to include a discussion of why the issues raised in the brief lacked merit. And in Smith v. Robbins, 528 U.S. 259 (2000), the Court upheld California's rule, which (unlike *Anders*) does not allow counsel to request withdrawal and requires counsel to remain silent on the merits of the case.

In the context of trial representation, it is a given that the ultimate decision on defense strategy belongs to the defendant (although good defense attorneys probably rarely, if ever, have much difficulty persuading a defendant to go along with the lawyer's view of sound strategy). But on appeal, there are limits to the defendant's ability to control counsel. In Jones v. Barnes, 463 U.S. 745 (1983), the Court rejected the defendant's assertion that "counsel has a constitutional duty to raise every non-frivolous issue requested by the defendant":

> . . . For judges to second-guess reasonable professional judgments and impose on appointed counsel a duty to raise every "colorable" claim suggested by a client would disserve the very goal of vigorous and effective advocacy that underlies *Anders*. Nothing in the Constitution or our interpretation of that document requires such a standard.

Interestingly, given *Faretta* as well as the Court's general view about defendant autonomy, a convicted defendant does *not* have the right to dispense with the assistance of counsel on appeal. See Martinez v. Court of Appeal of California, 528 U.S. 152, 159 (2000):

> No one, including Martinez and the *Faretta* majority, attempts to argue that as a rule pro se representation is wise, desirable or efficient.[10] Although we found in *Faretta* that the right to defend oneself at trial is "fundamental" in nature, 422 U.S., at 817, it is clear that it is representation by counsel that is the standard, not the exception. See Patterson v. Illinois, 487 U.S. 285, 307 (1988) (noting the "strong presumption against" waiver of right to counsel). Our experience has taught us that "a pro se defense is usually a bad defense, particularly when compared to a defense provided by an experienced criminal defense attorney."[11]
>
> . . . Even at the trial level . . . , the government's interest in ensuring the integrity and efficiency of the trial at times outweighs the defendant's interest in acting as his own lawyer. . . . In the appellate context, the balance between the two competing interests surely tips in favor of the State. The status of the accused defendant, who retains a presumption of innocence throughout the trial process, changes dramatically when a jury returns a guilty verdict. . . . In the words of the *Faretta* majority, appellate proceedings are simply not a case of "hal[ing] a person into its criminal courts.

NOTES ON COMPETENCY AND WAIVER

1. Is there, or ought there to be, a requirement of competency to waive counsel, separate from the issues of competency to proceed to trial and a voluntary waiver? The New York Court of Appeals answered the question negatively in the aptly named case of People v. Reason, 37 N.Y.2d 351 (1975). According to the court, "it would be difficult to say that a standard which was designed to determine whether

---

10. Some critics argue that the right to proceed pro se at trial in certain cases is akin to allowing the defendant to waive his right to a fair trial. See, e.g., United States v. Farhad, 190 F.3d 1097, 1106-1107 (CA9 1999) (Reinhardt, J., concurring specially).

11. Decker, The Sixth Amendment Right to Shoot Oneself in the Foot: An Assessment of the Guarantee of Self-Representation Twenty Years After *Faretta*, 6 Seton Hall Const. L.J. 483, 598 (1996).

a defendant was capable of defending himself, is inadequate when he chooses to conduct his own defense." Id., at 354. Bearing in mind the limits of anecdotal data, consider the decision in *Reason* in light of the following excerpts from Mr. Reason's opening and closing to the jury:

The Court: The order of business before the Court now, Mr. Reason, is your opening statement. Will you proceed and make it properly?

The Defendant: I will try to prove the existence of the dead, reincarnation of the realm of Todis, . . . Hays, . . . Hell, the underworld and the hushed truth of society based upon the entities of which our way of life is based. Fighting among themselves even for possession of the living and the dead and the association of whatever rationality or religion.

I will prove an angel, demon, a devil and a soul. Paradoxically I will introduce proof of police corruption, political control of government, criminal affairs according to certain arbitrations, abiding the way of life for a particular entity of homage of their dues for the bargaining of their souls. . . .

I will prove or I will disprove Christ as our God, saints, the devil and let these entities of the power to take human life and due — there is many deeply religious people that say it was the will of God who in many instances — it isn't always the will of God, but the will of other entities or as we read at the bottom of insurance contracts except by acts of God, sometimes by those acts of men too, by means of what may be considered a spiritual sort seemingly to have been of natural causes and often some that would have died by the cause of another is used as an instrument to die; that the other would be subject to the instrument of society such as fate, destiny, pre-destiny. But history is an accepted fact as disorderly as it may be which I will also attempt to prove, and historically men have proved, prayed to something of a greater competency, to Jehovah, Brahma, Ghatama, God and others. They believe, practice and perform rituals of sorcery, Budabo, witchcraft, Christianity, black magic, occult, Bubanza, . . . soothsayers, fortune tellers and priests. . . .

I will introduce the defendant's bad character to show his good intention or expose his entire criminal record, acts of his criminal importance, accomplishments, activities and disciplinary reports be considered. . . .

[In closing, the defendant argued in part:]

The issue of the dead belonged to God. It's in the bible. Each of the dead belong to God. God seeks the past. Life gives birth to time, time is passed, just passed, time passed, just passed. Anticipate time. Time is past. Hour has already been. I wrote right here, I would like to repeat that and I would, I would like to repeat that.

A long time ago, anticipating this, I would like to repeat that.

The issue of the dead belong of God. God seeks what is passed. Life gives birth to time. Time is past. We set time ahead of us confusing time and motion with duration. We are towards a delusion, perhaps, create illusion of a present that don't really exist; create instantaneous occurring successions on the same pattern offset by the evolving sun as time though it made difference to the sun how fast — (Unintelligible). Now, look at that, you people. I wrote it for you people. Memorized the whole thing if I had the time. This is not only pedantics, I quote Corinthian, Chapter 13, 8th Verse. . . .

2. In Godinez v. Moran, 509 U.S. 389 (1993), the Supreme Court held that the constitutional minimum standard for competency to waive the right to counsel, as well as to plead guilty, is no higher than the constitutional standard for competency to stand trial. That standard was established in Dusky v. United States, 420 U.S. 162 (1960): whether the defendant has "sufficient present ability to consult with his lawyer with a reasonable degree of rational understanding" and has "a rational as well as factual understanding of the proceedings against him." The *Moran* Court added:

> A finding that a defendant is competent to stand trial, however, is not all that is necessary before he may be permitted to plead guilty or waive his right to counsel. In addition to determining that a defendant who seeks to plead guilty or waive counsel is competent, a trial court must satisfy itself that the waiver of his constitutional rights is knowing and voluntary. Parke v. Raley, 506 U.S. 20, 28-29 (1992) (guilty plea); *Faretta*, supra, at 835 (waiver of counsel). In this sense there is a "heightened" standard for pleading guilty and for waiving the right to counsel, but it is not a heightened standard of *competence*.[12]
>
> This two-part inquiry is what we had in mind in [Westbrook v. Arizona, 384 U.S. 150 (1966) (per curiam)]. When we distinguished between "competence to stand trial" and "competence to waive [the] constitutional right to the assistance of counsel," 384 U.S., at 150, we were using "competence to waive" as a shorthand for the "intelligent and competent waiver" requirement of Johnson v. Zerbst. . . . Thus, *Westbrook* stands only for the unremarkable proposition that when a defendant seeks to waive his right to counsel, a determination that he is competent to stand trial is not enough; the waiver must also be intelligent and voluntary before it can be accepted.

Id., at 400-402. The Court also noted that states could choose to impose a higher standard of competency to stand trial than the one constitutionally mandated, under due process, by *Dusky*.

Some states, perhaps taking the hint from *Moran*, imposed restrictions on waiving the right to counsel that went beyond the bare-bones minimum of *Faretta*. One such state-law restriction reached the Court in the following case:

INDIANA v. EDWARDS, 554 U.S. 164 (2008): This case focuses upon a criminal defendant whom a state court found mentally competent to stand trial if represented by counsel but not mentally competent to conduct that trial himself. We must decide whether in these circumstances the Constitution forbids a State from insisting that the defendant proceed to trial with counsel, the State thereby denying the defendant the right to represent himself. . . . We conclude that the Constitution does not forbid a State so to insist.

. . . [I]n our view, a right of self-representation at trial will not "affirm the dignity" of a defendant who lacks the mental capacity to conduct his defense without the assistance of counsel. *Wiggins*, 465 U.S., at 176-177 ("Dignity" and "autonomy" of individual underlie self-representation right). To the contrary, given defendant's uncertain mental state, the spectacle that could well result from his self-representation at trial is at least as likely to prove humiliating as ennobling. Moreover, insofar as a defendant's lack of capacity threatens an improper conviction or sentence,

---

12. The focus of a competency inquiry is the defendant's mental capacity; the question is whether he has the ability to understand the proceedings. . . . The purpose of the "knowing and voluntary" inquiry, by contrast, is to determine whether the defendant actually does understand the significance and consequences of a particular decision and whether the decision is uncoerced. . . .

self-representation in that exceptional context undercuts the most basic of the Constitution's criminal law objectives, providing a fair trial. As Justice Brennan put it, "[t]he Constitution would protect none of us if it prevented the courts from acting to preserve the very processes that the Constitution itself prescribes." Illinois v. Allen, 397 U.S., at 350 (concurring opinion). See *Martinez*, 528 U.S., at 162 ("Even at the trial level . . . the government's interest in ensuring the integrity and efficiency of the trial at times outweighs the defendant's interest in acting as his own lawyer"). . . .

Further, proceedings must not only be fair, they must "appear fair to all who observe them." Wheat v. United States, 486 U.S. 153, 160. . . . An amicus brief reports one psychiatrist's reaction to having observed a patient (a patient who had satisfied *Dusky*) try to conduct his own defense: "[H]ow in the world can our legal system allow an insane man to defend himself?" Brief for Ohio et al. as Amici Curiae 24. . . . The application of *Dusky*'s basic mental competence standard can help in part to avoid this result. But given the different capacities needed to proceed to trial without counsel, there is little reason to believe that *Dusky* alone is sufficient. At the same time, the trial judge, particularly one such as the trial judge in this case, who presided over one of Edwards' competency hearings and his two trials, will often prove best able to make more fine-tuned mental capacity decisions, tailored to the individualized circumstances of a particular defendant.

We consequently conclude that . . . the Constitution permits States to insist upon representation by counsel for those competent enough to stand trial under *Dusky* but who still suffer from severe mental illness to the point where they are not competent to conduct trial proceedings by themselves.

Indiana has also asked us to adopt . . . a more specific standard that would "deny a criminal defendant the right to represent himself at trial where the defendant cannot communicate coherently with the court or a jury." Brief for Petitioner 20 (emphasis deleted). We are sufficiently uncertain, however, as to how that particular standard would work in practice to refrain from endorsing it as a federal constitutional standard here. We need not now, and we do not, adopt it. . . .

JUSTICE SCALIA, dissenting:

Beyond [forbidding a defendant to disrupt the courtroom], we have never constrained the ability of a defendant to retain "actual control over the case he chooses to present to the jury"—what we have termed "the core of the *Faretta* right." *Wiggins*, supra, at 178. . . .

. . . I would not adopt an approach to the right of self-representation that we have squarely rejected for other rights—allowing courts to disregard the right when doing so serves the purposes for which the right was intended. But if I were to adopt such an approach, I would remain in dissent, because I believe the Court's assessment of the purposes of the right of self-representation is inaccurate to boot. While there is little doubt that preserving individual "dignity" (to which the Court refers), is paramount among those purposes, there is equally little doubt that the loss of "dignity" the right is designed to prevent is not the defendant's making a fool of himself by presenting an amateurish or even incoherent defense. Rather, the dignity at issue is the supreme human dignity of being master of one's fate rather than a ward of the State—the dignity of individual choice. . . . In sum, if the Court is to honor the particular conception of "dignity" that underlies the self-representation right, it should respect the autonomy of the individual by honoring his choices knowingly and voluntarily made.

A further purpose that the Court finds is advanced by denial of the right of self-representation is the purpose of assuring that trials "appear fair to all who observe them." To my knowledge we have never denied a defendant a right simply on the ground that it would make his trial appear less "fair" to outside observers, and I would not inaugurate that principle here. But were I to do so, I would not apply it to deny a defendant the right to represent himself when he knowingly and voluntarily waives counsel. When Edwards stood to say that "I have a defense that I would like to represent or present to the Judge," it seems to me the epitome of both actual and apparent unfairness for the judge to say, I have heard "your desire to proceed by yourself and I've denied your request, so your attorney will speak for you from now on."

. . . The facts of this case illustrate this point with the utmost clarity. Edwards wished to take a self-defense case to the jury. His counsel preferred a defense that focused on lack of intent. Having been denied the right to conduct his own defense, Edwards was convicted without having had the opportunity to present to the jury the grounds he believed supported his innocence. I do not doubt that he likely would have been convicted anyway. But to hold that a defendant may be deprived of the right to make legal arguments for acquittal simply because a state-selected agent has made different arguments on his behalf is, as Justice Frankfurter [once] wrote, to "imprison a man in his privileges and call it the Constitution." In singling out mentally ill defendants for this treatment, the Court's opinion does not even have the questionable virtue of being politically correct. At a time when all society is trying to mainstream the mentally impaired, the Court permits them to be deprived of a basic constitutional right—for their own good.

NOTES AND QUESTIONS

1. After *Edwards*, apparently a state may permit a severely mentally ill defendant to commit judicial suicide but may also decline to do so. As interesting as this conclusion is the manner in which the Court reached it. *Faretta* is best understood as an exegesis on the significance of autonomy—the right to control oneself and one's decisions—for understanding the Sixth Amendment. Autonomy is one of three concepts that often are intermingled under the terms of the other two—privacy and dignity. Privacy refers to the right to control information about yourself, and dignity to the manner in which others must treat you. As can be seen in both *Wiggins* and *Edwards*, autonomy and dignity can be at odds with each other. Indeed, to some extent, *Wiggins* foreshadowed *Edwards* by suggesting that *Faretta*'s strong focus on autonomy must give way under the pressure of pragmatism to a focus on dignitary interests. This change allowed the Court ostensibly to protect *Faretta* rights while simultaneously protecting incompetent defendants from themselves.

2. Now consider the dissent. Isn't Justice Scalia right to be outraged by the notion that a state may hale a person into court to answer for a serious crime (because he *is* competent enough to stand trial), and also may force that person to be represented in court by a lawyer whom he doesn't want (because he *isn't* competent enough to represent himself)? How many defendants are likely to fall into that gap? And what do you think about Justice Scalia's argument that the defendant was actually deprived of the ability to make what he believed was his best defense?

3. Beyond the issue of competency, what does it mean that a waiver of counsel must be "knowing and intelligent"? Is that phrase internally inconsistent? If not, what are its referents? The Court in *Faretta* asserts that "technical knowledge" is

not even relevant to the inquiry and implies that on being convicted a technically incompetent individual may not assert ineffectiveness as a grounds for relief. How realistic is that? How would you react as a judge to a case in which an untrained person unknowingly forewent a potentially dispositive defense? If you believed that pro se representation had caused a false conviction, but recognized that no other legally adequate ground for reversal existed, would you feel bound by *Faretta*'s admonition that pro se litigants cannot claim error due to ineffectiveness? Might you be tempted to stretch other legal rules to reach the right result?

That is exactly what a number of courts have done, according to Sarah L. Allen, *Faretta*: Self-Representation, or Legal Misrepresentation? 90 Iowa L. Rev. 1553 (2005). The author searched for cases involving pro se representation that involved reversals of convictions, and in which there were dissents, the idea being that dissents might signal a majority stretching the law. A number of such cases were found with majority opinions fairly plainly stretching other legal rules to compensate for the inability to reverse on competency grounds.

4. Should a waiver of the Sixth Amendment right to counsel ever be allowed without first appointing counsel to discuss the matter with the defendant?

What if a defendant seeks to waive his right to counsel and plead guilty without the advice of counsel? Does the Constitution require that such a defendant be informed specifically by the trial judge, prior to entering the plea, that by virtue of waiving his right to counsel (1) he may wind up overlooking a viable defense, and (2) he may make an unwise decision about entering the plea? In Iowa v. Tovar, 541 U.S. 77 (2004), the Court rejected the claim that such warnings are essential to an intelligent and knowing waiver of the right to counsel, holding that in such a situation the Constitution requires knowledge of only the nature of charges, the right to be counseled about the plea, and the range of allowable punishments.

2.   The Right to Counsel of One's Choice

Throughout this chapter, there have been intimations that the Sixth Amendment might provide some protection for the right to counsel of one's choice, so long as either the defendant can afford an attorney or the attorney is otherwise willing to serve without reimbursement from the state for services provided. That issue came before the Court in the following case:

UNITED STATES v. GONZALEZ-LOPEZ

Certiorari to the United States Court of Appeals for the Eighth Circuit
548 U.S. 140 (2006)

JUSTICE SCALIA delivered the opinion of the Court.

We must decide whether a trial court's erroneous deprivation of a criminal defendant's choice of counsel entitles him to a reversal of his conviction.

I

Respondent Cuauhtemoc Gonzalez-Lopez was charged in the Eastern District of Missouri with conspiracy to distribute more than 100 kilograms of marijuana. His family hired attorney John Fahle to represent him. After the arraignment, respondent called a California attorney, Joseph Low, to discuss whether Low would represent him, either in addition to or instead of Fahle. Low flew from California to meet with respondent, who hired him. . . .

The following week, respondent informed Fahle that he wanted Low to be his only attorney. Low then filed an application for admission *pro hac vice*. The District Court denied his application without comment. A month later, Low filed a second application, which the District Court again denied without explanation. . . .

The case proceeded to trial, and Dickhaus represented respondent. Low again moved for admission and was again denied. The Court also denied Dickhaus's request to have Low at counsel table with him and ordered Low to sit in the audience and to have no contact with Dickhaus during the proceedings. To enforce the Court's order, a United States Marshal sat between Low and Dickhaus at trial. Respondent was unable to meet with Low throughout the trial, except for once on the last night. The jury found respondent guilty. . . .

Respondent appealed, and the Eighth Circuit vacated the conviction. The Court . . . held that the District Court erred in . . . its denials of [Low's] . . . motions, and violated respondent's Sixth Amendment right to paid counsel of his choosing. The court then concluded that this Sixth Amendment violation was not subject to harmless-error review. We granted certiorari.

II

. . . The Government here agrees, as it has previously, that "the Sixth Amendment guarantees the defendant the right to be represented by an otherwise qualified attorney whom that defendant can afford to hire, or who is willing to represent the defendant even though he is without funds." Caplin & Drysdale, Chartered v. United States, 491 U.S. 617, 624-625 (1989). To be sure, the right to counsel of choice "is circumscribed in several important respects." But the Government does not dispute the Eighth Circuit's conclusion in this case that the District Court erroneously deprived respondent of his counsel of choice.

The Government contends, however, that the Sixth Amendment violation is not "complete" unless the defendant can show that substitute counsel was ineffective within the meaning of Strickland v. Washington—i.e., that substitute counsel's performance was deficient and the defendant was prejudiced by it. In the alternative, the Government contends that the defendant must at least demonstrate that his counsel of choice would have pursued a different strategy that would have created a "reasonable probability that . . . the result of the proceedings would have been different,"—in other words, that he was prejudiced within the meaning of *Strickland* by the denial of his counsel of choice even if substitute counsel's performance was not constitutionally deficient.[1] To support these propositions, the Government points

---

1. The dissent proposes yet a third standard—viz., that the defendant must show "an identifiable difference in the quality of representation between the disqualified counsel and the attorney who represents the defendant at trial." (opinion of Alito, J.). That proposal suffers from the same infirmities (outlined later in text) that beset the Government's positions. In addition, however, it greatly impairs the clarity of the law. How is a lower-court judge to know what an "identifiable difference" consists of? Whereas the Government at least appeals to *Strickland* and the case law under it, the most the dissent can claim by way of precedential support for its rule is that it is "consistent with" cases that never discussed the issue of prejudice.

to our prior cases, which note that the right to counsel "has been accorded . . . not for its own sake, but for the effect it has on the ability of the accused to receive a fair trial." Mickens v. Taylor, 535 U.S. 162, 166 (2002). A trial is not unfair and thus the Sixth Amendment is not violated, the Government reasons, unless a defendant has been prejudiced.

Stated as broadly as this, the Government's argument in effect reads the Sixth Amendment as a more detailed version of the Due Process Clause—and then proceeds to give no effect to the details. It is true enough that the purpose of the rights set forth in that Amendment is to ensure a fair trial; but it does not follow that the rights can be disregarded so long as the trial is, on the whole, fair. . . .

. . . [T]he Sixth Amendment right to counsel of choice . . . commands, not that a trial be fair, but that a particular guarantee of fairness be provided—to wit, that the accused be defended by the counsel he believes to be best. "The Constitution guarantees a fair trial through the Due Process Clauses, but it defines the basic elements of a fair trial largely through the several provisions of the Sixth Amendment, including the Counsel Clause." *Strickland*, supra, at 684-685. In sum, the right at stake here is the right to counsel of choice, not the right to a fair trial; and that right was violated because the deprivation of counsel was erroneous. No additional showing of prejudice is required to make the violation "complete."

The cases the Government relies on involve the right to the effective assistance of counsel, the violation of which generally requires a defendant to establish prejudice. . . . The requirement that a defendant show prejudice in effective representation cases arises from the very nature of the specific element of the right to counsel at issue there—*effective* (not mistake-free) representation. Counsel cannot be "ineffective" unless his mistakes have harmed the defense (or, at least, unless it is reasonably likely that they have). Thus, a violation of the Sixth Amendment right to *effective* representation is not "complete" until the defendant is prejudiced.

The right to select counsel of one's choice, by contrast, has never been derived from the Sixth Amendment's purpose of ensuring a fair trial.[3] It has been regarded as the root meaning of the constitutional guarantee. Where the right to be assisted by counsel of one's choice is wrongly denied, therefore, it is unnecessary to conduct an ineffectiveness or prejudice inquiry to establish a Sixth Amendment violation. Deprivation of the right is "complete" when the defendant is erroneously prevented from being represented by the lawyer he wants, regardless of the quality of the representation he received. To argue otherwise is to confuse the right to counsel of choice—which is the right to a particular lawyer regardless of comparative effectiveness—with the right to effective counsel—which imposes a baseline requirement of competence on whatever lawyer is chosen or appointed.

III

Having concluded, in light of the Government's concession of erroneous deprivation, that the trial court violated respondent's Sixth Amendment right to counsel

3. In Wheat v. United States, 486 U.S. 153 (1988), where we formulated the right to counsel of choice and discussed some of the limitations upon it, we took note of the overarching purpose of fair trial in holding that the trial court has discretion to disallow a first choice of counsel that would create serious risk of conflict of interest. It is one thing to conclude that the right to counsel of choice may be limited by the need for fair trial, but quite another to say that the right does not exist unless its denial renders the trial unfair.

of choice, we must consider whether this error is subject to review for harmlessness. . . . [The general subject of harmless error is discussed in Chapter 17.—EDS.]

We have little trouble concluding that erroneous deprivation of the right to counsel of choice, "with consequences that are necessarily unquantifiable and indeterminate, unquestionably qualifies as 'structural error'" [not subject to harmless error review]. Different attorneys will pursue different strategies with regard to investigation and discovery, development of the theory of defense, selection of the jury, presentation of the witnesses, and style of witness examination and jury argument. And the choice of attorney will affect whether and on what terms the defendant cooperates with the prosecution, plea bargains, or decides instead to go to trial. In light of these myriad aspects of representation, the erroneous denial of counsel bears directly on the "framework within which the trial proceeds,"—or indeed on whether it proceeds at all. It is impossible to know what different choices the rejected counsel would have made, and then to quantify the impact of those different choices on the outcome of the proceedings. Many counseled decisions, including those involving plea bargains and cooperation with the government, do not even concern the conduct of the trial at all. Harmless-error analysis in such a context would be a speculative inquiry into what might have occurred in an alternate universe.

. . . To determine the effect of wrongful denial of choice of counsel, . . . we would not be looking for mistakes committed by the actual counsel, but for differences in the defense that would have been made by the rejected counsel—in matters ranging from questions asked on *voir dire* and cross-examination to such intangibles as argument style and relationship with the prosecutors. We would have to speculate upon what matters the rejected counsel would have handled differently—or indeed, would have handled the same but with the benefit of a more jury—pleasing courtroom style or a longstanding relationship of trust with the prosecutors. And then we would have to speculate upon what effect those different choices or different intangibles might have had. The difficulties of conducting the two assessments of prejudice are not remotely comparable.[5]

IV

Nothing we have said today casts any doubt or places any qualification upon our previous holdings that limit the right to counsel of choice and recognize the authority of trial courts to establish criteria for admitting lawyers to argue before them. As the dissent too discusses, the right to counsel of choice does not extend to defendants who require counsel to be appointed for them. Nor may a defendant insist on representation by a person who is not a member of the bar, or demand that a court honor his waiver of conflict-free representation. We have recognized a trial court's wide latitude in balancing the right to counsel of choice against the needs of fairness, and against the demands of its calendar. The court has, moreover, an "independent interest in ensuring that criminal trials are conducted within the

5. In its discussion of the analysis that would be required to conduct harmless-error review, the dissent focuses on which counsel was "better." This focus has the effect of making the analysis look achievable, but it is fundamentally inconsistent with the principle (which the dissent purports to accept for the sake of argument) that the Sixth Amendment can be violated without a showing of harm to the quality of representation. . . .

ethical standards of the profession and that legal proceedings appear fair to all who observe them." None of these limitations on the right to choose one's counsel is relevant here. This is not a case about a court's power to enforce rules or adhere to practices that determine which attorneys may appear before it, or to make scheduling and other decisions that effectively exclude a defendant's first choice of counsel. However broad a court's discretion may be, the Government has conceded that the District Court here erred when it denied respondent his choice of counsel. Accepting that premise, we hold that the error violated respondent's Sixth Amendment right to counsel of choice and that this violation is not subject to harmless-error analysis.

The judgment of the Court of Appeals is affirmed, and the case is remanded for further proceedings consistent with this opinion.

JUSTICE ALITO, with whom CHIEF JUSTICE ROBERTS, JUSTICE KENNEDY, and JUSTICE THOMAS join, dissenting.

I disagree with the Court's conclusion that a criminal conviction must automatically be reversed whenever a trial court errs in applying its rules regarding *pro hac vice* admissions and as a result prevents a defendant from being represented at trial by the defendant's first-choice attorney. Instead, a defendant should be required to make at least *some* showing that the trial court's erroneous ruling adversely affected the quality of assistance that the defendant received. In my view, the majority's contrary holding is based on an incorrect interpretation of the Sixth Amendment and a misapplication of harmless-error principles. I respectfully dissent.

I

The majority makes a subtle but important mistake at the outset in its characterization of what the Sixth Amendment guarantees. The majority states that the Sixth Amendment protects "the right of a defendant who does not require appointed counsel to choose who will represent him." What the Sixth Amendment actually protects, however, is the right to have *the assistance* that the defendant's counsel of choice is able to provide. It follows that if the erroneous disqualification of a defendant's counsel of choice does not impair the assistance that a defendant receives at trial, there is no violation of the Sixth Amendment.

The language of the Sixth Amendment supports this interpretation. The Assistance of Counsel Clause focuses on what a defendant is entitled to receive ("Assistance"), rather than on the identity of the provider. The background of the adoption of the Sixth Amendment points in the same direction. The specific evil against which the Assistance of Counsel Clause was aimed was the English common-law rule severely limiting a felony defendant's ability to be assisted by counsel. . . .

There is no doubt, of course, that the right "to have the Assistance of Counsel" carries with it a limited right to be represented by counsel of choice. At the time of the adoption of the Bill of Rights, when the availability of appointed counsel was generally limited, that is how the right inevitably played out: A defendant's right to have the assistance of counsel necessarily meant the right to have the assistance of whatever counsel the defendant was able to secure. But from the beginning, the right to counsel of choice has been circumscribed.

For one thing, a defendant's choice of counsel has always been restricted by the rules governing admission to practice before the court in question. . . .

The right to counsel of choice is also limited by conflict-of-interest rules. Even if a defendant is aware that his or her attorney of choice has a conflict, and even if the defendant is eager to waive any objection, the defendant has no constitutional right to be represented by that attorney.

Similarly, the right to be represented by counsel of choice can be limited by mundane case-management considerations. If a trial judge schedules a trial to begin on a particular date and defendant's counsel of choice is already committed for other trials until some time thereafter, the trial judge has discretion under appropriate circumstances to refuse to postpone the trial date and thereby, in effect, to force the defendant to forgo counsel of choice.

These limitations on the right to counsel of choice are tolerable because the focus of the right is the quality of the representation that the defendant receives, not the identity of the attorney who provides the representation. Limiting a defendant to those attorneys who are willing, available, and eligible to represent the defendant still leaves a defendant with a pool of attorneys to choose from—and, in most jurisdictions today, a large and diverse pool. Thus, these restrictions generally have no adverse effect on a defendant's ability to secure the best assistance that the defendant's circumstances permit.

Because the Sixth Amendment focuses on the quality of the assistance that counsel of choice would have provided, I would hold that the erroneous disqualification of counsel does not violate the Sixth Amendment unless the ruling diminishes the quality of assistance that the defendant would have otherwise received. This would not require a defendant to show that the second-choice attorney was constitutionally ineffective within the meaning of Strickland v. Washington. Rather, the defendant would be entitled to a new trial if the defendant could show "an identifiable difference in the quality of representation between the disqualified counsel and the attorney who represents the defendant at trial."

II

But even accepting, as the majority holds, that the erroneous disqualification of counsel of choice always violates the Sixth Amendment, it still would not follow that reversal is required in all cases. The Constitution, by its terms, does not mandate any particular remedy for violations of its own provisions. Instead, we are bound in this case by Federal Rule of Criminal Procedure 52(a), which instructs federal courts to "disregar[d]" "[a]ny error . . . which does not affect substantial rights." The only exceptions we have recognized to this rule have been for "a limited class of fundamental constitutional errors that 'defy analysis by "harmless error" standards.'" Neder v. United States, 527 U.S. 1, 7 (1999).

. . . Fundamental unfairness does not inexorably follow from the denial of first-choice counsel. The "decision to retain a particular lawyer" is "often uninformed"; a defendant's second-choice lawyer may thus turn out to be better than the defendant's first-choice lawyer. More often, a defendant's first- and second-choice lawyers may be simply indistinguishable. These possibilities would not justify violating the right to choice of counsel, but they do make me hard put to characterize the violation as "*always* render[ing] a trial unfair." Fairness may not limit the right, but it does inform the remedy.

Nor is it always or nearly always impossible to determine whether the first choice would have provided better representation than the second choice. There are undoubtedly cases in which the prosecution would have little difficulty showing that the second-choice attorney was better qualified than or at least as qualified as the defendant's initial choice, and there are other cases in which it will be evident to the trial judge that any difference in ability or strategy could not have possibly affected the outcome of the trial.

Requiring a defendant to fall back on a second-choice attorney is not comparable to denying a defendant the right to be represented by counsel at all. Refusing to permit a defendant to receive the assistance of any counsel is the epitome of fundamental unfairness, and as far as the effect on the outcome is concerned, it is much more difficult to assess the effect of a complete denial of counsel than it is to assess the effect of merely preventing representation by the defendant's first-choice attorney. To be sure, when the effect of an erroneous disqualification is hard to gauge, the prosecution will be unable to meet its burden of showing that the error was harmless beyond a reasonable doubt. But that does not justify eliminating the possibility of showing harmless error in all cases. . . .

III

Either of the two courses outlined above—requiring at least some showing of prejudice, or engaging in harmless-error review—would avoid the anomalous and unjustifiable consequences that follow from the majority's two-part rule of error without prejudice followed by automatic reversal.

Under the majority's holding, a defendant who is erroneously required to go to trial with a second-choice attorney is automatically entitled to a new trial even if this attorney performed brilliantly. By contrast, a defendant whose attorney was ineffective in the constitutional sense . . . cannot obtain relief without showing prejudice.

Under the majority's holding, a trial court may adopt rules severely restricting *pro hac vice* admissions, but if it adopts a generous rule and then errs in interpreting or applying it, the error automatically requires reversal of any conviction, regardless of whether the erroneous ruling had any effect on the defendant.

Under the majority's holding, some defendants will be awarded new trials even though it is clear that the erroneous disqualification of their first-choice counsel did not prejudice them in the least. Suppose, for example, that a defendant is initially represented by an attorney who previously represented the defendant in civil matters and who has little criminal experience. Suppose that this attorney is erroneously disqualified and that the defendant is then able to secure the services of a nationally acclaimed and highly experienced criminal defense attorney who secures a surprisingly favorable result at trial—for instance, acquittal on most but not all counts. Under the majority's holding, the trial court's erroneous ruling automatically means that the Sixth Amendment was violated—even if the defendant makes no attempt to argue that the disqualified attorney would have done a better job. In fact, the defendant would still be entitled to a new trial on the counts of conviction even if the defendant publicly proclaimed after the verdict that the second attorney had provided better representation than any other attorney in the country could have possibly done. . . .

Because I believe that some showing of prejudice is required to establish a violation of the Sixth Amendment, I would vacate and remand to let the Court of Appeals determine whether there was prejudice. However, assuming for the sake of argument that no prejudice is required, I believe that such a violation, like most constitutional violations, is amenable to harmless-error review. . . .

NOTES AND QUESTIONS

1. The majority opinion purports to be a straightforward application of the literal command of the Sixth Amendment, but is it? Where in the Amendment does it refer to the counsel the defendant "believes to be best"?

2. The dissent is surely correct that there is a critical distinction between right and remedy that the majority elides. But what about the dissent's view of the correct remedy? There is a certain intuitive appeal to the dissent's position that the focus should be on whether the disallowed counsel would have been better, but what exactly does that mean and how could it be implemented in fact? For example, how could it be shown that some other counsel might have been more effective in cross-examining a witness or making a closing argument? One cannot simply rely on reputation here; one needs evidence, but where would that evidence come from? If trial counsel were so bad as to meet the ineffectiveness standard, that would be one thing, but then the holding in *Gonzalez-Lopez* would be unnecessary.

Perhaps more troublesome, suppose trial counsel *did* botch a cross-examination. What about all the other examinations and cross-examinations counsel conducted? What if they were spectacularly effective? The measure of the quality of assistance is based not just on one discrete moment at trial, but on the trial as a whole. But if that is true, then the dissent implicitly calls for a complex comparison of how this trial actually went with how some counter-factual trial would have gone. Is that possible? Sensible?

3. On the one hand, given the curious linguistic difficulties of the majority's opinion and the practical difficulties of the dissent's, should the Court have simply focused on whether the defendant received constitutionally adequate representation and been done with it? On the other hand, wouldn't that approach (as the majority points out) effectively turn the Sixth Amendment's right to counsel into a mere bit player in support of the defendant's due process right to a fair trial? As we have seen throughout this chapter, one of the recurring themes in right to counsel cases is the effort to identify the core values that the Sixth Amendment serves: If it is about something more than fairness, what else is it about? Equality? Accuracy? Autonomy?

4. What effect, if any, will *Gonzalez-Lopez* have on substantive decisions concerning the right to counsel? The government conceded that the decision to deny Low's motions to represent the defendant was erroneous. Does the case increase the pressure on courts to find to the contrary simply to avoid automatic reversal?

5. If defendants who can afford counsel enjoy at least a limited right to counsel of their choice, and if *all* individuals have the right to proceed pro se as an implication of basic values of autonomy and dignity, should an indigent defendant also have the right to choose who is appointed to represent him? The general view is that there is no such right, the leading case being Drumgo v. Superior Court, 506 P.2d 1007, 106 Cal. Rptr. 631 (1973). Four years after *Drumgo*, the California Supreme Court held that failure to respect an indigent's choice of counsel may amount to an abuse of discretion by the trial court when there are objective circumstances making the defendant's request reasonable. Harris v. Superior Court, 19 Cal. 3d 786, 567 P.2d 750, 140 Cal. Rptr. 318 (1977).[20] The objective circumstances in *Harris* were that

---

20. The case involved William and Emily Harris, two leaders of the Symbionese Liberation Army, a radical left-wing organization responsible for a string of notorious crimes in California that included murder, bank robbery, and the kidnapping of newspaper heiress Patty Hearst.

the counsel the defendants wanted also represented them in related matters and were intimately acquainted with factual and legal matters likely to be relevant to the present litigation. Moreover, counsel appointed by the trial court were essentially ignorant of the case.

In Morris v. Slappy, 461 U.S. 1 (1983), the Supreme Court held that the Sixth Amendment does not guarantee a "meaningful relationship" between attorney and client. Therefore, it was not error to refuse to grant a continuance to allow one public defender, whom the defendant desired as counsel, rather than another to try the case. The primary issue, according to the Court, was whether the attorney who actually tried the case did so competently.

Does *Gonzalez-Lopez* in any way affect the holding in Morris v. Slappy? Should it?

NOTES ON FORFEITURE STATUTES AND THE RIGHT TO COUNSEL

1. In Caplin & Drysdale, Chartered v. United States, 491 U.S. 617 (1989), a well-known D.C. law firm sued the U.S. government for legal fees that it did not receive for defending one Charles Reckmeyer on charges of running a massive illegal drug operation. The reason the law firm did not get its money is that the government first "froze" it (before trial) and then "seized" it (after trial, at which Reckmeyer was convicted) through forfeiture, as authorized by the particular criminal statute under which Reckmeyer was charged. The law firm argued that this (1) effectively denied Reckmeyer (or, more precisely, would deny any future Reckmeyer) his Sixth Amendment right to counsel of choice; (2) violated due process, by allowing the prosecution to abuse its power and upset the "balance of forces" with the defense; and (3) created untenable conflicts of interest between Reckmeyer and his attorneys (e.g., because the attorneys had an incentive to encourage Reckmeyer to take any plea bargain that would include more prison time but avoid forfeiture).

The Court did not agree. Justice White, writing for a narrow 5-4 majority, found that Reckmeyer's right to counsel of choice was not infringed, mostly because the forfeited money was never really Reckmeyer's to begin with. Under "long-recognized and lawful practice," legal title to the "ill-gotten gains" vested in the government "at the time of the criminal act." This "relation-back" doctrine meant that Reckmeyer was basically in the same position as a bank robber seeking to use the bank's money to pay for his defense lawyer. And any future Reckmeyer who might prove unable to persuade paid counsel to take his case, due to the risk of forfeiture, would simply have to make do with court-appointed counsel—just like most other criminal defendants already do, even in complex cases.[21] On the due process claim, the Court acknowledged the possibility of prosecutorial abuse, but left it up to the lower courts to police such problems on a case-by-case basis. And the Court dismissed the conflict of interest arguments in a footnote as largely theoretical and speculative, also pointing out that *Strickland* remains available to deal with any such scenario, should it ever occur.

---

21. As the Court aptly put it in the companion case to *Caplin & Drysdale:* "In enacting [the forfeiture law,] Congress decided to give force to the old adage that 'crime does not pay.' We find no evidence that Congress intended to modify that . . . to read, 'crime does not pay, except for attorney's fees.'" See United States v. Monsanto, 491 U.S. 600 (1989).

Leaving aside the irony of Caplin & Drysdale using Reckmeyer's plight as grounds to seek almost $200,000 in legal fees from the government, what is the real issue in *Caplin & Drysdale*? Is it that the Reckmeyers of the world must (at least in the future) suffer the indignity of being represented by appointed counsel (or, maybe even worse, the public defender)? Or is it that prosecutors now have a potent new weapon in cases involving forfeiture statutes—namely, the ability to assert control over the defendant's choice of counsel? As Justice Blackmun argued, in dissent, "[t]he Government will be ever tempted to use the forfeiture weapon against a defense attorney who is particularly talented or aggressive on the client's behalf. . . ."

2. Does *Caplin & Drysdale* differ from most of the other cases in this chapter? Consider the following argument:

> One might view the ability to purchase lawyers' services as very much like the ability to acquire any other market commodity. Just as we strip Reckmeyer . . . of the ability to buy fancy houses, so, too, we deny [him] the right to hire fancy lawyers.
>
> But there is an alternative conception . . . under which lawyers are a very different kind of good. Under this conception, economic power serves as an *instrumentality* of criminal activity as well as a *proceed* from it. The complex criminal enterprise's wealth gives the enterprise opportunities for criminal activity that poorer entities do not have and gives it opportunities to evade liability that less affluent criminals lack. If the outcome of a criminal proceeding is positively correlated to the caliber of counsel appearing on a defendant's behalf, and if the caliber of counsel is positively related to the ability to retain the best counsel money can buy—both common assumptions—then the economic power acquired by a complex enterprise may enable the enterprise to stay in business by avoiding convictions and forfeitures. Economic power not only constitutes a *benefit* to the criminal; it also lessens her *costs* (because it lowers the probability that she will be detected or successfully prosecuted). The power to buy fancy lawyers may in fact be *worse* than the power to buy fancy houses, because the latter does not facilitate the commission of further crimes as the former can.

Pamela S. Karlan, Discrete and Relational Criminal Representation: The Changing Vision of the Right to Counsel, 105 Harv. L. Rev. 670, 709-710 (1992). If Professor Karlan is right, does that mean Sixth Amendment law should treat lawyers in organized crime cases differently than in more run-of-the-mill criminal cases?

3. In *Caplin & Drysdale*, the Court also rejected the argument (made by the American Bar Association as amicus curiae) that forcing defendants to use appointed counsel in complex criminal cases is a form of per se ineffective assistance. In the words of the Court, "we cannot say that the Sixth Amendment's guarantee of effective assistance of counsel is a guarantee of a privately-retained counsel in every complex case, irrespective of a defendant's ability to pay."

Why not? Remember that the *Caplin & Drysdale* problem is much more likely to arise in conspiracy and large-scale drug distribution cases (where forfeiture statutes are common) than in cases of ordinary "street crime" (where they are not). Such cases are likely to be expensive and time-consuming—perhaps a great deal more so than the average criminal case. Might the low pay, fee caps, and high caseloads of appointed defense counsel have a greater impact on the quality of representation in conspiracy-type cases than in run-of-the-mill criminal cases?

4. Most forfeiture statutes contain an "innocent owner" provision designed to protect those who engage in good-faith transactions with a person subsequently convicted of crimes involving forfeiture. But the courts have not been terribly forgiving.

See, e.g., United States v. 1977 Porsche Carrera 911 VIN 9117201924 License No. 459 DWR, 748 F. Supp. 1180 (W.D. Tex. 1990):

> If a lawyer receives property under suspicious circumstances, he has a duty to investigate further into the origin of the property in order to establish that he has not been "willfully blind" as to the illegal nature of the property. This Court is of the opinion that even in a case in which a lawyer is truly ignorant of any wrongdoing at the precise moment of acquisition of the property, but subsequently learns within a reasonable period . . . that the property is proceeds or has been used to facilitate a crime, that lawyer should not be considered an "innocent owner." . . .
>
> The Court is aware of the hardships this may impose on criminal defense lawyers, but such burden is contemplated by the asset forfeiture provisions, which aim to prevent criminals from using the proceeds of their illegal activities to obtain "the best defense counsel that money can buy." . . .

5. If requiring the forfeiture of assets that would have been used to pay for counsel does not violate any of the defendant's rights, what about searching a lawyer pursuant to a warrant while the lawyer's client is testifying before a grand jury? That's not a due process violation, said the Court in Conn v. Gabbert, 526 U.S. 286 (1999). Whether such a search might be unreasonable under the Fourth Amendment was not decided.

What about charging the attorney with a crime? The line between receiving legitimate fees and illegal money laundering may not always be clear. And defense attorneys have been indicted for their alleged involvement in criminal conspiracies based on allegations of money laundering. See, e.g., United States v. Abbell, 963 F. Supp. 1178 (S.D. Fla. 1997).

PART FOUR

THE ADJUDICATION PROCESS

Chapter 8

Bail and Pretrial Detention

The practice of admission to bail, as it has evolved in Anglo-American law, is not a device for keeping persons in jail upon mere accusation until it is found convenient to give them a trial. On the contrary, the spirit of the procedure is to enable them to stay out of jail until a trial has found them guilty. Without this conditional privilege, even those wrongly accused are punished by a period of imprisonment while awaiting trial and are handicapped in consulting counsel, searching for evidence and witnesses, and preparing a defense.

Justice Robert Jackson

For defendants who have been taken into custody and charged with a crime, an immediate and potentially crucial concern is whether, and under what circumstances, they can obtain release from custody until trial or some other resolution of the charges. This decision is often made by a magistrate judge at the defendant's first court appearance following an arrest, although sometimes a separate bail hearing is held.

Judges have broad discretion in making and shaping the pretrial release decision. The court may release the suspect based simply on a promise to show up for later court hearings—often called releasing the defendant on his "own recognizance," or "OR"—plus the suspect's promise not to commit any crimes while on release. Or the court may require the posting of bail—the pledging of money or a financial bond that the defendant will forfeit if he fails to show up as required, or if he otherwise violates the terms of his release. Whether the defendant is obligated to post bail or not, the court also may impose a series of nonfinancial conditions, such as the requirement that the suspect observe a curfew, refrain from contacting the victim, or enter a drug treatment program.

The traditional purpose of imposing bail and other release conditions is to ensure that the defendant appears in court when required, not to punish the accused or prejudge the merits of the case. Nonetheless, the type of crime a defendant is accused of committing undoubtedly plays a role in the bail decision. Most obviously, the more serious the charge the higher the potential sentence, and thus the greater incentive for a defendant to flee rather than stand trial. For this reason, in cases of very serious crimes pretrial release may be denied altogether, either by explicit judicial decision or by the less direct method of setting bail so high that the defendant is unable to post the necessary amount.

Even if a defendant is not a flight risk, judges also worry about the impact of releasing certain suspects back into the community. The fear that the accused will commit new crimes while awaiting trial is logically unrelated to whether the defendant will flee, but is nonetheless widely believed to influence the judge's decision.

As a result, over the past 30 years Congress and many state legislatures have enacted statutes that grant judges the authority to order the preventive detention of those who are a flight risk *or* whose pretrial release may pose a danger to the community.

The Constitution speaks directly but vaguely to the issue of bail in the Eighth Amendment, which says in part that "Excessive bail shall not be required." The first case in this section, Stack v. Boyle, deals with the interpretation of the "excessive bail clause." The second case, United States v. Salerno, resolves a constitutional challenge to the Bail Reform Act of 1984, 18 U.S.C. §§3141 et seq., the statute that authorizes federal judges to order preventive detention based on a prediction that the suspect will commit new crimes if released on bail.

A.   *Bail Amounts*

STACK v. BOYLE

Certiorari to the United States Court of Appeals for the Ninth Circuit
342 U.S. 1 (1951)

CHIEF JUSTICE VINSON delivered the opinion of the Court.

Indictments have been returned in the Southern District of California charging the twelve petitioners with conspiring to violate the Smith Act, 18 U.S.C. (Supp. IV) §§371, 2385.[*] Upon their arrest, bail was fixed for each petitioner in the widely varying amounts of $2,500, $7,500, $75,000, and $100,000. On motion of petitioner Schneiderman following arrest in the Southern District of New York, his bail was reduced to $50,000 before his removal to California. On motion of the Government to increase bail in the case of other petitioners, and after several intermediate procedural steps not material to the issues presented here, bail was fixed in the District Court for the Southern District of California in the uniform amount of $50,000 for each petitioner.

Petitioners moved to reduce bail on the ground that bail as fixed was excessive under the Eighth Amendment.[1] In support of their motion, petitioners submitted statements as to their financial resources, family relationships, health, prior criminal records, and other information. The only evidence offered by the Government was a certified record showing that four persons previously convicted under the Smith Act in the Southern District of New York had forfeited bail. No evidence was produced relating those four persons to the petitioners in this case. At a hearing on the motion, petitioners were examined by the District Judge and cross-examined by an attorney for the Government. Petitioners' factual statements stand uncontroverted.

After their motion to reduce bail was denied, petitioners filed applications for habeas corpus in the same District Court. Upon consideration of the record on the motion to reduce bail, the writs were denied. The Court of Appeals for the Ninth Circuit affirmed. 192 F.2d 56. . . .

---

[*] The Smith Act of 1940 prohibited advocacy of forceful or violent overthrow of the United States government. During the "Red Scare" of the late 1940s and early 1950s, it was the basis for numerous prosecutions of persons with actual or suspected ties to the Communist Party. — EDS.

1. "Excessive bail shall not be required, nor excessive fines imposed, nor cruel and unusual punishments inflicted." U.S. Const., Amend. VIII.

. . . From the passage of the Judiciary Act of 1789, 1 Stat. 73, 91, to the present Federal Rules of Criminal Procedure, Rule 46(a)(1), federal law has unequivocally provided that a person arrested for a non-capital offense *shall* be admitted to bail. This traditional right to freedom before conviction permits the unhampered preparation of a defense, and serves to prevent the infliction of punishment prior to conviction. . . . Unless this right to bail before trial is preserved, the presumption of innocence, secured only after centuries of struggle, would lose its meaning.

The right to release before trial is conditioned upon the accused's giving adequate assurance that he will stand trial and submit to sentence if found guilty. . . . Like the ancient practice of securing the oaths of responsible persons to stand as sureties for the accused, the modern practice of requiring a bail bond or the deposit of a sum of money subject to forfeiture serves as additional assurance of the presence of an accused. Bail set at a figure higher than an amount reasonably calculated to fulfill this purpose is "excessive" under the Eighth Amendment. . . .

Since the function of bail is limited, the fixing of bail for any individual defendant must be based upon standards relevant to the purpose of assuring the presence of that defendant. The traditional standards as expressed in the Federal Rules of Criminal Procedure[3] are to be applied in each case to each defendant. In this case petitioners are charged with offenses under the Smith Act and, if found guilty, their convictions are subject to review with the scrupulous care demanded by our Constitution. . . . Upon final judgment of conviction, petitioners face imprisonment of not more than five years and a fine of not more than $10,000. It is not denied that bail for each petitioner has been fixed in a sum much higher than that usually imposed for offenses with like penalties and yet there has been no factual showing to justify such action in this case. The Government asks the courts to depart from the norm by assuming, without the introduction of evidence, that each petitioner is a pawn in a conspiracy and will, in obedience to a superior, flee the jurisdiction. To infer from the fact of indictment alone a need for bail in an unusually high amount is an arbitrary act. Such conduct would inject into our own system of government the very principles of totalitarianism which Congress was seeking to guard against in passing the statute under which petitioners have been indicted.

If bail in an amount greater than that usually fixed for serious charges of crimes is required in the case of any of the petitioners, that is a matter to which evidence should be directed in a hearing so that the constitutional rights of each petitioner may be preserved. In the absence of such a showing, we are of the opinion that the fixing of bail before trial in these cases cannot be squared with the statutory and constitutional standards for admission to bail.

. . . The Court concludes that bail has not been fixed by proper methods in this case and that petitioners' remedy is by motion to reduce bail, with right of appeal to the Court of Appeals. Accordingly, the judgment of the Court of Appeals is vacated and the case is remanded to the District Court. . . .

[The separate opinion of Justice Jackson is omitted.]

---

3. Rule 46(c). "AMOUNT. If the defendant is admitted to bail, the amount thereof shall be such as in the judgment of the commissioner or court or judge or justice will insure the presence of the defendant, having regard to the nature and circumstances of the offense charged, the weight of the evidence against him, the financial ability of the defendant to give bail and the character of the defendant." [NOTE—This rule has been amended substantially since the Bail Reform Act of 1984. The current version of Rule 46 is set forth in the Supplement to this casebook.—EDS.]

NOTES AND QUESTIONS

1. What does it mean to say that bail is "excessive" within the meaning of the Eighth Amendment after Stack v. Boyle? If a judge set bail at $200 for a homeless man charged with breaking into a store, is that "excessive" if the man has only $10 in assets? Or, if a billionaire is charged with driving while intoxicated, is it excessive to set bail at $100 million? Courts would almost certainly conclude that bail was not excessive for the homeless man but was excessive for the billionaire. Can you articulate why this would be so?

2. Although the bail amounts can vary widely across jurisdictions, some statistics from the state courts provide a point of reference. A study of state felony defendants in the 75 largest counties in America found that in 2009, the median amount of bail for all defendants was $10,000. For murder, the median was $1,000,000; for drug trafficking, it was $20,000; and for property offenses, it was a mere $7,500. Among those defendants who could not (or did not) post bail, the median bail was set at $25,000, while for those who posted bail and were released, the median was $6,000. See Brian A. Reaves, Felony Defendants in Large Urban Counties, 2009 (2013), available at http://www.bjs.gov/content/pub/pdf/fdluc09.pdf.

Regardless of the amounts, many people end up staying in jail after arrest because they cannot afford to make bail. Consider the following from the *New York Times*:

> In a given year, city and county jails across the country admit between 11 million and 13 million people. In New York City, where courts use bail far less than in many jurisdictions, roughly 45,000 people are jailed each year simply because they can't pay their court-assigned bail. And while the city's courts set bail much lower than the national average, only one in 10 defendants is able to pay it at arraignment. To put a finer point on it: Even when bail is set comparatively low—at $500 or less, as it is in one-third of nonfelony cases—only 15 percent of defendants are able to come up with the money to avoid jail.

Nick Pinto, The Bail Trap, The New York Times Magazine (Aug. 13, 2015).

3. As Justice Jackson observed (see the opening quote of this chapter), being detained pending trial can have a prejudicial effect on the ability of the accused to mount a defense. One ten-year study conducted by the New York City Criminal Justice Agency supports this view:

> Multivariate models showed that pretrial detention increased the likelihood of conviction for both nonfelony and felony defendants, and the effect was statistically significant even after controlling for a wide range of case and defendant characteristics . . . . Pretrial detention alone had a strong effect on conviction, beyond what was explained by all the control variables in both nonfelony and felony models.

Mary T. Phillips, A Decade of Bail Research in New York City, Final Report, 116 (Aug. 2012), available at http://www.nycja.org/library.php. The study noted, for example, that in misdemeanor cases where the defendant was released at arraignment, the conviction rate was 50 percent; when the defendant was detained for part of the period prior to trial, the conviction rate was between 60 percent and 70 percent. And for those defendants who were detained until their case was resolved, the conviction rate was 92 percent. Id.

If lots of people are being detained because they can't afford bail, and if it is hurting their ability to defend themselves, what, if anything, should be done about it? Should courts simply release people who can't afford to pay? Lower bail to some amount that the defendant can afford? Or is this problem just an inevitable consequence of a system that processes such a large number of defendants?

4. Curiously, releasing more people on bail may actually *increase* the stress on the justice system rather than relieve it. The New York Times article cited above says the following: "The open secret is that in most jurisdictions, bail is the grease that keeps the gears of the overburdened system turning. Faced with the prospect of going to jail for want of bail, many defendants accept plea deals instead." Pinto, supra, The Bail Trap. In other words, if it were easier to make bail, fewer people would let the stress of being in jail compel them to take a plea deal and plead guilty—which in turn would make cases last longer and slow down the system. The New York City Study on bail concurs:

> The pressure on a jailed defendant to plead guilty seems a particularly compelling explanation for how detention could lead to a greater likelihood of conviction. A defendant who is facing a non-custodial sentence can be released immediately by pleading guilty, whereas holding out for acquittal may mean spending many more days, weeks, or months behind bars.

Phillips, supra, at 115. If this is true, can this be a legitimate way for the system to process cases?

5. One of the benefits of bail is that it reduces jail overcrowding, but in high crime jurisdictions, releasing a large number of people on bail also can create administrative headaches. The Philadelphia Inquirer studied that city's bail system and found that a high volume of arrestees, coupled with low funding to monitor them, meant that among all released suspects, more than 10 percent (a total of almost 47,000 people) became long-term fugitives, one of the worst rates in the nation. And while in theory the failure to appear meant that the city was entitled to keep the bail money, in practice, no real effort was made to collect the $1 billion in forfeited bail. See Dylan Purcell, Craig R. McCoy & Nancy Phillips, Violent Criminals Flout Broken Bail System, Philly.com (Dec. 15, 2009), available at www.philly.com/inquirer/special/20091215_Violent_Criminals_ Flout_Broken_Bail_System.html. The *Inquirer* study led to a significant overhaul in the bail system; changes included setting up a special bench warrant court, encouraging the use of private bail firms, and devoting resources to collect forfeited bail. One immediate result was that Philadelphia increase its collection of bail owed to the city from $39,000 in 2009 to $3 million in 2012, although this is still a small fraction of the amount due. See Craig R. McCoy, Philadelphia's New Bench Warrant Court is Cracking Down on Fugitives, http://www.philly.com/philly/news/special_packages/inquirer/courts-reform/20120506.

6. Stack v. Boyle emphasized that bail for each defendant "must be based upon standards relevant to the purpose of assuring the presence of that defendant." The Bail Reform Act of 1984, discussed below, lists several factors that courts are to consider when evaluating the flight risk: the nature and circumstances of the crime charged; the weight of the evidence; and the defendant's character, physical and mental condition, family ties, employment, finances, length of residence in the community, community ties, history of substance abuse, criminal history, record of court appearances, and status as a probationer or parolee. 18 U.S.C. §3142(g).

Should it matter if some of these factors correlate with race and ethnicity? A three-year study in the Second Circuit found that for many factors—including citizenship, home ownership, marital status, substance abuse, employment status, criminal history, time in the area, education, bail recommendations by pretrial service officers and prosecutors, and level of offense charged—"substantial differences between whites, African-Americans and Hispanics/Latinos were evident; for many of these factors, differences were also evident for Asian-Americans." The study concluded that, even after controlling for other characteristics, "race and ethnicity remained a statistically significant factor [in pretrial release decisions]." See Report of the Working Committees to the Second Circuit Task Force on Gender, Racial and Ethnic Fairness in the Courts, 1997 Ann. Surv. Am. L. 124, 311-320.

In contrast, a study commissioned by the Ninth Circuit's Task Force on Racial, Religious, and Ethnic Fairness, conducted by researchers from the Administrative Office of the U.S. Courts, concluded that "the results of the [study and analyses] consistently reveal that race/ethnicity is not a strong predictor of the decision to detain or release." See Thomas Bak, Pretrial Detention in the Ninth Circuit, 35 San Diego L. Rev. 993, 1033-1035 (1998).

In 2012, the percentage of African American suspects released on bail at some point prior to trial in the federal system was 44 percent, a higher release rate than for Whites (30 percent) and a much higher rate than for Hispanics (19 percent). See Bureau of Justice Statistics, Federal Justice Statistics, 2012—Statistical Tables at 14 (Table 3.3) (January 2015). What might explain the differences in these figures?

7. Does the defendant have a Sixth Amendment right to counsel at a bail hearing? The answer is surprisingly unclear. Coleman v. Alabama, 399 U.S. 1 (1970), held that the right to counsel applies to preliminary hearings, but Gerstein v. Pugh, 420 U.S. 103 (1975), found the right inapplicable to the immediate post-arrest probable cause hearings, where bail determinations are now made in many states. The Federal Rules of Criminal Procedure provide for appointed counsel at "every stage of the proceeding," including the initial appearance where bail is often set, see Fed. R. Crim. P. 44(a), but one study revealed that only eight states and the District of Columbia currently guarantee counsel at bail hearings. See Douglas L. Colbert, Thirty-Five Years After *Gideon*: The Illusory Right to Counsel at Bail Proceedings, [1998] U. Ill. L. Rev. 1.

Would defense lawyers at bail hearings make a difference? In another study of defendants charged with nonviolent crimes in Baltimore, the researchers found that defendants who were represented by counsel were more likely to be released on their own recognizance and more likely to have bail set at a lower amount than unrepresented defendants. The net effect was that represented defendants spent a median time of only two days in jail, as compared with nine days for unrepresented defendants. See Douglas L. Colbert, Ray Paternoster & Shawn Bushway, Do Attorneys Really Matter? The Empirical and Legal Case for the Right to Counsel at Bail, 23 Cardozo L. Rev. 1719 (2002).

8. Once the amount of bail is set, the defendant may be required to post the full amount with the court (a requirement called "full cash bond"), or may be required to post a "deposit bond" with the court, typically 10 percent of the bail amount, with the defendant being responsible for the full amount if he violates the terms of his release.

In some jurisdictions, however, a defendant may be required to obtain a surety bond from a third party—a bail bondsman—who will guarantee the payment of the full bail amount if the defendant fails to appear. The use of bail bondsmen is controversial. Once the defendant buys the bond and is released, his financial commitment is at an end: The cost of the surety bond is not refundable, and if the defendant fails to show up, it is the bondsman who is obligated to pay the full bail amount. So one concern is that bail bondsmen remove the financial incentive for defendant to appear—which is, of course, the purpose of setting bail in the first place.

But because bail bondsmen are now liable for the full bail amount, they have a great incentive to monitor the defendant while he is released and ensure the defendant appears at all court hearings. If the defendant flees, the bondsmen can hire "bounty hunters" (the subject of innumerable bad television shows, and one reasonably good movie: *Midnight Run* (1988)) to track down the fugitives and return them to court. Bounty hunters have been frequently criticized for their harsh, even violent, tactics, but courts often turn a blind eye to the methods used to return a fleeing fugitive. For a useful discussion of these issues, as well as an interesting analysis of whether the Uniform Criminal Extradition Act supersedes the bounty hunter's common law authority, see Milton Hirsch, *Midnight Run* Re-run: Bail Bondsmen, Bounty Hunters, and the Uniform Criminal Extradition Act, 62 U. Miami L. Rev. 59 (2007).

Two law-and-economics scholars have concluded that, even after controlling for selection variables (i.e., the fact that trial judges make different decisions about release conditions based on individual case and defendant characteristics), bail bond companies do a much better job than the government at controlling the behavior of released defendants:

> Defendants released on surety bond are 28 percent less likely to fail to appear than similar defendants released on their own recognizance, and if they do fail to appear, they are 53 percent less likely to remain at large for extended periods of time. Deposit bonds perform only marginally better than release on own recognizance. Requiring defendants to pay their bonds in cash can reduce the [failure-to-appear] rate similar to that for those released on surety bond. Given that a defendant skips town, however, the probability of recapture is much higher for those defendants released on surety bond. As a result, the probability of being a fugitive is 64 percent lower for those released on surety bond compared with those released on cash bond. These findings indicate that bond dealers and bail enforcement agents (bounty hunters) are effective at discouraging flight and at recapturing defendants. Bounty hunters, not public police, appear to be the true long arms of the law.

Eric Helland & Alexander Tabarrok, The Fugitive: Evidence on Public Versus Private Law Enforcement From Bail Jumping, 47 J. Law & Econ. 93, 118 (2004).

B. Preventive Detention

Although Stack v. Boyle discusses bail as if the only question is whether the defendant will flee, this has never been the sole basis for denying pretrial release. Courts have long assumed that if they find that the accused is likely to intimidate witnesses or tamper with evidence in his pending case, the Court can either deny bail or set conditions on release that are unrelated to the risk of flight, such as ordering the suspect not to make contact with witnesses or victims. The reasoning is that courts have the ability to preserve the integrity of the pending case, and a court's exercise of this authority is uncontroversial.

Whether the court can detain someone prior to trial simply because the judge thinks the suspect is dangerous in general is another matter. On the one hand, keeping someone in custody who was not a flight risk simply because they might commit other crimes if released sounds uncomfortably like punishment without a trial (and without even a crime yet). On the other hand, there is a widespread belief that certain defendants are simply too dangerous to release, and as a result, some courts would set bail at extremely high levels, not because of the flight risk, but because the judge knew the suspect could not afford the bail and thus would remain locked up.

The fear that some suspects were continuing to commit new crimes while out on bail, coupled with the unfairness of judges using high bail amounts as a sub rosa method of pretrial detention, led Congress to pass the Bail Reform Act of 1984, 18 U.S.C. §§3141 et seq. In general, the Act operates as follows:

- When an arrested defendant is brought before the court, the judicial officer (typically a magistrate judge) has four options:

    (1) Release the suspect on his own recognizance, or on a promise to pay money if he misses his court appearances. The simple promise to pay is often called an "unsecured bond," because it does not require the accused to post any money or collateral.

    (2) Release the person subject to financial conditions, nonfinancial conditions, or both. The conditions can include requiring that the suspect: post a percentage of the bail amount with the court or with a surety; agree to custodial supervision by a designated person; agree to keep or seek a job; participate in an educational program; agree to travel restrictions; agree not to contact witnesses or victims; report to designated authorities; abide by a curfew; agree not to possess weapons; abide by alcohol and drug restrictions; or seek medical or psychiatric treatment. 18 U.S.C. §3142(g). And of course, there is always a requirement that the accused not commit any crimes while out on bail.

    (3) Temporarily detain the suspect to allow the court to revoke the defendant's conditional release (if the defendant was already out on bail for another crime at the time of arrest, for example), or to permit the defendant to be deported.

    (4) Deny bail and order the suspect detained pending trial. 18 U.S.C. §3142(a).

- In determining whether the defendant is to be released or detained, the operative standard is whether the defendant is likely to appear at all required court appearances and whether his release will "endanger the safety of any other person or the community."

- Before a defendant can be detained, the court must hold a hearing, which may be called on motion of the prosecutor or by the court sua sponte. At the hearing, the accused has the right to counsel (including appointed counsel if he is indigent), has the right to testify, to present evidence, and to cross-examine the government's witnesses. For the accused to be detained, the court must find by clear and convincing evidence *either* that defendant is a flight risk *or* that no release conditions will ensure the safety of the community. 18 U.S.C. §3142(f).

- In some cases, a rebuttable presumption arises that the defendant should be detained. If the defendant has been arrested for certain serious drug crimes, for example, or if the defendant has previously been convicted of a serious crime while out on bail, the burden shifts to the accused to rebut the presumption that he should not be released. 18 U.S.C. §3142(e). Rebuttable presumptions are discussed further in the notes following the next case.

Not surprisingly, the notion that courts could detain a defendant based on the prediction that he would commit further crimes if released—that is, that he would "endanger the safety of the community"—was quickly challenged.

UNITED STATES v. SALERNO

Certiorari to the United States Court of Appeals for the Second Circuit
481 U.S. 739 (1987)

CHIEF JUSTICE REHNQUIST delivered the opinion of the Court.

The Bail Reform Act of 1984 (Act) allows a federal court to detain an arrestee pending trial if the Government demonstrates by clear and convincing evidence after an adversary hearing that no release conditions "will reasonably assure . . . the safety of any other person and the community." The United States Court of Appeals for the Second Circuit struck down this provision of the Act as facially unconstitutional, because, in that court's words, this type of pretrial detention violates "substantive due process." We granted certiorari because of a conflict among the Courts of Appeals regarding the validity of the Act. . . . We hold that, as against the facial attack mounted by these respondents, the Act fully comports with constitutional requirements. We therefore reverse.

I

Responding to "the alarming problem of crimes committed by persons on release," . . . Congress formulated the Bail Reform Act of 1984, 18 U.S.C. §3141 et seq. . . . , as the solution to a bail crisis in the federal courts. The Act represents the National Legislature's considered response to numerous perceived deficiencies in the federal bail process. By providing for sweeping changes in both the way federal courts consider bail applications and the circumstances under which bail is granted, Congress hoped to "give the courts adequate authority to make release decisions that give appropriate recognition to the danger a person may pose to others if released." . . .

To this end, §3141(a) of the Act requires a judicial officer to determine whether an arrestee shall be detained. Section 3142(e) provides that "[i]f, after a hearing pursuant to the provisions of subsection (f), the judicial officer finds that no condition or combination of conditions will reasonably assure the appearance of the person as required and the safety of any other person and the community, he shall order the detention of the person prior to trial." Section 3142(f) provides the arrestee with a number of procedural safeguards. He may request the presence of counsel at the detention hearing, he may testify and present witnesses in his behalf, as well as proffer evidence, and he may cross-examine other witnesses appearing at the hearing. If the judicial officer finds that no conditions of pretrial release can reasonably assure the safety of other persons and the community, he must state his findings of fact in writing, §3142(i), and support his conclusion with "clear and convincing evidence," §3142(f).

The judicial officer is not given unbridled discretion in making the detention determination. Congress has specified the considerations relevant to that decision. These factors include the nature and seriousness of the charges, the substantiality of the Government's evidence against the arrestee, the arrestee's background and characteristics, and the nature and seriousness of the danger posed by the suspect's release. §3142(g). Should a judicial officer order detention, the detainee is entitled to expedited appellate review of the detention order. §§3145(b), (c).

Respondents Anthony Salerno and Vincent Cafaro were arrested on March 21, 1986, after being charged in a 29-count indictment alleging various Racketeer Influenced and Corrupt Organizations Act (RICO) violations, mail and wire fraud offenses, extortion, and various criminal gambling violations. The RICO counts alleged 35 acts of racketeering activity, including fraud, extortion, gambling, and conspiracy to commit murder. At respondents' arraignment, the Government moved to have Salerno and Cafaro detained pursuant to §3142(e), on the ground that no condition of release would assure the safety of the community or any person. The District Court held a hearing at which the Government made a detailed proffer of evidence. The Government's case showed that Salerno was the "boss" of the Genovese crime family of La Cosa Nostra and that Cafaro was a "captain" in the Genovese family. According to the Government's proffer, based in large part on conversations intercepted by a court-ordered wiretap, the two respondents had participated in wide-ranging conspiracies to aid their illegitimate enterprises through violent means. The Government also offered the testimony of two of its trial witnesses, who would assert that Salerno personally participated in two murder conspiracies. Salerno opposed the motion for detention, challenging the credibility of the Government's witnesses. He offered the testimony of several character witnesses as well as a letter from his doctor stating that he was suffering from a serious medical condition. Cafaro presented no evidence at the hearing, but instead characterized the wiretap conversations as merely "tough talk."

The District Court granted the Government's detention motion, concluding that the Government had established by clear and convincing evidence that no condition or combination of conditions of release would ensure the safety of the community or any person. . . .

Respondents appealed, contending that to the extent that the Bail Reform Act permits pretrial detention on the ground that the arrestee is likely to commit future crimes, it is unconstitutional on its face. Over a dissent, the United States Court of Appeals for the Second Circuit agreed. 794 F.2d 64 (1986). . . .

II

A facial challenge to a legislative Act is, of course, the most difficult challenge to mount successfully, since the challenger must establish that no set of circumstances exists under which the Act would be valid. The fact that the Bail Reform Act might operate unconstitutionally under some conceivable set of circumstances is insufficient to render it wholly invalid, since we have not recognized an "overbreadth" doctrine outside the limited context of the First Amendment. . . . We think respondents have failed to shoulder their heavy burden to demonstrate that the Act is "facially" unconstitutional.

Respondents present two grounds for invalidating the Bail Reform Act's provisions permitting pretrial detention on the basis of future dangerousness. First, they rely upon the Court of Appeals' conclusion that the Act exceeds the limitations placed upon the Federal Government by the Due Process Clause of the Fifth Amendment. Second, they contend that the Act contravenes the Eighth Amendment's proscription against excessive bail. We treat these contentions in turn.

A

The Due Process Clause of the Fifth Amendment provides that "No person shall . . . be deprived of life, liberty, or property, without due process of law. . . ." This Court has held that the Due Process Clause protects individuals against two types of government action. So-called "substantive due process" prevents the government from engaging in conduct that "shocks the conscience," Rochin v. California, 342 U.S. 165, 172 (1952), or interferes with rights "implicit in the concept of ordered liberty," Palko v. Connecticut, 302 U.S. 319, 325-326 (1937). When government action depriving a person of life, liberty, or property survives substantive due process scrutiny, it must still be implemented in a fair manner. Mathews v. Eldridge, 424 U.S. 319, 335 (1976). This requirement has traditionally been referred to as "procedural" due process.

Respondents first argue that the Act violates substantive due process because the pretrial detention it authorizes constitutes impermissible punishment before trial. . . . The Government, however, has never argued that pretrial detention could be upheld if it were "punishment." The Court of Appeals assumed that pretrial detention under the Bail Reform Act is regulatory, not penal, and we agree that it is.

As an initial matter, the mere fact that a person is detained does not inexorably lead to the conclusion that the government has imposed punishment. . . . To determine whether a restriction on liberty constitutes impermissible punishment or permissible regulation, we first look to legislative intent. . . . Unless Congress expressly intended to impose punitive restrictions, the punitive/regulatory distinction turns on " 'whether an alternative purpose to which [the restriction] may rationally be connected is assignable for it, and whether it appears excessive in relation to the alternative purpose assigned [to it].' " [Schall v. Martin, 467 U.S. 253, 269 (1984)], quoting Kennedy v. Mendoza-Martinez, 372 U.S. 144, 168-169 (1963).

We conclude that the detention imposed by the Act falls on the regulatory side of the dichotomy. The legislative history of the Bail Reform Act clearly indicates that Congress did not formulate the pretrial detention provisions as punishment for dangerous individuals. . . . Congress instead perceived pretrial detention as a potential solution to a pressing societal problem. . . . There is no doubt that preventing danger to the community is a legitimate regulatory goal. . . .

Nor are the incidents of pretrial detention excessive in relation to the regulatory goal Congress sought to achieve. The Bail Reform Act carefully limits the circumstances under which detention may be sought to the most serious of crimes. See 18 U.S.C. §3142(f) (detention hearings available if case involves crimes of violence, offenses for which the sentence is life imprisonment or death, serious drug offenses, or certain repeat offenders). The arrestee is entitled to a prompt detention hearing, ibid., and the maximum length of pretrial detention is limited by the stringent time limitations of the Speedy Trial Act.[4] See 18 U.S.C. §3161 et seq. . . . Moreover, as in

_____

4. We intimate no view as to the point at which detention in a particular case might become excessively prolonged, and therefore punitive, in relation to Congress' regulatory goal.

Schall v. Martin, the conditions of confinement envisioned by the Act "appear to reflect the regulatory purposes relied upon by the" Government. 467 U.S., at 270. As in *Schall*, the statute at issue here requires that detainees be housed in a "facility separate, to the extent practicable, from persons awaiting or serving sentences or being held in custody pending appeal." 18 U.S.C. §3142(i)(2). We conclude, therefore, that the pretrial detention contemplated by the Bail Reform Act is regulatory in nature, and does not constitute punishment before trial in violation of the Due Process Clause.

The Court of Appeals nevertheless concluded that "the Due Process Clause prohibits pretrial detention on the ground of danger to the community as a regulatory measure, without regard to the duration of the detention." 794 F.2d, at 71. Respondents characterize the Due Process Clause as erecting an impenetrable "wall" in this area that "no governmental interest — rational, important, compelling or otherwise — may surmount." . . .

We do not think the Clause lays down any such categorical imperative. We have repeatedly held that the Government's regulatory interest in community safety can, in appropriate circumstances, outweigh an individual's liberty interest. For example, in times of war or insurrection, when society's interest is at its peak, the Government may detain individuals whom the Government believes to be dangerous. . . . Even outside the exigencies of war, we have found that sufficiently compelling governmental interests can justify detention of dangerous persons. Thus, we have found no absolute constitutional barrier to detention of potentially dangerous resident aliens pending deportation proceedings. . . . We have also held that the government may detain mentally unstable individuals who present a danger to the public, Addington v. Texas, 441 U.S. 418 (1979), and dangerous defendants who become incompetent to stand trial, Jackson v. Indiana, 406 U.S. 715, 731-739 (1972). . . . We have approved of postarrest regulatory detention of juveniles when they present a continuing danger to the community. Schall v. Martin, supra. Even competent adults may face substantial liberty restrictions as a result of the operation of our criminal justice system. If the police suspect an individual of a crime, they may arrest and hold him until a neutral magistrate determines whether probable cause exists. Gerstein v. Pugh, 420 U.S. 103 (1975). Finally, respondents concede and the Court of Appeals noted that an arrestee may be incarcerated until trial if he presents a risk of flight, see Bell v. Wolfish, 441 U.S. [520], at 534 [(1979)], or a danger to witnesses.

Respondents characterize all of these cases as exceptions to the "general rule" of substantive due process that the government may not detain a person prior to a judgment of guilt in a criminal trial. Such a "general rule" may freely be conceded, but we think that these cases show a sufficient number of exceptions to the rule that the congressional action challenged here can hardly be characterized as totally novel. Given the well-established authority of the government, in special circumstances, to restrain individuals' liberty prior to or even without criminal trial and conviction, we think that the present statute providing for pretrial detention on the basis of dangerousness must be evaluated in precisely the same manner that we evaluated the laws in the cases discussed above.

The government's interest in preventing crime by arrestees is both legitimate and compelling. . . . In *Schall*, supra, we recognized the strength of the State's interest in preventing juvenile crime. This general concern with crime prevention is no less compelling when the suspects are adults. Indeed, "[t]he harm suffered by the victim of a crime is not dependent upon the age of the perpetrator." Schall v. Martin, supra, at 264-265. The Bail Reform Act of 1984 responds to an even more particularized governmental interest than the interest we sustained in *Schall.* The statute we upheld in *Schall* permitted pretrial detention of any juvenile arrested on any charge after a showing that the individual might commit some undefined further crimes. The Bail Reform Act, in contrast, narrowly focuses on a particularly acute problem in which the Government interests are overwhelming. The Act operates only on individuals who have been arrested for a specific category of extremely serious offenses. 18 U.S.C. §3142(f). Congress specifically found that these individuals are far more likely to be responsible for dangerous acts in the community after arrest. . . . Nor is the Act by any means a scattershot attempt to incapacitate those who are merely suspected of these serious crimes. The Government must first of all demonstrate probable cause to believe that the charged crime has been committed by the arrestee, but that is not enough. In a full-blown adversary hearing, the Government must convince a neutral decision-maker by clear and convincing evidence that no conditions of release can reasonably assure the safety of the community or any person. 18 U.S.C. §3142(f). While the Government's general interest in preventing crime is compelling, even this interest is heightened when the Government musters convincing proof that the arrestee, already indicted or held to answer for a serious crime, presents a demonstrable danger to the community. Under these narrow circumstances, society's interest in crime prevention is at its greatest.

On the other side of the scale, of course, is the individual's strong interest in liberty. We do not minimize the importance and fundamental nature of this right. But, as our cases hold, this right may, in circumstances where the government's interest is sufficiently weighty, be subordinated to the greater needs of society. We think that Congress' careful delineation of the circumstances under which detention will be permitted satisfies this standard. . . .

Finally, we may dispose briefly of respondents' facial challenge to the procedures of the Bail Reform Act. To sustain them against such a challenge, we need only find them "adequate to authorize the pretrial detention of at least some [persons] charged with crimes," *Schall,* supra, at 264, whether or not they might be insufficient in some particular circumstances. We think they pass that test. As we stated in *Schall,* "there is nothing inherently unattainable about a prediction of future criminal conduct." 467 U.S., at 278. . . .

Under the Bail Reform Act, the procedures by which a judicial officer evaluates the likelihood of future dangerousness are specifically designed to further the accuracy of that determination. Detainees have a right to counsel at the detention hearing. 18 U.S.C. §3142(f). They may testify in their own behalf, present information by proffer or otherwise, and cross-examine witnesses who appear at the hearing. Ibid. The judicial officer charged with the responsibility of determining the appropriateness of detention is guided by statutorily enumerated factors, which include the nature and the circumstances of the charges, the weight of the evidence, the history and characteristics of the putative offender, and the danger to the community. §3142(g). The Government must prove its case by clear and convincing evidence. §3142(f). Finally, the judicial officer must include written findings of fact and a written statement of reasons for a decision to detain. §3142(i). The Act's review provisions, §3145(c), provide for immediate appellate review of the detention decision.

We think these extensive safeguards suffice to repel a facial challenge. The protections are more exacting than those we found sufficient in the juvenile context, see *Schall*, supra, at 275-281, and they far exceed what we found necessary to effect limited postarrest detention in Gerstein v. Pugh, 420 U.S. 103 (1975). Given the legitimate and compelling regulatory purpose of the Act and the procedural protections it offers, we conclude that the Act is not facially invalid under the Due Process Clause of the Fifth Amendment.

B

Respondents also contend that the Bail Reform Act violates the Excessive Bail Clause of the Eighth Amendment. The Court of Appeals did not address this issue because it found that the Act violates the Due Process Clause. We think that the Act survives a challenge founded upon the Eighth Amendment.

The Eighth Amendment addresses pretrial release by providing merely that "[e]xcessive bail shall not be required." This Clause, of course, says nothing about whether bail shall be available at all. Respondents nevertheless contend that this Clause grants them a right to bail calculated solely upon considerations of flight. They rely on Stack v. Boyle, 342 U.S. 1, 5 (1951), in which the Court stated that "[b]ail set at a figure higher than an amount reasonably calculated [to ensure the defendant's presence at trial] is 'excessive' under the Eighth Amendment." In respondents' view, since the Bail Reform Act allows a court essentially to set bail at an infinite amount for reasons not related to the risk of flight, it violates the Excessive Bail Clause. Respondents concede that the right to bail they have discovered in the Eighth Amendment is not absolute. A court may, for example, refuse bail in capital cases. And, as the Court of Appeals noted and respondents admit, a court may refuse bail when the defendant presents a threat to the judicial process by intimidating witnesses. . . . Respondents characterize these exceptions as consistent with what they claim to be the sole purpose of bail—to ensure the integrity of the judicial process.

While we agree that a primary function of bail is to safeguard the courts' role in adjudicating the guilt or innocence of defendants, we reject the proposition that the Eighth Amendment categorically prohibits the government from pursuing other admittedly compelling interests through regulation of pretrial release. The above-quoted dictum in Stack v. Boyle is far too slender a reed on which to rest this argument. The Court in *Stack* had no occasion to consider whether the Excessive Bail Clause requires courts to admit all defendants to bail, because the statute before the Court in that case in fact allowed the defendants to be bailed. Thus, the Court had to determine only whether bail, admittedly available in that case, was excessive if set at a sum greater than that necessary to ensure the arrestees' presence at trial. . . .

[W]e need not decide today whether the Excessive Bail Clause speaks at all to Congress' power to define the classes of criminal arrestees who shall be admitted to bail. For even if we were to conclude that the Eighth Amendment imposes some substantive limitations on the National Legislature's powers in this area, we would still hold that the Bail Reform Act is valid. Nothing in the text of the Bail Clause limits permissible Government considerations solely to questions of flight. The only arguable substantive limitation of the Bail Clause is that the Government's proposed conditions of release or detention not be "excessive" in light of the perceived evil. Of course, to determine whether the Government's response is excessive, we must compare that response against the interest the Government seeks to protect by means of that response. Thus, when the Government has admitted that its only interest is in preventing flight, bail must be set by a court at a sum designed to ensure that goal, and no more. Stack v. Boyle, supra. We believe that when Congress has mandated detention on the basis of a compelling interest other than prevention of flight, as it has here, the Eighth Amendment does not require release on bail.

III

In our society liberty is the norm, and detention prior to trial or without trial is the carefully limited exception. We hold that the provisions for pretrial detention in the Bail Reform Act of 1984 fall within that carefully limited exception. The Act authorizes the detention prior to trial of arrestees charged with serious felonies who are found after an adversary hearing to pose a threat to the safety of individuals or to the community which no condition of release can dispel. The numerous procedural safeguards detailed above must attend this adversary hearing. We are unwilling to say that this congressional determination, based as it is upon that primary concern of every government—a concern for the safety and indeed the lives of its citizens—on its face violates either the Due Process Clause of the Fifth Amendment or the Excessive Bail Clause of the Eighth Amendment.

The judgment of the Court of Appeals is therefore Reversed.

JUSTICE MARSHALL, with whom JUSTICE BRENNAN joins, dissenting.

This case brings before the Court for the first time a statute in which Congress declares that a person innocent of any crime may be jailed indefinitely, pending the trial of allegations which are legally presumed to be untrue, if the Government shows to the satisfaction of a judge that the accused is likely to commit crimes, unrelated to the pending charges, at any time in the future. Such statutes, consistent with the usages of tyranny and the excesses of what bitter experience teaches us to call the police state, have long been thought incompatible with the fundamental human rights protected by our Constitution. Today a majority of this Court holds otherwise. Its decision disregards basic principles of justice established centuries ago and enshrined beyond the reach of governmental interference in the Bill of Rights.

I

[This section, dealing with the procedural posture of the case, is omitted.—EDS.]

II

The majority approaches respondents' challenge to the Act by dividing the discussion into two sections, one concerned with the substantive guarantees implicit in the Due Process Clause, and the other concerned with the protection afforded by the Excessive Bail Clause of the Eighth Amendment. This is a sterile formalism, which divides a unitary argument into two independent parts and then professes to demonstrate that the parts are individually inadequate.

On the due process side of this false dichotomy appears an argument concerning the distinction between regulatory and punitive legislation. . . . The majority finds that "Congress did not formulate the pretrial detention provisions as punishment for dangerous individuals," but instead was pursuing the "legitimate regulatory goal" of "preventing danger to the community."[4] Concluding that pretrial detention is not an excessive solution to the problem of preventing danger to the community, the majority thus finds that no substantive element of the guarantee of due process invalidates the statute.

This argument does not demonstrate the conclusion it purports to justify. Let us apply the majority's reasoning to a similar, hypothetical case. After investigation, Congress determines (not unrealistically) that a large proportion of violent crime is perpetrated by persons who are unemployed. It also determines, equally reasonably, that much violent crime is committed at night. From amongst the panoply of "potential solutions," Congress chooses a statute which permits, after judicial proceedings, the imposition of a dusk-to-dawn curfew on anyone who is unemployed. Since this is not a measure enacted for the purpose of punishing the unemployed, and since the majority finds that preventing danger to the community is a legitimate regulatory goal, the curfew statute would, according to the majority's analysis, be a mere "regulatory" detention statute, entirely compatible with the substantive components of the Due Process Clause.

The absurdity of this conclusion arises, of course, from the majority's cramped concept of substantive due process. The majority proceeds as though the only substantive right protected by the Due Process Clause is a right to be free from punishment before conviction. The majority's technique for infringing this right is simple: merely redefine any measure which is claimed to be punishment as "regulation," and, magically, the Constitution no longer prohibits its imposition. Because, as I discuss in Part III, infra, the Due Process Clause protects other substantive rights which are infringed by this legislation, the majority's argument is merely an exercise in obfuscation.

The logic of the majority's Eighth Amendment analysis is equally unsatisfactory. The Eighth Amendment . . . states that "[e]xcessive bail shall not be required."

. . . If excessive bail is imposed the defendant stays in jail. The same result is achieved if bail is denied altogether. Whether the magistrate sets bail at $1 billion or refuses to set bail at all, the consequences are indistinguishable. It would be mere sophistry to suggest that the Eighth Amendment protects against the former decision, and not the latter. Indeed, such a result would lead to the conclusion that there was no need for Congress to pass a preventive detention measure of any kind; every federal magistrate and district judge could simply refuse, despite the absence of any evidence of risk of flight or danger to the community, to set bail. This would be entirely constitutional, since, according to the majority, the Eighth Amendment "says nothing about whether bail shall be available at all."

But perhaps, the majority says, this manifest absurdity can be avoided. Perhaps the Bail Clause is addressed only to the Judiciary. "[W]e need not decide today," the

---

4. . . . The Bail Reform Act does not limit its definition of dangerousness to the likelihood that the defendant poses a danger to others through the commission of *federal* crimes. Federal preventive detention may thus be ordered under the Act when the danger asserted by the Government is the danger that the defendant will violate state law. The majority nowhere identifies the constitutional source of congressional power to authorize the federal detention of persons whose predicted future conduct would not violate any federal statute and could not be punished by a federal court. I can only conclude that the Court's frequently expressed concern with the principles of federalism vanishes when it threatens to interfere with the Court's attainment of the desired result.

majority says, "whether the Excessive Bail Clause speaks at all to Congress' power to define the classes of criminal arrestees who shall be admitted to bail." The majority is correct that this question need not be decided today; it was decided long ago. Federal and state statutes which purport to accomplish what the Eighth Amendment forbids . . . may not stand. . . .

III

The essence of this case may be found, ironically enough, in a provision of the Act to which the majority does not refer. Title 18 U.S.C. §3142(j) . . . provides that "[n]othing in this section shall be construed as modifying or limiting the presumption of innocence." But the very pith and purpose of this statute is an abhorrent limitation of the presumption of innocence. The majority's untenable conclusion that the present Act is constitutional arises from a specious denial of the role of the Bail Clause and the Due Process Clause in protecting the invaluable guarantee afforded by the presumption of innocence.

   "The principle that there is a presumption of innocence in favor of the accused is the undoubted law, axiomatic and elementary, and its enforcement lies at the foundation of the administration of our criminal law." Coffin v. United States, 156 U.S. 432, 453 (1895). Our society's belief, reinforced over the centuries, that all are innocent until the state has proved them to be guilty, like the companion principle that guilt must be proved beyond a reasonable doubt, is "implicit in the concept of ordered liberty," Palko v. Connecticut, 302 U.S. 319, 325 (1937), and is established beyond legislative contravention in the Due Process Clause. . . .

   The statute now before us declares that persons who have been indicted may be detained if a judicial officer finds clear and convincing evidence that they pose a danger to individuals or to the community. The statute does not authorize the Government to imprison anyone it has evidence is dangerous; indictment is necessary. But let us suppose that a defendant is indicted and the Government shows by clear and convincing evidence that he is dangerous and should be detained pending a trial, at which trial the defendant is acquitted. May the Government continue to hold the defendant in detention based upon its showing that he is dangerous? The answer cannot be yes, for that would allow the Government to imprison someone for uncommitted crimes based upon "proof" not beyond a reasonable doubt. The result must therefore be that once the indictment has failed, detention cannot continue. But our fundamental principles of justice declare that the defendant is as innocent on the day before his trial as he is on the morning after his acquittal. Under this statute an untried indictment somehow acts to permit a detention, based on other charges, which after an acquittal would be unconstitutional. The conclusion is inescapable that the indictment has been turned into evidence, if not that the defendant is guilty of the crime charged, then that left to his own devices he will soon be guilty of something else. " 'If it suffices to accuse, what will become of the innocent?' " Coffin v. United States, supra, at 455 (quoting Ammianus Marcellinus, Rerum Gestarum Libri Qui Supersunt, L. XVIII, c. 1, A.D. 359). To be sure, an indictment is not without legal consequences. It establishes that there is probable cause to believe that an offense was committed, and that the defendant committed it. Upon probable cause a warrant for the defendant's arrest may issue; a period of administrative detention may occur before the evidence of probable cause is presented to a neutral magistrate. See Gerstein v. Pugh, 420 U.S. 103 (1975). Once a defendant has been committed for trial he may be detained in custody if the magistrate finds that no conditions of release will prevent him from becoming a fugitive. But in this connection the charging instrument is evidence of nothing more than the fact that there will be a trial. . . . The finding of probable cause conveys power to try, and the power to try imports of necessity the power to assure that the processes of justice will not be evaded or obstructed. . . . [But the] detention purportedly authorized by this statute bears no relation to the Government's power to try charges supported by a finding of probable cause, and thus the interests it serves are outside the scope of interests which may be considered in weighing the excessiveness of bail under the Eighth Amendment.

It is not a novel proposition that the Bail Clause plays a vital role in protecting the presumption of innocence. . . . As Chief Justice Vinson wrote for the Court in Stack v. Boyle, supra: "Unless th[e] right to bail before trial is preserved, the presumption of innocence, secured only after centuries of struggle, would lose its meaning." 342 U.S., at 4.

IV

There is a connection between the peculiar facts of this case and the evident constitutional defects in the statute which the Court upholds today. Respondent Cafaro was originally incarcerated for an indeterminate period at the request of the Government, which believed (or professed to believe) that his release imminently threatened the safety of the community. That threat apparently vanished, from the Government's point of view, when Cafaro agreed to act as a covert agent of the Government. There could be no more eloquent demonstration of the coercive power of authority to imprison upon prediction, or of the dangers which the almost inevitable abuses pose to the cherished liberties of a free society.

"It is a fair summary of history to say that the safeguards of liberty have frequently been forged in controversies involving not very nice people." United States v. Rabinowitz, 339 U.S. 56, 69 (1950) (Frankfurter, J., dissenting). Honoring the presumption of innocence is often difficult; sometimes we must pay substantial social costs as a result of our commitment to the values we espouse. But at the end of the day the presumption of innocence protects the innocent; the shortcuts we take with those whom we believe to be guilty injure only those wrongfully accused and, ultimately, ourselves.

Throughout the world today there are men, women, and children interned indefinitely, awaiting trials which may never come or which may be a mockery of the word, because their governments believe them to be "dangerous." Our Constitution, whose construction began two centuries ago, can shelter us forever from the evils of such unchecked power. Over 200 years it has slowly, through our efforts, grown more durable, more expansive, and more just. But it cannot protect us if we lack the courage, and the self-restraint, to protect ourselves. Today a majority of the Court applies itself to an ominous exercise in demolition. Theirs is truly a decision which will go forth without authority, and come back without respect.

I dissent.

JUSTICE STEVENS, dissenting.

There may be times when the Government's interest in protecting the safety of the community will justify the brief detention of a person who has not committed any crime. . . .[1] To use Judge Feinberg's example, it is indeed difficult to accept the proposition that the Government is without power to detain a person when it is a virtual certainty that he or she would otherwise kill a group of innocent people in the immediate future. United States v. Salerno, 794 F.2d 64, 77 (CA2 1986) (dissenting opinion). Similarly, I am unwilling to decide today that the police may never impose a limited curfew during a time of crisis. These questions are obviously not presented in this case, but they lurk in the background and preclude me from answering the question that is presented in as broad a manner as Justice Marshall has. Nonetheless, I firmly agree with Justice Marshall that the provision of the Bail Reform Act allowing pretrial detention on the basis of future dangerousness is unconstitutional. Whatever the answers are to the questions I have mentioned, it is clear to me that a pending indictment may not be given any weight in evaluating an individual's risk to the community or the need for immediate detention.

If the evidence of imminent danger is strong enough to warrant emergency detention, it should support that preventive measure regardless of whether the person has been charged, convicted, or acquitted of some other offense. In this case, for example, it is unrealistic to assume that the danger to the community that was present when respondents were at large did not justify their detention before they were indicted, but did require that measure the moment that the grand jury found probable cause to believe they had committed crimes in the past. It is equally unrealistic to assume that the danger will vanish if a jury happens to acquit them. Justice Marshall has demonstrated that the fact of indictment cannot, consistent with the presumption of innocence and the Eighth Amendment's Excessive Bail Clause, be used to create a special class, the members of which are, alone, eligible for detention because of future dangerousness. . . .

NOTES AND QUESTIONS

1. Recall in Stack v. Boyle the Court said that bail "serves to prevent the infliction of punishment prior to conviction." Tony Salerno claimed that to keep him in jail based on a prediction of dangerousness amounted to punishment for crimes that had not yet occurred. Is he right? Or is the Court correct that pretrial detention is a "regulatory" measure rather than punishment?

As the *Salerno* majority points out, there are familiar examples of regulatory measures that can result in confinement of a person, often in quite undesirable conditions. Most notably, a mentally ill person can be involuntarily confined to a psychiatric institution based on a prediction of future dangerousness. See Addington v. Texas, 441 U.S. 418 (1979). If you disagree with the result in *Salerno*, how would you distinguish this example? Or are those committed to a psychiatric hospital also being improperly "punished?" Does the Court's focus on the intent of Congress in permitting the confinement help draw a distinction? See generally Marc Miller & Martin Guggenheim, Pretrial Detention and Punishment, 75 Minn. L. Rev. 335,

---

1. "If the evidence overwhelmingly establishes that a skyjacker, for example, was insane at the time of his act, and that he is virtually certain to resume his violent behavior as soon as he is set free, must we then conclude that the only way to protect society from such predictable harm is to find an innocent man guilty of a crime he did not have the capacity to commit?" United States v. Greene, 497 F.2d [1068,] 1088 [(CA 7 1974)].

372 (1990), in which the authors claim that "the state cannot preventively detain a competent adult without making an implicit moral statement about the individual" and concluding that such a moral statement—when coupled with hard treatment, such as detention—constitutes "punishment."

2. It seems clear even after *Salerno* that there must be some triggering event that allows the government to make a prediction of dangerousness and then detain the person as a result. Before a person can be confined to a psychiatric institution, for example, there must be a finding of a mental illness. In the case of pretrial detention, the triggering event is the arrest—unless and until Tony Salerno is arrested, the government cannot snatch him up and detain him simply because they can confidently predict that he will commit future crimes. And of course, if Salerno were later acquitted, a court couldn't continue to hold him after trial, even if it has overwhelming evidence that he likely to resume his criminal career the next day. So there must be *something* about the arrest that moves Salerno into a different category, one that legitimizes the prediction of dangerousness and the resulting detention.

In the Court's view, what is it about an arrest that legitimizes the use of this power? An arrest can be based on probable cause, which is not a very exacting standard. One possible answer is found in a single line in the majority opinion: "Congress specifically found that these individuals [who are arrested for serious crimes] are far more likely to be responsible for dangerous acts in the community after arrest." Assuming the accuracy of this congressional finding, is this a sufficient basis for permitting preventive detention?

If so (or even if not), could Congress find that a *conviction* for a serious crime is sufficient to allow the preventive detention of someone, even after the person has served his sentence and is released from prison? In other words, after Tony Salerno is convicted and has done his time, could Congress permit the government to seek his continued confinement based on a prediction of future criminality? If you think the answer should be "no," consider Kansas v. Hendricks, 521 U.S. 346 (1997), and Kansas v. Crane, 534 U.S. 407 (2002), which upheld a Kansas statute that allowed for continued civil commitment of individuals who had already completed their sentence for sexual offenses based on a finding that they were likely to engage in future "predatory acts of sexual violence," as well as proof that the person currently has "serious difficulty in controlling behavior."

3. How confident should we be that trial courts can accurately predict the future dangerousness of a person? Few people doubted that Tony Salerno—the alleged boss of a New York crime family who would later be sentenced to 100 years in prison—would continue to commit offenses if released on bail. And the Supreme Court had taken the view, even before *Salerno*, that "there is nothing inherently unattainable about prediction of future criminal conduct." Schall v. Martin, 467 U.S. 253, 278 (1984). On the other hand, there is a great skepticism over the ability to predict future dangerous behavior accurately in more typical cases, and a great deal of concern about the potential for a high number of "false positives": conclusions that a person is dangerous to the community when he is not.

In a study that focused on the ability of judges to predict future dangerousness of juveniles, for example, Professors Fagan and Guggenheim concluded that "[t]he capacity [of judges] to select from among a group of accused delinquents those who pose an elevated risk of criminality in the legally critical interval following arrest is clear from the study. These results are all the more impressive given the limited nature of the information available to the judge at the time of the deten-tion decision." Nevertheless, they termed the overall results of their study "ambigu-ous," mostly because of the high incidence of false positives—almost 60 percent of the juveniles who were predicted to be dangerous (but were not detained for unre-lated reasons) were not rearrested for any crimes during the pretrial period, and more than 80 percent were not rearrested for any violent crimes. The researchers found the presence of these over-predictions of risk to be "at odds with constitutional concerns over false imprisonment and equal protection." Jeffrey Fagan & Martin Guggenheim, Preventive Detention and the Judicial Prediction of Dangerousness for Juveniles: A Natural Experiment, 86 J. Crim. L. & Criminology 415, 445-447 (1996).

4. At least some of the work of predicting future dangerousness (and flight risk) is done by statute. The Bail Reform Act provides that if the court finds after a hear-ing that there is probable cause to believe that the suspect committed certain seri-ous crimes—certain drug offenses, using a firearm during a crime of violence, or acts of international terrorism, for example—a rebuttable presumption arises that the defendant should be detained without bail. In addition, if the defendant has previously been convicted of certain serious crimes while he was out on bail fol-lowing an earlier arrest, a rebuttable presumption of dangerousness arises. See 18 U.S.C. §3142(e)(2), (3). Thus, the prosecutor can carry her claim (subject to rebut-tal) that the defendant is a future risk without making any individualized showing with respect to the particular defendant. Is this an appropriate use of rebuttable presumptions? Is a statutory presumption in favor of preventive detention consis-tent with the presumption of innocence?

5. Speaking of the presumption of innocence, Justice Marshall notes in his dis-sent that §3142(j) of the Bail Reform Act provides that "[n]othing in this section shall be construed as modifying or limiting the presumption of innocence." Is the dissent correct that very notion of "preventive detention" is inconsistent with this core principle of the criminal system? On the other hand, isn't every restraint on liberty after an arrest and before conviction—including any restrictions put on the accused as a condition of bail—similarly inconsistent, even if to a lesser degree? Although the majority did not address the point, can you articulate how the pre-sumption of innocence can be reconciled with the outcome in *Salerno*?

6. In a post-*Salerno* world, how many defendants are released prior to trial and how many are detained? Among federal defendants in fiscal year 2012, roughly one in three (33 percent) were released at some point prior to trial, with the rest being detained. See Bureau of Justice Statistics, Federal Justice Statistics, 2012—Statistical Tables at 13 (Table 3.1) (January 2015). This number reflects a decrease in the release rate of federal defendants from the earlier parts of the decade, where in 2006, 37 percent were released, and in 2001, 46 percent were admitted to bail. See http://bjs.ojp.usdoj.gov/content/pub/html/fjsst/2006/fjs06st.pdf (Table 3.1); http://www.albany.edu/sourcebook/pdf/t513.pd (Table 5.13). These figures stand in sharp contrast to State defendants charged with felonies: in 2009, 62 percent were released at some point prior to disposition. See http://www.bjs.gov/content/pub/pdf/fdluc09.pdf (Table 12).

As the *Salerno* majority notes, the concern that motivated the 1984 Bail Reform Act was not how many defendants were released, but rather, the behavior of those who were released. More than 35,000 federal defendants were released prior to trial in fiscal year 2012, and 83 percent complied with all conditions of their release (an improvement from 2006, where 78 percent had no violation), while the remaining

17 percent committed at least one violation. Of all the federal defendants released, only 1.4 percent failed to appear as required, and 9 percent had their release revoked. See Federal Justice Statistics, 2012, supra, at 15 (Table 3.3).

What do you make of these figures? Do they suggest that the bail system is working well, because a high percentage of defendants comply with all the conditions of release? Does the fact that two-thirds of the suspects are detained until disposition mean that the system is getting better at identifying risky bail candidates, or just that courts are becoming too cautious about who is released?

7. Even more than the number of fugitives, the drafters of the Bail Reform Act were worried about the amount of crime being committed by those on bail. On the federal side, only 1.6 percent of the released defendant were charged with a new felony while out on bail, id., and among state defendants, about 8 percent of those on pretrial release were rearrested for a new felony. See http://www.bjs.gov/content/pub/pdf/fdluc09.pdf (Table 19).

But even if a small *percentage* of defendants who are released on bail commit a new crime, the size of the crime problem in the country make the number of new victimizations significant. Consider the following:

> . . . [T]he present system of bail for those accused of violent crimes is responsible for some 122,000 violent crimes annually (and probably substantially more, given all the minimizing assumptions made [in this essay]) that would not have been committed had bail been denied to all those charged with a violent crime.
>
> The category of violent crimes, which is our focus here, includes a variety of sins, from homicide and rape to armed robbery and aggravated assault. Clearly, some of these crimes are much more egregious than others. In assessing the costs of current bail policies, it is important not to fall into the trap of assuming that such crimes as bailees commit are overwhelmingly of the less threatening variety. Indeed, bailees are unquestionably the most likely group—among those monitored by the criminal justice system—to commit homicides in the United States today; indeed, sixteen percent of all homicide arrests from 1990 to 2002 involved persons who were either on active bail or were fugitives from bail.

See Larry Laudan & Ronald J. Allen, Deadly Dilemmas II: Bail and Crime, 85 Chi.-Kent L. Rev. 23 (2010). How should we balance the costs of keeping more defendants detained prior to trial—including some who will turn out to be innocent—against the high costs of increased violent crime victimizations?

8. *Salerno* is one of the most important cases in criminal procedure, and its impact has been felt by a huge number of defendants. But the practical consequences may be somewhat less than meets the eye. Consider this observation by Professor Paul Robinson: "in some respects, one can argue that pretrial preventive detention is less objectionable than [the increasingly prevalent] prevention-based expansions of criminal liability and punishment," such as "three strikes" and sexual-predator laws. This is because most pretrial detainees are, in fact, convicted at trial, or more commonly by guilty plea, and the convicted defendant then receives credit against his or her sentence for the time spent in pretrial detention. Thus, "[a]t least theoretically, [the defendant] serves only the time deserved." Paul H. Robinson, Commentary: Punishing Dangerousness: Cloaking Preventive Detention as Criminal Justice, 114 Harv. L. Rev. 1429 (2001).

Chapter 9

The Charging Decision

A. Prosecutorial Discretion

Article II, Section 3 of the Constitution provides that the president "shall take Care that the Laws be faithfully executed." This clause, and those like it in state constitutions, has come to mean that the prosecutorial power is vested in the executive branch of government. In the federal system, prosecutions are conducted by 93 United States Attorneys, one for each judicial district,[1] and by the assistants who work for them. Unlike the chief prosecutors in most states, U.S. Attorneys are not elected; they are appointed by the president, and work under the direction of the Attorney General, the head of the Department of Justice.

It is hard to overstate the extent to which prosecutors control the initiation and direction of the criminal process. As the readings that follow show, decisions about whether to file criminal charges, which charges to file, and against whom charges should be brought, rest almost exclusively with the prosecutor and normally are not subject to judicial review.

This discretion gives prosecutors enormous power to decide what the criminal law really means in their jurisdiction. Despite the crime rate drop over the last two decades, there is still plenty of criminal behavior to prosecute—in 2013, there were over 1 million violent crimes in this country, including more than 14,000 murders and almost 80,000 rapes, as well as 8.6 million property crimes.[2] When these figures are combined with the perennial governmental problem of insufficient resources, the threshold question becomes how prosecutors decide which defendants to charge and what types of crimes to pursue.

Often, of course, there is no prosecutorial decision to make because the crime is never solved; a large number of crimes are never reported to law enforcement, and among those that are, the clearance rate on violent crimes is less than 50 percent, and the rate for property crimes is about 20 percent.[3] But there are still millions of arrests made every year, which means that at some point, the police and prosecutor have to decide when to move forward, when to seek a non-criminal alternative, and when to stand down. While it is impossible to say with precision how often

---

1. There are actually 94 judicial districts, but the District of Guam and the District of the Northern Mariana Islands share a U.S. Attorney.

2. FBI Uniform Crime Reports, Crime in the United States 2013, Table 1, www.fbi.gov/about-us/cjis/ucr/crime-in-the-u.s/2013/crime-in-the-u.s.-2013/offenses-known-to-law-enforcement/. All numbers in this section are approximate.

3. Id., Table 25.

prosecutors decide to forego a prosecution rather than file charges, some numbers from the federal system are suggestive.

In fiscal year 2012 the U.S. Marshall's service arrested and booked more than 170,000 suspects, half of them (85,000) for immigration offenses, and another 15 percent (26,000) for drug crimes.[4] Yet in that same year, federal prosecutors only filed charges against 93,000 defendants for all crimes, or about 54 percent of the number arrested.[5] Someone had to decide whether to move forward or not with those thousands of other suspects, and it seems quite likely that most of the time the decision was made by the prosecutor.

Why the prosecutor decides not to charge is also hard to quantify, although sometimes (but not always) the decision is memorialized in a declination report. In 2012, there were about 28,000 declination reports in the federal system; among the most popular explanations for not filing charges were:

- A determination that no crime was committed (28%)
- Weak evidence (23%)
- Defendant was already being prosecuted on other charges, or was being prosecuted by some other authority (9%)
- Lack of resources (4%)[6]

See also Michael Edmund O'Neill, Understanding Federal Prosecutorial Declinations: An Empirical Analysis of Predictive Factors, 41 Am. Crim. L. Rev. 1439 (2004). These numbers suggest two related points. First, that federal prosecutors can be and are highly selective in deciding when to file criminal charges. Second, because the prosecutor can be choosey, we would expect that once the charges are filed, the government would win most of the time.

On this last point the statistics are compelling. In 2012 in the federal system, there were over 96,000 criminal defendants whose case was processed to resolution. Of this group, 89 percent pled guilty, 8 percent had the charges dismissed, and 3 percent went to trial. Of those defendants who went to trial, more than four out of five (83%) were convicted. Adding the guilty pleas to the trial convictions results in an overall conviction rate for the federal government of 91 percent.[7]

Not all of these convictions lead to a harsh sentence. Almost one-half (47%) of all convicted federal defendants either served no prison time or were sentenced to 18 months in prison or less, often because the defense entered into a favorable plea bargain.[8] (On the state side, the estimated mean sentence of incarceration for *all* felonies is slightly more than 3 years, with a median sentence of less than 1.5 years, although there is wide variation by offense and location.)[9]

---

4. Bureau of Justice Statistics, Federal Justice Statistics Program 2012, Table 1.2 www.bjs.gov/index.cfm?ty=pbse&sid=62.

5. Id., Table 4.1.

6. Id., Table 2.3. There were also about 1,800 declination reports for which a reason not to prosecute could not be determined, for a total number of declination reports of 29,770.

7. Id., Table 4.2.

8. Bureau of Justice Statistics, Federal Criminal Case Processing Statistics, Query: Offenders Sentenced, 2012, Type of Sentence Imposed, http://www.bjs.gov/fjsrc/.

9. Felony Sentences in State Courts, 2006, Table 1.3 www.bjs.gov/index.cfm?ty =pbdetail&iid=2152.

Collectively these numbers suggest that "success" for a federal criminal suspect (and his lawyer) may come through avoiding formal charges in the first instance, or in striking a favorable deal to avoid a harsh sentence on conviction. But once the prosecutor decides to file charge, the likelihood of beating the rap entirely, especially by going to trial and being acquitted, is extremely small.

Control of the criminal process by professional prosecutors has not always been the norm. As recently as the early nineteenth century, a substantial fraction of criminal cases were litigated by private parties, usually crime victims or their families. At the founding of the republic, there were no professional police departments to investigate wrongdoing, not enough lawyers or money to staff even the judiciary, and most crimes in most places were relatively straightforward affairs. So if victims wanted to use the process to redress the wrongs against them, they needed to be self-starters, and sometimes brave as well.

There are many reasons why private control over criminal litigation gave way to public prosecution. In part, this development was a piece of a much larger phenomenon of growing professionalization (and bureaucratization) of criminal justice, a steady trend of the past 200 years. Police, judges, and prosecutors became full-time positions staffed by trained experts, leaving a diminished role for laypeople. Indeed, one might see the movement over the last two decades to protect the rights of crime victims, by giving them a quasi-official role in the plea negotiation or sentencing process, as a kind of rebellion against this professionalizing trend.

But two other reasons for the growth in power of professional prosecutors also deserve mention. The first is conceptual: Crime came to be seen, increasingly, not as a wrong to an individual victim but as a wrong against society as a whole. From this, it follows naturally that society's representative should act as the plaintiff, and ought to exercise the usual plaintiff's power of deciding whether to sue and what relief to seek. As Chief Justice Roberts has written, "Our entire criminal justice system is premised on the notion that a criminal prosecution pits the government against the governed, not one private citizen against another. . . . A basic step in organizing a civilized society is to take [the prosecution] sword out of private hands and turn it over to an organized government, acting on behalf of all the people." Robertson v. United States ex rel. Watson, 560 U.S. 272, 278, 282-283 (2010) (Roberts, C.J., dissenting from dismissal of certiorari as improvidently granted).

The second reason is practical. Some modern crimes are so complex, and the trail of evidence so hard to follow, that only a full-time prosecutor can hope to devote the resources needed to uncover the wrongdoing. Just as important, in a world in which a large slice of criminal behavior creates no identifiable victim with an incentive to bring the lawbreaker to justice, private prosecution might mean *no* prosecution. In recent years, for example, more than half of the federal criminal docket involved drug and immigration cases, two areas where private prosecutors would be hard to find.

Today, there is no dispute over the need for professional prosecutors, nor is there any serious question about the need for prosecutors to be vested with large amounts of discretion to manage their dockets—the size of the crime problem and institutional limits on the ability to process cases require prioritizing scarce resources. Whether that discretion should be subject to some form of judicial oversight remains an important question, however, as the materials that follow show.

1.   The Decision to Charge

INMATES OF ATTICA CORRECTIONAL FACILITY v. ROCKEFELLER

United States Court of Appeals for the Second Circuit
477 F.2d 375 (1973)

JUDGE MANSFIELD delivered the opinion of the court.

This appeal raises the question of whether the federal judiciary should, at the instance of victims, compel federal and state officials to investigate and prosecute persons who allegedly have violated certain federal and state criminal statutes. Plaintiffs in the purported class suit, which was commenced in the Southern District of New York against various state and federal officers, are certain present and former inmates of New York State's Attica Correctional Facility ("Attica"), the mother of an inmate who was killed when Attica was retaken after the inmate uprising in September 1971, and Arthur O. Eve, a New York State Assemblyman and member of the Subcommittee on Prisons. They appeal from an order of the district court, Lloyd F. MacMahon, Judge, dismissing their complaint. We affirm.

The complaint alleges that before, during, and after the prisoner revolt at and subsequent recapture of Attica in September 1971, which resulted in the killing of 32 inmates and the wounding of many others, the defendants, including the Governor of New York, the State Commissioner of Correctional Services, the Executive Deputy Commissioner of the State Department of Correctional Services, the Superintendent at Attica, and certain State Police, Corrections Officers, and other officials, either committed, conspired to commit, or aided and abetted in the commission of various crimes against the complaining inmates and members of the class they seek to represent. It is charged that the inmates were intentionally subjected to cruel and inhuman treatment prior to the inmate riot, that State Police, Troopers, and Correction Officers . . . intentionally killed some of the inmate victims without provocation during the recovery of Attica, that state officers . . . assaulted and beat prisoners after the prison had been successfully retaken and the prisoners had surrendered, . . . that personal property of the inmates was thereafter stolen or destroyed, and that medical assistance was maliciously denied to over 400 inmates wounded during the recovery of the prison.

The complaint further alleges that Robert E. Fischer, a Deputy State Attorney General specially appointed by the Governor . . . with a specially convened grand jury, to investigate crimes relating to the inmates' takeover of Attica and the resumption of control by the state authorities, . . . "has not investigated, nor does he intend to investigate, any crimes committed by state officers." . . .

With respect to the sole federal defendant, the United States Attorney for the Western District of New York, the complaint simply alleges that he has not arrested, investigated, or instituted prosecutions against any of the state officers accused of criminal violation of plaintiffs' federal civil rights, 18 U.S.C. §§241, 242, and he has thereby failed to carry out the duty placed upon him by 42 U.S.C. §1987, discussed below.

As a remedy for the asserted failure of the defendants to prosecute violations of state and federal criminal laws, plaintiffs request relief in the nature of mandamus (1) against state officials, requiring the State of New York to submit a plan for the independent and impartial investigation and prosecution of the offenses charged against the named and unknown state officers, and insuring the appointment of an impartial state prosecutor and state judge to "prosecute the defendants forthwith," and (2) against the United States Attorney, requiring him to investigate, arrest and prosecute the same state officers for having committed the federal offenses defined by 18 U.S.C. §§241 and 242. The latter statutes punish, respectively, conspiracies against a citizen's free exercise or enjoyment of rights secured by the Constitution and laws of the United States, . . . and the willful subjection of any inhabitant, under color of law, to the deprivation of such rights or to different punishment or penalties on account of alienage, color, or race than are prescribed for the punishment of citizens. . . .

The motions of the federal and state defendants to dismiss the complaint for failure to state claims upon which relief can be granted . . . were granted by Judge MacMahon without opinion. We agree that the extraordinary relief sought cannot be granted in the situation here presented. . . .

With respect to the defendant United States Attorney, plaintiffs seek mandamus to compel him to investigate and institute prosecutions against state officers, most of whom are not identified, for alleged violations of 18 U.S.C. §§241 and 242. Federal mandamus is, of course, available only "to compel an officer or employee of the United States . . . to perform a duty owed to the plaintiff." 28 U.S.C. §1361. And the legislative history of §1361 makes it clear that ordinarily the courts are "not to direct or influence the exercise of discretion of the officer or agency in the making of the decision," United States ex rel. Schonbrun v. Commanding Officer, 403 F.2d 371, 374 (2d Cir. 1968). More particularly, federal courts have traditionally and, to our knowledge, uniformly refrained from overturning, at the instance of a private person, discretionary decisions of federal prosecuting authorities not to prosecute persons regarding whom a complaint of criminal conduct is made. [There follows here a long string of case citations.—EDS.]

This judicial reluctance to direct federal prosecutions at the instance of a private party asserting the failure of United States officials to prosecute alleged criminal violations has been applied even in cases such as the present one where, according to the allegations of the complaint, which we must accept as true for purposes of this appeal, serious questions are raised as to the protection of the civil rights and physical security of a definable class of victims of crime and as to the fair administration of the criminal justice system. . . .

The primary ground upon which this traditional judicial aversion to compelling prosecutions has been based is the separation of powers doctrine.

> Although as a member of the bar, the attorney for the United States is an officer of the court, he is nevertheless an executive official of the Government, and it is as an officer of the executive department that he exercises a discretion as to whether or not there shall be a prosecution in a particular case. It follows, as an incident of the constitutional separation of powers, that the courts are not to interfere with the free exercise of the discretionary powers of the attorneys of the United States in their control over criminal prosecutions. United States v. Cox, 342 F.2d [167, 171 (5th Cir. 1965)].

. . . [In addition, in] the absence of statutorily defined standards governing reviewability, or regulatory or statutory policies of prosecution, the problems inherent in the task of supervising prosecutorial decisions do not lend themselves to resolution by the judiciary. The reviewing courts would be placed in the undesirable and injudicious posture of becoming "superprosecutors." In the normal case of review of executive acts of discretion, the administrative record is open, public and reviewable on the basis of what it contains. The decision not to prosecute, on the other hand, may be based upon the insufficiency of the available evidence, in which event the secrecy of the grand jury and of the prosecutor's file may serve to protect the accused's reputation from public damage based upon insufficient, improper, or even malicious charges. In camera review would not be meaningful without access by the complaining party to the evidence before the grand jury or U.S. Attorney. Such interference with the normal operations of criminal investigations, in turn, based solely upon allegations of criminal conduct, raises serious questions of potential abuse by persons seeking to have other persons prosecuted. Any person, merely by filing a complaint containing allegations in general terms (permitted by the Federal Rules) of unlawful failure to prosecute, could gain access to the prosecutor's file. . . .

Nor is it clear what the judiciary's role of supervision should be were it to undertake such a review. At what point would the prosecutor be entitled to call a halt to further investigation as unlikely to be productive? What evidentiary standard would be used to decide whether prosecution should be compelled? How much judgment would the United States Attorney be allowed? Would he be permitted to limit himself to a strong "test" case rather than pursue weaker cases? What collateral factors would be permissible bases for a decision not to prosecute, e.g., the pendency of another criminal proceeding elsewhere against the same parties? What sort of review should be available in cases like the present one where the conduct complained of allegedly violates state as well as federal laws? With limited personnel and facilities at his disposal, what priority would the prosecutor be required to give to cases in which investigation or prosecution was directed by the court?

These difficult questions engender serious doubts as to the judiciary's capacity to review and as to the problem of arbitrariness inherent in any judicial decision to order prosecution. On balance, we believe that substitution of a court's decision to compel prosecution for the U.S. Attorney's decision not to prosecute, even upon an abuse of discretion standard of review and even if limited to directing that a prosecution be undertaken in good faith, would be unwise.

Plaintiffs urge, however, that Congress withdrew the normal prosecutorial discretion for the kind of conduct alleged here by providing in 42 U.S.C. §1987[4] that the United States Attorneys are "authorized and required . . . to institute prosecutions against all persons violating any of the provisions of [18 U.S.C. §§241, 242]," and, therefore, that no barrier to a judicial directive to institute prosecutions remains. This contention must be rejected. The mandatory nature of the word "required" as it appears in §1987 is insufficient to evince a broad Congressional purpose to bar the exercise of executive discretion in the prosecution of federal civil rights crimes. . . .

---

4. §1987. Prosecution of violation of certain laws

The United States attorneys, marshals, and deputy marshals, the commissioners appointed by the district and territorial courts, with power to arrest, imprison, or bail offenders, and every other officer who is especially empowered by the President, are authorized and required, at the expense of the United States, to institute prosecutions against all persons violating any of the provisions of section 1990 of this title or of sections 5506 to 5516 and 5518 to 5532 of the Revised Statutes, and to cause such persons to be arrested, and imprisoned or bailed, for trial before the court of the United States or the territorial court having cognizance of the offense.

With respect to the state defendants, plaintiffs also seek prosecution of named and unknown persons for the violation of state crimes. However, they have pointed to no statutory language even arguably creating any mandatory duty upon the state officials to bring such prosecutions. To the contrary, New York law reposes in its prosecutors a discretion to decide whether or not to prosecute in a given case, which is not subject to review in the state courts. . . . Yet the federal district court is asked to compel state prosecutions and appoint an "impartial" state prosecutor and state judge to conduct them, as well as to require the submission of a plan for impartial investigation and prosecution of the alleged offenses, . . . in the context of a continuing grand jury investigation into criminal conduct connected with the Attica uprising, and where the state itself on September 30, 1971, appointed a Special Commission on Attica which has now published its findings. The very elaborateness of the relief believed by plaintiffs to be required indicates the difficulties inherent in judicial supervision of prosecutions, federal or state, which render such a course inadvisable. . . .

The order of the district court is affirmed.

NOTES AND QUESTIONS

1. Few cases squarely address the legal issue in *Inmates of Attica*, largely because the position the Second Circuit took is so well settled that few litigants bother to challenge it. Why is this so? Is it really self-evident, as the opinion suggests, that judges could not feasibly decide whether a given decision not to charge was fair?

The United States Attorney's Manual advises federal prosecutors that among the grounds for declining to file criminal charges is that "no substantial Federal interest would be served by prosecution." In assessing the federal interest in a case, the U.S. Attorney is to "weigh all relevant considerations, including: (1) Federal law enforcement priorities; (2) The nature and seriousness of the offense; (3) The deterrent effect of prosecution; (4) The person's culpability in connection with the offense; (5) The person's history with respect to criminal activity; (6) The person's willingness to cooperate in the investigation or prosecution of others; and (7) The probable sentence or other consequences if the person is convicted." U.S. Attorney's Manual §9-27.230, http://www.justice.gov/usam/united-states-attorneys-manual (visited September 10, 2015).

How difficult would it be for a judge to evaluate these factors? Note that courts now routinely review the decisions of administrative agencies, whose rulings often turn on highly technical and scientific evidence, as well as on the feasibility of the remedy and the opportunity costs of choosing one course of action over another. And while judicial review of administrative decisions is highly deferential, recall that *Inmates of Attica* rejected the notion of *any* such oversight, including a judicial check to ensure that prosecutors have made their decisions in good faith.

2. The separation of powers concerns that animated *Inmates of Attica* is more than a limit on the judicial power over the charging decision. Occasionally, a grand jury—the panel of citizens charged with reviewing the government's evidence and deciding if it is sufficient to proceed with a criminal charge (see Chapter 10)—will vote to return an indictment that the prosecutor believes is unjustified or unwise. The question then becomes whether the prosecutor must follow the grand jury's wishes and move the case forward, or whether she can ignore the grand jury and refuse to prosecute. Although the Supreme Court has observed that the grand jury

"has not been textually assigned . . . to any of the branches described in the first three Articles" of the Constitution and is thus "a constitutional fixture in its own right," United States v. Williams, 504 U.S. 36, 47 (1992), courts have consistently refused to intervene and require the prosecutor to follow the grand jury's wishes. Stated differently, it now seems settled that neither the grand jury nor a court can compel a federal prosecutor to sign and return an indictment against her wishes. See United States v. Cox, 342 F.2d 167, 171 (5th Cir. 1965).

3. Suppose you were a chief prosecutor in the *Inmates of Attica* case, and one of your assistants made the following argument: "Any prosecution of the prison guards will likely lead to an acquittal, because no upstate New York jury will convict a guard for violence against prisoners who had already killed another guard. So any prosecution would be a waste of the taxpayers' money and the resources of this office." If you believed that the guards had in fact committed crimes and thought that you had enough evidence to prove it, would this risk of "jury nullification"—where the jury acquits despite its belief that the defendant committed the crime—influence your decision to prosecute? Should it? Would it matter if you were elected to your office rather than appointed? The U.S. Attorney's Manual provides: "The potential that—despite the law and the facts that create a sound, prosecutable case—the factfinder is likely to acquit the defendant because of the unpopularity of some factor involved in the prosecution or because of the overwhelming popularity of the defendant or his/her cause, is not a factor prohibiting prosecution." §9-27.220 Comment. Notice that the Manual does not say that the risk of nullification *may* not be considered; it only says that the risk does not prohibit a prosecution.

4. One area where a decision not to file charges has received a great deal of attention is when a police officer uses deadly force against a citizen, and there are claims that the shooting was unjustified because the victim was unarmed or otherwise not a danger. Failure to prosecute the police officer in these cases—most famously, although not exclusively, in Ferguson, Missouri—has led to sharp, even violent protests, with critics claiming that prosecutors were too protective of police, especially when the victim was a minority-race citizen. The claims are that because of the close working relationship with law enforcement, prosecutors are too quick to believe the officer's version of events, and thus too slow to prosecute the use of excessive force.

Assume for the sake of discussion that the claims are true, and that prosecutors have an institutional bias that results in the under-enforcement of the criminal law against police officers. If courts can't compel a prosecution, what should the remedy be? One possible answer is to require that all officer-involved shootings be presented to a grand jury, to see if lay people agree with the decision not to charge. And in fact, for political reasons, many prosecutors will routinely present these cases to the grand jury, as was done in Ferguson. But as discussed in Chapter 10, it is widely believed that grand juries are so heavily influenced by the prosecutor that they are unlikely to impose enough pressure to compel a course of action that the prosecutor does not wish to take. And of course, as noted above, a grand jury can't force the filing of charges over the prosecutor's wishes.

Another possible solution is to require the appointment of a special prosecutor, someone with no ties to the local community, who could independently review the facts and decide whether the police officer should be charged. Would this solve the perceived conflict issue? Wouldn't an outside prosecutor (who is, after all, still a prosecutor) still likely to be biased in favor of law enforcement, even if she didn't know the officers personally? And if the independent prosecutor chose not to indict, who would the disappointed citizens have to blame?

A third possible solution is the political one—if the citizens of Ferguson do not like the way the District Attorney makes charging decisions, either in general or in a particular case, they can vote him out office. How often would you expect this to occur? Does the fact that the victims are often members of groups without much political clout mean that the political solution is not feasible?

Of course, on the federal level, U.S. Attorneys are not elected, and so do not even face the check of the ballot box. Consider a response to this concern offered by Justice Scalia in Morrison v. Olson, 487 U.S. 654 (1988), a case challenging the constitutionality of the appointment of independent counsels:

> Under our system of government, the primary check against prosecutorial abuse is a political one. The prosecutors who exercise this awesome discretion are selected and can be removed by a President, whom the people have trusted enough to elect. Moreover, when crimes are not investigated and prosecuted fairly, nonselectively, with a reasonable sense of proportion, the President pays the cost in political damage to his administration. If federal prosecutors "pick people that [they think they] should get, rather than cases that need to be prosecuted," if they amass many more resources against a particular prominent individual, or against a particular class of political protesters, or against members of a particular political party, than the gravity of the alleged offenses or the record of successful prosecutions seems to warrant, the unfairness will come home to roost in the Oval Office. . . . That result, of course, was precisely what the Founders had in mind when they provided that all executive powers would be exercised by a *single* Chief Executive. . . . The President is directly dependent on the people, and since there is only *one* President, *he* is responsible. The people know whom to blame. . . .

Id., at 729-730 (Scalia, J., dissenting). Are you persuaded? — Yes

5. Separation of powers is not the only barrier to judicial review of charging decisions. A second obstacle is standing. As the Supreme Court put it in Linda R. S. v. Richard D., 410 U.S. 614, 619 (1973), ordinarily "a private citizen lacks a judicially cognizable interest in the prosecution or nonprosecution of another." See also Allen v. Wright, 468 U.S. 737 (1984) (applying this principle to bar a suit by black parents seeking to force the Internal Revenue Service to revoke the tax-exempt status of allegedly discriminatory private schools). On this theory, *no one* can challenge a decision not to prosecute because, by definition, no one is harmed by such a decision. Does that position make sense? Are crime victims really uninjured by decisions not to charge their injurers? In a part of the opinion not excerpted above, the court of appeals in *Inmates of Attica* noted that standing was at least problematic in that case, but it did not resolve the issue.

2. Selecting the Charge

Beyond the decision of whether to file charges, prosecutors also have broad authority to decide which charges to file. Criminal statutes are sometimes written in expansive language, with the result that a defendant's alleged behavior often meets the definition of more than one offense. The power to decide whether certain conduct should be charged as a more serious or less serious crime is a matter of great strategic and systemic significance. As will been seen in the discussion of guilty pleas in Chapter 13, the ability to charge a defendant with a greater or lesser offense can give the government enormous leverage over the defendant during the plea bargaining process. The authority to charge identical conduct as a greater or lesser offense also raises concerns about unequal treatment of similarly situated defendants. Consider the Supreme Court's response to a defendant who challenged the prosecutor's exercise of the charge-selection power.

UNITED STATES v. BATCHELDER

Certiorari to the United States Court of Appeals for the Seventh Circuit
442 U.S. 114 (1979)

MR. JUSTICE MARSHALL delivered the opinion of the Court.

At issue in this case are two overlapping provisions of the Omnibus Crime Control and Safe Streets Act of 1968 (Omnibus Act). Both prohibit convicted felons from receiving firearms, but each authorizes different maximum penalties. We must determine whether a defendant convicted of the offense carrying the greater penalty may be sentenced only under the more lenient provision when his conduct violates both statutes.

I

Respondent, a previously convicted felon, was found guilty of receiving a firearm that had traveled in interstate commerce, in violation of 18 U.S.C. §922(h).[2] The District Court sentenced him under 18 U.S.C. §924(a) to five years' imprisonment, the maximum term authorized for violation of §922(h).[3]

The Court of Appeals affirmed the conviction but, by a divided vote, remanded for resentencing. The majority recognized that respondent had been indicted and convicted under §922(h) and that §924(a) permits five years' imprisonment for such violations. However, noting that the substantive elements of §922(h) and 18 U.S.C. App. §1202(a) are identical as applied to a convicted felon who unlawfully receives a firearm, the court interpreted the Omnibus Act to allow no more than

2. In pertinent part, 18 U.S.C. §922(h) provides:

It shall be unlawful for any person—
    (1) who is under indictment for, or who has been convicted in any court of, a crime punishable by imprisonment for a term exceeding one year;
    (2) who is a fugitive from justice;
    (3) who is an unlawful user of or addicted to marihuana or any depressant or stimulant drug . . . or narcotic drug . . . ; or
    (4) who has been adjudicated as a mental defective or who has been committed to any mental institution;
to receive any firearm or ammunition which has been shipped or transported in interstate or foreign commerce.

3. Title 18 U.S.C. §924(a) provides in relevant part:

Whoever violates any provision of this chapter . . . shall be fined not more than $5,000, or imprisoned not more than five years, or both, and shall become eligible for parole as the Board of Parole shall determine.

the 2-year maximum sentence provided by §1202(a).[4] In so holding, the Court of Appeals relied on three principles of statutory construction. Because, in its view, the "arguably contradict[ory]" penalty provisions for similar conduct and the "inconclusive" legislative history raised doubt whether Congress had intended the two penalty provisions to coexist, the court first applied the doctrine that ambiguities in criminal legislation are to be resolved in favor of the defendant. Second, the court determined that since §1202(a) was "Congress' last word on the issue of penalty," it may have implicitly repealed the punishment provisions of §924(a). Acknowledging that the "first two principles cannot be applied to these facts without some difficulty," the majority also invoked the maxim that a court should, if possible, interpret a statute to avoid constitutional questions. Here, the court reasoned, the "prosecutor's power to select one of two statutes that are identical except for their penalty provisions" implicated "important constitutional protections."

We granted certiorari, and now reverse the judgment vacating respondent's 5-year prison sentence.

II

This Court has previously noted the partial redundancy of §§922(h) and 1202(a), both as to the conduct they proscribe and the individuals they reach. See United States v. Bass, 404 U.S. 336, 341-343, and n. 9 (1971). However, we find nothing in the language, structure, or legislative history of the Omnibus Act to suggest that because of this overlap, a defendant convicted under §922(h) may be imprisoned for no more than the maximum term specified in §1202(a). As we read the Act, each substantive statute, in conjunction with its own sentencing provision, operates independently of the other.

While §§922 and 1202(a) both prohibit convicted felons such as petitioner from receiving firearms, each Title unambiguously specifies the penalties available to enforce its substantive proscriptions. Section 924(a) applies without exception to "[w]hoever violates any provision" of Title IV, and §922(h) is patently such a provision. See 18 U.S.C., ch. 44. Similarly, because Title VII's substantive prohibitions and penalties are both enumerated in §1202, its penalty scheme encompasses only criminal prosecutions brought under that provision. On their face, these statutes thus establish that §924(a) alone delimits the appropriate punishment for violations of §922(h).

In construing §1202(a) to override the penalties authorized by §924(a), the Court of Appeals relied, we believe erroneously, on three principles of statutory

---

4. Section 1202(a) states:

Any person who—

(1) has been convicted by a court of the United States or of a State or any political subdivision thereof of a felony, . . . or

(2) has been discharged from the Armed Forces under dishonorable conditions, or

(3) has been adjudged by a court of the United States or of a State or any political subdivision thereof of being mentally incompetent, or

(4) having been a citizen of the United States has renounced his citizenship, or

(5) being an alien is illegally or unlawfully in the United States,

and who receives, possesses, or transports in commerce or affecting commerce, after the date of enactment of this Act, any firearm shall be fined not more than $10,000 or imprisoned for not more than two years, or both.

interpretation. First, the court invoked the well-established doctrine that ambiguities in criminal statutes must be resolved in favor of lenity. Although this principle of construction applies to sentencing as well as substantive provisions, in the instant case there is no ambiguity to resolve. Respondent unquestionably violated §922(h), and §924(a) unquestionably permits five years' imprisonment for such a violation. That §1202(a) provides different penalties for essentially the same conduct is no justification for taking liberties with unequivocal statutory language.

Nor can §1202(a) be interpreted as implicitly repealing §924(a) whenever a defendant's conduct might violate both Titles. For it is "not enough to show that the two statutes produce differing results when applied to the same factual situation." *Radzanower v. Touche Ross & Co.*, 426 U.S. 148, 155 (1976). Rather, the legislative intent to repeal must be manifest in the "positive repugnancy between the provisions." *United States v. Borden Co.*, 308 U.S. 188 (1939). In this case, however, the penalty provisions are fully capable of coexisting because they apply to convictions under different statutes.

Finally, the maxim that statutes should be construed to avoid constitutional questions offers no assistance here. This "'cardinal principle' of statutory construction . . . is appropriate only when [an alternative interpretation] is 'fairly possible'" from the language of the statute. *Swain v. Pressley*, 430 U.S. 372, 378, n. 11 (1977). We simply are unable to discern any basis in the Omnibus Act for reading the term "five" in §924(a) to mean "two."

III

In resolving the statutory question, the majority below expressed "serious doubts about the constitutionality of two statutes that provide different penalties for identical conduct." Specifically, the court suggested that the statutes might (1) be void for vagueness, (2) implicate "due process and equal protection interest[s] in avoiding excessive prosecutorial discretion and in obtaining equal justice," and (3) constitute an impermissible delegation of congressional authority. We find no constitutional infirmities.

A

It is a fundamental tenet of due process that "[n]o one may be required at peril of life, liberty or property to speculate as to the meaning of penal statutes." *Lanzetta v. New Jersey*, 306 U.S. 451, 453 (1939). A criminal statute is therefore invalid if it "fails to give a person of ordinary intelligence fair notice that his contemplated conduct is forbidden." *United States v. Harriss*, 347 U.S. 612, 617 (1954). So too, vague sentencing provisions may post constitutional questions if they do not state with sufficient clarity the consequences of violating a given criminal statute. See *United States v. Evans*, 333 U.S. 483 (1948).

The provisions in issue here, however, unambiguously specify the activity proscribed and the penalties available upon conviction. That this particular conduct may violate both Titles does not detract from the notice afforded by each. Although the statutes create uncertainty as to which crime may be charged and therefore what penalties may be imposed, they do so to no greater extent than would a single statute authorizing various alternative punishments. So long as overlapping criminal provisions clearly define the conduct prohibited and the punishment authorized, the notice requirements of the Due Process Clause are satisfied.

B

This Court has long recognized that when an act violates more than one criminal statute, the Government may prosecutes under either so long as it does not discriminate against any class of defendants. See United States v. Beacon Brass Co., 344 U.S. 43, 45-46 (1952); Rosenberg v. United States, 346 U.S. 273, 294 (1953) (Clark, J., concurring, joined by five Members of the Court); Oyler v. Boles, 368 U.S. 448, 456 (1962); SEC v. National Securities, Inc., 393 U.S. 453, 468 (1969). Whether to prosecute and what charge to file or bring before a grand jury are decisions that generally rest in the prosecutor's discretion. See Confiscation Cases, 7 Wall. 454, 19 L. Ed. 196 (1869); United States v. Nixon, 418 U.S. 683, 693 (1974); Bordenkircher v. Hayes, 434 U.S. 357 (1978).

The Court of Appeals acknowledged this "settled rule" allowing prosecutorial choice. Nevertheless, relying on the dissenting opinion in Berra v. United States, 351 U.S. 131 (1956), the court distinguished overlapping statutes with identical standards of proof from provisions that vary in some particular. In the court's view, when two statutes prohibit "exactly the same conduct," the prosecutor's "selection of which of two penalties to apply" would be "unfettered." Because such prosecutorial discretion could produce "unequal justice," the court expressed doubt that this form of legislative redundancy was constitutional. We find this analysis factually and legally unsound.

Contrary to the Court of Appeals' assertions, a prosecutor's discretion to choose between §§922(h) and 1202(a) is not "unfettered." Selectivity in the enforcement of criminal laws is, of course, subject to constitutional constraints.[9] And a decision to proceed under §922(h) does not empower the Government to predetermine ultimate criminal sanctions. Rather, it merely enables the sentencing judge to impose a longer prison sentence than §1202(a) would permit and precludes him from imposing the greater fine authorized by §1202(a). More importantly, there is no appreciable difference between the discretion a prosecutor exercises when deciding whether to charge under one of two statutes with different elements and the discretion he exercises when choosing one of two statutes with identical elements. In the former situation, once he determines that the proof will support conviction under either statute, his decision is indistinguishable from the one he faces in the latter context. The prosecutor may be influenced by the penalties available upon conviction, but this fact, standing alone, does not give rise to a violation of the Equal Protection or Due Process Clause. Just as a defendant has no constitutional right to elect which of two applicable federal statutes shall be the basis of his indictment and prosecution neither is he entitled to choose the penalty scheme under which he will be sentenced.

Approaching the problem of prosecutorial discretion from a slightly different perspective, the Court of Appeals postulated that the statutes might impermissibly delegate to the Executive Branch the Legislature's responsibility to fix criminal penalties. We do not agree. The provisions at issue plainly demarcate the range of penalties that prosecutors and judges may seek and impose. In light of that specificity, the power that Congress has delegated to those officials is no broader than the

---

9. The Equal Protection Clause prohibits selective enforcement "based upon an unjustifiable standard such as race, religion, or other arbitrary classification." Oyler v. Boles, 368 U.S. 448, 456 (1962). Respondent does not allege that his prosecution was motivated by improper considerations.

authority they routinely exercise in enforcing the criminal laws. Having informed the courts, prosecutors, and defendants of the permissible punishment alternatives available under each Title, Congress has fulfilled its duty.

Accordingly, the judgment of the Court of Appeals is Reversed.

NOTES AND QUESTIONS

1. Justice Marshall's unanimous opinion for the Court seems to say that Congress is free to pass two statutes that punish identical conduct while providing for different sentences on conviction. Traditionally, it has been up to the legislature to decide on the range and contours of the sentence, and up to the judge to choose a more precise sentence within these limits. Doesn't *Batchelder* now give the prosecutor control over the potential sentencing range, at least in some cases? If so, on what basis should the prosecutor select a charge?

2. As the Court acknowledges in footnote 9, the prosecutor's charge-selecting power is still subject to the equal protection clause. Just as important, it is also subject to the Double Jeopardy Clause of the Fifth Amendment. A prosecutor may not, for example, spread several criminal charges over a series of trials if the crimes are related in a way that would make a second trial a re-litigation of issues decided in the first. Thus, where a defendant is accused of robbing six men at a single poker game and the prosecution elected to hold six separate trials, an acquittal at the first trial precludes any further trials, because the first jury has already determined that the defendant was not guilty of robbing the poker players. See Ashe v. Swenson, 397 U.S. 436 (1970), which is discussed in Chapter 16.

3. The prosecutor's authority over the selection of charges can create similar double jeopardy risks in drafting the indictment. A prosecutor might, for example, spread a single criminal charge over several counts in the indictment—charging a defendant who engaged in one fight with one person with simple assault, aggravated assault, assault with a deadly weapon, and assault with intent to kill. This is "multiplicitous" charging, and it creates a risk that a defendant will be punished more than once for a single crime.

A related but distinct problem occurs when a prosecutor charges multiple crimes in a single count of the indictment—charging a defendant with robbing two separate stores in a one-count indictment, for example. This is a "duplicitous" indictment, and it can harm the defendant because there is no way for the jury to convict of one count of robbery and acquit on another. A general verdict of guilt makes it appear (perhaps falsely) that the jury convicted on both, which can then prejudice the defendant at sentencing and on appeal.

Neither duplicity nor multiplicity is necessarily fatal to an indictment, but a court may at times require the government to choose a single criminal charge that is the basis of the prosecution and then tailor the evidence and jury instructions accordingly.

B. Limits on the Charging Power

The prosecutor's charging authority is extremely broad but not unlimited. The clearest restriction is that the government may not base its charging decision on race, ethnicity, political affiliation, or other constitutionally protected factors. But while this general point is obvious and uncontroversial, challenges to prosecutorial decision making on these grounds face significant practical and legal barriers.

Judge Mansfield's opinion in *Inmates of Attica* doesn't talk much about it, but race played a large role in that case. At the time of the riot, all but two members of the 500-plus-person prison staff were white, while more than 60 percent of the prisoners were black. See Leo Carroll, Race, Ethnicity and the Social Order of the Prison, in The Pains of Imprisonment 184 (Robert Johnson & Hans Toch eds., 1982). Black prisoners believed, with reason, that white guards treated them with special brutality. Anger at such treatment was one of the causes of the prisoners' riot. The guards were angry too: During the riot itself, a number of guards were taken prisoner, several were physically abused, and one was killed. The extreme violence with which the prison was retaken was, in part, a response to the violence of the prisoners' takeover. And that response had a racial cast.

The unrest that followed the decision not to indict the police officer involved in a fatal shooting of a black teenager in Ferguson, Missouri, in 2014 also was significantly affected by racial issues. After the shooting and the decision not to prosecute, the U.S. Department of Justice issued a scathing report about the police and municipal court system in Ferguson, concluding, among other things, that

> Ferguson's police and municipal court practices disproportionately harm African Americans. . . . The racially disparate impact of Ferguson's practices is driven, at least in part, by intentional discrimination in violation of the Equal Protection Clause of the Fourteenth Amendment. . . . [The] evidence includes: the consistency and magnitude of the racial disparities throughout Ferguson's police and court enforcement actions; the selection and execution of police and court practices that disproportionately harm African Americans and do little to promote public safety; the persistent exercise of discretion to the detriment of African Americans; the apparent consideration of race in assessing threat; and the historical opposition to having African Americans live in Ferguson, which lingers among some today.

U.S. Department of Justice Civil Rights Division, Investigation of the Ferguson Police Department 62, 63 (March 4, 2015), http://www.justice.gov/sites/default/files/opa/press-releases/attachments/2015/03/04/ferguson_police_department_report.pdf (visited August 26, 2015).

In such an environment it is no surprise that some defendants believe that the decision to charge them was motivated by race, and raise this claim as a defense to a criminal charge. These claims sound in equal protection, and require, among other things, proof that the prosecutor engaged in intentional discrimination by consciously treating blacks and whites differently. The fact that minority race citizens are disproportionately arrested, or charged, or convicted, is not enough on its own to prove discrimination, even if the prosecutors office is aware that focusing on a particular crime or adopting a particular enforcement practice will have a disparate impact. The Court has repeated on several occasions: "Discriminatory purpose . . . implies more than . . . intent as awareness of consequences. It implies that the decisionmaker . . . selected or reaffirmed a particular course of action at least in part 'because of,' not merely 'in spite of,' its adverse effects upon an identifiable group." Wayte v. United States, 470 U.S. 598, 610 (1985).

Of course, evidence of official intent is hard for defendants to gather. In a related context, the Supreme Court rejected an argument that intentional discrimination can be inferred from a sophisticated statistical study that showed racial bias by juries in the imposition of the death penalty, where the bias was correlated to the race of the murder victim. The Court noted that "Implementation of [the state's homicide] laws necessarily requires discretionary judgments. Because discretion is essential to the criminal justice process, we would demand exceptionally clear proof before we would infer that the discretion has been abused." The Court concluded that the statistical results were not the type "exceptionally clear proof" needed to create an inference of intentional discrimination. McCleskey v. Kemp, 481 U.S. 279 (1987).

A defendant who claims that the charges against him are tainted by racial considerations is raising a "selective prosecution" challenge. A person raising such a challenge has all the usual problems of proving intentional discrimination, but as the next case shows, he also has the related problem of gaining access to the information needed to prove the claim or, at least, to shift the burden to the government to justify the charges.

UNITED STATES v. ARMSTRONG

Certiorari to the United States Court of Appeals for the Ninth Circuit
517 U.S. 456 (1996)

CHIEF JUSTICE REHNQUIST delivered the opinion of the Court.

In this case, we consider the showing necessary for a defendant to be entitled to discovery on a claim that the prosecuting attorney singled him out for prosecution on the basis of his race. We conclude that respondents failed to satisfy the threshold showing: They failed to show that the Government declined to prosecute similarly situated suspects of other races.

In April 1992, respondents were indicted in the United States District Court for the Central District of California on charges of conspiring to possess with intent to distribute more than 50 grams of cocaine base (crack) and conspiring to distribute the same, in violation of 21 U.S.C. §§841 and 846, and federal firearms offenses. For three months prior to the indictment, agents of the Federal Bureau of Alcohol, Tobacco, and Firearms and the Narcotics Division of the Inglewood, California, Police Department had infiltrated a suspected crack distribution ring by using three confidential informants. On seven separate occasions during this period, the informants had bought a total of 124.3 grams of crack from respondents and witnessed respondents carrying firearms during the sales. The agents searched the hotel room in which the sales were transacted, arrested respondents Armstrong and Hampton in the room, and found more crack and a loaded gun. The agents later arrested the other respondents as part of the ring.

In response to the indictment, respondents filed a motion for discovery or for dismissal of the indictment, alleging that they were selected for federal prosecution because they are black. In support of their motion, they offered only an affidavit by a "Paralegal Specialist," employed by the Office of the Federal Public Defender representing one of the respondents. The only allegation in the affidavit was that, in every one of the 24 §841 or 846 cases closed by the office during 1991, the defendant was black. Accompanying the affidavit was a "study" listing the 24 defendants, their race, whether they were prosecuted for dealing cocaine as well as crack, and the status of each case.

The Government opposed the discovery motion, arguing, among other things, that there was no evidence or allegation "that the Government has acted unfairly or has prosecuted non-black defendants or failed to prosecute them." App. 150. The District Court granted the motion. It ordered the Government (1) to provide a list of all cases from the last three years in which the Government charged both cocaine and firearms offenses, (2) to identify the race of the defendants in those cases, (3) to identify what levels of law enforcement were involved in the investigations of those cases, and (4) to explain its criteria for deciding to prosecute those defendants for federal cocaine offenses.

[margin note: Gov't Argument]

The Government moved for reconsideration of the District Court's discovery order. With this motion it submitted affidavits and other evidence to explain why it had chosen to prosecute respondents and why respondents' study did not support the inference that the Government was singling out blacks for cocaine prosecution. The federal and local agents participating in the case alleged in affidavits that race played no role in their investigation. An Assistant United States Attorney explained in an affidavit that the decision to prosecute met the general criteria for prosecution, because

[margin note: Gov't justifications for why they Prosecuted]

> there was over 100 grams of cocaine base involved, over twice the threshold necessary for a ten year mandatory minimum sentence; there were multiple sales involving multiple defendants, thereby indicating a fairly substantial crack cocaine ring; . . . there were multiple federal firearms violations intertwined with the narcotics trafficking; the overall evidence in the case was extremely strong, including audio and videotapes of defendants; . . . and several of the defendants had criminal histories including narcotics and firearms violations. Id., at 81.

The Government also submitted sections of a published 1989 Drug Enforcement Administration report which concluded that "large-scale, interstate trafficking networks controlled by Jamaicans, Haitians and Black street gangs dominate the manufacture and distribution of crack." J. Featherly & E. Hill, Crack Cocaine Overview 1989; App. 103.

In response, one of respondents' attorneys submitted an affidavit alleging that an intake coordinator at a drug treatment center had told her that there are "an equal number of caucasian users and dealers to minority users and dealers." Id., at 138. Respondents also submitted an affidavit from a criminal defense attorney alleging that in his experience many nonblacks are prosecuted in state court for crack offenses, id., at 141, and a newspaper article reporting that Federal "crack criminals . . . are being punished far more severely than if they had been caught with powder cocaine, and almost every single one of them is black," Newton, Harsher Crack Sentences Criticized as Racial Inequity, Los Angeles Times, Nov. 23, 1992, p. 1.

The District Court denied the motion for reconsideration. When the Government indicated it would not comply with the court's discovery order, the court dismissed the case.[2]

---

2. We have never determined whether dismissal of the indictment, or some other sanction, is the proper remedy if a court determines that a defendant has been the victim of prosecution on the basis of his race. Here, "it was the government itself that suggested dismissal of the indictments to the district court so that an appeal might lie." 48 F.3d 1508, 1510 (CA9 1995).

A divided three-judge panel of the Court of Appeals for the Ninth Circuit reversed, holding that, because of the proof requirements for a selective-prosecution claim, defendants must "provide a colorable basis for believing that 'others similarly situated have not been prosecuted'" to obtain discovery. 21 F.3d 1431, 1436 (1994) (quoting United States v. Wayte, 710 F.2d 1385, 1387 (CA9 1983), aff'd, 470 U.S. 598 (1985)). The Court of Appeals voted to rehear the case en banc, and the en banc panel affirmed the District Court's order of dismissal, holding that "a defendant is not required to demonstrate that the government has failed to prosecute others who are similarly situated." 48 F.3d 1508, 1516 (1995) (emphasis deleted). We granted certiorari to determine the appropriate standard for discovery for a selective-prosecution claim. . . .

A selective-prosecution claim is not a defense on the merits to the criminal charge itself, but an independent assertion that the prosecutor has brought the charge for reasons forbidden by the Constitution. Our cases delineating the necessary elements to prove a claim of selective prosecution have taken great pains to explain that the standard is a demanding one. . . .

A selective-prosecution claim asks a court to exercise judicial power over a "special province" of the Executive. Heckler v. Chaney, 470 U.S. 821, 832 (1985). The Attorney General and United States Attorneys retain "broad discretion" to enforce the Nation's criminal laws. Wayte v. United States, 470 U.S. 598, 607 (1985). They have this latitude because they are designated by statute as the President's delegates to help him discharge his constitutional responsibility to "take Care that the Laws be faithfully executed." U.S. Const., Art. II, §3; see 28 U.S.C. §§516, 547. As a result, "the presumption of regularity supports" their prosecutorial decisions and "in the absence of clear evidence to the contrary, courts presume that they have properly discharged their official duties." United States v. Chemical Foundation, 272 U.S. 1, 14-15 (1926). In the ordinary case, "so long as the prosecutor has probable cause to believe that the accused committed an offense defined by statute, the decision whether or not to prosecute, and what charge to file or bring before a grand jury, generally rests entirely in his discretion." Bordenkircher v. Hayes, 434 U.S. 357, 364 (1978).

Of course, a prosecutor's discretion is "subject to constitutional constraints." United States v. Batchelder, 442 U.S. 114, 125 (1979). One of these constraints, imposed by the equal protection component of the Due Process Clause of the Fifth Amendment, is that the decision whether to prosecute may not be based on "an unjustifiable standard such as race, religion, or other arbitrary classification," Oyler v. Boles, 368 U.S. 448, 456 (1962). A defendant may demonstrate that the administration of a criminal law is "directed so exclusively against a particular class of persons . . . with a mind so unequal and oppressive" that the system of prosecution amounts to "a practical denial" of equal protection of the law. Yick Wo v. Hopkins, 118 U.S. 356, 373 (1886).

In order to dispel the presumption that a prosecutor has not violated equal protection, a criminal defendant must present "clear evidence to the contrary." Chemical Foundation, supra, at 14-15. We explained in Wayte why courts are "properly hesitant to examine the decision whether to prosecute." 470 U.S. at 608. Judicial deference to the decisions of these executive officers rests in part on an assessment of the relative competence of prosecutors and courts. "Such factors as the strength of the case, the prosecution's general deterrence value, the Government's enforcement priorities, and the case's relationship to the Government's overall enforcement plan are not readily susceptible to the kind of analysis the courts are competent to undertake." Id., at 607. It also stems from a concern not to unnecessarily impair the performance of a core executive constitutional function. "Examining the basis of a prosecution delays the criminal proceeding, threatens to chill law enforcement by subjecting the prosecutor's motives and decisionmaking to outside inquiry, and may undermine prosecutorial effectiveness by revealing the Government's enforcement policy." Ibid.

The requirements for a selective-prosecution claim draw on "ordinary equal protection standards." Id., at 608. The claimant must demonstrate that the federal prosecutorial policy "had a discriminatory effect and that it was motivated by a discriminatory purpose." Ibid. To establish a discriminatory effect in a race case, the claimant must show that similarly situated individuals of a different race were not prosecuted. This requirement has been established in our case law since Ah Sin v. Wittman, 198 U.S. 500 (1905). Ah Sin, a subject of China, petitioned a California state court for a writ of habeas corpus, seeking discharge from imprisonment under a San Francisco county ordinance prohibiting persons from setting up gambling tables in rooms barricaded to stop police from entering. Id., at 503. He alleged in his habeas petition "that the ordinance is enforced 'solely and exclusively against persons of the Chinese race and not otherwise.'" Id., at 507. We rejected his contention that this averment made out a claim under the Equal Protection Clause, because it did not allege "that the conditions and practices to which the ordinance was directed did not exist exclusively among the Chinese, or that there were other offenders against the ordinance than the Chinese as to whom it was not enforced." Id., at 507-508.

The similarly situated requirement does not make a selective-prosecution claim impossible to prove. Twenty years before *Ah Sin*, we invalidated an ordinance, also adopted by San Francisco, that prohibited the operation of laundries in wooden buildings. *Yick Wo*, 118 U.S. at 374. The plaintiff in error successfully demonstrated that the ordinance was applied against Chinese nationals but not against other laundry-shop operators. The authorities had denied the applications of 200 Chinese subjects for permits to operate shops in wooden buildings, but granted the applications of 80 individuals who were not Chinese subjects to operate laundries in wooden buildings "under similar conditions." Ibid.

. . . Having reviewed the requirements to prove a selective-prosecution claim, we turn to the showing necessary to obtain discovery in support of such a claim. If discovery is ordered, the Government must assemble from its own files documents which might corroborate or refute the defendant's claim. Discovery thus imposes many of the costs present when the Government must respond to a prima facie case of selective prosecution. It will divert prosecutors' resources and may disclose the Government's prosecutorial strategy. The justifications for a rigorous standard for the elements of a selective-prosecution claim thus require a correspondingly rigorous standard for discovery in aid of such a claim.

The parties, and the Courts of Appeals which have considered the requisite showing to establish entitlement to discovery, describe this showing with a variety of phrases, like "colorable basis," "substantial threshold showing," "substantial and concrete basis," or "reasonable likelihood." However, the many labels for this showing conceal the degree of consensus about the evidence necessary to meet it. The Courts of Appeals "require some evidence tending to show the existence of the essential elements of the defense," discriminatory effect and discriminatory intent. United States v. Berrios, 501 F.2d 1207, 1211 (CA2 1974).

In this case we consider what evidence constitutes "some evidence tending to show the existence" of the discriminatory effect element. The Court of Appeals held that a defendant may establish a colorable basis for discriminatory effect without evidence that the Government has failed to prosecute others who are similarly situated to the defendant. 48 F.3d at 1516. We think it was mistaken in this view. The vast majority of the Courts of Appeals require the defendant to produce some evidence that similarly situated defendants of other races could have been prosecuted, but were not, and this requirement is consistent with our equal protection case law. . . .

The Court of Appeals reached its decision in part because it started "with the presumption that people of all races commit all types of crimes—not with the premise that any type of crime is the exclusive province of any particular racial or ethnic group." 48 F.3d at 1516-1517. It cited no authority for this proposition, which seems contradicted by the most recent statistics of the United States Sentencing Commission. Those statistics show that: More than 90% of the persons sentenced in 1994 for crack cocaine trafficking were black, United States Sentencing Commn., 1994 Annual Report 107 (Table 45); 93.4% of convicted LSD dealers were white, ibid.; and 91% of those convicted for pornography or prostitution were white, id., at 41 (Table 13). Presumptions at war with presumably reliable statistics have no proper place in the analysis of this issue.

The Court of Appeals also expressed concern about the "evidentiary obstacles defendants face." 48 F.3d at 1514. But . . . respondents could have investigated whether similarly situated persons of other races were prosecuted by the State of California, were known to federal law enforcement officers, but were not prosecuted in federal court. We think the required threshold—a credible showing of different treatment of similarly situated persons—adequately balances the Government's interest in vigorous prosecution and the defendant's interest in avoiding selective prosecution.

In the case before us, respondents' "study" did not constitute "some evidence tending to show the existence of the essential elements of "a selective-prosecution claim. The study failed to identify individuals who were not black, could have been prosecuted for the offenses for which respondents were charged, but were not so prosecuted. This omission was not remedied by respondents' evidence in opposition to the Government's motion for reconsideration. The newspaper article, which discussed the discriminatory effect of federal drug sentencing laws, was not relevant to an allegation of discrimination in decisions to prosecute. Respondents' affidavits, which recounted one attorney's conversation with a drug treatment center employee and the experience of another attorney defending drug prosecutions in state court, recounted hearsay and reported personal conclusions based on anecdotal evidence. The judgment of the Court of Appeals is therefore reversed, and the case is remanded for proceedings consistent with this opinion.

[The concurring opinions of Justices Souter, Ginsburg, and Breyer are omitted.]

JUSTICE STEVENS, dissenting.

. . . The Court correctly concludes that in this case the facts presented to the District Court in support of respondents' claim that they had been singled out for prosecution because of their race were not sufficient to prove that defense. Moreover, I agree with the Court that their showing was not strong enough to give them a right to discovery. . . . [H]owever, I am persuaded that the District Judge did not abuse her discretion when she concluded that the factual showing was sufficiently disturbing to require some response from the United States Attorney's Office. Perhaps the discovery order was broader than necessary, but I cannot agree with the Court's apparent conclusion that no inquiry was permissible.

The District Judge's order should be evaluated in light of three circumstances that underscore the need for judicial vigilance over certain types of drug prosecutions. First, the Anti-Drug Abuse Act of 1986 and subsequent legislation established a regime of extremely high penalties for the possession and distribution of so-called "crack" cocaine. Those provisions treat one gram of crack as the equivalent of 100 grams of powder cocaine. The distribution of 50 grams of crack is thus punishable by the same mandatory minimum sentence of 10 years in prison that applies to the distribution of 5,000 grams of powder cocaine. The Sentencing Guidelines extend this ratio to penalty levels above the mandatory minimums: for any given quantity of crack, the guideline range is the same as if the offense had involved 100 times that amount in powder cocaine. These penalties result in sentences for crack offenders that average three to eight times longer than sentences for comparable powder offenders.[4]

Second, the disparity between the treatment of crack cocaine and powder cocaine is matched by the disparity between the severity of the punishment imposed by federal law and that imposed by state law for the same conduct. For a variety of reasons, often including the absence of mandatory minimums, the existence of parole, and lower baseline penalties, terms of imprisonment for drug offenses tend to be substantially lower in state systems than in the federal system. The difference is especially marked in the case of crack offenses. The majority of States draw no distinction between types of cocaine in their penalty schemes; of those that do, none has established as stark a differential as the Federal Government. For example, if respondent Hampton is found guilty, his federal sentence might be as long as a mandatory life term. Had he been tried in state court, his sentence could have been as short as 12 years, less worktime credits of half that amount.

Finally, it is undisputed that the brunt of the elevated federal penalties falls heavily on blacks. While 65% of the persons who have used crack are white, in 1993 they represented only 4% of the federal offenders convicted of trafficking in crack. Eighty-eight percent of such defendants were black. [United States Sentencing Commission, Special Report to Congress: Cocaine and Federal Sentencing Policy 39, 161 (Feb. 1995).] During the first 18 months of full guideline implementation, the sentencing disparity between black and white defendants grew from preguideline levels: blacks on average received sentences over 40% longer than whites. See Bureau of Justice Statistics, Sentencing in the Federal Courts: Does Race Matter? 6-7 (Dec. 1993). Those figures represent a major threat to the integrity of federal sentencing reform, whose main purpose was the elimination of disparity (especially racial) in sentencing. The Sentencing Commission acknowledges that the heightened crack penalties are a "primary cause of the growing disparity between sentences for Black and White federal defendants." Special Report 145. . . .

Respondents submitted a study showing that of all cases involving crack offenses that were closed by the Federal Public Defender's Office in 1991, 24 out of 24

---

4. Under the guidelines, penalties increase at a slower rate than drug quantities. For example, 5 grams of heroin result in a base offense level of 14 (15-21 months) while 10 grams of heroin (double the amount) result in an offense level of 16 (21-27 months). USSG §§2D1.1(c)(13), (12). Thus, the 100-to-1 ratio does not translate into sentences that are 100 times as long.

involved black defendants. To supplement this evidence, they submitted affidavits from two of the attorneys in the defense team. The first reported a statement from an intake coordinator at a local drug treatment center that, in his experience, an equal number of crack users and dealers were caucasian as belonged to minorities. App. 138. The second was from David R. Reed, counsel for respondent Armstrong. Reed was both an active court-appointed attorney in the Central District of California and one of the directors of the leading association of criminal defense lawyers who practice before the Los Angeles County courts. Reed stated that he did not recall "ever handling a [crack] cocaine case involving non-black defendants" in federal court, nor had he even heard of one. Id., at 140. He further stated that "there are many crack cocaine sales cases prosecuted in state court that do involve racial groups other than blacks." Id., at 141. . . .

The criticism that the affidavits were based on "anecdotal evidence" is . . . unpersuasive. I thought it was agreed that defendants do not need to prepare sophisticated statistical studies in order to receive mere discovery in cases like this one. Certainly evidence based on a drug counselor's personal observations or on an attorney's practice in two sets of courts, state and federal, can "tend to show the existence" of a selective prosecution.

Even if respondents failed to carry their burden of showing that there were individuals who were not black but who could have been prosecuted in federal court for the same offenses, it does not follow that the District Court abused its discretion in ordering discovery. There can be no doubt that such individuals exist, and indeed the Government has never denied the same. In those circumstances, I fail to see why the District Court was unable to take judicial notice of this obvious fact and demand information from the Government's files to support or refute respondents' evidence. The presumption that some whites are prosecuted in state court is not "contradicted" by the statistics the majority cites, which show only that high percentages of blacks are convicted of certain federal crimes, while high percentages of whites are convicted of other federal crimes. Those figures are entirely consistent with the allegation of selective prosecution. The relevant comparison, rather, would be with the percentages of blacks and whites who commit those crimes. But, as discussed above, in the case of crack far greater numbers of whites are believed guilty of using the substance. The District Court, therefore, was entitled to find the evidence before her significant and to require some explanation from the Government.[6]

In sum, I agree with the Sentencing Commission that "while the exercise of discretion by prosecutors and investigators has an impact on sentences in almost all cases to some extent, because of the 100-to-1 quantity ratio and federal mandatory minimum penalties, discretionary decisions in cocaine cases often have dramatic

---

6. Also telling was the Government's response to respondents' evidentiary showing. It submitted a list of more than 3,500 defendants who had been charged with federal narcotics violations over the previous 3 years. It also offered the names of 11 nonblack defendants whom it had prosecuted for crack offenses. All 11, however, were members of other racial or ethnic minorities. See 48 F.3d at 1511. The District Court was authorized to draw adverse inferences from the Government's inability to produce a single example of a white defendant, especially when the very purpose of its exercise was to allay the Court's concerns about the evidence of racially selective prosecutions. As another court has said: "Statistics are not, of course, the whole answer, but nothing is as emphatic as zero. . . ." United States v. Hinds County School Bd., 417 F.2d 852, 858 (CA5 1969) (per curiam).

effects." Special Report 138.[7] The severity of the penalty heightens both the danger of arbitrary enforcement and the need for careful scrutiny of any colorable claim of discriminatory enforcement. In this case, the evidence was sufficiently disturbing to persuade the District Judge to order discovery that might help explain the conspicuous racial pattern of cases before her Court. I cannot accept the majority's conclusion that the District Judge either exceeded her power or abused her discretion when she did so. I therefore respectfully dissent.

NOTES AND QUESTIONS

1. *Armstrong* purports to be solely about the standard for determining when defendants are entitled to discovery on a claim of discriminatory charging. But given the Court's ruling that a defendant must show that similarly situated white defendants could have been prosecuted, but were not, it would seem that obtaining discovery will be crucial in virtually every case like this. Can you think of other ways that a defense lawyer might be able to gather the necessary information to raise this type of claim?

If a defendant sets out to prove that similarly situated defendants have not been prosecuted, how many such cases should he have to identify? If the answer is one or two, perhaps *Armstrong* does not matter much. But if that is the answer, it is hard to understand why this threshold requirement is so important in the Court's analysis. Then again, if the answer for claims such as Armstrong's is a substantial number, how likely is it that any defendant will be able to satisfy this requirement and obtain discovery?

2. Reread footnote 2 in the majority opinion. Assume for the moment that Armstrong could prove his allegation that prosecutors were targeting blacks for prosecution and ignoring similar whites. What is the appropriate remedy? Dismissal of charges has an obvious advantage: It rewards successful claimants, and so encourages the bringing of valid claims, and so (presumably) checks prosecutorial misconduct. In contrast, if Armstrong can prove race discrimination and *fails* to get the charges against him dismissed, it is easy to predict that future victims of discriminatory prosecution will not go to the trouble of making the claim. But dismissal has an equally obvious disadvantage: Guilty defendants escape punishment because the prosecutor's office misbehaved.

The alternative is the remedy that was sought and rejected in *Inmates of Attica*: Compel prosecution of the white suspects who *weren't* prosecuted by the U.S. Attorney for the Central District of California. That remedy avoids giving guilty defendants a windfall, but it has all the disadvantages that troubled the court in *Inmates of Attica*. Time is a scarce commodity, and most prosecutor offices charge as

---

7. For this and other reasons, the Sentencing Commission in its Special Report to Congress "strongly recommended against a 100-to-1 quantity ratio." Special Report 198. The Commission shortly thereafter, by a 4-to-3 vote, amended the guidelines so as to equalize the treatment of crack and other forms of cocaine, and proposed modification of the statutory mandatory minimum penalties for crack offenses. See Statement of Commission Majority in Support of Recommended Changes in Cocaine and Federal Sentencing Policy (May 1, 1995). In October 1995, Congress overrode the Sentencing Commission's guideline amendments. See Pub. L. 104-38, 109 Stat. 334. Nevertheless, Congress at the same time directed the Commission to submit recommendations regarding changes to the statutory and guideline penalties for cocaine distribution, including specifically "revision of the drug quantity ratio of crack cocaine to powder cocaine." §2(a).

many cases as they can handle. It follows that compelling prosecution in one case means, as a practical matter, precluding prosecution somewhere else.

Suppose courts were to dismiss charges against successful discriminatory prosecution claimants. What then? Should all black defendants in crack cases have a right to dismissal until the Central District's U.S. Attorney prosecutes a given number of whites for crack violations?

3. Perhaps the prosecutorial patterns at issue in *Armstrong* are the consequence not of *prosecutors'* decisions, but of *police* decisions—choices made both by local police officers and by federal agents. As Daniel Richman has noted, police and prosecutors constitute what antitrust lawyers would call a "bilateral monopoly": Each must deal with the other, and neither side of this relationship can achieve its goals without the other side's cooperation. Daniel C. Richman, Prosecutors and Their Agents, Agents and Their Prosecutors, 103 Colum. L. Rev. 749 (2003). Prosecutors cannot prosecute unless the police bring them cases; and the police, who want to see their suspects punished, cannot make that happen without a decision to prosecute.

In some classes of federal criminal cases—including drug cases like the ones in *Armstrong*—the relationship is more complicated. Federal prosecutors ordinarily get their cases from federal agents. But many federal drug cases begin with an arrest by local police. The case is then turned over to federal prosecutors because the local district attorney lacks resources, or because the arrest arose out of a local-federal task force, or because local police are trying to play one prosecutor's office off against the other, or for a variety of other reasons. In these cases, the bilateral monopoly does not hold.

But for most cases, it *does* hold, which means that the biggest check on the power of prosecutors may be the police officers with whom they must deal—and vice versa. Note, in this connection, that prosecutors decline to prosecute a large fraction of the cases police officers bring them. The same dynamic is at work in federal cases, even when the crimes are the subject of intense public interest: Richman's article noted that in the six months after the terrorist attacks on September 11, 2001, federal prosecutors declined to prosecute 61 percent of the terrorism cases federal agents brought them. Id., at 765.

In short, one of the largest effects of the legal doctrine we see in *Inmates of Attica* and *Armstrong* is that no one, save the prosecutors, knows why they pursue the cases they pursue and decline the ones they decline. The decision to file criminal charges, or not, is one of the most important ways government officials exercise power. It is also one of the least transparent.

4. Sometimes defendants challenge prosecutors' charging decisions not on the ground that those decisions were selectively discriminatory, but on the ground that they were "vindictive." Vindictiveness has a special meaning here: It is not simply prosecutorial hostility; rather, it is prosecution aimed at punishing the exercise of a constitutional right. For a time in the 1970s, it appeared that "vindictive prosecution" claims would be both common and successful. Today, they are rarely made and even more rarely succeed. It is worth understanding why that is so.

Begin with Blackledge v. Perry, 417 U.S. 21 (1974). Perry, a state prisoner, was charged with misdemeanor assault for an altercation with another prisoner. After a bench trial at which he was convicted, Perry appealed and was victorious; under North Carolina law at the time, the victory entitled Perry to a new trial in a different state court. Perry's prosecutor responded to the appeal by charging Perry with felony assault with intent to kill. The Supreme Court invalidated the felony charges, stating: "[T]he Due Process Clause is not offended by all possibilities of increased punishment upon retrial after appeal, but only by those that pose a realistic likelihood of 'vindictiveness.'" Id., at 27. The Court explained:

> . . . A prosecutor clearly has a considerable stake in discouraging convicted misdemeanants from appealing and thus obtaining a trial de novo in the Superior Court, since such an appeal will clearly require increased expenditures of prosecutorial resources before the defendant's conviction becomes final, and may even result in a formerly convicted defendant's going free. And, if the prosecutor has the means readily at hand to discourage such appeals — by "upping the ante" through a felony indictment whenever a convicted misdemeanant pursues his statutory appellate remedy — the State can insure that only the most hardy defendants will brave the hazards of a de novo trial.
>
> . . . A person convicted of an offense is entitled to pursue his statutory right to a trial de novo, without apprehension that the State will retaliate by substituting a more serious charge for the original one, thus subjecting him to a significantly increased potential period of incarceration.
>
> Due process of law requires that such a potential for vindictiveness must not enter into North Carolina's two-tiered appellate process. We hold, therefore, that it was not constitutionally permissible for the State to respond to Perry's invocation of his statutory right to appeal by bringing a more serious charge against him prior to the trial de novo.

Id., at 27-29. *Blackledge* established a presumption of vindictiveness, but did not make clear the range of cases to which the presumption would apply.

Potentially, the range was huge. Millions of defendants have pled guilty to some criminal charges in exchange for a prosecutor's promise not to bring, or to drop, other charges. After *Blackledge*, some of those defendants started to claim that this ordinary plea bargaining practice amounted to vindictive prosecution, since prosecutors' bargaining position amounted to a threat to punish the exercise of the defendants' right to trial.

The Supreme Court rejected that argument in Bordenkircher v. Hayes, 434 U.S. 357 (1978). Hayes was indicted in Kentucky state court for "uttering a forged instrument in the amount of $88.30," a crime for which the permissible sentence was two to ten years in prison. The prosecutor offered him a plea bargain with a recommended five-year sentence. Hayes declined the offer, whereupon the prosecutor charged him under Kentucky's "three strikes" statute — Hayes had two prior felony convictions — which carried an automatic life sentence. Hayes was convicted and sentenced to life in prison, and he argued that this sentence was, in effect, a prosecutorial punishment for his exercise of his constitutional right to trial. The Supreme Court disagreed, in an opinion that emphasized prosecutors' power to add or withdraw charges as part of the plea bargaining process.

Four years after *Bordenkircher*, the Court curtailed vindictive prosecution claims even more sharply. The defendant in United States v. Goodwin, 457 U.S. 368 (1982), was charged with several misdemeanors and scheduled for trial before a magistrate. He invoked his right to a jury trial, whereupon the case was transferred to another prosecutor, who promptly added a felony charge. The defendant claimed that the felony charge amounted to punishment for his exercise of his right to a jury. The Court disagreed:

> . . . [A] presumption of vindictiveness is not warranted. A prosecutor should remain free before trial to exercise the broad discretion entrusted to him to determine the extent of the societal interest in prosecution. An initial decision should not freeze future conduct. As we made clear in *Bordenkircher*, the initial charges filed by a prosecutor may not reflect the extent to which an individual is legitimately subject to prosecution. . . .

Id., at 381-382. The Court concluded that "[t]he possibility" that the charges against Goodwin were "not in the public interest" but were instead designed as a penalty for the exercise of a constitutional right was "so unlikely that a presumption of vindictiveness certainly is not warranted." Id., at 384.

The bottom line after *Goodwin* is this: Most of the time a defendant's vindictive prosecution claim will not have the benefit of a presumption of vindictiveness, unless the case is factually on point with *Blackledge* (the defendant is convicted, is legally entitled to a new trial and exercises that right, after which the same prosecutor adds a more serious charge) or it closely approximates that setting. Consider, for example, the defendant who was charged with possession of child pornography and faced a zero to ten year sentence. Defendant filed a successful suppression motion, after which the government filed a superseding indictment that charged defendant with more serious crime, one that exposed defendant to a five to 25 year prison sentence. The Sixth Circuit found that because the government had the information on the more serious charge in its possession at the time it filed the original charge, the district court was well within its discretion to decide that in this setting a presumption of vindictiveness was warranted, and that the government failed to rebut the presumption that the higher charges were filed in retaliation for the successful suppression motion. United States v. LaDeau, 734 F.3d 561 (6th Cir. 2013). In almost all other cases, however, the presumption is that the prosecutor acted in good faith, and the defendant has the burden of proving an improper motive. In practice, that burden is rarely met, and successful vindictiveness claims are rare.

For a good discussion of the Supreme Court's vindictiveness jurisprudence, and arguments for a more robust doctrine, see Note, Vindicating Vindictiveness: Prosecutorial Discretion and Plea Bargaining, Past and Future, 123 Yale L.J. 1014 (2014).

5. Sometimes the charges filed by the prosecutor have little to do with the criminal conduct that gives rise to an investigation. The best-known example of these "pretext prosecutions" involved mob boss Al Capone, perhaps the most famous gangster in the country's history. Capone made most of his money through the sale of beer and liquor (those were illegal drugs in 1931), though he was also responsible for many other crimes, including several murders. But the federal agents who were busy trying to nail Capone couldn't prove those crimes in court, so they charged him with nonpayment of his income taxes. Capone was ultimately convicted and sent to prison. There are countless other examples: The owner of a nightclub where drugs are allegedly sold may be arrested for liquor law violations, or a CEO suspected of corporate fraud may be charged with lying to the FBI during the investigation if the more serious crimes are too difficult to prove.

Shortly after the terrorist attacks of September 11, 2001, then–Attorney General John Ashcroft praised that strategy and vowed to use it against suspected terrorists:

Attorney General [Robert] Kennedy made no apologies for using all of the available resources in the law to disrupt and dismantle organized crime networks. Very often, prosecutors were aggressive, using obscure statutes to arrest and detain suspected mobsters. One racketeer and his father were indicted for lying on a federal home loan application. A former gunman for the Capone mob was brought to court on a violation of the Migratory Bird Act. Agents found 563 game birds in his freezer—a mere 539 birds over the limit. . . .

The American people face a serious, immediate and ongoing threat from terrorism. At this moment, American service men and women are risking their lives to battle the enemy overseas. It falls to the men and women of Justice and law enforcement to engage terrorism at home. History's judgment will be harsh—and the people's judgment will be sure—if we fail to use every available resource to prevent future terrorist attacks.

Attorney General John Ashcroft, Prepared Remarks for the U.S. Mayors' Conference, Oct. 25, 2001, http://www.justice.gov/archive/ag/speeches/2001/agcrisis-remarks10_25.htm.

Is this good law enforcement policy?

6. Defendants in these pretext prosecutions have often raised equal protection claims, arguing that it is irrational and arbitrary to enforce crime X based on whether a defendant is suspected of crime Y. Those claims have generally failed. For a representative decision, see People v. Mantel, 388 N.Y.S.2d 565 (1976). The government charged Mantel with building and health code violations as part of an effort to "clean up" midtown Manhattan and, in particular, to go after the area's "sex-related establishments." Mantel argued that this constituted impermissibly arbitrary enforcement. The court disagreed:

> The city has found that efforts to curtail these illegal activities have been ineffective in the past because of fragmented efforts and serious manpower shortages in the various enforcement agencies. It was therefore determined to concentrate efforts on insuring compliance with safety and health related ordinances. . . . It is beyond doubt that health and building codes are well within the police power and necessary to regulate the public health, safety and welfare. Until the city has the financial, administrative and manpower resources to vigorously prosecute all such offenses, the selective enforcement decided upon herein would seem to be both rational and permissible.

Id., at 568-569.

7. Sometimes a defendant seeks redress for an unfounded criminal charge by suing the government actors who brought the charges; these civil actions are often called "malicious prosecution" claims. Consider the following scenario. Defendant does something to irritate an influential government official. That official, in turn, lobbies police and prosecutors to undertake an investigation, to try to find some crime they can pin on Defendant. (For fans of the HBO series *The Wire*, recall the second-season story of how the investigation of the dockworkers' union got started.) After some investigation the Defendant is charged, but thereafter, the charges are dropped or dismissed, or Defendant is acquitted. Now Defendant wants to sue. After all, he has been criminally prosecuted because he irritated a powerful government official—not the sort of thing that is supposed to happen in a just system.

That scenario describes Hartman v. Moore, 547 U.S. 250 (2006). Moore ran a firm that had developed multiline scanning technology for sorting mail— machines that could read addresses on letters and sort the letters properly. Moore lobbied the Postal Service to buy his technology; instead, the Postal Service temporarily adopted nine-digit ZIP codes, because those longer ZIP codes could be read without the equipment Moore was selling. Moore responded by turning his lobbying efforts to members of Congress and other government agencies. Eventually, in part because of Moore's efforts, the nine-digit zip code program was abandoned, and the Postal Service decided to purchase the multiline scanning technology—but from one of Moore's competitors. To add insult to injury, postal inspectors began a criminal investigation of Moore and his company, and both were later charged with criminal fraud. After a six-week trial, a federal district judge dismissed the charges. See United States v. Recognition Equipment Inc., 725 F. Supp. 587 (D.D.C. 1989). Moore sued six postal inspectors and one federal prosecutor, claiming he had been prosecuted for embarrassing the Postal Service.

After a litigation of Dickensian length—Justice Souter called it "a procedural history portending another Jarndyce v. Jarndyce"—the postal inspectors successfully moved for summary judgment, on the ground that the underlying criminal charges were supported by probable cause. By a vote of 5-2, the Supreme Court agreed. Here is the key passage from Justice Souter's majority opinion:

> In sum, the complexity of causation in a claim that prosecution was induced by an official bent on retaliation should be addressed specifically in defining the elements of the tort. Probable cause or its absence will be at least an evidentiary issue in practically all such cases. Because showing an absence of probable cause will have high probative force, and can be made mandatory with little or no added cost, it makes sense to require such a showing as an element of a plaintiff's case, and we hold that it must be pleaded and proven.

Justice Ginsburg's dissent, joined by Justice Breyer, began by stating:

> The Court of Appeals, reviewing the record so far made, determined that "the evidence of retaliatory motive [came] close to the proverbial smoking gun." The record also indicated that the postal inspectors engaged in "unusual prodding," strenuously urging a reluctant U.S. Attorney's Office to press charges against Moore.

The dissenters went on to argue that plaintiffs like Moore should prevail if they could show that, but for the retaliatory motive, they would not have been prosecuted—a showing that Moore probably could have made.

Who has the better of the argument? Is the probable-cause requirement, as Justice Souter contends, little more than a matter of legal bookkeeping that will have only slight effects on case outcomes? Or does the Court's decision amount to a blank check for government officials inclined to use criminal charges to harass their critics?

8. Although the prosecutor's decision to file one charge rather than another is an important one, note that in federal cases and in many states, even *uncharged* criminal conduct can influence a sentence following a conviction on other charges. In the federal system, if the defendant is convicted of crime *A* but the court is convinced by a preponderance of the evidence that the defendant also participated in crime *B*, an offense never charged in the indictment, the judge may consider crime *B* to be relevant conduct it can consider when setting the sentence for crime *A*. Thus, a

prosecutor's decision not to charge a certain offense, or to drop a charge in return for a guilty plea, may still lead to the defendant facing an increased prison sentence. For a useful discussion on the use of uncharged and acquitted conduct as a basis for sentencing, see David Yellen, Reforming the Federal Sentencing Guidelines' Misguided Approach to Real-Offense Sentencing, 58 Stan. L. Rev. 267 (2005); Julie R. O'Sullivan, In Defense of the U.S. Sentencing Guidelines Modified Real Offense System, 91 Nw. U. L. Rev. 1342 (1997).

Chapter 10

Pretrial Screening and the Grand Jury

A grand jury serves two functions. First, working under the direction of the prosecutor, the grand jury acts as a powerful investigative tool that unearths evidence of criminal behavior. It can require witnesses to appear before it and give testimony, and can compel those witnesses to produce documents and other physical evidence. The grand jury can exercise this power without having probable cause to believe that the compelled information will result in usable evidence at a trial—the subpoenas can issue without prior judicial approval, and as discussed below, challenges to a subpoena by the recipient will frequently fail.

Second, the grand jury must approve the prosecutor's proposed criminal charges. Before the federal government can file an indictment formally accusing someone of a felony, it must persuade a jury of 23 citizens (or at least, must persuade a majority of them) that there is sufficient evidence to send a case forward to trial. Here the grand jury acts as a screen against unfounded prosecutions: If the government has insufficient evidence of a suspect's guilt, the grand jury is supposed to prevent the case from continuing through the process.

How well the grand jury serves these two roles—often called the "sword" (i.e., investigative) and the "shield" (screening) function—is a source of debate, as the following materials show.

A. Background and Current Practice

The grand jury's English origins are commonly traced to the twelfth century, to the reign of Henry II. It began as an accusatory body of citizens drawn from nearby communities, whose task was to assist the Crown in instituting criminal cases. Local sheriffs had limited resources, and private criminal complaints were an unreliable way to ensure that bad behavior was detected, so the source of the incriminating information was often the jurors themselves; they were expected to bring to the jury room whatever evidence (or rumors and gossip) they possessed. The pressure on the grand jurors to inform on their neighbors was great, as fines could be imposed on a panel of jurors who failed to indict those whom the Crown considered guilty.

By the end of the seventeenth century, however, the grand jury had come to be viewed not as a convenient device for the lodging of criminal charges, but as a buffer between the state and the citizen, protecting the latter against unwarranted accusations. Although it is doubtful that the grand jury routinely or even frequently resisted royal pressure to indict, there were enough famous cases of the jurors' refusal to return charges against political opponents of the King to elevate the grand jury in the public mind to its role as a "bulwark against oppression."

It was this view of the institution that was transported to colonial America, where it took firm root in the years leading up to the Revolutionary War, when tensions between England and the colonies would often play out through disagreements over enforcement of the criminal laws. The most famous example occurred when the grand jury refused to indict the anti-royalist publisher John Peter Zenger for seditious libel, but there were also other, more mundane cases involving the Crown's frustrated efforts to enforce burdensome tax laws.

Grand juries were popular in early America for another reason. In many of the colonies, they served as a kind of running town meeting, a device by which the local population could ride herd on government officials of all sorts. Thus, a 1638 Massachusetts grand jury "rebuked the Town of Sandwich 'for not having their swine ringed,' complained of the lack of surveyors for repairing the highway, and questioned the right of the governor and assistants to sell land to certain persons." Richard D. Younger, The People's Panel 7 (1963). Late-seventeenth-century Pennsylvania grand juries "supervised all county expenditures and tax levies." Id., at 15. Far from being under the thumb of a local prosecutor or other local official, the very point of these grand juries was to serve as de facto local legislatures. The combination of refusals to indict in perceived political cases and its more general role as a watchdog over government officials helped pave the way for the inclusion of the grand jury guarantee in the Constitution.

In the nineteenth and twentieth centuries, the grand jury's role as a shield against oppression lost much of its luster. The increasing presence and professionalization of judges, prosecutors, and police, coupled with the increasing complexity of the criminal law, led to a diminishing role for the grand jury as an independent actor. There were still periodic stories of grand juries courageously investigating organized crime, and occasional cases of "runaway" grand juries that defied the prosecutor and pursued their own investigative course. But while these stories helped sustain the popular image of the "people's panel," in reality the grand jury had lost its ability to act independently of the prosecution. In fact, today it is hard to find any careful observer who will claim that the grand jury is truly an independent body—except for the Supreme Court, which as this Chapter shows, continues to insist that the grand jury is in control of, rather than controlled by, the prosecution.

The Fifth Amendment begins with the words, "No person shall be held to answer for a capital, or otherwise infamous crime, unless on a presentment or indictment of a Grand Jury, except in cases arising in the land or naval forces, or in the militia, when in actual service in time of war or public danger. . . ." The Supreme Court has assumed that the phrase "otherwise infamous crime" means felonies. See, e.g., Stirone v. United States, 361 U.S. 212, 215 (1961), and thus, the Constitution guarantees that no felony case can be prosecuted without the grand jury's approval.

The other mode of bringing charges mentioned in the Fifth Amendment, a "presentment," refers to a criminal charge brought directly by the grand jury and not by the prosecutor. Today, presentments virtually never occur and the practice is considered obsolete, despite arguments that grand juries should still have this power. See, e.g., Note, Renee B. Lettow, Reviving Federal Grand Jury Presentments, 103 Yale L.J. 1333 (1994). Indeed, should the grand jury vote to indict a defendant against the prosecutor's wishes, it seems clear that it would have no effect: An indictment must be signed by the prosecutor, Fed. R. Crim. P. 7(f), and lower courts have ruled that a judge may not force a prosecutor to proceed with a case. See Chapter 9 (discussing the prosecutor's charging discretion).

In his article Why Grand Juries Do Not (and Cannot) Protect the Accused, 80 Cornell L. Rev. 260, 265-266 (1995), Andrew Leipold offers a capsule summary of current grand jury procedure:

> The operation of a typical federal grand jury is straightforward. A pool of citizens is summoned at random from the judicial district where the jury will sit. From the group of qualified people who appear, twenty-three are chosen to serve on the jury. The jurors sit for an indefinite period not to exceed eighteen months; the number of days per month when they must actually appear depends on the prosecutor's case load. A district court judge administers the oath and gives the jurors general instructions about their duties. This marks the end of the judge's formal involvement in the process. From that point forward, the prosecutor dictates the course of the proceedings.
>
> The most striking feature of grand jury hearings is their secrecy. The press and public are barred from the proceedings, as are suspects and their counsel. Even judges are not allowed in the grand jury room; attendance is limited to the prosecutor, the jurors, the court reporter, and the single witness being questioned. Those who participate in the hearing are sworn to secrecy, and the court may use its contempt powers to ensure that this silence is maintained even after the case is resolved.
>
> Once in session, the grand jury's primary task is to review the cases presented to it by the government. The prosecutor calls and questions witnesses, and presents documentary evidence related to the crime in question. Unlike trial jurors, grand jurors may ask questions of the witness and may discuss the case with the prosecutor as evidence is submitted. After the case is presented, the prosecutor asks the jurors to vote to return an indictment accusing the defendant of a specific crime that the prosecutor believes is supported by the evidence. The jurors then deliberate in private. If at least twelve agree that there is probable cause to believe that the suspect committed the crime, the grand jury returns a "true bill" that, when signed by the prosecutor, becomes the indictment. If the grand jury concludes that the evidence is insufficient, it returns a "no bill" (or "no true bill"), and any preliminary charges filed against the suspect are dismissed.

Two features about current grand jury practice warrant special emphasis. First, witnesses who are called before a federal grand jury are not permitted to bring a lawyer with them into the hearing. A person who receives a grand jury subpoena may consult with a lawyer in advance, and may even bring counsel with her to the hallway outside the grand jury room. But when it is time to enter the room and testify, the witness goes in alone.

For a system that makes the right to the assistance of counsel a core value, this exclusion is puzzling to say the least. As a formal matter, the Sixth Amendment does not apply, because witnesses are not the "accused" in a criminal prosecution. But this hardly explains why a witness is forbidden to bring a lawyer with her if she can afford one, especially given the potential risks that a witness may be running. A witness can be asked questions whose answers would implicate her in a crime or would violate some other evidentiary privilege. And while the witness is always free to invoke a privilege and refuse to answer, this assumes that she will have both the presence of mind and the pluck to assert her right and remain silent. If a witness fails to assert the privilege and gives an incriminating answer, the prosecution is free to use that information in a later prosecution.

The situation in practice, however, is usually not as risky as the rules make it appear. Although the prosecution is not obligated to warn the witness in advance of the testimony of her right not to incriminate herself, it is the practice of the U.S. Attorneys to do so, just as it is considered ethical practice not to ask questions that obviously call for privileged information. In addition, if the witness is involved (or even may be involved) in criminal activity, a lawyer will advise the witness in advance to simply invoke the Fifth Amendment privilege in response to any questions the prosecutor asks. Finally, and most curiously, a witness who is unsure about a question is typically given the chance (with the prosecutor's/grand jurors' permission) to briefly leave the grand jury room, consult with her lawyer in the hallway, then return to the room and either answer or refuse to answer the question.

What explains this treatment of lawyers? Even if a lawyer in the grand jury room could not cross-examine a witness or object to a judge—there is no judge present—she could still provide valuable assistance by advising the client to invoke the Fifth Amendment or other privilege, much as lawyers do in police interrogations. Why should the grand jury room be different? Is it a fear that lawyers will complicate the proceedings, or is there something else at work? Note that many states with grand jury requirements allow counsel to be present, although their role is often limited. See, e.g., 725 Ill. Comp. Stat. 5/112-4.1 ("Any person appearing before the grand jury shall have the right to be accompanied by counsel who shall advise him of his rights but shall not participate in any other way.")

Historical inertia is surely part of the explanation, but another part may be skepticism that lawyers will always have the witness's best interest at heart. Consider a case where the grand jury is investigating a corporation and its CEO for possible fraud. The grand jury calls a staff accountant as a witness, and naturally the corporate lawyer would prefer to accompany the accountant into the grand jury room. The witness himself, however, might be chilled by having his employer's lawyer present because he knows that everything he says can be reported back to the CEO. By excluding all lawyers from the room, the witness still *may* report back to the lawyer what he told the grand jury, but he may also be freer to testify candidly and have his testimony remain at least temporarily secret.

The second feature worth considering is the limited reach of the constitutional grand jury clause: Unlike nearly every other provision of the Bill of Rights, the grand jury's protections do not apply to the States. In Hurtado v. California, 110 U.S. 516 (1884), the Supreme Court held that the grand jury clause of the Fifth Amendment is not incorporated into the Due Process Clause of the Fourteenth Amendment, and despite the wave of incorporation decisions in the last 60 years, *Hurtado* remains good law. As a result, more than half the states do not require a grand jury, or at least do not require it in many cases, and for those states that have the institution, their procedures need not and very often do not conform to federal practice. See 1 Sara Sun Beale & William C. Bryson, Grand Jury Law & Practice §§1.1, 1.5 (2d ed. 1997); see generally Federal Grand Jury, http://campus.udayton.edu/~grandjur/stategj/stateg.htm (also providing state grand jury information). So it is important to keep in mind that "grand jury law" differs widely between the state and federal systems, as well as among the various states.

Its insistence that the grand jury clause is not incorporated against the states may shed light on the Supreme Court's views of the institution's importance. In 2010 the Court ruled that the Second Amendment's right to keep and bear arms was incorporated because this right is "fundamental to a scheme of ordered liberty" and "deeply rooted in this Nation's history and tradition." McDonald v. City of Chicago, 561 U.S. 742 (2010). It can hardly be disputed that the grand jury is deeply rooted in our country's history, so is it fair to assume that the Supreme Court does *not* find the grand jury a necessary part of ordered liberty? As you consider the material in the following sections, you should notice how often the Court speaks in glowing terms about the role of the grand jury in the criminal process, and ask yourself why, if the institution is so important, the grand jury is treated so differently from other constitutional protections.

The materials below explore the scope of both the grand jury's investigative powers and its screening function. The next section, however, looks in more detail at one of the defining features of the grand jury: the requirement that the proceedings remain secret.

B.   *Grand Jury Secrecy*

1.   The Scope of the Secrecy Rule

Grand jury practice is governed by Federal Rule of Criminal Procedure 6, which is set forth in the Supplement. The rules making the grand jury proceedings secret are set out indirectly in Rule 6(d) and directly in Rule 6(e).

Rule 6(d) describes who may be present while the grand jury is in session. Only the jurors, the prosecutor, the witness being questioned, a court reporter, and an interpreter, if needed, may be in the room during a hearing. Once the evidence is presented and it is time for the grand jury to deliberate and vote, everyone else must leave and only the jurors remain (plus any interpreter).

For those permitted in the grand jury room, most are sworn to secrecy pursuant to Rule 6(e), which provides, in part, that jurors, the prosecutor, and the court reporter "must not disclose a matter occurring before the grand jury." (This information is often referred to in practice as "6(e) material.") Violations of Rule 6(e) can be punished as contempt, although, as the following material shows, what constitutes a "matter occurring before the grand jury" is hardly self-evident. The notable exception to this general rule is that *witnesses* are not required to keep confidential what they see and hear in the grand jury room, and they are free to discuss their grand jury testimony with anyone, including the target of the investigation.

At first blush, a secret proceeding seems antithetical to the American justice system, where so many of the events are presumptively open for press and public scrutiny: Arrests are matters of public record; bail hearings, arraignments, preliminary hearings, and plea hearings take place in open court. And, of course, the Sixth Amendment guarantees that the trial itself will be public.

What justifies this insistence on a closed hearing? The origins of the rule are easy enough to explain: If the goal was to place ordinary citizens between the accused and an overreaching crown, secrecy would help protect the jurors from royal unhappiness if they failed to abide by the king's wishes. But today the historical explanation rings hollow, as the image of a truly independent grand jury is hard to maintain when the government's representative, the prosecutor, now dominates the grand jury room (more on the prosecutor's role in Section C, below). Instead, the Supreme Court in the modern era has given the following justifications for keeping grand jury hearings a secret:

> (1) To prevent the escape of those whose indictment may be contemplated; (2) to insure the utmost freedom to the grand jury in its deliberations, and to prevent persons subject to indictment or their friends from importuning the grand jurors; (3) to prevent subornation of perjury or tampering with the witness who may testify before

the grand jury and later appear at the trial of those indicted by it; (4) to encourage free and untrammeled disclosures by persons who have information with respect to the commission of crimes; (5) to protect the innocent accused who is exonerated from disclosure of the fact that he has been under investigation, and from the expense of standing trial where there was no probability of guilt.

Douglas Oil Co. v. Petrol Oil Stops Northwest, 441 U.S. 211, 219, n. 10 (1979) (quotation marks omitted).

As persuasive as these reasons may be while the investigation is in progress, they lose at least some of their force after an indictment is returned. Once a defendant is charged and arrested, there is no more risk of flight or of pressuring the grand jurors, and the desire to protect the innocent from a false charge is removed by the indictment itself. And while protecting witnesses from tampering and encouraging cooperation are worthy goals, presumably many of the critical witnesses would be called to testify at trial and thus will be publicly identified at that point. Given this, how persuasive is it to claim that grand jury secrecy is critical even after the indictment, or better yet, after the entire case is over?

Note that there is no time limit on grand jury secrecy. In United States v. McDougal, 559 F.3d 837 (8th Cir. 2009), a defendant sought access to the grand jury material in her own case after the matter had ended and she had served her sentence, apparently because she wanted to write a novel or screenplay about the case. Although the woman argued that "[t]he reasons for sealing the record have now grown stale and disappeared," the court of appeals disagreed: "Although the interest in grand jury secrecy may be reduced after an investigation is completed, there is no provision in Rule 6(e) specifically authorizing disclosure at the conclusion of the proceedings." 559 F.3d, at 841.

Notice also that secrecy sometimes works against the interest of investigators. Selective disclosure of some investigative information "can place members of a targeted enterprise in a noncustodial 'prisoner's dilemma,' giving each person reason to fear that one of more of his comrades will race to the prosecutor's office to betray him in exchange for leniency, and therefore giving him reason to get there first." Daniel C. Richman, Grand Jury Secrecy: Plugging the Leaks in an Empty Bucket, 36 Am. Crim. L. Rev. 339, 346 (1999). So at least in some cases, prosecutors may wish they could reveal grand jury material because it could stimulate witnesses to come forward; stated differently, investigators might wish that they had a greater ability to barter such information to obtain access to evidence.

The law enforcement personnel participating in a grand jury investigation thus may have reasons either to adhere strictly to secrecy norms or to interpret those norms as narrowly as possible. Consider these conflicting incentives as you read the following case.

IN RE SEALED CASE NO. 99-3091

Appeal to the United States Court of Appeals for the D.C. Circuit
192 F.3d 995 (1999)

PER CURIAM:
The Office of Independent Counsel (OIC) seeks summary reversal of the district court's order to show cause why OIC should not be held in contempt for violating

the grand jury secrecy rule, and its order appointing the United States Department of Justice as prosecutor of OIC in a criminal contempt proceeding. In the alternative, OIC seeks a stay of those orders pending appeal. We conclude we have jurisdiction to consider the interlocutory appeal and grant the motion for summary reversal.

On January 31, 1999, while the Senate was trying President William J. Clinton on articles of impeachment, the New York Times published a front page article captioned "Starr is Weighing Whether to Indict Sitting President." As is relevant here, the article reported:

> Inside the Independent Counsel's Office, a group of prosecutors believes that not long after the Senate trial concludes, Mr. Starr should ask the grand jury of 23 men and women hearing the case against Mr. Clinton to indict him on charges of perjury and obstruction of justice, the associates said. The group wants to charge Mr. Clinton with lying under oath in his *Jones* deposition in January 1998 and in his grand jury testimony in August, the associates added.

The next day, the Office of the President (the White House) and Mr. Clinton jointly filed in district court a motion for an order to show cause why OIC, or the individuals therein, should not be held in contempt for disclosing grand jury material in violation of Federal Rule of Criminal Procedure 6(e). The White House and Mr. Clinton pointed to several excerpts from the article as evidence of OIC's violations of the grand jury secrecy rule.

OIC responded that the matters disclosed in the article merely rehashed old news reports and, in any event, did not fall within Rule 6(e)'s definition of "matters occurring before the grand jury." OIC also submitted a declaration from Charles G. Bakaly, III, then-Counselor to the Independent Counsel, regarding his communications with the author of the article, Don Van Natta, Jr. Bakaly declared, among other things, that in his conversations with Van Natta about whether the Independent Counsel could indict the President while still in office, "I refused to confirm or comment on what Judge Starr or the OIC was thinking or doing." According to OIC, the declaration was for the purpose of demonstrating that even if the matters disclosed were grand jury material, OIC was not the source of the information in the article.

Notwithstanding the foregoing, Independent Counsel Kenneth W. Starr asked the Federal Bureau of Investigation to provide OIC assistance in conducting an internal leak investigation. The Department of Justice authorized the FBI to do so, and as a result of the investigation, [ ].[2] Consequently, OIC took administrative action against Bakaly and referred the matter to the Department of Justice for a criminal investigation and decision. OIC informed the district court of these developments, withdrew Bakaly's declaration, and abandoned its argument that OIC was not the source of the information disclosed in the New York Times article. Although OIC noted that "the article regrettably discloses sensitive and confidential internal OIC information," it continued to maintain that the information was not protected by Rule 6(e).

Troubled by these developments, the district court ordered Bakaly and OIC to show cause why they should not be held in civil contempt for a violation of Rule 6(e), concluding that the portion of the New York Times article quoted above revealed

---

2. Bold brackets signify sealed material.

grand jury material and constituted a prima facie violation of Rule 6(e). [ ] The district court scheduled a consolidated show cause hearing, ordered the FBI and OIC to produce in camera all their relevant investigative reports, and required the FBI agents involved in the investigation to appear to testify. In accordance with this court's holding in In re Sealed Case No. 98-3077, 151 F.3d 1059, 1075-1076 (D.C. Cir. 1998), the district court ordered that the proceedings be closed and ex parte.

Convinced that the district court had misinterpreted this court's precedent, OIC and Bakaly asked the district court to certify for interlocutory appeal the question of the proper scope of Rule 6(e). The district court denied the request, referring only to its previous orders. . . .

One day later, on July 14th, the district court sua sponte issued an order appointing DOJ to serve as prosecutor of the contempt charges against Bakaly *and OIC.* The district court explained its unexpected inclusion of OIC in DOJ's prosecution: "DOJ's letter only refers to the contempt charges lodged against Mr. Bakaly. However, the Court also needs to resolve the closely related allegations against the OIC. The Court believes that these matters are best resolved through a single contempt proceeding involving both Mr. Bakaly and the OIC." Although the district court decided to afford Bakaly and OIC the protections of criminal law, it left open the possibility of civil, or a combination of civil and criminal, contempt sanctions. The district court also scheduled a pre-trial status conference for July 23. . . .

OIC filed an emergency motion to vacate the district court's July 14 order, [raising] numerous legal objections, including the argument that OIC is entitled to sovereign immunity from a criminal contempt proceeding. . . . To obtain an adversarial viewpoint on what we consider to be the dispositive issue in this case, we ordered Mr. Clinton and the White House, along with DOJ and OIC, to brief the question whether the alleged disclosures in the New York Times article relied upon by the district court in ordering a criminal contempt proceeding constitute a prima facie violation of Rule 6(e).

[Before reaching the Rule 6(e) issue, the court of appeals determined that by failing to respond to OIC's motion to vacate and allowing to stand its order requiring the OIC to appear as a criminal defendant at a status conference, the district court had conclusively rejected the OIC's claim of sovereign immunity. The court of appeals determined that this ruling was immediately appealable as a collateral order and that, in the circumstances of this case, taking pendent jurisdiction and disposing of the case on the merits of the Rule 6(e) issue was permissible and preferable to resolving the federal sovereign immunity issue.—EDS.]

Turning . . . to the merits of this case, we conclude that the disclosures made in the New York Times article do not constitute a prima facie violation of Rule 6(e). A prima facie violation based on a news report is established by showing that the report discloses "matters occurring before the grand jury" and indicates that sources of the information include government attorneys. Because OIC has withdrawn its argument that none of its attorneys was the source of the disclosures in the New York Times article at issue here, the only remaining issue is whether those disclosures qualify as "matters occurring before the grand jury." Fed. R. Crim. P. 6(e)(2).[8]

The district court concluded that only one excerpt from the New York Times article constituted a prima facie violation of Rule 6(e). That excerpt . . . disclosed

---

8. OIC contends that as an entity rather than an individual, it is not subject to Rule 6(e). It is unnecessary to decide this issue given our conclusion that there is no prima facie violation of Rule 6(e).

the desire of some OIC prosecutors to seek, not long after the conclusion of the Senate trial, an indictment of Mr. Clinton on perjury and obstruction of justice charges, including lying under oath in his deposition in the Paula Jones matter and in his grand jury testimony. These statements, according to the district court, reveal a specific time frame for seeking an indictment, the details of a likely indictment, and the direction a group of prosecutors within OIC believes the grand jury investigation should take. Not surprisingly, Mr. Clinton and the White House agree with the district court's expansive reading of Rule 6(e). OIC takes a narrow view of the Rule's coverage, arguing that matters occurring outside the physical presence of the grand jury are covered only if they reveal grand jury matters. DOJ generally supports OIC with respect to the Rule's coverage, but emphasizes the importance of the context and concreteness of disclosures.

The key to the district court's reasoning is its reliance on this court's definition of "matters occurring before the grand jury." In In re Motions of Dow Jones & Co., 142 F.3d 496, 500 (D.C. Cir. 1998), we noted that this phrase encompasses "not only what has occurred and what is occurring, but also what is likely to occur," including "the identities of witnesses or jurors, the substance of testimony as well as actual transcripts, the strategy or direction of the investigation, the deliberations or questions of jurors, and the like." Id. (internal quotation omitted). In the earlier contempt proceeding against Independent Counsel Starr, however, we cautioned the district court about "the problematic nature of applying so broad a definition, especially as it relates to the 'strategy or direction of the investigation,' to the inquiry as to whether a government attorney has made unauthorized disclosures." In re Sealed Case No. 98-3077, 151 F.3d at 1071 n. 12. Despite the seemingly broad nature of the statements in *Dow Jones*, we have never read Rule 6(e) to require that a "veil of secrecy be drawn over all matters occurring in the world that happen to be investigated by a grand jury." Securities & Exch. Commn. v. Dresser Indus., Inc., 628 F.2d 1368, 1382 (D.C. Cir. 1980) (en banc). Indeed, we have said that "[t]he disclosure of information 'coincidentally before the grand jury [which can] be revealed in such a manner that its revelation would not elucidate the inner workings of the grand jury' is not prohibited." Senate of Puerto Rico v. United States Dept. of Justice, 823 F.2d 574, 582 (D.C. Cir. 1987) (quoting Fund for Constitutional Govt. v. National Archives and Records Serv., 656 F.2d 856, 870 (D.C. Cir. 1981)). Thus, the phrases "likely to occur" and "strategy and direction" must be read in light of the text of Rule 6(e)—which limits the Rule's coverage to "matters occurring before the grand jury"—as well as the purposes of the Rule.

As we have recited on many occasions,

> Rule 6(e) . . . protects several interests of the criminal justice system: "First, if pre-indictment proceedings were made public, many prospective witnesses would be hesitant to come forward voluntarily, knowing that those against whom they testify would be aware of that testimony. Moreover, witnesses who appeared before the grand jury would be less likely to testify fully and frankly, as they would be open to retribution as well as to inducements. There also would be the risk that those about to be indicted would flee, or would try to influence individual grand jurors to vote against indictment. Finally, by preserving the secrecy of the proceedings, we assure that persons who are accused but exonerated by the grand jury will not be held up to public ridicule."

In re Sealed Case No. 98-3077, 151 F.3d 1059, 1070 (D.C. Cir. 1998) (quoting Douglas Oil Co. v. Petrol Stops Northwest, 441 U.S. 211, 219 (1979)). These purposes, as well as the text of the Rule itself, reflect the need to preserve the secrecy of the *grand jury* proceedings themselves. It is therefore necessary to differentiate between statements by a prosecutor's office with respect to its own investigation, and statements by a prosecutor's office with respect to a *grand jury's* investigation, a distinction of the utmost significance. . . .

Information actually presented to the grand jury is core Rule 6(e) material that is afforded the broadest protection from disclosure. Prosecutors' statements about their investigations, however, implicate the Rule only when they directly reveal grand jury matters. To be sure, we have recognized that Rule 6(e) would be easily evaded if a prosecutor could with impunity discuss with the press testimony about to be presented to a grand jury, so long as it had not yet occurred. Accordingly, we have read Rule 6(e) to cover matters "likely to occur." And even a discussion of "strategy and direction of the investigation" could include references to not yet delivered but clearly anticipated testimony. But that does not mean that *any* discussion of an investigation is violative of Rule 6(e). Indeed, the district court's Local Rule 308(b)(2), which governs attorney conduct in grand jury matters, recognizes that prosecutors often have a legitimate interest in revealing aspects of their investigations "to inform the public that the investigation is underway, to describe the general scope of the investigation, to obtain assistance in the apprehension of a suspect, to warn the public of any dangers, or otherwise aid in the investigation."

It may often be the case, however, that disclosures by the prosecution referencing its own investigation should not be made for tactical reasons, or are in fact prohibited by other Rules or ethical guidelines. For instance, prosecutors may be prohibited by internal guidelines, see, e.g., United States Attorney Manual §1-7.530, from discussing the strategy or direction of their investigation before an indictment is sought.[9] This would serve one of the same purposes as Rule 6(e): protecting the reputation of innocent suspects. But a court may not use Rule 6(e) to generally regulate prosecutorial statements to the press. The purpose of the Rule is only to protect the secrecy of grand jury proceedings.

Thus, internal deliberations of prosecutors that do not directly reveal grand jury proceedings are not Rule 6(e) material. As the Fifth Circuit stated in circumstances similar to those presented here,

> [a] discussion of actions taken by government attorneys or officials—e.g., a recommendation by the Justice Department attorneys to department officials that an indictment be sought against an individual—does not reveal any information about matters occurring before the grand jury. Nor does a statement of opinion as to an individual's potential criminal liability violate the dictates of Rule 6(e). This is so even though the opinion might be based on knowledge of the grand jury proceedings, provided, of course, the statement does not reveal the grand jury information on which it is based.

---

9. But see Eric H. Holder & Kevin A. Ohlson, Dealing with the Media in High-Profile White Collar Cases: The Prosecutor's Dilemma, in White Collar Crime, at B-1, B-1 to B-2 (1995) ("[I]n cases involving well-known people, the public has a right to be kept reasonably informed about what steps are being taken to pursue allegations of wrongdoing so that they can determine whether prosecutors are applying the law equally to all citizens. This point has become particularly pertinent in recent years because powerful figures increasingly seem to characterize criminal investigations of their alleged illegal conduct as 'political witch hunts.' This type of epithet only serves to unfairly impugn the motives of prosecutors and to undermine our legal system, and should not go unanswered.").

[In re Grand Jury Investigation [*Lance*], 610 F.2d 202, 217 (5th Cir. 1980).] It may be thought that when such deliberations include a discussion of whether an indictment should be sought, or whether a particular individual is potentially criminally liable, the deliberations have crossed into the realm of Rule 6(e) material. This ignores, however, the requirement that the matter occur before the grand jury. Where the reported deliberations do not reveal that an indictment *has been* sought or *will be* sought, ordinarily they will not reveal anything definite enough to come within the scope of Rule 6(e).

For these reasons, the disclosure that a group of OIC prosecutors "believe" that an indictment should be brought at the end of the impeachment proceedings does not on its face, or in the context of the article as a whole, violate Rule 6(e).[10] We acknowledge, as did OIC, that such statements are troubling, for they have the potential to damage the reputation of innocent suspects. But bare statements that some assistant prosecutors in OIC wish to seek an indictment do not implicate the grand jury; the prosecutors may not even be basing their opinion on information presented to a grand jury.

The fact that the disclosure also reveals a time period for seeking the indictment of "not long after the Senate trial concludes" does not in any way indicate what is "likely to occur" before the grand jury within the meaning of Rule 6(e). That disclosure reflects nothing more than a desire on the part of some OIC prosecutors to seek an indictment at that time, not a decision to do so. The general uncertainty as to whether an indictment would in fact be sought (according to the article, only some prosecutors in OIC thought one should be) leads us to conclude that this portion of the article did not reveal anything that was "occurring before the grand jury."

Nor does it violate the Rule to state the general grounds for such an indictment—here, lying under oath in a deposition and before the grand jury—where no secret grand jury material is revealed. In ordinary circumstances, Rule 6(e) covers the disclosure of the names of grand jury witnesses. Therefore, the statement that members of OIC wished to seek an indictment based on Mr. Clinton's alleged perjury before a grand jury would ordinarily be Rule 6(e) material. In this case, however, we take judicial notice that the President's status as a witness before the grand jury was a matter of widespread public knowledge well before the New York Times article at issue in this case was written; the President himself went on national television the day of his testimony to reveal this fact. Where the general public is already aware of the information contained in the prosecutor's statement, there is no additional harm in the prosecutor referring to such information.[11] Therefore, it cannot be said that OIC "disclosed" the name of a grand jury witness, in violation of Rule 6(e), by referring to the President's grand jury testimony.

Similarly, it would ordinarily be a violation of Rule 6(e) to disclose that a grand jury is investigating a particular person. Thus, the statement that a grand jury is "hearing the case against Mr. Clinton" would be covered by Rule 6(e) if it were not for the fact that the New York Times article did not reveal any secret, for it was already common knowledge well before January 31, 1999, that a grand jury

---

10. Indeed, the article stated that Independent Counsel Starr had not himself made any decision on whether to bring an indictment.

11. The prosecutor must still be careful, of course, when making such statements not to reveal some aspect of the grand jury investigation which is *itself* still cloaked in secrecy.

was investigating alleged perjury and obstruction of justice by the President. Once again, the President's appearance on national television confirmed as much.

In light of our conclusion that the excerpt from the New York Times article does not constitute a prima facie violation of Rule 6(e), we reverse and remand with instructions to dismiss the Rule 6(e) contempt proceedings against OIC. Because we have granted OIC's request for summary reversal, we dismiss as moot the alternative request for a stay. . . .

NOTES AND QUESTIONS

1. After the Rule 6(e) contempt proceeding against the OIC was dismissed, Bakaly stood trial and was found not guilty of criminal contempt in connection with the New York Times article. Given the ruling in In re Sealed Case No. 99-3091 that the information in the article did not constitute a prima facie violation of Rule 6(e), the charges against Bakaly did *not* involve such a violation, but instead the allegation that Bakaly had lied in the papers initially filed with the district court that explained his role in providing information for the article. As a Wall Street Journal article commented at the time of his acquittal, this created the unusual situation where "Mr. Bakaly was prosecuted for allegedly lying about leaking information that was legal to leak." Gary Fields, Starr Assistant Is Not Guilty of Contempt, Wall Street Journal, Oct. 9, 2000, at A26.

2. Independent Counsel Kenneth Starr's investigation highlighted some confusion in the law regarding grand jury secrecy. Do prosecutors violate Rule 6(e) when they reveal information about what witnesses have told FBI agents outside the grand jury? Are documents produced to the grand jury under compulsion of subpoena "matters occurring before the grand jury" for the purpose of Rule 6(e)? Professor Daniel Richman has proffered one explanation as to why Rule 6(e) doctrine is unsettled on these basic issues:

> Rule 6(e) does not establish a general regime of investigative secrecy for prosecutors and law enforcement agents. It addresses only what occurs "before the grand jury." As a matter of physical reality, however, the only thing that clearly occurs before a grand jury is testimony by a live witness, and sometimes the introduction of exhibits. Just about everything else generally occurs in a prosecutor's office or out in the field: deliberations about what investigations the grand jury will pursue, and which witnesses and documents will be subpoenaed in its name; interviews of potential witnesses conducted with an eye to deciding whether they will actually be brought before the grand jury; and receipt and review of documents obtained via grand jury subpoena. Particularly when prosecutors simultaneously develop a case in the grand jury and pursue other investigative options without using the grand jury, the language of Rule 6(e) provides all too little guidance as to what the government's secrecy obligations are. . . .

Daniel C. Richman, Grand Jury Secrecy: Plugging the Leaks in an Empty Bucket, 36 Am. Crim. L. Rev. 339, 341 (1999).

3. Investigations into to the source of a leak of grand jury materials are notoriously difficult to bring to a successful resolution, because often those most knowledgeable about the source of the leak—people in the media—are not compelled to disclose *their* sources. In addition, because grand jury witnesses are not generally bound by secrecy restrictions, there may be multiple ways in which information

about a grand jury investigation has legitimately entered the public domain—making even the identification of a breach of secrecy very difficult. In practice, this means that intentional leaks of grand jury material are nearly impossible to prove. Does this fact draw into question Rule 6(e)'s entire regime for grand jury secrecy? Or does Rule 6(e) serve its purpose by articulating a norm that will be at least partly internalized by investigative personnel?

4. If Rule 6(e)'s articulation of a norm of investigative secrecy is important, it's worth asking whether confining that norm to grand jury investigations is justified. After all, the subject of a traditional FBI investigation certainly suffers reputational injury when that fact becomes widely known—whether or not a grand jury has been convened. Professor Richman has gone even further to note that to the extent Rule 6(e) is about limiting the harms suffered by those who are the subject of a criminal investigation, the Rule may have the effect of showing special concern for the type of suspect who needs it least—the often well-heeled, white-collar suspect who is implicated in the sort of complex case most likely to be pursued in a grand jury:

> Does it make sense to have a system that in effect shows a special solicitude for targets and witnesses in white collar cases? Aren't these, in fact, the cases where, in the face of efforts by well-financed lawyers to impede information collection, the government is most in need of options that might include the selective dissemination of investigative data? One can also argue that the need for prosecutors to defend an investigation to the public while it is on-going is likely to be greater in white collar than in other contexts. After all, white collar targets are far better able to marshal support in the press and elsewhere than other targets—support that may impede the progress of an investigation and/or sway the potential jury pool.

Daniel C. Richman, Grand Jury Secrecy, supra, at 355. Does Rule 6(e) reflect nothing more than the political clout of white-collar defendants? Or are there other reasons for the law's special concern with investigative leaks in the grand jury context?

5. On the other hand, doesn't the secrecy rule sometimes *contribute* to the harm an innocent target suffers? Consider the police officer who shoots a fleeing suspect, or the politician who is suspected of taking bribes. The fact that the grand jury is looking at the case may become publicly known, but the actual evidence is typically kept secret. Suppose the grand jury decides not to indict because the shooting was justified or the bribe allegations were just false rumors spread by political opponents. Wouldn't the target prefer to have the grand jury information made public, to bolster the claim that no crime occurred?

Recall that after the grand jury refused to indict the police officer involved in a fatal shooting in Ferguson, Missouri, in 2014, the state prosecutor publicly revealed all of the grand jury information. Supporters thought this confirmed the officer's claim that no crime occurred, critics thought the information showed otherwise, but at least the debate was on the evidence itself and not on speculation. (The disclosures are posted at http://apps.stlpublicradio.org/ferguson-project/evidence.html). Is this a better way to proceed?

6. As noted, grand jury witnesses are not covered by Rule 6's secrecy rules. Indeed, a state law that prohibited a witness from publicly revealing his own grand jury testimony was struck down on by the Court on First Amendment grounds, Butterworth v. Smith, 494 U.S. 624 (1990), although by its terms, the decision was limited to an attempt to silence a witness after the grand jury had been discharged. Doesn't allowing witnesses to speak freely about the questions they were asked and the evidence

they were shown undermine at least some of the justifications for secrecy articulated above? If a witness is allowed to tip off the target about the grand jury's interest in him before the indictment is returned, doesn't that increase the risk of the target fleeing, or tampering with the jurors or the evidence? Also, if one purpose of the secrecy rule is to protect the target's reputation should the grand jury choose not to indict, doesn't allowing a witness to reveal the fact that the prosecutor was asking questions about the target subvert this goal, even after the grand jury has completed it work? For an interesting discussion on prosecutors' efforts to encourage grand jury witnesses not to reveal information, through cooperation agreements and otherwise, see R. Michael Cassidy, Silencing Grand Jury Witnesses, http://papers.ssrn. com/sol3/cf_dev/AbsByAuth.cfm? per_id=338839 (2015) (forthcoming 91 Ind. L. Rev. No. 4).

2. Exceptions to the Secrecy Rule

Despite a strong presumption of secrecy, Rule 6(e)(3) permits limited disclosure of grand jury material, typically in situations that recognize the needs and reality of prosecutorial practice. For example, 6(e) material may be disclosed by the prosecutor to a different federal grand jury, or to another prosecutor if the disclosure will assist in enforcing the federal criminal law. The material may also be disclosed to people who work with the prosecutor—paralegals, expert witnesses, law enforcement, secretaries—although the prosecutor must provide the court with a list of those who have been given access. These are perfectly sensible exceptions, because the prosecutor in the grand jury room will normally need the help of various non-prosecutors when putting a case together.

Beyond this narrow group, the list of exceptions is traditionally quite small. Consider the following situation: Suppose a U.S. Attorney, in the course of investigating a target for criminal fraud, uncovers information that would also give the government a strong claim for a civil action under the False Claims Act. The prosecutor would like to disclose the information to her civil counterparts at the Justice Department, and on examining Rule 6(e)(3), finds the following exceptions to the general secrecy rule:

> A) Disclosure of a grand-jury matter—other than the grand jury's deliberations or any grand juror's vote—may be made to:
>> (i) an attorney for the government for use in performing that attorney's duty; [or]
>> (ii) any government personnel . . . that an attorney for the government considers necessary to assist in performing that attorney's duty to enforce federal criminal law.

The Rule goes on to say that if proposed disclosure is not covered by one of these two sections (or by other provisions not relevant here), then the U.S. attorney must seek leave of court before turning the information over. So the question for the U.S. Attorney is whether she can just disclose the information to her civil counterpart, or must she obtain court permission first?

This was the question presented in United States v. Sells Engineering, 463 U.S. 418 (1983). The government quite plausibly argued that while Rule 6(e)(3)(A)(ii) was limited to disclosures that were necessary to helping the prosecutor "enforce federal criminal law," Rule 6(e)(3)(A)(i) was not so limited—all it says is that disclosure can be made to "an attorney for the government for use in performing that attorney's duty." Since all lawyers in the Justice Department, civil as well as criminal, come within the definition of "attorneys for the government,"[1] the prosecutor in *Sells* argued that the plain language of the Rule allows disclosure to a civil government attorney for purposes of enforcing the civil law.

A divided Supreme Court disagreed, and held that even Rule 6(e)(3)(A)(i) "is limited to use by those attorneys who conduct the criminal matters to which the materials pertain," despite the absence of this restriction in the text of the Rule. The majority found that "[t]his conclusion is mandated by the general purposes and policies of grand jury secrecy, by the limited policy reasons why government attorneys are granted access to grand jury materials for criminal use, and by the legislative history of Rule 6(e)." 463 U.S., at 427.

This narrow interpretation of the disclosure Rule would not be very significant if district courts were to freely grant a government motion to disclose grand jury material, but *Sells* made it clear that judges should be slow to do so. Courts should only grant a request to disclose, said the majority, where the party seeking disclosure has shown a "strong showing of particularized need" for the information. Quoting from an earlier opinion, the Court elaborated on this standard:

> Parties seeking grand jury transcripts under Rule 6(e) must show that the material they seek is needed to avoid a possible injustice in another judicial proceeding, that the need for disclosure is greater than the need for continued secrecy, and that their request is structured to cover only material so needed.

Id., at 443 (citation omitted). The Court in *Sells* added that even if the district court were to permit disclosure, the judge remained free to impose "protective limitations on the use of the disclosed material." Id.

There are other types of grand jury disclosure permitted by Rule 6(e)(3). The court may require disclosure at the request of a defendant who can show that grounds might exist for a motion to dismiss the indictment because of matters occurring before the grand jury. (Although as discussed below, the difficulties of making such a showing are considerable.) In addition, a court may order the disclosure of grand jury material in connection with some other judicial proceeding, or if the material shows a violation of state law, it may be given to state prosecutors. Importantly, however, these disclosures require judicial permission—the court continues to act as the gatekeeper and protector of grand jury information.

More recently, however, Congress has opened the disclosure door a bit wider, and has done so without requiring judicial approval. A few years after *Sells*, Congress provided, as part of a sweeping financial legislation, that U.S. Attorneys could, as a matter of course, disclose grand jury material to civil attorneys within the Justice Department to assist those attorneys in enforcing certain civil banking and civil forfeiture laws. This change is now reflected in Rule 6(e)(3)(A)(iii).

---

1. Federal Rule of Criminal Procedure 1(b)(1)(B) defines "attorney for the government" to mean, in part, "a United States attorney or an authorized assistant."

More importantly, in response to the terrorist attacks of September 11, 2001, Congress passed the USA PATRIOT Act, Pub. L. No. 107-56, 115 Stat. 272. The Act amended Rule 6 to provide that disclosure of matters occurring before the grand jury may also be made to any federal law enforcement, intelligence, protective, immigration, national defense, or national security official when such matters involve foreign intelligence or counterintelligence, in order to assist the official receiving the information in the performance of his official duties. Critically, there is no provision for prior court authorization, although the amended rule does provide that "[w]ithin a reasonable time after such disclosure, an attorney for the government must file under seal a notice with the court stating the fact that such information was disclosed and the departments, agencies, or entities to which the disclosure was made."

Are these changes to the traditional regime justifiable? As Sara Sun Beale and James Felman have pointed out, concerns with grand jury secrecy would not, in all cases, outweigh the need for broader use of national security-related information that might emerge in the course of a grand jury investigation. They go on to assert, however, that the PATRIOT Act's changes (particularly to the extent that these reforms downplay the role of the judiciary) raise concerns:

> The potential for a backdoor expansion of the grand jury's investigative jurisdiction is . . . problematic because it may increase the risk that the national defense and security institutions will be inappropriately involved in domestic affairs. Domestic law enforcement operates in a legal and constitutional culture that gives substantial weight to the rights of individuals. The relation of the government to its citizens is shaped by the constitutional requirement that the government respect each citizen's constitutional rights. The intelligence and military communities operate in a far different context than domestic law enforcement, and their institutional cultures and values have been shaped by their roles. Foreign powers, their agents, and their armies have no constitutional rights comparable to the rights identified by the Fourth, Fifth, and Sixth Amendments. In general, therefore, federal law has precluded the military from taking part in domestic law enforcement, and has drawn a sharp distinction between domestic and foreign intelligence surveillance. These limitations have been intended to reduce the likelihood that the military and foreign intelligence communities will erode the rights of American citizens. Particularly in the absence of judicial review, and in a context where the process operates in secret, arming these communities with the powers of the grand jury is highly problematic.

Sara Sun Beale & James E. Felman, The Consequences of Enlisting Federal Grand Juries in the War on Terrorism: Assessing the USA Patriot Act's Changes to Grand Jury Secrecy, 25 Harv. J.L. & Pub. Pol'y 699, 717-718 (2002). Do you agree? Is it likely that the military and the intelligence community will find it convenient to draw upon the powers of the grand jury in their counterterrorism work? Doesn't this depend, in part, on what alternative authorities these communities possess?

C.   The Investigative Power

In most cases, the suspect is arrested and a complaint is filed, and later the grand jury is asked to review the evidence and decide if there is enough evidence to indict. But as noted, there is another possible sequence of events, prototypically in a complex corporate matter or organized crime case. Here the government may believe that a crime has occurred or is ongoing, and may even know who the suspected criminals are. But because traditional law enforcement tools—witness interviews, search warrants, undercover police work—may be insufficient to gather the necessary evidence, the prosecutor turns to the grand jury to assist in the investigation. In this sequence the grand jury work occurs first, and the suspect is arrested only after the indictment is returned.

The grand jury carries out its investigation through the use of subpoenas—court orders directing a person to come before the grand jury and testify (subpoena ad testificandum) and to produce documents and other tangible items (subpoena duces tecum). The people receiving the subpoenas fall into one of three groups. The "target" is a person "as to whom the prosecutor or the grand jury has substantial evidence linking him or her to the commission of a crime and who, in the judgment of the prosecutor, is a putative defendant." A subpoenaed person is considered a "subject" of the investigation if his or her conduct comes within the scope of the grand jury's investigation, but the conduct is not enough to make the person a target. See U.S. Attorney's Manual 9-11.151. All others who are called before the grand jury are considered "witnesses."

In contrast to a police interrogation, the subpoenaed party need not be given the equivalent of *Miranda* warnings before testifying, see United States v. Mandujano, 425 U.S. 564 (1976) (plurality opinion). But like a police interrogation, the prosecutor need not inform the witness that she is the target of the investigation. See United States v. Washington, 431 U.S. 181 (1977). It is the policy of the Justice Department, however, to inform targets and subjects of their rights before they testify, and may, in certain circumstances, inform a person that he is in fact the target. U.S. Attorney's Manual 9-11.151, 9-11.153.

Once before the grand jury, the person is placed under oath and subject to questioning by the prosecutor. The rules of evidence do not apply (although the privilege rules do apply), which means that the prosecutor is not required to ask questions that would be permitted if they were asked at trial.

Although styled a "grand jury investigation," no one doubts that the prosecutor calls the shots. The prosecutor decides what matters to pursue, which targets to focus on, what witnesses to call, and what documents to subpoena. During the hearing, the prosecutor leads the questioning, and while grand jurors may ask questions of the their own and may even seek additional information, at the end of the process it is the prosecutor who decides which charges will be part of the proposed indictment on which the grand jury will vote.

The prosecutor's control over the grand jury raises an interesting legal question. Every year for the last few decades, the Supreme Court has spent an enormous amount of time and effort defining, limiting, and fine-tuning the constitutional limits on police officers' ability to investigate crime. Which of these limits, if any, should apply to a grand jury investigation? Although the grand jury is not part of law enforcement proper, it nevertheless works under the prosecutor's direction, gathers information that is often similar to what the police gather, and is backed by the court's enforcement power. Do the search and seizure rules apply? How about the Fifth Amendment limits on questioning? As you read the following material, ask yourself why the Court takes such a different approach to grand jury investigations.

1.   The Subpoena Power

UNITED STATES v. DIONISIO

Certiorari to the United States Court of Appeals for the Seventh Circuit
410 U.S. 1 (1973)

MR. JUSTICE STEWART delivered the opinion of the Court.

A special grand jury was convened in the Northern District of Illinois in February 1971, to investigate possible violations of federal criminal statutes relating to gambling. In the course of its investigation, the grand jury received in evidence certain voice recordings that had been obtained pursuant to court orders.

The grand jury subpoenaed approximately 20 persons, including the respondent Dionisio, seeking to obtain from them voice exemplars for comparison with the recorded conversations that had been received in evidence. . . . Dionisio and other witnesses refused to furnish the voice exemplars, asserting that these disclosures would violate their rights under the Fourth and Fifth Amendments. . . .

Following a hearing, the District Judge rejected the witnesses' constitutional arguments and ordered them to comply with the grand jury's request. . . . When Dionisio persisted in his refusal to respond to the grand jury's directive, the District Court adjudged him in civil contempt and ordered him committed to custody until he obeyed the court order, or until the expiration of 18 months.

The Court of Appeals for the Seventh Circuit reversed . . . [holding] that the Fourth Amendment required a preliminary showing of reasonableness before a grand jury witness could be compelled to furnish a voice exemplar, and that in this case the proposed "seizures" of the voice exemplars would be unreasonable because of the large number of witnesses summoned by the grand jury and directed to produce such exemplars. We disagree. . . .

[T]he obtaining of physical evidence from a person involves a potential Fourth Amendment violation at two different levels—the "seizure" of the "person" necessary to bring him into contact with government agents, and the subsequent search for and seizure of the evidence. . . . The constitutionality of the compulsory production of exemplars from a grand jury witness necessarily turns on [a] dual inquiry— whether either the initial compulsion of the person to appear before the grand jury, or the subsequent directive to make a voice recording is an unreasonable "seizure" within the meaning of the Fourth Amendment.

It is clear that a subpoena to appear before a grand jury is not a "seizure" in the Fourth Amendment sense, even though that summons may be inconvenient or burdensome. Last Term we again acknowledged what has long been recognized, that "[c]itizens generally are not constitutionally immune from grand jury subpoenas. . . ." Branzburg v. Hayes, 408 U.S. 665, 682. We concluded that:

> Although the powers of the grand jury are not unlimited and are subject to the supervision of a judge, the longstanding principle that "the public . . . has a right to every man's evidence," except for those persons protected by a constitutional, common law, or statutory privilege, is particularly applicable to grand jury proceedings.

Id., at 688.

These are recent reaffirmations of the historically grounded obligation of every person to appear and give his evidence before the grand jury. "The personal sacrifice involved is a part of the necessary contribution of the individual to the welfare of the public." Blair v. United States, 250 U.S. 273, 281. . . .

The compulsion exerted by a grand jury subpoena differs from the seizure effected by an arrest or even an investigative "stop" in more than civic obligation. For, as Judge Friendly wrote for the Court of Appeals for the Second Circuit:

> The latter is abrupt, is effected with force or the threat of it and often in demeaning circumstances, and, in the case of arrest, results in a record involving social stigma. A subpoena is served in the same manner as other legal process; it involves no stigma whatever; if the time for appearance is inconvenient, this can generally be altered; and it remains at all times under the control and supervision of a court.

United States v. Doe (Schwartz), 457 F.2d [895, 898].

Thus the Court of Appeals for the Seventh Circuit correctly recognized in a case subsequent to the one now before us, that a "grand jury subpoena to testify is not that kind of governmental intrusion on privacy against which the Fourth Amendment affords protection once the Fifth Amendment is satisfied." Fraser v. United States, 452 F.2d 616, 620.

This case is thus quite different from Davis v. Mississippi, supra, on which the Court of Appeals primarily relied.[2] For in *Davis* it was the initial seizure—the lawless dragnet detention—that violated the Fourth and Fourteenth Amendments, not the taking of the fingerprints. We noted that "[i]nvestigatory seizures would subject unlimited numbers of innocent persons to the harassment and ignominy incident to involuntary detention," 394 U.S., at 726, and we left open the question whether, consistently with the Fourth and Fourteenth Amendments, narrowly circumscribed procedures might be developed for obtaining fingerprints from people when there was no probable cause to arrest them. *Davis* is plainly inapposite to a case where the initial restraint does not itself infringe the Fourth Amendment.

This is not to say that a grand jury subpoena is some talisman that dissolves all constitutional protections. The grand jury cannot require a witness to testify against himself. It cannot require the production by a person of private books and records that would incriminate him. See Boyd v. United States, 116 U.S. 616, 633-635. The Fourth Amendment provides protection against a grand jury subpoena duces tecum too sweeping in its terms "to be regarded as reasonable." Hale v. Henkel, 201 U.S. 43, 76. . . .

But we are here faced with no such constitutional infirmities in the subpoena to appear before the grand jury or in the order to make the voice recordings. . . .

The Court of Appeals found critical significance in the fact that the grand jury had summoned approximately 20 witnesses to furnish voice exemplars. We think that fact is basically irrelevant to the constitutional issues here. The grand jury may

---

2. In Davis v. Mississippi, 394 U.S. 721 (1969), the Court held that it was error to admit the defendant's fingerprints into evidence at his trial for rape because they had been obtained in violation of the Fourth Amendment. The defendant was one of 25 young black men rounded up and detained for fingerprinting in connection with the crime. These detentions were done without the authorization of a warrant and in the absence of any probable cause. The Court held that the fingerprints were the fruit of an unlawful seizure of the defendant's person. —EDS.

have been attempting to identify a number of voices on the tapes in evidence, or it might have summoned the 20 witnesses in an effort to identify one voice. But whatever the case, "[a] grand jury's investigation is not fully carried out until every available clue has been run down and all witnesses examined in every proper way to find if a crime has been committed. . . ." United States v. Stone, 429 F.2d 138, 140. . . . The grand jury may well find it desirable to call numerous witnesses in the course of an investigation. It does not follow that each witness may resist a subpoena on the ground that too many witnesses have been called. Neither the order to Dionisio to appear nor the order to make a voice recording was rendered unreasonable by the fact that many others were subjected to the same compulsion.

But the conclusion that Dionisio's compulsory appearance before the grand jury was not an unreasonable "seizure" is the answer to only the first part of the Fourth Amendment inquiry here. Dionisio argues that the grand jury's subsequent directive to make the voice recording was itself an infringement of his rights under the Fourth Amendment. We cannot accept that argument.

In Katz v. United States, we said that the Fourth Amendment provides no protection for what "a person knowingly exposes to the public, even in his own home or office. . . ." 389 U.S. [347,] 351. The physical characteristics of a person's voice, its tone and manner, as opposed to the content of a specific conversation, are constantly exposed to the public. Like a man's facial characteristics, or handwriting, his voice is repeatedly produced for others to hear. No person can have a reasonable expectation that others will not know the sound of his voice, any more than he can reasonably expect that his face will be a mystery to the world. . . .

Since neither the summons to appear before the grand jury nor its directive to make a voice recording infringed upon any interest protected by the Fourth Amendment, there was no justification for requiring the grand jury to satisfy even the minimal requirement of "reasonableness" imposed by the Court of Appeals. A grand jury has broad investigative powers to determine whether a crime has been committed and who has committed it. The jurors may act on tips, rumors, evidence offered by the prosecutor, or their own personal knowledge. No grand jury witness is "entitled to set limits to the investigation that the grand jury may conduct." Blair v. United States, 250 U.S., at 282. . . . Since Dionisio raised no valid Fourth Amendment claim, there is no more reason to require a preliminary showing of reasonableness here than there would be in the case of any witness who, despite the lack of any constitutional or statutory privilege, declined to answer a question or comply with a grand jury request. Neither the Constitution nor our prior cases justify any such interference with grand jury proceedings.

The Fifth Amendment guarantees that no civilian may be brought to trial for an infamous crime "unless on a presentment or indictment of a Grand Jury." This constitutional guarantee presupposes an investigative body "acting independently of either prosecuting attorney or judge," Stirone v. United States, 361 U.S. 212, 218, whose mission is to clear the innocent, no less than to bring to trial those who may be guilty. Any holding that would saddle a grand jury with minitrials and preliminary showings would assuredly impede its investigation and frustrate the public's interest in the fair and expeditious administration of the criminal laws. The grand jury may not always serve its historic role as a protective bulwark standing solidly between the ordinary citizen and an overzealous prosecutor, but if it is even to approach the proper performance of its constitutional mission, it must be free to pursue its investigations unhindered by external influence or supervision so long as it does not trench upon the legitimate rights of any witness called before it.

Since the Court of Appeals found an unreasonable search and seizure where none existed, and imposed a preliminary showing of reasonableness where none was required, its judgment is reversed and this case is remanded to that court for further proceedings consistent with this opinion.

[The opinion of Justice Brennan, concurring in part and dissenting in part, and the dissenting opinion of Justice Douglas are omitted.]

MR. JUSTICE MARSHALL, dissenting.

. . . [T]he present case[] involve[s] official investigatory seizures that interfere with personal liberty. The Court considers dispositive, however, the fact that the seizures were effected by the grand jury, rather than the police. I cannot agree.

First, in Hale v. Henkel, 201 U.S. 43, 76 (1906), the Court held that a subpoena duces tecum ordering "the production of books and papers [before a grand jury] may constitute an unreasonable search and seizure within the Fourth Amendment," and on the particular facts of the case, it concluded that the subpoena was "far too sweeping in its terms to be regarded as reasonable." Considered alone, *Hale* would certainly seem to carry a strong implication that a subpoena compelling an individual's personal appearance before a grand jury, like a subpoena ordering the production of private papers, is subject to the Fourth Amendment standard of reasonableness. The protection of the Fourth Amendment is not, after all, limited to personal "papers," but extends also to "persons," "houses," and "effects." It would seem a strange hierarchy of constitutional values that would afford papers more protection from arbitrary governmental interference than people.

The Court, however, offers two interrelated justifications for excepting grand jury subpoenas directed at "persons," rather than "papers," from the constraints of the Fourth Amendment. These are a "historically grounded obligation of every person to appear and give his evidence before the grand jury," and the relative unintrusiveness of the grand jury subpoena on an individual's liberty.

In my view, the Court makes more of history than is justified. The Court treats the "historically grounded obligation" which it now discerns as extending to all "evidence," whatever its character. Yet, so far as I am aware, the obligation "to appear and give evidence" has heretofore been applied by this Court only in the context of testimonial evidence, either oral or documentary. . . .

The Court seems to reason that the exception to the Fourth Amendment for grand jury subpoenas directed at persons is justified by the relative unintrusiveness of the grand jury process on an individual's liberty. . . .

It may be that service of a grand jury subpoena does not involve the same potential for momentary embarrassment as does an arrest or investigatory "stop." But this difference seems inconsequential in comparison to the substantial stigma that—contrary to the Court's assertion—may result from a grand jury appearance as well as from an arrest or investigatory seizure. Public knowledge that a man has been summoned by a federal grand jury investigating, for instance, organized criminal activity can mean loss of friends, irreparable injury to business, and tremendous pressures on one's family life. Whatever nice legal distinctions may be drawn between police and prosecutor, on the one hand, and the grand jury, on the other, the public often treats an appearance before a grand jury as tantamount to a visit to the station house. Indeed, the former is frequently more damaging than the latter, for a grand jury appearance has an air of far greater gravity than a brief visit "downtown" for a "talk." The Fourth Amendment was placed in our Bill of Rights to protect the individual citizen from such potentially disruptive governmental intrusion into his private life. . . .

Nor do I believe that the constitutional problems inherent in such governmental interference with an individual's person are substantially alleviated because one may seek to appear at a "convenient time." . . . No matter how considerate a grand jury may be in arranging for an individual's appearance, the basic fact remains that his liberty has been officially restrained for some period of time. . . .

Of course, the Fourth Amendment does not bar all official seizures of the person, but only those that are unreasonable and are without sufficient cause. With this in mind, it is possible, at least, to explain, if not justify, the failure to apply the protection of the Fourth Amendment to grand jury subpoenas requiring individuals to appear and *testify*. . . .

Certainly the most celebrated function of the grand jury is to stand between the Government and the citizen and thus to protect the latter from harassment and unfounded prosecution. The grand jury does not shed those characteristics that give it insulating qualities when it acts in its investigative capacity. Properly functioning, the grand jury is to be the servant of neither the Government nor the courts, but of the people. As such, we assume that it comes to its task without bias or self-interest. Unlike the prosecutor or policeman, it has no election to win or executive appointment to keep. The anticipated neutrality of the grand jury, even when acting in its investigative capacity, may perhaps be relied upon to prevent unwarranted interference with the lives of private citizens and to ensure that the grand jury's subpoena powers over the person are exercised in only a reasonable fashion. Under such circumstances, it may be justifiable to give the grand jury broad personal subpoena powers that are outside the purview of the Fourth Amendment for—in contrast to the police—it is not likely that it will abuse those powers.

Whatever the present day validity of the historical assumption of neutrality which underlies the grand jury process, it must at least be recognized that if a grand jury is deprived of the independence essential to the assumption of neutrality—if it effectively surrenders that independence to a prosecutor—the dangers of excessive and unreasonable official interference with personal liberty are exactly those which the Fourth Amendment was intended to prevent. So long as the grand jury carries on its investigatory activities only through the mechanism of testimonial inquiries, the danger of such official usurpation of the grand jury process may not be unreasonably great. Individuals called to testify before the grand jury will have available their Fifth Amendment privilege against self-incrimination. . . .

But when we move beyond the realm of grand jury investigations limited to testimonial inquiries, as the Court does today, the danger increases that law enforcement officials may seek to usurp the grand jury process for the purpose of securing incriminating evidence from a particular suspect through the simple expedient of a subpoena. . . . Thus, if the grand jury may summon criminal suspects [to obtain voice exemplars] without complying with the Fourth Amendment, it will obviously present an attractive investigative tool to prosecutor and police. . . .

. . . [B]y holding that the grand jury's power to subpoena these respondents for the purpose of obtaining exemplars is completely outside the purview of the Fourth Amendment, the Court fails to appreciate the essential difference between real and testimonial evidence in the context of these cases, and thereby hastens the reduction of the grand jury into simply another investigative device of law enforcement officials. By contrast, the Court of Appeals, in proper recognition of these dangers, imposed narrow limitations on the subpoena power of the grand jury that are necessary to guard against unreasonable official interference with individual liberty but that would not impair significantly the traditional investigatory powers of that body. . . .

NOTES AND QUESTIONS

1. In addition to the majority's arguments, *Dionisio*'s distinction between a grand jury subpoena and a police seizure might be justified because the subpoenaed person has the chance to challenge it in court before being required to comply. But what if the subpoena requires the witness to appear before the grand jury or to produce documents or other evidence before the grand jury "forthwith"—i.e., immediately? Several courts have upheld the use of such subpoenas (often served when there is a threat that evidence sought by the subpoena will be destroyed) while noting that they may be misused and do not confer on police the authority to seize either the person who is commanded to appear or any items the subpoena may seek. See, e.g., United States v. Triumph Capital Group, Inc. 211 F.R.D. 31 (D. Conn. 2002).

2. *Dionisio* states that the Fourth Amendment has little application to a grand jury subpoena seeking testimony from a witness. The situation is somewhat (but only somewhat) different for a subpoena duces tecum. In Hale v. Henkel, 201 U.S. 43 (1906), the Court considered a challenge to a grand jury subpoena demanding the production of corporate documents as part of an antitrust investigation. The Court observed:

> [A]n order for the production of books and papers may constitute an unreasonable search and seizure within the Fourth Amendment. . . . Applying the test of reasonableness to the present case, we think the subpoena duces tecum is far too sweeping in its terms to be regarded as reasonable. It does not require the production of a single contract, or of contracts with a particular corporation, or a limited number of documents, but all understandings, contracts, or correspondence between the MacAndrews & Forbes Company, and no less than six different companies, as well as all reports made, and accounts rendered by such companies from the date of the organization of the MacAndrews & Forbes Company, as well as all letters received by that company since its organization from more than a dozen different companies, situated in seven different States in the Union.

Id., at 76-77. The Court went on to note that "[d]oubtless many, if not all, of these documents may ultimately be required, but some necessity should be shown . . . or some evidence of their materiality produced, to justify an order for the production of such a mass of papers." Id., at 77.

Hale's language is somewhat misleading—over the course of the past century, the Court's bark on this issue has been a good deal worse than its bite. Today, subpoenas are rarely quashed because they are, in the language of the *Hale* Court, "too sweeping . . . to be regarded as reasonable." It would be an exaggeration to say that there is *no* Fourth Amendment regulation of subpoenas. But it would not be much of an exaggeration.

Subpoena recipients may, however, argue that a grand jury request for documents violates Federal Rule of Criminal Procedure 17(c), which states that "A subpoena may order the witness to produce any books, papers, documents, data, or other objects the subpoena designates." Rule 17(c)(2) then says: "On motion made promptly, the court may quash or modify the subpoena if compliance would be unreasonable or oppressive." One interpretation of this Rule is that there is a "reasonableness requirement" that attaches to the grand jury subpoena power. Consider the Court's interpretation of this requirement in the next case.

UNITED STATES v. R. ENTERPRISES, INC.

Certiorari to the U.S. Court of Appeals for the Fourth Circuit
498 U.S. 292 (1991)

JUSTICE O'CONNOR delivered the opinion of the Court.*

This case requires the Court to decide what standards apply when a party seeks to avoid compliance with a subpoena duces tecum issued in connection with a grand jury investigation.

I

Since 1986, a federal grand jury sitting in the Eastern District of Virginia has been investigating allegations of interstate transportation of obscene materials. In early 1988, the grand jury issued a series of subpoenas to three companies—Model Magazine Distributors, Inc. (Model), R. Enterprises, Inc., and MFR Court Street Books, Inc. (MFR). Model is a New York distributor of sexually oriented paperback books, magazines, and videotapes. R. Enterprises, which distributes adult materials, and MFR, which sells books, magazines, and videotapes, are also based in New York. All three companies are wholly owned by Martin Rothstein. The grand jury subpoenas sought a variety of corporate books and records and, in Model's case, copies of 193 videotapes that Model had shipped to retailers in the Eastern District of Virginia. All three companies moved to quash the subpoenas, arguing that the subpoenas called for production of materials irrelevant to the grand jury's investigation and that the enforcement of the subpoenas would likely infringe their First Amendment rights.

The District Court, after extensive hearings, denied the motions to quash [on a variety of grounds]. . . . Notwithstanding these findings, the companies refused to comply with the subpoenas. The District Court found each in contempt and fined them $500 per day, but stayed imposition of the fine pending appeal.

The Court of Appeals for the Fourth Circuit upheld the business records subpoenas issued to Model, but remanded the motion to quash the subpoena for Model's videotapes. Of particular relevance here, the Court of Appeals quashed the business records subpoenas issued to R. Enterprises and MFR. In doing so, it applied the standards set out by this Court in United States v. Nixon, 418 U.S. 683, 699-700 (1974). The court recognized that *Nixon* dealt with a trial subpoena, not a grand jury subpoena, but determined that the rule was "equally applicable" in the grand jury

---

* Justice Scalia joins in all but Part III-B of this opinion.

context. Accordingly, it required the Government to clear the three hurdles that *Nixon* established in the trial context—relevancy, admissibility, and specificity—in order to enforce the grand jury subpoenas. The court concluded that the challenged subpoenas did not satisfy the *Nixon* standards, finding [in part that the subpoenas] . . . failed "to meet the requirements [*sic*] that any documents subpoenaed under [Federal] Rule [of Criminal Procedure] 17(c) must be admissible as evidence at trial." The Court of Appeals did not consider whether enforcement of the subpoenas duces tecum issued to respondents implicated the First Amendment.

We granted certiorari to determine whether the Court of Appeals applied the proper standard in evaluating the grand jury subpoenas issued to respondents. We now reverse.

II

The grand jury occupies a unique role in our criminal justice system. It is an investigatory body charged with the responsibility of determining whether or not a crime has been committed. Unlike this Court, whose jurisdiction is predicated on a specific case or controversy, the grand jury "can investigate merely on suspicion that the law is being violated, or even just because it wants assurance that it is not." United States v. Morton Salt Co., 338 U.S. 632, 642-643 (1950). The function of the grand jury is to inquire into all information that might possibly bear on its investigation until it has identified an offense or has satisfied itself that none has occurred. As a necessary consequence of its investigatory function, the grand jury paints with a broad brush. "A grand jury investigation 'is not fully carried out until every available clue has been run down and all witnesses examined in every proper way to find if a crime has been committed.'" Branzburg v. Hayes, 408 U.S. 665, 701 (1972), quoting United States v. Stone, 429 F.2d 138, 140 (CA2 1970).

A grand jury subpoena is thus much different from a subpoena issued in the context of a prospective criminal trial, where a specific offense has been identified and a particular defendant charged. "[T]he identity of the offender, and the precise nature of the offense, if there be one, normally are developed at the conclusion of the grand jury's labors, not at the beginning." Blair v. United States, 250 U.S. 273, 282 (1919). In short, the Government cannot be required to justify the issuance of a grand jury subpoena by presenting evidence sufficient to establish probable cause because the very purpose of requesting the information is to ascertain whether probable cause exists.

This Court has emphasized on numerous occasions that many of the rules and restrictions that apply at a trial do not apply in grand jury proceedings. This is especially true of evidentiary restrictions. The same rules that, in an adversary hearing on the merits, may increase the likelihood of accurate determinations of guilt or innocence do not necessarily advance the mission of a grand jury, whose task is to conduct an ex parte investigation to determine whether or not there is probable cause to prosecute a particular defendant. In Costello v. United States, 350 U.S. 359 (1956), this Court declined to apply the rule against hearsay to grand jury proceedings. Strict observance of trial rules in the context of a grand jury's preliminary investigation "would result in interminable delay but add nothing to the assurance of a fair trial." Id., at 364. In United States v. Calandra, 414 U.S. 338 (1974), we held that the Fourth Amendment exclusionary rule does not apply to grand jury proceedings. Permitting witnesses to invoke the exclusionary rule would "delay and disrupt grand jury proceedings" by requiring adversary hearings on peripheral matters, id., at 349, and would effectively transform such proceedings into preliminary trials on the merits, id., at 349-350. The teaching of the Court's decisions is clear: A grand jury "may compel the production of evidence or the testimony of witnesses as it considers appropriate, and its operation generally is unrestrained by the technical procedural and evidentiary rules governing the conduct of criminal trials," id., at 343.

This guiding principle renders suspect the Court of Appeals' holding that the standards announced in *Nixon* as to subpoenas issued in anticipation of trial apply equally in the grand jury context. The multifactor test announced in *Nixon* would invite procedural delays and detours while courts evaluate the relevancy and admissibility of documents sought by a particular subpoena. We have expressly stated that grand jury proceedings should be free of such delays. "Any holding that would saddle a grand jury with minitrials and preliminary showings would assuredly impede its investigation and frustrate the public's interest in the fair and expeditious administration of the criminal laws." United States v. Dionisio, 410 U.S. 1, 17 (1973). Additionally, application of the *Nixon* test in this context ignores that grand jury proceedings are subject to strict secrecy requirements. See Fed. Rule Crim. Proc. 6(e). Requiring the Government to explain in too much detail the particular reasons underlying a subpoena threatens to compromise "the indispensable secrecy of grand jury proceedings." United States v. Johnson, 319 U.S. 503, 513 (1943). Broad disclosure also affords the targets of investigation far more information about the grand jury's internal workings than the Federal Rules of Criminal Procedure appear to contemplate.

III

A

The investigatory powers of the grand jury are nevertheless not unlimited. Grand juries are not licensed to engage in arbitrary fishing expeditions, nor may they select targets of investigation out of malice or an intent to harass. In this case, the focus of our inquiry is the limit imposed on a grand jury by Federal Rule of Criminal Procedure 17(c), which governs the issuance of subpoenas duces tecum in federal criminal proceedings. The Rule provides that "[t]he court on motion made promptly may quash or modify the subpoena if compliance would be unreasonable or oppressive."

This standard is not self-explanatory. As we have observed, "what is reasonable depends on the context." New Jersey v. T.L.O., 469 U.S. 325, 337 (1985). In *Nixon*, this Court defined what is reasonable in the context of a jury trial. We determined that, in order to require production of information prior to trial, a party must make a reasonably specific request for information that would be both relevant and admissible at trial. 418 U.S., at 700. But, for the reasons we have explained above, the *Nixon* standard does not apply in the context of grand jury proceedings. In the grand jury context, the decision as to what offense will be charged is routinely not made until after the grand jury has concluded its investigation. One simply cannot know in advance whether information sought during the investigation will be relevant and admissible in a prosecution for a particular offense.

To the extent that Rule 17(c) imposes some reasonableness limitation on grand jury subpoenas, however, our task is to define it. In doing so, we recognize that a party to whom a grand jury subpoena is issued faces a difficult situation. As a rule, grand juries do not announce publicly the subjects of their investigations. A party who desires to challenge a grand jury subpoena thus may have no conception of the Government's purpose in seeking production of the requested information. Indeed, the party will often not know whether he or she is a primary target of the investigation or merely a peripheral witness. Absent even minimal information, the subpoena recipient is likely to find it exceedingly difficult to persuade a court that "compliance would be unreasonable." As one pair of commentators has summarized it, the challenging party's "unenviable task is to seek to persuade the court that the subpoena that has been served on [him or her] could not possibly serve any investigative purpose that the grand jury could legitimately be pursuing." 1 S. Beale & W. Bryson, Grand Jury Law and Practice §6:28 (1986).

Our task is to fashion an appropriate standard of reasonableness, one that gives due weight to the difficult position of subpoena recipients but does not impair the strong governmental interests in affording grand juries wide latitude, avoiding minitrials on peripheral matters, and preserving a necessary level of secrecy. We begin by reiterating that the law presumes, absent a strong showing to the contrary, that a grand jury acts within the legitimate scope of its authority. Consequently, a grand jury subpoena issued through normal channels is presumed to be reasonable, and the burden of showing unreasonableness must be on the recipient who seeks to avoid compliance. Indeed, this result is indicated by the language of Rule 17(c), which permits a subpoena to be quashed only "on motion" and "if *compliance* would be unreasonable" (emphasis added). To the extent that the Court of Appeals placed an initial burden on the Government, it committed error. Drawing on the principles articulated above, we conclude that where, as here, a subpoena is challenged on relevancy grounds, the motion to quash must be denied unless the district court determines that there is no reasonable possibility that the category of materials the Government seeks will produce information relevant to the general subject of the grand jury's investigation. Respondents did not challenge the subpoenas as being too indefinite nor did they claim that compliance would be overly burdensome.

B

It seems unlikely, of course, that a challenging party who does not know the general subject matter of the grand jury's investigation, no matter how valid that party's claim, will be able to make the necessary showing that compliance would be unreasonable. After all, a subpoena recipient "cannot put his whole life before the court in order to show that there is no crime to be investigated," Marston's, Inc. v. Strand, 114 Ariz. 260, 270, 560 P.2d 778, 788 (1977) (Gordon, J., specially concurring in part and dissenting in part). Consequently, a court may be justified in a case where unreasonableness is alleged in requiring the Government to reveal the general subject of the grand jury's investigation before requiring the challenging party to carry its burden of persuasion. We need not resolve this question in the present case, however, as there is no doubt that respondents knew the subject of the grand jury investigation pursuant to which the business records subpoenas were issued. In cases where the recipient of the subpoena does not know the nature of the investigation, we are confident that district courts will be able to craft appropriate procedures that balance the interests of the subpoena recipient against the strong governmental interests in maintaining secrecy, preserving investigatory flexibility, and avoiding procedural delays. For example, to ensure that subpoenas are not routinely challenged as a form of discovery, a district court may require that the Government reveal the subject of the investigation to the trial court *in camera*, so that the court may determine whether the motion to quash has a reasonable prospect for success before it discloses the subject matter to the challenging party.

IV

Applying these principles in this case demonstrates that the District Court correctly denied respondents' motions to quash. It is undisputed that all three companies—Model, R. Enterprises, and MFR—are owned by the same person, that all do business in the same area, and that one of the three, Model, has shipped sexually explicit materials into the Eastern District of Virginia. The District Court could have concluded from these facts that there was a reasonable possibility that the business records of R. Enterprises and MFR would produce information relevant to the grand jury's investigation into the interstate transportation of obscene materials. Respondents' blanket denial of any connection to Virginia did not suffice to render the District Court's conclusion invalid. A grand jury need not accept on faith the self-serving assertions of those who may have committed criminal acts. Rather, it is entitled to determine for itself whether a crime has been committed. . . .

The judgment is reversed insofar as the Court of Appeals quashed the subpoenas issued to R. Enterprises and MFR, and the case is remanded for further proceedings consistent with this opinion.

JUSTICE STEVENS, with whom JUSTICE MARSHALL and JUSTICE BLACKMUN join, concurring in part and concurring in the judgment.

Federal Rule of Criminal Procedure 17(c) authorizes a federal district court to quash or modify a grand jury subpoena duces tecum "if compliance would be unreasonable or oppressive." See United States v. Calandra, 414 U.S. 338, 346, n. 4 (1974). This Rule requires the district court to balance the burden of compliance, on the one hand, against the governmental interest in obtaining the documents on the other. A more burdensome subpoena should be justified by a somewhat higher degree of probable relevance than a subpoena that imposes a minimal or nonexistent burden. Against the procedural history of this case, the Court has attempted to define the term "reasonable" in the abstract, looking only at the relevance side of the balance. Because I believe that this truncated approach to the Rule will neither provide adequate guidance to the district court nor place any meaningful constraint on the overzealous prosecutor, I add these comments. . . .

The moving party has the initial task of demonstrating to the Court that he has some valid objection to compliance. This showing might be made in various ways. Depending on the volume and location of the requested materials, the mere cost in terms of time, money, and effort of responding to a dragnet subpoena could satisfy the initial hurdle. Similarly, if a witness showed that compliance with the subpoena would intrude significantly on his privacy interests, or call for the disclosure of trade secrets or other confidential information, further inquiry would be required. Or, as in this case, the movant might demonstrate that compliance would have First Amendment implications.

For the reasons stated by the Court, in the grand jury context the law enforcement interest will almost always prevail, and the documents must be produced. I stress, however, that the Court's opinion should not be read to suggest that the deferential relevance standard the Court has formulated will govern decision in every case, no matter how intrusive or burdensome the request.

I agree with the Court that what is "unreasonable or oppressive" in the context of a trial subpoena is not necessarily unreasonable or oppressive in the grand jury context. Although the same language of Rule 17(c) governs both situations, the teaching of United States v. Nixon, 418 U.S. 683 (1974), is not directly applicable to the very different grand jury context. Thus, I join in Parts I and II of the Court's opinion, and I am in accord with its decision to send the case back to the Court of Appeals.

NOTES AND QUESTIONS

1. *R. Enterprises* reaffirmed the traditional view that "A grand jury investigation is not fully carried out until every available clue has been run down and all witnesses examined in every proper way to find if a crime has been committed," and that a grand jury "can investigate merely on suspicion that the law is being violated, or even just because it wants assurance that it is not." Is it troublesome that the grand jury has, in some respects, more sweeping investigative powers than the police? Or, given that the prosecutor is in control of the grand jury process, is it preferable for an officer of the court to have this authority rather than the police? Does the answer depend on the extent to which we trust prosecutors more than we do the police not to use this power improperly?

2. What is the effect of *R. Enterprises*' relevance requirement? The Court says that one should start with a strong presumption in favor of the subpoena and then ask whether "there is no reasonable possibility that the category of materials the Government seeks will produce information relevant to the general subject of the grand jury's investigation." Can you hypothesize a case where the defendant will be able to show that the Court's standard is satisfied and the subpoena will be quashed?

3. Whatever the "reasonable possibility" standard means, it is plainly much less onerous than a probable cause standard. Why should the standards for obtaining documents by subpoena be so much more lax than the standards to justify a police search for those same documents?

Two possible answers are worth considering. The first bears on the law of search and seizure; it is laid out in Louis Michael Seidman, The Problems with Privacy's Problem, 93 Mich. L. Rev. 1079 (1993). Seidman's claim is that police searches always involve "collateral damage"—the officer sees things other than the things he is looking for, and the encounter between the officer and citizen often involves substantial coercion—and a large part of what the probable cause requirement protects against is that collateral harm. Subpoenas, he says, are different:

> Subpoenas amount to self-searches. They involve no violence, no disruption, no public humiliation or embarrassment. Like the required completion of tax returns, subpoenas invade informational privacy but impose no collateral damage. For precisely this reason, the Court treats them no differently from tax returns. So long as the subpoena is "reasonable" and not unduly burdensome, a defendant has no . . . right not to comply.

Id., at 1092.

The second reason relates to the historical origins of the grand jury. A probable cause standard and warrant requirement might be necessary means of checking the ability of government officials to use their coercive power improperly, a means of protecting, in the words of the Fourth Amendment, "the right of the people to be secure in their persons, houses, papers, and effects." But the grand jury, in its traditional conception, is not allied with government officials; it is *itself* "the people." This view of grand juries fits with a larger view of the original understanding of the Bill of Rights as a whole: not as a series of countermajoritarian rights, but as a series of *majoritarian* protections against official oppression. That understanding might explain the breadth of grand juries' power: Grand juries were a way that the people could check the power of government officials; the people were not themselves in need of checking.

4. Are you persuaded by this reasoning? Perhaps Professor Seidman's argument can be turned on its head. After all, it's one thing when police obtain and look through my appointment book because they have probable cause to believe it will reflect the payment of bribes to a local official. It's quite another, is it not, when my telephone records, bank records, and credit card receipts are perused by government prosecutors and laypeople who don't even know whether a crime has been committed? Consider the following analysis:

> [T]he federal subpoena power [is] something akin to a blank check. Prosecutors can go after whomever they like; they can be as intrusive as they choose; they can fight as hard as they want. Federal criminal law covers enough ground that if prosecutors look hard enough, they can find nearly anyone to have violated it. And prosecutors decide how hard to look. . . . Some sort of serious regulation is needed. The real question is, what form should it take? . . .
>
> An analogy to the civil process is useful. The rules for discovery in civil cases invite case-by-case adjustment based on the seriousness and scope of the case. Trial judges can give lawyers and litigants a lot of rope or a little. . . .
>
> If rough judgments about the importance of a case and the need for intrusive investigation are possible in civil cases, they are possible in white-collar criminal investigations as well. Indeed, the idea that unreasonably burdensome subpoenas should be quashed already exists in the law, and on occasion that idea translates into legally enforceable limits. What does not presently exist is the idea that the line between reasonable and unreasonable burdens should track the line between serious and less-than-serious crimes. . . . And that judgment ought to be made by courts, not by the prosecutors conducting the investigation.

William J. Stuntz, O.J. Simpson, Bill Clinton, and the Transsubstantive Fourth Amendment, 114 Harv. L. Rev. 842, 864-868 (2001).

2.   Limits on the Investigative Powers

Although the grand jury is a powerful investigative tool, there are some restrictions on its authority. The most obvious limit is a practical one: The grand jury is free to ask anyone, including suspects, to produce physical evidence, but if a person really has possession of the bloody knife used in the crime, he obviously won't produce it. From the suspect's perspective, going to jail for contempt of the grand jury is better than proving your own guilt of a murder, so for this kind of physical evidence, a search warrant executed by the police is required. The subpoena power is thus only useful when there is reason to believe that the person served will diligently search for and faithfully produce the requested material.

The ability to gather physical evidence through a subpoena may also be limited by the type of crime under investigation. Murders and drug deals do not usually leave paper trails. Physical evidence and live witnesses tend to be the keys to solving those crimes, and police tend to gather that evidence through searches and seizures and interrogations. White-collar criminal investigations are different. The police cannot feasibly search through hundreds of gigabytes of data looking for a single document, even though that document may be the key to proving that a crime occurred. So the government requires suspects (or witnesses, or custodians of relevant corporate documents) to do the work of searching through the file cabinets and assembling the relevant papers.

In addition, there are legal limits on the scope of the grand jury's investigation. The grand jury is free to subpoena a wide range of documents, but only until the indictment is returned. Once the defendant is formally charged, it is considered a misuse of the grand jury power to continue to gather evidence against the accused for use at trial. See United States v. Punn, 737 F.3d 1, 6 (2d Cir. 2013) ("The law is settled in this circuit and elsewhere that it is improper to utilize the Grand Jury for the sole or dominating purpose of preparing an already pending indictment for trial," although it may continue to investigate the defendant for possible new charges). So unlike traditional police methods of gathering information—search warrants, witness interviews—the investigative powers are limited to the purpose for which they are exercised, namely, to determine if the prosecutor has a sufficient case to justify a formal charge.

More importantly, the grand jury's subpoena power cannot compel the disclosure of privileged information. Although the rules of evidence do not apply to a grand jury proceeding, a grand jury witness need not disclose attorney-client communications, or information conveyed by the witness to a priest or physician. See Fed. R. Evid. 1101(d). And of course, the grand jury cannot compel a witness to testify or produce information in violation of the Fifth Amendment privilege against self-incrimination.

The Fifth Amendment privilege means that a grand jury witness cannot, by threat of contempt, be compelled to answer questions that would implicate him in a crime. The privilege allows the defendant to refuse to answer both direct questions ("Did you rob the bank?") and facially innocuous questions that might help the government to uncover evidence of the suspect's criminality ("Have you ever met Tony Salerno?"). As the Supreme Court has said, a suspect can refuse to provide information even if it would merely provide a "link in the chain of evidence needed to prosecute" the speaker for a federal crime. Hoffman v. United States, 341 U.S. 479, 486 (1951). This standard is sufficiently broad that once a suspect invokes the privilege, it is very difficult for the government to convince a court that the fear of self-incrimination is a sham.

On the other hand, a grand jury witness cannot refuse to answer questions simply because that answer is embarrassing, may cause the witness to lose his job, or might implicate some other person in a crime. Note that in this respect, the grand jury hearing is quite different from a suspect's refusal to answer questions during a police interrogation. In an interrogation, the suspect can refuse to answer any question for any reason, even a question that runs no risk of incriminating the speaker.

Before the grand jury, however, the subpoena obligates the witness to speak unless the answer is privileged.

The Fifth Amendment thus serves as a powerful protection for the individual defendant or, if you prefer, a significant limit on the government's investigative powers. The target of the investigation will almost certainly invoke the privilege rather than testify before the grand jury, so in a typical case, the target will not even be subpoenaed (although he might be invited to testify if he wishes to do so). Likewise, those who are involved in the transactions or who are part of the enterprise under investigation may well decide to stand on the privilege rather than testify, particularly since the grand jury hearings are secret and so no public stigma will attach to "taking the Fifth."

But critically, the prosecutor has a tool that allows her to overcome the suspect's privilege, albeit one that may come at a high cost. For the Fifth Amendment to apply, the testimony that the government is seeking to compel must incriminate the suspect in a crime *for which he can be prosecuted*. If there is no chance of prosecution, the suspect's privilege against self-incrimination disappears and a witness must testify, even about crimes that she committed, on pain of contempt. The next two sections discuss how a prosecutor might compel this testimony by using the power to immunize.

a.   *Immunizing Testimony*

Assume that a grand jury is investigating a case of suspected corporate fraud. The corporate records do not reveal any wrongdoing, but the prosecutor believes that most of the relevant evidence was destroyed by someone inside the company. The problem is that no one who is willing to testify knows anything, and those who are in a position to know the truth have all asserted the Fifth Amendment privilege. What can a prosecutor do to break this impasse?

Federal statutes provide one answer: Consider 18 U.S.C. §§6002 and 6003.

§6002. Immunity generally

Whenever a witness refuses, on the basis of his privilege against self-incrimination, to testify or provide other information in a proceeding before or ancillary to—

> (1) a court or grand jury of the United States,
>
> (2) an agency of the United States, or
>
> (3) either House of Congress, a joint committee of the two Houses, or a committee or a subcommittee of either House,

and the person presiding over the proceeding communicates to the witness an order issued under this title, the witness may not refuse to comply with the order on the basis of his privilege against self-incrimination; but no testimony or other information compelled under the order (or any information directly or indirectly derived from such testimony or other information) may be used against the witness in any criminal case, except a prosecution for perjury, giving a false statement, or otherwise failing to comply with the order.

§6003. Court and grand jury proceedings

(a) In the case of any individual who has been or may be called to testify or provide other information at any proceeding before or ancillary to a court of the United States or a grand jury of the United States, the United States district court for the judicial district in which the proceeding is or may be held shall issue, in accordance with subsection (b) of this section, upon the request of the United States attorney for such district, an order requiring such individual to give testimony or provide other information which he refuses to give or provide on the basis of his privilege against self-incrimination, such order to become effective as provided in section 6002 of this title.

(b) A United States attorney may, with the approval of the Attorney General, the Deputy Attorney General, the Associate Attorney General or any designated Assistant Attorney General or Deputy Assistant Attorney General, request an order under subsection (a) of this section when in his judgment—

(1) the testimony or other information from such individual may be necessary to the public interest; and

(2) such individual has refused or is likely to refuse to testify or provide other information on the basis of his privilege against self-incrimination.

There are several features to notice about these statutes. First, note the process Congress has prescribed for immunizing a witness. If a U.S. Attorney decides (with approval of the Justice Department) that obtaining a witness's testimony is in the public interest and that the witness is likely to invoke the Fifth Amendment privilege, the prosecutor simply requests a court order compelling the witness to testify, and the district court "shall issue" that order. In other words, the decision to obtain an immunity order requiring the witness to speak rests entirely with the prosecutor, with the court playing only an administrative role.

Why do you think that Congress entrusted the decision entirely to the executive branch? Shouldn't judges have at least some authority to decide what evidence should or should not be permitted in a trial or grand jury hearing? Or does the material on the prosecutor's charging discretion (see Chapter 9) provide an adequate justification for this process?

Second, there is nothing consensual or voluntary about a statutory immunity order; the witness must speak whether she wants to or not, and will be held in contempt if she refuses. Earlier in the development of the Fifth Amendment the Court concluded that the privilege helped protect an individual's dignitary interest in not being forced to provide evidence against herself, see, e.g., Murphy v. Waterfront Commission of New York Harbor, 378 U.S. 52 (1964) (Fifth Amendment privilege "reflects many of our fundamental values and most noble aspirations: . . . [including] our preference for an accusatorial rather than an inquisitorial system of criminal justice . . . [and] our respect for the inviolability of the human personality and of the right of each individual to a private enclave where he may lead a private life"). But §6002 makes it clear that prosecutors can overcome this interest simply by imposing an immunity order on the witness. As a result, the Court has more recently concluded that the Fifth Amendment is entirely about ensuring that a witness is free from prosecution that is based on self-incriminating testimony. See United States v. Balsys, 524 U.S. 666 (1998).

Third, the government's ability to compel self-incriminating testimony comes at a price. Although the government may force a witness to speak, "no testimony or other information compelled under the order (or any information directly or indirectly derived from such testimony or other information) may be used against the witness in any criminal case," except in cases of perjury or failing to comply with the court's order to testify.

Is this tradeoff—the witness loses his right to invoke the Fifth Amendment protection, and in return the prosecutor can't use that testimony to prosecute the witness—sufficient to protect the constitutional privilege? Your answer may depend in part on how broadly the courts construe the immunity grant, and in particular, the meaning of the phrase "any information directly or indirectly derived from such testimony." The contours of this phrase have proven to be one of the most complex areas of criminal procedure, as the following material reveals.

NOTES AND QUESTIONS

1. Although the ability to immunize witnesses to obtain their testimony has been around for a long time, the precise scope of an immunity grant remains a complex issue. For many years it was believed that if the government immunized a witness, it must provide "transactional" immunity—a blanket prohibition on prosecuting the witness for the crimes to which the testimony relates. Even if the police later learn about the witness's involvement in the bank robbery from a completely independent source, or even if the prosecutor already had enough information about the witness's involvement in the bank robbery to convict before granting the immunity, the witness is safe—the immunity makes the "transaction" (i.e., the bank robbery) off limits for prosecution.

Section 6002, however, only grants "use" immunity: it only prohibits the prosecutor from using the immunized testimony itself, directly or indirectly, to prosecute the testifying witness. If the prosecutor derives evidence from independent sources, the witness can still be prosecuted for the crime about which he was compelled to speak. This obviously provides less protection than transaction immunity, and so in Kastigar v. United States, 406 U.S. 441 (1972), the defendant challenged §6002 as being inconsistent with the Fifth Amendment. The Court disagreed, finding the "direct and indirect use" prohibition adequate to protect the defendant's interest. "[T]he immunity provided by 18 U.S.C. §6002 leaves the witness and the prosecutorial authorities in substantially the same position as if the witness had claimed the Fifth Amendment privilege," said the Court. "The immunity therefore is coextensive with the privilege and suffices to supplant it." Id., at 462.

2. Kastigar recognized, however, that the protection afforded by §6002 was only as good as the ability to ensure that immunized testimony was not somehow used in a later prosecution. Preventing the direct use is easy—if the witness testified under a grant of immunity, the prosecutor cannot use that testimony to prove the witness's guilt in a later trial, or even to impeach the witness. "Indirect" use of the testimony is a more difficult concept. We know from Kastigar that it prohibits "the use of compelled testimony as an 'investigatory lead,' and also bar[s] the use of any evidence obtained by focusing [the] investigation on a witness as a result of his compelled disclosures." Id., at 460 (footnote omitted). What else is meant by the indirect use of immunized testimony is explored below in the Hubbell case, although even after that decision the answer is far from clear.

Because of this uncertainty, one of the risks that the prosecutor incurs in immunizing through §§6002 and 6003 is that he will later be effectively precluded from prosecuting the witness at all. As soon as the prosecution charges a previously immunized witness, the defense will move to dismiss, and the court will hold a "Kastigar hearing" to decide whether the prosecutor is attempting to make direct or indirect use of the immunized evidence. Critically, the government bears the burden at that hearing; as the Court explained:

> Once a defendant demonstrates that he has testified, under a state grant of immunity, to matters related to the federal prosecution, the federal authorities have the burden of showing that their evidence is not tainted by establishing that they had an independent, legitimate source for the disputed evidence. This burden of proof, which we reaffirm as appropriate, is not limited to a negation of taint; rather, it imposes on the prosecution the affirmative duty to prove that the evidence it proposes to use is derived from a legitimate source wholly independent of the compelled testimony.

Id. (internal quotation marks and citation omitted).

If you were a prosecutor, how would you try to establish that the evidence you plan to use did *not* derive even indirectly from the immunized testimony? How would the timing and the identity of the law enforcement personnel involved in the evidence gathering affect your arguments?

3. Suppose Aaron and Betty are caught smuggling drugs from Canada into Maine. Believing that Aaron is the ringleader and that Betty is a peripheral player, the U.S. Attorney for Maine immunizes Betty under §§6002 and 6003 to obtain evidence against Aaron. Betty, however, refuses to testify, arguing that even if the federal prosecutors are barred from using her immunized testimony against her, she still faces a realistic threat of prosecution by the Maine *state* prosecutor as well as by Canadian authorities, neither of whom are bound by the federal statutes and are thus free to use Betty's immunized admissions to prosecute her. (Recall that under Criminal Rule 6(e)(3)(E), federal prosecutors may, with leave of court, disclose grand jury material to state or foreign prosecutors to assist with the enforcement of their respective criminal laws.) Thus, Betty argues, the scope of the immunity grant is *not* "substantially the same" as the Fifth Amendment privilege, *Kastigar* notwithstanding. Will this argument allow Betty to refuse to testify?

The Supreme Court has given a mixed answer to this question. In Murphy v. Waterfront Commission of New York Harbor, 378 U.S. 52, 78 (1964), the Court found that the Fifth Amendment privilege "protects a state witness against incrimination under federal as well as state law and a federal witness against incrimination under state as well as federal law." As a result, if a witness is immunized by a federal prosecutor in a federal case, a state prosecutor is barred from using that immunized testimony, directly or indirectly, against that witness to prosecute a state crime. Betty therefore cannot refuse to testify in the federal case, because the federal immunity protects against a state's use of the testimony. And while she still might be prosecuted under Maine law, the state district attorney will have to show that his evidence is not tainted by the immunized federal testimony.

Betty's worries about the Canadian prosecutors are a different matter. In United States v. Balsys, 524 U.S. 666 (1998), federal prosecutors issued an administrative subpoena to a resident alien, seeking to question him on whether he had lied in his immigration application about his activities during World War II. (The government suspected that Balsys had lied about working with the Nazis.) Balsys refused to answer, citing the Fifth Amendment privilege. Although the statute of limitations had run on any crimes arising from misstatements on the immigration forms— and thus any responses would not subject him to prosecution under U.S. law— Balsys claimed that his answers could subject him to prosecution under Israeli and Lithuanian law. The Court was unpersuaded, holding that the Fifth Amendment privilege did not protect against the threat of foreign prosecutions, and thus a witness could not refuse to comply with an immunity order on these grounds.

4. Statutory immunity under §§6002 and 6003 is not the only source of a prosecutor's power to immunize. A prosecutor and a witness might reach a separate agreement by which the witness will provide testimony, and, in return, the prosecutor will provide some level of immunity for that testimony. Under these "letter agreements" (sometimes called "pocket immunity"), the extent of the immunity will be whatever the parties agree to—if the witness has valuable information that is not otherwise available to the government, and if the witness is a relatively small player in a larger criminal enterprise, the prosecution might be willing to extend transaction immunity for the testimony. However, if the witness has relatively little bargaining power, the prosecutor might agree not to use the immunized testimony directly against the witness, but may reserve the right to use the testimony indirectly, say as a source of leads to other evidence. Because the immunity comes by way of agreement, the parties can include whatever terms they wish. But despite their non-statutory nature, courts will enforce these letter agreements as they would a grant of immunity under §§6002 and 6003.

Letter agreements obviously offer the prosecutor a great deal of flexibility, but from the government's perspective, they have at least one significant drawback: Unlike statutory immunity, the witness has to agree to the terms of the immunity. The only way to truly "compel" the witness to testify is through the §§6002 and 6003 process.

5. Having the power to immunize is one thing, using it is another, and many prosecutors are very reluctant to immunize witnesses. Why do you think this is so? One obvious concern is that the prosecutor might immunize the wrong person—the goal of immunity is to give something of value to the little fish in order to capture the big fish in the criminal scheme, but sometimes the prosecutor can't tell the size of the fish being immunized until after the evidence is gathered. So if he immunizes Betty to get Aaron, and the evidence later reveals that Betty is in fact the head of the smuggling ring, this is surely a bad day at the U.S. Attorney's office.

What other risks does the government run? In particular, ask yourself how an immunity order might affect the truthfulness of the witness's testimony as well as the jury's assessment of the witness's credibility.

6. The most common way for prosecutors to compel testimony from reluctant witnesses avoids granting "immunity" at all. In a large number of cases, the prosecutor will have sufficient leverage over one participant in a crime to induce that person to testify in return for reduced charges or sentencing considerations. These "cooperation agreements" typically require the reluctant witness to plead guilty to something, but spare the witness the risk of a more serious charge or punishment. These plea bargains (considered in more detail in Chapter 13) are conceptually just a variation on immunity agreements, with the main difference being that the "cost" to the prosecutor—the inability to prosecute the witness for the full degree of his involvement—is lower than for an immunity grant. Given this, can you articulate when a prosecutor still might need or prefer to immunize a witness?

b.   Documents and the Act of Production

Fifth Amendment complications arise when a witness is asked, not to testify directly, but to produce documents or other information that might be incriminating. Consider a case of suspected corporate fraud. The grand jury subpoenas the corporation's financial records, meaning that someone at the company—perhaps the bookkeeper—must cull through the documents, decide which ones are responsive, and produce them to the grand jury. Suppose the bookkeeper examines the relevant documents and realizes that they directly implicate him and the other officers in a scheme to defraud. Can the bookkeeper refuse to comply with the subpoena on Fifth Amendment grounds?

The answer can be complex. For over a century, the basic rule has been that corporations have no Fifth Amendment privilege, see Hale v. Henkel, 201 U.S. 43 (1906). As a result, corporate officers generally must produce corporate documents, whether or not those documents incriminate the corporation or even the officers themselves. So after *Hale*, it was easy to subpoena corporate documents, but still very hard to obtain documents from individual white-collar suspects.

Then came Fisher v. United States, 425 U.S. 391 (1976), which involved a subpoena for documents related to the defendant's income taxes. The documents had been prepared by the defendant's accountant and were in the defendant's possession until he gave them to his lawyer for safekeeping. The question before the Court was whether the lawyer had to hand over the documents. The Court held that, if the defendant would have had a valid Fifth Amendment objection to turning over the documents himself, the lawyer could raise that objection on his client's behalf. So, in a roundabout way, *Fisher* raised the question of whether the Fifth Amendment allowed a defendant to refuse to hand over incriminating documents that he owned and possessed. This was the same issue the Court had decided in the defendant's favor 90 years earlier in Boyd v. United States, 116 U.S. 616 (1886) (discussed in Chapter 4).

In *Fisher*, the Court went the other way. The Court held that, since the government had not compelled the defendant to *create* the documents, the documents themselves were not covered by the privilege. As a result, the law is now settled that the *contents* of documents—the information contained in them—are not protected from disclosure. (At least this is clearly so with respect to *business* documents; there remains some disagreement about whether *Fisher* applies in the same way to *personal* documents, such as diaries.) But even this principle is not as simple as it sounds.

Fisher went on to say that while the contents of the documents are not protected, the *act of producing* the documents might be. The physical act of producing the documents in response to a subpoena can itself be "testimonial," because it reveals to the government three things. First, the person producing the document "testifies" by his actions that the documents exist. Second, he testifies to the documents' authenticity—in effect, he says "these are the documents described in the subpoena." Third, he testifies to his possession of the documents. (If they were not in his control, he could not hand them over.) So under *Fisher*, this compelled testimony concerning the existence, authenticity, and possession of the subpoenaed documents is privileged, at least if it is incriminating. In such a case, the suspect can refuse to comply with a subpoena duces tecum, even though the information contained in the documents—which is what the prosecutor is really interested in—is not protected.

As if this formula were not complicated enough, *Fisher* articulated an additional qualification. Though the Court noted that every subpoena recipient "testifies" that the documents he hands over exist, are authentic, and were in his possession, the Court went on to say that, in some cases, one or more of those issues is a "foregone conclusion"—i.e., the government already knows and can prove that the documents exist, that they are what they purport to be, and that they were in the defendant's possession when the subpoena was issued. Where that is so, said *Fisher*, the Fifth Amendment "testimony" involved in handing over the documents is too insubstantial to merit constitutional protection.

Several commentators suggested that, in the wake of *Fisher*, the Court might hold that custodians of corporate documents can assert the privilege if the act of producing the documents would incriminate the custodian personally. In Braswell v. United States, 487 U.S. 99 (1988), a five-vote Court majority held otherwise. In the Court's view, "the custodian's act of production is not . . . a personal act, but rather an act of the corporation. Any claim of Fifth Amendment privilege asserted by [the custodian] would be tantamount to a claim of privilege by the corporation—which of course possesses no such privilege." Id., at 110.

But even where the act of producing documents is protected by the Fifth Amendment, the government still has options. Under 18 U.S.C. §§6002 and 6003, the prosecutor can immunize the "testimony" implicit in the act of production. Although this is sometimes called an "act of production immunity," in form and substance it is no different than the other types of immunity discussed above. If the government immunizes the act of production, it is then barred from making "direct or indirect" use of the statements that the documents exist, are authentic, and were within the control of the person producing them. The next case, involving a high-ranking official in the Justice Department under President Clinton, involves such an immunity grant, and shows the difficulty of determining the scope of the protection afforded by that immunity.

UNITED STATES v. HUBBELL

Certiorari to the United States Court of Appeals for the D.C. Circuit
530 U.S. 27 (2000)

JUSTICE STEVENS delivered the opinion of the Court.

The two questions presented concern the scope of a witness' protection against compelled self-incrimination: (1) whether the Fifth Amendment privilege protects a witness from being compelled to disclose the existence of incriminating documents that the Government is unable to describe with reasonable particularity; and (2) if the witness produces such documents pursuant to a grant of immunity, whether 18 U.S.C. §6002 prevents the Government from using them to prepare criminal charges against him.[3]

I

This proceeding arises out of the second prosecution of respondent, Webster Hubbell, commenced by the Independent Counsel appointed in August 1994 to investigate possible violations of federal law relating to the Whitewater Development Corporation. The first prosecution was terminated pursuant to a plea bargain. In December 1994, respondent pleaded guilty to charges of mail fraud and tax evasion

---

3. The text of §§6002 and 6003 are set forth supra in Section C.2.a of this Chapter.—EDS.

arising out of his billing practices as a member of an Arkansas law firm from 1989 to 1992, and was sentenced to 21 months in prison. In the plea agreement, respondent promised to provide the Independent Counsel with "full, complete, accurate, and truthful information" about matters relating to the Whitewater investigation.

The second prosecution resulted from the Independent Counsel's attempt to determine whether respondent had violated that promise. In October 1996, while respondent was incarcerated, the Independent Counsel served him with a subpoena duces tecum calling for the production of 11 categories of documents before a grand jury sitting in Little Rock, Arkansas. On November 19, he appeared before the grand jury and invoked his Fifth Amendment privilege against self-incrimination. In response to questioning by the prosecutor, respondent initially refused "to state whether there are documents within my possession, custody, or control responsive to the Subpoena." Thereafter, the prosecutor produced an order, which had previously been obtained from the District Court pursuant to 18 U.S.C. §6003(a), directing him to respond to the subpoena and granting him immunity "to the extent allowed by law." Respondent then produced 13,120 pages of documents and records and responded to a series of questions that established that those were all of the documents in his custody or control that were responsive to the commands in the subpoena, with the exception of a few documents he claimed were shielded by the attorney-client and attorney work-product privileges.

The contents of the documents produced by respondent provided the Independent Counsel with the information that led to this second prosecution. On April 30, 1998, a grand jury in the District of Columbia returned a 10-count indictment charging respondent with various tax-related crimes and mail and wire fraud. The District Court dismissed the indictment relying, in part, on the ground that the Independent Counsel's use of the subpoenaed documents violated §6002 because all of the evidence he would offer against respondent at trial derived either directly or indirectly from the testimonial aspects of respondent's immunized act of producing those documents. Noting that the Independent Counsel had admitted that he was not investigating tax-related issues when he issued the subpoena, and that he had "learned about the unreported income and other crimes from studying the records' contents," the District Court characterized the subpoena as "the quintessential fishing expedition."

The Court of Appeals vacated the judgment and remanded for further proceedings. The majority concluded that the District Court had incorrectly relied on the fact that the Independent Counsel did not have prior knowledge of the contents of the subpoenaed documents. The question the District Court should have addressed was the extent of the Government's independent knowledge of the documents' existence and authenticity, and of respondent's possession or control of them. It explained:

> On remand, the district court should hold a hearing in which it seeks to establish the extent and detail of the [G]overnment's knowledge of Hubbell's financial affairs (or of the paperwork documenting it) on the day the subpoena issued. It is only then that the court will be in a position to assess the testimonial value of Hubbell's response to the subpoena. Should the Independent Counsel prove capable of demonstrating with reasonable particularity a prior awareness that the exhaustive litany of documents sought in the subpoena existed and were in Hubbell's possession, then the wide distance evidently traveled from the subpoena to the substantive allegations contained in the indictment would be based upon legitimate intermediate steps. To the extent

that the information conveyed through Hubbell's compelled act of production provides the necessary linkage, however, the indictment deriving therefrom is tainted.

In the opinion of the dissenting judge, the majority failed to give full effect to the distinction between the contents of the documents and the limited testimonial significance of the act of producing them. In his view, as long as the prosecutor could make use of information contained in the documents or derived therefrom without any reference to the fact that respondent had produced them in response to a subpoena, there would be no improper use of the testimonial aspect of the immunized act of production. In other words, the constitutional privilege and the statute conferring use immunity would only shield the witness from the use of any information resulting from his subpoena response "beyond what the prosecutor would receive if the documents appeared in the grand jury room or in his office unsolicited and unmarked, like manna from heaven."

On remand, the Independent Counsel acknowledged that he could not satisfy the "reasonable particularity" standard prescribed by the Court of Appeals and entered into a conditional plea agreement with respondent. In essence, the agreement provides for the dismissal of the charges unless this Court's disposition of the case makes it reasonably likely that respondent's "act of production immunity" would not pose a significant bar to his prosecution. The case is not moot, however, because the agreement also provides for the entry of a guilty plea and a sentence that will not include incarceration if we should reverse and issue an opinion that is sufficiently favorable to the Government to satisfy that condition. Despite that agreement, we granted the Independent Counsel's petition for a writ of certiorari in order to determine the precise scope of a grant of immunity with respect to the production of documents in response to a subpoena. We now affirm. . . .

IV

The Government correctly emphasizes that the testimonial aspect of a response to a subpoena duces tecum does nothing more than establish the existence, authenticity, and custody of items that are produced. We assume that the Government is also entirely correct in its submission that it would not have to advert to respondent's act of production in order to prove the existence, authenticity, or custody of any documents that it might offer in evidence at a criminal trial; indeed, the Government disclaims any need to introduce any of the documents produced by respondent into evidence in order to prove the charges against him. It follows, according to the Government, that it has no intention of making improper "use" of respondent's compelled testimony.

The question, however, is not whether the response to the subpoena may be introduced into evidence at his criminal trial. That would surely be a prohibited "use" of the immunized act of production. But the fact that the Government intends no such use of the act of production leaves open the separate question whether it has already made "derivative use" of the testimonial aspect of that act in obtaining the indictment against respondent and in preparing its case for trial. It clearly has.

It is apparent from the text of the subpoena itself that the prosecutor needed respondent's assistance both to identify potential sources of information and to produce those sources. See Appendix, infra. Given the breadth of the description of the 11 categories of documents called for by the subpoena, the collection and production of the materials demanded was tantamount to answering a series of interrogatories asking a witness to disclose the existence and location of particular documents fitting certain broad descriptions. The assembly of literally hundreds of pages of material in response to a request for "any and all documents reflecting, referring, or relating to any direct or indirect sources of money or other things of value received by or provided to" an individual or members of his family during a 3-year period, is the functional equivalent of the preparation of an answer to either a detailed written interrogatory or a series of oral questions at a discovery deposition. Entirely apart from the contents of the 13,120 pages of materials that respondent produced in this case, it is undeniable that providing a catalog of existing documents fitting within any of the 11 broadly worded subpoena categories could provide a prosecutor with a "lead to incriminating evidence," or "a link in the chain of evidence needed to prosecute."

Indeed, the record makes it clear that that is what happened in this case. The documents were produced before a grand jury sitting in the Eastern District of Arkansas in aid of the Independent Counsel's attempt to determine whether respondent had violated a commitment in his first plea agreement. The use of those sources of information eventually led to the return of an indictment by a grand jury sitting in the District of Columbia for offenses that apparently are unrelated to that plea agreement. What the District Court characterized as a "fishing expedition" did produce a fish, but not the one that the Independent Counsel expected to hook. It is abundantly clear that the testimonial aspect of respondent's act of producing subpoenaed documents was the first step in a chain of evidence that led to this prosecution. The documents did not magically appear in the prosecutor's office like "manna from heaven." They arrived there only after respondent asserted his constitutional privilege, received a grant of immunity, and—under the compulsion of the District Court's order—took the mental and physical steps necessary to provide the prosecutor with an accurate inventory of the many sources of potentially incriminating evidence sought by the subpoena. It was only through respondent's truthful reply to the subpoena[23] that the Government received the incriminating documents of which it made "substantial use . . . in the investigation that led to the indictment." Brief for United States 3.

For these reasons, we cannot accept the Government's submission that respondent's immunity did not preclude its derivative use of the produced documents because its "possession of the documents [was] the fruit only of a simple physical act—the act of producing the documents." It was unquestionably necessary for respondent to make extensive use of "the contents of his own mind" in identifying the hundreds of documents responsive to the requests in the subpoena. The assembly of those documents was like telling an inquisitor the combination to a wall safe, not like being forced to surrender the key to a strongbox. The Government's anemic view of respondent's act of production as a mere physical act that is principally non-testimonial in character and can be entirely divorced from its "implicit"

---

23. See William J. Stuntz, Self-Incrimination and Excuse, 88 Colum. L. Rev. 1227, 1228-1229, 1256-1259, 1277-1279 (1988) (discussing the conceptual link between truth-telling and the privilege in the document production context); Samuel A. Alito, Jr., Documents and the Privilege Against Self-Incrimination, 48 U. Pitt. L. Rev. 27, 47 (1986); 8 J. Wigmore, Evidence §2264, p. 379 (J. McNaughton rev. 1961) (describing a subpoena duces tecum as "process relying on [the witness's] moral responsibility for truthtelling").

testimonial aspect so as to constitute a "legitimate, wholly independent source" (as required by *Kastigar*) for the documents produced simply fails to account for these realities.

In sum, we have no doubt that the constitutional privilege against self-incrimination protects the target of a grand jury investigation from being compelled to answer questions designed to elicit information about the existence of sources of potentially incriminating evidence. That constitutional privilege has the same application to the testimonial aspect of a response to a subpoena seeking discovery of those sources. Before the District Court, the Government arguably conceded that respondent's act of production in this case had a testimonial aspect that entitled him to respond to the subpoena by asserting his privilege against self-incrimination. See 167 F.3d, at 580 (noting District Court's finding that "Hubbell's compelled act of production required him to make communications as to the existence, possession, and authenticity of the subpoenaed documents"). On appeal and again before this Court, however, the Government has argued that the communicative aspect of respondent's act of producing ordinary business records is insufficiently "testimonial" to support a claim of privilege because the existence and possession of such records by any businessman is a "foregone conclusion" under our decision in Fisher v. United States. This argument both misreads *Fisher* and ignores our subsequent decision in United States v. Doe, 465 U.S. 605 (1984).

. . . *Fisher* involved summonses seeking production of working papers prepared by the taxpayers' accountants that the IRS knew were in the possession of the taxpayers' attorneys. In rejecting the taxpayers' claim that these documents were protected by the Fifth Amendment privilege, we stated:

> It is doubtful that implicitly admitting the existence and possession of the papers rises to the level of testimony within the protection of the Fifth Amendment. The papers belong to the *accountant*, were prepared by him, and are the kind usually prepared by an accountant working on the tax returns of his client. Surely the Government is in no way relying on the "truthtelling" of the *taxpayer* to prove the existence of or his access to the documents. . . . The existence and location of the papers are a foregone conclusion and the taxpayer adds little or nothing to the sum total of the Government's information by conceding that he in fact has the papers.

425 U.S., at 411 (emphases added).

Whatever the scope of this "foregone conclusion" rationale, the facts of this case plainly fall outside of it. While in *Fisher* the Government already knew that the documents were in the attorneys' possession and could independently confirm their existence and authenticity through the accountants who created them, here the Government has not shown that it had any prior knowledge of either the existence or the whereabouts of the 13,120 pages of documents ultimately produced by respondent. The Government cannot cure this deficiency through the over-broad argument that a businessman such as respondent will always possess general business and tax records that fall within the broad categories described in this subpoena. The *Doe* subpoenas also sought several broad categories of general business records, yet we upheld the District Court's finding that the act of producing those records would involve testimonial self-incrimination. Given our conclusion that respondent's act of production had a testimonial aspect, at least with respect to the existence and location of the documents sought by the Government's subpoena, respondent could not be compelled to produce those documents without first receiving a grant of immunity under §6003. As we construed §6002 in *Kastigar*, such immunity is co-extensive with the constitutional privilege. *Kastigar* requires that respondent's motion to dismiss the indictment on immunity grounds be granted unless the Government proves that the evidence it used in obtaining the indictment and proposed to use at trial was derived from legitimate sources "wholly independent" of the testimonial aspect of respondent's immunized conduct in assembling and producing the documents described in the subpoena. The Government, however, does not claim that it could make such a showing. Rather, it contends that its prosecution of respondent must be considered proper unless someone—presumably respondent—shows that "there is some substantial relation between the compelled testimonial communications implicit in the act of production (as opposed to the act of production standing alone) and some aspect of the information used in the investigation or the evidence presented at trial." Brief for United States 9. We could not accept this submission without repudiating the basis for our conclusion in *Kastigar* that the statutory guarantee of use and derivative-use immunity is as broad as the constitutional privilege itself. This we are not prepared to do.

Accordingly, the indictment against respondent must be dismissed. The judgment of the Court of Appeals is affirmed.

APPENDIX TO OPINION OF THE COURT

On October 31, 1996, upon application by the Independent Counsel, a subpoena was issued commanding respondent to appear and testify before the grand jury of the United States District Court for the Eastern District of Arkansas on November 19, 1996, and to bring with him various documents described in a "Subpoena Rider" as follows:

"A. Any and all documents reflecting, referring, or relating to any direct or indirect sources of money or other things of value received by or provided to Webster Hubbell, his wife, or children from January 1, 1993 to the present, including but not limited to the identity of employers or clients of legal or any other type of work.

"B. Any and all documents reflecting, referring, or relating to any direct or indirect sources of money or other things of value received by or provided to Webster Hubbell, his wife, or children from January 1, 1993 to the present, including but not limited to billing memoranda, draft statements, bills, final statements, and/or bills for work performed or time billed from January 1, 1993 to the present.

"C. Copies of all bank records of Webster Hubbell, his wife, or children for all accounts from January 1, 1993 to the present, including but not limited to all statements, registers and ledgers, cancelled checks, deposit items, and wire transfers.

"D. Any and all documents reflecting, referring, or relating to time worked or billed by Webster Hubbell from January 1, 1993 to the present, including but not limited to original time sheets, books, notes, papers, and/or computer records.

"E. Any and all documents reflecting, referring, or relating to expenses incurred by and/or disbursements of money by Webster Hubbell during the course of any work performed or to be performed by Mr. Hubbell from January 1, 1993 to the present.

"F. Any and all documents reflecting, referring, or relating to Webster Hubbell's schedule of activities, including but not limited to any and all calendars, daytimers, time books, appointment books, diaries, records of reverse telephone toll calls, credit card calls, telephone message slips, logs, other telephone records, minutes, databases, electronic mail messages, travel records, itineraries, tickets for transportation of any kind, payments, bills, expense backup documentation, schedules, and/or any other document or database that would disclose Webster Hubbell's activities from January 1, 1993 to the present.

"G. Any and all documents reflecting, referring, or relating to any retainer agreements or contracts for employment of Webster Hubbell, his wife, or his children from January 1, 1993 to the present.

"H. Any and all tax returns and tax return information, including but not limited to all W-2s, form 1099s, schedules, draft returns, work papers, and backup documents filed, created or held by or on behalf of Webster Hubbell, his wife, his children, and/or any business in which he, his wife, or his children holds or has held an interest, for the tax years 1993 to the present.

"I. Any and all documents reflecting, referring, or relating to work performed or to be performed or on behalf of the City of Los Angeles, California, the Los Angeles Department of Airports or any other Los Angeles municipal Governmental entity, Mary Leslie, and/or Alan S. Arkatov, including but not limited to correspondence, retainer agreements, contracts, time sheets, appointment calendars, activity calendars, diaries, billing statements, billing memoranda, telephone records, telephone message slips, telephone credit card statements, itineraries, tickets for transportation, payment records, expense receipts, ledgers, check registers, notes, memoranda, electronic mail, bank deposit items, cashier's checks, traveler's checks, wire transfer records and/or other records of financial transactions.

"J. Any and all documents reflecting, referring, or relating to work performed or to be performed by Webster Hubbell, his wife, or his children on the recommendation, counsel or other influence of Mary Leslie and/or Alan S. Arkatov, including but not limited to correspondence, retainer agreements, contracts, time sheets, appointment calendars, activity calendars, diaries, billing statements, billing memoranda, telephone records, telephone message slips, telephone credit card statements, itineraries, tickets for transportation, payment records, expense receipts, ledgers, check registers, notes, memoranda, electronic mail, bank deposit items, cashier's checks, traveler's checks, wire transfer records and/or other records of financial transactions.

"K. Any and all documents related to work performed or to be performed for or on behalf of Lippo Ltd. (formerly Public Finance (H.K.) Ltd.), the Lippo Group, the Lippo Bank, Mochtar Riady, James Riady, Stephen Riady, John Luen Wai Lee, John Huang, Mark W. Grobmyer, C. Joseph Giroir, Jr., or any affiliate, subsidiary, or corporation owned or controlled by or related to the aforementioned entities or individuals, including but not limited to correspondence, retainer agreements, contracts, time sheets, appointment calendars, activity calendars, diaries, billing statements, billing memoranda, telephone records, telephone message slips, telephone credit card statements, itineraries, tickets for transportation, payment records, expense receipts, ledgers, check registers, notes, memoranda, electronic mail, bank deposit items, cashier's checks, traveler's checks, wire transfer records and/or other records of financial transactions."

JUSTICE THOMAS, with whom JUSTICE SCALIA joins, concurring.

Our decision today involves the application of the act-of-production doctrine, which provides that persons compelled to turn over incriminating papers or other physical evidence pursuant to a subpoena duces tecum or a summons may invoke the Fifth Amendment privilege against self-incrimination as a bar to production only where the act of producing the evidence would contain "testimonial" features. I join the opinion of the Court because it properly applies this doctrine, but I write separately to note that this doctrine may be inconsistent with the original meaning of the Fifth Amendment's Self-Incrimination Clause. A substantial body of evidence suggests that the Fifth Amendment privilege protects against the compelled production not just of incriminating testimony, but of any incriminating evidence. In a future case, I would be willing to reconsider the scope and meaning of the Self-Incrimination Clause. . . .

This Court has not always taken the approach to the Fifth Amendment that we follow today. The first case interpreting the Self-Incrimination Clause—Boyd v. United States—was decided, though not explicitly, in accordance with the understanding that "witness" means one who gives evidence [whether in testimonial form or otherwise]. In *Boyd*, this Court unanimously held that the Fifth Amendment protects a defendant against compelled production of books and papers. And the Court linked its interpretation of the Fifth Amendment to the common-law understanding of the self-incrimination privilege.

But this Court's decision in Fisher v. United States rejected this understanding, permitting the Government to force a person to furnish incriminating physical evidence and protecting only the "testimonial" aspects of that transfer. In so doing, *Fisher* not only failed to examine the historical backdrop to the Fifth Amendment, it also required—as illustrated by extended discussion in the opinions below in this case—a difficult parsing of the act of responding to a subpoena duces tecum.

None of the parties in this case has asked us to depart from *Fisher*, but in light of the historical evidence that the Self-Incrimination Clause may have a broader reach than *Fisher* holds, I remain open to a reconsideration of that decision and its progeny in a proper case.

Chief Justice Rehnquist dissents and would reverse the judgment of the Court of Appeals in part, for the reasons given by Judge Williams in his dissenting opinion in that court, 167 F.3d 552, 597 (CADC 1999).

NOTES AND QUESTIONS

1. The critical question after *Hubbell* is much the same as it was beforehand: Under what circumstances can the grand jury subpoena records from a person and then use the contents of those documents to prosecute that person? Recall in *Fisher*, supra, the Court said that the act of production could implicate the Fifth Amendment, but where the existence of the documents was a foregone conclusion, the protection did not apply. *Hubbell* added another wrinkle—the government acknowledged that Mr. Hubbell could refuse to produce the documents on Fifth Amendment grounds, but then immunized the act of production. The question then became whether the government's reliance on the content of the documents to investigate and prosecute is the "direct or indirect use" of the three implicit statements Hubbell made when he turned over his boxes of documents.

The government rarely needs to make direct use of the three statements implicit in the act of production. Prosecutors in white-collar cases do not need to tell juries that the defendant handed over incriminating documents; they can authenticate documents through experts, and the documents prove their own existence. Thus, the government argued in *Hubbell*, as long as the prosecutor treats the documents as if they magically appeared in her office, with no use being made of where they came from, the government is free to use the contents of the documents.

Hubbell disagreed, finding that the prosecutors had made indirect use of the immunized statements, and did so in a way that tainted the contents of the documents. The Court's reasoning is deceptively simple: The government served a very broad subpoena on Mr. Hubbell, one that required a great deal of effort and thought to sort through a huge number of documents to find the ones that were responsive. When Hubbell produced the responsive documents under a grant of immunity—when he testified, in effect, that "these documents exist"—he was revealing information that had previously been unknown to prosecutors. As a result, when the government relied on the content of the documents to further its investigation, it was making indirect use of the immunized testimony—"but for" that implicit testimony, the prosecutor would have been unaware of the document's existence, and thus, its contents.

2. Although Mr. Hubbell's claim was upheld, applying the reasoning of the case is a challenge. The opinion emphasized that the act of production was not just a physical act, but instead, required Hubbell "to make extensive use of 'the contents of his own mind' in identifying the hundreds of documents responsive to the requests in the subpoena." More pointedly, (maybe) Justice Stevens indicates that it is any use of the defendant's mind that matters when he says, "The assembly of those [subpoenaed] documents was like telling an inquisitor the combination to a wall safe, not like being forced to surrender the key to a strongbox." This suggests that physical acts are unprotected while any communicative aspects of those acts that require access to the defendant's thoughts are protected. In another part of the *Hubbell* opinion not excerpted above, the Court reaffirmed its previous cases that held certain incriminating actions were not protected by the Fifth Amendment:

> [E]ven though the act may provide incriminating evidence, a criminal suspect may be compelled to put on a shirt, to provide a blood sample or handwriting exemplar, or to make a recording of his voice. The act of exhibiting such physical characteristics is not the same as a sworn communication by a witness that relates either express or implied assertions of fact or belief. Similarly, the fact that incriminating evidence may be the byproduct of obedience to a regulatory requirement, such as filing an income tax return, maintaining required records, or reporting an accident, does not clothe such required conduct with the testimonial privilege.

Hubbell, 530 U.S., at 35.

Is the act/statement distinction helpful? Is it clear, as the majority in *Hubbell* says, that the assembling of the documents called for by the subpoena was the "functional equivalent of the preparation of an answer to either a detailed written interrogatory or a series of oral questions at a discovery deposition" and therefore within the protections of the Fifth Amendment?

3. Going forward, the critical question would seem to be how certain the government must be of a subpoenaed document's existence before it can use the contents in a later prosecution. If the document's existence really is a "foregone conclusion," then *Fisher* holds that the Fifth Amendment doesn't apply at all, so there should be no occasion for the government to immunize the production. But the

kind of sweeping subpoena at issue in *Hubbell* will frequently result in the contents of the documents being tainted. As noted in the Supreme Court opinion, the court of appeals in *Hubbell* said that the government must be able to identify the document with "reasonable particularity" before issuing the subpoena to avoid making improper use of the act of production. Perhaps because the government acknowledged that it could not meet this test, the Supreme Court did not have occasion to discuss the standard further.

D.   *The Screening Function*

As Chapter 9 shows, prosecutors have very broad power to decide whom to charge and for what. But how long are those decisions beyond the courts' power to review? Does the authority to file charges entitle the government not only to file charges, but also to sustain a case until it is resolved at a trial or through a guilty plea? Or is the charging power qualified by some screening mechanism, some criminal procedure equivalent to summary judgment, by which bad charging decisions are separated from good ones?

The answer is layered. There is indeed a mechanism to review the prosecutor's charging decisions—in fact, there are two of them. In modern times, the preliminary hearing is often used as a judicial check on the charging decisions. In addition, both the historical and current function of the grand jury is to screen the charges, making sure that formal accusations are based on enough evidence to warrant a full trial. But as described below, sometimes the accused gets both a preliminary hearing and grand jury review; in many other cases, a defendant is not afforded a preliminary hearing but the grand jury reviews the case; and in still other cases, the defendant waives both the preliminary hearing and grand jury review, so he gets neither. More importantly, even when one or both of these procedures occur, there remains great skepticism about how effective a screen they are.

1.   Preliminary Hearings

In a typical case, after the suspect is arrested the police or prosecutor will file a criminal complaint, which is defined in Federal Rule of Criminal Procedure 3 as a "written statement of the essential facts constituting the offense charged." If the charge is a misdemeanor, the complaint may be the final charging instrument, but for felony charges, the complaint will, at some point, be replaced by a formal charging document, either an "information" or an "indictment." Each of these documents is prepared by the prosecutor and filed with the court, and each sets forth in some detail the crimes charged; the difference is that an indictment is a pleading approved by the grand jury, while an information is not subject to grand jury review.

Federal Rule 5.1 provides that at some point after a suspect is arrested and has had his first appearance before a judge, he is entitled to a preliminary hearing on the charges set forth in the complaint. This hearing is to be held no more than 14 days after the first appearance if the defendant is in custody, within 21 days if he is not. The purpose of the preliminary hearing is for the court to determine if there is "probable cause to believe that an offense has been committed and the defendant committed it." Rule 5.1(e).

Note that a defendant who is entitled to a preliminary hearing has, by definition, already been arrested, which means that a judicial finding of probable cause has already been made. If the arrest was pursuant to a warrant, the judge necessarily found, prior to the arrest, probable cause to believe the defendant committed the crime; if the arrest was made without a warrant, the defendant was entitled to a probable cause determination within 48 hours after the arrest. See County of Riverside v. McLaughlin, 500 U.S. 44 (1991). We might wonder, then, why a second probable cause hearing—a couple of weeks later at a preliminary hearing—is needed.

The answer is that, unlike the earlier probable cause determination, the preliminary hearing is adversarial. The probable cause finding for an arrest warrant is ex parte, and the finding at the first appearance is often perfunctory and made without defense counsel being present. But at a preliminary hearing, the defendant has the right to cross-examine witnesses and introduce evidence of his own, so now the government's claim of probable cause can, in theory, be vigorously challenged. Most important, the defendant is now represented by counsel. The Supreme Court concluded in Coleman v. Alabama, 399 U.S. 1 (1970), that a preliminary hearing is a "critical stage" to which the Sixth Amendment right attaches. Justice Brennan's plurality opinion highlighted the importance of both the adversarial process and the presence of a lawyer:

> Plainly the guiding hand of counsel at the preliminary hearing is essential to protect the indigent accused against an erroneous or improper prosecution. First, the lawyer's skilled examination and cross-examination of witnesses may expose fatal weaknesses in the State's case that may lead the magistrate to refuse to bind the accused over. Second, in any event, the skilled interrogation of witnesses by an experienced lawyer can fashion a vital impeachment tool for use in cross-examination of the state's witnesses at the trial, or preserve testimony favorable to the accused of a witness who does not appear at the trial. Third, trained counsel can more effectively discover the case the State has against his client and make possible the preparation of a proper defense to meet that case at the trial. Fourth, counsel can also be influential at the preliminary hearing in making effective arguments for the accused on such matters as the necessity for an early psychiatric examination or bail.

Id., at 9.

The government has the burden of persuasion at the preliminary hearing, and the prosecution presents its case through physical evidence and witnesses, much as it would at trial. The rules of evidence, however, are either relaxed or nonexistent, see Fed. R. Evid. 1101(d)(3), which means that hearsay information is likely to be freely admitted and heavily used. The ability to rely on hearsay is a great convenience for the government, because it means that it may not have to present the witnesses it will use at trial, and thus can avoid the possibility of cross-examination by the defense.

The defense can challenge the prosecutor's case, but whether it is wise to do so can raise hard strategic questions. On the one hand, the prosecutor's case will typically meet the probable cause threshold, and so defense counsel may be reluctant to cross-examine or introduce its own evidence that might reveal a defense strategy but is unlikely to change the result. Contesting the government's probable cause case might also reveal a hole in the prosecutor's case that, once revealed, can be fixed by the prosecutor prior to trial. On the other hand, discovery in criminal cases is often quite limited (see Chapter 12), and the defense may want to cross-examine a witness simply to learn something about the alleged facts and the government's theory of the case. Courts, however, are consistent in saying that preliminary hearings are not a discovery device, and so a judge may well cut off cross-examination if she believes the questions are irrelevant to the limited issue of probable cause.

But while courts are free to limit cross-examination in this way, lawyers on both sides need to be alert to the potential effect that such a decision can have. If the preliminary hearing witness later becomes unavailable to testify at trial, the inability of the defense to cross-examine fully may prevent the government from using the witness's preliminary hearing testimony as evidence. Under the Sixth Amendment Confrontation Clause, unless the defendant had a full chance to cross-examine the witness, the government is barred from using a transcript of the prior testimony as evidence at trial. See Crawford v. Washington, 541 U.S. 36 (2004) (testimonial evidence must be subject to confrontation to be admissible) (discussed in Chapter 14); Fed. R. Evid. 804(b)(1) (former testimony not excluded as hearsay if the opposing party had an "opportunity and similar motive" to cross-examine the declarant).

At the conclusion of the preliminary hearing, the magistrate judge will determine whether there is probable cause to move the case forward. If the judge finds no probable cause, she will dismiss the charges—but this does not prevent the government from filing new charges and putting the defendant through another preliminary hearing, or from seeking an indictment on the original charge from a grand jury. The bar on double jeopardy prevents the government from *trying* a defendant twice for the same crime, but not from *charging* him twice; this follows from the rule that "jeopardy" does not "attach" until either the trial jury is impaneled or the first witness is sworn. See Crist v. Bretz, 437 U.S. 28 (1978). But a preliminary hearing dismissal may, in practice, have more teeth than that rule might suggest: Most prosecutors will be wary of "going back to the well" on the precise charge that had been rejected at a preliminary hearing.

If, in a federal criminal case, the magistrate judge finds that probable cause exists, the case is then "bound over" to the grand jury, which will decide whether—you guessed it—there is probable cause to send the case forward to trial. If you wonder why there needs to be yet another probable cause determination, you need look no further than the Fifth Amendment, which, as noted, provides that in all felony cases the defendant has the right to grand jury review of the charges. So whether the defendant has a preliminary hearing or not, a federal prosecutor must present felony charges to the grand jury for a probable cause determination, unless the defendant waives that protection.

In contrast, the defendant has no constitutional right to a preliminary hearing; in fact, apart from the grand jury clause of the Fifth Amendment, there is no federal constitutional right to any review of a prosecutor's charging decision. See Gerstein v. Pugh, 420 U.S. 103, 119 (1975). And having still another proceeding to decide the same probable cause question really does seem duplicative. As a result, Federal Rule 5.1(a) provides that a defendant has a right to a preliminary hearing on felony charges *unless* the defendant waives that right *or* he is indicted by a grand jury before the preliminary hearing. Stated differently, the decision whether to afford the defendant a preliminary hearing rests largely in the prosecutor's hands—as long as there is a grand jury available that can return an indictment before the date of the preliminary hearing, the prosecutor can take the case directly to the grand jury and have the preliminary hearing canceled.

Why should this be so? If the purpose of the preliminary hearing is to review the prosecutor's charging decision, is it really appropriate to let that same prosecutor decide whether to let that review proceed? One response may be that the prosecutor is not avoiding a pretrial screen; he is just shifting the screening function from the preliminary hearing to the grand jury. But this, in turn, raises the obvious question of why there should be preliminary hearings at all.

At least superficially, the preliminary hearing would seem to offer a more effective method of screening charges. Preliminary hearings are open, adversarial, and the decision is made by a judge. Grand juries are secret, not adversarial, and decisions are made by the jurors. Recall also the discussion in *Coleman v. Alabama*, supra, about the importance of the guiding hand of counsel at the preliminary hearing, and recall that lawyers are not permitted to accompany their clients into the grand jury room. Given this, is it fair to view the two screening procedures as functional equivalents, as the rules do now?

Then again, if asked which procedure does a better job of eliminating weak charges, many observers would say "neither." Both procedures use the low "probable cause" threshold, both freely admit hearsay, and both fail to exclude illegally obtained and otherwise inadmissible evidence. In addition, experience has shown that both judges and grand juries approve the requested charges at very high rates. In the federal system, grand jurors return an indictment at the request of the prosecutor well over 99 percent of the time,[4] and while judges are somewhat more likely to reject a proposed charge at a preliminary hearing, it is unlikely the number of government failures here reach double digits.[5]

But it is important not to overread these figures, because the number of times a preliminary hearing or grand jury rejects a proposed criminal charge may tell us little about how often the prosecutor is deterred from bringing a weak charge. If the prosecutor knows that her proposed indictment or information will be rigorously tested, we would expect her not to pursue a weak case in the first place, which, in turn, should result in a very high approval rate. In short, it should be the *existence* of the review process, not its workings, that prevents the unfounded accusations.

One data point for measuring the effectiveness of preliminary hearings and/ or grand juries might be gleaned from the frequency with which defendants waive these protections. One practicing lawyer claims that in his jurisdiction, 90 percent of felony defendants waive preliminary hearings. See Michael J. Malkiewicz, Preliminary Hearing Can Improve Final Results in Criminal Cases, Del. Law., Winter 1989-1990, at 9. Other estimates are lower, but waiver clearly seems to be the rule rather than the exception. Of course, strength of the evidence is only one reason to waive. Malkiewicz goes on to list several others: Defense counsel lacks time or hasn't

---

4. See Andrew D. Leipold, Prosecutorial Charging Practices and Grand Jury Screening: Some Empirical Observations, in Roger A. Fairfax, Jr., ed., Grand Jury 2.0: Modern Perspectives on the Grand Jury (2010); Thomas P. Sullivan & Robert D. Nachman, If It Ain't Broke, Don't Fix It: Why the Grand Jury's Accusatory Function Should Not Be Changed, 75 J. Crim. L. & Criminology 1047, 1050, n. 16 (1984) (99.6 percent of federal grand jury returns were true bills).

5. Some older studies in state courts found preliminary hearing dismissal rates of three to eight percent. See Deborah Day Emerson & Nancy L. Ames, The Role of the Grand Jury and the Preliminary Hearing in Pretrial Screening 68 (1984); Kenneth Graham & Leon Letwin, The Preliminary Hearing in Los Angeles: Some Field Findings and Legal Policy Observations, 18 UCLA L. Rev. 635, 719-724 (1971).

been paid, limits on defense presentation of evidence make the allegation hard to refute, the prosecutor has told defense counsel that an indictment will issue even if the defense wins at the preliminary hearing, and the prosecutor offers defense counsel a copy of the police report in return for waiving the hearing. Last but not least, defense lawyers may think it more important to pursue a plea deal with a friendly and willing prosecutor than to force the prosecutor to show up for a preliminary hearing in anticipation of a trial that likely will never occur.

Grand jury review is waived less frequently, even though the rate at which the prosecutors' charges are approved is higher. In fiscal year 2012, there were over 83,000 federal felony defendants charged, and of this group, only 21 percent (roughly 17,000) were charged by information, indicating that they waived grand jury review.[6] It seems quite likely that those who proceeded by information planned to plead guilty eventually, as grand jury waivers are a frequent part of plea bargains made with the prosecutor.

Whether or not the government is worried about having charges rejected by the judge or a grand jury, there is also a significant amount of prosecutorial screening that goes on outside these procedures. In The Screening/Bargaining Tradeoff, 55 Stan. L. Rev. 29 (2002), Ronald Wright and Marc Miller discuss a screening system used by the District Attorney's office in New Orleans. Roughly 20 percent of the lawyers in the New Orleans D.A.'s office work in part of the office known as the Screening Section. After the bail hearing, every case is reviewed by that Section:

> . . . [D]esignated cases such as homicide or rape get assigned to screeners with special expertise. Drug cases and a few other high-volume cases go to a subgroup known as Expedited Screening. Ordinary cases go to the Screening Attorney on duty for that day. The screener reviews the investigation file, speaks to all the key witnesses and the victims (often by telephone, but sometimes in person), and generally gauges the strength of the case. If the police report neglects to mention a factual issue that is likely to arise at trial, the screening attorney will speak directly with the police officer to resolve it. There is a powerful office expectation that the Screening Attorney will make a decision within ten days of receiving the folder.

Id., at 63. This screening process is ex parte: Neither the defendant nor defense counsel is present. (For a sharp criticism of the New Orleans system on this ground, see Gerard Lynch, Screening Versus Plea Bargaining: Exactly What Are We Trading Off?, 55 Stan. L. Rev. 1399 (2003).) In New Orleans, the Screening Section has largely taken the place of preliminary hearings and grand juries. It has also, according to Wright and Miller, taken the place of most plea bargaining—a great advantage, in their view. The weeding-out that, elsewhere, takes place in formal legal screens and bargaining sessions is now performed almost entirely by the screeners in the D.A.'s office.

Professors Wright and Miller may be right that the New Orleans system is a model that other jurisdictions should copy. Or it could be that paper screening systems would be more suitable. Or perhaps grand juries and preliminary hearings are

---

6. These figures are derived from a dataset maintained by the Federal Justice Statistics Resource Center (FJSRC), a project of the Bureau of Justice Statistics. See BJS Federal Justice Statistics Program website (http://www.bjs.gov/fjsrc/). The data comes from the case management files of the Administrative Office of the U.S. Courts. The file from which the data are taken is listed on the FJSRC Web page as "Defendants Charged in Criminal Cases."

better screens than the conventional wisdom would have it. Regardless, one point seems clear: In a system that resolves a huge majority of cases without trials, the choice of how best to screen prosecutors' charging decisions is critically important to the quality of justice the system delivers.

2. Grand Jury Review

Even if the grand jury process makes it relatively easy for the prosecutor to obtain an indictment, meaningful pretrial screening might still occur if it were easy to challenge the indictment *after* it is returned. Perhaps it would make sense to give the prosecutors a free hand in getting a formal charge, but then once the government formally commits itself to prosecute, subject the indictment to judicial review after the fact. This section explores that issue.

Before turning to the substantive law, it is important to keep in mind the procedural setting in which the challenges to the grand jury arise. Because grand jury hearings are secret, defendants typically have no way of knowing what the prosecutor did or said in the grand jury room, making a motion to dismiss the indictment for irregularities in the process very difficult to sustain. Although Rule 6(e)(3)(E)(ii) says that a court can disclose grand jury material to "a defendant who shows that a ground may exist to dismiss the indictment because of a matter that occurred before the grand jury," it is often hard for the defendant to make even a preliminary showing of need without some access to the transcript of what took place. As you read the cases, notice how often the procedural posture of the case affects the rules the Court adopts for regulating grand jury practice.

COSTELLO v. UNITED STATES

Certiorari to the United States Court of Appeals for the Second Circuit
350 U.S. 359 (1956)

JUSTICE BLACK delivered the opinion of the Court.

We granted certiorari in this case to consider a single question: "May a defendant be required to stand trial and a conviction be sustained where only hearsay evidence was presented to the grand jury which indicted him?"

Petitioner, Frank Costello, was indicted for wilfully attempting to evade payment of income taxes due the United States for the years 1947, 1948, and 1949. The charge was that petitioner falsely and fraudulently reported less income than he and his wife actually received during the taxable years in question. Petitioner promptly filed a motion for inspection of the minutes of the grand jury and for a dismissal of the indictment. His motion was based on an affidavit stating that he was firmly convinced there could have been no legal or competent evidence before the grand jury which indicted him since he had reported all his income and paid all taxes due. The motion was denied. At the trial which followed the Government offered evidence designed to show increases in Costello's net worth in an attempt to prove that he had received more income during the years in question than he had reported. To establish its case the Government called and examined 144 witnesses and introduced 368 exhibits. All of the testimony and documents related to business transactions and expenditures by petitioner and his wife. The prosecution concluded its case by calling three government agents. Their investigations had produced the evidence used against petitioner at the trial. They were allowed to summarize the vast amount of evidence already heard and to introduce computations showing, if correct, that petitioner and his wife had received far greater income than they had reported. We have held such summarizations admissible in a "net worth" case like this. United States v. Johnson, 319 U.S. 503.

Counsel for petitioner asked each government witness at the trial whether he had appeared before the grand jury which returned the indictment. This cross-examination developed the fact that the three investigating officers had been the only witnesses before the grand jury. After the Government concluded its case, petitioner again moved to dismiss the indictment on the ground that the only evidence before the grand jury was "hearsay," since the three officers had no first-hand knowledge of the transactions upon which their computations were based. Nevertheless the trial court again refused to dismiss the indictment, and petitioner was convicted. The Court of Appeals affirmed, holding that the indictment was valid even though the sole evidence before the grand jury was hearsay. Petitioner here urges: (1) that an indictment based solely on hearsay evidence violates that part of the Fifth Amendment providing that "No person shall be held to answer for a capital, or otherwise infamous crime, unless on a presentment or indictment of a Grand Jury . . ." and (2) that if the Fifth Amendment does not invalidate an indictment based solely on hearsay we should now lay down such a rule for the guidance of federal courts.

The Fifth Amendment provides that federal prosecutions for capital or otherwise infamous crimes must be instituted by presentments or indictments of grand juries. But neither the Fifth Amendment nor any other constitutional provision prescribes the kind of evidence upon which grand juries must act. The grand jury is an English institution, brought to this country by the early colonists and incorporated in the Constitution by the Founders. There is every reason to believe that our constitutional grand jury was intended to operate substantially like its English progenitor. The basic purpose of the English grand jury was to provide a fair method for instituting criminal proceedings against persons believed to have committed crimes. Grand jurors were selected from the body of the people and their work was not hampered by rigid procedural or evidential rules. In fact, grand jurors could act on their own knowledge and were free to make their presentments or indictments on such information as they deemed satisfactory. Despite its broad power to institute criminal proceedings the grand jury grew in popular favor with the years. It acquired an independence in England free from control by the Crown or judges. Its adoption in our Constitution as the sole method for preferring charges in serious criminal cases shows the high place it held as an instrument of justice. And in this country as in England of old the grand jury has convened as a body of laymen, free from technical rules, acting in secret, pledged to indict no one because of prejudice and to free no one because of special favor. As late as 1927 an English historian could say that English grand juries were still free to act on their own knowledge if they pleased to do so. And in 1852 Mr. Justice Nelson on circuit could say "No case has been cited, nor have we been able to find any, furnishing an authority for looking into and revising the judgment of the grand jury upon the evidence, for the purpose of determining whether or not the finding was founded upon sufficient proof. . . ." United States v. Reed, 27 Fed. Cas. 727, 738.

In Holt v. United States, 218 U.S. 245, this Court had to decide whether an indictment should be quashed because supported in part by incompetent evidence. Aside from the incompetent evidence "there was very little evidence against the accused." The Court refused to hold that such an indictment should be quashed, pointing out that "The abuses of criminal practice would be enhanced if indictments could be upset on such a ground." 218 U.S., at 248. The same thing is true where as here all the evidence before the grand jury was in the nature of "hearsay." If indictments were to be held open to challenge on the ground that there was inadequate or incompetent evidence before the grand jury, the resulting delay would be great indeed. The result of such a rule would be that before trial on the merits a defendant could always insist on a kind of preliminary trial to determine the competency and adequacy of the evidence before the grand jury. This is not required by the Fifth Amendment. An indictment returned by a legally constituted and unbiased grand jury, like an information drawn by the prosecutor, if valid on its face, is enough to call for trial of the charge on the merits. The Fifth Amendment requires nothing more.

Petitioner urges that this Court should exercise its power to supervise the administration of justice in federal courts and establish a rule permitting defendants to challenge indictments on the ground that they are not supported by adequate or competent evidence. No persuasive reasons are advanced for establishing such a rule. It would run counter to the whole history of the grand jury institution, in which laymen conduct their inquiries unfettered by technical rules. Neither justice nor the concept of a fair trial requires such a change. In a trial on the merits, defendants are entitled to a strict observance of all the rules designed to bring about a fair verdict. Defendants are not entitled, however, to a rule which would result in interminable delay but add nothing to the assurance of a fair trial.

Affirmed.

JUSTICE CLARK and JUSTICE HARLAN took no part in the consideration or decision of this case.

JUSTICE BURTON, concurring.

I agree with the denial of the motion to quash the indictment. In my view, however, this case does not justify the breadth of the declarations made by the Court. I assume that this Court would not preclude an examination of grand-jury action to ascertain the existence of bias or prejudice in an indictment. Likewise, it seems to me that if it is shown that the grand jury had before it no substantial or rationally persuasive evidence upon which to base its indictment, that indictment should be quashed. To hold a person to answer to such an empty indictment for a capital or otherwise infamous federal crime robs the Fifth Amendment of much of its protective value to the private citizen.

Here, . . . substantial and rationally persuasive evidence apparently was presented to the grand jury. We may fairly assume that the evidence before that jury included much of the testimony later given at the trial by the three government agents who said that they had testified before the grand jury. At the trial, they summarized financial transactions of the accused about which they were not qualified to testify of their own knowledge. To use Justice Holmes' phrase in [Holt v. United States, 218 U.S. 245], such testimony, standing alone, was "incompetent by circumstances" (supra, at 248), and yet it was rationally persuasive of the crime charged and provided a substantial basis for the indictment. At the trial, with preliminary testimony laying the foundation for it, the same testimony constituted an important part of the competent evidence upon which the conviction was obtained.

To sustain this indictment under the above circumstances is well enough, but I agree with Judge Learned Hand that "if it appeared that no evidence had been offered that rationally established the facts, the indictment ought to be quashed; because then the grand jury would have in substance abdicated." 221 F.2d 668, 677. . . .

NOTES AND QUESTIONS

1. Frank Costello, the petitioner in Costello v. United States, was a celebrity of sorts. The alleged head of the Gambino crime family, Costello was called in 1951 to testify before the Kefauver Committee, a Senate committee investigating organized crime. As this was in the early days of television, the networks were scrambling to find programming to fill daytime slots; they seized on the public hearings and televised them in full, and the hearings attracted a nationwide audience. Costello, unlike some of the other witnesses the committee called, agreed initially to testify (i.e., he agreed not to invoke his privilege against self-incrimination), but only on the condition that the television cameras not show his face. The cameras instead zeroed in on Costello's hands, which fidgeted nervously throughout his testimony; Costello's fingers drumming and fists clenching made for far better theater than showing his face would have been. For a good, brief account, see William Manchester, The Glory and the Dream 734-735 (1973). To millions of Americans, Costello—or at least Costello's hands—became the personification of the Mob.

The hearings made Estes Kefauver, the chair of the investigating committee and a previously unknown senator from Tennessee, a national figure; in both 1952 and 1956, Kefauver narrowly missed winning the Democratic presidential nomination, and in the latter year he was the vice presidential nominee. They also led to Costello's successful prosecution for income tax evasion. That prosecution, in turn, produced what is still the leading decision defining the scope of the grand jury's authority to indict, and the limits of judicial authority to overturn indictments.

2. What exactly did the Court hold in Costello? The issue argued in the case was whether an indictment could be based wholly on evidence that would normally have been inadmissible hearsay at trial. (As a matter of evidence law, the agents' testimony in Costello was admissible at trial only because other witnesses with direct knowledge had testified to the same facts the agents were summarizing, but those other witnesses didn't testify before the grand jury.) Obviously, the Court resolved that question in the government's favor, but that was hardly a surprise; existing case law made the answer fairly clear even before Costello. The more important aspect of the decision is what it says about judicial review of the merits of the indictment—whether, for example, a court can dismiss an indictment because the evidence was insufficient (not just inadmissible). On that question, the Court says very little, but what it says is very important: Reread the last two paragraphs of Justice Black's opinion, and note especially the declaration that indictments that are valid on their face are valid, period.

3. Despite Justice Burton's attempt to limit the reach of *Costello*, the case has come to stand for the proposition that grand jury decisions to indict are largely unreviewable on the merits. What justifies that proposition? The Court's opinion suggests two reasons: (1) Review of decisions to indict would turn into a mini-trial prior to the real trial, and would thus be too administratively costly, and (2) review of decisions to indict would compromise the grand jury's independence.

How substantial are these justifications? As to the first, note that civil litigation has a fairly low-cost procedure for judicial resolution of clear cases without going through the trial process—summary judgment—and no one thinks *that* procedure is too difficult to administer. Why would review of decisions to indict be different? Isn't there something strange about the proposition that we take more seriously civil litigants' interest in being free from the burdens of civil trials than criminal defendants' interest in avoiding the costs and reputational harms associated with criminal trials? On the other hand, judicial review is unnecessary if grand juries already screen cases reasonably well. Do you read *Costello* as saying that as a matter of *fact*, grand juries eliminate weak cases?

As for the need to protect grand juries' independence, the relevant question is, independence from whom? *Costello* makes grand juries' decisions to indict independent of *judicial* control. But those decisions are, in practice, far from independent of *prosecutorial* control. Grand jury proceedings are conducted with little or no judicial oversight, and *Costello* reaffirms that the laws of evidence do not limit what evidence or argument prosecutors can present. In these circumstances, it is hardly surprising that prosecutors generally find it easy to obtain indictments when they want them; as Sol Wachtler, then–chief judge of the New York Court of Appeals, famously put it, a grand jury will indict a ham sandwich if so instructed by the prosecutor. (It should be noted that Wachtler later had some experience of his own with grand juries: He was indicted, and convicted, of making threats by mail in 1993 and served 13 months in federal prison.)

4. The concept of the grand jury as a truly independent entity is more plausible if one looks at the institution's history. Recall from Section A of this chapter that grand juries in colonial America often served as a monitor of government action and as an informal local legislative body. In addition, colonial grand juries could not possibly be dominated by professional prosecutors, because professional prosecutors did not exist. Indictments were regularly the product of the grand jurors' own information and their own investigation—and in a society where men tended to know a good deal about their neighbors, not much investigation was necessary. See Peter C. Hoffer & William B. Scott, Criminal Proceedings in Colonial Virginia xxvii-xxviii (1984).

Note the implication of this history for the kind of grand jury review at issue in *Costello*. The essence of the historical grand jury is the separation of charging from prosecution: Grand juries decided whom to charge and for what; prosecution was done by private parties, constables, or ad hoc public prosecutors. By the time of *Costello*, charging and prosecution were both jobs assigned to full-time professional prosecutors. Grand juries no longer seem to function as independent actors, but rather, serve as evaluators of the decisions that prosecutors make—a significantly different role. And the grand jury's sole source of information is the prosecutor whose decision it must evaluate.

Does that role make any sense today? If not, why have grand juries survived so long?

UNITED STATES v. WILLIAMS

Certiorari to the United States Court of Appeals for the Tenth Circuit
504 U.S. 36 (1992)

JUSTICE SCALIA delivered the opinion of the Court.

The question presented in this case is whether a district court may dismiss an otherwise valid indictment because the Government failed to disclose to the grand jury "substantial exculpatory evidence" in its possession.

I

On May 4, 1988, respondent John H. Williams, Jr., a Tulsa, Oklahoma, investor, was indicted by a federal grand jury on seven counts of "knowingly making [a] false statement or report . . . for the purpose of influencing . . . the action [of a federally insured financial institution]," in violation of 18 U.S.C. §1014. According to the indictment, between September 1984 and November 1985 Williams supplied four Oklahoma banks with "materially false" statements that variously overstated the value of his current assets and interest income in order to influence the banks' actions on his loan requests.

Williams' misrepresentation was allegedly effected through two financial statements provided to the banks, a "Market Value Balance Sheet" and a "Statement of Projected Income and Expense." The former included as "current assets" approximately $6 million in notes receivable from three venture capital companies. Though it contained a disclaimer that these assets were carried at cost rather than at market value, the Government asserted that listing them as "current assets"—i.e., assets quickly reducible to cash—was misleading, since Williams knew that none of the venture capital companies could afford to satisfy the notes in the short term. The second document—the Statement of Projected Income and Expense—allegedly misrepresented Williams' interest income, since it failed to reflect that the interest payments received on the notes of the venture capital companies were funded entirely by Williams' own loans to those companies. The Statement thus falsely implied, according to the Government, that Williams was deriving interest income from "an independent outside source."

Shortly after arraignment, the District Court granted Williams' motion for disclosure of all exculpatory portions of the grand jury transcripts. See Brady v. Maryland, 373 U.S. 83 (1963). Upon reviewing this material, Williams demanded that the District Court dismiss the indictment, alleging that the Government had failed to fulfill its obligation under the Tenth Circuit's prior decision in United States v. Page, 808 F.2d 723, 728 (1987), to present "substantial exculpatory evidence" to the grand jury (emphasis omitted). His contention was that evidence which the Government had chosen not to present to the grand jury—in particular, Williams' general ledgers and tax returns, and Williams' testimony in his contemporaneous Chapter 11 bankruptcy proceeding—disclosed that, for tax purposes and otherwise, he had regularly accounted for the "notes receivable" (and the interest on them) in a manner consistent with the Balance Sheet and the Income Statement. This, he contended, belied an intent to mislead the banks, and thus directly negated an essential element of the charged offense.

The District Court initially denied Williams' motion, but upon reconsideration ordered the indictment dismissed without prejudice. It found, after a hearing, that the withheld evidence was "relevant to an essential element of the crime charged," created "a reasonable doubt about [respondent's] guilt," and thus "rendered the grand jury's decision to indict gravely suspect." Upon the Government's appeal, the Court of Appeals affirmed the District Court's order. . . . It . . . found that the Government's behavior " 'substantially influenced'" the grand jury's decision to indict, or at the very least raised a " 'grave doubt that the decision to indict was free from such substantial influence.'" 899 F.2d, at 903 (quoting Bank of Nova Scotia v. United States, 487 U.S. 250, 263 (1988)). Under these circumstances, the Tenth Circuit concluded, it was not an abuse of discretion for the District Court to require the Government to begin anew before the grand jury. . . .

III

Respondent does not contend that the Fifth Amendment itself obliges the prosecutor to disclose substantial exculpatory evidence in his possession to the grand jury. Instead, building on our statement that the federal courts "may, within limits, formulate procedural rules not specifically required by the Constitution or the Congress," United States v. Hasting, 461 U.S. 499, 505 (1983), he argues that imposition of the Tenth Circuit's disclosure rule is supported by the courts' "supervisory power." We think not. *Hasting*, and the cases that rely upon the principle it expresses, deal strictly with the courts' power to control their own procedures. See, e.g., Jencks v. United States, 353 U.S. 657, 667-668 (1957); McNabb v. United States, 318 U.S. 332 (1943). That power has been applied not only to improve the truth-finding process of the trial, but also to prevent parties from reaping benefit or incurring harm from violations of substantive or procedural rules (imposed by the Constitution or laws) governing matters apart from the trial itself, see, e.g., Weeks v. United States, 232 U.S. 383 (1914). [*Weeks* is the case that established the exclusionary rule as a remedy for Fourth Amendment violations.—EDS.] Thus, Bank of Nova Scotia v. United States, 487 U.S. 250 (1988), makes clear that the supervisory power can be used to dismiss an indictment because of misconduct before the grand jury, at least where that misconduct amounts to a violation of one of those "few, clear rules which were carefully drafted and approved by this Court and by Congress to ensure the integrity of the grand jury's functions," United States v. Mechanik, 475 U.S. 66, 74 (1986) (O'Connor, J., concurring in judgment).[6]

We did not hold in *Bank of Nova Scotia*, however, that the courts' supervisory power could be used, not merely as a means of enforcing or vindicating legally compelled standards of prosecutorial conduct before the grand jury, but as a means of prescribing those standards of prosecutorial conduct in the first instance—just as it may be used as a means of establishing standards of prosecutorial conduct before the courts themselves. It is this latter exercise that respondent demands. Because the grand jury is an institution separate from the courts, over whose functioning

---

6. Rule 6 of the Federal Rules of Criminal Procedure contains a number of such rules, providing, for example, that "no person other than the jurors may be present while the grand jury is deliberating or voting," Rule 6(d), and placing strict controls on disclosure of "matters occurring before the grand jury," Rule 6(e); see generally United States v. Sells Engineering, Inc., 463 U.S. 418 (1983). Additional standards of behavior for prosecutors (and others) are set forth in the United States Code. See 18 U.S.C. §§6002, 6003 (setting forth procedures for granting a witness immunity from prosecution); §1623 (criminalizing false declarations before grand jury); §2515 (prohibiting grand jury use of unlawfully intercepted wire or oral communications); §1622 (criminalizing subornation of perjury).

the courts do not preside, we think it clear that, as a general matter at least, no such "supervisory" judicial authority exists, and that the disclosure rule applied here exceeded the Tenth Circuit's authority.

A

"Rooted in long centuries of Anglo-American history," Hannah v. Larche, 363 U.S. 420, 490 (1960) (Frankfurter, J., concurring in result), the grand jury is mentioned in the Bill of Rights, but not in the body of the Constitution. It has not been textually assigned, therefore, to any of the branches described in the first three Articles. . . . In fact the whole theory of its function is that it belongs to no branch of the institutional Government, serving as a kind of buffer or referee between the Government and the people. Although the grand jury normally operates, of course, in the courthouse and under judicial auspices, its institutional relationship with the Judicial Branch has traditionally been, so to speak, at arm's length. Judges' direct involvement in the functioning of the grand jury has generally been confined to the constitutive one of calling the grand jurors together and administering their oaths of office. See United States v. Calandra, 414 U.S. 338, 343 (1974); Fed. Rule Crim. Proc. 6(a).

The grand jury's functional independence from the Judicial Branch is evident both in the scope of its power to investigate criminal wrongdoing and in the manner in which that power is exercised. "Unlike [a] court, whose jurisdiction is predicated upon a specific case or controversy, the grand jury can investigate merely on suspicion that the law is being violated, or even because it wants assurance that it is not." United States v. R. Enterprises, Inc., 498 U.S. 292, 297 (1991). It need not identify the offender it suspects, or even "the precise nature of the offense" it is investigating. Blair v. United States, 250 U.S. 273, 282 (1919). The grand jury requires no authorization from its constituting court to initiate an investigation, nor does the prosecutor require leave of court to seek a grand jury indictment. And in its day-to-day functioning, the grand jury generally operates without the interference of a presiding judge. It swears in its own witnesses, Fed. Rule Crim. Proc. 6(c), and deliberates in total secrecy.

True, the grand jury cannot compel the appearance of witnesses and the production of evidence, and must appeal to the court when such compulsion is required. And the court will refuse to lend its assistance when the compulsion the grand jury seeks would override rights accorded by the Constitution, see, e.g., Gravel v. United States, 408 U.S. 606 (1972) (grand jury subpoena effectively qualified by order limiting questioning so as to preserve Speech or Debate Clause immunity), or even testimonial privileges recognized by the common law, see In re Grand Jury Investigation of Hugle, 754 F.2d 863 (CA9 1985) (opinion of Kennedy, J.) (same with respect to privilege for confidential marital communications). Even in this setting, however, we have insisted that the grand jury remain "free to pursue its investigations unhindered by external influence or supervision so long as it does not trench upon the legitimate rights of any witness called before it." United States v. Dionisio, 410 U.S. 1, 17-18 (1973). Recognizing this tradition of independence, we have said that the Fifth Amendment's "constitutional guarantee *presupposes* an investigative body 'acting independently of either prosecuting attorney *or judge*.' . . ." Id., at 16 (emphasis added).

No doubt in view of the grand jury proceeding's status as other than a constituent element of a "criminal prosecution," U.S. Const., Amdt. 6, we have said that certain constitutional protections afforded defendants in criminal proceedings have no application before that body. The Double Jeopardy Clause of the Fifth Amendment does not bar a grand jury from returning an indictment when a prior grand jury has refused to do so. See Ex parte United States, 287 U.S. 241, 250-251 (1932). We have twice suggested, though not held, that the Sixth Amendment right to counsel does not attach when an individual is summoned to appear before a grand jury, even if he is the subject of the investigation. See United States v. Mandujano, 425 U.S. 564, 581 (1976) (plurality opinion); In re Groban, 352 U.S. 330, 333 (1957); see also Fed. Rule Crim. Proc. 6(d). And although "the grand jury may not force a witness to answer questions in violation of [the Fifth Amendment's] constitutional guarantee" against self-incrimination, our cases suggest that an indictment obtained through the use of evidence previously obtained in violation of the privilege against self-incrimination "is nevertheless valid." *Calandra*, supra, at 346; see Lawn v. United States, 355 U.S. 339, 348-350 (1958).

Given the grand jury's operational separateness from its constituting court, it should come as no surprise that we have been reluctant to invoke the judicial supervisory power as a basis for prescribing modes of grand jury procedure. Over the years, we have received many requests to exercise supervision over the grand jury's evidence-taking process, but we have refused them all, including some more appealing than the one presented today. In United States v. Calandra, supra, a grand jury witness faced questions that were allegedly based upon physical evidence the Government had obtained through a violation of the Fourth Amendment; we rejected the proposal that the exclusionary rule be extended to grand jury proceedings, because of "the potential injury to the historic role and functions of the grand jury." 414 U.S. at 349. In Costello v United States, 350 U.S. 359 (1956), we declined to enforce the hearsay rule in grand jury proceedings, since that "would run counter to the whole history of the grand jury institution, in which laymen conduct their inquiries unfettered by technical rules." Id., at 364.

These authorities suggest that any power federal courts may have to fashion, on their own initiative, rules of grand jury procedure is a very limited one, not remotely comparable to the power they maintain over their own proceedings. It certainly would not permit judicial reshaping of the grand jury institution, substantially altering the traditional relationships between the prosecutor, the constituting court, and the grand jury itself. As we proceed to discuss, that would be the consequence of the proposed rule here.

B

Respondent argues that the Court of Appeals' rule can be justified as a sort of Fifth Amendment "common law," a necessary means of assuring the constitutional right to the judgment "of an independent and informed grand jury." Respondent makes a generalized appeal to functional notions: Judicial supervision of the quantity and quality of the evidence relied upon by the grand jury plainly facilitates, he says, the grand jury's performance of its twin historical responsibilities, i.e., bringing to trial those who may be justly accused and shielding the innocent from unfounded accusation and prosecution. We do not agree. The rule would neither preserve nor enhance the traditional functioning of the institution that the Fifth Amendment demands. To the contrary, requiring the prosecutor to present exculpatory as well as inculpatory evidence would alter the grand jury's historical role, transforming it from an accusatory to an adjudicatory body.

It is axiomatic that the grand jury sits not to determine guilt or innocence, but to assess whether there is adequate basis for bringing a criminal charge. That has always been so; and to make the assessment it has always been thought sufficient to hear only the prosecutor's side. As Blackstone described the prevailing practice in 18th-century England, the grand jury was "only to hear evidence on behalf of the prosecution[,] for the finding of an indictment is only in the nature of an enquiry or accusation, which is afterwards to be tried and determined." 4 W. Blackstone, Commentaries 300 (1769); see also 2 M. Hale, Pleas of the Crown 157 (1st Am. ed. 1847). So also in the United States. According to the description of an early American court, three years before the Fifth Amendment was ratified, it is the grand jury's function not "to enquire . . . upon what foundation [the charge may be] denied," or otherwise to try the suspect's defenses, but only to examine "upon what foundation [the charge] is made" by the prosecutor. Respublica v. Shaffer, 1 U.S. (1 Dall.) 236 (O. T. Phila. 1788); see also F. Wharton, Criminal Pleading and Practice §360, pp. 248-249 (8th ed. 1880). As a consequence, neither in this country nor in England has the suspect under investigation by the grand jury ever been thought to have a right to testify or to have exculpatory evidence presented.

Imposing upon the prosecutor a legal obligation to present exculpatory evidence in his possession would be incompatible with this system. If a "balanced" assessment of the entire matter is the objective, surely the first thing to be done—rather than requiring the prosecutor to say what he knows in defense of the target of the investigation—is to entitle the target to tender his own defense. To require the former while denying (as we do) the latter would be quite absurd. It would also be quite pointless, since it would merely invite the target to circumnavigate the system by delivering his exculpatory evidence to the prosecutor, whereupon it would have to be passed on to the grand jury—unless the prosecutor is willing to take the chance that a court will not deem the evidence important enough to qualify for mandatory disclosure. See, e.g., United States v. Law Firm of Zimmerman & Schwartz, P.C., 738 F. Supp. 407, 411 (D. Colo. 1990) (duty to disclose exculpatory evidence held satisfied when prosecution tendered to the grand jury defense-provided exhibits, testimony, and explanations of the governing law).

Respondent acknowledges (as he must) that the "common law" of the grand jury is not violated if the grand jury itself chooses to hear no more evidence than that which suffices to convince it an indictment is proper. Thus, had the Government offered to familiarize the grand jury in this case with the five boxes of financial statements and deposition testimony alleged to contain exculpatory information, and had the grand jury rejected the offer as pointless, respondent would presumably agree that the resulting indictment would have been valid. Respondent insists, however, that courts must require the modern prosecutor to alert the grand jury to the nature and extent of the available exculpatory evidence, because otherwise the grand jury "merely functions as an arm of the prosecution." We reject the attempt to convert a non-existent duty of the grand jury itself into an obligation of the prosecutor. The authority of the prosecutor to seek an indictment has long been understood to be "coterminous with the authority of the grand jury to entertain [the prosecutor's] charges." United States v. Thompson, 251 U.S. at 414. If the grand jury has no obligation to consider all "substantial exculpatory" evidence, we do not understand how the prosecutor can be said to have a binding obligation to present it.

There is yet another respect in which respondent's proposal not only fails to comport with, but positively contradicts, the "common law" of the Fifth Amendment grand jury. Motions to quash indictments based upon the sufficiency of the evidence relied upon by the grand jury were unheard of at common law in England, see, e.g., People v. Restenblatt, 1 Abb. Pr. 268, 269 (Ct. Gen. Sess. N.Y. 1855). And the traditional American practice was described by Justice Nelson, riding circuit in 1852, as follows:

> No case has been cited, nor have we been able to find any, furnishing an authority for looking into and revising the judgment of the grand jury upon the evidence, for the purpose of determining whether or not the finding was founded upon sufficient proof, or whether there was a deficiency in respect to any part of the complaint.

. . . United States v. Reed, 27 F. Cas. (2 Blatchf.) 727, 738 (No. 16,134) (CC NDNY 1852).

We accepted Justice Nelson's description in Costello v. United States, where we held that "it would run counter to the whole history of the grand jury institution" to permit an indictment to be challenged "on the ground that there was inadequate or incompetent evidence before the grand jury." 350 U.S. at 363-364. . . . It would make little sense, we think, to abstain from reviewing the evidentiary support for the grand jury's judgment while scrutinizing the sufficiency of the prosecutor's presentation. A complaint about the quality or adequacy of the evidence can always be recast as a complaint that the prosecutor's presentation was "incomplete" or "misleading." Our words in *Costello* bear repeating: Review of facially valid indictments on such grounds "would run counter to the whole history of the grand jury institution[,] [and] neither justice nor the concept of a fair trial requires [it]." 350 U.S. at 364.

Echoing the reasoning of the Tenth Circuit in United States v. Page, 808 F.2d at 728, respondent argues that a rule requiring the prosecutor to disclose exculpatory evidence to the grand jury would, by removing from the docket unjustified prosecutions, save valuable judicial time. That depends, we suppose, upon what the ratio would turn out to be between unjustified prosecutions eliminated and grand jury indictments challenged—for the latter as well as the former consume "valuable judicial time." We need not pursue the matter; if there is an advantage to the proposal, Congress is free to prescribe it. For the reasons set forth above, however, we conclude that courts have no authority to prescribe such a duty pursuant to their inherent supervisory authority over their own proceedings. The judgment of the Court of Appeals is accordingly reversed, and the cause is remanded for further proceedings consistent with this opinion.

JUSTICE STEVENS, with whom JUSTICE BLACKMUN, JUSTICE O'CONNOR, and JUSTICE THOMAS join, dissenting.

. . . Like the Hydra slain by Hercules, prosecutorial misconduct has many heads. Some are cataloged in Justice Sutherland's classic opinion for the Court in Berger v. United States, 295 U.S. 78 (1935):

> That the United States prosecuting attorney overstepped the bounds of that propriety and fairness which should characterize the conduct of such an officer in the prosecution of a criminal offense is clearly shown by the record. He was guilty of misstating the facts in his cross-examination of witnesses; of putting into the mouths of such witnesses things which they had not said; of suggesting by his questions that statements had been made to him personally out of court, in respect of which no proof was offered; of pretending to understand that a witness had said something which he

had not said and persistently cross-examining the witness upon that basis; of assuming prejudicial facts not in evidence; of bullying and arguing with witnesses; and in general, of conducting himself in a thoroughly indecorous and improper manner.

. . . The prosecuting attorney's argument to the jury . . . [contained] improper insinuations and assertions calculated to mislead the jury. Id., at 84-85.

. . . Nor has prosecutorial misconduct been limited to judicial proceedings: The reported cases indicate that it has sometimes infected grand jury proceedings as well. The cases contain examples of prosecutors presenting perjured testimony, United States v. Basurto, 497 F.2d 781, 786 (CA9 1974), questioning a witness outside the presence of the grand jury and then failing to inform the grand jury that the testimony was exculpatory, United States v. Phillips Petroleum, Inc., 435 F. Supp. 610, 615-617 (ND Okla. 1977), failing to inform the grand jury of its authority to subpoena witnesses, United States v. Samango, 607 F.2d 877, 884 (CA9 1979), operating under a conflict of interest, United States v. Gold, 470 F. Supp. 1336, 1346-1351 (ND Ill. 1979), misstating the law, United States v. Roberts, 481 F. Supp. 1385, 1389, and n. 10 (CD Cal. 1980), and misstating the facts on cross-examination of a witness, United States v. Lawson, 502 F. Supp. 158, 162, and nn. 6-7 (Md. 1980).

Justice Sutherland's identification of the basic reason why that sort of misconduct is intolerable merits repetition:

> The United States Attorney is the representative not of an ordinary party to a controversy, but of a sovereignty whose obligation to govern impartially is as compelling as its obligation to govern at all; and whose interest, therefore, in a criminal prosecution is not that it shall win a case, but that justice shall be done. As such, he is in a peculiar and very definite sense the servant of the law, the twofold aim of which is that guilt shall not escape or innocence suffer. He may prosecute with earnestness and vigor—indeed, he should do so. But, while he may strike hard blows, he is not at liberty to strike foul ones. It is as much his duty to refrain from improper methods calculated to produce a wrongful conviction as it is to use every legitimate means to bring about a just one. Berger v. United States, 295 U.S. at 88.

It is equally clear that the prosecutor has the same duty to refrain from improper methods calculated to produce a wrongful indictment. Indeed, the prosecutor's duty to protect the fundamental fairness of judicial proceedings assumes special importance when he is presenting evidence to a grand jury. As the Court of Appeals for the Third Circuit recognized, "the costs of continued unchecked prosecutorial misconduct" before the grand jury are particularly substantial because there

> the prosecutor operates without the check of a judge or a trained legal adversary, and virtually immune from public scrutiny. The prosecutor's abuse of his special relationship to the grand jury poses an enormous risk to defendants as well. For while in theory a trial provides the defendant with a full opportunity to contest and disprove the charges against him, in practice, the handing up of an indictment will often have a devastating personal and professional impact that a later dismissal or acquittal can never undo. Where the potential for abuse is so great, and the consequences of a mistaken indictment so serious, the ethical responsibilities of the prosecutor, and the obligation of the judiciary to protect against even the appearance of unfairness, are correspondingly heightened. United States v. Serubo, 604 F.2d 807, 817 (1979).

. . . In an opinion that I find difficult to comprehend, the Court today . . . seems to suggest that the court has no authority to supervise the conduct of the prosecutor in grand jury proceedings so long as he follows the dictates of the Constitution, applicable statutes, and Rule 6 of the Federal Rules of Criminal Procedure. The Court purports to support this conclusion by invoking the doctrine of separation of powers and citing a string of cases in which we have declined to impose categorical restraints on the grand jury. Needless to say, the Court's reasoning is unpersuasive.

Although the grand jury has not been "textually assigned" to "any of the branches described in the first three Articles" of the Constitution, it is not an autonomous body completely beyond the reach of the other branches. Throughout its life, from the moment it is convened until it is discharged, the grand jury is subject to the control of the court. As Judge Learned Hand recognized over 60 years ago, "a grand jury is neither an officer nor an agent of the United States, but a part of the court." Falter v. United States, 23 F.2d 420, 425 (CA2 1928). . . .

This Court has, of course, long recognized that the grand jury has wide latitude to investigate violations of federal law as it deems appropriate and need not obtain permission from either the court or the prosecutor. Correspondingly, we have acknowledged that "its operation generally is unrestrained by the technical procedural and evidentiary rules governing the conduct of criminal trials." *Calandra,* 414 U.S. at 343. But this is because Congress and the Court have generally thought it best not to impose procedural restraints on the grand jury; it is not because they lack all power to do so.

To the contrary, the Court has recognized that it has the authority to create and enforce limited rules applicable in grand jury proceedings. Thus, for example, the Court has said that the grand jury "may not itself violate a valid privilege, whether established by the Constitution, statutes, or the common law." Id., at 346. And the Court may prevent a grand jury from violating such a privilege by quashing or modifying a subpoena, id., at 346, n. 4, or issuing a protective order forbidding questions in violation of the privilege, Gravel v. United States, 408 U.S. 606, 628-629 (1972). Moreover, there are, as the Court notes, a series of cases in which we declined to impose categorical restraints on the grand jury. In none of those cases, however, did we question our power to reach a contrary result. . . .

We do not protect the integrity and independence of the grand jury by closing our eyes to the countless forms of prosecutorial misconduct that may occur inside the secrecy of the grand jury room. After all, the grand jury is not merely an investigatory body; it also serves as a "protector of citizens against arbitrary and oppressive governmental action." United States v. Calandra, 414 U.S. at 343. Explaining why the grand jury must be both "independent" and "informed," the Court wrote in Wood v. Georgia, 370 U.S. 375 (1962):

> Historically, this body has been regarded as a primary security to the innocent against hasty, malicious and oppressive persecution; it serves the invaluable function in our society of standing between the accuser and the accused, whether the latter be an individual, minority group, or other, to determine whether a charge is founded upon reason or was dictated by an intimidating power or by malice and personal ill will. Id., at 390.

It blinks reality to say that the grand jury can adequately perform this important historic role if it is intentionally misled by the prosecutor—on whose knowledge of the law and facts of the underlying criminal investigation the jurors will, of necessity, rely. . . .

What, then, is the proper disposition of this case? I agree with the Government that the prosecutor is not required to place all exculpatory evidence before the grand jury. A grand jury proceeding is an ex parte investigatory proceeding to determine whether there is probable cause to believe a violation of the criminal laws has occurred, not a trial. Requiring the prosecutor to ferret out and present all evidence that could be used at trial to create a reasonable doubt as to the defendant's guilt would be inconsistent with the purpose of the grand jury proceeding and would place significant burdens on the investigation. But that does not mean that the prosecutor may mislead the grand jury into believing that there is probable cause to indict by withholding clear evidence to the contrary. I thus agree with the Department of Justice that "when a prosecutor conducting a grand jury inquiry is personally aware of substantial evidence which directly negates the guilt of a subject of the investigation, the prosecutor must present or otherwise disclose such evidence to the grand jury before seeking an indictment against such a person." U.S. Dept. of Justice, United States Attorneys' Manual 9-11.233, p. 88 (1988).

Although I question whether the evidence withheld in this case directly negates respondent's guilt, I need not resolve my doubts because the Solicitor General did not ask the Court to review the nature of the evidence withheld. Instead, he asked us to decide the legal question whether an indictment may be dismissed because the prosecutor failed to present exculpatory evidence. Unlike the Court and the Solicitor General, I believe the answer to that question is yes, if the withheld evidence would plainly preclude a finding of probable cause. I therefore cannot endorse the Court's opinion. . . .

NOTES AND QUESTIONS

1. Williams made two kinds of arguments for a rule requiring disclosure of at least some exculpatory evidence to grand juries. First, he argued that such a rule should be imposed under the Court's "supervisory power"—that is, its power to make common law governing the operation of the federal court system. Justice Scalia answers that argument by pointing to grand juries' independence of the court system: he notes that the grand jury "has not been textually assigned . . . to any of the branches described in the first three Articles" of the Constitution. As a result, says the majority, the district court's supervisory power is "not remotely" as broad with respect to grand juries as it is with respect to ordinary court proceedings.

Second, Williams argued that his proposed rule should be imposed as part of a "Fifth Amendment common law" that would define and limit grand juries' role. Justice Scalia responds in part by noting that grand juries have traditionally been permitted to indict based on whatever evidence satisfied them; he goes on to say that prosecutors surely cannot be obliged to inform grand juries of things that grand juries themselves are free to ignore. In other words, prosecutors' obligation cannot exceed the obligation of the grand jurors themselves.

Both of Justice Scalia's responses envision grand juries as independent entities, with prosecutors as the grand jurors' servant, not their master. That may well have been the historical relationship, but few people would so characterize them today. What sense does it make to place so much emphasis on grand jury independence *now?* More broadly, what do cases like *Williams* make you think about "original intent" methods of constitutional interpretation? If grand juries played a different role at the time of the Founding than they do now, how should the difference be taken into account in defining the law that governs grand juries today? For a thoughtful and insightful discussion of the role of the grand jury, both historically and today, see Roger Fairfax, Jr., Grand Jury Discretion and Constitutional Design, 93 Cornell L. Rev. 703-763 (2008).

2. What about the more functional arguments offered by the Court? If prosecutors faced the obligation that Justice Stevens would impose, how would they behave? Might not Justice Stevens's regime invite a great deal of litigation about what evidence prosecutors did and didn't know about and how exculpatory it was? Would that be a good use of judicial and lawyer resources? Do you think defense counsel welcome the chance to litigate this additional set of issues?

3. But then, consider Justice Stevens's litany of different forms of prosecutorial manipulation of grand juries. How can grand juries do a decent job of screening prosecutorial charging decisions if prosecutors are free to withhold evidence that might show the case is likely to fail at trial?

4. After *Williams* significantly narrowed the grounds for challenging an indictment, there remain only a modest number of claims available to the defense. Footnote 6 of the majority opinion, as well as Justice Stevens's dissent in *Williams*, identifies various types of prosecutorial misbehavior about which the defense can justifiably complain. Rule 6 also makes clear that prosecutors may not be present while the grand jury is voting, they must present only one witness at a time, and they must keep grand jury material secret. And of course, no one thinks that a prosecutor is free to suborn perjury or present information known to be false to the grand jurors.

But even if a defendant learns of this type of prosecutorial misconduct (which is by no means certain), two barriers to a remedy remain. The first is the need to show prejudice. In Bank of Nova Scotia v. United States, 487 U.S. 250 (1988) (cited in *Williams*), the district court found that the prosecutor had, among other things, committed multiple violations of Rule 6(e), had presented misinformation to the grand jury, and had mistreated grand jury witnesses. Using his supervisory power, the district judge dismissed the indictment because of the government's misconduct. But the court of appeals reversed the dismissal and the Supreme Court affirmed, finding that, in the absence of demonstrated prejudice to the accused, grand jury errors are not a basis for dismissing the indictment. The Court pointed to Rule 52 of the Federal Rules, the "harmless error" provision, which provides that errors in the proceedings that do not affect the "substantial rights" of the accused are to be ignored, and said that judges may not avoid the harmless error rule simply to chastise prosecutorial overreaching. The Court acknowledged that there were a few cases where prejudice was not required to be shown—racial bias in the selection of the grand jury, for example—but these were the exception and not the rule. In most cases, said the Court, including the one before it, "dismissal of the indictment is appropriate only if it is established that the violation substantially influenced the grand jury's decision to indict, or if there is grave doubt that the decision to indict was free from the substantial influence of such violations." Id., at 255 (internal quotation marks omitted). The Court did not explain how such a showing could be made, and it is fair to say that few defendants have succeeded in showing how alleged errors influenced the grand jury's thinking.

Bank of Nova Scotia involved a challenge to the indictment that was raised *prior* to trial. This distinction is important, because the second barrier to an indictment challenge is that once the criminal case is over, the challenge becomes effectively moot. If the defendant is acquitted, there is obviously no challenge remaining, and if the defendant is convicted via guilty plea or trial, the Court has said that generally the error is per se harmless. In United States v. Mechanik, 475 U.S. 66 (1986), the defendant learned during his trial that the government had presented two witnesses to the grand jury simultaneously, in violation of Rule 6(d). The defendant moved promptly to dismiss; the judge took the motion under advisement, and after the defendant was convicted, the motion was denied. The Supreme Court assumed the violation of the Rule but concluded that once the trial jury convicted, any errors before the grand jury became harmless. "In courtroom proceedings as elsewhere," said the Court, "the moving finger writes; and, having writ, moves on." Thus, a defendant has limited access to the information needed to challenge the indictment, a high standard of prejudice to overcome if he can get the information, and now a limited window of time within which the challenge can be brought.

The combination of *Costello, Williams, Bank of Nova Scotia,* and *Mechanik* eliminates nearly all challenges to the grand jury's work. The Supreme Court seems largely unconcerned by the structural barriers (many of which it has built) that make it difficult for the grand jury to act as a shield; perhaps this is because most defendants will end up being convicted of something anyway, usually by a guilty plea, and perhaps because defendants retain the ability to force the case to trial, where the full range of procedural protections are available to them.

Given all this, is it realistic to think that the grand jury in fact restrains the prosecutors in making their charging decisions? If not, does the grand jury still serve a useful purpose in the criminal system?

Chapter 11

The Scope of the Prosecution

Selecting the proper target for prosecution and the proper charges are not the only critical pretrial decisions a prosecutor must make. Even before the grand jury returns an indictment, there are important choices required about the timing, location, and scope of the criminal case being considered. In the first instance, these are the prosecutor's decisions to make, but now—unlike the decision of whether and what charges to bring—there are meaningful legal constraints on the government's discretion.

This chapter looks at the "when, where, what, and who" of the criminal case. Section A looks at the constraints on when the government files charges. Generally, law enforcement and prosecutors can investigate as long as necessary and bring criminal charges anytime, provided they don't run afoul of the applicable statute of limitations. But once the decision to prosecute is put into action, either by arrest or by indictment, a clock starts ticking and the government's time frame to investigate and prepare a case narrows. The defendant has both a constitutional and a statutory right to a speedy trial, one that puts pressure on both prosecutors and courts to move a case forward.

Section B.1 looks at where a case must be filed—the venue of the trial. A defendant has a constitutional right to stand trial in the judicial district where the crime was committed, but this simple test can quickly become complicated. If the defendant transports drugs across the country, where was the crime committed? Where the trip started? Where it ended? In any state through which the defendant drove? Suppose a defendant in Maine is in a conspiracy with a defendant in California, and neither one has ever been to the other's state. Can the California defendant be transported to Maine for trial there? And what about crimes committed in cyberspace?

Section B.2 looks at venue from the other direction: When does the defendant have the right to a trial at some place *other* than where the crime was committed? Sometimes a crime is sufficiently notorious that the defendant fears he cannot get a fair trial in the district where the crime occurred, and will move for a change of venue. This section explores the competing interests at stake in such a motion, and asks how a judge should evaluate these interests.

Section C asks the "what" and the "who"—the issues of joinder and severance. If a defendant is accused of committing three bank robberies in three different towns on three different days, should all three charges be joined in a single indictment, and thus, be part of a single trial? Also, if more than one defendant is accused of robbing the same bank, should both defendants be considered in one trial, or should there be separate proceedings? Prosecutors and judges usually prefer a consolidated trial for efficiency reasons, but defendants will often argue that having a single jury hear about multiple charges and/or seeing multiple defendants in one case is highly prejudicial, and thus will move to sever the charges or defendants.

This section examines the circumstances under which trial judges should override the prosecutor's decision about the proper scope of the case.

A.   The Right to a Speedy Trial

When a defendant complains that his criminal case took too long to prosecute, the claim may derive from several sources. When the delay occurs between the crime and the commencement of formal legal proceedings, the defendant is protected primarily by the applicable state or federal statute of limitations. For a delay between the defendant's arrest or indictment and trial, the defendant is protected by: (1) the Speedy Trial Clause of the Sixth Amendment ("In all criminal prosecutions, the accused shall enjoy the right to a speedy and public trial. . . ."),[1] and similar speedy-trial provisions found in state constitutions; (2) state or federal statutes such as the federal Speedy Trial Act of 1974, 18 U.S.C. §§3161-3174 (1994) (comparable statutes have been enacted in most of the states); and (3) various court rules. Finally, excessive delay that is both unjust and prejudicial to the defendant may violate the Due Process Clause, regardless of whether such delay precedes or follows the defendant's arrest or indictment.

In the cases that follow, the Supreme Court faced claims of inordinate delay arising in different factual settings. As you read the cases, try to distinguish the various legal bases for the defendant's claim, and try to determine what interests are protected by the constitutional or statutory provisions involved.

BARKER v. WINGO

Certiorari to the United States Court of Appeals for the Sixth Circuit
407 U.S. 514 (1972)

JUSTICE POWELL delivered the opinion of the Court. Although a speedy trial is guaranteed the accused by the Sixth Amendment to the Constitution, this Court has dealt with that right on infrequent occasions. . . .

[I]n none of [our prior] cases have we attempted to set out the criteria by which the speedy trial right is to be judged. . . . This case compels us to make such an attempt.

I

On July 20, 1958, in Christian County, Kentucky, an elderly couple was beaten to death by intruders wielding an iron tire tool. Two suspects, Silas Manning and Willie Barker, the petitioner, were arrested shortly thereafter. The grand jury indicted them on September 15. Counsel was appointed on September 17, and Barker's trial was set for October 21. The Commonwealth had a stronger case against Manning, and it believed that Barker could not be convicted unless Manning testified against

---

1. The Supreme Court has applied the Speedy Trial Clause to the states; see Klopfer v. North Carolina, 386 U.S. 213, 222-223 (1967).

him. Manning was naturally unwilling to incriminate himself. Accordingly, on October 23, the day Silas Manning was brought to trial, the Commonwealth sought and obtained the first of what was to be a series of 16 continuances of Barker's trial. Barker made no objection. By first convicting Manning, the Commonwealth would remove possible problems of self-incrimination and would be able to assure his testimony against Barker.

The Commonwealth encountered more than a few difficulties in its prosecution of Manning. The first trial ended in a hung jury. A second trial resulted in a conviction, but the Kentucky Court of Appeals reversed because of the admission of evidence obtained by an illegal search. Manning v. Commonwealth, 328 S.W.2d 421 (1959). At his third trial, Manning was again convicted, and the Court of Appeals again reversed because the trial court had not granted a change of venue. Manning v. Commonwealth, 346 S.W.2d 755 (1961). A fourth trial resulted in a hung jury. Finally, after five trials, Manning was convicted, in March 1962, of murdering one victim, and after a sixth trial, in December 1962, he was convicted of murdering the other.

The Christian County Circuit Court holds three terms each year—in February, June, and September. Barker's initial trial was to take place in the September term of 1958. The first continuance postponed it until the February 1959 term. The second continuance was granted for one month only. Every term thereafter for as long as the Manning prosecutions were in process, the Commonwealth routinely moved to continue Barker's case to the next term. When the case was continued from the June 1959 term until the following September, Barker, having spent 10 months in jail, obtained his release by posting a $5,000 bond. He thereafter remained free in the community until his trial. Barker made no objection, through his counsel, to the first 11 continuances.

When on February 12, 1962, the Commonwealth moved for the twelfth time to continue the case until the following term, Barker's counsel filed a motion to dismiss the indictment. The motion to dismiss was denied two weeks later, and the Commonwealth's motion for a continuance was granted. The Commonwealth was granted further continuances in June 1962 and September 1962, to which Barker did not object.

In February 1963, the first term of court following Manning's final conviction, the Commonwealth moved to set Barker's trial for March 19. But on the day scheduled for trial, it again moved for a continuance until the June term. It gave as its reason the illness of the ex-sheriff who was the chief investigating officer in the case. To this continuance, Barker objected unsuccessfully.

The witness was still unable to testify in June, and the trial, which had been set for June 19, was continued again until the September term over Barker's objection. This time the court announced that the case would be dismissed for lack of prosecution if it were not tried during the next term. The final trial date was set for October 9, 1963. On that date, Barker again moved to dismiss the indictment, and this time specified that his right to a speedy trial had been violated. The motion was denied; the trial commenced with Manning as the chief prosecution witness; Barker was convicted and given a life sentence.

Barker appealed his conviction to the Kentucky Court of Appeals, relying in part on his speedy trial claim. The court affirmed. Barker v. Commonwealth, 385 S.W.2d 671 (1964). In February 1970 Barker petitioned for habeas corpus in the United States District Court for the Western District of Kentucky. Although the District

[handwritten margin note: Barker indicted on the 16th trial date continuance]

Court rejected the petition without holding a hearing, the Court granted petitioner leave to appeal in forma pauperis and a certificate of probable cause to appeal. On appeal, the Court of Appeals for the Sixth Circuit affirmed the District Court. 442 F.2d 1141 (1971). . . . We granted Barker's petition for certiorari.

II

The right to a speedy trial is generically different from any of the other rights enshrined in the Constitution for the protection of the accused. In addition to the general concern that all accused persons be treated according to decent and fair procedures, there is a societal interest in providing a speedy trial which exists separate from, and at times in opposition to, the interests of the accused. The inability of courts to provide a prompt trial has contributed to a large backlog of cases in urban courts which, among other things, enables defendants to negotiate more effectively for pleas of guilty to lesser offenses and otherwise manipulate the system. In addition, persons released on bond for lengthy periods awaiting trial have an opportunity to commit other crimes. It must be of little comfort to the residents of Christian County, Kentucky, to know that Barker was at large on bail for over four years while accused of a vicious and brutal murder of which he was ultimately convicted. Moreover, the longer an accused is free awaiting trial, the more tempting becomes his opportunity to jump bail and escape. Finally, delay between arrest and punishment may have a detrimental effect on rehabilitation.

If an accused cannot make bail, he is generally confined, as was Barker for 10 months, in a local jail. This contributes to the overcrowding and generally deplorable state of those institutions. Lengthy exposure to these conditions "has a destructive effect on human character and makes the rehabilitation of the individual offender much more difficult." At times the result may even be violent rioting. Finally, lengthy pretrial detention is costly. The cost of maintaining a prisoner in jail varies from $3 to $9 per day, and this amounts to millions across the Nation. In addition, society loses wages which might have been earned, and it must often support families of incarcerated breadwinners.

A second difference between the right to speedy trial and the accused's other constitutional rights is that deprivation of the right may work to the accused's advantage. Delay is not an uncommon defense tactic. As the time between the commission of the crime and trial lengthens, witnesses may become unavailable or their memories may fade. If the witnesses support the prosecution, its case will be weakened, sometimes seriously so. And it is the prosecution which carries the burden of proof. Thus, unlike the right to counsel or the right to be free from compelled self-incrimination, deprivation of the right to speedy trial does not per se prejudice the accused's ability to defend himself.

Finally, and perhaps most importantly, the right to speedy trial is a more vague concept than other procedural rights. It is, for example, impossible to determine with precision when the right has been denied. We cannot definitely say how long is too long in a system where justice is supposed to be swift but deliberate.[15] As a

---

15. "In large measure because of the many procedural safeguards provided an accused, the ordinary procedures for criminal prosecution are designed to move at a deliberate pace. A requirement of unreasonable speed would have a deleterious effect both upon the rights of the accused and upon the ability of society to protect itself." United States v. Ewell, 383 U.S. 116, 120 (1966).

consequence, there is no fixed point in the criminal process when the State can put the defendant to the choice of either exercising or waiving the right to a speedy trial. If, for example, the State moves for a 60-day continuance, granting that continuance is not a violation of the right to speedy trial unless the circumstances of the case are such that further delay would endanger the values the right protects. It is impossible to do more than generalize about when those circumstances exist. There is nothing comparable to the point in the process when a defendant exercises or waives his right to counsel or his right to a jury trial. Thus, . . . any inquiry into a speedy trial claim necessitates a functional analysis of the right in the particular context of the case. . . .

The amorphous quality of the right also leads to the unsatisfactorily severe remedy of dismissal of the indictment when the right has been deprived. This is indeed a serious consequence because it means that a defendant who may be guilty of a serious crime will go free, without having been tried. Such a remedy is more serious than an exclusionary rule or a reversal for a new trial, but it is the only possible remedy.

*[handwritten: * Severe remedy]*

III

Perhaps because the speedy trial right is so slippery, two rigid approaches are urged upon us as ways of eliminating some of the uncertainty which courts experience in protecting the right. The first suggestion is that we hold that the Constitution requires a criminal defendant to be offered a trial within a specified time period. The result of such a ruling would have the virtue of clarifying when the right is infringed and of simplifying courts' application of it. Recognizing this, some legislatures have enacted laws, and some courts have adopted procedural rules which more narrowly define the right. . . .

But such a result would require this Court to engage in legislative or rulemaking activity, rather than in the adjudicative process to which we should confine our efforts. We do not establish procedural rules for the States, except when mandated by the Constitution. We find no constitutional basis for holding that the speedy trial right can be quantified into a specified number of days or months. The States, of course, are free to prescribe a reasonable period consistent with constitutional standards, but our approach must be less precise.

[handwritten: Rejects 1) specified time rule ← 2) demand waiver doctrine]

The second suggested alternative would restrict consideration of the right to those cases in which the accused has demanded a speedy trial. Most States have recognized what is loosely referred to as the "demand rule," although eight States reject it. It is not clear, however, precisely what is meant by that term. Although every federal court of appeals that has considered the question has endorsed some kind of demand rule, some have regarded the rule within the concept of waiver, whereas others have viewed it as a factor to be weighed in assessing whether there has been a deprivation of the speedy trial right. We shall refer to the former approach as the demand-waiver doctrine. The demand-waiver doctrine provides that a defendant waives any consideration of his right to speedy trial for any period prior to which he has not demanded a trial. Under this rigid approach, a prior demand is a necessary condition to the consideration of the speedy trial right. . . .

Such an approach, by presuming waiver of a fundamental right from inaction, is inconsistent with this Court's pronouncements on waiver of constitutional rights. The Court has defined waiver as "an intentional relinquishment or abandonment of a known right or privilege." Johnson v. Zerbst, 304 U.S. 458, 464 (1938). Courts should "indulge every reasonable presumption against waiver," . . . and they should "not presume acquiescence in the loss of fundamental rights." . . .

In excepting the right to speedy trial from the rule of waiver we have applied to other fundamental rights, courts that have applied the demand-waiver rule have relied on the assumption that delay usually works for the benefit of the accused and on the absence of any readily ascertainable time in the criminal process for a defendant to be given the choice of exercising or waiving his right. But it is not necessarily true that delay benefits the defendant. There are cases in which delay appreciably harms the defendant's ability to defend himself. Moreover, a defendant confined to jail prior to trial is obviously disadvantaged by delay as is a defendant released on bail but unable to lead a normal life because of community suspicion and his own anxiety.

The nature of the speedy trial right does make it impossible to pinpoint a precise time in the process when the right must be asserted or waived, but that fact does not argue for placing the burden of protecting the right solely on defendants. A defendant has no duty to bring himself to trial; the State has that duty as well as the duty of insuring that the trial is consistent with due process. Moreover, for the reasons earlier expressed, society has a particular interest in bringing swift prosecutions, and society's representatives are the ones who should protect that interest.

It is also noteworthy that such a rigid view of the demand-waiver rule places defense counsel in an awkward position. Unless he demands a trial early and often, he is in danger of frustrating his client's right. If counsel is willing to tolerate some delay because he finds it reasonable and helpful in preparing his own case, he may be unable to obtain a speedy trial for his client at the end of that time. Since under the demand-waiver rule no time runs until the demand is made, the government will have whatever time is otherwise reasonable to bring the defendant to trial after a demand has been made. Thus, if the first demand is made three months after arrest in a jurisdiction which prescribes a six-month rule, the prosecution will have a total of nine months—which may be wholly unreasonable under the circumstances. The result in practice is likely to be either an automatic, pro forma demand made immediately after appointment of counsel or delays which, but for the demand-waiver rule, would not be tolerated. Such a result is not consistent with the interests of defendants, society, or the Constitution.

We reject, therefore, the rule that a defendant who fails to demand a speedy trial forever waives his right. This does not mean, however, that the defendant has no responsibility to assert his right. We think the better rule is that the defendant's assertion of or failure to assert his right to a speedy trial is one of the factors to be considered in an inquiry into the deprivation of the right. Such a formulation avoids the rigidities of the demand-waiver rule and the resulting possible unfairness in its application. It allows the trial court to exercise a judicial discretion based on the circumstances, including due consideration of any applicable formal procedural rule. It would permit, for example, a court to attach a different weight to a situation in which the defendant knowingly fails to object from a situation in which his attorney acquiesces in long delay without adequately informing his client, or from a situation in which no counsel is appointed. It would also allow a court to weigh the frequency and force of the objections as opposed to attaching significant weight to a purely pro forma objection.

In ruling that a defendant has some responsibility to assert a speedy trial claim, we do not depart from our holdings in other cases concerning the waiver of fundamental rights, in which we have placed the entire responsibility on the prosecution to show that the claimed waiver was knowingly and voluntarily made. Such cases have involved rights which must be exercised or waived at a specific time or under clearly identifiable circumstances, such as the rights to plead not guilty, to demand a jury trial, to exercise the privilege against self-incrimination, and to have the assistance of counsel. We have shown above that the right to a speedy trial is unique in its uncertainty as to when and under what circumstances it must be asserted or may be deemed waived. But the rule we announce today, which comports with constitutional principles, places the primary burden on the courts and the prosecutors to assure that cases are brought to trial. We hardly need add that if delay is attributable to the defendant, then his waiver may be given effect under standard waiver doctrine, the demand rule aside.

We, therefore, reject both of the inflexible approaches—the fixed-time period because it goes further than the Constitution requires; the demand-waiver rule because it is insensitive to a right which we have deemed fundamental. The approach we accept is a balancing test, in which the conduct of both the prosecution and the defendant are weighed.[29]

IV

A balancing test necessarily compels courts to approach speedy trial cases on an ad hoc basis. We can do little more than identify some of the factors which courts should assess in determining whether a particular defendant has been deprived of his right. Though some might express them in different ways, we identify four such factors: Length of delay, the reason for the delay, the defendant's assertion of his right, and prejudice to the defendant.

The length of the delay is to some extent a triggering mechanism. Until there is some delay which is presumptively prejudicial, there is no necessity for inquiry into the other factors that go into the balance. Nevertheless, because of the imprecision of the right to speedy trial, the length of delay that will provoke such an inquiry is necessarily dependent upon the peculiar circumstances of the case. To take but one example, the delay that can be tolerated for an ordinary street crime is considerably less than for a serious, complex conspiracy charge.

Closely related to length of delay is the reason the government assigns to justify the delay. Here, too, different weights should be assigned to different reasons. A deliberate attempt to delay the trial in order to hamper the defense should be weighted heavily against the government. A more neutral reason such as negligence or overcrowded courts should be weighted less heavily but nevertheless should be considered since the ultimate responsibility for such circumstances must rest with the government rather than with the defendant. Finally, a valid reason, such as a missing witness, should serve to justify appropriate delay.

We have already discussed the third factor, the defendant's responsibility to assert his right. Whether and how a defendant asserts his right is closely related to the other factors we have mentioned. The strength of his efforts will be affected by

29. Nothing we have said should be interpreted as disapproving a presumptive rule adopted by a court in the exercise of its supervisory powers which establishes a fixed time period within which cases must normally be brought.

the length of the delay, to some extent by the reason for the delay, and most particularly by the personal prejudice, which is not always readily identifiable, that he experiences. The more serious the deprivation, the more likely a defendant is to complain. The defendant's assertion of his speedy trial right, then, is entitled to strong evidentiary weight in determining whether the defendant is being deprived of the right. We emphasize that failure to assert the right will make it difficult for a defendant to prove that he was denied a speedy trial.

A fourth factor is prejudice to the defendant. Prejudice, of course, should be assessed in the light of the interests of defendants which the speedy trial right was designed to protect. This Court has identified three such interests: (i) to prevent oppressive pretrial incarceration; (ii) to minimize anxiety and concern of the accused; and (iii) to limit the possibility that the defense will be impaired. Of these, the most serious is the last, because the inability of a defendant adequately to prepare his case skews the fairness of the entire system. If witnesses die or disappear during a delay, the prejudice is obvious. There is also prejudice if defense witnesses are unable to recall accurately events of the distant past. Loss of memory, however, is not always reflected in the record because what has been forgotten can rarely be shown.

We have discussed previously the societal disadvantages of lengthy pretrial incarceration, but obviously the disadvantages for the accused who cannot obtain his release are even more serious. The time spent in jail awaiting trial has a detrimental impact on the individual. It often means loss of a job; it disrupts family life; and it enforces idleness. Most jails offer little or no recreational or rehabilitative programs. The time spent in jail is simply dead time. Moreover, if a defendant is locked up, he is hindered in his ability to gather evidence, contact witnesses, or otherwise prepare his defense.[35] Imposing those consequences on anyone who has not yet been convicted is serious. It is especially unfortunate to impose them on those persons who are ultimately found to be innocent. Finally, even if an accused is not incarcerated prior to trial, he is still disadvantaged by restraints on his liberty and by living under a cloud of anxiety, suspicion, and often hostility.

We regard none of the four factors identified above as either a necessary or sufficient condition to the finding of a deprivation of the right of speedy trial. Rather, they are related factors and must be considered together with such other circumstances as may be relevant. In sum, these factors have no talismanic qualities; courts must still engage in a difficult and sensitive balancing process. But, because we are dealing with a fundamental right of the accused, this process must be carried out with full recognition that the accused's interest in a speedy trial is specifically affirmed in the Constitution.

V

The difficulty of the task of balancing these factors is illustrated by this case, which we consider to be close. It is clear that the length of delay between arrest and

---

35. . . . There is statistical evidence that persons who are detained between arrest and trial are more likely to receive prison sentences than those who obtain pretrial release, although other factors bear upon this correlation. See Wald, Pretrial Detention and Ultimate Freedom: A Statistical Study, 39 N.Y.U. L. Rev. 631 (1964).

trial—well over five years—was extraordinary. Only seven months of that period can be attributed to a strong excuse, the illness of the ex-sheriff who was in charge of the investigation. Perhaps some delay would have been permissible under ordinary circumstances, so that Manning could be utilized as a witness in Barker's trial, but more than four years was too long a period, particularly since a good part of that period was attributable to the Commonwealth's failure or inability to try Manning under circumstances that comported with due process.

[handwritten margin note: time = too long]

Two counterbalancing factors, however, outweigh these deficiencies. The first is that prejudice was minimal. Of course, Barker was prejudiced to some extent by living for over four years under a cloud of suspicion and anxiety. Moreover, although he was released on bond for most of the period, he did spend 10 months in jail before trial. But there is no claim that any of Barker's witnesses died or otherwise became unavailable owing to the delay. The trial transcript indicates only two very minor lapses of memory—one on the part of a prosecution witness—which were in no way significant to the outcome.

[handwritten margin note: minimal prejudice]

More important than the absence of serious prejudice, is the fact that Barker did not want a speedy trial. Counsel was appointed for Barker immediately after his indictment and represented him throughout the period. No question is raised as to the competency of such counsel. Despite the fact that counsel had notice of the motions for continuances, the record shows no action whatever taken between October 21, 1958, and February 12, 1962, that could be construed as the assertion of the speedy trial right. On the latter date, in response to another motion for continuance, Barker moved to dismiss the indictment. The record does not show on what ground this motion was based, although it is clear that no alternative motion was made for an immediate trial. Instead the record strongly suggests that while he hoped to take advantage of the delay in which he had acquiesced, and thereby obtain a dismissal of the charges, he definitely did not want to be tried. Counsel conceded as much at oral argument: "Your honor, I would concede that Willie Mae Barker probably—I don't know this for a fact—probably did not want to be tried. I don't think any man wants to be tried. And I don't consider this a liability on his behalf. I don't blame him." Tr. of Oral Arg. 39.

[handwritten margin note: No assertion of speedy trial]

The probable reason for Barker's attitude was that he was gambling on Manning's acquittal. The evidence was not very strong against Manning, as the reversals and hung juries suggest, and Barker undoubtedly thought that if Manning were acquitted, he would never be tried. Counsel also conceded this: "Now, it's true that the reason for this delay was the Commonwealth of Kentucky's desire to secure the testimony of the accomplice, Silas Manning. And it's true that if Silas Manning were never convicted, Willie Mae Barker would never have been convicted. We concede this." Id., at 15.[39]

That Barker was gambling on Manning's acquittal is also suggested by his failure, following the pro forma motion to dismiss filed in February 1962, to object to the Commonwealth's next two motions for continuances. Indeed, it was not until March 1963, after Manning's convictions were final, that Barker, having lost his

39. Hindsight is, of course, 20/20, but we cannot help noting that if Barker had moved immediately and persistently for a speedy trial following indictment, and if he had been successful, he would have undoubtedly been acquitted since Manning's testimony was crucial to the Commonwealth's case. It could not have been anticipated at the outset, however, that Manning would have been tried six times over a four-year period. Thus, the decision to gamble on Manning's acquittal may have been a prudent choice at the time it was made.

gamble, began to object to further continuances. At that time, the Commonwealth's excuse was the illness of the ex-sheriff, which Barker has conceded justified the further delay.

We do not hold that there may never be a situation in which an indictment may be dismissed on speedy trial grounds where the defendant has failed to object to continuances. There may be a situation in which the defendant was represented by incompetent counsel, was severely prejudiced, or even cases in which the continuances were granted ex parte. But barring extraordinary circumstances, we would be reluctant indeed to rule that a defendant was denied this constitutional right on a record that strongly indicates, as does this one, that the defendant did not want a speedy trial. We hold, therefore, that Barker was not deprived of his due process right to a speedy trial.

The judgment of the Court of Appeals is Affirmed.

[The concurring opinion of Justice White is omitted.]

NOTES AND QUESTIONS

1. In *Barker*, the defendant apparently did not want a speedy trial for almost four years. Are there reasons a defendant might prefer delay, even if he is in jail prior to trial? Of course, even if the accused would prefer a leisurely trial to a speedy one, as the Court noted, there remains an independent societal interest in a prompt resolution of the charges. Are there other constitutional rights where the defendant's desire to forego a right will, at times, yield to society's interests in enforcement of the right, or is the speedy trial protection unique in this regard?

2. When discussing the four-part balancing test, the Court in *Barker* says "We regard none of the four factors identified above as *either a necessary or sufficient* condition to the finding of a deprivation of the right of speedy trial" (emphasis added). This statement should not be read too literally. The Court acknowledges that the length of delay "is to some extent a triggering mechanism," which really means that unless there is a significant time lag between the arrest and trial, even bad reasons for the delay and great prejudice will not support a constitutional speedy trial claim. Similarly, even if the length of the delay and the prejudice is great, if the reasons for the delay are attributable to the accused, the claim will almost certainly fail. With respect to the third factor, *Barker* "emphasize[d] that failure to assert the right will make it difficult for a defendant to prove that he was denied a speedy trial." And of course, if there is no prejudice caused by the delay, courts will rarely overturn a conviction simply because the trial was not speedy enough. And so while it remains true that for a speedy trial claim "courts must still engage in a difficult and sensitive balancing process," the absence of one or more of these factors will often be sufficient to defeat a Sixth Amendment challenge.

3. Suppose the "reasons for the delay"—the second *Barker* factor—are attributable, not to the defendant himself, but instead to defense *counsel*. Suppose further that defense counsel is appointed by, and paid by, the state, the entity that is responsible for bringing the defendant to trial promptly. Should these delays count heavily against a defendant who raises a constitutional speedy trial claim?

The Supreme Court has said that they do. In Vermont v. Brillon, 556 U.S. 81 (2009), the Court considered a Vermont Supreme Court decision that had reversed a conviction on Sixth Amendment Speedy Trial grounds, even though one significant cause of the delay was "the failure of several assigned counsel . . . to move [the defendant's] case forward." In an opinion by Justice Ginsburg, the Court rejected this interpretation of *Barker*, relying on the usual rule that the lawyer is the defendant's agent, and that his or her actions (or inactions) are attributable to the accused. The fact that defense counsel is paid by the government does not change the analysis, said the Court, because "[u]nlike a prosecutor or the court, assigned counsel is ordinarily not considered a state actor." The Court noted that the speedy trial calculations might be different if the defendant could show a "systemic breakdown in the public defender system" that resulted in delay, but no such evidence was presented.

✻ Vermont v. Brillon

4. Shortly after the Court's decision in *Barker*, Congress enacted the Speedy Trial Act of 1974, 18 U.S.C. §§3161-3174. Unlike the Sixth Amendment analysis, the Speedy Trial Act gives specific time limits within which certain events must occur. Once the defendant is arrested or served with a summons, says the Act, the prosecution has 30 days to file indictment or information. Also, the trial must be commenced within 70 days of the filing and making public of the information or indictment or the defendant's first appearance—whichever event happens later. Finally, if the defendant is continuously detained pending trial, the trial must begin within 90 days of the detention.

✻ Speedy Trial Act

This does not mean, however, that most federal trials actually take place within the 70-day and 90-day limits. The Act excludes from the time limits any delays caused by the unavailability of the defendant or a key witness, transportation needs, reasonable legal maneuvering by a codefendant, or "other proceedings" involving the defendant. The Act provides added flexibility by allowing trial courts to exclude delays caused by the granting of continuances based on the "ends of justice;" even delays caused by open-ended continuances are generally excluded. The result of these exclusions may well be that a trial begins weeks, even months, beyond the 70 day period set forth in the Act.

The Supreme Court has cautioned district courts that they must make case-specific findings that the ends of justice outweigh the need for speed, as the statute requires, see Bloate v. United States, 559 U.S. 196 (2010), but there is reason to think that courts do not always apply this requirement vigorously. For a harsh critique of how district courts have applied, even "abused," the ends of justice continuance, see Shon Hopwood, The Not So Speedy Trial Act, 89 Wash. L. Rev. 709, 719-729 (2014).

5. The goal of the Speedy Trial Act was to provide certainty about when trials were to begin. But like any legislation that regulates tens of thousands of cases each year, the text of the statute can't always be taken at face value. Consider United States v. Tinklenberg, 563 U.S. 647 (2011). Defendant's trial was to begin long after the 70-day period had run, so he moved to dismiss the indictment. The district court concluded that once certain days were properly excluded, the trial began on day 69. On appeal, the dispute centered on the propriety of excluding nine days during which the court had considered and resolved three pretrial motions. Defendant argued that these nine days should not be excluded from the Speedy Trial calculations, because under §3161(h)(1)(D), days are only excluded if they constitute "delay *resulting from* any pretrial motion, from the filing of the motion through the conclusion of the hearing, or other prompt disposition of such motion" (emphasis added). Defendant argued that the nine days that it took the court to resolve the three motions did not cause any delay, and thus should not be excluded. The Court of Appeals agreed.

Although the defendant's argument seemed to be supported by the text of the Speedy Trial Act—indeed, the Supreme Court found it "linguistically reasonable"—not a single Justice agreed with this reading. Instead, said the Court, when the party files a pretrial motion, the time it takes the judge to consider and resolve a motion is automatically excluded from the Act's 70-day period, regardless whether the motion causes any delay in the pretrial process. While Justice Breyer's opinion found this to be the better reading of the statutory language (and one that had been adopted by every other appellate court to consider the question), he also noted how administratively difficult it would be to figure out when a particular motion "caused" a delay. Given the frequency with which pretrial motions are filed, this was an additional burden that the Court was unwilling to impose on the district courts.

One ironic result of the Court's decision was that the three days it took the district court to consider and deny Mr. Tinklenberg's motion to dismiss the indictment because the Speedy Trial Act was violated were now excluded from the Speedy Trial Act calculation.

6. In the federal system the Speedy Trial Act of 1974 has largely supplanted the Sixth Amendment's Speedy Trial Clause as the basis for litigation about the defendant's right to a prompt disposition; in most cases, compliance with the statute will be interpreted as compliance with the constitutional provision. There remains, however, an important difference between the constitutional and the statutory right. As noted in *Barker*, if the defendant's Sixth Amendment right is violated, the "only possible remedy" is a dismissal of the charges with prejudice. In contrast, the remedy for a violation of the Act is dismissal of the charges, either with or without prejudice, based on the trial court's review of the seriousness of the crime charged, the circumstances surrounding the delay, and the potential effect of dismissal on the administration of justice. See United States v. Taylor, 487 U.S. 326 (1988) (reversing dismissal of charges because trial court was influenced primarily by government's "lackadaisical" attitude, instead of considering all relevant statutory factors).

Notice, however the potential oddity of the statutory remedy: If a court finds that the government has taken too long to bring the defendant to trial, the remedy may be that the case is dismissed without prejudice—meaning that the government is free to refile the case and begin again. The result, inevitably, is that it takes even longer to bring the defendant to trial, with all the negative consequences that can follow from that delay.

7. Like most protections, the speedy trial right can be waived. But how broad a waiver can the government obtain? In Zedner v. United States, 547 U.S. 489 (2006), in the midst of prolonged pretrial proceedings, the defendant agreed to waive "for all time" the application of the Speedy Trial Act. (He did so, in part, to buy himself time to try to prove that alleged counterfeit U.S. bonds, on which the charges against him were based, were actually authentic.) Thereafter, a 91-day delay ensued, and the defendant moved to dismiss the indictment for failure to comply with the Act. The district court denied the motion based on the earlier waiver, and the Second Circuit affirmed. But the Supreme Court reversed. According to the Court, the Act "comprehensively regulates the time within which a trial must begin," and makes no allowance for a "prospective" waiver of the kind purportedly signed by the defendant. Although the Act itself provides that a defendant may waive a completed violation of the Act by failing to move for dismissal prior to the start of the trial (or the entry of a guilty plea), the Court noted that "prospective" and "retrospective" waivers raise quite different concerns:

> [T]here is no reason to think that Congress wanted to treat prospective and retrospective waivers similarly. Allowing prospective waivers would seriously undermine the Act because there are many cases—like the case at hand—in which the prosecution, the defense, and the court would all be happy to opt out of the Act, to the detriment of the public interest. The sort of retrospective waiver allowed by [the Act] does not pose a comparable danger because the prosecution and the court cannot know until the trial actually starts or the guilty plea is actually entered whether the defendant will forgo moving to dismiss. As a consequence, the prosecution and the court retain a strong incentive to make sure that the trial begins on time.

Id., at 502. The Court rejected the government's alternative arguments, among which were a claim that the violation of the Act could still be found, on remand, to be "harmless error." The Court held that dismissal was required under the Act, and remanded the case solely for the purpose of allowing the trial court to determine whether the dismissal should be with or without prejudice. On remand, the district court ruled that the dismissal was without prejudice. United States v. Zedner, 2006 WL 6201406 (E.D.N.Y. 2006).

It is unclear how much effect *Zedner* has had in speeding up trials. For a claim that "defense lawyers continue to assert broad, open-ended speedy-trial waivers on behalf of their clients, and district courts continue to accept those waivers," see Hopwood, supra, 89 Wash. L. Rev. at 717 (footnotes omitted, citing cases).

8. The Speedy Trial Clause and supporting legislation like the Speedy Trial Act apply only to delay occurring between the defendant's arrest or indictment and trial. But what about delay between the crime and the initial filing of charges? Accusing a defendant long after the alleged events occurred can raise some of the same problems that worried the Court in Barker v. Wingo: Memories fade, witnesses can disappear, and physical evidence can be lost, all of which can make it much more difficult for the accused to put on a defense. If a defendant is prejudiced by a lengthy preindictment delay, can he raise a constitutional challenge?

The Court considered this issue in United States v. Lovasco, 431 U.S. 783 (1977). The defendant was accused of possessing eight firearms that had been stolen from the U.S. mail. Although it appeared that the government had sufficient evidence of the defendant's guilt on five of the weapons within 1 month of the crime, charges were not filed for 18 months after the offense allegedly occurred. The defendant moved to dismiss for excessive preindictment delay, claiming that, among other things, the delay had caused the defense to lose the testimony of two witnesses, both of whom had died several months after the crime took place. The district court granted the defendant's motion to dismiss, finding that the delay in taking the case to the grand jury was "unnecessary and unreasonable," and the court of appeals affirmed.

The Supreme Court, in an opinion by Justice Marshall, reversed. It began by noting the irrelevance of the constitutional Speedy Trial right to claims such as this, observing that until there has been a formal criminal charge filed, there is no "accused" or a "criminal prosecution" to implicate the Sixth Amendment. On the other hand, while the primary protection against preindictment delay is found in statutes of limitations, "the Due Process Clause has a limited role to play in protecting against oppressive delay." The Court went on to say:

> [T]he Due Process Clause does not permit courts to abort criminal prosecutions simply because they disagree with a prosecutor's judgment as to when to seek an

indictment. . . . We are to determine only whether the action complained of—here, compelling respondent to stand trial after the Government delayed indictment to investigate further—violates those "fundamental conceptions of justice which lie at the base of our civil and political institutions," Mooney v. Holohan, 294 U.S. 103, 112 (1935), and which define "the community's sense of fair play and decency," Rochin v. California, [342 U.S. 165, 173 (1952)].

[P]rosecutors are under no duty to file charges as soon as probable cause exists but before they are satisfied they will be able to establish the suspect's guilt beyond a reasonable doubt. To impose such a duty "would have a deleterious effect both upon the rights of the accused and upon the ability of society to protect itself." . . . From the perspective of potential defendants, requiring prosecutions to commence when probable cause is established is undesirable because it would increase the likelihood of unwarranted charges being filed, and would add to the time during which defendants stand accused but untried. . . . From the perspective of law enforcement officials, a requirement of immediate prosecution upon probable cause is equally unacceptable because it could make obtaining proof of guilt beyond a reasonable doubt impossible by causing potentially fruitful sources of information to evaporate before they are fully exploited. And from the standpoint of the courts, such a requirement is unwise because it would cause scarce resources to be consumed on cases that prove to be insubstantial, or that involve only some of the responsible parties or some of the criminal acts.

Although the Court cautioned that "delay undertaken by the Government solely to gain tactical advantage over the accused" was impermissible, it concluded that the mere fact of delay in filing the charges was not. "We therefore hold that to prosecute a defendant following investigative delay does not deprive him of due process, even if his defense might have been somewhat prejudiced by the lapse of time." *Lovasco*, 431 U.S. at 791-796.

9. Under *Lovasco*, prejudice to the defendant did not seem to play a significant role in the resolution of the due process challenge to pretrial delay. How does this compare to the role of prejudice under the Speedy Trial Clause? The next case addresses that issue.

DOGGETT v. UNITED STATES

Certiorari to the United States Court of Appeals for the Eleventh Circuit
505 U.S. 647 (1992)

JUSTICE SOUTER delivered the opinion of the Court.

In this case we consider whether the delay of 8 years between petitioner's indictment and arrest violated his Sixth Amendment right to a speedy trial. We hold that it did.

I

On February 22, 1980, petitioner Marc Doggett was indicted for conspiring with several others to import and distribute cocaine. See 84 Stat. 1265, 1291, as amended, 21 U.S.C. §§846, 963. Douglas Driver, the Drug Enforcement Administration's (DEA's) principal agent investigating the conspiracy, told the United States Marshal's Service that the DEA would oversee the apprehension of Doggett and his confederates. On

March 18, 1980, two police officers set out under Driver's orders to arrest Doggett at his parents' house in Raleigh, North Carolina, only to find that he was not there. His mother told the officers that he had left for Colombia four days earlier.

To catch Doggett on his return to the United States, Driver sent word of his outstanding arrest warrant to all United States Customs stations and to a number of law enforcement organizations. He also placed Doggett's name in the Treasury Enforcement Communication System (TECS), a computer network that helps Customs agents screen people entering the country, and in the National Crime Information Center computer system, which serves similar ends. The TECS entry expired that September, however, and Doggett's name vanished from the system.

In September 1981, Driver found out that Doggett was under arrest on drug charges in Panama and, thinking that a formal extradition request would be futile, simply asked Panama to "expel" Doggett to the United States. Although the Panamanian authorities promised to comply when their own proceedings had run their course, they freed Doggett the following July and let him go to Colombia, where he stayed with an aunt for several months. On September 25, 1982, he passed unhindered through Customs in New York City and settled down in Virginia. Since his return to the United States, he has married, earned a college degree, found a steady job as a computer operations manager, lived openly under his own name, and stayed within the law.

Doggett's travels abroad had not wholly escaped the Government's notice, however. In 1982, the American Embassy in Panama told the State Department of his departure to Colombia, but that information, for whatever reason, eluded the DEA, and Agent Driver assumed for several years that his quarry was still serving time in a Panamanian prison. Driver never asked DEA officials in Panama to check into Doggett's status, and only after his own fortuitous assignment to that country in 1985 did he discover Doggett's departure for Colombia. Driver then simply assumed Doggett had settled there, and he made no effort to find out for sure or to track Doggett down, either abroad or in the United States. Thus Doggett remained lost to the American criminal justice system until September 1988, when the Marshal's Service ran a simple credit check on several thousand people subject to outstanding arrest warrants and, within minutes, found out where Doggett lived and worked. On September 5, 1988, nearly 6 years after his return to the United States and 8½ years after his indictment, Doggett was arrested.

He naturally moved to dismiss the indictment, arguing that the Government's failure to prosecute him earlier violated his Sixth Amendment right to a speedy trial. The Federal Magistrate hearing his motion applied the criteria for assessing speedy trial claims set out in Barker v. Wingo, 407 U.S. 514 (1972). . . . The Magistrate found that the delay between Doggett's indictment and arrest was long enough to be "presumptively prejudicial," that the delay "clearly [was] attributable to the negligence of the government," and that Doggett could not be faulted for any delay in asserting his right to a speedy trial, there being no evidence that he had known of the charges against him until his arrest. The Magistrate also found, however, that Doggett had made no affirmative showing that the delay had impaired his ability to mount a successful defense or had otherwise prejudiced him. In his recommendation to the District Court, the Magistrate contended that this failure to demonstrate particular prejudice sufficed to defeat Doggett's speedy trial claim.

The District Court took the recommendation and denied Doggett's motion. Doggett then entered a conditional guilty plea under Federal Rule of Criminal

Procedure 11(a)(2), expressly reserving the right to appeal his ensuing conviction on the speedy trial claim.

A split panel of the Court of Appeals affirmed. . . .

II

The Sixth Amendment guarantees that, "[i]n all criminal prosecutions, the accused shall enjoy the right to a speedy . . . trial. . . ." On its face, the Speedy Trial Clause is written with such breadth that, taken literally, it would forbid the government to delay the trial of an "accused" for any reason at all. Our cases, however, have qualified the literal sweep of the provision by specifically recognizing the relevance of four separate enquiries: whether delay before trial was uncommonly long, whether the government or the criminal defendant is more to blame for that delay, whether, in due course, the defendant asserted his right to a speedy trial, and whether he suffered prejudice as the delay's result. See *Barker*, supra, at 530.

The first of these is actually a double enquiry. Simply to trigger a speedy trial analysis, an accused must allege that the interval between accusation and trial has crossed the threshold dividing ordinary from "presumptively prejudicial" delay, 407 U.S. at 530-531, since, by definition, he cannot complain that the government has denied him a "speedy" trial if it has, in fact, prosecuted his case with customary promptness. If the accused makes this showing, the court must then consider, as one factor among several, the extent to which the delay stretches beyond the bare minimum needed to trigger judicial examination of the claim. See id., at 533-534. This latter enquiry is significant to the speedy trial analysis because, as we discuss below, the presumption that pretrial delay has prejudiced the accused intensifies over time. In this case, the extraordinary 8½-year lag between Doggett's indictment and arrest clearly suffices to trigger the speedy trial enquiry;[1] its further significance within that enquiry will be dealt with later.

As for *Barker*'s second criterion, the Government claims to have sought Doggett with diligence. The findings of the courts below are to the contrary, however, and we review trial court determinations of negligence with considerable deference. . . . The Government gives us nothing to gainsay the findings that have come up to us, and we see nothing fatal to them in the record. For six years, the Government's investigators made no serious effort to test their progressively more questionable assumption that Doggett was living abroad, and, had they done so, they could have found him within minutes. While the Government's lethargy may have reflected no more than Doggett's relative unimportance in the world of drug trafficking, it was still findable negligence, and the finding stands.

The Government goes against the record again in suggesting that Doggett knew of his indictment years before he was arrested. Were this true, *Barker*'s third factor, concerning invocation of the right to a speedy trial, would be weighed heavily against him. But here again, the Government is trying to revisit the facts. At the

---

1. Depending on the nature of the charges, the lower courts have generally found post accusation delay "presumptively prejudicial" at least as it approaches one year. . . . We note that, as the term is used in this threshold context, "presumptive prejudice" does not necessarily indicate a statistical probability of prejudice; it simply marks the point at which courts deem the delay unreasonable enough to trigger the *Barker* enquiry. Cf. Uviller, Barker v. Wingo: Speedy Trial Gets a Fast Shuffle, 72 Colum. L. Rev. 1376, 1384-1385 (1972).

hearing on Doggett's speedy trial motion, it introduced no evidence challenging the testimony of Doggett's wife, who said that she did not know of the charges until his arrest, and of his mother, who claimed not to have told him or anyone else that the police had come looking for him. . . .

III

The Government is left, then, with its principal contention: that Doggett fails to make out a successful speedy trial claim because he has not shown precisely how he was prejudiced by the delay between his indictment and trial.

A

We have observed in prior cases that unreasonable delay between formal accusation and trial threatens to produce more than one sort of harm, including "oppressive pretrial incarceration," "anxiety and concern of the accused," and "the possibility that the [accused's] defense will be impaired" by dimming memories and loss of exculpatory evidence. *Barker*, 407 U.S. at 532. . . . Of these forms of prejudice, "the most serious is the last, because the inability of a defendant adequately to prepare his case skews the fairness of the entire system." 407 U.S. at 532. Doggett claims this kind of prejudice, and there is probably no other kind that he can claim, since he was subjected neither to pretrial detention nor, he has successfully contended, to awareness of unresolved charges against him.

The Government answers Doggett's claim by citing language in three cases, United States v. Marion, 404 U.S. 307, 320-323 (1971), United States v. MacDonald, 456 U.S. 1, 8 (1982), and United States v. Loud Hawk, 474 U.S. 302, 312 (1986), for the proposition that the Speedy Trial Clause does not significantly protect a criminal defendant's interest in fair adjudication. In so arguing, the Government asks us, in effect, to read part of *Barker* right out of the law, and that we will not do. In context, the cited passages support nothing beyond the principle . . . that the Sixth Amendment right of the accused to a speedy trial has no application beyond the confines of a formal criminal prosecution. Once triggered by arrest, indictment, or other official accusation, however, the speedy trial enquiry must weigh the effect of delay on the accused's defense just as it has to weigh any other form of prejudice that *Barker* recognized.[2] . . .

As an alternative to limiting *Barker*, the Government claims Doggett has failed to make any affirmative showing that the delay weakened his ability to raise specific defenses, elicit specific testimony, or produce specific items of evidence. Though Doggett did indeed come up short in this respect, the Government's argument takes it only so far: consideration of prejudice is not limited to the specifically demonstrable, and, as it concedes, . . . affirmative proof of particularized prejudice is not essential to every speedy trial claim. . . . *Barker* explicitly recognized that impairment of one's defense is the most difficult form of speedy trial prejudice to prove because time's erosion of exculpatory evidence and testimony "can rarely be shown." 407

---

2. Thus, we reject the Government's argument that the effect of delay on adjudicative accuracy is exclusively a matter for consideration under the Due Process Clause. We leave intact our earlier observation, see United States v. MacDonald, 456 U.S. 1, 7 (1982), that a defendant may invoke due process to challenge delay both before and after official accusation.

U.S. at 532. And though time can tilt the case against either side, . . . one cannot generally be sure which of them it has prejudiced more severely. Thus, we generally have to recognize that excessive delay presumptively compromises the reliability of a trial in ways that neither party can prove or, for that matter, identify. While such presumptive prejudice cannot alone carry a Sixth Amendment claim without regard to the other *Barker* criteria, . . . it is part of the mix of relevant facts, and its importance increases with the length of delay.

B

This brings us to an enquiry into the role that presumptive prejudice should play in the disposition of Doggett's speedy trial claim. We begin with hypothetical and somewhat easier cases and work our way to this one.

Our speedy trial standards recognize that pretrial delay is often both inevitable and wholly justifiable. The government may need time to collect witnesses against the accused, oppose his pretrial motions, or, if he goes into hiding, track him down. We attach great weight to such considerations when balancing them against the costs of going forward with a trial whose probative accuracy the passage of time has begun by degrees to throw into question. . . . Thus, in this case, if the Government had pursued Doggett with reasonable diligence from his indictment to his arrest, his speedy trial claim would fail. Indeed, that conclusion would generally follow as a matter of course however great the delay, so long as Doggett could not show specific prejudice to his defense.

The Government concedes, on the other hand, that Doggett would prevail if he could show that the Government had intentionally held back in its prosecution of him to gain some impermissible advantage at trial. . . . That we cannot doubt. *Barker* stressed that official bad faith in causing delay will be weighed heavily against the government, 407 U.S. at 531, and a bad-faith delay the length of this negligent one would present an overwhelming case for dismissal.

Between diligent prosecution and bad-faith delay, official negligence in bringing an accused to trial occupies the middle ground. While not compelling relief in every case where bad-faith delay would make relief virtually automatic, neither is negligence automatically tolerable simply because the accused cannot demonstrate exactly how it has prejudiced him. . . .

Barker made it clear that "different weights [are to be] assigned to different reasons" for delay. Ibid. Although negligence is obviously to be weighed more lightly than a deliberate intent to harm the accused's defense, it still falls on the wrong side of the divide between acceptable and unacceptable reasons for delaying a criminal prosecution once it has begun. And such is the nature of the prejudice presumed that the weight we assign to official negligence compounds over time as the presumption of evidentiary prejudice grows. Thus, our toleration of such negligence varies inversely with its protractedness, . . . and its consequent threat to the fairness of the accused's trial. Condoning prolonged and unjustifiable delays in prosecution would both penalize many defendants for the state's fault and simply encourage the government to gamble with the interests of criminal suspects assigned a low prosecutorial priority. The Government, indeed, can hardly complain too loudly, for persistent neglect in concluding a criminal prosecution indicates an uncommonly feeble interest in bringing an accused to justice; the more weight the Government attaches to securing a conviction, the harder it will try to get it.

To be sure, to warrant granting relief, negligence unaccompanied by particularized trial prejudice must have lasted longer than negligence demonstrably causing such prejudice. But even so, the Government's egregious persistence in failing to prosecute Doggett is clearly sufficient. The lag between Doggett's indictment and arrest was 8 years, and he would have faced trial 6 years earlier than he did but for the Government's inexcusable oversights. The portion of the delay attributable to the Government's negligence far exceeds the threshold needed to state a speedy trial claim; indeed, we have called shorter delays "extraordinary." See *Barker*, supra, at 533. When the Government's negligence thus causes delay six times as long as that generally sufficient to trigger judicial review, see n. 1, supra, and when the presumption of prejudice, albeit unspecified, is neither extenuated, as by the defendant's acquiescence, e.g., 407 U.S. at 534-536, nor persuasively rebutted,[4] the defendant is entitled to relief.

IV

We reverse the judgment of the Court of Appeals and remand the case for proceedings consistent with this opinion.

[The dissenting opinion of Justice O'Connor is omitted.]

JUSTICE THOMAS, with whom CHIEF JUSTICE REHNQUIST and JUSTICE SCALIA join, dissenting.

Just as "bad facts make bad law," so too odd facts make odd law. Doggett's 8-year odyssey from youthful drug dealing in the tobacco country of North Carolina, through stints in a Panamanian jail and in Colombia, to life as a computer operations manager, homeowner, and registered voter in suburban Virginia is extraordinary. But even more extraordinary is the Court's conclusion that the Government denied Doggett his Sixth Amendment right to a speedy trial despite the fact that he has suffered none of the harms that the right was designed to prevent. I respectfully dissent.

I

We have long identified the "major evils" against which the Speedy Trial Clause is directed as "undue and oppressive incarceration" and the "anxiety and concern accompanying public accusation." United States v. Marion, 404 U.S. 307, 320 (1971). The Court does not, and cannot, seriously dispute that those two concerns lie at the heart of the Clause, and that neither concern is implicated here. Doggett was neither in United States custody nor subject to bail during the entire 8½-year period at issue. Indeed, as this case comes to us, we must assume that he was blissfully unaware of his indictment all the while, and thus was not subject to the anxiety or humiliation that typically accompanies a known criminal charge.

Thus, this unusual case presents the question whether, independent of these core concerns, the Speedy Trial Clause protects an accused from two additional

---

4. While the Government ably counters Doggett's efforts to demonstrate particularized trial prejudice, it has not, and probably could not have, affirmatively proved that the delay left his ability to defend himself unimpaired. Cf. Uviller, 72 Colum. L. Rev., at 1394-1395.

harms: (1) prejudice to his ability to defend himself caused by the passage of time; and (2) disruption of his life years after the alleged commission of his crime. The Court today proclaims that the first of these additional harms is indeed an independent concern of the Clause, and on that basis compels reversal of Doggett's conviction and outright dismissal of the indictment against him. As to the second of these harms, the Court remains mum—despite the fact that we requested supplemental briefing on this very point.

I disagree with the Court's analysis. In my view, the Sixth Amendment's speedy trial guarantee does not provide independent protection against either prejudice to an accused's defense or the disruption of his life. I shall consider each in turn.

A

As we have explained, "the Speedy Trial Clause's core concern is impairment of *liberty*." United States v. Loud Hawk, 474 U.S. 302, 312 (1986) (emphasis added). Whenever a criminal trial takes place long after the events at issue, the defendant may be prejudiced in any number of ways. But "[t]he Speedy Trial Clause does not purport to protect a defendant from all effects flowing from a delay before trial." Id., at 311. The Clause is directed not generally against delay-related prejudice, but against delay-related prejudice to a defendant's liberty. "The speedy trial guarantee is designed to minimize the possibility of lengthy incarceration prior to trial, to reduce the lesser, but nevertheless substantial, impairment of liberty imposed on an accused while released on bail, and to shorten the disruption of life caused by arrest and the presence of unresolved criminal charges." United States v. MacDonald, 456 U.S. 1, 8 (1982). Thus, "when defendants are not incarcerated or subjected to other substantial restrictions on their liberty, a court should not weigh that time towards a claim under the Speedy Trial Clause." *Loud Hawk*, supra, at 312.

A lengthy pretrial delay, of course, may prejudice an accused's ability to defend himself. But, we have explained, prejudice to the defense is not the sort of impairment of liberty against which the Clause is directed. . . .

[P]rejudice to the defense stems from the interval between *crime* and trial, which is quite distinct from the interval between *accusation* and trial. If the Clause were indeed aimed at safeguarding against prejudice to the defense, then it would presumably limit *all* prosecutions that occur long after the criminal events at issue. A defendant prosecuted 10 years after a crime is just as hampered in his ability to defend himself whether he was indicted the week after the crime or the week before the trial—but no one would suggest that the Clause protects him in the latter situation. . . .

Although being an "accused" is necessary to trigger the Clause's protection, it is not sufficient to do so. The touchstone of the speedy trial right, after all, is the substantial deprivation of liberty that typically accompanies an "accusation," *not* the accusation itself. That explains why a person who has been arrested but not indicted is entitled to the protection of the Clause, . . . even though technically he has not been "accused" at all. And it explains why the lower courts consistently have held that, with respect to sealed (and hence secret) indictments, the protections of the Speedy Trial Clause are triggered *not* when the indictment is *filed*, but when it is *unsealed*. . . .

. . . *Barker*'s suggestion that preventing prejudice to the defense is a fundamental and independent objective of the Clause is plainly dictum. Never, until today, have we confronted a case where a defendant subjected to a lengthy delay after indictment nonetheless failed to suffer any substantial impairment of his liberty. I think it fair to say that *Barker* simply did not contemplate such an unusual situation. . . .

Just because the Speedy Trial Clause does not independently protect against prejudice to the defense does not, of course, mean that a defendant is utterly unprotected in this regard. To the contrary, "the applicable statute of limitations . . . is . . . the primary guarantee against bringing overly stale criminal charges," *Marion*, 404 U.S. at 322. . . .

Furthermore, the Due Process Clause always protects defendants against fundamentally unfair treatment by the government in criminal proceedings. See United States v. Lovasco, 431 U.S. 783 (1977). . . .

Therefore, I see no basis for the Court's conclusion that Doggett is entitled to relief under the Speedy Trial Clause *simply* because the Government was negligent in prosecuting him and because the resulting delay may have prejudiced his defense.

B

It remains to be considered, however, whether Doggett is entitled to relief under the Speedy Trial Clause because of the disruption of his life years after the criminal events at issue. In other words, does the Clause protect a right to repose, free from secret or unknown indictments? In my view, it does not, for much the same reasons set forth above.

The common law recognized no right of criminals to repose. "The maxim of our law has always been 'Nullum tempus occurrit regi,' ['time does not run against the king'], and as a criminal trial is regarded as an action by the king, it follows that it may be brought at any time." 2 J. Stephen, A History of the Criminal Law of England 1, 2 (1883) (noting examples of delays in prosecution ranging from 14 to 35 years). . . .

That is not to deny that our legal system has long recognized the value of repose, both to the individual and to society. But that recognition finds expression not in the sweeping commands of the Constitution, or in the common law, but in any number of specific statutes of limitations enacted by the federal and state legislatures. Such statutes not only protect a defendant from prejudice to his defense (as discussed above), but also balance his interest in repose against society's interest in the apprehension and punishment of criminals. . . . In general, the graver the offense, the longer the limitations period; indeed, many serious offenses, such as murder, typically carry no limitations period at all. . . . These statutes refute the notion that our society ever has recognized any general right of criminals to repose.

Doggett, however, asks us to hold that a defendant's interest in repose is a value independently protected by the Speedy Trial Clause. He emphasizes that at the time of his arrest he was "leading a normal, productive and law-abiding life," and that his "arrest and prosecution at this late date interrupted his life as a productive member of society and forced him to answer for actions taken in the distant past." . . . However uplifting this tale of personal redemption, our task is to illuminate the protections of the Speedy Trial Clause, not to take the measure of one man's life.

There is no basis for concluding that the disruption of an accused's life years after the commission of his alleged crime is an evil independently protected by the Speedy Trial Clause. Such disruption occurs *regardless* of whether the individual is under indictment during the period of delay. Thus, had Doggett been indicted shortly before his 1988 arrest rather than shortly after his 1980 crime, his repose would have been equally shattered—but he would not have even a colorable speedy trial claim. To recognize a constitutional right to repose is to recognize a right to be tried speedily *after the offense*. That would, of course, convert the Speedy Trial Clause into a constitutional statute of limitations—a result with no basis in the text or history of the Clause or in our precedents.

II

. . . The Court's error, in my view, lies not so much in its particular application of the *Barker* test to the facts of this case, but more fundamentally in its failure to recognize that the speedy trial guarantee cannot be violated—and thus *Barker* does not apply at all—when an accused is *entirely unaware* of a pending indictment against him. . . .

Today's opinion, I fear, will transform the courts of the land into boards of law enforcement supervision. For the Court compels dismissal of the charges against Doggett not because he was harmed in any way by the delay between his indictment and arrest,[6] but simply because the Government's efforts to catch him are found wanting. Indeed, the Court expressly concedes that "if the Government had pursued Doggett with reasonable diligence from his indictment to his arrest, his speedy trial claim would fail." . . . Our function, however, is not to slap the Government on the wrist for sloppy work or misplaced priorities, but to protect the legal rights of those individuals harmed thereby. By divorcing the Speedy Trial Clause from all considerations of prejudice to an accused, the Court positively invites the Nation's judges to indulge in ad hoc and result-driven second-guessing of the government's investigatory efforts. Our Constitution neither contemplates nor tolerates such a role. I respectfully dissent.

NOTES AND QUESTIONS

1. Why did Doggett win, while Barker and Lovasco lost? Was the government's conduct somehow worse in Doggett's case? Did he suffer greater harm as a result of the lengthy delay in bringing him to trial? How important was it that Doggett, at the time of his trial, had become a law-abiding family man with a good job and education? Should it matter, for purposes of a Speedy Trial claim, whether Doggett was an upstanding citizen or was still selling drugs at the time of his trial?

2. The dissent claims that "odd facts make odd law." Granting that *Doggett* presents odd facts, how does the case change the law on when the Sixth Amendment is violated? Consider the fourth Barker v. Wingo factor, prejudice to the accused from the delay. Did the majority adequately explain how Doggett was prejudiced? If he truly was unaware of the pending indictment, he could not have suffered the stress and public condemnation that comes from being accused of a crime, and the harm

---

6. It is quite likely, in fact, that the delay *benefited* Doggett. At the time of his arrest, he had been living an apparently normal, law-abiding life for some five years—a point not lost on the District Court Judge, who, instead of imposing a prison term, sentenced him to three years' probation and a $1,000 fine. . . . Thus, the delay gave Doggett the opportunity to prove what most defendants can only promise: that he no longer posed a threat to society. There can be little doubt that, had he been tried immediately after his cocaine-importation activities, he would have received a harsher sentence.

to the defendant's legal case was, as the Court recognized, "unspecified." So what is the standard of prejudice after *Doggett?*

3. *Doggett* is also an unusual case in that he had a claim under the Speedy Trial Clause of the Sixth Amendment but not a claim under the Speedy Trial Act. Can you articulate why Doggett's statutory claim was not viable?

4. Defendants are not the only ones with an interest in a speedy trial. Victims (or their survivors) may also have a strong desire to see justice dispensed swiftly. Under the Crime Victims' Rights law, 18 U.S.C. §3771, federal crime victims have the "right to proceedings free from unreasonable delay," and the court has a duty to "ensure that the crime victim is afforded [this] right[]."

These provisions suggest that victims could object to continuances or other delays in the progression of a criminal case. Do you think the effect of these objections is to ensure a more responsive criminal system? Or is the process more likely to be distorted by those victims with the knowledge and resources to make their voices heard?

B. Venue

1. Location of the Crime

Venue refers to the geographic location of the trial. Where the trial is to be held is set in the first instance by the government when it files the criminal charge. So the initial, and usually final, decision of where a defendant will be tried rests with the prosecution. If challenged by the defense, the prosecutor must prove at trial that venue is proper, although only by a preponderance of the evidence.

Venue may sound like a technical, administrative detail in the processing of a criminal case—after all, in the federal system the substantive criminal laws and procedures are the same whether the trial takes place in New York or Alaska. But in fact, the venue of a case can have an enormous impact on the accused. A defendant who must stand trial far from his home may be cut off from family, friends, and his job; he may not have ready access to his lawyer, or may have difficulty retaining unfamiliar local counsel; and, he may have a more difficult time gathering evidence and interviewing witnesses.

The practice of moving colonists accused of crimes to England to stand trial was one of the grievances against the king enumerated in the Declaration of Independence: "For transporting us beyond Seas to be tried for pretended offenses." Given this, it was no surprise that the Framers included a provision in Article III Section 2 of the Constitution that "The trial of all crimes, except in cases of impeachment . . . shall be held in the state where the said crime shall have been committed." The drafters of the Bill of Rights also were concerned about this issue, specifying in the Sixth Amendment that "In all criminal prosecutions, the accused shall enjoy the right to a speedy and impartial trial, by an impartial jury of the State and district wherein the crime shall have been committed." The Sixth Amendment requirement is referred to as the "vicinage" provision, as it refers to the place from where the jury is to be drawn, rather than specifying the location of the trial itself. These requirements were later incorporated into Federal Rule of Criminal Procedure 18, which provides in part: "Unless a statute or these rules permit otherwise, the government must prosecute an offense in a district where the offense was committed."

So to determine whether venue is proper, prosecutors and reviewing courts must determine where the crime charged was "committed." Note that this requirement does not necessarily relieve the accused of the burdens of defending himself in a location far from home. A California resident who commits a theft in Maine while on vacation will have to stand trial in Maine, regardless of the difficulties. (This type of case obviously was much less common at the time of the country's founding, when most crimes were quite local.) A guilty defendant can hardly complain about the inconvenience, although an innocent person might, but on balance it seems that Maine's interest in protecting its residents makes it fair to hold the trial there.

Often the place where the crime committed is obvious, and leaves no choice to the prosecution. When a defendant robs a bank in Texas and is arrested in Texas, venue is proper in the Texas judicial district where the bank is located. But suppose the Texas bank robber flees to Oklahoma, where he is arrested after a violent confrontation and is charged with both bank robbery and assaulting a federal agent. Is venue for both charges proper in either state, or must there be two trials? Or suppose a kidnapper in Ohio drives his victim to Pennsylvania; is venue for the kidnapping charge proper in West Virginia, through which the getaway car briefly drove?

Hard venue questions usually arise in the context of "continuing crimes," that is, offenses where some of the elements are committed in one state or district and other elements occur in other states or districts. Congress has addressed this issue in 18 U.S.C. §3237, which provides in part:

> (a) Except as otherwise expressly provided by enactment of Congress, any offense against the United States begun in one district and completed in another, or committed in more than one district, may be inquired of and prosecuted in any district in which such offense was begun, continued, or completed.

This broadly worded statute would appear to give prosecutors the maximum degree of flexibility in deciding where a case should be brought, but even this statute leaves room for disagreement, as the next case shows.

UNITED STATES v. RODRIGUEZ-MORENO

Certiorari to the United States Court of Appeals for the Third Circuit
526 U.S. 275 (1999)

JUSTICE THOMAS delivered the opinion of the Court.

This case presents the question whether venue in a prosecution for using or carrying a firearm "during and in relation to any crime of violence," in violation of 18 U.S.C. §924(c)(1), is proper in any district where the crime of violence was committed, even if the firearm was used or carried only in a single district.

I

During a drug transaction that took place in Houston, Texas, a New York drug dealer stole 30 kilograms of a Texas drug distributor's cocaine. The distributor hired respondent, Jacinto Rodriguez-Moreno, and others to find the dealer and to hold captive the middleman in the transaction, Ephrain Avendano, during the search. In pursuit of the dealer, the distributor and his henchmen drove from Texas to New Jersey with Avendano in tow. The group used Avendano's New Jersey apartment as a base for their operations for a few days. They soon moved to a house in New York and then to a house in Maryland, taking Avendano with them.

Shortly after respondent and the others arrived at the Maryland house, the owner of the home passed around a .357 magnum revolver and respondent took possession of the pistol. As it became clear that efforts to find the New York drug dealer would not bear fruit, respondent told his employer that he thought they should kill the middleman and end their search for the dealer. He put the gun to the back of Avendano's neck but, at the urging of his cohorts, did not shoot. Avendano eventually escaped through the back door and ran to a neighboring house. The neighbors called the Maryland police, who arrested respondent along with the rest of the kidnapers. The police also seized the .357 magnum, on which they later found respondent's fingerprint.

Rodriguez-Moreno and his codefendants were tried jointly in the United States District Court for the District of New Jersey. Respondent was charged with, inter alia, conspiring to kidnap Avendano, kidnapping Avendano, and using and carrying a firearm in relation to the kidnapping of Avendano, in violation of 18 U.S.C. §924(c)(1). At the conclusion of the Government's case, respondent moved to dismiss the §924(c)(1) count for lack of venue. He argued that venue was proper only in Maryland, the only place where the Government had proved he had actually used a gun. The District Court denied the motion, App. 54, and the jury found respondent guilty on the kidnaping counts and on the §924(c)(1) charge as well. He was sentenced to 87 months' imprisonment on the kidnapping charges, and was given a mandatory consecutive term of 60 months' imprisonment for committing the §924(c)(1) offense.

On a 2-to-1 vote, the Court of Appeals for the Third Circuit reversed respondent's §924(c)(1) conviction. A majority of the Third Circuit panel applied what it called the "verb test" to §924(c)(1), and determined that a violation of the statute is committed only in the district where a defendant "uses" or "carries" a firearm. Accordingly, it concluded that venue for the §924(c)(1) count was improper in New Jersey even though venue was proper there for the kidnapping of Avendano. The dissenting judge thought that the majority's test relied too much "on grammatical arcana," and argued that the proper approach was to "look at the substance of the statutes in question." In his view, the crime of violence is an essential element of the course of conduct that Congress sought to criminalize in enacting §924(c)(1), and therefore, "venue for a prosecution under [that] statute lies in any district in which the defendant committed the underlying crime of violence." The Government petitioned for review on the ground that the Third Circuit's holding was in conflict with a decision of the Court of Appeals for the Fifth Circuit. We granted certiorari, and now reverse.

II

Article III of the Constitution requires that "[t]he Trial of all Crimes . . . shall be held in the State where the said Crimes shall have been committed." Art. III, §2, cl. 3. Its command is reinforced by the Sixth Amendment's requirement that "[i]n all criminal prosecutions, the accused shall enjoy the right to a speedy and public trial, by an impartial jury of the State and district wherein the crime shall have been committed," and is echoed by Rule 18 of the Federal Rules of Criminal Procedure ("prosecution shall be had in a district in which the offense was committed").

As we confirmed just last Term, the "*locus delicti* [of the charged offense] must be determined from the nature of the crime alleged and the location of the act or acts constituting it." United States v. Cabrales, 524 U.S. 1, 6-7 (1998). In performing this inquiry, a court must initially identify the conduct constituting the offense (the nature of the crime) and then discern the location of the commission of the criminal acts.

At the time respondent committed the offense and was tried, 18 U.S.C. §924(c)(1) provided:

> Whoever, during and in relation to any crime of violence . . . for which he may be prosecuted in a court of the United States, uses or carries a firearm, shall, in addition to the punishment provided for such crime of violence . . . be sentenced to imprisonment for five years. . . .

The Third Circuit, as explained above, looked to the verbs of the statute to determine the nature of the substantive offense. But we have never before held, and decline to do so here, that verbs are the sole consideration in identifying the conduct that constitutes an offense. While the "verb test" certainly has value as an interpretative tool, it cannot be applied rigidly, to the exclusion of other relevant statutory language. The test unduly limits the inquiry into the nature of the offense and thereby creates a danger that certain conduct prohibited by statute will be missed.

In our view, the Third Circuit overlooked an essential conduct element of the §924(c)(1) offense. Section 924(c)(1) prohibits using or carrying a firearm "during and in relation to any crime of violence . . . for which [a defendant] may be prosecuted in a court of the United States." That the crime of violence element of the statute is embedded in a prepositional phrase and not expressed in verbs does not dissuade us from concluding that a defendant's violent acts are essential conduct elements. To prove the charged §924(c)(1) violation in this case, the Government was required to show that respondent used a firearm, that he committed all the acts necessary to be subject to punishment for kidnapping (a crime of violence) in a court of the United States, and that he used the gun "during and in relation to" the kidnaping of Avendano. In sum, we interpret §924(c)(1) to contain two distinct conduct elements—as is relevant to this case, the "using and carrying" of a gun and the commission of a kidnapping.[4]

Respondent, however, argues that for venue purposes "the New Jersey kidnapping is completely irrelevant to the firearm crime, because respondent did not *use* or *carry* a gun *during* the New Jersey crime." In the words of one amicus, §924(c)(1) is a "point-in-time" offense that only is committed in the place where the kidnapping and the use of a gun coincide. We disagree. Several Circuits have determined that kidnapping is

---

4. By way of comparison, last Term in United States v. Cabrales, 524 U.S. 1 (1998), we considered whether venue for money laundering was proper in Missouri, where the laundered proceeds were unlawfully generated, or rather, only in Florida, where the prohibited laundering transactions occurred. As we interpreted the laundering statutes at issue, they did not proscribe "the anterior criminal conduct that yielded the funds allegedly laundered." *Cabrales*, 524 U.S., at 7. The existence of criminally generated proceeds was a circumstance element of the offense but the proscribed conduct—defendant's money laundering activity—occurred " 'after the fact' of an offense begun and completed by others." Here, by contrast, given the "during and in relation to" language, the underlying crime of violence is a critical part of the §924(c)(1) offense.

a unitary crime, and we agree with their conclusion. A kidnapping, once begun, does not end until the victim is free. It does not make sense, then, to speak of it in discrete geographic fragments. Section 924(c)(1) criminalized a defendant's use of a firearm "during and in relation to" a crime of violence; in doing so, Congress proscribed both the use of the firearm *and* the commission of acts that constitute a violent crime. It does not matter that respondent used the .357 magnum revolver, as the Government concedes, only in Maryland because he did so "during and in relation to" a kidnapping that was begun in Texas and continued in New York, New Jersey, and Maryland. In our view, §924(c)(1) does not define a "point-in-time" offense when a firearm is used during and in relation to a continuing crime of violence.

As we said in United States v. Lombardo, 241 U.S. 73 (1916), "where a crime consists of distinct parts which have different localities the whole may be tried where any part can be proved to have been done." Id., at 77. The kidnapping, to which the §924(c)(1) offense is attached, was committed in all of the places that any part of it took place, and venue for the kidnapping charge against respondent was appropriate in any of them. (Congress has provided that continuing offenses can be tried "in any district in which such offense was begun, continued, or completed," 18 U.S.C. §3237(a).) Where venue is appropriate for the underlying crime of violence, so too it is for the §924(c)(1) offense. As the kidnapping was properly tried in New Jersey, the §924(c)(1) offense could be tried there as well.

* * *

We hold that venue for this prosecution was proper in the district where it was brought. The judgment of the Court of Appeals is therefore reversed.

JUSTICE SCALIA, with whom JUSTICE STEVENS joins, dissenting.

I agree with the Court that in deciding where a crime was committed for purposes of the venue provision of Article III, §2, of the Constitution, and the vicinage provision of the Sixth Amendment, we must look at "the nature of the crime alleged and the location of the act or acts constituting it." I disagree with the Court, however, that the crime defined in 18 U.S.C. §924(c)(1) is "committed" either where the defendant commits the predicate offense or where he uses or carries the gun. It seems to me unmistakably clear from the text of the law that this crime can be committed only where the defendant *both* engages in the acts making up the predicate offense *and* uses or carries the gun.

[Section 924(c)(1)] prohibits the act of using or carrying a firearm "during" (and in relation to) a predicate offense. The provisions of the United States Code defining the particular predicate offenses already punish all of the defendant's alleged criminal conduct except his use or carriage of a gun; §924(c)(1) itself criminalizes and punishes such use or carriage "during" the predicate crime, because that makes the crime more dangerous. This is a simple concept, and it is embodied in a straightforward text. To answer the question before us we need only ask where the defendant's alleged act of using a firearm during (and in relation to) a kidnaping occurred. Since it occurred only in Maryland, venue will lie only there.

The Court, however, relies on United States v. Lombardo, 241 U.S. 73, 77 (1916), for the proposition that "where a crime consists of distinct parts which have different localities the whole may be tried where any part can be proved to have been done." The fallacy in this reliance is that the crime before us does *not* consist of "distinct" parts that can occur in different localities. Its two parts are bound inseparably together by the word "during." Where the gun is being used, the predicate act must be occurring as well, and vice versa. The Court quite simply reads this requirement out of the statute—as though there were no difference between a statute making it a crime to steal a cookie and eat it (which could be prosecuted either in New Jersey, where the cookie was stolen, or in Maryland, where it was eaten) and a statute making it a crime to eat a cookie while robbing a bakery (which could be prosecuted only where the ingestive theft occurred).

The Court believes its holding is justified by the continuing nature of the kidnaping predicate offense, which invokes the statute providing that "any offense against the United States begun in one district and completed in another, or committed in more than one district, may be inquired of and prosecuted in any district in which such offense was begun, continued, or completed." 18 U.S.C. §3237(a). To disallow the New Jersey prosecution here, the Court suggests, is to convert §924(c)(1) from a continuing offense to a "point-in-time" offense. That is simply not so. I in no way contend that the kidnaping, or, for that matter, the use of the gun, can occur only at one point in time. Each can extend over a protracted period, and in many places. But §924(c)(1) is violated only so long as, *and where*, both continuing acts are being committed simultaneously. That is what the word "during" means. . . .

The short of the matter is that this defendant, who has a constitutional right to be tried in the State and district where his alleged crime was "committed," U.S. Const., Art. III, §2, cl. 3; Amdt. 6, has been prosecuted for using a gun during a kidnapping in a State and district where all agree he did not use a gun during a kidnapping. If to state this case is not to decide it, the law has departed further from the meaning of language than is appropriate for a government that is supposed to rule (and to be restrained) through the written word.

NOTES AND QUESTIONS

1. Was *Rodriguez-Moreno* correctly decided? Is it consistent with the intent of the constitutional protection for venue to say that the crime of using a firearm during a crime of violence took place in New Jersey, when there is no evidence that anyone possessed a gun there?

2. If you agree with the dissent that the weapons crime only occurred in Maryland, how would you distinguish the following case: The defendant steals a painting in Illinois, flees to Indiana, and is later charged with interstate transportation of stolen property. If he is charged with the crime in Illinois, can it fairly be said that the crime "occurred" there, before the stolen art actually moved across state lines? 18 U.S.C. §3237, which is quoted in the introduction to this section and mentioned in *Rodriguez-Moreno*, seems to say that venue would be proper in Illinois, but if so, why is *Rodriguez-Moreno* different?

3. In footnote 4 of *Rodriguez-Moreno*, the court distinguishes a venue case it had decided the previous term. In United States v. Cabrales, 524 U.S. 1 (1998), the defendant was charged with money laundering, as she allegedly had engaged in financial transactions that were both designed to avoid federal reporting requirements and that also involved criminally derived property. The "laundering" took place entirely in Florida; the money that was laundered came from cocaine sales that took place in Missouri. The question was whether venue for the money laundering charges was proper in Missouri.

The Court began by recognizing that where the crime occurred "must be determined from the nature of the crime alleged and the location of the act or acts constituting it." After examining the money laundering statutes, it concluded that they "interdict only the financial transactions (acts located entirely in Florida), not the anterior criminal conduct that yielded the funds allegedly laundered." The Court rejected the government's argument that these crimes were "continuing" offenses, ones that began with the accumulation of the illegal proceeds in Missouri. While the Court agreed that under the statutes "the money launderer must know she is dealing with funds derived from 'specified unlawful activity,' here, drug trafficking," it also concluded that the location of those unlawful activities was "of no moment" to the defendant. Under the statutes, the crime took place where the conduct occurred—the financial transactions themselves—not where the events giving rise to the circumstance element (the illegality of the funds) took place.

Is it possible to extract a consistent principle from *Rodriguez-Moreno* and *Cabrales?* Look again at the distinction between the two cases drawn in footnote 4 of *Rodriguez-Moreno.* Does the distinction between the circumstance element in *Cabrales* and the "critical part" of the statute in *Rodriguez-Moreno* provide some guidance?

4. One type of continuing crime that can easily raise venue questions is conspiracy. Because the essence of a conspiracy is the agreement to commit an offense, conspirators in large criminal enterprises can be scattered across the country. As will be seen in the section on joinder and severance (see Section C, below), a conspiracy charge is also one of the bases for joining multiple defendants into a single trial in a single location. So in a multistate conspiracy, where is venue proper?

The federal rule is quite expansive: Venue is proper in any jurisdiction where the agreement was made *or* where an overt act in furtherance of the conspiracy occurred. Thus, if *A* in Alaska, *B* in Idaho, and *C* in California agree by telephone to manufacture illegal drugs, and if *B* then goes to Montana to obtain a needed chemical, each of the three defendants could be required to stand trial for conspiracy in any of the four states.

Note, however, that the broad rule extends only to the conspiracy itself, and not necessarily to the crime that is the object of the conspiracy. In United States v. Walden, 464 F.2d 1015 (4th Cir. 1972), for example, the defendants were charged with both conspiracy to commit bank robbery and with the completed bank robbery. Both charges were filed in South Carolina, where overt acts in furtherance of the conspiracy had admittedly taken place. But the banks were located in other states, and the court found that venue for these robberies was proper only in those other states—that is, only in the states where the bank robbery actually occurred. Thus, a prosecutor who wants to bring both a conspiracy and a substantive charge in a single case must file the charges where venue is proper on the substantive counts.

5. 18 U.S.C. §3237 covers more than just venue for continuing offenses. The statute also provides:

> Any offense involving the use of the mails, transportation in interstate or foreign commerce, or the importation of an object or person into the United States is a continuing offense and, except as otherwise expressly provided by enactment of Congress, may be inquired of and prosecuted in any district from, through, or into which such commerce, mail matter, or imported object or person moves.

This provision is strikingly broad. Most notably, if an offense involves the use of the mails, venue is proper is any district from, *through*, or into which the mail travels.

Taken literally, a package of drugs that is mailed from Georgia to an addressee in Oregon would make venue proper in Utah if the mail happened to pass through there, even though the people of Utah would otherwise be unaffected by (and unaware of) the offense. In what respect can it be said that the crime "occurred" in Utah simply because the package passed through there, unopened, on its trip to the West Coast?

There is some reason to think that the statute should not be taken at face value. In United States v. Brennan, 183 F.3d 139 (2d Cir. 1999), the defendants were charged with mail fraud under 18 U.S.C. §1341. The allegedly fraudulent mailings were sent from the defendant's offices in the Southern District of New York, but the case was filed in the Eastern District of New York. The government defended its venue choice by showing that the fraudulent mailings would have gone through either Kennedy or LaGuardia airports, both of which were located in the Eastern District, and that the mail would have thus moved "through" there within the meaning of §3237. The Second Circuit rejected the argument, holding that "the mail fraud statute does not proscribe conduct involving 'the use of the mails' *within the meaning of §3237(a)*" (emphasis added). Although the Court admitted that this conclusion was "perhaps surprising," it went on to find that the "history and purpose" of §3237(a), and more important, the constitutional protection of defendants' "venue rights" showed that venue was improper. The court therefore reversed the convictions.

Whatever the merits of the Second Circuit's statutory interpretation, it is probably fair to read *Brennan* as a cautionary tale for prosecutors who are tempted to use the statutory venue powers to their fullest extent.

6. What about crimes committed in cyberspace? United States v. Auernheimer, 748 F.3d 525 (3d Cir. 2014), involved Andrew "weev" Auernheimer, an infamous computer "hacktivist." Working with a companion, "weev" managed to exploit a security flaw in AT&T's login software to obtain the e-mail addresses of 114,000 iPad owners; these e-mail addresses were disclosed to a news reporter, who proceeded to publish some of them. "weev" was indicted in the District of New Jersey on federal charges of conspiracy to violate both the Computer Fraud and Anti-Abuse Act (CFAA), 18 U.S.C. §1030(a)(5)(A), and a New Jersey computer-crime law, as well as federal identity theft in violation of 18 U.S.C. §1028(a)(7). "weev" was convicted and sentenced to 41 months in prison.

On appeal, the Third Circuit had to decide: What was the proper venue for the case? Was it where "weev" and his companion were located when they engaged in the behavior that constituted the crime? (This was Fayetteville, Arkansas, and San Francisco.) Was it where the AT&T servers that "weev" breached were located? (This was Dallas, Texas, and Atlanta, Georgia.) Was it where the reporter was based? (This was never proven at trial, but the Third Circuit concluded that it was *not* New Jersey.) Was it where the victims of the identity fraud lived? (This was potentially everywhere in the United States—including New Jersey, where about 4,500 of the victims lived.)

The Third Circuit reversed the convictions. The court first explained the task before it:

Venue in criminal cases is more than a technicality; it involves "matters that touch closely the fair administration of criminal justice and public confidence in it." United States v. Johnson, 323 U.S. 273, 276 (1944). This is especially true of computer crimes in the era of mass interconnectivity. . . .

Congress may prescribe specific venue requirements for particular crimes. Where it has not, as is the case here, we must determine the crime's locus delicti. "[T]he locus delicti must be determined from the nature of the crime alleged and the location of the act or acts constituting it." United States v. Anderson, 328 U.S. 699, 703 (1946). To perform this inquiry, we "must [1] initially identify the conduct constituting the offense . . . and then [2] discern the location of the commission of the criminal acts." *Rodriguez-Moreno*, 526 U.S. at 279. Venue should be narrowly construed. *Johnson*, 323 U.S. at 276. . . . In performing our venue inquiry, we must be careful to separate "essential conduct elements" from "circumstance element[s]." *Rodriguez-Moreno*, 526 U.S. at 280 & n. 4. . . . Only "essential conduct elements" can provide the basis for venue; "circumstance elements" cannot.

748 F.3d, at 529, 532-533.

The court analyzed each of the relevant crime statutes to determine the "essential conduct" prohibited. For conspiracy, this was either the "essential conduct" of the underlying crime(s), or any "overt act" in furtherance of the conspiracy. For the CFAA crime, it was "accessing [a computer] without authorization and obtaining information." For the New Jersey computer crime, it was "accessing [a computer] without authorization (or in excess of authorization) and disclosing data or personal identifying information." And for the federal identity theft crime, it was the "transfer, possession, or use [of the identity information], and doing so in connection with a federal crime or state felony."

Having identified the "essential conduct" prohibited, the court concluded that none of this conduct occurred in New Jersey. As for the two computer crimes, "[n]o protected computer was accessed and no data was obtained in New Jersey." As for the identity fraud crime, there was "no evidence that [the] transfer, possession, or use [of the information] occurred in New Jersey." Finally, none of the "overt acts alleged"—which included writing the program that obtained the e-mail addresses, deploying the program, and disclosing the e-mail addresses to the news reporter—occurred in New Jersey.

The court rejected the government's argument that, given the effects of the crime on New Jersey residents, an alternative "substantial contacts" test could be used to establish proper venue in New Jersey:

> Undoubtedly there are some instances where the location in which a crime's effects are felt is relevant to determining whether venue is proper. See *Rodriguez-Moreno*, 526 U.S. at 279 n. 2 (reserving the issue of whether venue may also be permissibly based on the location where a crime's effects are felt). But those cases are reserved for situations in which an essential conduct element is itself defined in terms of its effects. For example, in a prosecution for Hobbs Act robbery, venue may be proper in any district where commerce is affected because the terms of the act themselves forbid affecting commerce. See 18 U.S.C. §1951(a).

748 F.3d, at 537. The various crimes in *Auernheimer*, however, were not so defined by their effects. The court likewise rejected the government's argument that any error with respect to venue was "harmless," noting that (1) the Supreme Court has never held that venue errors are subject to "harmless error" analysis, and (2) in any event, the error was not "harmless" because it affected the defendant's "substantial right to be tried in the place where his alleged crime was committed." The court closed its opinion thusly:

> As we progress technologically, we must remain mindful that cybercrimes do not happen in some metaphysical location that justifies disregarding constitutional limits on venue. People and computers still exist in identifiable places in the physical world.

> When people commit crimes, we have the ability and obligation to ensure that they do not stand to account for those crimes in forums in which they performed no "essential conduct element" of the crimes charged. *Rodriguez-Moreno*, 526 U.S. at 280.

748 F.3d, at 541.

Clearly, cybercrime presents a daunting challenge for the courts in terms of determining the proper venue. Was the Third Circuit right to draw a line in the sand in *Auernheimer*? Or should cybercriminals be held to run the risk of being hauled into court wherever their victims may be found? Isn't that risk inherent (and obvious) in cybercrime?

2. Changes of Venue

A defendant has a constitutional right to have his case resolved where the crime was committed. But what if he doesn't *want* it there? Given the prosecutor's ability to set venue in some cases (discussed above), defendant's may believe that the place set for trial is prejudicial, because it is far removed from the defense witnesses and evidence. Some other crimes are sufficiently notorious in the place they occurred that a defendant might prefer to have the case tried elsewhere, where the facts are less well known and the passions of the potential jurors are less enflamed. The question then arises: When is a court permitted to, and when is it required to, grant a defense request to move the case?

The Federal Rules provide two avenues for a defendant who wishes to change venue. Rule 21(b) states:

> Upon the defendant's motion, the court may transfer the proceeding, or one or more counts, against that defendant to another district for the convenience of the parties and witnesses and in the interest of justice.

Notice that while the court is to consider the convenience of both parties and the witnesses in ruling on a motion, only the defendant can initiate the process. At its core, the Rule is designed to help the defendant who is prejudiced by having to defend himself in a remote location, which is the concern that lies at the heart of the constitutional venue protection.

A second ground for changing venue is found in Rule 21(a), which provides:

> Upon the defendant's motion, the court must transfer the proceeding against that defendant to another district if the court is satisfied that so great a prejudice against the defendant exists in the transferring district that the defendant cannot obtain a fair and impartial trial there.

Here the court "must" transfer a case on request if keeping the case where it was filed would deprive the defendant of a fair trial. Again, the focus is on the defendant—because the constitutional venue protections run to the accused, only the defense can seek a change of venue for unfair prejudice. This is so even though courts have recognized that the government itself has a compelling interest in a fair criminal proceeding, and even though, in some cases, community sentiment may run strongly in favor of the accused (the popular politician caught taking a bribe, for example). But even if there is a risk that the government's case will not be given unbiased consideration in the district where the crime occurred, a case cannot be transferred against the defendant's wishes.

Cases where the defendant seeks a change of venue for pretrial publicity are relatively rare, but in high-profile cases, involving prominent victims or defendants, or gruesome or sordid facts, the risks of a biased jury pool can be significant. Consider the Supreme Court's latest word on what type of showing it takes to demonstrate that pretrial publicity deprived the defendant of a fair trial.

SKILLING v. UNITED STATES

Certiorari to the United States Court of Appeals for the Fifth Circuit
561 U.S. 358 (2010)

JUSTICE GINSBURG delivered the opinion of the Court.

In 2001, Enron Corporation, then the seventh highest-revenue-grossing company in America, crashed into bankruptcy. We consider in this opinion two questions arising from the prosecution of Jeffrey Skilling, a longtime Enron executive, for crimes committed before the corporation's collapse. First, did pretrial publicity and community prejudice prevent Skilling from obtaining a fair trial? Second, did the jury improperly convict Skilling of conspiracy to commit "honest-services" wire fraud, 18 U.S.C. §§371, 1343, 1346?

Answering no to both questions, the Fifth Circuit affirmed Skilling's convictions. We conclude, in common with the Court of Appeals, that Skilling's fair-trial argument fails; Skilling, we hold, did not establish that a presumption of juror prejudice arose or that actual bias infected the jury that tried him. But we disagree with the Fifth Circuit's honest-services ruling. . . . We therefore affirm in part and vacate in part.[2]

I

Founded in 1985, Enron Corporation grew from its headquarters in Houston, Texas, into one of the world's leading energy companies. Skilling launched his career there in 1990 when Kenneth Lay, the company's founder, hired him to head an Enron subsidiary. Skilling steadily rose through the corporation's ranks, serving as president and chief operating officer, and then, beginning in February 2001, as chief executive officer. Six months later, on August 14, 2001, Skilling resigned from Enron.

Less than four months after Skilling's departure, Enron spiraled into bankruptcy. The company's stock, which had traded at $90 per share in August 2000, plummeted to pennies per share in late 2001. Attempting to comprehend what caused the corporation's collapse, the U.S. Department of Justice formed an Enron Task Force, comprising prosecutors and FBI agents from around the Nation. The Government's investigation uncovered an elaborate conspiracy to prop up Enron's short-run stock prices by overstating the company's financial well-being. In the years following Enron's bankruptcy, the Government prosecuted dozens of Enron employees who

---

2. The "honest services" portion of the Court's opinion is omitted. — EDS.

participated in the scheme. In time, the Government worked its way up the corporation's chain of command: On July 7, 2004, a grand jury indicted Skilling, Lay, and Richard Causey, Enron's former chief accounting officer.

These three defendants, the indictment alleged,

> engaged in a wide-ranging scheme to deceive the investing public, including Enron's shareholders, . . . about the true performance of Enron's businesses by: (a) manipulating Enron's publicly reported financial results; and (b) making public statements and representations about Enron's financial performance and results that were false and misleading.

Skilling and his co-conspirators, the indictment continued, "enriched themselves as a result of the scheme through salary, bonuses, grants of stock and stock options, other profits, and prestige."

In November 2004, Skilling moved to transfer the trial to another venue; he contended that hostility toward him in Houston, coupled with extensive pretrial publicity, had poisoned potential jurors. To support this assertion, Skilling, aided by media experts, submitted hundreds of news reports detailing Enron's downfall; he also presented affidavits from the experts he engaged portraying community attitudes in Houston in comparison to other potential venues.

The U.S. District Court for the Southern District of Texas, in accord with rulings in two earlier instituted Enron-related prosecutions, denied the venue-transfer motion. Despite "isolated incidents of intemperate commentary," the court observed, media coverage "ha[d][mostly] been objective and unemotional," and the facts of the case were "neither heinous nor sensational." Moreover, "courts ha[d] commonly" favored "effective voir dire . . . to ferret out any [juror] bias." Pretrial publicity about the case, the court concluded, did not warrant a presumption that Skilling would be unable to obtain a fair trial in Houston.

In the months leading up to the trial, the District Court solicited from the parties questions the court might use to screen prospective jurors. Unable to agree on a questionnaire's format and content, Skilling and the Government submitted dueling documents. On venire members' sources of Enron-related news, for example, the Government proposed that they tick boxes from a checklist of generic labels such as "[t]elevision," "[n]ewspaper," and "[r]adio"; Skilling proposed more probing questions asking venire members to list the specific names of their media sources and to report on "what st[ood] out in [their] mind[s]" of "all the things [they] ha[d] seen, heard or read about Enron."

The District Court rejected the Government's sparer inquiries in favor of Skilling's submission. Skilling's questions "[we]re more helpful," the court said, "because [they][we]re generally . . . open-ended and w[ould] allow the potential jurors to give us more meaningful information." The court converted Skilling's submission, with slight modifications, into a 77-question, 14-page document that asked prospective jurors about, inter alia, their sources of news and exposure to Enron-related publicity, beliefs concerning Enron and what caused its collapse, opinions regarding the defendants and their possible guilt or innocence, and relationships to the company and to anyone affected by its demise.

In November 2005, the District Court mailed the questionnaire to 400 prospective jurors and received responses from nearly all the addressees. The court granted hardship exemptions to approximately 90 individuals, and the parties, with the court's approval, further winnowed the pool by excusing another 119 for cause, hardship, or physical disability. The parties agreed to exclude, in particular, "each and every" prospective juror who said that a preexisting opinion about Enron or the defendants would prevent her from impartially considering the evidence at trial.

On December 28, 2005, three weeks before the date scheduled for the commencement of trial, Causey pleaded guilty. Skilling's attorneys immediately requested a continuance, and the District Court agreed to delay the proceedings until the end of January 2006. In the interim, Skilling renewed his change-of-venue motion, arguing that the juror questionnaires revealed pervasive bias and that news accounts of Causey's guilty plea further tainted the jury pool. If Houston remained the trial venue, Skilling urged that "jurors need to be questioned individually by both the Court *and* counsel" concerning their opinions of Enron and "publicity issues."

The District Court again declined to move the trial. Skilling, the court concluded, still had not "establish[ed] that pretrial publicity and/or community prejudice raise[d] a presumption of inherent jury prejudice." The questionnaires and voir dire, the court observed, provided safeguards adequate to ensure an impartial jury.

Denying Skilling's request for attorney-led voir dire, the court said that in 17 years on the bench:

> I've found . . . I get more forthcoming responses from potential jurors than the lawyers on either side. I don't know whether people are suspicious of lawyers—but I think if I ask a person a question, I will get a candid response much easier than if a lawyer asks the question.

But the court promised to give counsel an opportunity to ask follow-up questions, and it agreed that venire members should be examined individually about pretrial publicity. The court also allotted the defendants jointly 14 peremptory challenges, 2 more than the standard number prescribed by Federal Rule of Criminal Procedure 24(b)(2) and (c)(4)(B).

Voir dire began on January 30, 2006. The District Court first emphasized to the venire the importance of impartiality and explained the presumption of innocence and the Government's burden of proof. The trial, the court next instructed, was not a forum "to seek vengeance against Enron's former officers," or to "provide remedies for" its victims. "The bottom line," the court stressed, "is that we want . . . jurors who . . . will faithfully, conscientiously and impartially serve if selected." In response to the court's query whether any prospective juror questioned her ability to adhere to these instructions, two individuals indicated that they could not be fair; they were therefore excused for cause.

After questioning the venire as a group, the District Court brought prospective jurors one by one to the bench for individual examination. Although the questions varied, the process generally tracked the following format: The court asked about exposure to Enron-related news and the content of any stories that stood out in the prospective juror's mind. Next, the court homed in on questionnaire answers that raised a red flag signaling possible bias. The court then permitted each side to pose follow-up questions. Finally, after the venire member stepped away, the court entertained and ruled on challenges for cause. In all, the court granted one of the

Government's for cause challenges and denied four; it granted three of the defendants' challenges and denied six. The parties agreed to excuse three additional jurors for cause and one for hardship.

By the end of the day, the court had qualified 38 prospective jurors, a number sufficient, allowing for peremptory challenges, to empanel 12 jurors and 4 alternates. Before the jury was sworn in, Skilling objected to the seating of six jurors. He did not contend that they were in fact biased; instead, he urged that he would have used peremptories to exclude them had he not exhausted his supply by striking several venire members after the court refused to excuse them for cause. The court overruled this objection. . . .

Following a 4-month trial and nearly five days of deliberation, the jury found Skilling guilty of 19 counts, including the honest-services-fraud conspiracy charge, and not guilty of 9 insider-trading counts. The District Court sentenced Skilling to 292 months' imprisonment, 3 years' supervised release, and $45 million in restitution.

On appeal, Skilling raised a host of challenges to his convictions, including the fair-trial and honest-services arguments he presses here. Regarding the former, the Fifth Circuit initially determined that the volume and negative tone of media coverage generated by Enron's collapse created a presumption of juror prejudice. 554 F.3d 529, 559 (2009). The court also noted potential prejudice stemming from Causey's guilty plea and from the large number of victims in Houston—from the "[t]housands of Enron employees . . . [who] lost their jobs, and . . . saw their 401(k) accounts wiped out," to Houstonians who suffered spill-over economic effects.

The Court of Appeals stated, however, that "the presumption [of prejudice] is rebuttable," and it therefore examined the voir dire to determine whether "the District Court empaneled an impartial jury." The voir dire was, in the Fifth Circuit's view, "proper and thorough." Moreover, the court noted, Skilling had challenged only one seated juror—Juror 11—for cause. Although Juror 11 made some troubling comments about corporate greed, the District Court "observed [his] demeanor, listened to his answers, and believed he would make the government prove its case." In sum, the Fifth Circuit found that the Government had overcome the presumption of prejudice and that Skilling had not "show[n] that any juror who actually sat was prejudiced against him."

Arguing that the Fifth Circuit erred in its consideration of these claims, Skilling sought relief from this Court. We granted certiorari, 558 U.S. 945 (2009), and now affirm in part, vacate in part, and remand for further proceedings.

II

Pointing to "the community passion aroused by Enron's collapse and the vitriolic media treatment" aimed at him, Skilling argues that his trial "never should have proceeded in Houston." And even if it had been possible to select impartial jurors in Houston, "[t]he truncated voir dire . . . did almost nothing to weed out prejudices," he contends, so "[f]ar from rebutting the presumption of prejudice, the record below affirmatively confirmed it." Skilling's fair-trial claim thus raises two distinct questions. First, did the District Court err by failing to move the trial to a different venue based on a presumption of prejudice? Second, did actual prejudice contaminate Skilling's jury?

A

1

The Sixth Amendment secures to criminal defendants the right to trial by an impartial jury. By constitutional design, that trial occurs "in the State where the . . . Crimes . . . have been committed." Art. III, §2, cl. 3. See also Amdt. 6 (right to trial by "jury of the State and district wherein the crime shall have been committed"). The Constitution's place-of-trial prescriptions, however, do not impede transfer of the proceeding to a different district at the defendant's request if extraordinary local prejudice will prevent a fair trial—a "basic requirement of due process," In re Murchison, 349 U.S. 133, 136 (1955).[11]

2

"The theory of our [trial] system is that the conclusions to be reached in a case will be induced only by evidence and argument in open court, and not by any outside influence, whether of private talk or public print." Patterson v. Colorado ex rel. Attorney General of Colo., 205 U.S. 454, 462 (1907) (opinion for the Court by Holmes, J.). When does the publicity attending conduct charged as criminal dim prospects that the trier can judge a case, as due process requires, impartially, unswayed by outside influence? Because most cases of consequence garner at least some pretrial publicity, courts have considered this question in diverse settings. We begin our discussion by addressing the presumption of prejudice from which the Fifth Circuit's analysis in Skilling's case proceeded. The foundation precedent is Rideau v. Louisiana, 373 U.S. 723 (1963).

Wilbert Rideau robbed a bank in a small Louisiana town, kidnaped three bank employees, and killed one of them. Police interrogated Rideau in jail without counsel present and obtained his confession. Without informing Rideau, no less seeking his consent, the police filmed the interrogation. On three separate occasions shortly before the trial, a local television station broadcast the film to audiences ranging from 24,000 to 53,000 individuals. Rideau moved for a change of venue, arguing that he could not receive a fair trial in the parish where the crime occurred, which had a population of approximately 150,000 people. The trial court denied the motion, and a jury eventually convicted Rideau. The Supreme Court of Louisiana upheld the conviction.

We reversed. "What the people [in the community] saw on their television sets," we observed, "was Rideau, in jail, flanked by the sheriff and two state troopers, admitting in detail the commission of the robbery, kidnapping, and murder." "[T]o the tens of thousands of people who saw and heard it," we explained, the interrogation "in a very real sense *was* Rideau's trial—at which he pleaded guilty." We therefore "d[id] not hesitate to hold, without pausing to examine a particularized transcript of the voir dire," that "[t]he kangaroo court proceedings" trailing the televised confession violated due process.

---

11. Venue transfer in federal court is governed by Federal Rule of Criminal Procedure 21, which instructs that a "court must transfer the proceeding . . . to another district if the court is satisfied that so great a prejudice against the defendant exists in the transferring district that the defendant cannot obtain a fair and impartial trial there." . . . Skilling does not argue, distinct from his due process challenge, that the District Court abused its discretion under Rule 21 by declining to move his trial. We therefore review the District Court's venue-transfer decision only for compliance with the Constitution.

We followed *Rideau*'s lead in two later cases in which media coverage manifestly tainted a criminal prosecution. In Estes v. Texas, 381 U.S. 532, 538 (1965), extensive publicity before trial swelled into excessive exposure during preliminary court proceedings as reporters and television crews overran the courtroom and "bombard[ed] . . . the community with the sights and sounds of" the pretrial hearing. The media's overzealous reporting efforts, we observed, "led to considerable disruption" and denied the "judicial serenity and calm to which [Billie Sol Estes] was entitled."

Similarly, in Sheppard v. Maxwell, 384 U.S. 333 (1966), news reporters extensively covered the story of Sam Sheppard, who was accused of bludgeoning his pregnant wife to death. "[B]edlam reigned at the courthouse during the trial and newsmen took over practically the entire courtroom," thrusting jurors "into the role of celebrities." Pretrial media coverage, which we characterized as "months [of] virulent publicity about Sheppard and the murder," did not alone deny due process, we noted. But Sheppard's case involved more than heated reporting pretrial: We upset the murder conviction because a "carnival atmosphere" pervaded the trial.

In each of these cases, we overturned a "conviction obtained in a trial atmosphere that [was] utterly corrupted by press coverage"; our decisions, however, "cannot be made to stand for the proposition that juror exposure to . . . news accounts of the crime . . . alone presumptively deprives the defendant of due process." Murphy v. Florida, 421 U.S. 794, 798-799 (1975). See also, e.g., Patton v. Yount, 467 U.S. 1025 (1984).[13] Prominence does not necessarily produce prejudice, and juror *impartiality*, we have reiterated, does not require *ignorance*. Irvin v. Dowd, 366 U.S. 717, 722 (1961) (Jurors are not required to be "totally ignorant of the facts and issues involved"; "scarcely any of those best qualified to serve as jurors will not have formed some impression or opinion as to the merits of the case. A presumption of prejudice, our decisions indicate, attends only the extreme case.")

3

Relying on *Rideau*, *Estes*, and *Sheppard*, Skilling asserts that we need not pause to examine the screening questionnaires or the voir dire before declaring his jury's verdict void. We are not persuaded. Important differences separate Skilling's prosecution from those in which we have presumed juror prejudice.[14]

First, we have emphasized in prior decisions the size and characteristics of the community in which the crime occurred. In *Rideau*, for example, we noted that the murder was committed in a parish of only 150,000 residents. Houston, in contrast, is the fourth most populous city in the Nation: At the time of Skilling's trial, more than 4.5 million individuals eligible for jury duty resided in the Houston area. Given this large, diverse pool of potential jurors, the suggestion that 12 impartial

---

13. In *Yount*, the media reported on Jon Yount's confession to a brutal murder and his prior conviction for the crime, which had been reversed due to a violation of Miranda v. Arizona, 384 U.S. 436 (1966). During voir dire, 77% of prospective jurors acknowledged they would carry an opinion into the jury box, and 8 of the 14 seated jurors and alternates admitted they had formed an opinion as to Yount's guilt. Nevertheless, we rejected Yount's presumption-of-prejudice claim. The adverse publicity and community outrage, we noted, were at their height prior to Yount's first trial, four years before the second prosecution; time had helped "sooth[e] and eras[e]" community prejudice.

14. Skilling's reliance on *Estes* and *Sheppard* is particularly misplaced; those cases involved media interference with courtroom proceedings *during* trial. Skilling does not assert that news coverage reached and influenced his jury after it was empaneled.

individuals could not be empaneled is hard to sustain. See Mu'Min v. Virginia, 500 U.S. 415, 429 (1991) (potential for prejudice mitigated by the size of the "metropolitan Washington [D.C.] statistical area, which has a population of over 3 million, and in which, unfortunately, hundreds of murders are committed each year").

Second, although news stories about Skilling were not kind, they contained no confession or other blatantly prejudicial information of the type readers or viewers could not reasonably be expected to shut from sight. Rideau's dramatically staged admission of guilt, for instance, was likely imprinted indelibly in the mind of anyone who watched it. Pretrial publicity about Skilling was less memorable and prejudicial. No evidence of the smoking-gun variety invited prejudgment of his culpability. See United States v. Chagra, 669 F.2d 241, 251-252, n. 11 (CA5 1982) ("A jury may have difficulty in disbelieving or forgetting a defendant's opinion of his own guilt but have no difficulty in rejecting the opinions of others because they may not be well-founded.").

Third, unlike cases in which trial swiftly followed a widely reported crime, over four years elapsed between Enron's bankruptcy and Skilling's trial. Although reporters covered Enron-related news throughout this period, the decibel level of media attention diminished somewhat in the years following Enron's collapse.

Finally, and of prime significance, Skilling's jury acquitted him of nine insider-trading counts. Similarly, earlier instituted Enron-related prosecutions yielded no overwhelming victory for the Government. In *Rideau*, *Estes*, and *Sheppard*, in marked contrast, the jury's verdict did not undermine in any way the supposition of juror bias. It would be odd for an appellate court to presume prejudice in a case in which jurors' actions run counter to that presumption.

4

Skilling's trial, in short, shares little in common with those in which we approved a presumption of juror prejudice. The Fifth Circuit reached the opposite conclusion based primarily on the magnitude and negative tone of media attention directed at Enron. But "pretrial publicity—even pervasive, adverse publicity—does not inevitably lead to an unfair trial." Nebraska Press Assn. v. Stuart, 427 U.S. 539, 554 (1976). In this case, as just noted, news stories about Enron did not present the kind of vivid, unforgettable information we have recognized as particularly likely to produce prejudice, and Houston's size and diversity diluted the media's impact.

Nor did Enron's "sheer number of victims" trigger a presumption of prejudice. Although the widespread community impact necessitated careful identification and inspection of prospective jurors' connections to Enron, the extensive screening questionnaire and follow-up voir dire were well suited to that task. And hindsight shows the efficacy of these devices; as we discuss infra, . . . jurors' links to Enron were either nonexistent or attenuated.

Finally, although Causey's "well-publicized decision to plead guilty" shortly before trial created a danger of juror prejudice, the District Court took appropriate steps to reduce that risk. The court delayed the proceedings by two weeks, lessening the immediacy of that development. And during voir dire, the court asked about prospective jurors' exposure to recent publicity, including news regarding Causey. Only two venire members recalled the plea; neither mentioned Causey by name, and neither ultimately served on Skilling's jury. Although publicity about a codefendant's guilty plea calls for inquiry to guard against actual prejudice, it does not ordinarily—and, we are satisfied, it did not here—warrant an automatic presumption of prejudice.

Persuaded that no presumption arose,[18] we conclude that the District Court, in declining to order a venue change, did not exceed constitutional limitations.

B

We next consider whether actual prejudice infected Skilling's jury. Voir dire, Skilling asserts, did not adequately detect and defuse juror bias. "[T]he record . . . affirmatively confirm[s]" prejudice, he maintains, because several seated jurors "prejudged his guilt." We disagree with Skilling's characterization of the voir dire and the jurors selected through it.

1

No hard-and-fast formula dictates the necessary depth or breadth of voir dire. See United States v. Wood, 299 U.S. 123, 145-146 (1936) ("Impartiality is not a technical conception. It is a state of mind. For the ascertainment of this mental attitude of appropriate indifference, the Constitution lays down no particular tests and procedure is not chained to any ancient and artificial formula."). Jury selection, we have repeatedly emphasized, is "particularly within the province of the trial judge."

When pretrial publicity is at issue, "primary reliance on the judgment of the trial court makes [especially] good sense" because the judge "sits in the locale where the publicity is said to have had its effect" and may base her evaluation on her "own perception of the depth and extent of news stories that might influence a juror." *Mu'Min*, 500 U.S., at 427.

Reviewing courts are properly resistant to second-guessing the trial judge's estimation of a juror's impartiality, for that judge's appraisal is ordinarily influenced by a host of factors impossible to capture fully in the record—among them, the prospective juror's inflection, sincerity, demeanor, candor, body language, and apprehension of duty. In contrast to the cold transcript received by the appellate court, the in-the-moment voir dire affords the trial court a more intimate and immediate basis for assessing a venire member's fitness for jury service.

2

Skilling deems the voir dire insufficient because, he argues, jury selection lasted "just five hours," "[m]ost of the court's questions were conclusory[,] high-level, and failed adequately to probe jurors' true feelings," and the court "consistently took prospective jurors at their word once they claimed they could be fair, no matter what other indications of bias were present." Our review of the record, however, yields a different appraisal.[21]

---

18. The parties disagree about whether a presumption of prejudice can be rebutted, and, if it can, what standard of proof governs that issue. Because we hold that no presumption arose, we need not, and do not, reach these questions.

21. In addition to focusing on the adequacy of voir dire, our decisions have also "take[n] into account . . . other measures [that] were used to mitigate the adverse effects of publicity." Nebraska Press Assn. v. Stuart, 427 U.S. 539, 565 (1976). We have noted, for example, the prophylactic effect of "emphatic and clear instructions on the sworn duty of each juror to decide the issues only on evidence presented in open court." Id., at 564. Here, the District Court's instructions were unequivocal. . . . Peremptory challenges, too, "provid[e] protection against [prejudice]," United States ex rel. Darcy v. Handy, 351 U.S. 454, 462 (1956); the District Court, as earlier noted, exercised its discretion to grant the defendants two extra peremptories.

As noted, the District Court initially screened venire members by eliciting their responses to a comprehensive questionnaire drafted in large part by Skilling. That survey helped to identify prospective jurors excusable for cause and served as a springboard for further questions put to remaining members of the array. Voir dire thus was, in the court's words, the "culmination of a lengthy process."

The District Court conducted voir dire, moreover, aware of the greater-than-normal need, due to pretrial publicity, to ensure against jury bias. At Skilling's urging, the court examined each prospective juror individually, thus preventing the spread of any prejudicial information to other venire members. To encourage candor, the court repeatedly admonished that there were "no right and wrong answers to th[e] questions." The court denied Skilling's request for attorney-led voir dire because, in its experience, potential jurors were "more forthcoming" when the court, rather than counsel, asked the question. The parties, however, were accorded an opportunity to ask follow-up questions of every prospective juror brought to the bench for colloquy. Skilling's counsel declined to ask anything of more than half of the venire members questioned individually, including eight eventually selected for the jury, because, he explained, "the Court and other counsel have covered" everything he wanted to know.

Inspection of the questionnaires and voir dire of the individuals who actually served as jurors satisfies us that, notwithstanding the flaws Skilling lists, the selection process successfully secured jurors who were largely untouched by Enron's collapse. Eleven of the seated jurors and alternates reported no connection at all to Enron, while all other jurors reported at most an insubstantial link. As for pretrial publicity, 14 jurors and alternates specifically stated that they had paid scant attention to Enron-related news. The remaining two jurors indicated that nothing in the news influenced their opinions about Skilling.

The questionnaires confirmed that, whatever community prejudice existed in Houston generally, Skilling's jurors were not under its sway. Although many expressed sympathy for victims of Enron's bankruptcy and speculated that greed contributed to the corporation's collapse, these sentiments did not translate into animus toward Skilling. When asked whether they "ha[d] an opinion about . . . Jeffrey Skilling," none of the seated jurors and alternates checked the "yes" box. And in response to the question whether "any opinion [they] may have formed regarding Enron or [Skilling] [would] prevent" their impartial consideration of the evidence at trial, every juror—despite options to mark "yes" or "unsure"—instead checked "no."

The District Court, Skilling asserts, should not have "accept[ed] *at face value* jurors' promises of fairness." In Irvin v. Dowd, 366 U.S., at 727-728, Skilling points out, we found actual prejudice despite jurors' assurances that they could be impartial. Justice Sotomayor, in turn, repeatedly relies on *Irvin*, which she regards as closely analogous to this case. We disagree with that characterization of *Irvin*.

The facts of *Irvin* are worlds apart from those presented here. Leslie Irvin stood accused of a brutal murder and robbery spree in a small rural community. In the months before Irvin's trial, "a barrage" of publicity was "unleashed against him," including reports of his confessions to the slayings and robberies. This Court's description of the media coverage in *Irvin* reveals why the dissent's "best case" is not an apt comparison:

[S]tories revealed the details of [Irvin's] background, including a reference to crimes committed when a juvenile, his convictions for arson almost 20 years previously, for burglary and by a court-martial on AWOL charges during the war. He was accused of being a parole violator. The headlines announced his police line-up identification, that he faced a lie detector test, had been placed at the scene of the crime and that the six murders were solved but [he] refused to confess. Finally, they announced [Irvin's] confession to the six murders and the fact of his indictment for four of them in Indiana. They reported [Irvin's] offer to plead guilty if promised a 99-year sentence, but also the determination, on the other hand, of the prosecutor to secure the death penalty, and that [Irvin] had confessed to 24 burglaries (the modus operandi of these robberies was compared to that of the murders and the similarity noted). One story dramatically relayed the promise of a sheriff to devote his life to securing [Irvin's] execution. . . . Another characterized [Irvin] as remorseless and without conscience but also as having been found sane by a court-appointed panel of doctors. In many of the stories [Irvin] was described as the "confessed slayer of six," a parole violator and fraudulent-check artist. [Irvin's] court-appointed counsel was quoted as having received "much criticism over being Irvin's counsel" and it was pointed out, by way of excusing the attorney, that he would be subject to disbarment should he refuse to represent Irvin. On the day before the trial the newspapers carried the story that Irvin had orally admitted [to] the murder of [one victim] as well as "the robbery-murder of [a second individual]; the murder of [a third individual]; and the slaughter of three members of [a different family]."

Id., at 725-726.

"[N]ewspapers in which the[se] stories appeared were delivered regularly to 95% of the dwellings in" the county where the trial occurred, which had a population of only 30,000; "radio and TV stations, which likewise blanketed that county, also carried extensive newscasts covering the same incidents." Id., at 725.

Reviewing Irvin's fair-trial claim, this Court noted that "the pattern of deep and bitter prejudice" in the community "was clearly reflected in the sum total of the voir dire": "370 prospective jurors or almost 90% of those examined on the point . . . entertained some opinion as to guilt," and "[8] out of the 12 [jurors] thought [Irvin] was guilty." Although these jurors declared they could be impartial, we held that, "[w]ith his life at stake, it is not requiring too much that [Irvin] be tried in an atmosphere undisturbed by so huge a wave of public passion and by a jury other than one in which two-thirds of the members admit, before hearing any testimony, to possessing a belief in his guilt."

In this case, as noted, news stories about Enron contained nothing resembling the horrifying information rife in reports about Irvin's rampage of robberies and murders. Of key importance, Houston shares little in common with the rural community in which Irvin's trial proceeded, and circulation figures for Houston media sources were far lower than the 95% saturation level recorded in *Irvin*, see App. to Brief for United States 15a ("The Houston Chronicle . . . reaches less than one-third of occupied households in Houston."). Skilling's seated jurors, moreover, exhibited nothing like the display of bias shown in *Irvin*. In light of these large differences, the District Court had far less reason than did the trial court in *Irvin* to discredit jurors' promises of fairness.

The District Court, moreover, did not simply take venire members who proclaimed their impartiality at their word. As noted, all of Skilling's jurors had already affirmed on their questionnaires that they would have no trouble basing a verdict only on the evidence at trial. Nevertheless, the court followed up with each individually to uncover concealed bias. This face-to-face opportunity to gauge demeanor and credibility, coupled with information from the questionnaires regarding jurors' backgrounds, opinions, and sources of news, gave the court a sturdy foundation to assess fitness for jury service. The jury's not-guilty verdict on nine insider-trading counts after nearly five days of deliberation, meanwhile, suggests the court's assessments were accurate. Skilling, we conclude, failed to show that his voir dire fell short of constitutional requirements.

3

Skilling also singles out several jurors in particular and contends they were openly biased. See United States v. Martinez-Salazar, 528 U.S. 304, 316 (2000) ("[T]he seating of any juror who should have been dismissed for cause . . . require[s] reversal."). In reviewing claims of this type, the deference due to district courts is at its pinnacle: "A trial court's findings of juror impartiality may be overturned only for manifest error." *Mu'Min*, 500 U.S., at 428. Skilling, moreover, unsuccessfully challenged only one of the seated jurors for cause, "strong evidence that he was convinced the [other] jurors were not biased and had not formed any opinions as to his guilt." Beck v. Washington, 369 U.S. 541, 557-558 (1962).

Skilling contends that Juror 11 — the only seated juror he challenged for cause — "expressed the most obvious bias." Juror 11 stated that "greed on Enron's part" triggered the company's bankruptcy and that corporate executives, driven by avarice, "walk a line that stretches sometimes the legality of something." But, as the Fifth Circuit accurately summarized, Juror 11

> had "no idea" whether Skilling had "crossed that line," and he "didn't say that" every CEO is probably a crook. He also asserted that he could be fair and require the government to prove its case, that he did not believe everything he read in the paper, that he did not "get into the details" of the Enron coverage, that he did not watch television, and that Enron was "old news."

Despite his criticism of greed, Juror 11 remarked that Skilling "earned [his] salar[y]," and said he would have "no problem" telling his co-worker, who had lost 401(k) funds due to Enron's collapse, that the jury voted to acquit, if that scenario came to pass. The District Court, noting that it had "looked [Juror 11] in the eye and . . . heard all his [answers]," found his assertions of impartiality credible. . . .[33]

Skilling also objected at trial to the seating of six specific jurors whom, he said, he would have excluded had he not already exhausted his peremptory challenges. . . .

[For example, Skilling points to] Juror 63, who, Skilling points out, wrote on her questionnaire "that [Skilling] 'probably knew [he] w[as] breaking the law.'" During voir dire, however, Juror 63 insisted that she did not "really have an opinion [about Skilling's guilt] either way"; she did not "know what [she] was thinking" when she completed the questionnaire, but she "absolutely" presumed Skilling innocent and confirmed her understanding that the Government would "have to prove" his guilt, id. In response to follow-up questions from Skilling's counsel, she again stated she would not presume that Skilling violated any laws and could "[a]bsolutely" give her word that she could be fair. "Jurors," we have recognized, "cannot be expected

---

33. Skilling's trial counsel and jury consultants apparently did not regard Juror 11 as so "obvious[ly] bias[ed]," as to warrant exercise of a peremptory challenge.

invariably to express themselves carefully or even consistently." *Yount*, 467 U.S., at 1039. From where we sit, we cannot conclude that Juror 63 was biased.

The [ ] remaining jurors Skilling said he would have excluded with extra peremptory strikes exhibited no sign of prejudice we can discern. . . .

In sum, Skilling failed to establish that a presumption of prejudice arose or that actual bias infected the jury that tried him. Jurors, the trial court correctly comprehended, need not enter the box with empty heads in order to determine the facts impartially. "It is sufficient if the juror[s] can lay aside [their] impression[s] or opinion[s] and render a verdict based on the evidence presented in court." *Irvin*, 366 U.S., at 723. Taking account of the full record, rather than incomplete exchanges selectively culled from it, we find no cause to upset the lower courts' judgment that Skilling's jury met that measure.

* * *

For the foregoing reasons, we affirm the Fifth Circuit's ruling on Skilling's fair-trial argument, vacate its ruling on his conspiracy conviction, and remand the case for proceedings consistent with this opinion.

[The opinions of Justice Scalia, concurring in the Court's opinion on the pretrial publicity issue, and Justice Alito, concurring in part and concurring in the judgment, are omitted.]

JUSTICE SOTOMAYOR, with whom JUSTICE STEVENS and JUSTICE BREYER join, concurring in part and dissenting in part.

Under our relevant precedents, the more intense the public's antipathy toward a defendant, the more careful a court must be to prevent that sentiment from tainting the jury. In this case, passions ran extremely high. The sudden collapse of Enron directly affected thousands of people in the Houston area and shocked the entire community. The accompanying barrage of local media coverage was massive in volume and often caustic in tone. As Enron's one-time CEO, Skilling was at the center of the storm. Even if these extraordinary circumstances did not constitutionally compel a change of venue, they required the District Court to conduct a thorough voir dire in which prospective jurors' attitudes about the case were closely scrutinized. The District Court's inquiry lacked the necessary thoroughness and left serious doubts about whether the jury empaneled to decide Skilling's case was capable of rendering an impartial decision based solely on the evidence presented in the courtroom. Accordingly, I would grant Skilling relief on his fair-trial claim.

I

The majority understates the breadth and depth of community hostility toward Skilling and overlooks significant deficiencies in the District Court's jury selection process. The failure of Enron wounded Houston deeply. Virtually overnight, what had been the city's "largest, most visible, and most prosperous company," its "foremost social and charitable force," and "a source of civic pride" was reduced to a "shattered shell." Thousands of the company's employees lost their jobs and saw their retirement savings vanish. As the effects rippled through the local economy, thousands of additional jobs disappeared, businesses shuttered, and community groups that once benefited from Enron's largesse felt the loss of millions of dollars in contributions. Enron's community ties were so extensive that the entire local

U.S. Attorney's Office was forced to recuse itself from the Government's investigation into the company's fall.

With Enron's demise affecting the lives of so many Houstonians, local media coverage of the story saturated the community. According to a defense media expert, the Houston Chronicle—the area's leading newspaper—assigned as many as 12 reporters to work on the Enron story full time. The paper mentioned Enron in more than 4,000 articles during the 3-year period following the company's December 2001 bankruptcy filing. Hundreds of these articles discussed Skilling by name. Skilling's expert, a professional journalist and academic with 30 years' experience, could not "recall another instance where a local paper dedicated as many resources to a single topic over such an extended period of time as the Houston Chronicle . . . dedicated to Enron." Local television news coverage was similarly pervasive and, in terms of "editorial theme," "largely followed the Chronicle's lead." Between May 2002 and October 2004, local stations aired an estimated 19,000 news segments involving Enron, more than 1600 of which mentioned Skilling.

While many of the stories were straightforward news items, many others conveyed and amplified the community's outrage at the top executives perceived to be responsible for the company's bankruptcy. A Chronicle report on Skilling's 2002 testimony before Congress is typical of the coverage. It began, "Across Houston, Enron employees watched former chief executive Jeffrey Skilling's congressional testimony on television, turning incredulous, angry and then sarcastic by turns, as a man they knew as savvy and detail-oriented pleaded memory failure and ignorance about critical financial transactions at the now-collapsed energy giant." " 'He is lying; he knew everything,' said [an employee], who said she had seen Skilling frequently over her 18 years with the firm, where Skilling was known for his intimate grasp of the inner doings at the company. 'I am getting sicker by the minute.' "

Articles deriding Enron's senior executives were juxtaposed with pieces expressing sympathy toward and solidarity with the company's many victims. Skilling's media expert counted nearly a hundred victim-related stories in the Chronicle, including a "multi-page layout entitled 'The Faces of Enron,' " which poignantly described the gut-wrenching experiences of former employees who lost vast sums of money, faced eviction from their homes, could not afford Christmas gifts for their children, and felt "scared," "hurt," "humiliat[ed]," "helpless," and "betrayed."

When a federal grand jury indicted Skilling, Lay, and Richard Causey—Enron's former chief accounting officer—in 2004 on charges of conspiracy to defraud, securities fraud, and other crimes, the media placed them directly in its crosshairs. In the words of one article, "there was one thing those whose lives were touched by the once-exalted company all seemed to agree upon: The indictment of former Enron CEO Jeff Skilling was overdue." Scoffing at Skilling's attempts to paint himself as a "'victim' of his subordinates," the Chronicle derided "the doofus defense" that Lay and Skilling were expected to offer.

Citing the widely felt sense of victimhood among Houstonians and the voluminous adverse publicity, Skilling moved in November 2004 for a change of venue. The District Court denied the motion, characterizing the media coverage as largely "objective and unemotional." Voir dire, it concluded, would provide an effective means to "ferret out any bias" in the jury pool.

To that end, the District Court began the jury selection process by mailing screening questionnaires to 400 prospective jurors in November 2005. The completed questionnaires of the 283 respondents not excused for hardship dramatically illustrated the widespread impact of Enron's collapse on the Houston community and confirmed the intense animosity of Houstonians toward Skilling and his codefendants. More than one-third of the prospective jurors indicated that they or persons they knew had lost money or jobs as a result of the Enron bankruptcy. Two-thirds of the jurors expressed views about Enron or the defendants that suggested a potential predisposition to convict. In many instances, they did not mince words, describing Skilling as "smug," "arrogant," "brash," "conceited," "greedy," "deceitful," "totally unethical and criminal," "a crook," "the biggest liar on the face of the earth," and "guilty as sin" (capitalization omitted). Only about 5 percent of the prospective jurors did not read the Houston Chronicle, had not otherwise "heard or read about any of the Enron cases," were not connected to Enron victims, and gave no answers suggesting possible antipathy toward the defendants. The parties jointly stipulated to the dismissal of 119 members of the jury pool for cause, hardship, or disability, but numerous individuals who had made harsh comments about Skilling remained.[6]

On December 28, 2005, shortly after the questionnaires had been returned, Causey pleaded guilty. The plea was covered in lead newspaper and television stories. A front-page headline in the Chronicle proclaimed that "Causey's plea wreaks havoc for Lay, Skilling." A Chronicle editorial opined that "Causey's admission of securities fraud . . . makes less plausible Lay's claim that most of the guilty pleas were the result of prosecutorial pressure rather than actual wrongdoing."

I

The Court of Appeals incorporated the concept of presumptive prejudice into a burden-shifting framework: Once the defendant musters sufficient evidence of community hostility, the onus shifts to the Government to prove the impartiality of the jury. The majority similarly envisions a fixed point at which public passions become so intense that prejudice to a defendant's fair-trial rights must be presumed.

This Court has never treated the notion of presumptive prejudice so formalistically. Our decisions instead merely convey the commonsense understanding that

---

6. See, e.g., Juror 29 (Skilling is "[n]ot an honest man"); Juror 104 (Skilling "knows more than he's admitting"); Juror 211 ("I believe he was involved in wrong doings"); Juror 219 ("So many people lost their life savings because of the dishonesty of some members of the executive team"; Skilling was "[t]oo aggressive w[ith] accounting"); Juror 234 ("With his level of control and power, hard to believe that he was unaware and not responsible in some way"); Juror 240 (Skilling "[s]eems to be very much involved in criminal goings on"); Juror 255 ("[T]housands of people were taken advantage of by executives at Enron"; Skilling is "arrogant"; "Skilling was Andrew Fastow's immediate superior. Fastow has plead[ed] guilty to felony charges. I believe Skilling was aware of Fastow's illegal behavior"); Juror 263 ("Nice try resigning 6 months before the collaps[e], but again, he had to know what was going on"); Juror 272 (Skilling "[k]new he was getting out before the [d]am [b]roke"); Juror 292 (Skilling "[b]ailed out when he knew Enron was going down"); Juror 315 ("[H]ow could they not know and they seem to be lying about some things"); Juror 328 ("They should be held responsible as officers of this company for what happened"); Juror 350 ("I believe he greatly misused his power and affected hundreds of lives as a result"; "I believe they are all guilty. Their 'doings' affected not only those employed by Enron but many others as well"); Juror 360 ("I seem to remember him trying to claim to have mental or emotional issues that would remove him from any guilt. I think that is deceitful. It seems as though he is a big player in the downfall"); Juror 378 ("I believe he knew, and certainly should have known as the CEO, that illegal and improper [activities] were rampant in Enron"; "I believe all of them were instrumental, and were co-conspirators, in the massive fraud perpetrated at Enron").

as the tide of public enmity rises, so too does the danger that the prejudices of the community will infiltrate the jury. The underlying question has always been this: Do we have confidence that the jury's verdict was "induced only by evidence and argument in open court, and not by any outside influence, whether of private talk or public print"? Patterson v. Colorado ex rel. Attorney General of Colo., 205 U.S. 454, 462 (1907).

At one end of the spectrum, this Court has, on rare occasion, confronted such inherently prejudicial circumstances that it has reversed a defendant's conviction "without pausing to examine . . . the voir dire examination of the members of the jury." Rideau v. Louisiana, 373 U.S. 723, 727 (1963). In *Rideau*, repeated television broadcasts of the defendant's confession to murder, robbery, and kidnapping so thoroughly poisoned local sentiment as to raise doubts that even the most careful voir dire could have secured an impartial jury. A change of venue, the Court determined, was thus the only way to assure a fair trial.

Irvin [v. Dowd, 366 U.S. 717, 722 (1961),] offers an example of a case in which the trial court's voir dire did not suffice to counter the "wave of public passion" that had swept the community prior to the defendant's trial. The local news media had "extensively covered" the crimes (a murder spree), "arous[ing] great excitement and indignation." Following Irvin's arrest, the press "blanketed" the community with "a barrage of newspaper headlines, articles, cartoons and pictures" communicating numerous unfavorable details about Irvin, including that he had purportedly confessed. Nearly 90 percent of the 430 prospective jurors examined during the trial court's voir dire "entertained some opinion as to guilt-ranging in intensity from mere suspicion to absolute certainty." Of the 12 jurors seated, 8 "thought petitioner was guilty," although "each indicated that notwithstanding his opinion he could render an impartial verdict."

Despite the seated jurors' assurances of impartiality, this Court invalidated Irvin's conviction for want of due process. "It is not required," this Court declared, "that the jurors be totally ignorant of the facts and issues involved. . . . It is sufficient if the juror can lay aside his impression or opinion and render a verdict based on the evidence presented in court." The Court emphasized, however, that a juror's word on this matter is not decisive, particularly when "the build-up of prejudice [in the community] is clear and convincing."

III

A

Though the question is close, I agree with the Court that the prospect of seating an unbiased jury in Houston was not so remote as to compel the conclusion that the District Court acted unconstitutionally in denying Skilling's motion to change venue. Three considerations lead me to this conclusion. First, as the Court observes, the size and diversity of the Houston community make it probable that the jury pool contained a nontrivial number of persons who were unaffected by Enron's collapse, neutral in their outlook, and unlikely to be swept up in the public furor. Second, media coverage of the case, while ubiquitous and often inflammatory, did not, as the Court points out, contain a confession by Skilling or similar "smoking-gun" evidence of specific criminal acts. For many prospective jurors, the guilty plea of co-defendant and alleged co-conspirator Causey, along with the pleas and convictions of other Enron executives, no doubt suggested guilt by association. But reasonable minds exposed to such information would not necessarily have formed an indelible impression that Skilling himself was guilty as charged. Third, there is no suggestion that the courtroom in this case became, as in *Estes* and *Sheppard*, a "carnival" in which the "calmness and solemnity" of the proceedings was compromised. It is thus appropriate to examine the voir dire and determine whether it instills confidence in the impartiality of the jury actually selected.

B

In conducting this analysis, I am mindful of the "wide discretion" owed to trial courts when it comes to jury-related issues. Trial courts are uniquely positioned to assess public sentiment and the credibility of prospective jurors. Proximity to events, however, is not always a virtue. Persons in the midst of a tumult often lack a panoramic view. In particular, reviewing courts are well qualified to inquire into whether a trial court implemented procedures adequate to keep community prejudices from infecting the jury. If the jury selection process does not befit the circumstances of the case, the trial court's rulings on impartiality are necessarily called into doubt.

1

As the Court of Appeals apprehended, the District Court gave short shrift to the mountainous evidence of public hostility. For Houstonians, Enron's collapse was an event of once-in-a-generation proportions. Not only was the volume of media coverage "immense" and frequently intemperate, but "the sheer number of victims" created a climate in which animosity toward Skilling ran deep and the desire for conviction was widely shared.

The level of public animus toward Skilling dwarfed that present in cases such as *Murphy* and *Mu'Min*. . . . The much closer analogy is thus to *Irvin*, which similarly featured a "barrage" of media coverage and a "huge . . . wave of public passion," although even that case did not, as here, involve direct harm to entire segments of the community.

Attempting to distinguish *Irvin*, the majority suggests that Skilling's economic offenses were less incendiary than Irvin's violent crime spree and that "news stories about Enron contained nothing resembling the horrifying information rife in reports about Irvin's rampage of robberies and murders." Along similar lines, the District Court described "the facts of this case [as] neither heinous nor sensational." The majority also points to the four years that passed between Enron's declaration of bankruptcy and the start of Skilling's trial, asserting that "the decibel level of media attention diminished somewhat" over this time. Neither of these arguments is persuasive.

First, while violent crimes may well provoke widespread community outrage more readily than crimes involving monetary loss, economic crimes are certainly capable of rousing public passions, particularly when thousands of unsuspecting people are robbed of their livelihoods and retirement savings. Indeed, the record in this case is replete with examples of visceral outrage toward Skilling and other Enron executives. Houstonians compared Skilling to, among other things, a rapist, an axe murderer, and an Al Qaeda terrorist. . . . The bad blood was so strong that Skilling and other top executives hired private security to protect themselves from persons inclined to take the law into their own hands.

Second, the passage of time did little to soften community sentiment. . . . The Enron story was a continuing saga, and "publicity remained intense throughout." Not only did Enron's downfall generate wall-to-wall news coverage, but so too did a succession of subsequent Enron-related events. Of particular note is the highly publicized guilty plea of codefendant Causey just weeks before Skilling's trial. If anything, the time that elapsed between the bankruptcy and the trial made the task of seating an unbiased jury more difficult, not less.

2

Given the extent of the antipathy evident both in the community at large and in the responses to the written questionnaire, it was critical for the District Court to take "strong measures" to ensure the selection of "an impartial jury free from outside influences." *Sheppard*, 384 U.S., at 362. As this Court has recognized, "[i]n a community where most veniremen will admit to a disqualifying prejudice, the reliability of the others' protestations may be drawn into question." *Murphy*, 421 U.S., at 803. Perhaps because it had underestimated the public's antipathy toward Skilling, the District Court's 5-hour voir dire was manifestly insufficient to identify and remove biased jurors.

As an initial matter, important lines of inquiry were not pursued at all. The majority accepts, for instance, that "publicity about a codefendant's guilty plea calls for inquiry to guard against actual prejudice." Implying that the District Court undertook this inquiry, the majority states that "[o]nly two venire members recalled [Causey's] plea." In fact, the court asked very few prospective jurors any questions directed to their knowledge of or feelings about that event. Considering how much news the plea generated, many more than two venire members were likely aware of it. The lack of questioning, however, makes the prejudicial impact of the plea on those jurors impossible to assess.

The topics that the District Court did cover were addressed in cursory fashion. Most prospective jurors were asked just a few yes/no questions about their general exposure to media coverage and a handful of additional questions concerning any responses to the written questionnaire that suggested bias. In many instances, their answers were unenlightening. Yet the court rarely sought to draw them out with open-ended questions about their impressions of Enron or Skilling and showed limited patience for counsel's followup efforts.

These deficiencies in the form and content of the voir dire questions contributed to a deeper problem: The District Court failed to make a sufficiently critical assessment of prospective jurors' assurances of impartiality. Although the Court insists otherwise, the voir dire transcript indicates that the District Court essentially took jurors at their word when they promised to be fair. Indeed, the court declined to dismiss for cause any prospective juror who ultimately gave a clear assurance of impartiality, no matter how much equivocation preceded it.

Worse still, the District Court on a number of occasions accepted declarations of impartiality that were equivocal on their face. Prospective jurors who "hope[d]" they could presume innocence and did "not necessarily" think Skilling was guilty were permitted to remain in the pool. Juror 61, for instance, wrote of Lay on her questionnaire, "Shame on him." Asked by the court about this, she stated that, "innocent or guilty, he was at the helm" and "should have known what was going on at the company." The court then asked, "can you presume, as you start this trial, that

Mr. Lay is innocent?" She responded, "I hope so, but you know. I don't know. I can't honestly answer that one way or the other." Eventually, however, Juror 61 answered "Yes" when the court asked if she would be able to acquit if she had "a reasonable doubt that the defendants are guilty." Challenging her for cause, defense counsel insisted that they had not received "a clear and unequivocal answer" about her ability to be fair. The court denied the challenge, stating, "You know, she tried."

3

The majority suggests that the jury's decision to acquit Skilling on nine relatively minor insider trading charges confirms its impartiality. This argument, however, mistakes partiality with bad faith or blind vindictiveness. Jurors who act in good faith and sincerely believe in their own fairness may nevertheless harbor disqualifying prejudices. Such jurors may well acquit where evidence is wholly lacking, while subconsciously resolving closer calls against the defendant rather than giving him the benefit of the doubt.

* * *

Taken together, the District Court's failure to cover certain vital subjects, its superficial coverage of other topics, and its uncritical acceptance of assurances of impartiality leave me doubtful that Skilling's jury was indeed free from the deep-seated animosity that pervaded the community at large. "[R]egardless of the heinousness of the crime charged, the apparent guilt of the offender[,] or the station in life which he occupies," our system of justice demands trials that are fair in both appearance and fact. *Irvin*, 366 U.S., at 722. Because I do not believe Skilling's trial met this standard, I would grant him relief.

NOTES AND QUESTIONS

1. Who has the better of the argument in *Skilling*, the majority or the dissent? Both sides recognize that the collapse of Enron had far-reaching effects in Houston, and that the financial pain and accompanying anger caused by the event were deeply felt. In such a case, how realistic is it to think that a jury can close its ears to the outside discussion and consider only the evidence presented in court?

Part of the majority's reasoning was that the *Skilling* publicity was not like in cases such as *Rideau* and *Sheppard*, cases from an earlier age that involved violent crimes. But even acknowledging the differences in circumstances, isn't it fair to say that in modern times it is *easier* for potential jurors to be exposed to prejudicial pretrial publicity than it was when radio, television, and newspapers were the only credible sources of information?

More generally, why are courts so reluctant to grant a change of venue in high-profile cases? The convenience of the testifying witnesses and the need to transport potentially huge amounts of documents and physical evidence are part of the explanation, but is administrative efficiency an adequate answer? If you were a federal prosecutor arguing against Skilling's motion to transfer, what interests might you identify as to why the case should stay in Houston? See, e.g., Newton N. Minow (former Chair of the Federal Communications Commission) & Fred H. Cate, Who

Is an Impartial Juror in an Age of Mass Media?, 40 Am. U. L. Rev. 631, 647 (1991) ("Change of venue may also frustrate the local community's legitimate interests in resolving the case.").

On December 1, 2015, the U.S. District Court for the Eastern District of Massachusetts held a hearing on a motion for new trial filed by convicted (and death-sentenced) Boston Marathon bomber Dzhokhar Tsarnaev. Tsarnaev's motion was based in large part on the previous denial of his motion for a change of venue due to the "continuous and unrelenting publicity" about the case and the "extraordinary salience of the Marathon Bombing and their aftermath in the life of Boston and the surrounding communities." See http://www.bostonherald.com/news/local_coverage/2015/11/tsarnaev_gets_hearing_on_motion_for_new_trial. Surely Tsarnaev was correct in asserting that the crime generated massive publicity and produced city-wide (indeed, nation-wide) revulsion. If you were the judge, how would you rule?

2. Isn't the *Skilling* majority correct that prejudicial pretrial publicity claims are inherently fact-intensive questions, and that deference to the trial judge should be at its peak? Can the dissent realistically conclude, based on its reading of a paper record, that despite the district judge's factual findings, which were based on his observations, the jurors were not credible in their claims of being able to put their prior knowledge and feelings about the case aside?

3. How should the problem of prejudicial pretrial publicity be remedied? Two psychology professors have evaluated the available options, based on the results of numerous empirical studies. See Christina Studebaker & Steven Penrod, Pretrial Publicity: The Media, the Law, and Common Sense, 3 Psychol. Pub. Pol'y & L. 428 (1997). These options include (1) granting a continuance, in the hope that publicity will dissipate over time; (2) conducting extended voir dire to weed out prospective jurors who may have been influenced by publicity; (3) admonishing the jury not to be influenced by publicity; (4) encouraging the presentation of evidence at trial to counteract any impressions created by publicity; (5) relying on the jury's deliberations to overcome the effects of publicity; (6) changing the venire (i.e., bringing in jurors from another jurisdiction where there is less publicity); and (7) changing the venue (i.e., holding the trial in another jurisdiction).

Some of the findings collected by Studebaker and Penrod include the following: With respect to voir dire, "jurors who claimed that they could disregard the pretrial publicity simply did not—despite their apparent belief that they could." Id., at 441. With respect to judicial admonitions, "[t]he pre-trial publicity instruction did not reduce the biasing effect of exposure to either the 'factual' or 'emotional' pretrial publicity." Id., at 443. With respect to jury deliberations, "existing research on deliberation effects in the pretrial publicity arena is more supportive of the accentuation theory—jury deliberation appears to strengthen, not reduce, bias." Id., at 444. Studebaker and Penrod conclude that these three particular methods (voir dire, judicial admonitions, and jury deliberations) are especially unlikely to succeed because they "are based on removing bias after it has been developed"—indeed, they "require jurors to disregard pretrial publicity immediately after attention has been brought to it." Id., at 445. More promising are the approaches that seek "to select jurors who were never biased to begin with," such as a change of venire or a change of venue. Id.

C. Joinder and Severance

Part of the prosecutor's job when drafting the indictment is to decide what the potential trial will look like; in particular, she must decide (a) how many charges to bring against a defendant and (b) how many defendants to join in a single case. These questions raise joinder and severance issues.

In general, prosecutors prefer to resolve all related charges against all related defendants in a single trial. If the defendant stole a car in June, a car in July, and a car in August, the government is likely to seek a single three-count indictment, and thus resolve all three counts in one case. Similarly, if Marlo and Chris agree to sell drugs, the prosecution naturally would want to charge both with conspiracy and try the two together. Trials are expensive and time consuming, not only for the parties and court but also for witnesses and jurors. From an efficiency standpoint, presenting the full set of evidence once is obviously superior to holding multiple trials on similar issues.

Efficiency is the main reason for joinder, but there are others. A single case where evidence is presented on all parties and all counts will help paint a more complete picture for the jury, a picture that allows the jurors to better understand each defendant's conduct and intent when evidence on these points is revealed as part of a larger story. Jurors, who are unfamiliar with complex criminal transactions (one hopes), may have a hard time understanding the "relevant" evidence unless that evidence is placed in a broader context, much of which the law would label irrelevant if the matters were tried separately. In this respect, joint trials can increase the accuracy of the verdict.

There may also be some advantages to the defendant from joinder. The accused may prefer to have all three car theft charges resolved against him at one time rather than stand trial three times. Not only can this save the wear and tear of repeated proceedings and repeated lawyer fees, it also might prevent the prosecutor from getting multiple chances to strengthen her case from one trial to the next.

But more often, a defendant will prefer a separate trial, and so will at times file a motion to "sever" the different counts or the other defendants. Multiple charges can create an unfavorable "halo effect" in the minds of the jurors, leading them to assume that in a ten-count indictment the defendant surely must be guilty of *something*. Multiple counts that involve overlapping evidence also can confuse a jury, perhaps making it unclear whether there was sufficient evidence on each element of each count. (Was the handgun used in all three car thefts, or just in one?) Or, a defendant charged with multiple counts may face a dilemma on the question whether to testify on his own behalf. Perhaps he is not guilty of the first car theft, and even has an alibi to present, but he has no defense to the other two counts. In a single trial, he can't testify as to the first count without exposing himself to devastating cross-examination on the others.

The potential difficulties for an individual defendant in a multiparty trial are also significant. Consider the following description:

> An accused who sits at the defense table with other suspects risks being found guilty by association, especially if his co-defendants are charged with more serious crimes. In a joint trial the jury will be exposed to "spillover evidence," which might consist not only of information about co-defendant's crimes (which is bad enough), but also

evidence of defendant's own other bad acts, which now come to the jury's attention through the case against the co-defendants. The risk of juror confusion about which evidence applies against which suspect is also present, growing worse as the number of defendants increases. Co-defendants may present antagonistic defenses, or may make different decisions about whether to testify, making distinctions among the defendants stark. Co-defendants who take the stand are often sorely tempted to point the fingers at others, confronting a defendant with an additional layer of accusation he would not have faced had he been tried separately.

Andrew D. Leipold & Hossein A. Abbasi, The Impact of Joinder and Severance on Federal Criminal Cases: An Empirical Study, 59 Vand. L. Rev. 349, 357-358 (2006).

Federal Rule of Criminal Procedure 8 sets forth the circumstances under which the government may join charges and defendants in an indictment. Rule 14(a) then permits the court, either sua sponte or on motion of a party (almost always the defense), to sever.[3]

Rule 8. Joinder of Offenses and of Defendants

(a) *Joinder of Offenses.* The indictment or information may charge a defendant in separate counts with 2 or more offenses if the offenses charged—whether felonies or misdemeanors or both—are of the same or similar character, or are based on the same act or transaction, or are connected with or constitute parts of a common scheme or plan.

(b) *Joinder of Defendants.* The indictment or information may charge 2 or more defendants if they are alleged to have participated in the same act or transaction, or in the same series of acts or transactions, constituting an offense or offenses. The defendants may be charged in one or more counts together or separately. All defendants need not be charged in each count.

Rule 14. Relief from Prejudicial Joinder

(a) *Relief.* If the joinder of offenses or defendants in an indictment, an information, or a consolidation for trial appears to prejudice a defendant or the government, the court may order separate trials of counts, sever the defendants' trials, or provide any other relief that justice requires. . . .

A defendant who objects to a consolidated trial thus has two avenues of attack. Initially he can allege that the charges or defendants are not properly joined under Rule 8; that is, he can claim there was "misjoinder." In addition, or in the alternative, he can argue that even if the charges are properly joined, the court should sever the charges or defendants under Rule 14(a), because of the risk of unfair prejudice. The courts' interpretation of these rules and standards follows.

---

3. Federal Rule 13 also addresses joinder. It provides: "The court may order that separate cases be tried together as though brought in a single indictment or information if all offenses and all defendants could have been joined in a single indictment or information." This simply allows the consolidation of cases that were originally filed separately. For the court to join cases under Rule 13, however, it first must determine that they could have properly been joined under Rule 8. Rule 13 is thus a timing provision, one that adds nothing to the substance of the joinder or severance analysis.

UNITED STATES v. HAWKINS

United States Court of Appeals for the Fourth Circuit
776 F.3d 200 (2015)[4]

AGEE, Circuit Judge:

Collin Hawkins was indicted on separate counts related to a carjacking and a subsequent arrest as a felon in possession of a firearm. Prior to trial, Hawkins timely moved the court to sever the carjacking counts from the felon in possession charge on the grounds of improper joinder. The district court denied the motion and Hawkins was found guilty by a jury on all counts. For the reasons that follow, we affirm the judgment of the district court, in part, and vacate the judgment, in part.

I

Reuben King ("King") testified that on the evening of November 22, 2006, he was employed as a driver for Sedan Service in Baltimore, Maryland. That night, King received a phone call from a regular customer he knew as Warren, asking to be picked up at an apartment complex parking lot. When King arrived three persons entered his cab: Warren, the appellant Hawkins, and an unidentified female. At trial, King testified that he instantly recognized Hawkins, who sat next to him on the cab's front seat, from casual contact in the neighborhood over many years.

Warren instructed King that he needed to make three stops that night. During the first two stops, King explained that Warren got out of the car, talked to unidentified individuals for roughly ten to fifteen minutes, returned to the car, and then told King the intersection for the next stop. During the last stop, both Warren and Hawkins got out of the car for about ten or fifteen minutes, and then returned. Warren then instructed King to return to the apartment complex parking lot.

Once back in the parking lot King turned on the overhead dome light to calculate the fare and saw Hawkins holding a .357 caliber revolver only a few inches from his head, while Warren held a shotgun positioned to the back of King's head. According to King, Warren stated that if King moved, Warren would shoot him. King claimed that Hawkins then took two cell phones and roughly $400 in cash from him, and pushed King out of the driver's side door. Hawkins then pushed King in the direction of the trunk, during which time Hawkins emptied the remainder of King's pockets while Warren kept the shotgun pointed at King. Once they reached the trunk area, King testified that Hawkins told King to kneel down and keep his hands up. According to King, after he complied with the instruction, Hawkins then stated, "I'm not going to shoot you 'cause I know you."

King claimed he then heard footsteps going toward the car, the car doors closing, and the car pulling off. King testified that he then ran until he found police officers to whom he reported the carjacking.

---

4. The prior edition of this casebook set forth an earlier opinion in *Hawkins*, 589 F.3d 694 (4th Cir. 2009). In 2015 the Fourth Circuit issued this superseding opinion that amended the earlier decision to correct a factual error, but did not make any material change to the decision or the analysis. —EDS.

Shortly thereafter, King gave information about the carjacking to detectives and told them that Hawkins was involved. When shown a photo array King identified Hawkins as one of the perpetrators.

On December 9, 2006, Baltimore City police officers were investigating an unrelated incident in the same area of Baltimore, which they had reason to believe involved Hawkins. Acting on information that Hawkins would be arriving at a convenience store officers watched Hawkins approach the entrance of the store and tug at his waistband, indicating that he might be armed.

Officers entered the store and ordered Hawkins to the ground, but he refused to comply and started to slide his right hand up under his waistband. This caused officers to order Hawkins to keep his hands where they could be seen, but Hawkins refused to comply until he was physically subdued. A 9 millimeter pistol was retrieved from Hawkins' waistband when he was arrested.

On March 7, 2007, a federal grand jury in the District of Maryland indicted Hawkins on four counts. Count I alleged a carjacking based on the robbery of King's vehicle, in violation of 18 U.S.C. §2119 (2000). Count II alleged that Hawkins "did knowingly possess and brandish a firearm in furtherance of a crime of violence," the carjacking, in violation of 18 U.S.C. §924(c)(1)(A)(ii). J.A. 7. Count III alleged that Hawkins, "having been convicted of a crime punishable by imprisonment for a term exceeding one year, did knowingly and unlawfully possess a loaded firearm, to wit: a Bersa model Thunder 9 mm pistol" in violation of 18 U.S.C. §922(g)(1), the gun seized when he was arrested. Count IV alleged another felon in possession of a firearm charge, relating to a shotgun seized during a search of Hawkins' residence.

Prior to trial, Hawkins moved to sever Counts I and II (collectively the "carjacking counts") from Counts III and IV. Hawkins contended that Counts III and IV were improperly joined to Counts I and II under Federal Rule of Criminal Procedure 8(a). In the alternative, Hawkins argued severance was appropriate under Rule 14 because he "would be significantly prejudiced by a single trial" because "the jury may well conclude that Hawkins is guilty of one firearm count and then find him guilty of the others because of his criminal disposition." The district court denied Hawkins' motion because it could "discern no reason why a jury will not be able fairly and objectively to evaluate the evidence."

The Government elected not to proceed on Count IV and trial was held only on Counts I, II, and III. Hawkins pled not guilty to all three counts. However, as to Count III, Hawkins conceded his prior felony conviction and his possession of the .9 millimeter handgun at the time of his arrest both to the court prior to opening statements and again to the jury during opening statements.

Hawkins testified in his own defense and vigorously denied involvement in the carjacking. . . . His counsel actively cross-examined King and elicited various inconsistencies from his testimony on direct examination.

During closing argument, counsel for the Government mentioned that the carjacking was not the first time Hawkins had committed a crime against a person he knew, stating, "You heard yesterday the defendant admitted to police that he stole the 9 millimeter he was caught with on December 9th from his cousin." While the Government acknowledged that Hawkins had conceded his guilt to the felon-in-possession charge, it argued to the jury that it was a tactical admission:

U.S. ATTORNEY: Now, why would the defendant rob someone he knew? Well, as I indicated, this was not the first time he did that. He robbed, stole a gun from [his] cousin around December 9th.

These statements prompted Hawkins to move for a mistrial maintaining that the Government was attempting to persuade the jury to conclude Hawkins committed the carjacking based on the fact that he robbed his own cousin. The district court denied the motion. . . .

The jury found Hawkins guilty on all three counts. The district court sentenced Hawkins to 180 months for Count I, 120 months for Count II, and 120 months for Count III, for an aggregate term of incarceration of 360 months followed by three years of supervised release. Hawkins noted a timely appeal, and we have jurisdiction pursuant to 28 U.S.C. §1291 (2006).

II

Hawkins raises two primary issues on appeal. First, he contends that the district court erred in denying his motion to sever Counts I and II from Count III because Count III was improperly joined with Counts I and II under Rule 8.[3] Alternatively, Hawkins argues that if all three counts were properly joined for a single trial, the district court abused its discretion in denying his motion to sever under Rule 14 because the joinder of Count III with Counts I and II was unduly prejudicial. . . . .

III

Whether charges are properly joined in an indictment is a question of law that we review *de novo. See* United States v. Cardwell, 433 F.3d 378, 384-85 (4th Cir. 2005). "If the initial joinder was not proper, however, we review this nonconstitutional error for harmlessness, and reverse *unless* the misjoinder resulted in no 'actual prejudice' to the defendant [ ] 'because it had [no] substantial and injurious effect or influence in determining the jury's verdict.' " United States v. Mackins, 315 F.3d 399, 412 (4th Cir. 2003) (quoting United States v. Lane, 474 U.S. 438, 449 (1986)). If misjoinder is found, the Government bears the burden of demonstrating that any error resulting from the misjoinder was harmless. *Mackins,* 315 F.3d at 412.

A

Federal Rule of Criminal Procedure 8(a) provides:

Joinder of Offenses. The indictment or information may charge a defendant in separate counts with 2 or more offenses if the offenses charged — whether felonies or misdemeanors or both — are of the same or similar character, or are based on the same act or transaction, or are connected with or constitute parts of a common scheme or plan.

Fed. R. Crim. P. 8(a). Rule 8(a) permits "very broad joinder," *Mackins,* 315 F.3d at 412 (quoting 1A Charles Alan Wright, Federal Practice & Procedure §141 (3d

---

3. Hawkins does not argue on brief that he was harmed by the joinder as to Count III. Moreover, at oral argument he conceded that he was not contesting his conviction on Count III. Therefore, we will consider the issue abandoned and will affirm the conviction on Count III. Hawkins does contend he is entitled to resentencing on Count III because his sentence on that count was calculated in conjunction with and in reliance on the convictions for Counts I and II.

ed. 1999)), "because the prospect of duplicating witness testimony, impaneling additional jurors, and wasting limited judicial resources suggests that related offenses should be tried in a single proceeding." United States v. Mir, 525 F.3d 351, 357 (4th Cir. 2008). Thus, joinder is the "rule rather than the exception," United States v. Armstrong, 621 F.2d 951, 954 (9th Cir. 1980), "because of the efficiency in trying the defendant on related counts in the same trial." *Cardwell*, 433 F.3d at 385.

The requirements of Rule 8(a), however, " 'are not infinitely elastic,' " *Mackins*, 315 F.3d at 412, "and so 'cannot be stretched to cover offenses . . . which are discrete and dissimilar.' " *Id.* at 412. Joinder of unrelated charges "create[s] the possibility that a defendant will be convicted based on considerations other than the facts of the charged offense." *Cardwell*, 433 F.3d at 385.

In this case, the Government contends that the carjacking counts and possession of a firearm by a felon (Count III) are all offenses of the "same or similar character." The Government did not argue on brief, nor provide a rationale at oral argument, that joinder was proper either because the counts "are based on the same act" or "constitute parts of a common scheme or plan." Our review of the record substantiates the lack of a nexus between the carjacking counts and Count III which would reflect the charges to be the "same act" or a "common scheme or plan." Thus joinder rises and falls on whether Counts I and II are of a "same or similar character" to Count III.

Joinder of offenses that "are based on the same act or transaction or on two or more acts or transactions connected together or constituting parts of a common scheme or plan" presents the opportunity to submit evidence of one offense that ordinarily would be admissible at a separate trial for the other. United States v. Foutz, 540 F.2d 733, 737 (4th Cir. 1976). However, when offenses are joined based on their same or similar character, "admissibility at separate trials is not so clear." [Id.]

Hawkins admits that Counts I and II are properly joined because "they both related to the same carjacking that occurred on November 22, 200[6]." However, Hawkins argues that Count III "was entirely unrelated" to Counts I and II, in part because the felon-in-possession count "arose out of a distinct incident unrelated to the carjacking" and occurred seventeen days later. Hawkins emphasizes that there is no link between the carjacking counts and Count III because the handgun the police recovered from Hawkins' person on December 9 was *not* the same gun used in the carjacking. The fact that the carjacking and felon in possession counts involve *different* firearms is not contested by the Government.

The Government contends that all three counts were properly joined as offenses of the "same or similar character" for two reasons: first, because "all three were firearms offenses" and second, because "all these events occurred within a three-week period." In support of its argument, the government cites, inter alia, United States v. Cole, 857 F.2d 971 (4th Cir. 1988), and United States v. Rousseau, 257 F.3d 925 (9th Cir. 2001). These decisions, however, provide no help to the Government in this case.

In *Cole*, we held proper the joinder of various drug charges stemming from a large-scale cocaine distribution ring with the defendant's alien smuggling charges where the aliens smuggled into the country began to sell cocaine for his distribution ring after their arrival. We stated in *Cole* that "both the allegations in the indictment and the proof at trial were more than adequate to establish the connection between the drug conspiracy and the alien smuggling charges. . . . The Government alleges that this "analogous" case supports its argument because in *Cole,* we found "some connection" between the counts, and in balancing the possible prejudice in trying the counts together against the possible prejudice to the defendants, we found that the balance "tilted in favor of a joint trial."

However, the Government's argument fails to appreciate the extent of the connection we found in *Cole.* In *Cole,* the smuggled aliens worked in the drug distribution ring once they arrived in America. In effect, drug profits subsidized the illegal smuggling of aliens who, in turn, went to work in the drug conspiracy to generate further drug profits for the defendants. Indeed, there existed a logical and intimate connection between the offenses which made joinder proper.

There was not just "some connection" between the counts in *Cole;* instead, it was a strong connection. However, in the case at bar, the Government has proffered no evidence demonstrating a logical and close connection between the alleged carjacking and possession of a .357 caliber revolver on November 22, and Hawkins' possession of a .9 millimeter pistol on December 9.

Similarly, the Government's reliance on *Rousseau* is misplaced. In *Rousseau,* the defendant was charged with two counts of possession of a firearm by a convicted felon, although each arrest related to a different firearm. Prior to trial, Rousseau moved to sever the two felon-in-possession counts, but the court denied the motion. Based only upon its review of the face of the indictment, the Ninth Circuit found that both "incidents involved firearms charges," specifically felon-in-possession charges. Thus, the two offenses were of a "same or similar character."

The circumstances in *Rousseau* are easily distinguishable from the circumstances in the present case. In *Rousseau,* the defendant was charged with two counts of violating the *same* statute, 18 U.S.C. §922(g)(1), although the offenses occurred nearly six and a half months apart and the guns were different. But it is an unremarkable example of offenses of the "same or similar character" when the defendant is charged only with multiple violations of the same statute. See *Acker,* 52 F.3d at 514 ("Trial courts routinely allow joinder of different bank robbery counts against a single defendant in the same indictment.").

In the present case, however, Hawkins was charged with three *different* offenses: carjacking and possession of a firearm in furtherance of a crime of violence, and, about three weeks later, being a felon in possession of a different firearm. We perceive no similarity in the connection between these three *different* counts and the counts on the *same* offense found appropriate for joinder by the Ninth Circuit in *Rousseau.* . . .

[T]he only connection we discern between Count III and the carjacking counts is the appellant, Hawkins. We have held previously such a connection is not sufficient to sustain joinder. See *Cardwell,* 433 F.3d at 387 (requiring "additional facts" beyond the defendant as a basis for joinder of charges for defendant's participation in a murder-for-hire plot and for defendant's possession of a handgun when arrested for the murder-for-hire plot). Certainly, the indictment does not allege any explicit connection between the carjacking charges on November 26, 2006, and the felon-in-possession charge that stemmed from Hawkins' unrelated arrest on December 9, 2006. Nor do we find that the testimony at trial provides a basis by which to join the three counts as offenses of the "same or similar character." . . .

Moreover, the Government's reliance on the fact that all three offenses occurred during a three-week period will not sustain joinder, as we have held consistently that a mere temporal relationship is not sufficient to establish the propriety of joinder.[5]

Accordingly, we conclude that the district court erred in allowing joinder of Counts I and II with Count III because the charges are not of a same or similar character. We therefore turn to the question of whether this error requires reversal.

B

An error involving misjoinder "'affects substantial rights' and requires reversal *only* if the misjoinder results in actual prejudice because it 'had substantial and injurious effect or influence in determining the jury's verdict.'" United States v. Lane, 474 U.S. 438, 449 (1986). In assessing whether a misjoinder error results in actual prejudice, we are guided by the *Lane* Court's indicia of harmlessness:

> (1) whether the evidence of guilt was overwhelming and the concomitant effect of any improperly admitted evidence on the jury's verdict; (2) the steps taken to mitigate the effects of the error; and (3) the extent to which the improperly admitted evidence as to the misjoined counts would have been admissible at trial on the other counts.

Hawkins argues that if there had been separate trials, no evidence presented during a trial on Count III would have been admissible in the trial on Counts I and II, and vice versa. In particular, Hawkins avers that the Government's ability to present evidence on the unrelated charge of being a felon in possession to the same jury hearing the carjacking case "increase[d] the likelihood that . . . Hawkins would be convicted" of all three charges. Hawkins asserts that a jury hearing only Counts I and II would not hear evidence that Hawkins possessed a gun on December 9, 2006, that he had a prior felony conviction, that he sold drugs to support himself, and finally, that he had stolen the .9 millimeter gun from his cousin.

The Government responds that Hawkins suffered no undue prejudice from misjoinder because there was overwhelming evidence of Hawkins's guilt on each count, and because the evidence relating to Count III and the carjacking counts would have been mutually admissible under Rule 404(b). Furthermore, the Government contends "the district court took steps to eliminate any spillover effect as a result of the joinder."

The district court did provide a limiting instruction to the jury in its attempt to mitigate the effects of the joinder of all three counts. However, we conclude that, based on the other two indicia of harmlessness provided in *Lane*, the error in misjoinder affected Hawkins's substantial rights, and, furthermore, "'had substantial and injurious effect or influence in determining the jury's verdict.'" *Lane*, 474 U.S. at 449.

Although the Government argues to the contrary, we do not find that all of the evidence on Count III and that on Counts I and II would have been mutually admissible under Rule 404(b) if Hawkins had enjoyed the benefit of separate trials. Much

---

5. As we stated in *Cardwell*, allowing joinder based merely on a temporal relationship "would effectively read Rule 8(a) to allow limitless joinder whenever the charge resulted from the fruits of a single investigation." *Cardwell*, 433 F.3d at 386.

of the evidence presented to the jury on Count III would have been only marginally relevant, if relevant at all, to Counts I and II. There was simply nothing about
Hawkins being in possession of a different firearm in December that was related to
any of the elements of the carjacking counts.

Additionally, under a proper balancing analysis pursuant to Federal Rules of
Evidence 403 and 404(b), the probative value of the evidence would have been substantially outweighed by the danger of unfair prejudice to Hawkins. . . . Our point
is illustrated by the district court's statement from the bench denying Hawkins's
motion to exclude his admission that he had stolen the .9 millimeter pistol from
his cousin:

> COURT: This is very interesting because it clearly suggests that if he's willing to steal
> his cousin's gun, he's willing to steal anything from anybody. If he's willing to steal
> his cousin's gun, why wouldn't he be willing to steal money? His cousin's gun, why
> wouldn't he be willing [to] steal a car or cash or cell phones from some guy he just
> knows casually from the neighborhood?

In response, Hawkins's attorney stated:

> DEFENSE COUNSEL: That's exactly why we think it's not admissible, Your Honor.
> You're sort of making my point. If he's willing to steal from his cousin, you're telling
> the jury, look, what a bad guy he is.

This exchange reflects how unrelated bad conduct (the felon-in-possession of a
gun) offered in evidence on another charge (carjacking) to prove the defendant's
general propensity to commit crimes can have a " 'substantial and injurious effect
or influence in determining the jury's verdict,' " as with Counts I and II in the case
at bar. . . .

Additionally, . . . we are not persuaded that the evidence against Hawkins related
to the carjacking counts was overwhelming. . . . The only evidence against Hawkins
at trial on the carjacking counts was the testimony of the lone witness to the carjacking, King. Throughout the trial, counsel for Hawkins brought out multiple
inconsistencies prevalent in King's story about the carjacking. . . . The Government
produced no further corroborating evidence of Hawkins' guilt on that charge.
The .357 caliber revolver and shotgun allegedly used in the carjacking were never
found. Hawkins' accomplices, Warren and the unidentified female, were also never
found.

While the evidence against Hawkins as to Count III was overwhelming, the
Government's case against Hawkins on Counts I and II was not overwhelming and
"it is possible that the jury found him guilty of that crime under the rationale that
with so much smoke there must be fire." *Foutz,* 540 F.2d at 739. Had the three
offenses not been joined for trial, Count III's prejudicial evidence would not have
reached the jury, and Hawkins might well have been acquitted of Counts I and II.

IV

For the foregoing reasons, we affirm Hawkins' conviction on Count III as a convicted felon in possession of a firearm, but vacate his sentence on that count as it
was determined, in part, based on his convictions under Counts I and II. We vacate

Hawkins' convictions under Counts I and II. We remand this case to the district court for retrial on Counts I and II and for resentencing on Count III.

[The opinion by Judge Motz concurring in the judgment is omitted]

NOTES AND QUESTIONS

1. As *Hawkins* shows, one critical question that courts ask when faced with a severance request is the "cross admissibility" of evidence. If the evidence that would be presented on crime number three—here, the illegal gun possession at the convenience store—would be admissible for some reason in a separate trial on the first two crimes (the carjacking counts), then courts routinely conclude that there is no prejudice to the joinder, because the jury would hear the harmful evidence anyway.

Notice, however, that the opposite may not be true. Simply because evidence concerning count three (or concerning a codefendant) would be inadmissible in a separate trial does not itself compel severance. Many courts find that even if a jury is exposed to harmful evidence about other counts or other defendants, a joint trial is permitted if the evidence is simple and distinct enough that the jury can be trusted to keep straight which evidence relates to which counts or defendants. Moreover, judges put great faith in their own ability to instruct the jury on the proper and improper use of the evidence, and in jurors' ability to follow these instructions. See, e.g., United States v. Hill, 643 F.3d 807, 829 (11th Cir. 2011) ("we apply the strong presumption . . . that jurors are able to compartmentalize evidence by respecting limiting instructions specifying the defendants against whom the evidence may be considered" (internal quotation marks and citations omitted)). *Hawkins* is one of the relatively rare cases where, despite the trial court's limiting instructions, the appeals court found that the evidence on the misjoined count would not have been admissible in the carjacking case *and* that the jury might have been influenced by the spillover.

Is it realistic to believe that jurors segregate the evidence in this way during their deliberations? Or is Justice Jackson correct when he observed that in a joint conspiracy trial, "[t]here generally will be evidence of wrongdoing by somebody. It is difficult for the [defendant] to make his own case stand on its own merits in the minds of jurors who are ready to believe that birds of a feather are flocked together."? Krulewitch v. United States, 336 U.S. 440, 454 (1949) (Jackson, J. concurring).

2. The procedural posture of a joinder challenge matters a great deal. If the defendant shows *prior* to trial that the counts or defendants are not properly joined—and just as importantly, if the district judge finds that Rule 8 is not satisfied—the case should be severed, with no finding of prejudice required. But once the trial is held and the defendant is challenging the joinder on appeal, the appellate court will look for both a violation of Rule 8 and a showing of prejudice, as *Hawkins* shows. And while technically the prejudice showing for misjoinder (where the prosecution has the burden of persuasion) is different than the prejudice a defendant would have to show when claiming that the trial court erroneously failed to sever under Rule 14, in practice the inquiries look very similar.

3. Note that Rule 8 focuses on whether the criminal transactions at issue were "similar" (if the issue is joinder of offenses under 8(a)) or "the same" (joinder of defendants under 8(b)). Is that the right focus? Imagine a case in which three defendants—*X, Y,* and *Z*—are charged with robbery of a convenience store and

conspiracy to commit robbery. The evidence against *Y* and *Z* is very strong; the evidence against *X* is shaky. And *Y* and *Z* are alleged to have actually robbed the store. *X*, at most, drove the car to and from the crime scene. There is no doubt that *X*, *Y*, and *Z* satisfy the "same act or transaction" test of Rule 8(b). Does *X* nevertheless have a good argument that joinder is improper? Does that argument say anything about how to read Rule 14? Consider the following case.

ZAFIRO v. UNITED STATES

Certiorari to the United States Court of Appeals for the Seventh Circuit
506 U.S. 534 (1993)

JUSTICE O'CONNOR delivered the opinion of the Court.

Rule 8(b) of the Federal Rules of Criminal Procedure provides that defendants may be charged together "if they are alleged to have participated in the same act or transaction or in the same series of acts or transactions constituting an offense or offenses." Rule 14 of the Rules, in turn, permits a district court to grant a severance of defendants if "it appears that a defendant or the government is prejudiced by a joinder."[5] In this case, we consider whether Rule 14 requires severance as a matter of law when codefendants present "mutually antagonistic defenses."

I

Gloria Zafiro, Jose Martinez, Salvador Garcia, and Alfonso Soto were accused of distributing illegal drugs in the Chicago area, operating primarily out of Soto's bungalow in Chicago and Zafiro's apartment in Cicero, a nearby suburb. One day, government agents observed Garcia and Soto place a large box in Soto's car and drive from Soto's bungalow to Zafiro's apartment. The agents followed the two as they carried the box up the stairs. When the agents identified themselves, Garcia and Soto dropped the box and ran into the apartment. The agents entered the apartment in pursuit and found the four petitioners in the living room. The dropped box contained 55 pounds of cocaine. After obtaining a search warrant for the apartment, agents found approximately 16 pounds of cocaine, 25 grams of heroin, and 4 pounds of marijuana inside a suitcase in a closet. Next to the suitcase was a sack containing $22,960 in cash. Police officers also discovered 7 pounds of cocaine in a car parked in Soto's garage.

---

5. *Zafiro* was decided under an earlier version of Rules 8 and 14, but the differences in wording from the current version are purely stylistic, and have no effect on the substance of the analysis. The following is the text of Rule 14 that was in effect when *Zafiro* was decided:

Rule 14. Relief from Prejudicial Joinder

   If it appears that a defendant or the government is prejudiced by a joinder of offenses or of defendants in an indictment or information or by such joinder for trial together, the court may order an election or separate trials of counts, grant a severance of defendants or provide whatever other relief justice requires. In ruling on a motion by a defendant for severance the court may order the attorney for the government to deliver to the court for inspection in camera any statements or confessions made by the defendants which the government intends to introduce in evidence at the trial. —EDS.

The four petitioners were indicted and brought to trial together. At various points during the proceeding, Garcia and Soto moved for severance, arguing that their defenses were mutually antagonistic. Soto testified that he knew nothing about the drug conspiracy. He claimed that Garcia had asked him for a box, which he gave Garcia, and that he (Soto) did not know its contents until they were arrested. Garcia did not testify, but his lawyer argued that Garcia was innocent: The box belonged to Soto and Garcia was ignorant of its contents.

Zafiro and Martinez also repeatedly moved for severance on the ground that their defenses were mutually antagonistic. Zafiro testified that she was merely Martinez's girlfriend and knew nothing of the conspiracy. She claimed that Martinez stayed in her apartment occasionally, kept some clothes there, and gave her small amounts of money. Although she allowed Martinez to store a suitcase in her closet, she testified, she had no idea that the suitcase contained illegal drugs. Like Garcia, Martinez did not testify. But his lawyer argued that Martinez was only visiting his girlfriend and had no idea that she was involved in distributing drugs.

The District Court denied the motions for severance. The jury convicted all four petitioners of conspiring to possess cocaine, heroin, and marijuana with the intent to distribute. 21 U.S.C. §846. In addition, Garcia and Soto were convicted of possessing cocaine with the intent to distribute, §841(a)(1), and Martinez was convicted of possessing cocaine, heroin, and marijuana with the intent to distribute, ibid.

Petitioners appealed their convictions. Garcia, Soto, and Martinez claimed that the District Court abused its discretion in denying their motions to sever. (Zafiro did not appeal the denial of her severance motion, and thus, her claim is not properly before this Court.) . . . Noting that "mutual antagonism . . . and other . . . characterizations of the effort of one defendant to shift the blame from himself to a codefendant neither control nor illuminate the question of severance," 945 F.2d at 886, the Court of Appeals found that the defendants had not suffered prejudice and affirmed the District Court's denial of severance. We granted the petition for certiorari, and now affirm the judgment of the Court of Appeals.

II

. . . In interpreting Rule 14, the Courts of Appeals frequently have expressed the view that "mutually antagonistic" or "irreconcilable" defenses may be so prejudicial in some circumstances as to mandate severance. See, e.g., United States v. Benton, 852 F.2d 1456, 1469 (CA6 1988); United States v. Smith, 788 F.2d 663, 668 (CA10 1986); United States v. Magdaniel-Mora, 746 F.2d 715, 718 (CA11 1984); United States v. Berkowitz, 662 F.2d 1127, 1133-1134 (CA5 1981); United States v. Haldeman, 559 F.2d 31, 71-72 (CADC 1976). Notwithstanding such assertions, the courts have reversed relatively few convictions for failure to grant a severance on grounds of mutually antagonistic or irreconcilable defenses. The low rate of reversal may reflect the inability of defendants to prove a risk of prejudice in most cases involving conflicting defenses.

Nevertheless, petitioners urge us to adopt a bright-line rule, mandating severance whenever codefendants have conflicting defenses. We decline to do so. Mutually antagonistic defenses are not prejudicial per se. Moreover, Rule 14 does not require severance even if prejudice is shown; rather, it leaves the tailoring of the relief to be granted, if any, to the district court's sound discretion. See, e.g., United States v. Lane, 474 U.S. 438, 449 (1986).

We believe that, when defendants properly have been joined under Rule 8(b), a district court should grant a severance under Rule 14 only if there is a serious risk that a joint trial would compromise a specific trial right of one of the defendants, or prevent the jury from making a reliable judgment about guilt or innocence. Such a risk might occur when evidence that the jury should not consider against a defendant and that would not be admissible if a defendant were tried alone is admitted against a codefendant. For example, evidence of a codefendant's wrongdoing in some circumstances erroneously could lead a jury to conclude that a defendant was guilty. When many defendants are tried together in a complex case and they have markedly different degrees of culpability, this risk of prejudice is heightened. See Kotteakos v. United States, 328 U.S. 750, 774-775 (1946). Evidence that is probative of a defendant's guilt but technically admissible only against a codefendant also might present a risk of prejudice. See Bruton v. United States, 391 U.S. 123 (1968). Conversely, a defendant might suffer prejudice if essential exculpatory evidence that would be available to a defendant tried alone were unavailable in a joint trial. The risk of prejudice will vary with the facts in each case, and district courts may find prejudice in situations not discussed here. When the risk of prejudice is high, a district court is more likely to determine that separate trials are necessary, but . . . less drastic measures, such as limiting instructions, often will suffice to cure any risk of prejudice.

Turning to the facts of this case, we note that petitioners do not articulate any specific instances of prejudice. Instead they contend that the very nature of their defenses, without more, prejudiced them. Their theory is that when two defendants both claim they are innocent and each accuses the other of the crime, a jury will conclude (1) that both defendants are lying and convict them both on that basis, or (2) that at least one of the two must be guilty without regard to whether the Government has proved its case beyond a reasonable doubt.

As to the first contention, it is well settled that defendants are not entitled to severance merely because they may have a better chance of acquittal in separate trials. Rules 8(b) and 14 are designed "to promote economy and efficiency and to avoid a multiplicity of trials, [so long as] these objectives can be achieved without substantial prejudice to the right of the defendants to a fair trial." *Bruton*, 391 U.S. at 131, n. 6. . . . [A] fair trial does not include the right to exclude relevant and competent evidence. A defendant normally would not be entitled to exclude the testimony of a former codefendant if the district court did sever their trials, and we see no reason why relevant and competent testimony would be prejudicial merely because the witness is also a codefendant.

As to the second contention, the short answer is that petitioners' scenario simply did not occur here. The Government argued that all four petitioners were guilty and offered sufficient evidence as to all four petitioners; the jury in turn found all four petitioners guilty of various offenses. Moreover, even if there were some risk of prejudice, here it is of the type that can be cured with proper instructions, and "juries are presumed to follow their instructions." Richardson [v. Marsh, 481 U.S. 200, 211 (1987)]. The District Court properly instructed the jury that the Government had "the burden of proving beyond a reasonable doubt" that each defendant committed the crimes with which he or she was charged. The court then instructed the jury that it must "give separate consideration to each individual defendant and to each separate charge against him. Each defendant is entitled to have his or her case determined from his or her own conduct and from the evidence [that] may be applicable to him or to her." In addition, the District Court admonished the jury that opening and closing arguments are not evidence and that it should draw no inferences from a defendant's exercise of the right to silence. These instructions sufficed to cure any possibility of prejudice.

Rule 14 leaves the determination of risk of prejudice and any remedy that may be necessary to the sound discretion of the district courts. Because petitioners have not shown that their joint trial subjected them to any legally cognizable prejudice, we conclude that the District Court did not abuse its discretion in denying petitioners' motions to sever. The judgment of the Court of Appeals is affirmed.

[The opinion of Justice Stevens, concurring in the judgment, is omitted.]

NOTES AND QUESTIONS

1. *Zafiro* presents a common claim by defendants seeking to sever their trials, namely, that they have inconsistent and even antagonistic defenses. The Court clearly rejects the argument that antagonistic defenses are per se grounds for reversal, but goes on to describe the types of cases where severance would be proper: where "there is a serious risk that a joint trial would compromise a specific trial right of one of the defendants, or prevent the jury from making a reliable judgment about guilt or innocence."

2. The fear that the jury will be unable to "make a reliable judgment about guilt or innocence is closely tied to the number of counts and number of defendants, and the increased possibility of juror confusion if either number gets too high. But might the complexity of a multi-party or multi-count case also affect who is selected for the jury in first place? In United States v. Farano, the defendant argued that severance should have been granted because of the great complexity of the trial. The Seventh Circuit, per Judge Posner, observed:

> One can imagine a trial expected to be so long that no employed person could take the time off from his job to serve on the jury, with the result that the jury might be unrepresentative. "Professionals often cannot afford (or their employers will not abide) jury service on protracted cases. Consequently, courts frequently excuse them upon a showing of undue hardship or extreme inconvenience. The hardship results from the projected loss of pay over a lengthier trial. Collectively, these two practices combine to seriously suppress the percentage of persons with higher education who serve on juries in complex cases."

749 F.3d 658, 661 (7th Cir. 2014) (quoting Franklin Strier, The Educated Jury: A Proposal for Complex Litigation, 47 DePaul L. Rev. 49, 72-73 (1997)). On the facts, however, the court found "no indication that the jury was incompetent, by virtue of professional exemptions or hardship exclusions, to render a sound decision." Id.

Is this a serious concern? Should we assume that professionals are better, as a group, at evaluating complex cases? If so, should that enter the calculation on whether the defendant was prejudiced?

3. As to the second ground for severance identified in *Zafiro*, the Court did not go into detail about the "specific trial right[s]" that are to be protected by severance, but its citation to Bruton v. United States, 391 U.S. 123 (1968), is instructive. In a line of cases beginning with *Bruton*, the Court has said that a pretrial confession by a nontestifying codefendant (call him "*A*") cannot be admitted against *A* in a joint

trial if the confession implicates another defendant ("*B*") standing trial in the same case. If the prosecutor wants to use *A*'s confession against *A* at trial and *A* does not take the stand, the government generally must either redact the confession so it does not implicate *B* or must sever the cases. The *Bruton* doctrine is discussed further in the materials on the Confrontation Clause in Chapter 14.

4. One remarkable feature of joinder and severance decisions is the explicit tradeoff that courts make between fairness to the accused and efficiency of the trial process. This tradeoff is pervasive in the criminal system, of course, but courts are rarely as candid about it as they are when expressing a preference for joint trials. Thus, courts have said that Rule 8(a) "necessarily recognizes the adverse effect on the defendant by a joinder of counts, but considers this to be outweighed by gains in trial economy when one of the criteria of the rule are met," United States v. Werner, 620 F.2d 922, 929 (2d Cir. 1980), or that when charges or defendants are joined, "some prejudice almost necessarily results," but that "Rule 8(a) permits the first sort of prejudice and Rule 8(b) the second." Cupo v. United States, 359 F.2d 990, 993 (D.C. Cir. 1966). As a result, most courts seem to agree with Judge Richard Posner's statement: "The danger of prejudice to the least guilty, or perhaps prejudice to all from the sheer confusion of a multidefendant trial, is in all but the most unusual circumstances considered outweighed by the economies of a single trial in which all facets of the crime can be explored once and for all." United States v. Velasquez, 772 F.2d 1348 (7th Cir. 1985).

For the classic argument that this balance is wrong, see Robert O. Dawson, Joint Trials of Defendants in Criminal Cases: An Analysis of Efficiencies and Prejudices, 77 Mich. L. Rev. 1379 (1979):

> One supposed efficiency of joinder is a saving of the prosecutor's time because of the substantial overlap of evidence against the different defendants. But whether the trial is joint or individual affects only a small portion of the prosecutor's investment of time. It does not affect police investigation, which is usually completed before the prosecutor decides on charging and joinder. It should not affect plea bargaining—it is no more efficient for the prosecutor to plea bargain in a joined case than in one that has been severed. . . . It need not affect pretrial hearings, which may be held jointly, even when the trials are separate. It probably does not even make a substantial difference in the time the prosecutor spends preparing for trial. Whether trials are joint or separate, the prosecutor must review the evidentiary file and interview the witnesses. If separate trials are held, the prosecutor must review the file again, but would surely not need as much time as he would to prepare the case.
>
> A second presumed efficiency of joint trials is that they are more convenient for witnesses. In fact, however, the effect of joint trials on witnesses varies greatly from case to case and depends in part on whether the witness is a civilian or a professional. To involve lay witnesses in the prosecution of a case certainly forces real burdens upon them. They must leave work or home to testify, and an important witness may be required to remain at the courthouse throughout the trial. If the witness is a child or the victim of an alleged sex offense, we do not want him to repeat the trauma of testifying without excellent reasons. Most witnesses in criminal trials, however, are not civilians but professionals. The burden of presenting witnesses lies upon the government, whose witnesses are usually police officers, laboratory employees, prosecution investigators, and others whose jobs include testifying in court. While time away from the patrol beat or the laboratory is time away from important work, professional witnesses suffer little personal inconvenience or expense by testifying more than once. . . .

Furthermore, the parties can protect witnesses from multiple appearances by stipulating necessary but undisputed noncritical testimony. . . . Under appropriate circumstances, the trial court could even condition severance on stipulations of such testimony.

A third justification alleged for joint trials is that they conserve limited judicial resources. . . . But joint trials do not necessarily save judicial energy. They are far more difficult to schedule than individual trials. . . . In addition, once begun, joint trials are more complicated to conduct and take longer to complete than individual trials.

Id., at 1383-1386. Dawson went on to note that jury selection, the order of presentation of witnesses, and the adjudication of evidentiary objections are all much more difficult in joint trials than in individual trials.

5. How serious is the prejudicial effect of joinder? One study looked at nearly 20,000 federal criminal trials over a five-year period and tried to measure the effect of joinder on the outcome. After controlling for a variety of variables—jury trial versus bench trial, type and seriousness of case, appointed or retained lawyer, and geographic location of the trial—the study reached the following conclusions: (a) defendants who face more than one count at trial are about 10 percent more likely to be convicted of the most serious charge than defendants who stand trial on a single count; and (b) *in the aggregate*, multi-defendant trials have no impact on the outcome of cases. A defendant tried alone was just as likely to be convicted of the most serious charge as a defendant who stood trial with others.

This latter finding was somewhat surprising, as it is frequently assumed that joinder of defendants creates a higher risk of prejudice than the joinder of counts, but the data indicate otherwise. The study recognizes, however, that the lack of demonstrated effect from joined defendants may mask an important effect in individual cases—it may be that in a trial with several defendants, the more guilty parties are worse off because of the joinder, while the relatively less guilty parties get a benefit from being charged with more culpable parties. Over the run of cases, this could result in a net effect of zero, without undermining the conventional wisdom that joint trials can have a prejudicial effect, at least on some defendants. See Leipold & Abbasi, supra, 59 Vand. L. Rev., at 383-384.

Chapter 12

Discovery and Disclosure

The discovery and disclosure rules that regulate a party's access to information about the other side's case are of great importance to the fairness of the criminal process, and to its ability to generate accurate verdicts:

> Information is what trials are about. Trials are not about law. Disputes may arise on questions of law, trial judges may be called upon to make some dicey initial calls on legal issues, but the heart of the trial is the determination of who did what to whom and in what frame of mind. . . .
>
> So, understandably, at the trial stage, the parties are vitally interested in the raw factual data that can be produced in court.

H. Richard Uviller, The Tilted Playing Field 73 (1999). Access to information influences not only the criminal trial and the manner in which it unfolds, but also the plea bargaining process that may ultimately lead to a negotiated settlement of the case.

None of this is controversial. But just because there is widespread agreement on the importance of criminal discovery does not mean that there is comparable agreement on the appropriateness of any given discovery regime. Indeed, historically and today, the rules governing the exchange of information by parties in criminal cases have sparked considerable debate. Denying a defense motion to inspect grand jury minutes (at a time when discovery was all but unheard of in criminal cases), Judge Learned Hand articulated one view of discovery grounded in the prosecution's heavy burden at trial:

> Under our criminal procedure, the accused has every advantage. While the prosecution is held rigidly to the charge, he need not disclose the barest outline of his defense. He is immune from question or comment on his silence; he cannot be convicted when there is the least fair doubt in the minds of any one of the twelve. Why in addition he should in advance have the whole evidence against him to pick over at his leisure, and make his defense, fairly or foully, I have never been able to see.

United States v. Garsson, 291 F. 646, 649 (S.D.N.Y. 1923). Some 40 years later, Professor Abraham Goldstein took issue with Judge Hand; he focused on the prosecution's superior ability to employ police, grand juries, and other state resources in the investigation of crime:

> [P]retrial discovery by the prosecution is far-reaching. And it cannot in any sense be said to be matched by what is available to the defendant or by what he can keep from the prosecution—even when his "immunity" from self-incrimination is thrown into the scales. While the possibility that the defendant may produce a hitherto

undisclosed witness or theory of defense is always present, the opportunity for surprise is rendered practically illusory by the government's broad investigatory powers. . . . The sum of the matter is that the defendant is not an effective participant in the pretrial criminal process. It is to the trial alone that he must look for justice. Yet the imbalance of the pretrial period may prevent him from making the utmost of the critical trial date.

Abraham S. Goldstein, The State and the Accused: Balance of Advantage in Criminal Procedure, 69 Yale L.J. 1149, 1192 (1960).

It is only in the last 50-plus years that discovery has emerged as a basic component of the criminal adjudicative process. And while the trend since the 1960s has clearly been in the direction of more liberal disclosure by both prosecution and defense, discovery in criminal cases is still considerably narrower than civil discovery. In fact, the criminal discovery rules have been shaped by a debate between those who believe that broader, "civil-style" discovery would facilitate fairer and more accurate outcomes in criminal cases and those who believe that criminal cases are fundamentally different, requiring an altogether different (and more limited) discovery regime.

The proponents of liberal discovery often argue that the criminal defendant, lacking the state's resources to conduct a thorough factual investigation, must be afforded full notice of the prosecution's evidence so that this evidence can be adequately challenged. In recent years, some have pointed in particular to DNA exonerations—the uncovering of conclusive evidence that factually innocent people have been convicted—to argue that fuller disclosure of material in the prosecution's hands is needed to avoid wrongful convictions.

Opponents of "civil-style" discovery frequently cite the possibility that defendants will misuse discovery—to intimidate witnesses, obstruct justice, or concoct plausible but perjurious defenses that result in false acquittals. Complicating the debate is the question of reciprocity. Do the defendant's Fifth Amendment rights (or perhaps other constitutional protections afforded to him) limit the degree to which the prosecution can be granted reciprocal discovery from the defense? If so, how should this influence the overall shape of discovery rules?

Most discovery and disclosure rules have their basis in legislation or judicial rulings that vary substantially among jurisdictions. These rules are, however, shaped by limited but significant constitutional considerations. We begin by looking at the prosecution's disclosure obligations—not only those contained in discovery rules that differ from place to place, but also those that flow from overarching constitutional requirements that are not discovery rules in the formal sense, but that bind all prosecutors to disclose certain critical information—whatever the federal or local rules might require.

We then turn to the disclosure obligations imposed on the defense, with an emphasis on the Supreme Court decisions which concluded that defendants can be required to disclose information to the government without running afoul of the Fifth Amendment or otherwise making the proceedings fundamentally unfair. It is worth noting at the outset the importance of these cases, even beyond the particular disclosure required by the defense—as a political matter, the slow but steady growth in criminal disclosure by the *prosecution* in recent decades probably could not have occurred absent the reciprocal defense disclosure that the Supreme

Court has permitted. You should also note that the entire discussion in this chapter is shaped by the still unresolved question with which we began: whether broad or more limited discovery in criminal cases is the better rule.

A. *Disclosure by the Government*

1. The Prosecutor's General Discovery Obligations

Rule 16(a) of the Federal Rules of Criminal Procedure sets forth the federal prosecutor's basic disclosure obligations. Its requirements are significantly narrower than those found in many of the States, and thus it is important not to generalize too much about what "criminal discovery" is like outside the federal system. The federal model is still a good one to study, however, and not only because of the important role of federal prosecutions: Rule 16(a) has also served as one pattern for comprehensive discovery laws around the country and is roughly equivalent to the discovery rules to be found in over a dozen states. See Wayne R. LaFave, Jerold H. Israel, Nancy J. King & Orin S. Kerr, Criminal Procedure §20.2(b), at 364-365 (3d ed. 2007).

As you read the material that follows, ask yourself: How close does Rule 16 come to providing for full disclosure of prosecution evidence? Does it afford the defendant with sufficient discovery to prepare adequately for trial?

> **Rule 16. Discovery and Inspection**
>
> (a) Government's Disclosure.
>
>   (1) Information Subject to Disclosure.
>
>   (A) Defendant's Oral Statement. Upon a defendant's request, the government must disclose to the defendant the substance of any relevant oral statement made by the defendant, before or after arrest, in response to interrogation by a person the defendant knew was a government agent if the government intends to use the statement at trial.
>
>   (B) Defendant's Written or Recorded Statement. Upon a defendant's request, the government must disclose to the defendant, and make available for inspection, copying, or photographing, all of the following:
>
>   (i) any relevant written or recorded statement by the defendant if:
>   —the statement is within the government's possession, custody, or control; and
>   —the attorney for the government knows—or through due diligence could know—that the statement exists;
>
>   (ii) the portion of any written record containing the substance of any relevant oral statement made before or after arrest if the defendant made the statement in response to interrogation by a person the defendant knew was a government agent; and
>
>   (iii) the defendant's recorded testimony before a grand jury relating to the charged offense.
>
>   (C) Organizational Defendant. Upon a defendant's request, if the defendant is an organization, the government must disclose to the defendant any statement described in Rule 16(a)(1)(A) and (B) if the government contends that the person making the statement:

(i) was legally able to bind the defendant regarding the subject of the statement because of that person's position as the defendant's director, officer, employee, or agent; or

(ii) was personally involved in the alleged conduct constituting the offense and was legally able to bind the defendant regarding that conduct because of that person's position as the defendant's director, officer, employee, or agent.

(D) Defendant's Prior Record. Upon a defendant's request, the government must furnish the defendant with a copy of the defendant's prior criminal record that is within the government's possession, custody, or control if the attorney for the government knows—or through due diligence could know—that the record exists.

(E) Documents and Objects. Upon a defendant's request, the government must permit the defendant to inspect and to copy or photograph books, papers, documents, data, photographs, tangible objects, buildings or places, or copies or portions of any of these items, if the item is within the government's possession, custody, or control and:

(i) the item is material to preparing the defense;

(ii) the government intends to use the item in its case-in-chief at trial; or

(iii) the item was obtained from or belongs to the defendant.

(F) Reports of Examinations and Tests. Upon a defendant's request, the government must permit a defendant to inspect and to copy or photograph the results or reports of any physical or mental examination and of any scientific test or experiment if:

(i) the item is within the government's possession, custody, or control;

(ii) the attorney for the government knows—or through due diligence could know—that the item exists; and

(iii) the item is material to preparing the defense or the government intends to use the item in its case-in-chief at trial.

(G) Expert Witnesses. At the defendant's request, the government must give to the defendant a written summary of any [expert] testimony that the government intends to use . . . during its case-in-chief at trial. . . . The summary provided under this subparagraph must describe the witness's opinions, the bases and reasons for those opinions, and the witness's qualifications.

(2) Information Not Subject to Disclosure. Except as Rule 16(a)(1) provides otherwise, this rule does not authorize the discovery or inspection of reports, memoranda, or other internal government documents made by an attorney for the government or other government agent in connection with investigating or prosecuting the case. Nor does this rule authorize the discovery or inspection of statements made by prospective government witnesses except as provided in 18 U.S.C. §3500.[1] . . .

---

1. For a description of §3500, see infra, Note 2 in this section.—EDS.

NOTES AND QUESTIONS

1. *Nonexpert witnesses.* Notice that Rule 16 does not require the prosecution to disclose before trial any prior statements by nonexpert government witnesses on the subject matter of the testimony they will offer. From one perspective, this is extraordinary. Consider Professor Uviller's analysis:

> From the defendant's perspective—especially the perspective of the innocent defendant, learning the details of the accuser's story or the supporting evidence well before the trial begins is probably the only opportunity to check them out. Does the witness harbor a grudge? Does anything in his background caution against credence? Is the story inconsistent with, or contradicted by the accounts of others? Did the witness have the vantage claimed? Does the paper trail support the live recitals? These are some of the vital clues to testimonial error—and the guideposts for the construction of a persuasive alternative scenario—that can make the difference when the case plays out before the jury. If not afforded pretrial, the information can rarely be drawn from the witness when he gets up to render his smooth, coached, and well-defended account from the stand.

H. Richard Uviller, The Tilted Playing Field 93-94 (1999). Without disclosure of the witnesses' names and prior statements, a criminal defendant may have no avenue for learning the content of a witness's expected trial testimony. This creates a risk that the defense will be unable to counter a witness's trial testimony effectively simply because it lacks the time, skill, or resources to investigate, a risk that would diminished if this information was provided in pretrial discovery.

A small number of jurisdictions permit the defendant to depose witnesses before trial in certain circumstances, which obviously allows the defense time to prepare a response for trial. But in many jurisdictions, including the federal system, depositions in criminal cases are rarely permitted, and usually they are used to preserve the testimony of someone who is likely to be unavailable at trial; they are not available for routine discovery. Compounding the problem for the accused, witnesses frequently elect not to speak to the defense informally before trial—thus preventing defense counsel from obtaining the substance of a witness's testimony at all, at least while preparing for trial and negotiating plea deals.

2. On the other hand, both Federal Rule of Criminal Procedure 26.2 and the Jencks Act, 18 U.S.C. §3500, provide federal defendants the right to inspect certain witness statements, but *only* following the testimony of a government witness on direct examination. (The law specifically provides that before this point, "no statement . . . in the possession of the United States which was made by a Government witness or prospective Government witness . . . shall be the subject of subpoena, discovery, or inspection. . . .") The law defines "statement" to mean those declarations relating to the subject matter of the witness's testimony and constituting: (1) a written statement made by the witness and signed or otherwise adopted or approved by him; (2) a recording or transcription of an oral statement, provided that it is substantially verbatim and was recorded contemporaneously; and (3) any statement made to a grand jury.

Despite the language of the statute, however, in many federal courts it is the practice of prosecutors to provide "3500" or "Jencks material" to the defense shortly before trial begins or shortly before the witness testifies, rather than after the witness testifies on direct. See Ellen S. Podgor, Criminal Discovery of Jencks Witness

Statements: Timing Makes a Difference, 15 Ga. St. U. L. Rev. 651, 681-683 (1999). Regardless of how sensible this practice might be, is it appropriate for the lawyers and the courts to follow a practice that Congress apparently intended to prohibit?

3. One rationale for not disclosing the prior witness statements earlier is witness safety. Because the successful investigation and prosecution of criminal cases can depend heavily on the voluntary cooperation of witnesses, concerns with safety (and witness fears about safety) are important. According to a 1990 study by the Victim Services Agency of New York City, 36 percent of victims and witnesses interviewed in the Bronx Criminal Court had been threatened, and 57 percent of those who had not been threatened feared reprisals—stated differently, more than nine out of ten people involved in the process were worried about cooperating with the government. This study, as well as its own investigation, led the Office of Justice Programs of the U.S. Justice Department to find that "Prosecutors, police officers, judges, and victim advocates agree that witness intimidation is widespread, increasing, and having a serious impact on the prosecution of crime across the entire country." National Institute of Justice, Preventing Gang- and Drug-Related Witness Intimidation, at 1 (1996), https://www.ncjrs.gov/pdffiles/163067.pdf. Isn't this a sufficient justification for not disclosing witness names to the defense?

4. On the other side (and there's always another side), about two-thirds of the states provide for defense discovery of the names of prospective government witnesses, LaFave, et al., Criminal Procedure §20.3(h), at 411, with no apparent crippling of the criminal justice process. Does this suggest that the federal discovery rules are too limited? It may strengthen this argument further to note that the disclosure requirement is not absolute—judges in a mandatory disclosure regime can issue protective orders restricting discovery in appropriate cases. See Nora V. Demleitner, Witness Protection in Criminal Cases: Anonymity, Disguise or Other Options?, 46 Am. J. Comp. L. 641, 647 (1998) (noting that in states with expansive pretrial disclosure statutes, legislatures have generally afforded trial courts authority to issue protective orders to safeguard witnesses). Rule 16 itself provides for such orders: "At any time the court may, for good cause, deny, restrict, or defer discovery or inspection, or grant other appropriate relief. The court may permit a party to show good cause by a written statement that the court will inspect ex parte . . . ." Rule 16(d)(1).

5. Some of the difference between the federal approach and that of some states may be explained by the types of cases where witness intimidation is most prevalent. Consider the following from a 1995 Justice Department Report:

> A number of prosecutors linked the increase in violent victim and witness intimidation to the advent of gang-controlled crack sales in the mid- to late-1980's. As crack sales grew, some urban prosecutors noted an upturn in gang- and drug-related homicides. Several prosecutors estimated that today victim and witness intimidation is suspected in up to 75-100 percent of the violent crimes committed in some gang dominated neighborhoods.
>
> The 1992 National Crime Victimization Survey suggests that in neighborhoods not plagued by gangs and drug sales, fear and intimidation play a much less significant part in the failure to cooperate with police and prosecutors. The discrepancy between the perception of urban police and prosecutors and the findings of the National Crime Victimization Survey is important: victim and witness intimidation is *endemic* in neighborhoods infested with gang activity and drug sales and virtually *invisible* to people outside those neighborhoods.

National Institute of Justice, Victim and Witness Intimidation: New Developments and Emerging Responses, at 2 (1995) (footnotes omitted, emphasis in original), http://www.popcenter.org/problems/witness_intimidation/PDFs/Healey_1995.pdf. Although the Justice Department Report is now more than 20 years old, note that drug crimes still account for more than a quarter of federal prosecutions.

6. *Scientific evidence.* A substantial majority of discovery regimes contain some version of Rule 16's provision for turning over to the defense the results of scientific tests. Rule 16, as noted, also provides for disclosure of the substance of any expert testimony that the government intends to use during its case-in-chief. Do these provisions provide adequate discovery into the matters they regulate? Professor Giannelli thinks not:

> A discovery rule on scientific evidence should entail disclosure of all scientific reports. Rule 16 requires production only of reports by experts that the prosecution intends to call at trial, or reports that are material to the preparation of the defense. Consequently, if the prosecution receives an expert's report but does not intend to call that expert to the stand—the most intriguing situation from a defense perspective—the report is discoverable only if it is "material." The problem lies not with the materiality standard, but rather with the person who first applies that standard. Leaving the initial decision to the prosecutor to determine "materiality" is fraught with unnecessary risks, which often will lead to nondisclosure and needless litigation.

Paul C. Giannelli, Criminal Discovery, Scientific Evidence, and DNA, 44 Vand. L. Rev. 791, 808 (1991). Do you agree? Notice that Rule 16(a)(1)(E), providing for the inspection of documents and objects, contains an analogous "materiality" provision.

7. Some prosecutors have adopted an "open file" discovery practice in which they grant defense counsel access to most material about the case within the prosecutor's possession or control. There are strong arguments in favor of such discovery: "The beauty of open-file discovery is obvious as a remedy for the difficulty of subjective choice in a competitive adversarial environment. It does not require a prosecutor to make difficult discretionary decisions." Robert P. Mosteller, Exculpatory Evidence, Ethics, and the Road to the Disbarment of Mike Nifong: The Critical Importance of Full Open-File Discovery, 15 Geo. Mason L. Rev. 257, 309 (2008). Even noting the "modest but steady movement" in the direction of liberalizing discovery over the years, however, so far, few jurisdictions could be characterized as having true open file discovery regimes. Id., at 274. Would such an approach to discovery be preferable? Might its utility for criminal defendants depend in part on just what prosecutors and police record and place in the official file?

8. Whatever the merits of open file discovery are more generally, the case for liberalizing discovery may be particularly powerful with regard to scientific evidence—and perhaps most particularly, the evidence emanating from forensic labs nationwide. Consider Strengthening Forensic Science in the United States—A Path Forward, the 2009 study by the National Academy of Sciences ("NAS") on the current state of forensic science in the United States. Forensic science, according to the NAS, encompasses a broad range of disciplines, including those that are "laboratory based" such as "nuclear and mitochondrial DNA analysis, toxicology and drug analysis," and those "based on expert interpretation of observed patterns" in the analysis of fingerprints, writing samples, toolmarks, bite marks, hair specimens, and the like.

See id., at 7. The NAS reports that across these disciplines, "the integrity of crime laboratories [in the United States] increasingly has been called into question, with some highly publicized cases highlighting the sometimes lax standards of laboratories that have generated questionable or fraudulent evidence and that have lacked quality control measures that would have detected the questionable evidence." Id., at 44. The DNA exonerations helped provoke this scrutiny:

> The increased use of DNA analysis as a more reliable approach to matching crime scene evidence with suspects and victims has resulted in the reevaluation of older cases that retained biological evidence that could be analyzed by DNA. The number of exonerations resulting from the analysis of DNA has grown across the country in recent years, uncovering a disturbing number of wrongful convictions—some for capital crimes—and exposing serious limitations in some of the forensic science approaches commonly used in the United States.
>
> According to the Innocence Project, there have been 223 postconviction DNA exonerations in the United States since 1989 (as of November 2008).[2] Some have contested the percentage of exonerated defendants whose convictions allegedly were based on faulty science. Although the Innocence Project figures are disputed by forensic scientists who have reexamined the data, even those who are critical of the conclusions of The Innocence Project acknowledge that faulty forensic science has, on occasion, contributed to the wrongful conviction of innocent persons.
>
> The fact is that many forensic tests—such as those used to infer the source of toolmarks or bite marks—have never been exposed to stringent scientific scrutiny. Most of these techniques were developed in crime laboratories to aid in the investigation of evidence from a particular crime scene, and researching their limitations and foundations was never a top priority. . . . Before the first offering of the use of DNA in forensic science in 1986, no concerted effort had been made to determine the reliability of these tests, and some in the forensic science and law enforcement communities believed that scientists' ability to withstand cross-examination in court when giving testimony related to these tests was sufficient to demonstrate the tests' reliability. However, although the precise error rates of these forensic tests are still unknown, comparison of their results with DNA testing in some cases has revealed that some of these analyses, as currently performed, produce erroneous results. . . . Some non-DNA forensic tests do not meet the fundamental requirements of science, in terms of reproducibility, validity, and falsifiability.

Id., at 42. Would more liberal disclosure in criminal cases aid defense counsel in better exposing flaws in the forensic evidence offered against their clients? If so, what more information should the prosecutor disclose beyond the results? Compare Jim Dwyer, Peter Neufeld & Barry Scheck, Actual Innocence 257 (2000) (advocating "[c]omplete discovery of underlying data from forensic tests" and "comprehensible explanations of the work performed" as needed reform to help avoid wrongful convictions), with Paul Giannelli, Forensic Science: Scientific Evidence and Prosecutorial Misconduct in the Duke Lacrosse Rape Case, 45 Crim. L. Bull.

---

2. As of January 1, 2016, the number reported by the Innocence Project was 336 postconviction DNA exonerations. See http://www.innocenceproject.org/.—Eds.

4 (2009) (many attorneys "have neither the time nor the expertise to challenge scientific evidence").

9. Reconsider Judge Hand's famous statement that "the accused has every advantage" and "[w]hy in addition he should in advance have the whole evidence against him to pick over at his leisure, and make his defense, fairly or foully, I have never been able to see." Notably, Judge Hand also deemed "the ghost of the innocent man convicted . . . an unreal dream." *Garsson*, 291 F., at 649. Proponents of liberal discovery point to the growing number of postconviction exonerations from DNA to show that Judge Hand was wrong about the risk of wrongful conviction—and that, in fact, broad discovery is needed to protect the innocent. Does the argument on the other side amount, at least in part, to the claim that limited discovery is necessary so that the guilty can be convicted? And if so, is there any way to resolve *this* debate?

2. The Prosecutor's Constitutional Disclosure Obligations

KYLES v. WHITLEY

Certiorari to the United States Court of Appeals for the Fifth Circuit
514 U.S. 419 (1995)

JUSTICE SOUTER delivered the opinion of the Court. . . .

[A]t about 2:20 p.m. on Thursday, September 20, 1984, 60-year-old Dolores Dye left the Schwegmann Brothers' store (Schwegmann's) on Old Gentilly Road in New Orleans after doing some food shopping. As she put her grocery bags into the trunk of her red Ford LTD, a man accosted her and after a short struggle drew a revolver, fired into her left temple, and killed her. The gunman took Dye's keys and drove away in the LTD.

New Orleans police took statements from six eyewitnesses, who offered various descriptions of the gunman. They agreed that he was a black man, and four of them said that he had braided hair. The witnesses differed significantly, however, in their descriptions of height, age, weight, build, and hair length. Two reported seeing a man of 17 or 18, while another described the gunman as looking as old as 28. One witness described him as 5'4" or 5'5", medium build, 140-150 pounds; another described the man as slim and close to six feet. One witness said he had a mustache; none of the others spoke of any facial hair at all. One witness said the murderer had shoulder-length hair; another described the hair as "short."

Since the police believed the killer might have driven his own car to Schwegmann's and left it there when he drove off in Dye's LTD, they recorded the license numbers of the cars remaining in the parking lots around the store at 9:15 p.m. on the evening of the murder. . . .

At 5:30 p.m., on September 22, a man identifying himself as James Joseph called the police and reported that on the day of the murder he had bought a red Thunderbird from a friend named Curtis, whom he later identified as petitioner, Curtis Kyles. He said that he had subsequently read about Dye's murder in the newspapers and feared that the car he purchased was the victim's. He agreed to meet with the police.

A few hours later, the informant met New Orleans Detective John Miller, who was wired with a hidden body microphone, through which the ensuing conversation was recorded. The informant now said his name was Joseph Banks and that he was called Beanie. His actual name was Joseph Wallace.[3]

His story, as well as his name, had changed since his earlier call. In place of his original account of buying a Thunderbird from Kyles on Thursday, Beanie told Miller that he had not seen Kyles at all on Thursday, and had bought a red LTD the previous day, Friday. Beanie led Miller to the parking lot of a nearby bar, where he had left the red LTD, later identified as Dye's.

Beanie told Miller that he lived with Kyles's brother-in-law (later identified as Johnny Burns),[4] whom Beanie repeatedly called his "partner." Beanie described Kyles as slim, about 6-feet tall, 24 or 25 years old, with a "bush" hairstyle. When asked if Kyles ever wore his hair in plaits, Beanie said that he did but that he "had a bush" when Beanie bought the car.

During the conversation, Beanie repeatedly expressed concern that he might himself be a suspect in the murder. . . . Miller acknowledged that Beanie's possession of the car would have looked suspicious, but reassured him that he "didn't do anything wrong."

Beanie seemed eager to cast suspicion on Kyles, who allegedly made his living by "robbing people," and had tried to kill Beanie at some prior time. Beanie said that Kyles regularly carried two pistols, a .38 and a .32, and that if the police could "set him up good," they could "get that same gun" used to kill Dye. . . .

Beanie [said] that after he bought the car, he and his "partner" (Burns) drove Kyles to Schwegmann's about 9 p.m. on Friday evening to pick up Kyles's car, described as an orange four-door Ford.[5] When asked where Kyles's car had been parked, Beanie replied that it had been "[o]n the same side [of the lot] where the woman was killed at." [Miller and his supervisor, Sgt. James Eaton] later drove Beanie to Schwegmann's, where he indicated the space where he claimed Kyles's car had been parked. Beanie went on to say that when he and Burns had brought Kyles to pick up the car, Kyles had gone to some nearby bushes to retrieve a brown purse, which Kyles subsequently hid in a wardrobe at his apartment. Beanie said that Kyles had "a lot of groceries" in Schwegmann's bags and a new baby's potty "in the car." Beanie told Eaton that Kyles's garbage would go out the next day and that if Kyles was "smart" he would "put [the purse] in [the] garbage." Beanie made it clear that he expected some reward for his help, saying at one point that he was not "doing all of this for nothing." The police repeatedly assured Beanie that he would not lose the $400 he paid for the car.

After the visit to Schwegmann's, Eaton and Miller took Beanie to a police station where Miller interviewed him again on the record. . . . This statement, Beanie's third (the telephone call being the first, then the recorded conversation), repeats some of the essentials of the second one: that Beanie had purchased a red Ford LTD from Kyles for $400 on Friday evening; that Kyles had his hair "combed out" at the time of the sale; and that Kyles carried a .32 and a .38 with him "all the time."

---

3. Because the informant had so many aliases, we will follow the convention of the court below and refer to him throughout this opinion as Beanie.

4. Johnny Burns is the brother of a woman known as Pinky Burns. A number of trial witnesses referred to the relationship between Kyles and Pinky Burns as a common-law marriage (Louisiana's civil law notwithstanding). Kyles is the father of several of Pinky Burns's children.

5. . . . Kyles's car was actually a Mercury and . . . a two-door model.

Portions of the third statement, however, embellished or contradicted Beanie's preceding story and were even internally inconsistent. Beanie reported that after the sale, he and Kyles unloaded Schwegmann's grocery bags from the trunk and back seat of the LTD and placed them in Kyles's own car. Beanie said that Kyles took a brown purse from the front seat of the LTD and that they then drove in separate cars to Kyles's apartment, where they unloaded the groceries. Beanie also claimed that, a few hours later, he and his "partner" Burns went with Kyles to Schwegmann's, where they recovered Kyles's car and a "big brown pocket book" from "next to a building." Beanie did not explain how Kyles could have picked up his car and recovered the purse at Schwegmann's, after Beanie had seen Kyles with both just a few hours earlier. The police neither noted the inconsistencies nor questioned Beanie about them.

Although the police did not thereafter put Kyles under surveillance, they learned about events at his apartment from Beanie, who went there twice on Sunday. According to a fourth statement by Beanie, this one given to the chief prosecutor in November . . . , he first went to the apartment about 2 p.m., after a telephone conversation with a police officer who asked whether Kyles had the gun that was used to kill Dye. Beanie stayed in Kyles's apartment until about 5 p.m., when he left to call Detective John Miller. Then he returned about 7 p.m. and stayed until about 9:30 p.m., when he left to meet Miller, who also asked about the gun. According to this fourth statement, Beanie "rode around" with Miller until 3 a.m. on Monday, September 24. Sometime during those same early morning hours, detectives were sent . . . to pick up the rubbish outside Kyles's building. As Sgt. Eaton wrote in an interoffice memorandum, he had "reason to believe the victims [*sic*] personal papers and the Schwegmann's bags will be in the trash."

At 10:40 a.m., Kyles was arrested as he left the apartment, which was then searched under a warrant. Behind the kitchen stove, the police found a .32-caliber revolver containing five live rounds and one spent cartridge. Ballistics tests later showed that this pistol was used to murder Dye. In a wardrobe in a hallway leading to the kitchen, the officers found a homemade shoulder holster that fit the murder weapon. In a bedroom dresser drawer, they discovered two boxes of ammunition, one containing several .32-caliber rounds of the same brand as those found in the pistol. Back in the kitchen, various cans of cat and dog food, some of them of the brands Dye typically purchased, were found in Schwegmann's sacks. No other groceries were identified as possibly being Dye's, and no potty was found. Later that afternoon at the police station, police opened the rubbish bags and found the victim's purse, identification, and other personal belongings wrapped in a Schwegmann's sack.

The gun, the LTD, the purse, and the cans of pet food were dusted for fingerprints. The gun had been wiped clean. Several prints were found on the purse and on the LTD, but none was identified as Kyles's. Dye's prints were not found on any of the cans of pet food. Kyles's prints were found, however, on a small piece of paper taken from the front passenger-side floorboard of the LTD. The crime laboratory recorded the paper as a Schwegmann's sales slip, but without noting what had been printed on it, which was obliterated in the chemical process of lifting the fingerprints. A second Schwegmann's receipt was found in the trunk of the LTD, but Kyles's prints were not found on it. Beanie's fingerprints were not compared to any of the fingerprints found.

The lead detective on the case, John Dillman, put together a photo lineup that included a photograph of Kyles (but not of Beanie) and showed the array to five of the six eyewitnesses who had given statements. Three of them picked the photograph of Kyles; the other two could not confidently identify Kyles as Dye's assailant.

Kyles was indicted for first-degree murder. Before trial, his counsel filed a lengthy motion for disclosure by the State of any exculpatory or impeachment evidence. The prosecution responded that there was "no exculpatory evidence of any nature," despite the government's knowledge of the following evidentiary items: (1) the six contemporaneous eyewitness statements taken by police following the murder; (2) records of Beanie's initial call to the police; (3) the tape recording of the Saturday conversation between Beanie and officers Eaton and Miller; (4) the typed and signed statement given by Beanie on Sunday morning; (5) the computer print-out of license numbers of cars parked at Schwegmann's on the night of the murder, which did not list the number of Kyles's car; (6) the internal police memorandum calling for the seizure of the rubbish after Beanie had suggested that the purse might be found there; and (7) evidence linking Beanie to other crimes at Schwegmann's and to the unrelated murder of one Patricia Leidenheimer, committed in January before the Dye murder.

At the first trial, in November, the heart of the State's case was eyewitness testimony from four people who were at the scene of the crime (three of whom had previously picked Kyles from the photo lineup). Kyles . . . supplied an alibi that he had been picking up his children from school at the time of the murder. The theory of the defense was that Kyles had been framed by Beanie, who had planted evidence in Kyles's apartment and his rubbish for the purposes of shifting suspicion away from himself, removing an impediment to romance with Pinky Burns, and obtaining reward money. Beanie did not testify as a witness for either the defense or the prosecution.

[A]fter four hours of deliberation, the jury became deadlocked on the issue of guilt, and a mistrial was declared.

After the mistrial, the chief trial prosecutor, Cliff Strider, interviewed Beanie. Strider's notes show that Beanie again changed important elements of his story. He said that he went with Kyles to retrieve Kyles's car from the Schwegmann's lot on Thursday, the day of the murder, at some time between 5 and 7:30 p.m., not on Friday, at 9 p.m., as he had said in his second and third statements. (Indeed, in his second statement, Beanie said that he had not seen Kyles at all on Thursday.) He also said, for the first time, that when they had picked up the car they were accompanied not only by Johnny Burns but also by Kevin Black, who had testified for the defense at the first trial. Beanie now claimed that after getting Kyles's car they went to Black's house, retrieved a number of bags of groceries, a child's potty, and a brown purse, all of which they took to Kyles's apartment. Beanie also stated that on the Sunday after the murder he had been at Kyles's apartment two separate times. Notwithstanding the many inconsistencies and variations among Beanie's statements, neither Strider's notes nor any of the other notes and transcripts were given to the defense.

In December 1984, Kyles was tried a second time. Again, the heart of the State's case was the testimony of four eyewitnesses who positively identified Kyles in front of the jury. The prosecution also offered a blown-up photograph taken at the crime scene soon after the murder, on the basis of which the prosecutors argued that a seemingly two-toned car in the background of the photograph was Kyles's. . . . Once again, Beanie did not testify.

As in the first trial, the defense contended that the eyewitnesses were mistaken. Kyles's counsel called several individuals, including Kevin Black, who testified to seeing Beanie, with his hair in plaits, driving a red car similar to the victim's about an hour after the killing. Another witness testified that Beanie, with his hair in braids, had tried to sell him the car on Thursday evening, shortly after the murder. Another witness testified that Beanie, with his hair in a "Jheri curl," had attempted to sell him the car on Friday. One witness, Beanie's "partner," Burns, testified that he had seen Beanie on Sunday at Kyles's apartment, stooping down near the stove where the gun was eventually found, and the defense presented testimony that Beanie was romantically interested in Pinky Burns. To explain the pet food found in Kyles's apartment, there was testimony that Kyles's family kept a dog and cat and often fed stray animals in the neighborhood.

Finally, Kyles again took the stand. Denying any involvement in the shooting, he explained his fingerprints on the cash register receipt found in Dye's car by saying that Beanie had picked him up in a red car on Friday, September 21, and had taken him to Schwegmann's, where he purchased transmission fluid and a pack of cigarettes. He suggested that the receipt may have fallen from the bag when he removed the cigarettes.

On rebuttal, the prosecutor had Beanie brought into the courtroom. All of the testifying eyewitnesses, after viewing Beanie standing next to Kyles, reaffirmed their previous identifications of Kyles as the murderer. Kyles was convicted of first-degree murder and sentenced to death. . . .

The prosecution's affirmative duty to disclose evidence favorable to a defendant . . . is . . . most prominently associated with this Court's decision in Brady v. Maryland, 373 U.S. 83 (1963). *Brady* held "that the suppression by the prosecution of evidence favorable to an accused upon request violates due process where the evidence is material either to guilt or to punishment, irrespective of the good faith or bad faith of the prosecution." 373 U.S., at 87. . . .

In . . . United States v. Bagley, 473 U.S. 667 (1985), the Court disavowed any difference between exculpatory and impeachment evidence for *Brady* purposes, and it . . . held that regardless of request, favorable evidence is material, and constitutional error results from its suppression by the government, "if there is a reasonable probability that, had the evidence been disclosed to the defense, the result of the proceeding would have been different." 473 U.S., at 682 (opinion of Blackmun, J.); id., at 685 (White, J., concurring in part and concurring in judgment).

Four aspects of materiality under *Bagley* bear emphasis. Although the constitutional duty is triggered by the potential impact of favorable but undisclosed evidence, a showing of materiality does not require demonstration by a preponderance that disclosure of the suppressed evidence would have resulted ultimately in the defendant's acquittal (whether based on the presence of reasonable doubt or acceptance of an explanation for the crime that does not inculpate the defendant). *Bagley*'s touchstone of materiality is a "reasonable probability" of a different result, and the adjective is important. The question is not whether the defendant would more likely than not have received a different verdict with the evidence, but whether in its absence he received a fair trial, understood as a trial resulting in a verdict worthy of confidence. A "reasonable probability" of a different result is accordingly shown when the government's evidentiary suppression "undermines confidence in the outcome of the trial." *Bagley*, 473 U.S., at 678.

The second aspect of *Bagley* materiality bearing emphasis here is that it is not a sufficiency of evidence test. A defendant need not demonstrate that after discounting the inculpatory evidence in light of the undisclosed evidence, there would not have been enough left to convict. . . .

Third, we note that . . . once a reviewing court applying *Bagley* has found constitutional error there is no need for further harmless-error review. Assuming, arguendo, that a harmless-error enquiry were to apply, a *Bagley* error could not be treated as harmless, since "a reasonable probability that, had the evidence been disclosed to the defense, the result of the proceeding would have been different," necessarily entails the conclusion that the suppression must have had " 'substantial and injurious effect or influence in determining the jury's verdict,' " Brecht v. Abrahamson, 507 U.S. 619, 623 (1993), quoting Kotteakos v. United States, 328 U.S. 750, 776 (1946). . . .

The fourth and final aspect of *Bagley* materiality to be stressed here is its definition in terms of suppressed evidence considered collectively, not item by item. As Justice Blackmun emphasized in the portion of his opinion written for the Court, the Constitution is not violated every time the government fails or chooses not to disclose evidence that might prove helpful to the defense. 473 U.S., at 675 and n. 7. We have never held that the Constitution demands an open file policy (however such a policy might work out in practice), and the rule in *Bagley* (and, hence, in *Brady*) requires less of the prosecution than the ABA Standards for Criminal Justice, which call generally for prosecutorial disclosures of any evidence tending to exculpate or mitigate.

While the definition of *Bagley* materiality in terms of the cumulative effect of suppression must accordingly be seen as leaving the government with a degree of discretion, it must also be understood as imposing a corresponding burden. On the one side, showing that the prosecution knew of an item of favorable evidence unknown to the defense does not amount to a *Brady* violation, without more. But the prosecution, which alone can know what is undisclosed, must be assigned the consequent responsibility to gauge the likely net effect of all such evidence and make disclosure when the point of "reasonable probability" is reached. This in turn means that the individual prosecutor has a duty to learn of any favorable evidence known to the others acting on the government's behalf in the case, including the police. But whether the prosecutor succeeds or fails in meeting this obligation (whether, that is, a failure to disclose is in good faith or bad faith), the prosecution's responsibility for failing to disclose known, favorable evidence rising to a material level of importance is inescapable. . . .

[W]e were asked at oral argument to raise the threshold of materiality because the *Bagley* standard "makes it difficult . . . to know" from the "perspective [of the prosecutor at] trial . . . exactly what might become important later on." The State asks for "a certain amount of leeway in making a judgment call" as to the disclosure of any given piece of evidence.

Uncertainty about the degree of further "leeway" that might satisfy the State's request for a "certain amount" of it is the least of the reasons to deny the request. At bottom, what the State fails to recognize is that, with or without more leeway, the prosecution cannot be subject to any disclosure obligation without at some point having the responsibility to determine when it must act. . . .

This means, naturally, that a prosecutor anxious about tacking too close to the wind will disclose a favorable piece of evidence. This is as it should be. Such disclosure will serve to justify trust in the prosecutor as "the representative . . . of a sovereignty . . . whose interest . . . in a criminal prosecution is not that it shall win a case, but that justice shall be done." Berger v. United States, 295 U.S. 78, 88 (1935). And it will tend to preserve the criminal trial, as distinct from the prosecutor's private deliberations, as the chosen forum for ascertaining the truth about criminal accusations. . . .

In this case, disclosure of the suppressed evidence to competent counsel would have made a different result reasonably probable.

As the District Court put it, "the essence of the State's case" was the testimony of eyewitnesses, who identified Kyles as Dye's killer. Disclosure of their statements would have resulted in a markedly weaker case for the prosecution and a markedly stronger one for the defense. To begin with, the value of two of those witnesses would have been substantially reduced or destroyed.

The State rated Henry Williams as its best witness, who testified that he had seen the struggle and the actual shooting by Kyles. The jury would have found it helpful to probe this conclusion in the light of Williams's contemporaneous statement, in which he told the police that the assailant was "a black male, about 19 or 20 years old, about 5'4" or 5'5", 140 to 150 pounds, medium build" and that "his hair looked like it was platted." If cross-examined on this description, Williams would have had trouble explaining how he could have described Kyles, 6-feet tall and thin, as a man more than half a foot shorter with a medium build. Indeed, since Beanie was 22 years old, 5'5" tall, and 159 pounds, the defense would have had a compelling argument that Williams's description pointed to Beanie but not to Kyles.[13]

The trial testimony of a second eyewitness, Isaac Smallwood, was equally damning to Kyles. He testified that Kyles was the assailant, and that he saw him struggle with Dye. He said he saw Kyles take a ".32, a small black gun" out of his right pocket, shoot Dye in the head, and drive off in her LTD. When the prosecutor asked him whether he actually saw Kyles shoot Dye, Smallwood answered "Yeah."

Smallwood's statement taken at the parking lot, however, was vastly different. Immediately after the crime, Smallwood claimed that he had not seen the actual murder and had not seen the assailant outside the vehicle. "I heard a lound [*sic*] pop," he said. "When I looked around I saw a lady laying on the ground, and there was a red car coming toward me." Smallwood said that he got a look at the culprit, a black teenage male with a mustache and shoulder-length braided hair, as the victim's red Thunderbird passed where he was standing. When a police investigator specifically asked him whether he had seen the assailant outside the car, Smallwood answered that he had not; the gunman "was already in the car and coming toward me."

A jury would reasonably have been troubled by the adjustments to Smallwood's original story by the time of the second trial. The struggle and shooting, which

---

13. The defense could have further underscored the possibility that Beanie was Dye's killer through cross-examination of the police on their failure to direct any investigation against Beanie. If the police had disclosed Beanie's statements, they would have been forced to admit that their informant Beanie described Kyles as generally wearing his hair in a "bush" style (and so wearing it when he sold the car to Beanie), whereas Beanie wore his in plaits. There was a considerable amount of such *Brady* evidence on which the defense could have attacked the investigation as shoddy. The police failed to disclose that Beanie had charges pending against him for a theft at the same Schwegmann's store and was a primary suspect in the January 1984 murder of Patricia Leidenheimer, who, like Dye, was an older woman shot once in the head during an armed robbery. (Even though Beanie was a primary suspect in the Leidenheimer murder as early as September, he was not interviewed by the police about it until after Kyles's second trial in December. Beanie confessed his involvement in the murder, but was never charged in connection with it.) . . .

earlier he had not seen, he was able to describe with such detailed clarity as to identify the murder weapon as a small black .32-caliber pistol, which, of course, was the type of weapon used. His description of the victim's car had gone from a "Thunderbird" to an "LTD" and he saw fit to say nothing about the assailant's shoulder-length hair and moustache, details noted by no other eyewitness. These developments would have fueled a withering cross-examination, destroying confidence in Smallwood's story and raising a substantial implication that the prosecutor had coached him to give it.

Since the evolution over time of a given eyewitness's description can be fatal to its reliability, the Smallwood and Williams identifications would have been severely undermined by use of their suppressed statements. . . . Nor, of course, would the harm to the State's case on identity have been confined to their testimony alone. The fact that neither Williams nor Smallwood could have provided a consistent eyewitness description pointing to Kyles would have undercut the prosecution all the more because the remaining eyewitnesses called to testify (Territo and Kersh) had their best views of the gunman only as he fled the scene with his body partly concealed in Dye's car. . . .

Damage to the prosecution's case would not have been confined to evidence of the eyewitnesses, for Beanie's various statements would have raised opportunities to attack not only the probative value of crucial physical evidence and the circumstances in which it was found, but the thoroughness and even the good faith of the investigation, as well. . . . Beanie's statements to the police were replete with inconsistencies and would have allowed the jury to infer that Beanie was anxious to see Kyles arrested for Dye's murder. Their disclosure would have revealed a remarkably uncritical attitude on the part of the police. . . .

[T]he defense could have examined the police to good effect on their knowledge of Beanie's statements and so have attacked the reliability of the investigation in failing even to consider Beanie's possible guilt and in tolerating (if not countenancing) serious possibilities that incriminating evidence had been planted.

By demonstrating the detectives' knowledge of Beanie's affirmatively self-incriminating statements, the defense could have laid the foundation for a vigorous argument that the police had been guilty of negligence. In his initial meeting with police, Beanie admitted twice that he changed the license plates on the LTD. This admission enhanced the suspiciousness of his possession of the car; the defense could have argued persuasively that he was no bona fide purchaser. And when combined with his police record, evidence of prior criminal activity near Schwegmann's, and his status as a suspect in another murder, his devious behavior gave reason to believe that he had done more than buy a stolen car. There was further self-incrimination in Beanie's statement that Kyles's car was parked in the same part of the Schwegmann's lot where Dye was killed. Beanie's apparent awareness of the specific location of the murder could have been based, as the State contends, on television or newspaper reports, but perhaps it was not. . . . Since the police admittedly never treated Beanie as a suspect, the defense could thus have used his statements to throw the reliability of the investigation into doubt and to sully the credibility of Detective Dillman, who testified that Beanie was never a suspect, and that he had "no knowledge" that Beanie had changed the license plate.

The admitted failure of the police to pursue these pointers toward Beanie's possible guilt could only have magnified the effect on the jury of explaining how the purse and the gun happened to be recovered. In Beanie's original recorded statement, he told the police that "[Kyles's] garbage goes out tomorrow," and that "if he's smart he'll put [the purse] in [the] garbage." These statements, along with the internal memorandum stating that the police had "reason to believe" Dye's personal effects and Schwegmann's bags would be in the garbage, would have supported the defense's theory that Beanie was no mere observer, but was determining the investigation's direction and success. . . .

To the same effect would have been an enquiry based on Beanie's apparently revealing remark to police that "if you can set [Kyles] up good, you can get that same gun." While the jury might have understood that Beanie meant simply that if the police investigated Kyles, they would probably find the murder weapon, the jury could also have taken Beanie to have been making the more sinister suggestion that the police "set up" Kyles, and the defense could have argued that the police accepted the invitation. The prosecutor's notes of his interview with Beanie would have shown that police officers were asking Beanie the whereabouts of the gun all day Sunday, the very day when he was twice at Kyles's apartment and was allegedly seen by Johnny Burns lurking near the stove, where the gun was later found. Beanie's same statement, indeed, could have been used to cap an attack on the integrity of the investigation and on the reliability of Detective Dillman, who testified on cross-examination that he did not know if Beanie had been at Kyles's apartment on Sunday.

Next to be considered is the prosecution's list of the cars in the Schwegmann's parking lot at mid-evening after the murder. While its suppression does not rank with the failure to disclose the other evidence discussed here, it would have had some value as exculpation and impeachment, and it counts accordingly in determining whether *Bagley*'s standard of materiality is satisfied. On the police's assumption, argued to the jury, that the killer drove to the lot and left his car there during the heat of the investigation, the list without Kyles's registration would obviously have helped Kyles and would have had some value in countering an argument by the prosecution that a grainy enlargement of a photograph of the crime scene showed Kyles's car in the background. . . .

The State argues that the list was neither impeachment nor exculpatory evidence because Kyles could have moved his car before the list was created and because the list does not purport to be a comprehensive listing of all the cars in the Schwegmann's lot. Such argument, however, confuses the weight of the evidence with its favorable tendency. . . .

In assessing the significance of the evidence withheld, one must of course bear in mind that not every item of the State's case would have been directly undercut if the *Brady* evidence had been disclosed. It is significant, however, that the physical evidence remaining unscathed would . . . hardly have amounted to overwhelming proof that Kyles was the murderer. Ammunition and a holster were found in Kyles's apartment, but if the jury had suspected the gun had been planted the significance of these items might have been left in doubt. The fact that pet food was found in Kyles's apartment was consistent with the testimony of several defense witnesses that Kyles owned a dog and that his children fed stray cats. . . .

Similarly undispositive is the small Schwegmann's receipt on the front passenger floorboard of the LTD, the only physical evidence that bore a fingerprint identified as Kyles's. Kyles explained that Beanie had driven him to Schwegmann's on Friday to buy cigarettes and transmission fluid, and he theorized that the slip must have fallen out of the bag when he removed the cigarettes. This explanation is consistent with the location of the slip when found and with its small size. The State cannot very well argue that the fingerprint ties Kyles to the killing without also explaining how the 2-inch-long register slip could have been the receipt for a week's worth of groceries, which Dye had gone to Schwegmann's to purchase.

The inconclusiveness of the physical evidence does not, to be sure, prove Kyles's innocence, and the jury might have found the eyewitness testimony of Territo and Kersh sufficient to convict, even though less damning to Kyles than that of Smallwood and Williams. But the question is not whether the State would have had a case to go to the jury if it had disclosed the favorable evidence, but whether we can be confident that the jury's verdict would have been the same. . . .

"[F]airness" cannot be stretched to the point of calling this a fair trial. . . . The judgment of the Court of Appeals [affirming the denial of Kyles's petition for habeas corpus] is reversed, and the case is remanded for further proceedings consistent with this opinion. . . .

[The concurring opinion of Justice Stevens, joined by Justices Ginsburg and Breyer, is omitted.]

JUSTICE SCALIA, with whom the CHIEF JUSTICE, JUSTICE KENNEDY, and JUSTICE THOMAS join, dissenting. . . .

I am . . . forced to dissent . . . because, having improvidently decided to review the facts of this case, the Court goes on to get the facts wrong. Its findings are in my view clearly erroneous, and the Court's verdict would be reversed if there were somewhere further to appeal. . . .

[A] few general observations about the Court's methodology are appropriate. It is fundamental to the discovery rule of Brady v. Maryland, 373 U.S. 83 (1963), that the materiality of a failure to disclose favorable evidence "must be evaluated in the context of the entire record." United States v. Agurs, 427 U.S. 97, 112 (1976). It is simply not enough to show that the undisclosed evidence would have allowed the defense to weaken, or even to "destro[y]," the *particular* prosecution witnesses or items of prosecution evidence to which the undisclosed evidence relates. It is petitioner's burden to show that in light of all the evidence, including that untainted by the *Brady* violation, it is reasonably probable that a jury would have entertained a reasonable doubt regarding petitioner's guilt. . . .

In any analysis of this case, the desperate implausibility of the theory that petitioner put before the jury must be kept firmly in mind. The first half of that theory—designed to neutralize the physical evidence (Mrs. Dye's purse in his garbage, the murder weapon behind his stove) —was that petitioner was the victim of a "frame-up" by the police informer and evil genius, Beanie. Now, it is not unusual for a guilty person who knows that he is suspected of a crime to try to shift blame to someone else; and it is less common, but not unheard of, for a guilty person who is neither suspected nor subject to suspicion (because he has established a perfect alibi), to call attention to himself by coming forward to point the finger at an innocent person. But petitioner's theory is that the guilty Beanie, who *could* plausibly be accused of the crime . . . but who was *not* a suspect any more than Kyles was (the police as yet had no leads), injected both Kyles and himself into the investigation in order to get the innocent Kyles convicted. If this were not stupid enough, the wicked Beanie is supposed to have suggested that the police search his victim's premises *a full day before he got around to planting the incriminating evidence on the premises.*

The second half of petitioner's theory was that he was the victim of a quadruple coincidence, in which four eyewitnesses to the crime mistakenly identified him as the murderer—three picking him out of a photo array without hesitation, and all four affirming their identification in open court after comparing him with Beanie. The extraordinary mistake petitioner had to persuade the jury these four witnesses made was not simply to mistake the real killer, Beanie, for the very same innocent third party (hard enough to believe), but in addition to mistake him *for the very man Beanie had chosen to frame*—the last and most incredible level of coincidence. However small the chance that the jury would believe any one of those improbable scenarios, the likelihood that it would believe them all together is far smaller. . . .

[The] basic error of approaching the evidence piecemeal is . . . what accounts for the Court's obsessive focus on the credibility or culpability of Beanie, who did not even testify at trial and whose credibility or innocence the State has never once avowed. The Court's opinion reads as if either petitioner or Beanie must be telling the truth, and any evidence tending to inculpate or undermine the credibility of the one would exculpate or enhance the credibility of the other. But the jury verdict in this case said only that petitioner was guilty of the murder. That is perfectly consistent with the possibilities that Beanie repeatedly lied, that he was an accessory after the fact, or even that he planted evidence against petitioner. Even if the undisclosed evidence would have allowed the defense to thoroughly impeach Beanie and to suggest the above possibilities, the jury could well have believed *all* of those things and yet have condemned petitioner because it could not believe that *all four* of the eyewitnesses were similarly mistaken. . . .

The undisclosed evidence does not create a "'reasonable probability' of a different result." To begin with the eyewitness testimony. . . .

Territo, the first eyewitness called by the State, was waiting at a red light in a truck 30 or 40 yards from the Schwegmann's parking lot. He saw petitioner shoot Mrs. Dye, start her car, drive out onto the road, and pull up just behind Territo's truck. When the light turned green petitioner pulled beside Territo and stopped while waiting to make a turn. Petitioner looked Territo full in the face. . . . Territo also testified that a detective had shown him a picture of Beanie and asked him if the picture "could have been the guy that did it. I told him no." The second eyewitness, Kersh, also saw petitioner shoot Mrs. Dye. When asked whether she got "a good look" at him as he drove away, she answered "yes." . . . The third eyewitness, Smallwood, testified that he saw petitioner shoot Mrs. Dye, walk to the car, and drive away. Petitioner drove slowly by, within a distance of 15 or 25 feet, and Smallwood saw his face from the side. The fourth eyewitness, Williams, who had been working outside the parking lot, testified that "the gentleman came up the side of the car," struggled with Mrs. Dye, shot her, walked around to the driver's side of the car, and drove away. Williams not only "saw him before he shot her," but watched petitioner drive slowly by "within less than ten feet." When asked "[d]id you get an opportunity to look at him good?", Williams said, "I did."

The Court attempts to dispose of this direct, unqualified, and consistent eyewitness testimony in two ways. First, by relying on a theory so implausible that it was apparently not suggested by petitioner's counsel until the oral-argument-*cum*-evidentiary-hearing held before us, perhaps because it is a theory that only the most removed appellate court could love. This theory is that there is a reasonable probability that the jury would have changed its mind about the eyewitness identification because the *Brady* material would have permitted the defense to argue that the eyewitnesses only got a good look at the killer when he was sitting in Mrs. Dye's car, and thus could identify him, not by his height and build, but *only by his face*. Never mind, for the moment, that this is factually false, since the *Brady* material showed that only *one* of the four eyewitnesses, Smallwood, did not see the killer outside the car. And never mind, also, the dubious premise that the build of a man 6-feet tall (like petitioner) is indistinguishable, when seated behind the wheel, from that of a man less than 5 and one-half feet tall (like Beanie). To assert that unhesitant and categorical identification by four witnesses who viewed the killer, close-up and with the sun high in the sky, would not eliminate reasonable doubt if it were based *only* on *facial* characteristics, and not on height and build, is quite simply absurd. Facial features are *the primary means* by which human beings recognize one another. That is why police departments distribute "mug" shots of wanted felons, rather than Ivy-League-type posture pictures; it is why bank robbers wear stockings over their faces instead of floor-length capes over their shoulders; it is why the Lone Ranger wears a mask instead of a poncho; and it is why a criminal defense lawyer who seeks to destroy an identifying witness by asking "You admit that you saw only the killer's face?" will be laughed out of the courtroom.

It would be different, of course, if there were evidence that Kyles's and Beanie's faces looked like twins, or at least bore an unusual degree of resemblance. That facial resemblance *would* explain why, if Beanie committed the crime, all four witnesses picked out Kyles at first (though not why they continued to pick him out when he and Beanie stood side-by-side in court), and would render their failure to observe the height and build of the killer relevant. . . . *No* court has found that Kyles and Beanie bear any facial resemblance. In fact, quite the opposite: *every* federal and state court that has reviewed the record photographs, or seen the two men, has found that they do not resemble each other in any respect. . . .

The Court's second means of seeking to neutralize the impressive and unanimous eyewitness testimony uses the same "build-is-everything" theory to exaggerate the effect of the State's failure to disclose the contemporaneous statement of Henry Williams. That statement would assuredly have permitted a sharp cross-examination, since it contained estimations of height and weight that fit Beanie better than petitioner. But I think it is hyperbole to say that the statement would have "substantially reduced or destroyed" the value of Williams' testimony. Williams saw the murderer drive slowly by less than 10 feet away, and unhesitatingly picked him out of the photo lineup. The jury might well choose to give greater credence to the simple fact of identification than to the difficult estimation of height and weight.

The Court spends considerable time showing how Smallwood's testimony could have been discredited to such a degree as to "rais[e] a substantial implication that the prosecutor had coached him to give it." Perhaps so, but that is all irrelevant to this appeal, since all of that impeaching material (except the "facial identification" point I have discussed above) was available to the defense independently of the *Brady* material [based on inconsistencies between Smallwood's testimony at the first and second trials]. In sum, the undisclosed statements, credited with everything they could possibly have provided to the defense, leave two prosecution witnesses (Territo and Kersh) totally untouched; one prosecution witness (Smallwood) barely affected (he saw "only" the killer's face); and one prosecution witness (Williams) somewhat impaired (his description of the killer's height and weight did not match Kyles). We must keep all this in due perspective, remembering that the relevant question in the materiality inquiry is not how many points the defense could have scored off the prosecution witnesses, but whether it is reasonably probable that the new evidence would have caused the jury to accept the basic thesis that all four witnesses were mistaken. I think it plainly is not. . . .

The physical evidence confirms the immateriality of the nondisclosures. In a garbage bag outside petitioner's home the police found Mrs. Dye's purse and other belongings. Inside his home they found, behind the kitchen stove, the .32-caliber revolver used to kill Mrs. Dye; hanging in a wardrobe, a homemade shoulder holster that was "a perfect fit" for the revolver; in a dresser drawer in the bedroom, two boxes of gun cartridges, one containing only .32-caliber rounds of the same brand found in the murder weapon, another containing .22, .32, and .38-caliber rounds; in a kitchen cabinet, eight empty Schwegmann's bags; and in a cupboard underneath that cabinet, one Schwegmann's bag containing 15 cans of pet food. Petitioner's account at trial was that Beanie planted the purse, gun, and holster, that petitioner received the ammunition from Beanie as collateral for a loan, and that petitioner had bought the pet food the day of the murder. That account strains credulity to the breaking point.

The Court is correct that the *Brady* material would have supported the claim that Beanie planted Mrs. Dye's belongings in petitioner's garbage and (to a lesser degree) that Beanie planted the gun behind petitioner's stove. But we must see the whole story that petitioner presented to the jury. Petitioner would have it that Beanie did not plant the incriminating evidence until the day after he incited the police to search petitioner's home. Moreover, he succeeded in surreptitiously placing the gun behind the stove, and the matching shoulder holster in the wardrobe, while *at least 10 and as many as 19 people* were present in petitioner's small apartment. Beanie, who was wearing blue jeans and either a "tank-top" shirt or a short-sleeved shirt, would have had to be concealing about his person not only the shoulder holster and the murder weapon, but also a different gun with tape wrapped around the barrel that he showed to petitioner. Only appellate judges could swallow such a tale. Petitioner's only supporting evidence was Johnny Burns's testimony that he saw Beanie stooping behind the stove, presumably to plant the gun. Burns's credibility on the stand can perhaps best be gauged by observing that the state judge who presided over petitioner's trial stated, in a postconviction proceeding, that "[I] ha[ve] chosen to totally disregard everything that [Burns] has said." Burns, by the way, who repeatedly stated at trial that Beanie was his "best friend," has since been tried and convicted for killing Beanie.

Petitioner did not claim that the ammunition had been planted. The police found a .22-caliber rifle under petitioner's mattress and two boxes of ammunition, one containing .22, .32, and .38-caliber rounds, another containing only .32-caliber rounds of the same brand as those found loaded in the murder weapon. Petitioner's story was that Beanie gave him the rifle and the .32-caliber shells as security for a loan, but that he had taken the .22-caliber shells out of the box. Put aside that the latter detail was contradicted by the facts; but consider the inherent implausibility of Beanie's giving petitioner collateral in the form of a box containing *only* .32 shells, if it were true that petitioner did not own a .32-caliber gun. As the Fifth Circuit wrote, "[t]he more likely inference, apparently chosen by the jury, is that [petitioner] possessed .32 caliber ammunition because he possessed a .32-caliber firearm."

We come to the evidence of the pet food, so mundane and yet so very damning. Petitioner's confused and changing explanations for the presence of *15 cans* of pet food in a Schwegmann's bag under the sink must have fatally undermined his credibility before the jury. . . .

. . . Mr. and Mrs. Dye owned two cats and a dog, for which she regularly bought varying brands of pet food, several different brands at a time. Found in Mrs. Dye's home after her murder were the brands Nine Lives, Kalkan, and Puss n' Boots. Found in petitioner's home were eight cans of Nine Lives, four cans of Kalkan, and three cans of Cozy Kitten. Since we know that Mrs. Dye had been shopping that day and that the murderer made off with her goods, petitioner's possession of these items was powerful evidence that he was the murderer. Assuredly the jury drew that obvious inference. Pressed to explain why he just happened to buy 15 cans of pet food that very day (keep in mind that petitioner was a very poor man, who supported a common-law wife, a mistress, and four children), petitioner gave the reason that "it was on sale." The State, however, introduced testimony from the Schwegmann's advertising director that the pet food was not on sale that day. . . .

The State presented to the jury a massive core of evidence (including four eye-witnesses) showing that petitioner was guilty of murder, and that he lied about his guilt. The effect that the *Brady* materials would have had in chipping away at the edges of the State's case can only be called immaterial. . . .

I respectfully dissent.

NOTES AND QUESTIONS

1. How do the majority and the dissent reach such wildly different conclusions on the materiality of the prosecution's failure to disclose? Is it possible that they are addressing different questions? Justice Souter cites United States v. Bagley, 473 U.S. 667, 682 (1995), for the holding that the suppression of favorable evidence is material, for *Brady* purposes, "if there is a reasonable probability that, had the evidence been disclosed . . . the result of the proceeding would have been different." Is Justice Scalia asking this same question? Or is he asking whether there is a reasonable chance that the defendant did not commit the crime? Which is the better question on which to focus?

2. Kyles was tried for the murder three more times after the Supreme Court's decision. Each time, the jury deadlocked. Kyles was finally released in 1998—almost 15 years after his arrest. Does this subsequent history cast any light on the question whether the suppressed evidence created a "reasonable probability" of a different result?

3. The majority quotes famous language from Berger v. United States, 295 U.S. 78, 88 (1935), where Justice Sutherland noted that the government's interest in a criminal case "is not that it shall win a case, but that justice shall be done." Sutherland then went on to say:

> [The prosecutor] is in a peculiar and very definite sense the servant of the law, the twofold aim of which is that guilty shall not escape or innocence suffer. He may prosecute with earnestness and vigor—indeed he should do so. But while he may strike hard blows, he is not at liberty to strike foul ones. It is as much his duty to refrain from improper methods calculated to produce a wrongful conviction as it is to use every legitimate means to bring about a just one.

How easy is it for a prosecutor to fulfill this "peculiar" dual obligation? One of the challenges created by the *Brady* doctrine is that it places the prosecutor in a conflicted role—having to decide what information might help the defense beat the charges after she has convinced herself that the evidence as a whole proves guilt beyond a reasonable doubt. And the prosecutor must make the decision about what constitutes *Brady* material prior to trial, before knowing the details of the defendant's case. According to Professor Burke, applying the *Brady* standard prior to a trial thus "requires that prosecutors engage in a bizarre kind of anticipatory hindsight review." Alafair S. Burke, Improving Prosecutorial Decision Making: Some Lessons of Cognitive Science, 47 Wm. & Mary L. Rev. 1587, 1610 (2006). Professor Burke argues that due to cognitive bias, even the most conscientious prosecutor engaged in such review may prove unreliable in recognizing and producing *Brady* material:

> *Brady* requires a prosecutor who is determining whether to disclose a piece of evidence . . . to speculate first about how the remaining evidence will come together against the defendant at trial, and then about whether a reasonable probability exists that the piece of evidence at issue would affect the result of the trial. During the first step, a risk exists that prosecutors will engage in biased recall, retrieving from memory only those facts that tend to confirm the hypothesis of guilty. Moreover, because of selective information processing, the prosecutor will accept at face value the evidence she views as inculpatory, without subjecting it to the scrutiny that a defense attorney would encourage jurors to apply.
>
> Cognitive bias would also appear to taint the second speculative step of the *Brady* analysis. . . . Because of selective information processing, the prosecutor will look for weaknesses in evidence contradicting her existing belief in the defendant's guilt. In short, compared to a neutral decision maker, the prosecutor will overestimate the strength of the government's case against the defendant and underestimate the potential exculpatory value of the evidence whose disclosure is at issue. As a consequence, the prosecutor will fail to see materiality where it might in fact exist.

Id., at 1611-1612. How troublesome is this problem? Is there any practical way to avoid having the prosecutor, an advocate, make the *Brady* disclosure decisions?

4. Suppose that after making an arrest and after charges have been filed, the police learn of information that might be helpful to the prosecution, but also might be helpful to the defense — they learn that there was a previously undiscovered eyewitness, for example, or that a fingerprint was recovered from the scene that probably belonged to the perpetrator. Does *Brady* require the police and prosecutor to affirmatively pursue the new information, without knowing whether it is "favorable" to the defense or to the State?

This was the situation in Connick v. Thompson, 563 U.S. 51 (2011). The police recovered a blood sample at the scene of an armed robbery, and it was undisputed that the blood came from the perpetrator. But rather than test the sample against the defendant's blood, the prosecutor simply proceeded with the prosecution and obtained a conviction, never disclosing the sample to the defense, and not telling the defense that it knew the perpetrator's blood type (the prosecution claimed that it did not knew Thompson's blood type). Years later the defense found the report that revealed the perpetrator's blood type, which proved the defendant's innocence. The prosecutor conceded the *Brady* violation, and Thompson successfully sued under §1983. A divided Supreme Court ruled, however, that the defendant could not sustain a §1983 claim against the District Attorney under a "failure to train" theory and reversed the finding of liability.

[handwritten margin note: Problem w/ Brady is that it places the prosecutor in a conflicted role — having to decide what info might help the defense beat the charges after he has convinced himself that the evidence as a whole proves guilt beyond a reasonable doubt]

Because the District Attorney had conceded the *Brady* violation, the *Thompson* majority did not analyze whether the prosecution's ignorance about the character of the blood evidence (was it favorable or unfavorable to the accused?) was in fact a violation. But in his concurring opinion, Justice Scalia was not so reticent—he concluded "[t]here was probably no *Brady* violation at all" in the case, and certainly not one that the Supreme Court had ever recognized.

Can this be right? Can the prosecutor really just sit on evidence that might prove the defendant's innocence, not testing it, and not even telling the defense of its existence? If the prosecutor is so sure that defendant is guilty, what is she afraid of? On the other hand, is there anything in *Brady* that covers this case, assuming that the prosecutor is truly ignorant of what the evidence would show, if tested? How would you articulate what a prosecutor is obligated to do in a case like *Thompson*?

5. Although prosecutors make the threshold decision whether evidence constitutes *Brady* material, they must be fair-minded in how they evaluate conflicting evidence. In *Smith v. Cain*, 132 S. Ct. 627 (2012), the lone witness to a multiple murder told the police, both at the scene and several days later, that he could not identify the shooter. The witness subsequently changed his story and positively identified Smith as the killer, and testified to that effect at trial. The prosecutor did not, however, disclose the witness's earlier, inconsistent statements. Noting that the eyewitness testimony "was the only evidence linking Smith to the crime," the Supreme Court, 8-1, found a *Brady* violation in the withholding of the earlier statements and reversed the convictions. Chief Justice Roberts's majority opinion acknowledged that the witness's reluctance to identify the shooter right away *might* have been caused by a fear of retaliation by the shooter, as the State claimed, but found the State's argument on this point irrelevant. The proper course, the Court said, was for the government to disclose the conflicting information, let each side argue about the reason for the inconsistency, and let the jury sort things out.

Smith looks like an easy case, and the Court certainly treated it as such—the entire majority opinion is fewer than 1,000 words, and during the oral argument, the State's arguments for non-disclosure were so strained that Justice Kagan asked the Assistant District Attorney "did your office ever consider just confessing error in this case?" Given this, and given that the Court's opinion broke no new legal ground, why do you think the Court agreed to hear this case? Was it simply a belief that Mr. Smith was wrongly convicted? If so, consider a portion of Justice Scalia's dissent in Kyles v. Whitley, supra, that is not reproduced above. There Justice Scalia writes:

> The greatest puzzle of [the *Kyles*] decision is what could have caused *this* capital case to be singled out for favored treatment [by receiving Supreme Court review]. Perhaps it has been randomly selected as a symbol, to reassure America that the United States Supreme Court is reviewing capital convictions to make sure no factual error has been made. If so, it is a false symbol, for we assuredly do not do that. . . . The reality is that responsibility for factual accuracy, in capital cases as in other cases, rests elsewhere—with trial judges and juries, state appellate courts, and the lower federal courts; we do nothing but encourage foolish reliance to pretend otherwise.

Kyles, 514 U.S., at 457-458. Although *Smith* was not a capital case, does Justice Scalia's observation explain the Court's interest in the case? Does it—or should it—matter to the Supreme Court in deciding which cases to review that the District Attorney's Office that prosecuted Mr. Smith was the same one that violated *Brady* in Kyles v. Whitley, and that had conceded a *Brady* violation in Connick v. Thompson just one year before *Smith*?

6. The *Kyles* majority opinion noted two important qualifications on the scope of the *Brady* doctrine. The first was that the prosecutor is not only obligated to turn over information that is in her possession, but also "has a duty to learn of any favorable evidence known to the others acting on the government's behalf in the case, including the police." This means that it is no defense to an alleged *Brady* violation that the prosecutor did not realize the favorable evidence (say, a witness statement to the police that strongly supports the defense) existed—*Brady* imposes an obligation on the prosecutor to go looking for the information.

Second, and perhaps counter-intuitively, the good or bad faith of the prosecutor is legally irrelevant to the question of whether there was a *Brady* violation. The purpose of *Brady*, the Court has said, is to ensure a fair trial, and neither good faith errors nor intentional suppression of information should affect whether the information is material.

Compare this part of the *Brady* doctrine to the Court's treatment of the prosecutor's motives in the related context of the government's constitutional obligation to preserve evidence that might assist the defense. In Arizona v. Youngblood, 488 U.S. 51 (1988), police failed to properly preserve semen samples from the body and clothing of a ten-year-old victim of molestation and kidnapping. At trial, the defendant claimed that the child had erred in identifying him as the perpetrator and argued that if the evidence had been properly preserved, blood group tests performed on this evidence could have exonerated him. He was nevertheless convicted. The Court concluded that the state's failure to properly preserve this evidence for testing did not require reversal of the conviction in the absence of any showing that the police acted in bad faith:

> We think that requiring a defendant to show bad faith on the part of the police both limits the extent of the police's obligation to preserve evidence to reasonable bounds and confines it to that class of cases where the interests of justice most clearly require it, i.e., those cases in which the police themselves by their conduct indicate that the evidence could form a basis for exonerating the defendant. We therefore hold that unless a criminal defendant can show bad faith on the part of the police, failure to preserve potentially useful evidence does not constitute a denial of due process of law.

Id., at 58.

Is *Youngblood* consistent with *Brady*? Can you articulate why withheld information should be treated differently than a failure to preserve evidence? Note that after Youngblood served ten years in prison and was released, more sophisticated DNA tests were performed on the damaged evidence that was still in the possession of police, and Youngblood was exonerated. See Laurie P. Cohen, DNA Tests Free Man Imprisoned 10 Years, Wall Street Journal, Aug. 10, 2000, at B12.

7. *Brady* and its progeny clearly establish that due process requires prosecutors to turn over certain evidence in the interests of fair *trial*. That raises an obvious question: should *Brady* material also be produced during plea negotiations in the interests of a fair *conviction*? Consider the next case:

UNITED STATES v. RUIZ

Certiorari to the United States Court of Appeals for the Ninth Circuit
536 U.S. 622 (2002)

JUSTICE BREYER delivered the opinion of the Court.

In this case we primarily consider whether the Fifth and Sixth Amendments require federal prosecutors, before entering into a binding plea agreement with a criminal defendant, to disclose "impeachment information relating to any informants or other witnesses." App. to Pet. for Cert. 46a. We hold that the Constitution does not require that disclosure.

After immigration agents found 30 kilograms of marijuana in Angela Ruiz's luggage, federal prosecutors offered her what is known in the Southern District of California as a "fast track" plea bargain. That bargain—standard in that district—asks a defendant to waive indictment, trial, and an appeal. In return, the Government agrees to recommend to the sentencing judge a two-level departure downward from the otherwise applicable United States Sentencing Guidelines sentence. In Ruiz's case, a two-level departure downward would have shortened the ordinary Guidelines-specified 18-to-24-month sentencing range by 6 months, to 12-to-18-months. 241 F.3d 1157, 1161 (2001).

The prosecutors' proposed plea agreement contains a set of detailed terms. Among other things, it specifies that "any [known] information establishing the factual innocence of the defendant" "has been turned over to the defendant," and it acknowledges the Government's "continuing duty to provide such information." App. to Pet. for Cert. 45a-46a. At the same time it requires that the defendant "waive the right" to receive "impeachment information relating to any informants or other witnesses" as well as the right to receive information supporting any affirmative defense the defendant raises if the case goes to trial. Id., at 46a. Because Ruiz would not agree to this last-mentioned waiver, the prosecutors withdrew their bargaining offer. The Government then indicted Ruiz for unlawful drug possession. And despite the absence of any agreement, Ruiz ultimately pleaded guilty.

At sentencing, Ruiz asked the judge to grant her the same two-level downward departure that the Government would have recommended had she accepted the "fast track" agreement. The Government opposed her request, and the District Court denied it, imposing a standard Guideline sentence instead.

. . . Ruiz appealed her sentence to the United States Court of Appeals for the Ninth Circuit. The Ninth Circuit vacated the District Court's sentencing determination. The Ninth Circuit pointed out that the Constitution requires prosecutors to make certain impeachment information available to a defendant before trial. It decided that this obligation entitles defendants to receive that same information before they enter into a plea agreement. [241 F.3d, at 1164.] The Ninth Circuit also decided that the Constitution prohibits defendants from waiving their right to that information. Id., at 1165-1166. And it held that the prosecutors' standard "fast track" plea agreement was unlawful because it insisted upon that waiver. Id., at 1167. . . .

The constitutional question concerns a federal criminal defendant's waiver of the right to receive from prosecutors exculpatory impeachment material—a right that the Constitution provides as part of its basic "fair trial" guarantee. See U.S. Const., Amdts. 5, 6. See also Brady v. Maryland, 373 U.S. 83, 87 (1963) (due process requires prosecutors to "avoid . . . an unfair trial" by making available "upon request" evidence "favorable to an accused . . . where the evidence is material either to guilt or to punishment"); United States v. Agurs, 427 U.S. 97, 112-113 (1976) (defense request unnecessary); Kyles v. Whitley, 514 U.S. 419, 435 (1995) (exculpatory evidence is evidence the suppression of which would "undermine confidence in the verdict"); Giglio v. United States, 405 U.S. 150, 154 (1972) (exculpatory evidence includes "evidence affecting" witness "credibility," where the witness' "reliability" is likely "determinative of guilt or innocence").

When a defendant pleads guilty, he or she, of course, forgoes not only a fair trial, but also other accompanying constitutional guarantees. Given the seriousness of the matter, the Constitution insists, among other things, that the defendant enter a guilty plea that is "voluntary" and that the defendant must make related waivers "knowingly, intelligently, [and] with sufficient awareness of the relevant circumstances and likely consequences." Brady v. United States, 397 U.S. 742, 748 (1970).

In this case, the Ninth Circuit in effect held that a guilty plea is not "voluntary" (and that the defendant could not, by pleading guilty, waive his right to a fair trial) unless the prosecutors first made the same disclosure of material impeachment information that the prosecutors would have had to make had the defendant insisted upon a trial. We must decide whether the Constitution requires that pre-guilty plea disclosure of impeachment information. We conclude that it does not.

First, impeachment information is special in relation to the fairness of a trial, not in respect to whether a plea is voluntary ("knowing," "intelligent," and "sufficiently aware" . . .). Of course, the more information the defendant has, the more aware he is of the likely consequences of a plea, waiver, or decision, and the wiser that decision will likely be. But the Constitution does not require the prosecutor to share all useful information with the defendant. And the law ordinarily considers a waiver knowing, intelligent, and sufficiently aware if the defendant fully understands the nature of the right and how it would likely apply in general in the circumstances—even though the defendant may not know the specific detailed consequences of invoking it. A defendant, for example, may waive his right to remain silent, his right to a jury trial, or his right to counsel even if the defendant does not know the specific questions the authorities intend to ask, who will likely serve on the jury, or the particular lawyer the State might otherwise provide.

It is particularly difficult to characterize impeachment information as critical information of which the defendant must always be aware prior to pleading guilty given the random way in which such information may, or may not, help a particular defendant. The degree of help that impeachment information can provide will depend upon the defendant's own independent knowledge of the prosecution's potential case—a matter that the Constitution does not require prosecutors to disclose.

Second, we have found no legal authority embodied either in this Court's past cases or in cases from other circuits that provide significant support for the Ninth Circuit's decision. To the contrary, this Court has found that the Constitution, in respect to a defendant's awareness of relevant circumstances, does not require complete knowledge of the relevant circumstances, but permits a court to accept a guilty plea, with its accompanying waiver of various constitutional rights, despite various forms of misapprehension under which a defendant might labor. See Brady v. United States, 397 U.S., at 757 (defendant "misapprehended the quality of the State's case"); ibid. (defendant misapprehended "the likely penalties"); ibid.

(defendant failed to "anticipate a change in the law regarding" relevant "punishments"); McMann v. Richardson, 397 U.S. 759, 770 (1970) (counsel "misjudged the admissibility" of a "confession"); United States v. Broce, 488 U.S. 563, 573 (1989) (counsel failed to point out a potential defense); Tollett v. Henderson, 411 U.S. 258, 267 (1973) (counsel failed to find a potential constitutional infirmity in grand jury proceedings). It is difficult to distinguish, in terms of importance, a defendant's ignorance of grounds for impeachment of potential witnesses at a possible future trial from the varying forms of ignorance at issue in these cases.

Third, due process considerations, the very considerations that led this Court to find trial-related rights to exculpatory and impeachment information in *Brady* and *Giglio*, argue against the existence of the "right" that the Ninth Circuit found here. This Court has said that due process considerations include not only (1) the nature of the private interest at stake, but also (2) the value of the additional safeguard, and (3) the adverse impact of the requirement upon the Government's interests. Ake v. Oklahoma, 470 U.S. 68, 77 (1985). Here, as we have just pointed out, the added value of the Ninth Circuit's "right" to a defendant is often limited, for it depends upon the defendant's independent awareness of the details of the Government's case. And in any case, as the proposed plea agreement at issue here specifies, the Government will provide "any information establishing the factual innocence of the defendant" regardless. That fact, along with other guilty-plea safeguards, see Fed. Rule Crim. Proc. 11, diminishes the force of Ruiz's concern that, in the absence of impeachment information, innocent individuals, accused of crimes, will plead guilty.

At the same time, a constitutional obligation to provide impeachment information during plea bargaining, prior to entry of a guilty plea, could seriously interfere with the Government's interest in securing those guilty pleas that are factually justified, desired by defendants, and help to secure the efficient administration of justice. The Ninth Circuit's rule risks premature disclosure of Government witness information, which, the Government tells us, could "disrupt ongoing investigations" and expose prospective witnesses to serious harm. Brief for United States 25. And the careful tailoring that characterizes most legal Government witness disclosure requirements suggests recognition by both Congress and the Federal Rules Committees that such concerns are valid. See, e.g., 18 U.S.C. §3432 (witness list disclosure required in capital cases three days before trial with exceptions); §3500 (Government witness statements ordinarily subject to discovery only after testimony given); Fed. Rule Crim. Proc. 16(a)(2) (embodies limitations of 18 U.S.C. §3500).

Consequently, the Ninth Circuit's requirement could force the Government to abandon its "general practice" of not "disclosing to a defendant pleading guilty information that would reveal the identities of cooperating informants, undercover investigators, or other prospective witnesses." Brief for United States 25. It could require the Government to devote substantially more resources to trial preparation prior to plea bargaining, thereby depriving the plea-bargaining process of its main resource-saving advantages. Or it could lead the Government instead to abandon its heavy reliance upon plea bargaining in a vast number—90% or more—of federal criminal cases. We cannot say that the Constitution's due process requirement demands so radical a change in the criminal justice process in order to achieve so comparatively small a constitutional benefit.

These considerations, taken together, lead us to conclude that the Constitution does not require the Government to disclose material impeachment evidence prior to entering a plea agreement with a criminal defendant.

In addition, we note that the "fast track" plea agreement requires a defendant to waive her right to receive information the Government has regarding any "affirmative defense" she raises at trial. We do not believe the Constitution here requires provision of this information to the defendant prior to plea bargaining—for most (though not all) of the reasons previously stated. That is to say, in the context of this agreement, the need for this information is more closely related to the fairness of a trial than to the voluntariness of the plea; the value in terms of the defendant's added awareness of relevant circumstances is ordinarily limited; yet the added burden imposed upon the Government by requiring its provision well in advance of trial (often before trial preparation begins) can be serious, thereby significantly interfering with the administration of the plea bargaining process.

For these reasons the decision of the Court of Appeals for the Ninth Circuit is reversed.

JUSTICE THOMAS, concurring in the judgment.

I agree with the Court that the Constitution does not require the Government to disclose either affirmative defense information or impeachment information relating to informants or other witnesses before entering into a binding plea agreement with a criminal defendant. The Court, however, suggests that the constitutional analysis turns in some part on the "degree of help" such information would provide to the defendant at the plea stage, a distinction that is neither necessary nor accurate. To the extent that the Court is implicitly drawing a line based on a flawed characterization about the usefulness of certain types of information, I can only concur in the judgment. The principle supporting *Brady* was "avoidance of an unfair trial to the accused." *Brady v. Maryland*, 373 U.S. 83, 87 (1963). That concern is not implicated at the plea stage. . . .

NOTES AND QUESTIONS

1. The holding in *Ruiz* is limited to the failure to disclose impeachment evidence or evidence going to affirmative defenses before entering into a plea agreement. Recall that in *Kyles*, however, the Court drew no distinction between information that might impeach government witnesses and other sorts of exculpatory evidence. Indeed, the Court had explicitly rejected this distinction in Giglio v. United States, 405 U.S. 150, 154 (1972), a case cited with approval in *Ruiz*. Does *Ruiz* nonetheless recognize such a distinction? If so, does this suggest that in the *trial* context, failures to disclose impeachment evidence might be viewed by courts as less serious than other types of *Brady* violations? Or are you persuaded by the Court's explanation for why impeachment information is different in the context of a guilty plea?

2. What is the precise holding of *Ruiz*? Does the decision mean that there are now *three* classes of *Brady* information? The first, as described in the *Ruiz* opinion, includes information that the prosecutor "knows" establishes the defendant's "factual innocence." Although the government generously committed to provide such information even before a guilty plea, presumably there will *never* be material that fits this description—if the government knows the accused is factually innocent, the proper course is to dismiss the charges, not strike a plea deal.

The second category is impeachment material and information affecting affirmative defenses; here *Ruiz* is clear that the prosecutor has no duty to disclose prior to a guilty plea. But is there now a third category: information that neither establishes factual innocence nor goes to impeachment, but is still favorable and material to the defense? Information that points to an alternative suspect, or inconsistent lab results or fingerprint tests might qualify as this type of information, but *Ruiz* says nothing about a prosecutor's obligation with respect to this material. And while many lower courts have been unpersuaded by this distinction, and have read *Ruiz* to mean that *Brady* simply doesn't apply to the guilty plea stage, see, e.g., United States v. Conroy, 567 F.3d 174, 179 (5th Cir. 2009), a couple of lower courts have found that prosecutors still must disclose this type of *Brady* material prior to a guilty plea, see United States v. Danzi, 726 F. Supp. 2d 120 (D. Conn. 2010) (*Ruiz* did not alter Second Circuit precedent that required pre-plea disclosure of exculpatory *Brady* information), opinion clarified 2010 WL 3463272, or have at least have acknowledged the possibility. United States v. Moussaoui, 591 F.3d 263, 287-288 (4th Cir. 2010) (discussing the issue in *dicta* but not resolving the question). What do you think is the proper reading of *Ruiz* on this point?

3. One way to read *Ruiz* is that *Brady* rights, like other constitutional rights, are waivable. Should they be? Most rights that defendants waive when pleading guilty fall into one of two categories. The first consists of rights to some future benefit—say, a jury trial—about which the defendant is informed at the plea colloquy. The second category consists of rights to litigate some claim of past government misconduct—say, an improper police search—about which the defendant already knows. *Brady* claims are arguably different, because the defendant does not know about material exculpatory evidence in the government's possession unless and until such evidence is disclosed to him. Given this, is it appropriate to allow a defendant to waive a right when, by definition, he could not have known of the violation?

4. Perhaps the main goal of the *Brady* doctrine is to reduce the risk that an innocent person will be wrongfully convicted, by ensuring that the defense is aware of information that would help him prevail at trial. Is the same concern present for guilty pleas, where the defendant typically admits his criminal behavior? (Although see the discussion of innocent people pleading guilty in Chapter 13, at pages 1245-1247.) Does the holding of *Ruiz* seem less worrisome in this regard, given that the available information suggests that prosecutorial misconduct is a relatively infrequent cause of wrongful convictions, while faulty eyewitness identification and bad forensics are more common? See Brandon L. Garrett, Judging Innocence, 108 Colum. L. Rev. 55, 78 (2008). But cf. The Innocence Project, Causes of Wrongful Conviction, http://www.innocenceproject.org/causes-wrongful-conviction ("Evidence of fraud, negligence or misconduct by prosecutors or police is disturbingly not uncommon among the DNA exoneration cases," although bad identifications, forensics, confessions, and unreliable informants are the dominant causes).

Suppose *Ruiz* had held that prior to a guilty plea, *Brady* requires disclosure of any favorable, material evidence in the government's possession, and that the requirement cannot be waived. What effect would that ruling have on government evidence-gathering? One possibility is that the *Brady* right would make pre-plea investigation more expensive for the government; police or prosecutors might find evidence that would be helpful to the defense, in which case the evidence would have to be disclosed, possibly destroying any chance at reaching a plea bargain. At the margin, the government might decide to do less evidence-gathering prior to plea bargaining in order to reduce that risk. That does not sound like good news for innocent defendants, although it may help a guilty one if further investigation would have uncovered more criminal conduct. How should the law solve this problem?

B.   *Disclosure by the Defense*

1.   Defense Disclosure and the Constitution

WILLIAMS v. FLORIDA

Certiorari to the District Court of Appeal of Florida, Third District
399 U.S. 78 (1970)

MR. JUSTICE WHITE delivered the opinion of the Court.

Prior to his trial for robbery in the State of Florida, petitioner filed a "Motion for a Protective Order," seeking to be excused from the requirements of Rule 1.200 of the Florida Rules of Criminal Procedure. That rule requires a defendant, on written demand of the prosecuting attorney, to give notice in advance of trial if the defendant intends to claim an alibi, and to furnish the prosecuting attorney with information as to the place where he claims to have been and with the names and addresses of the alibi witnesses he intends to use. In his motion petitioner openly declared his intent to claim an alibi, but objected to the further disclosure requirements on the ground that the rule "compels the Defendant in a criminal case to be a witness against himself" in violation of his Fifth and Fourteenth Amendment rights. The motion was denied. . . . Petitioner was convicted as charged. . . . The District Court of Appeal affirmed. . . . We granted certiorari.

Florida's notice-of-alibi rule is in essence a requirement that a defendant submit to a limited form of pretrial discovery by the State whenever he intends to rely at trial on the defense of alibi. In exchange for the defendant's disclosure of the witnesses he proposes to use to establish that defense, the State in turn is required to notify the defendant of any witnesses it proposes to offer in rebuttal to that defense. Both sides are under a continuing duty promptly to disclose the names and addresses of additional witnesses bearing on the alibi as they become available. The threatened sanction for failure to comply is the exclusion at trial of the defendant's alibi evidence—except for his own testimony—or, in the case of the State, the exclusion of the State's evidence offered in rebuttal of the alibi.

In this case, following the denial of his Motion for a Protective Order, petitioner complied with the alibi rule and gave the State the name and address of one Mary Scotty. Mrs. Scotty was summoned to the office of the State Attorney on the morning of the trial, where she gave pretrial testimony. At the trial itself, Mrs. Scotty, petitioner, and petitioner's wife all testified that the three of them had been in Mrs. Scotty's apartment during the time of the robbery. On two occasions during cross-examination of Mrs. Scotty, the prosecuting attorney confronted her with her earlier deposition in which she had given dates and times that in some respects did not correspond with the dates and times given at trial. Mrs. Scotty adhered to her trial story, insisting that she had been mistaken in her earlier testimony. The State also offered in rebuttal the testimony of one of the officers investigating the robbery who claimed that Mrs. Scotty had asked him for directions on the afternoon in question during the time when she claimed to have been in her apartment with petitioner and his wife.

We need not linger over the suggestion that the discovery permitted the State against petitioner in this case deprived him of "due process" or a "fair trial." Florida law provides for liberal discovery by the defendant against the State, and the notice-of-alibi rule is itself carefully hedged with reciprocal duties requiring state disclosure to the defendant. Given the ease with which an alibi can be fabricated, the State's interest in protecting itself against an eleventh-hour defense is both obvious and legitimate. Reflecting this interest, notice-of-alibi provisions, dating at least from 1927, are now in existence in a substantial number of States. The adversary system of trial is hardly an end in itself; it is not yet a poker game in which players enjoy an absolute right always to conceal their cards until played. We find ample room in that system, at least as far as "due process" is concerned, for the instant Florida rule. . . .

Petitioner's major contention is that he was "compelled . . . to be a witness against himself" contrary to the commands of the Fifth and Fourteenth Amendments because the notice-of-alibi rule required him to give the State the name and address of Mrs. Scotty in advance of trial and thus to furnish the State with information useful in convicting him. No pretrial statement of petitioner was introduced at trial; but armed with Mrs. Scotty's name and address and the knowledge that she was to be petitioner's alibi witness, the State was able to take her deposition in advance of trial and to find rebuttal testimony. Also, requiring him to reveal the elements of his defense is claimed to have interfered with his right to wait until after the State had presented its case to decide how to defend against it. We conclude, however, as has apparently every other court that has considered the issue, that the privilege against self-incrimination is not violated by a requirement that the defendant give notice of an alibi defense and disclose his alibi witnesses.

The defendant in a criminal trial is frequently forced to testify himself and to call other witnesses in an effort to reduce the risk of conviction. When he presents his witnesses, he must reveal their identity and submit them to cross-examination which in itself may prove incriminating or which may furnish the State with leads to incriminating rebuttal evidence. That the defendant faces such a dilemma demanding a choice between complete silence and presenting a defense has never been thought an invasion of the privilege against compelled self-incrimination. The pressures generated by the State's evidence may be severe but they do not vitiate the defendant's choice to present an alibi defense and witnesses to prove it, even though the attempted defense ends in catastrophe for the defendant. However "testimonial" or "incriminating" the alibi defense proves to be, it cannot be considered "compelled" within the meaning of the Fifth and Fourteenth Amendments.

Very similar constraints operate on the defendant when the State requires pretrial notice of alibi and the naming of alibi witnesses. Nothing in such a rule requires the defendant to rely on an alibi or prevents him from abandoning the defense; these matters are left to his unfettered choice.[15] That choice must be

---

15. . . . The mere requirement that petitioner disclose in advance his intent to rely on an alibi in no way "fixed" his defense as of that point in time. The suggestion that the State, by referring to petitioner's proposed alibi in opening or closing statements might have "compelled" him to follow through with the defense in order to avoid an unfavorable inference is a hypothetical totally without support in this record. The first reference to the alibi came from petitioner's own attorney in his opening remarks; the State's response did not come until after the defense had finished direct examination of Mrs. Scotty. . . . On these facts, then, we simply are not confronted with the question of whether a defendant can be compelled in advance of trial to select a defense from which he can no longer deviate. We do not mean to suggest, though, that such a procedure must necessarily raise serious constitutional problems.

made, but the pressures that bear on his pretrial decision are of the same nature as those that would induce him to call alibi witnesses at the trial: the force of historical fact beyond both his and the State's control and the strength of the State's case built on these facts. Response to that kind of pressure by offering evidence or testimony is not compelled self-incrimination transgressing the Fifth and Fourteenth Amendments.

In the case before us, the notice-of-alibi rule by itself in no way affected petitioner's crucial decision to call alibi witnesses or added to the legitimate pressures leading to that course of action. At most, the rule only compelled petitioner to accelerate the timing of his disclosure, forcing him to divulge at an earlier date information that the petitioner from the beginning planned to divulge at trial. Nothing in the Fifth Amendment privilege entitles a defendant as a matter of constitutional right to await the end of the State's case before announcing the nature of his defense, any more than it entitles him to await the jury's verdict on the State's case-in-chief before deciding whether or not to take the stand himself.

Petitioner concedes that absent the notice-of-alibi rule the Constitution would raise no bar to the court's granting the State a continuance at trial on the ground of surprise as soon as the alibi witness is called. Nor would there be self-incrimination problems if, during that continuance, the State was permitted to do precisely what it did here prior to trial: take the deposition of the witness and find rebuttal evidence. But if so utilizing a continuance is permissible under the Fifth and Fourteenth Amendments, then surely the same result may be accomplished through pretrial discovery, as it was here, avoiding the necessity of a disrupted trial. We decline to hold that the privilege against compulsory self-incrimination guarantees the defendant the right to surprise the State with an alibi defense. . . .

Affirmed.

MR. JUSTICE BLACKMUN took no part in the consideration or decision of this case.

MR. CHIEF JUSTICE BURGER, concurring.

I join fully in Mr. Justice White's opinion for the Court. I see an added benefit to the notice-of-alibi rule in that it will serve important functions by way of disposing of cases without trial in appropriate circumstances—a matter of considerable importance when courts, prosecution offices, and legal aid and defender agencies are vastly overworked. The prosecutor upon receiving notice will, of course, investigate prospective alibi witnesses. If he finds them reliable and unimpeachable he will doubtless re-examine his entire case and this process would very likely lead to dismissal of the charges. . . .

On the other hand, inquiry into a claimed alibi defense may reveal it to be contrived and fabricated and the witnesses accordingly subject to impeachment or other attack. In this situation defense counsel would be obliged to re-examine his case and, if he found his client has proposed the use of false testimony, either seek to withdraw from the case or try to persuade his client to enter a plea of guilty, possibly by plea discussions which could lead to disposition on a lesser charge.

In either case the ends of justice will have been served and the processes expedited. These are the likely consequences of an enlarged and truly reciprocal pretrial disclosure of evidence and the move away from the "sporting contest" idea of criminal justice.

MR. JUSTICE BLACK, with whom MR. JUSTICE DOUGLAS joins . . . dissenting. . . .

The core of the majority's decision is an assumption that compelling a defendant to give notice of an alibi defense before a trial is no different from requiring a defendant, after the State has produced the evidence against him at trial, to plead alibi before the jury retires to consider the case. . . . That statement is plainly and simply wrong as a matter of fact and law, and the Court's holding based on that statement is a complete misunderstanding of the protections provided for criminal defendants by the Fifth Amendment and other provisions of the Bill of Rights.

When a defendant is required to indicate whether he might plead alibi in advance of trial, he faces a vastly different decision from that faced by one who can wait until the State has presented the case against him before making up his mind. Before trial the defendant knows only what the State's case might be. . . . At that time there is no certainty as to what kind of case the State will ultimately be able to prove at trial. Therefore any appraisal of the desirability of pleading alibi will be beset with guesswork and gambling far greater than that accompanying the decision at the trial itself. . . .

The Florida system, as interpreted by the majority, plays upon this inherent uncertainty in predicting the possible strength of the State's case in order effectively to coerce defendants into disclosing an alibi defense that may never be actually used. . . .

The Court apparently also assumes that a defendant who has given the required notice can abandon his alibi without hurting himself. Such an assumption is implicit in and necessary for the majority's argument that the pretrial decision is no different from that at the trial itself. I, however, cannot so lightly assume that pretrial notice will have no adverse effects on a defendant who later decides to forgo such a defense. Necessarily the defendant will have given the prosecutor the names of persons who may have some knowledge about the defendant himself or his activities. Necessarily the prosecutor will have every incentive to question these persons fully, and in doing so he may discover new leads or evidence. Undoubtedly there will be situations in which the State will seek to use such information—information it would probably never have obtained but for the defendant's coerced cooperation.

It is unnecessary for me, however, to engage in any such intellectual gymnastics concerning the practical effects of the notice-of-alibi procedure, because the Fifth Amendment itself clearly provides that "[n]o person . . . shall be compelled in any criminal case to be a witness against himself." If words are to be given their plain and obvious meaning, that provision, in my opinion, states that a criminal defendant cannot be required to give evidence, testimony, or any other assistance to the State to aid it in convicting him of crime. The Florida notice-of-alibi rule in my opinion is a patent violation of that constitutional provision because it requires a defendant to disclose information to the State so that the State can use that information to destroy him. It seems to me at least slightly incredible to suggest that this procedure may have some beneficial effects for defendants. . . . If a defendant thinks that making disclosure of an alibi before trial is in his best interests, he will obviously do so. And the only time the State needs the compulsion provided by this procedure is when the defendant has decided that such disclosure is likely to hurt his case.

It is no answer to this argument to suggest that the Fifth Amendment as so interpreted would give the defendant an unfair element of surprise, turning a trial into a "poker game" or "sporting contest," for that tactical advantage to the defendant is inherent in the type of trial required by our Bill of Rights. The Framers were well aware of the awesome investigative and prosecutorial powers of government and it was in order to limit those powers that they spelled out in detail in the Constitution the procedure to be followed in criminal trials. . . .

[The] constitutional right to remain absolutely silent cannot be avoided by superficially attractive analogies to any so-called "compulsion" inherent in the trial itself that may lead a defendant to put on evidence in his own defense. Obviously the Constitution contemplates that a defendant can be "compelled" to stand trial, and obviously there will be times when the trial process itself will require the defendant to do something in order to try to avoid a conviction. But nothing in the Constitution permits the State to add to the natural consequences of a trial and compel the defendant in advance of trial to participate in any way in the State's attempt to condemn him. . . .

On the surface this case involves only a notice-of-alibi provision, but in effect the decision opens the way for a profound change in one of the most important traditional safeguards of a criminal defendant. The rationale of today's decision is in no way limited to alibi defenses, or any other type or classification of evidence. The theory advanced goes at least so far as to permit the State to obtain under threat of sanction complete disclosure by the defendant in advance of trial of all evidence, testimony, and tactics he plans to use at that trial. In each case the justification will be that the rule affects only the "timing" of the disclosure, and not the substantive decision itself. . . .

NOTES AND QUESTIONS

1. Justice Black's prediction that the implications of *Williams* would reach far beyond notice-of-alibi rules (based on a broad reading of the majority opinion) proved prophetic. While it remains the case that prosecution disclosure is uniformly broader than defense disclosure, a "revolutionary expansion" in criminal disclosure to the prosecution occurred in the wake of *Williams*. Robert P. Mosteller, Discovery Against the Defense: Tilting the Adversarial Balance, 74 Cal. L. Rev. 1567, 1567-1570 (1986).

Consider Rule 16(b) of the Federal Rules of Criminal Procedure, the basic federal rule governing disclosure by the defense. It requires a defendant to disclose: (1) books, papers, documents, data, photographs, and tangible objects that are within his possession, custody, or control and that he intends to use in his case-in-chief at trial; (2) any results or reports of any physical or mental examinations, as well as any scientific tests or experiments, that are within his possession, custody, or control and that he intends to use in his case-in-chief or, with regard to reports, that were prepared by a witness he intends to call and that relate to the witness's testimony; and (3) a written summary of any expert testimony that he intends to use describing the opinions, bases, reasons for the opinions, and qualifications of the expert. (Note that the bulk of this disclosure is broadly conditioned on prior defense requests for the same type of discovery from the prosecution, and on the prosecution's compliance with these requests. In many states, however, the prosecution's entitlement to discovery into the defendant's case is automatic, and not conditioned on a prior defense request.)

In addition to Rule 16, the Federal Rules contain separate provisions providing for pretrial notice of alibi, insanity, and public authority defenses. See Rules

12.1, 12.2, and 12.3. Rule 26.2 also requires the defendant to provide certain witness statements to the government after a defense witness (excepting the defendant himself) has testified on direct examination at trial. See Rule 26.2.[4]

2. Defense disclosure in many states is broader than in the federal system, at times substantially so — some, for example, authorize the prosecution to obtain a specification of all defenses to be raised, the names and addresses of all defense witnesses to be called at trial, and all statements of defense witnesses, including memoranda of unsigned oral statements. Mosteller, supra, at 1570. Are such provisions consistent with the Fifth Amendment as merely examples of "accelerated disclosure"? Could the rules require the defense to tell the prosecutor prior to trial the order in which he intends to present his witnesses, or is this somehow different?

Setting aside items falling within the attorney-client or work product privilege, what about material the defense does *not* intend to introduce at trial? Are there any constitutional barriers to requiring the defendant to disclose scientific reports not intended to be used? What about documents or other physical evidence in the hands of the defense that are material to issues in the case? Or the identities of potential witnesses that the defendant does not intend to call? In other words, does the Fifth Amendment impose *any* constraints?

3. In Wardius v. Oregon, 412 U.S. 470, 474 (1973), the Court expanded on the summary due process analysis in *Williams*. The *Wardius* Court acknowledged that due process has little to say about the absolute amount of discovery provided in criminal cases. At the same time, however, the Court unanimously concluded that the Due Process Clause *does* "speak to the balance of forces between the accused and his accuser." The case invalidated a notice-of-alibi provision that did not provide for reciprocal discovery of the prosecution. Noting that the state "may not insist that trials be run as a 'search for truth' so far as defense witnesses are concerned, while maintaining 'poker game' secrecy for its own witnesses," the Court concluded that "[i]t is fundamentally unfair to require a defendant to divulge the details of his own case while at the same time subjecting him to the hazard of surprise concerning refutation of the very pieces of evidence which he disclosed to the State."

To comply with *Wardius*, rules providing for discovery into the defendant's case now commonly provide for reciprocal discovery from the prosecution. From the perspective of the criminal defendant, would it be fair to conclude that disclosure by the defense may be advantageous because it leads to broader government disclosure? Or are there reasons that a defense attorney might opt for *less* discovery from the government if she were also assured that the government could not seek disclosure of the defense case?

---

4. Rule 16(b) does not authorize pretrial discovery into statements made by the defendant or by prospective government or defense witnesses to the defendant, his agents, or his attorneys. The Rule also provides that "[e]xcept for scientific or medical reports, Rule 16(b)(1) does not authorize discovery or inspection of . . . reports, memoranda, or other documents made by the defendant, or the defendant's attorney or agent, during the case's investigation or defense." Rule 16(b)(2).

2. Sanctions for Nondisclosure

Sometimes the parties fail to provide the discovery required by Rule 16, either inadvertently or otherwise. In such a case, what remedies does a court have to correct the violation? Rule 16(d)(2) of the Federal Rules speaks to that question. It says that when a party has failed to comply with a discovery obligation, "the court may: (A) order that party to permit the discovery or inspection; specify its time, place, and manner; and prescribe other just terms and conditions; (B) grant a continuance; (C) prohibit that party from introducing the undisclosed evidence; or (D) enter any other order that is just under the circumstances."

There are two points to note about this provision. First, courts have a lot of latitude in deciding on a remedy—the authority to enter "any other order that is just" indicates as much. And so, for example, rather than prohibiting the offending party from introducing the undisclosed evidence under (d)(2)(C), the court may allow the evidence and give a jury instruction about the offending party's violation. Or, the court might declare a mistrial, so that in the new trial both sides would be working with the information that they were entitled to. See Robert M. Cary et al., Federal Criminal Discovery, 394-404 (ABA 2011).

Second, notice that Rule 16(d) by its terms speaks equally about sanctions for the prosecutor and the defense. While it may be sensible to give the judge equal authority over each party, should sanctions be imposed on a comparable basis? Should a prosecutor be sanctioned in a way that harms the government's (and thus, society's) interest in convicting the guilty? Should the defense be sanctioned in a way that harms defendant's ability to defend himself?

TAYLOR v. ILLINOIS

Certiorari to the Appellate Court of Illinois, First District
484 U.S. 400 (1988)

JUSTICE STEVENS delivered the opinion of the Court.

As a sanction for failing to identify a defense witness in response to a pretrial discovery request, an Illinois trial judge refused to allow the undisclosed witness to testify. The question presented is whether that refusal violated the petitioner's constitutional right to obtain the testimony of favorable witnesses. We hold that such a sanction is not absolutely prohibited by the Compulsory Process Clause of the Sixth Amendment and find no constitutional error on the specific facts of this case.

A jury convicted petitioner in 1984 of attempting to murder Jack Bridges in a street fight on the south side of Chicago on August 6, 1981. The conviction was supported by the testimony of Bridges, his brother, and three other witnesses. They described a 20-minute argument between Bridges and a young man named Derrick Travis, and a violent encounter that occurred over an hour later between several friends of Travis, including petitioner, on the one hand, and Bridges, belatedly aided by his brother, on the other. The incident was witnessed by 20 or 30 bystanders. It is undisputed that at least three members of the group which included Travis and petitioner were carrying pipes and clubs that they used to beat Bridges. Prosecution witnesses also testified that petitioner had a gun, that he shot Bridges in the back as he attempted to flee, and that, after Bridges fell, petitioner pointed the gun at Bridges' head but the weapon misfired.

Two sisters, who are friends of petitioner, testified on his behalf. In many respects their version of the incident was consistent with the prosecution's case, but they testified that it was Bridges' brother, rather than petitioner, who possessed a firearm and that he had fired into the group hitting his brother by mistake. No other witnesses testified for the defense.

Well in advance of trial, the prosecutor filed a discovery motion requesting a list of defense witnesses.[2] In his original response, petitioner's attorney identified the two sisters who later testified and two men who did not testify. On the first day of trial, defense counsel was allowed to amend his answer by adding the names of Derrick Travis and a Chicago police officer; neither of them actually testified.

On the second day of trial, after the prosecution's two principal witnesses had completed their testimony, defense counsel made an oral motion to amend his "Answer to Discovery" to include two more witnesses, Alfred Wormley and Pam Berkhalter. In support of the motion, counsel represented that he had just been informed about them and that they had probably seen the "entire incident."

In response to the court's inquiry about defendant's failure to tell him about the two witnesses earlier, counsel acknowledged that defendant had done so, but then represented that he had been unable to locate Wormley. After noting that the witnesses' names could have been supplied even if their addresses were unknown, the trial judge directed counsel to bring them in the next day, at which time he would decide whether they could testify. The judge indicated that he was concerned about the possibility "that witnesses are being found that really weren't there."

The next morning Wormley appeared in court with defense counsel.[7] After further colloquy about the consequences of a violation of discovery rules, counsel was permitted to make an offer of proof in the form of Wormley's testimony outside the presence of the jury. It developed that Wormley had not been a witness to the incident itself. He testified that prior to the incident he saw Jack Bridges and his brother with two guns in a blanket, that he heard them say "they were after Ray [petitioner] and the other people," and that on his way home he "happened to run into Ray and them" and warned them "to watch out because they got weapons." On cross-examination, Wormley acknowledged that he had first met defendant "about four months ago" (i.e., over two years after the incident). He also acknowledged that defense counsel had visited him at his home on the Wednesday of the week before the trial began. Thus, his testimony rather dramatically contradicted defense counsel's representations to the trial court.

After hearing Wormley testify, the trial judge concluded that the appropriate sanction for the discovery violation was to exclude his testimony. The judge explained:

---

2. Illinois Supreme Court Rule 413(d) provides in pertinent part:

Subject to constitutional limitations and within a reasonable time after the filing of a written motion by the State, defense counsel shall inform the State of any defenses which he intends to make at a hearing or trial and shall furnish the State with the following material and information within his possession or control:

> (i) *the names and last known addresses of persons he intends to call as witnesses* together with their relevant written or recorded statements, including memoranda reporting or summarizing their oral statements, any record of prior criminal convictions known to him . . . (emphasis added).

7. The record does not explain why Pam Berkhalter did not appear.

THE COURT: All right, I am going to deny Wormley an opportunity to testify here. He is not going to testify. I find this is a blatent [*sic*] violation of the discovery rules, willful violation of the rules. I also feel that defense attorneys have been violating discovery in this courtroom in the last three or four cases blatantly and I am going to put a stop to it and this is one way to do so.

Further, for whatever value it is, because this is a jury trial, I have a great deal of doubt in my mind as to the veracity of this young man that testified as to whether he was an eyewitness on the scene, sees guns that are wrapped up. He doesn't know Ray but he stops Ray.

At any rate, Mr. Wormley is not going to testify, be a witness in this courtroom.

The Illinois Appellate Court affirmed petitioner's conviction. . . . The Illinois Supreme Court denied leave to appeal and we granted the petition for certiorari.

In this Court petitioner makes two arguments. He first contends that the Sixth Amendment bars a court from ever ordering the preclusion of defense evidence as a sanction for violating a discovery rule. Alternatively, he contends that even if the right to present witnesses is not absolute, on the facts of this case the preclusion of Wormley's testimony was constitutional error. Before addressing these contentions, we consider the State's argument that the Compulsory Process Clause of the Sixth Amendment is merely a guarantee that the accused shall have the power to subpoena witnesses and simply does not apply to rulings on the admissibility of evidence.

In the State's view, no Compulsory Process Clause concerns are even raised by authorizing preclusion as a discovery sanction. . . . The State's argument is supported by the plain language of the Clause, by the historical evidence that it was intended to provide defendants with subpoena power that they lacked at common law, by some scholarly comment, and by a brief excerpt from the legislative history of the Clause. We have, however, consistently given the Clause the broader reading. . . .

As we noted just last Term, "[o]ur cases establish, at a minimum, that criminal defendants have the right to the government's assistance in compelling the attendance of favorable witnesses at trial and the right to put before a jury evidence that might influence the determination of guilt." Pennsylvania v. Ritchie, 480 U.S. 39, 56 (1987). Few rights are more fundamental than that of an accused to present witnesses in his own defense. . . . The right to compel a witness' presence in the courtroom could not protect the integrity of the adversary process if it did not embrace the right to have the witness' testimony heard by the trier of fact. The right to offer testimony is thus grounded in the Sixth Amendment even though it is not expressly described in so many words. . . .

Petitioner's claim that the Sixth Amendment creates an absolute bar to the preclusion of the testimony of a surprise witness is just as extreme and just as unacceptable as the State's position that the Amendment is simply irrelevant. The accused does not have an unfettered right to offer testimony that is incompetent, privileged, or otherwise inadmissible under standard rules of evidence. The Compulsory Process Clause provides him with an effective weapon, but it is a weapon that cannot be used irresponsibly. . . .

The principle that undergirds the defendant's right to present exculpatory evidence is also the source of essential limitations on the right. The adversary process could not function effectively without adherence to rules of procedure that govern the orderly presentation of facts and arguments to provide each party with a fair opportunity to assemble and submit evidence to contradict or explain the opponent's case. The trial process would be a shambles if either party had an absolute right to control the time and content of his witnesses' testimony. Neither may insist on the right to interrupt the opposing party's case, and obviously there is no absolute right to interrupt the deliberations of the jury to present newly discovered evidence. The State's interest in the orderly conduct of a criminal trial is sufficient to justify the imposition and enforcement of firm, though not always inflexible, rules relating to the identification and presentation of evidence.

The defendant's right to compulsory process is itself designed to vindicate the principle that the "ends of criminal justice would be defeated if judgments were to be founded on a partial or speculative presentation of the facts." Rules that provide for pretrial discovery of an opponent's witnesses serve the same high purpose. Discovery, like cross-examination, minimizes the risk that a judgment will be predicated on incomplete, misleading, or even deliberately fabricated testimony. The "State's interest in protecting itself against an eleventh-hour defense" is merely one component of the broader public interest in a full and truthful disclosure of critical facts.

To vindicate that interest we have held that even the defendant may not testify without being subjected to cross-examination. Moreover, in United States v. Nobles, 422 U.S. 225 (1975), we upheld an order excluding the testimony of an expert witness tendered by the defendant because he had refused to permit discovery of a "highly relevant" report. . . .

Petitioner does not question the legitimacy of a rule requiring pretrial disclosure of defense witnesses, but he argues that the sanction of preclusion of the testimony of a previously undisclosed witness is so drastic that it should never be imposed. He argues, correctly, that a less drastic sanction is always available. Prejudice to the prosecution could be minimized by granting a continuance or a mistrial to provide time for further investigation; moreover, further violations can be deterred by disciplinary sanctions against the defendant or defense counsel.

It may well be true that alternative sanctions are adequate and appropriate in most cases, but it is equally clear that they would be less effective than the preclusion sanction and that there are instances in which they would perpetuate rather than limit the prejudice to the State and the harm to the adversary process. One of the purposes of the discovery rule itself is to minimize the risk that fabricated testimony will be believed. Defendants who are willing to fabricate a defense may also be willing to fabricate excuses for failing to comply with a discovery requirement. The risk of a contempt violation may seem trivial to a defendant facing the threat of imprisonment for a term of years. A dishonest client can mislead an honest attorney, and there are occasions when an attorney assumes that the duty of loyalty to the client outweighs elementary obligations to the court.

. . . It is . . . reasonable to presume that there is something suspect about a defense witness who is not identified until after the 11th hour has passed. If a pattern of discovery violations is explicable only on the assumption that the violations were designed to conceal a plan to present fabricated testimony, it would be entirely appropriate to exclude the tainted evidence regardless of whether other sanctions would also be merited.

In order to reject petitioner's argument that preclusion is never a permissible sanction for a discovery violation it is neither necessary nor appropriate for us to attempt to draft a comprehensive set of standards to guide the exercise of discretion in every possible case. . . .

A trial judge may certainly insist on an explanation for a party's failure to comply with a request to identify his or her witnesses in advance of trial. If that explanation reveals that the omission was willful and motivated by a desire to obtain a tactical advantage that would minimize the effectiveness of cross-examination and the ability to adduce rebuttal evidence, it would be entirely consistent with the purposes of the Compulsory Process Clause simply to exclude the witness' testimony.[20] . . .

The simplicity of compliance with the discovery rule is also relevant. As we have noted, the Compulsory Process Clause cannot be invoked without the prior planning and affirmative conduct of the defendant. Lawyers are accustomed to meeting deadlines. Routine preparation involves location and interrogation of potential witnesses and the serving of subpoenas on those whose testimony will be offered at trial. The burden of identifying them in advance of trial adds little to these routine demands of trial preparation.

It would demean the high purpose of the Compulsory Process Clause to construe it as encompassing an absolute right to an automatic continuance or mistrial to allow presumptively perjured testimony to be presented to a jury. We reject petitioner's argument that a preclusion sanction is never appropriate no matter how serious the defendant's discovery violation may be.

Petitioner argues that the preclusion sanction was unnecessarily harsh in this case because the voir dire examination of Wormley adequately protected the prosecution from any possible prejudice resulting from surprise. Petitioner also contends that it is unfair to visit the sins of the lawyer upon his client. Neither argument has merit.

More is at stake than possible prejudice to the prosecution. We are also concerned with the impact of this kind of conduct on the integrity of the judicial process itself. The trial judge found that the discovery violation in this case was both willful and blatant.[22] In view of the fact that petitioner's counsel had actually interviewed Wormley during the week before the trial began and the further fact that he amended his Answer to Discovery on the first day of trial without identifying Wormley while he did identify two actual eyewitnesses whom he did not place on the stand, the inference that he was deliberately seeking a tactical advantage is inescapable. Regardless of whether prejudice to the prosecution could have been avoided in this particular case, it is plain that the case fits into the category of willful misconduct in which the severest sanction is appropriate. . . . The pretrial conduct revealed by the record in this case gives rise to a sufficiently strong inference that "witnesses are being found that really weren't there," to justify the sanction of preclusion.

The argument that the client should not be held responsible for his lawyer's misconduct strikes at the heart of the attorney-client relationship. Although there are

20. There may be cases in which a defendant has legitimate objections to disclosing the identity of a potential witness. Such objections, however, should be raised in advance of trial in response to the discovery request. . . . Under the Federal Rules of Criminal Procedure and under the rules adopted by most States, a party may request a protective order if he or she has just cause for objecting to a discovery request. In this case, there is no issue concerning the validity of the discovery requirement or petitioner's duty to comply with it. . . .

22. The trial judge also expressed concern about discovery violations in other trials. If those violations involved the same attorney, or otherwise contributed to a concern about the trustworthiness of Wormley's eleventh hour testimony, they were relevant. Unrelated discovery violations . . . would not, however, normally provide a proper basis for curtailing the defendant's constitutional right to present a complete defense.

basic rights that the attorney cannot waive without the fully informed and publicly acknowledged consent of the client,[24] the lawyer has — and must have — full authority to manage the conduct of the trial. The adversary process could not function effectively if every tactical decision required client approval. Moreover, given the protections afforded by the attorney-client privilege and the fact that extreme cases may involve unscrupulous conduct by both the client and the lawyer, it would be highly impracticable to require an investigation into their relative responsibilities before applying the sanction of preclusion. . . . In this case, petitioner has no greater right to disavow his lawyer's decision to conceal Wormley's identity until after the trial had commenced than he has to disavow the decision to refrain from adducing testimony from the eyewitnesses who were identified in the Answer to Discovery. Whenever a lawyer makes use of the sword provided by the Compulsory Process Clause, there is some risk that he may wound his own client.

The judgment of the Illinois Appellate Court is affirmed.

JUSTICE BRENNAN, with whom JUSTICE MARSHALL and JUSTICE BLACKMUN join, dissenting.

Criminal discovery is not a game. It is integral to the quest for truth and the fair adjudication of guilt or innocence. Violations of discovery rules thus cannot go uncorrected or undeterred without undermining the truthseeking process. The question in this case, however, is not whether discovery rules should be enforced but whether the need to correct and deter discovery violations requires a sanction that itself distorts the truthseeking process by excluding material evidence of innocence in a criminal case. . . .

. . . The question at the heart of this case . . . is whether precluding a criminal defense witness from testifying bears an arbitrary and disproportionate relation to the purposes of discovery, at least absent any evidence that the defendant was personally responsible for the discovery violations. This question is not answered by merely pointing out that discovery, like compulsory process, serves truthseeking interests. . . .

The use of the preclusion sanction as a corrective measure — that is, as a measure for addressing the adverse impact a discovery violation might have on truth-seeking in the case at hand — is asserted to have two justifications: (1) it bars the defendant from introducing testimony that has not been tested by discovery; and (2) it screens out witnesses who are inherently suspect because they were not disclosed until trial. The first justification has no bearing on this case because the defendant does not insist on a right to introduce a witness' testimony without giving the prosecution an opportunity for discovery. He concedes that the trial court was within its authority in requiring the witness to testify first out of the presence of the jury, and he concedes that the trial court could have granted the prosecution a continuance to give it sufficient time to conduct further discovery concerning the witness and the proffered

---

24. See, e.g., Brookhart v. Janis, 384 U.S. 1, 7-8 (1966) (defendant's constitutional right to plead not guilty and to have a trial where he could confront and cross-examine adversary witness could not be waived by his counsel without petitioner's consent); Doughty v. State, 470 N.E.2d 69, 70 (Ind. 1984) (record must show "personal communication of the defendant to the court that he chooses to relinquish the right [to a jury trial]"); Cross v. United States, 117 U.S. App. D.C. 56 (1963) (waiver of right to be present during trial).

testimony. He argues only that he should not be completely precluded from introducing the testimony. . . .

Nor, despite the Court's suggestions, is the preclusion at issue here justifiable on the theory that a trial court can exclude testimony that it presumes or finds suspect. . . .

[P]reventing a jury from hearing the proffered testimony based on its presumptive or apparent lack of credibility would be antithetical to the principles laid down in Washington v. Texas, 388 U.S. [14, 20-23 (1967) (invalidating a statute that disqualified accomplices from testifying for one another, but not for the state)], and reaffirmed in Rock v. Arkansas, 483 U.S. [44,] 53-55 [1987] [holding that a per se rule excluding all posthypnosis testimony impermissibly infringed on the defendant's right to testify]. . . . The Court in Washington v. Texas . . . concluded that "arbitrary rules that prevent whole categories of defense witnesses from testifying on the basis of a priori categories that presume them unworthy of belief" are unconstitutional. 388 U.S., at 22.

Although persons who are not identified as defense witnesses until trial may not be as trustworthy as other categories of persons, surely any presumption that they are so suspect that the jury can be prevented from even listening to their testimony is at least as arbitrary as presumptions excluding an accomplice's testimony, Washington v. Texas, supra, . . . or a defendant's posthypnosis testimony, *Rock*, supra. . . . The proper method, under Illinois law and Washington v. Texas, supra, for addressing the concern about reliability is for the prosecutor to inform the jury about the circumstances casting doubt on the testimony, thus allowing the jury to determine the credit and weight it wants to attach to such testimony. . . .

Of course, discovery sanctions must include more than corrective measures. They must also include punitive measures that can deter future discovery violations from taking place. . . .

In light of the availability of direct punitive measures, however, there is no good reason, at least absent evidence of the defendant's complicity, to countenance the arbitrary and disproportionate punishment imposed by the preclusion sanction. The central point to keep in mind is that witness preclusion operates as an effective deterrent only to the extent that it has a possible effect on the outcome of the trial. Indeed, it employs in part the possibility that a distorted record will cause a jury to convict a defendant of a crime he did not commit. Witness preclusion thus punishes discovery violations in a way that is both disproportionate—it might result in a defendant charged with a capital offense being convicted and receiving a death sentence he would not have received but for the discovery violation—and arbitrary—it might, in another case involving an identical discovery violation, result in a defendant suffering no change in verdict or, if charged with a lesser offense, being convicted and receiving a light or suspended sentence. In contrast, direct punitive measures (such as contempt sanctions or, if the attorney is responsible, disciplinary proceedings) can graduate the punishment to correspond to the severity of the discovery violation.

The arbitrary and disproportionate nature of the preclusion sanction is highlighted where the penalty falls on the defendant even though he bore no responsibility for the discovery violation. In this case, although there was ample evidence that the defense attorney willfully violated Rule 413(d), there was no evidence that the defendant played any role in that violation. . . .

Worse yet, the trial court made clear that it was excluding Wormley's testimony not only in response to the defense counsel's actions in this case but also in response to the actions of other defense attorneys in other cases. . . .

In the absence of any evidence that a defendant played any part in an attorney's willful discovery violation, directly sanctioning the attorney is not only fairer but *more* effective in deterring violations than excluding defense evidence. The threat of disciplinary proceedings, fines, or imprisonment will likely influence attorney behavior to a far greater extent than the rather indirect penalty threatened by evidentiary exclusion. . . .

The situation might be different if the defendant willfully caused the discovery violation because, as the Court points out, some defendants who face the prospect of a lengthy imprisonment are arguably impossible to deter with direct punitive sanctions such as contempt. But that is no explanation for allowing defense witness preclusion where there is no evidence that the defendant bore any responsibility for the discovery violation. . . . Deities may be able to visit the sins of the father on the son, but I cannot agree that courts should be permitted to visit the sins of the lawyer on the innocent client.

Nor is the issue resolved by analogizing to tactical errors an attorney might make such as failing to put witnesses on the stand that would have aided the defense. Although we have sometimes held a defendant bound by tactical errors his attorney makes that fall short of ineffective assistance of counsel, we have not previously suggested that a client can be punished for an attorney's *misconduct.* There are fundamental differences between attorney misconduct and tactical errors. . . . [T]he adversary system often cannot effectively deter attorney's tactical errors and does not want to deter tactical decisions. Thus, where a defense attorney makes a routine tactical decision not to introduce evidence at the proper time and the defense seeks to introduce the evidence later, deterrence measures may not be capable of preventing the untimely introduction of evidence from systemically disrupting trials, jury deliberations, or final verdicts. In those circumstances, treating the failure to introduce evidence at the proper time as a procedural default that binds the defendant is arguably the only means of systemically preventing such disruption — not because binding the defendant deters tactical errors any better than direct punitive sanctions but because binding the defendant to defense counsel's procedural default, by definition, eliminates the disruption. . . .

The rationales for binding defendants to attorneys' routine tactical errors do not apply to attorney misconduct. An attorney is never faced with a legitimate choice that includes misconduct as an option. Although it may be that "[t]he adversary process could not function effectively if every tactical decision required client approval," that concern is irrelevant here because a client has no authority to approve misconduct. Further, misconduct is not visible only with hindsight, as are many tactical errors. Consequently, misconduct is amenable to direct punitive sanctions against attorneys as a deterrent that can prevent attorneys from systemically engaging in misconduct that would disrupt the trial process. There is no need to take steps that will inflict the punishment on the defendant. . . .

In short, I can think of no scenario that does not involve a defendant's willful violation of a discovery rule where alternative sanctions would not fully vindicate the purposes of discovery without distorting the truthseeking process by excluding evidence of innocence. . . . Accordingly, absent evidence that the defendant was responsible for the discovery violation, the exclusion of criminal defense evidence is arbitrary and disproportionate to the purposes of discovery and criminal justice and should be per se unconstitutional. I thus cannot agree with the Court's case-by-case balancing approach or with its conclusion in this case that the exclusion was constitutional. . . .

NOTES AND QUESTIONS

1. Is it appropriate for a judge to preclude the use of evidence at trial as the remedy for defense discovery violations based on the *suspicion* that proffered evidence has been fabricated? Isn't this precisely what *Taylor* says? If a continuance would permit the prosecutor adequately to challenge such evidence and its admission would not otherwise prejudice her case, why should a court be making any judgment on the truth or falsity of the proposed testimony? Aren't such questions for the jury?

2. The majority in *Taylor* suggests that regardless whether prejudice to the prosecution could have been avoided, the "willful misconduct" in the case justified precluding Wormley's testimony. Assuming preclusion is a more appropriate sanction in cases of intentional misconduct as opposed to negligent discovery violations, how likely is it that a trial court will be able to distinguish between these cases? Will some of the factors that the Court in *Taylor* said were "relevant" to the sanction question—that a "judge may certainly insist on an explanation" for the discovery violation, for example, or the "simplicity of compliance with the discovery rule"—help courts determine the willfulness of the misconduct?

3. Sanctioning the defense is tricky, because, even beyond whether the violation was willful or negligent, the source of the problem may be impossible to determine. Sometimes the violations are entirely the fault of defense counsel—the lawyer forgot, was sloppy with information, was intentionally hiding the ball, and so on. But sometimes the fault lies with the accused. Perhaps he failed to recognize the importance of a piece of evidence and so never mentioned it, he hid information from his lawyer, or he simply made up some evidence (an alibi witness, for example). Should these cases be treated the same? If not, how can a court figure out who is at fault without digging deeply into attorney-client communications? And if a court can't reliably figure out who caused the violation, why shouldn't there be a default rule that the lawyer is to blame, and is the one who should bear the sanction?

4. Regardless of who is to blame for the violation, is exclusion *ever* appropriate if the evidence is reliable and potentially exculpatory? Consider the D.C. Circuit's response in United States v. Gray-Burriss, 791 F.3d 50, 56 (D.C. Cir. 2015). There the court found that the district judge abused his discretion in excluding defense evidence as a sanction for a clear discovery violation. Defendant had a document that strongly supported his innocence on a particular count, but although the government was entitled to the document in discovery, the defense did not produce it until the second week of trial. In finding that exclusion was not an permissible remedy, the court observed:

> . . . such a severe sanction would seldom be appropriate where . . . the trial court finds that [the party's] violation did not result from its bad faith and that a less drastic remedy (such as a continuance) will mitigate any unfair prejudice. This does not mean that exclusion is always unwarranted in the absence of bad faith or the presence of less drastic alternatives. Exclusion is inappropriate, however, when it would subvert[ ] one of Rule 16's goals: contributing to an accurate determination of the issue of guilt or innocence.

Id., at 56 (internal quotation marks and citations omitted). Is the D.C. Circuit saying, in effect, that before a court excludes evidence, it must find that the proffered evidence is unreliable? Is that consistent with *Taylor?*

5. One instance where a continuance will not solve the problem is when the other side has already acted on the assumption that the withheld evidence does not exist. Assume that a prosecutor has negligently failed to disclose discoverable material that proves that the defendant was present at the crime scene — say, a video from the lobby of a bank that was robbed. The defendant, unaware of the video, takes the stand at trial and falsely testifies that he was in another city on the day in question. The prosecution seeks to use the video to expose the defendant's lie, and defense objects, correctly noting that the government improperly failed to disclose the video. Should the court permit the evidence, on the theory that the defense has no protected right to commit perjury? Or should it exclude the evidence, reasoning that this is the only effective sanction for the government's failure to comply with the discovery rules, and that the defendant never would have perjured himself if the government had made the proper disclosure? See United States v. Noe, 821 F.2d 604 (11th Cir. 1987) ("Although [defendant] certainly does not have a right to 'fabricate' an alibi story, the Federal Rules of Criminal Procedure provide him a right to discover all statements that he made to law enforcement officials, and, correspondingly, to devise a defense strategy on the basis of the evidence disclosed.").

Chapter 13

Guilty Pleas and Plea Bargaining

After the defendant has been charged by indictment or by information, the next formal step in the process is the arraignment. Federal Rule 10 describes the arraignment as a simple, in-court process, where the defendant is informed of the charges against him and then asked whether he pleads guilty or not guilty.[1] (As described below, the defendant might also wish to plead "nolo contendere," or "no contest," but for the moment you can consider this just another form of a guilty plea.) At this stage many defendants will plead not guilty, but that state of affairs usually won't last for long. Before the case is finally resolved, the vast majority of defendants will plead guilty.

The criminal process that law students study, and movies and television celebrate, is formal, elaborate, and expensive. It involves a detailed examination of witnesses and physical evidence, tough adversarial argument from attorneys for the prosecution and defense, and fair-minded decision making from an impartial judge and jury. The heart of that process, of course, is the criminal trial.

For the huge majority of cases, the criminal process includes none of these things. Trials are, to put it mildly, exceptional. Of the nearly 49,000 defendants charged with felonies in the 75 most populous counties in the United States in 2009, about 64 percent pled guilty, another 25 percent had the charges dismissed, and most of the rest had some other non-adjudicative outcome (diversion or deferred prosecution, for example). Only about 3 percent of those 49,000 defendants went to trial, and of those who went to trial, two out of three were convicted.[2]

In federal cases there is a similar story. In 2012 there were over 96,000 defendants who had their cases resolved, 89 percent of whom pled guilty or nolo contendere. Another 8 percent had their charges dismissed prior to trial. Fewer than 3 percent of those charged with a federal offense went to trial and of those who did, more than 80 percent were convicted.[3]

---

1. Fed. R. Crim P. 10 provides in part:

    (a) IN GENERAL. An arraignment must be conducted in open court and must consist of:
        (1) ensuring that the defendant has a copy of the indictment or information;
        (2) reading the indictment or information to the defendant or stating to the defendant the substance of the charge; and then
        (3) asking the defendant to plead to the indictment or information.
    . . . .

The full text of Rule 10 is set forth in the Supplement.

2. U.S. Bureau of Justice Statistics, Felony Defendants in Large Urban Counties, 2009—Statistical Tables, Table 21 (Dec. 2013), http://www.bjs.gov/content/pub/pdf/fdluc09.pdf.

3. U.S. Bureau of Justice Statistics, Federal Justice Statistics, 2012—Statistical Tables, Table 4.2 (Jan. 2015), http://www.bjs.gov/content/pub/pdf/fjs12st.pdf.

If we focus only on those who were convicted, guilty pleas loom even larger. Over 97 percent of those convicted of a federal crime and those state defendants in the study cited above who ended their trip through the process with a conviction pled guilty. It follows that the huge majority of America's two-million-plus prison and jail inmates got where they are not by conviction at trial by a jury of their peers, or by a trial at all, but by admitting their guilt at a largely non-adversarial hearing. As the Supreme Court itself has acknowledged, "the reality [is] that the criminal justice system today is for the most part a system of pleas, not a system of trials." Lafler v. Cooper, 132 S. Ct. 1376, 1388 (2012).

That raises some fundamental questions: When is a guilty plea an adequate substitute for a formal decision by a qualified factfinder that the defendant is guilty of the crime charged beyond a reasonable doubt? In other words, what procedures are necessary to make guilty pleas sufficiently fair and accurate to justify dispensing with the trial process guaranteed by the Constitution? And what role do defense lawyers play in the plea process? A high percentage of criminal defendants receive appointed defense counsel, and appointed defense counsel operate under serious resource constraints, meaning that they cannot afford to go to trial in more than a small number of cases. How does that fact shape the plea process?

Notice that all of these questions are separate from the question of whether the state should be able to *induce* guilty pleas by making charging or sentencing concessions. Some defendants plead guilty without being offered any inducement by the prosecutor, but many more plead guilty because they get something in return from the government. To what extent should we tolerate (even embrace) the pervasive practice known as plea bargaining—a practice that, for better or for worse, produces the vast majority of the guilty pleas?

The materials in Section A of this chapter deal with the guilty plea process as a whole, including the consequences of entering a guilty plea—whether or not that guilty plea was induced by the State. Section B then examines the single dominant feature of the contemporary American criminal justice system: plea bargaining. Finally, Section C addresses the role of defense counsel in guilty pleas and plea bargaining.

A. The Guilty Plea

1. Rule 11 and the Plea Process

When a defendant pleads guilty, the case is effectively over. There are still some important steps that lie ahead—the defendant must be sentenced, and there might be an appeal—but a guilty plea resolves the charges against the accused, and after a valid plea is entered there is nothing left for the court to decide except the sentence. The court will enter a judgment of guilt, and the defendant stands convicted.

In a small number of cases the defendant may plead "nolo contendere" (no contest) instead of guilty, although the effect is largely the same, at least for criminal law purposes. A no contest plea is simply a declaration by the accused that, while he does not admit the charges against him, he will "not contest" the charges, and will permit the court to treat him as if he had pled guilty. The result of a nolo plea is a conviction. The court will sentence the defendant as if he had pled guilty, and the conviction will count for a later sentencing enhancement just as if it had followed a guilty plea. The primary distinction is that unlike a guilty plea, a no contest plea is not an admission of guilt, and if the defendant is later sued in a civil action (say, a wrongful death suit following a DUI conviction), he is not estopped from denying the facts on which the criminal charge was based. See Wright & Leipold, 1A Federal Practice and Procedure §175 (2008). But this plea is relatively rare—in 2012, there were only 134 nolo contendere pleas out of the 87, 908 felony convictions in federal court.[4] Nearly all defendants enter a traditional guilty plea.

As courts have noted, the guilty plea is a "grave and solemn act," to be accepted by the court "only with care and discernment." Brady v. United States, 397 U.S. 742, 748 (1970) (internal quotation marks and citation omitted). Because the judge has not played a role in the defendant's decision to plead guilty,[5] the court's sole opportunity to participate in the resolution of nearly all criminal cases comes when the defendant enters his guilty plea. Over the years, as guilty pleas have increased in importance, the proceeding where the court accepts a guilty plea has become more elaborate and more structured. Most, but not all, of that process is now captured in Federal Rule of Criminal Procedure 11. (The current version of Rule 11 appears in the Supplement, but note that several of the cases in this chapter refer to earlier versions of the rule.)

A defendant who wishes to plead guilty appears in open court, with counsel, along with the prosecutor. The judge is not required to place the defendant under oath, but it is considered better practice to do so; in theory a defendant who lies during the plea hearing could later be prosecuted for perjury, although in practice an obvious lie will more likely affect the eventual prison sentence. The judge then engages in a plea "colloquy" with the defendant personally—the judge speaks directly to the accused, to make sure the defendant is entering a valid guilty plea.

The requirements of a valid plea are set forth in Rule 11(b), although this part of the Rule has constitutional underpinnings. In Boykin v. Alabama, 395 U.S. 238, 242 (1969), the Court held that because a guilty plea is a waiver of a great many constitutional rights, including the right to trial, the right against self-incrimination, and the right to confront his accusers, there must be an *affirmative showing* in the record that the defendant entered the plea knowingly and voluntarily. Boykin's command spurred the Federal Rules Committee to action, and now Rule 11 sets forth an elaborate process by which the judge ensures that the defendant understands the scope and impact of his decision to plead guilty. The overlapping requirements of the Constitution and the Rules now provide that a valid guilty plea (1) must be made knowingly, (2) must be made voluntarily, and (3) has an adequate factual basis to support it. These requirements are discussed in the following sections.

a. Knowing

The plea colloquy can be quite wide-ranging. A court will often begin by asking the defendant about his age, his health, his education level, his employment status, his command of the English language, whether he has mental health or substance

---

4. Federal Justice Statistics, 2012—Statistical Tables, supra, Table 4.2.
5. Rule 11(c)(1) prohibits a federal judge from taking part in discussions between the parties about whether the defendant should plead guilty. This prohibition is not constitutionally based, however, and in many states, judges are permitted to participate in plea discussions. See Part B.2, below.

abuse problems, and whether he is currently taking any drugs or is under the influence of alcohol. The court is then likely to turn to the defense counsel and ask if she has any questions about the ability of the accused to understand the proceedings.

Rule 11(b)(1) then says that before a court can accept a guilty plea, the judge must inform the defendant of 14 items, and ensure that the defendant understands them. The first and most obvious item is that the defendant must be aware of the precise charge to which the defendant is pleading guilty, which typically means that he must be informed of the elements of the crime. The court then advises the defendant of some of the rights he is giving up if he pleads guilty:

- The right to plead not guilty
- The right to a jury trial
- The right to have a lawyer at every stage of the process, including the trial
- The right to confront his accusers

The court then informs the defendant of the impact of the guilty plea:

- The maximum possible penalty the accused faces on conviction
- Any mandatory minimum sentence that the judge will have to impose
- Any applicable forfeiture the defendant faces, and the court's authority to order restitution
- The court's duty to consider the sentencing range under the Federal Sentencing Guidelines
- If the defendant is pleading guilty pursuant to a plea agreement, and that agreement contains a waiver of the right to file an appeal or seek post conviction relief, the court must ensure that the defendant is aware of the waiver provision
- If the defendant is not a U.S. citizen, a conviction may have immigration or citizenship consequences

Only if the defendant personally affirms that he understands each of these points can the judge find that the guilty plea is made knowingly.

NOTES AND QUESTIONS

1. Rule 11(b) expressly requires that the judge "determine that the defendant understands" the information listed above. In practice, the plea colloquy makes that determination mechanical: Judges ask questions; defendants mostly say "yes." If that strikes you as inadequate, how could the inadequacy be corrected—or is this a problem that cannot be solved without turning the guilty plea process into a trial focused on the defendant's understanding?

2. Look carefully at what Rule 11 requires the court to tell the defendant before he pleads guilty. Keeping in mind that the purpose of the Rule is to ensure that the defendant is making an informed choice to plead guilty rather than go to trial, what, if anything, is missing from the list? If you were advising a client whether to plead guilty, what other information would you want to know?

Two items might make your list. The first, and perhaps the most obvious is the sentence the defendant will actually receive if he pleads guilty, versus the sentence we would face if he stood trial and lost. If the gap between the certain sentence following a guilty plea and the potential sentence after trial were small enough, a defendant might be more likely to roll the dice at trial; if the gap is quite large, the guilty plea might be more sensible. But notice that this precise piece of information is not given to the accused—he is only told of any mandatory minimum and the statutory maximum sentence he faces, not the sentence he will actually receive. This omission is best explained by the sentencing process, which can take weeks or months following a conviction, making it nearly impossible to know with any certainty the actual sentence that will follow a guilty plea. But the fact remains that the accused must normally make the plea decision without what may be the single most important piece of information.

A second item that the defendant might wish to know before pleading guilty is the impact of a plea on the rest of his life. Besides the possibility of prison, a fine, restitution, and forfeiture, there are lots of "collateral" consequences that follow a conviction. A felony conviction might deprive the defendant of the right to vote, to own a firearm, to live in certain public housing facilities, to contract with the government, to hold certain jobs, and to get student loans; in some cases, a conviction will require the accused to register as a sex offender, perhaps for the rest of his life. But courts have consistently found that the list of information that must be conveyed pursuant to Rule 11 is exhaustive; courts are under no duty to inform the accused of the other bad consequences that follow a conviction.

Telling the defendant about every negative impact of a conviction ("your wife's family will hate you") is obviously administratively impossible, and most are unlikely to be important enough to influence the decision whether to plead guilty. Look again at the list of collateral consequences described in the prior paragraph. Are there any there that you think are important enough, either in general or in particular cases, that if the defendant was not aware of them the plea could fairly be characterized as "not knowing"?

3. One result of a conviction that moved off the list of "collateral" consequences and on to the list of Rule 11 items the judge must tell the accused is the possible immigration effect on non-U.S. citizens. The fact that a non-citizen who was convicted of a crime might be deported could obviously be the most important effect of a conviction, and a defendant facing a removal might prefer to forego a plea and take even a slim chance at trial to avoid it. But courts had long treated the immigration consequences of a conviction as a collateral consequence, in part because immigration proceedings are civil in nature and thus outside the scope of the immediate criminal case.

In 2010, however, the Court concluded in Padilla v. Kentucky, 559 U.S. 356 (2010), that when a defense lawyer failed to give his non-citizen client the correct information about the deportation risks he ran by pleading guilty, this was "deficient performance" for purposes of an ineffective assistance of counsel claim under Strickland v. Washington, 466 U.S. 668 (1984) (a topic discussed in detail in Chapter 3). The Court's reasoning was based in part on the view that "[p]reserving the client's right to remain in the United States may be more important to the client than any potential jail sentence." The Federal Rules drafters agreed, and now Rule 11(b)(1)(O) provides that a judge must ensure that a defendant pleading guilty understands "that, if convicted, a defendant who is not a United States citizen may be removed from the United States, denied citizenship, and denied admission to the United States in the future."

Assume for the moment that the immigration effects of a conviction are important enough that they could routinely effect the decision whether to plead guilty or go to trial. Does the Rule tell the defendant what he needs to know? What other information, if any, do you think a court should tell a defendant to address this issue? Notice that the information in Rule 11(b)(1)(O) is to be told to every defendant, citizen and non-citizen alike. Why do you think the Rules drafters adopted this approach?

4. Because the warnings and advice required by Rule 11 are set forth explicitly, they are generally given correctly. But claims still do arise, most often because the judge failed to say something that Rule 11 required her to tell the defendant. Not surprisingly, the defendants in these cases virtually never objected to the omission at the time—if they had objected the court would have corrected the error—and so these challenges are subject to the demanding "plain error" standard on appeal (a topic discussed in Chapter 17). In United States v. Dominguez Benitez, 542 U.S. 74 (2004), the Supreme Court held that a defendant who is trying to undo his plea because of a defective Rule 11 colloquy can prevail only if they show that there is a reasonable probability that, but for error, the defendant would have decided not to plead guilty:

> . . . [T]he burden of establishing entitlement to relief for plain error is on the defendant claiming it, and for several reasons, we think that burden should not be too easy for defendants in Dominguez's position. First, the standard should . . . encourage timely objections and reduce wasteful reversals by demanding strenuous exertion to get relief for unpreserved error. Second, it should respect the particular importance of the finality of guilty pleas, which usually rest, after all, on a defendant's profession of guilt in open court, and are indispensable in the operation of the modern criminal justice system. See United States v. Timmreck, 441 U.S. 780, 784 (1979). And, in this case, these reasons are complemented by the fact . . . that the violation claimed was of Rule 11, not of due process.
>
> We hold, therefore, that a defendant who seeks reversal of his conviction after a guilty plea, on the ground that the district court committed plain error under Rule 11, must show a reasonable probability that, but for the error, he would not have entered the plea. A defendant must thus satisfy the judgment of the reviewing court, informed by the entire record, that the probability of a different result is "sufficient to undermine confidence in the outcome" of the proceeding. Strickland [v. Washington, 466 U.S. 668, 694 (1984)]. . . .

542 U.S., at 82-83. This standard is hard to meet. Precisely because the plea colloquy is such a formal exercise, few defendants can argue with a straight face that this same exercise was the motivating force behind their guilty pleas. The Court also has said that if there is evidence in the record that the omitted information was provided to the defendant by his lawyer prior to the guilty plea, the judge's failure to convey the Rule 11 information will be harmless. Bradshaw v. Stumpf, 545 U.S. 175 (2005).

b.   Voluntary

Rule 11(b)(2) says that a court must ensure that the guilty plea is "voluntary." On the surface this is sensible and unremarkable. No one thinks that a defendant who is tortured or otherwise coerced into pleading guilty should be convicted as a result, and history has shown that this risk is genuine. The Rule thus says, in part: "Before accepting a plea of guilty or nolo contendere, the court must address the defendant personally in open court and determine that the plea is voluntary and did not result from force [or] threats." So if the accused was coerced by the police or the prosecutor, he has the chance to reveal that fact in the safety of the courtroom.

The difficulty, of course, is deciding exactly what it means to "coerce" a guilty plea. In the early part of the last Century, courts found that confessions were not voluntary if they were "extracted by any sort of threats or violence, [or] obtained by *any direct or implied promises, however slight.*" See Bram v. United States, 168 U.S. 532, 542-543 (1897) (emphasis added, internal quotation marks and citation omitted). The problem was that this standard, if taken seriously, would jeopardize the growing practice of plea bargaining, which depended almost entirely on compelling the defendant to confess (plead guilty) in return for direct and implied threats ("we'll give you a more severe sentence if you go to trial and lose") and promises ("we'll drop some of the charges if you agree to plead guilty"), slight and otherwise. For many years this difficulty led to the unsavory spectacle of defendants telling the court that their plea was not induced by any threat or promise, the prosecutor agreeing, and the judge accepting the claim, even though everyone in the courtroom knew that the representation was false.

Finally, in Brady v. United States, 397 U.S. 742 (1970), the Supreme Court expressly held that plea bargaining did not itself render pleas involuntary, and the Rules of Procedure were changed accordingly. It is still impermissible to coerce a plea through force or threats, but the court now asks whether the guilty plea was induced by promises "other than promises in a plea agreement." As a result, since *Brady*, voluntariness challenges to guilty pleas have usually stemmed from claims that the government bargained improperly (for example, where the government made some impermissible threat in the course of bargaining for the plea). These claims are examined in Section B, below, in the material on plea bargaining.

c.   *Factual Basis*

Before accepting the defendant's guilty plea, the court is required by Rule 11(b)(3) to find a factual basis to support it. The obvious reason for this requirement is to protect the defendant from himself. The defendant knows what he did, and may well believe that what he did was a crime, but may not realize that his conduct is either no offense or a lesser offense that the one to which he is prepared to plead guilty. See, e.g., Henderson v. Morgan, 426 U.S. 637 (1976) (defendant pled guilty to second degree murder although there was nothing in the record to support the requirement that defendant have acted with intent; guilty plea held invalid).

Therefore, district judges must satisfy themselves that there is enough evidence of the defendant's guilt to justify entering a conviction on the crime in question. There is no standard of proof the court needs to satisfy, although it is understood that a valid factual basis can be found on far less than proof beyond a reasonable doubt. In finding the factual basis, the court is free to look to a wide variety of on-the-record sources: the judge can review the documentary evidence, question the prosecutor, question defense counsel, and review any presentence report. Often, however, the court will want to hear the information directly from the defendant, and ask the defendant to "allocute," and describe what he did and his relevant state of mind.

The judge need only find a factual basis for the elements of the crime; she need not make findings regarding affirmative defenses or potential punishment. In Libretti v. United States, 516 U.S. 29 (1995), for example, the defendant pled guilty to participation in a continuing criminal enterprise. As part of the plea agreement, he agreed to the forfeiture of a large amount of property. He then challenged the forfeiture portions of the plea agreement, arguing that they lacked a factual basis, and hence that the plea violated Rule 11. The Supreme Court rejected the claim, holding that the factual basis requirement applies only to the substantive charge to which the defendant pleads guilty, and that forfeiture is part of the punishment.

One curiosity about the factual basis requirement is that it does not apply to a plea of nolo contendere (discussed above in the introductory material to this Part). The justification for this exception is that there may be cases where the defendant is entirely innocent yet wants to dispose of the charges quickly, and that in such a case the defendant's interests are best served by dispensing with the factual basis finding. See Ranke v. U.S., 873 F.2d 1033, 1036 (7th Cir. 1989) (noting rationale).

Whether potentially innocent people should be permitted to plead guilty if they think it is in their best interests is a fascinating and important question. The next case raises this issue in an analogous situation, one that has come to bear the defendant's name — an "*Alford* plea."

NORTH CAROLINA v. ALFORD

Appeal from the United States Court of Appeals for the Fourth Circuit
400 U.S. 25 (1970)

JUSTICE WHITE delivered the opinion of the Court.

On December 2, 1963, Alford was indicted for first-degree murder, a capital offense under North Carolina law. The court appointed an attorney to represent him, and this attorney questioned all but one of the various witnesses who appellee said would substantiate his claim of innocence. The witnesses, however, did not support Alford's story but gave statements that strongly indicated his guilt. Faced with strong evidence of guilt and no substantial evidentiary support for the claim of innocence, Alford's attorney recommended that he plead guilty, but left the ultimate decision to Alford himself. The prosecutor agreed to accept a plea of guilty to a charge of second-degree murder, and on December 10, 1963, Alford pleaded guilty to the reduced charge.

Before the plea was finally accepted by the trial court, the court heard the sworn testimony of a police officer who summarized the State's case. Two other witnesses besides Alford were also heard. Although there was no eyewitness to the crime, the testimony indicated that shortly before the killing Alford took his gun from his house, stated his intention to kill the victim, and returned home with the declaration that he had carried out the killing. After the summary presentation of the State's case, Alford took the stand and testified that he had not committed the murder but that he was pleading guilty because he faced the threat of the death penalty if he did not do so.[2] In response to the questions of his counsel, he acknowledged that his counsel had informed him of the difference between second and first-degree murder and of his rights in case he chose to go to trial. The trial court then asked appellee if, in light of his denial of guilt, he still desired to plead guilty to second-degree murder and appellee answered, "Yes, sir. I plead guilty on—from the circumstances that he [Alford's attorney] told me." After eliciting information about Alford's prior criminal record, which was a long one,[4] the trial court sentenced him to 30 years' imprisonment, the maximum penalty for second-degree murder.

Alford sought post-conviction relief in the state court. Among the claims raised was the claim that his plea of guilty was invalid because it was the product of fear and coercion. After a hearing, the state court in 1965 found that the plea was "willingly, knowingly, and understandingly" made on the advice of competent counsel and in the face of a strong prosecution case. Subsequently, Alford petitioned for a writ of habeas corpus, first in the United States District Court for the Middle District of North Carolina, and then in the Court of Appeals for the Fourth Circuit. Both courts denied the writ on the basis of the state court's findings that Alford voluntarily and knowingly agreed to plead guilty. In 1967, Alford again petitioned for a writ of habeas corpus in the District Court for the Middle District of North Carolina. That court, without an evidentiary hearing, again denied relief on the grounds that the guilty plea was voluntary and waived all defenses and nonjurisdictional defects in any prior stage of the proceedings, and that the findings of the state court in 1965 clearly required rejection of Alford's claim that he was denied effective assistance of counsel prior to pleading guilty. On appeal, a divided panel of the Court of Appeals for the Fourth Circuit reversed on the ground that Alford's guilty plea was made involuntarily. 405 F.2d 340 (1968).

. . . We noted probable jurisdiction. We vacate the judgment of the Court of Appeals and remand the case for further proceedings.

We held in Brady v. United States, 397 U.S. 742 (1970), that a plea of guilty which would not have been entered except for the defendant's desire to avoid a possible death penalty and to limit the maximum penalty to life imprisonment or a term of years was not for that reason compelled within the meaning of the

---

2. After giving his version of the events of the night of the murder, Alford stated:

I pleaded guilty on second degree murder because they said there is too much evidence, but I ain't shot no man, but I take the fault for the other man. We never had an argument in our life and I just pleaded guilty because they said if I didn't they would gas me for it, and that is all.

In response to questions from his attorney, Alford affirmed that he had consulted several times with his attorney and with members of his family and had been informed of his rights if he chose to plead not guilty. Alford then reaffirmed his decision to plead guilty to second-degree murder:

Q   [by Alford's attorney]   And you authorized me to tender a plea of guilty to second degree murder before the court?
A   Yes, sir.
Q   And in doing that, that you have again affirmed your decision on that point?
A   Well, I'm still pleading that you all got me to plead guilty. I plead the other way, circumstantial evidence; that the jury will prosecute me on—on the second. You told me to plead guilty, right. I don't—I'm not guilty but I plead guilty.

4. Before Alford was sentenced, the trial judge asked Alford about prior convictions. Alford answered that, among other things, he had served six years of a ten-year sentence for murder, had been convicted nine times for armed robbery, and had been convicted for transporting stolen goods, forgery, and carrying a concealed weapon.

Fifth Amendment. . . . The standard was and remains whether the plea represents a voluntary and intelligent choice among the alternative courses of action open to the defendant. See Boykin v. Alabama, 395 U.S. 238, 242 (1969); Machibroda v. United States, 368 U.S. 487, 493 (1962); Kercheval v. United States, 274 U.S. 220, 223 (1927). That he would not have pleaded except for the opportunity to limit the possible penalty does not necessarily demonstrate that the plea of guilty was not the product of a free and rational choice, especially where the defendant was represented by competent counsel whose advice was that the plea would be to the defendant's advantage. . . .

As previously recounted, after Alford's plea of guilty was offered and the State's case was placed before the judge, Alford denied that he had committed the murder but reaffirmed his desire to plead guilty to avoid a possible death sentence and to limit the penalty to the 30-year maximum provided for second-degree murder. Ordinarily, a judgment of conviction resting on a plea of guilty is justified by the defendant's admission that he committed the crime charged against him and his consent that judgment be entered without a trial of any kind. The plea usually subsumes both elements, and justifiably so, even though there is no separate, express admission by the defendant that he committed the particular acts claimed to constitute the crime charged in the indictment. See Brady v. United States, supra, at 748. Here Alford entered his plea but accompanied it with the statement that he had not shot the victim.

If Alford's statements were to be credited as sincere assertions of his innocence, there obviously existed a factual and legal dispute between him and the State. Without more, it might be argued that the conviction entered on his guilty plea was invalid, since his assertion of innocence negatived any admission of guilt, which, as we observed last Term in *Brady*, is normally "central to the plea and the foundation for entering judgment against the defendant. . . ." 397 U.S., at 748.

In addition to Alford's statement, however, the court had heard an account of the events on the night of the murder, including information from Alford's acquaintances that he had departed from his home with his gun stating his intention to kill and that he had later declared that he had carried out his intention. Nor had Alford wavered in his desire to have the trial court determine his guilt without a jury trial. Although denying the charge against him, he nevertheless preferred the dispute between him and the State to be settled by the judge in the context of a guilty plea proceeding rather than by a formal trial. Thereupon, with the State's telling evidence and Alford's denial before it, the trial court proceeded to convict and sentence Alford for second-degree murder.

State and lower federal courts are divided upon whether a guilty plea can be accepted when it is accompanied by protestations of innocence and hence contains only a waiver of trial but no admission of guilt. Some courts, giving expression to the principle that "our law only authorizes a conviction where guilt is shown," Harris v. State, 76 Tex. Cr. R. 126, 131, 172 S.W. 975, 977 (1915), require that trial judges reject such pleas. But others have concluded that they should not "force any defense on a defendant in a criminal case," particularly when advancement of the defense might "end in disaster. . . ." Tremblay v. Overholser, 199 F. Supp. 569, 570 (DC 1961). They have argued that, since "guilt, or the degree of guilt, is at times uncertain and elusive," "an accused, though believing in or entertaining doubts respecting his innocence, might reasonably conclude a jury would be convinced of his guilt and that he would fare better in the sentence by pleading guilty. . . ." McCoy v. United

States, 363 F.2d 306, 308 (CADC 1966). As one state court observed nearly a century ago, "reasons other than the fact that he is guilty may induce a defendant to so plead, . . . [and] he must be permitted to judge for himself in this respect." State v. Kaufman, 51 Iowa 578, 580, 2 N.W. 275, 276 (1879) (dictum).

This Court has not confronted this precise issue, but prior decisions do yield relevant principles. . . . The issue in Hudson v. United States, 272 U.S. 451 (1926), was whether a federal court has power to impose a prison sentence after accepting a plea of nolo contendere, a plea by which a defendant does not expressly admit his guilt, but nonetheless waives his right to a trial and authorizes the court for purposes of the case to treat him as if he were guilty.[8] The Court held that a trial court does have such power, and . . . the federal courts have uniformly followed this rule, even in cases involving moral turpitude. Implicit in the nolo contendere cases is a recognition that the Constitution does not bar imposition of a prison sentence upon an accused who is unwilling expressly to admit his guilt but who, faced with grim alternatives, is willing to waive his trial and accept the sentence.

These cases would be directly in point if Alford had simply insisted on his plea but refused to admit the crime. The fact that his plea was denominated a plea of guilty rather than a plea of nolo contendere is of no constitutional significance with respect to the issue now before us, for the Constitution is concerned with the practical consequences, not the formal categorizations, of state law. Thus, while most pleas of guilty consist of both a waiver of trial and an express admission of guilt, the latter element is not a constitutional requisite to the imposition of a criminal penalty. An individual accused of crime may voluntarily, knowingly, and understandingly consent to the imposition of a prison sentence even if he is unwilling or unable to admit his participation in the acts constituting the crime.

Nor can we perceive any material difference between a plea that refuses to admit commission of the criminal act and a plea containing a protestation of innocence

---

8. Courts have defined the plea of nolo contendere in a variety of different ways, describing it, on the one hand, as "in effect, a plea of guilty," United States v. Food & Grocery Bureau, 43 F. Supp. 974, 979 (SD Cal. 1942), aff'd, 139 F.2d 973 (CA9 1943), and on the other, as a query directed to the court to determine the defendant's guilt. State v. Hopkins, 27 Del. 306, 88 A. 473 (1913). As a result, it is impossible to state precisely what a defendant does admit when he enters a nolo plea in a way that will consistently fit all the cases.

Hudson v. United States, supra, was also ambiguous. In one place, the Court called the plea "an admission of guilt for the purposes of the case," id., at 455, but in another, the Court quoted an English authority who had defined the plea as one "where a defendant, in a case not capital, doth not directly own himself guilty. . . ." Id., at 453, quoting 2 W. Hawkins, Pleas of the Crown 466 (8th ed. 1824).

The plea may have originated in the early medieval practice by which defendants wishing to avoid imprisonment would seek to make an end of the matter (finem facere) by offering to pay a sum of money to the king. See 2 F. Pollock & F. Maitland, History of English Law 517 (2d ed. 1909). An early fifteenth-century case indicated that a defendant did not admit his guilt when he sought such a compromise, but merely "that he put himself on the grace of our Lord, the King, and asked that he might be allowed to pay a fine (petit se admittit per finem)." Anon., Y. B. Hil. 9 Hen. 6, f. 59, pl. 8 (1431). . . .

[A]n eighteenth-century case distinguished between a nolo plea and a jury verdict of guilty, noting that in the former the defendant could introduce evidence of innocence in mitigation of punishment, whereas in the latter such evidence was precluded by the finding of actual guilt. Queen v. Templeman, 1 Salk. 55, 91 Eng. Rep. 54 (K.B. 1702).

Throughout its history, that is, the plea of nolo contendere has been viewed not as an express admission of guilt but as a consent by the defendant that he may be punished as if he were guilty and a prayer for leniency. Fed. Rule Crim. Proc. 11 preserves this distinction in its requirement that a court cannot accept a guilty plea unless it ["determine[s] that there is a factual basis for the plea"]; there is no similar requirement for pleas of nolo contendere, since it was thought desirable to permit defendants to plead nolo without making any inquiry into their actual guilt. See Notes of Advisory Committee to Rule 11.

when, as in the instant case, a defendant intelligently concludes that his interests require entry of a guilty plea and the record before the judge contains strong evidence of actual guilt. Here the State had a strong case of first-degree murder against Alford. Whether he realized or disbelieved his guilt, he insisted on his plea because in his view he had absolutely nothing to gain by a trial and much to gain by pleading. Because of the overwhelming evidence against him, a trial was precisely what neither Alford nor his attorney desired. Confronted with the choice between a trial for first-degree murder, on the one hand, and a plea of guilty to second-degree murder, on the other, Alford quite reasonably chose the latter and thereby limited the maximum penalty to a 30-year term. When his plea is viewed in light of the evidence against him, which substantially negated his claim of innocence and which further provided a means by which the judge could test whether the plea was being intelligently entered,[10] its validity cannot be seriously questioned. In view of the strong factual basis for the plea demonstrated by the State and Alford's clearly expressed desire to enter it despite his professed belief in his innocence, we hold that the trial judge did not commit constitutional error in accepting it.[11]

. . . Alford now argues in effect that the State should not have allowed him this choice but should have insisted on proving him guilty of murder in the first degree. The States in their wisdom may take this course by statute or otherwise and may prohibit the practice of accepting pleas to lesser included offenses under any circumstances. But this is not the mandate of the Fourteenth Amendment and the Bill of Rights. The prohibitions against involuntary or unintelligent pleas should not be relaxed, but neither should an exercise in arid logic render those constitutional guarantees counterproductive and put in jeopardy the very human values they were meant to preserve. . . .

[The concurring statement of Justice Black is omitted.]

JUSTICE BRENNAN, with whom JUSTICE DOUGLAS and JUSTICE MARSHALL join, dissenting.

Last Term, this Court held, over my dissent, that a plea of guilty may validly be induced by [a] threat to subject the defendant to the risk of death, so long as the plea is entered in open court and the defendant is represented by competent counsel who is aware of the threat. . . . Brady v. United States, 397 U.S. 742, 745-758 (1970). Today the Court makes clear that its previous holding was intended to apply

---

10. Because of the importance of protecting the innocent and of insuring that guilty pleas are a product of free and intelligent choice, various state and federal court decisions properly caution that pleas coupled with claims of innocence should not be accepted unless there is a factual basis for the plea, see, e.g., Griffin v. United States, 405 F.2d 1378, 1380 (CADC 1968); Commonwealth v. Cottrell, 433 Pa. 177, 249 A.2d 294 (1969); and until the judge taking the plea has inquired into and sought to resolve the conflict between the waiver of trial and the claim of innocence. See, e.g., People v. Serrano, 15 N.Y.2d 304, 308-309, 206 N.E.2d 330, 332 (1965).

In the federal courts, Fed. Rule Crim. Proc. 11 expressly provides that ["[b]efore entering judgment on a guilty plea, the court must determine that there is a factual basis for the plea"].

11. Our holding does not mean that a trial judge must accept every constitutionally valid guilty plea merely because a defendant wishes so to plead. A criminal defendant does not have an absolute right under the Constitution to have his guilty plea accepted by the court, although the States may by statute or otherwise confer such a right. Likewise, the States may bar their courts from accepting guilty pleas from any defendants who assert their innocence. Cf. [former] Fed. Rule Crim. Proc. 11, which gives a trial judge discretion to "refuse to accept a plea of guilty. . . ." We need not now delineate the scope of that discretion.

even when the record demonstrates that the actual effect of the unconstitutional threat was to induce a guilty plea from a defendant who was unwilling to admit his guilt.

. . . [W]ithout reaching the question whether due process permits the entry of judgment upon a plea of guilty accompanied by a contemporaneous denial of acts constituting the crime, I believe that at the very least such a denial of guilt is also a relevant factor in determining whether the plea was voluntarily and intelligently made. With these factors in mind, it is sufficient in my view to state that the facts set out in the majority opinion demonstrate that Alford was "so gripped by fear of the death penalty"[2] that his decision to plead guilty was not voluntary but was "the product of duress as much so as choice reflecting physical constraint." Haley v. Ohio, 332 U.S. 596, 606 (1948) (opinion of Frankfurter, J.). Accordingly, I would affirm the judgment of the Court of Appeals.

NOTES AND QUESTIONS

1. In cases in which a defendant is convicted at trial, the conviction rests on the judgment of a neutral factfinder that the prosecutor proved the defendant guilty of the crime charged beyond a reasonable doubt. In an ordinary guilty plea, the conviction rests on the defendant's confession in open court that he committed the crime charged. On what does Alford's conviction rest?

2. Although an "*Alford* plea" involves a defendant who protests his innocence, he is in fact pleading guilty. Stated differently, *Alford* pleas are *not* the same thing as a nolo contendere plea, even though in both the defendant refuses to admit guilt, and even though the Court in *Alford* used the existence of nolo pleas to justify accepting an *Alford* plea. (See footnote 8 of the Court's opinion.) Can you articulate why *Alford* pleas raise particular issues for the Rule 11 factual basis requirement?

3. Stephanos Bibas has argued that nolo pleas and *Alford* pleas are a mistake, because they undermine the moral values on which the criminal justice system is based:

> . . . *Alford* and nolo contendere pleas are unwise and should be abolished. These procedures may be constitutional and efficient, but they undermine key values served by admissions of guilt in open court. They undermine the procedural values of accuracy and public confidence in accuracy and fairness by convicting innocent defendants and creating the perception that innocent defendants are being pressured into pleading guilty. More basically, they allow guilty defendants to avoid accepting responsibility for their wrongs. Guilty defendants' refusals to admit guilt impede their repentance, education, and reform, as well as victims' healing process. In addition, pleas without confessions muddy the criminal law's moral message. Both kinds of pleas, but especially *Alford* pleas, equivocate; one might call them "guilty-but-not-guilty" pleas. They permit equivocation and ambiguity when clarity is essential. This equivocation, in turn, undermines denunciation of the defendant and vindication of the victim and the community's moral norms. Sacrificing these substantive goals is too high a price for an efficient plea procedure. Procedures that undercut substance have little point, as the point of procedure is to serve substance. Yet substantive values for the most part are not even on the proceduralists' radar screens. Thus, guilty

2. Brady v. United States, 397 U.S., at 750.

pleas should be reserved for those who confess. Jury trials should serve not only to acquit innocent defendants, but also to teach guilty defendants and vindicate their victims and the community's moral norms. They are morality plays. Because criminal law's norms include honesty and responsibility for one's actions, criminal procedure should not let guilty defendants dishonestly dodge responsibility and the truth.

Stephanos Bibas, Harmonizing Substantive-Criminal-Law Values and Criminal Procedure: The Case of *Alford* and Nolo Contendere Pleas, 88 Cornell L. Rev. 1361, 1363-1364 (2003). Bibas continues, id., at 1364-1366:

Consider the prominent example of Kathleen Soliah, which illustrates why unequivocal guilty-plea confessions serve these values better than equivocal *Alford* and nolo pleas. In the 1970s, Soliah belonged to the Symbionese Liberation Army, a radical San Francisco group that kidnapped Patricia Hearst and tried to kill government officials. Soliah fled to Minnesota and changed her name to Sara Jane Olson. For years, she denied belonging to the Symbionese Liberation Army or taking part in an attempt to bomb two police cars in 1975. Her lawyer expressed interest in negotiating an *Alford* or nolo contendere plea, but the judge and prosecutors would not countenance such a plea. Finally, on October 31, 2001, Olson clearly and unequivocally pleaded guilty to taking part in an attempt to bomb the two cars. Immediately afterwards, however, Olson told reporters that she had pleaded guilty to crimes of which she was innocent. Prosecutors speculated that Olson had changed her story to please her friends and family who had maintained her innocence.

Olson's judge, however, refused to countenance this express and instantaneous contradiction, noting that "the integrity of the criminal justice system is at stake." He called Olson in for another hearing and asked her whether she wanted her plea to stand. At that hearing, the judge confronted Olson and asked her, clearly and explicitly, if she was in fact guilty. She twice said yes and reaffirmed her plea. Five days later, Olson again publicly disavowed her guilt and moved to withdraw her plea. At the next court hearing, the judge noted that Olson found it psychologically very difficult to admit her crime to herself, her family, and her supporters. Relying on her previous admissions and pleas of guilt, the judge denied Olson's motion to withdraw her plea. Only after this final ruling did Olson tremble with emotion and say she was sorry for harming others.

An *Alford* or nolo plea in this case would have undercut important procedural and substantive values and norms. If Olson had entered an *Alford* plea and never admitted guilt, it would have been wrong to punish her without an authoritative trial verdict. Instead of eventually apologizing, she might well have persisted in her denials to herself and to others. Continued denials would have led her friends, her family, and the public to doubt the justice of the system. Punishment in these circumstances would undercut the norm of punishing only those known to be blameworthy. In addition, consistent protestations of innocence would hinder closure for the victims and the community. Here, in contrast, Olson clearly admitted guilt in court, making her later denials less credible. The public could more easily believe that she had falsely protested her innocence to save face. In addition, the court could justify its ruling by pointing to Olson's earlier admissions, on the advice of counsel, in open court. The court's action vindicated the norm of not going back on one's word. Furthermore, after the judge confronted her with her earlier admissions, Olson took the first steps toward apology and reconciliation. In short, Olson's admissions of guilt in open court were much firmer bases for conviction, repentance, and closure than an *Alford* or nolo plea would have been.

What do you think? Does your response to Bibas's argument change depending on how many of the defendants who claim innocence actually *are* innocent?

4. Note that even the U.S. Justice Department is squeamish about *Alford* pleas. Its Manual for Federal Prosecutors says the following:

> Despite the constitutional validity of *Alford* pleas, such pleas should be avoided except in the most unusual circumstances, even if no plea agreement is involved and the plea would cover all pending charges. Such pleas are particularly undesirable when entered as part of an agreement with the government. Involvement by attorneys for the government in the inducement of guilty pleas by defendants who protest their innocence may create an appearance of prosecutorial overreaching. . . . Consequently, it is preferable to have a jury resolve the factual and legal dispute between the government and the defendant, rather than have government attorneys encourage defendants to plead guilty under circumstances that the public might regard as questionable or unfair.

United States Attorney's Manual, §9-27.440, http://www.justice.gov/usam/usam-9-27000-principles-federal-prosecution#9-27.440 (visited Aug. 15, 2015).

5. On the other hand, if you think that *Alford* pleas are somehow unfair, ask yourself this: are defendants, as a group, better off or worse off when *Alford* pleas are permitted? If they were not allowed, an innocent defendant's only options would be to lie and admit guilt, or go to trial and hope the jury sees his innocence. Why should defendants be denied the third option that *Alford* provides—refuse to lie and admit guilt, but still take the benefit of the deal offered by the prosecutor, so at least he can avoid the risk of a very high sentence at trial?

6. Although Mr. Alford professed to be innocent of the crime charged, the rest of the available evidence strongly suggested that he was, in fact, guilty. One persistent theme in the scholarly literature on guilty pleas and plea bargaining is the unquantifiable but generally perceived risk that at least some *truly* innocent defendants—especially those facing the possibility of serious prison time coupled with substantial offers of leniency from the prosecution—may plead guilty to crimes they did not commit. Consider the following:

> In an ideal world, factually innocent defendants would not be charged with crimes they did not commit. In that same world, innocent defendants who were wrongly charged would never plead guilty, but would go to trial and be acquitted by a jury of their peers. But that is not the world we live in. We now know, for example, due to the availability of DNA testing, that at least twenty-nine individuals who pled guilty to crimes they did not commit served a combined total of more than one hundred and fifty years in prison before their exonerations. Why do they do it?
>
> There are three principal reasons why innocent defendants plead guilty. First, innocent persons charged with relatively minor offenses often plead guilty in order to get out of jail, to avoid the hassle of having criminal charges hanging over their heads, or to avoid being punished for exercising their right to trial. Second, defendants who were wrongfully convicted, but have their conviction vacated on direct appeal or in post-conviction review proceedings, plead guilty to receive a sentence of time served and obtain their immediate (or at least imminent) freedom. Third, some innocent defendants plead guilty due to the fear of a harsh alternative punishment.

John H. Blume & Rebecca K. Helm, The Unexonerated: Factually Innocent Defendants Who Plead Guilty, 100 Cornell L. Rev. 157, 172-173 (2014).

7. In the context of guilty pleas, part of this "innocence problem" is related to the fact that it is difficult for truly innocent defendants to reliably "signal"—to the prosecution, the trial judge, and perhaps even their own defense lawyer—that they are, in fact, innocent. The "system" generally assumes that most, if not all, defendants are factually guilty, an assumption thought to be confirmed by the extremely high rates at which defendants plead guilty. As a matter of strategy, it is clearly in the best interests of *all* defendants, whether guilty or not, to feign innocence until a sufficiently attractive plea offer is made by the prosecution. So what can a truly innocent defendant do to "signal" that fact, and thereby avoid eventually being pushed (by better and better plea offers) into pleading guilty?

Some scholars have argued that the signaling issue is largely insurmountable, given the strong incentives for guilty defendants to mimic the signaling behavior of truly innocent ones. See Robert E. Scott & William J. Stuntz, Plea Bargaining as Contract, 101 Yale L.J. 1909 (1992). Russell Covey asserts in response that effective signaling may be possible, but not necessarily within the plea negotiation process itself:

> For signaling to occur, at least one party must have private information and an economic incentive to communicate it. Those conditions are typical of plea bargaining. Defendants usually know if they are innocent or guilty, and innocent defendants have powerful incentives to communicate their private information to prosecutors. The ease by which guilty defendants can mimic nonverifiable innocence claims made by innocent defendants, however, prevents prosecutors from taking those claims seriously. Observing this, Dean Robert Scott and Professor William Stuntz characterize plea bargaining's innocence problem as, at bottom, a signaling defect. . . .
>
> Prosecutors cannot infer anything reliable about the defendant's private information based on their responses to plea offers because too many other factors influence plea evaluation. As Dean Scott and Professor Stuntz observe, the signal sent by innocent defendants through their higher price demands is indistinguishable from the comparatively higher price demands of those who heavily discount the future or who are less risk-averse. Since criminals likely are (almost by definition) less risk-averse and heavy discounters, the "innocence signal" implicit in the rejection of a plea offer is almost certain to be imperceptible to prosecutors. Accordingly, prosecutors cannot adjust plea prices based on unverified defendant signals of innocence. The plea bargaining "game" thus results in a "pooling equilibrium" in which defendant's private information is not incorporated into the price of the plea. . . .
>
> I argue that the procedural mechanism best suited to perform the separating function necessary to achieve the goal of more accurate pleapricing is interrogation. Building on the insights of Seidmann and Stein's pathbreaking game-theoretic analysis of the privilege against self-incrimination,[144] the Article argues that the decision to cooperate or not cooperate in the pretrial investigation satisfies (in a partial way) the essential prerequisites of a signaling mechanism. Submitting to interrogation is costly to criminal suspects, and that cost is imposed differentially. Interrogation is not cost-free for innocent suspects, but innocent suspects' costs are less—sometimes far less—in submitting to interrogation than those of guilty suspects. Moreover, the signal produced in interrogation—cooperation in the interrogation room—is logically related to the subject of the signal: The suspect's guilt or innocence. And interrogation is, or at least can be, an economically rational move for innocent suspects. . . .

---

144. See generally Daniel J. Seidmann & Alex Stein, The Right to Silence Helps the Innocent: A Game-Theoretic Analysis of the Fifth Amendment Privilege, 114 Harv. L. Rev. 430, 448-449 (2000).

> [P]lea bargain theory must be modified to account for the substantial likelihood that plea bargain prices are influenced by signaling. Pretrial interrogation creates an obvious dilemma for guilty suspects, and the defendant's response to interrogation generates a signal permitting some plea price differentiation to occur among guilty and innocent defendants, a prediction supported by the empirical data. Even apart from the substantive information obtained from interrogation, the choice to submit to interrogation serves as an important signal to police and prosecutors that is manifested in plea prices. In short, there is good reason to believe that plea bargains are negotiated not only in the shadows of trial, but also in the shadows of strategic choices made by suspects prior to trial and, especially, in the interrogation room.

Russell D. Covey, Signaling and Plea Bargaining's Innocence Problem, 66 Wash. & Lee L. Rev. 73 (2009).

Although Rule 11 imposes a significant check on the guilty plea process, it is important not to overstate its role as a source for defense challenges to guilty pleas. Guilty pleas are consensual transactions; a plea hearing is not an adversarial process, and neither the government nor the defense has any interest in raising objections while the proceeding is taking place. So mistakes, like the failure to scrupulously follow the dictates of Rule 11(b), may often pass unnoticed. As a result, guilty pleas are often very difficult to challenge on direct appeal; in the absence of a contemporaneous objections, Rule 11 violations may be waived entirely on appeal, or at best subject to plain error review. (These topics are covered in Chapter 17.) Defendants rarely win such claims.

2.   The Effect of a Guilty Plea

A guilty plea resolves the substantive charges against the accused, but it does much more than that. Rule 11(b)(1) contains a long list of rights that the defendant gives up by pleading guilty, but the defendant has many other rights that the Rule does not mention. If a defendant pled guilty, but prior to that had properly raised challenges based on, say, an illegal search, improper joinder, or a coerced confession, what is the effect of a plea on these claims? And what about claims whose factual bases defendants did not know? Do defendants waive or forfeit these claims when pleading guilty, or only those they already know about? These questions prompted a great deal of litigation in the first two decades of the modern era of guilty pleas (roughly the 1970s and early 1980s, after plea bargaining was approved in Brady v. United States, 397 U.S. 742, 748 (1970)). But most of these arguments have now been resolved in the government's favor, as the following case shows.

UNITED STATES v. BROCE

Certiorari to the United States Court of Appeals for the Tenth Circuit
488 U.S. 563 (1989)

JUSTICE KENNEDY delivered the opinion of the Court.

. . . Respondents, upon entering guilty pleas, were convicted of two separate counts of conspiracy, but contend now that only one conspiracy existed and that double jeopardy principles require the conviction and sentence on the second count to be set aside. . . . We hold that the double jeopardy challenge is foreclosed by the guilty pleas and the judgments of conviction. . . .

[Broce and a construction company that he owned were charged with two conspiracies to rig bids and suppress competition in violation of the Sherman Antitrust Act. Both Broce and his company pled guilty to both charges; defendants did not challenge either the sufficiency of the plea colloquy or the adequacy of advice they received from counsel. In separate litigation that took place at about the same time, another local construction company and its head, Robert Beachner, were charged with participation in another bid-rigging conspiracy. Beachner and his company took their case to trial and were acquitted. The government then brought charges against Beachner for yet other bid-rigging conspiracies. Beachner moved to dismiss those new charges, on the ground that they were really part of the same conspiracy the government had charged earlier, and for which Beachner had been acquitted—the new charges thus violated double jeopardy. Beachner's double jeopardy argument was successful; his motion to dismiss was granted.

Broce at this point sought to raise the same argument in connection with his guilty plea. The Court assumed for purposes of the analysis that, like Beachner, Broce had a possibly winning double jeopardy claim—the double jeopardy clause bars two convictions for one crime, so if Broce was guilty of one conspiracy rather than two, one of his convictions would have to be overturned. The Court then turned to whether Broce had waived his double jeopardy claim when he pled guilty to both conspiracy charges.—EDS.]

. . . Respondents had the opportunity, instead of entering their guilty pleas, to challenge the theory of the indictments and to attempt to show the existence of only one conspiracy in a trial-type proceeding. They chose not to, and hence relinquished that entitlement. In light of Beachner['s litigation], respondents may believe that they made a strategic miscalculation. Our precedents demonstrate, however, that such grounds do not justify setting aside an otherwise valid guilty plea.

. . . [W]e held in McMann v. Richardson, 397 U.S. 759 (1970), that a counseled defendant may not make a collateral attack on a guilty plea on the allegation that he misjudged the admissibility of his confession. "Waiving trial entails the inherent risk that the good-faith evaluations of a reasonably competent attorney will turn out to be mistaken either as to the facts or as to what a court's judgment might be on given facts." Id., at 770. See also Tollett v. Henderson, 411 U.S. 258, 267 (1973) ("[J]ust as it is not sufficient for the criminal defendant seeking to set aside such a plea to show that his counsel in retrospect may not have correctly appraised the constitutional significance of certain historical facts, it is likewise not sufficient that he show that if counsel had pursued a certain factual inquiry such a pursuit would have uncovered a possible constitutional infirmity in the proceedings.").

Respondents have submitted the affidavit of Kenneth F. Crockett, who served as their attorney when their pleas were entered. Crockett avers that he did not discuss double jeopardy issues with respondents prior to their pleas, and that respondents had not considered the possibility of raising a double jeopardy defense before pleading. Respondents contend that, under these circumstances, they cannot be held to have waived the right to raise a double jeopardy defense because there was no "intentional relinquishment or abandonment of a known right or privilege." Johnson v. Zerbst, 304 U.S. 458, 464 (1938).

Our decisions have not suggested that conscious waiver is necessary with respect to each potential defense relinquished by a plea of guilty. Waiver in that sense is not required. For example, the respondent in *Tollett* pleaded guilty to first-degree murder, and later filed a petition for habeas corpus contending that his plea should be set aside because black citizens had been excluded from the grand jury that indicted him. The collateral challenge was foreclosed by the earlier guilty plea. Although at the time of the indictment the facts relating to the selection of the grand jury were not known to respondent and his attorney, we held that to be irrelevant. . . .

The Crockett affidavit, as a consequence, has no bearing on whether respondents' guilty plea served as a relinquishment of their opportunity to receive a factual hearing on a double jeopardy claim. Relinquishment derives not from any inquiry into a defendant's subjective understanding of the range of potential defenses, but from the admissions necessarily made upon entry of a voluntary plea of guilty. The trial court complied with Rule 11 in ensuring that respondents were advised that, in pleading guilty, they were admitting guilt and waiving their right to a trial of any kind. A failure by counsel to provide advice may form the basis of a claim of ineffective assistance of counsel, but absent such a claim it cannot serve as the predicate for setting aside a valid plea. . . . Respondents have not called into question the voluntary and intelligent character of their pleas, and therefore are not entitled to the collateral relief they seek.

An exception to the rule barring collateral attack on a guilty plea was established by our decisions in Blackledge v. Perry, 417 U.S. 21 (1974), and Menna v. New York, supra, but it has no application to the case at bar.

The respondent in *Blackledge* had been charged in North Carolina with the state-law misdemeanor of assault with a deadly weapon. Pursuant to state procedures, he was tried in the county District Court without a jury, but was permitted, once he was convicted, to appeal to the county Superior Court and obtain a trial de novo. After the defendant filed an appeal, the prosecutor obtained an indictment charging felony assault with a deadly weapon with intent to kill and inflict serious bodily injury. The defendant pleaded guilty. We held that the potential for prosecutorial vindictiveness against those who seek to exercise their right to appeal raised sufficiently serious due process concerns to require a rule forbidding the State to bring more serious charges against defendants in that position. The plea of guilty did not foreclose a subsequent challenge because in *Blackledge* . . . the defendant's right was "the right not to be haled into court at all upon the felony charge. The very initiation of proceedings against him . . . thus operated to deny him due process of law." 417 U.S., at 30-31.

The petitioner in *Menna* had refused, after a grant of immunity, to obey a court order to testify before a grand jury. He was adjudicated in contempt of court and sentenced to a term in civil jail. After he was released, he was indicted for the same refusal to answer the questions. He pleaded guilty and was sentenced, but then appealed on double jeopardy grounds. The New York Court of Appeals concluded that Menna had waived his double jeopardy claim by pleading guilty. We reversed, citing *Blackledge* for the proposition that "[w]here the State is precluded by the United States Constitution from haling a defendant into court on a charge, federal law requires that a conviction on that charge be set aside even if the conviction was entered pursuant to a counseled plea of guilty." 423 U.S., at 62. We added, however, an important qualification:

> We do not hold that a double jeopardy claim may never be waived. We simply hold that a plea of guilty to a charge does not waive a claim that—judged on its face—the charge is one which the State may not constitutionally prosecute.

Id., at 63, n. 2.

In neither *Blackledge* nor *Menna* did the defendants seek further proceedings at which to expand the record with new evidence. In those cases, the determination that the second indictment could not go forward should have been made by the presiding judge at the time the plea was entered on the basis of the existing record. Both *Blackledge* and *Menna* could be (and ultimately were) resolved without any need to venture beyond that record. In *Blackledge*, . . . the constitutional infirmity in the proceedings lay in the State's power to bring any indictment at all. In *Menna*, the indictment was facially duplicative of the earlier offense of which the defendant had been convicted and sentenced so that the admissions made by Menna's guilty plea could not conceivably be construed to extend beyond a redundant confession to the earlier offense.

Respondents here, in contrast, pleaded guilty to indictments that on their face described separate conspiracies. They cannot prove their claim by relying on those indictments and the existing record. Indeed, . . . they cannot prove their claim without contradicting those indictments, and that opportunity is foreclosed by the admissions inherent in their guilty pleas. We therefore need not consider [the question whether the defendant's acceptance of] . . . a plea bargain [with] concessions by the Government . . . heightens the already substantial interest . . . in the finality of the plea. . . .

NOTES AND QUESTIONS

1. *Broce*, and a large number of lower court cases like it, stand for the proposition that a valid and unconditional plea waives all non-jurisdictional defects that may have occurred in the case. With a few exceptions, whether the claim was known to the defense or was unknown, constitutional or non-constitutional, the courts' response to a post-guilty plea challenge is the same: a guilty plea is a decision to forego the full process of a trial, including the right to appeal errors and defects in the process. The benefits of a guilty plea come at a cost, and one of those costs is the loss of the right to appeal alleged errors.

2. This rule is broad but not absolute: jurisdictional challenges survive a guilty plea, and the denial of defendant's right to counsel of his own choosing survives as well. But *Broce* makes it clear that these exceptions are narrow. Based on the Court's discussions of Blackledge v. Perry and Menna v. New York, it would appear that by pleading guilty, defendants lose all claims other than those that both (1) suggest the government lacks the power to punish the defendant at all, and (2) can be resolved without further fact finding. Does this distinction make sense, or is it just an effort to cabin *Blackledge* and *Menna* without overruling them?[6]

---

6. Actually, there is one other category of claims that defendants retain after pleading guilty: claims that arise after the guilty plea is entered. In Mitchell v. United States, 526 U.S. 314 (1999), the defendant pled guilty, but refused to testify at her sentencing hearing; the sentencing judge ruled that she had waived her Fifth Amendment privilege against self-incrimination by pleading guilty. The Supreme Court disagreed, holding that Mitchell's guilty plea did not waive her Fifth Amendment right at the sentencing hearing.

3. Even claims like Broce's are not necessarily lost. As discussed elsewhere, such claims simply must be converted into ineffective assistance of counsel claims—that is, someone in Broce's position would have to show that counsel's failure to raise the double jeopardy issue prior to the plea was constitutionally ineffective, and that this failure caused "prejudice" within the meaning of Strickland v. Washington, 466 U.S. 668 (1984) (see Chapter 3 and Chapter 17).

4. Imagine a drug prosecution in which the defendant claims that the key evidence against him was seized illegally and hence is inadmissible. The defendant raised the issue unsuccessfully in the district court, but believes he may well succeed in the court of appeals. If the defendant's claim prevails, the drug charge will be dismissed. Otherwise, the defendant will plead guilty because the evidence of guilt is clear. The norm in criminal procedure is not to allow interlocutory appeals, so now both the defense and prosecution are in an awkward position. Defendant doesn't want to waive his claim by pleading guilty, but it seems unnecessary and wasteful to hold a full blown trial, where guilt is a foregone conclusion, just to preserve the suppression issue for appeal.

The answer is a conditional guilty plea. Under Rule 11(a)(2), parties can agree that defendant will plead guilty, thus avoiding an unnecessary trial, while preserving one or two critical issues for appeal. If the defendant loses on appeal the plea and resulting conviction stand. If the defendant wins, he is allowed to withdraw his guilty plea.

Given that a conditional plea gives the defendant the potential benefit of a negotiated, and thus perhaps more favorable, plea, and the right to challenge pretrial errors, why wouldn't the defense seek a conditional plea in most cases? Note that Rule 11(a)(2) requires both "the consent of the court and the government" in such cases. When, if ever, should a court *not* consent to a conditional plea? And why allow the government to veto one?

B.   Plea Bargaining

1.   History and Practice

JOHN H. LANGBEIN, UNDERSTANDING THE SHORT HISTORY OF PLEA BARGAINING

13 Law & Soc'y Rev. 261, 261-270 (1979)

. . . [P]lea bargaining was unknown during most of the history of the common law. Only in the nineteenth century [is there] significant evidence of the practice in either England or America. These findings beckon to the legal historian for explanation. In modern times, plea bargaining has become the primary procedure through which we dispose of the vast proportion of cases of serious crime. How then could common law procedure function for so many centuries without a practice that is today so prevalent and seemingly so indispensable? . . .

The main historical explanation for the want of plea bargaining in former centuries is, I believe, simple and incontrovertible. When we turn back to the period before the middle of the eighteenth century, we find that common law trial procedure exhibited a degree of efficiency that we now expect only of our nontrial procedure. *Jury trial was a summary proceeding.* Over the intervening two centuries the rise of the adversary system and the related development of the law of evidence has caused the common law jury trial to undergo a profound transformation, robbing it of the wondrous efficiency that had characterized it for so many centuries.

The initial point to grasp . . . is how rapidly jury trials were conducted. The surviving sources show that well into the eighteenth century when the Old Bailey sat, it tried between twelve and twenty felony cases per day, and provincial assizes operated with similar dispatch. . . .

How could the Old Bailey of the 1730s process a dozen and more cases to full jury trial in one day, whereas in modern times the average jury trial requires several days of court time?

(1) The most important factor that expedited jury trial was the want of counsel. Neither prosecution nor defense was represented in ordinary criminal trials. The accused was forbidden counsel; the prosecution might be conducted by a lawyer, but in practice virtually never was. The victim or other complaining witness, sometimes aided by the law constable and the law justice of the peace, performed the role we now assign to the public prosecutor, gathering evidence and presenting it at trial. As a result, jury trial was not yet protracted by the motions, maneuvers, and speeches of counsel that afflict the modern trial.

(2) There was, for example, no voir dire of prospective jurors conducted by counsel. In practice the accused took the jury as he found it and virtually never employed his challenge rights. Indeed, at the Old Bailey only two twelve-man jury panels were used to discharge the entire caseload of as many as a hundred felony trials in a few days. Each jury usually heard several unrelated cases before deliberating on any. Often the juries rendered verdicts in these cases of life and death "at the bar," that is, so rapidly that they did not even retire from the courtroom to deliberate.

(3) The most efficient testimonial resource available to a criminal court is almost always the criminal defendant. He has, after all, been close enough to the events to get himself prosecuted. In modern Anglo-American procedure we have constructed the privilege against self-incrimination in a way that often encourages the accused to rely entirely upon the intermediation of counsel and say nothing in his own defense. But in the period before the accused had counsel, there could be no practical distinction between his roles as defender and as witness. The accused spoke continuously at the trial, replying to prosecution witnesses and giving his own version of the events.

(4) The presentation of evidence and the cross-examination of witnesses and accused took place in a fashion that was businesslike but lacked the time-consuming stiffness of a modern adversary trial. . . .

(5) The common law of evidence, which has injected such vast complexity into modern criminal trials, was virtually nonexistent as late as the opening decades of the eighteenth century. The trial judge had an alternative system of jury control that was both swifter and surer than the subsequent resort to rules of admissibility and exclusion. He had unrestricted powers of comment on the merits of criminal cases; he could reject a verdict that displeased him and require the jury to deliberate further; indeed, until 1670 he could fine a jury that persisted in acquitting against his wishes. . . .

(7) Finally, there was as yet virtually no appeal in criminal cases. Accordingly, the familiar modern machinations of counsel directed to provoking and preserving error for appeal were unknown.

It should surprise no one that in a system of trial as rough and rapid as this there was no particular pressure to develop nontrial procedure, or otherwise to encourage the accused to waive his right to jury trial. . . .

We should also not be surprised that this summary form of jury trial perished over the last two centuries. The level of safeguard against mistaken conviction was in several respects below what civilized people now require. The hard question, which remains unrescarched, is why the pressure for greater safeguard led in the Anglo-American procedure to the common law of evidence and dominance of the trial by lawyers, reforms that ultimately destroyed the system in the sense that they rendered trials unworkable as an ordinary or routine dispositive procedure for cases of serious crime. Similar pressures for safeguard were being felt in the Continental legal systems in the same period, but they led to reforms in nonadversarial procedure that preserved the institution of trial.

We think that we understand why there was no plea bargaining while jury trial retained its character as a summary proceeding. And we have no difficulty seeing that once jury trial had been overlaid with the complexity that characterizes it today, it could no longer be used as the exclusive dispositive proceeding for cases of serious crime. But these insights leave us still a good distance from explaining why the particular adaptation that resulted was plea bargaining. . . . We may, however, indicate some features of the earlier system of jury trial that predisposed Anglo-American procedure to plea bargaining.

The tradition of private prosecution has been a feature of English criminal procedure nearly as striking and tenacious as the jury trial. . . . Although the English did place some limits upon the power of the private prosecutor to compromise criminal litigation, the prosecutorial function nevertheless grew up steeped in the conceptual forms of private discretion as opposed to official duty. Even in America, where the public prosecutor has a longer history than in the mother jurisdiction, the district attorney fell heir to the discretion of the citizen prosecutor whom he succeeded. When, therefore, the transformation of jury trial left the trial system clogged, the pressure of caseloads could find release in the exercise of prosecutorial discretion much more naturally than on the Continent, where the prosecutorial function has for so long been performed by officials and where there has been constant concern to regulate their discretion.

. . . For many centuries [the criminal defendant], too, has had the civil litigant's right to concede liability without trial, through the use of the guilty plea. This device, now familiar to us as the doctrinal basis of our nontrial plea bargaining procedure, also turns out to be an Anglo-American peculiarity. In Continental legal systems someone who is accused of a serious crime may confess, but he will nevertheless go to trial. . . . [T]he common law treated confession as a waiver of trial, by contrast with the Continental practice of viewing it as merely evidence of the most cogent kind. . . .

An adaptation seemingly less radical than the nontrial procedure of plea bargaining would have been to institute trial without jury, what we now call bench trial, in cases of serious crime. Although it has become a familiar *via media* between jury trial and the guilty plea in our own day, in the nineteenth century bench trial was resisted. . . .

In England the great political trials associated with the fall of Stuart aristocracy and the evolution of the eighteenth-century constitution had sanctified jury trial in political theory. . . . In America, where the judiciary's association with the excesses of English colonial administration had led the framers to make jury trial a constitutional right, bench trial was all the harder to envision. . . .

Not only was the nontrial solution of plea bargaining more rapid than bench trial, it also protected the weak, elective American trial bench from the moral responsibility for adjudication and from the political liability of unpopular decisions. In an ideological milieu in which the mounting defects of adversary jury trial could not have been admitted and discussed even if they had been correctly understood, it was easier for the judiciary to tolerate trial waivers than jury waivers—easier, that is, for the judges to allow the prosecutor to wring out a plea concession than to bring themselves to insist on adjudication before condemnation. [Citations and footnotes omitted.]

NOTES AND QUESTIONS

1. Professor Langbein's article appeared as part of a symposium on plea bargaining; two other articles in that symposium also addressed plea bargaining's strange history. See Albert W. Alschuler, Plea Bargaining and Its History, 13 Law & Soc'y Rev. 211 (1979); Lawrence M. Friedman, Plea Bargaining in Historical Perspective, 13 Law & Soc'y Rev. 247 (1979).

2. On Langbein's account, plea bargaining arose out of the intersection of three phenomena: elaborate jury trials, the use of lawyers to present the prosecution and defense cases, and prosecutorial discretion. Perhaps that means that if we are to do away with plea bargaining, we need to do away with at least one of its three causes. Which one? Each has substantial merit, does it not? Elaborate jury trials are designed to provide much more accurate adjudication than the kind of slapdash Old Bailey proceedings Langbein describes. The use of lawyers is likewise designed to ensure accuracy—especially accuracy on the defendant's side, the accuracy of guilty verdicts. Prosecutorial discretion offers at least the opportunity for mercy and for treating different defendants differently, even if they engaged in the same conduct—no small thing in a world where criminal codes cover as much conduct as they do in the United States. If all those features of the criminal process are good and if plea bargaining follows from them, should we therefore keep plea bargaining?

3. The most detailed, and best, discussion of how plea bargaining came to dominate American criminal procedure is George Fisher, Plea Bargaining's Triumph, 109 Yale L.J. 857 (2000). Fisher focused his research on Middlesex County, Massachusetts; some of his conclusions may not be generalizable, though he maintains that most are. The following excerpt presents a rough sketch of his conclusions.

GEORGE FISHER, PLEA BARGAINING'S TRIUMPH

109 Yale L.J. 857, 864-868 (2000)

. . . [The] story of plea bargaining's rise begins in the opening decade of the nineteenth century. . . . Told chronologically, the story divides fairly neatly into two parts. During the first three-quarters or so of the nineteenth century, plea bargaining in Massachusetts advanced mainly in the realm of liquor-law prosecutions and murder cases, where . . . prosecutors had the power to negotiate pleas without any participation by the judge. These early deals took the form of *charge bargaining*—that is, in exchange for the defendant's plea to one or more of several charges, the prosecutor dropped the others or (in the case of murder) reduced the charge to a lesser offense. In the last quarter of the century, as judges converted to the cause, plea bargaining most often took the form of *sentence bargaining*, in which the defendant's plea won a reduced sentence. Backed by judges as well as prosecutors, plea bargaining now broke the narrow hold of liquor and murder prosecutions and conquered the whole penal territory—so that by century's close, guilty pleas accounted for some eighty-seven percent of criminal adjudications in Middlesex County. . . .

. . . My research in Middlesex County confirms earlier findings of a strikingly high rate of plea bargaining in Massachusetts liquor-law prosecutions in the early nineteenth century. Various . . . theories might explain a link between liquor prosecutions and plea bargaining, but the evidence overwhelmingly points to one—that the distinctive penalty scheme that the legislature created for the liquor laws, which assigned a fixed fine to almost every offense, deprived the judge of almost all sentencing discretion and put the prosecutor in a position to manipulate sentences by manipulating charges. Similarly, in capital [murder] cases, the prosecutor had the power to spare mandatory death by permitting them to plead guilty to a lesser charge. Prosecutors quickly exploited these narrow grants of sentencing authority and put in place a very modern practice of charge bargaining for pleas.

. . . [I]t is easy to see why prosecutors wanted to plea bargain. Prosecutors of the nineteenth century, like prosecutors today, plea bargained to ease their crushing workloads, made heavier in the nineteenth century both by their part-time status and utter lack of staff and by a caseload explosion perhaps set off by newly founded police forces and massive immigration. And of course they plea bargained to avoid the risk that wanton juries would spurn their painstakingly assembled cases. . . .

. . . Massachusetts legislators reacted sourly when they discovered how prosecutors were using the power unwittingly bestowed on them by the liquor law's rigid penalty scheme. At mid-century the legislature eliminated this power and very nearly succeeded in snuffing out prosecutorial plea bargaining in liquor cases. The legislature did not, however, disturb the prosecutor's power to conduct charge bargaining in murder cases, for there had been relatively few such bargains by mid-century. The result was that during the third quarter of the nineteenth century, plea bargaining advanced more dramatically in murder cases than in any other category. Even in liquor cases, the legislature's efforts to eradicate prosecutorial charge bargaining failed. After losing formal power to manipulate sentences in liquor cases, prosecutors retreated to the more covert and informal tactic of placing these cases "on file." This procedural maneuver, often done in exchange for a defendant's guilty plea, allowed prosecutors to elude altogether the legislature's sentencing provisions. The primitive device of *on-file plea bargaining* evolved directly into what we know today as probation. By the end of the century, probation had become one of plea bargaining's most dependable foot soldiers.

. . . [Now] consider the part played by defendants. It is not hard to see why defendants, given the chance, would plead guilty for a measure of leniency, but it is far less clear why their behavior on this score might change over time. Middlesex court records disclose that during the first half of the nineteenth century, decades before plea bargaining began its dramatic ascent, there had been a long decline in the proportion of non-liquor cases that ended in a plea. . . . [T]hese early guilty pleas were not plea bargains made in exchange for leniency, but rather the hopeless gestures of unrepresented defendants who properly saw that they had little chance of winning if they went to trial on their own. The gradual increase in the number of defendants who chose trial during the first part of the century therefore may mean that more and more defendants had counsel. Then, in the third quarter of the century, a sudden assault on the power of defendants to take their cases to trial may have reversed this course and helped to speed plea bargaining's rise. Laws passed in Massachusetts and elsewhere that gave defendants the right to testify at trial had the probably unintended effect of discouraging defendants with criminal pasts from going to trial. Seasoned criminals knew that if they took the stand to claim their innocence, the prosecutor could impeach their testimony with their old convictions and thereby destroy any real chance of acquittal. Yet if they failed to testify, defendants believed, juries would convict them for their silence. Together with the growing practice of probation, defendant-testimony laws confronted every defendant with a good reason to plea bargain. Defendant-testimony laws helped to persuade accomplished criminals to plead guilty, while the promise of probation, which was available almost exclusively to first offenders who pled guilty, served as an incentive for everyone else.

The combined willingness of all prosecutors and many defendants to bargain for pleas was not, however, enough for the practice to thrive outside the narrow context of liquor laws and murder cases. The statutory penalty structure for most crimes gave Massachusetts judges such great discretion in sentencing that the prosecutor typically could not unilaterally guarantee a low enough sentence to win the defendant's plea. Plea bargaining's sweeping triumph during the last quarter of the nineteenth century suggests, therefore, that judges had entered plea bargaining's ranks. . . . [A] caseload explosion on the civil side of Massachusetts courthouses helped force this change of judicial heart on the criminal side, for in Massachusetts, as in most American jurisdictions, the same judges sat on both civil and criminal cases. The industrial boom of the last part of the nineteenth century—and especially the spread of railroads and street cars—spawned a whole new strain of personal injury litigation that, case for case, absorbed far more time than the contractual nonpayment cases that once had filled the civil dockets. The figures in Massachusetts are clear: As judges devoted a hugely increasing proportion of their time to the civil caseload, they devoted a shrinking proportion to the criminal caseload, and they resolved more and more criminal cases by guilty plea. Judges apparently discovered that they had more power to spur pleas in criminal cases than to coerce settlements in civil cases. After all, a criminal court judge could credibly promise a reward in exchange for a plea or threaten a penalty for going to trial, but in civil court, the jury—not the judge—generally set the loser's penalty.

By century's end, all three of the courtroom's major actors—prosecutor, defendant, and judge—had found reasons to favor the plea-bargaining system. For prosecutor and judge, who together held most of the power that mattered, the spread of plea bargaining did not merely deliver marvelously efficient relief from a suffocating workload. It also spared the prosecutor the risk of loss and the judge the risk of reversal, and thereby protected the professional reputations of each. In fact, by erasing the possibility of either factual or legal error in the proceedings, plea bargains protected the reputation and hence the legitimacy of the system as a whole. . . .

. . . The power of the various actors who stood to gain from plea bargaining became, in a sense, plea bargaining's power. This collective, systemic interest in plea bargaining encouraged the rise of those institutions of criminal procedure that helped plea bargaining and hindered those that hurt it. In the nineteenth century, plea bargaining fostered probation's rise and thereby created a hugely versatile plea-bargaining tool. In the late nineteenth and early twentieth centuries, plea bargaining helped stave off the indeterminate sentence, which had threatened to halt plea bargaining's progress. And in the twentieth century, plea bargaining played a surprisingly direct role in assisting the creation of public defenders. In turn, these organizations for defense of the poor assured that in a majority of criminal cases, the defense lawyer would share the prosecutor's and judge's interests in maximizing systemic efficiency—and hence in plea bargaining. These examples of plea bargaining's influence over other institutions of criminal procedure are merely case studies within a larger trend. In fact, it is hard to think of a single enduring development in criminal procedure in the last 150 years that has not aided plea bargaining's cause.

Finally, [consider] how the power to plea bargain evolved in the late twentieth century. Before the advent of modern sentencing guidelines, both prosecutor and judge held some power to plea bargain without the other's cooperation. The result of their mutually independent bargaining strength was a certain balance of power, which to some degree protected defendants from abuses of power by either official. Today, however, sentencing guidelines have recast whole chunks of the criminal code in the mold of the old Massachusetts liquor laws. In the process, they have unsettled the balance of bargaining power by ensuring that the prosecutor, who always had the strongest interest in plea bargaining, now has the unilateral power to deal. . . . [Citations and footnotes omitted.]

NOTES AND QUESTIONS

1. Notice that while Professor Langbein emphasizes the role of jury trials and defense lawyers in plea bargaining's rise, Professor Fisher emphasizes the role of sentencing—Massachusetts prosecutors gained the power to bargain by gaining power over defendants' sentences, and that power has been reinforced by developments like probation and the rise of detailed sentencing guidelines. Who ought to have dominant power over sentencing? If prosecutors have the power to dismiss charges altogether—and with judges effectively disabled from reviewing such decisions, see Chapter 9—should prosecutors not also have the power to place a cap on the sentence a defendant can receive if he is convicted? If they can fix maximum sentences, why not minimum sentences? Is there a principled difference between ceilings and floors in this context?

2. Do you agree with the conclusion that "it is hard to think of a single enduring development in criminal procedure in the last 150 years that has not aided plea bargaining's cause"? What about the growth of a large and detailed body of search and seizure law enforced by the exclusionary rule? Assuming that development is "enduring"—it shows no signs of disappearing anytime soon—does it help plea bargaining or hinder it?

3. Whatever one may think about the causes of plea bargaining, there is little disagreement about its effects. The Supreme Court has quoted with approval the following apt description:

> To a large extent . . . horse trading [between prosecutor and defense counsel] determines who goes to jail and for how long. That is what plea bargaining is. It is not some adjunct to the criminal justice system; it *is* the criminal justice system.

Missouri v. Frye, 132 S. Ct. 1399, 1407 (2012), quoting Robert E. Scott and William J. Stuntz, Plea Bargaining as Contract, 101 Yale L.J. 1909, 1912 (1992).

4. There is an enormous literature on plea bargaining, but very little of it seeks to describe what defense attorneys and prosecutors actually do, and what they actually think about it. The best such description comes in an excellent short book by Milton Heumann, excerpted below. Heumann interviewed defense attorneys, prosecutors, and trial judges in three cities in Connecticut in the mid-1970s. Because the interviews took place decades ago, some of the examples are dated, and the sentences his interviewees discuss are lower than would be the case today; but the general picture still fits with the practice in many, probably most, jurisdictions.

The excerpt that follows begins with a discussion of how new criminal defense attorneys think about their jobs, then shifts to how they come to embrace plea bargaining, and finally closes with some discussion of how prosecutors think about and practice plea bargaining.

MILTON HEUMANN, PLEA BARGAINING: THE EXPERIENCES OF PROSECUTORS, JUDGES, AND DEFENSE ATTORNEYS

49-50, 57-59, 61-63, 76-78, 89, 100-103, 105-106
(1978)

[New criminal defense attorneys] shared several general expectations about what working in the criminal justice system would be like. They assumed that most cases would be given lengthy and detailed consideration. In law school, they had been trained to dissect appellate cases; their briefs on legal cases were finely honed pieces undertaken only after extensive research and deliberation. As one judge put it, they had learned to have a "romance with each case."

> You have a romance with each case. You're interested in the legal aspects, you go up to the stacks, you go to this book, that book, the index of legal periodicals. . . . You rewrite, and each one means something. And as you write, you change your style, and you find that there is a phrase here, or a phrase there, it's creativity that you are in love with. Each appellate case, each line, each finding, each paragraph would mean something.

Because of both substantive and procedural concerns, newcomers expected that their criminal court cases would require comparable time and effort. They assumed that disputable legal questions would characterize many of those cases.

> Q.   Did you think that legal issues would be more important in terms of the criminal cases you would be handling?
> A.   Well, I suppose, coming out of law school, you thought that justice . . . you know, we had some really good teachers; they talked about justice and the great principles of the Constitution to be upheld, and the great Fourth Amendment, and the Fifth, and the Sixth, and such. . . . I anticipated that I would be working on constitutional cases much more than has been the case. . . .

In the process of handling their cases, new defense attorneys learn that the reality of the court differs from what they had expected; through rewards and sanctions, they are also taught to proceed in a certain fashion. . . .

The most important thing the new defense attorney learns is that most of his clients are factually guilty. His raw material is not typically the railroaded innocent defendant; instead, it is an individual who, in all likelihood, is guilty as charged, or at least is guilty of an offense related to the charge. . . .

[These attorneys] learn of the defendant's guilt in several ways. Attorneys with primarily circuit court practices handle mostly misdemeanants.[7] These clients often perceive their own cases to be relatively minor, and they frequently and freely admit their guilt during the first or second meeting with the attorney. . . . [T]hey are more concerned about "getting it over with" than with disputing their own guilt. . . .

In superior court cases, defendants are less likely to own up to the offense in their initial contact with the defense attorney. Experienced defense attorneys posit that the defendant's reluctance is based on the belief that a defense attorney will work harder for a client that he assumes innocent. Whatever the explanation, the defendant at first offers a story that exculpates him. The newer the defense attorney, the more likely he is to believe the defendant's version of what happened. It is only when he confronts the state's attorney with the defendant's story that he learns that there is more to the matter than the defendant first led him to believe. . . . Skepticism in evaluating the defendant's story, then, is something new attorneys learn. Over time they become veritable cynics.

> Yeah, well, you know . . . the first year you practice law you believe everything your client tells you. The second year you practice, you believe everything that the other side tells you. The third year you don't know who's telling the truth. Most people tend not to believe their clients that much, justifiably.

. . . At the same time that he is learning piecemeal about the factual culpability of most defendants and the futility of legal challenge, the new defense attorney is forced to decide how to proceed in given cases. His options are twofold: He can opt for an adversary posture (motions and trials), or he can engage in plea bargaining. . . . He is taught the risks of being an adversary and the benefits of being a plea bargainer.

His education begins almost immediately. In every case the defense attorney needs certain information that the prosecutor possesses. This material includes the police report, the defendant's record, the basic facts of the case, and so on.

. . . [T]here is a formal way to obtain some of this material—through filing a Motion for Discovery and a Bill of Particulars. The new defense attorney assumes that these motions are in order in every case. What he is taught, though, is that the prosecutors resent these motions. Prosecutors prefer to communicate the information orally and informally, thus relieving themselves of the burden of preparing typewritten responses in every case. Since they assume that the case will be settled by a plea bargain, they feel a formal response to be an unwarranted waste of time. . . . The following remarks, by circuit and superior court prosecutors respectively, illustrate the hostility to these motions, and the sanctions that are brought to bear.

> And then we have the open-file policy for public defenders. They can look at all the files they want. There was a time when some new public defenders started filing

---

7. In Connecticut at the time of Heumann's study, circuit courts had jurisdiction over misdemeanors and some felonies; superior courts had jurisdiction over more serious felonies. —EDS.

Bills of Particulars. Now, if I am going to show you all my notes, why would you file a Bill of Particulars? If they handle us like that, close the files to them. Let them file their bills, and we'll argue the Bill of Particulars. Don't forget, they've got ten cases here and ten cases upstairs, and they've got to run up and down those stairs. Me, I'm in this one courtroom. I call the names, and I argue them. You know what I mean? So, they hassle you like that. . . . Same with private attorneys. There is an easy way and a hard way for them to get their fees. One way you can make the lawyer earn his fee; the other way you can have the lawyer come in, grab his thing, and run. If he wants to be a ball-breaker, I say, "File your motions, Pal." He has to file a Bill of Particulars, and then he'll have to come back to argue it. Then if he wants to put in a not-guilty plea to the jury, he comes back again. He comes back, and I say, "Oh, we have a case going on. You'll have to come back next week." So this guy is a private attorney, and he's running around trying to make money. He doesn't want to come to our court ten times for a lousy case. And with the public defenders, we control the docket in court, so you hassle them. You know, call one case, the guy upstairs runs downstairs, and back and forth. It's like a kid's game, but you know, I like to get along with people if I can, and I don't try to be obnoxious to people, but if a person hassles me, tries to make my life more difficult, I will make his more difficult.

. . . [W]hat I try to tell every new attorney who comes in . . . I try to "steer them straight." I'll call them in on the first case we're dealing with and say: "Look, there are two ways to practice law here. You can file all the motions you want, harass me any way you want, but you and your client in the long run are not going to gain anything. Or, do you want to come in, I'll tell you what my file has, I'll show you what my file has, and we can talk about the case. It's your choice." Now, he may give me a hard time the first or second time around, but, you know, the aggravations can be going both ways, and eventually most people come to the point where they'll prefer to sit down and see what I have rather than go into court and make a big production of everything.

. . . [In order to bargain successfully, defense attorneys] need to develop a sense of "what the case is worth." How are they to judge a prosecutor's offer which falls substantially below the maximum the charge allows? Is it a good deal? Could it be better? Is it in line with what other attorneys receive?

Newcomers learn to answer these questions through experience. All outside advice is sought and cherished. But, without exception, every attorney interviewed indicated the necessity of developing his own "feel for a case." . . . Essentially, it is an impressionistic multiple regression model carried in the attorney's head. It is a way of sorting and weighing the sundry factors that enter into a disposition. Attorneys believe it can be learned only through experience in negotiating cases. Once an attorney has a feel for cases, he knows whether to try or plea bargain a case; if he chooses plea bargaining, he knows how to weigh factors as diverse as the defendant's record, the facts of the case, the prosecutor's personality, the prosecutor's willingness to go to trial, the judge's reactions to specific types of crimes, the precedents in terms of prior dispositions for this type of offense, and so on. He is confident that he can predict early what disposition is obtainable. . . .

> You know, I think I know what I'm doing. . . . I've been a lawyer for a few years; I've specialized in criminal law. I can analyze a case; I can tell a defendant in a few minutes just what's going to happen, what should be done and all.
>
> I look at a file and I know I can beat it. So I know that maybe I'll have it continued, with a plea, and file motions, maybe one or two or three times, but I'm going to get it [dismissed]. Then on the other hand, you know, this guy has to plead to something.

You know that after you talk to him and read the sheet. You know he'll have to plead to something.

I can take twenty-five files and look them over and, maybe without even speaking to the defendant, predict what is likely to happen. It's difficult to think that you could do that, but you can read a police report and the facts of the case, and because you have read so many and know that this guy should do this, and the prosecutor should do that. You have a good idea completely ahead of time.

Q. How does a new attorney learn what a case is worth?

A. Well, the new guy is in trouble. He's got to learn the hard way, get battered around. . . . You've got to put together a lot of things. You got to start off with the offense and the circumstances surrounding the events, naturally. Then you got to take the defendant, his record, . . . his family situation, anything good that you have going for you. These are the textbook things to look for. Then you got things that aren't in the textbooks. The month of the year. I've always made it a practice to do great things in December. The courts are closing; you want to get people out of the jails. It's the season, to a certain extent. I always save some of my real problems for the last day of court before Christmas recess. Nobody's going to turn me down. One of the things you'll also acquire a feel for, you get to know the people that you're dealing with. We all have our hang-ups. Some prosecutors get very upset with certain types of crimes, certain types of defendants. Sometimes they had the guy before, so they know him too well. . . .

Q. How did you learn to plea bargain? How did you learn what a case is worth and what you could get?

A. Well, there are no courses given on it. It's like . . . Well, I guess you could analogize it to making love. You know, it's something you can't teach; you can't put it in a book; you can't give a lecture on it. But, like making love, you do it enough times, you learn to like it, and you'll get good at it. . . .

Q. So generally you'd opt for plea bargaining?

A. Well . . . let me say this. It isn't so much that I'm going to get screwed at trial . . . it's just that I can do so much without going to trial. It isn't even the fear of what happens to you after trial so much as the fact that it's almost an irrelevant consideration. The fact is that in the plea bargaining system—which is not so much an alternative to trial as the system—you get good results by plea bargaining.

. . . Prosecutors and state's attorneys learn that their roles primarily entail the processing of factually guilty defendants. Contrary to their expectations that problems of establishing factual guilt would be central to their job, they find that in most cases the evidence in the file is sufficient to conclude (and prove) that the defendant is factually guilty. For those cases where there is a substantial question as to factual guilt, the prosecutor has the power—and is inclined to exercise it—to . . . dismiss the case. . . .

Furthermore, [the prosecutor] finds that defense attorneys only infrequently contest the prosecutor's own conclusion that the defendant is guilty. In their initial approach to the prosecutor they may raise the possibility that the defendant is factually innocent, but in most subsequent discussions their advances focus on disposition and not on the problem of factual guilt. Thus, from the prosecutor's own reading of the file . . . and from comments of his "adversary," he learns that he begins with the upper hand. . . .

In addition to learning of the factual culpability of most defendants, the prosecutor also learns that defendants would be hard pressed to raise legal challenges to the state's case. . . . [M]ost cases are simply barren of any contestable legal issue, and nothing in the prosecutor's file or the defense attorney's arguments leads the prosecutor to conclude otherwise. . . . What remains problematic is the sentence the defendant will receive. . . .

Prosecutors and state's attorneys draw sharp distinctions between serious and nonserious cases. In both instances, they assume the defendant guilty, but they are looking for different types of dispositions, dependent upon their classification of the case. If it is a nonserious matter, they are amenable to defense requests for a small fine in the circuit court, some short, suspended sentence, or some brief period of probation; similarly, in a nonserious superior court matter the state's attorney is willing to work out a combination suspended sentence and probation. The central concern with these nonserious cases is to dispose of them quickly. . . .

On the other hand, if the case is serious, the prosecutor and state's attorney are likely to be looking for time. The serious case cannot be quickly disposed of by a no-time alternative. These are cases in which we would expect more involved and lengthy plea bargaining negotiations.

Whether the case is viewed as serious or nonserious depends on factors other than the formal charge(s) the defendant faces. For example, these non-formal considerations might include the degree of harm done the victim, the amount of violence employed by the defendant, the defendant's prior record, the characteristics of the victim and defendant, the defendant's motive; all are somewhat independent of formal charge, and yet all weigh heavily in the prosecutor's judgment of the seriousness of the case. Defendants facing the same formal charges, then, may find that prosecutors sort their cases into different categories. . . .

> After a matter of time you just see so much that you really . . . You must always remember there are always two sides to the story, even though somebody might've gotten belted with a pipe, and it is a serious offense, but there might be something in mitigation to that. You know, there are some statutes that are mandatory minimum time. Assault in the third degree with a dangerous weapon is mandatory time of one year. Now if we stuck to that statute and subsection, if we stuck to that, we'd be trying everything out there; there'd be a lot of people going away for a minimum of one year. But a lot of times we allow a little flexibility; we give them assault in the third but not with a dangerous weapon, and then we or the judge look at the facts. This kid today was, an example, the kid who hit the guy on the wrist with a pipe. Now technically he was guilty of assault with a dangerous weapon; he could have been charged with assault in the third with a dangerous weapon, and the mandatory minimum one year in jail. But the kid had a clean record, the fight was no big thing, so I gave him assault in the third, under subsection one, which is not with a dangerous weapon, and we were looking for a suspended sentence. That's what the judge did, thirty days suspended.

. . . In some serious cases, the prosecutor or state's attorney may not be looking for time. Generally, these are the cases in which the prosecutor has a problem establishing either the factual or legal guilt of the defendant, and thus is willing to settle for a plea to the charge and offer a recommendation of a suspended sentence. The logic is simple: The prosecutor feels the defendant is guilty of the offense but fears that if he insists on time, the defense attorney will go to trial and uncover the factual or legal defects of the state's case. Thus, the prosecutor "sweetens the deal" to extract a guilty plea and to decrease the likelihood that the attorney will gamble on complete vindication. . . .

NOTES AND QUESTIONS

1. If Heumann's picture is accurate, to what degree should we call plea bargaining "bargaining"? The label implies exchange, with each side giving something valuable to the other. It is easy to see what prosecutors give defendants. What do ordinary defendants — those who lack strong legal or factual claims — give prosecutors?

2. Defense attorneys and prosecutors alike seem convinced that the vast majority of defendants are guilty. Presumably, though, at least a few defendants are innocent of the charges brought against them. Who identifies those few defendants? How likely is it that this sorting process proceeds accurately?

3. Both prosecutors and defense attorneys regularly talk about customary "prices" for particular sorts of crime — the "feel" for what sentence a case would bring that lawyers acquired over time. Where do those customary prices come from? Who decides them, and how? What political or legal checks limit them?

4. The major point of Heumann's book is that the large majority of defense attorneys, prosecutors, and judges come to their jobs skeptical of plea bargaining but, over time, come to endorse the practice. One might argue that the breadth of that endorsement is itself a strong defense of plea bargaining — that if all the relevant actors (Heumann also notes that most *defendants* seem to embrace plea bargaining) find the practice acceptable and even a positive feature of the system, the rest of us should be untroubled by it. Are you persuaded? If not, why should the opinions of those who engage in this practice be disregarded?

5. The following sections deal with the law that surrounds plea bargaining. That law concerns three basic issues: the limits (if any) on the government's ability to threaten a defendant with serious adverse consequences for taking a case to trial; the limits (if any) on the subject matter of the bargain offered; and the manner in which the bargain is interpreted and enforced, both against the government and against the defense. As you read these materials, ask yourself whether, and if so how, these rules are likely to affect real-world behavior by the kind of lawyers Heumann interviewed.

Stop

2. Inducements to Plead

The next main case, Brady v. United States, marked the first time the Supreme Court approved the constitutionality of inducing a guilty plea through plea bargaining. As noted in Section A, above, prior to this time the practice of inducing pleas went forward but mostly under the table, with defendants proclaiming in open court that their pleas were the product of neither promises nor threats, and with courts declining to inquire into the presence or absence of any concessions by the prosecutor. *Brady*'s significance is thus twofold: First, the decision validates the legitimacy of bargaining for guilty pleas, and second, the decision brings that bargaining process into the open, and hence potentially under legal regulation. Plea bargaining is a market, but it is today a regulated market. Before *Brady*, it was mostly a black market.

Brady is also important, however, because of what it tells us about the degree of pressure the government can bring to bear to induce a guilty plea. As you read *Brady* and the material that follows it, ask whether a defendant who pleads guilty in response to the government's pressure has truly made a voluntary choice, and, relatedly, whether the pressure is the type that might induce an innocent person to plead guilty.

BRADY v. UNITED STATES

Certiorari to the United States Court of Appeals for the Tenth Circuit
397 U.S. 742 (1970)

JUSTICE WHITE delivered the opinion of the Court.

In 1959, petitioner was charged with kidnaping in violation of 18 U.S.C. §1201(a).[1] Since the indictment charged that the victim of the kidnaping was not liberated unharmed, petitioner faced a maximum penalty of death if the verdict of the jury should so recommend. Petitioner, represented by competent counsel throughout, first elected to plead not guilty. . . . Upon learning that his codefendant, who had confessed to the authorities, would plead guilty and be available to testify against him, petitioner changed his plea to guilty. His plea was accepted after the trial judge twice questioned him as to the voluntariness of his plea.[2] Petitioner was sentenced to 50 years' imprisonment, later reduced to 30.

In 1967, petitioner sought relief under 28 U.S.C. §2255, claiming that his plea of guilty was not voluntarily given because §1201(a) operated to coerce his plea, because his counsel exerted impermissible pressure upon him, and because his plea was induced by representations with respect to reduction of sentence and clemency. . . .

That a guilty plea is a grave and solemn act to be accepted only with care and discernment has long been recognized. Central to the plea and the foundation for entering judgment against the defendant is the defendant's admission in open court that he committed the acts charged in the indictment. He thus stands as a witness against himself and he is shielded by the Fifth Amendment from being compelled to do so—hence the minimum requirement that his plea be the voluntary expression

1. "Whoever knowingly transports in interstate or foreign commerce, any person who has been unlawfully seized, confined, inveigled, decoyed, kidnaped, abducted, or carried away and held for ransom or reward or otherwise, except, in the case of a minor, by a parent thereof, shall be punished (1) by death if the kidnaped person has not been liberated unharmed, and if the verdict of the jury shall so recommend, or (2) by imprisonment for any term of years or for life, if the death penalty is not imposed." [The death penalty provision in this statute was held unconstitutional by the Supreme Court in United States v. Jackson, 390 U.S. 570 (1968), two years before the Court's decision in *Brady*. See Note 2 following *Brady*.—EDS.]

2. Eight days after petitioner pleaded guilty, he was brought before the court for sentencing. At that time, the court questioned petitioner for a second time about the voluntariness of his plea:

> *The Court:* . . . Having read the presentence report and the statement you made to the probation officer, I want to be certain that you know what you are doing and you did know when you entered a plea of guilty the other day. Do you want to let that plea of guilty stand, or do you want to withdraw it and plead not guilty?
>
> *Defendant Brady:* I want to let that plea stand, sir.
>
> *The Court:* You understand that in doing that you are admitting and confessing the truth of the charge contained in the indictment and that you enter a plea of guilty voluntarily, without persuasion, coercion of any kind? Is that right?
>
> *Defendant Brady:* Yes, your Honor.
>
> *The Court:* And you do that?
>
> *Defendant Brady:* Yes, I do.
>
> *The Court:* You plead guilty to the charge?
>
> *Defendant Brady:* Yes, I do. [App. 29-30.]

of his own choice. But the plea is more than an admission of past conduct; it is the defendant's consent that judgment of conviction may be entered without a trial—a waiver of his right to trial before a jury or a judge. Waivers of constitutional rights not only must be voluntary but must be knowing, intelligent acts done with sufficient awareness of the relevant circumstances and likely consequences. On neither score was Brady's plea of guilty invalid.

The trial judge in 1959 found the plea voluntary before accepting it; the District Court in 1968, after an evidentiary hearing, found that the plea was voluntarily made; the Court of Appeals specifically approved the finding of voluntariness. We see no reason on this record to disturb the judgment of those courts. Petitioner, advised by competent counsel, tendered his plea after his codefendant, who had already given a confession, determined to plead guilty and became available to testify against petitioner. . . .

The voluntariness of Brady's plea can be determined only by considering all of the relevant circumstances surrounding it. One of these circumstances was the possibility of a heavier sentence following a guilty verdict after a trial. It may be that Brady, faced with a strong case against him and recognizing that his chances for acquittal were slight, preferred to plead guilty and thus limit the penalty to life imprisonment rather than to elect a jury trial which could result in a death penalty. But even if we assume that Brady would not have pleaded guilty except for the death penalty provision of §1201(a), this assumption merely identifies the penalty provision as a "but for" cause of his plea. That the statute caused the plea in this sense does not necessarily prove that the plea was coerced and invalid as an involuntary act.

The State to some degree encourages pleas of guilty at every important step in the criminal process. For some people, their breach of a State's law is alone sufficient reason for surrendering themselves and accepting punishment.

For others, apprehension and charge, both threatening acts by the Government, jar them into admitting their guilt. In still other cases, the post-indictment accumulation of evidence may convince the defendant and his counsel that a trial is not worth the agony and expense to the defendant and his family. All these pleas of guilty are valid in spite of the State's responsibility for some of the factors motivating the pleas; the pleas are no more improperly compelled than is the decision by a defendant at the close of the State's evidence at trial that he must take the stand or face certain conviction.

Of course, the agents of the State may not produce a plea by actual or threatened physical harm or by mental coercion overbearing the will of the defendant. But nothing of the sort is claimed in this case; nor is there evidence that Brady was so gripped by fear of the death penalty or hope of leniency that he did not or could not, with the help of counsel, rationally weigh the advantages of going to trial against the advantages of pleading guilty. Brady's claim is of a different sort: that it violates the Fifth Amendment to influence or encourage a guilty plea by opportunity or promise of leniency and that a guilty plea is coerced and invalid if influenced by the fear of a possibly higher penalty for the crime charged if a conviction is obtained after the State is put to its proof.

Insofar as the voluntariness of his plea is concerned, there is little to differentiate Brady from (1) the defendant, in a jurisdiction where the judge and jury have the same range of sentencing power, who pleads guilty because his lawyer advises him that the judge will very probably be more lenient than the jury; (2) the defendant, in a jurisdiction where the judge alone has sentencing power, who is advised by counsel that the judge is normally more lenient with defendants who plead guilty than with those who go to trial; (3) the defendant who is permitted by prosecutor and judge to plead guilty to a lesser offense included in the offense charged; and (4) the defendant who pleads guilty to certain counts with the understanding that other charges will be dropped. In each of these situations, as in Brady's case, the defendant might never plead guilty absent the possibility or certainty that the plea will result in a lesser penalty than the sentence that could be imposed after a trial and a verdict of guilty. We decline to hold, however, that a guilty plea is compelled and invalid under the Fifth Amendment whenever motivated by the defendant's desire to accept the certainty or probability of a lesser penalty rather than face a wider range of possibilities extending from acquittal to conviction and a higher penalty authorized by law for the crime charged.

The issue we deal with is inherent in the criminal law and its administration because guilty pleas are not constitutionally forbidden, because the criminal law characteristically extends to judge or jury a range of choice in setting the sentence in individual cases, and because both the State and the defendant often find it advantageous to preclude the possibility of the maximum penalty authorized by law. For a defendant who sees slight possibility of acquittal, the advantages of pleading guilty and limiting the probable penalty are obvious—his exposure is reduced, the correctional processes can begin immediately, and the practical burdens of a trial are eliminated. For the State there are also advantages—the more promptly imposed punishment after an admission of guilt may more effectively attain the objectives of punishment; and with the avoidance of trial, scarce judicial and prosecutorial resources are conserved for those cases in which there is a substantial issue of the defendant's guilt or in which there is substantial doubt that the State can sustain its burden of proof. It is this mutuality of advantage that perhaps explains the fact that at present well over three-fourths of the criminal convictions in this country rest on pleas of guilty, a great many of them no doubt motivated at least in part by the hope or assurance of a lesser penalty than might be imposed if there were a guilty verdict after a trial to judge or jury.

Of course, that the prevalence of guilty pleas is explainable does not necessarily validate those pleas or the system which produces them. But we cannot hold that it is unconstitutional for the State to extend a benefit to a defendant who in turn extends a substantial benefit to the State and who demonstrates by his plea that he is ready and willing to admit his crime and to enter the correctional system in a frame of mind that affords hope for success in rehabilitation over a shorter period of time than might otherwise be necessary.

A contrary holding would require the States and Federal Government to forbid guilty pleas altogether, to provide a single invariable penalty for each crime defined by the statutes, or to place the sentencing function in a separate authority having no knowledge of the manner in which the conviction in each case was obtained. In any event, it would be necessary to forbid prosecutors and judges to accept guilty pleas to selected counts, to lesser included offenses, or to reduced charges. The Fifth Amendment does not reach so far.

Bram v. United States, 168 U.S. 532 (1897), held that the admissibility of a confession depended upon whether it was compelled within the meaning of the Fifth Amendment. To be admissible, a confession must be "free and voluntary: that is, must not be extracted by any sort of threats or violence, nor obtained by any direct or implied promises, however slight, nor by the exertion of any improper influence." 168 U.S., at 542-543. . . .

Bram is not inconsistent with our holding that Brady's plea was not compelled even though the law promised him a lesser maximum penalty if he did not go to trial. *Bram* dealt with a confession given by a defendant in custody, alone and unrepresented by counsel. In such circumstances, even a mild promise of leniency was deemed sufficient to bar the confession, not because the promise was an illegal act as such, but because defendants at such times are too sensitive to inducement and the possible impact on them too great to ignore and too difficult to assess. But *Bram* and its progeny did not hold that the possibly coercive impact of a promise of leniency could not be dissipated by the presence and advice of counsel, any more than Miranda v. Arizona, 384 U.S. 436 (1966), held that the possibly coercive atmosphere of the police station could not be counteracted by the presence of counsel or other safeguards.

Brady's situation bears no resemblance to Bram's. Brady first pleaded not guilty; prior to changing his plea to guilty he was subjected to no threats or promises in face-to-face encounters with the authorities. He had competent counsel and full opportunity to assess the advantages and disadvantages of a trial as compared with those attending a plea of guilty; there was no hazard of an impulsive and improvident response to a seeming but unreal advantage. His plea of guilty was entered in open court and before a judge obviously sensitive to the requirements of the law with respect to guilty pleas. Brady's plea, unlike Bram's confession, was voluntary.

The standard as to the voluntariness of guilty pleas must be essentially that defined by Judge Tuttle of the Court of Appeals for the Fifth Circuit:

> A plea of guilty entered by one fully aware of the direct consequences, including the actual value of any commitments made to him by the court, prosecutor, or his own counsel, must stand unless induced by threats (or promises to discontinue improper harassment), misrepresentation (including unfulfilled or unfulfillable promises), or perhaps by promises that are by their nature improper as having no proper relationship to the prosecutor's business (e.g., bribes).

[Shelton v. United States, 246 F.2d 571, 572 n. 2 (5th Cir. 1957) (en banc), *rev'd on other grounds*, 356 U.S. 26 (1958).]

Under this standard, a plea of guilty is not invalid merely because entered to avoid the possibility of a death penalty.

The record before us also supports the conclusion that Brady's plea was intelligently made. He was advised by competent counsel, he was made aware of the nature of the charge against him, and there was nothing to indicate that he was incompetent or otherwise not in control of his mental faculties; once his confederate had pleaded guilty and became available to testify, he chose to plead guilty, perhaps to ensure that he would face no more than life imprisonment or a term of years. Brady was aware of precisely what he was doing when he admitted that he had kidnaped the victim and had not released her unharmed. . . .

We would have serious doubts about this case if the encouragement of guilty pleas by offers of leniency substantially increased the likelihood that defendants, advised by competent counsel, would falsely condemn themselves. But our view is to the contrary and is based on our expectations that courts will satisfy themselves that pleas of guilty are voluntarily and intelligently made by competent defendants with adequate advice of counsel and that there is nothing to question the accuracy and reliability of the defendants' admissions that they committed the crimes with which they are charged. In the case before us, nothing in the record impeaches Brady's plea or suggests that his admissions in open court were anything but the truth.

Although Brady's plea of guilty may well have been motivated in part by a desire to avoid a possible death penalty, we are convinced that his plea was voluntarily and intelligently made and we have no reason to doubt that his solemn admission of guilt was truthful. . . .

JUSTICE BLACK, while adhering to his belief that United States v. Jackson, 390 U.S. 570, was wrongly decided, concurs in the judgment and in substantially all of the opinion in this case.

[The opinion of Justice Brennan, joined by Justices Douglas and Marshall, concurring in the result, is omitted.]

NOTES AND QUESTIONS

1. Mr. Brady made two arguments as to why his guilty plea was invalid. First, he claimed that his plea was involuntary because it was made out of fear that a worse penalty (death) might be imposed on him if he took his case to trial. In response, Justice White repeatedly emphasized the fact that Brady was represented by counsel (see, for example, the discussion distinguishing Brady's situation from the one in *Bram*). This suggests a strong link between the Sixth Amendment right to counsel and the permissibility of plea bargaining. Is the link persuasive? How does the presence of counsel alter the decision that the defendant has to make?

2. Brady's second argument is that the plea was not "intelligent." This claim requires some explanation. In United States v. Jackson, 390 U.S. 570 (1968), the Supreme Court invalidated the death penalty provision of §1201, the statute under which Brady was convicted. Thus, the threatened penalty that prompted Brady's plea—a death sentence—could not have been legally imposed on him for reasons that became apparent only after the plea was entered. Brady argued, naturally enough, that this made his plea unintelligent, because it was based on incorrect legal assumptions. In a portion of the opinion not excerpted above, the Court responded to this claim as follows:

> Often the decision to plead guilty is heavily influenced by the defendant's appraisal of the prosecution's case against him and by the apparent likelihood of securing leniency should a guilty plea be offered and accepted. Considerations like these frequently present imponderable questions for which there are no certain answers; judgments may be made that in the light of later events seem improvident, although they were perfectly sensible at the time. The rule that a plea must be intelligently made to be valid does not require that a plea be vulnerable to later attack if the defendant did not correctly assess every relevant factor entering into his decision. A defendant is not entitled to withdraw his plea merely because he discovers long after the plea has been accepted that his calculus misapprehended the quality of the State's case or the likely penalties attached to alternative courses of action. More particularly, absent misrepresentation or other impermissible conduct by state agents, cf. Von Moltke v. Gillies, 332 U.S. 708 (1948), a voluntary plea of guilty intelligently made in the light of the then applicable law does not become vulnerable because later judicial decisions indicate that the plea rested on a faulty premise. A plea of guilty triggered by the expectations of a competently counseled defendant that the State will have a strong case against

him is not subject to later attack because the defendant's lawyer correctly advised him with respect to the then existing law as to possible penalties but later pronouncements of the courts, as in this case, hold that the maximum penalty for the crime in question was less than was reasonably assumed at the time the plea was entered.

Brady, 397 U.S. at 756-757. See also United States v. Ruiz, 536 U.S. 622 (2002) (the Constitution "permits a court to accept a guilty plea, with its accompanying waiver of various constitutional rights, despite various forms of misapprehension under which a defendant might labor").

What explains the Court's willingness to let a guilty plea stand despite defense counsel's misjudgments or changes in the law? Is it just about maintaining an efficient process, or is there something else at work here?

3. Why shouldn't the criminal system just ban plea bargaining? Why should the government "pay" defendants to plead guilty by reducing the charges or making sentencing concessions? If the prosecutor really has the evidence of defendant's guilt, shouldn't she insist the defendant either plead guilty to the full charges or else stand trial (perhaps agreeing to a slight sentence reduction for the defendant who pleads guilty and accepts responsibility, just to give some incentive to plead)? On the other hand, if the prosecutor does not have sufficient evidence, shouldn't she drop the charges rather than threatening the defendant with a huge potential sentence if he goes to trial?

Consider the following account of the likely consequences of forbidding plea bargaining:

First, the number of trials would increase sharply. Something in the neighborhood of ninety percent of cases now lead to pleas; if even one-third of those are the result of bargaining, prohibiting plea bargaining would quadruple the number of criminal trials. Second, the error rate of trials would rise. This follows from the first assumption. Trials are elaborate and costly affairs. Any reform that involves a several hundred percent increase in their number must necessarily involve economizing on the process, at least as long as one assumes a constant level of expenditures on the system. Reducing the process, in turn, logically implies increasing the rate of error. Third, the total number of convictions would fall, probably substantially. Abolition of plea bargaining would raise the average cost of prosecution because it would increase the percentage of cases that go to trial (and even slimmed-down, cheaper trials will be more expensive than bargained pleas). Given constant resources, this would mean a drop in the number of convictions. . . .

. . . [I]n a world without plea bargaining the average defendant would depend more heavily on his lawyer's expertise: the percentage of trials would sharply increase, and lawyers' skill surely matters more in a trial than in a plea bargaining session, particularly since the latter is likely to be constrained, to some extent, by customary "market" prices. This effect would be particularly pronounced in a trial system with a higher error rate than the current one, and with quicker, more slapdash preparation by the attorneys—a necessary consequence of vastly increasing the number of trials. The increased impact of skill differences among attorneys would adversely affect poor defendants, since they tend to have the worst lawyers. Thus, there is some ground for believing that a world without plea bargaining would disproportionately harm both the innocent and the poor, hardly a recipe for a more distributionally just system. . . .

Robert E. Scott & William J. Stuntz, Plea Bargaining as Contract, 101 Yale L.J. 1909, 1932-34 (1992).

4. What if the pressure to plead guilty comes from a source other than the prosecutor or police? Suppose the defendant agrees to plead guilty to one charge, but resists making a deal on the second charge. At a pretrial hearing, the judge urges the defendant to enter into a settlement with the government of all the charges against him. The judge hints that it would be in the defendant's interest to do so, because he might well receive a lower sentence than if he pled guilty to one charge and was convicted at trial on the other. The defendant then agrees to plead guilty to both charges. See United States v. Sanya, 774 F.3d 812, 817-818 (4th Cir. 2014). In such a case is the guilty plea voluntary?

As a matter of federal law the answer is a clear "no." Federal Rule 11(c)(1) says that a judge "must" not participate in plea discussions, and courts take this prohibition quite seriously. The fear is that, precisely because judges have the sentencing power, as well as the power to influence the course of trial through their rulings, defendants will feel coerced into pleading if they think the judge wants them to. How valid is this concern? It is plausible to assume that a defendant is not coerced into pleading guilty because of the threat of the death penalty (see *Brady*), but does feel impermissible pressure when a judge tells him—probably correctly—that his sentence will be lower if he pleads guilty than if he goes to trial and loses?

Notice that some states adopt a different approach and permit judges to engage in discussions with the parties about a plea deal, although often a new judge will hear the trial if the plea negotiations break down. Note also that even if a federal judge violates Rule 11(c)(1) and participates in the plea discussions, the violation will still be subject to harmless error analysis on appeal. United States v. Davila, 133 S. Ct. 2139 (2013).

5. Stephanos Bibas has sharply challenged the prevailing wisdom that plea bargains typically reflect an appropriately modified version of the result that a defendant would most likely obtain at a full-blown trial:

> [M]any plea bargains diverge from the shadows of trials. By "the shadows of trials," I mean the influence exerted by the strength of the evidence and the expected punishment after trial. Structural forces and psychological biases sometimes inefficiently prevent mutually beneficial bargains or induce harmful ones. Even when they do not harm efficiency, these legally irrelevant factors sometimes skew the fair allocation of punishment. As a result, some defendants strike skewed bargains. Other defendants plead when they would otherwise go to trial, or go to trial (and usually receive heavier sentences) when they would otherwise plead. Furthermore, some defendants' plea bargains diverge from trial shadows much more than others'. These divergent outcomes produce substantial sentencing inequities. Rather than basing sentences on the need for deterrence, retribution, incapacitation, or rehabilitation, plea bargaining effectively bases sentences in part on wealth, sex, age, education, intelligence, and confidence. Though trials allocate punishment imperfectly, plea bargaining adds another layer of distortions that warp the fair allocation of punishment. The shadow-of-trial model thus needs many refinements and nuances to make it more realistic. Plea-bargaining practices need many reforms to conform more closely to the shadows of trials and to iron out inequities.

Stephanos Bibas, Plea Bargaining Outside the Shadow of Trial, 117 Harv. L. Rev. 2463 (2004). What are the implications of this analysis? Are there corrective measures that can be taken to solve these problems, or are the problems inherent in any system of negotiated resolutions?

6. After *Brady* it is clear that an offer to lower the charge or sentence in return for a guilty plea does not render that plea involuntary. But suppose the prosecutor originally brings one charge (say, second degree murder), and then, when the defendant refuses to plead guilty, threatens to re-indict for a higher charge (first degree murder). Is the voluntariness analysis the same? The next case considers this issue.

BORDENKIRCHER v. HAYES

Certiorari to the United States Court of Appeals for the Sixth Circuit
434 U.S. 357 (1978)

JUSTICE STEWART delivered the opinion of the Court.

The question in this case is whether the Due Process Clause of the Fourteenth Amendment is violated when a state prosecutor carries out a threat made during plea negotiations to reindict the accused on more serious charges if he does not plead guilty to the offense with which he was originally charged.

The respondent, Paul Lewis Hayes, was indicted by a Fayette County, Ky., grand jury on a charge of uttering a forged instrument in the amount of $88.30, an offense then punishable by a term of 2 to 10 years in prison. Ky. Rev. Stat. §434.130 (1973) (repealed 1975). After arraignment, Hayes, his retained counsel, and the Commonwealth's Attorney met in the presence of the Clerk of the Court to discuss a possible plea agreement. During these conferences the prosecutor offered to recommend a sentence of five years in prison if Hayes would plead guilty to the indictment. He also said that if Hayes did not plead guilty and "saved the court the inconvenience and necessity of a trial," he would return to the grand jury to seek an indictment under the Kentucky Habitual Criminal Act, then Ky. Rev. Stat. §431.190 (1973) (repealed 1975), which would subject Hayes to a mandatory sentence of life imprisonment by reason of his two prior felony convictions.[2] Hayes chose not to plead guilty, and the prosecutor did obtain an indictment charging him under the Habitual Criminal Act. . . .

A jury found Hayes guilty on the principal charge of uttering a forged instrument and, in a separate proceeding, further found that he had twice before been convicted of felonies. As required by the habitual offender statute, he was sentenced to a life term in the penitentiary. The Kentucky Court of Appeals rejected Hayes' constitutional objections to the enhanced sentence, holding in an unpublished opinion that imprisonment for life with the possibility of parole was constitutionally permissible in light of the previous felonies of which Hayes had been convicted,[3] and that

---

2. At the time of Hayes' trial the statute provided that "[a]ny person convicted a . . . third time of felony . . . shall be confined in the penitentiary during his life." Ky. Rev. Stat. §431.190 (1973) (repealed 1975). That statute has been replaced by Ky. Rev. Stat. §532.080 (Supp. 1977) under which Hayes would have been sentenced to, at most, an indeterminate term of 10 to 20 years. §532.080(6)(b). In addition, under the new statute a previous conviction is a basis for enhanced sentencing only if a prison term of one year or more was imposed, the sentence or probation was completed within five years of the present offense, and the offender was over the age of 18 when the offense was committed. At least one of Hayes' prior convictions did not meet these conditions. See n. 3, infra.

3. According to his own testimony, Hayes had pleaded guilty in 1961, when he was 17 years old, to a charge of detaining a female, a lesser included offense of rape, and as a result had served five years in the state reformatory. In 1970 he had been convicted of robbery and sentenced to five years' imprisonment, but had been released on probation immediately.

the prosecutor's decision to indict him as a habitual offender was a legitimate use of available leverage in the plea bargaining process.

On Hayes' petition for a federal writ of habeas corpus, the United States District Court for the Eastern District of Kentucky agreed that there had been no constitutional violation in the sentence or the indictment procedure, and denied the writ. The Court of Appeals for the Sixth Circuit reversed. . . .

It may be helpful to clarify at the outset the nature of the issue in this case. While the prosecutor did not actually obtain the recidivist indictment until after the plea conferences had ended, his intention to do so was clearly expressed at the outset of the plea negotiations. Hayes was thus fully informed of the true terms of the offer when he made his decision to plead not guilty. This is not a situation, therefore, where the prosecutor without notice brought an additional and more serious charge after plea negotiations relating only to the original indictment had ended with the defendant's insistence on pleading not guilty. As a practical matter, in short, this case would be no different if the grand jury had indicted Hayes as a recidivist from the outset, and the prosecutor had offered to drop that charge as part of the plea bargain. . . .

This Court held in North Carolina v. Pearce, 395 U.S. 711, 725, that the Due Process Clause of the Fourteenth Amendment "requires that vindictiveness against a defendant for having successfully attacked his first conviction must play no part in the sentence he receives after a new trial." The same principle was later applied to prohibit a prosecutor from reindicting a convicted misdemeanant on a felony charge after the defendant had invoked an appellate remedy, since in this situation there was also a "realistic likelihood of 'vindictiveness.'" Blackledge v. Perry, 417 U.S. [21,] 27.

In those cases the Court was dealing with the State's unilateral imposition of a penalty upon a defendant who had chosen to exercise a legal right to attack his original conviction—a situation "very different from the give-and-take negotiation common in plea bargaining between the prosecution and defense, which arguably possess relatively equal bargaining power." Parker v. North Carolina, 397 U.S. 790, 809 (opinion of Brennan, J.). The Court has emphasized that the due process violation in cases such as *Pearce* and *Perry* lay not in the possibility that a defendant might be deterred from the exercise of a legal right, but rather in the danger that the State might be retaliating against the accused for lawfully attacking his conviction. See Blackledge v. Perry, supra, at 26-28.

To punish a person because he has done what the law plainly allows him to do is a due process violation of the most basic sort. . . . But in the "give-and-take" of plea bargaining, there is no such element of punishment or retaliation so long as the accused is free to accept or reject the prosecution's offer.

Plea bargaining flows from "the mutuality of advantage" to defendants and prosecutors, each with his own reasons for wanting to avoid trial. Brady v. United States, supra, at 752. Defendants advised by competent counsel and protected by other procedural safeguards are presumptively capable of intelligent choice in response to prosecutorial persuasion, and unlikely to be driven to false self-condemnation. Indeed, acceptance of the basic legitimacy of plea bargaining necessarily implies rejection of any notion that a guilty plea is involuntary in a constitutional sense simply because it is the end result of the bargaining process. By hypothesis, the plea may have been induced by promises of a recommendation of a lenient sentence or a reduction of charges, and thus by fear of the possibility of a greater penalty upon conviction after a trial.

While confronting a defendant with the risk of more severe punishment clearly may have a "discouraging effect on the defendant's assertion of his trial rights, the imposition of these difficult choices [is] an inevitable"—and permissible—"attribute of any legitimate system which tolerates and encourages the negotiation of pleas." Chaffin v. Stynchcombe, [412 U.S. 17, 31 (1973)]. It follows that, by tolerating and encouraging the negotiation of pleas, this Court has necessarily accepted as constitutionally legitimate the simple reality that the prosecutor's interest at the bargaining table is to persuade the defendant to forgo his right to plead not guilty.

It is not disputed here that Hayes was properly chargeable under the recidivist statute, since he had in fact been convicted of two previous felonies. In our system, so long as the prosecutor has probable cause to believe that the accused committed an offense defined by statute, the decision whether or not to prosecute, and what charge to file or bring before a grand jury, generally rests entirely in his discretion.[8] Within the limits set by the legislature's constitutionally valid definition of chargeable offenses, "the conscious exercise of some selectivity in enforcement is not in itself a federal constitutional violation" so long as "the selection was [not] deliberately based upon an unjustifiable standard such as race, religion, or other arbitrary classification." Oyler v. Boles, 368 U.S. 448, 456. To hold that the prosecutor's desire to induce a guilty plea is an "unjustifiable standard," which, like race or religion, may play no part in his charging decision, would contradict the very premises that underlie the concept of plea bargaining itself. Moreover, a rigid constitutional rule that would prohibit a prosecutor from acting forthrightly in his dealings with the defense could only invite unhealthy subterfuge that would drive the practice of plea bargaining back into the shadows from which it has so recently emerged.

There is no doubt that the breadth of discretion that our country's legal system vests in prosecuting attorneys carries with it the potential for both individual and institutional abuse. And broad though that discretion may be, there are undoubtedly constitutional limits upon its exercise. We hold only that the course of conduct engaged in by the prosecutor in this case, which no more than openly presented the defendant with the unpleasant alternatives of forgoing trial or facing charges on which he was plainly subject to prosecution, did not violate the Due Process Clause of the Fourteenth Amendment. . . .

[The dissenting opinion of Justice Blackmun, joined by Justices Brennan and Marshall, is omitted.]

JUSTICE POWELL, dissenting.

. . . Respondent was charged with the uttering of a single forged check in the amount of $88.30. Under Kentucky law, this offense was punishable by a prison term of from 2 to 10 years, apparently without regard to the amount of the forgery. During the course of plea bargaining, the prosecutor offered respondent a sentence of five years in consideration of a guilty plea. I observe, at this point, that five years in prison for the offense charged hardly could be characterized as a generous offer. Apparently respondent viewed the offer in this light and declined to accept it; he

---

8. This case does not involve the constitutional implications of a prosecutor's offer during plea bargaining of adverse or lenient treatment for some person other than the accused, see ALI Model Code of Pre-Arraignment Procedure, Commentary to §350.3, pp. 614-615 (1975), which might pose a greater danger of inducing a false guilty plea by skewing the assessment of the risks a defendant must consider.

protested that he was innocent and insisted on going to trial. Respondent adhered to this position even when the prosecutor advised that he would seek a new indictment under the State's Habitual Criminal Act which would subject respondent, if convicted, to a mandatory life sentence because of two prior felony convictions.

The prosecutor's initial assessment of respondent's case led him to forgo an indictment under the habitual criminal statute. The circumstances of respondent's prior convictions are relevant to this assessment and to my view of the case. Respondent was 17 years old when he committed his first offense. He was charged with rape but pleaded guilty to the lesser included offense of "detaining a female." One of the other participants in the incident was sentenced to life imprisonment. Respondent was sent not to prison but to a reformatory where he served five years. Respondent's second offense was robbery. This time he was found guilty by a jury and was sentenced to five years in prison, but he was placed on probation and served no time. Although respondent's prior convictions brought him within the terms of the Habitual Criminal Act, the offenses themselves did not result in imprisonment; yet the addition of a conviction on a charge involving $88.30 subjected respondent to a mandatory sentence of imprisonment for life. Persons convicted of rape and murder often are not punished so severely.

No explanation appears in the record for the prosecutor's decision to escalate the charge against respondent other than respondent's refusal to plead guilty. The prosecutor has conceded that his purpose was to discourage respondent's assertion of constitutional rights, and the majority accepts this characterization of events.

It seems to me that the question to be asked under the circumstances is whether the prosecutor reasonably might have charged respondent under the Habitual Criminal Act in the first place. The deference that courts properly accord the exercise of a prosecutor's discretion perhaps would foreclose judicial criticism if the prosecutor originally had sought an indictment under that Act, as unreasonable as it would have seemed.[2] But here the prosecutor evidently made a reasonable, responsible judgment not to subject an individual to a mandatory life sentence when his only new offense had societal implications as limited as those accompanying the uttering of a single $88 forged check and when the circumstances of his prior convictions confirmed the inappropriateness of applying the habitual criminal statute. I think it may be inferred that the prosecutor himself deemed it unreasonable and not in the public interest to put this defendant in jeopardy of a sentence of life imprisonment.

There may be situations in which a prosecutor would be fully justified in seeking a fresh indictment for a more serious offense. The most plausible justification might be that it would have been reasonable and in the public interest initially to have charged the defendant with the greater offense. In most cases a court could not know why the harsher indictment was sought, and an inquiry into the prosecutor's

---

2. The majority suggests that this case cannot be distinguished from the case where the prosecutor initially obtains an indictment under an enhancement statute and later agrees to drop the enhancement charge in exchange for a guilty plea. I would agree that these two situations would be alike only if it were assumed that the hypothetical prosecutor's decision to charge under the enhancement statute was occasioned not by consideration of the public interest but by a strategy to discourage the defendant from exercising his constitutional rights. In theory, I would condemn both practices. In practice, the hypothetical situation is largely unreviewable. The majority's view confuses the propriety of a particular exercise of prosecutorial discretion with its unreviewability. In the instant case, however, we have no problem of proof.

motive would neither be indicated nor likely to be fruitful. In those cases, I would agree with the majority that the situation would not differ materially from one in which the higher charge was brought at the outset.

But this is not such a case. Here, any inquiry into the prosecutor's purpose is made unnecessary by his candid acknowledgment that he threatened to procure and in fact procured the habitual criminal indictment because of respondent's insistence on exercising his constitutional rights. . . . I would affirm the opinion of the Court of Appeals on the facts of this case.

NOTES AND QUESTIONS

1. What do you make of Justice Powell's dissent? Should it really matter whether the prosecutor first charged Hayes with being a habitual offender and then offered to drop the charge, as opposed to charging him with "uttering a forged instrument" and then threatening to add the habitual offender charge if he refused to plead? Don't both scenarios amount to the same thing? Or does the sequence of charging and bargaining give us useful information about the prosecutor's motives in threatening to bring the higher charge?

2. The difference between the sentence offered in the plea deal and the expected sentence following a conviction at trial—in *Bordenkircher*, the difference between five years and life imprisonment—is sometimes described by scholars as a "trial penalty." (Or if you prefer, a "plea discount.") Although individual cases can vary widely, some studies have concluded that a federal defendant who goes to trial can generally expect to receive a sentence following a conviction that is about 15 percent higher than the likely sentence had he pled guilty. See, e.g., Jeffery T. Ulmer, James Eisenstein & Brian D. Johnson, Trial Penalties in Federal Sentencing: Extra-Guidelines Factors and District Variation, 27 Just. Q. 560, 575 (2010). Another scholar, critiquing the earlier studies, has concluded that the penalty is much higher, and that federal defendants who go to trial will receive on average a sentence that is more than 60 percent longer than a defendant who pled guilty. See Andrew Chongseh Kim, Underestimating the Trial Penalty: An Empirical Analysis of the Federal Trial Penalty and Critique of the Abrams Study, 85 Miss. L. Rev. 1195 (2015).

How much does the size of the penalty matter? Isn't the gap between the certain penalty following a plea and the expected penalty after trial *exactly* the type of leverage that is likely to induce an innocent person to plead guilty? Aren't innocent people more likely (or at least, more likely than the average guilty person) to be risk averse and plead guilty as the trial penalty grows? To ask the question differently, if *you* were accused of a crime that you did not commit, how confident are you that you would reject a plea deal that carried a very high trial penalty and trust the judicial process to recognize your innocence and acquit?[7]

Of course, if prosecutors are permitted to make these deals at all, some gap is clearly necessary; if the expected sentence were the same, few defendants would

---

7. This is basically the main theme of the award-winning HBO Films movie, Criminal Justice (1990), starring Forest Whitaker, Rosie Perez, Anthony LaPaglia, and Jennifer Grey. The movie—which is purely fictional, but which portrays quite accurately many of the key stages of both criminal investigation and criminal adjudication—is currently out of print, but can be viewed on YouTube.

forego even a small chance of acquittal at trial if there were no benefit to pleading guilty. But despite the holding in *Bordenkircher*, should there be some limit on the trial penalty? If so, what should that limit be? Or did *Bordenkircher* get it right in concluding that as a long as the defendant has the option of going to trial, there is no improper pressure in giving the defendant an extremely attractive alternative (relatively speaking) to trial?

3. If you think the prosecutor in *Bordenkircher* acted too aggressively, perhaps the problem lies less with the deal the defendant was offered — the prosecutor was arguably just making use of the tools she was given — and more with the breadth and lack of nuance of many criminal statutes. Consider the following:

> Suppose that Hayes' earlier convictions were fairly low-level felonies, a possibility that would tend to explain the relatively light sentences he had received. Suppose further that Kentucky's habitual criminal law had authorized a sentence of anywhere from ten years to life. The judge's sentence for the forgery charge would surely have fallen closer to the minimum than the maximum. And that conclusion is consistent with the decision the legislature made when it passed the habitual criminal statute. Felonies encompass a wide range of criminal behavior; the legislature made, at best, a roughly accurate categorical judgment. If the same legislators who passed the statute were to vote on sentences case by case, many defendants who qualify for habitual criminal sentencing would get far less than life in prison. . . . [T]he key point is that the legislature did not intend for the statute to be applied to every offender who might fall within its terms. Rather, the legislature implicitly relied on prosecutors to separate the wheat from the chaff — to exercise their discretion *not* to pursue habitual criminal sentencing for offenders who fell within the statute but seemed not to deserve such harsh treatment. *Bordenkircher* may well be such a case; that is, the legislature may have expected that prosecutors would not charge people like Hayes under the statute, though no enforcement mechanism backed up that expectation (because judicial review of charging decisions would be too costly).
>
>   The Kentucky statute thus gave the prosecutor a good deal of bargaining power over people like Hayes because it allowed him to threaten a sentence that, absent the statute, would have been implausible. . . . In a discretionary [sentencing] system, the choice might have been between a recommended five-year sentence and a likely ten or twelve years if the case went to trial. Given the statute, the choice was much more stark: five years or life. Hayes might not have accepted that deal, but every future defendant is likely to do so and do so quickly.

Scott & Stuntz, Plea Bargaining as Contract, 101 Yale L.J., at 1963-1964.

4. At the time *Bordenkircher* was decided, mandatory sentences were unusual; sentencing, in state and federal cases alike, was overwhelmingly discretionary with the court, with the governing statutes fixing very broad ranges within which sentences could permissibly fall.

That is not so today. Mandatory sentences have multiplied, at both state and federal levels. These contemporary mandatory sentences take two forms. The first is like the habitual offender statute at issue in *Bordenkircher*. Many states have mandatory recidivist sentencing statutes (some of which are popularly known as "three strikes" laws because, like the Kentucky statute in *Bordenkircher*, they require a long sentence as a consequence of a third felony conviction). A second popular variant is the so-called "mandatory minimum" statutes that require a high minimum sentence for, say, crimes involving the use of a gun, or for the possession or sale of a given quantity of drugs.

How do you suppose such mandatory sentencing statutes affect the plea bargaining process? The rest of the criminal process? The effects may be different than one would initially suppose:

> Research on mandatory sentencing laws during the 1970s and 1980s reveals a number of avoidance strategies. Boston police avoided application of a 1975 Massachusetts law calling for mandatory one-year sentences for persons convicted of carrying a gun by decreasing the number of arrests made for that offense and increasing (by 120 percent between 1974 and 1976) the number of weapons seizures without arrest. Prosecutors often avoid application of mandatory sentencing laws simply by filing charges for different, but roughly comparable, offenses that are not subject to mandatory sentences. Judges too can circumvent such laws. Detroit judges sidestepped a 1977 law requiring a two-year sentence for persons convicted of possession of a firearm in the commission of a felony by acquitting defendants of the gun charge (even though the evidence would support a conviction) or by decreasing the sentence they would otherwise impose by two years to offset the mandatory two-year term.
>
> Considerable recent research taken together . . . supports the following generalizations:
>
> 1. lawyers and judges will take steps to avoid application of laws they consider unduly harsh;
> 2. dismissal rates typically increase at early stages of the criminal justice process after effectuation of a mandatory penalty as practitioners attempt to shield some defendants from the law's reach;
> 3. defendants whose cases are not dismissed or diverted make more vigorous efforts to avoid conviction and to delay sentencing, which results in increased trial rates and case processing times increase;
> 4. defendants who are convicted of the target offense are often sentenced more severely than they would have been in the absence of the mandatory penalty provision; and
> 5. because declines in conviction rates for those arrested tend to offset increases in imprisonment rates for those convicted, often the overall probability that defendants will be incarcerated remains about the same after enactment of a mandatory sentence law.

Michael Tonry, Sentencing Matters 147-148 (1996) (citations omitted).

A second kind of sentencing policy that has affected plea bargaining involves sentencing guidelines (discussed in detail in Chapter 15). The federal system and a number of states now use such guidelines; they typically establish fairly narrow sentencing ranges for particular crimes, with limited flexibility for judicial departures from those ranges. Guideline systems sometimes incorporate "real offense" factors that are not easily subject to prosecutorial manipulation—for example, a state might have a guideline requiring a minimum sentence for robbery with a gun whether or not the gun element is part of the charged offense. But most sentences are anchored to the charged offense. The result is to give prosecutors a great deal more power over the ultimate sentence than in more discretionary systems.

How does this increased prosecutorial power over sentencing affect plea bargaining? Professor Jeffrey Standen offers the following answer:

> [T]he prosecutor is no longer the price taker but the price setter. Within the broad constraint of filing a charge upon which a jury will probably convict, the prosecutor may set the bargaining parameters as high or low as the facts permit, unrestricted

by the prospect of a judge re-examining the same course of conduct and making an independent determination. The bargaining that follows will not take place in light of the broad range of possible outcomes from sentences set independently by judges but instead according to the narrow, legislatively created sentencing range that attaches to the prosecutor's charge.

Jeffrey Standen, Plea Bargaining in the Shadow of the Guidelines, 81 Cal. L. Rev. 1471, 1513 (1993). Does this greater prosecutorial power undermine the voluntariness of guilty pleas? Or is all this simply a matter of sentencing policy to which the law of plea bargaining should be indifferent?

3.   The Subject Matter of Plea Bargaining

For the parties to strike a plea bargain, each side must have something to give that the other side wants. The most obvious item of value that the defendant has to offer is his willingness to plead guilty, to give the prosecutor a victory by ending the case with a conviction. Sometimes, however, the prosecutor is looking for more. Often the agreement to plead guilty is coupled with the defendant's agreement to cooperate with law enforcement, which typically includes the duty to provide information and evidence against other defendants. The defendant may have a few more bargaining chips to offer—compensation for the victims, the willingness to waive certain claims (discussed below)—but in general, prosecutors are interested in getting convictions, and in getting information that will lead to more convictions.

What can the defendant get from the prosecutor? Here the legal issues can become more interesting. As both *Brady* and Bordenkircher v. Hayes make clear, prosecutors can make offers or engage in bargaining behavior that "induce" or "encourage" a guilty plea, but they may not "compel" or "coerce" one. Drawing this line can raise some difficult legal and moral questions, as the materials below show.

Rule 11(c)(1) describes three types of permissible plea deals, set forth in subsections (c)(1)(A), (B), and (C); these deals are sometimes called (cleverly) "Type A," "Type B" and "Type C" agreements. A Type A agreement is common and straightforward. In return for a guilty plea to the charged crime, or to a lesser related crime, a prosecutor can agree not to file other charges or dismiss charges that are already filed. This is "charge bargaining"—defendant pleads guilty to one count of burglary in return for having the second count dismissed.

Under a Type B agreement, the defendant pleads guilty in return for a sentencing *recommendation* by the prosecutor, or an agreement not to oppose the sentence requested by the defense. Only the judge can fix a sentence, of course, and under a Type B agreement the defendant is bound to keep his part of the deal and plead guilty, even if the judge decides to reject the prosecutor's recommendation and sentence the defendant more severely than the parties contemplated. Stated differently, what the defendant is buying with his guilty plea is the expectation that the prosecutor's recommendation or acquiescence to a certain sentence will carry some weight with the court.

A Type C agreement gives the defendant more certainty about his eventual sentence, and thus requires the defense to have more leverage when negotiating an agreement. Here the parties agree that the defendant's guilty plea is expressly conditioned on the sentence the defendant receives being no higher than a fixed amount (or alternatively, that a particular provision of the Sentencing Guidelines or some sentencing factor does or does not apply). Again, only the judge can set the sentence, but now when the judge is considering the Type C plea agreement, she must make a decision. If she accepts the guilty plea and allows the defendant to plead guilty, she is then precluded from later imposing a sentence beyond the maximum agreed to by the parties. On the other hand, if the judge rejects the plea deal because she believes that the agreed-to sentence is too low, the defendant is no longer bound by the deal and is not obligated to plead guilty. Thus a defendant who pleads guilty pursuant to a Type C agreement can do so with confidence about the sentence he will actually receive.

The types of plea bargains listed in Rule 11 are not exhaustive; an effort to tailor the outcome of a case to its particular facts can lead to a range of other types of bargaining behavior and inducements. This in turn sometimes leads the defense to argue that the bargaining process was so unfair that it rendered the plea involuntary. One such claim was raised—and rejected—in *Brady,* and indirectly in *Bordenkircher:* that the gap between the sentence offered in return for a guilty plea and the potential sentence that could follow a trial was so extreme that no reasonable defendant could refuse the deal.

In other instances the claim is that the subject matter of the plea negotiations were improper—the defendant argues (after the fact) that certain subjects, not directly related to guilt or punishment, should be viewed as "off-limits" in negotiations. As you consider the materials that follow, ask yourself whether the inducements being offered the defendant should be considered proper or improper negotiating tactics, and once again, whether any of the inducements are sufficiently compelling that they are likely to lead an innocent defendant to plead guilty.

STOP

UNITED STATES v. HODGE

United States Court of Appeals for the Third Circuit
412 F.3d 479 (2005)

SMITH, CIRCUIT JUDGE.

Devin Hodge pleaded guilty to murdering the owner of a St. Thomas jewelry store. Devin's brother, Irvine, pleaded guilty to the same crime as part of a "package deal." The brothers were sentenced at the same proceeding to life in prison by the District Court of the Virgin Islands. Devin argues on appeal that the government breached its plea agreement, and that the District Court conducted a deficient plea colloquy in part because it was unaware that his plea was linked to his brother's. We hold that the government breached its plea agreement, and we will vacate Devin's sentence and remand for re-sentencing or withdrawal of his plea. We further hold that the District Court did not plainly err in conducting Devin's plea colloquy. We write to provide guidance for the District Court should a new plea colloquy be required on remand, and for other district courts faced with the sensitive task of testing voluntariness in package deal plea situations.

I

In May 1999, a federal grand jury indicted Devin Hodge, Irvine Hodge, and a third defendant for murder of the owner of the Emerald Lady Jewelry Store in Charlotte

Amalie, St. Thomas, and the theft of jewelry from the store. Devin pleaded not guilty. . . .

. . . In late-April 2000, the government sent Devin's attorney a draft plea agreement. The body of the cover letter stated:

> I am enclosing herewith a copy of a proposed plea agreement in the above captioned matter. The proposed agreement is the entire integrated agreement of the parties. Additionally, the plea offer from the government is a lock plea. That is, each of your clients must accept the plea as a condition of the government's acceptance of the plea. . . .

Four days after receiving this letter, Devin pleaded guilty. The written plea agreement provided that Devin would plead guilty to first degree murder, the second count of the Third Superseding Indictment. In return, the government agreed to "seek dismissal" at sentencing of the remaining counts, and to "recommend that [Devin] receive credit for acceptance of responsibility, assuming [Devin] does in fact clearly demonstrate acceptance of responsibility." While the government reserved its right to allocute at sentencing, it agreed "to make no specific sentencing recommendation other than to request that the sentence be within the guideline range."

The final paragraph of the written plea agreement provided that "[t]he parties agree that no other promises have been made in connection with this matter, and that this Plea Agreement constitutes the entire agreement between the United States Attorney for the District of the Virgin Islands and the defendant in the above-referenced case." The agreement did not mention that Devin's plea was "locked," or otherwise conditioned upon, Irvine's identical plea.

Later that month, the District Court held a joint change-of-plea hearing for Devin and Irvine. Devin's and Irvine's attorneys indicated that the pleas were identical and agreed to a "dual inquiry." . . .

Devin and Irvine were questioned separately regarding rights they were waiving by pleading guilty. Judge Moore asked: "Do you understand our system, and that you don't have to give [your rights] up, nobody can force you to give them up, but if you do waive those rights, what you'll do if you plead guilty, then they'll be waived and the next thing will be the sentencing?" The brothers each answered affirmatively. . . .

Judge Moore then homed in on voluntariness:

> The Court: Now, you are the only ones who can plead—change your plea to a charge, this Count 2, and it's—your plea [is] valid only if it's your free and voluntary act. So, Mr. Irvine Hodge, has anyone forced you in any way to enter a plea to this charge?
>
> Irvine: No, Your Honor.
>
> The Court: Anybody threatened you or promised you something?
>
> Irvine: No, Your Honor.
>
> The Court: When I say "promised," I'm talking about something other than what we went over in the plea agreement.
>
> Irvine: No, Your Honor.
>
> The Court: How about you, Mr. Devin Hodge; anyone forced you, forcing you now or bring any kind of pressure on you to coerce you in changing your plea?
>
> Hodge: No, Your Honor. I'm doing it of my own.

In March 2002, Devin, Irvine and their co-defendant were sentenced at the same hearing. . . . . [After the hearing], Judge Moore concluded that, in light of his knowledge of the case, what he had heard at the change-of-plea hearing, and the terms of the plea agreement, he had no alternative but to sentence both of the Hodge brothers to life in prison. . . .

II

A

[In this part of the opinion the court concluded that the government had breached its obligations under the plea agreement. Although the prosecutor agreed "to make no specific sentencing recommendation other than to request that the sentence be within the guideline range," the court found that the government's statements at sentencing were in fact advocating a life sentence. The court said the case would be remanded to the district court for a determination whether to grant specific performance or allow Devin to withdraw his guilty plea. Breaches of government promises made during plea negotiations are dealt with in Section B.4.c. of this chapter, below. — EDS.]

B

Devin further argues on appeal that the District Court's plea colloquy was deficient because the District Judge did not know Devin's plea was contingent on Irvine's identical plea, and vice versa. Had the District Court been properly informed about the package deal and had Devin been properly questioned, he contends that he would have been dissuaded from pleading guilty.

United States v. Vonn, 535 U.S. 55 (2002), held that a defendant who fails to object to Rule 11 error must carry the burden of showing on appeal that the error was "plain, prejudicial, and disreputable to the judicial system." Id. at 65. In other words, a defendant must show that: "(1) an error was committed; (2) the error was plain, that is, clear and obvious; and (3) the error affected the defendant's substantial rights. When those elements are satisfied, an appellate court in its discretion may order a correction if the error "seriously affects the fairness, integrity, or public reputation of judicial proceedings."

We conclude that the District Court did not commit plain error during the Rule 11 colloquy. Though the terms of the packaging agreement have not been disclosed to us, the government does not dispute that Devin's and Irvine's pleas were locked. And, indeed, the government's cover letter to the final draft plea agreement states that the pleas were "lock[ed]." As we explain below, other Courts of Appeals require disclosure of such arrangements to the district court, which must exercise special care at the Rule 11 colloquy to ensure that each participant pleads voluntarily. Until today, however, that was not the law in this Circuit. . . . [In addition,] even if the District Court had been informed that Devin's plea was packaged, we cannot say that failure to conduct Devin's colloquy with special care would have been "clear and obvious" error. It follows *a fortiori* that failure to provide special care was not clear and obvious error where, as here, the District Court was not informed of the package deal. . . .

While we hold that the District Court committed no plain error, we believe that determining voluntariness in package deal situations is an especially delicate matter.

We therefore write to provide guidance to the District Court should a new plea colloquy be necessary on remand, and to assist future district courts considering such pleas.

As their name suggests, package deal plea bargains exist where the government accepts a defendant's guilty plea on the condition that his co-defendant(s) also plead guilty. The incentive to join such arrangements is straightforward: the government offers defendants a "volume discount—a better deal than each could have gotten separately." United States v. Caro, 997 F.2d 657, 658 (9th Cir. 1993). Of course, the benefits of such deals are seldom distributed evenly, and every defendant may not be equally interested in bargain shopping. Familial or fraternal coercion of putative confederates in package plea deals is a serious concern, as to some extent is self-imposed pressure. Though reserving judgment on the question, the Supreme Court has warned that "offers of leniency or adverse treatment for some person other than the accused . . . might pose a greater danger of inducing a false guilty plea by skewing the assessment of the risks a defendant must consider." Bordenkircher v. Hayes, 434 U.S. 357, 365 n. 8 (1977). Mindful of these considerations, other Courts of Appeals widely require that (1) package plea deals be disclosed to the court[12] and (2) colloquies with package plea participants be conducted with special care.[13] We agree, and adopt these requirements for district courts in this Circuit considering packaged pleas.

There is no question that package deal plea bargains are constitutional. See [United States v. Pollard, 959 F.2d 1011, 1021-1022 (D.C. Cir. 1992)]. That conclusion is nearly axiomatic given the nature of our criminal justice system, of which plea bargains are an "essential part." "While confronting a defendant with the risk of more severe punishment clearly may have a discouraging effect on the defendant's assertion of his trial rights," the Supreme Court has explained, "the imposition of these difficult choices [is] an inevitable—and permissible—attribute of any legitimate system which tolerates and encourages the negotiation of pleas." Bordenkircher, 434 U.S. at 364. In turn, the Second Circuit has noted that, "[s]ince a defendant's plea is not rendered involuntary because he enters it to save himself many years in prison, it is difficult to see why the law should not permit a defendant to negotiate a plea that confers a similar benefit on others." [United States v. Marquez, 909 F.2d 738, 742 (2d Cir. 1990).] We agree and hold that package deal plea bargains are constitutionally permissible.

Though allowed, package deal pleas pose special risks, particularly when a trial court is unaware that defendants' pleas are tied together. The First Circuit, which

12. United States v. Daniels, 821 F.2d 76, 78-79 (1st Cir. 1987) (Breyer, J.) (holding that government failure to tell court at Rule 11 hearing that plea was packaged violated Rule 11); United States v. Clements, 992 F.2d 417, 419 (2d Cir. 1993) (per curiam) (stating that disclosure of plea packaging is the "preferred practice" and the "more prudent course," and that packaging "should be stated to the court."); United States v. Bennett, 332 F.3d 1094, 1101 (7th Cir.2003); United States v. Caro, 997 F.2d 657, 659-60 (9th Cir. 1993); United States v. Holland, 117 F.3d 589, 594 (D.C. Cir. 1997) (district court "should be informed" about plea packaging). [Further citations omitted.]

13. United States v. Tursi, 576 F.2d 396, 398 (1st Cir. 1978) (holding that "special care must be taken to ascertain the voluntariness of the [packaged] guilty plea"); Harman v. Mohn, 683 F.2d 834, 837-38 (4th Cir. 1982); [United States v. Usher, 703 F.2d 956, 958 (6th Cir. 1983);] Politte v. United States, 852 F.2d 924 (7th Cir. 1988); United States v. Castello, 724 F.2d 813, 815 (9th Cir. 1984). See United States v. Nuckols, 606 F.2d 566, 570 (5th Cir. 1979) (holding that special care must be taken to determine voluntariness where plea agreement is "made in consideration of lenient treatment as against third persons"). [Further citations omitted.]

has an extensive jurisprudence in this area, most often has reversed package deal pleas when the district court was not informed of the packaging. [United States v. Mescual-Cruz, 387 F.3d 1, 8 (1st Cir. 2004).] According to the First Circuit's sound reasoning, when a defendant's plea rests on a promise by the government that another defendant will benefit, that promise is a material term of the agreement. And, of course, "[f]ull disclosure to the district court of the material terms of plea agreements is necessary to insure that the Rule 11 colloquy is thorough and searching as to defendant's knowing, intelligent, and voluntary waiver of the right, among others, to a jury trial." [Id.] We therefore hold that the parties must notify the district court that a package deal exists and state to the court on the record the specific terms of that deal.[14]

Once a court has been told of a package deal, special care should be exercised during the Rule 11 plea colloquy to ensure that the defendant is pleading voluntarily. Other Courts of Appeals have studiously declined to dictate detailed "special care" marching orders. See, e.g., *Mescual-Cruz*, 387 F.3d at 8. We share their caution. More than three decades ago, the Supreme Court warned that the "[t]he nature of the inquiry required by Rule 11 must necessarily vary from case to case," McCarthy v. United States, 394 U.S. 459, 467 n. 20 (1969), and it recently reiterated that "Rule 11 should not be given such a crabbed interpretation that ceremony was exalted over substance." *Vonn*, 535 U.S. at 70. . . .

What then in general terms is "special care"? At the threshold, a district court notified of a package deal plea bargain should question counsel closely to ensure that the precise terms of the package plea deal are on the record. See Fed. R. Crim. P. 11(b)(2), 11(c)(2). Once it is clear exactly how a defendant's plea benefits his confederate(s), it may be helpful to ask who first proposed the package deal, see Politte v. United States, 852 F.2d 924, 930-931 (7th Cir. 1988), how extensively defense counsel was involved in developing the deal, and what benefit the defendant expects to gain from the deal. When asking whether a plea is a product of force, threats, or inducements and the like, a district court should take care not to ask only whether the *prosecutor* forced, threatened, or coerced the defendant, but whether anyone did so. United States v. Martinez-Molina, 64 F.3d 719, 734 (1st Cir. 1995). Having so inquired, the court should be particularly attuned to even mild expressions of reluctance by a defendant. *See* United States v. Farley, 72 F.3d 158, 164 (D.C. Cir. 1995). Such expressions always should trigger a more searching inquiry. See *Farley*, 72 F.3d at 164. On the other hand, as none of the defendants may be particularly eager to plead guilty, one defendant's expressions of reluctance should be compared to those of other defendants involved in the package deal.

---

14. Two Courts of Appeals have suggested that the duty to disclose plea packaging "falls with particular weight on prosecutors[,] who have a responsibility not merely to win, but to win fairly." [United States v. Caro, 997 F.2d 657, 659 n. 2 (9th Cir. 1993).]; [United States v. Clements, 992 F.2d 417, 419 (2d Cir. 1993).] (recommending prosecutorial disclosure as the "preferred practice"). Other Courts of Appeals expressly require prosecutorial disclosure yet are silent regarding defense counsel's commensurate duty, if any. *Mescual–Cruz*, 387 F.3d at 9 (requiring prosecutorial disclosure); [United States v. Bennett, 332 F.3d 1094, 1101 (7th Cir. 2003).] (same). We of course recognize that defendants, not prosecutors, face the danger of skewed assessment of risks when package deal plea bargains are at stake. See *Bordenkircher*, 434 U.S. at 365 n. 8. Descriptively, prosecutors thus may be more likely actually to disclose package deal pleas than their counterparts. But that does not absolve defense counsel from their express duty under Rule 11 to notify the court of the material terms of the plea agreement. Prescriptively, as officers of the court, defense counsel have no less of a duty to follow the rules of disclosure than prosecutors. That duty includes disclosing that a plea bargain is a package deal.

The foregoing is not a checklist that, if followed, automatically will prevent a Rule 11 colloquy from going awry. Rather, it is a summary of lessons drawn from colloquies evaluated by other Courts of Appeals. The overarching rule is that a district court considering a package plea deal should be particularly attentive to a defendant's responses to voluntariness questions throughout a plea colloquy. That being said, district courts of course should remember that package deal plea bargains are not inherently coercive, and that the judge's goal is not to doom the deal but simply to ensure that the defendant's plea is voluntary.

We recognize that Rule 11 colloquies have grown in length since their formal adoption, and we only cautiously augment their manifold considerations. Nevertheless, when the government risks inducing false guilty pleas by packaging pleas together, *Bordenkircher*, 434 U.S. at 365 n. 8, justice and prudence require that the district court be notified and pay special care.

NOTES AND QUESTIONS

1. Why should the prosecutor in *Hodge* be allowed to condition a plea offer to one defendant on the willingness of a second defendant to plead guilty? Defendants in these positions are, or at least should be, represented by separate counsel, which will often make it difficult for one defendant to control what the other will do. Is there any legitimate prosecutorial goal being served by packaged plea deals, or are they simply another lever for the prosecutor to pull to induce a guilty plea?

2. Although nearly all courts have found packaged plea deals (also called "tied" or "wired" plea agreements) constitutional, nearly all also find them worrisome, hence the discussion about the "special care" that must be taken when a court considers such a deal. As *Hodge* and other cases have recognized, there is a distinctive risk that packaged plea bargains will induce an innocent person to plead guilty, just to spare a loved one the trauma of the criminal process. Many people who could not otherwise imagine admitting to a crime that they did not commit might nonetheless be willing to plead guilty if the prosecutor said that the failure to plead would result in charges being filed against their child, their spouse, a sibling, or a parent.

This was the situation in United States v. Pollard, 959 F.2d 1011 (1992), where the D.C. Circuit affirmed the denial of habeas corpus relief for convicted spy Jonathan Pollard, who argued that he was unfairly pressured into pleading guilty (and cooperating with the government) by the desire to protect his wife, who was seriously ill at the time, from a possible life sentence as his alleged accomplice. Mr. Pollard agreed to plead guilty in return for the government's agreement to offer a lenient plea bargain to his wife, and was thereafter sentenced to life imprisonment. The court of appeals recognized the special risk this particular kind of plea deal created:

> To say that a practice is "coercive" or renders a plea "involuntary" means only that it creates improper pressure that would be likely to overbear the will of some innocent persons and cause them to plead guilty. . . .
>
> We can understand how it might be thought that a threat of long imprisonment for a loved one, particularly a spouse, would constitute even greater pressure on a defendant than a direct threat to him. Whether one could generalize as to that proposition depends, we suppose, on one's view of human nature.

Nonetheless, the court of appeals upheld the plea, concluding that the purported distinctive risks associated with protecting a family member "does not seem to be the sort of widely shared intuition upon which a constitutional rule should be based." The court was also unimpressed with the claimed additional pressures Pollard felt because of his wife's ill health.

> Nor do we believe that Mrs. Pollard's medical condition makes an otherwise acceptable linkage of their pleas unconstitutional. The appropriate dividing line between acceptable and unconstitutional plea wiring does not depend upon the physical condition or personal circumstances of the defendant; rather, it depends upon the conduct of the government. Where, as here, the government had probable cause to arrest and prosecute both defendants in a related crime, and there is no suggestion that the government conducted itself in bad faith in an effort to generate additional leverage over the defendant, we think a wired plea is constitutional.

Id., at 1021-1022.[8]

What is your "view of human nature"? Is it improper to put this kind of pressure on a defendant, or is it simply giving him the chance to purchase, through his guilty plea, something he may value more than dropped charges or sentencing concessions? Does your answer turn in part on how likely it is that, as noted in *Pollard*, the prosecution will "conduct[] itself in bad faith in an effort to generate additional leverage over the defendant"?

3. Suppose the defendant is charged with engaging in a drug sale while carrying a weapon, the penalty for which is much higher than it would be for a similar drug sale while unarmed. The defendant offers to plead guilty to the sale, but in return wants the prosecutor to stipulate that there was no weapon involved. Can the prosecutor engage in this kind of "fact bargaining?" If the parties make the deal, what would the lawyers say at the plea hearing if the judge asked whether the defendant was carrying a gun? The Justice Department has taken the position that "[s]tipulations to untrue facts are unethical," U.S. Attorney Manual 9-27.430, http://www.justice.gov/usam/usam-9-27000-principles-federal-prosecution#9-27.400. If so, is it permissible for the prosecutor to reduce a charge to petty theft to get a guilty plea when the value of the item stolen would make it grand theft? Reduce the claimed weight of the drugs the defendant was carrying to help bring about a lower sentence? Why or why not?

4. A guilty plea already has the effect of waiving most legal protections a criminal defendant has (see Section A, above). Can the prosecutor seek the waiver of even more rights, including those designed to protect the accuracy and integrity of the process?

One common provision in plea agreements is that the defendant agree to waive any appeal rights and postconviction challenges. Nearly every federal court of appeals has found these provisions valid, even though the waivers often cover challenges to the sentence that the defendant will later receive, and thus is unknown to the defendant at the time he makes the deal. Notice, however, that some courts have refused to enforce appeals waivers in limited circumstances, such as when the

[right margin handwritten note: Most federal appeals courts uphold validity of waiving appeals rights + postconviction challenges]

---

8. On July 28, 2015, Jonathan Pollard was granted parole; he was released on November 20, 2015, after having spent 30 years in prison. See http://www.cnn.com/2015/11/20/us/jonathan-pollard-israel-spy-release/.

district court failed to follow Rule 11 in taking the plea, the sentence imposed violated the plea agreement or the statute, or the prosecutor breached the plea agreement. See, e.g., United States v. Brizan, 709 F.3d 864, 866 (9th Cir. 2013).

5. Similarly, in United States v. Mezzanatto, 513 U.S. 196 (1996), the prosecutor was willing to discuss a cooperation agreement with the defense, but only if the defendant was willing waive the privilege to keep the negotiations confidential. Normally, under Federal Rule of Evidence 410, discussions during plea negotiations are inadmissible in a later trial against the accused if those discussions fail to result in a deal. In *Mezzanatto*, however, the government made it a condition of the discussions that the defendant waive this protection and allow the government to use his statements as impeachment evidence. Mr. Mezzanatto waived, negotiations broke down, and defendant's damaging admissions during the discussions were used to impeach his testimony at trial.

Defendant argued that the inadmissibility of plea discussions should be considered unwaivable, but the Supreme Court disagreed. Justice Thomas's opinion for the majority acknowledged that "[t]here may be some evidentiary provisions that are so fundamental to the reliability of the factfinding process that they may never be waived without irreparably discrediting the federal courts," but concluded that "enforcement of agreements like respondent's plainly will not have that effect. The admission of plea statements for impeachment purposes enhances the truth-seeking function of trials and will result in more accurate verdicts."[9]

The Court also rejected the argument that allowing prosecutors to insist on the waiver of rights would discourage plea bargaining. In language that could apply to a whole host of rights that defendant might be required to relinquish, the Court observed:

> [A]s a logical matter, it simply makes no sense to conclude that mutual settlement will be encouraged by precluding negotiation over an issue that may be particularly important to one of the parties to the transaction. A sounder way to encourage settlement is to permit the interested parties to enter into knowing and voluntary negotiations without any arbitrary limits on their bargaining chips. . . . A defendant can "maximize" what he has to "sell" only if he is permitted to offer what the prosecutor is most interested in buying.

Id., at 204, 206. Do you agree? Is it really in the defendant's interest to be able to bargain away all rights that he has in order to secure a plea deal? Can you identify some rights that a court might say *cannot* be waived, because that right is "so fundamental to the reliability of the factfinding process" that it would "discredit the federal courts" to allow the waiver?

6. Suppose the prosecutor attempts to use her leverage in the plea bargain process for purposes *other* than enforcement of the criminal law. The next case discusses this issue:

---

9. Lower federal courts have subsequently extended *Mezzanatto* to allow the prosecution to obtain, and enforce, a broader Rule 410 waiver that allows the defendant's statements made during failed plea negotiations to be used as part of the prosecution's case in chief. See United States v. Sylvester, 583 F.3d 285 (5th Cir. 2009); United States v. Burch, 156 F.3d 1315 (D.C. Cir. 1998).

NEWTON v. RUMERY

Certiorari to the United States Court of Appeals for the First Circuit
480 U.S. 386 (1987)

JUSTICE POWELL delivered the opinion of the Court with respect to Parts I, II, III-A, IV, and V, and an opinion with respect to Part III-B, in which CHIEF JUSTICE REHNQUIST, JUSTICE WHITE, and JUSTICE SCALIA joined.

The question in this case is whether a court properly may enforce an agreement in which a criminal defendant releases his right to file an action under 42 U.S.C. §1983 in return for a prosecutor's dismissal of pending criminal charges.

I

In 1983, a grand jury in Rockingham County, New Hampshire, indicted David Champy for aggravated felonious sexual assault. Respondent Bernard Rumery, a friend of Champy's, read about the charges in a local newspaper. Seeking information about the charges, he telephoned Mary Deary, who was acquainted with both Rumery and Champy. Coincidentally, Deary had been the victim of the assault in question and was expected to be the principal witness against Champy. The record does not reveal directly the date or substance of this conversation between Rumery and Deary, but Deary apparently was disturbed by the call. On March 12, according to police records, she called David Barrett, the Chief of Police for the town of Newton. She told him that Rumery was trying to force her to drop the charges against Champy. Rumery talked to Deary again on May 11. The substance of this conversation also is disputed. Rumery claims that Deary called him and that she raised the subject of Champy's difficulties. According to the police records, however, Deary told Chief Barrett that Rumery had threatened that, if Deary went forward on the Champy case, she would "end up like" two women who recently had been murdered in Lowell, Massachusetts. App. 49. Barrett arrested Rumery and accused him of tampering with a witness in violation of N.H. Rev. Stat. Ann. §641:5(I)(b) (1986), a Class B felony.

Rumery promptly retained Stephen Woods, an experienced criminal defense attorney. Woods contacted Brian Graf, the Deputy County Attorney for Rockingham County. He warned Graf that he "had better [dismiss] these charges, because we're going to win them and after that we're going to sue." App. 11. After further discussions, Graf and Woods reached an agreement, under which Graf would dismiss the charges against Rumery if Rumery would agree not to sue the town, its officials, or Deary for any harm caused by the arrest. All parties agreed that one factor in Graf's decision not to prosecute Rumery was Graf's desire to protect Deary from the trauma she would suffer if she were forced to testify. . . .

Woods drafted an agreement in which Rumery agreed to release any claims he might have against the town, its officials, or Deary if Graf agreed to dismiss the criminal charges (the release-dismissal agreement). After Graf approved the form of the agreement, Woods presented it to Rumery. Although Rumery's recollection of the events was quite different, the District Court found that Woods discussed the agreement with Rumery in his office for about an hour and explained to Rumery that he would forgo all civil actions if he signed the agreement. Three days later, on June 6, 1983, Rumery returned to Woods' office and signed the agreement. The criminal charges were dropped.

Ten months later, on April 13, 1984, Rumery filed an action under §1983 in the Federal District Court for the District of New Hampshire. He alleged that the town and its officers had violated his constitutional rights by arresting him, defaming him, and imprisoning him falsely. The defendants filed a motion to dismiss, relying on the release-dismissal agreement as an affirmative defense. Rumery argued that the agreement was unenforceable because it violated public policy. The court rejected Rumery's argument and concluded that a "release of claims under section 1983 is valid . . . if it results from a decision that is voluntary, deliberate and informed." . . . The court then dismissed Rumery's suit.

On appeal, the Court of Appeals for the First Circuit reversed. It adopted a per se rule invalidating release-dismissal agreements. . . . We reverse.

II

We begin by noting the source of the law that governs this case. The agreement purported to waive a right to sue conferred by a federal statute. The question whether the policies underlying that statute may in some circumstances render that waiver unenforceable is a question of federal law. We resolve this question by reference to traditional common-law principles, as we have resolved other questions about the principles governing §1983 actions. . . . The relevant principle is well established: A promise is unenforceable if the interest in its enforcement is outweighed in the circumstances by a public policy harmed by enforcement of the agreement.

III

The Court of Appeals concluded that the public interests related to release-dismissal agreements justified a per se rule of invalidity. . . . [A]lthough we agree that in some cases these agreements may infringe important interests of the criminal defendant and of society as a whole, we do not believe that the mere possibility of harm to these interests calls for a per se rule.

A

Rumery's first objection to release-dismissal agreements is that they are inherently coercive. He argues that it is unfair to present a criminal defendant with a choice between facing criminal charges and waiving his right to sue under §1983. We agree that some release-dismissal agreements may not be the product of an informed and voluntary decision. The risk, publicity, and expense of a criminal trial may intimidate a defendant, even if he believes his defense is meritorious. But this possibility does not justify invalidating all such agreements. In other contexts criminal defendants are required to make difficult choices that effectively waive constitutional rights. For example, it is well settled that plea bargaining does not violate the Constitution even though a guilty plea waives important constitutional rights. See Brady v. United States, 397 U.S. 742, 752-753 (1970).[3] . . . We see no reason to

---

3. We recognize that the analogy between plea bargains and release-dismissal agreements is not complete. The former are subject to judicial oversight. Moreover, when the State enters a plea bargain with a criminal defendant, it receives immediate and tangible benefits, such as promptly imposed punishment without the expenditure of prosecutorial resources, see Brady v. United States, 397 U.S., at 752. Also, the defendant's agreement to plead to some crime tends to ensure some satisfaction of the public's interest in the prosecution of crime and confirms that the prosecutor's charges have a basis in fact. The benefits the State may realize in particular cases from release-dismissal agreements may not be as tangible, but they are not insignificant.

believe that release-dismissal agreements pose a more coercive choice than other situations we have accepted. . . .

In many cases a defendant's choice to enter into a release-dismissal agreement will reflect a highly rational judgment that the certain benefits of escaping criminal prosecution exceed the speculative benefits of prevailing in a civil action. Rumery's voluntary decision to enter this agreement exemplifies such a judgment. Rumery is a sophisticated businessman. He was not in jail and was represented by an experienced criminal lawyer, who drafted the agreement. Rumery considered the agreement for three days before signing it. The benefits of the agreement to Rumery are obvious: He gained immunity from criminal prosecution in consideration of abandoning a civil suit that he may well have lost.

Because Rumery voluntarily waived his right to sue under §1983, the public interest opposing involuntary waiver of constitutional rights is no reason to hold this agreement invalid. Moreover, we find that the possibility of coercion in the making of similar agreements insufficient by itself to justify a per se rule against release-dismissal bargains. If there is such a reason, it must lie in some external public interest necessarily injured by release-dismissal agreements.

B

[T]he Court of Appeals held that all release-dismissal agreements offend public policy because it believed these agreements "tempt prosecutors to trump up charges in reaction to a defendant's civil rights claim, suppress evidence of police misconduct, and leave unremedied deprivations of constitutional rights." 778 F.2d, at 69. We can agree that in some cases there may be a substantial basis for this concern. It is true, of course, that §1983 actions to vindicate civil rights may further significant public interests. But it is important to remember that Rumery had no public duty to institute a §1983 action merely to further the public's interest in revealing police misconduct. . . .

We also believe the Court of Appeals misapprehended the range of public interests arguably affected by a release-dismissal agreement. The availability of such agreements may threaten important public interests. They may tempt prosecutors to bring frivolous charges, or to dismiss meritorious charges, to protect the interests of other officials. But a per se rule of invalidity fails to credit other relevant public interests and improperly assumes prosecutorial misconduct.

The vindication of constitutional rights and the exposure of official misconduct are not the only concerns implicated by §1983 suits. No one suggests that all such suits are meritorious. Many are marginal and some are frivolous. Yet even when the risk of ultimate liability is negligible, the burden of defending such lawsuits is substantial. . . . To the extent release-dismissal agreements protect public officials from the burdens of defending such unjust claims, they further this important public interest.

A per se rule invalidating release-dismissal agreements also assumes that prosecutors will seize the opportunity for wrongdoing. . . . [C]ourts normally must defer to prosecutorial decisions as to whom to prosecute. . . . Because these decisions "are not readily susceptible to the kind of analysis the courts are competent to undertake," we have been "properly hesitant to examine the decision whether to prosecute." [Wayte v. United States, 470 U.S. 598,] 607-608 [(1985)].

Against this background of discretion, the mere opportunity to act improperly does not compel an assumption that all—or even a significant number of—release-dismissal agreements stem from prosecutors abandoning "the independence of judgment required by [their] public trust," Imbler v. Pachtman, 424 U.S. 409, 423 (1976). Rather, tradition and experience justify our belief that the great majority of prosecutors will be faithful to their duty. Indeed, the merit of this view is illustrated by this case, where the only evidence of prosecutorial misconduct is the agreement itself.

Because release-dismissal agreements may further legitimate prosecutorial and public interests, we reject the Court of Appeals' holding that all such agreements are invalid per se.[8]

IV

Turning to the agreement presented by this case, we conclude that the District Court's decision to enforce the agreement was correct. As we have noted, . . . it is clear that Rumery voluntarily entered the agreement. Moreover, in this case the prosecutor had an independent, legitimate reason to make this agreement directly related to his prosecutorial responsibilities. The agreement foreclosed both the civil and criminal trials concerning Rumery, in which Deary would have been a key witness. She therefore was spared the public scrutiny and embarrassment she would have endured if she had had to testify in either of those cases. Both the prosecutor and the defense attorney testified in the District Court that this was a significant consideration in the prosecutor's decision.

In sum, we conclude that this agreement was voluntary, that there is no evidence of prosecutorial misconduct, and that enforcement of this agreement would not adversely affect the relevant public interests.[10]

V

We reverse the judgment of the Court of Appeals and remand the case to the District Court for dismissal of the complaint.

JUSTICE O'CONNOR, concurring in part and concurring in the judgment.

I join in Parts I, II, III-A, IV, and V of the Court's opinion. . . . I write separately, however, in order to set out the factors that lead me to conclude that this covenant should be enforced and to emphasize that it is the burden of those relying upon such covenants to establish that the agreement is neither involuntary nor the product of an abuse of the criminal process. . . .

---

8. Justice Stevens' evaluation of the public interests associated with release-dismissal agreements relies heavily on his view that Rumery is a completely innocent man. He rests this conclusion on the testimony Rumery and his attorney presented to the District Court, but fails to acknowledge that the District Court's factual findings gave little credence to this testimony. Justice Stevens also gives great weight to the fact that Rumery "must be presumed to be innocent." But this is not a criminal case. This is a civil case, in which Rumery bears the ultimate burden of proof.

10. We note that two Courts of Appeals have applied a voluntariness standard to determine the enforceability of agreements entered into after trial, in which the defendants released possible §1983 claims in return for sentencing considerations. See Bushnell v. Rossetti, 750 F.2d 298 (CA4 1984); Jones v. Taber, 648 F.2d 1201 (CA9 1981). We have no occasion in this case to determine whether an inquiry into voluntariness alone is sufficient to determine the enforceability of release-dismissal agreements. We also note that it would be helpful to conclude release-dismissal agreements under judicial supervision. Although such supervision is not essential to the validity of an otherwise-proper agreement, it would help ensure that the agreements did not result from prosecutorial misconduct.

[T]he defendants in a §1983 suit may establish that a particular release executed in exchange for the dismissal of criminal charges was voluntarily made, not the product of prosecutorial overreaching, and in the public interest. But they must prove that this is so; the courts should not presume it as I fear portions of Part III-B of the plurality opinion may imply.

Many factors may bear on whether a release was voluntary and not the product of overreaching, some of which come readily to mind. The knowledge and experience of the criminal defendant and the circumstances of the execution of the release, including, importantly, whether the defendant was counseled, are clearly relevant. The nature of the criminal charges that are pending is also important, for the greater the charge, the greater the coercive effect. The existence of a legitimate criminal justice objective for obtaining the release will support its validity. And, importantly, the possibility of abuse is clearly mitigated if the release-dismissal agreement is executed under judicial supervision.

Close examination of all the factors in this case leads me to concur in the Court's decision that this covenant not to sue is enforceable. There is ample evidence in the record concerning the circumstances of the execution of this agreement. Testimony of the prosecutor, defense counsel, and Rumery himself leave little doubt that the agreement was entered into voluntarily. While the charge pending against Rumery was serious—subjecting him to up to seven years in prison, N.H. Rev. Stat. Ann. §641:5(I)(b) (1986)—it is one of the lesser felonies under New Hampshire law, and a long prison term was probably unlikely given the absence of any prior criminal record and the weaknesses in the case against Rumery. Finally, as the Court correctly notes, the prosecutor had a legitimate reason to enter into this agreement directly related to his criminal justice function. . . . Mary Deary's emotional distress, her unwillingness to testify against Rumery, presumably in later civil as well as criminal proceedings, and the necessity of her testimony in the pending sexual assault case against David Champy all support the prosecutor's judgment that the charges against Rumery should be dropped if further injury to Deary, and therefore the Champy case, could thereby be avoided.

Against the convincing evidence that Rumery voluntarily entered into the agreement and that it served the public interest, there is only Rumery's blanket claim that agreements such as this one are inherently coercive. While it would have been preferable, and made this an easier case, had the release-dismissal agreement been concluded under some form of judicial supervision, I concur in the Court's judgment, and all but Part III-B of its opinion, that Rumery's §1983 suit is barred by his valid, voluntary release.

JUSTICE STEVENS, with whom JUSTICE BRENNAN, JUSTICE MARSHALL, and JUSTICE BLACKMUN join, dissenting.

The question whether the release-dismissal agreement signed by respondent is unenforceable is much more complex than the Court's opinion indicates. . . .

I

Respondent is an innocent man. As a matter of law, he must be presumed to be innocent. As a matter of fact, the uncontradicted sworn testimony of respondent, and his lawyer, buttressed by the circumstantial evidence, overwhelmingly attest to his innocence. There was no written statement by the alleged victim, sworn or unsworn, implicating respondent in any criminal activity. . . . Respondent was never indicted, and the warrant for his arrest was issued on the basis of a sketchy statement by Chief Barrett. . . . Prior to the arrest, and prior to the police chief's press conference concerning it, respondent was a respected member of a small community who had never been arrested, even for a traffic offense.

A few days before respondent was scheduled for a probable-cause hearing on the charge of witness tampering, respondent's attorney advised him to sign a covenant not to sue the town of Newton, its police officers, or the witness Deary in exchange for dismissal of the charge against him. The advice was predicated on the lawyer's judgment that the value of a dismissal outweighed the harmful consequences of an almost certain indictment on a felony charge together with the risk of conviction in a case in which the outcome would depend on the jury's assessment of the relative credibility of respondent and his alleged victim. The lawyer correctly advised respondent that even if he was completely innocent, there could be no guarantee of acquittal. He therefore placed a higher value on his client's interest in terminating the criminal proceeding promptly than on the uncertain benefits of pursuing a civil remedy against the town and its police department. After delaying a decision for three days, respondent reluctantly followed his lawyer's advice.

From respondent's point of view, it is unquestionably true that the decision to sign the release-dismissal agreement was, as the Court emphasizes, "voluntary, deliberate, and informed." I submit, however, that the deliberate and rational character of respondent's decision is not a sufficient reason for concluding that the agreement is enforceable. Otherwise, a promise to pay a state trooper $20 for not issuing a ticket for a traffic violation, or a promise to contribute to the police department's retirement fund in exchange for the dismissal of a felony charge, would be enforceable. Indeed, I would suppose that virtually all contracts that courts refuse to enforce nevertheless reflect perfectly rational decisions by the parties who entered into them. There is nothing irrational about an agreement to bribe a police officer, to enter into a wagering arrangement, to pay usurious rates of interests, or to threaten to indict an innocent man in order to induce him to surrender something of value.

The "voluntary, deliberate, and informed" character of a defendant's decision generally provides an acceptable basis for upholding the validity of a plea bargain. But it is inappropriate to assume that the same standard determines the validity of a quite different agreement to forgo a civil remedy for the violation of the defendant's constitutional rights in exchange for complete abandonment of a criminal charge.

The net result of every plea bargain is an admission of wrongdoing by the defendant and the imposition of a criminal sanction with its attendant stigma. Although there may be some cases in which an innocent person pleads guilty to a minor offense to avoid the risk of conviction on a more serious charge, it is reasonable to presume that such cases are rare and represent the exception rather than the rule. . . . Like a plea bargain, an agreement by the suspect to drop §1983 charges and to pay restitution to the victim in exchange for the prosecutor's termination of criminal proceedings involves an admission of wrongdoing by the defendant. The same cannot be said about an agreement that completely exonerates the defendant. Not only is such a person presumptively innocent as a matter of law; as a factual matter the prosecutor's interest in obtaining a covenant not to sue will be strongest in those cases in which he realizes that the defendant was innocent and was wrongfully accused. Moreover, the prosecutor will be most willing—indeed, he is ethically obligated—to drop charges when he believes that probable cause as established by the available, admissible evidence is lacking.

. . . A defendant entering a release-dismissal agreement is forced to waive claims based on official conduct under color of state law, in exchange merely for the assurance that the State will not prosecute him for conduct for which he has made no admission of wrongdoing. The State is spared the necessity of going to trial, but its willingness to drop the charge completely indicates that it might not have proceeded with the prosecution in any event. No social interest in the punishment of wrongdoers is satisfied; the only interest vindicated is that of resolving once and for all the question of §1983 liability.

Achieving this result has no connection with the give-and-take over the defendant's wrongdoing that is the essence of the plea-bargaining process, and thus cannot be justified by reference to the principles of mutual advantage that support plea bargaining. . . .

Thus, even though respondent's decision in this case was deliberate, informed, and voluntary, this observation does not address two distinct objections to enforcement of the release-dismissal agreement. The prosecutor's offer to drop charges if the defendant accedes to the agreement is inherently coercive; moreover, the agreement exacts a price unrelated to the character of the defendant's own conduct.

II

When the prosecutor negotiated the agreement with respondent, he represented three potentially conflicting interests. His primary duty, of course, was to represent the sovereign's interest in the evenhanded and effective enforcement of its criminal laws. In addition, as the covenant demonstrates, he sought to represent the interests of the town of Newton and its Police Department in connection with their possible civil liability to respondent. Finally, as the inclusion of Mary Deary as a covenantee indicates, the prosecutor also represented the interest of a potential witness who allegedly accused both respondent and a mutual friend of separate instances of wrongdoing. . . .

If we view the problem from the standpoint of the prosecutor's principal client, the State of New Hampshire, it is perfectly clear that the release-dismissal agreement was both unnecessary and unjustified. . . . The public is entitled to have the prosecutor's decision to go forward with a criminal case, or to dismiss it, made independently of his concerns about the potential damages liability of the Police Department. . . . At bottom, the Court's holding in this case seems to rest on concerns related to the potential witness, Mary Deary. . . . Arguably a special rule should be fashioned for witnesses who are victims of sexual assaults. The trauma associated with such an assault leaves scars that may make it especially difficult for a victim to press charges or to testify publicly about the event. It remains true, however, that uncorroborated, unsworn statements by persons who claim to have been victims of any crime, including such an assault, may be inaccurate, exaggerated, or incomplete—and sometimes even malicious. It is even more clear that hearsay descriptions of statements by such persons may be unreliable. Rather than adopting a general rule that upholds a release-dismissal agreement whenever the criminal charge was based on a statement by the alleged victim of a sexual assault, I believe the Court should insist upon a "close examination" of the facts that purportedly justified the agreement. . . .

Deary's unwillingness to testify against Rumery is perfectly obvious. That fact unquestionably supports the prosecutor's decision to dismiss the charge against respondent, but it is not a sufficient reason for exonerating police officers from the consequences of actions that they took when they must have known that Deary was unwilling to testify. . . . The need for Deary's testimony in the pending sexual assault case against Champy simply cannot justify denying this respondent a remedy for a violation of his Fourth Amendment rights. . . .

III

Because this is the first case of this kind that the Court has reviewed, I am hesitant to adopt an absolute rule invalidating all such agreements. I am, however, persuaded that the federal policies reflected in the enactment and enforcement of §1983 mandate a strong presumption against the enforceability of such agreements and that the presumption is not overcome in this case by the facts or by any of the policy concerns discussed by the plurality. . . .

Accordingly, although I am not prepared to endorse all of the reasoning of the Court of Appeals, I would affirm its judgment.

NOTES AND QUESTIONS

1. Because Justice O'Connor provided the crucial fifth vote for the outcome, her concurring opinion defines the enforceability of plea bargains containing release-dismissal agreements. What, exactly, is her position? How does it differ from the positions of Justice Powell and Justice Stevens?

2. Both the plurality and Justice O'Connor's opinion emphasize the public interest that can be furthered by release-dismissal agreements. In this regard, consider MacBoyle v. City of Panama, 384 F.3d 456 (6th Cir. 2004). The police were called to an apartment party because of a noise complaint, and once inside, observed possible underage drinking. According to the police, MacBoyle (who was not underage) became verbally abusive; according to MacBoyle, the police were verbally abusive and refused to leave. You know how the rest of the story goes — police arrest MacBoyle and charge him with resisting arrest and disorderly conduct; MacBoyle claims that he police used excessive force in making the arrest. The parties later entered into a release-dismissal agreement, where most of the charges were dismissed in return for MacBoyle's agreement not to sue. MacBoyle then changed his mind and brought a civil action for excessive force under 28 U.S.C. §1983.

Why should the courts enforce the agreement here? (Both the district court and court of appeals did so, and dismissed the civil action.) If Mr. MacBoyle resisted arrest and engaged in disorderly conduct, isn't the public interest best served if he is prosecuted, whether the police used excessive force or not? Alternatively, if it were the police who overreacted, or even if the prosecutor would normally just dismiss the charges because no real harm was done, shouldn't the criminal case be dismissed regardless of whether the defendant had a valid civil claim? On the other side, although MacBoyle is not obligated to bring a civil suit, if he wants to bring one, doesn't the public have an interest in seeing police officers who use excessive force held accountable? How then is the public interest being served by an agreement that may cover up *both* criminal behavior *and* police misconduct? If you represented the government in defending the agreement in *MacBoyle*, how would you articulate the public interest being served?

3. How far can the prosecutor go in using the plea bargain power to further the public interest? Suppose, for example, a mayor is caught engaging the services of a prostitute, which is a misdemeanor in the relevant jurisdiction. Can the prosecutor propose a deal whereby she will not file charges if the mayor resigns his office? Is it the prosecutor's place to decide whether the mayor should continue to serve, despite the (relatively minor) criminal charge, rather than the voters'? Compare United States v. Richmond, 550 F. Supp. 605 (E.D.N.Y. 1982) (invalidating portions of plea agreement related to the resignation from Congress and the agreement not to seek reelection), with U.S. Attorney's Manual, Criminal Resource Manual 624, http://www.justice.gov/usam/criminal-resource-manual-624-plea-negotiations-public-officials-us-v-richmond (visited Aug. 20, 2015) (disagreeing with *Richmond*, and encouraging federal prosecutors "to continue to consider voluntary offers of resignation from office as a desirable feature in plea agreements with elected and appointed public officials at all levels of government").

4. Plea Bargains as Contracts

It is often said that plea bargaining is a uniquely American institution. This statement, however, requires some important clarification. Virtually all systems of criminal justice throughout the world regularly provide defendants with a significant benefit (usually, more lenient punishment) if they concede, or at least do not contest, their guilt. And virtually all systems of criminal justice reserve the most elaborate kind of adjudicative proceeding available in such a system (e.g., a full-blown criminal trial) for a small subset of criminal cases, including those in which the defendants forego the aforementioned benefit and actively contest their guilt. These two key features of plea bargaining—encouragement for defendants to concede (or at least not to contest) their guilt, and corresponding conservation of systemic resources—are almost universal.

What is unusual about American-style plea bargaining, however, is the contract-like manner in which this incentive structure is implemented. In most other countries, it would be unthinkable (and often illegal) for the prosecution to engage in explicit negotiations with the defense for the purpose of entering into a binding agreement to trade favorable treatment for the defendant's trial rights.

As you read the following cases, you should think about the similarities—and the differences—between traditional contract law and the law and practice of plea bargaining.

a. *Contract Formation*

MABRY v. JOHNSON

Certiorari to the United States Court of Appeals for the Eighth Circuit
467 U.S. 504 (1984)

JUSTICE STEVENS delivered the opinion of the Court.

The question presented is whether a defendant's acceptance of a prosecutor's proposed plea bargain creates a constitutional right to have the bargain specifically enforced.

In the late evening of May 22, 1970, three members of a family returned home to find a burglary in progress. Shots were exchanged resulting in the daughter's death and the wounding of the father and respondent—one of the burglars. Respondent was tried and convicted on three charges: burglary, assault, and murder. The murder conviction was set aside by the Arkansas Supreme Court. Thereafter, plea negotiations ensued.

At the time of the negotiations respondent was serving his concurrent 21- and 12-year sentences on the burglary and assault convictions. On Friday, October 27, 1972, a deputy prosecutor proposed to respondent's attorney that in exchange for a plea of guilty to the charge of accessory after a felony murder, the prosecutor would recommend a sentence of 21 years to be served concurrently with the burglary and assault sentences. On the following day, counsel communicated the offer to respondent who agreed to accept it. On the next Monday the lawyer called the prosecutor "and communicated [respondent's] acceptance of the offer." App. 10. The prosecutor then told counsel that a mistake had been made and withdrew the offer. He proposed instead that in exchange for a guilty plea he would recommend a sentence of 21 years to be served consecutively to respondent's other sentences. Respondent rejected the new offer and elected to stand trial. On the second day of trial, the judge declared a mistrial and plea negotiations resumed, ultimately resulting in respondent's acceptance of the prosecutor's second offer. In accordance with the plea bargain, the state trial judge imposed a 21-year sentence to be served consecutively to the previous sentences.

After exhausting his state remedies, respondent filed a petition for a writ of habeas corpus under 28 U.S.C. §2254. The District Court dismissed the petition, finding that respondent had understood the consequences of his guilty plea, that he had received the effective assistance of counsel, and that because the evidence did not establish that respondent had detrimentally relied on the prosecutor's first proposed plea agreement, respondent had no right to enforce it. The Court of Appeals reversed. . . . The [court] concluded that "fairness" precluded the prosecution's withdrawal of a plea proposal once accepted by respondent. . . . We now reverse.

Respondent can obtain federal habeas corpus relief only if his custody is in violation of the Federal Constitution. A plea bargain standing alone is without constitutional significance; in itself it is a mere executory agreement which, until embodied in the judgment of a court, does not deprive an accused of liberty or any other constitutionally protected interest.[5] It is the ensuing guilty plea that implicates the Constitution. Only after respondent pleaded guilty was he convicted, and it is that conviction which gave rise to the deprivation of respondent's liberty at issue here.

It is well settled that a voluntary and intelligent plea of guilty made by an accused person, who has been advised by competent counsel, may not be collaterally attacked. It is also well settled that plea agreements are consistent with the requirements of voluntariness and intelligence—because each side may obtain advantages when a guilty plea is exchanged for sentencing concessions, the agreement is no less voluntary than any other bargained-for exchange. It is only when the consensual

---

5. Under Arkansas law, there is no entitlement to have the trial court impose a recommended sentence since a negotiated sentence recommendation does not bind the court, see Varnedare v. State, 264 Ark. 596, 599, 573 S.W.2d 57, 60 (1978); Marshall v. State, 262 Ark. 726, 561 S.W.2d 76 (1978); Ark. Rule Crim. Proc. 25.3(c); there is a critical difference between an entitlement and a mere hope or expectation that the trial court will follow the prosecutor's recommendation, see Olim v. Wakinekona, 461 U.S. 238, 248-251 (1983).

character of the plea is called into question that the validity of a guilty plea may be impaired. [See] Brady v. United States, 397 U.S. 742 (1970). . . .

Thus, only when it develops that the defendant was not fairly apprised of its consequences can his plea be challenged under the Due Process Clause. . . . It follows that when the prosecution breaches its promise with respect to an executed plea agreement, the defendant pleads guilty on a false premise, and hence his conviction cannot stand. . . .

. . . Respondent's plea was in no sense induced by the prosecutor's withdrawn offer; . . . at the time respondent pleaded guilty he knew the prosecution would recommend a 21-year consecutive sentence. Respondent does not challenge the District Court's finding that he pleaded guilty with the advice of competent counsel and with full awareness of the consequences—he knew that the prosecutor would recommend and that the judge could impose the sentence now under attack. Respondent's plea was thus in no sense the product of governmental deception; it rested on no "unfulfilled promise" and fully satisfied the test for voluntariness and intelligence.

Thus, because it did not impair the voluntariness or intelligence of his guilty plea, respondent's inability to enforce the prosecutor's offer is without constitutional significance. Neither is the question whether the prosecutor was negligent or otherwise culpable in first making and then withdrawing his offer relevant. The Due Process Clause is not a code of ethics for prosecutors; its concern is with the manner in which persons are deprived of their liberty. Here respondent was not deprived of his liberty in any fundamentally unfair way. Respondent was fully aware of the likely consequences when he pleaded guilty; it is not unfair to expect him to live with those consequences now. . . .

NOTES AND QUESTIONS

1. *Mabry* remains good law on the main legal issue presented, namely, that in the absence of detrimental reliance, a plea agreement reached by the parties does not become enforceable until the resulting guilty plea is accepted by the court.

If *Mabry* were an ordinary contracts case, how would it be decided? The standard contracts rule is that an executory contract is enforceable from the time the parties exchange promises. Once the government's offer to recommend concurrent sentences was accepted, that exchange had taken place—the government had promised a particular sentencing recommendation, and the defendant had promised to plead guilty. Then the government reneged. Why was the deal not enforceable?

2. Suppose the *defendant* had reneged: Suppose that, on the day of the plea, the defendant announced that he had changed his mind and no longer wished to plead guilty. Could the government hold him to his promise? If not, why not? Do your answers help resolve the question in the preceding note? Cf. Fed. R. Crim. P. 11(d)(1) ("A defendant may withdraw a plea of guilty or nolo contendere . . . before the court accepts the plea, for any reason or for no reason.").

3. Consistent with *Mabry*, courts routinely say that there is no enforceable plea agreement until the defendant actually pleads guilty or otherwise acts in detrimental reliance on the government's offer. What form might this detrimental reliance take? In United States v. Vizcarrondo-Casanova, 763 F.3d 89, 102-103 (1st Cir. 2014), for example, the defendant argued that once the government made the offer and the defendant accepted, he filed a motion to change his plea from not guilty to guilty, thereby signaling his guilt. The court of appeals found that although the

motion was filed in reasonable reliance on the apparent deal, there was no detriment to the defense when the government withdrew the offer, as simply filing the change of plea motion would not harm the defendant as the case moved forward.

So what would count as detrimental reliance? Suppose the defendant claimed that he stopped investigating once a deal was made, and that when the government reneged on the deal, his investigative leads were lost. Should the court find that at that point, the government could no longer withdraw the offer? Or suppose the plea deal included a provision that required the defendant to provide information against his accomplices, and before the defendant pled guilty, he began giving information to the prosecutor. Could the government avoid the detrimental reliance argument by agreeing not to use the information provided? Or is it too late at that point for the government to back out of the deal?

4. Most plea bargains involve a fairly simple exchange—the defendant agrees to plead guilty, and the government agrees to some charging or sentencing concessions. The chief issues in those bargains are of the sort that arise for any class of contracts: determining whether a bargain has been struck, interpreting the contract terms, and choosing a remedy in case of breach.

There is another class of bargains that raises a different set of issues. In many cases, the government is "buying" not only a guilty plea but also information (and typically courtroom testimony). That kind of bargain necessarily involves a good deal more uncertainty, on both sides, than is often the case with more conventional plea bargains. Consider the following discussion, taken from Daniel C. Richman, Cooperating Clients, 56 Ohio St. L.J. 69, 94-101 (1995):

> In contrast to the defendant choosing simply between plea and trial, the defendant who has testimony or information to "sell" must consider a leap into uncertainty. Everyone knows that, as a class, cooperators get big sentencing breaks. However, at the time he is contemplating whether to cooperate, a defendant typically will not know how large a discount he can expect, nor can he be sure that, were he to satisfy his part of the bargain, he would get a discount at all.
>
> Nothing about cooperation inherently compels this state of affairs. One can imagine a scheme in which a defendant interested in cooperating would give the government a summary of the information he has to sell, protected by a side agreement that would bar the government from using the information against him if negotiations break down. Alternatively, the defendant's lawyer could make a proffer of this information. Were the government willing to deal, an agreement could be struck obliging the defendant to plead guilty to certain charges and to testify or give information truthfully at the government's request; in exchange, the government would agree to make a sentencing presentation designed to give the defendant a precise discount commensurate with the value of his information. The defendant could then be sentenced before he actually testified in a single trial. If, thereafter, he reneged on his obligations, he could be prosecuted anew, for perjury in his trial testimony, for any charge dropped in consideration of his promise to cooperate, or for both.
>
> Such arrangements . . . are rarely available, because they do not serve the government's interests—and may not even serve most defendants' interests. Above all, the government's fear is that a defendant who has received his reward up front will perjure himself—give an account at odds with the "true" account that led the government to enter the cooperation agreement—when it comes time to testify against his former criminal associates. To deter defendants from "recanting," the government needs a mechanism . . . that promises swift and certain punishment for such conduct. An agreement that requires the government to pursue a defector in a separate criminal trial—and, for those charges dismissed pursuant to the agreement, to prove

breach of the agreement before even getting before a jury—does not fit this bill. The most efficient way for the government to keep some hold over the defendant is to postpone sentencing until after his cooperation.

A similar concern that a defendant have an incentive to testify "at his best" also leads the government to prefer an agreement that does not specify how much leniency a defendant can expect for his cooperation. Such vagueness allows . . . the government to avoid a stark choice between rewarding the defendant whose cooperation has been grudging and ripping up his agreement. . . .

The uncertainty that the government prefers in its cooperation agreements also reflects the fact that the document is designed to be seen not just by the parties but by the jury considering the cooperator's testimony. A vague agreement permits a witness who has admitted his involvement in heinous crimes to say, "I honestly don't know what sentence I will receive. I hope for leniency, but it's up to the judge." While defense counsel will try to educate the jury about the likelihood that the witness will receive exceptional lenience—and that the government will have considerable control over the extent of that lenience—the expectation is that jurors will be less likely to be put off by the "deal" than if the agreement set out a precise discount.

. . . The point is simply that the government will seek to keep the payout as uncertain as it can. Indeed, the government's risk aversion may lead defendants to prefer uncertainty as well, because if forced to commit himself . . . , a prosecutor would be less likely to be lenient, for fear that a defendant would renege or that the agreement would play badly before a jury.

The consequence of this convergence of interests is that cooperation agreements will typically be quite clear in setting out the charges a defendant will have to plead to and the scope of his immunity, but will often be quite vague as to what leniency the defendant can expect in exchange for his cooperation. . . . Typically, the defendant will broadly promise to testify truthfully, and to truthfully disclose all information concerning matters covered by the government's inquiries. Any effort to bind a cooperator to a particular "story" would be unseemly, and probably illegal. The government will reserve for itself the right to determine, prior to sentencing, whether the defendant has in fact cooperated fully and told the truth. Ordinarily, this reservation might simply mean that the government would retain control over what it tells the sentencing judge about the defendant's cooperation. Given that a judge would be likely to rely heavily on a prosecutor's assessment of such matters, this would be a substantial enforcement mechanism.

From the government's point of view, the great difficulty in dealing with potential "cooperators" is dealing with cases where defendants seek to renege on their end of the bargain by failing to provide the information or testimony the government expects. The next case deals with a variation on that problem—and with the question of what limits the law places on the government's ability to enforce compliance:

b. *Contract Interpretation*

RICKETTS v. ADAMSON

Certiorari to the United States Court of Appeals for the Ninth Circuit
483 U.S. 1 (1987)

JUSTICE WHITE delivered the opinion of the Court.

. . . In 1976, Donald Bolles, a reporter for the Arizona Republic, was fatally injured when a dynamite bomb exploded underneath his car. Respondent was arrested and charged with first-degree murder in connection with Bolles' death. Shortly after his trial had commenced, while jury selection was underway, respondent and the state prosecutor reached an agreement whereby respondent agreed to plead guilty to a charge of second-degree murder and to testify against two other individuals—Max Dunlap and James Robison—who were allegedly involved in Bolles' murder. Specifically, respondent agreed to "testify fully and completely in any Court, State or Federal, when requested by proper authorities against any and all parties involved in the murder of Don Bolles. . . ." The agreement provided that "[s]hould the defendant refuse to testify or should he at any time testify untruthfully . . . then this entire agreement is null and void and the original charge will be automatically reinstated."[1] The parties agreed that respondent would receive a prison sentence of 48-49 years, with a total incarceration time of 20 years and 2 months. In January 1977, the state trial court accepted the plea agreement and the proposed sentence, but withheld imposition of the sentence. Thereafter, respondent testified as obligated under the agreement, and both Dunlap and Robison were convicted of the first-degree murder of Bolles. While their convictions and sentences were on appeal, the trial court, upon motion of the State, sentenced respondent. In February 1980, the Arizona Supreme Court reversed the convictions of Dunlap and Robison and remanded their cases for retrial. State v. Dunlap, 125 Ariz. 104, 608 P.2d 41. This event sparked the dispute now before us.

The State sought respondent's cooperation and testimony in preparation for the retrial of Dunlap and Robison. On April 3, 1980, however, respondent's counsel informed the prosecutor that respondent believed his obligation to provide testimony under the agreement had terminated when he was sentenced. Respondent would again testify against Dunlap and Robison only if certain conditions were met, including, among others, that the State release him from custody following the retrial. 789 F.2d, at 733.[2] The State then informed respondent's attorney on April 9, 1980, that it deemed respondent to be in breach of the plea agreement. On April 18, 1980, the State called respondent to testify in pretrial proceedings. In response to questions, and upon advice of counsel, respondent invoked his Fifth Amendment privilege against self-incrimination. The trial judge, after respondent's counsel apprised him of the State's letter of April 9 indicating that the State considered respondent to be in breach of the plea agreement, refused to compel respondent to answer questions. The Arizona Supreme Court declined to accept jurisdiction of the State's petition for special action to review the trial judge's decision.

On May 8, 1980, the State filed a new information charging respondent with first-degree murder. Respondent's motion to quash the information on double jeopardy grounds was denied. Respondent challenged this decision by a special action in the Arizona Supreme Court. That court, after reviewing the plea agreement, the transcripts of the plea hearing and the sentencing hearing, respondent's April 3 letter

---

1. The agreement further provided that, in the event respondent refused to testify, he "will be subject to the charge of Open Murder, and if found guilty of First Degree Murder, to the penalty of death or life imprisonment requiring mandatory twenty-five years actual incarceration, and the State shall be free to file any charges, not yet filed as of the date of this agreement."

2. Respondent's other conditions—which he characterized as "demands"—included that he be held in a nonjail facility with protection during the retrials, that he be provided with new clothing, that protection be afforded his ex-wife and son, that a fund be provided for his son's education, that he be given adequate resources to establish a new identity outside Arizona following his release from custody, and that he be granted "full and complete immunity for any and all crimes in which he may have been involved."

to the state prosecutor, and the prosecutor's April 9 response to that letter, held with "no hesitation" that "the plea agreement contemplates availability of [respondent's] testimony whether at trial or retrial after reversal," Adamson v. Superior Court of Arizona, 125 Ariz. 579, 583, 611 P.2d 932, 936 (1980), and that respondent "violated the terms of the plea agreement." Ibid.[3] The court also rejected respondent's double jeopardy claim, holding that the plea agreement "by its very terms waives the defense of double jeopardy if the agreement is violated." Id., at 584, 611 P.2d, at 937. Finally, the court held that under state law and the terms of the plea agreement, the State should not have filed a new information, but should have merely reinstated the initial charge. Accordingly, the court vacated respondent's second-degree murder conviction, reinstated the original charge, and dismissed the new information.

After these rulings, respondent offered to testify at the retrials, but the State declined his offer. . . . Respondent was then convicted of first-degree murder and sentenced to death. The judgment was affirmed on direct appeal. . . . Respondent sought federal habeas corpus . . . asserting a number of claims relating to his trial and sentence. The District Court dismissed the petition; a Court of Appeals panel affirmed. 758 F.2d 441 (1985). The Court of Appeals went en banc, held that the State had violated respondent's rights under the Double Jeopardy Clause, and directed the issuance of a writ of habeas corpus. . . .

. . . Assuming . . . that under Arizona law second-degree murder is a lesser included offense of first-degree murder, the Double Jeopardy Clause, absent special circumstances, would have precluded prosecution of respondent for the greater charge on which he now stands convicted. Brown v. Ohio, 432 U.S. 161, 168 (1977). The State submits, however, that respondent's breach of the plea arrangement to which the parties had agreed removed the double jeopardy bar to prosecution of respondent on the first-degree murder charge. We agree with the State.

Under the terms of the plea agreement, both parties bargained for and received substantial benefits. The State obtained respondent's guilty plea and his promise to testify against "any and all parties involved in the murder of Don Bolles" and in certain specified other crimes. 789 F.2d, at 731. Respondent, a direct participant in a premeditated and brutal murder, received a specified prison sentence accompanied

---

3. The Arizona Supreme Court noted that at oral argument respondent explained for the first time the basis for his refusal to testify. Respondent relied on Paragraph 8 of the plea agreement, which provides: "All parties to this agreement hereby waive the time for sentencing and agree that the defendant will be sentenced at the conclusion of his testimony in all of the cases referred to in this agreement. . . ." In rejecting respondent's contention that this provision relieved him from his obligation to testify after he had already been sentenced, the court referred to the colloquy that occurred at the sentencing hearing. At that hearing, the prosecuting attorney stated that he had discussed with respondent's counsel the fact "that it may be necessary in the future to bring [respondent] back after sentencing for further testimony." 125 Ariz., at 583, 611 P.2d, at 936. Respondent's counsel indicated that they understood that future testimony may be necessary. The court concluded that whatever doubt was created by Paragraph 8 regarding respondent's obligation to testify after sentencing, the colloquy at the sentencing hearing evinced a "clear understanding" that respondent would be so obligated. Ibid. Respondent argued in the Court of Appeals—and renews the argument here—that the "further testimony" mentioned by the prosecutor at the sentencing hearing referred to testimony in a wholly separate prosecution that had yet to be tried. We will not second-guess the Arizona Supreme Court's construction of the language of the plea agreement. While we assess independently the plea agreement's effect on respondent's double jeopardy rights, the construction of the plea agreement and the concomitant obligations flowing therefrom are, within broad bounds of reasonableness, matters of state law, and we will not disturb the Arizona Supreme Court's reasonable disposition of those issues. . . .

with a guarantee that he would serve actual incarceration time of 20 years and 2 months. He further obtained the State's promise that he would not be prosecuted for his involvement in certain other crimes.

The agreement specifies in two separate paragraphs the consequences that would flow from respondent's breach of his promises. Paragraph 5 provides that if respondent refused to testify, "this entire agreement is null and void and the original charge will be *automatically* reinstated." Ibid. (emphasis added). Similarly, Paragraph 15 of the agreement states that "in the event this agreement becomes null and void, then the parties shall be returned to the positions they were in before this agreement." Id., at 732. Respondent unquestionably understood the meaning of these provisions. At the plea hearing, the trial judge read the plea agreement to respondent, line by line, and pointedly asked respondent whether he understood the provisions in Paragraphs 5 and 15. Respondent replied "Yes, sir," to each question. App. 23-24, 28-29. On this score, we do not find it significant, as did the Court of Appeals, that "double jeopardy" was not specifically waived by name in the plea agreement. . . . The terms of the agreement could not be clearer: in the event of respondent's breach occasioned by a refusal to testify, the parties would be returned to the status quo ante, in which case respondent would have no double jeopardy defense to waive. And, an agreement specifying that charges may be reinstated given certain circumstances is, at least under the provisions of this plea agreement, precisely equivalent to an agreement waiving a double jeopardy defense. . . .

We are also unimpressed by the [claim] that there was a good-faith dispute about whether respondent was bound to testify a second time and that until the extent of his obligation was decided, there could be no knowing and intelligent waiver of his double jeopardy defense. But respondent knew that if he breached the agreement he could be retried, and it is incredible to believe that he did not anticipate that the extent of his obligation would be decided by a court. Here he sought a construction of the agreement in the Arizona Supreme Court, and that court found that he had failed to live up to his promise. The result was that respondent was returned to the position he occupied prior to execution of the plea bargain: He stood charged with first-degree murder. Trial on that charge did not violate the Double Jeopardy Clause. United States v. Scott, 437 U.S. 82 (1978), supports this conclusion.

At the close of all the evidence in *Scott*, the trial judge granted defendant's motion to dismiss two counts of the indictment against him on the basis of pre-indictment delay. This Court held that the Double Jeopardy Clause did not bar the Government from appealing the trial judge's decision, because "in a case such as this the defendant, by deliberately choosing to seek termination of the proceedings against him on a basis unrelated to factual guilt or innocence of the offense of which he was accused, suffers no injury cognizable under the Double Jeopardy Clause. . . ." Id., at 98-99. . . . The respondent in this case had a similar choice. He could submit to the State's request that he testify at the retrial, and in so doing risk that he would be providing testimony that pursuant to the agreement he had no obligation to provide, or he could stand on his interpretation of the agreement, knowing that if he were wrong, his breach of the agreement would restore the parties to their original positions and he could be prosecuted for first-degree murder. Respondent chose the latter course, and the Double Jeopardy Clause does not relieve him from the consequences of that choice.

Respondent cannot escape the Arizona Supreme Court's interpretation of his obligations under the agreement. The State did not force the breach; respondent chose, perhaps for strategic reasons or as a gamble, to advance an interpretation of the agreement that proved erroneous. And, there is no indication that respondent did not fully understand the potential seriousness of the position he adopted. In the April 3 letter, respondent's counsel advised the prosecutor that respondent "is fully aware of the fact that your office may feel that he has not completed his obligations under the plea agreement . . . and, further, that your office may attempt to withdraw the plea agreement from him, [and] that he may be prosecuted for the killing of Donald Bolles on a first degree murder charge." 789 F.2d, at 733. This statement of respondent's awareness of the operative terms of the plea agreement only underscores that which respondent's plea hearing made evident: Respondent clearly appreciated and understood the consequences were he found to be in breach of the agreement.

Finally, it is of no moment that following the Arizona Supreme Court's decision respondent offered to comply with the terms of the agreement. At this point, respondent's second-degree murder conviction had already been ordered vacated and the original charge reinstated. The parties did not agree that respondent would be relieved from the consequences of his refusal to testify if he were able to advance a colorable argument that a testimonial obligation was not owing. The parties could have struck a different bargain, but permitting the State to enforce the agreement the parties actually made does not violate the Double Jeopardy Clause.

The judgment of the Court of Appeals is reversed.

JUSTICE BRENNAN, with whom JUSTICE MARSHALL, JUSTICE BLACKMUN, and JUSTICE STEVENS join, dissenting.

The critical question in this case is whether Adamson ever breached his plea agreement. Only by demonstrating that such a breach occurred can it plausibly be argued that Adamson waived his rights under the Double Jeopardy Clause. By simply assuming that such a breach occurred, the Court ignores the only important issue in this case. . . .

Without disturbing the conclusions of the Arizona Supreme Court as to the proper construction of the plea agreement, one may make two observations central to the resolution of this case. First, the agreement does not contain an explicit waiver of all double jeopardy protection. Instead, the Arizona Supreme Court found in the language of paras. 5 and 15 of the agreement only an implicit waiver of double jeopardy protection which was conditional on an act by Adamson that breached the agreement, such as refusing to testify as it required. Therefore, any finding that Adamson lost his protection against double jeopardy must be predicated on a finding that Adamson breached his agreement.

Second, Adamson's interpretation of the agreement—that he was not required to testify at the retrials of Max Dunlap and James Robison—was reasonable. Nothing in the plea agreement explicitly stated that Adamson was required to provide testimony should retrials prove necessary. Moreover, the agreement specifically referred in two separate paragraphs to events that would occur only after the conclusion of all testimony that Adamson would be required to give. Paragraph 8 stated that Adamson "will be sentenced at the conclusion of his testimony in all of the cases referred to in this agreement and Exhibits A and B, which accompany it." 789 F.2d 722, 732 (CA9 1986). At the time that the State demanded that Adamson testify in the retrials, he had been sentenced. Paragraph 18 stated that "the defendant is to remain in the custody of the Pima County Sheriff from the date of the entry of his plea until the conclusion of his testimony in all of the cases in which the defendant agrees to testify as a result of this agreement." Ibid. At the time the State demanded that Adamson testify in the retrials, Adamson had been transferred from the custody of the Pima County Sheriff. Adamson therefore could reasonably conclude that he had provided all the testimony required by the agreement, and that, as he communicated to the State by letter of April 3, 1980, the testimony demanded by the State went beyond his duties under the agreement. The Arizona Supreme Court rejected Adamson's construction. But even deferring to the state court's view that Adamson's interpretation was erroneous, one must also agree with the en banc Court of Appeals that Adamson's interpretation of the agreement was "reasonabl[e]," and was supported by the plain language of the agreement, "logic, and common sense." Id., at 729.

In sum, Adamson could lose his protection against double jeopardy only by breaching his agreement, and Adamson's interpretation of his responsibilities under the agreement, though erroneous, was reasonable. The next step in the analysis is to determine whether Adamson ever breached his agreement.

This Court has yet to address in any comprehensive way the rules of construction appropriate for disputes involving plea agreements. Nevertheless, it seems clear that the law of commercial contract may in some cases prove useful as an analogy or point of departure in construing a plea agreement, or in framing the terms of the debate. It is also clear, however, that commercial contract law can do no more than this, because plea agreements are constitutional contracts. The values that underlie commercial contract law, and that govern the relations between economic actors, are not coextensive with those that underlie the Due Process Clause, and that govern relations between criminal defendants and the State. Unlike some commercial contracts, plea agreements must be construed in light of the rights and obligations created by the Constitution.

The State argues and the Arizona Supreme Court seems to imply that a breach occurred when Adamson sent his letter of April 3, 1980, to the prosecutor in response to the State's demand for his testimony at the retrials of Dunlap and Robison. In this letter, Adamson stated that, under his interpretation of the agreement, he was no longer obligated to testify, and demanded additional consideration for any additional testimony.

Neither the State, the state courts, nor this Court has attempted to explain why this letter constituted a breach of the agreement. Of course, it could not plausibly be argued that merely sending such a letter constituted a breach by nonperformance, for nothing in the plea agreement states that Adamson shall not disagree with the State's interpretation of the plea agreement, or that Adamson shall not send the State a letter to that effect. But one might argue that, in the language of commercial contract law, the letter constituted a breach by anticipatory repudiation. Such a breach occurs when one party unequivocally informs the other that it no longer intends to honor their contract. "Where the contract is renounced before performance is due, and the renunciation goes to the whole contract, is absolute and unequivocal, the injured party may treat the breach as complete and bring his action at once." Roehm v. Horst, 178 U.S. 1, 7 (1900).[7] The reason for the rule is

7. See Restatement (Second) of Contracts §250 (1981); Uniform Commercial Code §2-610, 1A U. L. A. 321 (1976 and Supp. 1987); J. White & R. Summers, Uniform Commercial Code 212-214 (1980); 4 A. Corbin, Contracts §973 (1951); 2 S. Williston, Contracts §§1322, 1323 (3d ed. 1968).

plain: "announcing [one's] purpose to default" destroys the assurance of future performance that is central to a commercial contract.[8]

In the conventional case of anticipatory repudiation, therefore, the announcement of an intention to default on the contract constitutes a breach.[9] In his letter of April 3, however, Adamson did not announce such an intention. To the contrary, Adamson invoked the integrity of that agreement as a defense to what he perceived to be an unwarranted demand by the prosecutor that he testify at the retrials of Dunlap and Robison. And in insisting that he had no obligation to perform as the State demanded, Adamson advanced an objectively reasonable interpretation of his contract. . . .

. . . Even if one assumes, arguendo, that Adamson breached his plea agreement by offering an erroneous interpretation of that agreement, it still does not follow that the State was entitled to retry Adamson on charges of first-degree murder. As the Court acknowledges, immediately following the decision of the Arizona Supreme Court adopting the State's construction of the plea agreement, Adamson sent a letter to the State stating that he was ready and willing to testify. At this point, there was no obstacle to proceeding with the retrials of Dunlap and Robison; each case had been dismissed without prejudice to refiling, and only about one month's delay had resulted from the dispute over the scope of the plea agreement. Thus, what the State sought from Adamson—testimony in the Dunlap and Robison trials—was available to it.

The State decided instead to abandon the prosecution of Dunlap and Robison, and to capitalize on what it regarded as Adamson's breach by seeking the death penalty against him. . . . [E]ven in the world of commercial contracts it has long been settled that the party injured by a breach must nevertheless take all reasonable steps to minimize the consequent damage. . . .

Here it is macabre understatement to observe that the State needlessly exacerbated the liability of its contractual partner. The State suffered a 1-month delay in beginning the retrial of Dunlap and Robison, and incurred litigation costs. For these "losses," the State chose to make Adamson pay, not with a longer sentence, but with his life. A comparable result in commercial law, if one could be imagined, would not be enforced. The fundamental unfairness in the State's course of conduct here is even less acceptable under the Constitution. . . .

NOTES AND QUESTIONS

1. *Adamson*'s subsequent history is complicated but interesting. On remand, the Ninth Circuit decided that Adamson's death sentence was unconstitutionally arbitrary and hence a violation of due process; in the court's words, "Adamson was sentenced to death because he violated a contract." Adamson v. Ricketts, 865 F.2d

---

8. Equitable Trust Co. v. Western Pacific R. Co., 244 F. 485, 502 (SDNY 1917) (L. Hand, J.), *aff'd*, 250 F. 327 (CA2 1918).

9. The classic case is Hochster v. De la Tour, 2 El. & Bl. 678, 118 Eng. Rep. 922 (Q.B. 1853), from which the doctrine of breach by anticipatory repudiation evolved. In that case, De la Tour first contracted to hire Hochster, then prior to the starting date of employment sent Hochster a letter stating that his services would not be needed. The court held that the letter constituted a breach of the contract, and that Hochster did not need to wait until after the starting date to bring suit. In Roehm v. Horst, this Court discussed *Hochster* at length, and concluded that it provided "a reasonable and proper rule to be applied in this case and in many others." 178 U.S., at 20. Commentators continue to draw on *Hochster* to illustrate the principle. E.g., C. Fried, Contract as Promise 128-130, and n. 25 (1981).

1011, 1022 (9th Cir. 1988) (en banc). The Ninth Circuit also decided that Arizona's death penalty statute, under which Adamson was sentenced, (1) was unconstitutionally vague and (2) gave the sentencing judge authority that, under the Sixth Amendment, belonged to the jury. Id., at 1023-1038. Not surprisingly, the state again sought Supreme Court review.

In the meantime, the Supreme Court had granted certiorari in another case raising similar challenges to Arizona's death penalty statute. See Walton v. Arizona, 497 U.S. 639 (1990). As it usually does in such circumstances, the Court "held" the state's cert petition in Adamson's case—meaning that the Court simply left the petition undecided—until after it issued its decision in *Walton.* And in *Walton,* the Court upheld Arizona's death penalty statute and specifically rejected the arguments on which Adamson had prevailed in the Ninth Circuit. Ordinarily, the Court would have granted the state's petition in *Adamson,* vacated the Ninth Circuit's decision, and remanded for reconsideration in light of *Walton.* Three justices—Chief Justice Rehnquist and Justices White and Scalia—voted to do just that. But the other two justices in the *Walton* majority—Justices O'Connor and Kennedy— recused themselves (without explanation, per standard practice) in *Adamson,* and the *Walton* dissenters—Justices Brennan, Marshall, Blackmun, and Stevens (the same four who dissented in Ricketts v. Adamson)—voted to deny certiorari and let the Ninth Circuit's decision stand. Lewis v. Adamson, 497 U.S. 1031 (1990). So by a 4-3 vote, Adamson prevailed; his death penalty was overturned, even though all his arguments had just been rejected by a 5-4 decision of the Supreme Court. Technically, Arizona's death penalty statute was unconstitutional on its face *as to Adamson* (that sounds like a contradiction in terms, does it not?), but *not* as to anyone else.

The decision in *Walton* was later overruled, and the Arizona death penalty statute held unconstitutional (under the Sixth Amendment) as to *all* defendants in Ring v. Arizona, 536 U.S. 584 (2002).

2. What is the proper relationship between federal constitutional law and the law of contract in a case like *Ricketts*? The Court appears to hold that Arizona can permissibly define Adamson's conduct as a breach and can permissibly allow the government to rescind the plea agreement as a remedy. But Arizona is not *required* to define either breach or remedies in this way. What are the limits federal law places on states' definitions of the parties' obligations under plea agreements?

3. Put federalism issues to one side for the moment. Why is specific performance not an adequate remedy for Adamson's breach (assuming there was a breach)? Adamson could be directed to testify again, the government could immunize him for the relevant crimes, and Dunlap and Robison could presumably be convicted again, this time in a way that would be immune to appellate reversal. Doesn't that give the government the benefit of its bargain? Or is there something else the government has lost in this transaction?

4. *Ricketts* is clearly a case about contract interpretation. Adamson and the prosecution differed about the meaning of the contract; in the end, the Court holds that Adamson pursued his own interpretation at his peril, since "it is incredible to believe that he did not anticipate that the extent of his obligation would be decided by a court." What *should* Adamson have done, instead of essentially refusing to follow the prosecution's interpretation (a decision that was later construed, much to Adamson's dismay, as an anticipatory breach)? How could Adamson have signaled his disagreement with the prosecution's interpretation, and obtained a ruling on the issue, without risking a breach? Should defendants specifically reserve the right

to contest the interpretation of a plea agreement? Would prosecutors likely agree to such terms?

5. One blackletter principle of contract law is that ambiguities in the contract are construed against the drafter of the agreement, and virtually every federal court of appeals has agreed that when interpreting a plea agreement, ambiguities are to be construed against the government. See 1A Wright & Leipold, Federal Practice and Procedure 315 & n. 49 (2008) (collecting cases). Why wasn't this principle sufficient to resolve *Ricketts?* Aren't the competing positions in the case—and indeed, the differences between the majority and dissent—really about whether the contract required Adamson to testify at the retrial or not? And wasn't Adamson's position (that he was not required to do so), at least a reasonable interpretation of the agreement?

6. One of the most important issues in the interpretation of plea agreements is the question of the scope of immunity from prosecution the defendant enjoys by virtue of having pled guilty to the specified offenses. Many, perhaps most, plea bargains involve a guilty plea to some charges and the dismissal of others; presumably, the charges dismissed cannot be reinstated once the guilty plea is entered, at least not unless the plea agreement so specifies. How broadly does the immunity extend? Only to crimes listed in the agreement? To anything related to the criminal transaction that is the subject of the guilty plea? To any other crimes?

For a thorough and interesting discussion of this issue, see Daniel C. Richman, Bargaining About Future Jeopardy, 49 Vand. L. Rev. 1181 (1996). Richman summarizes the cases as follows:

> Some courts impose on prosecutors a reasonably narrow good faith obligation that bars sandbagging. These courts hold that the government may not intentionally nullify the explicit protections of a plea agreement by bringing a charge that it could easily have brought before and that is related to the offenses the agreement did address.[114] Other courts go beyond this focus on intent, extending default immunity to all charges that stem from the transactions referred to in the indictment and that the prosecution could have anticipated making when it entered into the agreement. Where a defendant pleads guilty pursuant to an agreement that makes no reference to possible murder charges and the victim later dies, for example, these courts bar the successive murder prosecution that could not even have been brought at the time of the defendant's plea.[115] At least one state court has gone further, presumptively barring any future charges that arise out of the transactions referenced in the charges to which the defendant pled.[116] Whether or not a prosecutor should have been able

114. See United States v. Burns, 990 F.2d 1426, 1435 (4th Cir. 1993) (concluding that the government would have violated Due Process Clause if, in the first case, it had deliberately delayed charging defendant with offense that it later brought in the second case, "in order to reap the benefits of his bargained guilty plea while denying him the opportunity to seek a concurrent sentence for related offenses").

115. See State v. Carpenter, 68 Ohio St. 3d 59, 623 N.E.2d 66, 68 (1993) (barring prosecution on greater charges following victim's death noting that all parties anticipated risk of this contingency); State v. Nelson, 23 Conn. App. 215, 579 A.2d 1104, 1106-1107 (1990) (same). But see People v. Latham, 609 N.Y.S.2d 141, 631 N.E.2d 83, 86 (1994) (finding no immunity for murder charges in absence of evidence that "both the defendant and the prosecution intended the plea to close the matter forever"). . . .

116. State v. Lordan, 116 N.H. 479, 363 A.2d 201, 203 (1976) ("Where the defendant commits several offenses in a single transaction and the prosecutor has knowledge of and jurisdiction over all these offenses and the defendant disposes of all charges then pending by a guilty plea to one or more of the charges, the prosecutor may not prefer additional charges arising from the same transaction unless either he has given notice on the record at the time of the plea of the possibility that he may prefer further charges or the defendant otherwise knows or ought reasonably to expect that further charges may be brought."). . . .

to anticipate making the successive charges does not appear to be relevant in this analysis.

Id., at 1211-1212. Which of these various approaches makes the most sense?

c.   Remedies for Breach of Contract

SANTOBELLO v. NEW YORK

Certiorari to the Appellate Division of the Supreme Court of New York
404 U.S. 257 (1971)

CHIEF JUSTICE BURGER delivered the opinion of the Court.

We granted certiorari in this case to determine whether the State's failure to keep a commitment concerning the sentence recommendation on a guilty plea required a new trial.

The facts are not in dispute. The State of New York indicted petitioner in 1969 on two felony counts, Promoting Gambling in the First Degree, and Possession of Gambling Records in the First Degree, N.Y. Penal Law §§225.10, 225.20. Petitioner first entered a plea of not guilty to both counts. After negotiations, the Assistant District Attorney in charge of the case agreed to permit petitioner to plead guilty to a lesser-included offense, Possession of Gambling Records in the Second Degree, N.Y. Penal Law §225.15, conviction of which would carry a maximum prison sentence of one year. The prosecutor agreed to make no recommendation as to the sentence.

On June 16, 1969, petitioner accordingly withdrew his plea of not guilty and entered a plea of guilty to the lesser charge. Petitioner represented to the sentencing judge that the plea was voluntary and that the facts of the case, as described by the Assistant District Attorney, were true. The court accepted the plea and set a date for sentencing. A series of delays followed, owing primarily to the absence of a presentence report, so that by September 23, 1969, petitioner had still not been sentenced. By that date petitioner acquired new defense counsel.

Petitioner's new counsel moved immediately to withdraw the guilty plea. In an accompanying affidavit, petitioner alleged that he did not know at the time of his plea that crucial evidence against him had been obtained as a result of an illegal search. The accuracy of this affidavit is subject to challenge since petitioner had filed and withdrawn a motion to suppress, before pleading guilty. In addition to his motion to withdraw his guilty plea, petitioner renewed the motion to suppress and filed a motion to inspect the grand jury minutes.

These three motions in turn caused further delay until November 26, 1969, when the court denied all three and set January 9, 1970, as the date for sentencing. On January 9 petitioner appeared before a different judge, the judge who had presided over the case to this juncture having retired. Petitioner renewed his motions, and the court again rejected them. The court then turned to consideration of the sentence.

At this appearance, another prosecutor had replaced the prosecutor who had negotiated the plea. The new prosecutor recommended the maximum one-year sentence. In making this recommendation, he cited petitioner's criminal record and alleged links with organized crime. Defense counsel immediately objected on the ground that the State had promised petitioner before the plea was entered that there would be no sentence recommendation by the prosecution. He sought to adjourn the sentence hearing in order to have time to prepare proof of the first prosecutor's promise. The second prosecutor, apparently ignorant of his colleague's commitment, argued that there was nothing in the record to support petitioner's claim of a promise, but the State, in subsequent proceedings, has not contested that such a promise was made.

The sentencing judge ended discussion with the following statement, quoting extensively from the presentence report:

> Mr. Aronstein [Defense Counsel], I am not at all influenced by what the District Attorney says, so that there is no need to adjourn the sentence, and there is no need to have any testimony. It doesn't make a particle of difference what the District Attorney says he will do, or what he doesn't do.
>
> I have here, Mr. Aronstein, a probation report. I have here a history of a long, long serious criminal record. I have here a picture of the life history of this man. . . .
>
> "He is unamenable to supervision in the community. He is a professional criminal." This is in quotes. "And a recidivist. Institutionalization"—that means, in plain language, just putting him away—"is the only means of halting his anti-social activities," and protecting you, your family, me, my family, protecting society. "Institutionalization." Plain language, put him behind bars.
>
> Under the plea, I can only send him to the New York City Correctional Institution for men for one year, which I am hereby doing.

The judge then imposed the maximum sentence of one year.

Petitioner sought and obtained a certificate of reasonable doubt and was admitted to bail pending an appeal. The Supreme Court of the State of New York, Appellate Division, First Department, unanimously affirmed petitioner's conviction, and petitioner was denied leave to appeal to the New York Court of Appeals. Petitioner then sought certiorari in this Court. . . .

Disposition of charges after plea discussions is not only an essential part of the process but a highly desirable part for many reasons. It leads to prompt and largely final disposition of most criminal cases; it avoids much of the corrosive impact of enforced idleness during pretrial confinement for those who are denied release pending trial; it protects the public from those accused persons who are prone to continue criminal conduct even while on pretrial release; and, by shortening the time between charge and disposition, it enhances whatever may be the rehabilitative prospects of the guilty when they are ultimately imprisoned. See Brady v. United States, 397 U.S. 742, 751-752 (1970).

However, all of these considerations presuppose fairness in securing agreement between an accused and a prosecutor. It is now clear, for example, that the accused pleading guilty must be counseled, absent a waiver. Moore v. Michigan, 355 U.S. 155 (1957). Fed. Rule Crim. Proc. 11, governing pleas in federal courts, now makes clear that the sentencing judge must develop, on the record, the factual basis for the plea, as, for example, by having the accused describe the conduct that gave rise to the charge. The plea must, of course, be voluntary and knowing and if it was induced by promises, the essence of those promises must in some way be made known. There is, of course, no absolute right to have a guilty plea accepted. Lynch v. Overholser, 369 U.S. 705, 719 (1962); Fed. Rule Crim. Proc. 11. A court may reject a plea in exercise of sound judicial discretion.

This phase of the process of criminal justice, and the adjudicative element inherent in accepting a plea of guilty, must be attended by safeguards to insure the defendant what is reasonably due in the circumstances. Those circumstances will vary, but a constant factor is that when a plea rests in any significant degree on a promise or agreement of the prosecutor, so that it can be said to be part of the inducement or consideration, such promise must be fulfilled.

On this record, petitioner "bargained" and negotiated for a particular plea in order to secure dismissal of more serious charges, but also on condition that no sentence recommendation would be made by the prosecutor. It is now conceded that the promise to abstain from a recommendation was made, and at this stage the prosecution is not in a good position to argue that its inadvertent breach of agreement is immaterial. The staff lawyers in a prosecutor's office have the burden of "letting the left hand know what the right hand is doing" or has done. That the breach of agreement was inadvertent does not lessen its impact.

We need not reach the question whether the sentencing judge would or would not have been influenced had he known all the details of the negotiations for the plea. He stated that the prosecutor's recommendation did not influence him and we have no reason to doubt that. Nevertheless, we conclude that the interests of justice and appropriate recognition of the duties of the prosecution in relation to promises made in the negotiation of pleas of guilty will be best served by remanding the case to the state courts for further consideration. The ultimate relief to which petitioner is entitled we leave to the discretion of the state court, which is in a better position to decide whether the circumstances of this case require only that there be specific performance of the agreement on the plea, in which case petitioner should be resentenced by a different judge, or whether, in the view of the state court, the circumstances require granting the relief sought by petitioner, i.e., the opportunity to withdraw his plea of guilty. We emphasize that this is in no sense to question the fairness of the sentencing judge; the fault here rests on the prosecutor, not on the sentencing judge.

The judgment is vacated and the case is remanded for reconsideration not inconsistent with this opinion.

JUSTICE DOUGLAS, concurring.

. . . I join the opinion of the Court and favor a constitutional rule for this as well as for other pending or oncoming [plea bargaining] cases. Where the "plea bargain" is not kept by the prosecutor, the sentence must be vacated and the state court will decide in light of the circumstances of each case whether due process requires (a) that there be specific performance of the plea bargain or (b) that the defendant be given the option to go to trial on the original charges. One alternative may do justice in one case, and the other in a different case. In choosing a remedy, however, a court ought to accord a defendant's preference considerable, if not controlling, weight inasmuch as the fundamental rights flouted by a prosecutor's breach of a plea bargain are those of the defendant, not of the State.

JUSTICE MARSHALL, with whom JUSTICE BRENNAN and JUSTICE STEWART join, concurring in part and dissenting in part.

I agree with much of the majority's opinion, but conclude that petitioner must be permitted to withdraw his guilty plea. This is the relief petitioner requested, and, on the facts set out by the majority, it is a form of relief to which he is entitled.

There is no need to belabor the fact that the Constitution guarantees to all criminal defendants the right to a trial by judge or jury, or, put another way, the "right not to plead guilty," United States v. Jackson, 390 U.S. 570, 581 (1968). This and other federal rights may be waived through a guilty plea, but such waivers are not lightly presumed and, in fact, are viewed with the "utmost solicitude." Boykin v. Alabama, 395 U.S. 238, 243 (1969). Given this, I believe that where the defendant presents a reason for vacating his plea and the government has not relied on the plea to its disadvantage, the plea may be vacated and the right to trial regained, at least where the motion to vacate is made prior to sentence and judgment. In other words, in such circumstances I would not deem the earlier plea to have irrevocably waived the defendant's federal constitutional right to a trial.

Here, petitioner never claimed any automatic right to withdraw a guilty plea before sentencing. Rather, he tendered a specific reason why, in his case, the plea should be vacated. His reason was that the prosecutor had broken a promise made in return for the agreement to plead guilty. When a prosecutor breaks the bargain, he undercuts the basis for the waiver of constitutional rights implicit in the plea. This, it seems to me, provides the defendant ample justification for rescinding the plea. Where a promise is "unfulfilled," Brady v. United States, 397 U.S. 742, 755 (1970), specifically denies that the plea "must stand." Of course, where the prosecutor has broken the plea agreement, it may be appropriate to permit the defendant to enforce the plea bargain. But that is not the remedy sought here. Rather, it seems to me that a breach of the plea bargain provides ample reason to permit the plea to be vacated. . . .

NOTES AND QUESTIONS

1. In a sense, *Santobello* is a natural companion case to Brady v. United States, which held that promising a defendant some charging or sentencing concession did not automatically render a guilty plea involuntary. *Santobello* holds that if the government promises such concessions, it has to keep its promises.

On the other hand, *Santobello* is quite different from *Brady* in one important respect. Recall that in *Brady*, the defendant must show that the withheld evidence harmed him, i.e., its disclosure would have created a reasonable probability of a different outcome. Even bad faith of the prosecutor, the Court has said, does not convert a failure to disclose into a *Brady* violation without a showing of harm. *Santobello*, in contrast, says that there is a violation even if the broken promise made no difference to the case—even if the trial judge was not influenced by the prosecutor's improper recommendation, defendant is entitled to some relief. Is there a distinction between the two types of cases that would justify this different treatment?

2. What is the legal source of *Santobello*'s holding? If the bargain between Santobello and the prosecutor is governed by the law of contract, the Supreme Court would appear to have no authority to determine either the presence of a breach or the range of appropriate remedies. Those matters would be determined by New York law. There is no federal rule or statute that governs such matters—Rule 11, recall, applies only to federal guilty pleas. So *Santobello* must be a constitutional decision, presumably a piece of law of due process. For an argument along these lines, see Peter Westen & David Westin, A Constitutional Law of Remedies for Broken Plea Bargains, 66 Cal. L. Rev. 471 (1978). Is that the right approach to developing

a law of plea bargaining? Is there any alternative if the voluntariness requirement is to have any meaning?

3. A claim under *Santobello* is one of the few claims that survives an unconditional guilty plea (see Section A of this chapter). As a result, there is a modest amount of litigation in the federal courts each year about whether the prosecutor fully lived up to her promises. And defendants occasionally win these claims. Here are some examples of where the prosecutors were found to be in breach, each involving a problem that arose during sentencing:

> (a) Defendant's reasonable interpretation of the plea agreement was that, when he gave assistance to the government as part of the deal, the information he provided would not be used by the prosecutor to argue for an increased sentence. The government then referred to the protected information at sentencing, which led to the case being remanded to a different judge for resentencing. U.S. v. Chavful, 781 F.3d 758 (5th Cir. 2015).
>
> (b) The prosecutor agreed to recommend a prison sentence at the low end of the Sentencing Guideline range. "The government breached its agreement, however, through its repeated and inflammatory references to [defendant's] criminal history in its sentencing memorandum. . . . The central theme of the government's sentencing position was that [defendant] was a dangerous recidivist who had spent twenty years flouting the law and menacing others. Whether intentional or not, the government breached the plea agreement by implicitly recommending a higher sentence than agreed upon." U.S. v. Heredia, 768 F.3d 1220, 1232-33 (9th Cir. 2014).
>
> (c) In the plea agreement the prosecutor agreed to recommend a certain sentence, but at the sentencing hearing he said that there were "problems" with the Sentencing Guidelines for this crime, that the Guidelines "did not make sense," and that the sentence was "way too low." The court found that this constituted a breach. "The government owes the defendant a duty to pay 'more than lip service' to a plea agreement. A plea agreement may be breached when '[t]he government's attorney . . . [i]s not only an unpersuasive advocate for the plea agreement, but, in effect, argue[s] against it.' . . . While a prosecutor normally need not present promised recommendations to the court with any particular degree of enthusiasm, it is improper for the prosecutor to inject material reservations about the agreement to which the government has committed itself." U.S. v. Cachucha, 484 F.3d 1266, 1270, 1271 (10th Cir. 2007) (internal quotation marks and citations omitted).

There are, of course, many more cases where claims of a breach are unsuccessful.

4. While the claims are less common, what happens if it is the *defendant* who breaches? Suppose that after the deal is reached and the defendant pleads guilty, he flees the country before sentencing. Later he is recaptured, and now the question is whether the plea deal is still in effect. It seems clear that becoming a fugitive was a material breach, whether the plea deal mentioned this possibility or not. See United States v. Munoz, 718 F.3d 726, 730 (7th Cir. 2013). But what effect does this have? Is the whole agreement void? Can the prosecutor insist on the enforcement of some provisions, say an appeal waiver? On these facts, the Seventh Circuit said that a selective enforcement remedy was appropriate.

> [A] classic rule of contract law, is that a party should be prevented from benefitting from its own breach. Thus, the fact that a party has breached a portion of a contract does not automatically result in the discharge of that party's remaining obligations. . . . Here, the government has elected to enforce the remaining provisions

of the plea agreements, including the appeal waivers. We see no reason why it should not be allowed to do so.

United States v. Hallahan, 756 F.3d 962, 973 (7th Cir. 2014) (internal quotation marks and citations omitted).

5. Why not give Santobello the right to choose his remedy—to choose between requiring the government to specifically perform the agreement and rescinding his guilty plea? If the goal is to put Santobello in the position he would have been in but for the broken promise, what remedy will best do that? Suppose the state of the evidence has changed in the meantime—some of the witnesses are no longer available, or physical evidence has been lost or mislaid. Will rescinding the plea fairly compensate for the breach? Will specific performance?

C. *The Role of Defense Counsel*

EDITORS' NOTE: In Missouri v. Frye, 132 S. Ct. 1399 (2012), and Lafler v. Cooper, 132 S. Ct. 1376 (2012), the U.S. Supreme Court held that the Sixth Amendment right to the effective assistance of counsel applies during the plea bargaining process. The Court further decided that defendants who, due to their own counsel's constitutional ineffectiveness, either choose to forgo an offered plea bargain or are never afforded the opportunity to accept the bargain may be provided a remedy by a reviewing court—including the possibility that the prosecutor may be required to re-offer the bargain, as well as the possibility that the court may unilaterally revise the defendant's sentence to reflect the bargain that never happened. (The Court suggested, unhelpfully, that the reviewing court may at its discretion give the defendant the sentence that was imposed after trial, the one that would have been imposed under the bargain, or "something in between.") The opinions in *Frye* and *Cooper*, and related notes, appear in connection with the materials on ineffective assistance of counsel in Part B.3 of Chapter 3, starting at page 203 and ending at page 226.

Do the decisions in Missouri v. Frye and Lafler v. Cooper suggest the possibility that the Court may become more receptive, in the future, to similarly creative remedies in cases involving breaches of plea bargains, such as the situation we saw in *Santobello*?

Chapter 14

The Jury and the Criminal Trial

A. The Right to a Trial by Jury

I consider trial by jury as the only anchor ever yet imagined by man, by which a government can be held to the principles of its constitution.

Thomas Jefferson (1788)

The right to a trial by jury in criminal cases, enshrined in Article III[1] and in the Sixth Amendment,[2] is one of the most revered civil liberties guaranteed by the United States Constitution. The jury trial (in a form that we might recognize as a direct predecessor to the modern jury trial) originated in England many centuries ago, with some scholars tracing its history back to Magna Carta or before[3] and a few finding analogues even in ancient Egypt[4] and Greece.[5] In any event, the right to jury trial in criminal cases was well established in the American colonies long before the Revolution. In fact, it was the only right that appeared in all 12 of the written state constitutions predating the Declaration of Independence.[6]

Two prominent pre-Revolution jury trials—one in England and the other in the colonies—helped lay the foundation for the Revolution itself. In 1670, 12 jurors who had refused to convict Quakers William Penn and William Mead for the crime of disturbing the peace by holding an unlawful assembly were themselves imprisoned under a writ of attaint, a procedure used at the time in England to punish jurors who "perjured" themselves by rendering a false verdict. One of the 12, Edward Bushell, challenged his imprisonment. In Bushell's Case, 124 Eng. Rep. 1006 (C.P. 1670), the Court of Common Pleas ordered Bushell's release, holding that no one has the right to question or second-guess a criminal jury's general verdict. Sixty-five years later, publisher John Peter Zenger was placed on trial in New York for the crime of seditious libel, based on newspaper stories critical of the royal governor. Andrew Hamilton volunteered in the middle of the trial to help defend Zenger.

---

1. "[T]he trial of all crimes, except in the cases of impeachment, shall be by jury; and such trial shall be held in the state where the said crimes shall have been committed." U.S. Const., Art. III, §2.

2. "In all criminal prosecutions, the accused shall enjoy the right to a speedy and public trial, by an impartial jury of the state and district wherein the crime shall have been committed." U.S. Const., Amdt. VI.

3. On the history of the jury trial in England, see generally 1 Sir Frederick Pollock & Frederic William Maitland, The History of English Law (1895); 1 W. C. Holdsworth, History of English Law (1922); 1 Winston Churchill, History of the English-Speaking People (1956).

4. See, e.g., J. Kendall Few, In Defense of Trial by Jury 12 (1993).

5. See, e.g., John Guinther, The Jury in America 2 (1988).

6. On the history of the jury trial in America, see generally Albert Alschuler & Andrew Deiss, A Brief History of the Criminal Jury in the United States, 61 U. Chi. L. Rev. 867 (1994).

Hamilton argued successfully that the jury should acquit because the stories were true, even though English libel law at the time did not recognize truth as a defense, citing Bushell's Case to the jurors as authority for their unreviewable power to do so. The widely publicized prosecution of Zenger, and his ultimate acquittal, served to underscore the deepening split between England and the colonies over freedom of speech and other civil liberties that became a catalyst for the Revolution.

Today it is well established that the proper role of the jury in a criminal trial is to determine the facts and apply the law—pursuant to instructions given by the trial judge—to those facts. In Sparf v. United States, 156 U.S. 51 (1895), the Supreme Court rejected the broad proposition that juries are free to "nullify" the law, i.e., to ignore the judge's instructions and proceed on their own view about what the law should be:

> We must hold firmly to the doctrine that in the courts of the United States it is the duty of juries in criminal cases to take the law from the court and apply that law to the facts as they find them to be from the evidence. Upon the court rests the responsibility of declaring the law; upon the jury, the responsibility of applying the law so declared to the facts as they, upon their conscience, believe them to be. Under any other system, the courts, although established in order to declare the law, would for every practical purpose be eliminated from our system of government as instrumentalities devised for the protection equally of society and of individuals in their essential rights. When that occurs our government will cease to be a government of laws, and become a government of men.

Id., at 102-103.

The *Sparf* Court carefully distinguished Bushell's Case, explaining that "the fundamental proposition decided [there] was that, in view of the different functions of court and jury, and because a general verdict of necessity resolves 'both law and fact complicately, and not the fact by itself,' it could never be proved, where the case went to the jury upon both law and facts, that the jurors did not proceed upon their view of the evidence." Id., at 90-91. In other words, the Court acknowledged that juries occasionally may refuse to convict guilty defendants[7] and that such verdicts are non-reviewable because the basis for them cannot be determined from the face of the verdict. But the practice of jury nullification is neither encouraged nor legally approved. Thus, prospective jurors who identify themselves, during jury selection, as potential nullifiers may be excluded from jury service. See, e.g., United States v. Thomas, 116 F.3d 606 (2d Cir. 1997). Trial judges routinely preclude defense lawyers from arguing (as Andrew Hamilton did in the *Zenger* case) that jurors should exercise their nullification power to acquit guilty defendants, as well as from presenting evidence to support a nullification defense. And jurors are universally instructed that it is their duty and obligation to obey the law as articulated by the judge.[8] See

---

7. For example, before the Civil War, some Northern antislavery juries refused to convict defendants charged with violations of the Fugitive Slave Law. After the war, it was Southern white juries that nullified the law, in cases involving prosecution of whites for the mistreatment of blacks. Similar situations have arisen during Prohibition (nullification of liquor laws), in pre- and post-statehood Utah (nullification, by Mormon juries, of bigamy and polygamy laws), and during the Vietnam War (refusal to convict draft dodgers and war protestors).

8. The Fully Informed Jury Association (FIJA) is a nonprofit organization that attempts to inform prospective jurors (and the public) about jury nullification through distribution of pamphlets and other methods. The activities of the FIJA have been most noticeable in the West and South, where antigovernment sentiment often tends to run higher than in the East or Midwest. For more information, see the FIJA website: http://www.fija.org.

generally Nancy J. King, Silencing Nullification Advocacy Inside the Jury Room and Outside the Courtroom, 65 U. Chi. L. Rev. 433 (1998). Perhaps the best explanation for this apparent conundrum was provided by Judge Leventhal of the U.S. Court of Appeals for the D.C. Circuit, who argued that jurors do not need formal instruction about their "freedom in an occasional case to depart from what the judge says"; instead, they learn about the nullification power through "informal communication from the total culture," including literature, movies, television, newspapers, magazines, and conversation. Anything more, Judge Leventhal claimed, would run an unacceptable risk of turning the jury into "a wildcat or runaway institution." See United States v. Dougherty, 473 F.2d 1113 (D.C. Cir. 1972).

The Sixth Amendment right to jury trial was applied to the states, by means of incorporation through the Fourteenth Amendment's Due Process Clause, in Duncan v. Louisiana, 391 U.S. 145 (1968). The *Duncan* case appears in Chapter 2, at page 79; at this point, you should read (or reread) it there. Notably, the Court in *Duncan* identified several reasons for believing that the right to jury trial in criminal cases is a "fundamental right" that must be recognized by the states: (1) it serves "to prevent oppression by the Government," protecting defendants against "unfounded criminal charges brought to eliminate enemies" and "judges too responsive to the voice of higher authority"; (2) it provides "an inestimable safeguard against the corrupt or overzealous prosecutor and against the compliant, biased, or eccentric judge"; (3) it gives defendants the opportunity to seek "the common-sense judgment of a jury" rather than "the more tutored but perhaps less sympathetic reaction of the single judge"; and (4) it reflects "a reluctance to entrust plenary powers over the life and liberty of the citizen to one judge or to a group of judges." Id., at 155-156.

The Court in *Duncan* acknowledged that there must be "a category of petty crimes or offenses which is not subject to the Sixth Amendment jury trial provision," see id., at 159; it declined, however, to fix the line between "serious" and "petty" crimes, holding only that Duncan's crime—which carried a possible two-year prison sentence—was non-petty. In Baldwin v. New York, 399 U.S. 117 (1970), the Court rejected the view that the line should be drawn between felonies and misdemeanors. Three justices (White, Brennan, and Marshall) concluded that "no offense can be deemed 'petty' for purposes of the right to trial by jury where imprisonment for more than six months is authorized." Id., at 69. Two other justices (Black and Douglas) wanted to go even further and apply the right to jury trial to all crimes. Id., at 74-76 (Black, J., concurring in the judgment).

What if the crime charged carries a maximum punishment of six months or less in prison? Can the defendant nevertheless claim a Sixth Amendment right to jury trial? There is a strong presumption against such claims unless the crime also involves "additional statutory penalties so severe as to indicate that the legislature considered the offense serious." See Lewis v. United States, 518 U.S. 322, 326 (1996). Thus, the Court has rejected jury-trial claims made by a defendant who received a mandatory two-day jail term for an otherwise petty crime, see Blanton v. City of North Las Vegas, 489 U.S. 538 (1989), and by a defendant who was charged in a single indictment with multiple petty crimes carrying an aggregate possible prison sentence of one year, see *Lewis*, supra. This last point may be particularly significant: Under *Lewis*, a defendant who faces a single misdemeanor charge that provides for up to one year of imprisonment is entitled to a jury trial, while a defendant charged with two misdemeanors that each carry a maximum six-month sentence is not entitled to a jury—even if after conviction the judge imposes consecutive sentences, so that the defendant spends a year in jail. Is this a sensible distinction?

Note that the existence of a right to jury trial does not mean that a jury trial necessarily will occur. In addition to the strong likelihood of a plea bargain, see Chapter 13, the defendant may waive his right to jury trial and request a bench trial. See Patton v. United States, 281 U.S. 276 (1930). The defendant does not, however, have the constitutional right to insist on a bench trial. In Singer v. United States, 380 U.S. 24 (1965), involving a challenge to a provision in the Federal Rules of Criminal Procedure requiring prosecutorial and judicial approval before a defendant could waive jury trial, the Court explained: "We find no constitutional impediment to conditioning a waiver of [the jury-trial] right on the consent of the prosecuting attorney and the trial judge when, if either refuses to consent, the result is simply that the defendant is subject to an impartial trial by jury—the very thing that the Constitution guarantees him." Id., at 36.

Once it has been determined that the right to jury trial applies to a particular case (and assuming that the defendant has not waived that right), then the next question becomes, what is the content of the right? What exactly is a "jury," within the meaning of the Sixth Amendment? This question involves several dimensions, including jury size, unanimity, and vicinage. The next case deals with the first dimension, size.

BALLEW v. GEORGIA

Certiorari to the Court of Appeals of Georgia
435 U.S. 223 (1978)

JUSTICE BLACKMUN announced the judgment of the Court and delivered an opinion in which JUSTICE STEVENS joined.

This case presents the issue whether a state criminal trial to a jury of only five persons deprives the accused of the right to trial by jury guaranteed to him by the Sixth and Fourteenth Amendments. Our resolution of the issue requires an application of principles enunciated in Williams v. Florida, 399 U.S. 78 (1970), where the use of a six-person jury in a state criminal trial was upheld against similar constitutional attack.

I

In November 1973 petitioner Claude Davis Ballew was the manager of the Paris Adult Theatre at 320 Peachtree Street, Atlanta, Ga. On November 9 two investigators from the Fulton County Solicitor General's office viewed at the theater a motion picture film entitled "Behind the Green Door." . . . After they had seen the film, they obtained a warrant for its seizure, returned to the theater, viewed the film once again, and seized it. . . . Petitioner and a cashier were arrested. Investigators returned to the theater on November 26, viewed the film in its entirety, secured still another warrant, and on November 27 once again viewed the motion picture and seized a second copy of the film. . . .

On September 14, 1974, petitioner was charged in a two-count misdemeanor accusation with [distributing obscene materials]. . . .

Petitioner was brought to trial in the Criminal Court of Fulton County. After a jury of 5 persons had been selected and sworn, petitioner moved that the court impanel a jury of 12 persons. . . . That court, however, tried its misdemeanor cases before juries of five persons. . . . Petitioner contended that for an obscenity trial, a jury of only five was constitutionally inadequate to assess the contemporary standards of the community. . . . He also argued that the Sixth and Fourteenth Amendments required a jury of at least six members in criminal cases. . . .

The motion for a 12-person jury was overruled, and the trial went on to its conclusion before the 5-person jury that had been impaneled. At the conclusion of the trial, the jury deliberated for 38 minutes and returned a verdict of guilty on both counts of the accusation. . . . The court imposed a sentence of one year and a $1,000 fine on each count, the periods of incarceration to run concurrently and to be suspended upon payment of the fines. . . . After a subsequent hearing, the court denied an amended motion for a new trial.

Petitioner took an appeal to the Court of Appeals of the State of Georgia. There he argued[, inter alia, that] the use of the five-member jury deprived him of his Sixth and Fourteenth Amendment right to a trial by jury. . . .

The Court of Appeals rejected petitioner's contentions. . . . In its consideration of the five-person-jury issue, the court noted that Williams v. Florida had not established a constitutional minimum number of jurors. Absent a holding by this Court that a five-person jury was constitutionally inadequate, the Court of Appeals considered itself bound by Sanders v. State, 234 Ga. 586, 216 S.E.2d 838 (1975), . . . where the constitutionality of the five-person jury had been upheld. . . .

In his petition for certiorari here, petitioner raised[, inter alia,] the unconstitutionality of the five-person jury. . . . We granted certiorari. 429 U.S. 1071 (1977). Because we now hold that the five member jury does not satisfy the jury trial guarantee of the Sixth Amendment, as applied to the States through the Fourteenth, we do not reach the other issues.

II

The Fourteenth Amendment guarantees the right of trial by jury in all state nonpetty criminal cases. Duncan v. Louisiana, 391 U.S. 145, 159-162 (1968). The Court in *Duncan* applied this Sixth Amendment right to the States because "trial by jury in criminal cases is fundamental to the American scheme of justice." Id., at 149. The right attaches in the present case because the maximum penalty for violating §26-2101, as it existed at the time of the alleged offenses, exceeded six months' imprisonment. . . .

In Williams v. Florida, 399 U.S., at 100, the Court reaffirmed that the "purpose of the jury trial, as we noted in *Duncan,* is to prevent oppression by the Government. 'Providing an accused with the right to be tried by a jury of his peers gave him an inestimable safeguard against the corrupt or overzealous prosecutor and against the compliant, biased, or eccentric judge.' Duncan v. Louisiana, [391 U.S.,] at 156." . . . This purpose is attained by the participation of the community in determinations of guilt and by the application of the common sense of laymen who, as jurors, consider the case. Williams v. Florida, 399 U.S., at 100.

Williams held that these functions and this purpose could be fulfilled by a jury of six members. As the Court's opinion in that case explained at some length, id., at 86-90, common-law juries included 12 members by historical accident, "unrelated to the great purposes which gave rise to the jury in the first place." Id., at 89-90. The Court's earlier cases that had *assumed* the number 12 to be constitutionally compelled were set to one side because they had not considered history and the function of the jury. Id., at 90-92. Rather than requiring 12 members, then, the Sixth Amendment mandated a jury only of sufficient size to promote group deliberation, to insulate members from outside intimidation, and to provide a representative cross-section of the community. Id., at 100. Although recognizing that by 1970 little empirical research had evaluated jury performance, the Court found no evidence that the reliability of jury verdicts diminished with six-member panels. Nor did the Court anticipate significant differences in result, including the frequency of "hung" juries. Id., at 101-102, and nn. 47 and 48. Because the reduction in size did not threaten exclusion of any particular class from jury roles, concern that the representative or cross-section character of the jury would suffer with a decrease to six members seemed "an unrealistic one." Id., at 102. As a consequence, the six-person jury was held not to violate the Sixth and Fourteenth Amendments.

III

When the Court in *Williams* permitted the reduction in jury size—or, to put it another way, when it held that a jury of six was not unconstitutional—it expressly reserved ruling on the issue whether a number smaller than six passed constitutional scrutiny. Id., at 91 n. 28.[9] The Court refused to speculate when this so-called "slippery slope" would become too steep. We face now, however, the two-fold question whether a further reduction in the size of the state criminal trial jury does make the grade too dangerous, that is, whether it inhibits the functioning of the jury as an institution to a significant degree, and, if so, whether any state interest counterbalances and justifies the disruption so as to preserve its constitutionality.

   Williams v. Florida and Colgrove v. Battin, 413 U.S. 149 (1973) (where the Court held that a jury of six members did not violate the Seventh Amendment right to a jury trial in a civil case), generated a quantity of scholarly work on jury size.[10] These writings do not draw or identify a bright line below which the number of jurors would not be able to function as required by the standards enunciated in *Williams*. On the other hand, they raise significant questions about the wisdom and constitutionality of a reduction below six. We examine these concerns:

   First, recent empirical data suggest that progressively smaller juries are less likely to foster effective group deliberation. At some point, this decline leads to inaccurate

9. In the cited footnote the Court said: "We have no occasion in this case to determine what minimum number can still constitute a 'jury,' but we do not doubt that six is above that minimum."

Respondent picks up the last phrase with absolute literalness here when it argues: "If six is above the minimum, five cannot be below the minimum. There is no number in between." . . . We, however, do not accept the proposition that by stating the number six was "above" the constitutional minimum the Court, by implication, held that at least the number five was constitutional. Instead, the Court was holding that six passed constitutional muster but was reserving judgment on any number less than six.

10. [Here the Court cited 19 separate books and articles reporting various social scientific studies of jury size conducted between 1971 and 1977.]

We have considered [these studies] carefully because they provide the only basis, besides judicial hunch, for a decision about whether smaller and smaller juries will be able to fulfill the purpose and functions of the Sixth Amendment. Without an examination about how juries and small groups actually work, we would not understand the basis for the conclusion of Mr. Justice Powell that a "line has to be drawn somewhere." . . .

factfinding and incorrect application of the common sense of the community to the facts. Generally, a positive correlation exists between group size and the quality of both group performance and group productivity. A variety of explanations have been offered for this conclusion. Several are particularly applicable in the jury setting. The smaller the group, the less likely are members to make critical contributions necessary for the solution of a given problem. Because most juries are not permitted to take notes, . . . memory is important for accurate jury deliberations. As juries decrease in size, then, they are less likely to have members who remember each of the important pieces of evidence or argument. Furthermore, the smaller the group, the less likely it is to overcome the biases of its members to obtain an accurate result. When individual and group decisionmaking were compared, it was seen that groups performed better because prejudices of individuals were frequently counterbalanced, and objectivity resulted. Groups also exhibited increased motivation and self-criticism. All these advantages, except, perhaps, self-motivation, tend to diminish as the size of the group diminishes. Because juries frequently face complex problems laden with value choices, the benefits are important and should be retained. In particular, the counterbalancing of various biases is critical to the accurate application of the common sense of the community to the facts of any given case.

Second, the data now raise doubts about the accuracy of the results achieved by smaller and smaller panels. Statistical studies suggest that the risk of convicting an innocent person (Type I error) rises as the size of the jury diminishes. Because the risk of not convicting a guilty person (Type II error) increases with the size of the panel, an optimal jury size can be selected as a function of the interaction between the two risks. Nagel and Neef concluded that the optimal size, for the purpose of minimizing errors, should vary with the importance attached to the two types of mistakes. After weighting Type I error as 10 times more significant than Type II, perhaps not an unreasonable assumption, they concluded that the optimal jury size was between six and eight. As the size diminished to five and below, the weighted sum of errors increased because of the enlarging risk of the conviction of innocent defendants. [See Nagel & Neef, Deductive Modeling to Determine an Optimum Jury Size and Fraction Required to Convict, [1975] Wash. U. L.Q. 933, 946-948, 956, 975.]

Another doubt about progressively smaller juries arises from the increasing inconsistency that results from the decreases. Saks argued that the "more a jury type fosters consistency, the greater will be the proportion of juries which select the correct (i.e., the same) verdict and the fewer 'errors' will be made." [M. Saks, Jury Verdicts 86-87 (1977).] . . . Working with statistics described in H. Kalven & H. Zeisel, The American Jury 460 (1966), Nagel and Neef tested the average conviction propensity of juries, that is, the likelihood that any given jury of a set would convict the defendant. [See Nagel & Neef, supra, at 952, 971.] They found that half of all 12-person juries would have average conviction propensities that varied by no more than 20 points. Half of all six-person juries, on the other hand, had average conviction propensities varying by 30 points, a difference they found significant in both real and percentage terms. Lempert reached similar results when he considered the likelihood of juries to compromise over the various views of their members, an important phenomenon for the fulfillment of the common-sense function. . . . [See Lempert, Undiscovering "Nondiscernible" Differences: Empirical Research and the Jury-Size Cases, 73 Mich. L. Rev. 643, 680 (1975).] And he predicted that compromises would be more consistent when larger juries were employed. For example,

12-person juries could be expected to reach extreme compromises in 4% of the cases, while 6-person panels would reach extreme results in 16%. All three of these post-*Williams* studies, therefore, raise significant doubts about the consistency and reliability of the decisions of smaller juries.

Third, the data suggest that the verdicts of jury deliberation in criminal cases will vary as juries become smaller, and that the variance amounts to an imbalance to the detriment of one side, the defense. Both Lempert and Zeisel found that the number of hung juries would diminish as the panels decreased in size. Zeisel said that the number would be cut in half—from 5% to 2.4% with a decrease from 12 to 6 members. [See Zeisel, . . . And Then There Were None: The Diminution of the Federal Jury, 38 U. Chi. L. Rev. 710, 720 (1971).] Both studies emphasized that juries in criminal cases generally hang with only one, or more likely two, jurors remaining unconvinced of guilt. Also, group theory suggests that a person in the minority will adhere to his position more frequently when he has at least one other person supporting his argument. . . . As the numbers [on the jury] diminish below six, . . . fewer panels would have one member with the minority viewpoint and still fewer would have two. The chance for hung juries would decline accordingly.

Fourth, what has just been said about the presence of minority viewpoint as juries decrease in size foretells problems not only for jury decisionmaking, but also for the representation of minority groups in the community. The Court repeatedly has held that meaningful community participation cannot be attained with the exclusion of minorities or other identifiable groups from jury service. . . . Although the Court in *Williams* concluded that the six-person jury did not fail to represent adequately a cross-section of the community, the opportunity for meaningful and appropriate representation does decrease with the size of the panels. Thus, if a minority group constitutes 10% of the community, 53.1% of randomly selected six-member juries could be expected to have no minority representative among their members, and 89% not to have two. Further reduction in size will erect additional barriers to representation.

Fifth, several authors have identified in jury research methodological problems tending to mask differences in the operation of smaller and larger juries. . . . Studies that aggregate data also risk masking case-by-case differences in jury deliberations. . . .

IV

While we adhere to, and reaffirm our holding in Williams v. Florida, these studies, most of which have been made since *Williams* was decided in 1970, lead us to conclude that the purpose and functioning of the jury in a criminal trial is seriously impaired, and to a constitutional degree, by a reduction in size to below six members. We readily admit that we do not pretend to discern a clear line between six members and five. But the assembled data raise substantial doubt about the reliability and appropriate representation of panels smaller than six. Because of the fundamental importance of the jury trial to the American system of criminal justice, any further reduction that promotes inaccurate and possibly biased decisionmaking, that causes untoward differences in verdicts, and that prevents juries from truly representing their communities, attains constitutional significance.

Georgia here presents no persuasive argument that a reduction to five does not offend important Sixth Amendment interests. First, its reliance on Johnson v.

Louisiana, 406 U.S. 356 (1972), for the proposition that the Court previously has approved the five-person jury is misplaced. In *Johnson* the petitioner . . . contended that requiring only nine members of a 12-person panel to convict in a felony case was a deprival of equal protection when a unanimous verdict was required from the 5-member panel used in a misdemeanor trial. The Court held merely that the classification was not invidious. Id., at 364. Because the issue of the constitutionality of the five-member jury was not then before the Court, it did not rule upon it.

Second, Georgia argues that its use of five-member juries does not violate the Sixth and Fourteenth Amendments because they are used only in misdemeanor cases. If six persons may constitutionally assess the felony charge in *Williams*, the State reasons, five persons should be a constitutionally adequate number for a misdemeanor trial. The problem with this argument is that the purpose and functions of the jury do not vary significantly with the importance of the crime. . . . In the present case the possible deprivation of liberty is substantial. . . . We cannot conclude that there is less need for the imposition and the direction of the sense of the community in this case than when the State has chosen to label an offense a felony. The need for an effective jury here must be judged by the same standards announced and applied in Williams v. Florida.

Third, the retention by Georgia of the unanimity requirement does not solve the Sixth and Fourteenth Amendment problem. Our concern has to do with the ability of the smaller group to perform the functions mandated by the Amendments. That a five-person jury may return a unanimous decision does not speak to the questions whether the group engaged in meaningful deliberation, could remember all the important facts and arguments, and truly represented the sense of the entire community. . . .

Fourth, Georgia submits that the five-person jury adequately represents the community because there is no arbitrary exclusion of any particular class. We agree that it has not been demonstrated that the Georgia system violates the Equal Protection Clause by discriminating on the basis of race or some other improper classification. . . . But the data outlined above raise substantial doubt about the ability of juries truly to represent the community as membership decreases below six. . . . Not only is the representation of racial minorities threatened in such circumstances, but also majority attitude or various minority positions may be misconstrued or misapplied by the smaller groups. . . .

Fifth, the empirical data cited by Georgia do not relieve our doubts. . . . Methodological problems prevent reliance on the three studies that do purport to bolster Georgia's position. The reliability of the two Michigan studies cited by the State has been criticized elsewhere. [See Saks, supra, at 43-46; Zeisel & Diamond, "Convincing Empirical Evidence" on the Six Member Jury, 41 U. Chi. L. Rev. 281, 286-290 (1974); Diamond, A Jury Experiment Reanalyzed, 7 U. Mich. J.L. Reform 520 (1974).] The Davis study . . . also presented an extreme set of facts so that none of the panels rendered a guilty verdict. [See Saks, supra, at 49-51.] None of these three reports, therefore, convinces us that a reduction in the number of jurors below six will not affect to a constitutional degree the functioning of juries in criminal trials.

V

With the reduction in the number of jurors below six creating a substantial threat to Sixth and Fourteenth Amendment guarantees, we must consider whether any interest of the State justifies the reduction. We find no significant state advantage in reducing the number of jurors from six to five.

The States utilize juries of less than 12 primarily for administrative reasons. Savings in court time and in financial costs are claimed to justify the reductions. The financial benefits of the reduction from 12 to 6 are substantial; this is mainly because fewer jurors draw daily allowances as they hear cases. On the other hand, the asserted saving in judicial time is not so clear. . . . [In one study,] [t]otal trial time did not diminish, and court delays and backlogs improved very little. [See Pabst, Statistical Studies of the Costs of Six-Man Versus Twelve-Man Juries, 14 Wm. & Mary L. Rev. 326 (1972).] The point that is to be made, of course, is that a reduction in size from six to five or four or even three would save the States little. . . . Perhaps this explains why only two States, Georgia and Virginia, have reduced the size of juries in certain nonpetty criminal cases to five. In short, the State has offered little or no justification for its reduction to five members.

Petitioner, therefore, has established that his trial on criminal charges before a five-member jury deprived him of the right to trial by jury guaranteed by the Sixth and Fourteenth Amendments.

VI

The judgment of the Court of Appeals is reversed, and the case is remanded for further proceedings not inconsistent with this opinion.

[Justice Brennan, in an opinion joined by Justices Stewart and Marshall, joined Justice Blackmun's lead opinion "insofar as it holds that the Sixth and Fourteenth Amendments require juries in criminal trials to contain more than five persons," but argued that the defendant should not undergo a new trial because the Georgia obscenity statute was unconstitutionally overbroad. The opinions of Justice Stevens, concurring, and Justice White, concurring in the judgment, are omitted.]

JUSTICE POWELL, with whom CHIEF JUSTICE BURGER and JUSTICE REHNQUIST join, concurring in the judgment.

I concur in the judgment, as I agree that use of a jury as small as five members, with authority to convict for serious offenses, involves grave questions of fairness. As the opinion of Mr. Justice Blackmun indicates, the line between five- and six-member juries is difficult to justify, but a line has to be drawn somewhere if the substance of jury trial is to be preserved.

I do not agree, however, that every feature of jury trial practice must be the same in both federal and state courts. . . . Also, I have reservations as to the wisdom — as well as the necessity — of Mr. Justice Blackmun's heavy reliance on numerology derived from statistical studies. Moreover, neither the validity nor the methodology employed by the studies cited was subjected to the traditional testing mechanisms of the adversary process. The studies relied on merely represent unexamined findings of persons interested in the jury system. . . .

NOTES AND QUESTIONS

1. With one exception, all of the empirical studies cited by the Court in *Ballew* involved a comparison between six-member juries and 12-member juries. As noted by the Court, the studies established that six-member juries are inferior in almost

every respect to 12-member juries. Why, then, did the Court "adhere to, and reaffirm" its decision in Williams v. Florida, upholding the use of six-member juries? Would it not have made much more sense for the Court simply to overrule *Williams* and hold that any jury with *six or fewer* members—including Ballew's five-member jury—violates the Sixth Amendment?

As for the specific question before the Court in *Ballew*—namely, whether five-member juries can function as well as the six-member juries that had been upheld in Williams v. Florida—only one cited study even touched on that subject. On what basis, then, did the Court conclude that there is a constitutional difference between five-member and six-member juries? Did the Court have sufficient empirical evidence to support that proposition? Was the Court justified in simply extrapolating the results of the studies of six-member juries? Even if hard lines must sometimes be drawn, shouldn't the Court draw those lines in a logical and empirically supportable manner?

2. *Ballew* is a rare example of a case in which the Supreme Court relied on empirical evidence (or, as Justice Powell dismissively described it, "numerology") to establish constitutional doctrine. Social scientists tend to view *Ballew* with a combination of pride and outrage—pride that empirical social-science research, for once, made a difference to the Court, coupled with outrage that the Court so obviously missed (or ignored) the entire message of the studies. See, e.g., sources collected in Myron Jacobstein & Roy M. Mersky, Jury Size: Articles and Bibliography from the Literature of Law and the Social and Behavioral Sciences (1998).

The Court's almost universal reluctance to rely on empirical social-science research is itself a subject worthy of study. Why is empirical evidence relatively rare in Court opinions? Is it because the Court does not understand such evidence? Because the Court feels incompetent to weigh and evaluate it? Because the Court does not want to rely on such evidence, based on fear of losing control over the legal outcome? Or because the Court generally knows where it wants to go with a case and does not want to be bothered with empirical evidence that might point in the opposite direction? See J. Alexander Tanford, The Limits of a Scientific Jurisprudence: The Supreme Court and Psychology, 66 Ind. L.J. 137 (1990).

Given the presence of important empirical issues in so many of the constitutional cases that come before the Court, and the unavoidable necessity to resolve such empirical issues in the course of making a decision, what generally takes the place of empirical evidence in the Court's analysis? Professor Richard Lempert has suggested the following:

> . . . Courts are influenced . . . by popular knowledge, and judges as part of an educated elite are influenced by social science learning to the extent it penetrates their elite culture. . . .
>
> It is . . . likely that appellate judges are most influenced by freelance research published in popular publications read by the educated elite or in publications specifically designed for lawyers, and to a lesser extent by the kinds of summary talks that social scientists sometimes give at bar association meetings, judicial conferences, continuing education programs for judges and the like.

Richard Lempert, "Between Cup and Lip": Social Science Influences on Law and Policy, 10 Law & Pol'y 167, 188, 190-191(1988). In other words, instead of relying on empirical evidence that might be submitted by the parties, or by an amicus curiae, the justices may be more likely to base their empirical judgments on whatever social science they have read about in the *New York Times* or the *ABA Journal*.

3. Note that the justifications given for trial by jury do not include accurate adjudication, although perhaps a right to see the "common-sense judgment of the jury" edges up to the point. In fact, there is reason to believe that group decisionmaking may have epistemological advantages in certain circumstances. Long ago, the Marquis de Condorcet proved, interestingly in the context of justifying jury decision making in capital cases, "that if the probable truth of an enlightened voter's opinion is greater than one-half when choosing between one of two alternatives, then the larger the group of such voters, the greater the probability that a majority decision will be true." Ronald J. Allen & Sarah A. Jehl, Burdens of Persuasion in Civil Cases: Algorithms v. Explanations, 4 Mich. St. L. Rev. 893, 906 (2003). The modern heir to Condorcet is a body of research commonly known as "the wisdom of the crowd," in honor of the book that brought the issue into public awareness, James Surowiecki, The Wisdom of Crowds: Why the Many Are Smarter Than the Few and How Collective Wisdom Shapes Business, Economies, Societies, and Nations (2004). The conditions under which these effects occur are stringent, however, including well-informed, independent, and unbiased voters. Recent work has begun exploring how often those conditions are met in real work decision context and the detrimental consequences for accurate decisionmaking when they are not. See, e.g., Vassilis Kostakos: Is the Crowd's Wisdom Biased? A Quantitative Analysis of Three Online Communities, 4 Computational Science & Engineering 251-255 (2009), and the MIT Technology Review: http://www.technologyreview.com/web/23477/?a=f. Nonetheless, jurors, and thus juries, may often meet these conditions, although majority voting is not the decision rule.

Other empirical work may also bear on the wisdom of jury decisionmaking, but less optimistically so. Group deliberation seems, in many instances, to have a polarizing effect, moving bodies that deliberate toward more extreme positions than their initial starting points would suggest. This effect is discussed in Cass Sunstein, The Law of Group Polarization, 10 J. Pol. Phil. 175 (2002). Some jury trials may well reflect this phenomenon, such as death penalty cases involving controversial issues and, literally, life or death.

Should any of this matter to constitutional adjudication?

4. In Apodaca v. Oregon, 406 U.S. 404 (1972), the Court addressed the issue of jury unanimity in the context of the traditional 12-member jury. Four justices took the position that the Sixth Amendment requirement must be the same for both state and federal criminal cases and that jury unanimity is required in both contexts. Four other justices agreed that the Sixth Amendment requirement must be the same for both state and federal criminal cases, but felt that jury unanimity is not required in either context. The ninth justice, Justice Powell, claimed that due process incorporation does not require imposition of the same Sixth Amendment rule in both state and federal criminal cases. Justice Powell concluded that, even though the Sixth Amendment guarantees a unanimous jury in federal criminal cases, the states may dispense with unanimity without violating due process. The confusing end result: Eight justices agreed that the Sixth Amendment must mean the same thing in both state and federal criminal cases, and five justices agreed that the Sixth Amendment requires jury unanimity. Yet, because of Justice Powell's idiosyncratic view about due process incorporation, the states nevertheless were permitted to dispense with unanimity.

If a state chooses to reduce the size of its juries to six members, pursuant to Williams v. Florida, then unanimity is required. See Burch v. Louisiana, 441 U.S. 130 (1979).

Kim Taylor-Thompson defends the unanimity requirement because it forces the jury to reach "complete consensus," which "at least provide[s] an impetus to stretch beyond group experiences and loyalties" and thus helps to ensure that minority voices on the jury will be heard. In contrast, with non-unanimous juries "the majority could ignore minority views by simply outvoting dissenters." Kim Taylor-Thompson, Empty Votes in Jury Deliberations, 113 Harv. L. Rev. 1261, 1264 (2000). Interestingly, very few states have instituted non-unanimity voting rules for juries. One reason is the perception that the unanimity requirement does not lead too frequently to hung juries, and thus there is no good reason to jettison it. See, e.g., the empirical study done for the National Center for State Courts: Paula L. Hannaford-Agor, Valerie P. Hans, Nicole L. Mott & G. Thomas Munsterman, Are Hung Juries a Problem? (2002). The rate for hung juries fluctuates around 5-6 percent in both state and federal felony courts, although there are numerous difficulties in obtaining and classifying the data (e.g., how does one classify a case in which a jury hangs on one but not another count?). As the authors point out, the implications of hung jurors may have been even less than meets the eye: "The limited data we were able to obtain suggest that juror deadlock often forces prosecutors and defense counsel to reassess the relative strengths and weaknesses of their cases and agree on a non-trial disposition. Over half of the cases that originally hung ultimately resulted in a plea agreement or a dismissal. Only one-third of trials that resulted in a hung jury were retried to a new jury. Dispositions in the retrials mirrored the original distribution of jury trial outcomes almost perfectly—a fact which belies the popular contention that these cases would have resulted in a conviction but for the unreasonable behavior of one or two holdout jurors." Id., at 82-83.

5. Article III of the Constitution contains a venue clause, requiring that "the trial of all crimes . . . shall be held in the state where the said crimes shall have been committed." In addition, the Sixth Amendment requires that juries be "of the state and district wherein the crime shall have been committed," a requirement usually referred to as vicinage. Application of these two constitutional requirements depends on an analysis of the elements of the particular crime involved. Venue and vicinage are discussed in Chapter 11. See, e.g., United States v. Rodriguez-Moreno, 526 U.S. 275 (1999) (defendant charged with using or carrying a firearm "during and in relation to any crime of violence," in violation of 18 U.S.C. §924(c)(1), may be tried, consistently with vicinage and venue requirements, in any district where the crime of violence was committed, even if no firearm was used therein); United States v. Cabrales, 524 U.S. 1 (1998) (defendant charged with money laundering offenses, in violation of 18 U.S.C. §§1956(a)(1)(B)(ii) and 1957, may not be tried in Missouri because, although the money allegedly derived from illegal sales of cocaine in Missouri, the alleged acts of money laundering by the defendant occurred entirely in Florida).

B. Jury Composition

There are three central issues concerning the composition of a criminal jury: (1) Was the jury impartial, within the meaning of the Sixth Amendment? (2) Was the jury selected from a venire that represented a "fair cross section" of the community, an implied requirement under the Sixth Amendment? (3) Was the jury selected in a nondiscriminatory way in compliance with the requirements of the Equal Protection Clause of the Fourteenth Amendment (or, in federal cases, the equivalent requirements imposed under the Fifth Amendment's Due Process Clause)?

The first stage of jury selection, and thus the first step toward vindicating these requirements, involves the compilation by the jury commissioner (or equivalent official) of a large *master list* of prospective jurors. In the (not so distant) past, many jurisdictions employed a "key man" system, under which community leaders would identify those thought qualified to serve on a jury. Today, however, master lists are usually derived from a combination of voter registration lists, telephone books, drivers' license lists, lists of public utility customers, and even welfare rolls.

From the master list, random processes are used to select a subset of names for the *venire*, a smaller list from which prospective jurors will be called to serve in an individual case (or, in some jurisdictions, for a term of weeks or months, during which the same venire remains subject to being called for jury duty). When members of the venire are contacted by the jury commissioner for possible jury service, they are asked to supply basic information about themselves. This information may result in the prospective juror being disqualified or exempted. *Disqualifications* are based on such matters as lack of citizenship, underage status, illiteracy, or the existence of a prior felony conviction. *Exemptions* are based largely on occupation; in most jurisdictions, for example, doctors and members of the clergy are exempted.[9]

Many prospective jurors who are neither disqualified nor exempt claim that jury service would be a personal hardship for them. This claim, if persuasive, may lead to the granting of an excuse, either by the jury commissioner or (at a later stage of the selection process) by the trial judge. *Excuses* are often based on advanced age, physical infirmity, financial hardship, transportation problems, or the need to care for young children. Even within a particular jurisdiction, the likelihood of obtaining an excuse may vary with the receptivity of the trial judge to the prospective juror's claim of hardship.

After the venire has been culled by disqualifications, exemptions, and excuses, the next stage of jury selection consists of voir dire. During *voir dire* (from the French, "to see, to speak"), prospective jurors are asked questions, in person, so that the trial judge, prosecutor, and defense attorney can learn more about them. Depending on the jurisdiction, voir dire may be conducted by the lawyers, by the judge, or by both the lawyers and the judge. Even where the judge conducts voir dire, often the lawyers will be allowed to submit questions to be asked by the judge. The scope of voir dire questioning is determined, in general, by the local legal culture (i.e., in some areas, prolonged and probing voir dire is a routine occurrence, while in others, the customary practice is to ask only a few brief questions) and, in specific cases, by limits set by the judge.

Voir dire serves three important purposes. First, the Sixth Amendment guarantees every defendant the right to be tried by an impartial jury, and voir dire

9. Under the federal Jury Selection and Service Act, 28 U.S.C. §1863(b)(6), active-duty service members, police officers and firefighters, and "persons either elected to public office or directly appointed by a person elected to public office" who "are actively engaged in the performance of official duties" are exempt and therefore "barred from jury service" in federal cases.

provides the lawyers and the judge with information that allows for the *exclusion* of prospective jurors who may be disinterested for one reason or another. For example, if a prospective juror, in response to voir dire questioning, states that she is closely related to a police officer and, as a result, cannot fairly and impartially evaluate the defendant's claim that a police officer fabricated evidence against him, then that prospective juror would likely be excluded. The potential sources of lack of impartiality are as wide ranging as humanity is complex—financial interest, emotional attachment or its opposite, ideological commitments, and so on.

The primary mechanism for the exclusion of potential jurors lacking impartiality is the *challenge for cause.* During or after voir dire, the prosecutor and defense attorney have an unlimited opportunity to make challenges for cause against prospective jurors they believe to be biased. These challenges must be resolved by the trial judge, based on information obtained from the prospective juror. Even in the absence of a challenge for cause, however, the judge must exclude, on her own motion, any prospective juror whom the judge believes to be biased.

A second purpose for voir dire is to provide the lawyers with information that can be used in the exercise of another means of excluding potential jurors, called the *peremptory challenge.* These challenges are granted in limited number, according to the law of the jurisdiction (usually the same number for both sides, although sometimes the defense is granted more than the prosecution), and—subject to narrow exceptions discussed below—can be exercised for any reason at all (or even without any stated reason). The idea behind the peremptory challenge is that a lawyer may sometimes feel that a prospective juror would be adverse to her side of the case, yet be unable to establish that the prospective juror is biased; indeed, it may be impossible (or impolitic, in the presence of other prospective jurors) for the lawyer even to state the basis for her feelings. The peremptory challenge allows the lawyer to act on such feelings, and to exclude such prospective jurors, without the need to explain. For example, if a prospective juror, in response to voir dire questioning, states that he often got into trouble as a teenager, this would probably be insufficient to show bias but might provide the basis for the exercise of a peremptory challenge by the prosecutor, who might fear that such a prospective juror would be more likely than others to sympathize with the defendant.

The third purpose for voir dire, especially in those jurisdictions where lawyers play a prominent role in voir dire, is to provide prospective jurors with their first exposure to the issues in the case. Often, prosecutors and defense attorneys will use voir dire as an opportunity to begin the process of educating the jury about the case—from their own respective perspectives, of course. For example, a defense lawyer who plans to contest an eyewitness account of the crime may ask prospective jurors at voir dire if they have ever known of an instance where an eyewitness to an event turned out to be mistaken about the identity of the parties involved. It has been estimated that such attempts to sensitize the jury may occur in 40 to 80 percent of criminal trials. See R. W. Balch, Curt Taylor Griffiths, Edwin L. Hall & L. Thomas Winfree, The Socialization of Jurors, 4 J. Crim. Just. 271-283 (1976).

At the conclusion of voir dire, after all challenges for cause have been ruled upon and all peremptory challenges have been exercised (or waived), what remains is the jury that will be sworn to decide the case. In the Notes and Questions that follow, we first examine more carefully the requirement of impartiality. We then turn to the remaining two issues. The *Duren* case and the materials following it examine the meaning of a "fair cross section of the community" for purposes of the right to trial by jury, and *Batson* and the related material examine the potential discriminatory use of peremptory challenges.

NOTES AND QUESTIONS ON THE IMPARTIALITY REQUIREMENT

1. The impartiality requirement does not mean that prospective jurors must be completely uninformed about the facts of the case; in modern society, it might not be possible to find jurors who have not heard something about a high-profile case from television, newspapers, or social media. The impartiality requirement also does not mean that prospective jurors must be completely without opinions or must start out precisely evenhanded in their views about the case. Rather, it is only "those strong and deep impressions which close the mind against the testimony that may be offered in opposition to them, which will combat that testimony and resist its force, [that] constitute a sufficient objection." Reynolds v. United States, 98 U.S. 145, 155 (1879). To put it another way, a prospective juror lacks impartiality only if he or she has views about the case strong enough to "prevent or substantially impair the performance of his [or her] duties as a juror" in accordance with the law. See Wainwright v. Witt, 469 U.S. 412, 424 (1985).

2. Several leading Supreme Court impartiality cases have involved claims that jurors were biased because of racial prejudice. Instructive in this regard are Ham v. South Carolina, 409 U.S. 524 (1973), and Ristaino v. Ross, 424 U.S. 589 (1976). In *Ham*, the defendant was a young, bearded black man who was active in the civil rights movement in Florence, South Carolina. He was charged with marijuana possession, and he claimed to have been framed by the police because of his race and his civil rights activism. His lawyer asked the trial judge to question the prospective jurors at voir dire about their possible racial biases, but the request was denied, and Ham was convicted. The Court found a constitutional violation; although "the trial judge was not required to put the question in any particular form," the defendant must be "permitted to have the jurors interrogated on the issue of racial bias." Id., at 527.

In *Ross*, the defendant was a black man from Massachusetts charged with armed robbery, assault, and battery by means of a dangerous weapon, and assault and battery with intent to murder, in connection with an attack on a white Boston University security guard. His lawyer sought to have the trial judge ask the prospective jurors the following voir dire question: "Are there any of you who believe that a white person is more likely to be telling the truth than a black person?" The trial judge refused, and Ross was convicted. The Court affirmed the conviction, explaining that *Ham* "did not announce a requirement of universal applicability. Rather, it reflected an assessment of whether under all circumstances presented there was a constitutionally significant likelihood that, absent questioning about racial prejudice, the jurors would not be [impartial]." Id., at 596.

As the Court has acknowledged, "[I]t is plain that there is some risk of racial prejudice influencing a jury whenever there is a crime involving interracial violence." Turner v. Murray, 476 U.S. 28, 36, n. 8 (1986) (plurality opinion of Justice White). What, then, is the constitutional distinction between *Ham* and *Ross*?

The critical factor present in *Ham*, but not present in [*Ross*], was that racial issues were "inextricably bound up with the conduct of the trial," and the consequent need, under all the circumstances, specifically to inquire into possible racial prejudice in order to assure an impartial jury. . . . Although [*Ross*] involved an alleged criminal confrontation between a black assailant and a white victim, that fact pattern alone did not create a need of "constitutional dimensions" to question the jury concerning racial prejudice. . . . There is no constitutional presumption of juror bias for or against members of any particular racial or ethnic groups. . . . Only when there are more substantial indications of the likelihood of racial or ethnic prejudice affecting the jurors in a particular case does the trial court's denial of a defendant's request to examine the jurors' ability to deal impartially with this subject amount to an unconstitutional abuse of discretion.

Rosales-Lopez v. United States, 451 U.S. 182, 190 (plurality opinion of Justice White).

See also Turner v. Murray, supra, where the Court applied *Ham*, not *Ross*, to hold that "a *capital* defendant accused of an interracial crime is entitled to have prospective jurors informed of the race of the victim and questioned on the issue of racial bias," id., at 36-37 (emphasis added). In a separate, plurality portion of Justice White's lead opinion in *Turner*, he reiterated that "[t]he fact of interracial violence alone is not a 'special circumstance' entitling the defendant to have prospective jurors questioned about racial prejudice," id., at 35, n. 7 (plurality opinion of Justice White). Nevertheless, Turner's death sentence (but not his guilty verdict) had to be overturned because of the combination of three such "special circumstances": (1) that "the crime charged involved interracial violence," (2) "the broad discretion given the jury at the death-penalty hearing," and (3) "the special seriousness of the risk of improper sentencing in a capital case." Id., at 37 (plurality opinion of Justice White).

3. Another important line of Supreme Court impartiality decisions involves juror attitudes about the death penalty. In Witherspoon v. Illinois, 391 U.S. 510 (1968), the Court declared that persons opposed to the death penalty could be excluded, on impartiality grounds, from juries in capital cases only if they made it "unmistakably clear (1) that they would *automatically* vote against the imposition of capital punishment without regard to any evidence that might be developed at the trial of the case before them, or (2) that their attitude toward the death penalty would prevent them from making an impartial decision as to the defendant's *guilt*." Id., at 522, n. 21 (emphasis in original).

In Wainwright v. Witt, 469 U.S. 412 (1985), however, the Court modified the *Witherspoon* standard, explaining that—in capital and noncapital cases alike—"the quest is for jurors who will conscientiously apply the law and find the facts." Id., at 423. The Court held:

> [T]he proper standard for determining when a prospective juror may be excluded for cause because of his or her views on capital punishment . . . is whether the juror's views would "prevent or substantially impair the performance of his [or her] duties as a juror in accordance with his [or her] instructions and his [or her] oath." We note that, in addition to dispensing with *Witherspoon*'s reference to "automatic" decision-making, this standard likewise does not require that a juror's bias be proved with "unmistakable clarity." This is because determinations of juror bias cannot be reduced to question-and-answer sessions which obtain results in the manner of a catechism. What common sense should have realized experience has proved: many veniremen simply cannot be asked enough questions to reach the point where their bias has been made "unmistakably clear"; these veniremen may not know how they will react when faced with imposing the death sentence, or may be unable to articulate, or may wish

New std.

> to hide their true feelings. Despite this lack of clarity in the printed record, however, there will be situations where the trial judge is left with the definite impression that a prospective juror would be unable to faithfully and impartially apply the law. . . . [T]his is why deference must be paid to the trial judge who sees and hears the juror.

Id., at 424-426. See also Uttecht v. Brown, 551 U.S. 1 (2007), where the Court, by 5-4, held that the *Witt* standard must be applied by federal habeas courts with a kind of "double" deference: deference to the trial court that had the chance to judge the demeanor of the prospective juror in the first instance, as well as the mandatory deference owed to state courts by all federal habeas courts.

One year later, in Lockhart v. McCree, 476 U.S. 162 (1986), the Court faced a novel twist on the impartiality argument. The defendant in *McCree* claimed, inter alia, that the exclusion, prior to the start of his capital trial, of prospective jurors who would have been impartial as to guilt or innocence but who were biased as to capital sentencing (under the old *Witherspoon* standard) violated his right to an impartial jury. The claim was based on extensive empirical research concerning the impact of such exclusion on the guilt-innocence determination. As the *McCree* dissenters put it:

> The perspectives on the criminal justice system of jurors who survive death qualification are systematically different from those of the excluded jurors. Death-qualified jurors are, for example, more likely to believe that a defendant's failure to testify is indicative of his guilt, more hostile to the insanity defense, more mistrustful of defense attorneys, and less concerned about the danger of erroneous convictions. . . . This proprosecution bias is reflected in the greater readiness of death-qualified jurors to convict or to convict on more serious charges.

Id., at 188 (Marshall, J., dissenting).

The Court "assume[d] for purposes of this opinion that the studies are both methodologically valid and adequate to establish that 'death qualification' in fact produces juries somewhat more 'conviction-prone' than 'non-death-qualified' juries." Id., at 173. Nevertheless, the Court rejected the impartiality claim:

> McCree concedes that the individual jurors who served at his trial were impartial, as that term [has been] defined by this Court. . . . Instead, McCree argues that his jury lacked impartiality because the absence of "*Witherspoon*-excludables" "slanted" the jury in favor of conviction.
>
> We do not agree. McCree's "impartiality" argument apparently is based on the theory that, because all individual jurors are to some extent predisposed towards one result or another, a constitutionally impartial *jury* can be constructed only by "balancing" the various predispositions of the individual *jurors*. Thus, according to McCree, when the State "tips the scales" by excluding prospective jurors with a particular viewpoint, an impermissibly partial jury results. We have consistently rejected this view of jury impartiality, including as recently as last Term when we squarely held that an impartial *jury* consists of nothing more than "*jurors* who will conscientiously apply the law and find the facts." Wainwright v. Witt, 469 U.S. 412, 423 (1985) (emphasis added). . . .
>
> The view of jury impartiality urged upon us by McCree is both illogical and hopelessly impractical. . . . McCree admits that exactly the same 12 individuals could have ended up on his jury through the "luck of the draw," without in any way violating the constitutional guarantee of impartiality. Even accepting McCree's position that we

should focus on the *jury* rather than the individual *jurors*, it is hard for us to understand the logic of the argument that a given jury is unconstitutionally partial when it results from a state-ordained process, yet impartial when exactly the same jury results from mere chance. On a more practical level, if it were true that the Constitution required a certain mix of individual viewpoints on the jury, then trial judges would be required to undertake the Sisyphean task of "balancing" juries, making sure that each contains the proper number of Democrats and Republicans, young persons and old persons, white-collar executives and blue-collar laborers, and so on. Adopting McCree's concept of jury impartiality would also likely require the elimination of peremptory challenges, which are commonly used by both the State and the defendant to attempt to produce a jury favorable to the challenger. . . .

In our view, it is simply not possible to define jury impartiality, for constitutional purposes, by reference to some hypothetical mix of individual viewpoints. . . . [T]he Constitution presupposes that a jury selected from a fair cross section of the community is impartial, regardless of the mix of individual viewpoints actually represented on the jury, so long as the jurors can conscientiously and properly carry out their sworn duty to apply the law to the facts of the particular case.

Id., at 177-179, 183-184.

Are you persuaded by the Court's reasoning in *McCree*? Does it seem fair to you that the defendant—in a capital case, no less—was convicted by a jury that the empirical studies showed, and that the Court admitted (for purposes of its opinion), was more prone to convict than the average, non-death-qualified jury? Even if, as the Court noted, the same conviction-prone jury could have occurred by chance, should it not matter that in McCree's case it was the product of a deliberate prosecution strategy to exclude death-penalty opponents from the jury? Would it affect your view to know that at least some prosecutors are alleged to seek the death penalty in at least some murder cases mostly so that they will be able to "death-qualify" the jury, only to drop the request for the death penalty later in the case? See *McCree*, 476 U.S., at 176, n. 16 (declining to address this argument because the prosecutor did not waive the death penalty in McCree's case); id., at 188, n. 4 (Marshall, J., dissenting) (citing examples of this practice).

Is the problem simply that McCree's argument did not fit into the Court's existing case law on jury impartiality? Maybe what McCree needed was a new constitutional doctrine designed to prohibit the prosecution from systematically skewing juries in its favor. Could this doctrine be implied in the Sixth Amendment? Or could it be derived from more general notions of "fundamental fairness" under the Due Process Clause?

What other common practices might be affected by such a doctrine? What about the now-pervasive use of jury-selection experts—at least in a context where the prosecutor has superior resources to hire such experts, as compared with the defense lawyer? What about the practice, common in many prosecutors' offices, of keeping records about the verdicts rendered by past juries, so that such records can be used in the future to exclude (usually through peremptories) jurors who previously voted in favor of acquitting a defendant? Note that defense lawyers usually do not have an equal opportunity to maintain such jury records because they are not "repeat players" to the same extent as the prosecutor; in any given jurisdiction, the prosecutor is involved in every criminal case, whereas even the public defender will be involved in only a smaller subset of the cases.

Although they derive from separate constitutional sources, the remaining two issues—the "fair cross section" and the equal protection requirements—combine to serve the single goal of ensuring that juries reflect the diversity of the American people. In reading the cases and notes that follow, you should ask yourself several questions: Does diversity matter? If so, why does it matter? What is the proper role of the jury in a diverse (and often divided) society? Finally, and most controversially, should jurors represent their diverse genders, races, ethnicities, religions, and/or sexual orientations, or should they strive to overcome their differences and become a "melting pot" jury?

1. The Requirement of a Fair Cross Section

DUREN v. MISSOURI

Certiorari to the Supreme Court of Missouri
439 U.S. 357 (1979)

JUSTICE WHITE delivered the opinion of the Court.

In Taylor v. Louisiana, 419 U.S. 522 (1975), this Court held that systematic exclusion of women during the jury-selection process, resulting in jury pools not "reasonably representative" of the community, denies a criminal defendant his right, under the Sixth and Fourteenth Amendments, to a petit jury selected from a fair cross section of the community.[1] Under the system invalidated in *Taylor*, a woman could not serve on a jury unless she filed a written declaration of her willingness to do so. As a result, although 53% of the persons eligible for jury service were women, less than 1% of the 1,800 persons whose names were drawn from the jury wheel during the year in which appellant Taylor's jury was chosen were female. Id., at 524.

At the time of our decision in *Taylor*, no other State provided that women could not serve on a jury unless they volunteered to serve. However, five States, including Missouri, provided an automatic exemption from jury service for any women requesting not to serve. Subsequent to *Taylor*, three of these States eliminated this exemption. Only Missouri, respondent in this case, and Tennessee continue to exempt women from jury service upon request. Today we hold that such systematic exclusion of women that results in jury venires averaging less than 15% female violates the Constitution's fair-cross-section requirement.

I

Petitioner Duren was indicted in 1975 in the Circuit Court of Jackson County, Mo., for first-degree murder and first-degree robbery. In a pretrial motion to quash his petit jury panel, and again in a post-conviction motion for a new trial, he contended that his right to trial by a jury chosen from a fair cross section of his community was denied by provisions of Missouri law granting women who so request an automatic exemption from jury service. Both motions were denied.

---

1. See Taylor v. Louisiana, 419 U.S., at 526-531, 538; Duncan v. Louisiana, 391 U.S. 145 (1968). A criminal defendant has standing to challenge exclusion resulting in a violation of the fair-cross-section requirement, whether or not he is a member of the excluded class. See *Taylor*, supra, at 526.

At hearings on these motions, petitioner established that the jury-selection process in Jackson County begins with the annual mailing of a questionnaire to persons randomly selected from the Jackson County voter registration list. Approximately 70,000 questionnaires were mailed in 1975. The questionnaire contains a list of occupations and other categories which are the basis under Missouri law for either disqualification or exemption from jury service. Included on the questionnaire is a paragraph prominently addressed "TO WOMEN" that states in part:

> Any woman who elects not to serve will fill out this paragraph and mail this questionnaire to the jury commissioner at once.

A similar paragraph is addressed "TO MEN OVER 65 YEARS OF AGE," who are also statutorily exempt upon request.

The names of those sent questionnaires are placed in the master jury wheel for Jackson County, except for those returning the questionnaire who indicate disqualification or claim an applicable exemption. Summonses are mailed on a weekly basis to prospective jurors randomly drawn from the jury wheel. The summons, like the questionnaire, contains special directions to men over 65 and to women, this time advising them to return the summons by mail if they desire not to serve. The practice also is that even those women who do not return the summons are treated as having claimed exemption if they fail to appear for jury service on the appointed day. Other persons seeking to claim an exemption at this stage must make written or personal application to the court.

Petitioner established that according to the 1970 census, 54% of the adult inhabitants of Jackson County were women. He also showed that for the periods June-October 1975 and January-March 1976, 11,197 persons were summoned and that 2,992 of these, or 26.7%, were women. Of those summoned, 741 women and 4,378 men appeared for service. Thus, 14.5% (741 of 5,119) of the persons on the postsummons weekly venires during the period in which petitioner's jury was chosen were female. In March 1976, when petitioner's trial began, 15.5% of those on the weekly venires were women (110 of 707). Petitioner's jury was selected from a 53-person panel on which there were 5 women; all 12 jurors chosen were men. None of the foregoing statistical evidence was disputed.

In affirming petitioner's conviction, the Missouri Supreme Court questioned two aspects of his statistical presentation. First, it considered the census figures inadequate because they were six years old and might not precisely mirror the percentage of women registered to vote. Second, petitioner had not unequivocally demonstrated the extent to which the low percentage of women appearing for jury service was due to the automatic exemption for women, rather than to sex-neutral exemptions such as that for persons over age 65.

The court went on to hold, however, that even accepting petitioner's statistical proof, "the number of female names in the wheel, those summoned and those appearing were well above acceptable constitutional standards." . . .[19] We granted certiorari, . . . because of concern that the decision below is not consistent with our decision in *Taylor*.

---

19. The decision below also rejected petitioner's challenge under the Equal Protection Clause of the Fourteenth Amendment. This challenge has not been renewed before this Court.

II

We think that in certain crucial respects the Missouri Supreme Court misconceived the nature of the fair-cross-section inquiry set forth in Taylor. In holding that "petit juries must be drawn from a source fairly representative of the community," 419 U.S., at 538, we explained that "jury wheels, pools of names, panels, or venires from which juries are drawn must not systematically exclude distinctive groups in the community and thereby fail to be reasonably representative thereof." Ibid.[20]

In order to establish a prima facie violation of the fair-cross-section requirement, the defendant must show (1) that the group alleged to be excluded is a "distinctive" group in the community; (2) that the representation of this group in venires from which juries are selected is not fair and reasonable in relation to the number of such persons in the community; and (3) that this underrepresentation is due to systematic exclusion of the group in the jury-selection process.

A

With respect to the first part of the prima facie test, *Taylor* without doubt established that women "are sufficiently numerous and distinct from men" so that "if they are systematically eliminated from jury panels, the Sixth Amendment's fair-cross-section requirement cannot be satisfied." Id., at 531.

B

The second prong of the prima facie case was established by petitioner's statistical presentation. Initially, the defendant must demonstrate the percentage of the community made up of the group alleged to be underrepresented, for this is the conceptual benchmark for the Sixth Amendment fair-cross-section requirement. In *Taylor*, the State had stipulated that 53% of the population eligible for jury service was female, while petitioner Duren has relied upon a census measurement of the actual percentage of women in the community (54%). In the trial court, the State of Missouri never challenged these data. Although the Missouri Supreme Court speculated that changing population patterns between 1970 and 1976 and unequal voter registration by men and women rendered the census figures a questionable frame of reference, there is no evidence whatsoever in the record to suggest that the 1970 census data significantly distorted the percentage of women in Jackson County at the time of trial. Petitioner's presentation was clearly adequate prima facie evidence of population characteristics for the purpose of making a fair-cross-section violation.

Given petitioner's proof that in the relevant community slightly over half of the adults are women, we must disagree with the conclusion of the court below that jury venires containing approximately 15% women are "reasonably representative" of this community. If the percentage of women appearing on jury pools in Jackson County had precisely mirrored the percentage of women in the population, more than one of every two prospective jurors would have been female. In fact, less than one of every six prospective jurors was female; 85% of the average jury was male. Such a gross discrepancy between the percentage of women in jury venires and the

---

20. We further explained that this requirement does not mean "that petit juries actually chosen must mirror the community," 419 U.S., at 538.

percentage of women in the community requires the conclusion that women were not fairly represented in the source from which petit juries were drawn in Jackson County.

C

Finally, in order to establish a prima facie case, it was necessary for petitioner to show that the underrepresentation of women, generally and on his venire, was due to their systematic exclusion in the jury-selection process. Petitioner's proof met this requirement. His undisputed demonstration that a large discrepancy occurred not just occasionally, but in every weekly venire for a period of nearly a year manifestly indicates that the cause of the underrepresentation was systematic—that is, inherent in the particular jury-selection process utilized.

Petitioner Duren's statistics and other evidence also established when in the selection process the systematic exclusion took place. There was no indication that underrepresentation of women occurred at the first stage of the selection process—the questionnaire canvass of persons randomly selected from the relevant voter registration list. The first sign of a systematic discrepancy is at the next stage—the construction of the jury wheel from which persons are randomly summoned for service. Less than 30% of those summoned were female, demonstrating that a substantially larger number of women answering the questionnaire claimed either ineligibility or exemption from jury service. Moreover, at the summons stage women were not only given another opportunity to claim exemption, but also were presumed to have claimed exemption when they did not respond to the summons. Thus, the percentage of women at the final, venire, stage (14.5%) was much lower than the percentage of women who were summoned for service (26.7%).

The resulting disproportionate and consistent exclusion of women from the jury wheel and at the venire stage was quite obviously due to the system by which juries were selected. Petitioner demonstrated that the underrepresentation of women in the final pool of prospective jurors was due to the operation of Missouri's exemption criteria—whether the automatic exemption for women or other statutory exemptions—as implemented in Jackson County. Women were therefore systematically underrepresented within the meaning of *Taylor*.

III

The demonstration of a prima facie fair-cross-section violation by the defendant is not the end of the inquiry into whether a constitutional violation has occurred. We have explained that "States remain free to prescribe relevant qualifications for their jurors and to provide reasonable exemptions so long as it may be fairly said that the jury lists or panels are representative of the community." *Taylor*, 419 U.S., at 538. However, we cautioned that "[t]he right to a proper jury cannot be overcome on merely rational grounds," id., at 534. Rather, it requires that a significant state interest be manifestly and primarily advanced by those aspects of the jury-selection process, such as exemption criteria, that result in the disproportionate exclusion of a distinctive group.

The Supreme Court of Missouri suggested that the low percentage of women on jury venires in Jackson County may have been due to a greater number of women than of men qualifying for or claiming permissible exemptions, such as those for persons over 65, teachers, and government workers. . . . Respondent further argues that petitioner has not proved that the exemption for women had "any effect" on or was responsible for the underrepresentation of women on venires. . . .

However, once the defendant has made a prima facie showing of an infringement of his constitutional right to a jury drawn from a fair cross section of the community, it is the State that bears the burden of justifying this infringement by showing attainment of a fair cross section to be incompatible with a significant state interest. See *Taylor*, 419 U.S., at 533-535. Assuming, arguendo, that the exemptions mentioned by the court below would justify failure to achieve a fair community cross section on jury venires, the State must demonstrate that these exemptions caused the underrepresentation complained of. The record contains no such proof, and mere suggestions or assertions to that effect are insufficient.

The other possible cause of the disproportionate exclusion of women on Jackson County jury venires is, of course, the automatic exemption for women. Neither the Missouri Supreme Court nor respondent in its brief has offered any substantial justification for this exemption. In response to questioning at oral argument, counsel for respondent ventured that the only state interest advanced by the exemption is safeguarding the important role played by women in home and family life. But exempting all women because of the preclusive domestic responsibilities of some women is insufficient justification for their disproportionate exclusion on jury venires. What we stated in *Taylor* with respect to the system there challenged under which women could "opt in" for jury service is equally applicable to Missouri's "opt out" exemption:

> It is untenable to suggest these days that it would be a special hardship for each and every woman to perform jury service or that society cannot spare *any* women from their present duties. This may be the case with many, and it may be burdensome to sort out those who should be exempted from those who should serve. But that task is performed in the case of men, and the administrative convenience in dealing with women as a class is insufficient justification for diluting the quality of community judgment represented by the jury in criminal trials. . . .
>
> If it was ever the case that women were unqualified to sit on juries or were so situated that none of them should be required to perform jury service, that time has long since passed.

419 U.S., at 534-535, 537 (footnote omitted).

We recognize that a State may have an important interest in assuring that those members of the family responsible for the care of children are available to do so. An exemption appropriately tailored to this interest would, we think, survive a fair-cross-section challenge. We stress, however, that the constitutional guarantee to a jury drawn from a fair cross section of the community requires that States exercise proper caution in exempting broad categories of persons from jury service. Although most occupational and other reasonable exemptions may inevitably involve some degree of overinclusiveness or underinclusiveness, any category expressly limited to a group in the community of sufficient magnitude and distinctiveness so as to be within the fair-cross-section requirement—such as women—runs the danger of resulting in underrepresentation sufficient to constitute a prima facie violation of that constitutional requirement. We also repeat the observation made in *Taylor* that it is unlikely that reasonable exemptions, such as those based on special hardship, incapacity, or community needs, "would pose substantial threats that the remaining pool of jurors would not be representative of the community." Id., at 534.

The judgment of the Missouri Supreme Court is reversed, and the case is remanded for further proceedings not inconsistent with this opinion.

JUSTICE REHNQUIST, dissenting.

. . . The Constitution does not require, and our jurisprudence is ill served, by a hybrid doctrine such as that developed in *Taylor*, and in this case.*

Even if I were able to reconcile the Court's agile amalgamation of the Due Process Clause and the Equal Protection Clause of the Fourteenth Amendment in deciding this case and *Taylor*, I have no little concern about where the road upon which the Court has embarked will ultimately lead. . . .

Eventually the Court either will insist that women be treated identically to men for purposes of jury selection . . . , or in some later sequel to this line of cases will discover some peculiar magic in the number 15 that will enable it to distinguish between such a percentage and a higher percentage less than 50. But whichever of these routes the Court chooses to travel when the question is actually presented, its decision today puts state legislators and local jury commissioners at a serious disadvantage wholly unwarranted by the constitutional provisions upon which it relies. If the Court ultimately concludes that men and women must be treated exactly alike for purposes of jury service, it will have imposed substantial burdens upon many women, particularly in less populated areas, without necessarily producing any corresponding increase in the representative character of jury panels. If it ultimately concludes that a percentage of women on jury panels greater than 15 but substantially less than 50 is permissible even though the State's jury selection system permits women but not men to "opt out" of jury service, it is simply playing a constitutional numbers game. . . .

The probability, then, is that today's decision will cause States to abandon not only gender-based but also occupation-based classifications for purposes of jury service. Doctors and nurses, though virtually irreplaceable in smaller communities,

---

* . . . If . . . men and women are essentially fungible for purposes of jury duty, the question arises how underrepresentation of either sex on the jury or the venire infringes on a defendant's right to have his fate decided by an impartial tribunal. Counsel for petitioner, when asked at oral argument to explain the difference, from the defendant's point of view, between men and women jurors, offered: "It is that indefinable something— . . . I think that we perhaps all understand it when we see it and when we feel it, but it is not that easy to describe; yes, there is a difference." . . . But close analysis of the fair-cross-section doctrine demonstrates that the Court itself does not really believe in such mysticism. For if "that indefinable something" were truly an essential element of the due process right to trial by an impartial jury, a defendant would be entitled to a jury composed of men and women in perfect proportion to their numbers in the community. Yet in *Taylor*, supra, at 538, the majority stressed: "Defendants are not entitled to a jury of any particular composition, . . . but the jury wheels, pools of names, panels, or venires from which juries are drawn must not systematically exclude distinctive groups in the community and thereby fail to be reasonably representative thereof." Thus, a defendant's constitutional right to an impartial jury is protected so long as "that indefinable something" supposedly crucial to impartiality is adequately represented on the jury venire; that the petit jury ultimately struck is composed of one sex is irrelevant.

The Sixth and Fourteenth Amendments guarantee a criminal defendant the right to be tried by an impartial jury. If impartiality is not lost because a particular class or group represented in the community is unrepresented on the petit jury, it is certainly not lost because the class or group is underrepresented on the jury venire. It is therefore clear that the majority's fair-cross-section rationale is not concerned with the defendant's due process right to an impartial jury at all. Instead, the requirement that distinct segments of the community be represented on jury venires is concerned with the equal protection right of the excluded class to participate in the judicial process through jury service. . . .

may ultimately be held by the Court to bring their own "flavor" or "indefinable something" to a jury venire. . . . If so, they could then be exempted from jury service only on a case-by-case basis, and would join others with skills much less in demand whiling away their time in jury rooms of countless courthouses.

No one but a lawyer could think that this was a managerially sound solution to an important problem of judicial administration, and no one but a lawyer thoroughly steeped in the teachings of cases such as *Taylor* [and the Court's recent Equal Protection decisions] could think that such a solution was mandated by the United States Constitution. . . .

NOTES AND QUESTIONS

1. Why must a jury be drawn from a fair cross section of the community? In *Taylor*, the Court identified three primary reasons: (1) "guard[ing] against the exercise of arbitrary power," (2) preserving "public confidence in the fairness of the criminal justice system," and (3) implementing the belief that "sharing in the administration of justice is a phase of civic responsibility." 419 U.S., at 530-531. The Court emphasized, however, that "in holding that petit juries must be drawn from a source fairly representative of the community we impose no requirement that petit juries actually chosen must mirror the community and reflect the various distinctive groups in the population." Id., at 538.

2. In Lockhart v. McCree, discussed supra at page 1332 in the context of impartiality, the defendant also claimed that the "death qualification" of his jury violated the fair-cross-section requirement. The Court rejected this claim as well, on two grounds. First, "[w]e have never invoked the fair-cross-section principle to invalidate the use of either for-cause or peremptory challenges to prospective jurors, or to require petit juries, as opposed to jury panels or venires, to reflect the composition of the community at large." 476 U.S., at 173. Second, "groups defined solely in terms of shared attitudes that would prevent or substantially impair members of the group from performing one of their duties as jurors, such as the '*Witherspoon*-excludables' at issue here, are not 'distinctive groups' for fair-cross-section purposes." Id., at 174. The Court asserted that the exclusion of "*Witherspoon*-excludables"—unlike the exclusion of blacks, women, or Latinos—does not contravene any of the three purposes of the fair-cross-section requirement identified in *Taylor*. (1) Because "*Witherspoon*-excludables" are excluded for a legally valid reason (i.e., their bias with respect to capital sentencing), there is little danger of "arbitrarily skew[ing]" the jury; (2) because they are excluded for a reason arguably within their control, there is no "appearance of unfairness"; and (3) because they may serve as jurors in other, noncapital cases, there is no "substantial deprivation of their basic rights of citizenship." Id., at 175-176.

3. The Court has also, on occasion, addressed similar claims of jury non-representativeness under the Equal Protection Clause. See, e.g., Castaneda v. Partida, 430 U.S. 482 (1977) (finding equal protection violation when Texas "key man" system for selecting grand juries produced only 39 percent Mexican-Americans, compared to county population of 79.1 percent Mexican-Americans); Vasquez v. Hillery, 474 U.S. 254 (1986) (finding equal protection violation when no black had ever served on grand jury in Kings County, California, from 1900 to 1962, the year when defendant was indicted).

2. Equal Protection and the Peremptory Challenge

In the early 1980s, numerous constitutional attacks were made against the common practice of prosecutors using their peremptory challenges to remove all or most prospective black jurors in cases involving black defendants. These attacks were based primarily on the fair-cross-section requirement because most defendants believed that they could not satisfy the tougher burden of proof for establishing an equal protection violation. See, e.g., Booker v. Jabe, 775 F.2d 762 (6th Cir. 1985); McCray v. Abrams, 750 F.2d 1113 (2d Cir. 1984). In the next case, however, the Supreme Court—over the defendant's objection—recharacterized the claim as one based on equal protection and proceeded to make peremptory challenges a little less "peremptory."

BATSON v. KENTUCKY

Certiorari to the Supreme Court of Kentucky
476 U.S. 79 (1986)

JUSTICE POWELL delivered the opinion of the Court.

This case requires us to reexamine that portion of Swain v. Alabama, 380 U.S. 202 (1965), concerning the evidentiary burden placed on a criminal defendant who claims that he has been denied equal protection through the State's use of peremptory challenges to exclude members of his race from the petit jury.

I

Petitioner, a black man, was indicted in Kentucky on charges of second-degree burglary and receipt of stolen goods. On the first day of trial in Jefferson Circuit Court, the judge conducted voir dire examination of the venire, excused certain jurors for cause, and permitted the parties to exercise peremptory challenges. The prosecutor used his peremptory challenges to strike all four black persons on the venire, and a jury composed only of white persons was selected. Defense counsel moved to discharge the jury before it was sworn on the ground that the prosecutor's removal of the black veniremen violated petitioner's rights under the Sixth and Fourteenth Amendments to a jury drawn from a cross section of the community, and under the Fourteenth Amendment to equal protection of the laws. Counsel requested a hearing on his motion. Without expressly ruling on the request for a hearing, the trial judge observed that the parties were entitled to use their peremptory challenges to "strike anybody they want to." The judge then denied petitioner's motion, reasoning that the cross-section requirement applies only to selection of the venire and not to selection of the petit jury itself.

The jury convicted petitioner on both counts. On appeal to the Supreme Court of Kentucky, petitioner pressed, among other claims, the argument concerning the prosecutor's use of peremptory challenges. Conceding that Swain v. Alabama, supra, apparently foreclosed an equal protection claim based solely on the prosecutor's conduct in this case, petitioner urged the court . . . to hold that such conduct violated his rights under the Sixth Amendment and §11 of the Kentucky Constitution to a jury drawn from a cross section of the community. Petitioner also contended that the facts showed that the prosecutor had engaged in a "pattern" of discriminatory challenges in this case and established an equal protection violation under *Swain.*

The Supreme Court of Kentucky affirmed. . . . We granted certiorari . . . and now reverse.

II

In Swain v. Alabama, this Court recognized that a "State's purposeful or deliberate denial to Negroes on account of race of participation as jurors in the administration of justice violates the Equal Protection Clause." 380 U.S., at 203-204. This principle has been "consistently and repeatedly" reaffirmed, id., at 204, in numerous decisions of this Court both preceding and following *Swain.* We reaffirm the principle today.[4]

A

More than a century ago, the Court decided that the State denies a black defendant equal protection of the laws when it puts him on trial before a jury from which members of his race have been purposefully excluded. Strauder v. West Virginia, 100 U.S. 303 (1880). That decision laid the foundation for the Court's unceasing efforts to eradicate racial discrimination in the procedures used to select the venire from which individual jurors are drawn. In *Strauder,* the Court explained that the central concern of the recently ratified Fourteenth Amendment was to put an end to governmental discrimination on account of race. Id., at 306-307. Exclusion of black citizens from service as jurors constitutes a primary example of the evil the Fourteenth Amendment was designed to cure.

In holding that racial discrimination in jury selection offends the Equal Protection Clause, the Court in *Strauder* recognized, however, that a defendant has no right to a "petit jury composed in whole or in part of persons of his own race." Id., at 305. . . .[6] But the defendant does have the right to be tried by a jury whose members are selected pursuant to non-discriminatory criteria. . . . The Equal Protection Clause guarantees the defendant that the State will not exclude members of his race from the jury venire on account of race, *Strauder,* supra, at 305, or on the false assumption that members of his race as a group are not qualified to serve as jurors. . . .

4. In this Court, petitioner has argued that the prosecutor's conduct violated his rights under the Sixth and Fourteenth Amendments to an impartial jury and to a jury drawn from a cross section of the community. Petitioner has framed his argument in these terms in an apparent effort to avoid inviting the Court directly to reconsider one of its own precedents. On the other hand, the State has insisted that petitioner is claiming a denial of equal protection and that we must reconsider *Swain* to find a constitutional violation on this record. We agree with the State that resolution of petitioner's claim properly turns on application of equal protection principles and express no view on the merits of any of petitioner's Sixth Amendment arguments.

6. Similarly, though the Sixth Amendment guarantees that the petit jury will be selected from a pool of names representing a cross section of the community, Taylor v. Louisiana, 419 U.S. 522 (1975), we have never held that the Sixth Amendment requires that "petit juries actually chosen must mirror the community and reflect the various distinctive groups in the population," id., at 538. Indeed, it would be impossible to apply a concept of proportional representation to the petit jury in view of the heterogeneous nature of our society. Such impossibility is illustrated by the Court's holding that a jury of six persons is not unconstitutional. Williams v. Florida, 399 U.S. 78, 102-103 (1970).

Purposeful racial discrimination in selection of the venire violates a defendant's right to equal protection because it denies him the protection that a trial by jury is intended to secure. "The very idea of a jury is a body . . . composed of the peers or equals of the person whose rights it is selected or summoned to determine; that is, of his neighbors, fellows, associates, persons having the same legal status in society as that which he holds." *Strauder*, supra, at 308. . . . The petit jury has occupied a central position in our system of justice by safeguarding a person accused of crime against the arbitrary exercise of power by prosecutor or judge. Duncan v. Louisiana, 391 U.S. 145, 156 (1968). Those on the venire must be "indifferently chosen," to secure the defendant's right under the Fourteenth Amendment to "protection of life and liberty against race or color prejudice." *Strauder*, supra, at 309.

Racial discrimination in selection of jurors harms not only the accused whose life or liberty they are summoned to try. Competence to serve as a juror ultimately depends on an assessment of individual qualifications and ability impartially to consider evidence presented at a trial. . . . A person's race simply "is unrelated to his fitness as a juror." . . . As long ago as *Strauder*, therefore, the Court recognized that by denying a person participation in jury service on account of his race, the State unconstitutionally discriminated against the excluded juror. 100 U.S., at 308. . . .

The harm from discriminatory jury selection extends beyond that inflicted on the defendant and the excluded juror to touch the entire community. Selection procedures that purposefully exclude black persons from juries undermine public confidence in the fairness of our system of justice. . . . Discrimination within the judicial system is most pernicious because it is "a stimulant to that race prejudice which is an impediment to securing to [black citizens] that equal justice which the law aims to secure to all others." *Strauder*, 100 U.S., at 308.

B

In *Strauder*, the Court invalidated a state statute that provided that only white men could serve as jurors. Id., at 305. We can be confident that no State now has such a law. The Constitution requires, however, that we look beyond the face of the statute defining juror qualifications and also consider challenged selection practices to afford "protection against action of the State through its administrative officers in effecting the prohibited discrimination." . . . Thus, the Court has found a denial of equal protection where the procedures implementing a neutral statute operated to exclude persons from the venire on racial grounds, and has made clear that the Constitution prohibits all forms of purposeful racial discrimination in selection of jurors. While decisions of this Court have been concerned largely with discrimination during selection of the venire, the principles announced there also forbid discrimination on account of race in selection of the petit jury. Since the Fourteenth Amendment protects an accused throughout the proceedings bringing him to justice, . . . the State may not draw up its jury lists pursuant to neutral procedures but then resort to discrimination at "other stages in the selection process." . . .

Accordingly, the component of the jury selection process at issue here, the State's privilege to strike individual jurors through peremptory challenges, is subject to the commands of the Equal Protection Clause.[12] Although a prosecutor ordinarily is

---

12. We express no views on whether the Constitution imposes any limit on the exercise of peremptory challenges by defense counsel. . . .

entitled to exercise permitted peremptory challenges "for any reason at all, as long as that reason is related to his view concerning the outcome" of the case to be tried, . . . the Equal Protection Clause forbids the prosecutor to challenge potential jurors solely on account of their race or on the assumption that black jurors as a group will be unable impartially to consider the State's case against a black defendant.

III

The principles announced in *Strauder* never have been questioned in any subsequent decision of this Court. Rather, the Court has been called upon repeatedly to review the application of those principles to particular facts. A recurring question in these cases, as in any case alleging a violation of the Equal Protection Clause, was whether the defendant had met his burden of proving purposeful discrimination on the part of the State. . . . That question also was at the heart of the portion of Swain v. Alabama we reexamine today.

A

Swain required the Court to decide, among other issues, whether a black defendant was denied equal protection by the State's exercise of peremptory challenges to exclude members of his race from the petit jury. 380 U.S., at 209-210. The record in *Swain* showed that the prosecutor had used the State's peremptory challenges to strike the six black persons included on the petit jury venire. Id., at 210. While rejecting the defendant's claim for failure to prove purposeful discrimination, the Court nonetheless indicated that the Equal Protection Clause placed some limits on the State's exercise of peremptory challenges. Id., at 222-224.

The Court sought to accommodate the prosecutor's historical privilege of peremptory challenge free of judicial control, id., at 214-220, and the constitutional prohibition on exclusion of persons from jury service on account of race, id., at 222-224. While the Constitution does not confer a right to peremptory challenges, id., at 219 . . . those challenges traditionally have been viewed as one means of assuring the selection of a qualified and unbiased jury, 380 U.S., at 219. To preserve the peremptory nature of the prosecutor's challenge, the Court in *Swain* declined to scrutinize his actions in a particular case by relying on a presumption that he properly exercised the State's challenges. Id., at 221-222.

The Court went on to observe, however, that a State may not exercise its challenges in contravention of the Equal Protection Clause. . . . For example, an inference of purposeful discrimination would be raised on evidence that a prosecutor, "in case after case, whatever the circumstances, whatever the crime and whoever the defendant or the victim may be, is responsible for the removal of Negroes who have been selected as qualified jurors by the jury commissioners and who have survived challenges for cause, with the result that no Negroes ever serve on petit juries." Id., at 223. . . .

B

Since the decision in *Swain*, we have explained that our cases concerning selection of the venire reflect the general equal protection principle that the "invidious quality" of governmental action claimed to be racially discriminatory "must ultimately be traced to a racially discriminatory purpose." Washington v. Davis, 426 U.S.

229, 240 (1976). As in any equal protection case, the "burden is, of course," on the defendant who alleges discriminatory selection of the venire "to prove the existence of purposeful discrimination." . . . Circumstantial evidence of invidious intent may include proof of disproportionate impact. Washington v. Davis, 426 U.S., at 242. We have observed that under some circumstances proof of discriminatory impact "may for all practical purposes demonstrate unconstitutionality because in various circumstances the discrimination is very difficult to explain on nonracial grounds." Ibid. For example, "total or seriously disproportionate exclusion of Negroes from jury venires," ibid., "is itself such an 'unequal application of the law . . . as to show intentional discrimination,'" id., at 241. . . .

Moreover, since *Swain*, we have recognized that a black defendant alleging that members of his race have been impermissibly excluded from the venire may make out a prima facie case of purposeful discrimination by showing that the totality of the relevant facts gives rise to an inference of discriminatory purpose. Washington v. Davis, supra, at 239-242. Once the defendant makes the requisite showing, the burden shifts to the State to explain adequately the racial exclusion. . . . The State cannot meet this burden on mere general assertions that its officials did not discriminate or that they properly performed their official duties. . . . Rather, the State must demonstrate that "permissible racially neutral selection criteria and procedures have produced the monochromatic result." . . .

The showing necessary to establish a prima facie case of purposeful discrimination in selection of the venire may be discerned in this Court's decisions. . . . The defendant initially must show that he is a member of a racial group capable of being singled out for differential treatment. . . . In combination with that evidence, a defendant may then make a prima facie case by proving that in the particular jurisdiction members of his race have not been summoned for jury service over an extended period of time. . . . Proof of systematic exclusion from the venire raises an inference of purposeful discrimination because the "result bespeaks discrimination." . . .

Since the ultimate issue is whether the State has discriminated in selecting the defendant's venire, however, the defendant may establish a prima facie case "in other ways than by evidence of long-continued unexplained absence" of members of his race "from many panels." . . .

Thus, since the decision in *Swain*, this Court has recognized that a defendant may make a prima facie showing of purposeful racial discrimination in selection of the venire by relying solely on the facts concerning its selection in *his* case. These decisions are in accordance with the proposition, articulated in Arlington Heights v. Metropolitan Housing Development Corp., 429 U.S. 252, 266 (1977), that "a consistent pattern of official racial discrimination" is not "a necessary predicate to a violation of the Equal Protection Clause. A single invidiously discriminatory governmental act" is not "immunized by the absence of such discrimination in the making of other comparable decisions." 429 U.S., at 266, n. 14. For evidentiary requirements to dictate that "several must suffer discrimination" before one could object, . . . would be inconsistent with the promise of equal protection to all.

C

. . . These principles support our conclusion that a defendant may establish a prima facie case of purposeful discrimination in selection of the petit jury solely on evidence concerning the prosecutor's exercise of peremptory challenges at the defendant's trial. To establish such a case, the defendant first must show that he is a member of a cognizable racial group, . . . and that the prosecutor has exercised peremptory challenges to remove from the venire members of the defendant's race. Second, the defendant is entitled to rely on the fact, as to which there can be no dispute, that peremptory challenges constitute a jury selection practice that permits "those to discriminate who are of a mind to discriminate." . . . Finally, the defendant must show that these facts and any other relevant circumstances raise an inference that the prosecutor used that practice to exclude the veniremen from the petit jury on account of their race. This combination of factors in the empaneling of the petit jury, as in the selection of the venire, raises the necessary inference of purposeful discrimination.

In deciding whether the defendant has made the requisite showing, the trial court should consider all relevant circumstances. For example, a "pattern" of strikes against black jurors included in the particular venire might give rise to an inference of discrimination. Similarly, the prosecutor's questions and statements during voir dire examination and in exercising his challenges may support or refute an inference of discriminatory purpose. These examples are merely illustrative. We have confidence that trial judges, experienced in supervising voir dire, will be able to decide if the circumstances concerning the prosecutor's use of peremptory challenges creates a prima facie case of discrimination against black jurors.

Once the defendant makes a prima facie showing, the burden shifts to the State to come forward with a neutral explanation for challenging black jurors. Though this requirement imposes a limitation in some cases on the full peremptory character of the historic challenge, we emphasize that the prosecutor's explanation need not rise to the level justifying exercise of a challenge for cause. . . . But the prosecutor may not rebut the defendant's prima facie case of discrimination by stating merely that he challenged jurors of the defendant's race on the assumption—or his intuitive judgment—that they would be partial to the defendant because of their shared race. . . . Just as the Equal Protection Clause forbids the States to exclude black persons from the venire on the assumption that blacks as a group are unqualified to serve as jurors, . . . so it forbids the States to strike black veniremen on the assumption that they will be biased in a particular case simply because the defendant is black. The core guarantee of equal protection, ensuring citizens that their State will not discriminate on account of race, would be meaningless were we to approve the exclusion of jurors on the basis of such assumptions, which arise solely from the jurors' race. Nor may the prosecutor rebut the defendant's case merely by denying that he had a discriminatory motive or "affirm[ing] [his] good faith in making individual selections." . . . If these general assertions were accepted as rebutting a defendant's prima facie case, the Equal Protection Clause "would be but a vain and illusory requirement." . . . The prosecutor therefore must articulate a neutral explanation related to the particular case to be tried.[20] The trial court then will have the duty to determine if the defendant has established purposeful discrimination[21]. . . .

20. The Court of Appeals for the Second Circuit [has] observed . . . that "[t]here are any number of bases" on which a prosecutor reasonably may believe that it is desirable to strike a juror who is not excusable for cause. As we explained in another context, however, the prosecutor must give a "clear and reasonably specific" explanation of his "legitimate reasons" for exercising the challenges. . . .

21. In a recent Title VII sex discrimination case, we stated that "a finding of intentional discrimination is a finding of fact" entitled to appropriate deference by a reviewing court. . . . Since the trial judge's findings in the context under consideration here largely will turn on evaluation of credibility, a reviewing court ordinarily should give those findings great deference. . . .

V

In this case, petitioner made a timely objection to the prosecutor's removal of all black persons on the venire. Because the trial court flatly rejected the objection without requiring the prosecutor to give an explanation for his action, we remand this case for further proceedings. If the trial court decides that the facts establish, prima facie, purposeful discrimination and the prosecutor does not come forward with a neutral explanation for his action, our precedents require that petitioner's conviction be reversed. . . .

It is so ordered.

[The concurring opinions of Justice White, Justice Stevens (with whom Justice Brennan joined), and Justice O'Connor are omitted.]

JUSTICE MARSHALL, concurring.

. . . The decision today will not end the racial discrimination that peremptories inject into the jury-selection process. That goal can be accomplished only by eliminating peremptory challenges entirely.

I . . .

Misuse of the peremptory challenge to exclude black jurors has become both common and flagrant. . . .

The Court's discussion of the utter unconstitutionality of that practice needs no amplification. . . . [T]he Equal Protection Clause prohibits a State from taking any action based on crude, inaccurate racial stereotypes—even an action that does not serve the State's interests. Exclusion of blacks from a jury, solely because of race, can no more be justified by a belief that blacks are less likely than whites to consider fairly or sympathetically the State's case against a black defendant than it can be justified by the notion that blacks lack the "intelligence, experience, or moral integrity" . . . to be entrusted with that role.

II

I wholeheartedly concur in the Court's conclusion that use of the peremptory challenge to remove blacks from juries, on the basis of their race, violates the Equal Protection Clause. I would go further, however, in fashioning a remedy adequate to eliminate that discrimination. Merely allowing defendants the opportunity to challenge the racially discriminatory use of peremptory challenges in individual cases will not end the illegitimate use of the peremptory challenge.

. . . First, defendants cannot attack the discriminatory use of peremptory challenges at all unless the challenges are so flagrant as to establish a prima facie case. This means, in those States, that where only one or two black jurors survive the challenges for cause, the prosecutor need have no compunction about striking them from the jury because of their race. . . . Prosecutors are left free to discriminate against blacks in jury selection provided that they hold that discrimination to an "acceptable" level.

Second, when a defendant can establish a prima facie case, trial courts face the difficult burden of assessing prosecutors' motives. . . . Any prosecutor can easily assert facially neutral reasons for striking a juror, and trial courts are ill equipped to second-guess those reasons. How is the court to treat a prosecutor's statement that he struck a juror because the juror had a son about the same age as defendant, . . .

or seemed "uncommunicative," . . . or "never cracked a smile" and, therefore "did not possess the sensitivities necessary to realistically look at the issues and decide the facts in this case" . . . ? If such easily generated explanations are sufficient to discharge the prosecutor's obligation to justify his strikes on non-racial grounds, then the protection erected by the Court today may be illusory. . . .

I applaud the Court's holding that the racially discriminatory use of peremptory challenges violates the Equal Protection Clause, and I join the Court's opinion. However, only by banning peremptories entirely can such discrimination be ended.

[The dissenting opinion of Chief Justice Burger is omitted.]

JUSTICE REHNQUIST, with whom CHIEF JUSTICE BURGER joins, dissenting. . . .

In *Swain*, this Court carefully distinguished two possible scenarios involving the State's use of its peremptory challenges to exclude blacks from juries in criminal cases. In Part III of the majority opinion, the *Swain* Court concluded that the first of these scenarios, namely, the exclusion of blacks "for reasons wholly unrelated to the outcome of the particular case on trial . . . to deny the Negro the same right and opportunity to participate in the administration of justice enjoyed by the white population," 380 U.S., at 224, might violate the guarantees of equal protection. See id., at 222-228. The Court felt that the important and historic purposes of the peremptory challenge were not furthered by the exclusion of blacks "in case after case, whatever the circumstances, whatever the crime *and whoever the defendant or the victim may be.*" Id., at 223 (emphasis added). Nevertheless, the Court ultimately held that "the record in this case is not sufficient to demonstrate that [this] rule has been violated. . . . Petitioner has the burden of proof and he has failed to carry it." Id., at 224, 226. Three Justices dissented, arguing that the petitioner's evidentiary burden was satisfied by testimony that no black had ever served on a petit jury in the relevant county. See id., at 228-247 (Goldberg, J., joined by Warren, C.J., and Douglas, J., dissenting).

Significantly, the *Swain* Court reached a very different conclusion with respect to the second kind of peremptory-challenge scenario. In Part II of its opinion, the Court held that the State's use of peremptory challenges to exclude blacks from a particular jury based on the assumption or belief that they would be more likely to favor a black defendant does not violate equal protection. . . .

Even the *Swain* dissenters did not take issue with the majority's position that the Equal Protection Clause does not prohibit the State from using its peremptory challenges to exclude blacks based on the assumption or belief that they would be partial to a black defendant. . . .

The Court today asserts, however, that "the Equal Protection Clause forbids the prosecutor to challenge potential jurors solely . . . on the assumption that black jurors as a group will be unable impartially to consider the State's case against a black defendant." . . . Later, in discussing the State's need to establish a nondiscriminatory basis for striking blacks from the jury, the Court states that "the prosecutor may not rebut the defendant's prima facie case of discrimination by stating merely that he challenged jurors of the defendant's race on the assumption — or his intuitive judgment — that they would be partial to the defendant because of their shared race." . . . [B]oth statements are directly contrary to the view of the Equal Protection Clause shared by the majority and the dissenters in *Swain*. . . .

I cannot subscribe to the Court's unprecedented use of the Equal Protection Clause to restrict the historic scope of the peremptory challenge, which has been described as "a necessary part of trial by jury." *Swain*, 380 U.S., at 219. In my view, there is simply nothing "unequal" about the State's using its peremptory challenges to strike blacks from the jury in cases involving black defendants, so long as such challenges are also used to exclude whites in cases involving white defendants, Hispanics in cases involving Hispanic defendants, Asians in cases involving Asian defendants, and so on. This case-specific use of peremptory challenges by the State does not single out blacks, or members of any other race for that matter, for discriminatory treatment. Such use of peremptories is at best based upon seat-of-the-pants instincts, which are undoubtedly crudely stereotypical and may in many cases be hopelessly mistaken. But as long as they are applied across-the-board to jurors of all races and nationalities, I do not see—and the Court most certainly has not explained—how their use violates the Equal Protection Clause.

Nor does such use of peremptory challenges by the State infringe upon any other constitutional interests. The Court does not suggest that exclusion of blacks from the jury through the State's use of peremptory challenges results in a violation of either the fair-cross-section or impartiality component of the Sixth Amendment. . . . And because the case-specific use of peremptory challenges by the State does not deny blacks the right to serve as jurors in cases involving non-black defendants, it harms neither the excluded jurors nor the remainder of the community. . . .

The use of group affiliations, such as age, race, or occupation, as a "proxy" for potential juror partiality, based on the assumption or belief that members of one group are more likely to favor defendants who belong to the same group, has long been accepted as a legitimate basis for the State's exercise of peremptory challenges. See *Swain*, supra. . . . Indeed, given the need for reasonable limitations on the time devoted to voir dire, the use of such "proxies" by both the State and the defendant may be extremely useful in eliminating from the jury persons who might be biased in one way or another. The Court today holds that the State may not use its peremptory challenges to strike black prospective jurors on this basis without violating the Constitution. But I do not believe there is anything in the Equal Protection Clause, or any other constitutional provision, that justifies such a departure from the substantive holding contained in Part II of *Swain*. . . .

NOTES AND QUESTIONS

1. What is the rationale for the Court's decision in *Batson*? Justice Powell's majority opinion seems to equate (for purposes of applying the Equal Protection Clause) two situations: (1) the use of peremptories (in *Batson*) to remove all blacks from the jury in a particular criminal case involving a black defendant, on the assumption that they would tend to favor the black defendant more than white jurors would, and (2) the previous practice (prior to *Swain*) of excluding all blacks from the venire in all cases, on the assumption that they were unqualified as a class to serve as jurors. Are the two situations really analogous?

Surely there is simply no correlation between race and qualification to serve as a juror, but is the use of race-based peremptories in particular cases similarly irrational? Do you think that jury verdicts are unaffected by the racial composition of the juries that render those verdicts? Are black jurors and white jurors fungible? In a society that continues to be plagued by serious racial disparities, it seems highly unlikely that this would be so. And public opinion surveys routinely reveal large differences in how blacks and whites perceive at least some criminal justice issues and cases. For example, in 2013, a Gallup poll showed that 54 percent of non-Hispanic whites felt that the acquittal of George Zimmerman in the shooting death of Trayvon Martin was "right," while only 30 percent thought the verdict was "wrong"; for non-Hispanic blacks, only 5 percent felt that the acquittal was "right," while 85 percent thought it was "wrong."

Empirical evidence lends support to the conclusion that, at least sometimes, race does matter in the jury room. See, e.g., Deborah Ramirez, Affirmative Jury Selection: A Proposal to Advance Both the Deliberative Ideal and Jury Diversity, 1998 U. Chi. Legal F. 161, 165-166 (citing studies) ("[I]t is not surprising that the empirical evidence shows in some close cases, where small differences in perspective matter, the racial composition of the jury affects substantive outcomes and verdicts. . . . [I]n those close cases where the verdict is properly in doubt when the deliberations begin, the different perspectives and dynamics of a racially mixed jury can generate results that are different from those reached by homogenous juries.").

If, in fact, black jurors and white jurors sometimes *do* tend to have different perspectives about the same case and if, in fact, racially mixed juries sometimes *do* reach different results than racially homogenous juries, then we must return to the original question: What is the rationale for the Court's decision in *Batson*? Was there an alternative approach in *Batson* that would have allowed the Court to recognize the existence of a correlation between race and juror behavior, but nevertheless prohibit prosecutors from using such a correlation as the basis for exercising peremptories?

2. Why does the rationale matter? The answer to this question requires consideration of traditional equal protection analysis. This analysis often depends heavily on the Court's choice of a review standard for the challenged government action: Under the "strict scrutiny" standard generally applicable to race-based government action, the government usually loses, whereas under the "rational basis" standard applicable to most non-race-based government action, the government usually wins. What equal protection standard is used by the Court in *Batson*? Does Justice Powell ever identify the applicable standard?

If *Batson* is based on the notion that the prosecutor's race-based use of peremptories is irrational and contrary to fact (because black jurors and white jurors are fungible), then, of course, the result of the case would be the same under either the "rational basis" or the "strict scrutiny" standard. But what about other possible constitutional challenges to peremptories? If the Court in *Batson* is saying that race-based peremptories fail to meet even the "rational basis" standard, then how can age-based peremptories (which are presumably no more "rational" than race-based ones) survive a constitutional challenge? Or occupation-based peremptories? Or any other use of peremptories based on loose correlations rather than provable biases of an individual prospective juror—a category that basically includes all peremptories? Does *Batson* logically lead to the abolition of all peremptories?

3. What about gender-based use of peremptories? In J. E. B. v. Alabama ex rel. T. B., 511 U.S. 127 (1994), the Court—in a paternity case where nine out of the ten male prospective jurors were removed by state peremptory challenges—held that gender-based use of peremptories violates the Equal Protection Clause:

> Under our equal protection jurisprudence, gender-based classifications require "an exceedingly persuasive justification" in order to survive constitutional scrutiny. See

Personnel Administrator of Mass. v. Feeney, 442 U.S. 256, 273 (1979).[10] . . . Thus, the only question is whether discrimination on the basis of gender in jury selection substantially furthers the State's legitimate interest in achieving a fair and impartial trial. . . .

Far from proffering an exceptionally persuasive justification for its gender-based peremptory challenges, respondent maintains that its decision to strike virtually all the males from the jury in this case "may reasonably have been based upon the perception, supported by history, that men otherwise totally qualified to serve upon a jury in any case might be more sympathetic and receptive to the arguments of a man alleged in a paternity action to be the father of an out-of-wedlock child, while women equally qualified to serve upon a jury might be more sympathetic and receptive to the arguments of the complaining witness who bore the child." . . .

We shall not accept as a defense to gender based-peremptory challenges "the very stereotype the law condemns." . . . Respondent's rationale, not unlike those regularly expressed for gender-based strikes, is reminiscent of the arguments advanced to justify the total exclusion of women from juries. Respondent offers virtually no support for the conclusion that gender alone is an accurate predictor of juror's attitudes; yet it urges this Court to condone the same stereotypes that justified the wholesale exclusion of women from juries and the ballot box. Respondent seems to assume that gross generalizations that would be deemed impermissible if made on the basis of race are somehow permissible when made on the basis of gender. . . .

. . . Striking individual jurors on the assumption that they hold particular views simply because of their gender is "practically a brand upon them, affixed by the law, an assertion of their inferiority." Strauder v. West Virginia, 100 U.S., at 308. It denigrates the dignity of the excluded juror, and, for a woman, reinvokes a history of exclusion from political participation. The message it sends to all those in the courtroom, and all those who may later learn of the discriminatory act, is that certain individuals, for no reason other than gender, are presumed unqualified by state actors to decide important questions upon which reasonable persons could disagree. . . .

In light of *Batson*, the result in *J. E. B.* was perhaps not surprising. What *was* interesting, however, was the apparent ambivalence of the *J. E. B.* majority on the question of whether or not gender-based peremptories are inevitably irrational or contrary to fact. Just after denigrating the state for failing to demonstrate that "gender alone is an accurate predictor of juror's attitudes," see supra, Justice Blackmun, writing for the majority, added the following important words in a footnote:

> Even if a measure of truth can be found in some of the gender stereotypes used to justify gender-based peremptory challenges, that fact alone cannot support discrimination on the basis of gender in jury selection. We have made abundantly clear in past cases that gender classifications that rest on impermissible stereotypes violate the Equal Protection Clause, even when some statistical support can be conjured up for the generalization. . . . The generalization advanced by Alabama in support of its asserted right to discriminate on the basis of gender is, at the least, overbroad, and serves only to perpetuate the same "outmoded notions of the relative capabilities of men and women" . . . that we have invalidated in other contexts. . . . The Equal Protection Clause, as interpreted by decisions of this Court, acknowledges that a shred of truth may be contained in some stereotypes, but requires that state actors look beyond the surface before making judgments about people that are likely to stigmatize as well as to perpetuate historical patterns of discrimination.

10. This equal protection standard for gender-based classifications, falling somewhere between "strict scrutiny" and "rational basis," is often referred to as "intermediate scrutiny." — EDS.

Id., at 139, n. 11. Justice O'Connor, who provided the crucial fifth vote for Justice Blackmun's majority opinion, made the same point, but much more emphatically, in her separate opinion:

> . . . We know that like race, gender matters. A plethora of studies make clear that in rape cases, for example, female jurors are somewhat more likely to vote to convict than male jurors. See R. Hastie, S. Penrod, & N. Pennington, Inside the Jury 140-141 (1983) (collecting and summarizing empirical studies). Moreover, though there have been no similarly definitive studies regarding, for example, sexual harassment, child custody, or spousal or child abuse, one need not be a sexist to share the intuition that in certain cases a person's gender and resulting life experience will be relevant to his or her view of the case. "Jurors are not expected to come into the jury box and leave behind them all that their human experience has taught them." . . . Individuals are not expected to ignore as jurors what they know as men—or women.
>
> Today's decision severely limits a litigant's ability to act on this intuition, for the import of our holding is that any correlation between a juror's gender and attitudes is irrelevant as a matter of constitutional law. But to say that gender makes no difference as a matter of law is not to say that gender makes no difference as a matter of fact. I previously have said with regard to *Batson*: "That the Court will not tolerate prosecutors' racially discriminatory use of the peremptory challenge, in effect, is a special rule of relevance, a statement about what this Nation stands for, rather than a statement of fact." . . . Today's decision is a statement that, in an effort to eliminate the potential discriminatory use of the peremptory, . . . gender is now governed by the special rule of relevancy formerly reserved for race. . . . In extending *Batson* to gender we have . . . diminished the ability of litigants to act on sometimes accurate gender-based assumptions about juror attitudes.

Id., at 149-150 (O'Connor, J., concurring).

Do these remarks by Justice Blackmun (for the majority) and Justice O'Connor signify a subtle yet significant shift in the rationale for invalidating certain peremptories under the Equal Protection Clause? Do they suggest that the state's gender-based use of peremptories might be rational, yet nevertheless unconstitutional—under the "intermediate scrutiny" given to gender-based classifications? In light of *J. E. B.*, should *Batson* be interpreted as a "strict scrutiny" rather than a "rational basis" case? And, if so, can the Court hold the line on *Batson* in the future by limiting its application to those few classifications (like race and gender) that trigger heightened levels of equal protection scrutiny, while refusing to extend it to other situations (such as age-based and occupation-based peremptories) that would have to be evaluated under the lower, "rational basis" standard?

4. If the underlying premise of the fair-cross-section cases, and of *Batson*, is that race sometimes *does* matter, and if we are serious about ensuring that black defendants receive a fair trial, then should we recognize a black defendant's affirmative right to have blacks on the actual jury? After all, even after *Batson*, and based on the racial demographics of most jurisdictions, it is unlikely that—absent such an affirmative right—the usual random process of jury selection will produce a jury with significant black representation. This idea has been advocated by Deborah Ramirez, Affirmative Jury Selection: A Proposal to Advance Both the Deliberative Ideal and Jury Diversity, 1998 U. Chi. Legal F. 161. Professor Ramirez argues that "a racially diverse jury is more likely to render a race-neutral verdict, because it is more likely to suppress racial bias in deliberations and to challenge inferences based on thoughtless racial stereotypes." Id., at 161. She acknowledges "the danger that jurors who are chosen in part because

of their racial, religious, or ethnic affiliation may come to believe that they have a duty to represent their particular group in some fashion," id., at 162, but suggests that the particular procedures used to achieve racially mixed juries could help to minimize this danger (e.g., using "affirmative peremptory choices," through which the inclusion of prospective jurors of different races would be achieved by means of secret decisions by the litigants, as opposed to using open racial quotas). For a contrary view, see Jeffrey Abramson, Two Ideals of Jury Deliberation, 1998 U. Chi. Legal F. 125; see also Hiroshi Fukurai & Darryl Davies, Affirmative Action in Jury Selection: Racially Representative Juries, Racial Quotas, and Affirmative Juries of the Hennepin Model and the Jury De Medietatae Linguae, 4 Va. J. Soc. Pol'y & L. 645 (1997); Nancy J. King, Racial Jurymandering: Cancer or Cure? A Contemporary Review of Affirmative Action in Jury Selection, 68 N.Y.U. L. Rev. 707 (1993).

An even more controversial suggestion has been made by Professor Paul Butler. He argues that black jurors should, at least in some cases, use the nullification power to find guilty black defendants not guilty:

> . . . Let us assume that there is a black defendant who, the evidence suggests, is guilty of the crime with which he has been charged, and a black juror who thinks that there are too many black men in prison. The black juror has two choices: She can vote for conviction, thus sending another black man to prison and implicitly allowing her presence to support public confidence in the system that puts him there, or she can vote "not guilty," thereby acquitting the defendant, or at least causing a mistrial. In choosing the latter, the juror makes a decision not to be a passive symbol of support for a system for which she has no respect. Rather than signaling her displeasure with the system by breaching "community peace," the black juror invokes the political nature of her role in the criminal justice system and votes "no." In a sense, the black juror engages in an act of civil disobedience, except that her choice is better than civil disobedience because it is lawful. Is the black juror's race-conscious act moral? Absolutely. It would be farcical for her to be the sole color-blind actor in the criminal process, especially when it is her blackness that advertises the system's fairness. At this point, every African-American should ask herself whether the operation of the criminal law in the United States advances the interests of black people. If it does not, the doctrine of jury nullification affords African-American jurors the opportunity to control the authority of the law over some African-American criminal defendants. In essence, black people can "opt out" of American criminal law.

Paul Butler, Racially Based Jury Nullification: Black Power in the Criminal Justice System, 105 Yale L.J. 677, 714 (1995). For a contrary view, see Andrew D. Leipold, The Dangers of Race-Based Jury Nullification: A Response to Professor Butler, 44 UCLA L. Rev. 109 (1996); see also Elissa Krauss & Martha Schulman, The Myth of Black Juror Nullification: Racism Dressed Up in Jurisprudential Clothing, 7 Cornell J.L. & Pub. Pol'y 57 (1997).

What do you think of these proposals? Is it possible to select a neutral jury without taking account of the race of the jurors? Is it possible to use race in jury selection without fostering even greater race-consciousness within the jury? If not, then what is the future of the jury in our racially diverse society?

5. *Batson* left numerous other important questions unanswered:

A. Can a white defendant challenge the prosecutor's use of peremptories to strike black prospective jurors? In Holland v. Illinois, 493 U.S. 474 (1990), the white defendant, concerned that he might lack standing to raise a *Batson* equal protection claim, argued instead that the prosecutor's removal of black prospective jurors violated his Sixth Amendment fair-cross-section right. The Court disagreed, reiterating its view that the fair-cross-section right applies only to the venire, and not to the actual jury. Just one year later, in Powers v. Ohio, 499 U.S. 400 (1991), the Court held that a white defendant indeed has standing to raise a *Batson* equal protection claim. Such standing was based on (1) the view (expressed for the first time in *Powers*) that the *Batson* right belongs not only to the defendant, but also to the excluded prospective jurors, see id., at 406-409, and (2) the holding that, under traditional rules of standing to raise constitutional claims, defendants can assert jus tertii (third-party) standing to raise the *Batson* rights of excluded prospective jurors of a different race, see id., at 410-415.

B. Does *Batson* apply to peremptories exercised by defendants? The Court addressed this question in Georgia v. McCollum, 505 U.S. 42 (1992), but the answer was already largely predetermined by two earlier decisions. One was Powers v. Ohio, where (as noted above) the Court recognized the concept of third-party standing (in a white defendant) to assert the *Batson* rights of black prospective jurors. The other was Edmonson v. Leesville Concrete Co., 500 U.S. 614 (1991), where the Court held that *Batson* applies to civil cases on the ground that "state action" (a requirement for an equal protection claim) can be found in the judicial system's close supervision of jury selection and peremptory challenges (even if both litigants are private parties). After *Powers* and *Edmonson*, *McCollum* was an easy case—there was "state action" even if the defendant was the party exercising the peremptory challenges, and the prosecutor could claim third-party standing to raise the *Batson* rights of the excluded prospective jurors.

In *J. E. B.*, supra, Justice O'Connor, who had dissented in *Edmonson* and *McCollum*, repeated her assertion that "the Equal Protection Clause does not limit the exercise of peremptory challenges by private civil litigants and criminal defendants." 511 U.S., at 151 (O'Connor, J., concurring). She added:

> Will we, in the name of fighting gender discrimination, hold that the battered wife—on trial for wounding her abusive husband—is a state actor? Will we preclude her from using her peremptory challenges to ensure that the jury of her peers contains as many women members as possible? I assume we will, but I hope we will not.

Ibid.

What if a defendant seeks to exercise a peremptory challenge against a juror who would not be subject to a for-cause challenge, and the peremptory challenge is erroneously denied by the trial judge based on *Batson* and *McCollum*? Does the seating of such a challenged juror violate the constitutional rights of the defendant, and if so, does it require automatic reversal of the resulting conviction? In Rivera v. Illinois, 556 U.S. 148 (2009), the Court unanimously held that such an error does not require automatic reversal as a matter of federal law. The Court noted that peremptory challenges are not themselves of constitutional status; moreover, because the challenged juror was unbiased, there was no violation of the defendant's constitutional right to an impartial jury. In the end, the Court held that it was up to each state to decide—as a matter of state law—whether the erroneous denial of a peremptory challenge should lead to automatic reversal or be subjected to harmless-error analysis.

C. Perhaps the key issue, in terms of *Batson*'s significance to the real world of criminal jury trials, is how the lower courts should interpret and apply the *Batson* standard to prosecutorial (and, after *McCollum*, defense) peremptory challenges. Justice

Marshall, in his *Batson* dissent, argued that the standard would not limit prosecutors who wished to discriminate because it would be all too easy to come up with "race-neutral" explanations for any contested challenges. The *Batson* majority, however, placed its faith in the lower courts to police the prosecutorial abuse of peremptories. Subsequent developments seemed to indicate that perhaps Marshall was right.

In Hernandez v. New York, 500 U.S. 352 (1991), the prosecutor used peremptories in a manner that disproportionately excluded Latinos. The offered reason for the strikes was that they were based not on ethnicity, but instead on the prosecutor's perception (derived from voir dire) that the challenged individuals, who were bilingual, would find it difficult to accept the court translator's official English version of the Spanish-language testimony to be given during the trial. The trial judge rejected the defendant's *Batson* claim, and the Supreme Court affirmed. Justice Kennedy, writing for a four-justice plurality, found the offered reason to be "race neutral." He concluded that "the challenges rested neither on the intention to exclude Latino or bilingual jurors, nor on stereotypical assumptions about Latinos or bilinguals. . . . While the prosecutor's criterion might well result in the disproportionate removal of prospective Latino jurors, that disproportionate impact does not turn the prosecutor's actions into a per se violation of the Equal Protection Clause." Justice Kennedy added, however, that trial judges may consider such disproportionate impact as evidence that the offered reason might be a pretext for racial discrimination. Justice O'Connor, joined by Justice Scalia, concurred on the ground that the trial judge had made a factual finding, not clearly erroneous, that the offered reason was race neutral and thus satisfied *Batson*.

In Purkett v. Elem, 514 U.S. 765 (1995), the prosecutor used peremptories to strike two black prospective jurors. When the trial judge requested an explanation, the prosecutor answered that he struck the first juror because of his long, curly, "unkempt" hair and the second because of his mustache and goatee-type beard. The trial judge found these answers satisfactory under *Batson*, but a federal appeals court, sitting in habeas, later concluded that they were pretextual because the prosecutor never explained why hair length or facial hair should matter to a juror's qualifications. A per curiam Supreme Court reversed. The Court found that the prosecutor's explanations, whether reasonable or not, were race neutral and thus satisfied step two of the *Batson* inquiry. Turning to step three of the inquiry, the habeas court never offered any valid basis for overturning the trial judge's factual finding of "no racial motive" for the peremptories. The Court emphasized that, in step three, the proper focus is on the *genuineness* of the proponent's alleged race-neutral motive rather than its *reasonableness*.

After *Hernandez* and *Purkett*, many believed that *Batson*'s promise would go unfulfilled. If it was really so easy for prosecutors to explain their peremptories in race-neutral terms, and thereby avoid a *Batson* reversal, then what was the point of the whole exercise in the first place?

Possibly for this reason, some lower courts began to screen *Batson* claims more aggressively at the initial stage of the three-stage inquiry, eliminating many claims before ever reaching the second, "race-neutral explanation" stage. These courts (utilizing the flexibility that the Supreme Court appeared to grant them in implementing *Batson*'s mandate) held that, at the initial stage of the inquiry, the defendant must meet a prima facie burden of proving, by a preponderance of the evidence, that the prosecutor's use of peremptories gives rise to an inference of racial discrimination. Otherwise, there is nothing for the prosecutor to rebut at the second stage.

In Johnson v. California, 545 U.S. 162 (2005), the Supreme Court, by 8-1, soundly rejected this interpretation of *Batson*. According to the Court:

> [W]e assumed in *Batson* that the trial judge would have the benefit of all relevant circumstances, including the prosecutor's explanation, before deciding whether it was more likely than not that the challenge was improperly motivated. We did not intend the first step to be so onerous that a defendant would have to persuade the judge on the basis of all the facts, some of which are impossible for the defendant to know with certainty—that the challenge was more likely than not the product of purposeful discrimination. Instead, a defendant satisfies the requirements of *Batson*'s first step by producing evidence sufficient to permit the trial judge to draw an inference that discrimination has occurred.

In a footnote, the Court pointed out what perhaps should have been obvious—that even if a defendant's *Batson* claim is relatively weak, there might nevertheless be some value in requiring the prosecution to respond. The clear message of *Johnson* seems to be that most *Batson* claims (i.e., all those that are not facially implausible) should survive the first stage of the *Batson* analysis and proceed to the second and third stages. But that may still beg the question. What happens when those claims get to the later stages of the analysis? How aggressive should the lower courts be, in reviewing the prosecutor's asserted race-neutral reasons for the challenged peremptory strikes?

Two Supreme Court decisions—in the same case—seem, at least on the surface, to suggest that such review should be fairly aggressive. In the first decision, Miller-El v. Cockrell, 537 U.S. 322 (2003), the Court (with only Justice Thomas dissenting) overturned the Fifth Circuit's denial of a "certificate of appealability" to review a *Batson* claim made by a Dallas County, Texas, death-row inmate in a federal habeas corpus petition. The Court concluded that Miller-El's evidence was more than adequate to raise an inference of prosecutorial race discrimination, and thus met the test of habeas appealability, which requires a "substantial showing of the denial of a constitutional right." The Court also found the lower court's reliance on the prosecution's alleged race-neutral reasons unwarranted, especially given that "the application of these rationales to the venire might have been selective and based on racial considerations." Id., at 343.

The Fifth Circuit, on remand, issued the "certificate of appealability," but then (somewhat inexplicably, given the Supreme Court's tone in Miller-El v. Cockrell) rejected Miller-El's underlying *Batson* claim on the merits. The case then returned to the Supreme Court.

MILLER-EL v. DRETKE

Certiorari to the U.S. Court of Appeals for the Fifth Circuit
545 U.S. 231 (2005)

JUSTICE SOUTER delivered the opinion of the Court.

Two years ago, we ordered that a certificate of appealability, under 28 U.S.C. §2253(c), be issued to habeas petitioner Miller-El, affording review of the District Court's rejection of the claim that prosecutors in his capital murder trial made peremptory strikes of potential jurors based on race. Today we find Miller-El entitled to prevail on that claim and order relief under §2254.

I

In the course of robbing a Holiday Inn in Dallas, Texas in late 1985, Miller-El and his accomplices bound and gagged two hotel employees, whom Miller-El then shot, killing one and severely injuring the other. During jury selection in Miller-El's trial for capital murder, prosecutors used peremptory strikes against 10 qualified black venire members. Miller-El objected that the strikes were based on race and could not be presumed legitimate, given a history of excluding black members from criminal juries by the Dallas County District Attorney's Office. The trial court received evidence of the practice alleged but found no "systematic exclusion of blacks as a matter of policy" by that office, and therefore no entitlement to relief under Swain v. Alabama, 380 U.S. 202 (1965), the case then defining and marking the limits of relief from racially biased jury selection. The court denied Miller-El's request to pick a new jury, and the trial ended with his death sentence for capital murder.

While an appeal was pending, this Court decided Batson v. Kentucky, 476 U.S. 79 (1986), which replaced *Swain*'s threshold requirement to prove systemic discrimination under a Fourteenth Amendment jury claim, with the rule that discrimination by the prosecutor in selecting the defendant's jury sufficed to establish the constitutional violation. The Texas Court of Criminal Appeals then remanded the matter to the trial court to determine whether Miller-El could show that prosecutors in his case peremptorily struck prospective black jurors because of race. Miller-El v. State, 748 S.W.2d 459 (1988).

The trial court found no such demonstration. After reviewing the voir dire record of the explanations given for some of the challenged strikes, and after hearing one of the prosecutors, Paul Macaluso, give his justification for those previously unexplained, the trial court accepted the stated race-neutral reasons for the strikes, which the judge called "completely credible [and] sufficient" as the grounds for a finding of "no purposeful discrimination." The Court of Criminal Appeals affirmed, stating it found "ample support" in the voir dire record for the race-neutral explanations offered by prosecutors for the peremptory strikes.

Miller-El then sought habeas relief under 28 U.S.C. §2254, again pressing his *Batson* claim, among others not now before us. The District Court denied relief, and the Court of Appeals for the Fifth Circuit precluded appeal by denying a certificate of appealability, Miller-El v. Johnson, 261 F.3d 445 (2001). We granted certiorari to consider whether Miller-El was entitled to review on the *Batson* claim, Miller-El v. Cockrell, 534 U.S. 1122 (2002), and reversed the Court of Appeals. After examining the record of Miller-El's extensive evidence of purposeful discrimination by the Dallas County District Attorney's Office before and during his trial, we found an appeal was in order, since the merits of the *Batson* claim were, at the least, debatable by jurists of reason. Miller-El v. Cockrell, 537 U.S. 322 (2003). After granting a certificate of appealability, the Fifth Circuit rejected Miller-El's *Batson* claim on the merits. 361 F.3d 849 (2004). We again granted certiorari, and again we reverse.

II

A

"It is well known that prejudices often exist against particular classes in the community, which sway the judgment of jurors, and which, therefore, operate in some cases to deny to persons of those classes the full enjoyment of that protection which others enjoy." Strauder v. West Virginia, 100 U.S. 303, 309 (1880). . . .

The rub has been the practical difficulty of ferreting out discrimination in selections discretionary by nature, and choices subject to myriad legitimate influences, whatever the race of the individuals on the panel from which jurors are selected. . . . The *Swain* court tried to relate peremptory challenge to equal protection by presuming the legitimacy of prosecutors' strikes except in the face of a longstanding pattern of discrimination. . . . [380 U.S.,] at 223-224.

Swain's demand to make out a continuity of discrimination over time, however, turned out to be difficult to the point of unworkable, and in Batson v. Kentucky, we . . . held that a defendant could make out a prima facie case of discriminatory jury selection by "the totality of the relevant facts" about a prosecutor's conduct during the defendant's own trial. 476 U.S., at 94, 96. . . .

Although the move from *Swain* to *Batson* left a defendant free to challenge the prosecution without having to cast *Swain*'s wide net, the net was not entirely consigned to history, for *Batson*'s individualized focus came with a weakness of its own, owing to its very emphasis on the particular reasons a prosecutor might give. If any facially neutral reason sufficed to answer a *Batson* challenge, then *Batson* would not amount to much more than *Swain*. Some stated reasons are false, and although some false reasons are shown up within the four corners of a given case, sometimes a court may not be sure unless it looks beyond the case at hand. Hence *Batson*'s explanation that a defendant may rely on "all relevant circumstances" to raise an inference of purposeful discrimination. 476 U.S., at 96-97.

B

This case comes to us on review of a denial of habeas relief sought under 28 U.S.C. §2254, following the Texas trial court's prior determination of fact that the State's race-neutral explanations were true, see Purkett v. Elem, 514 U.S. 765, 769 (1995) (per curiam); Batson v. Kentucky, supra, at 98, n. 21.

Under the Antiterrorism and Effective Death Penalty Act of 1996, Miller-El may obtain relief only by showing the Texas conclusion to be "an unreasonable determination of the facts in light of the evidence presented in the State court proceeding." 28 U.S.C. §2254(d)(2). Thus we presume the Texas court's factual findings to be sound unless Miller-El rebuts the "presumption of correctness by clear and convincing evidence." §2254(e)(1). The standard is demanding but not insatiable; as we said the last time this case was here, "deference does not by definition preclude relief." Miller-El v. Cockrell, 537 U.S., at 340.

III

A

The numbers describing the prosecution's use of peremptories are remarkable. Out of 20 black members of the 108-person venire panel for Miller-El's trial, only 1 served. Although 9 were excused for cause or by agreement, 10 were peremptorily struck by the prosecution. Id., at 331. "The prosecutors used their peremptory strikes to exclude 91% of the eligible African-American venire members. . . . Happenstance is unlikely to produce this disparity." Id., at 342.

More powerful than these bare statistics, however, are side-by-side comparisons of some black venire panelists who were struck and white panelists allowed to serve. If a prosecutor's proffered reason for striking a black panelist applies just as well to an otherwise similar nonblack who is permitted to serve, that is evidence tending to prove purposeful discrimination to be considered at *Batson*'s third step. . . . While we did not develop a comparative juror analysis last time, we did note that the prosecution's reasons for exercising peremptory strikes against some black panel members appeared equally on point as to some white jurors who served. Miller-El v. Cockrell, supra, at 343. The details of two panel member comparisons bear this out.

The prosecution used its second peremptory strike to exclude Billy Jean Fields, a black man who expressed unwavering support for the death penalty. On the questionnaire filled out by all panel members before individual examination on the stand, Fields said that he believed in capital punishment, and during questioning he disclosed his belief that the State acts on God's behalf when it imposes the death penalty. "Therefore, if the State exacts death, then that's what it should be." App. 174. He testified that he had no religious or philosophical reservations about the death penalty and that the death penalty deterred crime. Id., at 174-175. He twice averred, without apparent hesitation, that he could sit on Miller-El's jury and make a decision to impose this penalty. Id., at 176-177.

Although at one point in the questioning, Fields indicated that the possibility of rehabilitation might be relevant to the likelihood that a defendant would commit future acts of violence, id., at 183, he responded to ensuing questions by saying that although he believed anyone could be rehabilitated, this belief would not stand in the way of a decision to impose the death penalty:

> Based on what you [the prosecutor] said as far as the crime goes, there are only two things that could be rendered, death or life in prison. If for some reason the testimony didn't warrant death, then life imprisonment would give an individual an opportunity to rehabilitate. But, you know, you said that the jurors didn't have the opportunity to make a personal decision in the matter with reference to what I thought or felt, but it was just based on the questions according to the way the law has been handed down.

Id., at 185 (alteration omitted).

Fields also noted on his questionnaire that his brother had a criminal history. During questioning, the prosecution went into this, too:

> *Q.* Could you tell me a little bit about that?
> *A.* He was arrested and convicted on [a] number of occasions for possession of a controlled substance.
> *Q.* Was that here in Dallas?
> *A.* Yes.
> *Q.* Was he involved in any trials or anything like that?
> *A.* I suppose of sorts. I don't really know too much about it.
> *Q.* Was he ever convicted?
> *A.* Yeah, he served time.
> *Q.* Do you feel that that would in any way interfere with your service on this jury at all?
> *A.* No.

App. 190.

Fields was struck peremptorily by the prosecution, with prosecutor James Nelson offering a race-neutral reason:

> We . . . have concern with reference to some of his statements as to the death penalty in that he said that he could only give death if he thought a person could not be rehabilitated and he later made the comment that any person could be rehabilitated if they find God or are introduced to God and the fact that we have a concern that his religious feelings may affect his jury service in this case.

Id., at 197 (alteration omitted).

Thus, Nelson simply mischaracterized Fields's testimony. He represented that Fields said he would not vote for death if rehabilitation was possible, whereas Fields unequivocally stated that he could impose the death penalty regardless of the possibility of rehabilitation. Perhaps Nelson misunderstood, but unless he had an ulterior reason for keeping Fields off the jury we think he would have proceeded differently. In light of Fields's outspoken support for the death penalty, we expect the prosecutor would have cleared up any misunderstanding by asking further questions before getting to the point of exercising a strike.

If, indeed, Fields's thoughts on rehabilitation did make the prosecutor uneasy, he should have worried about a number of white panel members he accepted with no evident reservations. Sandra Hearn said that she believed in the death penalty "if a criminal cannot be rehabilitated and continues to commit the same type of crime." Id., at 429. Hearn went so far as to express doubt that at the penalty phase of a capital case she could conclude that a convicted murderer "would probably commit some criminal acts of violence in the future." Id., at 440. "People change," she said, making it hard to assess the risk of someone's future dangerousness. "The evidence would have to be awful strong." Ibid. But the prosecution did not respond to Hearn the way it did to Fields, and without delving into her views about rehabilitation with any further question, it raised no objection to her serving on the jury. White panelist Mary Witt said she would take the possibility of rehabilitation into account in deciding at the penalty phase of the trial about a defendant's probability of future dangerousness, 6 Record of *Voir Dire* 2433 (hereinafter Record), but the prosecutors asked her no further question about her views on reformation, and they accepted her as a juror. Id., at 2464-2465.[4] Latino venireman Fernando Gutierrez, who served on the jury, said that he would consider the death penalty for someone who could not be rehabilitated, App. 777, but the prosecutors did not question him further about this view. In sum, nonblack jurors whose remarks on rehabilitation could well have signaled a limit on their willingness to impose a death sentence were not questioned further and drew no objection, but the prosecution expressed apprehension about a black juror's belief in the possibility of reformation even though he repeatedly stated his approval of the death penalty and testified that he could impose it according to state legal standards even when the alternative sentence of life imprisonment would give a defendant (like everyone else in the world) the opportunity to reform.[5]

4. Witt ultimately did not serve because she was peremptorily struck by the defense. 6 Record 2465. The fact that Witt and other venire members discussed here were peremptorily struck by the defense is not relevant to our point. For each of them, the defense did not make a decision to exercise a peremptory until after the prosecution decided whether to accept or reject, so each was accepted by the prosecution before being ultimately struck by the defense. . . .

5. Prosecutors did exercise peremptory strikes on Penny Crowson and Charlotte Whaley, who expressed views about rehabilitation similar to those of Witt and Gutierrez. App. 554, 715.

The unlikelihood that his position on rehabilitation had anything to do with the peremptory strike of Fields is underscored by the prosecution's response after Miller-El's lawyer pointed out that the prosecutor had misrepresented Fields's responses on the subject. A moment earlier the prosecutor had finished his misdescription of Fields's views on potential rehabilitation with the words, "Those are our reasons for exercising our . . . strike at this time." Id., at 197. When defense counsel called him on his misstatement, he neither defended what he said nor withdrew the strike. Id., at 198. Instead, he suddenly came up with Fields's brother's prior conviction as another reason for the strike. Id., at 199.

It would be difficult to credit the State's new explanation, which reeks of afterthought. While the Court of Appeals tried to bolster it with the observation that no seated juror was in Fields's position with respect to his brother, 361 F.3d, at 859-860, the court's readiness to accept the State's substitute reason ignores not only its pretextual timing but the other reasons rendering it implausible. Fields's testimony indicated he was not close to his brother, App. 190 ("I don't really know too much about it"), and the prosecution asked nothing further about the influence his brother's history might have had on Fields, as it probably would have done if the family history had actually mattered. See, e.g., Ex parte Travis, 776 So. 2d 874, 881 (Ala. 2000) ("The State's failure to engage in any meaningful voir dire examination on a subject the State alleges it is concerned about is evidence suggesting that the explanation is a sham and a pretext for discrimination"). There is no good reason to doubt that the State's afterthought about Fields's brother was anything but makeweight. . . .

In sum, when we look for nonblack jurors similarly situated to Fields, we find strong similarities as well as some differences.[6] But the differences seem far from significant, particularly when we read Fields's voir dire testimony in its entirety. Upon that reading, Fields should have been an ideal juror in the eyes of a prosecutor seeking a death sentence, and the prosecutors' explanations for the strike cannot reasonably be accepted. See Miller-El v. Cockrell, 537 U.S., at 339 (the credibility of reasons given can be measured by "how reasonable, or how improbable, the explanations are; and by whether the proffered rationale has some basis in accepted trial strategy").

The prosecution's proffered reasons for striking Joe Warren, another black venireman, are comparably unlikely. Warren gave this answer when he was asked what the death penalty accomplished:

> I don't know. It's really hard to say because I know sometimes you feel that it might help to deter crime and then you feel that the person is not really suffering. You're taking the suffering away from him. So it's like I said, sometimes you have mixed feelings about whether or not this is punishment or, you know, you're relieving personal punishment.

App. 205; 3 Record 1532.

---

6. The dissent contends that there are no white panelists similarly situated to Fields and to panel member Joe Warren because " 'similarly situated' does not mean matching any one of several reasons the prosecution gave for striking a potential juror—it means matching *all* of them." Post, at 19 (quoting Miller-El v. Cockrell, 537 U.S., at 362-363 (Thomas, J., dissenting)). None of our cases announces a rule that no comparison is probative unless the situation of the individuals compared is identical in all respects, and there is no reason to accept one. Nothing in the combination of Fields's statements about rehabilitation and his brother's history discredits our grounds for inferring that these purported reasons were pretextual. A per se rule that a defendant cannot win a *Batson* claim unless there is an exactly identical white juror would leave *Batson* inoperable; potential jurors are not products of a set of cookie cutters.

The prosecution said nothing about these remarks when it struck Warren from the panel, but prosecutor Paul Macaluso referred to this answer as the first of his reasons when he testified at the later *Batson* hearing:

I thought [Warren's statements on voir dire] were inconsistent responses. At one point he says, you know, on a case-by-case basis and at another point he said, well, I think—I got the impression, at least, that he suggested that the death penalty was an easy way out, that they should be made to suffer more.

App. 909.

On the face of it, the explanation is reasonable from the State's point of view, but its plausibility is severely undercut by the prosecution's failure to object to other panel members who expressed views much like Warren's. [For example,] Sandra Jenkins, whom the State accepted (but who was then struck by the defense) testified that she thought "a harsher treatment is life imprisonment with no parole." Id., at 542. Leta Girard, accepted by the State (but also struck by the defense) gave her opinion that "living sometimes is a worse—is worse to me than dying would be." Id., at 624. The fact that Macaluso's reason also applied to these other panel members, most of them white, none of them struck, is evidence of pretext.

The suggestion of pretext is not, moreover, mitigated much by Macaluso's explanation that Warren was struck when the State had 10 peremptory challenges left and could afford to be liberal in using them. Id., at 908. If that were the explanation for striking Warren and later accepting panel members who thought death would be too easy, the prosecutors should have struck Sandra Jenkins, whom they examined and accepted before Warren. . . . Yet the prosecutors accepted the white panel member Jenkins and struck the black venireman Warren.

Macaluso's explanation that the prosecutors grew more sparing with peremptory challenges as the jury selection wore on does, however, weaken any suggestion that the State's acceptance of [Troy] Woods, the one black juror, shows that race was not in play. Woods was the eighth juror, qualified in the fifth week of jury selection. Joint Lodging 125. When the State accepted him, 11 of its 15 peremptory strikes were gone, 7 of them used to strike black panel members. The juror questionnaires show that at least three members of the venire panel yet to be questioned on the stand were opposed to capital punishment, Janice Mackey, id., at 79; Paul Bailey, id., at 63; and Anna Keaton, id., at 55. With at least three remaining panel members highly undesirable to the State, the prosecutors had to exercise prudent restraint in using strikes. This late-stage decision to accept a black panel member willing to impose a death sentence does not, therefore, neutralize the early-stage decision to challenge a comparable venireman, Warren. In fact, if the prosecutors were going to accept any black juror to obscure the otherwise consistent pattern of opposition to seating one, the time to do so was getting late. . . .

[T]he rule in *Batson* provides an opportunity to the prosecutor to give the reason for striking the juror, and it requires the judge to assess the plausibility of that reason in light of all evidence with a bearing on it. 476 U.S., at 96-97; Miller-El v. Cockrell, 537 U.S., at 339. It is true that peremptories are often the subjects of instinct, Batson v. Kentucky, 476 U.S., at 106 (Marshall, J., concurring), and it can sometimes be hard to say what the reason is. But when illegitimate grounds like race are in issue, a prosecutor simply has got to state his reasons as best he can and stand or fall on the plausibility of the reasons he gives. A *Batson* challenge does not call for a mere exercise in thinking up any rational basis. If the stated reason does not hold up, its pretextual significance does not fade because a trial judge, or an appeals court, can imagine a reason that might not have been shown up as false. The Court of Appeals's and the dissent's substitution of a reason for eliminating Warren does nothing to satisfy the prosecutors' burden of stating a racially neutral explanation for their own actions.

The whole of the voir dire testimony subject to consideration casts the prosecution's reasons for striking Warren in an implausible light. Comparing his strike with the treatment of panel members who expressed similar views supports a conclusion that race was significant in determining who was challenged and who was not.

B

The case for discrimination goes beyond these comparisons to include broader patterns of practice during the jury selection. The prosecution's shuffling of the venire panel, its enquiry into views on the death penalty, its questioning about minimum acceptable sentences: all indicate decisions probably based on race. Finally, the appearance of discrimination is confirmed by widely known evidence of the general policy of the Dallas County District Attorney's Office to exclude black venire members from juries at the time Miller-El's jury was selected.

The first clue to the prosecutors' intentions, distinct from the peremptory challenges themselves, is their resort during voir dire to a procedure known in Texas as the jury shuffle. In the State's criminal practice, either side may literally reshuffle the cards bearing panel members' names, thus rearranging the order in which members of a venire panel are seated and reached for questioning. Once the order is established, the panel members seated at the back are likely to escape voir dire altogether, for those not questioned by the end of the week are dismissed. . . .

In this case, the prosecution and then the defense shuffled the cards at the beginning of the first week of voir dire; the record does not reflect the changes in order. App. 113-114. At the beginning of the second week, when a number of black members were seated at the front of the panel, the prosecution shuffled. 2 Record 836-837. At the beginning of the third week, the first four panel members were black. The prosecution shuffled, and these black panel members ended up at the back. Then the defense shuffled, and the black panel members again appeared at the front. The prosecution requested another shuffle, but the trial court refused. App. 124-132. Finally, the defense shuffled at the beginning of the fourth and fifth weeks of voir dire; the record does not reflect the panel's racial composition before or after those shuffles. Id., at 621-622; 9 Record 3585.

The State notes in its brief that there might be racially neutral reasons for shuffling the jury, and we suppose there might be. But no racially neutral reason has ever been offered in this case, and nothing stops the suspicion of discriminatory intent from rising to an inference.

The next body of evidence that the State was trying to avoid black jurors is the contrasting voir dire questions posed respectively to black and nonblack panel members, on two different subjects. First, there were the prosecutors' statements preceding questions about a potential juror's thoughts on capital punishment. Some of these prefatory statements were cast in general terms, but some followed the so-called graphic script, describing the method of execution in rhetorical and clinical detail. It is intended, Miller-El contends, to prompt some expression of hesitation to consider the death penalty and thus to elicit plausibly neutral grounds for a peremptory strike of a potential juror subjected to it, if not a strike for cause. If the graphic script is given to a higher proportion of blacks than whites, this is evidence that prosecutors more often wanted blacks off the jury, absent some neutral and extenuating explanation.

As we pointed out last time, for 94% of white venire panel members, prosecutors gave a bland description of the death penalty before asking about the individual's feelings on the subject. Miller-El v. Cockrell, 537 U.S., at 332. . . . Only 6% of white venire panelists, but 53% of those who were black, heard [the much more graphic] description of the death penalty before being asked their feelings about it. . . .

The State concedes that this disparate questioning did occur but argues that use of the graphic script turned not on a panelist's race but on expressed ambivalence about the death penalty in the preliminary questionnaire. Prosecutors were trying, the argument goes, to weed out noncommittal or uncertain jurors, not black jurors. And while some white venire members expressed opposition to the death penalty on their questionnaires, they were not read the graphic script because their feelings were already clear. The State says that giving the graphic script to these panel members would only have antagonized them. Brief for Respondent 27-32.

This argument, however, first advanced in dissent when the case was last here, Miller-El v. Cockrell, supra, at 364-368 (opinion of Thomas, J.), and later adopted by the State and the Court of Appeals, simply does not fit the facts. Looking at the answers on the questionnaires, and at voir dire testimony expressly discussing answers on the questionnaires, we find that black venire members were more likely than nonblacks to receive the graphic script regardless of their expressions of certainty or ambivalence about the death penalty, and the State's chosen explanation for the graphic script fails in the cases of four out of the eight black panel members who received it. Two of them, Janice Mackey and Anna Keaton, clearly stated opposition to the death penalty but they received the graphic script, while the black panel members Wayman Kennedy and Jeannette Butler were unambiguously in favor but got the graphic description anyway. The State's explanation does even worse in the instances of the five nonblacks who received the graphic script, missing the mark four times out of five: Vivian Sztybel and Filemon Zablan received it, although each was unambiguously in favor of the death penalty, while Dominick Desinise and Clara Evans unambiguously opposed it but were given the graphic version. . . .

The State's attempt at a race-neutral rationalization thus simply fails to explain what the prosecutors did. But if we posit instead that the prosecutors' first object was to use the graphic script to make a case for excluding black panel members opposed to or ambivalent about the death penalty, there is a much tighter fit of fact and explanation. Of the 10 nonblacks whose questionnaires expressed ambivalence or opposition, only 30% received the graphic treatment. But of the seven blacks who expressed ambivalence or opposition, 86% heard the graphic script. As between the State's ambivalence explanation and Miller-El's racial one, race is much the better, and the reasonable inference is that race was the major consideration when the prosecution chose to follow the graphic script.

The same is true for another kind of disparate questioning, which might fairly be called trickery. The prosecutors asked members of the panel how low a sentence they would consider imposing for murder. Most potential jurors were first told that Texas law provided for a minimum term of five years, but some members of the panel were not, and if a panel member then insisted on a minimum above five years, the prosecutor would suppress his normal preference for tough jurors and claim cause to strike [on the ground of protecting defendants from overzealous jurors]. Two Terms ago, we described how this disparate questioning was correlated with race:

> Ninety-four percent of whites were informed of the statutory minimum sentence, compared [with] only twelve and a half percent of African-Americans. No explanation is proffered for the statistical disparity. . . . Indeed, while petitioner's appeal was pending before the Texas Court of Criminal Appeals, that court found a *Batson* violation where this precise line of disparate questioning on mandatory minimums was employed by one of the same prosecutors who tried the instant case. Chambers v. State, 784 S.W.2d 29, 31 (Tex. Crim. App. 1989).

Miller-El v. Cockrell, 537 U.S., at 345.

The State concedes that the manipulative minimum punishment questioning was used to create cause to strike, but now it offers the extenuation that prosecutors omitted the 5-year information not on the basis of race, but on stated opposition to the death penalty, or ambivalence about it, on the questionnaires and in the voir dire testimony. . . . But the State's rationale flatly fails to explain why most white panel members who expressed similar opposition or ambivalence were not subjected to it. . . . [O]nly 27% of nonblacks questioned on the subject who expressed these views were subjected to the trick question, as against 100% of black members. Once again, the implication of race in the prosecutors' choice of questioning cannot be explained away.

There is a final body of evidence that confirms this conclusion. We know that for decades leading up to the time this case was tried prosecutors in the Dallas County office had followed a specific policy of systematically excluding blacks from juries, as we explained the last time the case was here.

> . . . [T]he defense presented evidence that the District Attorney's Office had adopted a formal policy to exclude minorities from jury service. . . . A manual entitled "Jury Selection in a Criminal Case" [sometimes known as the Sparling Manual] was distributed to prosecutors. It contained an article authored by a former prosecutor (and later a judge) under the direction of his superiors in the District Attorney's Office, outlining the reasoning for excluding minorities from jury service. Although the manual was written in 1968, it remained in circulation until 1976, if not later, and was available at least to one of the prosecutors in Miller-El's trial.

Miller-El v. Cockrell, 537 U.S., at 334-335.

Prosecutors here "marked the race of each prospective juror on their juror cards." Id., at 347.[38]

The Court of Appeals concluded that Miller-El failed to show by clear and convincing evidence that the state court's finding of no discrimination was wrong, whether his evidence was viewed collectively or separately. 361 F.3d, at 862. We find this conclusion as unsupportable as the "dismissive and strained interpretation" of his evidence that we disapproved when we decided Miller-El was entitled to a certificate

---

38. The State claimed at oral argument that prosecutors could have been tracking jurors' races to be sure of avoiding a *Batson* violation. Tr. of Oral Arg. 44. *Batson*, of course, was decided the month after Miller-El was tried.

of appealability. See Miller-El v. Cockrell, supra, at 344. It is true, of course, that at some points the significance of Miller-El's evidence is open to judgment calls, but when this evidence on the issues raised is viewed cumulatively its direction is too powerful to conclude anything but discrimination.

In the course of drawing a jury to try a black defendant, 10 of the 11 qualified black venire panel members were peremptorily struck. At least two of them, Fields and Warren, were ostensibly acceptable to prosecutors seeking a death verdict, and Fields was ideal. The prosecutors' chosen race-neutral reasons for the strikes do not hold up and are so far at odds with the evidence that pretext is the fair conclusion, indicating the very discrimination the explanations were meant to deny.

The strikes that drew these incredible explanations occurred in a selection process replete with evidence that the prosecutors were selecting and rejecting potential jurors because of race. At least two of the jury shuffles conducted by the State make no sense except as efforts to delay consideration of black jury panelists to the end of the week, when they might not even be reached. The State has in fact never offered any other explanation. Nor has the State denied that disparate lines of questioning were pursued: 53% of black panelists but only 3% of nonblacks were questioned with a graphic script meant to induce qualms about applying the death penalty (and thus explain a strike), and 100% of blacks but only 27% of nonblacks were subjected to a trick question about the minimum acceptable penalty for murder, meant to induce a disqualifying answer. The State's attempts to explain the prosecutors' questioning of particular witnesses on nonracial grounds fit the evidence less well than the racially discriminatory hypothesis.

If anything more is needed for an undeniable explanation of what was going on, history supplies it. The prosecutors took their cues from a 20-year-old manual of tips on jury selection, as shown by their notes of the race of each potential juror. By the time a jury was chosen, the State had peremptorily challenged 12% of qualified nonblack panel members, but eliminated 91% of the black ones.

It blinks reality to deny that the State struck Fields and Warren, included in that 91%, because they were black. The strikes correlate with no fact as well as they correlate with race, and they occurred during a selection infected by shuffling and disparate questioning that race explains better than any race-neutral reason advanced by the State. The State's pretextual positions confirm Miller-El's claim, and the prosecutors' own notes proclaim that the Sparling Manual's emphasis on race was on their minds when they considered every potential juror.

The state court's conclusion that the prosecutors' strikes of Fields and Warren were not racially determined is shown up as wrong to a clear and convincing degree; the state court's conclusion was unreasonable as well as erroneous. The judgment of the Court of Appeals is reversed, and the case is remanded for entry of judgment for petitioner together with orders of appropriate relief.

JUSTICE BREYER, concurring.

In Batson v. Kentucky, 476 U.S. 79 (1986), the Court adopted a burden-shifting rule designed to ferret out the unconstitutional use of race in jury selection. In his separate opinion, Justice Thurgood Marshall predicted that the Court's rule would not achieve its goal. The only way to "end the racial discrimination that peremptories inject into the jury-selection process," he concluded, was to "eliminate peremptory challenges entirely." Id., at 102-103 (concurring opinion). Today's case reinforces Justice Marshall's concerns.

I

To begin with, this case illustrates the practical problems of proof that Justice Marshall described. . . .

At *Batson*'s first step, litigants remain free to misuse peremptory challenges as long as the strikes fall *below* the prima facie threshold level. . . . At *Batson*'s second step, prosecutors need only tender a neutral reason, not a "persuasive, or even plausible" one. . . . And most importantly, at step three, *Batson* asks judges to engage in the awkward, sometime hopeless, task of second-guessing a prosecutor's instinctive judgment—the underlying basis for which may be invisible even to the prosecutor exercising the challenge. . . .

Given the inevitably clumsy fit between any objectively measurable standard and the subjective decision making at issue, I am not surprised to find studies and anecdotal reports suggesting that, despite *Batson*, the discriminatory use of peremptory challenges remains a problem. See, e.g., Baldus, Woodworth, Zuckerman, Weiner, & Broffitt, The Use of Peremptory Challenges in Capital Murder Trials: A Legal and Empirical Analysis, 3 U. Pa. J. Const. L. 3, 52-53, 73, n. 197 (2001) (in 317 capital trials in Philadelphia between 1981 and 1997, prosecutors struck 51% of black jurors and 26% of nonblack jurors; defense counsel struck 26% of black jurors and 54% of nonblack jurors; and race-based uses of prosecutorial peremptories declined by only 2% after *Batson*); Rose, The Peremptory Challenge Accused of Race or Gender Discrimination? Some Data from One County, 23 Law & Hum. Behav. 695, 698-699 (1999) (in one North Carolina county, 71% of excused black jurors were removed by the prosecution; 81% of excused white jurors were removed by the defense); Tucker, In Moore's Trials, Excluded Jurors Fit Racial Pattern, Washington Post, Apr. 2, 2001, p. A1 (in a D. C. murder case spanning four trials, prosecutors excused 41 blacks or other minorities and 6 whites; defense counsel struck 29 whites and 13 black venire members); Mize, A Legal Discrimination; Juries Are Not Supposed to be Picked on the Basis of Race and Sex, But It Happens All the Time, Washington Post, Oct. 8, 2000, p. B8 (authored by judge on the D.C. Superior Court); see also Melilli, *Batson* in Practice: What We Have Learned About *Batson* and Peremptory Challenges, 71 Notre Dame L. Rev. 447, 462-464 (1996) (finding *Batson* challenges' success rates lower where peremptories were used to strike black, rather than white, potential jurors); Brand, The Supreme Court, Equal Protection and Jury Selection: Denying That Race Still Matters, 1994 Wis. L. Rev. 511, 583-589 (examining judicial decisions and concluding that few *Batson* challenges succeed); Note, Batson v. Kentucky and J. E. B. v. Alabama ex rel. T. B.: Is the Peremptory Challenge Still Preeminent? 36 Boston College L. Rev. 161, 189, and n. 303 (1994) (same); Montoya, The Future of the Post-*Batson* Peremptory Challenge: Voir Dire by Questionnaire and the "Blind" Peremptory Challenge, 29 U. Mich. J.L. Reform 981, 1006, nn. 126-127, 1035 (1996) (reporting attorneys' views on the difficulty of proving *Batson* claims).

II

Practical problems of proof to the side, peremptory challenges seem increasingly anomalous in our judicial system. On the one hand, the Court has widened and deepened *Batson*'s basic constitutional rule [by applying it to criminal defendants, private litigants, cases in which defendants and excluded jurors are of different races, and peremptory challenges based on gender].

On the other hand, the use of race- and gender-based stereotypes in the jury-selection process seems better organized and more systematized than ever before. See, e.g., Post, A Loaded Box of Stereotypes: Despite "Batson," Race, Gender Play Big Roles in Jury Selection., Nat'l L.J., Apr. 25, 2005, pp. 1, 18 (discussing common reliance on race and gender in jury selection). For example, one jury-selection guide counsels attorneys to perform a "demographic analysis" that assigns numerical points to characteristics such as age, occupation, and marital status—in addition to race as well as gender. See V. Starr & A. McCormick, Jury Selection 193-200 (3d ed. 2001). Thus, in a hypothetical dispute between a white landlord and an African-American tenant, the authors suggest awarding two points to an African-American venire member while subtracting one point from her white counterpart. Id., at 197-199.

For example, a bar journal article counsels lawyers to "rate" potential jurors "demographically (age, gender, marital status, etc.) and mark who would be under stereotypical circumstances [their] natural *enemies* and *allies*." Drake, The Art of Litigating: Deselecting Jurors Like the Pros, 34 Md. Bar J. 18, 22 (Mar.-Apr. 2001) (emphasis in original).

For example, materials from a legal convention, while noting that "nationality" is less important than "once was thought," and emphasizing that "the answers a prospective juror gives to questions are much more valuable," still point out that "stereotypically" those of "Italian, French, and Spanish" origin "are thought to be pro-plaintiff as well as other minorities, such as Mexican and Jewish[;] persons of German, Scandinavian, Swedish, Finnish, Dutch, Nordic, British, Scottish, Oriental, and Russian origin are thought to be better for the defense"; African-Americans "have always been considered good for the plaintiff," and "more politically conservative minorities will be more likely to lean toward defendants." Blue, Mirroring, Proxemics, Nonverbal Communication and Other Psychological Tools, Advocacy Track—Psychology of Trial, Association of Trial Lawyers of America Annual Convention Reference Materials, 1 Ann. 2001 ATLA-CLE 153, available at WESTLAW, ATLACLE database (June 8, 2005). . . .

These examples reflect a professional effort to fulfill the lawyer's obligation to help his or her client. Cf. *J. E. B.*, supra, at 148-149 (O'Connor, J., concurring) (observing that jurors' race and gender may inform their perspective). Nevertheless, the outcome in terms of jury selection is the same as it would be were the motive less benign. And as long as that is so, the law's antidiscrimination command and a peremptory jury-selection system that permits or encourages the use of stereotypes work at cross-purposes.

Finally, a jury system without peremptories is no longer unthinkable. Members of the legal profession have begun serious consideration of that possibility. See, e.g., Allen v. Florida, 596 So. 2d 1083, 1088-1089 (Fla. App. 1992) (Hubbart, J., concurring). . . . And England, a common-law jurisdiction that has eliminated peremptory challenges, continues to administer fair trials based largely on random jury selection. See Criminal Justice Act, 1988, ch. 33, §118(1), 22 Halsbury's Statutes 357 (4th ed. 2003 reissue) (U.K.); see also 2 Jury Service in Victoria, Final Report, ch. 5, p. 165 (Dec. 1997) (1993 study of English barristers showed majority support for system without peremptory challenges).

III

I recognize that peremptory challenges have a long historical pedigree. They may help to reassure a party of the fairness of the jury. But long ago, Blackstone recognized the peremptory challenge as an "arbitrary and capricious species of [a] challenge." 4 W. Blackstone, Commentaries on the Laws of England 346 (1769). . . .

. . . In light of the considerations I have mentioned, I believe it necessary to reconsider *Batson*'s test and the peremptory challenge system as a whole. With that qualification, I join the Court's opinion.

JUSTICE THOMAS, with whom CHIEF JUSTICE REHNQUIST and JUSTICE SCALIA join, dissenting.

. . . Miller-El's cumulative evidence does not come remotely close to clearly and convincingly establishing that the state court's factual finding was unreasonable. [This case involves] four types of evidence: (1) the alleged disparate treatment and (2) disparate questioning of black and white veniremen; (3) the prosecution's jury shuffles; and (4) historical discrimination by the D.A.'s Office in the selection of juries. Although each type of evidence "is open to judgment calls," supra, the majority finds that a succession of unpersuasive arguments amounts to a compelling case. In the end, the majority's opinion is its own best refutation: It strains to demonstrate what should instead be patently obvious.

The majority devotes the bulk of its opinion to a side-by-side comparison of white panelists who were allowed to serve and two black panelists who were struck, Billy Jean Fields and Joe Warren. Ante, at 7-19. The majority argues that the prosecution's reasons for striking Fields and Warren apply equally to whites who were permitted to serve, and thus those reasons must have been pretextual. The voir dire transcript reveals that the majority is mistaken.

It is worth noting at the outset, however, that Miller-El's and the Court's claims have always been a moving target. Of the 20 black veniremen at Miller-El's trial, 9 were struck for cause or by the parties' agreement, and 1 served on the jury. Miller-El claimed at the *Batson* hearing that all 10 remaining black veniremen were dismissed on account of race. That number dropped to 7 on appeal, and then again to 6 during his federal habeas proceedings. . . .

The majority now focuses exclusively on Fields and Warren. But Warren was obviously equivocal about the death penalty. In the end, the majority's case reduces to a single venireman, Fields, and its reading of a 20-year-old voir dire transcript that is ambiguous at best. This is the antithesis of clear and convincing evidence.

From the outset of questioning, Warren did not specify when he would vote to impose the death penalty. When asked by prosecutor Paul Macaluso about his ability to impose the death penalty, Warren stated, "There are some cases where I would agree, you know, and there are others that I don't." 3 Record 1526. Macaluso then explained at length the types of crimes that qualified as capital murder under Texas law, and asked whether Warren would be able to impose the death penalty for those types of heinous crimes. Id., at 1527-1530. Warren continued to hedge: "I would say it depends on the case and the circumstances involved at the time." Id., at 1530. He offered no sense of the circumstances that would lead him to conclude that the death penalty was an appropriate punishment.

Macaluso then changed tack and asked whether Warren believed that the death penalty accomplished any social purpose. Id., at 1531-1532. Once again, Warren proved impossible to pin down: "Yes and no. Sometimes I think it does and sometimes I think it don't. Sometimes you have mixed feelings about things like that." Id., at 1532. Macaluso then focused on what the death penalty accomplished in those cases where Warren believed it useful. Ibid. Even then, Warren expressed no firm view:

"I don't know. It's really hard to say because I know sometimes you feel that it might help to deter crime and then you feel that the person is not really suffering. You're taking the suffering away from him. So it's like I said, sometimes you have mixed feelings about whether or not this is punishment or, you know, you're relieving personal punishment." Ibid.

While Warren's ambivalence was driven by his uncertainty that the death penalty was severe enough, that is beside the point. Throughout the examination, Warren gave no indication whether or when he would prefer the death penalty to other forms of punishment, specifically life imprisonment. 3 Record 1532-1533. To prosecutors seeking the death penalty, the reason for Warren's ambivalence was irrelevant. . . .

According to the majority, Macaluso testified that he struck Warren for his statement that the death penalty was "an easy way out," ante, at 14 (quoting App. 909), and not for his ambivalence about the death penalty, ante, at 17. This grossly mischaracterizes the record. Macaluso specifically testified at the *Batson* hearing that he was troubled by the "*inconsistency*" of Warren's responses. App. 909 (emphasis added). Macaluso was speaking of Warren's ambivalence about the death penalty, a reason wholly unrelated to race. This was Macaluso's "stated reason," and Macaluso ought to "stand or fall on the plausibility" of this reason—not one concocted by the majority. Ante, at 18.

The majority points to four other panel members—Kevin Duke, Troy Woods, Sandra Jenkins, and Leta Girard—who supposedly expressed views much like Warren's, but who were not struck by the State. According to the majority, this is evidence of pretext. But the majority's premise is faulty. None of these veniremen was as difficult to pin down on the death penalty as Warren. For instance, Duke supported the death penalty. App. 373 ("I've always believed in having the death penalty. I think it serves a purpose"); ibid. ("I mean, it's a sad thing to see, to have to kill someone, but they shouldn't have done the things that they did. Sometimes they deserve to be killed"); id., at 394 ("If I feel that I can answer all three of these [special-issue] questions yes and I feel that he's done a crime worthy of the death penalty, yes, I will give the death penalty"). By contrast, Warren never expressed a firm view one way or the other. . . .

Nevertheless, even assuming that any of these veniremen expressed views similar to Warren's, Duke, Woods, and Girard were questioned much later in the jury selection process, when the State had fewer peremptories to spare. Only Sandra Jenkins was questioned early in the voir dire process, and thus only Jenkins was even arguably similarly situated to Warren. However, Jenkins and Warren were different in important respects. Jenkins expressed no doubt whatsoever about the death penalty. She testified that she had researched the death penalty in high school, and she said in response to questioning by both parties that she strongly believed in the death penalty's value as a deterrent to crime. 3 Record 1074-1075, 1103-1104. This alone explains why the State accepted Jenkins as a juror, while Miller-El struck her. In addition, Jenkins did not have a relative who had been convicted of a crime, but Warren did. At the *Batson* hearing, Macaluso testified that he struck Warren both for Warren's inconsistent responses regarding the death penalty and for his brother's conviction.

The majority thinks it can prove pretext by pointing to white veniremen who match only one of the State's proffered reasons for striking Warren. This defies logic. "'Similarly situated' does not mean matching any one of several reasons the prosecution gave for striking a potential juror—it means matching *all* of them." *Miller-El I*, 537 U.S., at 362-363 (Thomas, J., dissenting). Given limited peremptories, prosecutors often must focus on the potential jurors most likely to disfavor their case. By ignoring the totality of reasons that a prosecutor strikes any particular venireman, it is the majority that treats potential jurors as "products of a set of cookie cutters"—as if potential jurors who share only some among many traits must be treated the same to avoid a *Batson* violation. Of course jurors must not be "identical in all respects" to gauge pretext, but to isolate race as a variable, the jurors must be comparable in all respects that the prosecutor proffers as important. This does not mean "that a defendant cannot win a *Batson* claim unless there is an exactly identical white juror." It means that a defendant cannot support a *Batson* claim by comparing veniremen of different races unless the veniremen are truly similar. . . .

The second black venireman on whom the majority relies is Billy Jean Fields. Fields expressed support for the death penalty, App. 174-175, but Fields also expressed views that called into question his ability to impose the death penalty. Fields was a deeply religious man, id., at 173-174, 192-194, and prosecutors feared that his religious convictions might make him reluctant to impose the death penalty. Those fears were confirmed by Fields' view that all people could be rehabilitated if introduced to God, a fear that had special force considering the special-issue questions necessary to impose the death penalty in Texas. One of those questions asked whether there was a probability that the defendant would engage in future violence that threatened society. When they reached this question, Macaluso and Fields had the following exchange:

> [*MACALUSO:*]   What does that word probability mean to you in that connotation?
> [*FIELDS:*]   Well, it means is there a possibility that [a defendant] will continue to lead this type of life, will he be rehabilitated or does he intend to make this a life-long ambition.
> [*MACALUSO:*]   Let me ask you, Mr. Fields, do you feel as though some people simply cannot be rehabilitated?
> [*FIELDS:*]   No.
> [*MACALUSO:*]   You think everyone can be rehabilitated?
> [*FIELDS:*]   Yes.

Id., at 183-184.

Thus, Fields indicated that the possibility of rehabilitation was ever-present and relevant to whether a defendant might commit future acts of violence. In light of that view, it is understandable that prosecutors doubted whether he could vote to impose the death penalty.

Fields did testify that he could impose the death penalty, even on a defendant who could be rehabilitated. Id., at 185. For the majority, this shows that the State's reason was pretextual. But of course Fields said that he could fairly consider the death penalty—if he had answered otherwise, he would have been challengeable *for cause*. The point is that Fields' earlier answers cast significant doubt on whether he could impose the death penalty. The very purpose of peremptory strikes is to allow parties to remove potential jurors whom they suspect, but cannot prove, may exhibit a particular bias. See *Swain*, 380 U.S., at 220; J. E. B. v. Alabama ex rel. T. B., 511 U.S. 127, 148 (1994) (O'Connor, J., concurring). Based on Fields' voir dire testimony, it was perfectly reasonable for prosecutors to suspect that Fields might be swayed by a penitent defendant's testimony. The prosecutors may have been worried for nothing about Fields' religious sentiments, but that does not mean they were instead worried about Fields' race. . . .

Miller-El's claims of disparate questioning [involving use of the so-called "graphic script"] also do not fit the facts. . . . The State questioned panelists differently when their questionnaire responses indicated ambivalence about the death penalty. Any racial disparity in questioning resulted from the reality that more nonblack veniremen favored the death penalty and were willing to impose it.

Miller-El also alleges that the State employed two different scripts on the basis of race when asking questions about imposition of the minimum sentence. This disparate-questioning argument is even more flawed than the last one. The evidence confirms that, as the State argues, prosecutors used different questioning on minimum sentences to create cause to strike veniremen who were ambivalent about or opposed to the death penalty. . . .

Miller-El's argument that prosecutors shuffled the jury to remove blacks is pure speculation. At the *Batson* hearing, Miller-El did not raise, nor was there any discussion of, the topic of jury shuffling as a racial tactic. The record shows only that the State shuffled the jury during the first three weeks of jury selection, while Miller-El shuffled the jury during each of the five weeks. This evidence no more proves that prosecutors sought to eliminate blacks from the jury, than it proves that Miller-El sought to eliminate whites even more often. *Miller-El I*, 537 U.S., at 360 (Thomas, J., dissenting).

Miller-El notes that the State twice shuffled the jury (in the second and third weeks) when a number of blacks were seated at the front of the panel. According to the majority, this gives rise to an "inference" that prosecutors were discriminating. But Miller-El should not be asking this Court to draw "inferences"; he should be asking it to examine clear and convincing proof. And the inference is not even a strong one. We do not know if the nonblacks near the front shared characteristics with the blacks near the front, providing race-neutral reasons for the shuffles. We also do not know the racial composition of the panel during the first week when the State shuffled, or during the fourth and fifth weeks when it did not.

More important, any number of characteristics other than race could have been apparent to prosecutors from a visual inspection of the jury panel. Granted, we do not know whether prosecutors relied on racially neutral reasons, but that is because Miller-El never asked at the *Batson* hearing. It is Miller-El's burden to prove racial discrimination, and the jury-shuffle evidence itself does not provide such proof.

The majority's speculation would not be complete, however, without its discussion (block-quoted from *Miller-El I*) of the history of discrimination in the D.A.'s Office. This is nothing more than guilt by association that is unsupported by the record. Some of the witnesses at the *Swain* hearing did testify that individual prosecutors had discriminated. However, no one testified that the prosecutors in Miller-El's trial—Norman Kinne, Paul Macaluso, and Jim Nelson—had ever been among those to engage in racially discriminatory jury selection.

The majority then tars prosecutors with a manual entitled Jury Selection in a Criminal Case (hereinafter Manual or Sparling Manual), authored by John Sparling, a former Dallas County prosecutor. There is no evidence, however, that Kinne, Macaluso, or Nelson had ever read the Manual—which was written in 1968, almost two decades before Miller-El's trial. The reason there is no evidence on the question is that Miller-El never asked. During the entire *Batson* hearing, there is no mention of the Sparling Manual. Miller-El never questioned Macaluso about it, and he never questioned Kinne or Nelson at all. The majority simply assumes that all Dallas County prosecutors were racist and remained that way through the mid-1980's.

Nor does the majority rely on the Manual for anything more than show. The Manual contains a single, admittedly stereotypical line on race: "Minority races almost always empathize with the Defendant." App. 102. Yet the Manual also tells prosecutors not to select "anyone who had a close friend or relative that was prosecuted by the State." Id., at 112. That was true of both Warren and Fields, and yet the majority cavalierly dismisses as "makeweight" the State's justification that Warren and Fields were struck because they were related to individuals convicted of crimes. . . .

Finally, the majority notes that prosecutors "marked the race of each prospective juror on their juror cards." Ante, at 31 (quoting *Miller-El I*, supra, at 347). This suffers from the same problems as Miller-El's other evidence. Prosecutors did mark the juror cards with the jurors' race, sex, and juror number. We have no idea—and even the majority cannot bring itself to speculate—whether this was done merely for identification purposes or for some more nefarious reason. The reason we have no idea is that the juror cards were never introduced before the state courts, and thus prosecutors were never questioned about their use of them.

* * *

. . . Miller-El has not established, much less established by clear and convincing evidence, that prosecutors racially discriminated in the selection of his jury—and he certainly has not done so on the basis of the evidence presented to the Texas courts. On the basis of facts and law, rather than sentiments, Miller-El does not merit the writ. I respectfully dissent.

What message can be drawn from the *Miller-El* saga? Is the Supreme Court trying to signal to the lower courts that *Batson* review, especially at stages two and three, should be conducted more aggressively than *Hernandez* and *Purkett* suggested? The outcome of *Miller-El* would seem to so indicate.

But what, exactly, is the nature of *Batson* review, as contemplated by the Court? One of the most striking aspects of *Miller-El* is the extent to which both the majority and the dissent become caught up in lengthy and complicated arguments over the facts of the case. (Indeed, in its original form, *Miller-El* is far more lengthy and complicated than the version that appears above; radical editing was necessary in order to fit the opinion into the casebook.) It is far from clear that, on balance, the majority has the better of the factual argument.

Why spend so much time and energy arguing about the meaning of specific words used by each prospective juror during voir dire? Or about subtle comparisons of one juror's views with another's? Or about the nuances of the prosecutor's explanations for challenged peremptory strikes? Can these fact-based arguments ever really settle the question whether the prosecutor's strikes were motivated by discrimination?

From an epistemological point of view, the problem is that, in the absence of such things as direct admission of racist motivation, particular facts acquire meaning only when viewed in the context of patterns of behavior. Such patterns emerge only from analyzing behavior in the aggregate. To put it bluntly, without the evidence provided by the raw numbers in *Miller-El* (11 qualified black venire members, 10 of whom were eliminated by prosecution peremptory challenges) — together with the racially disparate use of different questioning "scripts," *and* the apparently long-standing prosecutorial abuse of the bizarre Texas "jury-shuffling" procedure, *and* the long history of racial discrimination by Dallas County prosecutors — would the peremptory strikes of Fields and Warren have been enough to prove discrimination in the case? The answer is almost certainly no, especially in light of the fact that, with even slightly more plausible race-neutral explanations, the prosecutors might well have prevailed *despite* such evidence.

Consider the data Justice Breyer cites to in his concurrence, supra. The single most striking thing is that the parties are discriminating in mirror image ways. In one study, in 317 capital trials in Philadelphia between 1981 and 1997, prosecutors struck 51 percent of black jurors and 26 percent of nonblack jurors; defense counsel struck 26 percent of black jurors and 54 percent of nonblack jurors; in another, 71 percent of excused black jurors were removed by the prosecution; 81 percent of excused white jurors were removed by the defense; and in yet another, in a D.C. murder case spanning four trials, prosecutors excused 41 blacks or other minorities and 6 whites; defense counsel struck 29 whites and 13 black venire members. If entering into voir dire both black and whites have about an equal chance of being stricken "because of their color," then how is a member of either race being discriminated against? What about the correlates of race such as education, social standing, income, and the like? How can one sort these out in the causal chain from a racial animus? One answer may be that, in cases such as *Miller-El*, those other variables seemed to be applied only with respect to one race but not others, but how can one even know that? Any particular variable will be in almost infinitely complex relationships with a large number of other variables, and their interaction may be the cause of any particular outcome.

This leads us (and the Court) back to the basic issue: How does one prove discrimination in a particular case? *Batson* was designed to free defendants (and, after *McCollum*, prosecutors as well) from the necessity of conducting sophisticated statistical studies to identify patterns of discriminatory behavior. The *Batson* Court apparently believed that discrimination could be proved simply by examining the facts of a particular case. *Miller-El* (together with its predecessors, *Hernandez* and *Purkett*) demonstrates, however, that such fact-based inquiry is destined to be meaningless without context — the very kind of context provided by statistical studies. Absent the statistical studies, the Court is forced to rely on "statistics-lite" (some raw numbers, a little history) as a weak substitute.

Two post-*Miller-El* decisions reveal the kind of judicial confusion that can result whenever such "statistics-lite" are absent, or when context is similarly lacking. In Rice v. Collins, 546 U.S. 333 (2006), a unanimous Court overturned the Ninth Circuit's decision to find a *Batson* violation on habeas review. The Ninth Circuit's ruling was based on its rejection of the race-neutral reasons offered by the prosecutor for striking a prospective juror. Those reasons (which had been accepted by all previous state and federal courts to review the case) included that the prospective juror was young, single, lacked ties to the community, and had "rolled her eyes" in response to a voir dire question. The Court explained: "The panel majority's attempt to use a set of debatable inferences to set aside the conclusion reached by the state court does not satisfy [the] requirements for granting a writ of habeas corpus." Id., at 342. In a separate concurrence, Justice Breyer, joined by Justice Souter, reiterated his view (first expressed in *Miller-El II*) that *Batson* itself might need to be revisited, and peremptory challenges might need to be abolished, because of the "unresolvable tension between, on the one hand, what Blackstone called an inherently 'arbitrary and capricious' peremptory challenge system, . . . and, on the other hand, the Constitution's nondiscrimination command." Id., at 344 (Breyer, J., concurring).

The second case was Snyder v. Louisiana, 552 U.S. 472 (2008). There, the defendant complained about the peremptory strike of two black prospective jurors, Mr. Brooks and Ms. Scott. The Court noted that *Miller-El* "made it clear that in considering a *Batson* objection, or in reviewing a ruling claimed to be *Batson* error, all of the circumstances that bear upon the issue of racial animosity must be consulted. . . . Here, as just one example, if there were persisting doubts as to the outcome, a court would be required to consider the strike of Ms. Scott for the bearing it might have upon the strike of Mr. Brooks." But the Court ultimately ruled (by 7-2, with Justices Scalia and Thomas dissenting) that the strike of Mr. Brooks failed on its own, because it was based on an asserted rationale (the prosecutor's claim that Mr. Brooks was a student-teacher who might be "nervous" about the impact of a lengthy jury trial on his teaching job) that could equally have applied to numerous white prospective jurors who were not struck. The Court acknowledged that the trial judge, who had rejected the *Batson* challenge, usually would be in the best position to evaluate the credibility of the rationale proffered by the prosecutor, but explained that in the instant case, the trial judge made no findings on the record about Mr. Brooks's demeanor. Thus, the Court reversed Snyder's conviction.

In the end, can the *Batson/Miller-El* approach—well-intentioned though it may be—ever produce a truly satisfying conclusion about the existence (or non-existence) of discrimination in a particular case?

C. The Defendant's Trial Rights

1. The Right to Be Present, to Testify, to Obtain Evidence, and to Present a Defense

Although neither the Constitution nor any provision of the Bill of Rights says so explicitly, the Supreme Court has rendered a series of decisions essentially generalizing various specific rights into a right to present a defense. For example, in Illinois v. Allen, 397 U.S. 337 (1970), the Court concluded that a defendant has the right to be present during the trial. In *Allen*, the defendant argued with the trial judge "in a most abusive and disrespectful manner," used vile and abusive language, and engaged in disruptive behavior (including throwing papers on the floor). After being warned by the judge that another outburst would lead to his removal from the courtroom, Allen continued to behave badly. The judge ordered him removed, and the trial proceeded without him up to the conclusion of the prosecution's case. At that point, Allen agreed to settle down, and he was allowed to stay in the courtroom for the remainder of the trial. The Court held that "trial judges confronted with disruptive, contumacious, stubbornly defiant defendants must be given sufficient discretion to meet the circumstances of each case." Id., at 343. The Court cited with approval three possible remedies: (1) binding and gagging the unruly defendant, (2) holding him in contempt, and (3) removing him from the courtroom until he agrees to behave properly. The Court affirmed Allen's conviction, finding that the trial judge did not abuse his discretion. See also Holbrook v. Flynn, 475 U.S. 560 (1986), holding that due process was not violated when the defendant was surrounded for security purposes, in the courtroom, by numerous uniformed state troopers and other police officers. The *Flynn* Court distinguished strong police presence, which "need not be interpreted [by jurors] as a sign that [the defendant] is particularly dangerous or culpable," id., at 569, from the constitutionally disapproved practice of forcing a defendant to wear prison clothes before the jury, which serves as a "constant reminder of the accused's condition" and thus "may affect a juror's judgment," id., at 568, citing Estelle v. Williams, 425 U.S. 501 (1976).

The Court revisited the right to be present in Kentucky v. Stincer, 482 U.S. 730 (1987). There the defendant was excluded from a witness-competency hearing, held in the trial judge's chambers, for two young girls who were scheduled to testify against him on sodomy charges. The Court held that the right to be present, which is protected by the Due Process Clause, is limited to "any stage of the criminal proceeding that is critical to its outcome if [the defendant's] presence would contribute to the fairness of the procedure." Id., at 745. Because the girls would not give any substantive testimony at the hearing, but only would answer questions designed to determine their ability to testify factually and truthfully, and because the defendant "has given no indication that his presence . . . would have been useful in ensuring a more reliable determination as to whether the witnesses were competent to testify," the Court rejected the defendant's claim. Id., at 745-747.

The defendant not only has the right to be present at his trial, but also the right to take the stand and testify on his own behalf if he wants to. This was not always the rule. In Rock v. Arkansas, 483 U.S. 44 (1987), the Supreme Court referred to the "historic common-law view . . . that all parties to litigation, including criminal defendants, were disqualified from testifying because of their interest in the outcome of the trial." But in the modern world, said the Court, "there [i]s no rational justification for prohibiting the sworn testimony of the accused, who above all others may be in a position to meet the prosecution's case." Id. at 50.

In *Rock*, the Court found the right to testify to be implied by several constitutional provisions: (1) Due Process "fundamental fairness" includes not only the defendant's right to notice of the charges against him, but also the right "to be heard." (2) The Compulsory Process clause of the Sixth Amendment, which provides that an accused has the right to call "witnesses in his favor," implies the defendant's right to call himself as a witness. (3) The Fifth Amendment's guarantee against compelled self-incrimination—which protects the defendant's choice *not* to testify at trial—implies a corollary right to choose *to* testify. (4) The Sixth Amendment right of the accused to represent himself at trial, see Faretta v. California, 422 U.S. 806 (1975) (discussed in Chapter 3), includes the right "to present his own version of events in his own words." See *Rock*, 483 U.S. at 51-53.

The right to present a defense would seem to suggest a right to have access to evidence, although it is important not to overstate the scope of any such right. The Compulsory Process clause ensures that witnesses can be subpoenaed to appear at trial and testify for the defense, but it does not require witnesses to cooperate with the defense beforehand. A co-defendant may have information that is critical to the accused, but a defendant cannot compel the prosecutor to give a co-defendant immunity so that he can safely testify on the accused's behalf. As discussed in Chapter 12, the accused has a constitutional right to the disclosure of material exculpatory information within the prosecutor's control (the *Brady* doctrine), as well as rule-based rights to some pretrial discovery, but these rights are limited — for example, there is no right to receive *Brady* information during plea negotiations, and no right to obtain prosecution witness statements before trial. Such limits are not overcome by a defendant's generalized claim that he is entitled to evidence to support his defense.

Note also that a defendant's access to evidence may be undermined — often without legal recourse — by the government's behavior. Recall the discussion in Chapter 12 (at page 1209) of the *Youngblood* case, where the government failed to properly preserve physical evidence that could have exonerated the defendant of a child rape. The Court found no due process violation because the government did not act in bad faith when it destroyed the evidence. Modern DNA testing eventually led Arizona prosecutors to admit that Youngblood was completely innocent — after he had already spent many years behind bars for the crime. If trials are supposed to be a search for the truth, should defendants enjoy a more robust right of access to evidence? For more on the subject of criminal trials and factual accuracy, see Section F., infra, at page 1458.

Two significant differences between criminal trials and civil trials are that (1) criminal defendants cannot be called to the stand by the government, see Griffin v. California, 380 U.S. 609 (1965), discussed below; and (2) discovery rights are more limited in criminal cases, as discussed in Chapter 12. This creates the possibility, or at least fear, that defendants will try to manipulate matters either by not disclosing information and then surprising the government at trial, or by tailoring their testimony to that of the other witnesses in the case. This, in turn, has led to a number of efforts to limit their ability to do so. Based on concern about perjured testimony, Georgia law forbad a defendant's lawyer from guiding the defendant on direct examination, which the Court struck down as violating the right to counsel. Ferguson v. Georgia, 365 U.S. 570 (1961). Tennessee required that a defendant testify before any other defense witnesses are called, out of a concern that the defendant would tailor the testimony in light of the testimony of the other witness. Finding that such a requirement violated both the defendant's right to remain silent (he had to choose whether to testify at an inopportune time) and the right to counsel (the decision had to be made without counsel having full knowledge of the evidence), the Court struck down the statute in Brooks v. Tennessee, 406 U.S. 605 (1972).

Efforts to restrict defense proffers have met similar fates. In Holmes v. South Carolina, 547 U.S. 319 (2006), the defendant was precluded from introducing evidence that another man possibly had committed the crime with which he was charged. The exclusion was based on an odd South Carolina rule stating that evidence of third-party guilt is admissible only if it raises a "reasonable inference" of the defendant's innocence. The South Carolina Supreme Court held that such an inference could not be raised in the instant case because the prosecution's evidence of Holmes's guilt was strong; the court therefore did not even consider the probative value of Holmes's proffered third-party-guilt evidence in making its admissibility decision. The U.S. Supreme Court unanimously reversed. In an opinion by Justice Alito, the Court held that the South Carolina rule was "arbitrary" and "does not rationally serve the end" of excluding non-probative evidence. Therefore, the rule denied Holmes his right to "a meaningful opportunity to present a complete defense." Id., at 331. In Rock v. Arkansas, mentioned above, a per se exclusion of the defendant's hypnotically refreshed testimony was held to violate the due process rights to be heard and to offer testimony, Sixth Amendment right to compulsory process, and Fifth Amendment Self-Incrimination Clause, under which the defendant's "opportunity to testify is a necessary corollary to the . . . guarantee against compelled testimony."

One should not conclude that the state is powerless to enforce reasonable rules governing evidence, however. In Taylor v. Illinois, 484 U.S. 400 (1988), discussed in Chapter 12, the Court upheld the refusal to allow a witness to testify as a sanction for the defendant having failed to identify the witness in a pretrial discovery request. In United States v. Nobles, 422 U.S. 225 (1975), the exclusion of a defense expert was upheld where the defense refused to disclose his report, and in Michigan v. Lucas, 500 U.S. 145 (1991), the Court concluded that the Constitution did not necessarily forbid exclusion as a sanction for failure to put the government on notice of the defendant's intent to introduce past sexual behavior of a rape complainant, as required by state law.

As the holdings discussed above suggest, there is almost an infinite variety of ways that evidentiary proffers can raise constitutional questions. The best generalization is that the probability of upholding a state's exclusion of evidence as a sanction for a defendant's failure to abide by procedural requirements increases as the evidence gets further away from the defendant and as the defendant's (or lawyer's) behavior is increasingly obstreperous.

There is one other evidentiary matter that has systematically caused difficulties, and that is whether juries should be precluded from drawing certain inferences, and the associated question whether the government should be precluded from arguing those inferences in closing. In *Griffin*, supra, the prosecutor, at closing, made several disparaging comments to the jury about the fact that the defendant had failed to take the stand to explain his presence in the alley where the murder victim's body was found. The trial judge's instructions lent support to the prosecutor's comments, stating that "if [the defendant] does not testify . . . the jury may take that failure into consideration as tending to indicate . . . that among the inferences that may be reasonably drawn therefrom those unfavorable to the defendant are the more probable." 380 U.S. at 610. The Court held that any such comment on the defendant's silence, by either the prosecutor or the judge, violates the Self-Incrimination Clause of the Fifth Amendment because "[i]t is a penalty imposed by courts for exercising a constitutional privilege." Id., at 614. The Court acknowledged that juries might draw negative inferences from a defendant's silence at trial, even without improper comments, but nevertheless found it unacceptable for the trial judge to "solemnize[] the silence of the accused into evidence against him." Id. See also Carter v. Kentucky, 450 U.S. 288 (1981) (holding that the trial judge must, upon the defendant's request, instruct the jury not to draw any adverse inferences from the defendant's silence).

Following *Griffin*, the Court used similar reasoning to invalidate other practices that imposed burdens on the defendants' constitutional rights. For example, in United States v. Jackson, 390 U.S. 570 (1968), the Federal Kidnapping Act provided for the possibility of a death sentence for defendants who were convicted at a jury trial, but only a maximum sentence of life imprisonment for defendants who pleaded guilty or were convicted in a bench trial. The Court, citing *Griffin*, found that the statute "needlessly encouraged" waivers of the constitutional rights to jury trial and to remain silent, and therefore invalidated the death-penalty provision contained in the statute. In Doyle v. Ohio, 426 U.S. 610 (1976), the Court relied on *Griffin* to hold that a defendant's post-arrest silence, after receiving *Miranda* warnings, cannot be used against the defendant in the prosecution's case-in-chief at trial.

The *Griffin* doctrine has come under significant pressure. In Mitchell v. United States, 526 U.S. 314 (1999), the defendant pleaded guilty to several drug crimes, but reserved the right to contest the amount of the drugs attributable to her. At the sentencing hearing, the trial judge found, based on the testimony of several witnesses, that the defendant had sold enough cocaine to qualify for a ten-year mandatory minimum sentence. The judge told the defendant, "I held it against you that you didn't come forward today and tell me that you really only did this a couple of times. . . . I'm taking the position that you should come forward and explain your side of this issue." Id., at 319. The Court held that such use of the defendant's silence, at sentencing, violates the Fifth Amendment under *Griffin*. But Justice Scalia, in a strongly worded dissent joined by three other justices, argued that *Griffin* was unsupportable by logic or history:

> The illogic of the *Griffin* line is plain, for it runs exactly counter to normal evidentiary inferences: If I ask my son whether he saw a movie I had forbidden him to watch, and he remains silent, the import of his silence is clear. . . . And as for history, *Griffin's* pedigree is equally dubious. . . . [T]he text and history of the Fifth Amendment give no indication that there is a federal *constitutional* prohibition on the use of the defendant's silence as demeanor evidence. . . . To my mind, *Griffin* was a wrong turn—which is not cause enough to overrule it, but is cause enough to resist its extension.

Id., at 332, 335-336 (Scalia, J., dissenting).

In Portuondo v. Agard, 529 U.S. 61 (2000), the court considered "whether it was constitutional for a prosecutor, in her summation, to call the jury's attention to the fact that the defendant had the opportunity to hear all other witnesses testify and to tailor his testimony accordingly." The Court concluded this did not violate the Constitution:

> Lacking any historical support for the constitutional rights that he asserts, respondent must rely entirely upon our opinion in *Griffin*. That case is a poor analogue, however, for several reasons. What we prohibited the prosecutor from urging the jury to do in *Griffin* was something *the jury is not permitted to do*. The defendant's right to hold the prosecution to proving its case without his assistance is not to be impaired by the jury's counting the defendant's silence at trial against him—and upon request the court must instruct the jury to that effect. See Carter v. Kentucky, 450 U.S. 288 (1981). It is reasonable enough to expect a jury to comply with that instruction since, as we observed in *Griffin*, the inference of guilt from silence is not always "natural or irresistible." 380 U.S., at 615. A defendant might refuse to testify simply out of fear that he will be made to look bad by clever counsel, or fear "that his prior convictions will prejudice the jury." Ibid. . . . By contrast, it *is* natural and irresistible for a jury, in evaluating the relative credibility of a defendant who testifies last, to have in mind and weigh in the balance the fact that he heard the testimony of all those who preceded him. It is one thing (as *Griffin* requires) for the jury to evaluate all the *other* evidence in the case without giving any effect to the defendant's refusal to testify; it is something else (and quite impossible) for the jury to evaluate the credibility of the defendant's testimony while blotting out from its mind the fact that before giving the

testimony the defendant had been sitting there listening to the other witnesses. Thus, the principle respondent asks us to adopt here differs from what we adopted in *Griffin* in one or the other of the following respects: It either prohibits inviting the jury to do what the jury is perfectly entitled to do; or it requires the jury to do what is practically impossible.

Second, *Griffin* prohibited comments that suggest a defendant's silence is "evidence of *guilt*." 380 U.S., at 615 (emphasis added). . . . The prosecutor's comments in this case, by contrast, concerned respondent's *credibility as a witness*, and were therefore in accord with our longstanding rule that when a defendant takes the stand, "his credibility may be impeached and his testimony assailed like that of any other witness." . . .

Respondent points to our opinion in Geders v. United States, 425 U.S. 80, 87-91 (1976), which held that the defendant must be treated differently from other witnesses insofar as sequestration orders are concerned, since sequestration for an extended period of time denies the Sixth Amendment right to counsel. With respect to issues of credibility, however, no such special treatment has been accorded. Jenkins v. Anderson, 447 U.S. 231 (1980), illustrates the point. There the prosecutor in a first-degree murder trial, during cross-examination and again in closing argument, attempted to impeach the defendant's claim of self-defense by suggesting that he would not have waited two weeks to report the killing if that was what had occurred. In an argument strikingly similar to the one presented here, the defendant in *Jenkins* claimed that commenting on his prearrest silence violated his Fifth Amendment privilege against self-incrimination because "a person facing arrest will not remain silent if his failure to speak later can be used to impeach him." Id., at 236. The Court noted that it was not clear whether the Fifth Amendment protects prearrest silence, id., at 236, n. 2, but held that, *assuming it does*, the prosecutor's comments were constitutionally permissible. "[T]he Constitution does not forbid 'every government-imposed choice in the criminal process that has the effect of discouraging the exercise of constitutional rights.'" Id., at 236. . . . Once a defendant takes the stand, he is "subject to cross-examination impeaching his credibility just like any other witness." *Jenkins*, 447 U.S., at 235-236. . . .

Agard, 529 U.S., at 67-70.

Justice Ginsburg, in dissent, argued that

> The Court today transforms a defendant's presence at trial from a Sixth Amendment right into an automatic burden on his credibility. . . .
>
> The burden today's decision imposes on the exercise of Sixth Amendment rights is justified, the Court maintains, because "the central function of the trial . . . is to discover the truth." . . . A trial ideally is a search for the truth, but I do not agree that the Court's decision advances that search. The generic accusation that today's decision permits the prosecutor to make on summation does not serve to distinguish guilty defendants from innocent ones. Every criminal defendant, guilty or not, has the [Sixth Amendment] right to attend his trial. . . . Indeed, as the Court grants, . . . New York law *requires* defendants to be present when tried. It follows that every defendant who testifies is equally susceptible to a generic accusation about his opportunity for tailoring. The prosecutorial comment at issue, tied only to the defendant's presence in the courtroom and not to his actual testimony, tarnishes the innocent no less than the guilty.

529 U.S., at 76, 77-78.

Agard, decided just one year after *Mitchell*, reaffirmed *Griffin*—but refused to extend it to bar prosecutorial comment on the defendant's choice to testify last at trial. Why the refusal? Notice that there has always been a latent ambiguity in *Griffin*: Is *Griffin* based on the idea that the inference of guilt from the defendant's silence is unfair because there exist other *equally likely* reasons (i.e., other than guilt) for a defendant to remain silent at trial? Or is the inference improper *even if it accurately reflects the most likely reason* for the defendant to remain silent? Under the first interpretation, only empirically unsupportable burdens on constitutional rights would be invalid, whereas under the second, all burdens would be invalid unless strictly necessary, whether or not they are based on empirically accurate assumptions. The potential scope of the *Griffin* doctrine, of course, is much broader under the second interpretation than under the first.

Does *Agard* suggest that the Court may now be edging toward adopting the narrower, first interpretation of *Griffin*? Is that not precisely why the Court refuses to extend *Griffin* to the situation presented in *Agard*—i.e., because the inference in *Agard* is empirically supportable and therefore not "unfair"?

The approach taken by the Court in *Agard* leads to the following provocative question: If a prosecutor promises a defendant that prior convictions will not be introduced against him, can the prosecutor then comment on the defendant's silence at trial—because, having eliminated the most likely non-guilt reason for the defendant's silence, such adverse comment will no longer be "unfair"?

2.   The Confrontation Clause

There are three major lines of Supreme Court decisions dealing with the Confrontation Clause ("in all criminal prosecutions, the accused shall enjoy the right . . . to be confronted with the witnesses against him"). The first involves the specific procedures that must be followed when a witness testifies at trial. The second involves the admission, at trial, of prior statements of witnesses who do not testify at trial and thus are not subject to confrontation and cross-examination. The third involves the special problems posed by the admission, at a joint trial, of prior statements by non-testifying codefendants.

With respect to in-court procedures, Maryland v. Craig, 497 U.S. 836 (1990), and Coy v. Iowa, 487 U.S. 1012 (1988), together stand for the proposition that "a defendant's right to confront accusatory witnesses may be satisfied absent a physical, face-to-face confrontation at trial only where denial of such confrontation is necessary to further an important public policy and only where the reliability of the testimony is otherwise assured," *Craig*, 497 U.S., at 850. Thus, in *Coy*, where a child witness testified from behind a screen and no necessity for this particular procedure was shown, the right of confrontation was violated; but in *Craig*, where a child witness testified on closed-circuit television after a showing of necessity, the right was not violated.

The next two sections address the second and third line of cases on the confrontation clause: the admission of prior statements generally, and the admission of a codefendant's prior statements in a joint trial.

a.   The Crawford *Revolution*

With respect to the general issue of prior statements, the Supreme Court has signaled a major change from its previous approach, as represented by cases such as

White v. Illinois, 502 U.S. 346 (1992); Idaho v. Wright, 497 U.S. 805 (1990); Bourjaily v. United States, 483 U.S. 171 (1987); Lee v. Illinois, 476 U.S. 530 (1986); United States v. Inadi, 475 U.S. 387 (1986); and Ohio v. Roberts, 448 U.S. 56 (1980). The previous rule, as outlined in *Roberts*, was that a prior statement of a witness who did not testify at trial (and therefore was not subject to cross-examination by the defendant) nevertheless could be introduced at trial if (1) the witness was "unavailable" to testify at trial, and (2) the prior statement bore adequate "indicia of reliability" to substitute for the missing cross-examination. *Roberts*, 448 U.S., at 66. Such reliability, in turn, could be inferred if (1) the prior statement fell within a "firmly rooted" hearsay exception, such as spontaneous declarations or statements made in the course of receiving medical care, see *White*, 502 U.S., at 355, n. 8, or coconspirator statements, see *Bourjaily*, 483 U.S., at 183, or if (2) the prior statement was supported by "particularized guarantees of trustworthiness," see *Roberts*, 448 U.S., at 66. *Inadi* and *White* later softened the "unavailability" requirement by holding it inapplicable to at least some out-of-court prior statements, such as excited utterances, that would tend to be even more probative than similar statements made by the same witness in court. See *White*, 502 U.S., at 356.

The approach of *Roberts*, and the entire line of cases following it, was squarely rejected by the Court in the following case:

CRAWFORD v. WASHINGTON

Certiorari to the Supreme Court of Washington
541 U.S. 36 (2004)

Petitioner Michael Crawford stabbed a man who allegedly tried to rape his wife, Sylvia. At his trial, the State played for the jury Sylvia's tape-recorded statement to the police describing the stabbing, even though he had no opportunity for cross-examination. The Washington Supreme Court upheld petitioner's conviction after determining that Sylvia's statement was reliable. The question presented is whether this procedure complied with the Sixth Amendment's guarantee that, "[i]n all criminal prosecutions, the accused shall enjoy the right . . . to be confronted with the witnesses against him."

I

On August 5, 1999, Kenneth Lee was stabbed at his apartment. Police arrested petitioner later that night. After giving petitioner and his wife *Miranda* warnings, detectives interrogated each of them twice. Petitioner eventually confessed that he and Sylvia had gone in search of Lee because he was upset over an earlier incident in which Lee had tried to rape her. The two had found Lee at his apartment, and a fight ensued in which Lee was stabbed in the torso and petitioner's hand was cut. Petitioner gave the following account of the fight:

> Q. Okay. Did you ever see anything in [Lee's] hands?
> A. I think so, but I'm not positive.
> Q. Okay, when you think so, what do you mean by that?
> A. I coulda swore I seen him goin' for somethin' before, right before everything happened. He was like reachin', fiddlin' around down here and stuff . . . and I just

> . . . I don't know, I think, this is just a possibility, but I think, I think that he pulled somethin' out and I grabbed for it and that's how I got cut . . . but I'm not positive. I, I, my mind goes blank when things like this happen. I mean, I just, I remember things wrong, I remember things that just doesn't, don't make sense to me later.

App. 155 (punctuation added).

Sylvia generally corroborated petitioner's story about the events leading up to the fight, but her account of the fight itself was arguably different—particularly with respect to whether Lee had drawn a weapon before petitioner assaulted him:

> Q. Did Kenny do anything to fight back from this assault?
> A. (pausing) I know he reached into his pocket . . . or somethin' . . . I don't know what.
> Q. After he was stabbed?
> A. He saw Michael coming up. He lifted his hand . . . his chest open, he might [have] went to go strike his hand out or something and then (inaudible).
> Q. Okay, you, you gotta speak up.
> A. Okay, he lifted his hand over his head maybe to strike Michael's hand down or something and then he put his hands in his . . . put his right hand in his right pocket . . . took a step back . . . Michael proceeded to stab him . . . then his hands were like . . . how do you explain this . . . open arms . . . with his hands open and he fell down . . . and we ran (describing subject holding hands open, palms toward assailant).
> Q. Okay, when he's standing there with his open hands, you're talking about Kenny, correct?
> A. Yeah, after, after the fact, yes.
> Q. Did you see anything in his hands at that point?
> A. (pausing) um um (no).

Id., at 137 (punctuation added).

The State charged petitioner with assault and attempted murder. At trial, he claimed self-defense. Sylvia did not testify because of the state marital privilege, which generally bars a spouse from testifying without the other spouse's consent. See Wash. Rev. Code §5.60.060(1) (1994). In Washington, this privilege does not extend to a spouse's out-of-court statements admissible under a hearsay exception, . . . so the State sought to introduce Sylvia's tape-recorded statements to the police as evidence that the stabbing was not in self-defense. Noting that Sylvia had admitted she led petitioner to Lee's apartment and thus had facilitated the assault, the State invoked the hearsay exception for statements against penal interest, Wash. Rule Evid. 804(b)(3) (2003). . . .

[Petitioner objected on Confrontation Clause grounds, but the trial court admitted Sylvia's statement pursuant to Ohio v. Roberts, 448 U.S. 56 (1980), on the grounds that (1) the wife was "unavailable" (due to the defendant's invocation of the spousal privilege), and (2) the prior statement bore "particularized guarantees of trustworthiness," specifically, it interlocked in several respects with the defendant's own statements. Petitioner was convicted of assault. — EDS.]

II

The Sixth Amendment's Confrontation Clause provides that, "[i]n all criminal prosecutions, the accused shall enjoy the right . . . to be confronted with the witnesses against him." We have held that this bedrock procedural guarantee applies to both federal and state prosecutions. Pointer v. Texas, 380 U.S. 400, 406 (1965). As noted above, *Roberts* says that an unavailable witness's out-of-court statement may be admitted so long as it has adequate indicia of reliability—i.e., falls within a "firmly rooted hearsay exception" or bears "particularized guarantees of trustworthiness." 448 U.S., at 66. Petitioner argues that this test strays from the original meaning of the Confrontation Clause and urges us to reconsider it.

[Here, Justice Scalia reviewed the original intent behind the Confrontation Clause, and the relation between the Clause and the common law of hearsay.—EDS.]

III

This history supports two inferences about the meaning of the Sixth Amendment.

A

First, the principal evil at which the Confrontation Clause was directed was the civil-law mode of criminal procedure, and particularly its use of ex parte examinations as evidence against the accused. . . . The Sixth Amendment must be interpreted with this focus in mind.

Accordingly, we once again reject the view that the Confrontation Clause applies of its own force only to in-court testimony. . . . Leaving the regulation of out-of-court statements to the law of evidence would render the Confrontation Clause powerless to prevent even the most flagrant inquisitorial practices. . . . This focus also suggests that not all hearsay implicates the Sixth Amendment's core concerns. An off-hand, overheard remark might be unreliable evidence and thus a good candidate for exclusion under hearsay rules, but it bears little resemblance to the civil-law abuses the Confrontation Clause targeted. On the other hand, ex parte examinations might sometimes be admissible under modern hearsay rules, but the Framers certainly would not have condoned them.

The text of the Confrontation Clause reflects this focus. It applies to "witnesses" against the accused—in other words, those who "bear testimony." 1 N. Webster, An American Dictionary of the English Language (1828). "Testimony," in turn, is typically "[a] solemn declaration or affirmation made for the purpose of establishing or proving some fact." Ibid. An accuser who makes a formal statement to government officers bears testimony in a sense that a person who makes a casual remark to an acquaintance does not. The constitutional text, like the history underlying the common-law right of confrontation, thus reflects an especially acute concern with a specific type of out-of-court statement.

Various formulations of this core class of "testimonial" statements exist: "ex parte in-court testimony or its functional equivalent—that is, material such as affidavits, custodial examinations, prior testimony that the defendant was unable to cross-examine, or similar pretrial statements that declarants would reasonably expect to be used prosecutorially," Brief for Petitioner 23; "extrajudicial statements . . . contained in formalized testimonial materials, such as affidavits, depositions, prior testimony, or confessions," White v. Illinois, 502 U.S. 346, 365 (1992) (Thomas, J., joined by Scalia, J., concurring in part and concurring in judgment); "statements that were made under circumstances which would lead an objective witness reasonably to believe that the statement would be available for use at a later trial," Brief for

National Association of Criminal Defense Lawyers et al. as Amici Curiae 3. These formulations all share a common nucleus and then define the Clause's coverage at various levels of abstraction around it. Regardless of the precise articulation, some statements qualify under any definition—for example, ex parte testimony at a preliminary hearing.

Statements taken by police officers in the course of interrogations are also testimonial under even a narrow standard. Police interrogations bear a striking resemblance to examinations by justices of the peace in England. The statements are not *sworn* testimony, but the absence of oath was not dispositive. . . .

That interrogators are police officers rather than magistrates does not change the picture either. Justices of the peace conducting examinations under the Marian statutes were not magistrates as we understand that office today, but had an essentially investigative and prosecutorial function. See 1 Stephen, Criminal Law of England, at 221; Langbein, Prosecuting Crime in the Renaissance, at 34-45. England did not have a professional police force until the 19th century, see 1 Stephen, supra, at 194-200, so it is not surprising that other government officers performed the investigative functions now associated primarily with the police. The involvement of government officers in the production of testimonial evidence presents the same risk, whether the officers are police or justices of the peace.

In sum, even if the Sixth Amendment is not solely concerned with testimonial hearsay, that is its primary object, and interrogations by law enforcement officers fall squarely within that class.[4]

B

The historical record also supports a second proposition: that the Framers would not have allowed admission of testimonial statements of a witness who did not appear at trial unless he was unavailable to testify, and the defendant had had a prior opportunity for cross-examination. The text of the Sixth Amendment does not suggest any open-ended exceptions from the confrontation requirement to be developed by the courts. Rather, the "right . . . to be confronted with the witnesses against him," Amdt. 6, is most naturally read as a reference to the right of confrontation at common law, admitting only those exceptions established at the time of the founding. See Mattox v. United States, 156 U.S. 237, 243 (1895). . . .

[T]he common law in 1791 conditioned admissibility of an absent witness's examination on unavailability and a prior opportunity to cross-examine. The Sixth Amendment therefore incorporates those limitations. The numerous early state decisions applying the same test confirm that these principles were received as part of the common law in this country.

We do not read the historical sources to say that a prior opportunity to cross-examine was merely a sufficient, rather than a necessary, condition for admissibility of testimonial statements. They suggest that this requirement was dispositive, and not merely one of several ways to establish reliability. This is not to deny . . . that

4. We use the term "interrogation" in its colloquial, rather than any technical legal, sense. Cf. Rhode Island v. Innis, 446 U.S. 291, 300-301 (1980). Just as various definitions of "testimonial" exist, one can imagine various definitions of "interrogation," and we need not select among them in this case. Sylvia's recorded statement, knowingly given in response to structured police questioning, qualifies under any conceivable definition.

"[t]here were always exceptions to the general rule of exclusion" of hearsay evidence. Several had become well established by 1791. See 3 Wigmore §1397, at 101; Brief for United States as Amicus Curiae 13, n. 5. But there is scant evidence that exceptions were invoked to admit *testimonial* statements against the accused in a *criminal* case.[6] Most of the hearsay exceptions covered statements that by their nature were not testimonial—for example, business records or statements in furtherance of a conspiracy. We do not infer from these that the Framers thought exceptions would apply even to prior testimony. Cf. Lilly v. Virginia, 527 U.S. 116, 134 (1999) (plurality opinion) ("[A]ccomplices' confessions that inculpate a criminal defendant are not within a firmly rooted exception to the hearsay rule").

IV

Our case law has been largely consistent with these two principles. . . .

[Here, Justice Scalia reviewed the case law back to the late 1800s, to show that the results in the cases generally conformed to the two historical principles described above. He noted only one exception: White v. Illinois, 502 U.S. 346 (1992), in which the Court approved the admission, under the "spontaneous declaration" hearsay exception, of prior statements by a child victim to an investigating police officer. He described *White* as being "arguably in tension with the rule requiring a prior opportunity for cross-examination when the proffered statement is testimonial."—EDS.]

Our cases have thus remained faithful to the Framers' understanding: Testimonial statements of witnesses absent from trial have been admitted only where the declarant is unavailable, and only where the defendant has had a prior opportunity to cross-examine.[9]

V

Although the results of our decisions have generally been faithful to the original meaning of the Confrontation Clause, the same cannot be said of our rationales. *Roberts* conditions the admissibility of all hearsay evidence on whether it falls under a "firmly rooted hearsay exception" or bears "particularized guarantees of trustworthiness." 448 U.S., at 66. This test departs from the historical principles identified above in two respects. First, it is too broad: It applies the same mode of analysis whether or not the hearsay consists of ex parte testimony. This often results in close constitutional scrutiny in cases that are far removed from the core concerns of the

---

6. The one deviation we have found involves dying declarations. The existence of that exception as a general rule of criminal hearsay law cannot be disputed. See, e.g., Mattox v. United States, 156 U.S. 237, 243-244 (1895); King v. Reason, 16 How. St. Tr. 1, 24-38 (K.B. 1722). . . . Although many dying declarations may not be testimonial, there is authority for admitting even those that clearly are. . . . We need not decide in this case whether the Sixth Amendment incorporates an exception for testimonial dying declarations. If this exception must be accepted on historical grounds, it is sui generis.

9. . . . [W]e reiterate that, when the declarant appears for cross-examination at trial, the Confrontation Clause places no constraints at all on the use of his prior testimonial statements. See California v. Green, 399 U.S. 149, 162 (1970). It is therefore irrelevant that the reliability of some out-of-court statements "'cannot be replicated, even if the declarant testifies to the same matters in court.'" . . . (quoting United States v. Inadi, 475 U.S. 387, 395 (1986)). The Clause does not bar admission of a statement so long as the declarant is present at trial to defend or explain it. (The Clause also does not bar the use of testimonial statements for purposes other than establishing the truth of the matter asserted. See Tennessee v. Street, 471 U.S. 409, 414 (1985).)

Clause. At the same time, however, the test is too narrow: It admits statements that *do* consist of ex parte testimony upon a mere finding of reliability. This malleable standard often fails to protect against paradigmatic confrontation violations. . . .

A

Where testimonial statements are involved, we do not think the Framers meant to leave the Sixth Amendment's protection to the vagaries of the rules of evidence, much less to amorphous notions of "reliability." Certainly none of the authorities discussed above acknowledges any general reliability exception to the common-law rule. Admitting statements deemed reliable by a judge is fundamentally at odds with the right of confrontation. To be sure, the Clause's ultimate goal is to ensure reliability of evidence, but it is a procedural rather than a substantive guarantee. It commands, not that evidence be reliable, but that reliability be assessed in a particular manner: by testing in the crucible of cross-examination. The Clause thus reflects a judgment, not only about the desirability of reliable evidence (a point on which there could be little dissent), but about how reliability can best be determined. Cf. 3 Blackstone, Commentaries, at 373 ("This open examination of witnesses . . . is much more conducive to the clearing up of truth"); M. Hale, History and Analysis of the Common Law of England 258 (1713) (adversarial testing "beats and bolts out the Truth much better").

The *Roberts* test allows a jury to hear evidence, untested by the adversary process, based on a mere judicial determination of reliability. It thus replaces the constitutionally prescribed method of assessing reliability with a wholly foreign one. . . .

Dispensing with confrontation because testimony is obviously reliable is akin to dispensing with jury trial because a defendant is obviously guilty. This is not what the Sixth Amendment prescribes.

B

The legacy of *Roberts* in other courts vindicates the Framers' wisdom in rejecting a general reliability exception. The framework is so unpredictable that it fails to provide meaningful protection from even core confrontation violations.

Reliability is an amorphous, if not entirely subjective, concept. There are countless factors bearing on whether a statement is reliable; the nine-factor balancing test applied by the Court of Appeals below is representative. . . . Whether a statement is deemed reliable depends heavily on which factors the judge considers and how much weight he accords each of them. Some courts wind up attaching the same significance to opposite facts. For example, . . . [t]he Virginia Court of Appeals found a statement more reliable because the witness was in custody and charged with a crime (thus making the statement more obviously against her penal interest), see Nowlin v. Commonwealth, 40 Va. App. 327, 335-338, 579 S.E.2d 367, 371-372 (2003), while the Wisconsin Court of Appeals found a statement more reliable because the witness was *not* in custody and *not* a suspect, see State v. Bintz, 2002 WI App. 204, P13, 257 Wis. 2d 177, 187, 650 N.W.2d 913, 918. . . .

The unpardonable vice of the *Roberts* test, however, is not its unpredictability, but its demonstrated capacity to admit core testimonial statements that the Confrontation Clause plainly meant to exclude. Despite the plurality's speculation in *Lilly*, 527 U.S., at 137, that it was "highly unlikely" that accomplice confessions implicating the accused could survive *Roberts*, courts continue routinely to admit them. . . . One recent study found that, after *Lilly*, appellate courts admitted accomplice statements to the authorities in 25 out of 70 cases—more than one-third of the time. Kirst, Appellate Court Answers to the Confrontation Questions in Lilly v. Virginia, 53 Syracuse L. Rev. 87, 105 (2003). Courts have invoked *Roberts* to admit other sorts of plainly testimonial statements despite the absence of any opportunity to cross-examine. See United States v. Aguilar, 295 F.3d 1018, 1021-1023 (CA9 2002) (plea allocution showing existence of a conspiracy); United States v. Papajohn, 212 F.3d 1112, 1118-1120 (CA8 2000) (grand jury testimony); *Bintz*, supra, PP15-22, 257 Wis. 2d, at 188-191, 650 N.W. 2d, at 918-920 (prior trial testimony).

To add insult to injury, some of the courts that admit untested testimonial statements find reliability in the very factors that *make* the statements testimonial. As noted earlier, one court relied on the fact that the witness's statement was made to police while in custody on pending charges—the theory being that this made the statement more clearly against penal interest and thus more reliable. *Nowlin*, supra, at 335-338, 579 S.E.2d, at 371-372. Other courts routinely rely on the fact that a prior statement is given under oath in judicial proceedings. . . . That inculpating statements are given in a testimonial setting is not an antidote to the confrontation problem, but rather the trigger that makes the Clause's demands most urgent. It is not enough to point out that most of the usual safeguards of the adversary process attend the statement, when the single safeguard missing is the one the Confrontation Clause demands.

C

Roberts' failings were on full display in the proceedings below. Sylvia Crawford made her statement while in police custody, herself a potential suspect in the case. Indeed, she had been told that whether she would be released "depend[ed] on how the investigation continues." App. 81. In response to often leading questions from police detectives, she implicated her husband in Lee's stabbing and at least arguably undermined his self-defense claim. Despite all this, the trial court admitted her statement, listing several reasons why it was reliable. In its opinion reversing, the Court of Appeals listed several *other* reasons why the statement was *not* reliable. Finally, the State Supreme Court relied exclusively on the interlocking character of the statement and disregarded every other factor the lower courts had considered. The case is thus a self-contained demonstration of *Roberts*' unpredictable and inconsistent application.

Each of the courts also made assumptions that cross-examination might well have undermined. . . . We readily concede that we could resolve this case by simply reweighing the "reliability factors" under *Roberts* and finding that Sylvia Crawford's statement falls short. But we view this as one of those rare cases in which the result below is so improbable that it reveals a fundamental failure on our part to interpret the Constitution in a way that secures its intended constraint on judicial discretion. Moreover, to reverse the Washington Supreme Court's decision after conducting our own reliability analysis would perpetuate, not avoid, what the Sixth Amendment condemns. The Constitution prescribes a procedure for determining the reliability of testimony in criminal trials, and we, no less than the state courts, lack authority to replace it with one of our own devising.

We have no doubt that the courts below were acting in utmost good faith when they found reliability. The Framers, however, would not have been content to indulge this assumption. They knew that judges, like other government officers, could not always be trusted to safeguard the rights of the people. . . . They were loath to leave too much discretion in judicial hands. Cf. U.S. Const., Amdt. 6 (criminal jury trial); Amdt. 7 (civil jury trial); Ring v. Arizona, 536 U.S. 584, 611-612 (2002) (Scalia, J., concurring). By replacing categorical constitutional guarantees with open-ended balancing tests, we do violence to their design. Vague standards are manipulable, and, while that might be a small concern in run-of-the-mill assault prosecutions like this one, the Framers had an eye toward politically charged cases . . . —great state trials where the impartiality of even those at the highest levels of the judiciary might not be so clear. It is difficult to imagine *Roberts* providing any meaningful protection in those circumstances. . . .

Where nontestimonial hearsay is at issue, it is wholly consistent with the Framers' design to afford the States flexibility in their development of hearsay law—as does *Roberts*, and as would an approach that exempted such statements from Confrontation Clause scrutiny altogether. Where testimonial evidence is at issue, however, the Sixth Amendment demands what the common law required: unavailability and a prior opportunity for cross-examination. We leave for another day any effort to spell out a comprehensive definition of "testimonial."[10] Whatever else the term covers, it applies at a minimum to prior testimony at a preliminary hearing, before a grand jury, or at a former trial; and to police interrogations. These are the modern practices with closest kinship to the abuses at which the Confrontation Clause was directed. In this case, the State admitted Sylvia's testimonial statement against petitioner, despite the fact that he had no opportunity to cross-examine her. That alone is sufficient to make out a violation of the Sixth Amendment. *Roberts* notwithstanding, we decline to mine the record in search of indicia of reliability. Where testimonial statements are at issue, the only indicium of reliability sufficient to satisfy constitutional demands is the one the Constitution actually prescribes: confrontation.

The judgment of the Washington Supreme Court is reversed, and the case is remanded for further proceedings not inconsistent with this opinion.

[Chief Justice Rehnquist and Justice O'Connor concurred in the judgment, agreeing that the wife's statement should have been excluded, but finding that result to be properly dictated by *Roberts*, and expressing the view that adoption of a new approach "is not backed by sufficiently persuasive reasoning to overrule long-established precedent."]

Crawford, although subsequently held *not* to apply retroactively to convicted defendants whose criminal cases were already final, see Whorton v. Bockting, 549 U.S. 406 (2006), nevertheless impacted the world of criminal trials like a bombshell, not least because of the singular lack of guidance provided by Justice Scalia about the meaning of the crucial term, "testimony." Does the following followup case help?

---

10. We acknowledge the Chief Justice's objection, that our refusal to articulate a comprehensive definition in this case will cause interim uncertainty. But it can hardly be any worse than the status quo. . . . The difference is that the *Roberts* test is *inherently*, and therefore *permanently*, unpredictable.

DAVIS v. WASHINGTON

Certiorari to the Supreme Court of Washington
547 U.S. 813 (2006)

JUSTICE SCALIA delivered the opinion of the Court. These cases require us to determine when statements made to law enforcement personnel during a 911 call or at a crime scene are "testimonial" and thus subject to the requirements of the Sixth Amendment's Confrontation Clause.

I

A

The relevant statements in Davis v. Washington, No. 05-5224, were made to a 911 emergency operator on February 1, 2001. When the operator answered the initial call, the connection terminated before anyone spoke. She reversed the call, and Michelle McCottry answered. In the ensuing conversation, the operator ascertained that McCottry was involved in a domestic disturbance with her former boyfriend Adrian Davis, the petitioner in this case:

> 911 Operator: Hello.
> Complainant: Hello.
> 911 Operator: What's going on?
> Complainant: He's here jumpin' on me again.
> 911 Operator: Okay. Listen to me carefully. Are you in a house or an apartment?
> Complainant: I'm in a house.
> 911 Operator: Are there any weapons?
> Complainant: No. He's usin' his fists.
> 911 Operator: Okay. Has he been drinking?
> Complainant: No.
> 911 Operator: Okay, sweetie. I've got help started. Stay on the line with me, okay?
> Complainant: I'm on the line.
> 911 Operator: Listen to me carefully. Do you know his last name?
> Complainant: It's Davis.
> 911 Operator: Davis? Okay, what's his first name?
> Complainant: Adran.
> 911 Operator: What is it?
> Complainant: Adrian.
> 911 Operator: Adrian?
> Complainant: Yeah.
> 911 Operator: Okay. What's his middle initial?
> Complainant: Martell. He's runnin' now.

App. in No. 05-5224, pp. 8-9.

As the conversation continued, the operator learned that Davis had "just run out the door" after hitting McCottry, and that he was leaving in a car with someone else. McCottry started talking, but the operator cut her off, saying, "Stop talking and answer my questions." She then gathered more information about Davis (including his birthday) and learned that Davis had told McCottry that his purpose in coming to the house was "to get his stuff," since McCottry was moving. McCottry described the context of the assault, after which the operator told her that the police were on their way. "They're gonna check the area for him first," the operator said, "and then they're gonna come talk to you." Id., at 12-13.

The police arrived within four minutes of the 911 call and observed McCottry's shaken state, the "fresh injuries on her forearm and her face," and her "frantic efforts to gather her belongings and her children so that they could leave the residence." 154 Wash. 2d 291, 296, 111 P.3d 844, 847 (2005) (en banc).

The State charged Davis with felony violation of a domestic no-contact order. "The State's only witnesses were the two police officers who responded to the 911 call. Both officers testified that McCottry exhibited injuries that appeared to be recent, but neither officer could testify as to the cause of the injuries." Ibid. McCottry presumably could have testified as to whether Davis was her assailant, but she did not appear. Over Davis's objection, based on the Confrontation Clause of the Sixth Amendment, the trial court admitted the recording of her exchange with the 911 operator, and the jury convicted him. The Washington Court of Appeals affirmed, 116 Wash. App. 81, 64 P.3d 661 (2003). The Supreme Court of Washington, with one dissenting justice, also affirmed, concluding that the portion of the 911 conversation in which McCottry identified Davis was not testimonial, and that if other portions of the conversation were testimonial, admitting them was harmless beyond a reasonable doubt. 154 Wash. 2d, at 305, 111 P.3d, at 851. We granted certiorari.

B

In Hammon v. Indiana, No. 05-5705, police responded late on the night of February 26, 2003, to a "reported domestic disturbance" at the home of Hershel and Amy Hammon. 829 N.E.2d 444, 446 (Ind. 2005). They found Amy alone on the front porch, appearing "somewhat frightened," but she told them that "nothing was the matter," id., at 446, 447. She gave them permission to enter the house, where an officer saw "a gas heating unit in the corner of the living room" that had "flames coming out of the . . . partial glass front. There were pieces of glass on the ground in front of it and there was flame emitting from the front of the heating unit." App. in No. 05-5705, p. 16.

Hershel, meanwhile, was in the kitchen. He told the police "that he and his wife had 'been in an argument' but 'everything was fine now' and the argument 'never became physical.'" 829 N.E.2d, at 447. By this point Amy had come back inside. One of the officers remained with Hershel; the other went to the living room to talk with Amy, and "again asked [her] what had occurred." Ibid. Hershel made several attempts to participate in Amy's conversation with the police, but was rebuffed. The officer later testified that Hershel "became angry when I insisted that [he] stay separated from Mrs. Hammon so that we can investigate what had happened." After hearing Amy's account, the officer "had her fill out and sign a battery affidavit." Amy handwrote the following: "Broke our Furnace & shoved me down on the floor into the broken glass. Hit me in the chest and threw me down. Broke our lamps & phone. Tore up my van where I couldn't leave the house. Attacked my daughter." [App. in No. 05-5705,] at 2.

The State charged Hershel with domestic battery and with violating his probation. Amy was subpoenaed, but she did not appear at his subsequent bench trial. The State called the officer who had questioned Amy, and asked him to recount what Amy told him and to authenticate the affidavit. Hershel's counsel repeatedly objected to the admission of this evidence. At one point, after hearing the prosecutor defend the affidavit because it was made "under oath," defense counsel said, "That doesn't give us the opportunity to cross examine [the] person who allegedly drafted it. Makes me mad." Nonetheless, the trial court admitted the affidavit as a "present sense impression," and Amy's statements as "excited utterances" that "are expressly permitted in these kinds of cases even if the declarant is not available to testify." The officer thus testified that Amy

> informed me that she and Hershel had been in an argument. That he became irrate [*sic*] over the fact of their daughter going to a boyfriend's house. The argument became . . . physical after being verbal and she informed me that Mr. Hammon, during the verbal part of the argument was breaking things in the living room and I believe she stated he broke the phone, broke the lamp, broke the front of the heater. When it became physical he threw her down into the glass of the heater. . . .
>
> She informed me Mr. Hammon had pushed her onto the ground, had shoved her head into the broken glass of the heater and that he had punched her in the chest twice I believe.

Id., at 17-18.

The trial judge found Hershel guilty on both charges, and the Indiana Court of Appeals affirmed in relevant part, 809 N.E.2d 945 (2004). The Indiana Supreme Court also affirmed, concluding that Amy's statement was admissible for state-law purposes as an excited utterance, 829 N.E. 2d, at 449; that "a 'testimonial' statement is one given or taken in significant part for purposes of preserving it for potential future use in legal proceedings," where "the motivations of the questioner and declarant are the central concerns," id., at 456, 457; and that Amy's oral statement was not "testimonial" under these standards, id., at 458. It also concluded that, although the affidavit was testimonial and thus wrongly admitted, it was harmless beyond a reasonable doubt, largely because the trial was to the bench. Id., at 458-459. We granted certiorari.

II

The Confrontation Clause of the Sixth Amendment provides: "In all criminal prosecutions, the accused shall enjoy the right . . . to be confronted with the witnesses against him." In Crawford v. Washington, 541 U.S. 36, 53-54 (2004), we held that this provision bars "admission of testimonial statements of a witness who did not appear at trial unless he was unavailable to testify, and the defendant had had a prior opportunity for cross-examination." A critical portion of this holding, and the portion central to resolution of the two cases now before us, is the phrase "testimonial statements." Only statements of this sort cause the declarant to be a "witness" within the meaning of the Confrontation Clause. See id., at 51. It is the testimonial character of the statement that separates it from other hearsay that, while subject to traditional limitations upon hearsay evidence, is not subject to the Confrontation Clause.

Our opinion in *Crawford* set forth "various formulations" of the core class of "testimonial" statements, ibid., but found it unnecessary to endorse any of them, because "some statements qualify under any definition," id., at 52. Among those, we said, were "statements taken by police officers in the course of interrogations," ibid.; see also id., at 53. The questioning that generated the deponent's statement in *Crawford*—which was made and recorded while she was in police custody, after having been given *Miranda* warnings as a possible suspect herself—"qualifies under any conceivable definition" of an "interrogation," 541 U.S., at 53, n. 4. We therefore did not define that term, except to say that "we use [it] . . . in its colloquial, rather than any technical legal, sense," and that "one can imagine various definitions . . . , and we need not select among them in this case." Ibid. The character of the statements in the present cases is not as clear, and these cases require us to determine more precisely which police interrogations produce testimony.

Without attempting to produce an exhaustive classification of all conceivable statements—or even all conceivable statements in response to police interrogation—as either testimonial or nontestimonial, it suffices to decide the present cases to hold as follows: Statements are nontestimonial when made in the course of police interrogation under circumstances objectively indicating that the primary purpose of the interrogation is to enable police assistance to meet an ongoing emergency. They are testimonial when the circumstances objectively indicate that there is no such ongoing emergency, and that the primary purpose of the interrogation is to establish or prove past events potentially relevant to later criminal prosecution.[1]

III

A

In *Crawford*, it sufficed for resolution of the case before us to determine that "even if the Sixth Amendment is not solely concerned with testimonial hearsay, that is its primary object, and interrogations by law enforcement officers fall squarely within that class." Id., at 53. Moreover, as we have just described, the facts of that case spared us the need to define what we meant by "interrogations." The *Davis* case today does not permit us this luxury of indecision. The inquiries of a police operator in the course of a 911 call[2] are an interrogation in one sense, but not in a sense that "qualifies under any conceivable definition." We must decide, therefore, whether the Confrontation Clause applies only to testimonial hearsay; and, if so, whether the recording of a 911 call qualifies.

The answer to the first question was suggested in *Crawford*, even if not explicitly held:

---

1. Our holding refers to interrogations because, as explained below, the statements in the cases presently before us are the products of interrogations—which in some circumstances tend to generate testimonial responses. This is not to imply, however, that statements made in the absence of any interrogation are necessarily nontestimonial. The Framers were no more willing to exempt from cross-examination volunteered testimony or answers to open-ended questions than they were to exempt answers to detailed interrogation. (Part of the evidence against Sir Walter Raleigh was a letter from Lord Cobham that was plainly not the result of sustained questioning. Raleigh's Case, 2 How. St. Tr. 1, 27 (1603).) And of course even when interrogation exists, it is in the final analysis the declarant's statements, not the interrogator's questions, that the Confrontation Clause requires us to evaluate.

2. If 911 operators are not themselves law enforcement officers, they may at least be agents of law enforcement when they conduct interrogations of 911 callers. For purposes of this opinion (and without deciding the point), we consider their acts to be acts of the police. As in Crawford v. Washington, 541 U.S. 36 (2004), therefore, our holding today makes it unnecessary to consider whether and when statements made to someone other than law enforcement personnel are "testimonial."

> The text of the Confrontation Clause reflects this focus [on testimonial hearsay]. It applies to "witnesses" against the accused—in other words, those who "bear testimony." 1 N. Webster, An American Dictionary of the English Language (1828). "Testimony," in turn, is typically "a solemn declaration or affirmation made for the purpose of establishing or proving some fact." Ibid. An accuser who makes a formal statement to government officers bears testimony in a sense that a person who makes a casual remark to an acquaintance does not.

541 U.S., at 51.

A limitation so clearly reflected in the text of the constitutional provision must fairly be said to mark out not merely its "core," but its perimeter.

[Justice Scalia next cited numerous early and modern cases to show that the Confrontation Clause has—with one exception, White v. Illinois, 502 U.S. 346 (1992), discussed and implicitly criticized in *Crawford*—been applied by the Court only in cases that "clearly involve testimony."—EDS.]

Most of the American cases applying the Confrontation Clause or its state constitutional or common-law counterparts involved testimonial statements of the most formal sort—sworn testimony in prior judicial proceedings or formal depositions under oath—which invites the argument that the scope of the Clause is limited to that very formal category. But the English cases that were the progenitors of the Confrontation Clause did not limit the exclusionary rule to prior court testimony and formal depositions, see *Crawford*, supra, at 52, and n. 3. In any event, we do not think it conceivable that the protections of the Confrontation Clause can readily be evaded by having a note-taking policeman *recite* the unsworn hearsay testimony of the declarant, instead of having the declarant sign a deposition. Indeed, if there is one point for which no case—English or early American, state or federal—can be cited, that is it.

The question before us in *Davis*, then, is whether, objectively considered, the interrogation that took place in the course of the 911 call produced testimonial statements. When we said in *Crawford*, supra, at 53, that "interrogations by law enforcement officers fall squarely within [the] class" of testimonial hearsay, we had immediately in mind (for that was the case before us) interrogations solely directed at establishing the facts of a past crime, in order to identify (or provide evidence to convict) the perpetrator. The product of such interrogation, whether reduced to a writing signed by the declarant or embedded in the memory (and perhaps notes) of the interrogating officer, is testimonial. It is, in the terms of the 1828 American dictionary quoted in *Crawford*, "[a] solemn declaration or affirmation made for the purpose of establishing or proving some fact." 541 U.S., at 51. (The solemnity of even an oral declaration of relevant past fact to an investigating officer is well enough established by the severe consequences that can attend a deliberate falsehood. See, e.g., United States v. Stewart, 433 F.3d 273, 288 (CA2 2006) (false statements made to federal investigators violate 18 U.S.C. §1001); State v. Reed, 2005 WI 53, ¶30, 280 Wis. 2d 68, 695 N.W.2d 315, 323 (state criminal offense to "knowingly give false information to [an] officer with [the] intent to mislead the officer in the performance of his or her duty").) A 911 call, on the other hand, and at least the initial interrogation conducted in connection with a 911 call, is ordinarily not designed primarily to "establish or prove" some past fact, but to describe current circumstances requiring police assistance.

The difference between the interrogation in *Davis* and the one in *Crawford* is apparent on the face of things. In *Davis*, McCottry was speaking about events *as they were actually happening*, rather than "describing past events," Lilly v. Virginia, 527 U.S. 116, 137 (1999) (plurality opinion). Sylvia Crawford's interrogation, on the other hand, took place hours after the events she described had occurred. Moreover, any reasonable listener would recognize that McCottry (unlike Sylvia Crawford) was facing an ongoing emergency. Although one *might* call 911 to provide a narrative report of a crime absent any imminent danger, McCottry's call was plainly a call for help against bona fide physical threat. Third, the nature of what was asked and answered in *Davis*, again viewed objectively, was such that the elicited statements were necessary to be able to *resolve* the present emergency, rather than simply to learn (as in *Crawford*) what had happened in the past. That is true even of the operator's effort to establish the identity of the assailant, so that the dispatched officers might know whether they would be encountering a violent felon. See, e.g., Hiibel v. Sixth Judicial Dist. Court of Nev., Humboldt Cty., 542 U.S. 177, 186 (2004). And finally, the difference in the level of formality between the two interviews is striking. Crawford was responding calmly, at the station house, to a series of questions, with the officer-interrogator taping and making notes of her answers; McCottry's frantic answers were provided over the phone, in an environment that was not tranquil, or even (as far as any reasonable 911 operator could make out) safe.

We conclude from all this that the circumstances of McCottry's interrogation objectively indicate its primary purpose was to enable police assistance to meet an ongoing emergency. She simply was not acting as a *witness*; she was not *testifying*. What she said was not "a weaker substitute for live testimony" at trial, United States v. Inadi, 475 U.S. 387, 394 (1986), like Lord Cobham's statements in Raleigh's Case, 2 How. St. Tr. 1 (1603), or Jane Dingler's ex parte statements against her husband in King v. Dingler, 2 Leach 561, 168 Eng. Rep. 383 (1791), or Sylvia Crawford's statement in *Crawford*. In each of those cases, the ex parte actors and the evidentiary products of the ex parte communication aligned perfectly with their courtroom analogues. McCottry's emergency statement does not. No "witness" goes into court to proclaim an emergency and seek help.

Davis seeks to cast McCottry in the unlikely role of a witness by pointing to English cases. None of them involves statements made during an ongoing emergency. In King v. Brasier, 1 Leach 199, 168 Eng. Rep. 202 (1779), for example, a young rape victim, "immediately on her coming home, told all the circumstances of the injury" to her mother. Id., at 200, 168 Eng. Rep., at 202. The case would be helpful to Davis if the relevant statement had been the girl's screams for aid as she was being chased by her assailant. But by the time the victim got home, her story was an account of past events.

This is not to say that a conversation which begins as an interrogation to determine the need for emergency assistance cannot, as the Indiana Supreme Court put it, "evolve into testimonial statements," 829 N.E. 2d, at 457, once that purpose has been achieved. In this case, for example, after the operator gained the information needed to address the exigency of the moment, the emergency appears to have ended (when Davis drove away from the premises). The operator then told McCottry to be quiet, and proceeded to pose a battery of questions. It could readily be maintained that, from that point on, McCottry's statements were testimonial, not unlike the "structured police questioning" that occurred in *Crawford*, 541 U.S., at 53, n. 4. This presents no great problem. Just as, for Fifth Amendment purposes, "police officers can and will distinguish almost instinctively between questions necessary to secure their own safety or the safety of the public and questions designed solely to elicit testimonial evidence from a suspect," New York v. Quarles, 467 U.S. 649, 658-659 (1984), trial courts will recognize the point at which, for Sixth Amendment purposes, statements in response to interrogations become testimonial. Through in limine procedure, they should redact or exclude the portions of any statement that have become testimonial, as they do, for example, with unduly prejudicial portions of otherwise admissible evidence. Davis's jury did not hear the *complete* 911 call, although it may well have heard some testimonial portions. We were asked to classify only McCottry's early statements identifying Davis as her assailant, and we agree with the Washington Supreme Court that they were not testimonial. That court also concluded that, even if later parts of the call were testimonial, their admission was harmless beyond a reasonable doubt. Davis does not challenge that holding, and we therefore assume it to be correct.

B

Determining the testimonial or nontestimonial character of the statements that were the product of the interrogation in *Hammon* is a much easier task, since they were not much different from the statements we found to be testimonial in *Crawford.* It is entirely clear from the circumstances that the interrogation was part of an investigation into possibly criminal past conduct—as, indeed, the testifying officer expressly acknowledged, App. in No. 05-5705, at 25, 32, 34. There was no emergency in progress; the interrogating officer testified that he had heard no arguments or crashing and saw no one throw or break anything. When the officers first arrived, Amy told them that things were fine, and there was no immediate threat to her person. When the officer questioned Amy for the second time, and elicited the challenged statements, he was not seeking to determine (as in *Davis*) "what is happening," but rather "what happened." Objectively viewed, the primary, if not indeed the sole, purpose of the interrogation was to investigate a possible crime—which is, of course, precisely what the officer *should* have done.

It is true that the *Crawford* interrogation was more formal. It followed a *Miranda* warning, was tape-recorded, and took place at the station house, see 541 U.S., at 53, n. 4. While these features certainly strengthened the statements' testimonial aspect—made it more objectively apparent, that is, that the purpose of the exercise was to nail down the truth about past criminal events—none was essential to the point. It was formal enough that Amy's interrogation was conducted in a separate room, away from her husband (who tried to intervene), with the officer receiving her replies for use in his "investigation." App. in No. 05-5705, at 34. What we called the "striking resemblance" of the *Crawford* statement to civil-law ex parte examinations, 541 U.S., at 52, is shared by Amy's statement here. Both declarants were actively separated from the defendant—officers forcibly prevented Hershel from participating in the interrogation. Both statements deliberately recounted, in response to police questioning, how potentially criminal past events began and progressed. And both took place some time after the events described were over. Such statements under official interrogation are an obvious substitute for live testimony, because they do precisely *what a witness does* on direct examination; they are inherently testimonial.[5]

Both Indiana and the United States as amicus curiae argue that this case should be resolved much like *Davis*. For the reasons we find the comparison to *Crawford* compelling, we find the comparison to *Davis* unpersuasive. The statements in *Davis* were taken when McCottry was alone, not only unprotected by police (as Amy Hammon was protected), but apparently in immediate danger from Davis. She was seeking aid, not telling a story about the past. McCottry's present-tense statements showed immediacy; Amy's narrative of past events was delivered at some remove in time from the danger she described. And after Amy answered the officer's questions, he had her execute an affidavit, in order, he testified, "to establish events that have occurred previously." App. in No. 05-5705, at 18.

Although we necessarily reject the Indiana Supreme Court's implication that virtually any "initial inquiries" at the crime scene will not be testimonial, see 829 N.E. 2d, at 453, 457, we do not hold the opposite—that *no* questions at the scene will yield nontestimonial answers. We have already observed of domestic disputes that "officers called to investigate . . . need to know whom they are dealing with in order to assess the situation, the threat to their own safety, and possible danger to the potential victim." *Hiibel*, 542 U.S., at 186. Such exigencies may *often* mean that "initial inquiries" produce nontestimonial statements. But in cases like this one, where Amy's statements were neither a cry for help nor the provision of information enabling officers immediately to end a threatening situation, the fact that they were given at an alleged crime scene and were "initial inquiries" is immaterial. Cf. *Crawford*, supra, at 52, n. 3.[6]

IV

Respondents in both cases, joined by a number of their amici, contend that the nature of the offenses charged in these two cases—domestic violence—requires

---

5. The dissent criticizes our test for being "neither workable nor a targeted attempt to reach the abuses forbidden by the [Confrontation] Clause," post, at 9 (opinion of Thomas, J.). As to the former: We have acknowledged that our holding is not an "exhaustive classification of all conceivable statements—or even all conceivable statements in response to police interrogation," supra, at 7, but rather a resolution of the cases before us and those like them. For those cases, the test is objective and quite "workable." . . .

As for the charge that our holding is not a "targeted attempt to reach the abuses forbidden by the [Confrontation] Clause," which the dissent describes as the depositions taken by Marian magistrates, characterized by a high degree of formality, see post, at 2-3: We do not dispute that formality is indeed essential to testimonial utterance. But we no longer have examining Marian magistrates; and we do have, as our 18th-century forebears did not, examining police officers, see L. Friedman, Crime and Punishment in American History 67-68 (1993)—who perform investigative and testimonial functions once performed by examining Marian magistrates, see J. Langbein, The Origins of Adversary Criminal Trial 41 (2003). It imports sufficient formality, in our view, that lies to such officers are criminal offenses. Restricting the Confrontation Clause to the precise forms against which it was originally directed is a recipe for its extinction. Cf. Kyllo v. United States, 533 U.S. 27 (2001).

6. Police investigations themselves are, of course, in no way impugned by our characterization of their fruits as testimonial. Investigations of past crimes prevent future harms and lead to necessary arrests. While prosecutors may hope that inculpatory "nontestimonial" evidence is gathered, this is essentially beyond police control. Their saying that an emergency exists cannot make it be so. The Confrontation Clause in no way governs police conduct, because it is the trial use of, not the investigatory *collection* of, ex parte testimonial statements which offends that provision. But neither can police conduct govern the Confrontation Clause; testimonial statements are what they are.

greater flexibility in the use of testimonial evidence. This particular type of crime is notoriously susceptible to intimidation or coercion of the victim to ensure that she does not testify at trial. When this occurs, the Confrontation Clause gives the criminal a windfall. We may not, however, vitiate constitutional guarantees when they have the effect of allowing the guilty to go free. Cf. Kyllo v. United States, 533 U.S. 27 (2001) (suppressing evidence from an illegal search). But when defendants seek to undermine the judicial process by procuring or coercing silence from witnesses and victims, the Sixth Amendment does not require courts to acquiesce. While defendants have no duty to assist the State in proving their guilt, they *do* have the duty to refrain from acting in ways that destroy the integrity of the criminal-trial system. We reiterate what we said in *Crawford*: that "the rule of forfeiture by wrongdoing . . . extinguishes confrontation claims on essentially equitable grounds." 541 U.S., at 62 (citing *Reynolds*, 98 U.S., at 158-159). That is, one who obtains the absence of a witness by wrongdoing forfeits the constitutional right to confrontation.

We take no position on the standards necessary to demonstrate such forfeiture, but federal courts using Federal Rule of Evidence 804(b)(6), which codifies the forfeiture doctrine, have generally held the Government to the preponderance-of-the-evidence standard, see, e.g., United States v. Scott, 284 F.3d 758, 762 (CA7 2002). State courts tend to follow the same practice, see, e.g., Commonwealth v. Edwards, 444 Mass. 526, 542, 830 N.E.2d 158, 172 (2005). Moreover, if a hearing on forfeiture is required, *Edwards*, for instance, observed that "hearsay evidence, including the unavailable witness's out-of-court statements, may be considered." Id., at 545, 830 N.E.2d, at 174. . . .

We have determined that, absent a finding of forfeiture by wrongdoing, the Sixth Amendment operates to exclude Amy Hammon's affidavit. The Indiana courts may (if they are asked) determine on remand whether such a claim of forfeiture is properly raised and, if so, whether it is meritorious.

* * *

We affirm the judgment of the Supreme Court of Washington in No. 05-5224. We reverse the judgment of the Supreme Court of Indiana in No. 05-5705, and remand the case to that Court for proceedings not inconsistent with this opinion.

JUSTICE THOMAS, concurring in the judgment in part and dissenting in part.

In Crawford v. Washington, 541 U.S. 36 (2004), we abandoned the general reliability inquiry we had long employed to judge the admissibility of hearsay evidence under the Confrontation Clause, describing that inquiry as "*inherently*, and therefore *permanently*, unpredictable." Id., at 68, n. 10 (emphasis in original). Today, a mere two years after the Court decided *Crawford*, it adopts an equally unpredictable test, under which district courts are charged with divining the "primary purpose" of police interrogations. Besides being difficult for courts to apply, this test characterizes as "testimonial," and therefore inadmissible, evidence that bears little resemblance to what we have recognized as the evidence targeted by the Confrontation Clause. Because neither of the cases before the Court today would implicate the Confrontation Clause under an appropriately targeted standard, I concur only in the judgment in Davis v. Washington, No. 05-5224, and dissent from the Court's resolution of Hammon v. Indiana, No. 05-5705.

I

A

The Confrontation Clause provides that "in all criminal prosecutions, the accused shall enjoy the right . . . to be confronted with the witnesses against him. . . ." U.S. Const., Amdt. 6. We have recognized that the operative phrase in the Clause, "witnesses against him," could be interpreted narrowly, to reach only those witnesses who actually testify at trial, or more broadly, to reach many or all of those whose out-of-court statements are offered at trial. *Crawford*, supra, at 42-43; White v. Illinois, 502 U.S. 346, 359-363 (1992) (Thomas, J., concurring in part and concurring in judgment). Because the narrowest interpretation of the Clause would conflict with both the history giving rise to the adoption of the Clause and this Court's precedent, we have rejected such a reading. See *Crawford*, supra, at 50-51; *White*, supra, at 360 (opinion of Thomas, J.).

Rejection of the narrowest view of the Clause does not, however, require the broadest application of the Clause to exclude otherwise admissible hearsay evidence. The history surrounding the right to confrontation supports the conclusion that it was developed to target particular practices that occurred under the English bail and committal statutes passed during the reign of Queen Mary, namely, the "civil-law mode of criminal procedure, and particularly its use of ex parte examinations as evidence against the accused." *Crawford*, supra, at 43, 50; *White*, supra, at 361-362 (opinion of Thomas, J.); Mattox v. United States, 156 U.S. 237, 242 (1895). "The predominant purpose of the [Marian committal] statute was to institute *systematic* questioning of the accused and the witnesses." J. Langbein, Prosecuting Crime in the Renaissance 23 (1974) (emphasis added). The statute required an oral examination of the suspect and the accusers, transcription within two days of the examinations, and physical transmission to the judges hearing the case. Id., at 10, 23. These examinations came to be used as evidence in some cases, in lieu of a personal appearance by the witness. *Crawford*, supra, at 43-44; 9 W. Holdsworth, A History of English Law 223-229 (1926). Many statements that would be inadmissible as a matter of hearsay law bear little resemblance to these evidentiary practices, which the Framers proposed the Confrontation Clause to prevent. See, e.g., *Crawford*, supra, at 51 (contrasting "an off-hand, overheard remark" with the abuses targeted by the Confrontation Clause). Accordingly, it is unlikely that the Framers intended the word "witness" to be read so broadly as to include such statements. Cf. Dutton v. Evans, 400 U.S. 74, 94 (1970) (Harlan, J., concurring in result) (rejecting the "assumption that the core purpose of the Confrontation Clause of the Sixth Amendment is to prevent overly broad exceptions to the hearsay rule").

In *Crawford*, we recognized that this history could be squared with the language of the Clause, giving rise to a workable, and more accurate, interpretation of the Clause. "Witnesses," we said, are those who " 'bear testimony.' " 541 U.S., at 51 (quoting 1 N. Webster, An American Dictionary of the English Language (1828)). And " 'testimony' " is " '[a] solemn declaration or affirmation made for the purpose of establishing or proving some fact.' " Ibid. (quoting Webster, supra). Admittedly, we did not set forth a detailed framework for addressing whether a statement is "testimonial" and thus subject to the Confrontation Clause. But the plain terms of the "testimony" definition we endorsed necessarily require some degree of solemnity before a statement can be deemed "testimonial."

This requirement of solemnity supports my view that the statements regulated by the Confrontation Clause must include "extrajudicial statements . . . contained in formalized testimonial materials, such as affidavits, depositions, prior testimony, or confessions." *White*, supra, at 365 (opinion of Thomas, J.). Affidavits, depositions, and prior testimony are, by their very nature, taken through a formalized process. Likewise, confessions, when extracted by police in a formal manner, carry sufficient indicia of solemnity to constitute formalized statements and, accordingly, bear a "striking resemblance," *Crawford*, supra, at 52, to the examinations of the accused and accusers under the Marian statutes.[1] See generally Langbein, supra, at 21-34.

Although the Court concedes that the early American cases invoking the right to confrontation or the Confrontation Clause itself all "clearly involved testimony" as defined in *Crawford*, it fails to acknowledge that all of the cases it cites fall within the narrower category of formalized testimonial materials I have proposed.[2] Interactions between the police and an accused (or witnesses) resemble Marian proceedings—and these early cases—only when the interactions are somehow rendered "formal." In *Crawford*, for example, the interrogation was custodial, taken after warnings given pursuant to Miranda v. Arizona, 384 U.S. 436 (1966). 541 U.S., at 38. *Miranda* warnings, by their terms, inform a prospective defendant that " 'anything he says can be used against him in a court of law.' " Dickerson v. United States, 530 U.S. 428, 435 (2000) (quoting *Miranda*, supra, at 479). This imports a solemnity to the process that is not present in a mere conversation between a witness or suspect and a police officer.[3]

The Court all but concedes that no case can be cited for its conclusion that the Confrontation Clause also applies to informal police questioning under certain circumstances. Instead, the sole basis for the Court's conclusion is its apprehension that the Confrontation Clause will "readily be evaded" if it is only applicable to formalized testimonial materials. But the Court's proposed solution to the risk of evasion is needlessly overinclusive. Because the Confrontation Clause sought to regulate prosecutorial abuse occurring through use of ex parte statements as evidence against the accused, it also reaches the use of technically informal statements when used to evade the formalized process. That is, even if the interrogation itself is not formal, the production of evidence by the prosecution at trial would resemble the abuses targeted by the Confrontation Clause if the prosecution attempted to use out-of-court statements as a means of circumventing the literal right of confrontation, see Coy v. Iowa, 487 U.S. 1012 (1988). In such a case, the Confrontation Clause could fairly be applied to exclude the hearsay statements offered by the prosecution, preventing evasion without simultaneously excluding evidence offered by the prosecution in good faith.

The Court's standard is not only disconnected from history and unnecessary to prevent abuse; it also yields no predictable results to police officers and prosecutors

---

1. Like the Court, I presume the acts of the 911 operator to be the acts of the police. Accordingly, I refer to both the operator in *Davis* and the officer in *Hammon*, and their counterparts in similar cases, collectively as "the police."

2. Our more recent cases, too, nearly all hold excludable under the Confrontation Clause materials that are plainly highly formal. . . .

3. The possibility that an oral declaration of past fact to a police officer, if false, could result in legal consequences to the speaker, may render honesty in casual conversations with police officers important. It does not, however, render those conversations solemn or formal in the ordinary meanings of those terms.

attempting to comply with the law. Cf. *Crawford*, supra, at 68, n. 10 (criticizing unpredictability of the pre-*Crawford* test); *White*, 502 U.S., at 364-365 (Thomas, J., concurring in part and concurring in judgment) (limiting the Confrontation Clause to the discrete category of materials historically abused would "greatly simplify" application of the Clause). In many, if not most, cases where police respond to a report of a crime, whether pursuant to a 911 call from the victim or otherwise, the purposes of an interrogation, viewed from the perspective of the police, are *both* to respond to the emergency situation *and* to gather evidence. See New York v. Quarles, 467 U.S. 649, 656 (1984) ("Undoubtedly most police officers [deciding whether to give *Miranda* warnings in a possible emergency situation] would act out of a host of different, instinctive, and largely unverifiable motives—their own safety, the safety of others, and perhaps as well the desire to obtain incriminating evidence from the suspect"). Assigning one of these two "largely unverifiable motives," primacy requires constructing a hierarchy of purpose that will rarely be present—and is not reliably discernible. It will inevitably be, quite simply, an exercise in fiction.

The Court's repeated invocation of the word "objective" to describe its test, however, suggests that the Court may not mean to reference purpose at all, but instead to inquire into the function served by the interrogation. Certainly such a test would avoid the pitfalls that have led us repeatedly to reject tests dependent on the subjective intentions of police officers.[4] It would do so, however, at the cost of being even more disconnected from the prosecutorial abuses targeted by the Confrontation Clause. Additionally, it would shift the ability to control whether a violation occurred from the police and prosecutor to the judge, whose determination as to the "primary purpose" of a particular interrogation would be unpredictable and not necessarily tethered to the actual purpose for which the police performed the interrogation.

B

Neither the 911 call at issue in *Davis* nor the police questioning at issue in *Hammon* is testimonial under the appropriate framework. Neither the call nor the questioning is itself a formalized dialogue.[5] Nor do any circumstances surrounding the taking of the statements render those statements sufficiently formal to resemble the Marian examinations; the statements were neither Mirandized nor custodial, nor accompanied by any similar indicia of formality. Finally, there is no suggestion that the prosecution attempted to offer the women's hearsay evidence at trial in order to evade confrontation. See 829 N.E.2d 444, 447 (Ind. 2005) (prosecution subpoenaed Amy Hammon to testify, but she was not present); 154 Wash. 2d 291, 296, 111 P.3d 844, 847 (2005) (en banc) (State was unable to locate Michelle McCottry at the time of trial). Accordingly, the statements at issue in both cases are nontestimonial and admissible under the Confrontation Clause.

---

4. See New York v. Quarles, 467 U.S. 649, 655-656, and n. 6 (1984) (subjective motivation of officer not relevant in considering whether the public safety exception to Miranda v. Arizona, 384 U.S. 436 (1966), is applicable); Rhode Island v. Innis, 446 U.S. 291, 301 (1980) (subjective intent of police officer to obtain incriminatory statement not relevant to whether an interrogation has occurred); Whren v. United States, 517 U.S. 806, 813 (1996) (refusing to evaluate Fourth Amendment reasonableness in light of the officers' actual motivations).

5. Although the police questioning in *Hammon* was ultimately reduced to an affidavit, all agree that the affidavit is inadmissible per se under our definition of the term "testimonial." Brief for Respondent in No. 05-5705, p. 46; Brief for United States as Amicus Curiae in No. 05-5705, p. 14.

The Court's determination that the evidence against Hammon must be excluded extends the Confrontation Clause far beyond the abuses it was intended to prevent. When combined with the Court's holding that the evidence against Davis is perfectly admissible, however, the Court's *Hammon* holding also reveals the difficulty of applying the Court's requirement that courts investigate the "primary purposes" of the investigation. The Court draws a line between the two cases based on its explanation that *Hammon* involves "no emergency in progress," but instead, mere questioning as "part of an investigation into possibly criminal past conduct," and its explanation that *Davis* involves questioning for the "primary purpose" of "enabling police assistance to meet an ongoing emergency." But the fact that the officer in *Hammon* was investigating Mr. Hammon's past conduct does not foreclose the possibility that the primary purpose of his inquiry was to assess whether Mr. Hammon constituted a continuing danger to his wife, requiring further police presence or action. It is hardly remarkable that Hammon did not act abusively towards his wife in the presence of the officers, and his good judgment to refrain from criminal behavior in the presence of police sheds little, if any, light on whether his violence would have resumed had the police left without further questioning, transforming what the Court dismisses as "past conduct" back into an "ongoing emergency."[6] Nor does the mere fact that McCottry needed emergency aid shed light on whether the "primary purpose" of gathering, for example, the name of her assailant was to protect the police, to protect the victim, or to gather information for prosecution. In both of the cases before the Court, like many similar cases, pronouncement of the "primary" motive behind the interrogation calls for nothing more than a guess by courts.

II

Because the standard adopted by the Court today is neither workable nor a targeted attempt to reach the abuses forbidden by the Clause, I concur only in the judgment in Davis v. Washington, No. 05-5224, and respectfully dissent from the Court's resolution of Hammon v. Indiana, No. 05-5705.

NOTES AND QUESTIONS

1. Who's got the better of the argument here? Justice Scalia, whose definition of "testimony" seems to depend mostly on whether the statements at issue dealt with contemporaneous or past events? Or Justice Thomas, whose test would depend on the "formality" of the circumstances under which the statements were made? What, if anything, do either of these competing approaches have to do with the underlying purpose of the Confrontation Clause, which is (presumably) to help ensure that trial testimony is adequately tested and, therefore, can be trusted as reasonably reliable? In particular, isn't it a little strange that, under both tests, most 911 calls

---

6. Some of the factors on which the Court relies to determine that the police questioning in *Hammon* was testimonial apply equally in *Davis*. For example, while Hammon was "actively separated from the [victim]" and thereby "prevented . . . from participating in the interrogation," Davis was apart from McCottry while she was questioned by the 911 operator and thus unable to participate in the questioning. Similarly, "the events described [by McCottry] were over" by the time she recounted them to the 911 operator.

(which are usually made under highly stressful, if not downright dangerous, circumstances that seem very likely to affect the witness's perceptions) will turn out to be non-problematic under the Confrontation Clause (and thus admissible without cross-examination, assuming all other requirements for admissibility are met)?

2. There is an interesting tension in the majority opinion in *Davis*. Why does Justice Scalia spend so much time discussing the behavior and purposes of the relevant government agents, if as he states, see footnote 1, it's the nature of the declarant's statements that matters to the application of the Confrontation Clause, and not the nature of the interrogator's questions? For example, if the 911 operator in *Davis* had asked no questions at all, but simply had listened quietly and patiently while Michelle McCottry blurted out her statements, would the result in the case have been any different? Wouldn't the Confrontation Clause have kicked in at exactly the same point—i.e., the moment when McCottry stated that "[h]e's runnin' now," thus indicating that the immediate emergency had passed? Why should the "primary purpose of the interrogation" matter at all, given that (to use Justice Scalia's own words, in footnote 6) "police conduct [cannot] govern the Confrontation Clause; testimonial statements are what they are"?

3. In *Davis*, the Court noted that a defendant can lose his Confrontation Clause protection through the equitable doctrine of "forfeiture by wrongdoing." Does the act of "wrongdoing" have to be for the purpose of preventing the witness from testifying? Or is any act of "wrongdoing" sufficient, as long as it has the effect of preventing the witness from testifying?

In Giles v. California, 554 U.S. 353 (2008), the defendant was accused of murdering his wife, and the prosecution was allowed to use the "forfeiture by wrongdoing" exception to introduce prior unconfronted testimonial statements, made by the wife, accusing her husband of domestic violence. A fractured Court (in a lead opinion by Justice Scalia that garnered majority support for all but one section) held that the forfeiture exception applies "only when the defendant engaged in conduct *designed* to prevent the witness from testifying." Although this required reversal of the conviction, Scalia noted that on remand, an inquiry could be made into whether there might be evidence sufficient to show that the defendant did, indeed, murder his wife for the purpose of silencing her. Such evidence might include, for example, "[e]arlier abuse, or threats of abuse, intended to dissuade the victim from resorting to outside help," as well as "evidence of ongoing criminal proceedings at which the victim would have been expected to testify," all of which would be "highly relevant" to the key issue of whether the defendant's crime "expressed the intent to isolate the victim and to stop her from reporting abuse to the authorities or cooperating with a criminal prosecution." Justices Thomas and Alito joined the lead opinion, but wrote separately to express the view that, although not an issue properly before the Court, the contested statements might not even be "testimonial" in the first place (since they were not closely analogous to in-court witness statements). Justices Souter and Ginsburg joined all but one section of the lead opinion (a section that contained exceptionally strong rhetoric about the role of history and original intent in interpreting the Confrontation Clause, and correspondingly strong denigration of the dissenters' policy-oriented jurisprudence). Justices Breyer, Stevens, and Kennedy dissented, largely on the grounds that the Court's decision would allow domestic abusers to benefit from the violent results of their abuse.

4. Note Justice Scalia's back-of-the-hand dismissal of the concern that *Davis* will undermine the factual accuracy of criminal adjudication, especially in domestic

violence cases: "When this occurs, the Confrontation Clause gives the criminal a windfall. We may not, however, vitiate constitutional guarantees when they have the effect of allowing the guilty to go free."

How can such a view be squared with, for example, the Court's decision during the same Term in House v. Bell, 547 U.S. 518 (2006), discussed at page 1458, infra, a decision clearly motivated by the desire to improve factual accuracy in criminal cases (or, more specifically, to remedy factual *in*-accuracy)? How can it be squared with Holmes v. South Carolina, also discussed at page 1458? Should constitutional criminal procedure rules be designed and applied with a primary focus on enhancing factual accuracy, or are some procedural rules an end in themselves—even when they may sometimes work *against* accuracy, as in *Crawford* and *Davis*?

It is undoubtedly true that procedural justice and factual accuracy often complement each other. But when these two values come into conflict, how should the Court choose between them? Does an absolutist statement like the one quoted in the preceding paragraph seem like the best way to resolve such a conflict? Do you think Justice Scalia really meant what he said?

5. Apparently Justice Scalia was quite serious. In an astonishing elevation of form over both substance and good sense, the same five-person majority, with Scalia writing the opinion, held in Melendez-Diaz v. Massachusetts, 557 U.S. 305 (2009), that a certificate from a state laboratory after chemical testing certifying the contents and quantity of a seized substance was a "testimonial" statement, and thus within the rule in *Crawford* requiring the opportunity to cross-examine the maker of the statement.

To the majority, the "case involves little more than the application of our holding in *Crawford*. . . . The Sixth Amendment does not permit the prosecution to prove its case via ex parte out-of-court affidavits. . . ." In a biting and powerful dissent, however, Justice Kennedy pointed out that, regardless whether *Crawford* may stand for that proposition, the Sixth Amendment does not. It does not prohibit "ex parte affidavits"; it provides a right to confront the witnesses against you. The question is not what is "testimonial"; the question is, who are the witnesses the Sixth Amendment refers to? As the dissent pointed out, there is virtually nothing in the constitutional language, history, precedent, or good sense justifying the majority's reworking of long-settled procedural and evidentiary rules that exempted such people as lab technicians from being called by the state in order to admit their lab results. The concern of the Sixth Amendment, according to the dissent, is the key factual witnesses against a defendant, with respect to whom face-to-face confrontation may make a difference. Face-to-face confrontation with lab technicians is highly unlikely to be of any benefit to the defense and will impose serious costs on the state. To be sure, errors are made by lab technicians, and it is not inconceivable that, in a small number of cases, cross-examining the lab technician may point out a problem. However, defendants now have the right under the Compulsory Process Clause to subpoena whomever they like, including lab technicians, and examine them at trial.

Against the minimal benefits to factual accuracy of the Court's approach, consider the costs. As the dissent argued in passages to which the majority did not respond:

> The Court says that, before the results of a scientific test may be introduced into evidence, the defendant has the right to confront the "analyst." One must assume that this term, though it appears nowhere in the Confrontation Clause, nevertheless has

some constitutional substance that now must be elaborated in future cases. There is no accepted definition of analyst, and there is no established precedent to define that term.

Consider how many people play a role in a routine test for the presence of illegal drugs. One person prepares a sample of the drug, places it in a testing machine, and retrieves the machine's printout—often, a graph showing the frequencies of radiation absorbed by the sample or the masses of the sample's molecular fragments. . . . A second person interprets the graph the machine prints out—perhaps by comparing that printout with published, standardized graphs of known drugs. Meanwhile, a third person—perhaps an independent contractor—has calibrated the machine and, having done so, has certified that the machine is in good working order. Finally, a fourth person—perhaps the laboratory's director—certifies that his subordinates followed established procedures.

It is not at all evident which of these four persons is the analyst to be confronted under the rule the Court announces today. If all are witnesses who must appear for in-court confrontation, then the Court has, for all practical purposes, forbidden the use of scientific tests in criminal trials. . . . [R]equiring even one of these individuals to testify threatens to disrupt if not end many prosecutions where guilt is clear but a newly found formalism now holds sway.

The Federal Government may face even graver difficulties than the States because its operations are so widespread. For example, the FBI laboratory at Quantico, Virginia, supports federal, state, and local investigations across the country. Its 500 employees conduct over one million scientific tests each year. . . . The Court's decision means that before any of those million tests reaches a jury, at least one of the laboratory's analysts must board a plane, find his or her way to an unfamiliar courthouse, and sit there waiting to read aloud notes made months ago.

The Court purchases its meddling with the Confrontation Clause at a dear price, a price not measured in taxpayer dollars alone. Guilty defendants will go free, on the most technical grounds, as a direct result of today's decision, adding nothing to the truth-finding process. The analyst will not always make it to the courthouse in time. He or she may be ill; may be out of the country; may be unable to travel because of inclement weather; or may at that very moment be waiting outside some other courtroom for another defendant to exercise the right the Court invents today. If for any reason the analyst cannot make it to the courthouse in time, then, the Court holds, the jury cannot learn of the analyst's findings (unless, by some unlikely turn of events, the defendant previously cross-examined the analyst). The result, in many cases, will be that the prosecution cannot meet its burden of proof, and the guilty defendant goes free on a technicality that, because it results in an acquittal, cannot be reviewed on appeal.

557 U.S., at 332-333, 342-343.

6. *Melendez-Diaz* and its "dear price" led to much hand-wringing, and the development of creative strategies, by prosecutors trying to avoid its impacts. One of those strategies was to designate a single lab technician to go to court and testify in person about the lab reports filed in many different criminal cases—lab reports in the preparation of which the "testifying" lab technician did not participate.

In Bullcoming v. New Mexico, 131 S. Ct. 2705 (2011), the Court took up the following issue: "[W]hether the Confrontation Clause permits the prosecution to introduce a forensic laboratory report containing a testimonial certification—made for the purpose of proving a particular fact—through the in-court testimony of a scientist who did not sign the certification or perform or observe the test reported in the certification." In a 5-4 decision, the Court held that the answer is "emphatically

'No'": "The accused's right is to be confronted with the analyst who made the certi-fication, unless that analyst is unavailable at trial, and the accused had an opportu-nity, pretrial, to cross-examine that particular scientist." Id. at 2715.

Justice Ginsburg, joined in full by Justice Scalia and in large part by Justices Thomas, Sotomayor, and Kagan, explained for the majority why the appearance in court of forensic scientist Gerasimos Razatos could not substitute for the appear-ance of Curtis Caylor, the analyst who had actually conducted the blood-alcohol test (BAC) in question (and who happened to be on unpaid leave at the time of Bullcoming's trial):

> [T]he New Mexico Supreme Court believed that Razatos could substitute for Caylor because Razatos "qualified as an expert witness with respect to the gas chro-matograph machine and the SLD's laboratory procedures." But surrogate testimony of the kind Razatos was equipped to give could not convey what Caylor knew or observed about the events his certification concerned, i.e., the particular test and testing process he employed. Nor could such surrogate testimony expose any lapses or lies on the certifying analyst's part. Significant here, Razatos had no knowledge of the reason why Caylor had been placed on unpaid leave. With Caylor on the stand, Bullcoming's counsel could have asked questions designed to reveal whether incom-petence, evasiveness, or dishonesty accounted for Caylor's removal from his work sta-tion. Notable in this regard, the State never asserted that Caylor was "unavailable"; the prosecution conveyed only that Caylor was on uncompensated leave. Nor did the State assert that Razatos had any "independent opinion" concerning Bullcoming's BAC. In this light, Caylor's live testimony could hardly be typed "a hollow formality."
>
> More fundamentally, as this Court stressed in *Crawford*, "[t]he text of the Sixth Amendment does not suggest any open-ended exceptions from the confrontation requirement to be developed by the courts." 541 U.S., at 54. Nor is it "the role of courts to extrapolate from the words of the [Confrontation Clause] to the values behind it, and then to enforce its guarantees only to the extent they serve (in the courts' views) those underlying values." Giles v. California, 554 U.S. 353, 375 (2008). Accordingly, the Clause does not tolerate dispensing with confrontation simply because the court believes that questioning one witness about another's testimonial statements provides a fair enough opportunity for cross-examination. . . .
>
> In short, when the State elected to introduce Caylor's certification, Caylor became a witness Bullcoming had the right to confront. Our precedent cannot sensibly be read any other way. See *Melendez-Diaz*, 557 U.S., at ___ (Kennedy, J., dissenting) (Court's holding means "the . . . analyst who must testify is the person who signed the certificate").

Bullcoming, 131 S. Ct., at 2715-2716. Another portion of Justice Ginsburg's majority opinion concluded that the lab report in question was "testimonial," finding that "[i]n all material respects, the laboratory report in this case resembles those in *Melendez-Diaz*."

In a separate concurring opinion, Justice Sotomayor identified four issues *not* addressed or resolved in *Bullcoming*:

> First, this is not a case in which the State suggested an alternate purpose, much less an alternate primary purpose, for the BAC report. For example, the State has not claimed that the report was necessary to provide Bullcoming with medical treatment. . . .
>
> Second, this is not a case in which the person testifying is a supervisor, reviewer, or someone else with a personal, albeit limited, connection to the scientific test at

issue. . . . . We need not address what degree of involvement is sufficient because here Razatos had no involvement whatsoever in the relevant test and report.

Third, this is not a case in which an expert witness was asked for his independent opinion about underlying testimonial reports that were not themselves admitted into evidence. . . . We would face a different question if asked to determine the constitutionality of allowing an expert witness to discuss others' testimonial statements if the testimonial statements were not themselves admitted as evidence.

Finally, this is not a case in which the State introduced only machine-generated results, such as a printout from a gas chromatograph. . . . Thus, we do not decide whether, as the New Mexico Supreme Court suggests, a State could introduce (assuming an adequate chain of custody foundation) raw data generated by a machine in conjunction with the testimony of an expert witness.

131 S. Ct., at 2722-2723 (Sotomayor, J., concurring).

In dissent, Justice Kennedy, joined by Chief Justice Roberts, Justice Breyer, and Justice Alito, bemoaned the Court's decision:

> Whether or not one agrees with the reasoning and the result in *Melendez-Diaz*, the Court today takes the new and serious misstep of extending that holding to instances like this one. . . .
>
> . . . From 2008 to 2010, subpoenas requiring New Mexico analysts to testify in impaired-driving cases rose 71%, to 1,600— or 8 or 9 every workday. In a State that is the Nation's fifth largest by area and that employs just 10 total analysts, each analyst in blood alcohol cases recently received 200 subpoenas per year. The analysts now must travel great distances on most working days. The result has been, in the laboratory's words, "chaotic." And if the defense raises an objection and the analyst is tied up in another court proceeding; or on leave; or absent; or delayed in transit; or no longer employed; or ill; or no longer living, the defense gets a windfall. As a result, good defense attorneys will object in ever-greater numbers to a prosecution failure or inability to produce laboratory analysts at trial. The concomitant increases in subpoenas will further impede the state laboratory's ability to keep pace with its obligations. Scarce state resources could be committed to other urgent needs in the criminal justice system.
>
> Seven years after its initiation, it bears remembering that the *Crawford* approach was not preordained. This Court's missteps have produced an interpretation of the word "witness" at odds with its meaning elsewhere in the Constitution, including elsewhere in the Sixth Amendment, see Amar, Sixth Amendment First Principles, 84 Geo. L.J. 641, 647, 691-696 (1996), and at odds with the sound administration of justice. It is time to return to solid ground. A proper place to begin that return is to decline to extend *Melendez-Diaz* to bar the reliable, commonsense evidentiary framework the State sought to follow in this case.

Bullcoming, 131 S. Ct., at 2728 (Kennedy, J., dissenting).

7. One year after *Bullcoming*, the Court returned to the subject of lab reports in Williams v. Illinois, 132 S. Ct. 2221 (2012). The facts, according to the Court, were:

> In petitioner's bench trial for rape, the prosecution called an expert [a forensic specialist at the Illinois State Police lab] who testified that a DNA profile produced by an outside laboratory, Cellmark, matched a profile produced by the state police lab using a sample of petitioner's blood. On direct examination, the expert testified that Cellmark was an accredited laboratory and that Cellmark provided the police with a DNA profile. The expert also explained the notations on documents admitted as

> business records, stating that, according to the records, vaginal swabs taken from the victim were sent to and received back from Cellmark. The expert made no other statement that was offered for the purpose of identifying the sample of biological material used in deriving the profile or for the purpose of establishing how Cellmark handled or tested the sample. Nor did the expert vouch for the accuracy of the profile that Cellmark produced. Nevertheless, petitioner contends that the expert's testimony violated the Confrontation Clause as interpreted in *Crawford*.

Id., at 2227.

The hypothetical sane observer obviously would have concluded that this was an easy case, given *Bullcoming*'s "emphatic no," as the answer to whether a lab report may be admitted if the person signing it is not produced for cross-examination. The sane observer would notice that a certified lab report is most likely more reliable than an uncertified, more or less anonymous, report from a faceless organization. In any sane world, there is greater reason to insist on cross-examination in *Williams* than in *Bullcoming*.

But, confirming that the legal world is on occasion a wondrous sight to behold, the Court upheld the admission of the lab report in a 4-1-4 split that may go down in history as one of the Court's most peculiar decisions. A four-person plurality, authored by Justice Alito and joined by Chief Justice Roberts and Justices Kennedy and Breyer, issued a tortured opinion focusing on why the report was not being admitted for its truth, and therefore there was no constitutional problem. Justice Thomas concurred in the result on the (now-familiar, for him) ground that the Confrontation Clause is limited to formal, affidavit-like documents ("a narrow class of statements bearing indicia of solemnity"), which excluded this unsworn document from its coverage. In passing, Thomas rejected every proposition uttered by the plurality and the dissent. A four-person dissent, authored by Justice Kagan, and joined by Justices Scalia, Ginsburg, and Sotomayor, expressed a continued willingness to make it cost- prohibitive to enforce much of the criminal law, and in passing rejected every proposition offered in both the plurality and the concurrence. The result was that five of the Justices rejected the plurality's arguments, five of the Justices rejected the dissent's arguments, and eight of the Justices rejected the concurrence's arguments, yet future cases now will be decided largely by Justice Thomas's solo view as to the formalities of the evidentiary proffer.

Although it is a parlous enterprise to divine the actual states of mind of Supreme Court Justices, the plurality opinion in *Williams* is so strained that the obvious inference is that those Justices who joined it were looking for any way to cut back on the destructive effect of the *Crawford* line of cases. The first argument, as noted above, involved whether the lab report was being offered for its truth. In an opinion that would make the old masters of the common law of evidence proud, the plurality said "no." The witness was only asked whether there was a match between the Cellmark report and a separate DNA analysis done by the state from a sample taken from Williams. She was not asked if the Cellmark report was based on a sample that came from defendant. Thus, she was not relying on the Cellmark report to show that it was reporting tests of a sample from Williams. Other evidence made it clear that this sample had come from Williams and had been reliably done. There was conventional chain-of-custody evidence, and the match itself was "circumstantial evidence" that the sample came from Williams. "In contrast, Cellmark's report was considered for the limited purpose of seeing whether it matched something else, and the relevance of that match was established by independent circumstantial evidence showing that the report was based on a sample from the crime scene." The trouble with this entire line of reasoning is that, without the actual findings in the report, there is nothing to match, and thus there is no relevance to Lambatos' testimony. There is nothing but the report that details the DNA profile in the sample tested by Cellmark. For a discussion of this problem, and its contemporary manifestations in the law of hearsay, see Ronald J. Allen, et al., Evidence: Text, Problems, and Cases 686-693 (5th ed. 2011).

Perhaps not content with its own reasoning about the hearsay rule, the plurality went on to make the claim that there was no Confrontation Clause violation in any event:

> In *Melendez-Diaz* and *Bullcoming*, the Court held that the particular forensic reports at issue qualified as testimonial statements, but the Court did not hold that all forensic reports fall into the same category. Introduction of the reports in those cases ran afoul of the Confrontation Clause because they were the equivalent of affidavits made for the purpose of proving the guilt of a particular criminal defendant at trial. There was nothing resembling an ongoing emergency, as the suspects in both cases had already been captured, and the tests in question were relatively simple and can generally be performed by a single analyst. In addition, the technicians who prepared the reports must have realized that their contents (which reported an elevated blood-alcohol level and the presence of an illegal drug) would be incriminating. . . .
>
> The Cellmark report is very different. It plainly was not prepared for the primary purpose of accusing a targeted individual. In identifying the primary purpose of an out-of-court statement, we apply an objective test. We look for the primary purpose that a reasonable person would have ascribed to the statement, taking into account all of the surrounding circumstances.
>
> Here, the primary purpose of the Cellmark report, viewed objectively, was not to accuse petitioner or to create evidence for use at trial. When the ISP lab sent the sample to Cellmark, its primary purpose was to catch a dangerous rapist who was still at large, not to obtain evidence for use against petitioner, who was neither in custody nor under suspicion at that time. Similarly, no one at Cellmark could have possibly known that the profile that it produced would turn out to inculpate petitioner—or for that matter, anyone else whose DNA profile was in a law enforcement database. Under these circumstances, there was no "prospect of fabrication" and no incentive to produce anything other than a scientifically sound and reliable profile.

Williams, 132 S. Ct., at 2243-2244. Given Justice Thomas's concurrence, the lesson to the states seems to be that by eliminating any formal certification process, and by keeping lab technicians in the dark as to what they are doing (which actually would be a good thing in any event, to avoid various biases), the states may be able to avoid the exclusionary effect on lab reports of the *Crawford* line of cases.

8. As if *Crawford, Davis, Hammon, Melendez-Diaz,* and *Bullcoming* weren't quite enough to addle the minds of judges and litigants across the land, the Supreme Court made matters even worse when it reviewed a Michigan case involving a classic "dying declaration" by a murder victim identifying his killer. Recall that, in footnote 6 of *Crawford*, the Court suggested that "dying declarations" might be a "sui generis" exception from the new regime altogether, on purely historical grounds, see supra at page 1386. But the Michigan murder case couldn't be resolved by means of the "dying declaration" exception because the state courts had failed to make a finding that the relevant victim statement really *was* a "dying declaration," and the prosecution had failed to preserve the issue. That led to the following decision.

MICHIGAN v. BRYANT

Certiorari to the Supreme Court of Michigan
562 U.S. 344 (2011)

JUSTICE SOTOMAYOR delivered the opinion of the Court.

At respondent Richard Bryant's trial, the court admitted statements that the victim, Anthony Covington, made to police officers who discovered him mortally wounded in a gas station parking lot. A jury convicted Bryant of, inter alia, second-degree murder. On appeal, the Supreme Court of Michigan held that the Sixth Amendment's Confrontation Clause, as explained in our decisions in Crawford v. Washington, 541 U.S. 36 (2004), and Davis v. Washington, 547 U.S. 813 (2006), rendered Covington's statements inadmissible testimonial hearsay, and the court reversed Bryant's conviction. We granted the State's petition for a writ of certiorari to consider whether the Confrontation Clause barred the admission at trial of Covington's statements to the police. We hold that the circumstances of the interaction between Covington and the police objectively indicate that the "primary purpose of the interrogation" was "to enable police assistance to meet an ongoing emergency." *Davis,* 547 U.S., at 822. Therefore, Covington's identification and description of the shooter and the location of the shooting were not testimonial statements, and their admission at Bryant's trial did not violate the Confrontation Clause. We vacate the judgment of the Supreme Court of Michigan and remand.

I

Around 3:25 a.m. on April 29, 2001, Detroit, Michigan police officers responded to a radio dispatch indicating that a man had been shot. At the scene, they found the victim, Anthony Covington, lying on the ground next to his car in a gas station parking lot. Covington had a gunshot wound to his abdomen, appeared to be in great pain, and spoke with difficulty.

The police asked him "what had happened, who had shot him, and where the shooting had occurred." Covington stated that "Rick" shot him at around 3 a.m. He also indicated that he had a conversation with Bryant, whom he recognized based on his voice, through the back door of Bryant's house. Covington explained that when he turned to leave, he was shot through the door and then drove to the gas station, where police found him.

Covington's conversation with the police ended within 5 to 10 minutes when emergency medical services arrived. Covington was transported to a hospital and died within hours. The police left the gas station after speaking with Covington, called for backup, and traveled to Bryant's house. They did not find Bryant there but did find blood and a bullet on the back porch and an apparent bullet hole in the back door. Police also found Covington's wallet and identification outside the house.

At trial, which occurred prior to our decisions in *Crawford,* 541 U.S. 36, and *Davis,* 547 U.S. 813, the police officers who spoke with Covington at the gas station testified about what Covington had told them. The jury returned a guilty verdict on charges of second-degree murder, being a felon in possession of a firearm, and possession of a firearm during the commission of a felony.

Bryant appealed, and the Michigan Court of Appeals affirmed his conviction. Bryant then appealed to the Supreme Court of Michigan, arguing that the trial court erred in admitting Covington's statements to the police. The Supreme Court of Michigan eventually remanded the case to the Court of Appeals for reconsideration in light of our 2006 decision in *Davis*. On remand, the Court of Appeals again affirmed, holding that Covington's statements were properly admitted because they were not testimonial. Bryant again appealed to the Supreme Court of Michigan, which reversed his conviction. . . . [It] held that the admission of Covington's statements constituted prejudicial plain error warranting reversal and ordered a new trial. The court did not address whether, absent a Confrontation Clause bar, the statements' admission would have been otherwise consistent with Michigan's hearsay rules or due process.[1]

. . . We granted certiorari to determine whether the Confrontation Clause barred admission of Covington's statements.

II

. . . *Crawford* examined the common-law history of the confrontation right. . . . In light of this history, we emphasized the word "witnesses" in the Sixth Amendment, defining it as "those who 'bear testimony.' " 541 U.S., at 51. . . . We noted that "[a]n accuser who makes a formal statement to government officers bears testimony in a sense that a person who makes a casual remark to an acquaintance does not." We therefore limited the Confrontation Clause's reach to testimonial statements. . . .

In 2006, the Court in Davis v. Washington and Hammon v. Indiana, 547 U.S. 813, . . . explained that when *Crawford* said that

> " 'interrogations by law enforcement officers fall squarely within [the] class' of testimonial hearsay, we had immediately in mind (for that was the case before us) interrogations solely directed at establishing the facts of a past crime, in order to identify (or provide evidence to convict) the perpetrator. The product of such interrogation, whether reduced to a writing signed by the declarant or embedded in the memory (and perhaps notes) of the interrogating officer, is testimonial." *Davis*, 547 U.S., at 826.

We thus made clear in *Davis* that not all those questioned by the police are witnesses and not all "interrogations by law enforcement officers," *Crawford*, 541 U.S., at 53, are subject to the Confrontation Clause.

Davis and *Hammon* were both domestic violence cases. . . . To address the facts of both cases, we expanded upon the meaning of "testimonial" that we first employed in *Crawford* and discussed the concept of an ongoing emergency. We explained:

> "Statements are nontestimonial when made in the course of police interrogation under circumstances objectively indicating that the primary purpose of the interrogation is to enable police assistance to meet an ongoing emergency. They are testimonial when the circumstances objectively indicate that there is no such ongoing emergency, and that the primary purpose of the interrogation is to establish or prove past events potentially relevant to later criminal prosecution." *Davis*, 547 U.S., at 822.

Examining the *Davis* and *Hammon* statements in light of those definitions, we held that the statements at issue in *Davis* were nontestimonial and the statements in

---

1. The Supreme Court of Michigan held that the question whether the victim's statements would have been admissible as "dying declarations" was not properly before it. . . . Because of the State's failure to preserve its argument with regard to dying declarations, we similarly need not decide that question here.

Hammon were testimonial. We distinguished the statements in *Davis* from the testimonial statements in *Crawford* on several grounds, including that the victim in *Davis* was "speaking about events *as they were actually happening*, rather than 'describ[ing] past events,'" that there was an ongoing emergency, that the "elicited statements were necessary to be able to *resolve* the present emergency," and that the statements were not formal. 547 U.S., at 827. In *Hammon*, on the other hand, we held that, "[i]t is entirely clear from the circumstances that the interrogation was part of an investigation into possibly criminal past conduct." Id., at 829. There was "no emergency in progress." Ibid. . . .

. . . The basic purpose of the Confrontation Clause was to "targe[t]" the sort of "abuses" exemplified at the notorious treason trial of Sir Walter Raleigh. *Crawford*, 541 U.S., at 51. Thus, the most important instances in which the Clause restricts the introduction of out-of-court statements are those in which state actors are involved in a formal, out-of-court interrogation of a witness to obtain evidence for trial. . . . When, as in *Davis*, the primary purpose of an interrogation is to respond to an "ongoing emergency," its purpose is not to create a record for trial and thus is not within the scope of the Clause. But there may be *other* circumstances, aside from ongoing emergencies, when a statement is not procured with a primary purpose of creating an out-of-court substitute for trial testimony. In making the primary purpose determination, standard rules of hearsay, designed to identify some statements as reliable, will be relevant. Where no such primary purpose exists, the admissibility of a statement is the concern of state and federal rules of evidence, not the Confrontation Clause.

Deciding this case also requires further explanation of the "ongoing emergency" circumstance addressed in *Davis*. Because *Davis* and *Hammon* arose in the domestic violence context, that was the situation "we had immediately in mind (for that was the case before us)." 547 U.S., at 826. We now face a new context: a nondomestic dispute, involving a victim found in a public location, suffering from a fatal gunshot wound, and a perpetrator whose location was unknown at the time the police located the victim. Thus, we confront for the first time circumstances in which the "ongoing emergency" discussed in *Davis* extends beyond an initial victim to a potential threat to the responding police and the public at large. This new context requires us to provide additional clarification with regard to what *Davis* meant by "the primary purpose of the interrogation is to enable police assistance to meet an ongoing emergency."

III

To determine whether the "primary purpose" of an interrogation is "to enable police assistance to meet an ongoing emergency," *Davis*, 547 U.S., at 822, which would render the resulting statements nontestimonial, we objectively evaluate the circumstances in which the encounter occurs and the statements and actions of the parties.

A

The Michigan Supreme Court correctly understood that this inquiry is objective. 483 Mich., at 142, 768 N.W.2d, at 70. *Davis* uses the word "objective" or "objectively" no fewer than eight times in describing the relevant inquiry. . . .

An objective analysis of the circumstances of an encounter and the statements and actions of the parties to it provides the most accurate assessment of the "primary purpose of the interrogation." The circumstances in which an encounter occurs—e.g., at or near the scene of the crime versus at a police station, during an ongoing emergency or afterwards—are clearly matters of objective fact. The statements and actions of the parties must also be objectively evaluated. That is, the relevant inquiry is not the subjective or actual purpose of the individuals involved in a particular encounter, but rather the purpose that reasonable participants would have had, as ascertained from the individuals' statements and actions and the circumstances in which the encounter occurred.[7]

B

As our recent Confrontation Clause cases have explained, the existence of an "ongoing emergency" at the time of an encounter between an individual and the police is among the most important circumstances informing the "primary purpose" of an interrogation. See *Davis*, 547 U.S., at 828-830; *Crawford*, 541 U.S., at 65. The existence of an ongoing emergency is relevant to determining the primary purpose of the interrogation because an emergency focuses the participants on something other than "prov[ing] past events potentially relevant to later criminal prosecution."[8] *Davis*, 547 U.S., at 822. Rather, it focuses them on "end[ing] a threatening situation." Id., at 832. Implicit in *Davis* is the idea that because the prospect of fabrication in statements given for the primary purpose of resolving that emergency is presumably significantly diminished, the Confrontation Clause does not require such statements to be subject to the crucible of cross-examination.

This logic is not unlike that justifying the excited utterance exception in hearsay law. Statements "relating to a startling event or condition made while the declarant was under the stress of excitement caused by the event or condition," Fed. Rule Evid. 803(2); see also Mich. Rule Evid. 803(2) (2010), are considered reliable because the declarant, in the excitement, presumably cannot form a falsehood. See Idaho v. Wright, 497 U.S. 805, 820 (1990) ("The basis for the 'excited utterance' exception . . . is that such statements are given under circumstances that eliminate

7. This approach is consistent with our rejection of subjective inquiries in other areas of criminal law. See, e.g., Whren v. United States, 517 U.S. 806, 813 (1996) (refusing to evaluate Fourth Amendment reasonableness subjectively in light of the officers' actual motivations); New York v. Quarles, 467 U.S. 649, 655-656, and n. 6 (1984) (holding that an officer's subjective motivation is irrelevant to determining the applicability of the public safety exception to Miranda v. Arizona, 384 U.S. 436 (1966)); Rhode Island v. Innis, 446 U.S. 291, 301-302 (1980) (holding that a police officer's subjective intent to obtain incriminatory statements is not relevant to determining whether an interrogation has occurred).

8. The existence of an ongoing emergency must be objectively assessed from the perspective of the parties to the interrogation at the time, not with the benefit of hindsight. If the information the parties knew at the time of the encounter would lead a reasonable person to believe that there was an emergency, even if that belief was later proved incorrect, that is sufficient for purposes of the Confrontation Clause. The emergency is relevant to the "primary purpose of the interrogation" because of the effect it has on the parties' purpose, not because of its actual existence.

the possibility of fabrication, coaching, or confabulation. . . ."). An ongoing emergency has a similar effect of focusing an individual's attention on responding to the emergency.[9]

Following our precedents, the court below correctly began its analysis with the circumstances in which Covington interacted with the police. But in doing so, the court construed *Davis* to have decided more than it did and thus employed an unduly narrow understanding of "ongoing emergency" that *Davis* does not require.

First, the Michigan Supreme Court repeatedly and incorrectly asserted that *Davis* "defined" "'ongoing emergency.'" In fact, *Davis* did not even define the extent of the emergency in that case. The Michigan Supreme Court erroneously read *Davis* as deciding that "the statements made after the defendant stopped assaulting the victim and left the premises did *not* occur during an 'ongoing emergency.'" We explicitly explained in *Davis*, however, that we were asked to review only the testimonial nature of Michelle McCottry's initial statements during the 911 call; we therefore merely *assumed* the correctness of the Washington Supreme Court's holding that admission of her other statements was harmless, without deciding whether those subsequent statements were also made for the primary purpose of resolving an ongoing emergency.

Second, by assuming that *Davis* defined the outer bounds of "ongoing emergency," the Michigan Supreme Court failed to appreciate that whether an emergency exists and is ongoing is a highly context-dependent inquiry. *Davis* and *Hammon* involved domestic violence, a known and identified perpetrator, and, in *Hammon*, a neutralized threat. Because *Davis* and *Hammon* were domestic violence cases, we focused only on the threat to the victims and assessed the ongoing emergency from the perspective of whether there was a continuing threat *to them.*

Domestic violence cases like *Davis* and *Hammon* often have a narrower zone of potential victims than cases involving threats to public safety. An assessment of whether an emergency that threatens the police and public is ongoing cannot narrowly focus on whether the threat solely to the first victim has been neutralized because the threat to the first responders and public may continue. See Brief for United States as Amicus Curiae 19-20 ("An emergency posed by an unknown shooter who remains at large does not automatically abate just because the police can provide security to his first victim").

---

9. Many other exceptions to the hearsay rules similarly rest on the belief that certain statements are, by their nature, made for a purpose other than use in a prosecution and therefore should not be barred by hearsay prohibitions. See, e.g., Fed. Rule Evid. 801(d)(2)(E) (statement by a co-conspirator during and in furtherance of the conspiracy); 803(4) (Statements for Purposes of Medical Diagnosis or Treatment); 803(6) (Records of Regularly Conducted Activity); 803(8) (Public Records and Reports); 803(9) (Records of Vital Statistics); 803(11) (Records of Religious Organizations); 803(12) (Marriage, Baptismal, and Similar Certificates); 803(13) (Family Records); 804(b)(3) (Statement Against Interest); see also Melendez-Diaz v. Massachusetts, 557 U.S. __, __ (2009) ("Business and public records are generally admissible absent confrontation not because they qualify under an exception to the hearsay rules, but because—having been created for the administration of an entity's affairs and not for the purpose of establishing or proving some fact at trial—they are not testimonial"); Giles v. California, 554 U.S., at 376 (noting in the context of domestic violence that "[s]tatements to friends and neighbors about abuse and intimidation and statements to physicians in the course of receiving treatment would be excluded, if at all, only by hearsay rules"); *Crawford*, 541 U.S., at 56 ("Most of the hearsay exceptions covered statements that by their nature were not testimonial—for example, business records or statements in furtherance of a conspiracy").

The Michigan Supreme Court also did not appreciate that the duration and scope of an emergency may depend in part on the type of weapon employed. The court relied on *Davis* and *Hammon*, in which the assailants used their fists, as controlling the scope of the emergency here, which involved the use of a gun. The problem with that reasoning is clear when considered in light of the assault on Amy Hammon. Hershel Hammon was armed only with his fists when he attacked his wife, so removing Amy to a separate room was sufficient to end the emergency. If Hershel had been reported to be armed with a gun, however, separation by a single household wall might not have been sufficient to end the emergency.

The Michigan Supreme Court's failure to focus on the context-dependent nature of our *Davis* decision also led it to conclude that the medical condition of a declarant is irrelevant. . . . But *Davis* and *Hammon* did not present medical emergencies, despite some injuries to the victims. Thus, we have not previously considered, much less ruled out, the relevance of a victim's severe injuries to the primary purpose inquiry.

. . . The medical condition of the victim is important to the primary purpose inquiry to the extent that it sheds light on the ability of the victim to have any purpose at all in responding to police questions and on the likelihood that any purpose formed would necessarily be a testimonial one. The victim's medical state also provides important context for first responders to judge the existence and magnitude of a continuing threat to the victim, themselves, and the public.

. . . [N]one of this suggests that an emergency is ongoing in every place or even just surrounding the victim for the entire time that the perpetrator of a violent crime is on the loose. As we recognized in *Davis*, "a conversation which begins as an interrogation to determine the need for emergency assistance" can "evolve into testimonial statements." This evolution may occur if, for example, a declarant provides police with information that makes clear that what appeared to be an emergency is not or is no longer an emergency or that what appeared to be a public threat is actually a private dispute. It could also occur if a perpetrator is disarmed, surrenders, is apprehended, or, as in *Davis*, flees with little prospect of posing a threat to the public. Trial courts can determine in the first instance when any transition from nontestimonial to testimonial occurs, and exclude "the portions of any statement that have become testimonial, as they do, for example, with unduly prejudicial portions of otherwise admissible evidence."

Finally, our discussion of the Michigan Supreme Court's misunderstanding of what *Davis* meant by "ongoing emergency" should not be taken to imply that the existence *vel non* of an ongoing emergency is dispositive of the testimonial inquiry. As *Davis* made clear, whether an ongoing emergency exists is simply one factor—albeit an important factor—that informs the ultimate inquiry regarding the "primary purpose" of an interrogation. Another factor the Michigan Supreme Court did not sufficiently account for is the importance of *informality* in an encounter between a victim and police. Formality is not the sole touchstone of our primary purpose inquiry because, although formality suggests the absence of an emergency and therefore an increased likelihood that the purpose of the interrogation is to "establish or prove past events potentially relevant to later criminal prosecution," informality does not necessarily indicate the presence of an emergency or the lack of testimonial intent. The court below, however, too readily dismissed the informality of the circumstances in this case in a single brief footnote and in fact seems to have suggested that the encounter in this case was formal, 768 N.W.2d, at 75, n. 16.

As we explain further below, the questioning in this case occurred in an exposed, public area, prior to the arrival of emergency medical services, and in a disorganized fashion. All of those facts make this case distinguishable from the formal station-house interrogation in *Crawford*. . . .

C

In addition to the circumstances in which an encounter occurs, the statements and actions of both the declarant and interrogators provide objective evidence of the primary purpose of the interrogation. See, e.g., *Davis*, 547 U.S., at 827 ("[T]he nature of what was *asked and answered* in *Davis*, again viewed objectively, was such that the elicited statements were necessary to be able to *resolve* the present emergency, rather than simply to learn (as in *Crawford*) what had happened in the past" (first emphasis added)). . . .

. . . *Davis* requires a combined inquiry that accounts for both the declarant and the interrogator.[11] In many instances, the primary purpose of the interrogation will be most accurately ascertained by looking to the contents of both the questions and the answers. To give an extreme example, if the police say to a victim, "Tell us who did this to you so that we can arrest and prosecute them," the victim's response that "Rick did it," appears purely accusatory because by virtue of the phrasing of the question, the victim necessarily has prosecution in mind when she answers.

The combined approach also ameliorates problems that could arise from looking solely to one participant. Predominant among these is the problem of mixed motives on the part of both interrogators and declarants. Police officers in our society function as both first responders and criminal investigators. Their dual responsibilities may mean that they act with different motives simultaneously or in quick succession.

Victims are also likely to have mixed motives when they make statements to the police. During an ongoing emergency, a victim is most likely to want the threat to her and to other potential victims to end, but that does not necessarily mean that the victim wants or envisions prosecution of the assailant. A victim may want the attacker to be incapacitated temporarily or rehabilitated. Alternatively, a severely injured victim may have no purpose at all in answering questions posed; the answers may be simply reflexive. The victim's injuries could be so debilitating as to prevent her from thinking sufficiently clearly to understand whether her statements are for the purpose of addressing an ongoing emergency or for the purpose of future

---

11. Some portions of *Davis*, however, have caused confusion about whether the inquiry prescribes examination of one participant to the exclusion of the other. *Davis*' language indicating that a statement's testimonial or nontestimonial nature derives from "the primary purpose *of the interrogation*," 547 U.S., at 822 (emphasis added), could be read to suggest that the relevant purpose is that of the interrogator. In contrast, footnote 1 in *Davis* explains, "it is in the final analysis the declarant's statements, not the interrogator's questions, that the Confrontation Clause requires us to evaluate." Id., at 822-823, n. 1. . . . But this statement in footnote 1 of *Davis* merely acknowledges that the Confrontation Clause is not implicated when statements are offered "for purposes other than establishing the truth of the matter asserted." *Crawford*, 541 U.S., at 60, n. 9. An interrogator's questions, unlike a declarant's answers, do not assert the truth of any matter. The language in the footnote was not meant to determine *how* the courts are to assess the nature of the declarant's purpose, but merely to remind readers that it is the statements, and not the questions, that must be evaluated under the Sixth Amendment.

prosecution.[12] Taking into account a victim's injuries does not transform this objective inquiry into a subjective one. The inquiry is still objective because it focuses on the understanding and purpose of a reasonable victim in the circumstances of the actual victim—circumstances that prominently include the victim's physical state.

The dissent suggests that we intend to give controlling weight to the "intentions of the police." . . . That is a misreading of our opinion. At trial, the declarant's statements, not the interrogator's questions, will be introduced to "establis[h] the truth of the matter asserted," *Crawford*, 541 U.S., at 60, n. 9, and must therefore pass the Sixth Amendment test. In determining whether a declarant's statements are testimonial, courts should look to all of the relevant circumstances. Even Justice Scalia concedes that the interrogator is relevant to this evaluation, and we agree that "[t]he identity of an interrogator, and the content and tenor of his questions," can illuminate the "primary purpose of the interrogation." The dissent criticizes the complexity of our approach, but we, at least, are unwilling to sacrifice accuracy for simplicity. Simpler is not always better, and courts making a "primary purpose" assessment should not be unjustifiably restrained from consulting all relevant information, including the statements and actions of interrogators. . . .

IV

As we suggested in *Davis*, when a court must determine whether the Confrontation Clause bars the admission of a statement at trial, it should determine the "primary purpose of the interrogation" by objectively evaluating the statements and actions of the parties to the encounter, in light of the circumstances in which the interrogation occurs. The existence of an emergency or the parties' perception that an emergency is ongoing is among the most important circumstances that courts must take into account in determining whether an interrogation is testimonial because statements made to assist police in addressing an ongoing emergency presumably lack the testimonial purpose that would subject them to the requirement of confrontation. As the context of this case brings into sharp relief, the existence and duration of an emergency depend on the type and scope of danger posed to the victim, the police, and the public. . . .

We first examine the circumstances in which the interrogation occurred. The parties disagree over whether there was an emergency when the police arrived at the gas station. Bryant argues, and the Michigan Supreme Court accepted, that there was no ongoing emergency because "there . . . was no criminal conduct occurring. No shots were being fired, no one was seen in possession of a firearm, nor were any witnesses seen cowering in fear or running from the scene." Bryant, while conceding that "a serious or life-threatening injury creates a medical emergency for a victim," further argues that a declarant's medical emergency is not relevant to the ongoing emergency determination.

In contrast, Michigan and the Solicitor General explain that when the police responded to the call that a man had been shot and found Covington bleeding on the gas station parking lot, "they did not know who Covington was, whether the

---

12. In such a situation, the severe injuries of the victim would undoubtedly also weigh on the credibility and reliability that the trier of fact would afford to the statements. . . .

shooting had occurred at the gas station or at a different location, who the assailant was, or whether the assailant posed a continuing threat to Covington or others."

The Michigan Supreme Court stated that the police asked Covington, "what had happened, who had shot him, and where the shooting had occurred." . . . The officers basically agree on what information they learned from Covington, but not on the order in which they learned it or on whether Covington's statements were in response to general or detailed questions. They all agree that the first question was "what happened?" The answer was either "I was shot" or "Rick shot me."

. . . Nothing Covington said to the police indicated that the cause of the shooting was a purely private dispute or that the threat from the shooter had ended. The record reveals little about the motive for the shooting. The police officers who spoke with Covington at the gas station testified that Covington did not tell them what words Covington and Rick had exchanged prior to the shooting. What Covington did tell the officers was that he fled Bryant's back porch, indicating that he perceived an ongoing threat. The police did not know, and Covington did not tell them, whether the threat was limited to him. The potential scope of the dispute and therefore the emergency in this case thus stretches more broadly than those at issue in *Davis* and *Hammon* and encompasses a threat potentially to the police and the public.

This is also the first of our post-*Crawford* Confrontation Clause cases to involve a gun. The physical separation that was sufficient to end the emergency in *Hammon* was not necessarily sufficient to end the threat in this case; Covington was shot through the back door of Bryant's house. Bryant's argument that there was no ongoing emergency because "[n]o shots were being fired," surely construes ongoing emergency too narrowly. An emergency does not last only for the time between when the assailant pulls the trigger and the bullet hits the victim. . . .

. . . At bottom, there was an ongoing emergency here where an armed shooter, whose motive for and location after the shooting were unknown, had mortally wounded Covington within a few blocks and a few minutes of the location where the police found Covington.

This is not to suggest that the emergency continued until Bryant was arrested in California a year after the shooting. We need not decide precisely when the emergency ended because Covington's encounter with the police and all of the statements he made during that interaction occurred within the first few minutes of the police officers' arrival and well before they secured the scene of the shooting—the shooter's last known location.

. . . The circumstances of the encounter provide important context for understanding Covington's statements to the police. When the police arrived at Covington's side, their first question to him was "What happened?"[18] Covington's response was either "Rick shot me" or "I was shot," followed very quickly by an identification of "Rick" as the shooter. In response to further questions, Covington explained that the shooting occurred through the back door of Bryant's house and provided a physical description of the shooter. When he made the statements, Covington was lying in a gas station parking lot bleeding from a mortal gunshot wound to his abdomen. His answers to the police officers' questions were punctuated with questions

---

18. Although the dissent claims otherwise, at least one officer asked Covington something akin to "how was he doing." App. 131 (testimony of Officer Stuglin). . . .

about when emergency medical services would arrive. He was obviously in considerable pain and had difficulty breathing and talking. From this description of his condition and report of his statements, we cannot say that a person in Covington's situation would have had a "primary purpose" "to establish or prove past events potentially relevant to later criminal prosecution." *Davis*, 547 U.S., at 822.

For their part, the police responded to a call that a man had been shot. As discussed above, they did not know why, where, or when the shooting had occurred. Nor did they know the location of the shooter or anything else about the circumstances in which the crime occurred.[19] The questions they asked . . . were the exact type of questions necessary to allow the police to " 'assess the situation, the threat to their own safety, and possible danger to the potential victim' " and to the public, *Davis*, 547 U.S., at 832. In other words, they solicited the information necessary to enable them "to meet an ongoing emergency."

Nothing in Covington's responses indicated to the police that, contrary to their expectation upon responding to a call reporting a shooting, there was no emergency or that a prior emergency had ended. . . . The initial inquiries in this case resulted in the type of nontestimonial statements we contemplated in *Davis*.

Finally, we consider the informality of the situation and the interrogation. This situation is more similar, though not identical, to the informal, harried 911 call in *Davis* than to the structured, station-house interview in *Crawford*. As the officers' trial testimony reflects, the situation was fluid and somewhat confused: the officers arrived at different times; apparently each, upon arrival, asked Covington "what happened?"; and, contrary to the dissent's portrayal, they did not conduct a structured interrogation. The informality suggests that the interrogators' primary purpose was simply to address what they perceived to be an ongoing emergency, and the circumstances lacked any formality that would have alerted Covington to or focused him on the possible future prosecutorial use of his statements. . . .

* * *

For the foregoing reasons, we hold that Covington's statements were not testimonial and that their admission at Bryant's trial did not violate the Confrontation Clause. We leave for the Michigan courts to decide on remand whether the statements' admission was otherwise permitted by state hearsay rules. The judgment of the Supreme Court of Michigan is vacated, and the case is remanded for further proceedings not inconsistent with this opinion.

JUSTICE KAGAN took no part in the consideration or decision of this case.

JUSTICE THOMAS, concurring in the judgment.

I agree with the Court that the admission of Covington's out-of-court statements did not violate the Confrontation Clause, but I reach this conclusion because Covington's questioning by police lacked sufficient formality and solemnity for his

---

19. Contrary to the dissent's suggestion, and despite the fact that the record was developed prior to *Davis'* focus on the existence of an "ongoing emergency," the record contains some testimony to support the idea that the police officers were concerned about the location of the shooter when they arrived on the scene and thus to suggest that the purpose of the questioning of Covington was to determine the shooter's location.

statements to be considered "testimonial." See Crawford v. Washington, 541 U.S. 36 (2004). . . .

JUSTICE SCALIA, dissenting.

Today's tale—a story of five officers conducting successive examinations of a dying man with the primary purpose, not of obtaining and preserving his testimony regarding his killer, but of protecting him, them, and others from a murderer somewhere on the loose—is so transparently false that professing to believe it demeans this institution. But reaching a patently incorrect conclusion on the facts is a relatively benign judicial mischief; it affects, after all, only the case at hand. In its vain attempt to make the incredible plausible, however—or perhaps as an intended second goal—today's opinion distorts our Confrontation Clause jurisprudence and leaves it in a shambles. Instead of clarifying the law, the Court makes itself the obfuscator of last resort. Because I continue to adhere to the Confrontation Clause that the People adopted, as described in Crawford v. Washington, 541 U.S. 36 (2004), I dissent.

I

A

. . . *Crawford* and *Davis* did not address whose perspective matters—the declarant's, the interrogator's, or both—when assessing "the primary purpose of [an] interrogation." In those cases the statements were testimonial from any perspective. I think the same is true here, but because the Court picks a perspective so will I: The declarant's intent is what counts. In-court testimony is more than a narrative of past events; it is a solemn declaration made in the course of a criminal trial. For an out-of-court statement to qualify as testimonial, the declarant must intend the statement to be a solemn declaration rather than an unconsidered or offhand remark; and he must make the statement with the understanding that it may be used to invoke the coercive machinery of the State against the accused.[1] See Friedman, Grappling with the Meaning of "Testimonial," 71 Brooklyn L. Rev. 241, 259 (2005). That is what distinguishes a narrative told to a friend over dinner from a statement to the police. See *Crawford*, supra, at 51. The hidden purpose of an interrogator cannot substitute for the declarant's intentional solemnity or his understanding of how his words may be used.

A declarant-focused inquiry is also the only inquiry that would work in every fact pattern implicating the Confrontation Clause. The Clause applies to volunteered testimony as well as statements solicited through police interrogation. See *Davis*, supra, at 822-823, n. 1. An inquiry into an officer's purposes would make no sense when a declarant blurts out "Rick shot me" as soon as the officer arrives on the scene. I see no reason to adopt a different test—one that accounts for an officer's intent—when the officer asks "what happened" before the declarant makes his accusation. (This does not mean the interrogator is irrelevant. The identity of an interrogator, and the content and tenor of his questions, can bear upon whether

---

1. I remain agnostic about whether and when statements to nonstate actors are testimonial. See Davis v. Washington, 547 U.S. 813, 823, n. 2 (2006).

a declarant intends to make a solemn statement, and envisions its use at a criminal trial. But none of this means that the interrogator's purpose matters.)

In an unsuccessful attempt to make its finding of emergency plausible, the Court instead adopts a test that looks to the purposes of both the police and the declarant. It claims that this is demanded by necessity, fretting that a domestic-violence victim may want her abuser briefly arrested—presumably to teach him a lesson—but not desire prosecution. I do not need to probe the purposes of the police to solve that problem. Even if a victim speaks to the police "to establish or prove past events" solely for the purpose of getting her abuser arrested, she surely knows her account is "potentially relevant to later criminal prosecution" should one ensue. *Davis*, supra, at 822.

The Court also wrings its hands over the possibility that "a severely injured victim" may lack the capacity to form a purpose, and instead answer questions "reflexive[ly]." How to assess whether a declarant with diminished capacity bore testimony is a difficult question, and one I do not need to answer today. But the Court's proposed answer—to substitute the intentions of the police for the missing intentions of the declarant—cannot be the correct one. When the declarant has diminished capacity, focusing on the interrogators make less sense, not more. The inquiry under *Crawford* turns in part on the actions and statements of a declarant's audience only because they shape the declarant's perception of why his audience is listening and therefore influence *his purpose* in making the declaration. But a person who cannot perceive his own purposes certainly cannot perceive why a listener might be interested in what he has to say. . . .

The only virtue of the Court's approach (if it can be misnamed a virtue) is that it leaves judges free to reach the "fairest" result under the totality of the circumstances. If the dastardly police trick a declarant into giving an incriminating statement against a sympathetic defendant, a court can focus on the police's intent and declare the statement testimonial. If the defendant "deserves" to go to jail, then a court can focus on whatever perspective is necessary to declare damning hearsay nontestimonial. And when all else fails, a court can mix-and-match perspectives to reach its desired outcome. Unfortunately, under this malleable approach "the guarantee of confrontation is no guarantee at all." Giles v. California, 554 U.S. 353, 375 (2008) (plurality).

B

Looking to the declarant's purpose (as we should), this is an absurdly easy case. Roughly 25 minutes after Anthony Covington had been shot, Detroit police responded to a 911 call reporting that a gunshot victim had appeared at a neighborhood gas station. They quickly arrived at the scene, and in less than 10 minutes five different Detroit police officers questioned Covington about the shooting. Each asked him a similar battery of questions: "what happened" and when, "who shot" the victim, and "where" did the shooting take place. After Covington would answer, they would ask follow-up questions, such as "how tall is" the shooter, "[h]ow much does he weigh," what is the exact address or physical description of the house where the shooting took place, and what chain of events led to the shooting. The battery relented when the paramedics arrived and began tending to Covington's wounds.

From Covington's perspective, his statements had little value except to ensure the arrest and eventual prosecution of Richard Bryant. He knew the "threatening situation," *Davis*, 547 U.S., at 832, had ended six blocks away and 25 minutes earlier when he fled from Bryant's back porch. Bryant had not confronted him face-to-face before he was mortally wounded, instead shooting him through a door. Even if Bryant had pursued him (unlikely), and after seeing that Covington had ended up at the gas station was unable to confront him there before the police arrived (doubly unlikely), it was entirely beyond imagination that Bryant would again open fire while Covington was surrounded by five armed police officers. And Covington knew the shooting was the work of a drug dealer, not a spree killer who might randomly threaten others. . . .

Covington's pressing medical needs do not suggest that he was responding to an emergency, but to the contrary reinforce the testimonial character of his statements. He understood the police were focused on investigating a past crime, not his medical needs. None of the officers asked Covington how he was doing, attempted more than superficially to assess the severity of his wounds, or attempted to administer first aid.[2] They instead primarily asked questions with little, if any, relevance to Covington's dire situation. Police, paramedics, and doctors do not need to know the address where a shooting took place, the name of the shooter, or the shooter's height and weight to provide proper medical care. . . .

Neither Covington's statements nor the colloquy between him and the officers would have been out of place at a trial; it would have been a routine direct examination. Like a witness, Covington recounted in detail how a past criminal event began and progressed, and like a prosecutor, the police elicited that account through structured questioning. . . . Ex parte examinations raise the same constitutional concerns whether they take place in a gas-station parking lot or in a police interrogation room.

C

Worse still for the repute of today's opinion, this is an absurdly easy case even if one (erroneously) takes the interrogating officers' purpose into account. The five officers interrogated Covington primarily to investigate past criminal events. . . .

D

A final word about the Court's active imagination. The Court invents a world where an ongoing emergency exists whenever "an armed shooter, whose motive for and location after the shooting [are] unknown, . . . mortally wound[s]" one individual "within a few blocks and [25] minutes of the location where the police" ultimately find that victim. Breathlessly, it worries that a shooter could leave the scene armed and ready to pull the trigger again. Nothing suggests the five officers in this case shared the Court's dystopian view of Detroit, where drug dealers hunt their shooting victim down and fire into a crowd of police officers to finish him off,

---

2. Officer Stuglin's testimony does not undermine my assessment of the officers' behavior, although the Court suggests otherwise. Officer Stuglin first testified that he "asked something like what happened or are you okay, something to that line." When pressed on whether he asked "how are you doing?," he responded, "Well, basically . . . what's wrong." Other officers were not so equivocal: They admitted they had no need to "ask him how he was doing. . . . It was very obvious how he was doing."

or where spree killers shoot through a door and then roam the streets leaving a trail of bodies behind. Because almost 90 percent of murders involve a single victim, it is much more likely—indeed, I think it certain—that the officers viewed their encounter with Covington for what it was: an investigation into a past crime with no ongoing or immediate consequences.

The Court's distorted view creates an expansive exception to the Confrontation Clause for violent crimes. Because Bryant posed a continuing threat to public safety in the Court's imagination, the emergency persisted for confrontation purposes at least until the police learned his "motive for and location after the shooting." . . . This is a dangerous definition of emergency. Many individuals who testify against a defendant at trial first offer their accounts to police in the hours after a violent act. If the police can plausibly claim that a "potential threat to . . . the public" persisted through those first few hours, . . . a defendant will have no constitutionally protected right to exclude the uncross-examined testimony of such witnesses. His conviction could rest (as perhaps it did here) solely on the officers' recollection at trial of the witnesses' accusations. . . .

II

A

But today's decision is not only a gross distortion of the facts. It is a gross distortion of the law—a revisionist narrative in which reliability continues to guide our Confrontation Clause jurisprudence, at least where emergencies and faux emergencies are concerned. . . .

The Court announces that in future cases it will look to "standard rules of hearsay, designed to identify some statements as reliable," when deciding whether a statement is testimonial. Ohio v. Roberts, 448 U.S. 56 (1980) said something remarkably similar: An out-of-court statement is admissible if it "falls within a firmly rooted hearsay exception" or otherwise "bears adequate 'indicia of reliability.'" Id., at 66. We tried that approach to the Confrontation Clause for nearly 25 years before *Crawford rejected* it as an unworkable standard unmoored from the text and the historical roots of the Confrontation Clause. . . .

The Court attempts to fit its resurrected interest in reliability into the *Crawford* framework, but the result is incoherent. Reliability, the Court tells us, is a good indicator of whether "a statement is . . . an out-of-court substitute for trial testimony." That is patently false. Reliability tells us *nothing* about whether a statement is testimonial. Testimonial and nontestimonial statements alike come in varying degrees of reliability. An eyewitness's statements to the police after a fender-bender, for example, are both reliable and testimonial. Statements to the police from one driver attempting to blame the other would be similarly testimonial but rarely reliable.

The Court suggests otherwise because it "misunderstands the relationship" between qualification for one of the standard hearsay exceptions and exemption from the confrontation requirement. Melendez-Diaz v. Massachusetts, 557 U.S. ___, ___ (2009). That relationship is not a causal one. Hearsay law exempts business records, for example, because businesses have a financial incentive to keep reliable records. See Fed. Rule Evid. 803(6). The Sixth Amendment also generally admits business records into evidence, but not because the records are reliable or because hearsay law says so. It admits them "because—having been created for the administration of an entity's affairs and not for the purpose of establishing or proving some fact at trial—they are not" weaker substitutes for live testimony. *Melendez-Diaz*, 557 U.S., at ___. . . .

Is it possible that the Court does not recognize the contradiction between its focus on reliable statements and *Crawford*'s focus on testimonial ones? Does it not realize that the two cannot coexist? Or does it intend, by following today's illogical roadmap, to resurrect *Roberts* by a thousand unprincipled distinctions without ever explicitly overruling *Crawford*? After all, honestly overruling *Crawford* would destroy the illusion of judicial minimalism and restraint. And it would force the Court to explain how the Justices' preference comports with the meaning of the Confrontation Clause that the People adopted—or to confess that only the Justices' preference really matters.

B

The Court recedes from *Crawford* in a second significant way. It requires judges to conduct "open-ended balancing tests" and "amorphous, if not entirely subjective," inquiries into the totality of the circumstances bearing upon reliability. 541 U.S., at 63, 68. Where the prosecution cries "emergency," the admissibility of a statement now turns on "a highly context-dependent inquiry," into the type of weapon the defendant wielded; the type of crime the defendant committed; the medical condition of the declarant; if the declarant is injured, whether paramedics have arrived on the scene; whether the encounter takes place in an "exposed public area"; whether the encounter appears disorganized; whether the declarant is capable of forming a purpose; whether the police have secured the scene of the crime; the formality of the statement; and finally, whether the statement strikes us as reliable. This is no better than the nine-factor balancing test we rejected in *Crawford*, 541 U.S., at 63. I do not look forward to resolving conflicts in the future over whether knives and poison are more like guns or fists for Confrontation Clause purposes, or whether rape and armed robbery are more like murder or domestic violence.

It can be said, of course, that under *Crawford* analysis of whether a statement is testimonial requires consideration of all the circumstances, and so is also something of a multifactor balancing test. But the "reliability" test does not replace that analysis; it supplements it. As I understand the Court's opinion, even when it is determined that no emergency exists (or perhaps before that determination is made) the statement would be found admissible as far as the Confrontation Clause is concerned if it is not testimonial.

In any case, we did not disavow multifactor balancing for reliability in *Crawford* out of a preference for rules over standards. We did so because it "d[id] violence to" the Framers' design. . . .

* * *

Judicial decisions, like the Constitution itself, are nothing more than "parchment barriers," 5 Writings of James Madison 269, 272 (G. Hunt ed. 1901). Both depend on a judicial culture that understands its constitutionally assigned role, has the courage to persist in that role when it means announcing unpopular decisions, and has the modesty to persist when it produces results that go against the judges' policy preferences. Today's opinion falls far short of living up to that obligation—short on the facts, and short on the law.

For all I know, Bryant has received his just deserts. But he surely has not received them pursuant to the procedures that our Constitution requires. And what has been taken away from him has been taken away from us all.

[Justice Ginsburg's dissenting opinion is omitted]

NOTES AND QUESTIONS

1. OMG! What's going on in *Bryant?* How can lower courts possibly make sense out of *Bryant*, given the prior decisions in *Crawford, Davis, Hammon,* and *Melendez-Diaz*, and especially given the *subsequent* decision—rendered less than four months after *Bryant*—in *Bullcoming?*

Perhaps it might help to think about *Crawford* doctrine in terms of the evolving views of the individual Justices. Although Justice Scalia enjoyed strong majorities in *Crawford* (seven Justices) and *Davis/Hammon* (eight Justices), he lost a couple of votes when Justice Stevens and Justice Souter left the Court. And *Melendez-Diaz* marked a key turning point; as a result of that case, four of the other Justices who had supported Justice Scalia in *Davis/Hammon* suddenly woke up and realized the absurd lengths to which *Crawford* doctrine eventually might go.

At this point, it seems that there remain only two "true believers" in the hard-core revolutionary vision of the Confrontation Clause represented by *Crawford, Davis/Hammon,* and *Melendez-Diaz*: Justice Scalia (the author of the majority opinion in each of those cases) and Justice Ginsburg. Justice Thomas was never entirely on board; he joined *Crawford*, but his unique emphasis on "formality" as the key to the Confrontation Clause means that he has always held a much narrower view of that decision than Justice Scalia. Then there are the four "counterreactionaries," who turned sharply against Justice Scalia's view in *Melendez-Diaz*, and who are now committed to limiting *Crawford* as much as humanly possible: Chief Justice Roberts, Justice Kennedy, Justice Breyer, and Justice Alito. Finally, the two newest Justices—Justice Sotomayor and (as far as we can tell, on limited data) Justice Kagan—appear to be pragmatists who prefer a case-by-case and issue-by-issue approach to one based on abstract principles. In fact, Justice Sotomayor—at least in light of her majority opinion in *Bryant*—seems to long for a return to the fact-specific, contextual doctrine of Ohio v. Roberts. Given this line-up, is there much hope for coherence in the Court's Confrontation Clause decisions?

2. Perhaps there is some hope, even if it is faint. In Ohio v. Clark, 135 S. Ct. 2173 (2015), the Court considered whether the Confrontation Clause barred the introduction of statements by a three-year-old child identifying Clark, the child's mother's boyfriend, as the one who committed the abuse against the child and his infant sister. The statements were made in response to questioning by the child's teachers; the teachers promptly reported the statements to the police, as they were required to do by state law, and the statements were later used at trial to convict Clark of various crimes.

All nine Justices agreed that the child's statements were admissible. Justice Alito wrote a majority opinion that managed to garner six votes. Justice Scalia (joined by Justice Ginsburg) and Justice Thomas each concurred in the judgment. According to the majority:

> Because neither the child nor his teachers had the primary purpose of assisting in Clark's prosecution, the child's statements do not implicate the Confrontation Clause and therefore were admissible at trial.

. . . In Davis v. Washington and Hammon v. Indiana, 547 U.S. 813 (2006), . . . [we announced] what has come to be known as the "primary purpose" test. . . . "Statements are nontestimonial when made in the course of police interrogation under circumstances objectively indicating that the primary purpose of the interrogation is to enable police assistance to meet an ongoing emergency. They are testimonial when the circumstances objectively indicate that there is no such ongoing emergency, and that the primary purpose of the interrogation is to establish or prove past events potentially relevant to later criminal prosecution." Because the cases involved statements to law enforcement officers, we reserved the question whether similar statements to individuals other than law enforcement officers would raise similar issues under the Confrontation Clause.

In Michigan v. Bryant, 562 U.S. 344 (2011), we further expounded on the primary purpose test. The inquiry, we emphasized, must consider "all of the relevant circumstances." And we reiterated our view in *Davis* that, when "the primary purpose of an interrogation is to respond to an 'ongoing emergency,' its purpose is not to create a record for trial and thus is not within the scope of the [Confrontation] Clause." 562 U.S., at 358. At the same time, we noted that "there may be *other* circumstances, aside from ongoing emergencies, when a statement is not procured with a primary purpose of creating an out-of-court substitute for trial testimony." "[T]he existence *vel non* of an ongoing emergency is not the touchstone of the testimonial inquiry." Instead, "whether an ongoing emergency exists is simply one factor . . . that informs the ultimate inquiry regarding the 'primary purpose' of an interrogation." Id., at 366.

One additional factor is "the informality of the situation and the interrogation." Id., at 377. A "formal station-house interrogation," like the questioning in *Crawford*, is more likely to provoke testimonial statements, while less formal questioning is less likely to reflect a primary purpose aimed at obtaining testimonial evidence against the accused. And in determining whether a statement is testimonial, "standard rules of hearsay, designed to identify some statements as reliable, will be relevant." In the end, the question is whether, in light of all the circumstances, viewed objectively, the "primary purpose" of the conversation was to "creat[e] an out-of-court substitute for trial testimony." Id., at 358. . . .

Thus, under our precedents, a statement cannot fall within the Confrontation Clause unless its primary purpose was testimonial. "Where no such primary purpose exists, the admissibility of a statement is the concern of state and federal rules of evidence, not the Confrontation Clause." But that does not mean that the Confrontation Clause bars every statement that satisfies the "primary purpose" test. We have recognized that the Confrontation Clause does not prohibit the introduction of out-of-court statements that would have been admissible in a criminal case at the time of the founding. See Giles v. California, 554 U.S. 353-359 (2008); *Crawford*, 541 U.S., at 56, n. 6, 62. Thus, the primary purpose test is a necessary, but not always sufficient, condition for the exclusion of out-of-court statements under the Confrontation Clause.

In this case, we consider statements made to preschool teachers, not the police. We are therefore presented with the question we have repeatedly reserved: whether statements to persons other than law enforcement officers are subject to the Confrontation Clause. Because at least some statements to individuals who are not law enforcement officers could conceivably raise confrontation concerns, we decline to adopt a categorical rule excluding them from the Sixth Amendment's reach. Nevertheless, such statements are much less likely to be testimonial than statements to law enforcement officers. And considering all the relevant circumstances here, [the child's] statements clearly were not made with the primary purpose of creating evidence for Clark's prosecution. Thus, their introduction at trial did not violate the Confrontation Clause.

135 S. Ct., at 2177, 2179-2181. The majority identified the following as "relevant circumstances": (1) the teachers were investigating an ongoing emergency, and were

motivated primarily by their desire to protect the child from his abuser; (2) the questioning by the teachers occurred in the "informal setting of a preschool lunchroom and classroom"; (3) the child's age made it "extremely unlikely" that the child "would intend his statements to be a substitute for trial testimony"; (4) historical evidence supported the conclusion that similar statements "were admissible at common law"[11]; and (5) "although we decline to adopt a rule that statements to individuals who are not law enforcement officers are categorically outside the Sixth Amendment, the fact that [the child] was speaking to his teachers remains highly relevant. . . . Statements made to someone who is not principally charged with uncovering and prosecuting criminal behavior are significantly less likely to be testimonial than statements given to law enforcement officers." The defendant argued that four additional circumstances should cut the other way: (1) the fact that the teachers were legally required to report the statements to the police; (2) the fact that the actions of the teachers had the "natural tendency" to lead to Clark's prosecution and conviction; (3) the fact that the child would have been incompetent to testify at trial; and (4) the fact that the jury likely perceived the child's statements as "the functional equivalent of testimony." The majority, however, found these additional circumstances *not* relevant to the Confrontation Clause outcome.

Justice Scalia (joined by Justice Ginsburg) concurred in the judgment:

> I agree with the Court's holding, and with its refusal to decide two questions quite unnecessary to that holding: what effect Ohio's mandatory-reporting law has in transforming a private party into a state actor for Confrontation Clause purposes, and whether a more permissive Confrontation Clause test—one less likely to hold the statements testimonial—should apply to interrogations by private actors. The statements here would not be testimonial under the usual test applicable to informal police interrogation.
>
> . . . I write separately, however, to protest the Court's shoveling of fresh dirt upon the Sixth Amendment right of confrontation so recently rescued from the grave in Crawford v. Washington, 541 U.S. 36 (2004). . . .
>
> Take, for example, the opinion's statement that the primary-purpose test is merely *one* of several heretofore unmentioned conditions ("necessary, but not always sufficient") that must be satisfied before the Clause's protections apply. That is absolutely false, and has no support in our opinions. The Confrontation Clause categorically entitles a defendant *to be confronted with the witnesses against him*; and the primary-purpose test sorts out, among the many people who interact with the police informally, *who is acting as a witness and who is not.* Those who fall into the former category bear testimony, and are therefore acting as "witnesses," subject to the right of confrontation. There are no other mysterious requirements that the Court declines to name.
>
> The opinion asserts that future defendants, and future Confrontation Clause majorities, must provide "evidence that the adoption of the Confrontation Clause was understood to require the exclusion of evidence that was regularly admitted in criminal cases at the time of the founding." This dictum gets the burden precisely backwards—which is of course precisely the idea. Defendants may invoke their Confrontation Clause rights once they have established that the state seeks

---

11. For this proposition, the Court cited Lyon & LaMagna, The History of Children's Hearsay: From Old Bailey to Post-*Davis*, 82 Ind. L.J. 1029, 1030 (2007) (examining child rape cases from 1687 to 1788), and J. Langbein, The Origins of Adversary Criminal Trial 239 (2003) (concluding that Old Bailey in 18th-century London "tolerated flagrant hearsay in rape prosecutions involving a child victim who was not competent to testify because she was too young to appreciate the significance of her oath").

to introduce testimonial evidence against them in a criminal case without unavailability of the witness and a previous opportunity to cross-examine. The burden is upon the prosecutor who seeks to introduce evidence *over* this bar to prove a long-established practice of introducing *specific* kinds of evidence, such as dying declarations, see *Crawford*, supra, for which cross-examination was not typically necessary. A suspicious mind (or even one that is merely not naïve) might regard this distortion as the first step in an attempt to smuggle longstanding hearsay exceptions back into the Confrontation Clause—in other words, an attempt to return to Ohio v. Roberts.

But the good news is that there are evidently not the votes to return to that halcyon era for prosecutors; and that dicta, even calculated dicta, are nothing but dicta. They are enough, however, combined with the peculiar phenomenon of a Supreme Court opinion's aggressive hostility to precedent that it purports to be applying, to prevent my joining the writing for the Court. I concur only in the judgment.

135 S. Ct., at 2183-2185 (Scalia, J., concurring in the judgment).
Justice Thomas also concurred in the judgment:

I agree with the Court that Ohio mandatory reporters are not agents of law enforcement, that statements made to private persons or by very young children will rarely implicate the Confrontation Clause, and that the admission of the statements at issue here did not implicate that constitutional provision. I nonetheless cannot join the majority's analysis. In the decade since we first sought to return to the original meaning of the Confrontation Clause, see Crawford v. Washington, 541 U.S. 36 (2004), we have carefully reserved consideration of that Clause's application to statements made to private persons for a case in which it was squarely presented.

This is that case; yet the majority does not offer clear guidance on the subject, declaring only that "the primary purpose test is a necessary, but not always sufficient, condition" for a statement to fall within the scope of the Confrontation Clause. The primary purpose test, however, is just as much "an exercise in fiction . . . disconnected from history" for statements made to private persons as it is for statements made to agents of law enforcement, if not more so. See *Bryant*, supra, at 379 (Thomas, J., concurring in judgment) (internal quotation marks omitted). I would not apply it here. Nor would I leave the resolution of this important question in doubt.

Instead, I would use the same test for statements to private persons that I have employed for statements to agents of law enforcement, assessing whether those statements bear sufficient indicia of solemnity to qualify as testimonial. . . .

135 S. Ct., at 2185-2186 (Thomas, J., concurring in the judgment).
Notwithstanding the discomfort of Justices Scalia, Ginsburg, and Thomas, does *Clark* mean there might be some light at the end of the tunnel? Could we be witnessing the rise of a new, multi-factor test that might lead to a more factually nuanced definition of "testimony"? Will such a test allow the new-found Court majority to ameliorate some of the more harsh and rigid practical consequences of *Crawford*? Only time will tell.

3. Note two interesting aspects of the Court's opinions in this area. First, they were prompted, in part, by the ambiguities in the *Roberts* line of cases, suggesting at a minimum that the *Crawford* replacement should be easier to apply. Second, they consistently refuse to take account of the implications of modern-day social, economic, scientific, and justice system realities, and insist instead upon the application of a formal test mandated by the constitutional text as "the Framers" understood it.

On the first issue, it is fair to say that, rather than calming the waters disturbed by *Roberts, Crawford* threw the criminal justice process into turmoil. Within two years of the cases, over 6,000 cases had cited to it, and now tens of thousands have. See, e.g., Jennifer A. Lindt, Protecting the Most Vulnerable Victims: Prosecution of Child Sex Offenses in Illinois Post Crawford v. Washington, 27 N. Ill. U. L. Rev. 95 (2006).

On the second issue, the Court's version of history has systematically been shown to be in error, which calls into question a method of constitutional interpretation so dependent on historical analysis. Consider the following from Thomas Y. Davies, Not "The Framers' Design": How the Framing-Era Ban Against Hearsay Evidence Refutes the *Crawford-Davis* "Testimonial" Formulation of the Scope of the Original Confrontation Clause, 15 J.L. & Pol'y 349-350 (2007):

> According to proponents, an originalist approach to constitutional interpretation injects discipline into constitutional decision-making. At least in criminal procedure, this claim is unrealistic. Instead, the originalist claims that have appeared in recent criminal procedure decisions have usually reflected the ideological proclivities of the justices who made them, but have rarely resembled the historical legal doctrines that actually shaped the Framers' understanding.
>
> The divergence between originalist claims and historical doctrine has been particularly apparent in two recent decisions that construed the Sixth Amendment Confrontation Clause with regard to the admission of hearsay evidence in criminal trials. In the 2004 decision Crawford v. Washington, and again in the 2006 decision Davis v. Washington, Justice Scalia asserted in opinions for the Court that "the Framers' design" for the scope of the confrontation right was that the right should regulate the admission as evidence in criminal trials of only "testimonial" out-of-court statements, but not apply at all to less formal, "nontestimonial" hearsay evidence.
>
> As a practical matter, it seems likely that the narrow scope accorded to the confrontation right in *Crawford* will allow prosecutors considerable room to use hearsay evidence in criminal cases rather than produce the person who made the out-of-court statement as a trial witness, even when the person who made the hearsay statement is readily available to be called. Thus, the *Crawford* formulation of the limited scope of the right appears to mean that criminal defendants will often be deprived of meeting face to face the available declarant who made the out-of-court statement and will also be deprived of cross-examining the declarant in the view of the jury. Is that outcome really consistent with the framing-era doctrine that shaped the Framers' understanding of the confrontation right?
>
> Plainly not. Although Justice Scalia endorsed formulating the Confrontation Clause to permit "only those [hearsay] exceptions established at the time of the founding," he did not follow through on identifying such exceptions in *Crawford* or *Davis*. If he had actually canvassed the framing-era evidence authorities, he would have discovered that framing-era evidence doctrine imposed a virtually total ban against using unsworn hearsay evidence to prove a criminal defendant's guilt. Although framing-era law did permit some hearsay evidence to be admitted regarding certain specific issues in civil lawsuit trials, those exceptions were not understood to apply to criminal trials. Instead, as of 1789, a dying declaration of a murder victim was the only kind of unsworn out-of-court statement that could be admitted in a criminal trial to prove the guilt of the defendant. Otherwise, the hearsay "exceptions" that now constitute a prominent feature of criminal evidence law had not yet been invented. Instead, nineteenth-century judges invented the hearsay exceptions that now apply to criminal trials only after the framing. Hence, it is clear that the Framers did not design the Confrontation Clause so as to accommodate the admission of unsworn hearsay statements.

Indeed, the framing-era authorities indicate that admission of hearsay statements would have violated basic principles of common-law criminal evidence. In particular, the framing-era sources indicate that the confrontation right itself prohibited the use of hearsay statements as evidence of the defendant's guilt. The condemnations of hearsay that appeared in prominent and widely used framing-era authorities typically recognized that the admission of a hearsay statement would deprive the defendant of the opportunity to cross-examine the speaker in the presence of the trial jury, and that opportunity to cross-examine was understood to be a salient aspect of the confrontation right. Thus, the framing-era sources actually suggest that the Framers would not have approved of the hearsay exceptions that were later invented because the Framers would have perceived such exceptions to violate a defendant's confrontation right.

Hence, *Crawford's* testimonial formulation of the scope of the confrontation right does not reflect "the Framers' design." Rather, *Crawford's* permissive allowance of unsworn hearsay is inconsistent with the basic premises that shaped the Framers' understanding of the right. Thus, whatever might be said for or against *Crawford's* formulation as a matter of contemporary constitutional policy, the fictional character of the historical claims made in that opinion constitute further evidence that originalism is a defective approach to constitutional decision-making. . . .

b. *The* Bruton *Rule*

Prior statements by a codefendant that are *not* admissible against the defendant as coconspirator statements, but that *are* admissible against the codefendant who made the statements, create special problems during a joint trial because of their potentially devastating impact on the jury with respect to the guilt of both defendants. This has led the Court to develop a special prophylactic rule—the *Bruton* rule—generally barring the admission of such statements. The next case deals with the scope of this rule.

GRAY v. MARYLAND

Certiorari to the Court of Appeals of Maryland
523 U.S. 185 (1998)

JUSTICE BREYER delivered the opinion of the Court.

The issue in this case concerns the application of Bruton v. United States, 391 U.S. 123 (1968). *Bruton* involved two defendants accused of participating in the same crime and tried jointly before the same jury. One of the defendants had confessed. His confession named and incriminated the other defendant. The trial judge issued a limiting instruction, telling the jury that it should consider the confession as evidence only against the codefendant who had confessed and not against the defendant named in the confession. *Bruton* held that, despite the limiting instruction, the Constitution forbids the use of such a confession in the joint trial.

The case before us differs from *Bruton* in that the prosecution here redacted the codefendant's confession by substituting for the defendant's name in the confession a blank space or the word "deleted." We must decide whether these substitutions make a significant legal difference. We hold that they do not and that *Bruton*'s protective rule applies.

I

In 1993, Stacy Williams died after a severe beating. Anthony Bell gave a confession, to the Baltimore City police, in which he said that he (Bell), Kevin Gray, and Jacquin "Tank" Vanlandingham had participated in the beating that resulted in Williams' death. Vanlandingham later died. A Maryland grand jury indicted Bell and Gray for murder. The State of Maryland tried them jointly.

The trial judge, after denying Gray's motion for a separate trial, permitted the State to introduce Bell's confession into evidence at trial. But the judge ordered the confession redacted. Consequently, the police detective who read the confession into evidence said the word "deleted" or "deletion" whenever Gray's name or Vanlandingham's name appeared. Immediately after the police detective read the redacted confession to the jury, the prosecutor asked, "after he gave you that information, you subsequently were able to arrest Mr. Kevin Gray; is that correct?" The officer responded, "That's correct." . . . The State also introduced into evidence a written copy of the confession with those two names omitted, leaving in their place blank white spaces separated by commas. . . . The State produced other witnesses, who said that six persons (including Bell, Gray, and Vanlandingham) participated in the beating. Gray testified and denied his participation. Bell did not testify.

When instructing the jury, the trial judge specified that the confession was evidence only against Bell; the instructions said that the jury should not use the confession as evidence against Gray. The jury convicted both Bell and Gray. Gray appealed.

Maryland's intermediate appellate court accepted Gray's argument that *Bruton* prohibited use of the confession and set aside his conviction. . . . Maryland's highest court disagreed and reinstated the conviction. . . . We granted certiorari in order to consider *Bruton*'s application to a redaction that replaces a name with an obvious blank space or symbol or word such as "deleted."

II

In deciding whether *Bruton*'s protective rule applies to the redacted confession before us, we must consider both *Bruton*, and a later case, Richardson v. Marsh, 481 U.S. 200 (1987), which limited *Bruton*'s scope. We shall briefly summarize each of these two cases.

Bruton, as we have said, involved two defendants—Evans and Bruton—tried jointly for robbery. Evans did not testify, but the Government introduced into evidence Evans' confession, which stated that both he (Evans) and Bruton together had committed the robbery. 391 U.S., at 124. The trial judge told the jury it could consider the confession as evidence only against Evans, not against Bruton. Id., at 125.

This Court held that, despite the limiting instruction, the introduction of Evans' out-of-court confession at Bruton's trial had violated Bruton's right, protected by the Sixth Amendment, to cross-examine witnesses. Id., at 137. The Court recognized that in many circumstances a limiting instruction will adequately protect one defendant from the prejudicial effects of the introduction at a joint trial of evidence intended for use only against a different defendant. Id., at 135. But it said that

[T]here are some contexts in which the risk that the jury will not, or cannot, follow instructions is so great, and the consequences of failure so vital to the defendant, that the practical and human limitations of the jury system cannot be ignored. Such a context is presented here, where the powerfully incriminating extrajudicial statements of a codefendant, who stands accused side-by-side with the defendant, are deliberately spread before the jury in a joint trial. Not only are the incriminations devastating to the defendant but their credibility is inevitably suspect. . . . The unreliability of such evidence is intolerably compounded when the alleged accomplice, as here, does not testify and cannot be tested by cross-examination.

Id., at 135-136 (citations omitted).

The Court found that Evans' confession constituted just such a "powerfully incriminating extrajudicial statemen[t]," and that its introduction into evidence, insulated from cross-examination, violated Bruton's Sixth Amendment rights. Id., at 135.

In Richardson v. Marsh, . . . the Court considered a redacted confession. The case involved a joint murder trial of Marsh and Williams. The State had redacted the confession of one defendant, Williams, so as to "omit all reference" to his codefendant, Marsh— "indeed, to omit all indication that *anyone* other than . . . Williams" and a third person had "participated in the crime." [481 U.S.], at 203 (emphasis in original). The trial court also instructed the jury not to consider the confession against Marsh. Id., at 205. As redacted, the confession indicated that Williams and the third person had discussed the murder in the front seat of a car while they traveled to the victim's house. Id., at 203-204, n. 1. The redacted confession contained no indication that Marsh—or any other person—was in the car. Ibid. Later in the trial, however, Marsh testified that she was in the back seat of the car. Id., at 204. For that reason, in context, the confession still could have helped convince the jury that Marsh knew about the murder in advance and therefore had participated knowingly in the crime.

The Court held that this redacted confession fell outside *Bruton*'s scope and was admissible (with appropriate limiting instructions) at the joint trial. The Court distinguished Evans' confession in *Bruton* as a confession that was "incriminating on its face," and which had "expressly implicate[d]" *Bruton*. 481 U.S. 200, at 208. By contrast, Williams' confession amounted to "evidence requiring linkage" in that it "became" incriminating in respect to Marsh "only when linked with evidence introduced later at trial." Ibid. The Court held

that the Confrontation Clause is not violated by the admission of a nontestifying codefendant's confession with a proper limiting instruction when, as here, the confession is redacted to eliminate not only the defendant's name, but any reference to his or her existence.

Id., at 211.

The Court added: "We express no opinion on the admissibility of a confession in which the defendant's name has been replaced with a symbol or neutral pronoun." Id., at 211, n. 5.

III

Originally, the codefendant's confession in the case before us, like that in *Bruton*, referred to, and directly implicated another defendant. The State, however, redacted that confession by removing the nonconfessing defendant's name. Nonetheless, unlike *Richardson*'s redacted confession, this confession refers directly to the "existence" of the nonconfessing defendant. The State has simply replaced the nonconfessing defendant's name with a kind of symbol, namely the word "deleted" or a blank space set off by commas. The redacted confession, for example, responded to the question "Who was in the group that beat Stacey," with the phrase, "Me, _____, and a few other guys." . . . And when the police witness read the confession in court, he said the word "deleted" or "deletion" where the blank spaces appear. We therefore must decide a question that *Richardson* left open, namely whether redaction that replaces a defendant's name with an obvious indication of deletion, such as a blank space, the word "deleted," or a similar symbol, still falls within *Bruton*'s protective rule. We hold that it does.

Bruton, as interpreted by *Richardson*, holds that certain "powerfully incriminating extrajudicial statements of a codefendant" — those naming another defendant — considered as a class, are so prejudicial that limiting instructions cannot work. *Richardson*, 481 U.S., at 207; *Bruton*, 391 U.S., at 135. Unless the prosecutor wishes to hold separate trials or to use separate juries or to abandon use of the confession, he must redact the confession to reduce significantly or to eliminate the special prejudice that the *Bruton* Court found. Redactions that simply replace a name with an obvious blank space or a word such as "deleted" or a symbol or other similarly obvious indications of alteration, however, leave statements that, considered as a class, so closely resemble *Bruton*'s unredacted statements that, in our view, the law must require the same result.

For one thing, a jury will often react similarly to an unredacted confession and a confession redacted in this way, for the jury will often realize that the confession refers specifically to the defendant. This is true even when the State does not blatantly link the defendant to the deleted name, as it did in this case by asking whether Gray was arrested on the basis of information in Bell's confession as soon as the officer had finished reading the redacted statement. Consider a simplified but typical example, a confession that reads "I, Bob Smith, along with Sam Jones, robbed the bank." To replace the words "Sam Jones" with an obvious blank will not likely fool anyone. A juror somewhat familiar with criminal law would know immediately that the blank, in the phrase "I, Bob Smith, along with _____, robbed the bank," refers to defendant Jones. A juror who does not know the law and who therefore wonders to whom the blank might refer need only lift his eyes to Jones, sitting at counsel table, to find what will seem the obvious answer, at least if the juror hears the judge's instruction not to consider the confession as evidence against Jones, for that instruction will provide an obvious reason for the blank. A more sophisticated juror, wondering if the blank refers to someone else, might also wonder how, if it did, the prosecutor could argue the confession is reliable, for the prosecutor, after all, has been arguing that Jones, not someone else, helped Smith commit the crime.

For another thing, the obvious deletion may well call the jurors' attention specially to the removed name. By encouraging the jury to speculate about the reference, the redaction may overemphasize the importance of the confession's accusation — once the jurors work out the reference. . . .

Finally, *Bruton*'s protected statements and statements redacted to leave a blank or some other similarly obvious alteration, function the same way grammatically. They are directly accusatory. Evans' statement in *Bruton* used a proper name to point explicitly to an accused defendant. And *Bruton* held that the "powerfully incriminating" effect of what Justice Stewart called "an out-of-court accusation," 391 U.S., at 138 (concurring opinion), creates a special, and vital, need for cross-examination—a need that would be immediately obvious had the codefendant pointed directly to the defendant in the courtroom itself. The blank space in an obviously redacted confession also points directly to the defendant, and it accuses the defendant in a manner similar to Evans' use of Bruton's name or to a testifying codefendant's accusatory finger. By way of contrast, the factual statement at issue in *Richardson*—a statement about what others said in the front seat of a car—differs from directly accusatory evidence in this respect, for it does not point directly to a defendant at all.

We concede certain differences between *Bruton* and this case. A confession that uses a blank or the word "delete" (or, for that matter, a first name or a nickname) less obviously refers to the defendant than a confession that uses the defendant's full and proper name. Moreover, in some instances the person to whom the blank refers may not be clear: Although the follow-up question asked by the State in this case eliminated all doubt, the reference might not be transparent in other cases in which a confession, like the present confession, uses two (or more) blanks, even though only one other defendant appears at trial, and in which the trial indicates that there are more participants than the confession has named. Nonetheless, as we have said, we believe that, considered as a class, redactions that replace a proper name with an obvious blank, the word "delete," a symbol, or similarly notify the jury that a name has been deleted are similar enough to *Bruton*'s unredacted confessions as to warrant the same legal results.

IV

. . . We concede that *Richardson* placed outside the scope of *Bruton*'s rule those statements that incriminate inferentially. 481 U.S., at 208. We also concede that the jury must use inference to connect the statement in this redacted confession with the defendant. But inference pure and simple cannot make the critical difference, for if it did, then *Richardson* would also place outside *Bruton*'s scope confessions that use shortened first names, nicknames, descriptions as unique as the "redhaired, bearded, one-eyed man-with-a-limp," United States v. Grinnell Corp., 384 U.S. 563, 591 (1966) (Fortas, J., dissenting), and perhaps even full names of defendants who are always known by a nickname. This Court has assumed, however, that nicknames and specific descriptions fall inside, not outside, *Bruton*'s protection. . . .

That being so, *Richardson* must depend in significant part upon the *kind* of, not the simple *fact* of, inference. *Richardson*'s inferences involved statements that did not refer directly to the defendant himself and which became incriminating "only when linked with evidence introduced later at trial." 481 U.S., at 208. The inferences at issue here involve statements that, despite redaction, obviously refer directly to someone, often obviously the defendant, and which involve inferences that a jury ordinarily could make immediately, even were the confession the very first item introduced at trial. Moreover, the redacted confession with the blank prominent on its face, in *Richardson*'s words, "*facially* incriminat[es]" the codefendant. Id., at 209 (emphasis added). Like the confession in *Bruton* itself, the accusation that the redacted confession makes "is more vivid than inferential incrimination, and hence more difficult to thrust out of mind." 481 U.S., at 208.

Nor are the policy reasons that *Richardson* provided in support of its conclusion applicable here. *Richardson* expressed concern lest application of *Bruton*'s rule apply where "redaction" of confessions, particularly "confessions incriminating by connection," would often "not [be] possible," thereby forcing prosecutors too often to abandon use either of the confession or of a joint trial. 481 U.S., at 209. Additional redaction of a confession that uses a blank space, the word "delete," or a symbol, however, normally is possible. Consider as an example a portion of the confession before us: The witness who read the confession told the jury that the confession (among other things) said,

> *Question:*   Who was in the group that beat Stacey?
> *Answer:*   Me, deleted, deleted, and a few other guys. . . .

Why could the witness not, instead, have said:

> *Question:*   Who was in the group that beat Stacey?
> *Answer:*   Me and a few other guys.

The *Richardson* Court also feared that the inclusion, within *Bruton*'s protective rule, of confessions that incriminated "by connection" too often would provoke mistrials, or would unnecessarily lead prosecutors to abandon the confession or joint trial, because neither the prosecutors nor the judge could easily predict, until after the introduction of all the evidence, whether or not *Bruton* had barred use of the confession. 481 U.S., at 209. To include the use of blanks, the word "delete," symbols, or other indications of redaction, within *Bruton*'s protections, however, runs no such risk. Their use is easily identified prior to trial and does not depend, in any special way, upon the other evidence introduced in the case. We also note that several Circuits have interpreted *Bruton* similarly for many years, . . . yet no one has told us of any significant practical difficulties arising out of their administration of that rule.

For these reasons, we hold that the confession here at issue, which substituted blanks and the word "delete" for the respondent's proper name, falls within the class of statements to which *Bruton*'s protections apply.

The judgment of the Court of Appeals is vacated, and the case is remanded for further proceedings not inconsistent with this opinion.

JUSTICE SCALIA, with whom CHIEF JUSTICE REHNQUIST, JUSTICE KENNEDY, and JUSTICE THOMAS join, dissenting.

In Richardson v. Marsh, 481 U.S. 200 (1987), we declined to extend the "narrow exception" of Bruton v. United States, 391 U.S. 123 (1968), beyond confessions that facially incriminate a defendant. Today the Court "concede[s] that *Richardson* placed outside the scope of *Bruton*'s rule those statements that incriminate inferentially," . . . "concede[s] that the jury must use inference to connect the statement in this redacted confession with the defendant," . . . but nonetheless extends *Bruton* to confessions that have been redacted to delete the defendant's name. Because I believe the line drawn in *Richardson* should not be changed, I respectfully dissent.

The almost invariable assumption of the law is that jurors follow their instructions. . . . This rule "is a pragmatic one, rooted less in the absolute certitude that the presumption is true than in the belief that it represents a reasonable practical accommodation of the interests of the state and the defendant in the criminal justice process." *Richardson*, 481 U.S., at 211. . . . The same applies to codefendant confessions: "[A] witness whose testimony is introduced at a joint trial is not considered to be a witness 'against' a defendant if the jury is instructed to consider that testimony only against a codefendant." *Richardson*, supra, at 206. In *Bruton*, we recognized a "narrow exception" to this rule. . . .

We declined in *Richardson*, however, to extend *Bruton* to confessions that incriminate only by inference from other evidence. . . . Today the Court struggles to decide whether a confession redacted to omit the defendant's name is incriminating on its face or by inference. On the one hand, the Court "concede[s] that the jury must use inference to connect the statement in this redacted confession with the defendant," . . . but later asserts, on the other hand, that "the redacted confession with the blank prominent on its face . . .'*facially* incriminat[es]'" him. . . . The Court should have stopped with its concession: the statement "Me, deleted, deleted, and a few other guys" does not facially incriminate anyone but the speaker. The Court's analogizing of "deleted" to a physical description that clearly identifies the defendant . . . does not survive scrutiny. By "facially incriminating," we have meant incriminating independent of other evidence introduced at trial. *Richardson*, supra, 481 U.S. 200, at 208-209. Since the defendant's appearance at counsel table is not evidence, the description "red-haired, bearded, one-eyed man-with-a-limp," . . . would be facially incriminating—unless, of course, the defendant had dyed his hair black and shaved his beard before trial, and the prosecution introduced evidence concerning his former appearance. Similarly, the statement "Me, Kevin Gray, and a few other guys" would be facially incriminating, unless the defendant's name set forth in the indictment was not Kevin Gray, and evidence was introduced to the effect that he sometimes used "Kevin Gray" as an alias. By contrast, the person to whom "deleted" refers in "Me, deleted, deleted, and a few other guys" is not apparent from anything the jury knows independent of the evidence at trial. Though the jury may speculate, the statement expressly implicates no one but the speaker.

Of course the Court is correct that confessions redacted to omit the defendant's name are more likely to incriminate than confessions redacted to omit any reference to his existence. But it is also true—and more relevant here—that confessions redacted to omit the defendant's name are *less* likely to incriminate than confessions that expressly state it. The latter are "powerfully incriminating" as a class, *Bruton*, supra, at 124, n. 1, 135; the former are not so. . . . The issue [here] is not whether the confession incriminated petitioner, but whether the incrimination is so "powerful" that we must depart from the normal presumption that the jury follows its instructions. *Richardson*, supra, at 208, n. 3. I think it is not—and I am certain that drawing the line for departing from the ordinary rule at the *facial identification* of the defendant makes more sense than drawing it anywhere else.

The Court's extension of *Bruton* to name-redacted confessions "as a class" will seriously compromise "society's compelling interest in finding, convicting, and punishing those who violate the law." Moran v. Burbine, 475 U.S. 412, 426 (1986) (citation omitted). . . . The Court minimizes the damage that it does by suggesting that "[a]dditional redaction of a confession that uses a blank space, the word 'delete,' or a symbol . . . normally is possible." In the present case, it asks, why could the police officer not have testified that Bell's answer was "Me and a few other guys"? . . . The answer, it seems obvious to me, is because that is not what Bell said. Bell's answer was "Me, Tank, Kevin and a few other guys." Introducing the statement with full disclosure of deletions is one thing; introducing as the complete statement what was in fact only a part is something else. And of course even concealed deletions from the text will often not do the job that the Court demands. For inchoate offenses—conspiracy in particular—redaction to delete all reference to a confederate would often render the confession nonsensical. If the question was "Who agreed to beat Stacey?" and the answer was "Me and Kevin," we might redact the answer to "Me and [deleted]," or perhaps to "Me and somebody else," but surely not to just "Me"—for that would no longer be a confession to the conspiracy charge, but rather the foundation for an insanity defense. To my knowledge we have never before endorsed—and to my strong belief we ought not endorse—the redaction of a statement by some means other than the deletion of certain words, with the fact of the deletion shown.[1] The risk to the integrity of our system (not to mention the increase in its complexity) posed by the approval of such free-lance editing seems to me infinitely greater than the risk posed by the entirely honest reproduction that the Court disapproves.

The United States Constitution guarantees, not a perfect system of criminal justice (as to which there can be considerable disagreement), but a minimum standard of fairness. Lest we lose sight of the forest for the trees, it should be borne in mind that federal and state rules of criminal procedure—which can afford to seek perfection because they can be more readily changed—exclude nontestifying codefendant confessions even where the Sixth Amendment does not. Under the Federal Rules of Criminal Procedure (and Maryland's), a trial court may order separate trials if joinder will prejudice a defendant. See Fed. Rule Crim. Proc. 14; Md. Crim. Rule 4-253(c) (1998). . . . The federal rule expressly contemplates that in ruling on a severance motion the court will inspect "in camera any statements or confessions made by the defendants which the government intends to introduce in evidence at the trial." Fed. Rule Crim. Proc. 14. Federal and most state trial courts (including Maryland's) also have the discretion to exclude unfairly prejudicial (albeit probative) evidence. Fed. Rule Evid. 403; Md. Rule Evid. 5-403 (1998). Here, petitioner moved for a severance on the ground that the admission of Bell's confession would be unfairly prejudicial. The trial court denied the motion, explaining that where a confession names two others, and the evidence is that five or six others participated, redaction of petitioner's name would not leave the jury with the "unavoidable inference" that Bell implicated Gray. . . .

I do not understand the Court to disagree that the redaction itself left unclear to whom the blank referred.[2] . . . That being so, the rule set forth in *Richardson* applies, and the statement could constitutionally be admitted with limiting instruction. This remains, insofar as the Sixth Amendment is concerned, the most "reasonable

---

1. The Court is mistaken to suggest that in Richardson v. Marsh, 481 U.S. 200 (1987), we endorsed rewriting confessions as a proper method of redaction. . . . There the parties agreed to the method of redaction, . . . and we had no occasion to address the propriety of editing confessions without showing the nature of the editing.

2. The Court does believe, however, that the answer to a "follow-up question"—"All right, now, officer, after he gave you that information, you subsequently were able to arrest Mr. Kevin Gray; is that correct?" ("That's correct")—"eliminated all doubt" as to the subject of the redaction. Ante, at 2, 8. That is probably not so, and is certainly far from clear. . . . But if the question *did* bring the redaction home to the defendant, surely that shows the impropriety of the question rather than of the redaction—*and the question was not objected to.* The failure to object deprives petitioner of the right to complain. . . . Of course the Court's reliance upon this testimony belies its contention that name-redacted confessions are powerfully incriminating "as a class." . . .

practical accommodation of the interests of the state and the defendant in the criminal justice process." *Richardson*, 481 U.S., at 211. For these reasons, I would affirm the judgment of the Court of Appeals of Maryland.

NOTES AND QUESTIONS

1. Keep in mind that the issue in *Gray* is not whether the codefendant statement should be admissible against the defendant—everyone agrees that it should not be—but rather how the courts should address and remedy this recurring problem. Does it seem strange that the Court should rely so heavily on the (probably overrated) power of curative instructions to solve similar problems in other contexts, as we have already seen, yet adopt a strict prophylactic rule against admissibility of codefendant statements based on a lack of confidence in curative instructions? Does the Court have any empirical evidence to support the implicit conclusion that codefendant statements are uniquely prejudicial, so much so that they deserve to be treated as a special exception to the usual rule about curative instructions?

2. What about the not uncommon situation of "interlocking confessions," where the confession of the codefendant overlaps in significant respects with a statement made by the defendant himself? In Parker v. Randolph, 442 U.S. 62 (1979), a plurality of the Court suggested that the codefendant's confessions need not be excluded under *Bruton*, on the ground that they "will seldom, if ever, be of the 'devastating' character referred to in *Bruton* when the incriminated defendant has admitted his own guilt." See *Randolph*, 442 U.S., at 73. Thus, impeaching the codefendant "would likely yield small advantage." Id.

But in Cruz v. New York, 481 U.S. 186 (1987), a majority of the Court came out the other way on the issue. In *Cruz*, the defendant, Eulogio Cruz, was under investigation along with his brother, Benjamin Cruz, for the murder of Jerry Cruz (who was not related to Eulogio and Benjamin). During the investigation, Norberto Cruz, Jerry's brother, told the police about incriminating statements that Eulogio and Benjamin had previously made to him, concerning the murder of a Bronx gas-station attendant. When the police questioned Benjamin about Jerry's murder, he denied any involvement in it. But he confessed, on videotape, to the gas-station murder. Eulogio and Benjamin were charged with the gas-station murder. At a joint trial, the prosecution introduced Benjamin's confession and also called Norberto as a witness to testify about the statements made by Eulogio and Benjamin. Eulogio's lawyer argued that Norberto's testimony was false and stemmed from Norberto's belief that Eulogio had killed his brother, Jerry. Both Eulogio and Benjamin were convicted.

The Court reversed the convictions. In an opinion by Justice Scalia, the Court explained:

> [I]t seems to us that "interlocking" bears a positively inverse relationship to devastation. A codefendant's confession will be relatively harmless if the incriminating story it tells is different from that which the defendant himself is alleged to have told, but enormously damaging if it confirms, in all essential respects, the defendant's alleged confession. It might be otherwise if the defendant were *standing by* his confession, in which case it could be said that the codefendant's confession does no more than support the defendant's very own case. But in the real world of criminal litigation, the defendant is seeking to *avoid* his own confession—on the ground that it was not

accurately reported, or that it was not really true when made. In the present case, for example, [Eulogio] sought to establish that Norberto had a motive for falsely reporting a confession that never in fact occurred. In such circumstances a codefendant's confession that corroborates the defendant's confession significantly harms the defendant's case, whereas one that is positively incompatible gives credence to the defendant's assertion that his own alleged confession was nonexistent or false.

Id., at 192.

3. As noted by the *Gray* dissent, the *Bruton* problem is one reason why trial courts sometimes grant severance motions under Federal Rule of Criminal Procedure 14. See also Chapter 11. One prominent example of this occurred in the Oklahoma City bombing case, where the trial court granted a motion to sever the trials of Timothy McVeigh and Terry Nichols on the ground that the admission of out-of-court statements by Nichols (which could not effectively be redacted), at a joint trial, would "profoundly prejudice[]" McVeigh. See United States v. McVeigh, 169 F.R.D. 362 (1996).

D. *Influences Upon the Jury*

Although jury trials may be revered in American history, juries are not perfect. Indeed, the use of juries in criminal cases creates special problems—problems that would not arise if the system relied on bench trials exclusively. Precisely because of the jury's amateur status, it is peculiarly susceptible to certain improper influences that would be less likely to affect the decisions of a professionally trained and experienced trial judge. In Chapter 11, we considered the effect of pretrial publicity on the location of the trial. Here we address the issues of improper prosecutorial argument.

DARDEN v. WAINWRIGHT

Certiorari to the United States Court of Appeals for the Eleventh Circuit
477 U.S. 168 (1986)

JUSTICE POWELL delivered the opinion of the Court.

This case presents three questions concerning the validity of petitioner's criminal conviction and death sentence: (i) whether the exclusion for cause of a member of the venire violated the principles announced in Wainwright v. Witt, 469 U.S. 412 (1985); (ii) whether the prosecution's closing argument during the guilt phase of a bifurcated trial rendered the trial fundamentally unfair and deprived the sentencing determination of the reliability required by the Eighth Amendment; and (iii) whether petitioner was denied effective assistance of counsel at the sentencing phase of his trial.

I

Petitioner was tried and found guilty of murder, robbery, and assault with intent to kill in the Circuit Court for Citrus County, Florida, in January 1974. Pursuant to Florida's capital sentencing statute, the same jury that convicted petitioner heard further testimony and argument in order to make a nonbinding recommendation as to whether a death sentence should be imposed. The jury recommended a death sentence, and the trial judge followed that recommendation. On direct appeal, the Florida Supreme Court affirmed the conviction and the sentence. Petitioner made several of the same arguments in that appeal that he makes here. With respect to the prosecutorial misconduct claim, the court disapproved of the closing argument, but reasoned that the law required a new trial "only in those cases in which it is reasonably evident that the remarks might have influenced the jury to reach a more severe verdict of guilt . . . or in which the comment is unfair." . . . It concluded that the comments had not rendered petitioner's trial unfair. . . . This Court granted certiorari, . . . limited the grant to the claim of prosecutorial misconduct, . . . heard oral argument, and dismissed the writ as improvidently granted, 430 U.S. 704 (1977).

Petitioner then sought federal habeas corpus relief, raising the same claims he raises here. The District Court denied the petition. . . . A divided panel of the Court of Appeals for the Eleventh Circuit affirmed. . . . The Court of Appeals granted rehearing en banc, and affirmed the District Court by an equally divided court. . . . Following a second rehearing en banc the Court of Appeals reversed on the claim of improper excusal of a member of the venire. . . . This Court granted the State's petition for certiorari on that claim, vacated the Court of Appeals' judgment, and remanded for reconsideration in light of Wainwright v. Witt, 469 U.S. 1202 (1985). On remand, the en banc court denied relief. . . . Petitioner filed an application for a stay of his execution that this Court treated as a petition for certiorari and granted, at the same time staying his execution. . . . We now affirm.

II

Because of the nature of petitioner's claims, the facts of this case will be stated in more detail than is normally necessary in this Court. On September 8, 1973, at about 5:30 p.m., a black adult male entered Carl's Furniture Store near Lakeland, Florida. The only other person in the store was the proprietor, Mrs. Turman, who lived with her husband in a house behind the store. Mr. Turman, who worked nights at a juvenile home, had awakened at about 5 p.m., had a cup of coffee at the store with his wife, and returned home to let their dogs out for a run. Mrs. Turman showed the man around the store. He stated that he was interested in purchasing about $600 worth of furniture for a rental unit, and asked to see several different items. He left the store briefly, stating that his wife would be back to look at some of the items.

The same man returned just a few minutes later asking to see some stoves, and inquiring about the price. When Mrs. Turman turned toward the adding machine, he grabbed her and pressed a gun to her back, saying "Do as I say and you won't get hurt." He took her to the rear of the store and told her to open the cash register. He took the money, then ordered her to the part of the store where some box springs and mattresses were stacked against the wall. At that time Mr. Turman appeared at the back door. Mrs. Turman screamed while the man reached across her right shoulder and shot Mr. Turman between the eyes. Mr. Turman fell backwards, with one foot partially in the building. Ordering Mrs. Turman not to move, the man tried to pull Mr. Turman into the building and close the door, but could not do so because one of Mr. Turman's feet was caught in the door. The man left Mr. Turman faceup in the rain, and told Mrs. Turman to get down on the floor approximately five feet from where her husband lay dying. While she begged to go to her husband, he told her to remove her false teeth. He unzipped his pants, unbuckled his belt, and demanded that Mrs. Turman perform oral sex on him. She began to cry "Lord, have mercy." He told her to get up and go towards the front of the store.

Meanwhile, a neighbor family, the Arnolds, became aware that something had happened to Mr. Turman. The mother sent her 16-year-old son Phillip, a part-time employee at the furniture store, to help. When Phillip reached the back door he saw Mr. Turman lying partially in the building. When Phillip opened the door to take Turman's body inside, Mrs. Turman shouted "Phillip, no, go back." Phillip did not know what she meant and asked the man to help get Turman inside. He replied, "Sure, buddy, I will help you." As Phillip looked up, the man was pointing a gun in his face. He pulled the trigger and the gun misfired; he pulled the trigger again and shot Phillip in the mouth. Phillip started to run away, and was shot in the neck. While he was still running, he was shot a third time in the side. Despite these wounds, Phillip managed to stumble to the home of a neighbor, Mrs. Edith Hill. She had her husband call an ambulance while she tried to stop Phillip's bleeding. While she was helping Phillip, she saw a late model green Chevrolet leave the store and head towards Tampa on State Highway 92. Phillip survived the incident; Mr. Turman, who never regained consciousness, died later that night.

Minutes after the murder petitioner was driving towards Tampa on Highway 92, just a few miles away from the furniture store. He was out on furlough from a Florida prison, and was driving a car borrowed from his girl friend in Tampa. He was driving fast on a wet road. Petitioner testified that as he came up on a line of cars in his lane, he was unable to slow down. He attempted to pass, but was forced off the road to avoid a head-on collision with an oncoming car. Petitioner crashed into a telephone pole. The driver of the oncoming car, John Stone, stopped his car and went to petitioner to see if he could help. Stone testified that as he approached the car, petitioner was zipping up his pants and buckling his belt. Police at the crash site later identified petitioner's car as a 1969 Chevrolet Impala of greenish golden brown color. Petitioner paid a bystander to give him a ride to Tampa. Petitioner later returned with a wrecker, only to find that the car had been towed away by the police.

By the time the police arrived at the scene of the accident, petitioner had left. The fact that the car matched the description of the car leaving the scene of the murder, and that the accident had occurred within three and one-half miles of the furniture store and within minutes of the murder, led police to suspect that the car was driven by the murderer. They searched the area. An officer found a pistol—a revolver—about 40 feet from the crash site. The arrangement of shells within the chambers exactly matched the pattern that should have been found in the murder weapon: one shot, one misfire, followed by three shots, with a live shell remaining in the next chamber to be fired. A specialist for the Federal Bureau of Investigation examined the pistol and testified that it was a Smith & Wesson .38 special revolver. It had been manufactured as a standard .38; it later was sent to England to be rebored, making it a much rarer type of gun than the standard .38. An examination of the bullet that killed Mr. Turman revealed that it came from a .38 Smith & Wesson special.

On the day following the murder petitioner was arrested at his girl friend's house in Tampa. A few days later Mrs. Turman identified him at a preliminary hearing as her husband's murderer. Phillip Arnold selected petitioner's picture out of a spread of six photographs as the man who had shot him.[1] By that time, a Public Defender had been appointed to represent petitioner.

As petitioner's arguments all relate to incidents in the course of his trial, they will be taken up, together with the relevant facts, in chronological order.

III

[This section of the Court's opinion, rejecting the defendant's claim of improper exclusion of a prospective juror, is omitted.]

IV

Petitioner next contends that the prosecution's closing argument at the guilt-innocence stage of the trial rendered his conviction fundamentally unfair and deprived the sentencing determination of the reliability that the Eighth Amendment requires.

It is helpful as an initial matter to place these remarks in context. Closing argument came at the end of several days of trial. Because of a state procedural rule petitioner's counsel had the opportunity to present the initial summation as well as a rebuttal to the prosecutors' closing arguments. The prosecutors' comments must be evaluated in light of the defense argument that preceded it, which blamed the Polk County Sheriff 's Office for a lack of evidence,[5] alluded to the death penalty,[6] characterized the perpetrator of the crimes as an "animal,"[7] and contained counsel's personal opinion of the strength of the State's evidence.[8]

---

1. There are some minor discrepancies in the eyewitness identification. Mrs. Turman first described her assailant immediately after the murder while her husband was being taken to the emergency room. She told the investigating officer that the attacker was a heavy-set man. . . . When asked if he was "neat in his appearance, clean-looking, clean-shaven," she responded "[a]s far as I can remember, yes, sir." Ibid. She also stated to the officer that she thought that the attacker was about her height, 5' 6" tall, and that he was wearing a pullover shirt with a stripe around the neck. . . . The first time she saw petitioner after the attack was when she identified him at the preliminary hearing. She had not read any newspaper accounts of the crime, nor had she seen any picture of petitioner. When she was asked if petitioner was the man who had committed the crimes, she said yes. She also repeatedly identified him at trial.

Phillip Arnold first identified petitioner in a photo lineup while in the hospital. He could not speak at the time, and in response to the written question whether petitioner had a mustache, Phillip wrote back "I don't think so." . . . Phillip also testified at trial that the attacker was a heavy-set man wearing a dull, light color knit shirt with a ring around the neck. . . . He testified that the man was almost his height, about 6' 2" tall.

A motorist who stopped at the scene of the accident testified that petitioner was wearing a white or off-grey button-down shirt and that he had a slight mustache. . . . In fact, the witness stated that he "didn't know it was that [the mustache] or the raindrops on him or not. I couldn't really tell that much to it, it was real thin, that's all." . . . Petitioner is about 5' 10" tall, and at the time of trial testified that he weighed about 175 pounds.

5. "The Judge is going to tell you to consider the evidence or the lack of evidence. We have a lack of evidence, almost criminally negligent on the part of the Polk County Sheriff 's Office in this case. You could go on and on about it." . . .

6. "They took a coincidence and magnified that into a capital case. And they are asking you to kill a man on coincidence." . . .

7. "The first witness that you saw was Mrs. Turman, who was a pathetic figure; who worked and struggled all of her life to build what little she had, the little furniture store; and a woman who was robbed, sexually assaulted, and then had her husband slaughtered before her eyes, by what would have to be a vicious animal." . . . "And this murderer ran after him, aimed again, and this poor kid with half his brains blown away. . . . It's the work of an animal, there's no doubt about it." . . .

8. "So they come on up here and ask Citrus County people to kill the man. You will be instructed on lesser included offenses. . . . The question is, do they have enough evidence to kill that man, enough evidence? And I honestly do not think they do." . . .

The prosecutors then made their closing argument. That argument deserves the condemnation it has received from every court to review it, although no court has held that the argument rendered the trial unfair. Several comments attempted to place some of the blame for the crime on the Division of Corrections, because Darden was on weekend furlough from a prison sentence when the crime occurred.[9] Some comments implied that the death penalty would be the only guarantee against a future similar act.[10] Others incorporated the defense's use of the word "animal."[11] Prosecutor McDaniel made several offensive comments reflecting an emotional reaction to the case.[12] These comments undoubtedly were improper. But as both the District Court and the original panel of the Court of Appeals (whose opinion on this issue still stands) recognized, it "is not enough that the prosecutors' remarks were undesirable or even universally condemned." . . . The relevant question is whether the prosecutors' comments "so infected the trial with unfairness as to make the resulting conviction a denial of due process." Donnelly v. DeChristoforo, 416 U.S. 637 (1974). . . .

Under this standard of review, we agree with the reasoning of every court to consider these comments that they did not deprive petitioner of a fair trial.[13] The prosecutors' argument did not manipulate or misstate the evidence, nor did it implicate other specific rights of the accused such as the right to counsel or the right to remain silent. . . . Much of the objectionable content was invited by or was responsive to the opening summation of the defense. As we explained in United States v. Young, 470 U.S. 1 (1985), the idea of "invited response" is used not to excuse improper comments, but to determine their effect on the trial as a whole. Id., at 13. The trial court instructed the jurors several times that their decision was to be made on the basis of the evidence alone, and that the arguments of counsel were not evidence. The weight of the evidence against petitioner was heavy; the "overwhelming eyewitness and circumstantial evidence to support a finding of guilt

9. "As far as I am concerned, there should be another Defendant in this courtroom, one more, and that is the division of corrections, the prisons. . . . Can we expect him to stay in a prison when they go there? Can't we expect them to stay locked up once they go there? Do we know that they're going to be out on the public with guns, drinking?" . . . "Yes, there is another Defendant, but I regret that I know of no charges to place upon him, except the public condemnation of them, condemn them." . . .

10. "I will ask you to advise the Court to give him death. That's the only way that I know that he is not going to get out on the public. It's the only way I know. It's the only way I can be sure of it. It's the only way that anybody can be sure of it now, because the people that turned him loose—." . . .

11. "As far as I am concerned, and as Mr. Maloney said as he identified this man, this person as an animal, this animal was on the public for one reason." . . .

12. "He shouldn't be out of his cell unless he has a leash on him and a prison guard at the other end of that leash." . . . "I wish [Mr. Turman] had had a shotgun in his hand when he walked in the back door and blown his [Darden's] face off. I wish that I could see him sitting here with no face, blown away by a shotgun." . . . "I wish someone had walked in the back door and blown his head off at that point." . . . "He fired in the boy's back, number five, saving one. Didn't get a chance to use it. I wish he had used it on himself." . . . "I wish he had been killed in the accident, but he wasn't. Again, we are unlucky that time." . . . "[D]on't forget what he has done according to those witnesses, to make every attempt to change his appearance from September the 8th, 1973. The hair, the goatee, even the moustache and the weight. The only thing he hasn't done that I know of is cut his throat." . . . After this, the last in a series of such comments, defense counsel objected for the first time.

13. Justice Blackmun's dissenting opinion argues that because of prosecutorial misconduct petitioner did not receive a fair trial. The dissent states that the Court is "willing to tolerate not only imperfection but a level of fairness and reliability so low it should make conscientious prosecutors cringe." . . . We agree that the argument was, and deserved to be, condemned. . . . Conscientious prosecutors will recognize, however, that *every court* that criticized the argument went on to hold that the *fairness* of petitioner's trial was not affected by the prosecutors' argument. . . .

on all charges," . . . reduced the likelihood that the jury's decision was influenced by argument. Finally, defense counsel made the tactical decision not to present any witness other than petitioner. This decision not only permitted them to give their summation prior to the prosecution's closing argument, but also gave them the opportunity to make a final rebuttal argument. Defense counsel were able to use the opportunity for rebuttal very effectively, turning much of the prosecutors' closing argument against them by placing many of the prosecutors' comments and actions in a light that was more likely to engender strong disapproval than result in inflamed passions against petitioner.[14] For these reasons, we agree with the District Court below that "Darden's trial was not perfect—few are—but neither was it fundamentally unfair." . . .[15]

V

[This section of the Court's opinion, rejecting the defendant's claim of ineffective assistance of counsel based on failure to develop mitigating evidence at the capital sentencing phase of the trial, is omitted.]

VI

The judgment of the Court of Appeals is affirmed, and the case is remanded for proceedings consistent with this opinion.

[The concurring opinion of Chief Justice Burger and the dissenting opinion of Justice Brennan are omitted.]

JUSTICE BLACKMUN, with whom JUSTICE BRENNAN, JUSTICE MARSHALL, and JUSTICE STEVENS join, dissenting.

Although the Constitution guarantees a criminal defendant only "a fair trial [and] not a perfect one," . . . this Court has stressed repeatedly in the decade since Gregg v. Georgia, 428 U.S. 153 (1976), that the Eighth Amendment requires a heightened degree of reliability in any case where a State seeks to take the defendant's life. Today's opinion, however, reveals a Court willing to tolerate not only imperfection but a level of fairness and reliability so low it should make conscientious prosecutors cringe.

---

14. "Mr. McDaniel made an impassioned plea . . . how many times did he repeat [it]? I wish you had been shot, I wish they had blown his face away. My God, I get the impression he would like to be the man that stands there and pulls the switch on him." . . .

One of Darden's counsel testified at the habeas corpus hearing that he made the tactical decision not to object to the improper comments. Based on his long experience with prosecutor McDaniel, he knew McDaniel would "get much more vehement in his remarks if you allowed him to go on." By not immediately objecting, he hoped to encourage the prosecution to commit reversible error. . . .

15. Justice Blackmun's dissenting opinion mistakenly argues that the Court today finds, in essence, that any error was harmless, and then criticizes the Court for not applying the harmless-error standard. . . . We do not decide the claim of prosecutorial misconduct on the ground that it was harmless error. In our view of the case, that issue is not presented. Rather, we agree with the holding of every court that has addressed the issue, that the prosecutorial argument, in the context of the facts and circumstances of this case, did not render petitioner's trial unfair—i.e., that it was not constitutional error.

I

A

The Court's discussion of Darden's claim of prosecutorial misconduct is noteworthy for its omissions. Despite the fact that earlier this Term the Court relied heavily on standards governing the professional responsibility of defense counsel in ruling that an attorney's actions did not deprive his client of any constitutional right, see Nix v. Whiteside, 475 U.S. 157, 166-171 (1986), today it entirely ignores standards governing the professional responsibility of prosecutors in reaching the conclusion that the summations of Darden's prosecutors did not deprive him of a fair trial. . . .

The prosecutors' remarks in this case reflect behavior as to which "virtually all the sources speak with one voice," Nix v. Whiteside, supra, at 166, that is, a voice of strong condemnation. The following brief comparison of established standards of prosecutorial conduct with the prosecutors' behavior in this case merely illustrates, but hardly exhausts, the scope of the misconduct involved:

1. "A lawyer shall not . . . state a personal opinion as to . . . the credibility of a witness . . . or the guilt or innocence of an accused." Model Rules of Professional Conduct, Rule 3.4(e) (1984); see also Code of Professional Responsibility, DR 7-106(C)(4) (1980); ABA Standards for Criminal Justice 3-5.8(b) (2d ed. 1980). Yet one prosecutor, White, stated: "I am convinced, as convinced as I know I am standing before you today, that Willie Jasper Darden is a murderer, that he murdered Mr. Turman, that he robbed Mrs. Turman and that he shot to kill Phillip Arnold. I will be convinced of that the rest of my life." . . . And the other prosecutor, McDaniel, stated, with respect to Darden's testimony: "Well, let me tell you something: If I am ever over in that chair over there, facing life or death, life imprisonment or death, I guarantee you I will lie until my teeth fall out." . . .

2. "The prosecutor should refrain from argument which would divert the jury from its duty to decide the case on the evidence, by injecting issues broader than the guilt or innocence of the accused under the controlling law, or by making predictions of the consequences of the jury's verdict." ABA Standards for Criminal Justice 3-5.8(d) (2d ed. 1980); cf. Model Rules of Professional Conduct, Rule 3.4(e); Code of Professional Responsibility, DR 7-106(C)(7); ABA Standards for Criminal Justice 3-6.1(c) (2d ed. 1980). Yet McDaniel's argument was filled with references to Darden's status as a prisoner on furlough who "shouldn't be out of his cell unless he has a leash on him." . . . Again and again, he sought to put on trial an absent "defendant," the State Department of Corrections that had furloughed Darden. . . . He also implied that defense counsel would use improper tricks to deflect the jury from the real issue. . . . Darden's status as a furloughed prisoner, the release policies of the Department of Corrections, and his counsel's anticipated tactics obviously had no legal relevance to the question the jury was being asked to decide: whether he had committed the robbery and murder at the Turmans' furniture store. Indeed, the State argued before this Court that McDaniel's remarks were harmless precisely because he "failed to discuss the issues, the weight of the evidence, or the credibility of the witnesses." . . .

3. "The prosecutor should not use arguments calculated to inflame the passions or prejudices of the jury." ABA Standards for Criminal Justice 3-5.8(c) (2d ed. 1980). . . . Yet McDaniel repeatedly expressed a wish "that I could see [Darden] sitting here with no face, blown away by a shotgun." . . . Indeed, I do not think McDaniel's summation, taken as a whole, can accurately be described as anything but a relentless and single-minded attempt to inflame the jury.

B

The Court . . . relies on the standard established in Donnelly v. DeChristoforo, 416 U.S. 637, 643 (1974), for deciding when a prosecutor's comments at a state trial render that trial fundamentally unfair. It omits, however, any discussion of the facts, so different from those in this case, that led the Court to conclude in *DeChristoforo* that that defendant had not been deprived of a fair trial.

DeChristoforo concerned "two remarks made by the prosecutor during the course of his rather lengthy closing argument to the jury." Id., at 640. One remark was "but one moment of an extended trial." Id., at 645. And even the more objectionable remark was so "ambiguous," ibid., that it provided no basis for inferring either that the prosecutor "intend[ed] [it] to have its most damaging meaning or that a jury, sitting through lengthy exhortation, [would] draw that meaning from the plethora of less damaging interpretations," id., at 647. Finally, the trial judge in *DeChristoforo* expressly instructed the jury to disregard the improper statements. Id., at 645. This Court's holding thus rested on its conclusion that the prosecutor's comments were neither so extensive nor so improper as to violate the Constitution.

Far from involving "ambiguous" statements that "might or might not" affect the jury, id., at 647, the remarks at issue here were "focused, unambiguous, and strong." Caldwell v. Mississippi, 472 U.S. 320, 340 (1985). It is impossible to read the transcript of McDaniel's summation without seeing it as a calculated and sustained attempt to inflame the jury. Almost every page contains at least one offensive or improper statement; some pages contain little else. The misconduct here was not "slight or confined to a single instance, but . . . was pronounced and persistent, with a probable cumulative effect upon the jury which cannot be disregarded as inconsequential." . . .

C

The Court presents what is, for me, an entirely unpersuasive one-page laundry list of reasons for ignoring this blatant misconduct. First, the Court says that the summations "did not manipulate or misstate the evidence [or] . . . implicate other specific rights of the accused such as the right to counsel or the right to remain silent." . . . With all respect, that observation is quite beside the point. The "solemn purpose of endeavoring to ascertain the truth . . . is the sine qua non of a fair trial," Estes v. Texas, 381 U.S. 532, 540 (1965), and the summations cut to the very heart of the Due Process Clause by diverting the jury's attention "from the ultimate question of guilt or innocence that should be the central concern in a criminal proceeding." . . .

Second, the Court says that "[m]uch of the objectionable content was invited by or was responsive to the opening summation of the defense." . . . The Court identifies four portions of the defense summation that it thinks somehow "invited" McDaniel's sustained barrage. The State, however, did not object to any of these statements, and, to my mind, none of them is so objectionable that it would have justified a tactical decision to interrupt the defense summation and perhaps irritate the jury. . . .

The Court begins by stating that defense counsel "blamed" the Sheriff's Office for a lack of evidence. . . . The Court does not identify which, if any, of McDaniel's remarks represented a response to this statement. I cannot believe that the Court is suggesting, for example, that defense counsel's one mention of the "almost crimina[l] negligen[ce] on the part of the Polk County Sheriff's Office," . . . justified McDaniel's express and repeated wish that he could try the Department of Corrections for murder. . . .

Next, the Court notes that defense counsel "alluded" to the death penalty. . . . While this allusion might have justified McDaniel's statement that "you are merely to determine his innocence or guilt, nothing else," . . . it could hardly justify, for example, McDaniel's expressions of his personal wish that Darden be "blown away by a shotgun." . . .

Moreover, the Court says, defense counsel twice referred to the perpetrator as an "animal." . . . It is entirely unclear to me why this characterization called for any response from the prosecutor at all. Taken in context, defense counsel's statements did nothing more than tell the jury that, although everyone agreed that a heinous crime had been committed, the issue on which it should focus was whether Darden had committed it.

Finally, the Court finds that Darden brought upon himself McDaniel's tirade because defense counsel gave his "personal opinion of the strength of the State's evidence." . . . Again, the Court gives no explanation of how the statement it quotes—a single, mild expression of defense counsel's overall assessment of the evidence—justified the "response" that followed, which consisted, to the extent it represented a comment on the evidence at all, of accusations of perjury, . . . and personal disparagements of opposing counsel. . . . In sum, McDaniel went so far beyond "respond[ing] substantially in order to 'right the scale,'" *Young*, 470 U.S., at 13, that the reasoning in *Young* provides no basis at all for the Court's holding today.

The third reason the Court gives for discounting the effects of the improper summations is the supposed curative effect of the trial judge's instructions: The judge had instructed the jury that it was to decide the case on the evidence and that the arguments of counsel were not evidence. . . . But the trial court overruled Darden's objection to McDaniel's repeated expressions of his wish that Darden had been killed, . . . thus perhaps leaving the jury with the impression that McDaniel's comments were somehow relevant to the question before them. The trial judge's instruction that the attorneys were "trained in the law," and thus that their "analysis of the issues" could be "extremely helpful," . . . might also have suggested to the jury that the substance of McDaniel's tirade was pertinent to their deliberations.

Fourth, the Court suggests that because Darden enjoyed the tactical advantage of having the last summation, he was able to "tur[n] much of the prosecutors' closing argument against them." . . . Since Darden was ultimately convicted, it is hard to see what basis the Court has for its naked assertion that "[d]efense counsel were able to use the opportunity for rebuttal very effectively." . . .

Fifth, the Court finds, in essence, that any error was harmless . . . but it does not identify the standard it [uses] to decide the harmlessness of the error. . . .

Regardless of which test is used, I simply do not believe the evidence in this case was so overwhelming that this Court can conclude, on the basis of the written record before it, that the jury's verdict was not the product of the prosecutors' misconduct. The three most damaging pieces of evidence—the identifications of Darden by Phillip Arnold and Helen Turman and the ballistics evidence—are all sufficiently problematic that they leave me unconvinced that a jury not exposed to McDaniel's egregious summation would necessarily have convicted Darden.

Arnold first identified Darden in a photo array shown to him in the hospital. The trial court suppressed that out-of-court identification following a long argument concerning the reliability and constitutionality of the procedures by which it was obtained. . . .

Mrs. Turman's initial identification was made under even more suggestive circumstances. She testified at trial that she was taken to a preliminary hearing at which Darden appeared in order "[t]o identify him." . . . Instead of being asked to view Darden in a lineup, Mrs. Turman was brought into the courtroom, where Darden apparently was the only black man present. . . . Over defense counsel's objection, after the prosecutor asked her whether "this man sitting here" was "the man that shot your husband," . . . she identified Darden.[5] . . .

Finally, the ballistics evidence is hardly overwhelming. The purported murder weapon was tied conclusively neither to the crime nor to Darden. Special Agent Cunningham of the Federal Bureau of Investigation's Firearms Identification Unit testified that the bullets recovered at the scene of the crime "could have been fired" from the gun, but he was unwilling to say that they in fact had come from that weapon. . . . He also testified, contrary to the Court's assertion, that rebored Smith & Wessons were fairly common. . . . Deputy Sheriff Weatherford testified that the gun was discovered in a roadside ditch adjacent to where Darden had wrecked his car on the evening of the crime. But the gun was discovered the next day, . . . and the ditch was also next to a bar's parking lot. . . .

Darden testified at trial on his own behalf and denied any involvement in the robbery and murder. . . . His account of his actions on the day of the crime was contradicted only by Mrs. Turman's and Arnold's identifications. Indeed, a number of the State's witnesses corroborated parts of Darden's account. The trial judge who had seen and heard Darden testify found that he "emotionally and with what appeared on its face to be sincerity, proclaimed his innocence." . . . In setting sentence, he viewed the fact that Darden "repeatedly professed his complete innocence of the charges" as a mitigating factor. . . .

Thus, at bottom, this case rests on the jury's determination of the credibility of three witnesses—Helen Turman and Phillip Arnold, on the one side, and Willie Darden, on the other. I cannot conclude that McDaniel's sustained assault on Darden's very humanity did not affect the jury's ability to judge the credibility

---

5. Mrs. Turman's identification took place after the following colloquy between the court, the prosecutor (Mr. Mars), and the defense attorney (Mr. Hill):

The Court: Ask her to identify.
Mr. Mars: Yes, sir.
Q: Can you see this man sitting here?
Mr. Hill: Your Honor, I am going to object to that type of identification.
The Court: I am not. Sit down.
Mr. Hill: Judge—
The Court: Not under these circumstances, Mr. Hill.
Mr. Hill: Judge, even as a defense attorney, that shows no respect in court, much less for the Court, and I—
The Court: I appreciate—
Mr. Hill: And the objection, I want on the record.
The Court: I appreciate that. It's on the record. This woman has had a traumatic experience and she—
Mr. Hill: Judge, I appreciate that. I still have an obligation to my client.
The Court: I appreciate that. Now if you want to be held in contempt, you pardon me. Alright, go ahead.
Q: Is this the man that shot your husband?
A: Yes, sir. . . .

question on the real evidence before it. Because I believe that he did not have a trial that was fair, I would reverse Darden's conviction; I would not allow him to go to his death until he has been convicted at a fair trial.

II

[This section of the dissenting opinion, addressing the defendant's claim of improper exclusion of a prospective juror, is omitted.]

III

Twice during the past year—in United States v. Young, 470 U.S. 1 (1985), and again today—this Court has been faced with clearly improper prosecutorial misconduct during summations. Each time, the Court has condemned the behavior but affirmed the conviction. Forty years ago, Judge Jerome N. Frank, in dissent, discussed the Second Circuit's similar approach in language we would do well to remember today:

> This court has several times used vigorous language in denouncing government counsel for such conduct as that of the [prosecutor] here. But, each time, it has said that, nevertheless, it would not reverse. Such an attitude of helpless piety is, I think, undesirable. It means actual condonation of counsel's alleged offense, coupled with verbal disapprobation. If we continue to do nothing practical to prevent such conduct, we should cease to disapprove it. For otherwise it will be as if we declared in effect, "Government attorneys, without fear of reversal, may say just about what they please in addressing juries, for our rules on the subject are pretend-rules. If prosecutors win verdicts as a result of 'disapproved' remarks, we will not deprive them of their victories; we will merely go through the form of expressing displeasure. The deprecatory words we use in our opinions on such occasions are purely ceremonial." Government counsel, employing such tactics, are the kind who, eager to win victories, will gladly pay the small price of a ritualistic verbal spanking. The practice of this court—recalling the bitter tear shed by the Walrus as he ate the oysters—breeds a deplorably cynical attitude towards the judiciary (footnote omitted).

United States v. Antonelli Fireworks Co., 155 F.2d 631, 661 . . . (1946).

I believe this Court must do more than wring its hands when a State uses improper legal standards to select juries in capital cases and permits prosecutors to pervert the adversary process. I therefore dissent.

NOTES AND QUESTIONS

1. On the general subject of prosecutorial misconduct, consider once again the famous words from Berger v. United States, 295 U.S. 78, 88 (1935) (previously discussed in Chapter 12, at page 1206), on the prosecutor as "servant of the law":

> He may prosecute with earnestness and vigor—indeed, he should do so. But while he may strike hard blows, he is not at liberty to strike foul ones. It is as much his duty to refrain from improper methods calculated to produce a wrongful conviction as it is to use every legitimate means to bring about a just one. . . . It is fair to say that the average jury, in a greater or lesser degree, has confidence that these obligations, which so

plainly rest upon the prosecuting attorney, will be faithfully observed. Consequently, improper suggestions, insinuations, and, especially, assertions of personal knowledge are apt to carry much weight against the accused when they should properly carry none.

Notice the *Berger* Court's special concern about the potential impact of prosecutorial misconduct on the jury.

2. *Darden* relied heavily on three previous Court decisions involving challenges to prosecutorial arguments before the jury:

In Donnelly v. DeChristoforo, 416 U.S. 637, 643 (1974), the defendant and a codefendant were charged with first-degree murder. In the midst of the joint trial, the codefendant pleaded guilty to second-degree murder, and the jury was so informed. In closing argument, the prosecutor told the jury, "I honestly and sincerely believe that there is no doubt in this case, none whatsoever." In addition, the prosecutor stated: "[The defendant and his lawyer] said they hope that you find him not guilty. I quite frankly think that they hope that you find him guilty of something a little less than first-degree murder." The defendant was convicted of first-degree murder, and the Supreme Court affirmed. The Court noted that the trial judge acted quickly to inform the jury that the prosecutor's comments were not evidence, and concluded that the overall impact of the comments was insufficient to make out a due process violation.

In United States v. Young, 470 U.S. 1 (1985), the defense lawyer, in summation, intimated that the prosecution had deliberately withheld exculpatory evidence, charged the prosecution with "reprehensible" conduct, and stated, "I submit to you that there's not a person in this courtroom including [the prosecution] who think that [the defendant] intended to defraud [the victim]." The prosecutor did not object, but in his rebuttal argument responded by expressing his own opinion about the defendant's guilt and telling the jurors that, if they acquitted the defendant, "I don't think you're doing your job as jurors. . . ." The defense did not object, and the defendant was convicted. The Supreme Court affirmed, despite lamenting that "[t]he kind of advocacy shown by this record has no place in the administration of justice." The Court noted that the prosecutor's comments were a form of "invited response" to the defense lawyer's prior improper comments. However, the Court stressed that "the issue is not the prosecutor's license to make otherwise improper arguments, but whether the prosecutor's 'invited response,' taken in context, unfairly prejudiced the defendant." The Court concluded that the prosecutor's comments "went beyond what was necessary to 'right the scale' in the wake of defense counsel's misconduct." Nevertheless, the prosecutor's error "was not 'plain error' warranting the court to overlook the absence of any objection by the defense."

In Caldwell v. Mississippi, 472 U.S. 320 (1985), the prosecutor, in the sentencing phase of a capital case, responded to the defense lawyer's plea for mercy by telling the jury at closing:

Now, they would have you believe that you're going to kill this man and they know—they know that your decision is not the final decision. My God, how unfair can you be? Your job is reviewable. . . . They said, "Thou shalt not kill," If that applies to him, it applies to you, insinuating that your decision is the final decision and that they're gonna take [the defendant] out in front of this Courthouse in moments and string him up and that is terribly, terribly unfair. For they know, as I know, and as

Judge Baker has told you, that the decision you render is automatically reviewable by the Supreme Court. Automatically, and I think it's unfair and I don't mind telling them so.

Id., at 325-326. The Supreme Court held that this argument violated the Eighth Amendment's Cruel and Unusual Punishment Clause because it led the jury to believe "that the responsibility for determining the appropriateness of the defendant's death rests elsewhere." The Court rejected the contention that the prosecutor's comments about appellate review were an "invited response," noting that they had little to do directly with the defense lawyer's mercy plea. Justice O'Connor, in concurrence, emphasized that the prosecutor's comments were not only potentially highly prejudicial, but also inaccurate, because appellate review in capital cases is limited and cannot revisit the merits of the jury's verdict.

3. In addition to publicity and improper prosecutorial argument, similar concerns about jury influence arise in the context of admission of tainted evidence. This is yet another area in which judges and lawyers tend to follow the traditional approach, which consists of giving a curative instruction to tell the jury not to rely on the improper evidence. Empirical research, however, demonstrates that such curative instructions do not usually have the desired effect on jury behavior — perhaps lending credence to the folk wisdom about what happens if you tell someone not to think about pink elephants:

> [P]eople find it very difficult to actively suppress a thought upon instruction, particularly when that thought is vivid or emotionally arousing. Indeed, the harder people try to control a thought, the less likely they are to succeed.

Christina Studebaker & Steven Penrod, Pretrial Publicity: The Media, the Law, and Common Sense, 3 Psychol. Pub. Pol'y & L. 428, 446 (1997), citing D. M. Wegner, White Bears and Other Unwanted Thoughts: Suppression, Obsession, and the Psychology of Mental Control (1989); see also Thompson, Fong & Rosenhan, Inadmissible Evidence and Juror Verdicts, 40 J. Personality & Soc. Psychol. 453, 461 (1981) (jurors tend to ignore curative instructions to disregard inadmissible evidence); Brooks & Doob, Justice and the Jury, J. Soc. Issues, Summer 1975, at 176-177 (jurors tend to ignore curative instructions limiting use of previous convictions to impeach defendant's credibility); cf. Tanford & Penrod, Social Inference Processes in Juror Judgments of Multiple Offense Trials, 47 J. Personality & Soc. Psychol. 749 (1984) (joinder of charges increases likelihood of conviction on particular charge, and curative instructions do not remedy problem).

E.   *Proof and Verdict Issues*

At the close of the trial, the case will be submitted to the factfinder for a decision. In a jury trial, the trial judge will instruct the jury in a detailed manner about the law pertaining to the case, and the jury will then retire to deliberate in secrecy about whether to convict or acquit. Several important procedural issues relate to the standards by which the jury (or trial judge, in a bench trial) must make this decision, the nature and form of the verdict by which the decision is announced, and permissible challenges to the verdict.

1. The Burden of Proof

In the landmark case of In re Winship, 397 U.S. 358 (1970), the Supreme Court declared (in a juvenile delinquency case) that, under the Due Process Clause, a criminal conviction cannot be based on any standard less than proof of every element of the crime "beyond a reasonable doubt." "Reasonable doubt" has never been clearly defined by the Court. In Cage v. Louisiana, 498 U.S. 39 (1990) (per curiam), the Court rejected (as too pro-prosecution) jury instructions defining "reasonable doubt" as "a grave uncertainty" and "an actual substantial doubt," and describing the proper standard as one of "moral certainty." In the companion cases of Victor v. Nebraska and Sandoval v. California, 511 U.S. 1 (1994), however, the Court approved jury instructions stating that a "reasonable doubt" exists whenever, after "consideration of all the evidence," the juror lacks "an abiding conviction, to a moral certainty," of the defendant's guilt. The Court reiterated its displeasure with such phrases as "substantial doubt" and "moral certainty," but concluded that the instructions, in their entirety, provided sufficient context to explain to the jurors the true meaning of "reasonable doubt"—which, the Court suggested, is doubt "that would cause a reasonable person to hesitate to act." Id., at 20. See also Jackson v. Virginia, 443 U.S. 307, 317, n. 9 (1979) (describing "reasonable doubt" as doubt "based on reason which arises from the evidence or lack of evidence").

Under *Winship*, it is clear that the prosecution must bear the burden of proving all elements of a crime beyond a reasonable doubt. See also Sandstrom v. Montana, 442 U.S. 510 (1979), holding that *Winship* prohibits a jury instruction creating a presumption with respect to an element of a crime; Francis v. Franklin, 471 U.S. 307 (1985), holding that *Winship* and *Sandstrom* prohibit not only conclusive, but also rebuttable, presumptions. But what are the elements of a crime?

In Mullaney v. Wilbur, 421 U.S. 684 (1975), a unanimous Court held that *Winship* prohibits a legislature from placing on the defendant in a homicide case the burden of proving by a preponderance of the evidence, in order to reduce the crime from murder to manslaughter, that the killing had occurred in the heat of passion. The Court explained that *Winship* cannot be "limited to those facts that constitute a crime as defined by state law"; otherwise, the legislature could "undermine many of the interests that decision sought to protect" by "redefin[ing] the elements that constitute different crimes, characterizing them [instead] as factors that bear solely on the extent of punishment." Id., at 698.

Just two years after *Mullaney*, however, in Patterson v. New York, 432 U.S. 197 (1977), the Court upheld a similar statute placing on the defendant the burden of proving, in a second-degree murder case, the "affirmative defense" that the killing was the result of "extreme emotional disturbance for which there was a reasonable explanation or excuse"; such proof had the effect of reducing the crime from second-degree murder to manslaughter. The Court distinguished *Mullaney* on the ground that the statute in *Patterson* did not make the absence of "extreme emotional disturbance" an element of second degree murder, but instead provided only that the existence of such a factor would serve as an "affirmative defense" to the crime. The Court drew an analogy to the insanity defense, which previously had been held by the Court to be an "affirmative defense" that the defendant could constitutionally be required to prove, and noted that a contrary result might cause legislatures to eliminate such defenses entirely. The Court concluded:

. . . [E]ven if we were to hold that a State must prove sanity to convict once that fact is put in issue, it would not necessarily follow that a State must prove beyond a reasonable doubt every fact, the existence or nonexistence of which it is willing to recognize as an exculpatory or mitigating circumstance affecting the degree of culpability or the severity of the punishment. . . .

We thus decline to adopt as a constitutional imperative, operative countrywide, that a State must disprove beyond a reasonable doubt every fact constituting any and all affirmative defenses related to the culpability of an accused. . . .

This view may seem to permit state legislatures to reallocate burdens of proof by labeling as affirmative defenses at least some of the elements of the crimes now defined in their statutes. But there are obviously constitutional limits beyond which the States may not go in this regard. . . .

Id., at 207, 210.

What are these "constitutional limits" on legislative reshaping of the elements of a crime? The *Patterson* Court identified only one—that the legislature cannot "declare an individual guilty or presumptively guilty of a crime." Id., at 210. Nonetheless, in Martin v. Ohio, 480 U.S. 228 (1987), the Court upheld a statute placing on the defendant the burden of proving by a preponderance of the evidence, as an "affirmative defense" to a murder charge, that the killing was committed in self-defense—even though 48 out of the 50 states treated the absence of self-defense as an element of the crime of murder.

The Court's burden-of-proof cases—and especially *Patterson*—have been sharply criticized by commentators on the ground that they elevate form over substance in determining exactly what are the "elements" of a crime. The best of these commentaries have suggested that, at a minimum, the prosecution should be required to prove beyond a reasonable doubt any facts that would be necessary in order for the statutorily authorized range of punishments to satisfy the Eighth Amendment's proportionality requirement. See, e.g., Ronald J. Allen, Foreword: Montana v. Egelhoff—Reflections on the Limits of Legislative Imagination and Judicial Authority, 87 J. Crim. L. & Criminology 633 (1997); John C. Jeffries & Paul B. Stephan, Defenses, Presumptions, and Burden of Proof in the Criminal Law, 88 Yale L.J. 1325 (1979); Ronald J. Allen, Mullaney v. Wilbur, the Supreme Court, and the Substantive Criminal Law—An Examination of the Limits of Legitimate Intervention, 55 Tex. L. Rev. 269 (1977).

The *Winship/Mullaney/Patterson* problem has recently recurred with a vengeance, in the different context of burdens of proof with respect to so-called "sentencing factors." See Chapter 15. In fact, the problem is ubiquitous in criminal litigation. It affects statutory inferences, presumptions, comment on the evidence, judicial notice, instructions on defenses and lesser-included counts, and affirmative defenses, because each of these intersects with burdens of persuasion in one manner or another. This leads to very strange results. For example, a legislature may not create a "presumption" of an element upon proof of some other fact, because that would adversely affect proof beyond reasonable doubt, yet the legislature almost surely could eliminate the "presumed" element entirely, or make it into an affirmative defense. The Court has never noticed the interconnectedness of the various categories noted above that intersect the burden of persuasion, and thus it has never addressed the somewhat internally inconsistent, if not paradoxical, jurisprudence it has created in this area. For a thorough discussion, see Ronald J.

Allen, Structuring Jury Decisionmaking in Criminal Cases: A Unified Constitutional Analysis of Evidentiary Devices, 94 Harv. L. Rev. 321-368 (1980).

2. Unanimity of the Verdict

As noted at the beginning of this chapter, the Sixth Amendment has been held not to require unanimous verdicts, at least in the context of 12-member juries. Nevertheless, unanimity is still required in the federal system and in most states. Does the unanimity requirement, where it exists, mean that the jurors must all agree on one particular theory of the case? Or on one particular way of establishing one of the elements of the crime?

In Schad v. Arizona, 501 U.S. 624 (1991), the Court affirmed a state conviction for first-degree murder despite the fact that the jury may not have been unanimous on whether the defendant acted with premeditation or was guilty of felony murder. But in Richardson v. United States, 526 U.S. 813 (1999), the Court reversed a federal conviction because the jury was not required to reach a unanimous verdict with respect to the defendant's commission of numerous specific violations of federal drug laws that were alleged to be part of a "series of violations" needed to establish the larger crime of operating a "continuing criminal enterprise." The *Richardson* Court explained that resolving this question requires close examination of the statutory elements of the crime charged:

> . . . Where, for example, an element of robbery is force or the threat of force, some jurors might conclude that the defendant used a knife to create the threat; others might conclude he used a gun. But that disagreement—a disagreement about means— would not matter as long as all 12 jurors unanimously concluded that the Government had proved the necessary related element, namely that the defendant has threatened force. . . .
>
> In this case, we must decide whether the statute's phrase "series of violations" refers to one element, namely, a "series," in respect to which the "violations" constitute the underlying brute facts or means, or whether the words create several elements, namely the several "violations," in respect to *each* of which the jury must agree unanimously and separately.

Id., at 817-818. Ultimately, the Court's statutory analysis led it to conclude that each alleged violation constituted a separate element of the "continuing criminal enterprise" crime and thus had to be found unanimously. Id., at 818-820.

What can the trial judge do to prod the jury to reach a unanimous verdict? In Allen v. United States, 164 U.S. 492 (1896), the Court upheld the giving of an instruction, in the midst of a prolonged period of jury deliberation, designed to encourage any jurors still in the minority to reconsider the reasonableness of their views. (This is now called an "*Allen* charge" or, sometimes, a "dynamite charge.") The Court explained that "[i]t certainly cannot be the law that each juror should not listen with deference to the arguments and with a distrust of his own judgment, if he finds a large majority of the jury taking a different view of the case from what he does himself." Id., at 501. But in Jenkins v. United States, 380 U.S. 445 (1965) (per curiam), the Court found a due process violation when the trial judge instructed the jury that "[y]ou have got to reach a decision in this case." Id., at 446.

The constitutionality of an *Allen* charge was also at issue in Lowenfield v. Phelps, 484 U.S. 231 (1988). There the trial judge gave an instruction not specifically addressed to jurors who were in the minority, but urging all of the jurors to rethink their views. The judge also polled the jury, twice, to see whether the jurors believed that further deliberations would be productive. (This procedure is not allowed in federal cases; see Brasfield v. United States, 272 U.S. 448 (1926).) The Court concluded that, on the facts, "the combination of the polling of the jury and the supplemental instruction was not 'coercive' in such a way as to deny [the defendant] any constitutional right." Id., at 241.

On the empirical effects of "dynamite charges," see Vicki Smith & Saul Kassin, Effects of the Dynamite Charge on the Deliberations of Deadlocked Mock Juries, 17 Law & Hum. Behav. 625 (1993) (concluding that the "dynamite charge" moved deadlocked juries toward unanimity by increasing pressure on jurors in the minority, but not on those in the majority, to change their votes).

3.   Consistency of the Verdict; General Verdicts

The general rule is that no constitutional issue is created by the return of inconsistent verdicts because such verdicts may be simply the product of permissible leniency. Thus, for example, a defendant can be convicted of armed robbery but acquitted of possessing a firearm. See, e.g., Harris v. Rivera, 454 U.S. 339 (1981) (per curiam) (upholding conviction by inconsistent verdicts in bench trial in state court); United States v. Powell, 469 U.S. 57 (1984) (same result, in jury trial in federal court).

Although the almost universal practice in America is for criminal cases to be decided by general verdict, without any indication of the reasons underlying the verdict, such practice is currently under attack in Europe as a possible violation of human rights. Article 6 of the European Convention on Human Rights (ECHR) provides that all criminal defendants are entitled to a trial before an independent and impartial tribunal, whose judgments must be delivered in public. Some have argued that general jury verdicts are not the kind of reasoned judgments contemplated by the ECHR.

Andrew Leipold has argued that defendants who are acquitted of a crime should have a statutory right to ask the jury (or the judge, in a bench trial) to determine, in addition to his *legal* guilt or innocence, whether or not he is *factually* innocent. According to Leipold, the "innocent, acquitted defendant"—although obviously far less deserving of society's sympathy than an innocent, convicted defendant—nevertheless suffers several demonstrable harms:

> My thesis is that while innocent people who are arrested, charged, and acquitted of crimes have far fewer problems than the wrongfully convicted, their burdens are still substantial and still worthy of attention. Many of these problems, such as cost and the risk of an erroneous outcome, are faced by every party in any legal proceeding, but others are unique. In particular, a factually innocent defendant confronts the problem of being publicly accused by the government of criminal behavior with no real prospect of ever being officially vindicated. An innocent suspect may have the charges dismissed or may be acquitted, but the sequella of an indictment may leave the defendant's reputation, personal relationships, and ability to earn a living so badly damaged that he may never be able to return to the life he knew before being accused. More subtly, a person who was once charged with a crime is put on a different (and far

less desirable) track in the legal system than someone who has never been arrested. A later acquittal or dismissal does surprisingly little to relieve an innocent defendant of the resulting burdens.

Andrew D. Leipold, The Problem of the Innocent, Acquitted Defendant, 94 Nw. U. L. Rev. 1297, 1299 (2000). Leipold acknowledges numerous practical problems with his proposal, including the nature and allocation of the burden of proof with respect to factual innocence, but concludes that "[l]eaving the most important decision that courts make, and the most important decision in some defendants' lives, shrouded in mystery can hardly be the right outcome for a system that prizes fair and equal treatment under the law." Id., at 1356.

4. Impeachment of the Verdict

Once the jury has reached its verdict, the rule is that no impeachment of the verdict by a juror will be allowed, except for the rare case in which a juror testifies that some *external* influence affected the jury's deliberations. This rule is strictly applied. In Tanner v. United States, 483 U.S. 107 (1987), a juror in a federal fraud trial volunteered, after the conclusion of the trial, information that several of the jurors consumed alcohol during lunch breaks, causing them to sleep through the afternoon sessions of the trial. Later, another juror volunteered that "the jury was on one big party"; he stated that seven of the jurors drank alcohol during lunch breaks, that four of the jurors (including himself) often drank from one to three pitchers of beer, that several other jurors also consumed mixed drinks, that four of the jurors (again, including himself) smoked marijuana regularly during the trial, that one juror ingested cocaine five times and another juror did so two or three times, and that one juror sold a quarter-pound of marijuana to another juror during the trial and brought drug paraphernalia into the courthouse. The Court held that this information was of no legal consequence:

> There is little doubt that postverdict investigation into juror misconduct would in some instances lead to the invalidation of verdicts reached after irresponsible or improper juror behavior. It is not at all clear, however, that the jury system could survive such efforts to perfect it. Allegations of juror misconduct, incompetency, or inattentiveness, raised for the first time days, weeks, or months after the verdict, seriously disrupt the finality of the process. . . . Moreover, full and frank discussion in the jury room, jurors' willingness to return an unpopular verdict, and the community's trust in a system that relies on the decisions of laypeople would all be undermined by a barrage of postverdict scrutiny of juror conduct. . . .

Id., at 120-121.

Does this remind you, just a little bit, of the adage about ostriches who bury their heads in the sand? Is there no possibility of an alternative approach that would insulate jury decisionmaking from review in most cases, but allow for correction of the most egregious instances of juror (or, apparently, in the *Tanner* case, jury) misconduct?

In Regina v. Connor and Regina v. Mirze, [2004] UKHL 2, the United Kingdom's House of Lords considered the possibility that traditional jury secrecy might violate the aforementioned Article 6 of the European Convention on Human Rights. Both cases involved defendants who claimed misconduct by the juries that convicted them. In one case, a juror allegedly held the use of an interpreter against the defendant; in the other case, a juror accused other jurors of not giving proper consideration to the verdict. A majority of the Lords declined to abrogate the common-law rule of secrecy of jury deliberations on the alleged facts of the two cases. But the Lords also acknowledged that modern human-rights law, as expressed in the ECHR, might require abrogation of jury secrecy in exceptional cases, especially if the allegations of jury misconduct were made before the verdict was reached. The Lords also recommended improvements to the British jury system, including better jury instructions and better factual reporting about trials from trial judges to appellate courts.

5.   **Post-Verdict Motions**

After the jury's verdict has been announced, and assuming that the defendant has been convicted, there are several procedural routes by which the defendant may seek to overturn the verdict in the trial court. The defendant may file a motion for a judgment of acquittal, on the ground that the evidence presented during the trial was legally insufficient for a conviction (i.e., the evidence did not meet the legal standard of proof of guilt "beyond a reasonable doubt"). The trial judge has the authority to enter a judgment of acquittal notwithstanding the jury's verdict, if the judge finds the evidence legally insufficient—although the fact that the jury reached the opposite conclusion will inevitably weigh heavily on the judge's mind. (This is one reason why many defendants file an initial motion for a judgment of acquittal immediately after the conclusion of the prosecution's case-in-chief, before the jury has a chance to render its verdict.) In addition, the trial judge must view the evidence in the light most favorable to the prosecution, further reducing the likelihood of the defendant's success.

The defendant may also file a motion for a new trial, either on the ground of newly discovered evidence or on some other ground (often including the "interests of justice"). In the case of newly discovered evidence, most states and the federal system limit the time period after judgment during which such evidence can be used to seek a new trial. See, e.g., Fed. R. Crim. P. 33 (3-year limit); Ariz. Rule Crim. Proc. 24.2(a) (60-day limit); Minn. Rule Crim. Proc. 26.04(3) (15-day limit). Moreover, to qualify as "newly discovered," such evidence generally must have been unavailable to the defendant, even assuming the exercise of "due diligence," at the time of the trial.

In the case of a motion for a new trial based on grounds other than newly discovered evidence, the defendant may raise any number of procedural trial errors; some states actually require the filing of such a motion in order to preserve procedural issues for appeal. The defendant may also ask the trial judge to order a new trial on the ground that the jury's verdict was contrary to the weight of the evidence; because the remedy of a new trial is less disruptive than the remedy of a court-directed acquittal, the standard for granting such a motion is somewhat more favorable to the defendant, as compared to the aforementioned motion for a judgment of acquittal. A motion for a new trial based on grounds other than newly discovered evidence, however, is often subject to very strict time limits, see, e.g., Fed. R. Crim. P. 33 (14-day time limit).

F. Criminal Trials and Factual Accuracy

To what extent should criminal trials (and, more generally, criminal justice — including the full range of pretrial proceedings, trials, direct appeals, and postconviction proceedings) be designed to ensure, as much as humanly possible, factually accurate results? Should our choices about the structure and procedural rules of the criminal justice system be made mostly, or even exclusively, on the basis of whether those choices will further both the conviction of the guilty and the acquittal of the innocent (which are, after all, two sides of the very same coin)? Or are there other important values — such as autonomy, privacy, equality, fairness, respect for the individual — that deserve equal treatment?

In recent years, the Supreme Court has seemed increasingly ambivalent about where the primary emphasis should lie. On the one hand, the Court has manifested a growing discomfort about the number of criminal cases in which potentially innocent defendants have been found guilty of serious, and sometimes even capital, crimes. This concern about factual inaccuracy can clearly be seen in such decisions as Holmes v. South Carolina, 547 U.S. 319 (2006) (reversing a conviction because the defendant was precluded from introducing evidence at trial that pointed to a different suspect); Youngblood v. West Virginia, 547 U.S. 867 (2006) (reversing and remanding a potentially meritorious *Brady* claim to the state courts for further review); and especially House v. Bell, 547 U.S. 518 (2006).

In *House*, the Court (by 5-3, with Justice Alito not participating) reversed the Sixth Circuit, and allowed a Death Row inmate's habeas corpus action to proceed despite the petitioner's failure to follow the applicable procedural rules in state court, because the Court found that the petitioner's newly discovered evidence of factual innocence (specifically, DNA test results) was strong enough that "it is more likely than not that no reasonable juror would have found petitioner guilty beyond a reasonable doubt" if the evidence had been available at trial. The Court's emphatic conclusion was based not only on the new DNA evidence itself, but also on the "evidentiary disarray" (which was described in great detail, and at great length, in Justice Breyer's majority opinion) surrounding the prosecution's forensic evidence at trial. Upon consideration of all of the evidence (including the new DNA evidence), the Court held that although the case was not one of "conclusive exoneration," it nevertheless qualified as one of those "rare case[s]" meriting habeas review despite the petitioner's procedural default. See Joseph L. Hoffmann, House v. Bell and the Death of Innocence, in Death Penalty Stories, John Blume & Jordan Steiker, eds. (2009).

On the other hand, the Court has also decided several recent cases in ways that seemingly ignored or downplayed the issue of factual accuracy in favor of something else. For example, in Davis v. Washington, 547 U.S. 813 (2006), the Court continued its development of a brand new Confrontation Clause approach that elevates the Framers' views about what kinds of evidence must be subjected to cross-examination (specifically, evidence resembling that which was introduced under certain English statutes passed during the reign of Queen Mary) over more functional considerations about whether, and to what extent, cross-examination might actually contribute to the reliability of evidence (and thus the factual accuracy of trials). Along somewhat similar lines, see Oregon v. Guzek, 546 U.S. 517 (2006) (holding that a capital defendant has no constitutional right to introduce evidence of his innocence at a capital sentencing hearing, once he has been found guilty at the trial stage of the case); United States v. Ruiz, 536 U.S. 622 (2002) (holding that prosecutors need not disclose to defendants, prior to accepting a guilty plea, evidence that would impeach prosecution informants or witnesses).

Is there a way to reconcile these apparent inconsistencies in approach? Is this a simple case of two different factions on the Court disagreeing about what matters most in criminal cases? Or does this confusing situation possibly reflect, instead, a gradual shift from the largely procedural emphasis of the Court during much of the 1960s and 1970s to a new and more substantive approach—perhaps motivated by the recent, highly publicized spate of DNA exonerations (especially in capital cases)? Will we see in the near future, perhaps, additional decisions by the Court along the lines of House v. Bell, opening up new avenues of opportunity for defendants with claims of factual innocence to challenge their convictions?

Any perception of a trend in this direction may have been dashed, at least temporarily, by the Court's ruling in District Attorney's Office for the Third Judicial District v. Osborne, 557 U.S. 52 (2009). Osborne was convicted of kidnapping, sexual assault, and assault (but acquitted of attempted murder) in connection with a brutal 1993 attack on a prostitute, and was sentenced to 26 years in prison. Although Osborne's conviction and sentence were affirmed on appeal, and also in state and federal postconviction review, he continued to profess his innocence. Osborne eventually filed a §1983 petition in federal court, seeking access to physical evidence in the state's possession so that he could have it tested by advanced DNA methods. His petition was premised on the argument that such access should be guaranteed by the Due Process Clause—in either the procedural sense, by analogy to the defendant's right to be notified of material exculpatory evidence under Brady v. Maryland, 373 U.S. 83 (1969), or in the substantive sense.

The Court, in a 5-4 decision, rejected both versions of the argument. According to the Court, claims of factual innocence made after conviction entitle the claimant to less stringent procedural protections than would attach to such claims made at trial, thus making *Brady* inapposite. "The State accordingly has more flexibility in deciding what procedures are needed in the context of postconviction relief. . . . Federal courts may upset a State's postconviction relief procedures only if they are fundamentally inadequate to vindicate the substantive rights provided. . . . We see nothing inadequate about the procedures Alaska has provided to vindicate its state right to postconviction relief in general, and nothing inadequate about how those procedures apply to those who seek access to DNA evidence." 557 U.S., at 69. The Court also rejected Osborne's substantive due process argument, based on both the argument's "novelty" as well as the fact that it would embroil the Court in difficult policy choices (such as whether, and for how long, states should be required to preserve evidence for possible future testing). In the end, the Court concluded:

> DNA evidence will undoubtedly lead to changes in the criminal justice system. It has done so already. The question is whether further change will primarily be made by legislative revision and judicial interpretation of the existing system, or whether the Federal Judiciary must leap ahead—revising (or even discarding) the system by creating a new constitutional right and taking over responsibility for refining it.

Id., at 74.

PART FIVE

POSTTRIAL PROCEEDINGS

Chapter 15

Sentencing

A. Introduction to Sentencing

1. Sentencing Options

A defendant who has been convicted of a crime may be sentenced to a variety of different punishments. Almost all felony crimes are punishable by a sentence of confinement in a state or federal prison, or in a local jail, and/or by a period of probation. At the extreme, in many jurisdictions, some murders are punishable by a sentence of death. Monetary punishments, such as fines, orders of restitution, and criminal forfeitures, are common, either separately or in combination with other punishments. Between incarceration and probation lie intermediate sanctions including house arrest, inpatient treatment programs, "boot camps," electronic monitoring, day-reporting programs, furlough programs, and community service.

In terms of per capita incarceration rates, the United States is one of the most punitive nations in the world.[1] A few other outliers like North Korea, the Seychelles, and Turkmenistan have roughly similar incarceration rates, but the U.S. incarceration rate of 698 prisoners per 100,000 population (at the end of 2013) vastly exceeds that of virtually every other nation, including Brazil (301), South Africa (292), Mexico (212), Australia (151), United Kingdom (148), Canada (106), Germany (78), Japan (49), and India (33). Even Russia (450), Belarus (306), and China (165) do not imprison nearly as many people (on a per capita basis) as we do.

How did we get here? The incarceration rate in the United States, as can be seen in Figure 15.1 below, increased dramatically from 1980 to 2009 before starting to decline slightly. At year-end 2014, an estimated 1,561,500 persons were incarcerated in federal and state prisons and jails; this number represented a 1 percent decrease from year-end 2013, and a decline of 3.3 percent from the high point at year-end 2009. About 97 percent of all prisoners were serving sentences of more than one year. At year-end 2013, the total number of persons under the supervision of the adult criminal justice system (including those on parole or probation) was 6,899,000, or 1 out of every 35 adults in the United States.

---

1. The statistics in this introductory section are reported in "Highest to Lowest: Prison Population Rate," an online report by the World Prison Brief, Institute for Criminal Policy Research at Birkbeck, University of London, available online at http://www.prisonstudies.org/highest-to-lowest/prison_population_rate; "The Growth of Incarceration in the United States: Exploring Causes and Consequences," Jeremy Travis and Bruce Western (eds.), National Research Council (2014), see http://www.nap.edu/download.php?record_id=18613; and various statistical publications by the U.S. Department of Justice, Bureau of Justice Statistics, available online at http://bjs.ojp.usdoj.gov/. The death penalty statistics at the end of this section are reported in NAACP Legal Defense Fund, Death Row U.S.A., Winter 2015, available online at http://www.naacpldf.org/files/publications/DRUSA_Winter_2015.pdf.

Figure 15.1 – U.S. Incarcerations by Year

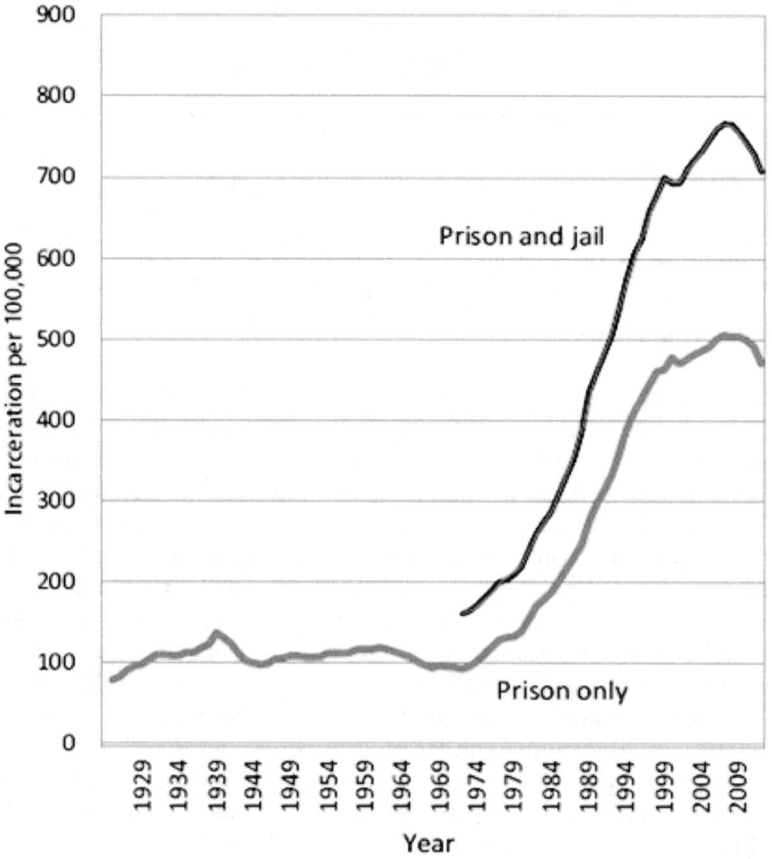

Source: National Research Council (2014)

The causes of the dramatic rise in incarceration in America since 1980 are debated. Certainly the "war on drugs," including the proliferation of "mandatory minimum" prison sentences, had a lot to do with it. Substantial increases in punishments for violent crimes, including "three strikes" laws that target repeat offenders, also played a role. Some argue that the increased incarceration rate reflects misguided public anxiety over crime, fueled by media hype and racial and ethnic stereotyping. Others note that the modern sharp decline in crime rates in America (e.g., the U.S. homicide rate dropped from 9.5 per 100,000 in 1993, to 4.5 per 100,000 in 2013) has roughly coincided with the increase in incarceration, and contend that there is a causal effect. As with much of criminology, the evidence seems largely ambiguous.

The slight recent decline in imprisonment has coincided with the stirrings of a new national conversation about penal policy and the myriad costs of mass incarceration—including not only the obvious impact on those incarcerated and their loved ones, but also the costs to the larger society, including both financial costs (in 2012, the states spent more than $50 billion on imprisonment; in 2014, 18 states and the federal government were operating their prison systems at more than 100% of capacity) and social costs (e.g., the disruptive effects in many poor communities, and communities of color, as huge numbers of adult males are placed behind bars, thereby dramatically restricting their opportunities for future economic, social, and political participation). Mass incarceration has produced a severely disparate impact based on race and ethnicity, as illustrated by Figure 15.2, below. Minorities now constitute 60 percent of the American prison population; the imprisonment rate for black men age 30-39 (6%) is substantially higher than that for Hispanics (2%) and whites (1%). Black men under the age of 35 without a high-school diploma are now more likely to be in prison than employed in the labor market. These kinds of statistics, and the human toll that lies beneath them, have helped to stimulate a robust political discussion about whether the costs are worth whatever benefits may be generated by mass incarceration. As then-U.S. Attorney General Eric Holder argued in September 2014:

> [T]he United States will never be able to prosecute or incarcerate its way to becoming a safer nation. We must never, and we will never, stop being vigilant against crime—and the conditions and choices that breed it. But, for far too long—under well-intentioned policies designed to be "tough" on criminals—our system has perpetuated a destructive cycle of poverty, criminality, and incarceration that has trapped countless people and weakened entire communities—particularly communities of color.
>
> In recent decades, the effects of these policies—and the impact of the "truth-in-sentencing" mindset—have been dramatic. Although the United States comprises just 5 percent of the world's population, we incarcerate almost a quarter of its prisoners. The entire United States population has increased by about a third since 1980. But the federal prison population has grown by almost 800 percent over the same period. Spending on corrections, incarceration, and law enforcement has exploded, consuming $260 billion per year nationwide. And the Bureau of Prisons currently commands about a third of the Justice Department's overall budget.
>
> Perhaps most troubling is the fact that this astonishing rise in incarceration—and the escalating costs it has imposed on our country, in terms both economic and human—have not measurably benefited our society. We can *all* be proud of the progress that's been made at reducing the crime rate over the past two decades—thanks to the tireless work of prosecutors and the bravery of law enforcement officials across America. But statistics have shown—and all of us have seen—that high incarceration rates and longer-than-necessary prison terms *have not* played a significant role in materially improving public safety, reducing crime, or strengthening communities.
>
> In fact, the opposite is often true. Two weeks ago, the *Washington Post* reported that new analysis of crime data and incarceration rates—performed by the Pew Charitable Trusts, and covering the period of 1994 to 2012—shows that states with the most significant drops in crime *also* saw reductions in their prison populations. States that took drastic steps to reduce their prison populations—in many cases by percentages well into the double digits—saw crime go down as well. And the one state—West Virginia—with the greatest increase in its incarceration rate actually experienced an *uptick* in crime.
>
> As the *Post* makes clear: "To the extent that there is any trend here, it's actually that states incarcerating people have seen *smaller* decreases in crime." And this has been borne out at the national level, as well. . . .
>
> We know that over-incarceration crushes opportunity. We know it prevents people, and entire communities, from getting on the right track. And we've seen that—as more and more government leaders have gradually come to recognize—at a fundamental level, it challenges our commitment to the cause of justice. . . .

Figure 15.2 – U.S. Incarcerations by Race and Ethnicity

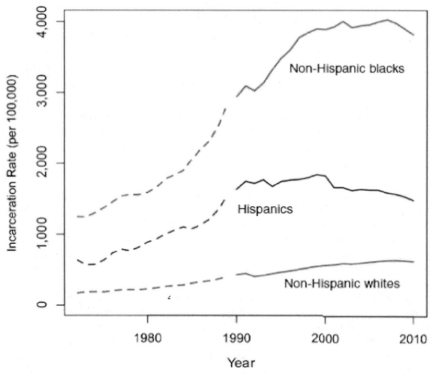

Source: National Resource Council (2014)

See Eric H. Holder, Jr., Keynote Address at the Brennan Center for Justice, September 23, 2014, available online at https://www.brennancenter.org/analysis/keynote-address-shifting-law-enforcement-goals-to-reduce-mass-incarceration.

There are no comparable comprehensive studies of intermediate sanctions, but the available evidence suggests that—especially as prison capacities are more frequently exceeded—such punishments are becoming increasingly popular with tax-conscious legislatures and sentencing judges. "Intermediate sanctions have been seen as a way both to reduce the need for prison beds and to provide a continuum of sanctions that satisfies the just deserts concern for proportionality in punishment." See Michael Tonry, Intermediate Sanctions in Sentencing Reform, 2 U. Chi. L. Sch. Roundtable 391 (1995). Although occasional notorious failures (like the Willie Horton prison-furlough debacle that contributed to the downfall of Democratic presidential candidate Michael Dukakis in 1988) have led public officials to underutilize such sanctions, or to limit their use to offenders who would not have been imprisoned anyway, nevertheless such sanctions "can be used to save money and prison use, without significant sacrifices in public safety." See Michael Tonry, Intermediate Sanctions in Sentencing Guidelines, 23 Crime & Just. 199 (1998).

At the apex of the sentencing pyramid lies the most extreme punishment—the death penalty. Prior to 1972, the death penalty was imposed by juries that were given virtually no guidance as to how the decision should be made. In Furman v. Georgia, 408 U.S. 238 (1972), the Supreme Court held that such open-ended discretion in death sentencing violates the Eighth Amendment's "cruel and unusual punishment" clause, because it tends to produce arbitrary, capricious, and often discriminatory results. All death sentences imposed prior to *Furman* were therefore reversed. After *Furman*, however, many states enacted new death-penalty statutes designed to guide the jury's exercise of sentencing discretion, primarily through statutory lists of "aggravating circumstances" (that weighed in favor of a death sentence) and "mitigating circumstances" (that weighed against it). In Gregg v. Georgia, 428 U.S. 153 (1976), the Court held that these new "guided discretion" statutes complied with the Eighth Amendment, and allowed capital punishment to resume. In Lockett v. Ohio, 438 U.S. 586 (1978), the Court clarified that defendants cannot be limited to the "mitigating circumstances" listed in the relevant statute; rather, the Eighth Amendment requires that all relevant mitigating evidence must be considered by the jury.

Despite the Court's efforts in *Furman* and *Gregg* to bring rationality and fairness to capital sentencing, the problem of disparate application persists. In McCleskey v. Kemp, 481 U.S. 279 (1987), the death penalty in Georgia was challenged on equal protection and Eighth Amendment grounds, based on a landmark study by Professor David Baldus establishing that defendants who killed white victims were significantly more likely to receive the death penalty than those who killed black victims. The Court, in a 5-4 decision, rejected the challenge, finding that the discrepancies identified in the Baldus study were the inevitable result of necessary discretion in capital sentencing, and did not rise to the level of "the major systemic defects identified in *Furman*." Id., at 313. Subsequent empirical studies have found similar race-of-the-victim disparity in other death penalty jurisdictions.

In the United States today, the death penalty is effectively limited to intentional murders or felony murders during which the defendant exhibited at least a "reckless disregard for human life." See Kennedy v. Louisiana, 554 U.S. 407 (2008) (death penalty for rape of child held unconstitutional); Tison v. Arizona, 481 U.S. 137 (1987) (death penalty permitted for some felony murderers); Coker v. Georgia, 433 U.S. 584 (1977) (death penalty for rape of adult woman held unconstitutional).[2] Thirty-two states and the federal government currently authorize the imposition of the death penalty for some murders. As of January 1, 2015, a total of 3,019 persons were on death row, and 1,394 persons had been executed since the resumption of capital punishment in 1976. Of those on death row in January 2015, 43.0 percent were white, 41.6 percent were black, and 12.8 percent were of Hispanic origin. Death row populations steadily increased from 1976 through the end of 2002, but have slightly decreased since then. Much of this decrease occurred in January 2003, when the lame-duck Governor of Illinois, George Ryan, commuted all of the death sentences in that state. California has the largest current death row, at 743 persons, followed by Florida (403) and Texas (276). Texas, however, has executed far more persons than any other state since 1976—a total of 518 executions as of January 2015, or more than 37 percent of the entire national total. Other states with relatively large numbers of executions include Oklahoma (111), Virginia (110), Florida (89), and Missouri (80); by contrast, California—despite its huge death row—has executed only 13 persons since 1976.

---

2. Federal law continues to authorize the death penalty for certain crimes of treason or espionage, but these statutes have not been tested in the Supreme Court, and their constitutional validity remains unanswered.

In recent years, perhaps due to the national publicity surrounding the high-profile exonerations of death-row inmates in Illinois and elsewhere, or perhaps due to the extremely high costs of litigating a capital case to conclusion, the numbers of both new death sentences and executions have declined. In 2014, 35 persons were executed nationwide; this was the smallest number in 20 years, down substantially from the modern peak of 98 executions in 1999. And only 72 new death sentences were imposed in 2014, as compared with 315 new death sentences in 1996. Since 2007, seven states have abolished capital punishment, either by statute or by judicial decision (and either retroactively, sparing all persons then on death row, or prospectively only). And four current Supreme Court Justices are now on record as being significantly concerned about the death penalty's constitutionality.[3] Are we witnessing the gradual elimination of capital punishment in America?

2. Sentencing Considerations

The Supreme Court has addressed several constitutional challenges to the consideration of particular kinds of information at sentencing. Some of the most important rulings include the following:

Past Criminal Conduct.   Such information generally may be considered at sentencing. On the one hand, sentences may not be increased on the basis of prior felony convictions obtained in violation of the Sixth Amendment right to appointed counsel under Gideon v. Wainwright, 372 U.S. 335 (1963). See United States v. Tucker, 404 U.S. 443 (1972); Burgett v. Texas, 389 U.S. 109 (1967). On the other hand, uncounseled misdemeanor convictions, in cases where the defendant had no Sixth Amendment right to appointed counsel in the first place, may be considered at sentencing. See Nichols v. United States, 511 U.S. 738 (1994).

Future Dangerousness.   Psychiatric testimony about the defendant's future dangerousness may be considered at sentencing, even in a death penalty case where the need for reliability is greatest. See Barefoot v. Estelle, 463 U.S. 880 (1983); Jurek v. Texas, 428 U.S. 262 (1976).[4]

False Testimony at Trial.   The fact that the defendant committed perjury at trial may be considered at sentencing, and such consideration does not place an

---

3. The states that have recently abolished the death penalty are New York (2007), New Jersey (2007), New Mexico (2009), Illinois (2011), Connecticut (2012), Maryland (2013), and Nebraska (2015). The Supreme Court case in which four current Justices — Breyer, Ginsburg, Sotomayor, and Kagan — all indicated varying levels of discomfort with the constitutionality of the death penalty was Glossip v. Gross, 135 S. Ct. 1885 (2015).

4. Pennsylvania is currently engaged in the first major initiative to build "risk assessment" (i.e., predictions of future criminal behavior based on statistical analysis of various risk factors, such as demographic info, family history, education, work history, and criminal history) into criminal sentencing. The state legislature, back in 2010, mandated the Pennsylvania Commission on Sentencing to incorporate risk assessment into the state's sentencing guidelines, see 2010 Act 95, available online at http://www.legis. state.pa.us/cfdocs/legis/li/uconsCheck.cfm?yr=2010&sessInd=0&act=9, and the Commission is finally getting close to completing the required revisions. The Pennsylvania initiative is controversial, see, e.g., Anna Maria Barry-Jester, Ben Casselman & Dana Goldstein, "Should Prison Sentences Be Based On Crimes That Haven't Been Committed Yet?" (August 24, 2015), available online at http://fivethirtyeight. com/features/prison-reform-risk-assessment/, and it is not yet known whether the Supreme Court ultimately will find the new approach to be constitutional.

unconstitutional burden on the defendant's right to testify at trial. See United States v. Dunnigan, 507 U.S. 87 (1993); United States v. Grayson, 438 U.S. 41 (1978).

Silence at Sentencing. The fact that the defendant chose not to testify at a sentencing hearing may not be considered in determining the defendant's sentence, because such use would violate the defendant's Fifth Amendment privilege against self-incrimination. This is true even if the defendant pleaded guilty to the crime. See Mitchell v. United States, 526 U.S. 314 (1999).

Racial Bias. The fact that a defendant was motivated by racial hatred to commit a crime may be considered at sentencing. See Wisconsin v. Mitchell, 508 U.S. 476 (1993); Barclay v. Florida, 463 U.S. 939 (1983). But a defendant's abstract beliefs, including membership in a racist group, are protected by the First Amendment and may not be considered unless directly relevant to the sentencing proceeding. See Dawson v. Delaware, 503 U.S. 159 (1992).

Judicial Vindictiveness. A defendant's sentence may not be increased after a retrial simply because the defendant chose to challenge his conviction by means of an appeal or postconviction proceeding. And, in order to protect defendants against the fear of such judicial vindictiveness, any trial judge who wishes to impose a harsher sentence after a retrial must set forth, on the record, the legitimate reasons supporting such a sentence. See North Carolina v. Pearce, 395 U.S. 711 (1969). These legitimate reasons may include information about the defendant's conduct occurring after the time of the original sentencing hearing, see *Pearce*, or other information that is similarly not susceptible to judicial manipulation, such as the fact that the defendant was later convicted on charges that were pending at the time of the original sentencing hearing, see Wasman v. United States, 468 U.S. 559 (1984). Moreover, the prophylactic protection of *Pearce* is quite limited in scope. It does not apply to resentencing at a trial de novo following a challenge to a misdemeanor conviction, see Colten v. Kentucky, 407 U.S. 104 (1972); to resentencing by a second jury, in a case involving jury sentencing, see Chaffin v. Stynchcombe, 412 U.S. 17 (1973); to resentencing by a trial judge after an original sentence that was imposed by a jury, see Texas v. McCullough, 475 U.S. 134 (1986); or to resentencing by a trial judge after the vacation of a guilty plea, see Alabama v. Smith, 490 U.S. 794 (1989). In each of these situations, the Court found that the circumstances generally did not warrant an inference of likely judicial vindictiveness.

Victim Impact Statements. Statements from crime victims (or their survivors) about the impact of the crime generally may be considered at sentencing, even in a death penalty case, as long as those statements are not so prejudicial as to violate either the general rules of evidence or the Due Process Clause. In a death penalty case, however, such statements may not include the opinions of the survivors about whether or not the defendant should receive a death sentence. See Payne v. Tennessee, 501 U.S. 808 (1991).

3. Substantive Limits on Sentencing — Eighth Amendment Proportionality

The Eighth Amendment provides: "Excessive bail shall not be required, nor excessive fines imposed, nor cruel and unusual punishments inflicted." Although it is generally agreed that the Eighth Amendment absolutely prohibits certain kinds of "cruel and unusual" punishments (e.g., in modern American society, drawing and quartering would be unconstitutional), there is far less agreement about whether, and to what extent, the Eighth Amendment also regulates the *relationship* between crimes and punishments. Does the Eighth Amendment contain an implied requirement of proportionality (i.e., that the punishment must fit the particular crime)? Under such a view, a punishment that is constitutional for one crime might be unconstitutional for another, less serious crime. Can life imprisonment, even if it is a constitutional punishment for the crime of murder, be imposed for the crime of driving without a valid driver's license? Or for an overtime parking violation?

In the special context of capital punishment, the Supreme Court has long acknowledged—and continues to acknowledge—the existence of an Eighth Amendment proportionality requirement. Thus, in Coker v. Georgia, 433 U.S. 584 (1977), the Court held that the death penalty was disproportionate to the crime of rape of an adult woman. In Tison v. Arizona, 481 U.S. 137 (1987), the Court held that the death penalty was disproportionate for the crime of felony murder, unless the defendant exhibited at least "reckless disregard for human life."

Outside the capital punishment context, however, the Court has been much less willing to engage in extended Eighth Amendment proportionality review of sentences.

EWING v. CALIFORNIA

Certiorari to the Court of Appeal of California, Second Appellate District
538 U.S. 11 (2003)

JUSTICE O'CONNOR announced the judgment of the Court and delivered an opinion in which CHIEF JUSTICE REHNQUIST and JUSTICE KENNEDY join.

In this case, we decide whether the Eighth Amendment prohibits the State of California from sentencing a repeat felon to a prison term of 25 years to life under the State's "Three Strikes and You're Out" law.

I

California's three strikes law reflects a shift in the State's sentencing policies toward incapacitating and deterring repeat offenders who threaten the public safety. The law was designed "to ensure longer prison sentences and greater punishment for those who commit a felony and have been previously convicted of serious and/ or violent felony offenses." Cal. Penal Code Ann. §667(b) (West 1999). [In early 1993, the bill that would later become the three strikes law was defeated in a legislative committee.] Public outrage over the defeat sparked a voter initiative to add Proposition 184, based loosely on the bill, to the ballot in the November 1994 general election.

On October 1, 1993, while Proposition 184 was circulating, 12-year-old Polly Klaas was kidnaped from her home in Petaluma, California. Her admitted killer, Richard Allen Davis, had a long criminal history that included two prior kidnaping convictions. Davis had served only half of his most recent sentence (16 years for kidnaping, assault, and burglary). Had Davis served his entire sentence, he would still have been in prison on the day that Polly Klaas was kidnaped.

Polly Klaas' murder galvanized support for the three strikes initiative. Within days, Proposition 184 was on its way to becoming the fastest qualifying initiative in California history. [It passed both houses of the legislature by wide margins, and was signed into law on March 7, 1994.] California voters approved Proposition 184 by a margin of 72 to 28 percent on November 8, 1994.

California thus became the second State to enact a three strikes law. In November 1993, the voters of Washington State approved their own three strikes law, Initiative 593, by a margin of 3 to 1. U.S. Dept. of Justice, National Institute of Justice, J. Clark, J. Austin, & D. Henry, "Three Strikes and You're Out": A Review of State Legislation 1 (Sept. 1997). Between 1993 and 1995, 24 States and the Federal Government enacted three strikes laws. Ibid. Though the three strikes laws vary from State to State, they share a common goal of protecting the public safety by providing lengthy prison terms for habitual felons.

B

California's current three strikes law [(which is at Cal. Penal Code Ann. §§667 and 1170)] consists of two virtually identical statutory schemes "designed to increase the prison terms of repeat felons." When a defendant is convicted of a felony, and he has previously been convicted of one or more prior felonies defined as "serious" or "violent" in Cal. Penal Code Ann. §§667.5 and 1192.7 (West Supp. 2002), sentencing is conducted pursuant to the three strikes law. Prior convictions must be alleged in the charging document, and the defendant has a right to a jury determination that the prosecution has proved the prior convictions beyond a reasonable doubt. §1025; §1158 (West 1985).

If the defendant has one prior "serious" or "violent" felony conviction, he must be sentenced to "twice the term otherwise provided as punishment for the current felony conviction." If the defendant has two or more prior "serious" or "violent" felony convictions, he must receive "an indeterminate term of life imprisonment." Defendants sentenced to life under the three strikes law become eligible for parole on a date calculated by reference to a "minimum term," which is the greater of (a) three times the term otherwise provided for the current conviction, (b) 25 years, or (c) the term determined by the court pursuant to §1170 for the underlying conviction, including any enhancements. . . .

C

On parole from a 9-year prison term, petitioner Gary Ewing walked into the pro shop of the El Segundo Golf Course in Los Angeles County on March 12, 2000. He walked out with three golf clubs, priced at $399 apiece, concealed in his pants leg. A shop employee, whose suspicions were aroused when he observed Ewing limp out of the pro shop, telephoned the police. The police apprehended Ewing in the parking lot.

Ewing is no stranger to the criminal justice system. [Here, Justice O'Connor reviewed Ewing's criminal history *prior* to the specific crimes that triggered the three strikes law in the instant case. This history included convictions for felony grand theft auto (later dismissed), theft (twice), petty theft, battery, burglary, possession of drug paraphernalia, appropriating lost property, unlawful possession of a firearm, and trespassing. —EDS.]

In October and November 1993, Ewing committed three burglaries and one robbery at a Long Beach, California, apartment complex over a 5-week period. He awakened one of his victims, asleep on her living room sofa, as he tried to disconnect her video cassette recorder from the television in that room. When she screamed, Ewing ran out the front door. On another occasion, Ewing accosted a victim in the mailroom of the apartment complex. Ewing claimed to have a gun and ordered the victim to hand over his wallet. When the victim resisted, Ewing produced a knife and forced the victim back to the apartment itself. While Ewing rifled through the bedroom, the victim fled the apartment screaming for help. Ewing absconded with the victim's money and credit cards.

On December 9, 1993, Ewing was arrested [at the same apartment complex]. A jury convicted Ewing of first-degree robbery and three counts of residential burglary. Sentenced to nine years and eight months in prison, Ewing was paroled in 1999.

Only 10 months later, Ewing stole the golf clubs at issue in this case. He was charged with, and ultimately convicted of, one count of felony grand theft of personal property in excess of $400. As required by the three strikes law, the prosecutor formally alleged, and the trial court later found, that Ewing had been convicted previously of four serious or violent felonies for the three burglaries and the robbery in the Long Beach apartment complex. . . .

. . . . Before sentencing Ewing, the trial court took note of his entire criminal history, including the fact that he was on parole when he committed his latest offense. The court also heard arguments from defense counsel and a plea from Ewing himself.

. . . . As a newly convicted felon with two or more "serious" or "violent" felony convictions in his past, Ewing was sentenced under the three strikes law to 25 years to life.

The California Court of Appeal affirmed in an unpublished opinion. . . . The Supreme Court of California denied Ewing's petition for review, and we granted certiorari. We now affirm.

II

A

The Eighth Amendment, which forbids cruel and unusual punishments, contains a "narrow proportionality principle" that "applies to noncapital sentences." Harmelin v. Michigan, 501 U.S. 957, 996-997 (1991) (Kennedy, J., concurring in part and concurring in judgment). . . . We have most recently addressed the proportionality principle as applied to terms of years in a series of cases beginning with Rummel v. Estelle, [445 U.S. 263 (1980)].

In *Rummel*, we held that it did not violate the Eighth Amendment for a State to sentence a three-time offender to life in prison with the possibility of parole. Like Ewing, Rummel was sentenced to a lengthy prison term under a recidivism statute. Rummel's two prior offenses were a 1964 felony for "fraudulent use of a credit card to obtain $80 worth of goods or services," and a 1969 felony conviction for "passing a forged check in the amount of $28.36." His triggering offense was a conviction for felony theft—"obtaining $120.75 by false pretenses."

This Court ruled that "having twice imprisoned him for felonies, Texas was entitled to place upon Rummel the onus of one who is simply unable to bring his conduct within the social norms prescribed by the criminal law of the State." [445 U.S.,] at 284. The recidivism statute "is nothing more than a societal decision that when such a person commits yet another felony, he should be subjected to the admittedly serious penalty of incarceration for life, subject only to the State's judgment as to whether to grant him parole." Id., at 278. We noted that this Court "has on occasion stated that the Eighth Amendment prohibits imposition of a sentence that is grossly disproportionate to the severity of the crime." Id., at 271. But "outside the context of capital punishment, successful challenges to the proportionality of particular sentences have been exceedingly rare." Id., at 272. Although we stated that the proportionality principle "would . . . come into play in the extreme example . . . if a legislature made overtime parking a felony punishable by life imprisonment," id., at 274, n. 11, we held that "the mandatory life sentence imposed upon this petitioner does not constitute cruel and unusual punishment under the Eighth and Fourteenth Amendments" id., at 285.

In Hutto v. Davis, 454 U.S. 370 (1982) (per curiam), the defendant was sentenced to two consecutive terms of 20 years in prison for possession with intent to distribute nine ounces of marijuana and distribution of marijuana. We held that such a sentence was constitutional: "In short, *Rummel* stands for the proposition that federal courts should be reluctant to review legislatively mandated terms of imprisonment, and that successful challenges to the proportionality of particular sentences should be exceedingly rare." Id., at 374 (citations and internal quotation marks omitted).

Three years after *Rummel*, in Solem v. Helm, 463 U.S. 277, 279 (1983), we held that the Eighth Amendment prohibited "a life sentence without possibility of parole for a seventh nonviolent felony." The triggering offense in *Solem* was "uttering a 'no account' check for $100." We specifically stated that the Eighth Amendment's ban on cruel and unusual punishments "prohibits . . . sentences that are disproportionate to the crime committed," and that the "constitutional principle of proportionality has been recognized explicitly in this Court for almost a century." Id., at 284, 286. The *Solem* Court then explained that three factors may be relevant to a determination of whether a sentence is so disproportionate that it violates the Eighth Amendment: "(i) the gravity of the offense and the harshness of the penalty; (ii) the sentences imposed on other criminals in the same jurisdiction; and (iii) the sentences imposed for commission of the same crime in other jurisdictions." Id., at 292.

Applying these factors in *Solem*, we struck down the defendant's sentence of life without parole. We specifically noted the contrast between that sentence and the sentence in *Rummel*, pursuant to which the defendant was eligible for parole. 463 U.S., at 297. . . . Indeed, we explicitly declined to overrule *Rummel*. . . .

Eight years after *Solem*, we grappled with the proportionality issue again in *Harmelin*, supra. *Harmelin* was not a recidivism case, but rather involved a first-time offender convicted of possessing 672 grams of cocaine. He was sentenced to life in prison without possibility of parole. A majority of the Court rejected Harmelin's claim that his sentence was so grossly disproportionate that it violated the Eighth Amendment. The Court, however, could not agree on why his proportionality argument failed. Justice Scalia, joined by Chief Justice Rehnquist, wrote that the proportionality principle was "an aspect of our death penalty jurisprudence, rather than a generalizable aspect of Eighth Amendment law." Id., at 994. He would thus have declined to apply gross disproportionality principles except in reviewing capital sentences.

Justice Kennedy, joined by two other Members of the Court, concurred in part and concurred in the judgment. Justice Kennedy specifically recognized that "the Eighth

Amendment proportionality principle also applies to noncapital sentences." Id., at 997. He then identified four principles of proportionality review—"the primacy of the legislature, the variety of legitimate penological schemes, the nature of our federal system, and the requirement that proportionality review be guided by objective factors"—that "inform the final one: The Eighth Amendment does not require strict proportionality between crime and sentence. Rather, it forbids only extreme sentences that are 'grossly disproportionate' to the crime." Id., at 1001 (citing *Solem*, supra, at 288). Justice Kennedy's concurrence also stated that *Solem* "did not mandate" comparative analysis "within and between jurisdictions." 501 U.S., at 1004-1005.

The proportionality principles in our cases distilled in Justice Kennedy's concurrence guide our application of the Eighth Amendment in the new context that we are called upon to consider.

B

For many years, most States have had laws providing for enhanced sentencing of repeat offenders. . . . Yet between 1993 and 1995, three strikes laws effected a sea change in criminal sentencing throughout the Nation.[1] These laws responded to widespread public concerns about crime by targeting the class of offenders who pose the greatest threat to public safety: career criminals. As one of the chief architects of California's three strikes law has explained: "Three Strikes was intended to go beyond simply making sentences tougher. It was intended to be a focused effort to create a sentencing policy that would use the judicial system to reduce serious and violent crime." Ardaiz, California's Three Strikes Law: History, Expectations, Consequences 32 McGeorge L. Rev. 1, 12 (2000).

Throughout the States, legislatures enacting three strikes laws made a deliberate policy choice that individuals who have repeatedly engaged in serious or violent criminal behavior, and whose conduct has not been deterred by more conventional approaches to punishment, must be isolated from society in order to protect the public safety. Though three strikes laws may be relatively new, our tradition of deferring to state legislatures in making and implementing such important policy decisions is longstanding. . . .

Our traditional deference to legislative policy choices finds a corollary in the principle that the Constitution "does not mandate adoption of any one penological theory." Id., at 999 (Kennedy, J., concurring in part and concurring in judgment). A sentence can have a variety of justifications, such as incapacitation, deterrence, retribution, or rehabilitation. . . . Some or all of these justifications may play a role in a State's sentencing scheme. Selecting the sentencing rationales is generally a policy choice to be made by state legislatures, not federal courts.

When the California Legislature enacted the three strikes law, it made a judgment that protecting the public safety requires incapacitating criminals who have already been convicted of at least one serious or violent crime. Nothing in the Eighth Amendment prohibits California from making that choice. . . . Recidivism has long been recognized as a legitimate basis for increased punishment. . . .

---

1. It is hardly surprising that the statistics relied upon by Justice Breyer show that prior to the enactment of the three strikes law, "*no* one like Ewing could have served more than *10* years in prison." Profound disappointment with the perceived lenity of criminal sentencing (especially for repeat felons) led to passage of three strikes laws in the first place. . . .

California's justification is no pretext. Recidivism is a serious public safety concern in California and throughout the Nation. According to a recent report, approximately 67 percent of former inmates released from state prisons were charged with at least one "serious" new crime within three years of their release. See U.S. Dept. of Justice, Bureau of Justice Statistics, P. Langan & D. Levin, Special Report: Recidivism of Prisoners Released in 1994, p. 1 (June 2002). In particular, released property offenders like Ewing had higher recidivism rates than those released after committing violent, drug, or public-order offenses. Id., at 8. Approximately 73 percent of the property offenders released in 1994 were arrested again within three years, compared to approximately 61 percent of the violent offenders, 62 percent of the public-order offenders, and 66 percent of the drug offenders.

In 1996, when the Sacramento Bee studied 233 three strikes offenders in California, it found that they had an aggregate of 1,165 prior felony convictions, an average of 5 apiece. . . . The Sacramento Bee concluded, based on its investigation, that "in the vast majority of the cases, regardless of the third strike, the [three strikes] law is snaring [the] long-term habitual offenders with multiple felony convictions. . . ." [See Furillo, Three Strikes—The Verdict's In: Most Offenders Have Long Criminal Histories, Sacramento Bee, Mar. 31, 1996, p. A1.]

The State's interest in deterring crime also lends some support to the three strikes law. We have long viewed both incapacitation and deterrence as rationales for recidivism statutes. . . . Four years after the passage of California's three strikes law, the recidivism rate of parolees returned to prison for the commission of a new crime dropped by nearly 25 percent. California Dept. of Justice, Office of the Attorney General, "Three Strikes and You're Out"—Its Impact on the California Criminal Justice System After Four Years 10 (1998). Even more dramatically:

> an unintended but positive consequence of "Three Strikes" has been the impact on parolees leaving the state. More California parolees are now leaving the state than parolees from other jurisdictions entering California. This striking turnaround started in 1994. It was the first time more parolees left the state than entered since 1976. This trend has continued and in 1997 more than 1,000 net parolees left California.

Ibid.

To be sure, California's three strikes law has sparked controversy. Critics have doubted the law's wisdom, cost-efficiency, and effectiveness in reaching its goals. See, e.g., Zimring, Hawkins, & Kamin, Punishment and Democracy: Three Strikes and You're Out in California (2001); Vitiello, Three Strikes: Can We Return to Rationality? 87 J. Crim. L. & Criminology 395, 423 (1997). This criticism is appropriately directed at the legislature, which has primary responsibility for making the difficult policy choices that underlie any criminal sentencing scheme. We do not sit as a "superlegislature" to second-guess these policy choices. It is enough that the State of California has a reasonable basis for believing that dramatically enhanced sentences for habitual felons "advances the goals of [its] criminal justice system in any substantial way." See *Solem*, 463 U.S., at 297, n. 22.

III

Against this backdrop, we consider Ewing's claim that his three strikes sentence of 25 years to life is unconstitutionally disproportionate to his offense of "shoplifting three golf clubs." We first address the gravity of the offense compared to the harshness of the penalty. At the threshold, we note that Ewing incorrectly frames the issue. The gravity of his offense was not merely "shoplifting three golf clubs." Rather, Ewing was convicted of felony grand theft for stealing nearly $1,200 worth of merchandise after previously having been convicted of at least two "violent" or "serious" felonies. Even standing alone, Ewing's theft should not be taken lightly. His crime was certainly not "one of the most passive felonies a person could commit." *Solem*, supra, at 296 (internal quotation marks omitted). . . .

In weighing the gravity of Ewing's offense, we must place on the scales not only his current felony, but also his long history of felony recidivism. . . . In imposing a three strikes sentence, the State's interest is not merely punishing the offense of conviction, or the "triggering" offense: "It is in addition the interest . . . in dealing in a harsher manner with those who by repeated criminal acts have shown that they are simply incapable of conforming to the norms of society as established by its criminal law." See *Rummel*, 445 U.S., at 276; *Solem*, supra, at 296. To give full effect to the State's choice of this legitimate penological goal, our proportionality review of Ewing's sentence must take that goal into account.

Ewing's sentence is justified by the State's public-safety interest in incapacitating and deterring recidivist felons, and amply supported by his own long, serious criminal record. Ewing has been convicted of numerous misdemeanor and felony offenses, served nine separate terms of incarceration, and committed most of his crimes while on probation or parole. His prior "strikes" were serious felonies including robbery and three residential burglaries. To be sure, Ewing's sentence is a long one. But it reflects a rational legislative judgment, entitled to deference, that offenders who have committed serious or violent felonies and who continue to commit felonies must be incapacitated. . . . Ewing's is not "the rare case in which a threshold comparison of the crime committed and the sentence imposed leads to an inference of gross disproportionality." *Harmelin*, 501 U.S., at 1005 (Kennedy, J., concurring in part and concurring in judgment).

We hold that Ewing's sentence of 25 years to life in prison, imposed for the offense of felony grand theft under the three strikes law, is not grossly disproportionate and therefore does not violate the Eighth Amendment's prohibition on cruel and unusual punishments. The judgment of the California Court of Appeal is affirmed.

JUSTICE SCALIA, concurring in the judgment.

. . . Out of respect for the principle of stare decisis, I might [accept the] holding of Solem v. Helm, 463 U.S. 277 (1983) — that the Eighth Amendment contains a narrow proportionality principle — if I felt I could intelligently apply it. This case demonstrates why I cannot.

Proportionality — the notion that the punishment should fit the crime — is inherently a concept tied to the penological goal of retribution. . . . In the present case, the game is up once the plurality has acknowledged that "the Constitution does not mandate adoption of any one penological theory," and that a "sentence can have a variety of justifications, such as incapacitation, deterrence, retribution, or rehabilitation." . . .

. . . Perhaps the plurality should revise its terminology, so that what it reads into the Eighth Amendment is not the unstated proposition that all punishment should be reasonably proportionate to the gravity of the offense, but rather the unstated proposition that all punishment should reasonably pursue the multiple purposes of the criminal law. That formulation would make it clearer than ever, of course, that the plurality is not applying law but evaluating policy.

Because I agree that petitioner's sentence does not violate the Eighth Amendment's prohibition against cruel and unusual punishments, I concur in the judgment.

JUSTICE THOMAS, concurring in the judgment.

I agree with Justice Scalia's view that the proportionality test announced in Solem v. Helm, 463 U.S. 277 (1983), is incapable of judicial application. Even were *Solem*'s test perfectly clear, however, I would not feel compelled by stare decisis to apply it. In my view, the Cruel and Unusual Punishments Clause of the Eighth Amendment contains no proportionality principle. . . .

JUSTICE STEVENS, with whom JUSTICE SOUTER, JUSTICE GINSBURG, and JUSTICE BREYER join, dissenting.

Justice Breyer has cogently explained why the sentence imposed in this case is both cruel and unusual.[1] The concurrences prompt this separate writing to emphasize that proportionality review is not only capable of judicial application but also required by the Eighth Amendment. . . .

The absence of a black-letter rule does not disable judges from exercising their discretion in construing the outer limits on sentencing authority that the Eighth Amendment imposes. . . .

Throughout most of the Nation's history—before guideline sentencing became so prevalent—federal and state trial judges imposed specific sentences pursuant to grants of authority that gave them uncabined discretion within broad ranges. See K. Stith & J. Cabranes, Fear of Judging: Sentencing Guidelines in the Federal Courts 9 (1998) (hereinafter Stith & Cabranes). . . . In exercising their discretion, sentencing judges wisely employed a proportionality principle that took into account all of the justifications for punishment—namely, deterrence, incapacitation, retribution and rehabilitation. See Stith & Cabranes 14. Likewise, I think it clear that the Eighth Amendment's prohibition of "cruel and unusual punishments" expresses a broad and basic proportionality principle that takes into account all of the justifications for penal sanctions. . . .

Accordingly, I respectfully dissent.

JUSTICE BREYER, with whom JUSTICE STEVENS, JUSTICE SOUTER, and JUSTICE GINSBURG join, dissenting.

The constitutional question is whether the "three strikes" sentence imposed by California upon repeat-offender Gary Ewing is "grossly disproportionate" to his crime. The sentence amounts to a real prison term of at least 25 years. The sentence-triggering criminal conduct consists of the theft of three golf clubs priced at a total of $1,197. The offender has a criminal history that includes four felony convictions arising out of three separate burglaries (one armed). In Solem v. Helm, 463 U.S.

---

1. I agree with Justice Breyer that Ewing's sentence is grossly disproportionate even under *Harmelin*'s narrow proportionality framework. However, it is not clear that this case is controlled by *Harmelin*, which considered the proportionality of a life sentence imposed on a drug offender who had no prior felony convictions. Rather, the three-factor analysis established in Solem v. Helm, 463 U.S. 277, 290-291 (1983), which specifically addressed recidivist sentencing, seems more directly on point.

277 (1983), the Court found grossly disproportionate a somewhat longer sentence imposed on a recidivist offender for triggering criminal conduct that was somewhat less severe. In my view, the differences are not determinative, and the Court should reach the same ultimate conclusion here.

I

... I believe that the case before us is a "rare" case—one in which a court can say with reasonable confidence that the punishment is "grossly disproportionate" to the crime.

II

Ewing's claim crosses the gross disproportionality "threshold." First, precedent makes clear that Ewing's sentence raises a serious disproportionality question. Ewing is a recidivist. Hence the two cases most directly in point are those in which the Court considered the constitutionality of recidivist sentencing: *Rummel* and *Solem*. Ewing's claim falls between these two cases. It is stronger than the claim presented in *Rummel*, where the Court upheld a recidivist's sentence as constitutional. It is weaker than the claim presented in *Solem*, where the Court struck down a recidivist sentence as unconstitutional.

Three kinds of sentence-related characteristics define the relevant comparative spectrum: (a) the length of the prison term in real time, i.e., the time that the offender is likely actually to spend in prison; (b) the sentence-triggering criminal conduct, i.e., the offender's actual behavior or other offense-related circumstances; and (c) the offender's criminal history. . . .

The third factor, prior record, cannot explain the difference [between *Rummel* and *Solem*]. The offender's prior record was *worse* in *Solem*, where the Court found the sentence too long, than in *Rummel*, where the Court upheld the sentence. The second factor, offense conduct, cannot explain the difference. The nature of the triggering offense—viewed in terms of the actual monetary loss—in the two cases was about the same. The one critical factor that explains the difference in the outcome is the length of the likely prison term measured in real time. In *Rummel*, where the Court upheld the sentence, the state sentencing statute authorized parole for the offender, Rummel, after 10 or 12 years. In *Solem*, where the Court struck down the sentence, the sentence required the offender, Helm, to spend the rest of his life in prison.

Now consider the present case. The third factor, *offender characteristics*—i.e., prior record—does not differ significantly here from that in *Solem*. . . . The second factor, *offense behavior*, is worse than that in *Solem*, but only to a degree. . . . [T]he difference lies in the *value* of the goods obtained. That difference, measured in terms of the most relevant feature (loss to the victim, i.e., wholesale value) and adjusted for the irrelevant feature of inflation, comes down (in 1979 values) to about $379 here compared with $100 in *Solem*, or (in 1973 values) to $232 here compared with $120.75 in *Rummel*. . . .

The difference in *length* of the real prison term—the first, and critical, factor in *Solem* and *Rummel*—is considerably more important. Ewing's sentence here amounts, in real terms, to at least 25 years without parole or good-time credits. That sentence is considerably shorter than Helm's sentence in *Solem*, which amounted, in real terms, to life in prison. Nonetheless Ewing's real prison term is more than twice as long as the term at issue in *Rummel*, which amounted, in real terms, to at least 10 or 12 years. And, Ewing's sentence, unlike Rummel's (but like Helm's sentence in *Solem*), is long enough to consume the productive remainder of almost any offender's life. (It means that Ewing himself, seriously ill when sentenced at age 38, will likely die in prison.)

The upshot is that the length of the real prison term—the factor that explains the *Solem/Rummel* difference in outcome—places Ewing closer to *Solem* than to *Rummel*, though the greater value of the golf clubs that Ewing stole moves Ewing's case back slightly in *Rummel*'s direction. Overall, the comparison places Ewing's sentence well within the twilight zone between *Solem* and *Rummel*—a zone where the argument for unconstitutionality is substantial, where the cases themselves cannot determine the constitutional outcome.

Second, Ewing's sentence on its face imposes one of the most severe punishments available upon a recidivist who subsequently engaged in one of the less serious forms of criminal conduct. I do not deny the seriousness of shoplifting, which an amicus curiae tells us costs retailers in the range of $30 billion annually. . . . [But] the sentence-triggering behavior here ranks well toward the bottom of the criminal conduct scale. . . .

Third, some objective evidence suggests that many experienced judges would consider Ewing's sentence disproportionately harsh. The United States Sentencing Commission . . . does not include shoplifting (or similar theft-related offenses) among the crimes that might trigger especially long sentences for recidivists, see USSG §4B1.1 (Nov. 2002). . . .

Taken together, these three circumstances make clear that Ewing's "gross disproportionality" argument is a strong one. That being so, his claim *must* pass the "threshold" test. If it did not, what would be the function of the test? . . . A threshold test that blocked every ultimately invalid constitutional claim—even strong ones—would not be a *threshold* test but a *determinative* test. And, it would be a *determinative* test that failed to take account of highly pertinent sentencing information, namely, comparison with other sentences. . . .

III

Believing Ewing's argument a strong one, sufficient to pass the threshold, I turn to the comparative analysis. A comparison of Ewing's sentence with other sentences requires answers to two questions. First, how would other jurisdictions (or California at other times, i.e., without the three strikes penalty) punish the *same offense conduct*? Second, upon what other conduct would other jurisdictions (or California) impose the *same prison term*? Moreover, since hypothetical punishment is beside the point, the relevant prison time, for comparative purposes, is real prison time, i.e., the time that an offender must *actually serve*. . . .

As to California itself, we know the following: First, between the end of World War II and 1994 (when California enacted the three strikes law), *no one* like Ewing could have served more than *10* years in prison. . . .

Second, statistics suggest that recidivists *of all sorts* convicted during that same time period in California served a small fraction of Ewing's real-time sentence. On average, recidivists served three to four additional (recidivist-related) years in prison, with 90 percent serving less than an additional real seven to eight years. . . .

Third, we know that California has reserved, and still reserves, Ewing-type prison time, i.e., at least 25 real years in prison, for criminals convicted of crimes far worse than was Ewing's. Statistics for the years 1945 to 1981, for example, indicate that typical (nonrecidivist) male first-degree murderers served between 10 and 15 real years in prison, with 90 percent of all such murderers serving less than 20 real years. . . . Moreover, California, which has moved toward a real-time sentencing system (where the statutory punishment approximates the time served), still punishes far less harshly those who have engaged in far more serious conduct. . . . It reserves the sentence that it here imposes upon (former-burglar-now-golf-club-thief) Ewing, for nonrecidivist, first-degree murderers. See §190(a) (West Supp. 2003) (sentence of 25 years to life for first-degree murder).

As to other jurisdictions, we know the following: The United States, bound by the federal Sentencing Guidelines, would impose upon a recidivist, such as Ewing, a sentence that, in any ordinary case, would not exceed 18 months in prison. USSG §2B1.1(a) (Nov. 1999). . . . [T]he law would make it legally impossible for a Ewing-type offender to serve more than 10 years in prison in 33 jurisdictions, as well as the federal courts, more than 15 years in 4 other States, and more than 20 years in 4 additional States. In nine other States, the law *might* make it legally possible to impose a sentence of 25 years or more—though that fact by itself, of course, does not mean that judges have actually done so. . . .

The upshot is that comparison of other sentencing practices, both in other jurisdictions and in California at other times (or in respect to other crimes), validates what an initial threshold examination suggested. . . . Outside the California three strikes context, Ewing's recidivist sentence is virtually unique in its harshness for his offense of conviction, and by a considerable degree.

IV

[In this section, Justice Breyer rejected the argument that California's three strikes law might nevertheless be justified on grounds of administrative efficiency, because the law could have specified the triggering crimes and thereby avoided the anomaly of including persons like Ewing. He also rejected the claim that the law might be justified by deterrence, concluding that it "amounts to overkill."—Eds.]

V

Justice Scalia and Justice Thomas argue that we should not review for gross disproportionality a sentence to a term of years. . . . I concede that a bright-line rule would give legislators and sentencing judges more guidance. But application of the Eighth Amendment to a sentence of a term of years requires a case-by-case approach. And, in my view, like that of the plurality, meaningful enforcement of the Eighth Amendment demands that application—even if only at sentencing's outer bounds. . . .

In sum, even if I accept for present purposes the plurality's analytical framework, Ewing's sentence (life imprisonment with a minimum term of 25 years) is grossly disproportionate to the triggering offense conduct—stealing three golf clubs—Ewing's recidivism notwithstanding.

For these reasons, I dissent.

NOTES AND QUESTIONS

1. Do you agree with the conclusion reached by a majority of the Justices in *Ewing* that the Eighth Amendment is not offended by a sentence of 25 years to life in prison for a "triggering crime" of stealing three golf clubs? How is your analysis affected by the knowledge that—even with the recent trend toward increased criminal punishments—no other state would appear to allow such severe punishment for a defendant like Ewing? Or that California generally reserves such punishment exclusively for murderers? How, if at all, is your analysis affected by the fact that Ewing was "seriously ill" at the time of his sentencing, and would "likely die in prison"?

Does Justice Breyer's alternative, highly detailed (and, at points, highly mathematical) analysis seem like a better way for the Court to apply the Eighth Amendment? Or would it simply produce a flood of costly and time-consuming appellate litigation?

2. After *Harmelin* and *Ewing*, what is left of the Eighth Amendment proportionality requirement in noncapital cases? According to Justice Kennedy's *Harmelin* concurrence (which controls, given the fragmented Court lineup—remember that three Justices in *Ewing* adopted Justice Kennedy's *Harmelin* position, while two other Justices would have gone even further and eliminated all proportionality review), no comparative analysis need be performed unless "a threshold comparison of the crime committed and the sentence imposed leads to an inference of gross disproportionality." Based on the results in *Harmelin* and *Ewing*, however, would any sentence of imprisonment, no matter how long, ever be likely to cross this threshold?

3. The Supreme Court's decision in *Harmelin* turned out not to be the last word on that particular statute. One year later, the Michigan Supreme Court held that the mandatory-life-without-parole statute, as applied to simple possession of narcotics, violated a provision in the Michigan state constitution prohibiting "cruel *or* unusual" punishments. See People v. Bullock, 485 N.W.2d 866 (Mich. 1992). But the statute remained in effect for those convicted of manufacture, distribution, or possession with intent to manufacture or distribute narcotics. By 1997, 205 prisoners in Michigan were serving life sentences without parole under the statute involved in *Harmelin* and *Bullock*. Of these, 173 had no prior criminal record.

In July 1998, the Michigan legislature enacted an amendment to the statute allowing for the possibility of parole, after 15 years, for first-time, nonviolent offenders who agreed to cooperate fully with the prosecutor. See Brian M. Thomas, Note, Recent Legislation: Criminal Procedure—Parole Eligibility—Michigan Eliminates Mandatory Drug Sentences and Allows Parole for Possession of 650 or More Grams of Cocaine or Heroin, 76 U. Det. Mercy L. Rev. 679 (1999).

4. What about the excessive fines clause of the Eighth Amendment? How does the analysis of a monetary punishment under that provision compare with the *Harmelin/Ewing* analysis of prison sentences under the cruel and unusual punishments clause?

In United States v. Bajakajian, 524 U.S. 321 (1998), the Supreme Court—for the first time—applied the excessive fines clause to invalidate a monetary punishment. The defendant was convicted of willfully violating the law that requires anyone leaving the United States to report if they are carrying more than $10,000 in currency, see 31 U.S.C. §§5316(a)(1)(A) and 5322(a). In fact, the defendant was carrying a total of $357,144. The government sought forfeiture of the entire amount, as authorized by 18 U.S.C. §982(a)(1), but the defendant claimed that such a forfeiture would violate the excessive fines clause.

The Court agreed with the defendant that forfeiture of the entire $357,144 would violate the excessive fines clause. Justice Thomas, writing for the majority, explained:

> The touchstone of the constitutional inquiry under the Excessive Fines Clause is the principle of proportionality: The amount of the forfeiture must bear some relationship to the gravity of the offense that it is designed to punish. . . . Until today, however, we have not articulated a standard for determining whether a punitive forfeiture is constitutionally excessive. We now hold that a punitive forfeiture violates the Excessive Fines Clause if it is grossly disproportional to the gravity of a defendant's offense.
>
> The text and history of the Excessive Fines Clause demonstrate the centrality of proportionality to the excessiveness inquiry; nonetheless, they provide little guidance as to how disproportional a punitive forfeiture must be to the gravity of an offense in order to be "excessive." . . .
>
> We must therefore rely on other considerations in deriving a constitutional excessiveness standard, and there are two that we find particularly relevant. The first . . . is that judgments about the appropriate punishment for an offense belong in the first instance to the legislature. See, e.g., Solem v. Helm, 463 U.S. 277 (1983). . . . The second is that any judicial determination regarding the gravity of a particular criminal offense will be inherently imprecise. Both of these principles counsel against requiring strict proportionality between the amount of a punitive forfeiture and the gravity of a criminal offense, and we therefore adopt the standard of gross disproportionality articulated in our Cruel and Unusual Punishments Clause precedents. . . .
>
> Under this standard, the forfeiture of respondent's entire $357,144 would violate the Excessive Fines Clause. Respondent's crime was solely a reporting offense. It was permissible to transport the currency out of the country so long as he reported it. . . . Furthermore, as the District Court found, respondent's violation was unrelated to any other illegal activities. . . . Whatever his other vices, respondent does not fit into the class of persons for whom the statute was principally designed: He is not a money launderer, a drug trafficker, or a tax evader. . . .
>
> Comparing the gravity of respondent's crime with the $357,144 forfeiture the Government seeks, we conclude that such a forfeiture would be grossly disproportionate to the gravity of his offense. . . . [I]t bears no articulable correlation to any injury suffered by the Government.

524 U.S., at 334-340.

Note that the *Bajakajian* Court purported to apply the same "gross disproportionality" standard as in *Harmelin* and *Ewing.* Yet the result reached was different. The *Bajakajian* dissenters argued that "[t]he crime of smuggling or failing to report cash is more serious than the Court is willing to acknowledge. The drug trade, money laundering, and tax evasion all depend in part on smuggled and unreported cash. . . . Money launderers will rejoice to know they face forfeitures of less than 5% of the money transported, provided they hire accomplished liars to carry their money for them." 524 U.S., at 351, 354 (Kennedy, J., dissenting). Shouldn't the *Bajakajian* Court have granted more deference to the judgment of Congress about the seriousness of the crime, as well as about the appropriate level of monetary punishment?

5. In *Harmelin* and *Ewing,* the Court basically declined the invitation to engage in meaningful substantive review of noncapital prison sentences. This reluctance may have its roots in legitimacy concerns related to the Court's basic counter-majoritarian

dilemma, which may be intensified in the particular legal and historical context of the Eighth Amendment. See Joseph L. Hoffmann, "The 'Cruel and Unusual Punishment' Clause: A Significant Limit on the Government's Power to Punish, or Mere Constitutional Rhetoric?" in The Bill of Rights in Modern America (D. Bodenhamer & J. Ely, Jr., eds., rev. ed. 2008). Or it may stem from the realization that the Court has few, if any, anchors to prevent substantive review of criminal sentences from devolving into standardless pronouncements of the Justices' own personal moral beliefs. Or it may reflect simply the Court's relative lack of experience, and thus lack of expertise, in such substantive review. See Ronald J. Allen & Ethan A. Hastert, From *Winship* to *Apprendi* to *Booker*: Constitutional Command or Constitutional Blunder?, 58 Stan. L. Rev. 195-216 (2005).

In any event, it is hard not to be struck by the stark contrast between the Court's cautious approach to Eighth Amendment substantive review of noncapital sentences and its much more aggressive approach to substantive review of capital sentences.

ROPER v. SIMMONS

Certiorari to the Supreme Court of Missouri
543 U.S. 551 (2005)

JUSTICE KENNEDY delivered the opinion of the Court.

This case requires us to address, for the second time in a decade and a half, whether it is permissible under the Eighth and Fourteenth Amendments to the Constitution of the United States to execute a juvenile offender who was older than 15 but younger than 18 when he committed a capital crime. In Stanford v. Kentucky, 492 U.S. 361 (1989), a divided Court rejected the proposition that the Constitution bars capital punishment for juvenile offenders in this age group. We reconsider the question.

I

[This section, detailing the brutal facts of the murder that was planned by Simmons, and that was committed by him and two younger accomplices, is omitted.—EDS.]

II

The Eighth Amendment provides: "Excessive bail shall not be required, nor excessive fines imposed, nor cruel and unusual punishments inflicted." The provision is applicable to the States through the Fourteenth Amendment. As the Court explained in Atkins [v. Virginia, 536 U.S. 304 (2002)], the Eighth Amendment guarantees individuals the right not to be subjected to excessive sanctions. The right flows from the basic " 'precept of justice that punishment for crime should be graduated and proportioned to [the] offense.' " 536 U.S., at 311 (quoting Weems v. United States, 217 U.S. 349, 367 (1910)). By protecting even those convicted of heinous crimes, the Eighth Amendment reaffirms the duty of the government to respect the dignity of all persons.

The prohibition against "cruel and unusual punishments," like other expansive language in the Constitution, must be interpreted according to its text, by considering history, tradition, and precedent, and with due regard for its purpose and function in the constitutional design. To implement this framework we have established the propriety and affirmed the necessity of referring to "the evolving standards of decency that mark the progress of a maturing society" to determine which punishments are so disproportionate as to be cruel and unusual. Trop v. Dulles, 356 U.S. 86, 100-101 (1958) (plurality opinion).

In Thompson v. Oklahoma, 487 U.S. 815 (1988), a plurality of the Court determined that our standards of decency do not permit the execution of any offender under the age of 16 at the time of the crime. . . . With Justice O'Connor concurring in the judgment on narrower grounds, id., at 848-859, the Court set aside the death sentence that had been imposed on the 15-year-old offender.

The next year, in Stanford v. Kentucky, 492 U.S. 361 (1989), the Court, over a dissenting opinion joined by four Justices, referred to contemporary standards of decency in this country and concluded the Eighth and Fourteenth Amendments did not proscribe the execution of juvenile offenders over 15 but under 18. The Court noted that 22 of the 37 death penalty States permitted the death penalty for 16-year-old offenders, and, among these 37 States, 25 permitted it for 17-year-old offenders. These numbers, in the Court's view, indicated there was no national consensus "sufficient to label a particular punishment cruel and unusual." . . .

The same day the Court decided *Stanford*, it held that the Eighth Amendment did not mandate a categorical exemption from the death penalty for the mentally retarded. Penry v. Lynaugh, 492 U.S. 302 (1989). . . .

Three Terms ago the subject was reconsidered in *Atkins*. We held that standards of decency have evolved since *Penry* and now demonstrate that the execution of the mentally retarded is cruel and unusual punishment. The Court noted objective indicia of society's standards, as expressed in legislative enactments and state practice with respect to executions of the mentally retarded. When *Atkins* was decided only a minority of States permitted the practice, and even in those States it was rare. On the basis of these indicia the Court determined that executing mentally retarded offenders "has become truly unusual, and it is fair to say that a national consensus has developed against it." [536 U.S.,] at 316.

The inquiry into our society's evolving standards of decency did not end there. . . . Mental retardation, the Court said, diminishes personal culpability even if the offender can distinguish right from wrong. The impairments of mentally retarded offenders make it less defensible to impose the death penalty as retribution for past crimes and less likely that the death penalty will have a real deterrent effect. Based on these considerations and on the finding of national consensus against executing the mentally retarded, the Court ruled that the death penalty constitutes an excessive sanction for the entire category of mentally retarded offenders. . . .

Just as the *Atkins* Court reconsidered the issue decided in *Penry*, we now reconsider the issue decided in *Stanford*. The beginning point is a review of objective indicia of consensus, as expressed in particular by the enactments of legislatures that have addressed the question. This data gives us essential instruction. We then must determine, in the exercise of our own independent judgment, whether the death penalty is a disproportionate punishment for juveniles.

III

A

The evidence of national consensus against the death penalty for juveniles is similar, and in some respects parallel, to the evidence *Atkins* held sufficient to demonstrate a national consensus against the death penalty for the mentally retarded. When *Atkins* was decided, 30 States prohibited the death penalty for the mentally retarded. This number comprised 12 that had abandoned the death penalty altogether, and 18 that maintained it but excluded the mentally retarded from its reach. By a similar calculation in this case, 30 States prohibit the juvenile death penalty, comprising 12 that have rejected the death penalty altogether and 18 that maintain it but, by express provision or judicial interpretation, exclude juveniles from its reach. *Atkins* emphasized that even in the 20 States without formal prohibition, the practice of executing the mentally retarded was infrequent. Since *Penry*, only five States had executed offenders known to have an IQ under 70. In the present case, too, even in the 20 States without a formal prohibition on executing juveniles, the practice is infrequent. Since *Stanford*, six States have executed prisoners for crimes committed as juveniles. In the past 10 years, only three have done so: Oklahoma, Texas, and Virginia. See V. Streib, The Juvenile Death Penalty Today: Death Sentences and Executions for Juvenile Crimes, January 1, 1973-December 31, 2004, No. 76, p. 4 (2005), available at http://www.law.onu.edu/faculty/streib/documents/JuvDeathDec2004.pdf (last updated Jan. 31, 2005) (as visited Feb. 25, 2005, and available in the Clerk of Court's case file). . . .

. . . The number of States that have abandoned capital punishment for juvenile offenders since *Stanford* is smaller than the number of States that abandoned capital punishment for the mentally retarded after *Penry*; yet we think the same consistency of direction of change has been demonstrated. Since *Stanford*, no State that previously prohibited capital punishment for juveniles has reinstated it. This fact, coupled with the trend toward abolition of the juvenile death penalty, carries special force in light of the general popularity of anticrime legislation, *Atkins*, supra, at 315, and in light of the particular trend in recent years toward cracking down on juvenile crime in other respects. . . . Any difference between this case and *Atkins* with respect to the pace of abolition is thus counterbalanced by the consistent direction of the change.

The slower pace of abolition of the juvenile death penalty over the past 15 years, moreover, may have a simple explanation. When we heard *Penry*, only two death penalty States had already prohibited the execution of the mentally retarded. When we heard *Stanford*, by contrast, 12 death penalty States had already prohibited the execution of any juvenile under 18, and 15 had prohibited the execution of any juvenile under 17. If anything, this shows that the impropriety of executing juveniles between 16 and 18 years of age gained wide recognition earlier than the impropriety of executing the mentally retarded. . . .

As in *Atkins*, the objective indicia of consensus in this case—the rejection of the juvenile death penalty in the majority of States; the infrequency of its use even where it remains on the books; and the consistency in the trend toward abolition of the practice—provide sufficient evidence that today our society views juveniles, in the words *Atkins* used respecting the mentally retarded, as "categorically less culpable than the average criminal." 536 U.S., at 316.

B

A majority of States have rejected the imposition of the death penalty on juvenile offenders under 18, and we now hold this is required by the Eighth Amendment.

Because the death penalty is the most severe punishment, the Eighth Amendment applies to it with special force. *Thompson*, 487 U.S., at 856 (O'Connor, J., concurring in judgment). Capital punishment must be limited to those offenders who commit "a narrow category of the most serious crimes" and whose extreme culpability makes them "the most deserving of execution." *Atkins*, supra, at 319. . . .

Three general differences between juveniles under 18 and adults demonstrate that juvenile offenders cannot with reliability be classified among the worst offenders. First, as any parent knows and as the scientific and sociological studies respondent and his amici cite tend to confirm, "[a] lack of maturity and an underdeveloped sense of responsibility are found in youth more often than in adults and are more understandable among the young. These qualities often result in impetuous and ill-considered actions and decisions." Johnson [v. Texas, 509 U.S. 350,] 367 [(1993)]. . . . It has been noted that "adolescents are overrepresented statistically in virtually every category of reckless behavior." Arnett, Reckless Behavior in Adolescence: A Developmental Perspective, 12 Developmental Review 339 (1992). In recognition of the comparative immaturity and irresponsibility of juveniles, almost every State prohibits those under 18 years of age from voting, serving on juries, or marrying without parental consent. . . .

The second area of difference is that juveniles are more vulnerable or susceptible to negative influences and outside pressures, including peer pressure. . . . This is explained in part by the prevailing circumstance that juveniles have less control, or less experience with control, over their own environment. See Steinberg & Scott, Less Guilty by Reason of Adolescence: Developmental Immaturity, Diminished Responsibility, and the Juvenile Death Penalty, 58 Am. Psychologist 1009, 1014 (2003) (hereinafter Steinberg & Scott) ("[A]s legal minors, [juveniles] lack the freedom that adults have to extricate themselves from a criminogenic setting").

The third broad difference is that the character of a juvenile is not as well formed as that of an adult. The personality traits of juveniles are more transitory, less fixed. See generally E. Erikson, Identity: Youth and Crisis (1968).

These differences render suspect any conclusion that a juvenile falls among the worst offenders. The susceptibility of juveniles to immature and irresponsible behavior means "their irresponsible conduct is not as morally reprehensible as that of an adult." *Thompson*, supra, at 835 (plurality opinion). Their own vulnerability and comparative lack of control over their immediate surroundings mean juveniles have a greater claim than adults to be forgiven for failing to escape negative influences in their whole environment. See *Stanford*, 492 U.S., at 395 (Brennan, J., dissenting). The reality that juveniles still struggle to define their identity means it is less supportable to conclude that even a heinous crime committed by a juvenile is evidence of irretrievably depraved character. From a moral standpoint it would be misguided to equate the failings of a minor with those of an adult, for a greater possibility exists that a minor's character deficiencies will be reformed. Indeed, "[t]he relevance of youth as a mitigating factor derives from the fact that the signature qualities of youth are transient; as individuals mature, the impetuousness and recklessness that may dominate in younger years can subside." *Johnson*, supra, at 368; see also Steinberg & Scott 1014 ("For most teens, [risky or antisocial] behaviors are fleeting; they cease with maturity as individual identity becomes settled. Only a relatively small proportion of adolescents who experiment in risky or illegal activities develop entrenched patterns of problem behavior that persist into adulthood").

In *Thompson*, a plurality of the Court recognized the import of these characteristics with respect to juveniles under 16, and relied on them to hold that the Eighth

Amendment prohibited the imposition of the death penalty on juveniles below that age. We conclude the same reasoning applies to all juvenile offenders under 18.

Once the diminished culpability of juveniles is recognized, it is evident that the penological justifications for the death penalty apply to them with lesser force than to adults. We have held there are two distinct social purposes served by the death penalty: "retribution and deterrence of capital crimes by prospective offenders." *Atkins*, 536 U.S., at 319. . . .

Whether viewed as an attempt to express the community's moral outrage or as an attempt to right the balance for the wrong to the victim, the case for retribution is not as strong with a minor as with an adult. Retribution is not proportional if the law's most severe penalty is imposed on one whose culpability or blameworthiness is diminished, to a substantial degree, by reason of youth and immaturity.

As for deterrence, it is unclear whether the death penalty has a significant or even measurable deterrent effect on juveniles, as counsel for the petitioner acknowledged at oral argument. Tr. of Oral Arg. 48. In general we leave to legislatures the assessment of the efficacy of various criminal penalty schemes, see Harmelin v. Michigan, 501 U.S. 957, 998-999 (1991) (Kennedy, J., concurring in part and concurring in judgment). Here, however, the absence of evidence of deterrent effect is of special concern because the same characteristics that render juveniles less culpable than adults suggest as well that juveniles will be less susceptible to deterrence. . . . To the extent the juvenile death penalty might have residual deterrent effect, it is worth noting that the punishment of life imprisonment without the possibility of parole is itself a severe sanction, in particular for a young person.

In concluding that neither retribution nor deterrence provides adequate justification for imposing the death penalty on juvenile offenders, we cannot deny or overlook the brutal crimes too many juvenile offenders have committed. Certainly it can be argued, although we by no means concede the point, that a rare case might arise in which a juvenile offender has sufficient psychological maturity, and at the same time demonstrates sufficient depravity, to merit a sentence of death. . . . A central feature of death penalty sentencing is a particular assessment of the circumstances of the crime and the characteristics of the offender. The system is designed to consider both aggravating and mitigating circumstances, including youth, in every case. Given this Court's own insistence on individualized consideration, petitioner maintains that it is both arbitrary and unnecessary to adopt a categorical rule barring imposition of the death penalty on any offender under 18 years of age.

We disagree. The differences between juvenile and adult offenders are too marked and well understood to risk allowing a youthful person to receive the death penalty despite insufficient culpability. An unacceptable likelihood exists that the brutality or cold-blooded nature of any particular crime would overpower mitigating arguments based on youth as a matter of course, even where the juvenile offender's objective immaturity, vulnerability, and lack of true depravity should require a sentence less severe than death. In some cases a defendant's youth may even be counted against him. In this very case, as we noted above, the prosecutor argued Simmons' youth was aggravating rather than mitigating. While this sort of overreaching could be corrected by a particular rule to ensure that the mitigating force of youth is not overlooked, that would not address our larger concerns.

It is difficult even for expert psychologists to differentiate between the juvenile offender whose crime reflects unfortunate yet transient immaturity, and the rare juvenile offender whose crime reflects irreparable corruption. See Steinberg &

Scott 1014-1016. As we understand it, this difficulty underlies the rule forbidding psychiatrists from diagnosing any patient under 18 as having antisocial personality disorder, a disorder also referred to as psychopathy or sociopathy, and which is characterized by callousness, cynicism, and contempt for the feelings, rights, and suffering of others. American Psychiatric Association, Diagnostic and Statistical Manual of Mental Disorders 701-706 (4th ed. text rev. 2000); see also Steinberg & Scott 1015. If trained psychiatrists with the advantage of clinical testing and observation refrain, despite diagnostic expertise, from assessing any juvenile under 18 as having antisocial personality disorder, we conclude that States should refrain from asking jurors to issue a far graver condemnation—that a juvenile offender merits the death penalty. When a juvenile offender commits a heinous crime, the State can exact forfeiture of some of the most basic liberties, but the State cannot extinguish his life and his potential to attain a mature understanding of his own humanity.

Drawing the line at 18 years of age is subject, of course, to the objections always raised against categorical rules. The qualities that distinguish juveniles from adults do not disappear when an individual turns 18. By the same token, some under 18 have already attained a level of maturity some adults will never reach. For the reasons we have discussed, however, a line must be drawn. . . . The age of 18 is the point where society draws the line for many purposes between childhood and adulthood. It is, we conclude, the age at which the line for death eligibility ought to rest. . . .

IV

Our determination that the death penalty is disproportionate punishment for offenders under 18 finds confirmation in the stark reality that the United States is the only country in the world that continues to give official sanction to the juvenile death penalty. This reality does not become controlling, for the task of interpreting the Eighth Amendment remains our responsibility. Yet at least from the time of the Court's decision in *Trop*, the Court has referred to the laws of other countries and to international authorities as instructive for its interpretation of the Eighth Amendment's prohibition of "cruel and unusual punishments."

As respondent and a number of amici emphasize, Article 37 of the United Nations Convention on the Rights of the Child, which every country in the world has ratified save for the United States and Somalia, contains an express prohibition on capital punishment for crimes committed by juveniles under 18. United Nations Convention on the Rights of the Child, Art. 37, Nov. 20, 1989, 1577 U.N.T.S. 3, 28 I.L.M. 1448, 1468-1470 (entered into force Sept. 2, 1990); Brief for Respondent 48; Brief for European Union et al. as Amici Curiae 12-13; Brief for President James Earl Carter, Jr., et al. as Amici Curiae 9; Brief for Former U.S. Diplomats Morton Abramowitz et al. as Amici Curiae 7; Brief for Human Rights Committee of the Bar of England and Wales et al. as Amici Curiae 13-14. No ratifying country has entered a reservation to the provision prohibiting the execution of juvenile offenders. Parallel prohibitions are contained in other significant international covenants.

Respondent and his amici have submitted, and petitioner does not contest, that only seven countries other than the United States have executed juvenile offenders since 1990: Iran, Pakistan, Saudi Arabia, Yemen, Nigeria, the Democratic Republic of Congo, and China. Since then each of these countries has either abolished capital punishment for juveniles or made public disavowal of the practice. Brief for

Respondent 49-50. In sum, it is fair to say that the United States now stands alone in a world that has turned its face against the juvenile death penalty.

Though the international covenants prohibiting the juvenile death penalty are of more recent date, it is instructive to note that the United Kingdom abolished the juvenile death penalty before these covenants came into being. The United Kingdom's experience bears particular relevance here in light of the historic ties between our countries and in light of the Eighth Amendment's own origins. The Amendment was modeled on a parallel provision in the English Declaration of Rights of 1689, which provided: "[E]xcessive Bail ought not to be required nor excessive Fines imposed; nor cruel and unusual Punishments inflicted." 1 W. & M., ch. 2, §10, in 3 Eng. Stat., at Large 441 (1770). As of now, the United Kingdom has abolished the death penalty in its entirety; but, decades before it took this step, it recognized the disproportionate nature of the juvenile death penalty; and it abolished that penalty as a separate matter. . . .

It is proper that we acknowledge the overwhelming weight of international opinion against the juvenile death penalty, resting in large part on the understanding that the instability and emotional imbalance of young people may often be a factor in the crime. See Brief for Human Rights Committee of the Bar of England and Wales et al. as Amici Curiae 10-11. The opinion of the world community, while not controlling our outcome, does provide respected and significant confirmation for our own conclusions.

Over time, from one generation to the next, the Constitution has come to earn the high respect and even, as Madison dared to hope, the veneration of the American people. See The Federalist No. 49, p. 314 (C. Rossiter ed. 1961). The document sets forth, and rests upon, innovative principles original to the American experience, such as federalism; a proven balance in political mechanisms through separation of powers; specific guarantees for the accused in criminal cases; and broad provisions to secure individual freedom and preserve human dignity. These doctrines and guarantees are central to the American experience and remain essential to our present-day self-definition and national identity. Not the least of the reasons we honor the Constitution, then, is because we know it to be our own. It does not lessen our fidelity to the Constitution or our pride in its origins to acknowledge that the express affirmation of certain fundamental rights by other nations and peoples simply underscores the centrality of those same rights within our own heritage of freedom.

* * *

The Eighth and Fourteenth Amendments forbid imposition of the death penalty on offenders who were under the age of 18 when their crimes were committed. The judgment of the Missouri Supreme Court setting aside the sentence of death imposed upon Christopher Simmons is affirmed.

JUSTICE STEVENS, with whom JUSTICE GINSBURG joins, concurring.

Perhaps even more important than our specific holding today is our reaffirmation of the basic principle that informs the Court's interpretation of the Eighth Amendment. If the meaning of that Amendment had been frozen when it was originally drafted, it would impose no impediment to the execution of 7-year-old children today. See Stanford v. Kentucky, 492 U.S. 361, 368 (1989) (describing the common law at the time of the Amendment's adoption). The evolving standards of decency that have driven our construction of this critically important part of the Bill of Rights foreclose any such reading of the Amendment. In the best tradition of the common law, the pace of that evolution is a matter for continuing debate; but that our understanding of the Constitution does change from time to time has been settled since John Marshall breathed life into its text. If great lawyers of his day—Alexander Hamilton, for example—were sitting with us today, I would expect them to join Justice Kennedy's opinion for the Court. In all events, I do so without hesitation.

JUSTICE O'CONNOR, dissenting.

The Court's decision today establishes a categorical rule forbidding the execution of any offender for any crime committed before his 18th birthday, no matter how deliberate, wanton, or cruel the offense. Neither the objective evidence of contemporary societal values, nor the Court's moral proportionality analysis, nor the two in tandem suffice to justify this ruling.

. . . [T]he rule decreed by the Court rests, ultimately, on its independent moral judgment that death is a disproportionately severe punishment for any 17-year-old offender. I do not subscribe to this judgment. . . .

It is beyond cavil that juveniles as a class are generally less mature, less responsible, and less fully formed than adults, and that these differences bear on juveniles' comparative moral culpability. But even accepting this premise, the Court's proportionality argument fails to support its categorical rule.

First, the Court adduces no evidence whatsoever in support of its sweeping conclusion . . . that it is only in "rare" cases, if ever, that 17-year-old murderers are sufficiently mature and act with sufficient depravity to warrant the death penalty. The fact that juveniles are generally *less* culpable for their misconduct than adults does not necessarily mean that a 17-year-old murderer cannot be *sufficiently* culpable to merit the death penalty. . . . Similarly, the fact that the availability of the death penalty may be *less* likely to deter a juvenile from committing a capital crime does not imply that this threat cannot *effectively* deter some 17-year-olds from such an act. Surely there is an age below which no offender, no matter what his crime, can be deemed to have the cognitive or emotional maturity necessary to warrant the death penalty. But at least at the margins between adolescence and adulthood . . . the relevant differences between "adults" and "juveniles" appear to be a matter of degree, rather than of kind. . . .

The Court's proportionality argument suffers from a second and closely related defect: It fails to establish that the differences in maturity between 17-year-olds and young "adults" are both universal enough and significant enough to justify a bright-line prophylactic rule against capital punishment of the former. . . . In short, the class of offenders exempted from capital punishment by today's decision is too broad and too diverse to warrant a categorical prohibition. Indeed, the age-based line drawn by the Court is indefensibly arbitrary—it quite likely will protect a number of offenders who are mature enough to deserve the death penalty and may well leave vulnerable many who are not.

For purposes of proportionality analysis, 17-year-olds as a class are qualitatively and materially different from the mentally retarded. "Mentally retarded" offenders, as we understood that category in *Atkins,* are *defined* by precisely the characteristics which render death an excessive punishment. . . . There is no such inherent or accurate fit between an offender's chronological age and the personal limitations which the Court believes make capital punishment excessive for 17-year-old murderers. . . .

The proportionality issues raised by the Court clearly implicate Eighth Amendment concerns. But these concerns may properly be addressed not by means of an arbitrary, categorical age-based rule, but rather through individualized sentencing in which juries are required to give appropriate mitigating weight to the defendant's immaturity, his susceptibility to outside pressures, his cognizance of the consequences of his actions, and so forth. In that way the constitutional response can be tailored to the specific problem it is meant to remedy. . . .

Because I do not believe that a genuine *national* consensus against the juvenile death penalty has yet developed, and because I do not believe the Court's moral proportionality argument justifies a categorical, age-based constitutional rule, I can assign no . . . *confirmatory* role to the international consensus described by the Court. . . .

Nevertheless, I disagree with Justice Scalia's contention that foreign and international law have no place in our Eighth Amendment jurisprudence. . . . Obviously, American law is distinctive in many respects, not least where the specific provisions of our Constitution and the history of its exposition so dictate. But this Nation's evolving understanding of human dignity certainly is neither wholly isolated from, nor inherently at odds with, the values prevailing in other countries. On the contrary, we should not be surprised to find congruence between domestic and international values, especially where the international community has reached clear agreement—expressed in international law or in the domestic laws of individual countries—that a particular form of punishment is inconsistent with fundamental human rights. At least, the existence of an international consensus of this nature can serve to confirm the reasonableness of a consonant and genuine American consensus. The instant case presents no such domestic consensus, however, and the recent emergence of an otherwise global consensus does not alter that basic fact. . . .

JUSTICE SCALIA, with whom CHIEF JUSTICE REHNQUIST and JUSTICE THOMAS join, dissenting.

In urging approval of a constitution that gave life-tenured judges the power to nullify laws enacted by the people's representatives, Alexander Hamilton assured the citizens of New York that there was little risk in this, since "[t]he judiciary . . . ha[s] neither FORCE nor WILL but merely judgment." The Federalist No. 78, p. 465 (C. Rossiter ed. 1961). But Hamilton had in mind a traditional judiciary, "bound down by strict rules and precedents which serve to define and point out their duty in every particular case that comes before them." Id., at 471. Bound down, indeed. What a mockery today's opinion makes of Hamilton's expectation, announcing the Court's conclusion that the meaning of our Constitution has changed over the past 15 years—not, mind you, that this Court's decision 15 years ago was *wrong*, but that the Constitution *has changed.* The Court reaches this implausible result by purporting to advert, not to the original meaning of the Eighth Amendment, but to "the evolving standards of decency" of our national society. It then finds, on the flimsiest of grounds, that a national consensus which could not be perceived in our people's laws barely 15 years ago now solidly exists. Worse still, the Court says in so many words that what our people's laws say about the issue does not, in the last analysis, matter. The Court thus proclaims itself sole arbiter of our Nation's moral standards—and in the course of discharging that awesome responsibility purports to take guidance from the views of foreign courts and legislatures. Because I do not believe that the meaning of our Eighth Amendment, any more than the meaning of other provisions of our Constitution, should be determined by the subjective views of five Members of this Court and like-minded foreigners, I dissent.

I

In determining that capital punishment of offenders who committed murder before age 18 is "cruel and unusual" under the Eighth Amendment, the Court first considers, in accordance with our modern (though in my view mistaken) jurisprudence, whether there is a "national consensus" that laws allowing such executions contravene our modern "standards of decency." . . . As in Atkins v. Virginia, 536 U.S. 304, 312 (2002), the Court dutifully recites this test and claims halfheartedly that a national consensus has emerged since our decision in *Stanford*, because 18 States — or 47% of States that permit capital punishment — now have legislation prohibiting the execution of offenders under 18, and because all of four States have adopted such legislation since *Stanford*.

Words have no meaning if the views of less than 50% of death penalty States can constitute a national consensus. Our previous cases have required overwhelming opposition to a challenged practice, generally over a long period of time. . . .

In an attempt to keep afloat its implausible assertion of national consensus, the Court throws overboard a proposition well established in our Eighth Amendment jurisprudence. . . . *None* of our cases dealing with an alleged constitutional limitation upon the death penalty has counted, as States supporting a consensus in favor of that limitation, States that have eliminated the death penalty entirely. And with good reason. Consulting States that bar the death penalty concerning the necessity of making an exception to the penalty for offenders under 18 is rather like including old-order Amishmen in a consumer-preference poll on the electric car. Of *course* they don't like it, but that sheds no light whatever on the point at issue. That 12 States favor *no* executions says something about consensus against the death penalty, but nothing — absolutely nothing — about consensus that offenders under 18 deserve special immunity from such a penalty. . . . What might be relevant, perhaps, is how many of those States permit 16- and 17-year-old offenders to be treated as adults with respect to noncapital offenses. (They all do; indeed, some even *require* that juveniles as young as 14 be tried as adults if they are charged with murder.) The attempt by the Court to turn its remarkable minority consensus into a faux majority by counting Amishmen is an act of nomological desperation.

Recognizing that its national-consensus argument was weak compared with our earlier cases, the *Atkins* Court found additional support in the fact that 16 States had prohibited execution of mentally retarded individuals since Penry v. Lynaugh, 492 U.S. 302 (1989). . . . Now, the Court says a legislative change in four States is "significant" enough to trigger a constitutional prohibition. It is amazing to think that this subtle shift in numbers can take the issue entirely off the table for legislative debate.

I also doubt whether many of the legislators who voted to change the laws in those four States would have done so if they had known their decision would (by the pronouncement of this Court) be rendered irreversible. After all, legislative support for capital punishment, in any form, has surged and ebbed throughout our Nation's history. . . .

Relying on such narrow margins is especially inappropriate in light of the fact that a number of legislatures and voters have expressly affirmed their support for capital punishment of 16- and 17-year-old offenders since *Stanford*. Though the Court is correct that no State has lowered its death penalty age, both the Missouri and Virginia Legislatures—which, at the time of *Stanford*, had no minimum age requirement—expressly established 16 as the minimum. Mo. Rev. Stat. §565.020.2 (2000); Va. Code Ann. §18.2-10(a) (Lexis 2004). The people of Arizona and Florida have done the same by ballot initiative. Thus, even States that have not executed an under-18 offender in recent years unquestionably favor the possibility of capital punishment in some circumstances. . . .

II

Of course, the real force driving today's decision is not the actions of four state legislatures, but the Court's "own judgment" that murderers younger than 18 can never be as morally culpable as older counterparts. . . . If the Eighth Amendment set forth an ordinary rule of law, it would indeed be the role of this Court to say what the law is. But the Court having pronounced that the Eighth Amendment is an ever-changing reflection of "the evolving standards of decency" of our society, it makes no sense for the Justices then to *prescribe* those standards rather than discern them from the practices of our people. On the evolving-standards hypothesis, the only legitimate function of this Court is to identify a moral consensus of the American people. By what conceivable warrant can nine lawyers presume to be the authoritative conscience of the Nation?[8]

. . . Today's opinion provides a perfect example of why judges are ill equipped to make the type of legislative judgments the Court insists on making here. To support its opinion that States should be prohibited from imposing the death penalty on anyone who committed murder before age 18, the Court looks to scientific and sociological studies, picking and choosing those that support its position. It never explains why those particular studies are methodologically sound; none was ever entered into evidence or tested in an adversarial proceeding. . . .

That "almost every State prohibits those under 18 years of age from voting, serving on juries, or marrying without parental consent," is patently irrelevant. . . . As we explained in *Stanford*, 492 U.S., at 374, it is "absurd to think that one must be mature enough to drive carefully, to drink responsibly, or to vote intelligently, in order to be mature enough to understand that murdering another human being is profoundly wrong, and to conform one's conduct to that most minimal of all civilized standards." Serving on a jury or entering into marriage also involve decisions far more sophisticated than the simple decision not to take another's life.

. . . In other contexts where individualized consideration is provided, we have recognized that at least some minors will be mature enough to make difficult decisions that involve moral considerations. For instance, we have struck down abortion statutes that do not allow minors deemed mature by courts to bypass parental notification provisions. See, e.g., Bellotti v. Baird, 443 U.S. 622, 643-644 (1979) (opinion of Powell, J.); Planned Parenthood of Central Mo. v. Danforth, 428 U.S. 52,

---

8. Justice O'Connor agrees with our analysis that no national consensus exists here. She is nonetheless prepared (like the majority) to override the judgment of America's legislatures if it contradicts her own assessment of "moral proportionality." She dissents here only because it does not. The votes in today's case demonstrate that the offending of selected lawyers' moral sentiments is not a predictable basis for law—much less a democratic one.

74-75 (1976). It is hard to see why this context should be any different. Whether to obtain an abortion is surely a much more complex decision for a young person than whether to kill an innocent person in cold blood.

The Court concludes, however, that juries cannot be trusted with the delicate task of weighing a defendant's youth along with the other mitigating and aggravating factors of his crime. This startling conclusion undermines the very foundations of our capital sentencing system. . . . The Court says that juries will be unable to appreciate the significance of a defendant's youth when faced with details of a brutal crime. This assertion is based on no evidence; to the contrary, the Court itself acknowledges that the execution of under-18 offenders is "infrequent" even in the States "without a formal prohibition on executing juveniles," suggesting that juries take seriously their responsibility to weigh youth as a mitigating factor. . . .

III

Though the views of our own citizens are essentially irrelevant to the Court's decision today, the views of other countries and the so-called international community take center stage.

. . . [T]he basic premise of the Court's argument—that American law should conform to the laws of the rest of the world—ought to be rejected out of hand. In fact the Court itself does not believe it. In many significant respects the laws of most other countries differ from our law—including not only such explicit provisions of our Constitution as the right to jury trial and grand jury indictment, but even many interpretations of the Constitution prescribed by this Court itself. The Court-pronounced exclusionary rule, for example, is distinctively American. When we adopted that rule in Mapp v. Ohio, 367 U.S. 643, 655 (1961), it was "unique to American Jurisprudence." Bivens v. Six Unknown Fed. Narcotics Agents, 403 U.S. 388, 415 (1971) (Burger, C.J., dissenting). Since then a categorical exclusionary rule has been "universally rejected" by other countries, including those with rules prohibiting illegal searches and police misconduct, despite the fact that none of these countries "appears to have any alternative form of discipline for police that is effective in preventing search violations." Bradley, *Mapp* Goes Abroad, 52 Case W. Res. L. Rev. 375, 399-400 (2001). . . .

The Court has been oblivious to the views of other countries when deciding how to interpret our Constitution's requirement that "Congress shall make no law respecting an establishment of religion. . . ." Amdt. 1. Most other countries—including those committed to religious neutrality—do not insist on the degree of separation between church and state that this Court requires. . . .

And let us not forget the Court's abortion jurisprudence, which makes us one of only six countries that allow abortion on demand until the point of viability. See Larsen, Importing Constitutional Norms from a "Wider Civilization": *Lawrence* and the Rehnquist Court's Use of Foreign and International Law in Domestic Constitutional Interpretation, 65 Ohio St. L.J. 1283, 1320 (2004); Center for Reproductive Rights, The World's Abortion Laws (June 2004), http://www.reproductiverights.org/pub_fac_abortion_laws.html. Though the Government and amici in cases following Roe v. Wade, 410 U.S. 113 (1973), urged the Court to follow the international community's lead, these arguments fell on deaf ears. . . .

The Court's special reliance on the laws of the United Kingdom is perhaps the most indefensible part of its opinion. It is of course true that we share a common history with the United Kingdom, and that we often consult English sources when asked to discern the meaning of a constitutional text written against the backdrop of 18th-century English law and legal thought. If we applied that approach today, our task would be an easy one. As we explained in Harmelin v. Michigan, 501 U.S. 957, 973-974 (1991), the "Cruell and Unusuall Punishments" provision of the English Declaration of Rights was originally meant to describe those punishments "out of [the Judges'] Power" — that is, those punishments that were not authorized by common law or statute, but that were nonetheless administered by the Crown or the Crown's judges. Under that reasoning, the death penalty for under-18 offenders would easily survive this challenge. The Court has, however — I think wrongly — long rejected a purely originalist approach to our Eighth Amendment, and that is certainly not the approach the Court takes today. Instead, the Court undertakes the majestic task of determining (and thereby prescribing) *our* Nation's *current* standards of decency. It is beyond comprehension why we should look, for that purpose, to a country that has developed, in the centuries since the Revolutionary War — and with increasing speed since the United Kingdom's recent submission to the jurisprudence of European courts dominated by continental jurists — a legal, political, and social culture quite different from our own. If we took the Court's directive seriously, we would also consider relaxing our double jeopardy prohibition, since the British Law Commission recently published a report that would significantly extend the rights of the prosecution to appeal cases where an acquittal was the result of a judge's ruling that was legally incorrect. See Law Commission, Double Jeopardy and Prosecution Appeals, LAW COM No. 267, Cm 5048, p. 6, P 1.19 (Mar. 2001); J. Spencer, The English System in European Criminal Procedures 142, 204, and n. 239 (M. Delmas-Marty & J. Spencer eds. 2002). We would also curtail our right to jury trial in criminal cases since, despite the jury system's deep roots in our shared common law, England now permits all but the most serious offenders to be tried by magistrates without a jury. See D. Feldman, England and Wales, in Criminal Procedure: A Worldwide Study 91, 114-115 (C. Bradley ed. 1999).

The Court should either profess its willingness to reconsider all these matters in light of the views of foreigners, or else it should cease putting forth foreigners' views as part of the *reasoned basis* of its decisions. To invoke alien law when it agrees with one's own thinking, and ignore it otherwise, is not reasoned decisionmaking, but sophistry.

. . . I do not believe that approval by "other nations and peoples" should buttress our commitment to American principles any more than (what should logically follow) disapproval by "other nations and peoples" should weaken that commitment. More importantly, however, the Court's statement flatly misdescribes what is going on here. Foreign sources are cited today, *not* to underscore our "fidelity" to the Constitution, our "pride in its origins," and "our own [American] heritage." To the contrary, they are cited *to set aside* the centuries-old American practice — a practice still engaged in by a large majority of the relevant States — of letting a jury of 12 citizens decide whether, in the particular case, youth should be the basis for withholding the death penalty. What these foreign sources "affirm," rather than repudiate, is the Justices' own notion of how the world ought to be, and their diktat that it shall be so henceforth in America. The Court's parting attempt to downplay the significance of its extensive discussion of foreign law is unconvincing. "Acknowledgment" of foreign approval has no place in the legal opinion of this Court *unless it is part of the basis for the Court's judgment* — which is surely what it parades as today.

IV

To add insult to injury, the Court affirms the Missouri Supreme Court without even admonishing that court for its flagrant disregard of our precedent in *Stanford*. . . .

. . . [T]his is no way to run a legal system. . . . To allow lower courts to behave as we do, "updating" the Eighth Amendment as needed, destroys stability and makes our case law an unreliable basis for the designing of laws by citizens and their representatives, and for action by public officials. The result will be to crown arbitrariness with chaos.

NOTES AND QUESTIONS

1. Other than the recognized fact that "death is different," see Gregg v. Georgia, 428 U.S. 153, 188 (1976), is there any way to explain the dramatic divergence, in both result and Eighth Amendment methodology, between *Harmelin* and *Ewing*, on the one hand, and *Simmons*, on the other? Even if death *is* different, is that a satisfactory explanation for the divergence? Why is a marginal "national consensus" of either 30 states (per Justice Kennedy) or 18 states (per Justice Scalia) sufficient to establish a categorical Eighth Amendment rule in *Simmons*, whereas a consensus of 49 states was held insufficient in both *Harmelin* and *Ewing*? (Recall that, in both of those cases, the relevant states stood alone in the harshness of the prison sentences they imposed.) Why are the views of the United Kingdom and the European Union relevant to the Eighth Amendment issue in *Simmons*, but not even mentioned in *Harmelin* and *Ewing*? Isn't there a consistency problem with the Court's view that 17-year-olds, as a class, are insufficiently mature and responsible to commit crimes that might justify capital punishment, but sufficiently mature and responsible to exercise the right to an abortion without parental consent?

Might the result in *Simmons* simply reflect the Court's seemingly growing concern with the morality of capital punishment itself? If so, then wouldn't it be better for the Court to 'fess up and address the problem in a more direct and honest manner?

2. Do the above questions, and apparent inconsistencies, provide further evidence in support of Justice Scalia's claim that the Court should (as it seemed to do in *Harmelin* and *Ewing*) get out of the business of Eighth Amendment proportionality review entirely? Is this one of those areas of constitutional adjudication—like substantive due process—in which the Court's decisions are destined, at least much of the time, to appear arbitrary and lawless? Or is there another possible approach to proportionality review that would offer greater predictability and doctrinal stability?

3. In Kennedy v. Louisiana, 554 U.S. 407 (2008), the Court, by 5-4, struck down the death penalty as a punishment for the rape of a child that does not result in the victim's death. The majority opinion acknowledged that, since 1995, six states (including Louisiana) had enacted legislation authorizing the death penalty for child rape, while five others were considering similar legislation, but found this trend insufficient to outweigh the fact that—at least as of the time of the decision—44 states (including the 12 states that had no death penalty at all) would not allow a defendant to be executed for such a crime. The Court also emphasized that the Eighth Amendment is measured by the "evolving standards of human decency," and expressed the view that "decency, in its essence, presumes respect for the individual and thus moderation or restraint in the application of capital punishment."

4. Just how "different" *is* death, anyway, in Eighth Amendment proportionality terms? The Court injected more than a little bit of uncertainty into the answer to this question in Graham v. Florida, 130 S. Ct. 2011 (2010). There, the Court held, per Justice Kennedy, that juveniles convicted of a non-homicide crime may not be sentenced to life in prison without possibility of parole, but instead must be provided with "some meaningful opportunity to obtain release based on demonstrated maturity and rehabilitation." Id., at 2030. The decision was based on a categorical analysis of crime and punishment essentially identical to those in the capital cases of *Atkins, Roper,* and *Kennedy,* and drew heavily on similar "objective" indicia of an emerging "national consensus." The *Graham* Court, like the *Roper* Court, also engaged in a detailed and lengthy discussion of the reduced maturity and moral responsibility of juveniles, and cited extensively the views of other nations.

Justice Thomas, joined by Justices Scalia and Alito, sharply dissented:

> The question of what acts are "deserving" of what punishments is bound so tightly with questions of morality and social conditions as to make it, almost by definition, a question for legislative resolution. It is true that the Court previously has relied on the notion of proportionality in holding certain classes of offenses categorically exempt from capital punishment. But never before today has the Court relied on its own view of just deserts to impose a categorical limit on the imposition of a lesser punishment. Its willingness to cross that well-established boundary raises the question whether any democratic choice regarding appropriate punishment is safe from the Court's ever-expanding constitutional veto.

Id., at 2056.

5. In Miller v. Alabama, 132 S. Ct. 2455 (2012) (decided together with the companion case of Jackson v. Hobbs), a narrowly divided 5-4 Court—relying heavily on the same social-science evidence as in *Graham*—held that juveniles who commit homicides may not be sentenced to life imprisonment without possibility of parole *under mandatory sentencing schemes* (i.e., under sentencing statutes that require the imposition of an LWOP sentence without allowing the sentencer to consider possible mitigating or extenuating circumstances). Media accounts of the *Miller* decision, unfortunately, were largely inaccurate. Despite the facial similarity to *Graham, Miller* is *not* a proportionality case, and the Court did *not* rule in *Miller* that juveniles cannot receive LWOP sentences. Instead, *Miller* is a case about the *procedure* that a jurisdiction must follow, before it can sentence a juvenile defendant to life without parole. At the same time, the Court in *Miller* clearly signalled its general discomfort with such sentences:

> [W]e do not consider Jackson's and Miller's alternative argument that the Eighth Amendment requires a categorical bar on life without parole for juveniles, or at least for those 14 and younger. But given all we have said in *Roper, Graham,* and this decision about children's diminished culpability and heightened capacity for change, we think appropriate occasions for sentencing juveniles to this harshest possible penalty will be uncommon. . . . Although we do not foreclose a sentencer's ability to make that judgment in homicide cases, we require it to take into account how children are different, and how those differences counsel against irrevocably sentencing them to a lifetime in prison.

Id., at 2469. Will *Miller* lead, eventually, to an Eighth Amendment proportionality decision barring life without parole for all juveniles? We'll have to wait and see.

B.   Discretion and Rules in Sentencing

In the middle of the twentieth century, American trial judges were vested with broad discretion to determine the appropriate sentence for a defendant who was convicted of a crime, and the exercise of this discretion—within the limits set by the legislature in the relevant crime statute—was virtually unreviewable. There was no requirement for the judge to state publicly the reasons for imposing a particular sentence. In short, traditional discretionary sentencing operated in a virtual "black box"; information about the crime and about the defendant would enter on one side, and the sentence would emerge from the other side, usually without explanation.

By the 1960s, virtually every state had also adopted a system of indeterminate sentences, meaning that a defendant's release date was determined not by the trial judge, but through the further exercise of discretion by a parole board or probation agency. Such indeterminate sentences were thought to be more consistent with the rehabilitative ideal that generally prevailed at the time in American penological theory.

One of the most prominent critics of discretionary and indeterminate sentencing, U.S. District Judge Marvin Frankel of the Southern District of New York, wrote about some of the problems with the traditional approach.

MARVIN FRANKEL, LAWLESSNESS IN SENTENCING

41 U. Cin. L. Rev. 1, 4-6, 29-31, 51 (1972)

The common form of criminal penalty provision confers upon the sentencing judge an enormous range of choice. The scope of what we call "discretion" permits imprisonment for anything from a day to one, five, 10, 20, or more years. . . .

The statutes granting such powers characteristically say nothing about the factors to be weighed in moving to either end of the spectrum or to some place between. It might be supposed by some stranger arrived in our midst that the criteria for measuring a particular sentence would be discoverable outside the narrow limits of the statutes and would be known to the judicial experts rendering the judgments. But the supposition would lack substantial foundation. Even the most basic sentencing principles are not prescribed or stated with persuasive authority. . . .

Moving upward from what should be the philosophical axioms of a rational scheme of sentencing law, we have no structure of rules, or even guidelines, affecting other elements arguably pertinent to the nature or severity of the sentence. . . .

What factors should be assessed—and where, if anywhere, are comparisons to be sought—in gauging the relative seriousness of the specific offense and offender as against the spectrum of offenses by others in the same legal category? . . .

With the delegation of power so unchanneled, it is surely no overstatement to say that "the new penology has resulted in vesting in judges and parole and probation agencies the greatest degree of uncontrolled power over the liberty of human beings that one can find in the legal system." The process would be totally unruly even if judges were superbly and uniformly trained for the solemn work of sentencing. As everyone knows, however, they are not trained at all. . . .

The basic premise of the indeterminate sentence is the modern conception that rehabilitation is the paramount goal in sentencing. . . . I do not argue that the indeterminate sentence is always and everywhere inappropriate. I believe, however, that its unqualified use rests upon undemonstrated premises; that the premises, even if sound, should not have the sweeping application they are given; and that the excessive extension of indeterminacy has probably resulted in much cruelty and injustice, rather than the great goods its proponents envisage. . . .

. . . I propose that there be established a National Commission charged with permanent responsibility for (1) the study of sentencing, corrections, and parole; (2) the formulation of laws and rules to which the results of such study may lead; and (3) the actual enactment of rules subject to congressional veto. . . .

. . . [T]he stakes of everyone in a system of rational sentencing are too great for contentment with the disheveled status quo. The improvements needed will not be achieved through fitful bursts of activity. The task requires the continuous attention of a respected agency. . . .

———————————

Within a few years, Judge Frankel's proposal for the creation of a national "sentencing commission" began to take root. Meanwhile, by the late 1970s, with crime rates rising and empirical studies documenting the inability of penological experts to rehabilitate most offenders, the rehabilitative ideal began to fade from the American penological scene. See generally Francis A. Allen, The Decline of the Rehabilitative Ideal: Penal Policy and Social Purpose (1981). In 1976, Andrew von Hirsch wrote an influential book, Doing Justice, advocating a retributive theory of punishment based on Kantian "just deserts." The book, together with Judge Frankel's proposal, served as the catalyst for many of the sentencing reforms that followed.

SPECIAL REPORT: "TRUTH IN SENTENCING IN STATE PRISONS"

U.S. Department of Justice, Bureau of Justice Statistics
January 1999

Sentencing reform policies have paralleled the mood of the country on crime and punishment, shifting between requiring a fixed prison time prior to release or allowing discretionary release of offenders by judges, parole boards, or corrections officials. Over the last two decades, sentencing requirements and release policies have become more restrictive, primarily in response to widespread "get tough on crime" attitudes in the Nation. . . .

In the early 1970s, States generally permitted parole boards to determine when an offender would be released from prison. In addition, good-time reductions for satisfactory prison behavior, earned-time incentives for participation in work or educational programs, and other time reductions to control prison crowding resulted in the early release of prisoners. These policies permitted officials to individualize the amount of punishment or leniency an offender received and provided means to manage the prison population.

Such discretion in sentencing and release policies led to criticism that some offenders were punished more harshly than others for similar offenses and to complaints that overall sentencing and release laws were too soft on criminals. By the late 1970s and early 1980s, States began developing sentencing guidelines, enacting mandatory minimum sentences and adopting other sentencing reforms to reduce disparity in sentencing and to toughen penalties for certain offenses, specifically drug offenses (as part of the "war on drugs"), offenses with weapons, and offenses committed by repeat or habitual criminals.

States continued to increase the severity of sentencing laws (primarily for violent offenders) by enacting restrictions on the possibility of early release, which became known as truth in sentencing. Truth-in-sentencing laws require offenders to serve a substantial portion of the prison sentence imposed by the court before being eligible for release. Previous policies which reduced the amount of time an offender served on a sentence, such as good-time, earned-time and parole board release, are restricted or eliminated under truth-in-sentencing laws. The definition of truth in sentencing varies among the States, as do the percent of sentence required to be served and the crimes covered by the laws. Most States have targeted violent offenders under truth in sentencing. . . .

Fourteen States have abolished early release by discretion of a parole board for all offenders. Seven States abolished parole board release within the last 10 years. Eight States abolished parole board release during the same year a truth-in-sentencing law was passed. . . . Parole boards still have discretion over inmates who were sentenced for crimes committed prior to the effective date of the law that eliminated parole board release. . . .

A few other States have abolished parole board release for certain violent or felony offenders . . . or for certain crimes against a person. . . . California allows discretionary release by a parole board only for offenders with indeterminate life sentences. In general, States restrict the possibility of parole board release based on the offender's criminal history or the circumstances of the offense. . . .

The first legislatively created sentencing commission was formed in Minnesota in 1978. At the federal level, in 1984, Congress enacted the Sentencing Reform Act, 18 U.S.C. §§3551 et seq., and 28 U.S.C. §§991-998, thereby transferring much of the control over federal criminal sentencing from trial judges to a newly created United States Sentencing Commission. U.S. Circuit Judge Deanell Reece Tacha of the U.S. Court of Appeals for the Tenth Circuit, who served on the original Commission, explained the basic operation of the new system:

DEANELL REECE TACHA, SERVING THIS TIME: EXAMINING THE FEDERAL SENTENCING GUIDELINES AFTER A DECADE OF EXPERIENCE

62 Mo. L. Rev. 471 (1997)

In 1984, after more than ten years of study and debate, Congress overwhelmingly passed the Sentencing Reform Act, which brought about the most farreaching reforms in federal sentencing that this nation has ever seen. The Sentencing Reform Act abolished parole and introduced a comprehensive new sentencing scheme to ensure that federal sentencing satisfied the goals of certainty, uniformity and fairness, while furthering the traditional purposes of criminal punishment: deterrence, incapacitation, just punishment and rehabilitation.

To achieve these goals, the Sentencing Reform Act created the United States Sentencing Commission, which in turn created the federal sentencing guidelines. The guidelines went into effect in 1987 and, although they have been amended more than 500 times, the basic structure and operation has remained intact. The guidelines are designed so that a judge measures the seriousness of a defendant's offense and the extent of his criminal history in order to select the sentence he should receive. The seriousness of the offense is based on a combination of factors, including:

- the offense of conviction (e.g., robbery, drug trafficking, fraud);
- specific aggravating or mitigating conduct that occurs during the offense of conviction (e.g., the amount of money taken, use of a gun, bodily injury); and
- other adjustments for factors that are relevant regardless of the type of offense involved (e.g., the victim's vulnerability, the defendant's role in the offense, obstruction of justice, acceptance of responsibility). A defendant's criminal history score reflects the number, seriousness and recency of his prior offenses.

These two considerations—offense seriousness and criminal history—are represented along the two axes of the sentencing table, which judges use to select a final sentence. The table is a grid with the offense levels running along the vertical axis and the criminal history levels running along the horizontal axis. The point at which a given offense level and criminal history score intersect on the grid shows the range of months from which the judge can choose a specific sentence.

The judge may depart from the sentencing range and impose a higher or lower sentence only if there are aggravating or mitigating circumstances that have not been adequately taken into account by the Commission in formulating the guidelines. On the rationale that it would undermine the principal goals of the Sentencing Reform Act, a judge may not depart simply because she thinks the final sentencing range is too harsh or too lenient. However, she is given flexibility to depart when faced with an extraordinary or atypical case.

Finally, the judge must determine whether the guideline sentence is consistent with the statutory maximum and minimum sentences mandated by Congress. The guidelines were drafted to achieve some parity with mandatory sentences, but if the guideline sentence is inconsistent with a mandatory sentence, the mandatory sentence will trump the guidelines.

The Federal Sentencing Guidelines, together with their counterparts in the roughly one-half of the states that have adopted similar guidelines, were designed primarily to reduce disparity in sentencing. But the federal guidelines achieved this goal by shifting sentencing discretion from trial judges to prosecutors, whose discretionary charging decisions now largely determine (together with the guidelines themselves and the relevant facts about the crime and the defendant) the sentence that a defendant will receive upon conviction. This led to sharp criticism of the federal guidelines by numerous judges and scholars; see, e.g., Kate Stith & Jose Cabranes, Fear of Judging: Sentencing Guidelines in the Federal Courts (1998); Michael Tonry, Sentencing Matters (1996); Doris Marie Provine, Too Many Black Men: The Sentencing Judge's Dilemma, 23 Law & Soc. Inquiry 823 (1998); Daniel J. Freed, Federal Sentencing in the Wake of Guidelines: Unacceptable Limits on the Discretion of Sentencers, 101 Yale L.J. 1681 (1992); Donald P. Lay, Rethinking the Guidelines: A Call for Cooperation, 101 Yale L.J. 1755 (1992); Gerald W. Heaney, The Reality of Guidelines Sentencing: No End to Disparity, 28 Am. Crim. L. Rev. 161 (1991).

One unanticipated consequence of the federal guidelines has been a dramatic increase in sentencing litigation. Sentencing issues that previously were nonreviewable, in the era of "black-box" discretionary sentencing, have now emerged into the light of day to become the basis for sentencing appeals and petitions to vacate sentences. Between 1987 (when the Federal Sentencing Guidelines first went into effect) and 1999, while the overall number of case filings in the federal appellate courts grew by about 50 percent, the number of petitions in those same courts seeking to vacate a sentence grew by almost 500 percent.[5]

C.   Do the Rules of Constitutional Criminal Procedure Apply to Sentencing?

The single most important procedural issue in sentencing law today is whether, and to what extent, sentencing proceedings are subject to the rules of constitutional criminal procedure that apply to the determination of a defendant's guilt or innocence at trial. Until recently, the answer was relatively clear. Traditional discretionary sentencing has long been viewed as sufficiently distinct from the guilt-innocence determination to warrant different constitutional treatment. Thus, although a few constitutional rules, such as the right to counsel, have been applied equally to trials and sentencing proceedings, other rules, such as the right to confrontation, have not. The next case, although predating the constitutionalization of most criminal procedure rules, still represents the leading exposition of the reasoning behind the traditional approach.

WILLIAMS v. NEW YORK

Appeal from the Court of Appeals of New York
337 U.S. 241 (1949)

JUSTICE BLACK delivered the opinion of the Court.

A jury in a New York state court found appellant guilty of murder in the first degree. The jury recommended life imprisonment, but the trial judge imposed sentence of death. In giving his reasons for imposing the death sentence the judge

---

5. These percentages may be even higher today; during the one-year period ending September 30, 2006, more than 82.8 percent of all criminal appeals terminated in the federal courts included a sentencing issue. See Mark Motivans, Federal Justice Statistics, 2006 (NCJ 225711, May 2009).

discussed in open court the evidence upon which the jury had convicted stating that this evidence had been considered in the light of additional information obtained through the court's "Probation Department, and through other sources." Consideration of this additional information was pursuant to §482 of New York Criminal Code which provides:

> . . . Before rendering judgment or pronouncing sentence the court shall cause the defendant's previous criminal record to be submitted to it, including any reports that may have been made as a result of a mental, phychiatric [*sic*] or physical examination of such person, and may seek any information that will aid the court in determining the proper treatment of such defendant.

The Court of Appeals of New York affirmed the conviction and sentence over the contention that as construed and applied the controlling penal statutes are in violation of the due process clause of the Fourteenth Amendment of the Constitution of the United States "in that the sentence of death was based upon information supplied by witnesses with whom the accused had not been confronted and as to whom he had no opportunity for cross-examination or rebuttal. . . ." Because the statutes were sustained over this constitutional challenge the case is here on appeal under 28 U.S.C. §1257(2).

The narrow contention here makes it unnecessary to set out the facts at length. The record shows a carefully conducted trial lasting more than two weeks in which appellant was represented by three appointed lawyers who conducted his defense with fidelity and zeal. The evidence proved a wholly indefensible murder committed by a person engaged in a burglary. The judge instructed the jury that if it returned a verdict of guilty as charged, without recommendation for life sentence, "The Court must impose the death penalty," but if such recommendation was made, "the Court may impose a life sentence." The judge went on to emphasize that "the Court is not bound to accept your recommendation."

About five weeks after the verdict of guilty with recommendation of life imprisonment, and after a statutory pre-sentence investigation report to the judge, the defendant was brought to court to be sentenced. Asked what he had to say, appellant protested his innocence. After each of his three lawyers had appealed to the court to accept the jury's recommendation of a life sentence, the judge gave reasons why he felt that the death sentence should be imposed. He narrated the shocking details of the crime as shown by the trial evidence, expressing his own complete belief in appellant's guilt. He stated that the pre-sentence investigation revealed many material facts concerning appellant's background which though relevant to the question of punishment could not properly have been brought to the attention of the jury in its consideration of the question of guilt. He referred to the experience appellant "had had on thirty other burglaries in and about the same vicinity" where the murder had been committed. The appellant had not been convicted of these burglaries although the judge had information that he had confessed to some and had been identified as the perpetrator of some of the others. The judge also referred to certain activities of appellant as shown by the probation report that indicated appellant possessed "a morbid sexuality" and classified him as a "menace to society." The accuracy of the statements made by the judge as to appellant's background and past practices was not challenged by appellant or his counsel, nor was the judge asked to disregard any of them or to afford appellant a chance to refute or discredit any of them by cross-examination or otherwise.

The case presents a serious and difficult question. The question relates to the rules of evidence applicable to the manner in which a judge may obtain information to guide him in the imposition of sentence upon an already convicted defendant. Within limits fixed by statutes, New York judges are given a broad discretion to decide the type and extent of punishment for convicted defendants. Here, for example, the judge's discretion was to sentence to life imprisonment or death. To aid a judge in exercising this discretion intelligently the New York procedural policy encourages him to consider information about the convicted person's past life, health, habits, conduct, and mental and moral propensities. The sentencing judge may consider such information even though obtained outside the courtroom from persons whom a defendant has not been permitted to confront or cross-examine. It is the consideration of information obtained by a sentencing judge in this manner that is the basis for appellant's broad constitutional challenge to the New York statutory policy.

Appellant urges that the New York statutory policy is in irreconcilable conflict with the underlying philosophy of a second procedural policy grounded in the due process of law clause of the Fourteenth Amendment. That policy . . . is in part that no person shall be tried and convicted of an offense unless he is given reasonable notice of the charges against him and is afforded an opportunity to examine adverse witnesses. That the due process clause does provide these salutary and time-tested protections where the question for consideration is the guilt of a defendant seems entirely clear from the genesis and historical evolution of the clause. . . .

Tribunals passing on the guilt of a defendant always have been hedged in by strict evidentiary procedural limitations. But both before and since the American colonies became a nation, courts in this country and in England practiced a policy under which a sentencing judge could exercise a wide discretion in the sources and types of evidence used to assist him in determining the kind and extent of punishment to be imposed within limits fixed by law. Out-of-court affidavits have been used frequently, and of course in the smaller communities sentencing judges naturally have in mind their knowledge of the personalities and backgrounds of convicted offenders. A recent manifestation of the historical latitude allowed sentencing judges appears in Rule 32 of the Federal Rules of Criminal Procedure. That rule provides for consideration by federal judges of reports made by probation officers containing information about a convicted defendant, including such information "as may be helpful in imposing sentence or in granting probation or in the correctional treatment of the defendant. . . ."

In addition to the historical basis for different evidentiary rules governing trial and sentencing procedures there are sound practical reasons for the distinction. In a trial before verdict the issue is whether a defendant is guilty of having engaged in certain criminal conduct of which he has been specifically accused. Rules of evidence have been fashioned for criminal trials which narrowly confine the trial contest to evidence that is strictly relevant to the particular offense charged. These rules rest in part on a necessity to prevent a time-consuming and confusing trial of collateral issues. They were also designed to prevent tribunals concerned solely with the issue of guilt of a particular offense from being influenced to convict for that offense by evidence that the defendant had habitually engaged in other misconduct. A sentencing judge, however, is not confined to the narrow issue of guilt. His task within fixed statutory or constitutional limits is to determine the type and extent of punishment after the issue of guilt has been determined. Highly relevant—if not essential—to his selection of an appropriate sentence is the possession of the fullest information possible concerning the defendant's life and characteristics. And modern concepts individualizing punishment have made it all the more necessary that a sentencing judge not be denied an opportunity to obtain pertinent information by a requirement of rigid adherence to restrictive rules of evidence properly applicable to the trial.

Undoubtedly the New York statutes emphasize a prevalent modern philosophy of penology that the punishment should fit the offender and not merely the crime. . . . The belief no longer prevails that every offense in a like legal category calls for an identical punishment without regard to the past life and habits of a particular offender. This whole country has traveled far from the period in which the death sentence was an automatic and commonplace result of convictions—even for offenses today deemed trivial. Today's philosophy of individualizing sentences makes sharp distinctions for example between first and repeated offenders. Indeterminate sentences the ultimate termination of which are sometimes decided by non-judicial agencies have to a large extent taken the place of the old rigidly fixed punishments. The practice of probation which relies heavily on non-judicial implementation has been accepted as a wise policy. Execution of the United States parole system rests on the discretion of an administrative parole board. . . . Retribution is no longer the dominant objective of the criminal law. Reformation and rehabilitation of offenders have become important goals of criminal jurisprudence.

Modern changes in the treatment of offenders make it more necessary now than a century ago for observance of the distinctions in the evidential procedure in the trial and sentencing processes. For indeterminate sentences and probation have resulted in an increase in the discretionary powers exercised in fixing punishments. In general, these modern changes have not resulted in making the lot of offenders harder. On the contrary a strong motivating force for the changes has been the belief that by careful study of the lives and personalities of convicted offenders many could be less severely punished and restored sooner to complete freedom and useful citizenship. This belief to a large extent has been justified.

Under the practice of individualizing punishments, investigational techniques have been given an important role. Probation workers making reports of their investigations have not been trained to prosecute but to aid offenders. Their reports have been given a high value by conscientious judges who want to sentence persons on the best available information rather than on guesswork and inadequate information. To deprive sentencing judges of this kind of information would undermine modern penological procedural policies that have been cautiously adopted throughout the nation after careful consideration and experimentation. We must recognize that most of the information now relied upon by judges to guide them in the intelligent imposition of sentences would be unavailable if information were restricted to that given in open court by witnesses subject to cross-examination. And the modern probation report draws on information concerning every aspect of a defendant's life.[15] The type and extent of this information make totally impractical

---

15. A publication circulated by the Administrative Office of the United States Courts contains a suggested form for all United States probation reports and serves as an example of the type of information contained in the reports. This form consists of thirteen "marginal headings": (1) Offense; (2) Prior Record; (3) Family History; (4) Home and Neighborhood; (5) Education; (6) Religion; (7) Interests and Activities; (8) Health (physical and mental); (9) Employment; (10) Resources; (11) Summary; (12) Plan; and (13) Agencies Interested. Each of the headings is further broken down into subheadings. The form represents a framework into which information can be inserted to give the sentencing judge a composite picture of the defendant. Administrative Office of the United States Courts, The Presentence Investigation Report, Pub. No. 101 (1943).

if not impossible open court testimony with cross-examination. Such a procedure could endlessly delay criminal administration in a retrial of collateral issues.

The considerations we have set out admonish us against treating the due process clause as a uniform command that courts throughout the Nation abandon their age-old practice of seeking information from out-of-court sources to guide their judgment toward a more enlightened and just sentence. New York criminal statutes set wide limits for maximum and minimum sentences. Under New York statutes a state judge cannot escape his grave responsibility of fixing sentence. In determining whether a defendant shall receive a one-year minimum or a twenty-year maximum sentence, we do not think the Federal Constitution restricts the view of the sentencing judge to the information received in open court. The due process clause should not be treated as a device for freezing the evidential procedure of sentencing in the mold of trial procedure. So to treat the due process clause would hinder if not preclude all courts—state and federal—from making progressive efforts to improve the administration of criminal justice.

It is urged, however, that we should draw a constitutional distinction as to the procedure for obtaining information where the death sentence is imposed. We cannot accept the contention. Leaving a sentencing judge free to avail himself of out-of-court information in making such a fateful choice of sentences does secure to him a broad discretionary power, one susceptible of abuse. But in considering whether a rigid constitutional barrier should be created, it must be remembered that there is possibility of abuse wherever a judge must choose between life imprisonment and death. And it is conceded that no federal constitutional objection would have been possible if the judge here had sentenced appellant to death because appellant's trial manner impressed the judge that appellant was a bad risk for society, or if the judge had sentenced him to death giving no reason at all. We cannot say that the due process clause renders a sentence void merely because a judge gets additional out-of-court information to assist him in the exercise of this awesome power of imposing the death sentence.

Appellant was found guilty after a fairly conducted trial. His sentence followed a hearing conducted by the judge. Upon the judge's inquiry as to why sentence should not be imposed, the defendant made statements. His counsel made extended arguments. The case went to the highest court in the state, and that court had power to reverse for abuse of discretion or legal error in the imposition of the sentence. That court affirmed. We hold that appellant was not denied due process of law.

Affirmed.

[The dissenting opinion of Justice Murphy is omitted.]

NOTES AND QUESTIONS

1. In Gardner v. Florida, 430 U.S. 349 (1977), the Court held that modern capital sentencing—where the sentencer's discretion must, in order to comply with the Eighth Amendment, be guided by statutory "aggravating circumstances"—requires a higher level of procedural protection for the defendant than does traditional discretionary sentencing under *Williams*. Thus, in a post-*Furman* capital case, the defendant was denied due process "when the death sentence was imposed, at least in part, on the basis of information which he had no opportunity to deny or explain." Id., at 362.

In Ring v. Arizona, 536 U.S. 584 (2002), the Court went even further in applying the constitutional rules of criminal procedure to capital sentencing, holding that "aggravating circumstances" are the functional equivalents of elements of a crime, and thus must be found beyond reasonable doubt by a jury. *Ring* is discussed infra, at page 1511.

2. Does the decision in *Williams* represent a normative statement by the Court that criminal sentencing *should not* be subject to all of the same procedural rules that apply to criminal trials? Or does the decision reflect merely the Court's recognition of the practical reality that—in a world of "black box" discretionary sentencing—much of what happens *cannot* effectively be governed by such procedural rules, since in most cases there will be no practical way to determine whether those rules have been followed?

3. The Supreme Court in *Williams* held that at least some of the constitutional rules of criminal procedure applicable to criminal trials—specifically, in that case, the right to confront adverse witnesses—do not apply to traditional discretionary criminal sentencing. But what about nontraditional forms of criminal sentencing? In the late twentieth century, the legislatures of many states and the federal government—wanting to be seen as "tough on crime"—began to experiment with "mandatory minimum" sentencing. Under such statutes, all defendants convicted of certain designated crimes (or of crimes committed under certain designated factual circumstances, such as the defendant's use of a gun) must serve a fixed minimum prison term before becoming eligible for parole or other release.

In Chapter 14, at page 1452, you first encountered the *Winship/Mullaney/Patterson* line of cases dealing with burdens of proof and the elements of a crime. In McMillan v. Pennsylvania, 477 U.S. 79 (1986), the Court squarely addressed, for the first time, the potential implications of the *Winship/Mullaney/Patterson* line of cases for "mandatory minimum" sentencing. *McMillan* involved a Pennsylvania statute that mandated a minimum five-year prison sentence for any defendant who "visibly possessed a firearm" during the commission of certain enumerated felonies. Under the statute, the presence of this special sentencing factor was determined by the sentencing judge, on a "preponderance of the evidence" standard, based on all of the evidence introduced either at trial or during a separate sentencing hearing. The defendant, McMillan, received the mandatory five-year prison sentence; on appeal, he argued that because the "visible firearm possession" sentencing factor was the functional equivalent of an element of the crime for which he was ultimately sentenced, due process—as interpreted by *Winship* and its progeny—required proof "beyond a reasonable doubt" (or, at least, some standard of proof more rigorous than mere "preponderance of the evidence").

The Supreme Court, in a 5-4 majority opinion by Justice Rehnquist, upheld the constitutionality of the statute. The Court relied heavily on *Patterson*, where it had explained that "the state legislature's definition of the elements of the offense is usually dispositive." While noting—as it had in *Patterson*—that "there are obviously constitutional limits beyond which the States may not go in this regard," the Court found Pennsylvania's statute to fall within those still-undefined limits: The statute did not create any impermissible presumptions, it did not change the definitions of any existing crimes (but merely "dictated the precise weight" to be given one particular sentencing factor), and—perhaps most important—it did not provide for a mandatory minimum sentence larger than the sentences already authorized for the underlying substantive crimes to which the statute applied. In the Court's words, "The statute gives no impression of having been tailored to permit the visible possession finding to be a tail which wags the dog of the substantive offense." Having found no constitutional defect in the statute's treatment of "visible possession" as a sentencing factor (rather than an element of the crime), the Court handily dismissed McMillan's objections to the preponderance standard, citing *Williams* for the proposition that "[s]entencing courts have traditionally heard evidence and found facts without any prescribed burden of proof at all." Finally, the Court noted a logical flaw in McMillan's argument:

> Petitioners apparently concede that Pennsylvania's scheme would pass constitutional muster if only it did not remove the sentencing court's discretion, i.e., if the legislature had simply directed the court to *consider* visible possession in passing sentence. . . . We have some difficulty fathoming why the due process calculus would change simply because the legislature has seen fit to provide sentencing courts with additional guidance.

Id., at 92.

Justice Stevens dissented,[6] pointing out that the majority's position suffered from its own logical flaw:

> It would demean the importance of the reasonable-doubt standard — indeed, it would demean the Constitution itself — if the substance of the standard could be avoided by nothing more than a legislative declaration that prohibited conduct is not an "element" of a crime. A legislative definition of an offense named "assault" could be broad enough to encompass every intentional infliction of harm by one person upon another, but surely the legislature could not provide that only that fact must be proved beyond a reasonable doubt and then specify a range of increased punishments if the prosecution could show by a preponderance of the evidence that the defendant robbed, raped, or killed his victim "during the commission of the offense."
>
> . . . I submit . . . that if a State provides that a specific component of a prohibited transaction shall give rise both to a special stigma and to a special punishment, that component must be treated as a "fact necessary to constitute the crime" within the meaning of our holding in In re Winship.

Id., at 102-103.

4. In Walton v. Arizona, 497 U.S. 639 (1990), the Court — in another 5-4 decision, with virtually the same lineup as in *McMillan*[7] upheld the Arizona death penalty statute against, inter alia, a challenge that it violated the Sixth Amendment's right to trial by jury by giving to the trial judge (instead of a jury) the responsibility of finding the "aggravating circumstances" that could lead to imposition of a death sentence.

The majority, in an opinion by Justice White, explained that under Arizona law "[a]ggravating circumstances are not separate penalties or offenses, but are 'standards to guide the making of [the] choice' between the alternative verdicts of death and life imprisonment. Thus, . . . the judge's finding of any particular aggravating circumstance does not of itself 'convict' a defendant (i.e., require the death

---

6. There was also a separate dissent by Justice Marshall, which was joined by Justices Brennan and Blackmun.

7. The only difference was that Justice Scalia replaced the retired Justice Powell on the winning side of the case.

penalty), and the failure to find any particular aggravating circumstance does not 'acquit' a defendant (i.e., preclude the death penalty)." *Walton*, 497 U.S., at 648.

In dissent on this issue, Justice Stevens[8] pointed out that "under Arizona law, . . . a first-degree murder is not punishable by a death sentence until at least one statutory aggravating circumstance has been proved," and argued that such aggravating circumstances thus "operate as statutory 'elements' of capital murder," id., at 709, and n. 1. He concluded—in language that now seems all too prescient:

> By stretching the limits of sentencing determinations that are made by judges . . . , these decisions have encroached on the factfinding function that has so long been entrusted to the jury. Further distorting the sentencing function to encompass findings of factual elements necessary to establish a capital offense is the unhappy product of the gradual "increase and spread" of these precedents, "to the utter disuse of juries in questions of the most momentous concern." . . . [I]t is not too late to change our course. . . .

Id., at 713-714.

NOTES ON DETERMINATE SENTENCING AND THE CONSTITUTION

Does the recent shift from traditional discretionary sentencing to determinate sentencing, as described above at pages 1498-1502, necessitate reexamination of the basic principles underlying *Williams* and *McMillan*? The answer, perhaps surprisingly, turns out to be "yes." In Apprendi v. New Jersey, 530 U.S. 466 (2000), the Supreme Court rocked the world of criminal sentencing by holding that at least some of the factors relied upon in determinate sentencing are the functional equivalents of elements of a new crime, and thus must be found by a jury beyond a reasonable doubt. This holding, if extended by the Court to its logical limits, may bring about the demise of determinate sentencing altogether—or at least of the particular form of determinate sentencing that has been implemented in most jurisdictions over the past 20 years. To understand *Apprendi* and its potential consequences, however, we must first survey the pre-*Apprendi* jurisprudential landscape.

1. The Supreme Court's first major constitutional encounter with determinate sentencing came in Mistretta v. United States, 488 U.S. 361 (1989). *Mistretta* involved a broad claim that the Sentencing Reform Act of 1984, which created the United States Sentencing Commission and charged that body with the responsibility to draft sentencing guidelines for federal crimes, violated the constitutional doctrine of separation of powers and involved excessive delegation of legislative powers to a nonlegislative body. The Court, by 8-1, disagreed. In an opinion by Justice Blackmun, the Court carefully reviewed the Act and the Guidelines promulgated thereunder, and held that the Act's delegation of Congressional powers was "sufficiently specific and detailed" to meet constitutional requirements. Although the *Mistretta* Court did not decide any particular constitutional issues relating to the operation of the Guidelines, neither did it signal any serious concerns about how those Guidelines operated.

---

8. Justices Brennan, Marshall, and Blackmun dissented on other grounds.

2. During the next decade or so, the Court addressed—and mostly rejected—a series of narrower and more specific constitutional challenges to particular aspects or applications of the Federal Sentencing Guidelines. In Witte v. United States, 515 U.S. 389 (1995), for example, the Court rejected a claim that reliance on uncharged conduct to enhance a defendant's sentence under the Guidelines precluded, under the Double Jeopardy Clause, a subsequent criminal prosecution based on that same conduct. In United States v. Watts, 519 U.S. 148 (1997), the Court held, in a per curiam opinion, that even alleged crimes for which the defendant previously was acquitted could be used, without violating due process, to enhance his sentence for a later crime under the Guidelines. Although neither *Witte* nor *Watts* dealt with the constitutional right to jury trial, both cases seemed to signify that the Constitution generally did not prohibit judges from increasing defendants' sentences based on judicial findings of facts that were never found by the jury.

Perhaps more significant, in Edwards v. United States, 523 U.S. 511 (1998), the Court flatly rejected a statutory and constitutional challenge to the imposition of a higher Guideline sentence for conspiracy to possess crack cocaine, despite the fact that the jury's general verdict might have been based solely on a conspiracy involving powder cocaine (which would have produced a lower sentence). The defendant in *Edwards* argued unsuccessfully that the trial judge should have been limited to sentencing him for the kind of conspiracy that necessarily was found by the jury. According to Justice Breyer's opinion for a unanimous Court: "The Sentencing Guidelines instruct *the judge* in a case like this one to determine both the amount and the kind of 'controlled substances' for which a defendant should be held accountable—and then to impose a sentence that varies depending upon amount and kind."[9]

3. In another case decided the same Term as *Edwards*, however, the constitutional worm began to turn. In Almendarez-Torres v. United States, 523 U.S. 224 (1998), the Court faced for the first time a claim that one of the factors identified in the Federal Sentencing Guidelines as the basis for an increased sentence—specifically, the defendant's prior criminal convictions—should be viewed as the functional equivalent of an element of a new crime. The defendant argued that, under the Fifth Amendment, his prior criminal convictions (to which he had admitted at his plea hearing) were required to be alleged in the indictment. The Court rejected this claim, but the case was close (5-4), and the four dissenters—Justices Stevens, Scalia, Souter, and Ginsburg—expressed "serious doubt as to whether the statute as interpreted by the Court in the present case is constitutional." In the prophetic words of Justice Scalia: "[I]t is genuinely doubtful whether the Constitution permits a judge (rather than a jury) to determine by a mere preponderance of the evidence (rather than beyond a reasonable doubt) a fact that increases the maximum penalty to which a criminal defendant is subject. . . ."

One year later, in Jones v. United States, 526 U.S. 227 (1999), the Court considered the Government's contention that the federal carjacking statute did not require a jury finding, beyond a reasonable doubt, on the factual issue whether the defendant's crime caused "serious bodily injury" to the victim (a fact that increased the defendant's maximum sentence from 15 years to 25 years in prison). Justice Thomas joined the four *Almendarez-Torres* dissenters to produce the *Jones* majority,

---

9. Note that Justice Breyer, before being appointed to the Supreme Court (i.e., when he was still a Circuit Judge), served as one of the original members of the United States Sentencing Commission that drafted the original Federal Sentencing Guidelines.

which concluded: "[U]nder the Due Process Clause of the Fifth Amendment and the notice and jury trial guarantees of the Sixth Amendment, any fact (other than prior conviction) that increases the maximum penalty for a crime must be charged in an indictment, submitted to a jury, and proven beyond a reasonable doubt. Because our prior cases suggest rather than establish this principle, our concern about the Government's reading of the statute rises only to the level of doubt, not certainty." In order to avoid this "constitutional doubt," the *Jones* Court, in an opinion by Justice Souter, construed the statute to require "serious bodily injury" to be alleged in the indictment, and found by a jury at trial beyond a reasonable doubt.

4. That led directly to the momentous decision in Apprendi v. New Jersey, 530 U.S. 466 (2000). In *Apprendi*, the defendant pled guilty to possessing a firearm for an unlawful purpose, a crime carrying a statutory sentence of between five and ten years in prison. During the defendant's sentencing hearing, however, the trial judge found, by a preponderance of the evidence, that the crime was committed for the purpose of intimidation based on the race of the victim. This judicial finding triggered the New Jersey "hate crime" statute, which provided for an "extended term" of imprisonment—doubling the normal sentencing range—for any such "hate crime." Under the "hate crime" statute, the judge was authorized to impose a sentence of up to 20 years, and sentenced the defendant to 12 years in prison.

In an opinion by Justice Stevens (the author of the primary dissent in *McMillan*), joined by Justices Scalia, Souter, Thomas, and Ginsburg, the Court held that this situation violated the Constitution by depriving the defendant of his right to have pretrial notice of all elements of the crime with which he was charged, and to have those elements found at trial by a jury beyond a reasonable doubt. According to the Court: "Other than the fact of a prior conviction [as in *Almendarez-Torres*], any fact that increases the penalty for a crime beyond the prescribed statutory maximum must be submitted to a jury, and proved beyond a reasonable doubt. . . ." Rejecting New Jersey's argument that the "hate crime" enhancement was a "sentencing factor" under *McMillan*, rather than an "element" of a new crime, the Court described the proffered distinction as "constitutionally novel and elusive," and explained: "[T]he relevant inquiry is one not of form, but of effect—does the required finding expose the defendant to a greater punishment than that authorized by the jury's guilty verdict?"

5. *Apprendi* was a significant enough decision in its own right; for example, it led some federal courts to begin invalidating sentences imposed for drug crimes where the jury did not make factual findings about the amount of drugs sold or possessed. See, e.g., Nordby v. United States, 225 F.3d 1053 (9th Cir. 2000). But even more significant were the questions left unanswered by *Apprendi*.

For example, what did *Apprendi* mean for capital sentencing? In Ring v. Arizona, 536 U.S. 584 (2002), the Court held that the prior *Walton* decision (upholding judicial factfinding of the aggravating circumstances necessary to impose a death sentence) was incompatible with *Apprendi*. In response to Arizona's contention that *Apprendi* did not apply because the statutory range of punishment for first-degree murder in Arizona included death (and thus the defendant was not sentenced above the statutory maximum), the *Ring* Court explained: "In effect, 'the required finding [of an aggravating circumstance] expose[d] [Ring] to a greater punishment than that authorized by the jury's guilty verdict.' The Arizona first-degree murder statute 'authorizes a maximum punishment of death only in a formal sense.' . . . Because Arizona's enumerated aggravating factors operate as 'the functional equivalent of a greater offense,' . . . the Sixth Amendment requires that they be found by a jury."

Another unanswered question was whether *McMillan* itself could survive *Apprendi*. In Harris v. United States, 536 U.S. 545 (2002), the Court—by 5-4, and without a complete majority opinion—reaffirmed (at least temporarily) the validity of *McMillan*. (*Harris*, and by extension *McMillan*, were both later overruled. See infra, at page 1547.)

6. The "big question" that loomed after *Apprendi*, however, was whether that decision would lead to the invalidation of the Federal Sentencing Guidelines and similar state-law determinate-sentencing schemes—none of which required jury determination of all facts that triggered increases in guideline sentences. In *Apprendi*, both Justice Stevens's majority opinion and Justice Thomas's concurrence explicitly declined to discuss the possible impact of *Apprendi* on the Guidelines, while Justice O'Connor's dissent suggested that, in light of *Apprendi*, the Guidelines must be viewed as constitutionally suspect. Meanwhile, Justice Breyer (one of the drafters of the original Guidelines) wrote a separate dissent in *Apprendi* for the sole purpose of defending the Guidelines against what he perceived to be a thinly veiled threat to their constitutionality. This provoked Justice Scalia to accuse Justice Breyer of succumbing to the "erroneous and all-too-common assumption that the Constitution means what we think it ought to mean."

On June 24, 2004, after four years of significant uncertainty in the lower courts (and, no doubt, significant anxiety in Justice Breyer as well), the Court—in a majority opinion by Justice Scalia—took a big step toward answering the "big question."

BLAKELY v. WASHINGTON, 542 U.S. 296 (2004): Petitioner Ralph Howard Blakely, Jr., pleaded guilty to the kidnaping of his estranged wife. The facts admitted in his plea, standing alone, supported a maximum sentence of 53 months. Pursuant to state law, the court imposed an "exceptional" sentence of 90 months after making a judicial determination that he had acted with "deliberate cruelty." We consider whether this violated petitioner's Sixth Amendment right to trial by jury. . . .

This case requires us to apply the rule we expressed in Apprendi v. New Jersey, 530 U.S. 466, 490 (2000): "Other than the fact of a prior conviction, any fact that increases the penalty for a crime beyond the prescribed statutory maximum must be submitted to a jury, and proved beyond a reasonable doubt." This rule reflects two longstanding tenets of common-law criminal jurisprudence: that the "truth of every accusation" against a defendant "should afterwards be confirmed by the unanimous suffrage of twelve of his equals and neighbours," 4 W. Blackstone, Commentaries on the Laws of England 343 (1769), and that "an accusation which lacks any particular fact which the law makes essential to the punishment is . . . no accusation within the requirements of the common law, and it is no accusation in reason," 1 J. Bishop, Criminal Procedure §87, p. 55 (2d ed. 1872). These principles have been acknowledged by courts and treatises since the earliest days of graduated sentencing; we compiled the relevant authorities in *Apprendi*, see 530 U.S., at 476-483, 489-490, n. 15; id., at 501-518, (Thomas, J., concurring), and need not repeat them here.[6] . . .

[In both *Apprendi* and Ring v. Arizona, 536 U.S. 584 (2002),] we concluded that the defendant's constitutional rights had been violated because the judge had imposed a sentence greater than the maximum he could have imposed under state law without the challenged factual finding.

---

6. [In dissent,] Justice O'Connor does not even provide a coherent alternative meaning for the jury-trial guarantee, unless one considers "whatever the legislature chooses to leave to the jury, so long as it does not go too far" coherent.

In this case, petitioner was sentenced to more than three years above the 53-month statutory maximum of the standard range because he had acted with "deliberate cruelty." The facts supporting that finding were neither admitted by petitioner nor found by a jury. The State nevertheless contends that there was no *Apprendi* violation because the relevant "statutory maximum" is not 53 months, but the 10-year maximum for class B felonies in §9A.20.021(1)(b). . . . Our precedents make clear, however, that the "statutory maximum" for *Apprendi* purposes is the maximum sentence a judge may impose solely on the basis of the facts reflected in the jury verdict or admitted by the defendant. See *Ring*, supra, at 602 ("'the maximum he would receive if punished according to the facts reflected in the jury verdict alone'" (quoting *Apprendi*, supra, at 483)). . . . In other words, the relevant "statutory maximum" is not the maximum sentence a judge may impose after finding additional facts, but the maximum he may impose without any additional findings. When a judge inflicts punishment that the jury's verdict alone does not allow, the jury has not found all the facts "which the law makes essential to the punishment," Bishop, supra, §87, at 55, and the judge exceeds his proper authority. . . .

[T]he State tries to distinguish *Apprendi* and *Ring* by pointing out that the enumerated grounds for departure in its regime are illustrative rather than exhaustive. This distinction is immaterial. Whether the judge's authority to impose an enhanced sentence depends on finding a specified fact (as in *Apprendi*), one of several specified facts (as in *Ring*), or any aggravating fact (as here), it remains the case that the jury's verdict alone does not authorize the sentence. The judge acquires that authority only upon finding some additional fact.[8]

Because the State's sentencing procedure did not comply with the Sixth Amendment, petitioner's sentence is invalid.[9]

Our commitment to *Apprendi* in this context reflects not just respect for long-standing precedent, but the need to give intelligible content to the right of jury trial. That right is no mere procedural formality, but a fundamental reservation of power in our constitutional structure. Just as suffrage ensures the people's ultimate control in the legislative and executive branches, jury trial is meant to ensure their control in the judiciary. . . . *Apprendi* carries out this design by ensuring that the judge's authority to sentence derives wholly from the jury's verdict. Without that restriction, the jury would not exercise the control that the Framers intended.

Those who would reject *Apprendi* are resigned to one of two alternatives. The first is that the jury need only find whatever facts the legislature chooses to label elements of the crime, and that those it labels sentencing factors—no matter how much they may increase the punishment—may be found by the judge. This would mean, for example, that a judge could sentence a man for committing murder even if the jury convicted him only of illegally possessing the firearm used to commit it—or of making an illegal lane change while fleeing the death scene. Not even *Apprendi*'s critics would advocate this absurd result. . . . The jury could not function as circuitbreaker

8. Nor does it matter that the judge must, after finding aggravating facts, make a judgment that they present a compelling ground for departure. He cannot make that judgment without finding some facts to support it beyond the bare elements of the offense. Whether the judicially determined facts require a sentence enhancement or merely allow it, the verdict alone does not authorize the sentence.

9. The United States, as amicus curiae, urges us to affirm. It notes differences between Washington's sentencing regime and the Federal Sentencing Guidelines but questions whether those differences are constitutionally significant. See Brief for United States as Amicus Curiae 25-30. The Federal Guidelines are not before us, and we express no opinion on them.

in the State's machinery of justice if it were relegated to making a determination that the defendant at some point did something wrong, a mere preliminary to a judicial inquisition into the facts of the crime the State actually seeks to punish.[10]

The second alternative is that legislatures may establish legally essential sentencing factors within limits—limits crossed when, perhaps, the sentencing factor is a "tail which wags the dog of the substantive offense." *McMillan*, 477 U.S., at 88. What this means in operation is that the law must not go too far—it must not exceed the judicial estimation of the proper role of the judge.

The subjectivity of this standard is obvious . . . Whether the Sixth Amendment incorporates this manipulable standard rather than *Apprendi*'s bright-line rule depends on the plausibility of the claim that the Framers would have left definition of the scope of jury power up to judges' intuitive sense of how far is too far. We think that claim not plausible at all, because the very reason the Framers put a jury-trial guarantee in the Constitution is that they were unwilling to trust government to mark out the role of the jury.

Justice O'Connor argues that, because determinate sentencing schemes involving judicial factfinding entail less judicial discretion than indeterminate schemes, the constitutionality of the latter implies the constitutionality of the former. This argument is flawed on a number of levels. First, the Sixth Amendment by its terms is not a limitation on judicial power, but a reservation of jury power. It limits judicial power only to the extent that the claimed judicial power infringes on the province of the jury. Indeterminate sentencing does not do so. It increases judicial discretion, to be sure, but not at the expense of the jury's traditional function of finding the facts essential to lawful imposition of the penalty. . . .

But even assuming that restraint of judicial power unrelated to the jury's role is a Sixth Amendment objective, it is far from clear that *Apprendi* disserves that goal. Determinate judicial-factfinding schemes entail less judicial power than indeterminate schemes, but more judicial power than determinate jury-factfinding schemes. Whether *Apprendi* increases judicial power overall depends on what States with determinate judicial-factfinding schemes would do, given the choice between the two alternatives. Justice O'Connor simply assumes that the net effect will favor judges, but she has no empirical basis for that prediction. . . .

Justice Breyer argues that *Apprendi* works to the detriment of criminal defendants who plead guilty by depriving them of the opportunity to argue sentencing factors to a judge. But nothing prevents a defendant from waiving his *Apprendi* rights. When a defendant pleads guilty, the State is free to seek judicial sentence enhancements so long as the defendant either stipulates to the relevant facts or consents to judicial factfinding. . . .

Nor do we see any merit to Justice Breyer's contention that *Apprendi* is unfair to criminal defendants because, if States respond by enacting "17-element robbery crimes," prosecutors will have more elements with which to bargain. . . . [G]iven the sprawling scope of most criminal codes, and the power to affect sentences by making (even nonbinding) sentencing recommendations, there is already no shortage

---

10. Justice O'Connor believes that a "built-in political check" will prevent lawmakers from manipulating offense elements in this fashion. But the many immediate practical advantages of judicial factfinding . . . suggest that political forces would, if anything, pull in the opposite direction. In any case, the Framers' decision to entrench the jury-trial right in the Constitution shows that they did not trust government to make political decisions in this area.

of in terrorem tools at prosecutors' disposal. See King & Klein, *Apprendi* and Plea Bargaining, 54 Stan. L. Rev. 295, 296 (2001) ("Every prosecutorial bargaining chip mentioned . . . existed pre-*Apprendi* exactly as it does post-*Apprendi*").

Justice Breyer's more general argument—that *Apprendi* undermines alternatives to adversarial factfinding—is not so much a criticism of *Apprendi* as an assault on jury trial generally. His esteem for "non-adversarial" truth-seeking processes . . . supports just as well an argument against either. Our Constitution and the common-law traditions it entrenches, however, do not admit the contention that facts are better discovered by judicial inquisition than by adversarial testing before a jury. See 3 Blackstone, Commentaries, at 373-374, 379-381. Justice Breyer may be convinced of the equity of the regime he favors, but his views are not the ones we are bound to uphold.

Ultimately, our decision cannot turn on whether or to what degree trial by jury impairs the efficiency or fairness of criminal justice. One can certainly argue that both these values would be better served by leaving justice entirely in the hands of professionals; many nations of the world, particularly those following civil-law traditions, take just that course. There is not one shred of doubt, however, about the Framers' paradigm for criminal justice: not the civil-law ideal of administrative perfection, but the common-law ideal of limited state power accomplished by strict division of authority between judge and jury. As *Apprendi* held, every defendant has the right to insist that the prosecutor prove to a jury all facts legally essential to the punishment. Under the dissenters' alternative, he has no such right. That should be the end of the matter.

Notwithstanding the careful language of footnote 9 in *Blakely*, the potential import of the decision for the Federal Sentencing Guidelines (and all state guideline systems other than Washington's) was readily apparent to all. Most observers stubbornly refused to believe that the Court would, after 20 years, throw out the Federal Guidelines, and predicted instead that relevant distinctions with the Washington state guideline system would be found. A few sages warned of looming chaos and disaster. On January 12, 2005, the Court finally addressed the uncertainty over the application of *Apprendi* and *Blakely* to the Federal Sentencing Guidelines. But the Court's decision managed to create even more uncertainty than it resolved.

UNITED STATES v. BOOKER

Certiorari to the United States Court of Appeals for the Seventh Circuit
543 U.S. 220 (2005)

JUSTICE STEVENS delivered the opinion of the Court in part.[10]

The question presented in each of these cases[11] is whether an application of the Federal Sentencing Guidelines violated the Sixth Amendment. In each case,

---

10. Justice Stevens was joined in this part by Justices Scalia, Souter, Thomas, and Ginsburg.—EDS.

11. *Booker* was decided together with United States v. Fanfan, on certiorari before judgment to the United States Court of Appeals for the First Circuit.—EDS.

the courts below held that binding rules set forth in the Guidelines limited the severity of the sentence that the judge could lawfully impose on the defendant based on the facts found by the jury at his trial. In both cases the courts rejected, on the basis of our decision in Blakely v. Washington, 542 U.S. 296 (2004), the Government's recommended application of the Sentencing Guidelines because the proposed sentences were based on additional facts that the sentencing judge found by a preponderance of the evidence. We hold that both courts correctly concluded that the Sixth Amendment as construed in *Blakely* does apply to the Sentencing Guidelines. In a separate opinion authored by Justice Breyer, the Court concludes that in light of this holding, two provisions of the Sentencing Reform Act of 1984 (SRA) that have the effect of making the Guidelines mandatory must be invalidated in order to allow the statute to operate in a manner consistent with congressional intent.

I

[In this section, Justice Stevens reviewed the facts of the two cases. Booker was found, by a jury, to have possessed with intent to distribute 92.5 grams of crack cocaine, which authorized a Guideline sentence of 210 to 262 months. At sentencing, the judge found by a preponderance that Booker actually possessed an additional 566 grams of crack, raising the Guideline sentence to 360 months to life in prison. Booker received a sentence of 360 months. The Seventh Circuit, relying on *Blakely*, reversed.

Fanfan was convicted by a jury of conspiracy to distribute more than 500 grams of cocaine, which authorized a maximum Guideline sentence of 78 months. At sentencing, the judge found by a preponderance that Fanfan actually controlled a much greater quantity of various illegal drugs, and that he was a leader of the operation, raising the Guideline maximum to 16 years. Relying on *Blakely*, however, the judge imposed the lower Guideline sentence authorized by the jury's verdict. The government appealed and also filed a petition for certiorari before judgment, which the Supreme Court granted. —EDS.]

II

It has been settled throughout our history that the Constitution protects every criminal defendant "against conviction except upon proof beyond a reasonable doubt of every fact necessary to constitute the crime with which he is charged." In re Winship, 397 U.S. 358, 364 (1970). It is equally clear that the "Constitution gives a criminal defendant the right to demand that a jury find him guilty of all the elements of the crime with which he is charged." United States v. Gaudin, 515 U.S. 506, 511 (1995). These basic precepts, firmly rooted in the common law, have provided the basis for recent decisions interpreting modern criminal statutes and sentencing procedures. . . .

[T]here is no distinction of constitutional significance between the Federal Sentencing Guidelines and the Washington procedures at issue in [*Blakely*]. . . . This conclusion rests on the premise, common to both systems, that the relevant sentencing rules are mandatory and impose binding requirements on all sentencing judges.

If the Guidelines as currently written could be read as merely advisory provisions that recommended, rather than required, the selection of particular sentences in response to differing sets of facts, their use would not implicate the Sixth Amendment. We have never doubted the authority of a judge to exercise broad discretion in imposing a sentence within a statutory range. See Apprendi [v. New Jersey,] 530 U.S. [466,] 481; Williams v. New York, 337 U.S. 241, 246 (1949). . . .

The Guidelines as written, however, are not advisory; they are mandatory and binding on all judges. . . . [18 U.S.C. §3553](b) directs that the court "*shall* impose a sentence of the kind, and within the range" established by the Guidelines, subject to departures in specific, limited cases. . . .

The availability of a departure in specified circumstances does not avoid the constitutional issue. . . . At first glance, one might believe that the ability of a district judge to depart from the Guidelines means that she is bound only by the statutory maximum. Were this the case, there would be no *Apprendi* problem. Importantly, however, departures are not available in every case, and in fact are unavailable in most. In most cases, as a matter of law, the Commission will have adequately taken all relevant factors into account, and no departure will be legally permissible. In those instances, the judge is bound to impose a sentence within the Guidelines range. . . .

In his dissent, Justice Breyer . . . points to traditional judicial authority to increase sentences to take account of any unusual blameworthiness in the manner employed in committing a crime, an authority that the Guidelines require to be exercised consistently throughout the system. This tradition, however, does not provide a sound guide to enforcement of the Sixth Amendment's guarantee of a jury trial in today's world.

In 1986, [we] first recognized a new trend in the legislative regulation of sentencing when we considered the significance of facts selected by legislatures that not only authorized, or even mandated, heavier sentences than would otherwise have been imposed, but increased the range of sentences possible for the underlying crime. See McMillan v. Pennsylvania, 477 U.S. 79, 87-88 (1986). Provisions for such enhancements of the permissible sentencing range reflected growing and wholly justified legislative concern about the proliferation and variety of drug crimes and their frequent identification with firearms offences.

The effect of the increasing emphasis on facts that enhanced sentencing ranges, however, was to increase the judge's power and diminish that of the jury. It became the judge, not the jury, that determined the upper limits of sentencing, and the facts determined were not required to be raised before trial or proved by more than a preponderance.

As the enhancements became greater, the jury's finding of the underlying crime became less significant. And the enhancements became very serious indeed. . . .

As it thus became clear that sentencing was no longer taking place in the tradition that Justice Breyer invokes, the Court was faced with the issue of preserving an ancient guarantee under a new set of circumstances. The new sentencing practice forced the Court to address the question how the right of jury trial could be preserved, in a meaningful way guaranteeing that the jury would still stand between the individual and the power of the government under the new sentencing regime. And it is the new circumstances, not a tradition or practice that the new circumstances have superseded, that have led us to the answer. . . . It is an answer not motivated by Sixth Amendment formalism, but by the need to preserve Sixth Amendment substance.

III

[Here, Justice Stevens considered, and rejected, arguments made by the government that *Blakely* should not apply to the Federal Guidelines because (1) they were drafted by a commission, rather than by the legislature itself; (2) prior Court decisions had upheld the constitutionality of the Guidelines; and (3) doing so would violate the principle of separation of powers, because it would effectively convert the Guidelines (which were not written by Congress) into new criminal statutes. — EDS.]

IV

All of the foregoing support our conclusion that our holding in *Blakely* applies to the Sentencing Guidelines. We recognize . . . that in some cases jury factfinding may impair the most expedient and efficient sentencing of defendants. But the interest in fairness and reliability protected by the right to a jury trial — a common-law right that defendants enjoyed for centuries and that is now enshrined in the Sixth Amendment — has always outweighed the interest in concluding trials swiftly. *Blakely*, 542 U.S. 296. As Blackstone put it:

> However *convenient* these [new methods of trial] may appear at first (as doubtless all arbitrary powers, well executed, are the most *convenient*) yet let it be again remembered, that delays, and little inconveniences in the forms of justice, are the price that all free nations must pay for their liberty in more substantial matters; that these inroads upon this sacred bulwark of the nation are fundamentally opposite to the spirit of our constitution; and that, though begun in trifles, the precedent may gradually increase and spread, to the utter disuse of juries in questions of the most momentous concerns.

4 Commentaries on the Laws of England 343-344 (1769).

Accordingly, we reaffirm our holding in *Apprendi*: Any fact (other than a prior conviction) which is necessary to support a sentence exceeding the maximum authorized by the facts established by a plea of guilty or a jury verdict must be admitted by the defendant or proved to a jury beyond a reasonable doubt.

JUSTICE BREYER delivered the opinion of the Court in part.[12]

. . . We answer the question of remedy by finding the provision of the federal sentencing statute that makes the Guidelines mandatory, 18 U.S.C. §3553(b)(1), incompatible with today's constitutional holding. We conclude that this provision must be severed and excised, as must one other statutory section, §3742(e), which depends upon the Guidelines' mandatory nature. So modified, the Federal Sentencing Act makes the Guidelines effectively advisory. It requires a sentencing court to consider Guidelines ranges, but it permits the court to tailor the sentence in light of other statutory concerns as well.

I

We answer the remedial question by looking to legislative intent. . . . We seek to determine what "Congress would have intended" in light of the Court's constitutional

___

12. Justice Breyer was joined in this part by Chief Justice Rehnquist and Justices O'Connor, Kennedy, and Ginsburg. — EDS.

holding. Denver Area Ed. Telecommunications Consortium, Inc. v. FCC, 518 U.S. 727, 767 (1996) (plurality opinion). . . . In this instance, we must determine which of the two following remedial approaches is the more compatible with the legislature's intent as embodied in the 1984 Sentencing Act.

One approach, that of Justice Stevens' dissent, would retain the Sentencing Act (and the Guidelines) as written, but would engraft onto the existing system today's Sixth Amendment "jury trial" requirement. The addition would change the Guidelines by preventing the sentencing court from increasing a sentence on the basis of a fact that the jury did not find (or that the offender did not admit).

The other approach, which we now adopt, would (through severance and excision of two provisions) make the Guidelines system advisory while maintaining a strong connection between the sentence imposed and the offender's real conduct—a connection important to the increased uniformity of sentencing that Congress intended its Guidelines system to achieve.

Both approaches would significantly alter the system that Congress designed. But today's constitutional holding means that it is no longer possible to maintain the judicial factfinding that Congress thought would underpin the mandatory Guidelines system that it sought to create. . . . Hence we must decide whether we would deviate less radically from Congress' intended system (1) by superimposing the constitutional requirement announced today or (2) through elimination of some provisions of the statute. . . .

In today's context—a highly complex statute, interrelated provisions, and a constitutional requirement that creates fundamental change—we cannot assume that Congress, if faced with the statute's invalidity in key applications, would have preferred to apply the statute in as many other instances as possible. Neither can we determine likely congressional intent mechanically. We cannot simply approach the problem grammatically, say, by looking to see whether the constitutional requirement and the words of the Act are linguistically compatible.

Nor do simple numbers provide an answer. It is, of course, true that the numbers show that the constitutional jury trial requirement would lead to additional decisionmaking by juries in only a minority of cases. . . . Prosecutors and defense attorneys would still resolve the lion's share of criminal matters through plea bargaining, and plea bargaining takes place without a jury. Many of the rest involve only simple issues calling for no upward Guidelines adjustment. And in at least some of the remainder, a judge may find adequate room to adjust a sentence within the single Guidelines range to which the jury verdict points, or within the overlap between that range and the next highest.

But the constitutional jury trial requirement would nonetheless affect every case. It would affect decisions about whether to go to trial. It would affect the content of plea negotiations. It would alter the judge's role in sentencing. Thus we must determine likely intent not by counting proceedings, but by evaluating the consequences of the Court's constitutional requirement in light of the Act's language, its history, and its basic purposes.

While reasonable minds can, and do, differ about the outcome, we conclude that the constitutional jury trial requirement is not compatible with the Act as written and that some severance and excision are necessary. . . . [I]n light of today's holding, we compare maintaining the Act as written with jury factfinding added (the dissenters' proposed remedy) to the total invalidation of the statute, and conclude that Congress would have preferred the latter. We then compare our own remedy to the total invalidation of the statute, and conclude that Congress would have preferred our remedy.

II

[Here, Justice Breyer explained that Congress relied heavily on judicial factfinding in the Sentencing Reform Act, especially for the purpose of ensuring that sentences would uniformly reflect the defendant's "real conduct," and not merely what was charged and proved at trial. Engrafting a jury-trial requirement onto the Guideline system (as the dissenters would do) would make it impossible to achieve this goal, and Congress thus would have preferred to have no Guidelines at all.—EDS.]

III

We now turn to the question of *which* portions of the sentencing statute we must sever and excise as inconsistent with the Court's constitutional requirement. Although, as we have explained, we believe that Congress would have preferred the total invalidation of the statute to the dissenters' remedial approach, we nevertheless do not believe that the entire statute must be invalidated. . . . Most of the statute is perfectly valid. . . . And we must "refrain from invalidating more of the statute than is necessary." . . . Indeed, we must retain those portions of the Act that are (1) constitutionally valid, (2) capable of "functioning independently," and (3) consistent with Congress' basic objectives in enacting the statute. [See Alaska Airlines, Inc. v. Brock, 480 U.S. 678 (1987); Regan v. Time, Inc., 468 U.S. 641 (1984) (plurality opinion).]

Application of these criteria indicates that we must sever and excise two specific statutory provisions: the provision that requires sentencing courts to impose a sentence within the applicable Guidelines range (in the absence of circumstances that justify a departure), see 18 U.S.C. §3553(b)(1), and the provision that sets forth standards of review on appeal, including de novo review of departures from the applicable Guidelines range, see §3742(e). With these two sections excised . . . , the remainder of the Act satisfies the Court's constitutional requirements.

As the Court today recognizes in its first opinion in these cases, the existence of §3553(b)(1) is a necessary condition of the constitutional violation. . . .

The remainder of the Act "functions independently." Without the "mandatory" provision, the Act nonetheless requires judges to take account of the Guidelines together with other sentencing goals. See 18 U.S.C. §3553 (a). The Act nonetheless requires judges to consider the Guidelines "sentencing range established for . . . the applicable category of offense committed by the applicable category of defendant," the pertinent Sentencing Commission policy statements, the need to avoid unwarranted sentencing disparities, and the need to provide restitution to victims. And the Act nonetheless requires judges to impose sentences that reflect the seriousness of the offense, promote respect for the law, provide just punishment, afford adequate deterrence, protect the public, and effectively provide the defendant with needed educational or vocational training and medical care. . . .

Moreover, despite the absence of §3553(b)(1), the Act continues to provide for appeals from sentencing decisions (irrespective of whether the trial judge sentences within or outside the Guidelines range in the exercise of his discretionary power under §3553(a)). See §3742(a) (appeal by defendant); §3742(b) (appeal by

Government). We concede that the excision of §3553(b)(1) requires the excision of a different, appeals-related section, namely §3742(e), which sets forth standards of review on appeal. That section contains critical cross-references to the (now-excised) §3553(b)(1) and consequently must be severed and excised for similar reasons.

Excision of §3742(e), however, does not pose a critical problem for the handling of appeals. That is because, as we have previously held, a statute that does not *explicitly* set forth a standard of review may nonetheless do so *implicitly*. See Pierce v. Underwood, 487 U.S. 552, 558-560 (1988) (adopting a standard of review, where "neither a clear statutory prescription nor a historical tradition" existed, based on the statutory text and structure, and on practical considerations). . . . We infer appropriate review standards from related statutory language, the structure of the statute, and the "sound administration of justice." *Pierce*, supra, at 559-560. And in this instance those factors . . . imply a practical standard of review already familiar to appellate courts: review for "unreasonableness." 18 U.S.C. §3742(e)(3).

. . . Section 3553(a) remains in effect, and sets forth numerous factors that guide sentencing. Those factors in turn will guide appellate courts, as they have in the past, in determining whether a sentence is unreasonable.

Taking into account the factors set forth in *Pierce*, we read the statute as implying this appellate review standard. . . . Justice Scalia believes that only in "Wonderland" is it possible to infer a standard of review after excising §3742(e). But our application of *Pierce* does not justify that characterization. *Pierce* requires us to judge the appropriateness of our inference based on the statute's language and basic purposes. We believe our inference a fair one linguistically, and one consistent with Congress' intent to provide appellate review. . . .

Nor do we share the dissenters' doubts about the practicality of a "reasonableness" standard of review. "Reasonableness" standards are not foreign to sentencing law. The Act has long required their use in important sentencing circumstances—both on review of departures, . . . and on review of sentences imposed where there was no applicable Guideline. . . . Together, these cases account for about 16.7% of sentencing appeals. . . . That is why we think it fair . . . to assume judicial familiarity with a "reasonableness" standard. And that is why we believe that appellate judges will prove capable of facing with greater equanimity than would Justice Scalia what he calls the "daunting prospect" of applying such a standard across the board.

Neither do we share Justice Scalia's belief that use of a reasonableness standard "will produce a discordant symphony" leading to "excessive sentencing disparities," and "wreak havoc" on the judicial system. The Sentencing Commission will continue to collect and study appellate court decisionmaking. It will continue to modify its Guidelines in light of what it learns, thereby encouraging what it finds to be better sentencing practices. It will thereby promote uniformity in the sentencing process. . . .

Regardless, in this context, we must view fears of a "discordant symphony," "excessive disparities," and "havoc" (if they are not themselves "gross exaggerations") with a comparative eye. We cannot and do not claim that use of a "reasonableness" standard will provide the uniformity that Congress originally sought to secure. Nor do we doubt that Congress wrote the language of the appellate provisions to correspond with the mandatory system it intended to create. . . . But, as by now should be clear, that mandatory system is no longer an open choice. And the remedial question we must ask here (as we did in respect to §3553(b)(1)) is, which alternative adheres more closely to Congress' original objective: (1) retention of sentencing appeals, or (2) invalidation of the entire Act, including its appellate provisions? The former, by providing appellate review, would tend to iron out sentencing differences; the latter would not. Hence we believe Congress would have preferred the former to the latter—even if the former means that some provisions will apply differently from the way Congress had originally expected. . . .

. . . Congress sought to "provide certainty and fairness in meeting the purposes of sentencing, [while] avoiding unwarranted sentencing disparities . . . [and] maintaining sufficient flexibility to permit individualized sentences when warranted." 28 U.S.C. §991(b)(1)(B). . . . The system remaining after excision, while lacking the mandatory features that Congress enacted, retains other features that help to further these objectives.

As we have said, the Sentencing Commission remains in place, writing Guidelines, collecting information about actual district court sentencing decisions, undertaking research, and revising the Guidelines accordingly. . . . The district courts, while not bound to apply the Guidelines, must consult those Guidelines and take them into account when sentencing. But compare post, at 4 (Scalia, J., dissenting) (claiming that the sentencing judge has the same discretion "he possessed before the Act was passed"). The courts of appeals review sentencing decisions for unreasonableness. These features of the remaining system, while not the system Congress enacted, nonetheless continue to move sentencing in Congress' preferred direction, helping to avoid excessive sentencing disparities while maintaining flexibility sufficient to individualize sentences where necessary. . . . We can find no feature of the remaining system that tends to hinder, rather than to further, these basic objectives. Under these circumstances, why would Congress not have preferred excision of the "mandatory" provision to a system that engrafts today's constitutional requirement onto the unchanged pre-existing statute—a system that, in terms of Congress' basic objectives, is counterproductive?

We do not doubt that Congress, when it wrote the Sentencing Act, intended to create a form of mandatory Guidelines system. But, we repeat, given today's constitutional holding, that is not a choice that remains open. Hence we have examined the statute in depth to determine Congress' likely intent *in light of today's holding.* . . . And we have concluded that today's holding is fundamentally inconsistent with the judge-based sentencing system that Congress enacted into law. In our view, it is more consistent with Congress' likely intent in enacting the Sentencing Reform Act (1) to preserve important elements of that system while severing and excising two provisions (§§3553(b)(1) and 3742(e)) than (2) to maintain all provisions of the Act and engraft today's constitutional requirement onto that statutory scheme.

Ours, of course, is not the last word: The ball now lies in Congress' court. The National Legislature is equipped to devise and install, long-term, the sentencing system, compatible with the Constitution, that Congress judges best for the federal system of justice.

IV

[Here, Justice Breyer considered, and rejected, arguments made by the parties for other remedies, including (1) rendering the Guidelines advisory in any case where their mandatory application would violate the Sixth Amendment (but retaining them as mandatory otherwise), and (2) excising only the provisions of the statute that require judicial factfinding.—Eds.]

V

In respondent Booker's case, . . . [w]e affirm the judgment of the Court of Appeals and remand the case. On remand, the District Court should impose a sentence in accordance with today's opinions, and, if the sentence comes before the Court of Appeals for review, the Court of Appeals should apply the review standards set forth in this opinion.

. . . Fanfan's sentence does not violate the Sixth Amendment. Nonetheless, the Government (and the defendant should he so choose) may seek resentencing under the system set forth in today's opinions. Hence we vacate the judgment of the District Court and remand the case for further proceedings consistent with this opinion.

As these dispositions indicate, we must apply today's holdings—both the Sixth Amendment holding and our remedial interpretation of the Sentencing Act—to all cases on direct review. See Griffith v. Kentucky, 479 U.S. 314, 328 (1987). . . . That fact does not mean that we believe that every sentence gives rise to a Sixth Amendment violation. Nor do we believe that every appeal will lead to a new sentencing hearing. That is because we expect reviewing courts to apply ordinary prudential doctrines, determining, for example, whether the issue was raised below and whether it fails the "plain-error" test. It is also because, in cases not involving a Sixth Amendment violation, whether resentencing is warranted or whether it will instead be sufficient to review a sentence for reasonableness may depend upon application of the harmless-error doctrine.

JUSTICE STEVENS, dissenting in part.

Neither of the two Court opinions that decide these cases finds any constitutional infirmity inherent in any provision of the Sentencing Reform Act of 1984 (SRA) or the Federal Sentencing Guidelines. Specifically, neither 18 U.S.C. §3553(b)(1), which makes application of the Guidelines mandatory, nor §3742(e), which authorizes appellate review of departures from the Guidelines, is even arguably unconstitutional. Neither the Government, nor the respondents, nor any of the numerous amici has suggested that there is any need to invalidate either provision in order to avoid violations of the Sixth Amendment in the administration of the Guidelines. The Court's decision to do so represents a policy choice that Congress has considered and decisively rejected. While it is perfectly clear that Congress has ample power to repeal these two statutory provisions if it so desires, this Court should not make that choice on Congress' behalf. I respectfully dissent from the Court's extraordinary exercise of authority. . . .

JUSTICE SCALIA, dissenting in part.

. . . I write separately mainly to add some comments regarding the change that the remedial majority's handiwork has wrought (or perhaps—who can tell?—has not wrought) upon appellate review of federal sentencing.

The remedial majority takes as the North Star of its analysis the fact that Congress enacted a "judge-based sentencing system." That seems to me quite misguided. Congress did indeed expect judges to make the factual determinations to which the Guidelines apply, just as it expected the Guidelines to be mandatory. But which of those expectations was central to the congressional purpose is not hard to determine. No headline describing the Sentencing Reform Act of 1984 (Act) would have read "Congress reaffirms judge-based sentencing" rather than "Congress prescribes standardized sentences." Justice Breyer's opinion for the Court repeatedly acknowledges that the primary objective of the Act was to reduce sentencing disparity. Inexplicably, however, the opinion concludes that the *manner* of achieving uniform sentences was more important to Congress than actually achieving uniformity—that Congress was so attached to having *judges* determine "real conduct" on the basis of bureaucratically prepared, hearsay-riddled presentence reports that it would rather lose the binding nature of the Guidelines than adhere to the old-fashioned process of having *juries* find the facts that expose a defendant to increased prison time. The majority's remedial choice is thus wonderfully ironic: In order to rescue from nullification a statutory scheme designed to eliminate discretionary sentencing, it discards the provisions that eliminate discretionary sentencing.

That is the plain effect of the remedial majority's decision to excise 18 U.S.C. §3553(b)(1). . . . District judges will no longer be told they "shall impose a sentence . . . within the range" established by the Guidelines. §3553(b)(1). Instead, under §3553(a), they will need only to "consider" that range as one of many factors, including "the need for the sentence . . . to provide just punishment for the offense," "to afford adequate deterrence to criminal conduct," and "to protect the public from the further crimes of the defendant." The statute provides no order of priority among all those factors, but since the three just mentioned are the fundamental criteria governing penology, the statute—absent the mandate of §3553(b)(1)—authorizes the judge to apply his own perceptions of just punishment, deterrence, and protection of the public even when these differ from the perceptions of the Commission members who drew up the Guidelines. Since the Guidelines are not binding, in order to comply with the (oddly) surviving requirement that the court set forth "the specific reason for the imposition of a sentence different from that described" in the Guidelines, §3553(c)(2), the sentencing judge need only state that "this court does not believe that the punishment set forth in the Guidelines is appropriate for this sort of offense." That is to say, . . . the sentencing judge, after considering the recited factors (including the Guidelines), has full discretion, as full as what he possessed before the Act was passed, to sentence anywhere within the statutory range. If the majority thought otherwise—if it thought the Guidelines not only had to be "considered" (as the amputated statute requires) but had generally to be followed—its opinion would surely say so.

As frustrating as this conclusion is to the Act's purpose of uniform sentencing, it at least establishes a clear and comprehensible regime—essentially the regime that existed before the Act became effective. That clarity is eliminated, however, by the remedial majority's surgery on 18 U.S.C. §3742, the provision governing appellate review of sentences. Even the most casual reading of this section discloses that its purpose—its *only* purpose—is to enable courts of appeals to enforce conformity with the Guidelines. . . . If the Guidelines are no longer binding, one would think that the provision designed to ensure compliance with them would, in its totality, be inoperative. The Court holds otherwise. Like a black-robed Alexander cutting the Gordian knot, it simply severs the purpose of the review provisions from their text, holding that only subsection (e), which sets forth the determinations that the court of appeals must make, is inoperative, whereas all the rest of §3742 subsists. . . . This is rather like deleting the ingredients portion of a recipe and telling the cook to proceed with the preparation portion.

The Court claims that "a statute that does not *explicitly* set forth a standard of review may nonetheless do so *implicitly*." Perhaps so. But we have before us a statute that *does* explicitly set forth a standard of review. The question is, when the Court has *severed* that standard of review (contained in §3742(e)), does it make any sense to look for some congressional "implication" of a *different* standard of review in the remnants of the statute that the Court has left standing? Only in Wonderland. (This may explain in part why . . . *none* of the numerous persons and organizations filing briefs as parties or amici in these cases—all of whom filed this side of the looking-glass—proposed, or I think even imagined, the remedial majority's wonderful disposition.) . . . The Court's need to create a new, "implied" standard of review—however "linguistically" "fair"—amounts to a confession that it has exceeded its powers. . . .

There can be no doubt that the Court's severability analysis has produced a scheme dramatically different from anything Congress has enacted since 1984. Sentencing courts are told to "provide just punishment" (among other things), and appellate courts are told to ensure that district judges are not "unreasonable." The worst feature of the scheme is that no one knows—and perhaps no one is meant to know—how advisory Guidelines and "unreasonableness" review will function in practice. . . .

[A]ny system which held it per se unreasonable (and hence reversible) for a sentencing judge to reject the Guidelines is indistinguishable from the mandatory Guidelines system that the Court today holds unconstitutional. But the remedial majority's gross exaggerations (it says that the "practical standard of review" it prescribes is "already familiar to appellate courts" . . .) may lead some courts of appeals to conclude—may indeed be designed to lead courts of appeals to conclude—that little has changed . . . ([i.e.,] within the correct Guidelines range, affirm; outside the range without adequate explanation, vacate and remand). . . . At the other extreme, a court of appeals might . . . approv[e] virtually any sentence within the statutory range . . . , so long as the district judge goes through the appropriate formalities, such as expressing his consideration of and disagreement with the Guidelines sentence. What I anticipate will happen is that "unreasonableness" review will produce a discordant symphony of different standards, varying from court to court and judge to judge. . . .

. . . Will appellate review for "unreasonableness" preserve de facto mandatory Guidelines by discouraging district courts from sentencing outside Guidelines ranges? Will it simply add another layer of unfettered judicial discretion to the sentencing process? Or will it be a mere formality, used by busy appellate judges only to ensure that busy district judges say all the right things when they explain how they have exercised their newly restored discretion? Time may tell, but today's remedial majority will not.

I respectfully dissent.

Justice Breyer, dissenting in part.

. . . The Court holds that the Sixth Amendment requires a jury, not a judge, to find sentencing facts—facts about the *way* in which an offender committed the crime—where those facts would move an offender from lower to higher Guidelines ranges. I disagree with the Court's conclusion. I find nothing in the Sixth Amendment that forbids a sentencing judge to determine (as judges at sentencing have traditionally determined) the *manner* or *way* in which the offender carried out the crime of which he was convicted. . . .

[Justice Thomas, dissenting in part, argued that 18 U.S.C. §3553(b)(1), and related portions of the Federal Guidelines, should be invalidated as applied to *Booker* (and all similar cases involving Guideline sentences based on judicial fact-finding), but should be upheld as constitutional in all other cases (including *Fanfan*), where application of the Guidelines as written would not violate the Sixth Amendment. — EDS.]

NOTES AND QUESTIONS

1. The combined effects of *Blakely* and *Booker* reverberated like shock waves through the federal and state criminal justice systems. Some jurisdictions decided to completely rewrite their sentencing laws in an attempt to conform to *Apprendi*; others took the position (perhaps just wishful thinking?) that their sentencing schemes could still be distinguished from those at issue in *Blakely* and *Booker*, and thus could be spared from the *Apprendi* avalanche. See, e.g., Cunningham v. California, 549 U.S. 270 (2007), in which California's determinate sentencing law was struck down by 6-3 (with Justices Kennedy, Breyer, and Alito dissenting); the Court, in a majority opinion written by Justice Ginsburg, rejected California's claim that its sentencing law could survive *Blakely/Booker* because it did not specify the particular "aggravating" facts necessary for a trial judge to move a defendant up from the "middle term" sentence to the "upper term" sentence for the crime of conviction, but instead left such factual findings to the "broad discretion" of the trial judge. Still other jurisdictions took a "wait and see" attitude, apparently waiting for the next shoe to drop from the Supreme Court. For a helpful summary account of the post-*Booker* landscape, see Joshua Dressler, Understanding Criminal Procedure: Adjudication 366-375 (2006); for a set of insightful scholarly contributions on the subject, see the aptly titled special issue The *Booker* Aftershock, 17 Fed. Sent. Rep., 231-290 (2005).

At least two important subsidiary questions were answered helpfully by the Court. On the same day as *Blakely*, the Court also held (by a 5-4 vote) that Ring v. Arizona — and thus, by extension, *Apprendi*, *Blakely*, and *Booker* (all three of which derived from the same source) — did *not* apply retroactively to cases litigated on federal habeas corpus review. The Court's decision in Schriro v. Summerlin, 542 U.S. 348 (2004), helped to keep *Blakely/Booker* from impacting literally hundreds of thousands of determinate sentences previously imposed in the federal and state criminal justice systems.

Moreover, *Blakely/Booker* errors *can* be held "harmless." In Washington v. Recuenco, 548 U.S. 212 (2006), the Court, in a 7-2 majority opinion written by Justice Thomas (with Justices Stevens and Ginsburg dissenting), rejected the defendant's argument that failure to submit a sentencing factor to a jury determination, under a "beyond reasonable doubt" standard, is the kind of "structural error" that automatically requires reversal in every case. The Court relied heavily on the case of Neder v. United States, 527 U.S. 1 (1999), which held that a trial court's erroneous failure to submit an element of a crime (in that case, the "materiality" of an alleged mail and wire fraud) to the jury could be subjected to "harmless error" review, because such an error "does not *necessarily* render a criminal trial fundamentally unfair or an unreliable vehicle for determining guilt or innocence." Id., at 9. The Court in *Recuenco* concluded that *Blakely/Booker* errors are "indistinguishable" from the kind of error involved in *Neder*, and thus require the same result with respect to "harmless error" analysis. Harmless error doctrine, both on direct appeal and in habeas corpus proceedings, is considered further in Chapter 17.

2. Does *Booker* reflect well on the Court? Consider the Justices' handiwork: Two majority opinions—both of whose authors also authored *dissenting* opinions. A right and a remedy that eight of the nine Justices find utterly inconsistent—and not a single word from the one Justice who believes in both. A major federal statute rewritten to require a standard of review that Congress has repeatedly rejected—all justified by the need to defer to Congress's wishes. These are not characteristics one would generally associate with wise judging. Does *Booker* seem wise to you? Does Justice Ginsburg's position?

Justice Scalia appears to be exercised about his colleagues' lack of deference to Congress. How deferential is Justice Scalia? Had his position prevailed, some sentencing factors—but only some—would have shifted from the sentencing proceeding to the trial, with a different decisionmaker and a different burden of proof. Facts that triggered a rise in the maximum sentence would be treated very differently than facts that triggered a fall, or (under *Harris*, see supra, at page 1512) that triggered a mandatory minimum sentence. No one in Congress ever proposed such a system. It does seem fair to charge Justice Breyer with rewriting the federal sentencing laws; at the same time, Justices Stevens and Scalia seemed bent on doing some considerable rewriting of their own. No one in *Booker* can fairly claim to have shown much deference to the legislative branch.

3. *Booker* took yet another step down the path the Supreme Court first trod with its decision in Apprendi v. New Jersey, see supra, at page 1509. Where does that path lead? *Apprendi* and *Blakely* were written as ringing defenses of the right to trial by jury. Sentencing guidelines and other mandatory sentencing rules supposedly threatened that right, by basing the defendant's punishment on facts found not by a jury but by a trial judge. *Apprendi* and its progeny were supposed to block that threat, to right the balance of power between judge and jury by shifting facts that bear on the defendant's culpability from the judge-controlled sentencing proceeding to the trial, where the jury would rule.

How does that balance of power look after *Booker*? Under Justice Breyer's newly voluntary Guidelines, judges will do just as much factfinding as they did before the Court's decision. Indeed, they will probably do even *more* factfinding, since judges can now base their sentences on facts other than those the Guidelines deemed relevant: yet more facts for judges to consider, as long as their sentencing decisions are "reasonable" (whatever that means). The scope of jury power does not seem any greater the day after *Booker* than it was the day before. If anything, juries are less powerful. Judges appear to be the real winners: trial judges who now have a great deal more sentencing discretion than they had before, and federal Court of Appeals judges who may now, in the guise of fleshing out Breyer's "reasonableness" standard of review, create something like a common law of sentencing.

4. Whatever the long-term practical effects of *Apprendi/Blakely/Booker* prove to be, the fact remains that the most important initiative in the realm of constitutional criminal procedure over the past two decades is the Court's expansion into sentencing law of the right to a jury trial. Is that the right that most needs expanding? The idea behind constitutional protections for criminal defendants is that minorities need protection from the majority. That idea seems especially powerful given the hugely disproportionate number of African Americans in our 2-million-plus inmate population—and the long history of abuse of black suspects and defendants by

white-dominated law enforcement agencies. If ever there were a place for strong constitutional protection of minority rights, it would seem to be America's criminal justice system.

But the jury is a very odd way to protect those rights. Juries are fundamentally majoritarian. At the time of the Founding (which, needless to say, was not a time when anyone was particularly worried about protecting the rights of black Americans), juries were seen as a way that the people — the *majority* of the people — could rein in the power of distant rulers, not a means by which discrete and insular minorities would be protected from a majority bent on locking them up. (For the classic discussion, see Akhil Reed Amar, The Bill of Rights as a Constitution, 100 Yale L.J. 1131 (1991).) Throughout the long reign of Jim Crow, the criminal jury was one of the bulwarks of white supremacy, a story well told in Michael J. Klarman, From Jim Crow to Civil Rights: The Supreme Court and the Struggle for Racial Equality (2004). Robert Caro's biography of Lyndon Johnson offers a telling example. In 1957, Congress looked likely to pass major voting rights legislation. Southern Senators could not block the legislation, so they sought a means of rendering it toothless. They found what they were looking for: The bill was amended to require a right to jury trial for any officials charged with violating black voting rights. The Southern Senators understood that no white Southern jury (blacks were kept off juries at the time) would convict in such a case. The bill was passed with the jury provision, and Southern blacks continued to be denied the right to vote. Robert A. Caro, The Years of Lyndon Johnson: Master of the Senate 944-989 (2002). Given that history, isn't it more than a little strange that the jury would wind up at the center of constitutional regulation of American criminal justice?

5. Consider another angle on the problem. Juries are supposed to be a democratic check on the criminal justice system. But why, exactly, is the criminal justice system in need of more democracy? America is the only country in the developed world that elects its prosecutors. (The vast majority of criminal prosecutions are brought by local district attorneys, nearly all of whom are elected by the counties in which they work.) That is not all: A large proportion of local trial judges are elected too, as are most of the appellate judges who review criminal convictions. The system hardly seems to suffer from a lack of democratic checks.

Given the breadth of American criminal codes and the range of the sentencing options those codes offer, it is, for the most part, relatively easy for prosecutors to convict the people they want, and to put them away for as long as they want. Or, rather, it is easy to convict and punish the people the *voters* want convicted and punished. The danger in such a system is that the voters will want to punish the wrong people, and will want to punish the right people too severely. How is that danger best addressed? Juries? Better procedural rules? Perhaps the real need is for better *substantive* rules — criminal codes and sentencing rules that define the worst and most harmful conduct and assign fair sentences. *Apprendi/Blakely/Booker* does nothing to advance *that* goal.

How is the goal best advanced? How can we make sentencing more fair? How can we make criminal justice more just?

6. Justice Breyer's majority opinion in *Booker* almost immediately gave rise to a new question: To what extent should the judicial "common law" of sentencing be influenced by the newly "voluntary" Guidelines — especially in light of Justice Breyer's remarkably opaque invitation for federal appellate courts to review sentences, post-*Booker*, for "unreasonableness"? Consider the following scenarios:

(a) What if a particular federal district judge believes (as many do) that certain personal characteristics of the defendant (e.g., the defendant's age, education, mental and physical condition, employment record, family ties, and socioeconomic status)—which the Guidelines *specifically exclude* from sentencing consideration, see U.S.S.G. §5H1—are, in fact, relevant to the goals of criminal sentencing? Justice Breyer says that judges "must consult th[e] Guidelines and take them into account when sentencing." If a judge requests, and considers, the Guideline-prohibited information at sentencing, and imposes a sentence based on such information, has she complied with Breyer's opinion? Does she have to explain (in every such case) why she is disobeying the clear mandate of the Guidelines? How should the appellate court respond?

A few days after *Booker* was decided, U.S. District Judge Lynn Adelman imposed a sentence less than one-third of what the Guidelines would have required, based on information that the defendant was a 50-year-old "devoted family man," with a solid employment history, who was responsible for the care and support of his elderly parents—all information that was excluded from consideration by the Guidelines. Judge Adelman went so far as to say that she was *required* to consider this information, because the underlying statute (18 U.S.C. §3553(a)—note that this is the very same statute upon which Breyer bases his "unreasonableness" standard of review), which remains binding, identifies "the history and characteristics of the defendant" as relevant to the goals of federal sentencing, whereas the exclusionary Guidelines provision, after *Booker*, is no longer binding. See United States v. Ranum, No. 04-CR-31 (E.D. Wis. Jan. 19, 2005).

(b) What if a particular federal district judge believes (as many do) that the Guidelines are simply too harsh (or, as is less frequently the case, too lenient) for some crime or category of crimes? Can the judge ignore the Guidelines? Does she have to explain (in every such case) why she believes the Guidelines are wrong? Is this what Breyer means by "consult[ing] the Guidelines and tak[ing] them into account"? How should the appellate court respond?

(c) What if a particular federal district judge believes (as at least some do) that sentences should be based solely on criminal conduct that is charged and proven, beyond a reasonable doubt, at trial, and should not be based on uncharged criminal conduct proven by a preponderance of the evidence at sentencing? Despite the Guidelines' central reliance on "real conduct" factors, can the judge refuse to consider any such factors offered by the prosecution at sentencing, and sentence the defendant based solely on the criminal conduct that was charged and proven at trial? Does the judge have to explain (in every such case) why she is unwilling to consider such factors? Wouldn't this be a mortal blow to the sentencing uniformity that Breyer is so desperately trying to preserve? How should the appellate court respond?

It is in this sense that *Booker* actually introduced a whole new kind of uncertainty into the old world of discretionary sentencing. In the old days, the problem was sentencing variation based on differing judicial views about sentencing policy; after *Booker*, we also began to experience sentencing variation based on differing judicial views about the binding-ness of the newly "voluntary" Guidelines.

In *Booker*, Justice Breyer seemed perfectly willing to let Congress resolve the standard of review issue: "The ball now lies in Congress' court." Congress, however, has declined to take up Justice Breyer's suggestion in any meaningful way, shape, or form. Indeed, the silence from Capitol Hill on the issue has been deafening. Does that make you feel more, or less, sanguine about what the Court did in *Booker*?

7. Unlike Justice Breyer, who (perhaps deliberately) supplied almost no content to his "unreasonableness" standard of review in *Booker*, Justice Scalia had a clear answer for the questions raised in the preceding note: "[T]he sentencing judge, after considering the recited factors (including the Guidelines), has full discretion, as full as what he possessed before the Act was passed, to sentence anywhere within the statutory range." In Scalia's view of the post-*Booker* world, in other words, the federal appellate court has no meaningful role to play, and the Guidelines are basically dead.

Aggressive appellate review, according to Scalia, would effectively re-create a quasi-mandatory Guideline system flatly inconsistent with the *other* part of the majority opinion in *Booker* (the part written by Stevens, and joined by Scalia): "[A]ny system which held it per se unreasonable (and hence reversible) for a sentencing judge to reject the Guidelines is indistinguishable from the mandatory Guidelines system that the Court today holds unconstitutional." Of course, Scalia is exactly right about this—automatic appellate reversals *would* mean that the Guidelines remain binding in effect—and it would therefore be exceedingly difficult, if not impossible, for appellate judges *both* to exert meaningful pressure on trial judges to conform to the new advisory Guidelines, *and* at the same time to avoid converting those Guidelines into unconstitutional, quasi-mandatory ones.

Is it possible for a federal district judge to have complete sentencing discretion (as apparently required by the Stevens majority opinion), but yet *not* to have it (as apparently required by the Breyer majority opinion)? Or is discretion like an on-off switch—you either have it, or you don't?

Note that even discretionary decisions traditionally are subject to the deferential "abuse of discretion" standard of review. Would it have been more acceptable, under Scalia's view, for Breyer's majority opinion in *Booker* to adopt the "abuse of discretion" standard for appellate review of sentences, rather than the "unreasonableness" one? Would this have made any difference? Don't all of the same tough questions from the preceding note inevitably arise, even under an "abuse of discretion" standard? Does this mean Scalia's position is ultimately untenable?

8. So, in the end, what *does* "reasonableness" in appellate review really mean? Does it mean a presumption in favor of within-Guidelines sentences, and against outside-Guideline sentences? If so, doesn't that essentially re-create the constitutional problem the Court faced in *Blakely* and *Booker*? But if not, aren't we right back to the "old days" of unfettered sentencing discretion, which led to the Guidelines in the first place?

GALL v. UNITED STATES

Certiorari to the United States Court of Appeals for the Eighth Circuit
552 U.S. 38 (2007)

JUSTICE STEVENS delivered the opinion of the Court.

In two cases argued on the same day last Term we considered the standard that courts of appeals should apply when reviewing the reasonableness of sentences imposed by district judges. The first, Rita v. United States, 551 U.S. 338 (2007), involved a sentence *within* the range recommended by the Federal Sentencing Guidelines; we held that when a district judge's discretionary decision in a particular case accords with the sentence the United States Sentencing Commission deems appropriate "in the mine run of cases," the court of appeals may presume that the sentence is reasonable. Id., at 347, 351.

The second case, Claiborne v. United States, involved a sentence *below* the range recommended by the Guidelines, and raised the converse question whether a court of appeals may apply a "proportionality test," and require that a sentence that constitutes a substantial variance from the Guidelines be justified by extraordinary circumstances. We did not have the opportunity to answer this question because the case was mooted by Claiborne's untimely death. Claiborne v. United States, 549 U.S. 1016 (2007) (per curiam). We granted certiorari in the case before us today in order to reach that question, left unanswered last Term. We now hold that, while the extent of the difference between a particular sentence and the recommended Guidelines range is surely relevant, courts of appeals must review all sentences—whether inside, just outside, or significantly outside the Guidelines range—under a deferential abuse-of-discretion standard. We also hold that the sentence imposed by the experienced District Judge in this case was reasonable.

I

In February or March 2000, petitioner Brian Gall, a second-year college student at the University of Iowa, was invited by Luke Rinderknecht to join an ongoing enterprise distributing a controlled substance popularly known as "ecstasy." Gall—who was then a user of ecstasy, cocaine, and marijuana—accepted the invitation. During the ensuing seven months, Gall delivered ecstasy pills, which he received from Rinderknecht, to other conspirators, who then sold them to consumers. He netted over $30,000.

A month or two after joining the conspiracy, Gall stopped using ecstasy. A few months after that, in September 2000, he advised Rinderknecht and other co-conspirators that he was withdrawing from the conspiracy. He has not sold illegal drugs of any kind since. He has, in the words of the District Court, "self-rehabilitated." App. 75. He graduated from the University of Iowa in 2002, and moved first to Arizona, where he obtained a job in the construction industry, and later to Colorado, where he earned $18 per hour as a master carpenter. He has not used any illegal drugs since graduating from college.

After Gall moved to Arizona, he was approached by federal law enforcement agents who questioned him about his involvement in the ecstasy distribution conspiracy. Gall admitted his limited participation in the distribution of ecstasy, and the agents took no further action at that time. On April 28, 2004—approximately a year and a half after this initial interview, and three and a half years after Gall withdrew from the conspiracy—an indictment was returned in the Southern District of Iowa charging him and seven other defendants with participating in a conspiracy to distribute ecstasy, cocaine, and marijuana, that began in or about May 1996 and continued through October 30, 2002. The Government has never questioned the truthfulness of any of Gall's earlier statements or contended that he played any role in, or had any knowledge of, other aspects of the conspiracy described in the indictment. When he received notice of the indictment, Gall moved back to Iowa and surrendered to the authorities. While free on his own recognizance, Gall started his own business in the construction industry, primarily engaged in subcontracting for the installation of windows and doors. In his first year, his profits were over $2,000 per month.

Gall entered into a plea agreement with the Government, stipulating that he was "responsible for, but did not necessarily distribute himself, at least 2,500 grams of [ecstasy], or the equivalent of at least 87.5 kilograms of marijuana." Id., at 25. In the agreement, the Government acknowledged that by "on or about September of 2000," Gall had communicated his intent to stop distributing ecstasy to Rinderknecht and other members of the conspiracy. Ibid. The agreement further provided that recent changes in the Guidelines that enhanced the recommended punishment for distributing ecstasy were not applicable to Gall because he had withdrawn from the conspiracy prior to the effective date of those changes.

In her presentence report, the probation officer concluded that Gall had no significant criminal history; that he was not an organizer, leader, or manager; and that his offense did not involve the use of any weapons. The report stated that Gall had truthfully provided the Government with all of the evidence he had concerning the alleged offenses, but that his evidence was not useful because he provided no new information to the agents. The report also described Gall's substantial use of drugs prior to his offense and the absence of any such use in recent years. The report recommended a sentencing range of 30 to 37 months of imprisonment.

The record of the sentencing hearing held on May 27, 2005, includes a "small flood" of letters from Gall's parents and other relatives, his fiance, neighbors, and representatives of firms doing business with him, uniformly praising his character and work ethic. . . . The [federal prosecutor] did not contest any of the evidence concerning Gall's law-abiding life during the preceding five years, but urged that "the Guidelines are appropriate and should be followed," and requested that the court impose a prison sentence within the Guidelines range. Id., at 93. He mentioned that two of Gall's co-conspirators had been sentenced to 30 and 35 months, respectively, but upon further questioning by the District Court, he acknowledged that neither of them had voluntarily withdrawn from the conspiracy.

The District Judge sentenced Gall to probation for a term of 36 months. In addition to making a lengthy statement on the record, the judge filed a detailed sentencing memorandum explaining his decision, and provided the following statement of reasons in his written judgment:

> The Court determined that, considering all the factors under 18 U.S.C. 3553(a), the Defendant's explicit withdrawal from the conspiracy almost four years before the filing of the Indictment, the Defendant's post-offense conduct, especially obtaining a college degree and the start of his own successful business, the support of family and friends, lack of criminal history, and his age at the time of the offense conduct, all warrant the sentence imposed, which was sufficient, but not greater than necessary to serve the purposes of sentencing.

Id., at 117.

At the end of both the sentencing hearing and the sentencing memorandum, the District Judge reminded Gall that probation, rather than "an act of leniency," is a "substantial restriction of freedom." Id., at 99, 125. In the memorandum, he emphasized:

> [Gall] will have to comply with strict reporting conditions along with a three-year regime of alcohol and drug testing. He will not be able to change or make

decisions about significant circumstances in his life, such as where to live or work, which are prized liberty interests, without first seeking authorization from his Probation Officer or, perhaps, even the Court. Of course, the Defendant always faces the harsh consequences that await if he violates the conditions of his probationary term.

Id., at 125.

Finally, the District Judge explained why he had concluded that the sentence of probation reflected the seriousness of Gall's offense and that no term of imprisonment was necessary:

Any term of imprisonment in this case would be counter effective by depriving society of the contributions of the Defendant who, the Court has found, understands the consequences of his criminal conduct and is doing everything in his power to forge a new life. The Defendant's post-offense conduct indicates neither that he will return to criminal behavior nor that the Defendant is a danger to society. In fact, the Defendant's post-offense conduct was not motivated by a desire to please the Court or any other governmental agency, but was the pre-Indictment product of the Defendant's own desire to lead a better life.

Id., at 125-126.

II

The Court of Appeals reversed and remanded for resentencing. Relying on its earlier opinion in United States v. Claiborne, 439 F.3d 479 (8th Cir. 2006), it held that a sentence outside of the Guidelines range must be supported by a justification that " ' "is proportional to the extent of the difference between the advisory range and the sentence imposed." ' " 446 F.3d 884, 889 (8th Cir. 2006) (quoting Claiborne, 439 F.3d, at 481, in turn quoting United States v. Johnson, 427 F.3d 423, 426-427 (7th Cir. 2005)). Characterizing the difference between a sentence of probation and the bottom of Gall's advisory Guidelines range of 30 months as "extraordinary" because it amounted to "a 100% downward variance," 446 F.3d, at 889, the Court of Appeals held that such a variance must be—and here was not—supported by extraordinary circumstances.

Rather than making an attempt to quantify the value of the justifications provided by the District Judge, the Court of Appeals identified what it regarded as five separate errors in the District Judge's reasoning: (1) He gave "too much weight to Gall's withdrawal from the conspiracy"; (2) given that Gall was 21 at the time of his offense, the District Judge erroneously gave "significant weight" to studies showing impetuous behavior by persons under the age of 18; (3) he did not "properly weigh" the seriousness of Gall's offense; (4) he failed to consider whether a sentence of probation would result in "unwarranted" disparities; and (5) he placed "too much emphasis on Gall's post-offense rehabilitation." Id., at 889-890. As we shall explain, we are not persuaded that these factors, whether viewed separately or in the aggregate, are sufficient to support the conclusion that the District Judge abused his discretion. As a preface to our discussion of these particulars, however, we shall explain why the Court of Appeals' rule requiring "proportional" justifications for departures from the Guidelines range is not consistent with our remedial opinion in United States v. Booker, 543 U.S. 220 (2005).

III

In *Booker* we invalidated both the statutory provision, 18 U.S.C. §3553(b)(1), which made the Sentencing Guidelines mandatory, and §3742(e), which directed appellate courts to apply a de novo standard of review to departures from the Guidelines. As a result of our decision, the Guidelines are now advisory, and appellate review of sentencing decisions is limited to determining whether they are "reasonable." Our explanation of "reasonableness" review in the *Booker* opinion made it pellucidly clear that the familiar abuse-of-discretion standard of review now applies to appellate review of sentencing decisions. See 543 U.S., at 260-262; see also *Rita*, 551 U.S., at 360 (Stevens, J., concurring).

It is also clear that a district judge must give serious consideration to the extent of any departure from the Guidelines and must explain his conclusion that an unusually lenient or an unusually harsh sentence is appropriate in a particular case with sufficient justifications. For even though the Guidelines are advisory rather than mandatory, they are, as we pointed out in *Rita*, the product of careful study based on extensive empirical evidence derived from the review of thousands of individual sentencing decisions. Id., at 349.

In reviewing the reasonableness of a sentence outside the Guidelines range, appellate courts may therefore take the degree of variance into account and consider the extent of a deviation from the Guidelines. We reject, however, an appellate rule that requires "extraordinary" circumstances to justify a sentence outside the Guidelines range. We also reject the use of a rigid mathematical formula that uses the percentage of a departure as the standard for determining the strength of the justifications required for a specific sentence.

As an initial matter, the approaches we reject come too close to creating an impermissible presumption of unreasonableness for sentences outside the Guidelines range. See id. ("The fact that we permit courts of appeals to adopt a presumption of reasonableness does not mean that courts may adopt a presumption of unreasonableness"). Even the Government has acknowledged that such a presumption would not be consistent with *Booker*. See Brief for United States in Rita v. United States, O.T. 2006, No. 06-5754, pp. 34-35.

The mathematical approach also suffers from infirmities of application. On one side of the equation, deviations from the Guidelines range will always appear more extreme—in percentage terms—when the range itself is low, and a sentence of probation will always be a 100% departure regardless of whether the Guidelines range is 1 month or 100 years. Moreover, quantifying the variance as a certain percentage of the maximum, minimum, or median prison sentence recommended by the Guidelines gives no weight to the "substantial restriction of freedom" involved in a term of supervised release or probation. App. 95.

We recognize that custodial sentences are qualitatively more severe than probationary sentences of equivalent terms. Offenders on probation are nonetheless subject to several standard conditions that substantially restrict their liberty. . . . Probationers may not leave the judicial district, move, or change jobs without notifying, and in some cases receiving permission from, their probation officer or the court. They must report regularly to their probation officer, permit unannounced visits to their homes, refrain from associating with any person convicted of a felony, and refrain from excessive drinking. USSG §5B1.3. Most probationers are also subject to individual "special conditions" imposed by the court. Gall, for instance, may not patronize any establishment that derives more than 50% of its revenue from the sale of alcohol, and must submit to random drug tests as directed by his probation officer. App. 109.

On the other side of the equation, the mathematical approach assumes the existence of some ascertainable method of assigning percentages to various justifications. Does withdrawal from a conspiracy justify more or less than, say, a 30% reduction? Does it matter that the withdrawal occurred several years ago? Is it relevant that the withdrawal was motivated by a decision to discontinue the use of drugs and to lead a better life? What percentage, if any, should be assigned to evidence that a defendant poses no future threat to society, or to evidence that innocent third parties are dependent on him? The formula is a classic example of attempting to measure an inventory of apples by counting oranges.

Most importantly, both the exceptional circumstances requirement and the rigid mathematical formulation reflect a practice—common among courts that have adopted "proportional review"—of applying a heightened standard of review to sentences outside the Guidelines range. This is inconsistent with the rule that the abuse-of-discretion standard of review applies to appellate review of all sentencing decisions—whether inside or outside the Guidelines range.

As we explained in *Rita*, a district court should begin all sentencing proceedings by correctly calculating the applicable Guidelines range. See 551 U.S., at 351. As a matter of administration and to secure nationwide consistency, the Guidelines should be the starting point and the initial benchmark. The Guidelines are not the only consideration, however. Accordingly, after giving both parties an opportunity to argue for whatever sentence they deem appropriate, the district judge should then consider all of the §3553(a) factors to determine whether they support the sentence requested by a party.[6] In so doing, he may not presume that the Guidelines range is reasonable. See id. He must make an individualized assessment based on the facts presented. If he decides that an outside-Guidelines sentence is warranted, he must consider the extent of the deviation and ensure that the justification is sufficiently compelling to support the degree of the variance. We find it uncontroversial that a major departure should be supported by a more significant justification than a minor one. After settling on the appropriate sentence, he must adequately explain the chosen sentence to allow for meaningful appellate review and to promote the perception of fair sentencing. Id., at 356-358.

Regardless of whether the sentence imposed is inside or outside the Guidelines range, the appellate court must review the sentence under an abuse-of-discretion standard. It must first ensure that the district court committed no significant procedural error, such as failing to calculate (or improperly calculating) the Guidelines range, treating the Guidelines as mandatory, failing to consider the §3553(a) factors, selecting a sentence based on clearly erroneous facts, or failing to adequately explain the chosen sentence—including an explanation for any deviation from the Guidelines range. Assuming that the district court's sentencing decision is procedurally sound, the appellate court should then consider the substantive reasonableness of the sentence imposed under an abuse-of-discretion standard. When conducting this review, the court will, of course, take into account the totality of the circumstances, including the extent of any variance from the Guidelines range.

---

6. . . . The fact that §3553(a) explicitly directs sentencing courts to consider the Guidelines supports the premise that district courts must begin their analysis with the Guidelines and remain cognizant of them throughout the sentencing process.

If the sentence is within the Guidelines range, the appellate court may, but is not required to, apply a presumption of reasonableness. Id., at 347. But if the sentence is outside the Guidelines range, the court may not apply a presumption of unreasonableness. It may consider the extent of the deviation, but must give due deference to the district court's decision that the §3553(a) factors, on a whole, justify the extent of the variance. The fact that the appellate court might reasonably have concluded that a different sentence was appropriate is insufficient to justify reversal of the district court.

Practical considerations also underlie this legal principle. "The sentencing judge is in a superior position to find facts and judge their import under §3553(a) in the individual case. The judge sees and hears the evidence, makes credibility determinations, has full knowledge of the facts and gains insights not conveyed by the record." Brief for Federal Public and Community Defenders et al. as Amici Curiae 16. "The sentencing judge has access to, and greater familiarity with, the individual case and the individual defendant before him than the Commission or the appeals court." *Rita*, 551 U.S., at 357-358. Moreover, "district courts have an institutional advantage over appellate courts in making these sorts of determinations, especially as they see so many more Guidelines sentences than appellate courts do." Koon v. United States, 518 U.S. 81, 98 (1996).[7]

"It has been uniform and constant in the federal judicial tradition for the sentencing judge to consider every convicted person as an individual and every case as a unique study in the human failings that sometimes mitigate, sometimes magnify, the crime and the punishment to ensue." Id., at 113.[8] The uniqueness of the individual case, however, does not change the deferential abuse-of-discretion standard of review that applies to all sentencing decisions. As we shall now explain, the opinion of the Court of Appeals in this case does not reflect the requisite deference and does not support the conclusion that the District Court abused its discretion.

IV

As an initial matter, we note that the District Judge committed no significant procedural error. He correctly calculated the applicable Guidelines range, allowed both parties to present arguments as to what they believed the appropriate sentence should be, considered all of the §3553(a) factors, and thoroughly documented his reasoning. The Court of Appeals found that the District Judge erred in failing to give proper weight to the seriousness of the offense, as required by §3553(a)(2)(A), and failing to consider whether a sentence of probation would create unwarranted disparities, as required by §3553(a)(6). We disagree.

. . . The Court of Appeals concluded that "the district court did not properly weigh the seriousness of Gall's offense" because it "ignored the serious health risks

---

7. District judges sentence, on average, 117 defendants every year. Administrative Office of United States Courts, 2006 Federal Court Management Statistics 167. . . .

8. It is particularly revealing that when we adopted an abuse-of-discretion standard in *Koon*, we explicitly rejected the Government's argument that "de novo review of departure decisions is necessary 'to protect against unwarranted disparities arising from the differing sentencing approaches of individual district judges.'" 518 U.S., at 97 (quoting Brief for United States in O.T. 1995, No. 94-1664, p. 12). Even then we were satisfied that a more deferential abuse-of-discretion standard could successfully balance the need to "reduce unjustified disparities" across the Nation and "consider every convicted person as an individual." 518 U.S., at 113.

ecstasy poses." 446 F.3d, at 890. Contrary to the Court of Appeals' conclusion, the District Judge plainly did consider the seriousness of the offense. . . . It is true that the District Judge did not make specific reference to the (unquestionably significant) health risks posed by ecstasy, but the prosecutor did not raise ecstasy's effects at the sentencing hearing. Had the prosecutor raised the issue, specific discussion of the point might have been in order, but it was not incumbent on the District Judge to raise every conceivably relevant issue on his own initiative.

The Government's legitimate concern that a lenient sentence for a serious offense threatens to promote disrespect for the law is at least to some extent offset by the fact that seven of the eight defendants in this case have been sentenced to significant prison terms. Moreover, the unique facts of Gall's situation provide support for the District Judge's conclusion that, in Gall's case, "a sentence of imprisonment may work to promote not respect, but derision, of the law if the law is viewed as merely a means to dispense harsh punishment without taking into account the real conduct and circumstances involved in sentencing." Id., at 126.

Section 3553(a)(6) requires judges to consider "the need to avoid unwarranted sentence disparities among defendants with similar records who have been found guilty of similar conduct." . . . [A]voidance of unwarranted disparities was clearly considered by the Sentencing Commission when setting the Guidelines ranges. Since the District Judge correctly calculated and carefully reviewed the Guidelines range, he necessarily gave significant weight and consideration to the need to avoid unwarranted disparities.

Moreover, . . . it seems that the judge gave specific attention to the issue of disparity when he inquired about the sentences already imposed by a different judge on two of Gall's codefendants. . . . [I]t is perfectly clear that the District Judge considered the need to avoid unwarranted disparities, but also considered the need to avoid unwarranted *similarities* among other co-conspirators who were not similarly situated. The District Judge regarded Gall's voluntary withdrawal as a reasonable basis for giving him a less severe sentence than the three codefendants . . . , who neither withdrew from the conspiracy nor rehabilitated themselves as Gall had done. We also note that neither the Court of Appeals nor the Government has called our attention to a comparable defendant who received a more severe sentence.

Since the District Court committed no procedural error, the only question for the Court of Appeals was whether the sentence was reasonable—i.e., whether the District Judge abused his discretion in determining that the §3553(a) factors supported a sentence of probation and justified a substantial deviation from the Guidelines range. As we shall now explain, the sentence was reasonable. The Court of Appeals' decision to the contrary was incorrect and failed to demonstrate the requisite deference to the District Judge's decision.

V

The Court of Appeals gave virtually no deference to the District Court's decision that the §3553(a) factors justified a significant variance in this case. Although the Court of Appeals correctly stated that the appropriate standard of review was abuse of discretion, it engaged in an analysis that more closely resembled de novo review of the facts presented and determined that, in its view, the degree of variance was not warranted.

The Court of Appeals thought that the District Court "gave too much weight to Gall's withdrawal from the conspiracy because the court failed to acknowledge the significant benefit Gall received from being subject to the 1999 Guidelines."[10] 446 F.3d, at 889. This criticism is flawed in that it ignores the critical relevance of Gall's voluntary withdrawal, a circumstance that distinguished his conduct not only from that of all his codefendants, but from the vast majority of defendants convicted of conspiracy in federal court. The District Court quite reasonably attached great weight to the fact that Gall voluntarily withdrew from the conspiracy after deciding, on his own initiative, to change his life. This lends strong support to the District Court's conclusion that Gall is not going to return to criminal behavior and is not a danger to society. See 18 U.S.C. §§3553(a)(2)(B), (C). Compared to a case where the offender's rehabilitation occurred after he was charged with a crime, the District Court here had greater justification for believing Gall's turnaround was genuine, as distinct from a transparent attempt to build a mitigation case.

The Court of Appeals thought the District Judge "gave significant weight to an improper factor" when he compared Gall's sale of ecstasy when he was a 21-year-old adult to the "impetuous and ill-considered" actions of persons under the age of 18. 446 F.3d, at 890. The appellate court correctly observed that the studies cited by the District Judge do not explain how Gall's "specific behavior in the instant case was impetuous or ill-considered." Ibid.

In that portion of his sentencing memorandum, however, the judge was discussing the "character of the defendant," not the nature of his offense. App. 122. He noted that Gall's criminal history included a ticket for underage drinking when he was 18 years old and possession of marijuana that was contemporaneous with his offense in this case. In summary, the District Judge observed that all of Gall's criminal history "including the present offense, occurred when he was twenty-one-years old or younger" and appeared "to stem from his addictions to drugs and alcohol." Id., at 123. . . .

Given the dramatic contrast between Gall's behavior before he joined the conspiracy and his conduct after withdrawing, it was not unreasonable for the District Judge to view Gall's immaturity at the time of the offense as a mitigating factor, and his later behavior as a sign that he had matured and would not engage in such impetuous and ill-considered conduct in the future. Indeed, his consideration of that factor finds support in our cases. See, e.g., Johnson v. Texas, 509 U.S. 350, 367 (1993) (holding that a jury was free to consider a 19-year-old defendant's youth when determining whether there was a probability that he would continue to commit violent acts in the future and stating that " 'youth is more than a chronological fact. It is a time and condition of life when a person may be most susceptible to influence and to psychological damage' " (quoting Eddings v. Oklahoma, 455 U.S. 104, 115 (1982))).

Finally, the Court of Appeals thought that, even if Gall's rehabilitation was dramatic and permanent, a sentence of probation for participation as a middle-man in a conspiracy distributing 10,000 pills of ecstasy "lies outside the range of choice dictated by the facts of the case." 446 F.3d, at 890. If the Guidelines were

---

10. The Court of Appeals explained that under the current Guidelines, which treat ecstasy more harshly, Gall's base offense level would have been 32, eight levels higher than the base offense level imposed under the 1999 Guidelines.

still mandatory, and assuming the facts did not justify a Guidelines-based downward departure, this would provide a sufficient basis for setting aside Gall's sentence because the Guidelines state that probation alone is not an appropriate sentence for comparable offenses. But the Guidelines are not mandatory, and thus the "range of choice dictated by the facts of the case" is significantly broadened. Moreover, the Guidelines are only one of the factors to consider when imposing sentence, and §3553(a)(3) directs the judge to consider sentences other than imprisonment.

We also note that the Government did not argue below, and has not argued here, that a sentence of probation could never be imposed for a crime identical to Gall's. Indeed, it acknowledged that probation could be permissible if the record contained different—but in our view, no more compelling—mitigating evidence. Tr. of Oral Arg. 37-38 (stating that probation could be an appropriate sentence, given the exact same offense, if "there are compelling family circumstances where individuals will be very badly hurt in the defendant's family if no one is available to take care of them"). . . .

The Court of Appeals clearly disagreed with the District Judge's conclusion that consideration of the §3553(a) factors justified a sentence of probation; it believed that the circumstances presented here were insufficient to sustain such a marked deviation from the Guidelines range. But it is not for the Court of Appeals to decide de novo whether the justification for a variance is sufficient or the sentence reasonable. On abuse-of-discretion review, the Court of Appeals should have given due deference to the District Court's reasoned and reasonable decision that the §3553(a) factors, on the whole, justified the sentence. Accordingly, the judgment of the Court of Appeals is reversed.

JUSTICE SCALIA, concurring.

I join the opinion of the Court.

In Rita v. United States, 551 U.S. 338 (2007), I wrote separately to state my view that any appellate review of sentences for substantive reasonableness will necessarily result in a sentencing scheme constitutionally indistinguishable from the mandatory Guidelines struck down in United States v. Booker, 543 U.S. 220 (2005). Whether a sentencing scheme uses mandatory Guidelines, a "proportionality test" for Guidelines variances, or a deferential abuse-of-discretion standard, there will be some sentences upheld only on the basis of additional judge-found facts.

Although I continue to believe that substantive-reasonableness review is inherently flawed, I give stare decisis effect to the statutory holding of *Rita.* The highly deferential standard adopted by the Court today will result in far fewer unconstitutional sentences than the proportionality standard employed by the Eighth Circuit. Moreover, as I noted in *Rita,* the Court has not foreclosed as-applied constitutional challenges to sentences. The door therefore remains open for a defendant to demonstrate that his sentence, whether inside or outside the advisory Guidelines range, would not have been upheld but for the existence of a fact found by the sentencing judge and not by the jury.

JUSTICE SOUTER, concurring.

I join the Court's opinion here, as I do in today's companion case of Kimbrough v. United States, 552 U.S. 85 (2007), which follow United States v. Booker, 543 U.S. 220 (2005), and Rita v. United States, 551 U.S. 338 (2007). My disagreements with holdings in those earlier cases are not the stuff of formally perpetual dissent, but I see their objectionable points hexing our judgments today, see id., at 384 (Souter, J., dissenting), and *Booker,* supra, at 272 (Stevens, J., dissenting in part). After *Booker's* remedial holding, I continue to think that the best resolution of the tension between substantial consistency throughout the system and the right of jury trial would be a new Act of Congress: reestablishing a statutory system of mandatory sentencing guidelines (though not identical to the original in all points of detail), but providing for jury findings of all facts necessary to set the upper range of sentencing discretion. See *Rita,* supra, at 392.

JUSTICE THOMAS, dissenting.
Consistent with my dissenting opinion in Kimbrough v. United States, 552 U.S. 85 (2007), I would affirm the judgment of the Court of Appeals because the District Court committed statutory error when it departed below the applicable Guidelines range.

JUSTICE ALITO, dissenting.
The fundamental question in this case is whether, under the remedial decision in United States v. Booker, 543 U.S. 220 (2005), a district court must give the policy decisions that are embodied in the Sentencing Guidelines at least some significant weight in making a sentencing decision. I would answer that question in the affirmative and would therefore affirm the decision of the Court of Appeals.

I

In *Booker,* . . . the lower federal courts were instructed that the Guidelines must be regarded as "effectively advisory," *Booker,* 543 U.S., at 245, and that individual sentencing decisions are subject to appellate review for "reasonableness." Id., at 262. The *Booker* remedial opinion did not explain exactly what it meant by a system of "advisory" guidelines or by "reasonableness" review, and the opinion is open to different interpretations.

It is possible to read the opinion to mean that district judges, after giving the Guidelines a polite nod, may then proceed essentially as if the Sentencing Reform Act had never been enacted. This is how two of the dissents interpreted the Court's opinion. . . .

While this is a possible understanding of the remedial opinion, a better reading is that sentencing judges must still give the Guidelines' policy decisions some significant weight and that the courts of appeals must still police compliance. . . . [Under such a reading], district courts are still required to give some deference to the policy decisions embodied in the Guidelines and . . . appellate review must monitor compliance. District courts must not only "consult" the Guidelines, they must "take them into account." Id., at 264. In addition, the remedial majority [in *Booker* distanced itself] from Justice Scalia's position that, under an advisory Guidelines scheme, a district judge would have "discretion to sentence anywhere within the ranges authorized by statute" so long as the judge "stated that 'this court does not believe that the punishment set forth in the Guidelines is appropriate for this sort of offense.'" Id., at 305 (opinion dissenting in part).

[I]n the remedial opinion, the Court expressed confidence that appellate review for reasonableness would help to avoid "excessive sentencing disparities" and "would tend to iron out sentencing differences." Id., at 263. Indeed, a major theme of the remedial opinion, as well as our decision last Term in Rita v. United States, 551 U.S. 338 (2007), was that the post-*Booker* sentencing regime would still promote the Sentencing Reform Act's goal of reducing sentencing disparities. . . .

It is unrealistic to think this goal can be achieved over the long term if sentencing judges need only give lip service to the Guidelines. The other sentencing factors set out in §3553(a) are so broad that they impose few real restraints on sentencing judges. See id., at 305 (Scalia, J., dissenting in part). Thus, if judges are obligated to do no more than consult the Guidelines before deciding upon the sentence that is, in their independent judgment, sufficient to serve the other §3553(a) factors, federal sentencing will not "move . . . in Congress' preferred direction." Id., at 264 (opinion of the Court). On the contrary, sentencing disparities will gradually increase. Appellate decisions affirming sentences that diverge from the Guidelines (such as the Court's decision today) will be influential, and the sentencing habits developed during the pre-*Booker* era will fade.

Finally, in reading the *Booker* remedial opinion, we should not forget the decision's constitutional underpinnings. *Booker* and its antecedents are based on the Sixth Amendment right to trial by jury. . . . It is telling that the rules set out in the Court's opinion in the present case have nothing to do with juries or factfinding and, indeed, that not one of the facts that bears on petitioner's sentence is disputed. What is at issue, instead, is the allocation of the authority to decide issues of substantive sentencing policy, an issue on which the Sixth Amendment says absolutely nothing. The yawning gap between the Sixth Amendment and the Court's opinion should be enough to show that the *Blakely/Booker* line of cases has gone astray. . . .

I recognize that the Court is committed to the *Blakely/Booker* line of cases, but we are not required to continue along a path that will take us further and further off course. Because the *Booker* remedial opinion may be read to require sentencing judges to give weight to the Guidelines, I would adopt that interpretation and thus minimize the gap between what the Sixth Amendment requires and what our cases have held.

II

[In this last section, which is omitted, Justice Alito found "no evidence that the District Court deferred to the Guidelines to any significant degree," but instead simply "determined what it thought was appropriate under the circumstances and sentenced petitioner accordingly." He noted that "abuse-of-discretion review is not toothless," and ultimately agreed with the Eighth Circuit that "the District Court did not properly exercise its discretion."—EDS.]

NOTES AND QUESTIONS

1. Does *Gall* resolve the conflict between Justice Breyer and Justice Scalia over the proper standard of review for Guideline cases? Or does it leave the issue still unsettled? Does the fact that both Breyer and Scalia joined the majority opinion help you to answer these questions?

2. In Kimbrough v. United States, 552 U.S. 85 (2007), the companion case to *Gall*, the Supreme Court upheld as "reasonable" a district judge's decision to deviate from the Guidelines based on the judge's disagreement with the wide sentencing

disparity between crimes involving crack cocaine and powder cocaine. The Court, in a majority opinion by Justice Ginsburg, explained that "closer review may be in order when the sentencing judge varies from the Guidelines based solely on the judge's view that the Guidelines range 'fails properly to reflect §3553(a) considerations' even in a mine-run case," but concluded that the instant case "presents no occasion for elaborative discussion of this matter," because the Guidelines for crack cocaine crimes "do not exemplify the Commission's exercise of its characteristic institutional role." Instead, those Guidelines, according to the Court, were more or less forced upon the Sentencing Commission by Congress's failure properly to address the crack/powder distinction in several statutes creating mandatory minimum sentences. Justice Scalia joined the majority opinion, but also added, in concurrence, that nothing in *Kimbrough* should be read as inconsistent with prior Court decisions holding that "the district court is free to make its own reasonable application of the §3553(a) factors, and to reject (after due consideration) the advice of the Guidelines."

For a helpful analysis of *Kimbrough* and its confusing consequences in the federal appellate courts, see Carissa Byrne Hessick, Appellate Review of Sentencing Policy Decisions After *Kimbrough*, 93 Marq. L. Rev. 717 (2009). As Professor Hessick explains:

> In light of the ambiguous language contained in the *Kimbrough* decision and the criticism that can be leveled at the opinion, it may come as no surprise that the circuits have taken several different approaches to reviewing district court policy determinations after *Kimbrough*. Indeed, the Court has already decided an additional case in order to clarify some ambiguous dicta from *Kimbrough* that led several circuits to permit district courts to vary from the crack cocaine Guidelines based only on individual case or defendant characteristics, rather than based on categorical policy disagreements. Spears v. United States[, 129 S. Ct. 840 (2009),] confirmed that "district courts are entitled to reject and vary categorically from the crack-cocaine Guidelines based on a policy disagreement with those Guidelines," as opposed to case-specific criteria. But several other points of contention remain, including whether to follow the closer review dictum, what effect *Kimbrough* had on prior circuit precedent, and whether certain Guidelines represent policy choices by the Commission or by Congress. The circuits disagree on each of these questions. . . .
>
> The Court's decision in *Kimbrough* was designed to clarify uncertainty surrounding the new form of appellate sentencing review established in *Booker*. It appears, however, that *Kimbrough* may have actually resulted in more appellate uncertainty. Some of this uncertainty is attributable to the Court's dicta suggesting the level of appellate scrutiny of district court disagreement with Guidelines' policy may depend on whether a particular Guideline is the product of "empirical data and national experience." But, even without such dicta, appellate review of district court sentencing decisions is likely to occur differently in different circuits. That is because the *Booker* remedy—solving the Sixth Amendment problem by restoring district court discretion while, at the same time, seeking to preserve some adherence to the Guidelines through appellate review—is internally inconsistent and thus inherently unstable. Some circuits are inevitably going to prioritize one facet of the *Booker* remedy over the other, and thus circuit conflict is likely to continue.

Id., at 733, 749. For another helpful article examining the impact of *Blakely/Booker* in the state courts, see John F. Pfaff, The Future of Appellate Sentencing Review: *Booker* in the States, 93 Marq. L. Rev. 683 (2009).

3. In the first major empirical study to compare the actual sentencing behavior of federal district judges before and after the Court's decisions in *Gall* and *Kimbrough*, Professor Ryan W. Scott examined a unique data set of federal criminal cases from the District of Massachusetts, the only federal district in the United States that reports publicly the "Statement of Reasons" for almost all sentencing decisions[13] including the offense level, criminal history, Guideline range, any statutory minimum sentence, and the basis for any departure from the Guidelines. Scott was able to match this case-specific sentencing information with corresponding information from public docket entries, thereby identifying the specific judges who rendered each particular sentence. After limiting the study to those judges who (1) drew their cases randomly from the same shared pool and (2) imposed at least 25 sentences between October 1, 2001, and September 30, 2008, Scott ended up with a data set of 2,262 sentences imposed by ten district judges. Comparing individual judicial sentencing behavior during three separate time periods—before *Booker*, between *Booker* and *Gall/Kimbrough*, and after *Gall/Kimbrough*—Scott reports:

Analysis of the Boston data reveals a clear increase in inter-judge sentencing disparity, both in sentence length and in guideline sentencing patterns. The effect of the judge on sentence length has doubled in strength since *Kimbrough* and *Gall*. And in their guideline sentencing patterns, judges have responded in starkly different ways to *Booker*, with some following a "free at last" pattern and others a "business as usual" pattern. . . .

Among Boston judges as a whole, average sentence length has increased since *Booker*. . . . Average sentence length climbed from 47.7 months before *Booker*, to 58.3 months in the years following *Booker*, to 63.7 months after *Kimbrough* and *Gall*. Excluding cases subject to a mandatory minimum, the increase is more gradual, from 30.8 months before *Booker*, to 33.7 months after *Booker*, to 35.5 months after *Kimbrough* and *Gall*.

But average sentence length for the district as a whole masks significant variation among individual judges. . . . Although the difference between the highest and lowest averages remains essentially unchanged between periods, the distribution of averages has widened compared to the pre-*Booker* period. After *Kimbrough* and *Gall*, in particular, two clusters of judges are readily apparent: one cluster following the trend toward higher sentences with averages around 70 months, and another cluster splitting off with averages around 45 months.

Statistical analysis confirms that the effect of the judge on sentence length has grown stronger since *Kimbrough* and *Gall*. . . . [T]he regression models indicate a delayed reaction, but ultimately a sharp uptick in inter-judge sentencing disparity since *Booker*. In the years before the decision, the percentage of variance in sentence length explained by the identity of the judge stood at 2.9%. Immediately after *Booker*, the rate actually declined slightly to 2.5%. But in the *Kimbrough/Gall* period, it rose sharply to 6.1%. That means the effect of the judge on sentence length is now more than twice as strong as in the three years before *Booker*.

The increase in inter-judge disparity is even clearer in cases not governed by a mandatory minimum sentence. . . . For cases not subject to a mandatory minimum, the trend is unmistakable. The distribution of average sentences among judges has grown substantially wider since *Booker*: from a total spread of 15 months before *Booker*, to almost 30 months after *Booker*, to almost 40 months in the wake of *Kimbrough* and *Gall*.

---

13. The "Statement of Reasons" is not made public if the presiding judge orders it sealed.

The stark differences between judges have real consequences for criminal defendants. Before *Booker*, regardless of the judge, a defendant in Boston not facing a mandatory minimum could expect that the judge's average sentence would fall between 25.9 months and 40.2 months. Today, after *Kimbrough* and *Gall*, three judges on the court are imposing average sentences of 25.5 months or less, while two other judges on the court are imposing average sentences of 51.4 months or more. That is an average difference of more than two years in prison, depending on which judge is assigned to the case. . . .

Statistical analysis of how far, on average, each judge has sentenced from the guideline range confirms an increase in inter-judge disparity in guideline sentencing. . . . Under the mandatory Guidelines in 2002-2003, average distance from the guideline range was tightly clustered within a range of 4.5 months. . . . But after *Booker*, the distribution has widened dramatically and grown broader in every period. In the most recent period, following *Kimbrough* and *Gall*, average distances from the Guidelines span 20.0 months, ranging from 4.2 months to a remarkable 24.2 months.

As expected, the trend is even more pronounced for "discretionary" sentences in which the sentencing judge was free, as a legal and practical matter, to sentence outside the guideline range. . . . For criminal defendants in the 80% of cases where the judge has full discretion to sentence outside the guideline range, [i.e., those that did not involve the constraints of a mandatory minimum, time already served that exceeded the Guideline minimum sentence, or a Guideline recommendation of probation,] the difference between judges has serious consequences. Under the mandatory Guidelines in 2002-2003, regardless of the judge assigned to the case, a criminal defendant could expect an average sentence 7.8 months or less [in terms of distance] from the Guidelines. Today, in the wake of *Kimbrough* and *Gall*, three judges in Boston continue to sentence on average 6.1 months or less from the guideline range. But a different group of three Boston judges sentences, on average, 24.6 months or more from the guideline range. That is an average difference of more than a year and a half in prison, depending on the judge.

Ryan W. Scott, Inter-Judge Sentencing Disparity After *Booker*: A First Look, 63 Stan. L. Rev. 1 (2010), available online at http://papers.ssrn.com/sol3/papers. cfm?abstract_id=1446744.

Does Professor Scott's study suggest that Justice Breyer's attempt to keep the Guidelines "semi-binding" has proved at least partially effective, because at least *some* district judges continue to sentence mostly according to the Guidelines? Or does Justice Scalia get the last laugh, because *other* district judges now feel "free at last" to disobey the Guidelines? Does adding a brand new source of sentencing disparity—i.e., the extent to which a particular district judge, after *Booker*, *Gall*, and *Kimbrough*, now views the Guidelines as "semi-binding" (per Breyer) or "advisory only" (per Scalia)—to all of the traditional sources of sentencing disparity seem like a move in the right direction?

4. *Booker*, *Gall*, and *Kimbrough* might be viewed as calling into question the fundamental premises underlying *Apprendi* and *Blakely*, because they each approved a remedial scheme that (at least in the view of Justice Scalia, the author of *Blakely* and thus the chief architect of the prevailing *Apprendi* doctrine) seems incompatible with those premises. But those three cases did not directly challenge the *Apprendi* doctrine itself. Then along came the case of Oregon v. Ice, 555 U.S. 160 (2009). Under Oregon law, Ice—who was convicted of multiple crimes in a single trial—was subject to consecutive rather than concurrent sentences only if the trial judge made a factual finding that the crimes involved separate incidents, or if (in

the same incident) the defendant manifested a "willingness to commit more than one criminal offense" or the crimes created a risk of "greater or qualitatively different loss, injury or harm to the victim." The judge made such factual findings in Ice's case, and Ice was given consecutive sentences that totaled 340 months in prison.

The Court held that Ice's consecutive sentencing did not violate *Apprendi* or *Blakely/Booker.* In a majority opinion by Justice Ginsburg, joined by Justices Stevens, Kennedy, Breyer, and Alito, the Court explained:

> This case concerns the scope of the Sixth Amendment's jury-trial guarantee, as construed in Apprendi v. New Jersey, 530 U.S. 466 (2000), and Blakely v. Washington, 542 U.S. 296 (2004). Those decisions are rooted in the historic jury function—determining whether the prosecution has proved each element of an offense beyond a reasonable doubt. They hold that it is within the jury's province to determine any fact (other than the existence of a prior conviction) that increases the maximum punishment authorized for a particular offense. Thus far, the Court has not extended the *Apprendi* and *Blakely* line of decisions beyond the offense-specific context that supplied the historic grounding for the decisions. The question here presented concerns a sentencing function in which the jury traditionally played no part: When a defendant has been tried and convicted of multiple offenses, each involving discrete sentencing prescriptions, does the Sixth Amendment mandate jury determination of any fact declared necessary to the imposition of consecutive, in lieu of concurrent, sentences? . . .
>
> Our application of *Apprendi*'s rule must honor the "long-standing common-law practice" in which the rule is rooted. . . . The rule's animating principle is the preservation of the jury's historic role as a bulwark between the State and the accused at the trial for an alleged offense. See *Apprendi*, 530 U.S., at 477. Guided by that principle, our opinions make clear that the Sixth Amendment does not countenance legislative encroachment on the jury's traditional domain. See id., at 497. We accordingly considered whether the finding of a particular fact was understood as within "the domain of the jury . . . by those who framed the Bill of Rights." Harris v. United States, 536 U.S. 545, 557 (2002) (plurality opinion). In undertaking this inquiry, we remain cognizant that administration of a discrete criminal justice system is among the basic sovereign prerogatives States retain. See, e.g., Patterson v. New York, 432 U.S. 197, 201 (1977).
>
> These twin considerations—historical practice and respect for state sovereignty—counsel against extending *Apprendi*'s rule to the imposition of sentences for discrete crimes. The decision to impose sentences consecutively is not within the jury function that "extends down centuries into the common law." *Apprendi*, 530 U.S., at 477. Instead, specification of the regime for administering multiple sentences has long been considered the prerogative of state legislatures.
>
> Members of this Court have warned against "wooden, unyielding insistence on expanding the *Apprendi* doctrine far beyond its necessary boundaries." Cunningham [v. California], 549 U.S. [270], 295 (Kennedy, J., dissenting). The jury-trial right is best honored through a "principled rationale" that applies the rule of the *Apprendi* cases "within the central sphere of their concern." 549 U.S., at 295. Our disposition today—upholding an Oregon statute that assigns to judges a decision that has not traditionally belonged to the jury—is faithful to that aim.

Id., at 163, 167-168, 172. Justice Scalia, predictably, was not amused:

> [T]he Court attempts to distinguish Oregon's sentencing scheme by reasoning that the rule of *Apprendi* applies only to the length of a sentence for an individual crime and not to the total sentence for a defendant. I cannot understand why we would make such a strange exception to the treasured right of trial by jury. Neither the

reasoning of the *Apprendi* line of cases, nor any distinctive history of the factfinding necessary to imposition of consecutive sentences, nor (of course) logic supports such an odd rule. . . .

To support its distinction-without-a-difference, the Court puts forward the same (the *very* same) arguments regarding the history of sentencing that were rejected by *Apprendi*. Here, it is entirely irrelevant that common-law judges had discretion to impose either consecutive or concurrent sentences, just as there it was entirely irrelevant that common-law judges had discretion to impose greater or lesser sentences (within the prescribed statutory maximum) for individual convictions. . . . Our concern here is precisely the same as our concern in *Apprendi*: What happens when a State breaks from the common-law practice of discretionary sentences and permits the imposition of an elevated sentence only upon the showing of extraordinary facts? In such a system, the defendant "is *entitled* to" the lighter sentence "and by reason of the Sixth Amendment[,] the facts bearing upon that entitlement must be found by a jury." *Blakely*, 542 U.S., at 309. . . .

Today's opinion muddies the waters, and gives cause to doubt whether the Court is willing to stand by *Apprendi*'s interpretation of the Sixth Amendment's jury-trial guarantee.

Id., at 173-175, 178. Does *Ice* truly represent the beginning of the end for the *Apprendi/Blakely/Booker* doctrine? Or is it a one-off exception that leaves the core of the rule unscathed?

5. In Southern Union Co. v. United States, 132 S. Ct. 2344 (2012), the Court addressed the issue whether *Apprendi* doctrine applies to the imposition of criminal fines. In a (remarkably historically detailed) majority opinion by Justice Sotomayor, joined by Chief Justice Roberts and Justices Scalia, Thomas, Ginsburg, and Kagan, the Court held that the answer is "yes"—so long as the criminal fine in question is substantial enough to render the relevant criminal case "non-petty," and thereby trigger the Sixth Amendment's right to jury trial, on which *Apprendi* is largely based. [A quick editorial aside: Does the due process component of *Apprendi* doctrine, which requires all facts that determine the defendant's maximum sentence to be found "beyond a reasonable doubt," apply even to those "non-petty" criminal cases to which the Sixth Amendment's right to jury trial is inapplicable? That's a pretty interesting question, and one about which the Court does not yet seem to have carefully thought.] In *Southern Union Co.*, the Court explicitly rejected the argument of the dissenters—Justice Breyer, joined by Justices Kennedy and Alito—that *Ice* was good precedent for refusing to extend *Apprendi* to contexts beyond the "central sphere of [its] concern." According to the majority: "While the punishments at stake in [prior] cases were imprisonment or a death sentence, we see no principled basis under *Apprendi* for treating criminal fines differently. . . . In stating *Apprendi*'s rule, we have never distinguished one form of punishment from another. Instead, our decisions broadly prohibit judicial factfinding that increases maximum criminal 'sentence[s],' 'penalties,' or 'punishment[s]'—terms that each undeniably embrace fines."

6. In Peugh v. United States, 133 S. Ct. 1310 (2013), the Court ruled by 5-4 that the Federal Sentencing Guidelines—notwithstanding their "advisory" nature, ever since *Booker*—carry sufficiently persuasive force with sentencing judges to trigger the protection of the Ex Post Facto Clause. Thus, when an applicable sentencing guideline was increased after the defendant's commission of the crime, but before his sentencing, the defendant was entitled to be sentenced under the prior version. Justice Sotomayor's lead opinion was joined by Justices Ginsburg, Breyer, and Kagan in full,

and by Justice Kennedy with the exception of a section that discussed broadly the "animating principles" of "fundamental justice" that underlie the Ex Post Facto Clause.

7. In Alleyne v. United States, 133 S. Ct. 2151 (2013), the Court returned once again to the subject of mandatory minimum sentences. By a margin of 5-4, and with five separate opinions, the Court in *Alleyne* overruled Harris v. United States, the 2002 decision that reaffirmed McMillan v. Pennsylvania, the 1986 decision that upheld the constitutionality of allowing judges to make the factual findings upon which "mandatory minimum" sentences were based. Justice Thomas wrote, in a portion of his lead opinion that managed to garner five votes:

> It is indisputable that a fact triggering a mandatory minimum alters the prescribed range of sentences to which a criminal defendant is exposed. *Apprendi*, supra, at 490; *Harris*, 536 U.S., at 575, 582 (Thomas, J., dissenting). . . .
>
> It is impossible to dissociate the floor of a sentencing range from the penalty affixed to the crime. See *Harris*, supra, at 569 (Breyer, J., concurring in part and concurring in judgment) (facts increasing the minimum and facts increasing the maximum cannot be distinguished "in terms of logic"). Indeed, criminal statutes have long specified both the floor and ceiling of sentence ranges, which is evidence that both define the legally prescribed penalty. . . . This historical practice allowed those who violated the law to know, ex ante, the contours of the penalty that the legislature affixed to the crime—and comports with the obvious truth that the floor of a mandatory range is as relevant to wrongdoers as the ceiling. A fact that increases a sentencing floor, thus, forms an essential ingredient of the offense.
>
> Moreover, it is impossible to dispute that facts increasing the legally prescribed floor aggravate the punishment. *Harris*, supra, at 579 (Thomas, J., dissenting). . . . Elevating the low-end of a sentencing range heightens the loss of liberty associated with the crime: the defendant's "expected punishment has increased as a result of the narrowed range" and "the prosecution is empowered, by invoking the mandatory minimum, to require the judge to impose a higher punishment than he might wish." *Apprendi*, supra, at 522 (Thomas, J., concurring). Why else would Congress link an increased mandatory minimum to a particular aggravating fact other than to heighten the consequences for that behavior? . . . This reality demonstrates that the core crime and the fact triggering the mandatory minimum sentence together constitute a new, aggravated crime, each element of which must be submitted to the jury.[2]
>
> Defining facts that increase a mandatory statutory minimum to be part of the substantive offense enables the defendant to predict the legally applicable penalty from the face of the indictment. See *Apprendi*, 530 U.S., at 478-479. It also preserves the historic role of the jury as an intermediary between the State and criminal defendants. . . .
>
> Because there is no basis in principle or logic to distinguish facts that raise the maximum from those that increase the minimum, *Harris* was inconsistent with *Apprendi*. It is, accordingly, overruled.[5]

2. Juries must find any facts that increase either the statutory maximum or minimum because the Sixth Amendment applies where a finding of fact both alters the legally prescribed range and does so in a way that aggravates the penalty. Importantly, this is distinct from factfinding used to guide judicial discretion in selecting a punishment "within limits fixed by law." Williams v. New York, 337 U.S. 241, 246 (1949). While such findings of fact may lead judges to select sentences that are more severe than the ones they would have selected without those facts, the Sixth Amendment does not govern that element of sentencing. Infra, at 15-17, and n. 6.

5. The force of stare decisis is at its nadir in cases concerning procedural rules that implicate fundamental constitutional protections. Because *Harris* is irreconcilable with the reasoning of *Apprendi* and the original meaning of the Sixth Amendment, we follow the latter.

Id., at 2160-2162. Chief Justice Roberts, joined by Justices Scalia and Kennedy, dissented on the grounds that the majority was taking *Apprendi* doctrine too far, thus demonstrating a fundamental lack of understanding of the doctrine:

> Suppose a jury convicts a defendant of a crime carrying a sentence of five to ten years. And suppose the judge says he would sentence the defendant to five years, but because he finds that the defendant used a gun during the crime, he is going to add two years and sentence him to seven. No one thinks that this violates the defendant's right to a jury trial in any way.
>
> Now suppose the legislature says that two years should be added to the five year minimum, if the judge finds that the defendant used a gun during the crime. Such a provision affects the role of the judge—limiting his discretion—but has no effect on the role of the jury. And because it does not affect the jury's role, it does not violate the jury trial guarantee of the Sixth Amendment.
>
> The Framers envisioned the Sixth Amendment as a protection for defendants from the power of the Government. The Court transforms it into a protection for judges from the power of the legislature. For that reason, I respectfully dissent.

Id., at 2167-2168. Justice Alito also dissented, in an opinion that seemed to presage continuing instability in the federal constitutional law of sentencing:

> . . . If the Court is of a mind to reconsider existing precedent, a prime candidate should be Apprendi v. New Jersey, 530 U.S. 466 (2000). . . .
>
> The Court's decision creates a precedent about precedent that may have greater precedential effect than the dubious decisions on which it relies.*

Id., at 2172-2173.

8. After *Alleyne,* is there any kind of judicial factfinding at sentencing that still survives the *Apprendi/Blakely/Booker* onslaught? Perhaps there is one: Judicial factfinding about a defendant's prior criminal record, which apparently still remains permissible under *Almendarez-Torres* (see supra, at page 1510). Is it only stare decisis that keeps *Almendarez-Torres* alive? Does stare decisis really seem to matter very much in this particular context, given how often the Court has reversed course on more important constitutional questions related to *Apprendi* over the past several years?

---

* . . . [O]ther than the fact that there are currently five Justices willing to vote to overrule *Harris,* and not five Justices willing to overrule *Apprendi,* there is no compelling reason why the Court overrules the former rather than the latter. If the opportunity arises in the future to overrule *Apprendi* or the present case . . . the precedent the Court sets today will be relevant to the issue of stare decisis.

Chapter 16

Double Jeopardy

The double jeopardy clause of the Fifth Amendment provides, "[N]or shall any person be subject for the same offence to be twice put in jeopardy of life or limb." That simple phrase has produced a varied set of legal doctrines of astonishing complexity. While most of the doctrines themselves are settled—relatively few issues in double jeopardy law are up for grabs at the present time—there is no agreed-upon theory that unites them. As you work through the doctrinal tangles below, ask yourself two questions: (1) What is the purpose of the ban on double jeopardy in this context? (2) How does this legal rule further that purpose?

Begin with the fact that the ban on double jeopardy "consist[s] of three separate constitutional protections. It protects against a second prosecution for the same offense after acquittal. It protects against a second prosecution for the same offense after conviction. And it protects against multiple punishments for the same offense." North Carolina v. Pearce, 395 U.S. 711, 717 (1969). Actually, there is a fourth protection: The double jeopardy clause also protects the defendant's interest in having his case decided by a particular judge or jury. The need to protect that interest explains the rule banning retrial after a mistrial, unless the mistrial was justified by what the Court calls "manifest necessity." None of these protections is absolute; each exists within a network of exceptions and conditions—the rationales for which are often obscure.

The material below is divided into four sections. First, in Section A, we take up the meaning of the phrase "twice put in jeopardy," and the two major doctrines that phrase has spawned: double jeopardy's "acquittal rule" and the presumptive ban on prosecution after a mistrial. Next, in Section B, the chapter turns to the meaning of the other key phrase of the double jeopardy clause: "for the same offence." That has been the locus of most double jeopardy litigation over the past two decades. Section C discusses the "dual sovereignty" doctrine, which holds that multiple prosecutions for the same crime by different sovereigns—different states, or a state and the federal government—are permissible. Section D concludes with an important boundary question: What counts as a criminal prosecution for purposes of double jeopardy law?

A.   *"Twice Put in Jeopardy"*

1.   Acquittals

FONG FOO v. UNITED STATES

Certiorari to the United States Court of Appeals for the First Circuit
369 U.S. 141 (1962)

PER CURIAM.

The petitioners, a corporation and two of its employees, were brought to trial before a jury in a federal district court upon an indictment charging a conspiracy and the substantive offense of concealing material facts in a matter within the jurisdiction of an agency of the United States, in violation of 18 U.S.C. §§371 and 1001. After seven days of what promised to be a long and complicated trial, three government witnesses had appeared and a fourth was in the process of testifying. At that point the district judge directed the jury to return verdicts of acquittal as to all the defendants, and a formal judgment of acquittal was subsequently entered.

The record shows that the district judge's action was based upon one or both of two grounds: supposed improper conduct on the part of the Assistant United States Attorney who was prosecuting the case, and a supposed lack of credibility in the testimony of the witnesses for the prosecution who had testified up to that point.

The Government filed a petition for a writ of mandamus in the Court of Appeals for the First Circuit, praying that the judgment of acquittal be vacated and the case reassigned for trial. The court granted the petition, upon the ground that under the circumstances revealed by the record the trial court was without power to direct the judgment in question. Judge Aldrich concurred separately, finding that the directed judgment of acquittal had been based solely on the supposed improper conduct of the prosecutor, and agreeing with his colleagues that the district judge was without power to direct an acquittal on that ground. 286 F.2d 556. We granted certiorari to consider a question of importance in the administration of justice in the federal courts.

In holding that the District Court was without power to direct acquittals under the circumstances disclosed by the record, the Court of Appeals relied primarily upon two decisions of this Court, Ex parte United States, 242 U.S. 27, and Ex parte United States, 287 U.S. 241. In the first of these cases it was held that a district judge had no power to suspend a mandatory prison sentence, and that a writ of mandamus would lie to require the judge to vacate his erroneous order of suspension. In the second case the Court issued a writ of mandamus ordering a district judge to issue a bench warrant which he had refused to do, in the purported exercise of his discretion, for a person under an indictment returned by a properly constituted grand jury.

Neither of those decisions involved the guaranty of the Fifth Amendment that no person shall "be subject for the same offence to be twice put in jeopardy of life or limb." That constitutional provision is at the very root of the present case, and we cannot but conclude that the guaranty was violated when the Court of Appeals set aside the judgment of acquittal and directed that the petitioners be tried again for the same offense.

The petitioners were tried under a valid indictment in a federal court which had jurisdiction over them and over the subject matter. The trial did not terminate prior to the entry of judgment, as in Gori v. United States, 367 U.S. 364. It terminated with the entry of a final judgment of acquittal as to each petitioner. The Court of Appeals thought, not without reason, that the acquittal was based upon an egregiously erroneous foundation. Nevertheless, "[t]he verdict of acquittal was final, and could not be reviewed . . . without putting [the petitioners] twice in jeopardy, and thereby violating the Constitution." United States v. Ball, 163 U.S. 662, 671. . . .

MR. JUSTICE HARLAN, concurring.

Were I able to find, as Judge Aldrich did, that the District Court's judgment of acquittal was based solely on the Assistant United States Attorney's *alleged* misconduct, I would think that a retrial of the petitioners would not be prevented by the Double Jeopardy Clause of the Fifth Amendment. Even assuming that a trial court may have power, in extreme circumstances, to direct a judgment of acquittal, instead of declaring a mistrial, because of a prosecutor's misconduct—a proposition which I seriously doubt—I do not think that such power existed in the circumstances of this case. But since an examination of the record leaves me unable, as it did the majority of the Court of Appeals, to attribute the action of the District Court to this factor alone, I concur in the judgment of reversal.

MR. JUSTICE CLARK, dissenting.

The Court speaks with such expanse that I am obliged to dissent. It says that because "a final judgment of acquittal" was entered pursuant to a directed verdict the propriety of such "acquittal" cannot be reviewed even though the Government had not concluded its main case at the time the verdict was directed. The District Court under the circumstances here clearly had no power to direct a verdict of acquittal or to enter a judgment thereon. In my view when a trial court has no power to direct such a verdict, the judgment based thereon is a nullity. The word "acquittal" in this context is no magic open sesame freeing in this case two persons and absolving a corporation from serious grand jury charges of fraud upon the Government.

On the record before us it matters not whether the so-called acquittal was pursuant to the trial court's conclusion that the Government's witnesses up to that point lacked credibility or was based on the alleged misconduct of the prosecution.

On the first point, the Government had only examined three of its witnesses and was in the process of examining a fourth when the acquittal was entered. . . .

It is fundamental in our criminal jurisprudence that the public has a right to have a person who stands legally indicted by a grand jury publicly tried on the charge. No judge has the power before hearing the testimony proffered by the Government or at least canvassing the same to enter a judgment of acquittal and thus frustrate the Government in the performance of its duty to prosecute those who violate its law.

. . . As the majority of the Court of Appeals observed, the District Court:

> abruptly terminated the Government's case . . . long before the Government had had an opportunity to show whether or not it had a case; and, moreover, he did so in ignorance of either the exact nature or the cogency of the specific evidence of guilt which Government's counsel said he had available and was ready to present. 286 F.2d, at 562-563.

At such a stage of the case the District Court had no power to prejudge the Government's proof—find it insufficient or unconvincing—and set the petitioners free.

On the second point, even if there were misconduct, the court still had no power to punish the Government because of the indiscretion of its lawyer. As this Court said in McGuire v. United States, 273 U.S. 95, 99 (1927), "A criminal prosecution is more than a game in which the Government may be checkmated and the game lost merely because its officers have not played according to rule." At most, if there had been misconduct, the remedy would have been to declare a mistrial and impose appropriate punishment upon the Assistant United States Attorney, rather than upon the public. In my view the judgment of the Court of Appeals should, therefore, be affirmed.

NOTES ON THE SPECIAL STATUS OF ACQUITTALS

Fong Foo stands for the proposition that acquittals are final, even when clearly mistaken. This proposition is as much of an absolute as you are likely to find anywhere in the law. There is only one scenario that has ever been held (and only by an intermediate appellate court, not by the Supreme Court) to be an exception to that proposition: when the acquittal was obtained by bribing or coercing the decision maker. Consider the highly unusual case of Aleman v. Judges of the Circuit Court of Cook County, 138 F.3d 302 (7th Cir. 1998). Harry Aleman—also known as the "Pizza Guy" (don't you love Mafia aliases?)—was charged with murdering a local Teamsters official. Aleman was tried by a Cook County, Illinois judge (no jury); the defendant paid the judge $10,000 to acquit him, which the judge then did. (When he received his payment, the bribed judge said, in classic Chicago style: "That's all I get is ten thousand dollars? I think I deserve more.") The government discovered the bribe, re-charged Aleman with the same murder, and argued that double jeopardy did not apply because Aleman was never really in "jeopardy" of a conviction at the original trial, because it was rigged. The Court of Appeals for the Seventh Circuit agreed; the Supreme Court denied Aleman's writ of certiorari. Is *Aleman* consistent with *Fong Foo*?

Bribery aside, the proposition that acquittals are final entails another proposition: The government "has no right of appeal in a criminal case, absent explicit statutory authority." United States v. Scott, 437 U.S., at 84-85. A federal statute, 18 U.S.C. §3731, permits a government appeal in a federal criminal case except "where the double jeopardy clause of the United States Constitution prohibits further prosecution." Many states have similar statutes. As you read the notes that follow, remember that the definition of "acquittal" also determines the boundaries of the government's right to appeal adverse judgments.

Identity of the Decisionmaker—Jury or Judge. Juries are, of course, free to acquit in criminal cases, even when the evidence justifies a conviction. That power is generally discouraged: Jurors are not told they may acquit for any reason—frequently they are told the opposite—and the literature on jury nullification is largely critical of the practice. See, e.g., Andrew D. Leipold, Rethinking Jury Nullification, 82 Va. L. Rev. 253 (1996). Yet *Fong Foo* seems to give trial judges the same nullification power that criminal juries have. Why? One can readily imagine arguments for giving 12 ordinary citizens the right to decide that a given criminal statute is too harsh to be applied in a given context. But why should *judges* have that right?

Whatever its merits, the rule *Fong Foo* established was reaffirmed in Sanabria v. United States, 437 U.S. 54 (1978). *Sanabria's* facts are unusually complicated. Along with a number of codefendants, Sanabria was charged with conducting an illegal gambling business in violation of 18 U.S.C. §1955; the federal crime was defined to include only gambling businesses that were unlawful in the state in which they took place. As to Sanabria, the government's evidence tended to establish his participation in a numbers business but not his participation in a business involving gambling on horse races (the latter was the business most of Sanabria's codefendants allegedly operated). During the course of the trial, defense counsel moved for a judgment of acquittal as to Sanabria, on the ground that the indictment referred to a Massachusetts statute that forbade gambling on horse races but not numbers businesses. (Another state statute covered numbers businesses; that is, the error in the indictment was apparently technical only. See 437 U.S., at 58-59.) The trial court struck all evidence concerning the numbers operation, and then granted the motion for judgment of acquittal.

The government appealed, arguing that the ruling in *Sanabria* was not really an acquittal but merely a dismissal for error in the indictment. The Supreme Court disagreed. In an opinion by Justice Marshall, the Court held that even assuming the trial judge's decision was erroneous, the judgment was final. The Court called the rule barring any appeal of acquittals "the most fundamental rule of double jeopardy jurisprudence," id., at 64 (quotation omitted), and, quoting *Fong Foo*, added: "The fundamental nature of this rule is manifested by its explicit extension to situations where an acquittal is 'based upon an egregiously erroneous foundation.'" Id.

In 2013, the Court once again reaffirmed that an acquittal is the end of the case, even if it was entered by a judge who made a legal error. In Evans v. Michigan, 133 S. Ct. 1069 (2013), the trial judge mistakenly thought that the crime charged required proof of a certain element, and since the prosecutor had not proven that element, granted a directed verdict for defendant. The state court of appeals agreed with the government that the trial judge has misinterpreted the statute, and remanded for further prosecution. The Supreme Court, with only one dissent, said that double jeopardy should have barred the State's appeal, and now barred a retrial. Cases such as *Fong Foo* and *Sanabria*, said the Court, firmly established that an acquittal, even one that was based on a judicial misinterpretation of the criminal statute, was entitled to the full measure of double jeopardy protection.

With *Fong Foo*, *Sanabria*, and *Evans*, compare Wilson v. United States, 420 U.S. 332 (1975). Wilson was charged with illegally converting union funds to his personal use; his case went to trial before a jury. The jury convicted. The trial judge then granted a defense motion to dismiss the charges against Wilson due to excessive preindictment delay by the government. The government appealed, and the defense argued that the trial judge's ruling was an acquittal and was therefore final and unchallengeable. The Supreme Court, once again speaking through Justice Marshall, concluded otherwise:

> . . . [W]here there is no threat of either multiple punishment or successive prosecutions, the Double Jeopardy Clause is not offended. . . . Although review of any ruling of law discharging a defendant obviously enhances the likelihood of conviction and subjects him to continuing expense and anxiety, a defendant has no legitimate claim to benefit from an error of law when that error could be corrected without subjecting him to a second trial before a second trier of fact.

Id., at 344-345. Note the Court's emphasis on the fact that no second trial would be necessary; presumably, the idea is that if the government's appeal were successful,

Wilson would stand convicted based on the jury verdict. Note too that the Court did not address the subject matter of the trial judge's ruling; it appears that the *Wilson* result would hold even if the judge had found the defendant factually innocent of the charges against him. Does that make sense?

Finally, consider United States v. Martin Linen Supply Co., 430 U.S. 564 (1977). Two corporations and their individual owner were tried for criminal contempt. The jury deadlocked and was dismissed. At that point, the defendant filed a motion for judgment of acquittal, which the district judge granted. As in the cases discussed above, the issue before the Supreme Court was whether the government could appeal this ruling. The Court held it could not, in an opinion that relied heavily on *Fong Foo.* Justice Brennan's majority opinion emphasized the impermissibility of a second trial following an acquittal—and the district judge's order unquestionably qualified as an acquittal.

What is the point of these cases? It is often said that they are designed to protect the defendant's interest in finality—hence the emphasis in *Wilson* and *Martin Linen Supply* on whether a retrial would be necessary if the government's appeal were successful. But as Peter Westen noted in a famously interesting article, this argument fails to explain why the finality interest is protected *absolutely*—why acquittals are deemed final "even where the prosecution is acknowledged to have acted in good faith and even where the acquittals are known to be 'egregiously erroneous.'" Peter Westen, The Three Faces of Double Jeopardy: Reflections on Government Appeals of Criminal Sentences, 78 Mich. L. Rev. 1001, 1006-1007 (1980) (quoting *Fong Foo*). As Westen further notes (and as the materials below explore), the finality interest is not deemed powerful enough to bar retrials after an appellate reversal or (at least in some circumstances) a mistrial.

The better argument, Westen contends, is that the finality of acquittals is tied to the jury's right to nullify:

> To say that a verdict is erroneous means that it is the end product of a trial that did not conform to the rules governing opening statements, evidence, jury instructions, closing statements, and so forth. The purpose of such rules is to insure that a case is tried in accord with the legislative standard governing guilt or innocence. Yet as long as the criminal jury has authority to acquit against the evidence, viz., authority to alter legislative standards in favor of more lenient standards of its own, trial errors of that kind may be immaterial. One cannot tell whether an "erroneous" acquittal is the product of legal error, or whether it is the fruit of the jury's desire to nullify the law by which the case was tried. Since the jury verdict itself is opaque, and since the jury cannot be easily examined about its verdict without skewing its deliberations, two alternatives remain: either to reject all "erroneous" jury verdicts, knowing full well that some of them will be based on the jury's desire to nullify, or to accept all such verdicts, knowing that some of them will be the product of legal errors. As between the two alternatives, the jury-acquittal rule opts for the latter, reflecting the judgment that it is ultimately better to err in favor of nullification than against it.

Id., at 1018. Of course, as Westen recognizes, that explains the jury's prerogative, not the judge's. But as Westen and coauthor Richard Drubel argue in another article,

> [T]here are . . . good reasons to vest trial judges with the authority to acquit against the evidence. It enables the judicial system to temper the legislature's generalized

standards of criminal responsibility with lenity in particular cases. It also places bench trials on an equal footing with jury trials. . . .

Peter Westen & Richard Drubel, Toward a General Theory of Double Jeopardy, [1978] Sup. Ct. Rev. 81, 134 (1979). Are those reasons powerful enough to justify constitutionally protecting nullification from the bench? (Westen and Drubel think not. See id., at 134-135.)

One way to reconcile the cases discussed above is to say that criminal defendants are entitled to one potential "nullifier"—the jury if the jury comes to a final decision, but the judge if the trial is to the bench or if the jury deadlocks. Is that a sensible entitlement? Is it important that criminal defendants have some opportunity to make nonlegal arguments (e.g., whatever the law says, this conduct does not deserve to be criminally punished)? Are judges likely to do a good job of evaluating such arguments?

Timing. The constitutional bar on defendants' being "twice put in jeopardy" for the same crime is, in part, a rule about timing. For a defendant to be "twice put in jeopardy," (1) he must be "in jeopardy," (2) he must have been in some *other* "jeopardy"—i.e., there must be more than one "jeopardy," and (3) these multiple "jeopardies" must be "for the same offence." The first two of these three conditions depend in large part on when a given "jeopardy" begins and when it ends.

In Crist v. Bretz, 437 U.S. 28 (1978), the Court held that in jury trials, jeopardy begins or "attaches" when the jury is impanelled and sworn. The Court justified its conclusion by

> the need to protect the interest of an accused in retaining a chosen jury. That interest was described in Wade v. Hunter, [336 U.S. 684, 689,] as a defendant's "valued right to have his trial completed by a particular tribunal." It is an interest with roots deep in the historic development of trial by jury in the Anglo-American system of criminal justice. Throughout that history there ran a strong tradition that once banded together a jury should not be discharged until it had completed its solemn task of announcing a verdict.

Id., at 35-36. Note that this conclusion bars the use of double jeopardy doctrine as a vehicle to prevent multiple or harassing criminal investigations, since a mere investigation does not constitute "jeopardy." Consider Serfass v. United States, 420 U.S. 377 (1975). There, the defendant was charged with criminal draft evasion; the district court granted a pretrial motion to dismiss the charge on the ground that the defendant had established conscientious objector status—seemingly the equivalent of a ruling that the government lacked sufficient evidence to prosecute. The Supreme Court held that the government could appeal from the district court's ruling, even though the appeal could lead to a trial, because jeopardy had not yet attached when the district court's ruling was made.

When does a given jeopardy end? Obviously, it ends with an acquittal—*Fong Foo* holds as much. Does it end with the reversal of a conviction? In Ball v. United States, 163 U.S. 662, 672 (1896), the Court held that "it is quite clear that a defendant, who procures a judgment against him upon an indictment to be set aside, may be tried anew upon the same indictment . . . for the same offence of which he had been convicted." Under *Ball,* a second trial is permitted following the reversal of the defendant's conviction because the second trial does not constitute a new "jeopardy," but simply a continuation of the same jeopardy that began with the first trial. See also United States v. Tateo, 377 U.S. 463 (1964), holding the *Ball* rule applicable to reversals on collateral review.

Appellate "Acquittals."   The *Ball* rule establishes that at least some appellate reversals do not bar retrial. In Burks v. United States, 437 U.S. 1 (1978), the Court held that an appellate holding that the evidence was insufficient to convict *does* bar retrial:

> [S]uch an appellate reversal means that the government's case was so lacking that it should not have even been *submitted* to the jury. Since we necessarily afford absolute finality to a jury's *verdict* of acquittal—no matter how erroneous its decision—it is difficult to conceive how society has any greater interest in retrying a defendant when, on review, it is decided as a matter of law that the jury could not properly have returned a verdict of guilty.

Id., at 16 (emphasis in original). Suppose an intermediate appellate court finds the evidence insufficient, and the government wishes to appeal *that* ruling to the state supreme court. Is the appeal permissible? In other words, does the appellate acquittal have the same standing as a jury acquittal? Recall Wilson v. United States, 420 U.S. 332 (1975), where the Court upheld an appeal from a trial court dismissal after a jury verdict of guilty had been returned. *Wilson* might suggest that judicial acquittals are less final than jury acquittals. But then, the trial court in *Wilson* did not squarely find that the evidence was insufficient to convict, so maybe the court's ruling was not an "acquittal" after all.

In some jurisdictions, appellate judges have the authority to order new trials when they disagree with the jury's verdict, even if the verdict was legally supportable. These "thirteenth juror" reversals do not bar retrial under *Burks*. See Tibbs v. Florida, 457 U.S. 31 (1982).

Acquittals and Dismissals.   As the preceding note suggests, double jeopardy doctrine places a great deal of emphasis on whether a given appellate ruling was or was not the equivalent of an acquittal. The same is true of trial court rulings. In United States v. Scott, 437 U.S. 82 (1978), the defendant was charged with three counts of drug distribution. The defense moved to dismiss two of the three counts for prejudicial preindictment delay by the government. At the close of the evidence, the district judge granted the defense motion. (The third count went to the jury, which acquitted.) The government sought to appeal the district judge's ruling; the defendant argued that that ruling was final, since a reversal would necessarily require another trial. The Court held that appeal from dismissals of this sort were permissible, even if they might result in a second trial. The Court analogized the issue to the cases involving appellate reversal:

> The successful appeal of a judgment of conviction, on any ground other than the insufficiency of the evidence to support the verdict, Burks v. United States, [437 U.S. 1 (1978),] poses no bar to further prosecution on the same charge. A judgment of acquittal, whether based on a jury verdict of not guilty or on a ruling by the court that the evidence is insufficient to convict, may not be appealed and terminates the prosecution when a second trial would be necessitated by a reversal. What may seem superficially to be a disparity in the rules governing a defendant's liability to be tried again is explainable by reference to the underlying purposes of the Double Jeopardy

Clause. As . . . *Fong Foo* illustrate[s], the law attaches particular significance to an acquittal. To permit a second trial after an acquittal, however mistaken the acquittal may have been, would present an unacceptably high risk that the Government, with its vastly superior resources, might wear down the defendant so that "even though innocent he may be found guilty." Green [v. United States, 355 U.S. 184, 188 (1957)]. On the other hand, to require a criminal defendant to stand trial again after he has successfully invoked a statutory right of appeal to upset his first conviction is not an act of governmental oppression of the sort against which the Double Jeopardy Clause was intended to protect. . . .

. . . [Here], the dismissal of an indictment for preindictment delay represents a legal judgment that a defendant, although criminally culpable, may not be punished because of a supposed constitutional violation.

We think that in a case such as this the defendant, by deliberately choosing to seek termination of the proceedings against him on a basis unrelated to factual guilt or innocence of the offense of which he is accused, suffers no injury cognizable under the Double Jeopardy Clause if the Government is permitted to appeal from such a ruling of the trial court in favor of the defendant.

Id., at 90-91, 98-99. Elsewhere in its opinion, the Court sought to define which trial court rulings would constitute an acquittal:

[A] defendant is acquitted only when the ruling of the judge, whatever its label, actually represents a resolution in the defendant's favor, correct or not, of some or all of the factual elements of the offense charged. Where the court, before the jury returns a verdict, enters a judgment of acquittal pursuant to Fed. Rule Crim. Proc. 29, appeal will be barred only when it is plain that the District Court evaluated the Government's evidence and determined that it was legally insufficient to sustain a conviction.

Id., at 97 (quotations and citations omitted). Review the statement of facts in *Fong Foo*; does the trial judge's acquittal in that case plainly satisfy the standard in *Scott*?

In Smith v. Massachusetts, 543 U.S. 462 (2005), at the close of the prosecution's evidence, the defense moved for a required finding of "not guilty" on one count—involving unlawful possession of a firearm—based on the prosecution's alleged failure to prove an element of the crime. The trial judge granted the defense motion, and the ruling was entered on the docket. Later, just before closing arguments, the prosecution pointed out to the judge that a state-law precedent rendered the earlier ruling incorrect. At that point, the judge announced that she was "reversing" her ruling, and allowed the firearms charge to go to the jury. The defendant was convicted on all counts.

On appeal, the defendant raised a double jeopardy claim, based in part on Massachusetts Rule of Criminal Procedure 25(a), which provides: "The judge . . . shall enter a finding of not guilty . . . if the evidence is insufficient as a matter of law to sustain a conviction. If a defendant's motion for a required finding of not guilty is made at the close of the Commonwealth's evidence, it shall be ruled upon at that time." The Appeals Court of Massachusetts held that Rule 25(a) did not preclude the judge from reconsidering an insufficiency decision previously made, and affirmed the firearms conviction.

The Supreme Court, in a 5-4 decision, reversed. All nine Justices agreed that the finding made by the trial judge was based on insufficiency of the evidence, and thus was tantamount to an acquittal. All nine Justices also agreed that the states possess the power to authorize—by statute, court rule, or judicial decision—trial judges to reconsider midtrial insufficiency-of-the-evidence rulings, and that such reconsideration itself would not violate double jeopardy. (But compare *Evans*, supra, at page 1553.) The majority and dissent parted company, however, over whether Smith should nevertheless prevail because his case was the first in Massachusetts to authorize midtrial reconsideration of an acquittal based on insufficiency of the evidence; the majority felt that this unexpected development might have prejudiced Smith, in terms of affecting his presentation of his defense at trial, while the dissenters found no such prejudice — especially given that the trial judge's original insufficiency ruling was plainly erroneous.

Should federal double jeopardy claims turn on the clarity (or lack thereof) of state law? Suppose Massachusetts law, *prior* to Smith's case, had clearly authorized reconsideration of midtrial insufficiency rulings. Now suppose the trial judge in *Smith* had dismissed the firearms charge and said "this decision is final and irrevocable. I will not, under any circumstances, entertain a motion for reconsideration." Later in the trial, the prosecution moves to reconsider, points out the relevant state precedent, and the judge corrects her mistake. Would Smith have a valid double jeopardy claim? Does *Fong Foo* bear on this question?

Consider one more hypothetical. Suppose *Smith* were a bench trial, not a jury trial; suppose further that, at the trial's conclusion, the judge acquitted Smith, after which the prosecution immediately moved for reconsideration. Finally, suppose the judge granted the prosecutor's motion, vacated her own judgment of acquittal, and entered a new judgment of conviction. Assuming that Massachusetts law clearly authorized such a procedure, would Smith have a valid double jeopardy claim? Should he?

Implied Acquittals.   In Green v. United States, 355 U.S. 184 (1957), the defendant was charged with arson and murder in the first degree. At trial, the judge also instructed the jury on the lesser-included offense of murder in the second degree. The jury found Green guilty of arson and second-degree murder, but its verdict was silent on the first-degree murder charge. Green successfully appealed the murder conviction on the ground that the evidence did not support the charge of second-degree murder, and the case was remanded for a new trial. At the second trial, Green was once again prosecuted for first-degree murder; this time, he was convicted, and he received a death sentence.

The Supreme Court held that the second trial on the charge of first-degree murder was a violation of Green's double jeopardy rights:

> Green was in direct peril of being convicted and punished for first degree murder at his first trial. He was forced to run the gantlet once on that charge and the jury refused to convict him. When given the choice between finding him guilty of either first or second degree murder it chose the latter. In this situation the great majority of cases in this country have regarded the jury's verdict as an implicit acquittal on the charge of first degree murder. But the result in this case need not rest alone on the assumption, which we believe legitimate, that the jury for one reason or another acquitted Green of murder in the first degree. For here, the jury was dismissed without returning any express verdict on that charge and without Green's consent. Yet it was given a full opportunity to return a verdict and no extraordinary circumstances appeared which prevented it from doing so. Therefore it seems clear, under established principles of former jeopardy, that Green's jeopardy for first degree murder came to an end when the jury was discharged so that he could not be retried for that

offense. In brief, we believe this case can be treated no differently, for purposes of former jeopardy, than if the jury had returned a verdict which expressly read: "We find the defendant not guilty of murder in the first degree but guilty of murder in the second degree."

Id., at 190-191. The Court also held that Green did not waive his double jeopardy rights by appealing his conviction on the charge of second-degree murder.

In Blueford v. Arkansas, 132 S. Ct. 2044 (2012), the Court refused to apply *Green* to a case involving lesser-included offenses in which a mistrial was declared because the jury was deadlocked. Blueford was charged in the alternative with capital murder, first-degree murder, manslaughter, and negligent homicide. The trial judge instructed the jury to consider the charges by starting with the most serious (i.e., capital murder), and then progressing to a less serious charge only if they found reasonable doubt on the more serious charge. The verdict forms allowed the jury either to acquit on all charges, or to convict on any one charge, but did not allow for any combination of acquittals and convictions. After a few hours of deliberation, the jury reported that it was deadlocked. In response to an inquiry from the trial judge, the foreperson explained that the jury was unanimous in agreeing that the defendant should be acquitted of capital murder and first-degree murder, was deadlocked on the manslaughter charge, and had not yet voted on the negligent homicide charge. The judge instructed the jury to continue deliberating, but declined a defense request to give the jury an additional verdict form that would have allowed for an acquittal on some but not all of the charges. After another half-hour of deliberation, the jury remained deadlocked, and the judge declared a mistrial. The Court held that Blueford could be retried on all of the charges:

> The foreperson's report was not a final resolution of anything. When the foreperson told the court how the jury had voted on each offense, the jury's deliberations had not yet concluded. The jurors in fact went back to the jury room to deliberate further, even after the foreperson had delivered her report. When they emerged a half hour later, the foreperson stated only that they were unable to reach a verdict. She gave no indication whether it was still the case that all 12 jurors believed Blueford was not guilty of capital or first-degree murder, that 9 of them believed he was guilty of manslaughter, or that a vote had not been taken on negligent homicide. The fact that deliberations continued after the report deprives that report of the finality necessary to constitute an acquittal on the murder offenses.

Id., at 2050. The Court also rejected Blueford's alternative argument that, before declaring a mistrial, the trial judge should have been required—as a matter of double jeopardy law—to give the jury the requested additional verdict form.

Protecting Acquittals. An acquittal represents a judgment that the defendant should not be convicted of a particular crime. The most obvious way to undermine that judgment is to prosecute the defendant a second time for the same crime—a course of action barred, quite plainly, by the double jeopardy clause. But suppose the government's behavior is more subtle. Suppose it charges the defendant with another crime that, though different, turns on facts common to the charge for which the defendant was acquitted. If the second charge stands, the government can, in effect, relitigate the case that it lost—the very thing cases like *Fong Foo* purport to forbid. Consider the next case.

ASHE v. SWENSON

Certiorari to the United States Court of Appeals for the Eighth Circuit
397 U.S. 436 (1970)

MR. JUSTICE STEWART delivered the opinion of the Court.

[Six men playing poker in the early morning of January 10, 1960, were robbed by "three or four masked men"; the robbers escaped in a car belonging to one of the victims. Later that morning, police found the stolen car abandoned in a field, and three men were arrested nearby. Ashe was arrested "some distance away" from the car. In May 1960, Ashe was tried for the robbery of Donald Knight, one of the poker players. The testimony of the four prosecution witnesses at trial — Knight and three other poker players — established clearly that Knight and the others had been robbed. Their testimony was "weak," however, on the issue of whether Ashe was one of the robbers; two of them "could not identify" Ashe, the third stated only that Ashe's voice "sounded very much like" one of the robbers, and the fourth identified Ashe only by his "size and height, and his actions." Cross-examination was "brief," focusing entirely on the identification issue. The defense presented no testimony and waived final argument. — EDS.]

The trial judge instructed the jury that if it found that the petitioner was one of the participants in the armed robbery, the theft of "any money" from Knight would sustain a conviction. He also instructed the jury that if the petitioner was one of the robbers, he was guilty under the law even if he had not personally robbed Knight. The jury — though not instructed to elaborate upon its verdict — found the petitioner "not guilty due to insufficient evidence."

Six weeks later the petitioner was brought to trial again, this time for the robbery of another participant in the poker game, a man named Roberts. The petitioner filed a motion to dismiss, based on his previous acquittal. The motion was overruled, and the second trial began. The witnesses were for the most part the same, though this time their testimony was substantially stronger on the issue of the petitioner's identity. . . . The State further refined its case at the second trial by declining to call one of the participants in the poker game whose identification testimony at the first trial had been conspicuously negative. The case went to the jury on instructions virtually identical to those given at the first trial. This time the jury found the petitioner guilty, and he was sentenced to a 35-year term in the state penitentiary. . . .

"Collateral estoppel" is an awkward phrase, but it stands for an extremely important principle in our adversary system of justice. It means simply that when an issue of ultimate fact has once been determined by a valid and final judgment, that issue cannot again be litigated between the same parties in any future lawsuit. Although first developed in civil litigation, collateral estoppel has been an established rule of federal criminal law at least since this Court's decision more than 50 years ago in United States v. Oppenheimer, 242 U.S. 85. As Mr. Justice Holmes put the matter in that case, "It cannot be that the safeguards of the person, so often and so rightly mentioned with solemn reverence, are less than those that protect from a liability in debt." 242 U.S., at 87. As a rule of federal law, therefore, "[i]t is much too late to suggest that this principle is not fully applicable to a former judgment in a criminal case, either because of lack of 'mutuality' or because the former judgment may reflect only a belief that the Government had not met the higher burden of proof exacted in such cases. . . ." United States v. Kramer, 289 F.2d 909, 913.

The federal decisions have made clear that the rule of collateral estoppel in criminal cases is not to be applied with the hypertechnical and archaic approach of a 19th century pleading book, but with realism and rationality. Where a previous judgment of acquittal was based upon a general verdict, as is usually the case, this approach requires a court to "examine the record of a prior proceeding, taking into account the pleadings, evidence, charge, and other relevant matter, and conclude whether a rational jury could have grounded its verdict upon an issue other than that which the defendant seeks to foreclose from consideration." The inquiry "must be set in a practical frame and viewed with an eye to all the circumstances of the proceedings." Sealfon v. United States, 332 U.S. 575, 579 . . . .

Straightforward application of the federal rule to the present case can lead to but one conclusion. For the record is utterly devoid of any indication that the first jury could rationally have found that an armed robbery had not occurred, or that Knight had not been a victim of that robbery. The single rationally conceivable issue in dispute before the jury was whether the petitioner had been one of the robbers. And the jury by its verdict found that he had not. The federal rule of law, therefore, would make a second prosecution for the robbery of Roberts wholly impermissible.

The ultimate question to be determined, then, in the light of Benton v. Maryland, [395 U.S. 784],[1] is whether this established rule of federal law is embodied in the Fifth Amendment guarantee against double jeopardy. We do not hesitate to hold that it is. For whatever else that constitutional guarantee may embrace, it surely protects a man who has been acquitted from having to "run the gantlet" a second time. Green v. United States, 355 U.S. 184, 190.

The question is not whether Missouri could validly charge the petitioner with six separate offenses for the robbery of the six poker players. It is not whether he could have received a total of six punishments if he had been convicted in a single trial of robbing the six victims. It is simply whether, after a jury determined by its verdict that the petitioner was not one of the robbers, the State could constitutionally hale him before a new jury to litigate that issue again. . . .

In this case the State in its brief has frankly conceded that following the petitioner's acquittal, it treated the first trial as no more than a dry run for the second prosecution: "No doubt the prosecutor felt the state had a provable case on the first charge and, when he lost, he did what every good attorney would do—he refined his presentation in light of the turn of events at the first trial." But this is precisely what the constitutional guarantee forbids.

The judgment is reversed, and the case is remanded to the Court of Appeals for the Eighth Circuit for further proceedings consistent with this opinion.

[The concurring opinions of Justice Black, Justice Harlan, and Justice Brennan, and the dissenting opinion of Chief Justice Burger, are omitted.]

NOTES AND QUESTIONS

1. The majority in *Ashe* assumed that collateral estoppel couldn't possibly be applied in the *government's* favor. Is that sensible?

---

1. In Benton v. Maryland, 395 U.S. 784 (1969), the Supreme Court held that the Double Jeopardy Clause applied to the states through the Due Process Clause of the Fourteenth Amendment.—EDS.

In fact, in a few cases, criminal defendants *have* been precluded from litigating an issue resolved against them in an earlier criminal trial. In United States v. Rangel-Perez, 179 F. Supp. 619 (S.D. Cal. 1959), the defendant was charged with being a deported alien found in the United States; the court barred relitigation by the defense of the defendant's alien status, based on an earlier conviction for a similar offense where that element had been proved. In United States v. Levasseur, 699 F. Supp. 965 (D. Mass.), *rev'd on other grounds,* 846 F.2d 786 (1st Cir. 1988), the court barred several defendants from relitigating the legality of a police search, where the defendants had lost a suppression motion in another criminal case based on the same search. At least one state supreme court has gone farther, albeit in dicta: In People v. Ford, 416 P.2d 132 (Cal. 1966), the California Supreme Court stated that it was proper to instruct the jury in a felony murder prosecution that the defendant had already been convicted of the underlying felony. These and other cases are collected in Richard B. Kennelly, Jr., Note, Precluding the Accused: Offensive Collateral Estoppel in Criminal Cases, 80 Va. L. Rev. 1379 (1994).

2. Notwithstanding the cases in the preceding note, the general assumption remains that collateral estoppel in criminal cases is asymmetric—that it bars the government from relitigation but does not apply to the defense. That is a strong disincentive to litigating a crime like the one in *Ashe* serially: "If a prosecutor wins the first trial, she will have to prove everything all over again in a second criminal case; but if she loses on any issue, she loses that issue forever. . . ." Akhil Reed Amar, Double Jeopardy Law Made Simple, 106 Yale L.J. 1807, 1828 (1997). Actually, even without *Ashe,* serial prosecutions would be rare. Recall the discussion of joinder in Chapter 11. In joinder cases, the usual assumption is that prosecutors gain from bringing as many charges (and as many defendants) as possible in *one* proceeding. If that gain is real, the risk of serial prosecution must be small.

3. In Yeager v. United States, 557 U.S. 110 (2009), the Court held that acquittals that otherwise qualify for *Ashe*'s preclusive effect do not become disqualified simply because the jury also became hung on other related counts:

> A hung count is not a "relevant" part of the "record of [the] prior proceeding." See *Ashe,* 397 U.S., at 444. Because a jury speaks only through its verdict, its failure to reach a verdict cannot—by negative implication—yield a piece of information that helps put together the trial puzzle. A mistried count is therefore nothing like the other forms of record material that *Ashe* suggested should be part of the preclusion inquiry. . . .
> . . . [W]e hold that the consideration of hung counts has no place in the issue-preclusion analysis. Indeed, if it were relevant, the fact that petitioner has already survived one trial should be a factor cutting in favor of, rather than against, applying a double jeopardy bar. To identify what a jury necessarily determined at trial, courts should scrutinize a jury's decisions, not its failures to decide.

Id., at 2367-2368. *Ashe* already imposes an almost insurmountable burden on a defendant seeking preclusion, in the sense that the defendant must demonstrate that the previous jury's acquittal verdict (which, of course, generally carries no explanation) necessarily was based on the same factual issue that he now seeks to treat as resolved. *Yeager* represents a decision by the Court not to make that burden any more insurmountable than it already is: After *Yeager,* at least the defendant does not *also* have to overcome speculation about why the jury *didn't* reach a verdict on some of the other charges against him.

4. Does *Ashe* affect the way the law ought to construe plea bargains? Many, perhaps most, plea bargains involve an agreement by the defendant to plead guilty in return for an agreement by the government to forgo pressing certain charges. Should the defendant be treated as having been "impliedly acquitted" of the forgone charges? Compare Green v. United States, 355 U.S. 184 (1957) (cited in *Ashe,* and discussed supra, at page 1558). Why or why not? For an insightful analysis of the relationship between double jeopardy doctrine and plea bargaining, especially with respect to defendants who may face future prosecutions for crimes not yet charged, see Daniel C. Richman, Bargaining About Future Jeopardy, 49 Vanderbilt L. Rev. 1181 (1996).

2. Mistrials

OREGON v. KENNEDY

Certiorari to the Court of Appeals of Oregon
456 U.S. 667 (1982)

JUSTICE REHNQUIST delivered the opinion of the Court.

The Oregon Court of Appeals decided that the Double Jeopardy Clause of the Fifth Amendment to the United States Constitution barred respondent's retrial after his first trial ended in a mistrial granted on his own motion. 49 Ore. App. 415, 619 P.2d 948 (1980). The Court of Appeals concluded that retrial was barred because the prosecutorial misconduct that occasioned the mistrial in the first instance amounted to "overreaching." Because that court took an overly expansive view of the application of the Double Jeopardy Clause following a mistrial resulting from the defendant's own motion, we reverse its judgment.

Respondent was charged with the theft of an oriental rug. During his first trial, the State called an expert witness on the subject of Middle Eastern rugs to testify as to the value and the identity of the rug in question. On cross-examination, respondent's attorney apparently attempted to establish bias on the part of the expert witness by asking him whether he had filed a criminal complaint against respondent. The witness eventually acknowledged this fact, but explained that no action had been taken on his complaint. On redirect examination, the prosecutor sought to elicit the reasons why the witness had filed a complaint against respondent, but the trial court sustained a series of objections to this line of inquiry.[1] The following colloquy then ensued:

> *Prosecutor.* Have you ever done business with the Kennedys?
> *Witness.* No, I have not.
> *Prosecutor.* Is that because he is a crook?

The trial court then granted respondent's motion for a mistrial.

When the State later sought to retry respondent, he moved to dismiss the charges because of double jeopardy. After a hearing at which the prosecutor testified, the

---

1. The Court of Appeals later explained that respondent's "objections were not well taken, and the judge's rulings were probably wrong." 49 Ore. App. 415, 417, 619 P.2d 948, 949 (1980).

trial court[2] found as a fact that "it was not the intention of the prosecutor in this case to cause a mistrial." 49 Ore. App., at 418, 619 P.2d, at 949. On the basis of this finding, the trial court held that double jeopardy principles did not bar retrial, and respondent was then tried and convicted.

Respondent then successfully appealed to the Oregon Court of Appeals, which sustained his double jeopardy claim. . . . The Court of Appeals accepted the trial court's finding that it was not the intent of the prosecutor to cause a mistrial. Nevertheless, the court held that retrial was barred because the prosecutor's conduct in this case constituted what it viewed as "overreaching." . . . [T]he Court of Appeals expressed the view that [the prosecutor's] personal attack left respondent with a "Hobson's choice—either to accept a necessarily prejudiced jury, or to move for a mistrial and face the process of being retried at a later time." Id., at 418, 619 P.2d, at 950. . . .

Where the trial is terminated over the objection of the defendant, the classical test for lifting the double jeopardy bar to a second trial is the "manifest necessity" standard first enunciated in Justice Story's opinion for the Court in United States v. Perez, 9 Wheat. 579, 580 (1824). *Perez* dealt with the most common form of "manifest necessity": a mistrial declared by the judge following the jury's declaration that it was unable to reach a verdict. While other situations have been recognized by our cases as meeting the "manifest necessity" standard, the hung jury remains the prototypical example. See, e.g., Arizona v. Washington, 434 U.S. 497, 509 (1978); Illinois v. Somerville, 410 U.S. 458, 463 (1973). The "manifest necessity" standard provides sufficient protection to the defendant's interests in having his case finally decided by the jury first selected while at the same time maintaining "the public's interest in fair trials designed to end in just judgments." Wade v. Hunter, [336 U.S. 684, 689 (1949)].

But in the case of a mistrial declared at the behest of the defendant, quite different principles come into play. Here the defendant himself has elected to terminate the proceedings against him, and the "manifest necessity" standard has no place in the application of the Double Jeopardy Clause. United States v. Dinitz, [424 U.S. 600, 607-610 (1976)]. . . .

Our cases, however, have indicated that even where the defendant moves for a mistrial, there is a narrow exception to the rule that the Double Jeopardy Clause is no bar to retrial. The circumstances under which respondent's first trial was terminated require us to delineate the bounds of that exception more fully than we have in previous cases.

Since one of the principal threads making up the protection embodied in the Double Jeopardy Clause is the right of the defendant to have his trial completed before the first jury empaneled to try him, it may be wondered as a matter of original inquiry why the defendant's election to terminate the first trial by his own motion should not be deemed a renunciation of that right for all purposes. We have recognized, however, that there would be great difficulty in applying such a rule where the prosecutor's actions giving rise to the motion for mistrial were done "in order to goad the [defendant] into requesting a mistrial." United States v. Dinitz, supra, at 611. In such a case, the defendant's valued right to complete his trial before the

---

2. These proceedings were not conducted by the same trial judge who presided over respondent's initial trial.

first jury would be a hollow shell if the inevitable motion for mistrial were held to prevent a later invocation of the bar of double jeopardy in all circumstances. But the precise phrasing of the circumstances which *will* allow a defendant to interpose the defense of double jeopardy . . . have been stated with less than crystal clarity in our cases. . . . In United States v. Dinitz, 424 U.S., at 611, we said:

> The Double Jeopardy Clause does protect a defendant against governmental actions intended to provoke mistrial requests and thereby to subject defendants to the substantial burdens imposed by multiple prosecutions.

. . . But immediately following the quoted language we went on to say:

> [The Double Jeopardy Clause] bars retrials where "bad-faith conduct by judge or prosecutor," threatens the "[harassment] of an accused by successive prosecutions or declaration of a mistrial so as to afford the prosecution a more favorable opportunity to convict" the defendant. United States v. Dinitz, 424 U.S., at 611 (citation omitted).

The language just quoted would seem to broaden the test from one of *intent* to provoke a motion for a mistrial to a more generalized standard of "bad faith conduct" or "harassment" on the part of the judge or prosecutor. . . .

The difficulty with the more general standards which would permit a broader exception than one merely based on intent is that they offer virtually no standards for their application. Every act on the part of a rational prosecutor during a trial is designed to "prejudice" the defendant by placing before the judge or jury evidence leading to a finding of his guilt. Given the complexity of the rules of evidence, it will be a rare trial of any complexity in which some proffered evidence by the prosecutor or by the defendant's attorney will not be found objectionable by the trial court. Most such objections are undoubtedly curable by simply refusing to allow the proffered evidence to be admitted, or in the case of a particular line of inquiry taken by counsel with a witness, by an admonition to desist from a particular line of inquiry.

More serious infractions on the part of the prosecutor may provoke a motion for mistrial on the part of the defendant, and may in the view of the trial court warrant the granting of such a motion. The "overreaching" standard applied by the court below . . . , however, would add another classification of prosecutorial error, one requiring dismissal of the indictment, but without supplying any standard by which to assess that error.

By contrast, a standard that examines the intent of the prosecutor, though certainly not entirely free from practical difficulties, is a manageable standard to apply. It merely calls for the court to make a finding of fact. Inferring the existence or nonexistence of intent from objective facts and circumstances is a familiar process in our criminal justice system. When it is remembered that resolution of double jeopardy questions by state trial courts are reviewable not only within the state court system, but in the federal court system on habeas corpus as well, the desirability of an easily applied principle is apparent.

Prosecutorial conduct that might be viewed as harassment or overreaching, even if sufficient to justify a mistrial on defendant's motion, therefore, does not bar retrial absent intent on the part of the prosecutor to subvert the protections afforded by the Double Jeopardy Clause. A defendant's motion for a mistrial constitutes "a deliberate election on his part to forgo his valued right to have his guilt or innocence determined before the first trier of fact." United States v. Scott, 437 U.S. 82, 93 (1978). Where prosecutorial error even of a degree sufficient to warrant a mistrial has occurred, "[the] important consideration, for purposes of the Double Jeopardy Clause, is that the defendant retain primary control over the course to be followed in the event of such error." United States v. Dinitz, supra, at 609. Only where the governmental conduct in question is intended to "goad" the defendant into moving for a mistrial may a defendant raise the bar of double jeopardy to a second trial after having succeeded in aborting the first on his own motion.

Were we to embrace the broad and somewhat amorphous standard adopted by the Oregon Court of Appeals, we are not sure that criminal defendants as a class would be aided. Knowing that the granting of the defendant's motion for mistrial would all but inevitably bring with it an attempt to bar a second trial on grounds of double jeopardy, the judge presiding over the first trial might well be more loath to grant a defendant's motion for mistrial. If a mistrial were in fact warranted under the applicable law, of course, the defendant could in many instances successfully appeal a judgment of conviction on the same grounds that he urged a mistrial, and the Double Jeopardy Clause would present no bar to retrial. But some of the advantages secured to him by the Double Jeopardy Clause—the freedom from extended anxiety, and the necessity to confront the government's case only once—would be to a large extent lost in the process of trial to verdict, reversal on appeal, and subsequent retrial. . . .

. . . We do not by this opinion lay down a flat rule that where a defendant in a criminal trial successfully moves for a mistrial, he may not thereafter invoke the bar of double jeopardy against a second trial. But we do hold that the circumstances under which such a defendant may invoke the bar of double jeopardy in a second effort to try him are limited to those cases in which the conduct giving rise to the successful motion for a mistrial was intended to provoke the defendant into moving for a mistrial.

Since the Oregon trial court found, and the Oregon Court of Appeals accepted, that the prosecutorial conduct culminating in the termination of the first trial in this case was not so intended by the prosecutor, that is the end of the matter for purposes of the Double Jeopardy Clause of the Fifth Amendment to the United States Constitution. . . .

[A concurring opinion by Justice Powell and opinions concurring in the judgment by Justice Brennan and Justice Stevens are omitted.]

NOTES AND QUESTIONS

1. What is the proper standard to adopt in a case like *Kennedy*? Here as elsewhere, intentional misconduct can be very hard to establish. Perhaps, then, *Kennedy* comes close in practice to a rule that mistrials sought by the defense always permit retrial. That seems insufficiently protective of the defendant's interest in being tried by *this* jury. But what is the alternative? Is this a matter best left to the judgment of trial judges?

2. Why does the defendant have such a strong interest in being tried by a particular jury (or a particular judge) in the first place? As long as the jury that convicts or acquits him is properly selected and impartial, why does it matter which jury it is? Perhaps it doesn't. The problem in mistrial cases may be not protecting the defendant's interest in a particular decision maker, but guarding against both sides' efforts to relitigate jury selection, by prompting mistrial motions when the selection process has gone badly. Does *Kennedy* adequately guard against that problem?

3. *Kennedy* deals with mistrials prompted by prosecutorial conduct, but the issue can arise from defense conduct as well. In Arizona v. Washington, 434 U.S. 497 (1978), the defendant was convicted of murder, but his conviction was overturned on appeal on the ground that the government had improperly withheld exculpatory evidence. In his opening statement at the defendant's second trial, defense counsel stated to the jury:

> You will hear testimony that notwithstanding the fact that we had a trial in May of 1971 in this matter, that the prosecutor hid those statements and . . . didn't give those statements at all, hid them.
>
>   You will hear that that evidence was suppressed and hidden by the prosecutor in that case. You will hear that that evidence was purposely withheld. You will hear that because of the misconduct of the County Attorney at that time and because he withheld evidence, that the Supreme Court of Arizona granted a new trial in this case.

Id., at 499. After opening statements were completed, the prosecutor sought and was granted a mistrial. The Supreme Court held that retrial was permissible—that the mistrial had satisfied the "manifest necessity" standard—though the Court stressed that the case was a close one:

> We recognize that the extent of the possible bias cannot be measured, and that the District Court was quite correct in believing that some trial judges might have proceeded with the trial after giving the jury appropriate cautionary instructions. In a strict, literal sense, the mistrial was not "necessary." Nevertheless, the overriding interest in the evenhanded administration of justice requires that we accord the highest degree of respect to the trial judge's evaluation of the likelihood that the impartiality of one or more jurors may have been affected by the improper comment.

Id., at 511. Is *Washington* consistent with *Kennedy*?

4. In the "prototypical" scenario described in *Kennedy*, where the trial judge finds "manifest necessity" and declares a mistrial due to a "hung" or deadlocked jury, under what standard should that decision be reviewed? In Renico v. Lett, 130 S. Ct. 1855 (2010), the Court made clear that the standard is both flexible and highly deferential:

> We have expressly declined to require the "mechanical application" of any "rigid formula" when trial judges decide whether jury deadlock warrants a mistrial. . . . We have also explicitly held that a trial judge declaring a mistrial is not required to make explicit findings of "manifest necessity" nor to "articulate on the record all the factors which informed the deliberate exercise of his discretion." [Arizona v.] Washington, [434 U.S. 497,] 517 [(1978)]. And we have never required a trial judge, before declaring a mistrial based on jury deadlock, to force the jury to deliberate for a minimum period of time, to question the jurors individually, to consult with (or obtain the consent of) either the prosecutor or defense counsel, to issue a supplemental jury instruction, or to consider any other means of breaking the impasse. In 1981, then-Justice Rehnquist noted that this Court had never "overturned a trial court's declaration of a mistrial after a jury was unable to reach a verdict on the ground that the 'manifest necessity' standard had not been met." Winston v. Moore, 452 U.S. 944, 947 (opinion dissenting from denial of certiorari). The same remains true today, nearly 30 years later.

Id., at 1863-1864.

B.   "For the Same Offence"

The Double Jeopardy Clause bars prosecuting or punishing someone twice for a single crime. What that clause means depends critically on what counts as a single crime—or, to use the constitutional language, "the same offence." The issue arises in three settings: (1) The defendant is acquitted, and the government tries to prosecute him again for the same crime. (2) The defendant is convicted, and the government tries to prosecute him again for the same crime. (3) The government tries to punish the defendant twice for the same crime in a single proceeding.

Most of this section is devoted to the second scenario, but we begin with a few comments on the first and the third. The first scenario, acquittal followed by reprosecution, is governed by Ashe v. Swenson, 397 U.S. 436 (1970). In practice, it rarely arises—perhaps because the government feels politically constrained not to challenge jury verdicts. The third scenario likewise produces little litigation, because the relevant double jeopardy rule is so lax. In "multiple punishment" cases—the government brings two charges against a defendant in one proceeding, and the defendant claims the two charges are the same—double jeopardy is a rule of legislative intent. As the Supreme Court put it in Missouri v. Hunter, 459 U.S. 359, 366 (1983): "With respect to cumulative sentences imposed in a single trial, the Double Jeopardy Clause does no more than prevent the sentencing court from prescribing greater punishment than the legislature intended." The defendant in *Hunter* was charged, in the same proceeding, with robbing a supermarket and with "armed criminal action" (he used a gun in the robbery). The Missouri legislature created the latter crime in order to raise the sentence of anyone who used a dangerous weapon to commit a crime: precisely what happened in *Hunter*. Consequently, the Court found no double jeopardy violation. That is the usual bottom line in "multiple punishment" cases. See Anne Bowen Poulin, Double Jeopardy and Multiple Punishment: Cutting the Gordian Knot, 77 U. Colo. L. Rev. 595 (2006).

The doctrine is both more demanding and much more complicated in the second scenario: A defendant is prosecuted and convicted, and the government wants to prosecute him again for (the defendant claims) "the same offence." Consider the following simple hypothetical: Suppose the defendant assaults the victim with a knife. The government prosecutes and convicts the defendant of simple assault; the defendant is sentenced to six months in the local jail. Then, the same prosecutor's office charges the defendant with assault with a deadly weapon, based on the same incident; the sentencing range for that crime is two to five years in the state penitentiary. The defendant challenges the second charge on double jeopardy grounds; as we shall see, the defendant's claim succeeds on these facts. Before taking up the doctrine, however, it helps to think about two questions: (1) Why does the government want to prosecute a defendant again for the same crime, after having already convicted him once? (2) What interest of the defendant does the law of double jeopardy protect in this situation?

There are several reasons why a prosecutor's office might wish to proceed in this way. The prosecutor might be unhappy with the sentence the judge imposed in the first proceeding. The prosecutor may not have correctly understood the facts before the first trial; given a better understanding now, she may believe the more severe charge is appropriate. The first charge may have been a bureaucratic error: Office policy required a more severe charge, but the assistant district attorney handling the case misunderstood the policy. All these possibilities (and there are others) are variations on a single theme: The government wishes to relitigate the defendant's sentence.

Of course, the defendant has an obvious interest in *not* relitigating his sentence. A large part of that interest is captured by the term "repose": At some point, the defendant needs to know that the incident in question is closed—that he has received his punishment, and there will be no more. Double jeopardy law protects this interest in repose with a constitutional finality rule. Another possibility is more substantive: Nancy King has suggested that *successive* prosecution tends to produce excessive punishment—that, for example, two assault sentences in the hypothetical above will be harsher than a single sentence for the more severe assault charge. See Nancy J. King, Portioning Punishment: Constitutional Limits on Successive and Excessive Penalties, 144 U. Pa. L. Rev. 101 (1995). If King is right, double jeopardy serves as an adjunct to the Eighth Amendment's ban on "cruel and unusual punishment."

The double jeopardy case law does not embrace any of these theories, or any other theory for that matter. For the most part, double jeopardy doctrine is fairly stable (though that has not always been the case). But the doctrine is not well theorized; courts agree on the correct outcomes, but pay surprisingly little attention to the reasons behind those outcomes. As you read the cases that follow, ask yourself what theory best explains the doctrine—and what theory makes the most sense.

NOTES ON THE RISE, FALL, AND RISE OF THE *BLOCKBURGER* TEST

1. The defendant in Blockburger v. United States, 284 U.S. 299 (1932), was charged under the old Harrison Act, the first major federal drug legislation. The Harrison Act didn't ban drug sales altogether, but it did impose strict licensing and tax requirements that, in practice, functioned as a prohibition. Blockburger was charged with selling morphine outside the original stamped package in violation of the Act, and also with selling the drug without a written order from the buyer, which violated another provision of the Act. Blockburger argued that the two charges were "the same" for double jeopardy purposes.

The Supreme Court disagreed. Writing for a unanimous Court, Justice Sutherland concluded:

> The applicable rule is that where the same act or transaction constitutes a violation of two distinct statutory provisions, the test to be applied to determine whether there are two offenses or only one, is whether each provision requires proof of a fact which the other does not.

Id., at 304. Applying that formula to Blockburger's claim, the Court concluded that the two crimes were different. The first required proof that the morphine was outside the original stamped package, while the second didn't. The second crime required proof that the sale was not pursuant to a buyer's written order; the first crime didn't. Consequently, Blockburger could be prosecuted for both—in the same proceeding or in two separate trials.

Blockburger turns double jeopardy law into an exercise in high-school algebra. Imagine a defendant charged and convicted of a crime with elements *A, B, C,* and *D.* Now imagine that the prosecutor wants to bring a new charge against this same defendant, arising out of the same incident. The new crime has elements *B, C, D,* and *E.* Under *Blockburger,* the new charge is permissible: The first crime required proof of element *A* and the second one did not, while the second required proof of element *E*, which was outside the scope of the first crime. If the government had instead brought a second charge with elements *B*, *C*, and *D* only, that charge *would* be barred by double jeopardy: One of the two crimes has a unique element (*A*) but the other one doesn't; *B*, *C*, and *D* are common to both crimes. This conclusion is important: It means that lesser-included offenses are barred by the prosecution of greater offenses—and vice versa.

So, under *Blockburger*, if a defendant is convicted of manslaughter, he may not then be prosecuted for murdering the same victim. If the defendant is convicted of assault with a deadly weapon, he may not then be prosecuted for simple assault (again assuming the victim and date of the crime remain the same). But the same defendant *may* be charged with, say, assault with a deadly weapon and assault with intent to kill in separate proceedings—even though the time, place, victim, and perpetrator are all the same. The first crime requires proof that a deadly weapon was used and the second doesn't (one can intend to kill without using a deadly weapon); the second crime requires proof of intent to kill and the first doesn't (one can use a deadly weapon without intending to kill).

Notice three features of this exercise. First, the double jeopardy issue can be decided on the face of the charging document—no evidence need be taken; it does not matter how the government intends to prove the second charge. The question is resolved based on the elements of the two crimes. Second, the size of the overlap between the two crimes makes no difference. In the first algebraic example, three of the four elements of each crime were common to both crimes, and both crimes happened at the same time and were committed by the same person. It could easily be the case that both crimes were proved by precisely the same evidence. Under *Blockburger*, the government still wins. Third, the sentencing consequences of the two crimes are irrelevant. Successive prosecution and multiple punishment cases arise in the first place because prosecutors wish to impose a different sentence than a single charge would yield. One would think that double jeopardy law would therefore pay some attention to sentencing: It is, after all, the point of the exercise. Under *Blockburger*, though, sentencing consequences are beside the point. Double jeopardy is a matter of form, not substance.

One more aspect of *Blockburger* deserves mention: The defendant's claim was multiple punishment, not successive prosecution; the two drug charges were both brought in the same case. Most of the cases discussed in the notes that follow involve defendants who were prosecuted twice, and who claim that the second prosecution was barred by the first. It is worth remembering that throughout the relevant time period, most courts applied *Blockburger*'s test to multiple punishment cases—where the two charges are brought in a single prosecution—as well as to successive prosecution cases. There is an important difference, however: Under Missouri v. Hunter, 459 U.S. 359 (1983), *Blockburger* is nothing more than a rule of statutory interpretation in the multiple punishment context. In the successive prosecution cases, *Blockburger* is a constitutional requirement.

2. *Blockburger*'s algebraic approach governed the "same offence" issue for the next several decades. For most of that time, the issue did not attract much litigation, because the Double Jeopardy Clause only applied to the federal government, and most criminal prosecutions happened in state courts. Benton v. Maryland, 395 U.S. 784 (1969), held that the ban on double jeopardy applied to state cases, because that ban was one of the fundamental liberties incorporated into the Due

Process Clause in the Fourteenth Amendment. After *Benton*, *Blockburger*'s boundaries were frequently tested—and the Court's commitment to the algebraic approach wavered, as the following cases show.

3. One of the most important tests came in Brown v. Ohio, 432 U.S. 161 (1977). The facts in *Brown* were as follows:

> On November 29, 1973, the petitioner, Nathaniel Brown, stole a 1965 Chevrolet from a parking lot in East Cleveland, Ohio. Nine days later, on December 8, 1973, Brown was caught driving the car in Wickliffe, Ohio. The Wickliffe police charged him with "joyriding"—taking or operating the car without the owner's consent—in violation of Ohio Rev. Code Ann. §4549.04(D). . . . Brown pleaded guilty to this charge and was sentenced to 30 days in jail and a $1,000 fine.
>
> Upon his release from jail on January 8, 1974, Brown was returned to East Cleveland to face further charges, and on February 5 he was indicted by the Cuyahoga County grand jury. The indictment was in two counts, the first charging the theft of the car "on or about the 29th day of November 1973," in violation of Ohio Rev. Code Ann. §4549.04(A) (1973), and the second charging joyriding on the same date in violation of §4549.04(D).

Id., at 162-163. The joyriding prohibition read: "No person shall purposely take, operate, or keep any motor vehicle without the consent of its owner." The auto theft statute was simpler: "No person shall steal any motor vehicle." According to the Ohio Court of Appeals, auto theft was joyriding plus the intent to permanently deprive the owner of his car. Thus, joyriding was a lesser-included version of auto theft, meaning the two crimes were "the same offence" under *Blockburger*. The state nevertheless claimed they *weren't* the same offense as far as Brown was concerned, because the first joyriding charge was based on Brown's behavior on December 8, 1973, while the auto theft charge was based on his conduct on November 29, 1973—the day Brown took the car. The different dates meant that each crime required proof of a fact that the other didn't.

The Supreme Court rejected the state's argument:

> After correctly holding that joyriding and auto theft are the same offense under the Double Jeopardy Clause, the Ohio Court of Appeals nevertheless concluded that Nathaniel Brown could be convicted of both crimes because the charges against him focused on different parts of his 9-day joyride. We hold a different view. The Double Jeopardy Clause is not such a fragile guarantee that prosecutors can avoid its limitations by the simple expedient of dividing a single crime into a series of temporal or spatial units. The applicable Ohio statutes, as written and as construed in this case, make the theft and operation of a single car a single offense. Although the Wickliffe and East Cleveland authorities may have had different perspectives on Brown's offense, it was still only one offense under Ohio law. Accordingly, the specification of different dates in the two charges on which Brown was convicted cannot alter the fact that he was placed twice in jeopardy for the same offense in violation of the Fifth and Fourteenth Amendments.

Id., at 169-170. Justice Powell, author of the *Brown* majority opinion, dropped a footnote qualifying the language just quoted:

> We would have a different case if the Ohio Legislature had provided that joyriding is a separate offense for each day in which a motor vehicle is operated without the

owner's consent. We also would have a different case if in sustaining Brown's second conviction the Ohio courts had construed the joyriding statute to have that effect. . . .

Id., at 169, n. 8. Doesn't this mean that prosecutors *can* avoid double jeopardy "by the simple expedient of dividing a single crime into a series of temporal . . . units"—as long as the state legislature drafts or the state appellate courts construe the relevant statutes to do just that?

4. Harris v. Oklahoma, 433 U.S. 682 (1977) (per curiam), was decided two weeks after *Brown*. The Court's opinion was brief, but important:

> A clerk in a Tulsa, Oklahoma grocery store was shot and killed by a companion of petitioner in the course of a robbery of the store by the two men. Petitioner was convicted of felony murder in Oklahoma State court. The opinion of the Oklahoma Court of Criminal Appeals in this case states that "[i]n a felony murder case, the proof of the underlying felony [here robbery with firearms] is needed to prove the intent necessary for a felony murder conviction." 555 P.2d 76, 80-81 (1976). Petitioner nevertheless was thereafter brought to trial and convicted on a separate information charging the robbery with firearms, after denial of his motion to dismiss on the ground that this prosecution violated the Double Jeopardy Clause of the Fifth Amendment because he had been already convicted of the offense in the felony-murder trial. The Oklahoma Court of Criminal Appeals affirmed.
>
> When, as here, conviction of a greater crime, murder, cannot be had without conviction of the lesser crime, robbery with firearms, the Double Jeopardy Clause bars prosecution for the lesser crime after conviction of the greater one.[*] In re Nielsen, 131 U.S. 176 (1889); cf. Brown v. Ohio, 432 U.S. 161 (1977). "[A] person [who] has been tried and convicted for a crime which has various incidents included in it, . . . cannot be a second time tried for one of those incidents without being twice put in jeopardy for the same offence." In re Nielsen, supra, at 188.

Id., at 682-683.

At first blush, *Harris* seems squarely at odds with *Blockburger*. Felony murder does not require proof of robbery, and armed robbery does not require proof that the defendant caused the victim's death, so the two crimes cannot be "the same" for double jeopardy purposes. But perhaps the cases are consistent after all. Felony murder is a crime that incorporates a set of other crimes. It could be expressed as a list: murder during the course of a robbery, murder during the course of a rape, murder during the course of a kidnapping, and so on. When deciding double jeopardy cases under *Blockburger*, perhaps such crimes should be considered *as if the legislature had enacted the relevant list* rather than a single criminal statute. *Harris* then becomes an easy case—for the defense. After all, armed robbery is plainly a lesser-included offense relative to murder during the course of an armed robbery.

As the cases in the notes that follow indicate, there are a number of crimes like felony murder—crimes that incorporate a list of other crimes; sometimes the list is specified, sometimes not. Should all such criminal statutes be read the way the Court read the felony murder law in *Harris*? If not, how are courts supposed to know when to follow *Harris* and when to ignore it?

---

* The State conceded in its response to the petition for certiorari that "in the Murder case, it was necessary for all the ingredients of the underlying felony of Robbery with Firearms to be proved. . . ."

5. *Harris* had disturbing implications for enterprise crimes like RICO (Racketeer Influenced and Corrupt Organizations Act, 18 U.S.C. §§1961-1968) and CCE (the "continuing criminal enterprise" statute, 21 U.S.C. §848). (Both of the statutes just cited are federal, but similar statutes exist in many state codes.) These statutes have two goals. First, as the label suggests, they aim to define criminal enterprises and punish those who operate them. The second goal is related: to punish career criminals by identifying various "predicate crimes" that such criminals typically commit. RICO is the classic example of an enterprise crime. The most commonly used provision in the RICO statute covers anyone who operates a criminal enterprise "through a pattern of racketeering activity." 18 U.S.C. §1962(c). "Pattern" basically means two or more acts of "racketeering activity," which the statute defines by giving a long list of predicate crimes — ranging from drugs to violent crimes to white-collar offenses. Similarly, the CCE statute seeks to punish "drug kingpins." The statute does this by listing qualifying drug crimes; anyone who commits such crimes is, by definition, a "drug kingpin," and may be punished for a CCE violation. As these examples suggest, enterprise crimes bear some similarity to status offenses: a famous article by Judge (then Professor) Gerard Lynch labeled RICO "the crime of being a criminal." Gerard E. Lynch, RICO: The Crime of Being a Criminal, Parts I and II, 87 Colum. L. Rev. 661 (1987). Lynch's title is apt because of the huge role predicate crimes play in RICO (or CCE) analysis.

Often, defendants prosecuted for enterprise crimes have already been charged and convicted for one or more of the predicate crimes on which the government relies for the enterprise charge. If enterprise crimes are treated as felony murder was treated in *Harris*, those prosecutions would all be invalid. *Harris* held that felony murder statutes should be read as lists: murder during the course of a rape, murder during the course of a robbery, and so forth. Enterprise crimes could plausibly be read the same way: a continuing enterprise that combined drug crimes *A, B,* and *C*; a continuing enterprise that combined drug crimes *B, C,* and *D*; a continuing enterprise that combined drug crimes *A, B,* and *D*; and so on. On that construction, any one predicate crime would be a lesser-included offense (just as armed robbery was in *Harris*), and prosecution for the greater offense — the enterprise crime — would be barred.

The Supreme Court found that result unacceptable. The defendant in Garrett v. United States, 471 U.S. 773 (1985), was charged and convicted of importing marijuana; the charge involved a large shipment that Garrett helped unload from a ship at Neah Bay, Washington. Two months after that conviction, Garrett was charged in a federal CCE indictment in Florida; the Washington marijuana importation was one of three predicate crimes charged in the Florida indictment. The Court found no double jeopardy bar to the second charge. Then-Justice Rehnquist's majority opinion noted that there was a "good deal of difference" between the "classic" lesser-included-offense situation and the one presented in *Garrett*, because — unlike joyriding and automobile theft, where each moment of criminal conduct simultaneously violates both statutes — CCE defines an ongoing crime; Garrett's CCE offense was not complete when he imported marijuana in Washington. (In fact, as the Court noted, the CCE offense was still not complete when the indictment was returned for the Washington crime.) As Rehnquist artfully put it: "One who insists that the music stop and the piper be paid at a particular point must at least have stopped dancing himself before he may seek such an accounting." Id., at 790.

The Court's analysis in *Garrett* was consistent with *Blockburger* itself: The CCE statute did not require proof of marijuana importation — that was just one of a list of predicate crimes—and marijuana importation obviously did not require proof of a "continuing criminal enterprise." But *Garrett* could not easily be squared with *Harris*. At the least, *Garrett* stands for the proposition that *Harris* does not apply to enterprise crimes. The upshot is that such crimes almost never raise serious double jeopardy problems.

That last sentence applies to conspiracy prosecutions as well. Criminal defendants are often charged with both a particular substantive crime and with conspiracy to commit that crime, sometimes in a single prosecution and sometimes in separate prosecutions. In United States v. Felix, 503 U.S. 378 (1992), the Court held that "a substantive crime and a conspiracy to commit that crime are not the 'same offence' for double jeopardy purposes." The majority opinion in *Felix*, again authored by Chief Justice Rehnquist, explained that holding as follows:

> In a related context, we recently cautioned against the "ready transposition of the 'lesser included offense' principles of double jeopardy from the classically simple situation presented in Brown v. Ohio to the multilayered conduct, both as to time and to place, involved in [CCE prosecutions]." [Garrett v. United States, 441 U.S.,] at 789. The great majority of conspiracy prosecutions involve similar allegations of multi-layered conduct as to time and place; the conspiracy charge against Felix is a perfect example. Reliance on the lesser included offense analysis, however useful in the context of a "single course of conduct," is therefore much less helpful in analyzing subsequent conspiracy prosecutions that are supported by previously prosecuted overt acts, just as it falls short in examining CCE offenses that are based on previously prosecuted predicate acts. Id., at 788-789.

503 U.S., at 389-390. As the passage just quoted indicates, the *Felix* Court cited *Garrett* extensively.

6. Even before *Felix*, the *Blockburger* test seemed unstable. Cases like *Brown*, *Harris*, and *Garrett* suggested that the Court was looking for a better approach to "same offence" cases. So it did not come as a complete surprise when, in Grady v. Corbin, 495 U.S. 508 (1990), the Court decided simply to do away with *Blockburger*.

Grady arose out of a miscommunication. Corbin was a drunk driver; he drove his car across the double yellow line of a state highway in upstate New York, and struck two cars traveling in the other direction. The driver of one of those two cars was killed, and a passenger in that same car was seriously injured. A blood alcohol test showed that Corbin had nearly twice the legal limit of alcohol in his blood. On these facts, the local district attorney's office could be expected to seek an indictment for manslaughter and felony assault—which shortly happened. In the meantime, though, Corbin was served with two traffic tickets, charging him with driving while intoxicated and "failing to keep right of the median." Three weeks after the accident, Corbin pled guilty to those charges—with no one from the District Attorney's office present. Three weeks after the guilty plea, Corbin received his sentence: a $350 fine and a six-month revocation of his driver's license. An Assistant District Attorney did show up for Corbin's sentencing, but she had not read the file, was not aware that anyone had been killed or injured in the accident, and did not know that a grand jury would soon be investigating the relevant events.

Two months later, Corbin was indicted for manslaughter, reckless assault, and driving while intoxicated. The prosecution "filed a bill of particulars that identified the three reckless or negligent acts on which it would rely to prove the homicide and assault charges":

(1) operating a motor vehicle on a public highway in an intoxicated condition, (2) failing to keep right of the median, and (3) driving approximately 45 to 50 miles per Comprehensive hour in heavy rain, "which was a speed too fast for the weather and road conditions then pending." App. 20. Respondent moved to dismiss the indictment on . . . double jeopardy grounds.

Id., at 514.

On a straightforward application of *Blockburger*, Corbin seemed to have a weak case. Manslaughter and assault did not require proof that Corbin had failed to keep his car on the right side of the road, and the traffic charge did not require proof of injury or death. The New York Court of Appeals nevertheless found Corbin's double jeopardy claim valid—and, by a 5-4 vote in an opinion by Justice Brennan, the Supreme Court agreed:

> [A] subsequent prosecution must do more than merely survive the *Blockburger* test. . . . [T]he Double Jeopardy Clause bars any subsequent prosecution in which the government, to establish an essential element of an offense charged in that prosecution, will prove conduct that constitutes an offense for which the defendant has already been prosecuted.[11] This is not an "actual evidence" or "same evidence" test. The critical inquiry is what conduct the State will prove, not the evidence the State will use to prove that conduct. As we have held, the presentation of specific evidence in one trial does not forever prevent the government from introducing that same evidence in a subsequent proceeding. See Dowling v. United States, 493 U.S. 342 (1990). On the other hand, a State cannot avoid the dictates of the Double Jeopardy Clause merely by altering in successive prosecutions the evidence offered to prove the same conduct. For example, if two bystanders had witnessed Corbin's accident, it would make no difference to our double jeopardy analysis if the State called one witness to testify in the first trial that Corbin's vehicle crossed the median (or if nobody testified in the first trial because Corbin, as he did, pleaded guilty) and called the other witness to testify to the same conduct in the second trial.

495 U.S., at 521-522. Having articulated a new constitutional test for successive prosecutions, Justice Brennan then proceeded to apply that test to the facts of Corbin's case. Because of the filing of the bill of particulars, it was relatively easy for the Court to determine exactly what the state intended to prove in order to obtain a conviction on the manslaughter and assault charges—and to conclude that those charges, under the state's current theory of the case, were barred by double jeopardy.

Justice Brennan's opinion noted that Corbin could be prosecuted for manslaughter and assault by using a different theory of the case: "This holding would not bar a subsequent prosecution on the homicide and assault charges if the bill of particulars revealed that the State would not rely on proving the conduct for which Corbin had already been convicted (i.e., if the State relied solely on Corbin's driving too

---

11. Similarly, if in the course of securing a conviction for one offense the State necessarily has proved the conduct comprising all of the elements of another offense not yet prosecuted (a "component offense"), the Double Jeopardy Clause would bar subsequent prosecution of the component offense. See Harris v. Oklahoma, 433 U.S. 682 (1977) ("When, as here, conviction of a greater crime, murder, cannot be had without conviction of the lesser crime, robbery with firearms, the Double Jeopardy Clause bars prosecution for the lesser crime after conviction of the greater one") (footnote omitted); cf. *Brown*, 432 U.S., at 168 (noting that it is irrelevant for the purposes of the Double Jeopardy Clause whether the conviction of the greater offense precedes the conviction of the lesser offense or vice versa).

fast in heavy rain to establish recklessness or negligence)." Justice Brennan stressed that the Court was *not* adopting a "same transaction" test—i.e., a requirement that all crimes related to a given transaction or incident be charged in a single prosecution. Still, *Grady* was a sharp departure from previous double jeopardy cases—and a major expansion of the meaning of "the same offence."[2]

Justice Scalia wrote the chief dissent in *Grady*. (He was joined by Chief Justice Rehnquist and Justice Kennedy; Justice O'Connor dissented separately.) After defending the *Blockburger* test, Scalia opined that the effect of the Court's ruling in *Grady* would be to force the states into adopting the "same transaction" approach—because otherwise, they would be barred from using, in a later prosecution, potentially persuasive evidence of substantive crimes that were proved in a prior prosecution, even if those earlier crimes were not elements of the later crime. Justice Scalia also noted some practical difficulties in applying Justice Brennan's new rule—especially the bar on introduction, during a second prosecution, of evidence that would "prove conduct that constitutes an offense for which the defendant has already been prosecuted":

> Apart from the lack of rational basis for this latter limitation, I am greatly perplexed (as will be the unfortunate trial court judges who must apply today's rootless decision) as to what precisely it means. It is not at all apparent how a court is to go about deciding whether the evidence that has been introduced (or that will be introduced) at the second trial "proves conduct" that constitutes an offense for which the defendant has already been prosecuted. Is the judge in the second trial supposed to pretend that he is the judge in the first one, and to let the second trial proceed only if the evidence would not be enough to go to the jury on the earlier charge? Or (as the language of the Court's test more readily suggests) is the judge in the second trial supposed to decide on his own whether the evidence before him really "proves" the earlier charge (perhaps beyond a reasonable doubt)? Consider application of the Court's new rule in the unusually simple circumstances of the present case: Suppose that, in the trial upon remand, the prosecution's evidence shows, among other things, that when the vehicles came to rest after the collision they were located on what was, for the defendant's vehicle, the wrong side of the road. The prosecution also produces a witness who testifies that prior to the collision the defendant's vehicle was "weaving back and forth"—*without* saying, however, that it was weaving back and forth over the center line. Is this enough to meet today's requirement of "proving" the offense of operating a vehicle on the wrong side of the road? If not, suppose in addition that defense counsel asks the witness on cross-examination, "When you said the defendant's vehicle was 'weaving back and forth,' did you mean weaving back and forth across the center line?"—to which the witness replies "yes." Will this self-inflicted wound count for purposes of determining what the prosecution has "proved"? If so, can the prosecution then seek to impeach its own witness by showing that his recollection of the vehicle's crossing the center line was inaccurate? Or can it at least introduce another witness to establish that fact? There are many questions here, and the answers to all of them are ridiculous. Whatever line is selected as the criterion of "proving" the prior offense—enough evidence to go to the jury, more likely than not, or beyond a reasonable doubt—the prosecutor in the second trial will presumably seek to introduce

---

2. Technically, Justice Brennan's opinion in *Grady* did not overrule *Blockburger*—rather, the Court added a new double jeopardy requirement *in addition to* the *Blockburger* test. The effect, however, was the same as if *Blockburger* had been overruled. On the one hand, in any case in which the state satisfies *Grady*'s requirements, *Blockburger* will be satisfied as well. On the other hand, there are a great many cases that satisfy *Blockburger* but flunk *Grady*. The upshot is that, as long as *Grady* was good law, *Blockburger* did not work.

as much evidence as he can without crossing that line; and the defense attorney will presumably seek to provoke the prosecutor into (or assist him in) proving the defendant guilty of the earlier crime. This delicious role reversal, discovered to have been mandated by the Double Jeopardy Clause lo these 200 years, makes for high comedy but inferior justice. . . . Even if we had no constitutional text and no prior case law to rely upon, rejection of today's opinion is adequately supported by the modest desire to protect our criminal legal system from ridicule.

Id., at 540-542 (Scalia, J., dissenting).

The opinions in *Grady* contain a great deal of discussion of the merits of different double jeopardy rules. But there is very little discussion of the justice of Corbin's claim. Suppose the state had been allowed to proceed with the manslaughter and assault charges. Would Corbin have been the victim of an injustice? Certainly not by reference to the results in factually similar cases. The only way any defendant could walk away with a modest fine on facts like those in *Grady* was through the kind of bureaucratic mistake that characterized Corbin's first "prosecution." Why should Corbin benefit from the government's error? Corbin seems more the beneficiary of official ineptitude than the victim of government oppression.

Consider another angle on the case. Suppose Corbin was indeed prosecuted twice—once for the traffic offenses, once for manslaughter and assault; suppose further that that course of action is indeed unjust. How can the injustice best be remedied? The Court assumes the only possible remedy is to dismiss the indictment for manslaughter and assault. But there is another possibility: Why not give Corbin his $350 back, rescind the license revocation, and let the prosecution for manslaughter and assault go forward? In other words, why not eliminate punishment for the traffic offense, rather than for manslaughter and assault? The answer is that, traditionally, double jeopardy law does not work that way; once one "jeopardy" is complete, the only available remedy is dismissal of charges that produce a second "jeopardy" for the same crime. Still, tradition is not much of an answer. Grady v. Corbin may be a case in which the defendant's interest in being punished once—not twice—for his crime *and* the state's interest in punishing homicides could have been protected. But that could only happen if the courts focused attention not just on the scope of the double jeopardy right, but on the proper remedy for its violation.

7. In the three years following *Grady*, the Supreme Court saw two personnel changes. Justice Brennan retired and was replaced by Justice Souter; and Justice Marshall retired and was replaced by Justice Thomas. In 1993, the Court revisited *Grady*—only this time, Justice Thomas lined up with the *Grady* dissenters. The *Blockburger* test rose from the ashes.

The case was United States v. Dixon, 509 U.S. 688 (1993). *Dixon* was actually two companion cases—Alvin Dixon and Michael Foster were both convicted of criminal contempt; in both cases, the government proceeded to indict the defendants for the same conduct that formed the basis of the contempt charges. Foster's case required the Court either to apply *Grady* or overrule it; the Court chose the latter path, and reinstated the *Blockburger* test as governing double jeopardy law. Dixon's case raised questions about the nature and meaning of the *Blockburger* test. Though the Court dealt with the two cases in a single set of opinions, they are best understood separately. We excerpt the Court's discussion of Dixon's case below. But first, consider Foster's double jeopardy claim.

Michael Foster was an abusive husband; his repeated assaults led his wife, Ana Foster, to obtain a civil protection order (CPO) against him. That order required that Foster not "molest, assault, or in any manner threaten or physically abuse" Ana. After repeatedly violating the CPO, Foster was charged with criminal contempt—the elements of which were the same as the crime of simple assault plus knowing violation of the CPO. He was convicted, and received a total sentence of 600 days of incarceration. Later, Foster was indicted for, inter alia, "threatening to injure another" and assault with intent to kill.

All nine Justices agreed that, on these facts, Foster did not have a valid double jeopardy claim under *Blockburger*. Eight of the nine agreed that Foster *did* have a valid claim under Grady v. Corbin. (Justice Blackmun disagreed: He thought there was no double jeopardy violation even under *Grady*, because of the special status of contempt proceedings.) Thus, Foster's case squarely posed the question whether *Grady* should remain good law. Justice Scalia wrote for a five-vote majority—the four *Grady* dissenters plus Justice Thomas:

> . . . We have concluded . . . that *Grady* must be overruled. Unlike *Blockburger* analysis, whose definition of what prevents two crimes from being the "same offence" has deep historical roots and has been accepted in numerous precedents of this Court, *Grady* lacks constitutional roots. The "same-conduct" rule it announced is wholly inconsistent with earlier Supreme Court precedent and with the clear common-law understanding of double jeopardy. . . .
>
> . . . *Grady* was not only wrong in principle; it has already proved unstable in application. Less than two years after it came down, in United States v. Felix, 503 U.S. 378 (1992), we were forced to recognize a large exception to it. There we concluded that a subsequent prosecution for conspiracy to manufacture, possess, and distribute methamphetamine was not barred by a previous conviction for attempt to manufacture the same substance. We offered as a justification for avoiding a "literal" (i.e., faithful) reading of *Grady* "longstanding authority" to the effect that prosecution for conspiracy is not precluded by prior prosecution for the substantive offense. *Felix*, supra, at 388-391. Of course the very existence of such a large and longstanding "exception" to the *Grady* rule gave cause for concern that the rule was not an accurate expression of the law. . . .
>
> . . . [W]e think it time to acknowledge what is now, three years after *Grady*, compellingly clear: The case was a mistake. We do not lightly reconsider a precedent, but, because *Grady* contradicted an "unbroken line of decisions," contained "less than accurate" historical analysis, and has produced "confusion," we do so here. Solorio v. United States, 483 U.S. 435, 439, 442, 450 (1987). . . .

Dixon, 509 U.S., at 703-711. Justice Souter was *Grady*'s chief defender:

> . . . [W]hile the government may punish a person separately for each conviction of at least as many different offenses as meet the *Blockburger* test, we have long held that it must sometimes bring its prosecutions for these offenses together. If a separate prosecution were permitted for every offense arising out of the same conduct, the government could manipulate the definitions of offenses, creating fine distinctions among them and permitting a zealous prosecutor to try a person again and again for essentially the same criminal conduct. . . .
>
> An example will show why this [position is correct]. Assume three crimes: robbery with a firearm, robbery in a dwelling, and simple robbery. The elements of the three crimes are the same, except that robbery with a firearm has the element that a firearm be used in the commission of the robbery while the other two crimes do not, and robbery in a dwelling has the element that the robbery occur in a dwelling while the other two crimes do not.

If a person committed a robbery in a dwelling with a firearm and was prosecuted for simple robbery, all agree he could not be prosecuted subsequently for either of the greater offenses of robbery with a firearm or robbery in a dwelling. Under the lens of *Blockburger*, however, if that same person were prosecuted first for robbery with a firearm, he could be prosecuted subsequently for robbery in a dwelling, even though he could not subsequently be prosecuted on the basis of that same robbery for simple robbery. This is true simply because neither of the crimes, robbery with a firearm and robbery in a dwelling, is either identical to or a lesser-included offense of the other. But since the purpose of the Double Jeopardy Clause's protection against successive prosecutions is to prevent repeated trials in which a defendant will be forced to defend against the same charge again and again, . . . it should be irrelevant that the second prosecution would require the defendant to defend himself not only from the charge that he committed the robbery, but also from the charge of some additional fact, in this case, that the scene of the crime was a dwelling. If, instead, protection against successive prosecution were as limited as it would be by *Blockburger* alone, the doctrine would be as striking for its anomalies as for the limited protection it would provide. . . .

Id., at 747-749 (Souter, J., concurring in the judgment in part and dissenting in part). Justice Scalia responded to Souter's argument as follows:

The centerpiece of Justice Souter's analysis is an appealing theory of a "successive prosecution" strand of the Double Jeopardy Clause that has a different meaning from its supposed "successive punishment" strand. We have often noted that the Clause serves the function of preventing both successive punishment and successive prosecution, but there is no authority, except *Grady*, for the proposition that it has different meanings in the two contexts. That is perhaps because it is embarrassing to assert that the single term "same offence" (the words of the Fifth Amendment at issue here) has two different meanings—that what is the same offense is yet not the same offense. Justice Souter provides no authority whatsoever (and we are aware of none) for the bald assertion that "we have long held that [the government] must sometimes bring its prosecutions for [separate] offenses together." The collateral-estoppel effect attributed to the Double Jeopardy Clause, see Ashe v. Swenson, 397 U.S. 436 (1970), may bar a later prosecution for a separate offense where the Government has lost an earlier prosecution involving the same facts. But this does not establish that the Government "must . . . bring its prosecutions . . . together." It is entirely free to bring them separately, and can win convictions in both. Of course the collateral-estoppel issue is not raised in this case. . . .

Id., at 704-705.

Who has the better of this debate?

8. Given the Court's decision to abandon *Grady*, *Blockburger* is once again binding law. The precise boundaries of the *Blockburger* test are now a matter of great doctrinal importance. Consider what *Dixon* says about *that* issue.

UNITED STATES v. DIXON

Certiorari to the District of Columbia Court of Appeals
509 U.S. 688 (1993)

JUSTICE SCALIA announced the judgment of the Court and delivered the opinion of the Court with respect to Parts I, II, and IV. . . .

I

Respondent Alvin Dixon was arrested for second-degree murder and was released on bond. Consistent with the District of Columbia's bail law authorizing the judicial officer to impose any condition that "will reasonably assure the appearance of the person for trial or the safety of any other person or the community," D.C. Code Ann. §23-1321(a) (1989), Dixon's release form specified that he was not to commit "any criminal offense," and warned that any violation of the conditions of release would subject him "to revocation of release, an order of detention, and prosecution for contempt of court." See §23-1329(a) (authorizing those sanctions).

While awaiting trial, Dixon was arrested and indicted for possession of cocaine with intent to distribute, in violation of D.C. Code Ann. §33-541(a)(1) (1988). The court issued an order requiring Dixon to show cause why he should not be held in contempt or have the terms of his pretrial release modified. At the show-cause hearing, four police officers testified to facts surrounding the alleged drug offense; Dixon's counsel cross-examined these witnesses and introduced other evidence. The court concluded that the Government had established "beyond a reasonable doubt that [Dixon] was in possession of drugs and that those drugs were possessed with the intent to distribute." 598 A.2d 724, 728 (D.C. 1991). The court therefore found Dixon guilty of criminal contempt under §23-1329(c), which allows contempt sanctions after expedited proceedings without a jury and "in accordance with principles applicable to proceedings for criminal contempt." For his contempt, Dixon was sentenced to 180 days in jail. D.C. Code §23-1329(c) (maximum penalty of six months' imprisonment and $1000 fine). He later moved to dismiss the cocaine indictment on double jeopardy grounds; the trial court granted the motion. . . .

The Government appealed the double jeopardy ruling in *Dixon.* . . . The District of Columbia Court of Appeals . . . , relying on our recent decision in Grady v. Corbin, 495 U.S. 508 (1990), ruled that [the second prosecution for cocaine possession was] barred by the Double Jeopardy Clause. 598 A.2d, at 725. In its petition for certiorari, the Government presented the sole question "whether the Double Jeopardy Clause bars prosecution of a defendant on substantive criminal charges based upon the same conduct for which he previously has been held in criminal contempt of court." . . .

II

[Justice Scalia began by reviewing the history of the contempt power, noting that the specific kinds of contempt orders issued herein would have been impossible at common law, or in the nineteenth century American judicial system.]

We have held that constitutional protections for criminal defendants other than the double jeopardy provision apply in nonsummary criminal contempt prosecutions just as they do in other criminal prosecutions. See, e.g., Gompers v. Bucks Stove & Range Co., 221 U.S. 418, 444 (1911) (presumption of innocence, proof beyond a reasonable doubt, and guarantee against self-incrimination); Cooke v. United States, 267 U.S. 517, 537 (1925) (notice of charges, assistance of counsel, and right to present a defense); In re Oliver, 333 U.S. 257, 278 (1948) (public trial). We think it obvious, and today hold, that the protection of the Double Jeopardy Clause likewise attaches.

In both the multiple punishment and multiple prosecution contexts, this Court has concluded that where the two offenses for which the defendant is punished or tried cannot survive the "same-elements" test, the double jeopardy bar applies. See, e.g., Brown v. Ohio, 432 U.S. 161, 168-169 (1977); Blockburger v. United States, 284 U.S. 299, 304 (1932) (multiple punishment); Gavieres v. United States, 220 U.S. 338, 342 (1911) (successive prosecutions). The same-elements test, sometimes referred to as the "Blockburger" test, inquires whether each offense contains an element not contained in the other; if not, they are the "same offence" and double jeopardy bars additional punishment and successive prosecution. In a case such as [State v. Yancy, 4 N.C. 133 (1814)], for example, in which the contempt prosecution was for disruption of judicial business, the same-elements test would not bar subsequent prosecution for the criminal assault that was part of the disruption, because the contempt offense did not require the element of criminal conduct, and the criminal offense did not require the element of disrupting judicial business. . . .

III

. . . The statute applicable in Dixon's contempt prosecution provides that "[a] person who has been conditionally released . . . and who has violated a condition of release shall be subject to . . . prosecution for contempt of court." §23-1329(a). Obviously, Dixon could not commit an "offence" under this provision until an order setting out conditions was issued. The statute by itself imposes no legal obligation on anyone. Dixon's cocaine possession, although an offense under [the D.C. Code], was not an offense under §23-1329 until a judge incorporated the statutory drug offense into his release order.

In this situation, in which the contempt sanction is imposed for violating the order through commission of the incorporated drug offense, the later attempt to prosecute Dixon for the drug offense resembles the situation that produced our judgment of double jeopardy in Harris v. Oklahoma, 433 U.S. 682 (1977) (per curiam). There we held that a subsequent prosecution for robbery with a firearm was barred by the Double Jeopardy Clause, because the defendant had already been tried for felony murder based on the same underlying felony. We have described our terse per curiam in *Harris* as standing for the proposition that, for double jeopardy purposes, "the crime generally described as felony murder" is not "a separate offense distinct from its various elements." Illinois v. Vitale, 447 U.S. 410, 420-421 (1980). So too here. . . . The Dixon court order incorporated the entire governing criminal code in the same manner as the *Harris* felony-murder statute incorporated the several enumerated felonies. Here, as in *Harris*, the underlying substantive criminal offense is "a species of lesser-included offense." *Vitale*, supra, at 420. . . .

. . . Because Dixon's drug offense did not include any element not contained in his previous contempt offense, his subsequent prosecution violates the Double Jeopardy Clause . . .

IV

[This part of Justice Scalia's opinion, joined by a majority of the Justices, discussed Michael Foster's claims. The Court concluded that those claims failed under the *Blockburger* test, but would succeed under Grady v. Corbin. The Court then went on to explain why *Grady* should be overruled.]

CHIEF JUSTICE REHNQUIST, with whom JUSTICE O'CONNOR and JUSTICE THOMAS join, concurring in part and dissenting in part.

. . . I do not join Part III of Justice Scalia's opinion because I think that none of the criminal prosecutions in this case were barred under *Blockburger*. I must then confront the expanded version of double jeopardy embodied in *Grady*. For the reasons set forth in the *Grady* dissent (Scalia, J., dissenting), . . . I, too, think that *Grady* must be overruled. I . . . write separately to express my disagreement with Justice Scalia's application of Blockburger in Part III.

In my view, *Blockburger*'s same-elements test requires us to focus not on the terms of the particular court orders involved, but on the elements of contempt of court in the ordinary sense. Relying on Harris v. Oklahoma, 433 U.S. 682 (1977), a three-paragraph per curiam in an unargued case, Justice Scalia concludes otherwise today, and thus incorrectly finds in Part III of his opinion that the subsequent prosecution[] of Dixon for drug distribution . . . violated the Double Jeopardy Clause. In so doing, Justice Scalia rejects the traditional view—shared by every federal court of appeals and state supreme court that addressed the issue prior to *Grady*—that, as a general matter, double jeopardy does not bar a subsequent prosecution based on conduct for which a defendant has been held in criminal contempt. I cannot subscribe to a reading of *Harris* that upsets this previously well-settled principle of law. Because the generic crime of contempt of court has different elements than the substantive criminal charges in this case, I believe that they are separate offenses under *Blockburger*. I would therefore limit *Harris* to the context in which it arose: where the crimes in question are analogous to greater and lesser-included offenses. The crimes at issue here bear no such resemblance. . . .

Close inspection of the crimes at issue in *Harris* reveals, moreover, that our decision in that case was not a departure from *Blockburger*'s focus on the statutory elements of the offenses charged. In *Harris*, we held that a conviction for felony murder based on a killing in the course of an armed robbery foreclosed a subsequent prosecution for robbery with a firearm. Though the felony-murder statute in *Harris* did not require proof of armed robbery, it did include as an element proof that the defendant was engaged in the commission of some felony. We construed this generic reference to some felony as incorporating the statutory elements of the various felonies upon which a felony-murder conviction could rest. The criminal contempt provision involved here, by contrast, contains no such generic reference which by definition incorporates the statutory elements of assault or drug distribution.

Unless we are to accept the extraordinary view that the three-paragraph per curiam in *Harris* was intended to overrule sub silentio our previous decisions that looked to the statutory elements of the offenses charged in applying *Blockburger*, we are bound to conclude . . . that the ratio decidendi of our *Harris* decision was that the two crimes there were akin to greater and lesser included offenses. The crimes at issue here, however, cannot be viewed as greater and lesser included offenses, either intuitively or logically. A crime such as possession with intent to distribute cocaine is a serious felony that cannot easily be conceived of as a lesser included offense of criminal contempt, a relatively petty offense as applied to the conduct in this case. See D.C. Code Ann. §33-541(a)(2)(A) (Supp. 1992) (the maximum sentence for possession with intent to distribute cocaine is 15 years in prison). Indeed, to say that criminal contempt is an aggravated form of that offense defies common sense. . . .

But there is a more fundamental reason why the offenses in this case are not analogous to greater and lesser included offenses. A lesser included offense is defined as one that is "necessarily included" within the statutory elements of another offense. See Fed. Rule Crim. Proc. 31(c). Taking the facts of *Harris* as an example, a defendant who commits armed robbery necessarily has satisfied one of the statutory elements of felony murder. The same cannot be said, of course, about this case: A defendant who is guilty of possession with intent to distribute cocaine or of assault has not necessarily satisfied any statutory element of criminal contempt. Nor, for that matter, can it be said that a defendant who is held in criminal contempt has necessarily satisfied any element of those substantive crimes. In short, the offenses for which Dixon [was] prosecuted in this case cannot be analogized to greater and lesser included offenses; hence, they are separate and distinct for double jeopardy purposes.

The following analogy, raised by the Government at oral argument, helps illustrate the absurd results that Justice Scalia's *Harris/Blockburger* analysis could in theory produce. Suppose that the offense in question is failure to comply with a lawful order of a police officer, see, e.g., Ind. Code §9-21-8-1 (Supp. 1992), and that the police officer's order was, "Don't shoot that man." Under Justice Scalia's flawed reading of *Harris*, the elements of the offense of failure to obey a police officer's lawful order would include, for purposes of *Blockburger*'s same-elements test, the elements of, perhaps, murder or manslaughter, in effect converting those felonies into a lesser included offense of the crime of failure to comply with a lawful order of a police officer. . . .

JUSTICE WHITE, with whom JUSTICE STEVENS joins, concurring in the judgment in part and dissenting in part.

. . . [M]y view is that the subsequent prosecutions in both *Dixon* and *Foster* were impermissible as to *all* counts. I reach this conclusion because the offenses at issue in the contempt proceedings were either identical to, or lesser included offenses of, those charged in the subsequent prosecutions. . . .

The contempt orders in *Foster* and *Dixon* referred in one case to the District's laws regarding assaults and threats, and, in the other, to the criminal code in its entirety. The prohibitions imposed by the court orders, in other words, duplicated those already in place by virtue of the criminal statutes. Aside from differences in the sanctions inflicted, the distinction between being punished for violation of the criminal laws and being punished for violation of the court orders, therefore, is simply this: Whereas in the former case "the entire population" is subject to prosecution, in the latter such authority extends only to "those particular persons whose legal obligations result from their earlier participation in proceedings before the court." [Young v. United States ex rel. Vuitton et Fils, 481 U.S. 787, 800, n. 10 (1987).] But the *offenses* that are to be sanctioned in either proceeding must be similar, since the contempt orders incorporated, in full or in part, the criminal code.

Thus, in this case, the offense for which Dixon was held in contempt was possession with intent to distribute drugs. Since he previously had been indicted for precisely the same offense, the double jeopardy bar should apply. . . .[8]

---

8. Therefore, I obviously disagree with the Chief Justice's Blockburger v. United States, 284 U.S. 299 (1932), analysis which would require overruling not only Grady v. Corbin, 495 U.S. 508 (1990), but, as Justice Scalia explains, Harris v. Oklahoma, 433 U.S. 682 (1977), as well. At the very least, where conviction of the crime of contempt cannot be had without conviction of a statutory crime forbidden by court order, the Double Jeopardy Clause bars prosecution for the latter after acquittal or conviction of the former.

JUSTICE SOUTER, with whom JUSTICE STEVENS joins, concurring in the judgment in part and dissenting in part.

. . . I would . . . apply our successive prosecution decisions . . . to conclude that the prosecutions below were barred by the Double Jeopardy Clause. Dixon was prosecuted for violating a court order to "[r]efrain from committing any criminal offense." The contempt prosecution proved beyond a reasonable doubt that he had possessed cocaine with intent to distribute it. His prosecution, therefore, for possession with intent to distribute cocaine based on the same incident is barred. It is of course true that the elements of the two offenses can be treated as different. In the contempt conviction, the government had to prove knowledge of the court order as well as Dixon's commission of some criminal offense. In the subsequent prosecution, the government would have to prove possession of cocaine with intent to distribute. In any event, because the government has already prosecuted Dixon for the possession of cocaine at issue here, Dixon cannot be tried for that incident a second time. . . .

[The opinion of Justice Blackmun, concurring in part and dissenting in part, is omitted.]

NOTES AND QUESTIONS

1. Where does the law stand after *Dixon*? The answer is complicated, because *Dixon* produced two different, overlapping majorities. First, one majority of the Justices decided that Dixon's two crimes—contempt of court and possession of cocaine—were "the same." Justices Scalia and Kennedy see those crimes as "the same" because the contempt charge, in their view, is analogous to the felony murder law in Harris v. Oklahoma, 433 U.S. 682 (1977). Justices White and Stevens agree; notice footnote 8 in Justice White's opinion. That amounts to four votes for the *Blockburger* test coupled with a broad reading of *Harris*. Justice Souter, the fifth vote to bar Dixon's drug charge, has a different view: He sees the contempt charge and the cocaine charge as "the same" because they were based on the same conduct and would be proved by the same evidence—the approach mandated by Grady v. Corbin, 495 U.S. 508 (1990), which *Dixon* overrules.

That is the first *Dixon* majority. Then there is the second *Dixon* majority, the one that overruled *Grady*. Justices Scalia and Kennedy belong to that majority, as do the Chief Justice and Justices O'Connor and Thomas. These five Justices believe *Blockburger* and not *Grady* defines the meaning of "same offence." But they do not agree about what *Blockburger* means, nor about whether Dixon should win. Scalia and Kennedy take a broad view of *Harris* and vote to strike down Dixon's drug charge; Rehnquist, O'Connor, and Thomas would limit *Harris* to its facts and would permit the drug charge to go forward. As this confusing head count indicates, the key to the disagreement is the legal status of *Harris*. The Court has given that case a narrow reading in Garrett v. United States, 471 U.S. 773 (1985), and United States v. Felix, 503 U.S. 378 (1992)—the cases that apply double jeopardy analysis to enterprise crimes and conspiracy cases. Now, a four-Justice plurality has given that case a broad reading in *Dixon*. What the proper reading of *Harris* is today is anyone's guess.

2. Professor Erin Murphy notes that *Dixon* seems to have had little effect on the growing popularity, at least in the states, of contempt charges as a means to enforce conformity with legal and social norms:

Although *Dixon* might have stalled the use of contempt charges in state courts, that does not seem to be the case. In ruling that double jeopardy precluded only charges based on identical elements, the Court left open a fairly wide swath of terrain. One of the defendants discussed in *Dixon*, for instance, could not be tried for simple assault after having been convicted for contempt on that basis, but he could still be tried for the more serious offenses of assault with intent to kill and several counts of threats. Moreover, in many cases, bringing contempt charges may be appealing as a means of inducing plea bargaining with regard to other substantive counts.

For instance, domestic violence prosecutors have increasingly used contempt charges in order to secure convictions in otherwise difficult to prosecute cases. . . .

But contempt prosecutions are not confined only to the realm of domestic violence. Perhaps in response to the widespread formation of pretrial services agencies across the nation, conditions of release such as drug testing, job or educational training, and rehabilitative programs have become standard parts of release. In some jurisdictions, imposition of a "stay away" from a block or area has become a regular bail term.

And, of course, as release conditions have proliferated, so too have reported violations of those conditions. In 2000, for instance, 32% of released felony defendants in the seventy-five most populous counties committed some misconduct while in a release status, including failure to appear, arrest for a new offense, or [another violation of release conditions]. And, in general, the use of contempt as a means of enforcing such release conditions has become quite common.

Erin Murphy, Manufacturing Crime: Process, Pretext, and Criminal Justice, 97 Georgetown L.J. 1435 (2009); see also Jeannie Suk, Criminal Law Comes Home, 116 Yale L.J. 2 (2006) (discussing prevalence of protective orders, and associated criminal contempt prosecutions, as a means of addressing the problem of domestic violence).

3. *Dixon* involves successive prosecution claims. What rules apply to multiple punishment claims? Recall that in Missouri v. Hunter, 459 U.S. 359 (1983), the Court held that the Double Jeopardy Clause does not limit legislatures' ability to punish a defendant more than once for the same crime in the same proceeding. In multiple punishment cases, *Hunter* holds, double jeopardy law functions as a rule of statutory interpretation: We presume the legislature does not intend double punishment, but it is only a presumption. Then, in *Dixon*, Justice Scalia (in the portion of his opinion that was joined by a majority) writes that "there is no authority, except *Grady*, for the proposition that" the Double Jeopardy Clause means something different in multiple punishment cases than in successive prosecution cases. "[I]t is embarrassing to assert that the single term 'same offence' . . . has two different meanings—that what is the same offense is yet not the same offense." 509 U.S., at 704. It sounds like *Hunter* and *Dixon* are at odds.

The Court addressed this issue in a backhanded way in Rutledge v. United States, 517 U.S. 292 (1996). Rutledge was charged with conspiracy to distribute cocaine; he was also charged with operating a continuing criminal enterprise (CCE). The "enterprise" was cocaine distribution. One of the elements of the CCE charge was that Rutledge acted "in concert with" others—i.e., that Rutledge conspired with others. The Court held that that made CCE and conspiracy greater- and lesser-included offenses under *Blockburger*. The Court stated the relevant double jeopardy rule as follows: "[W]e presume that where two statutory provisions proscribe the 'same offense,' a legislature does not intend to impose two punishments for that offense." Id., at 297 (citation omitted). So "same offence" means the same thing in multiple punishment and successive prosecution cases; the governing test is *Blockburger*. But that test operates as a rule of statutory construction in multiple punishment cases. It is a constitutional requirement in successive prosecution cases.

4. What is the point of the *Blockburger* test? If the goal is to limit excessive punishment, the law surely fails: No attention is paid in these cases to the fairness (or not) of the aggregate sentence the defendants receive. If the goal is to guarantee finality, so that when a defendant once faces prosecution for a criminal incident, he can know that he will not face it again (at least not for that same incident), again the law fails. *Blockburger* makes charge-stacking easy. Most criminal codes have multiple versions of every major crime; those different prohibitions generally share most elements, but each has at least one unique element. Thus, a single criminal incident can easily yield a half-dozen criminal charges, either in one prosecution or spread across multiple prosecutions. *Blockburger* does nothing to prevent that. None of this is to say that defendants never prevail under *Blockburger*. Clearly, they do. But when they do, it is usually a sign that the prosecution made a foolish mistake, charged crimes *A* and *B* when they should have charged crimes *B* and *C* instead — or that one part of the district attorney's office failed to inform another part of the same office about a pending case: the scenario that produced Grady v. Corbin.

In short, "same offence" doctrine is not merely an instance of placing form over substance, though it is surely that. The larger problem with the doctrine is that the form bears no relation to the substance. Charge-stacking and prosecutorial harassment may be large problems in America's criminal justice system. If they are, there is no reason to believe that double jeopardy law does anything to make those problems smaller.

NOTES ON SENTENCING AND THE MEANING OF "THE SAME OFFENCE"

1. The traditional view about sentencing and double jeopardy was that the latter had nothing to do with the former. Double jeopardy applied to prosecutions, not to sentences. Therefore, relitigation of issues resolved in previous sentencing proceedings was fine — regardless of what the issue was or who won in the earlier proceeding. Neither *Blockburger* nor Ashe v. Swenson nor any of the doctrines surrounding double jeopardy's "acquittal rule" applied to sentencing.

That was the traditional rule. That rule began to bend in Bullington v. Missouri, 451 U.S. 430 (1981). Bullington was convicted of capital murder. At the close of the sentencing proceeding that followed, the jury determined that he should be sentenced to life in prison rather than death. Bullington's conviction was later overturned due to an error in jury selection, and he was again tried for capital murder. Bullington objected that he had been "acquitted" of the death penalty, and consequently could not be placed in jeopardy of receiving it again. By a 5-4 vote, the Supreme Court agreed. In several more recent cases, the Court has explained the *Bullington* rule. "[A]n acquittal on the merits by the sole decision-maker in the [capital sentencing] proceeding is final and bars retrial on the same charge." Arizona v. Rumsey, 467 U.S. 203, 211 (1984). A capital murder defendant wins an "acquittal on the merits" with respect to the death penalty when the sentencer (judge or jury) "decides that the prosecution has not proved its case that the death penalty is appropriate." Poland v. Arizona, 476 U.S. 147, 155 (1986) (emphasis deleted). Absent an "acquittal on the merits" — if, for example, the sentencing jury hangs, see

Sattazahn v. Pennsylvania, 537 U.S. 101 (2003) — relitigation of the death penalty is permissible.

These rules apply to the death penalty. Until recently, it was taken for granted that noncapital sentencing did not implicate the double jeopardy guarantee. The defendant in Witte v. United States, 515 U.S. 389 (1995), was charged and convicted of conspiring to distribute marijuana. Under the Federal Sentencing Guidelines, Witte's sentence was raised considerably based on other, uncharged drug violations, including a conspiracy to import a large quantity of cocaine. (His ultimate sentence on the marijuana charge was 12 years in prison.) While Witte was serving his sentence, another federal grand jury indicted him for importing that same large quantity of cocaine. Naturally, Witte claimed that this chain of events violated double jeopardy, since he had already been punished for the cocaine violation. The Supreme Court decided otherwise—the Court held that his entire 12-year sentence constituted "punishment" only for the marijuana charge. Since the cocaine charge was plainly not "the same" as the marijuana charge, the second prosecution was permissible.

2. Then came the Court's decisions in Apprendi v. New Jersey, 530 U.S. 466 (2000), Blakely v. Washington, 542 U.S. 296 (2004), and United States v. Booker, 543 U.S. 220 (2005). *Apprendi* held that any fact that increases the defendant's sentence beyond the statutory maximum functions as an element of an aggravated crime, and must therefore be found beyond a reasonable doubt by a jury. *Blakely* and *Booker* held that the *Apprendi* rule applies as well to any fact that is necessary in order to increase the defendant's maximum lawful sentence under a particular jurisdiction's sentencing guidelines (*Booker* involved the Federal Sentencing Guidelines, while *Blakely* dealt with the guidelines in the state of Washington).

If *Apprendi*, *Blakely*, and *Booker* hold that certain sentencing facts are to be treated as elements of crimes for purposes of the Sixth Amendment's jury trial guarantee and the Due Process Clause's standard of proof beyond a reasonable doubt, are they also elements of crimes for purposes of the Fifth Amendment's ban on double jeopardy? If so, the *Blockburger* test will be even more forgiving than it was before. *Apprendi/Blakely/Booker* means that ordinary crimes in guidelines jurisdictions now have many more "elements" than they once did. The *Blockburger* test says that any two crimes are different as long as each has at least one "element" that the other lacks. In a world where crimes have not three or four elements but a dozen or more, it will presumably be easier to find those unique elements—and it was already fairly easy.

The story may be the same in capital murder cases—or it may be different. The Court has not yet spoken, but Justice Scalia—*Blakely*'s author—offered his view of the matter in a plurality opinion in Sattazahn v. Pennsylvania, 537 U.S. 101 (2003):

> . . . Our decision in Apprendi v. New Jersey, 530 U.S. 466 (2000), clarified what constitutes an "element" of an offense for purposes of the Sixth Amendment's jury-trial guarantee. Put simply, if the existence of any fact (other than a prior conviction) increases the maximum punishment that may be imposed on a defendant, that fact—no matter how the State labels it—constitutes an element, and must be found by a jury beyond a reasonable doubt.
>
> Just last Term we recognized the import of *Apprendi* in the context of capital-sentencing proceedings. In Ring v. Arizona, [536 U.S. 584] (2002), we held that aggravating circumstances that make a defendant eligible for the death penalty "operate as 'the functional equivalent of an element of a *greater offense*.'" Id., at [608] (emphasis added). That is to say, for purposes of the Sixth Amendment's jury-trial guarantee, the underlying offense of "murder" is a distinct, lesser included offense of "murder plus

one or more aggravating circumstances": Whereas the former exposes a defendant
to a maximum penalty of life imprisonment, the latter increases the maximum permissible sentence to death. Accordingly, we held that the Sixth Amendment requires
that a jury, and not a judge, find the existence of any aggravating circumstances, and
that they be found, not by a mere preponderance of the evidence, but beyond a reasonable doubt. We can think of no principled reason to distinguish, in this context,
between what constitutes an offense for purposes of the Sixth Amendment's jury-trial
guarantee and what constitutes an "offence" for purposes of the Fifth Amendment's
Double Jeopardy Clause. . . . If a jury unanimously concludes that a State has failed to
meet its burden of proving the existence of one or more aggravating circumstances,
double-jeopardy protections attach to that "acquittal" on the offense of "murder plus
aggravating circumstance(s)." . . .

 For purposes of the Double Jeopardy Clause, then, "first-degree murder" under
Pennsylvania law—the offense of which petitioner was convicted during the guilt
phase of his proceedings—is properly understood to be a lesser included offense
of "first-degree murder plus aggravating circumstance(s)." Thus, if petitioner's first
sentencing jury had unanimously concluded that Pennsylvania failed to prove any
aggravating circumstances, that conclusion would operate as an "acquittal" of the
greater offense—which would bar Pennsylvania from retrying petitioner on that
greater offense (and thus, from seeking the death penalty) on retrial.

Id., at 111-112. Notice that Justice Scalia characterizes the crime of capital murder
as "murder plus one or more aggravating circumstances." There is another way that
crime might be defined for double jeopardy purposes, consistent with *Apprendi*:
murder plus the *particular* aggravating circumstance that the prosecution seeks to
prove in each particular case. Suppose, as is common, that a given state's capital
murder statute says that the prosecution must prove at least one aggravating factor in order for the defendant to receive the death penalty; suppose further that
the statute lists a dozen different aggravating factors. Can the state now prosecute
a single capital murder a dozen times, as long as it alleges a different aggravating
factor in each prosecution? Stay tuned.

C.   Double Jeopardy and the "Dual Sovereignty" Doctrine

HEATH v. ALABAMA

Certiorari to the Supreme Court of Alabama
474 U.S. 82 (1985)

JUSTICE O'CONNOR delivered the opinion of the Court.

 The question before the Court is whether the Double Jeopardy Clause of the
Fifth Amendment bars Alabama from trying petitioner for the capital offense of
murder during a kidnaping after Georgia has convicted him of murder based on
the same homicide. In particular, this case presents the issue of the applicability of
the dual sovereignty doctrine to successive prosecutions by two States.

I

[Heath paid two men $2,000 to kill his wife, Rebecca, who was then nine months
pregnant. Heath, who lived together with his wife in Alabama, met with the two

men in Georgia to give them the keys to his car and his house, and led them back to his house. The two men kidnapped Rebecca, drove her to Georgia, and murdered and buried her there. Georgia and Alabama conducted parallel investigations of the crime. Heath was indicted for "malice murder" in Georgia; facing a risk of the death penalty, he pleaded guilty in exchange for a life sentence. Three months later, Alabama indicted Heath for the capital offense of murder during a kidnaping. Heath challenged the Alabama indictment on jurisdictional and double jeopardy grounds, but the trial court rejected both challenges. (On the jurisdictional issue, the trial court concluded that, under Alabama law, any crime that commences in Alabama may be prosecuted in Alabama.) Heath was convicted and sentenced to death, and the Alabama Court of Criminal Appeals and Alabama Supreme Court both affirmed. The U.S. Supreme Court granted review, limited to the double jeopardy issue. — Eds.]

II

Successive prosecutions are barred by the Fifth Amendment only if the two offenses for which the defendant is prosecuted are the "same" for double jeopardy purposes. Respondent does not contravene petitioner's contention that the offenses of "murder during a kidnaping" and "malice murder," as construed by the courts of Alabama and Georgia respectively, may be considered greater and lesser offenses and, thus, the "same" offense under Brown v. Ohio, supra, absent operation of the dual sovereignty principle. See id., at 169; Illinois v. Vitale, 447 U.S. 410 (1980). We therefore assume, arguendo, that, had these offenses arisen under the laws of one State and had petitioner been separately prosecuted for both offenses in that State, the second conviction would have been barred by the Double Jeopardy Clause.

The sole remaining question upon which we granted certiorari is whether the dual sovereignty doctrine permits successive prosecutions under the laws of different States which otherwise would be held to "subject [the defendant] for the same offence to be twice put in jeopardy." Although we have not previously so held, we believe the answer to this query is inescapable. The dual sovereignty doctrine, as originally articulated and consistently applied by this Court, compels the conclusion that successive prosecutions by two States for the same conduct are not barred by the Double Jeopardy Clause.

The dual sovereignty doctrine is founded on the common-law conception of crime as an offense against the sovereignty of the government. When a defendant in a single act violates the "peace and dignity" of two sovereigns by breaking the laws of each, he has committed two distinct "offences." United States v. Lanza, 260 U.S. 377, 382 (1922). As the Court explained in Moore v. Illinois, 14 How. 13, 19 (1852), "[an] offence, in its legal signification, means the transgression of a law." Consequently, when the same act transgresses the laws of two sovereigns, "it cannot be truly averred that the offender has been twice punished for the same offence; but only that by one act he has committed two offences, for each of which he is justly punishable." Id., at 20.

In applying the dual sovereignty doctrine, then, the crucial determination is whether the two entities that seek successively to prosecute a defendant for the same course of conduct can be termed separate sovereigns. This determination turns on whether the two entities draw their authority to punish the offender from distinct sources of power. See, e.g., United States v. Wheeler, 435 U.S. 313, 320 (1978);

Waller v. Florida, 397 U.S. 387, 393 (1970); Puerto Rico v. Shell Co., 302 U.S. 253, 264-265 (1937); *Lanza,* supra, at 382; Grafton v. United States, 206 U.S. 333, 354-355 (1907). Thus, the Court has uniformly held that the States are separate sovereigns with respect to the Federal Government because each State's power to prosecute is derived from its own "inherent sovereignty," not from the Federal Government. *Wheeler,* supra, at 320, n. 14. See Abbate v. United States, 359 U.S. 187, 193-194 (1959) (collecting cases); *Lanza,* supra. As stated in *Lanza,* supra, at 382:

> Each government in determining what shall be an offense against its peace and dignity is exercising its own sovereignty, not that of the other.
>
> It follows that an act denounced as a crime by both national and state sovereignties is an offense against the peace and dignity of both and may be punished by each.

See also Bartkus v. Illinois, 359 U.S. 121 (1959); Westfall v. United States, 274 U.S. 256, 258 (1927) (Holmes, J.) (the proposition that the State and Federal Governments may punish the same conduct "is too plain to need more than statement").

The States are no less sovereign with respect to each other than they are with respect to the Federal Government. Their powers to undertake criminal prosecutions derive from separate and independent sources of power and authority originally belonging to them before admission to the Union and preserved to them by the Tenth Amendment. See *Lanza,* supra, at 382. The States are equal to each other "in power, dignity and authority, each competent to exert that residuum of sovereignty not delegated to the United States by the Constitution itself." Coyle v. Oklahoma, 221 U.S. 559, 567 (1911). See Skiriotes v. Florida, 313 U.S. 69, 77 (1941). Thus, "[e]ach has the power, inherent in any sovereign, independently to determine what shall be an offense against its authority and to punish such offenses, and in doing so each 'is exercising its own sovereignty, not that of the other.'" *Wheeler,* supra, at 320 (quoting *Lanza,* supra, at 382).

The cases in which the Court has applied the dual sovereignty principle outside the realm of successive federal and state prosecutions illustrate the soundness of this analysis. United States v. Wheeler, supra, is particularly instructive because there the Court expressly refused to find that only the State and Federal Governments could be considered distinct sovereigns with respect to each other for double jeopardy purposes, stating that "so restrictive a view of [the dual sovereignty] concept . . . would require disregard of the very words of the Double Jeopardy Clause." Id., at 330. Instead, the *Wheeler* Court reiterated the principle that the sovereignty of two prosecuting entities for these purposes is determined by "the ultimate source of the power under which the respective prosecutions were undertaken." Id., at 320. On the basis of this reasoning, the Court held that the Navajo Tribe, whose power to prosecute its members for tribal offenses is derived from the Tribe's "primeval sovereignty" rather than a delegation of federal authority, is an independent sovereign from the Federal Government for purposes of the dual sovereignty doctrine. Id., at 328.

In those instances where the Court has found the dual sovereignty doctrine inapplicable, it has done so because the two prosecuting entities did not derive their powers to prosecute from independent sources of authority. Thus, the Court has held that successive prosecutions by federal and territorial courts are barred because such courts are "creations emanating from the same sovereignty." *Puerto Rico,* 302 U.S., at 264. See id., at 264-266. See also *Grafton,* supra (the Philippine

Islands). Similarly, municipalities that derive their power to try a defendant from the same organic law that empowers the State to prosecute are not separate sovereigns with respect to the State. See, e.g., *Waller*, supra. These cases confirm that it is the presence of independent sovereign authority to prosecute, not the relation between States and the Federal Government in our federalist system, that constitutes the basis for the dual sovereignty doctrine. . . .

III

Petitioner invites us to restrict the applicability of the dual sovereignty principle to cases in which two governmental entities, having concurrent jurisdiction and pursuing quite different interests, can demonstrate that allowing only one entity to exercise jurisdiction over the defendant will interfere with the unvindicated interests of the second entity and that multiple prosecutions therefore are necessary for the satisfaction of the legitimate interests of both entities. This balancing of interests approach, however, cannot be reconciled with the dual sovereignty principle. This Court has plainly and repeatedly stated that two identical offenses are *not* the "same offence" within the meaning of the Double Jeopardy Clause if they are prosecuted by different sovereigns. See, e.g., United States v. Lanza, 260 U.S. 377 (1922) (same conduct, indistinguishable statutes, same "interests"). If the States are separate sovereigns, as they must be under the definition of sovereignty which the Court consistently has employed, the circumstances of the case are irrelevant. . . .

It is axiomatic that "[i]n America, the powers of sovereignty are divided between the government of the Union, and those of the States. They are each sovereign, with respect to the objects committed to it, and neither sovereign with respect to the objects committed to the other." McCulloch v. Maryland, 4 Wheat. 316, 410 (1819). It is as well established that the States, "as political communities, [are] distinct and sovereign, and consequently foreign to each other." Bank of United States v. Daniel, 12 Pet. 32, 54 (1838). See also Skiriotes v. Florida, 313 U.S., at 77; Coyle v. Oklahoma, 221 U.S., at 567. The Constitution leaves in the possession of each State "certain exclusive and very important portions of sovereign power." The Federalist No. 9, p. 55 (J. Cooke ed. 1961). Foremost among the prerogatives of sovereignty is the power to create and enforce a criminal code. See, e.g., Alfred L. Snapp & Son, Inc. v. Puerto Rico ex rel. Barez, 458 U.S. 592, 601 (1982); *McCulloch*, supra, at 418. To deny a State its power to enforce its criminal laws because another State has won the race to the courthouse "would be a shocking and untoward deprivation of the historic right and obligation of the States to maintain peace and order within their confines." *Bartkus*, 359 U.S., at 137.

Such a deprivation of a State's sovereign powers cannot be justified by the assertion that under "interest analysis" the State's legitimate penal interests will be satisfied through a prosecution conducted by another State. A State's interest in vindicating its sovereign authority through enforcement of *its* laws by definition can never be satisfied by another State's enforcement of its own laws. Just as the Federal Government has the right to decide that a state prosecution has not vindicated a violation of the "peace and dignity" of the Federal Government, a State must be entitled to decide that a prosecution by another State has not satisfied its legitimate sovereign interest. In recognition of this fact, the Court consistently has endorsed the principle that a single act constitutes an "offence" against each sovereign whose laws are violated by that act. The Court has always understood the words of the

Double Jeopardy Clause to reflect this fundamental principle, and we see no reason why we should reconsider that understanding today.

The judgment of the Supreme Court of Alabama is affirmed.

[The dissenting opinion of Justice Brennan is omitted.]

JUSTICE MARSHALL, with whom JUSTICE BRENNAN joins, dissenting.

Seizing upon the suggestion in past cases that every "independent" sovereign government may prosecute violations of its laws even when the defendant has already been tried for the same crime in another jurisdiction, the Court today gives short shrift to the policies underlying those precedents. The "dual sovereignty" doctrine, heretofore used to permit federal and state prosecutions for the same offense, was born of the need to accommodate complementary state and federal concerns within our system of concurrent territorial jurisdictions. It cannot justify successive prosecutions by different States. Moreover, even were the dual sovereignty doctrine to support successive state prosecutions as a general matter, it simply could not legitimate the collusion between Georgia and Alabama in this case to ensure that petitioner is executed for his crime.

I

[This section, in which Justice Marshall describes in detail the investigative cooperation between the Georgia and Alabama authorities, and the intense publicity surrounding the murder of Rebecca Heath, is omitted. — EDS.]

II

Had the Georgia authorities suddenly become dissatisfied with the life sentence petitioner received in their courts and reindicted petitioner in order to seek the death penalty once again, that indictment would without question be barred by the Double Jeopardy Clause of the Fifth Amendment, as applied to the States by the Fourteenth Amendment, Benton v. Maryland, 395 U.S. 784 (1969). Whether the second indictment repeated the charge of malice murder or instead charged murder in the course of a kidnaping, it would surely, under any reasonable constitutional standard, offend the bar to successive prosecutions for the same offense. See Brown v. Ohio, 432 U.S. 161, 166 (1977); id., at 170 (Brennan, J., concurring).

The only difference between this case and such a hypothetical volte-face by Georgia is that here Alabama, not Georgia, was offended by the notion that petitioner might not forfeit his life in punishment for his crime. The only reason the Court gives for permitting Alabama to go forward is that Georgia and Alabama are separate sovereigns.

The dual sovereignty theory posits that where the same act offends the laws of two sovereigns, "it cannot be truly averred that the offender has been twice punished for the same offence; but only that by one act he has committed two offences, for each of which he is justly punishable." Moore v. Illinois, 14 How. 13, 20 (1852). Therefore, "prosecutions under the laws of separate sovereigns do not, in the language of the Fifth Amendment, 'subject [the defendant] for the same offence to be twice put in jeopardy.'" United States v. Wheeler, 435 U.S. 313, 317 (1978). Mindful of the admonitions of Justice Black, we should recognize this exegesis of the Clause as, at best, a useful fiction and, at worst, a dangerous one. See Bartkus

v. Illinois, 359 U.S. 121, 158 (1959) (Black, J., dissenting). No evidence has ever been adduced to indicate that the Framers intended the word "offence" to have so restrictive a meaning.

This strained reading of the Double Jeopardy Clause has survived and indeed flourished in this Court's cases not because of any inherent plausibility, but because it provides reassuring interpretivist support for a rule that accommodates the unique nature of our federal system. Before this rule is extended to cover a new class of cases, the reasons for its creation should therefore be made clear.

Under the constitutional scheme, the Federal Government has been given the exclusive power to vindicate certain of our Nation's sovereign interests, leaving the States to exercise complementary authority over matters of more local concern. The respective spheres of the Federal Government and the States may overlap at times, and even where they do not, different interests may be implicated by a single act. See, e.g., Abbate v. United States, 359 U.S. 187 (1959) (conspiracy to dynamite telephone company facilities entails both destruction of property and disruption of federal communications network). Yet were a prosecution by a State, however zealously pursued, allowed to preclude further prosecution by the Federal Government for the same crime, an entire range of national interests could be frustrated. The importance of those federal interests has thus quite properly been permitted to trump a defendant's interest in avoiding successive prosecutions or multiple punishments for the same crime. See Screws v. United States, 325 U.S. 91, 108-110, and n. 10 (1945) (plurality opinion). Conversely, because "the States under our federal system have the principal responsibility for defining and prosecuting crimes," Abbate v. United States, supra, at 195, it would be inappropriate—in the absence of a specific congressional intent to pre-empt state action pursuant to the Supremacy Clause—to allow a federal prosecution to preclude state authorities from vindicating "the historic right and obligation of the States to maintain peace and order within their confines," Bartkus v. Illinois, supra, at 137.

The complementary nature of the sovereignty exercised by the Federal Government and the States places upon a defendant burdens commensurate with concomitant privileges. Past cases have recognized that the special ordeal suffered by a defendant prosecuted by both federal and state authorities is the price of living in a federal system, the cost of dual citizenship. Every citizen, the Court has noted, "owes allegiance to the two departments, so to speak, and within their respective spheres must pay the penalties which each exacts for disobedience to its laws. In return, he can demand protection from each within its own jurisdiction." United States v. Cruikshank, 92 U.S. 542, 551 (1876). See Moore v. Illinois, supra, at 20 ("Every citizen . . . may be said to owe allegiance to two sovereigns, and may be liable to punishment for an infraction of the laws of either.").

. . . Where two States seek to prosecute the same defendant for the same crime in two separate proceedings, the justifications found in the federal-state context for an exemption from double jeopardy constraints simply do not hold. Although the two States may have opted for different policies within their assigned territorial jurisdictions, the sovereign concerns with whose vindication each State has been charged are identical. Thus, in contrast to the federal-state context, barring the second prosecution would still permit one government to act upon the broad range of sovereign concerns that have been reserved to the States by the Constitution. The compelling need in the federal-state context to subordinate double jeopardy concerns is thus considerably diminished in cases involving successive prosecutions by different States. Moreover, from the defendant's perspective, the burden of successive prosecutions cannot be justified as the quid pro quo of dual citizenship.

To be sure, a refusal to extend the dual sovereignty rule to state-state prosecutions would preclude the State that has lost the "race to the courthouse" from vindicating legitimate policies distinct from those underlying its sister State's prosecution. But as yet, I am not persuaded that a State's desire to further a particular policy should be permitted to deprive a defendant of his constitutionally protected right not to be brought to bar more than once to answer essentially the same charges.

III

Having expressed my doubts as to the Court's ill-considered resolution of the dual sovereignty question in this case, I must confess that my quarrel with the Court's disposition of this case is based less upon how this question was resolved than upon the fact that it was considered at all. Although, in granting Heath's petition for certiorari, this Court ordered the parties to focus upon the dual sovereignty issue, I believe the Court errs in refusing to consider the fundamental unfairness of the process by which petitioner stands condemned to die.

Even where the power of two sovereigns to pursue separate prosecutions for the same crime has been undisputed, this Court has barred both governments from combining to do together what each could not constitutionally do on its own. See Murphy v. Waterfront Comm'n, 378 U.S. 52 (1964); Elkins v. United States, 364 U.S. 206 (1960).[3] And just as the Constitution bars one sovereign from facilitating another's prosecution by delivering testimony coerced under promise of immunity or evidence illegally seized, I believe that it prohibits two sovereigns from combining forces to ensure that a defendant receives only the trappings of criminal process as he is sped along to execution.

While no one can doubt the propriety of two States cooperating to bring a criminal to justice, the cooperation between Georgia and Alabama in this case went far beyond their initial joint investigation. Georgia's efforts to secure petitioner's execution did not end with its acceptance of his guilty plea. Its law enforcement officials went on to play leading roles as prosecution witnesses in the Alabama trial. Indeed, had the Alabama trial judge not restricted the State to one assisting officer at the prosecution's table during trial, a Georgia officer would have shared the honors with an Alabama officer. Although the record does not reveal the precise nature of the assurances made by Georgia authorities that induced petitioner to plead guilty in the first proceeding against him, I cannot believe he would have done so had he

---

3. To be sure, *Murphy*, which bars a State from compelling a witness to give testimony that might be used against him in a federal prosecution, and *Elkins*, which bars the introduction in a federal prosecution of evidence illegally seized by state officers, do not necessarily undermine the basis of the rule allowing successive state and federal prosecutions. It is one thing to bar a sovereign from using certain evidence and quite another to bar it from prosecuting altogether. But these cases can be read to suggest that despite the independent sovereign status of the Federal and State Governments, courts should not be blind to the impact of combined federal-state law enforcement on an accused's constitutional rights. See Note, Double Prosecution by State and Federal Governments: Another Exercise in Federalism, 80 Harv. L. Rev. 1538, 1547 (1967). Justice Harlan's belief that *Murphy* "abolished the 'two sovereignties' rule," Stevens v. Marks, 383 U.S. 234, 250 (1966) (Harlan, J., concurring in part, dissenting in part), was thus well founded.

been aware that the officials whose forbearance he bought in Georgia with his plea would merely continue their efforts to secure his death in another jurisdiction. Cf. Santobello v. New York, 404 U.S. 257, 262 (1971).

Even before the Fourteenth Amendment was held to incorporate the protections of the Double Jeopardy Clause, four Members of this Court registered their outrage at "an instance of the prosecution being allowed to harass the accused with repeated trials and convictions on the same evidence, until it [achieved] its desired result of a capital verdict." Ciucci v. Illinois, 356 U.S. 571, 573 (1958). Such "relentless prosecutions," they asserted, constituted "an unseemly and oppressive use of a criminal trial that violates the concept of due process contained in the Fourteenth Amendment, whatever its ultimate scope is taken to be." Id., at 575. The only differences between the facts in *Ciucci* and those in this case are that here the relentless effort was a cooperative one between two States and that petitioner sought to avoid trial by pleading guilty. Whether viewed as a violation of the Double Jeopardy Clause or simply as an affront to the due process guarantee of fundamental fairness, Alabama's prosecution of petitioner cannot survive constitutional scrutiny. I therefore must dissent.

NOTES AND QUESTIONS

1. The history of double jeopardy doctrine does not support the Court's position in *Heath*. In English law, the principle that no one should be prosecuted twice for the same crime dates to the twelfth century:

> In the twelfth century a major element of the conflict between Thomas Becket and Henry II was the king's desire to have clerics who had been convicted in ecclesiastical courts turned over to civil tribunals for further prosecution. Henry conceded the point in 1176 following Becket's martyrdom. The king's concession is significant because the royal and ecclesiastical courts obviously did not draw their power from the same sovereign. The application of the double jeopardy bar to successive religious and secular prosecutions demonstrates that the focus of the prohibition was the defendant, not the prosecutor.

Ronald J. Allen & John P. Ratnaswamy, Heath v. Alabama: A Case Study of Doctrine and Rationality in the Supreme Court, 76 J. Crim. L. & Criminology 801, 807 (1985). Allen and Ratnaswamy go on to note that the dual-sovereignty concept entered American law in the mid-nineteenth century, at a time when conflict between state and federal governments was at its height; the focus was on state-federal coordination, not on state-state prosecutions as in *Heath*:

> In the middle of the nineteenth century the conception of the double jeopardy clause as prohibiting successive prosecutions by any prosecuting authority was questioned by dicta in a series of [Supreme Court] cases. These cases were not motivated by mystical conceptions of "sovereignty"; instead, they were motivated by concerns about the different roles of the two levels of American government and by a growing realization that something had to be done to prevent conflict between the states and the national government. Those considerations led to the discussion in these cases of a dual sovereignty exception to the double jeopardy clause, and it is those concerns, along with the individual interests protected by the clause, that should control the scope of any such exception. . . .

[The key case was] Moore v. Illinois, [55 U.S. 13 (1852),] [where] the Court for the first time directly discussed the problem of duplicate state and federal prosecutions for the same crime. Moore was convicted under an Illinois statute proscribing the harboring or secreting of fugitive slaves. Moore's principal argument was preemption of the state law by the federal Fugitive Slave Act, but he also objected to the possible double jeopardy problem of prosecution under both the state and federal statutes. The Supreme Court found that the Illinois and federal statutes were dissimilar in their essential underlying purpose, in their definition of the offense, and in the nature of the punishment which they authorized. The purpose of the federal government was protection of the property interests of slave owners, while the state's goal was to bar black persons, whether slave or free, from the state's territory. Despite these differences, the Court nevertheless proceeded to articulate for the first time the dual sovereignty theory. . . .

The decision was an inevitable consequence of its historical context. In *Moore*, the Court was asked to strike down a type of state statute that was at the heart of a dispute over the scope of states' rights, a dispute so serious that it would lead to the Civil War. The Court was being asked to do so not only where the laws of neither "sovereign" impinged upon the legitimate interests of the other, but where the Court was beginning to realize that state and federal criminal statutes were going to overlap and intersect in unpredictable ways. Moreover, none of the alternatives available to the Court were feasible, except for the creation of a dual sovereignty exception to the double jeopardy prohibition. . . .

"Dual sovereignty," in short, arose as an exception to the normal rules of double jeopardy for certain fundamental reasons related to the structure of American government. Unless there is some other justification for the theory, it should apply only where the reasons which gave rise to it are present: where two governmental entities pursuing quite diverse interests share substantially overlapping territorial jurisdictions, where there is a substantial risk of interference by one governmental entity in the affairs of another, and where multiple prosecutions are necessary for the satisfaction of the legitimate purposes of each governmental unit. The Court in *Heath* virtually ignored these considerations . . .

76 J. Crim. L. & Criminology, at 811-814.

2. There are few cases like *Heath*. Double prosecution by state and federal officials is more common. The prosecutions of the police officers who beat Rodney King in March 1991 offer a famous example. King, a black man, was apprehended after a high-speed chase through Los Angeles. Four police officers beat him brutally; a nearby civilian captured the beating on videotape. The officers were charged with felony assault in California state court. Before trial, the case was moved to Simi Valley—a nearly all-white community with one of the highest concentrations of retired police officers in the United States. The jury acquitted three of the four defendants on all charges; a single charge against one defendant produced a hung jury. There were no convictions. The verdict triggered massive rioting in Los Angeles; at least 40 people died in the course of the riots and the police efforts to quell them.

The federal government then prosecuted the four officers for willfully depriving King of his constitutional rights (in particular, his right to be free from excessive police use of force under the Fourth Amendment). Two of the officers—Timothy Wind and Ted Briseno—were again acquitted. The other two—Stacey Koon and Lawrence Powell—were convicted. Their convictions were affirmed on appeal; the case went up to the Supreme Court, though not on any issues related to double jeopardy. See Koon v. United States, 518 U.S. 81 (1996) (discussing standard of review in sentencing decisions under the Federal Sentencing Guidelines).

Another example was Terry Nichols. Nichols was Timothy McVeigh's codefendant in the Oklahoma City terrorist bombing case. The federal government prosecuted both Nichols and McVeigh in federal court; the government sought the death penalty as to both defendants. McVeigh was convicted and sentenced to death. Nichols was convicted and sentenced to life in prison. Oklahoma wanted another shot at the death penalty for Nichols, so he was tried again in state court, for capital murder. (Once again, he escaped a death sentence.) Does that process sound fair? Are your reactions to the Rodney King and the Oklahoma City bombing cases consistent?

3. There is an obvious functional concern underlying the dual prosecutions in *Koon.* The federal government has a strong interest in protecting its citizens from deprivations of constitutional rights by state and local officials—that, after all, was one of the driving forces behind the Fourteenth Amendment. If federal prosecution is barred by a state prosecution, local district attorneys might prosecute halfheartedly or even purposely try to produce an acquittal, thereby insulating defendants from criminal punishment. Is that problem serious enough to justify dual sovereignty doctrine? Keep in mind that there is also a troubling scenario on the other side of the scale: A defendant is prosecuted in state court and wins; the federal government then prosecutes him again in response to political pressure. Is *that* problem serious enough to suggest that dual sovereignty doctrine is a mistake?

For insightful analyses of these and other questions, see Akhil Reed Amar & Jonathan L. Marcus, Double Jeopardy after Rodney King, 95 Colum. L. Rev. 1 (1995); Paul Cassell, The Rodney King Trials and the Double Jeopardy Clause: Some Observations on Original Meaning and the ACLU's Schizophrenic Views of the Dual Sovereignty Doctrine, 41 UCLA L. Rev. 693 (1994); Susan Herman, Double Jeopardy All Over Again: Dual Sovereignty, Rodney King, and the ACLU, 41 UCLA L. Rev. 609 (1994).

D. Double Jeopardy and the Criminal-Civil Divide

The government sometimes fights crime in proceedings that are, at least nominally, civil rather than criminal. Civil fines, forfeitures of personal and real property, punitive damages, and even some kinds of taxes are used to deter and, at least in the popular sense of the word, punish crime. These practices raise a host of issues, some deeply philosophical. For a fascinating exploration of those issues, see generally Carol S. Steiker, Punishment and Procedure: Punishment Theory and the Criminal-Civil Procedural Divide, 85 Geo. L.J. 775 (1997) (seeking to develop philosophical basis for determining whether particular sanctions are "civil" or "criminal").

These not-quite-criminal proceedings can raise double jeopardy concerns. The Supreme Court has followed a meandering path in dealing with those concerns. The defendant in United States v. Halper, 490 U.S. 435 (1989) was the manager of a New York medical laboratory that served Medicare patients. He was charged under the criminal false-claims statute, 18 U.S.C. §287, with 65 separate counts of filing falsely inflated claims for Medicare reimbursement of patient expenses. The total amount of the overbilling was $585. Halper was convicted on all counts, sentenced to two years in prison, and fined $5,000. The government then filed a lawsuit against Halper under the civil False Claims Act, 31 U.S.C. §§3729-3731, seeking the maximum statutory remedy of $2,000 per violation, plus twice the amount of actual damages sustained by the government and litigation costs. The district court entered summary judgment against Halper on liability, on the basis of the prior criminal proceeding. But the court ultimately concluded that a civil sanction of more than $130,000 against Halper would constitute a second "punishment" for the "same offense" for which he had already been punished, in violation of the Double Jeopardy Clause, and thus reduced the government's award to double-damages plus costs.

A unanimous Supreme Court agreed. The Court saw the question as "[w]hether and under what circumstances a civil penalty may constitute punishment for the purpose of the Double Jeopardy Clause." The Court rejected the government's contention that "whether proceedings are criminal or civil is a matter of statutory construction," finding such a view "not well suited to the context of the 'humane interests' safeguarded by the Double Jeopardy Clause's proscription of multiple punishments." Instead, the Court explained:

> What we announce now is a rule for the rare case, the case such as the one before us, where a fixed-penalty provision subjects a prolific but small-gauge offender to a sanction overwhelmingly disproportionate to the damages he has caused. The rule is one of reason: Where a defendant previously has sustained a criminal penalty and the civil penalty sought in the subsequent proceeding bears no rational relation to the goal of compensating the Government for its loss, but rather appears to qualify as "punishment" in the plain meaning of the word, then the defendant is entitled to an accounting of the Government's damages and costs to determine if the penalty sought in fact constitutes a second punishment.

490 U.S., at 449-450. The Court concluded that the statutorily authorized award of more than $130,000 would be so excessive, compared to the government's actual damages, as to constitute "punishment" for double jeopardy purposes, but remanded the case for additional findings on the amount of those actual damages.

In Department of Revenue of Montana v. Kurth Ranch, 511 U.S. 767 (1994), the Court faced a different configuration of criminal and civil proceedings. In 1987, Montana enacted a "Dangerous Drug Tax Act," which imposed a tax on the "possession and storage of dangerous drugs," defined as drugs whose possession can lead to criminal prosecution and seizure under Montana law. The tax was set at a relatively high rate—10 percent of the assessed market value of the drugs, or a specified amount (e.g., $100 per ounce for marijuana), whichever is greater.[3] Two weeks after this new tax law became effective, six members of the Kurth family were charged with conspiracy to possess drugs with intent to sell, based on accusations that they were cultivating marijuana on their family farm. All pled guilty. In addition, the government filed a civil forfeiture action seeking recovery of all cash and equipment used in the Kurth's marijuana operation; this action was settled when the Kurths agreed to the forfeiture of $18,016.83 in cash and equipment. Shortly after the conclusion of the criminal case and civil forfeiture proceeding, the state Department of Revenue assessed almost $900,000 in tax liability against the Kurths under the new tax law. The Kurths filed for bankruptcy and objected to the DOR's claim for

---

3. For some components of a marijuana plant, such as the stems, leaves, and other loose parts known collectively as "shake," the minimum tax of $100 per ounce amounted to approximately eight times the market value of the drug itself.

unpaid drug taxes. The bankruptcy court held the Montana tax law unconstitutional under the double jeopardy clause and *Halper*, and the district and appellate courts affirmed.

The Supreme Court, in a 5-4 decision, likewise ruled in the Kurths' favor, although for somewhat different reasons. Justice Stevens' majority opinion noted that *Halper* dealt with a civil penalty and not a tax, and explained that *Halper*'s "method of determining whether the exaction was remedial or punitive"—i.e., a method that focuses on the costs of investigation and prosecution, and on other actual damages suffered by the government—"simply does not work in the case of a tax statute," where the purposes of the law (e.g., raising revenue) are so different. In this instance, the high rate of taxation and the obvious deterrent purpose did not "automatically" render the legislation punitive. But the fact that the drug tax was assessed only against "persons who have been arrested" for a crime, combined with the further fact that it was levied on "goods that the taxpayer neither owns nor possesses when the tax is imposed," led the Court to conclude that "this drug tax is a concoction of anomalies, too far-removed in crucial respects from a standard tax assessment to escape characterization as punishment for the purpose of Double Jeopardy analysis." The Court expressly limited its constitutional holding to the situation where such a punitive tax is levied after the conclusion of the criminal case, reserving the reverse situation (as well as the situation of criminal and tax sanctions imposed in the same proceeding) for another day.

There were three dissenting opinions. Chief Justice Rehnquist, joined by Justices O'Connor and Scalia, agreed with the Court that the *Halper* test did not apply to tax statutes, but disagreed with the Court's conclusion that the "anomalies" in the Montana statute made it unconstitutional. Justice O'Connor found the *Halper* test applicable and would have upheld the Montana statute based on the government's need for funds to offset the high costs of drug interdiction and prosecution. Finally, Justice Scalia, joined by Justice Thomas, took a broader approach:

> The difficulty of applying *Halper*'s analysis to Montana's Dangerous Drug Tax has prompted me to focus on the antecedent question whether there is a multiple-punishments component of the Double Jeopardy Clause. As indicated above, I have concluded . . . that there is not. Instead, the Due Process Clause keeps punishment within the bounds established by the legislature, and the Cruel and Unusual Punishments and Excessive Fines Clauses place substantive limits upon what those legislated bounds may be. . . .
>
> It is time to put the *Halper* genie back in the bottle, and to acknowledge what the text of the Constitution makes perfectly clear: the Double Jeopardy Clause prohibits successive prosecution, not successive punishment. Multiple punishment is of course restricted by the Cruel and Unusual Punishments Clause insofar as its nature is concerned, and by the Excessive Fines Clause insofar as its cumulative extent is concerned. Its multiplicity qua multiplicity, however, is restricted only by the Double Jeopardy Clause's requirement that there be no successive criminal prosecution, and by the Due Process Clause's requirement that the cumulative punishments be in accord with the law of the land, i.e., authorized by the legislature.

511 U.S., at 802-805 (Scalia, J., dissenting).

Having dispensed with the "multiple punishment" aspect of double jeopardy, Justice Scalia then turned his attention to the "successive prosecution" aspect, which the majority had also found to be implicated by the combination of the criminal prosecution of the Kurths and the subsequent civil proceedings growing out of the tax assessment:

Although a few of our cases include statements to the effect that a proceeding in which punishment is imposed is criminal, see, e.g., Kennedy v. Mendoza-Martinez, 372 U.S. 144, 167 (1963), the criterion of "punishment" for that purpose is significantly different (and significantly more deferential to the government) than the criterion applied in *Halper*. United States v. Ward, 448 U.S. 242 (1980), put it this way:

> Where Congress has indicated an intention to establish a civil penalty, we have inquired further whether the statutory scheme was so punitive either in purpose or effect as to negate that intention. In regard to this latter inquiry, we have noted that "only the clearest proof could suffice to establish the unconstitutionality of a statute on such a ground."

Id., at 248-249, quoting Flemming v. Nestor, 363 U.S. 603, 617 (1960) (citation omitted).

Halper's focus on whether the sanction serves the goals of "retribution and deterrence" is just one factor in the *Kennedy-Ward* test, see 372 U.S., at 168-169, and one factor alone is not dispositive, see *Ward*, 448 U.S., at 250-251. . . .

511 U.S., at 805-806. Justice Scalia concluded that, under the *Kennedy-Ward* test, the Montana drug tax law did not impose "punishment" in a manner violative of the "successive prosecution" aspect of double jeopardy. Though that position did not carry the day in *Kurth Ranch*, it did a good deal better in the next case.

UNITED STATES v. URSERY

Certiorari to the United States Court of Appeals for the Sixth Circuit
518 U.S. 267 (1996)

[This case was decided together with United States v. $405,089.23 in United States Currency et al., on certiorari to the United States Court of Appeals for the Ninth Circuit. — EDS.]

CHIEF JUSTICE REHNQUIST delivered the opinion of the Court.

In separate cases, the United States Court of Appeals for the Sixth Circuit and the United States Court of Appeals for the Ninth Circuit held that the Double Jeopardy Clause prohibits the Government from both punishing a defendant for a criminal offense and forfeiting his property for that same offense in a separate civil proceeding. We consolidated those cases for our review, and now reverse. These civil forfeitures (and civil forfeitures generally), we hold, do not constitute "punishment" for purposes of the Double Jeopardy Clause.

I

No. 95-345: Michigan Police found marijuana growing adjacent to respondent Guy Ursery's house, and discovered marijuana seeds, stems, stalks, and a grow-light within the house. The United States instituted civil forfeiture proceedings against the house, alleging that the property was subject to forfeiture under 84 Stat. 1276, as amended, 21 U.S.C. §881(a)(7) because it had been used for several years to facilitate the unlawful processing and distribution of a controlled substance. Ursery ultimately paid the United States $13,250 to settle the forfeiture claim in full. Shortly before the settlement was consummated, Ursery was indicted for manufacturing marijuana, in violation of §841(a)(1). A jury found him guilty, and he was sentenced to 63 months in prison.

The Court of Appeals for the Sixth Circuit by a divided vote reversed Ursery's criminal conviction, holding that the conviction violated the Double Jeopardy Clause of the Fifth Amendment of the United States Constitution. 59 F.3d 568 (1995). The court based its conclusion in part upon its belief that our decisions in United States v. Halper, 490 U.S. 435 (1989), and Austin v. United States, 509 U.S. 602 (1993), meant that any civil forfeiture under §881(a)(7) constitutes punishment for purposes of the Double Jeopardy Clause. Ursery, in the court's view, had therefore been "punished" in the forfeiture proceeding against his property, and could not be subsequently criminally tried for violation of 21 U.S.C. §841(a)(1).

No. 95-346: Following a jury trial, Charles Wesley Arlt and James Wren were convicted of: conspiracy to aid and abet the manufacture of methamphetamine, in violation of 21 U.S.C. §846; conspiracy to launder monetary instruments, in violation of 18 U.S.C. §371; and numerous counts of money laundering, in violation of §1956. The District Court sentenced Arlt to life in prison and a 10-year term of supervised release, and imposed a fine of $250,000. Wren was sentenced to life imprisonment and a 5-year term of supervised release.

Before the criminal trial had started, the United States had filed a civil in rem complaint against various property seized from, or titled to, Arlt and Wren, or Payback Mines, a corporation controlled by Arlt. The complaint alleged that each piece of property was subject to forfeiture both under 18 U.S.C. §981(a)(1)(A), which provides that "[a]ny property . . . involved in a transaction or attempted transaction in violation of" §1956 (the money-laundering statute) "is subject to forfeiture to the United States"; and under 21 U.S.C. §881(a)(6), which provides for the forfeiture of (i) "[a]ll . . . things of value furnished or intended to be furnished by any person in exchange for" illegal drugs, (ii) "all proceeds traceable to such an exchange," and (iii) "all moneys, negotiable instruments, and securities used or intended to be used to facilitate" a federal drug felony. The parties agreed to defer litigation of the forfeiture action during the criminal prosecution. More than a year after the conclusion of the criminal trial, the District Court granted the Government's motion for summary judgment in the civil forfeiture proceeding.

Arlt and Wren appealed the decision in the forfeiture action, and the Court of Appeals for the Ninth Circuit reversed, holding that the forfeiture violated the Double Jeopardy Clause. 33 F.3d 1210 (1994). The court's decision was based in part upon the same view as that expressed by the Court of Appeals for the Sixth Circuit in Ursery's case—that our decisions in *Halper* and *Austin* meant that, as a categorical matter, forfeitures under §§981(a)(1)(A) and 881(a)(6) always constitute "punishment."

We granted the Government's petition for certiorari in each of the two cases, and we now reverse. 516 U.S. 1070 (1996).

II

The Double Jeopardy Clause provides: "[N]or shall any person be subject for the same offence to be twice put in jeopardy of life or limb." U.S. Const., Amdt. 5. The Clause serves the function of preventing both "successive punishments and . . . successive prosecutions." United States v. Dixon, 509 U.S. 688, 696 (1993), citing

North Carolina v. Pearce, 395 U.S. 711 (1969). The protection against multiple punishments prohibits the Government from "'punishing twice, or attempting a second time to punish criminally for the same offense.'" Witte v. United States, 515 U.S. 389, 396 (1995) (emphasis deleted), quoting Helvering v. Mitchell, 303 U.S. 391, 399 (1938).

In the decisions that we review, the Courts of Appeals held that the civil forfeitures constituted "punishment," making them subject to the prohibitions of the Double Jeopardy Clause. The Government challenges that characterization of the forfeitures, arguing that the courts were wrong to conclude that civil forfeitures are punitive for double jeopardy purposes.

A

Since the earliest years of this Nation, Congress has authorized the Government to seek parallel in rem civil forfeiture actions and criminal prosecutions based upon the same underlying events. See, e.g., Act of July 31, 1789, ch. 5, §12, 1 Stat. 39 (goods unloaded at night or without a permit subject to forfeiture and persons unloading subject to criminal prosecution); §25, id., at 43 (persons convicted of buying or concealing illegally imported goods subject to both monetary fine and in rem forfeiture of the goods); §34, id., at 46 (imposing criminal penalty and in rem forfeiture where person convicted of relanding goods entitled to drawback); see also The Palmyra, 25 U.S. 1, 12 Wheat. 1, 14-15 (1827) ("Many cases exist, where there is both a forfeiture in rem and a personal penalty"). . . . And, in a long line of cases, this Court has considered the application of the Double Jeopardy Clause to civil forfeitures, consistently concluding that the Clause does not apply to such actions because they do not impose punishment.

[The Court then discussed two of its earlier cases involving the relationship between the double jeopardy clause and civil forfeiture. The first case, Various Items of Personal Property v. United States, 282 U.S. 577 (1931), held that the clause was inapplicable to civil forfeiture actions because the forfeiture proceeding was in rem and thus not any part of the punishment imposed against the individual for the criminal offense. The second case, One Lot Emerald Cut Stones v. United States, 409 U.S. 232 (1972) (per curiam), reaffirmed the rule of *Various Items*, emphasizing that the statutory forfeiture provision was codified separately from the parallel criminal provisions and thus constituted a civil sanction rather than a second punishment. The Court also noted that the decisions in *Various Items* and *Emerald Cut Stones* were consistent with the long-standing common law rule that civil forfeiture *could not* proceed until *after* the offender was convicted of the parallel crime. —EDS.]

In our most recent decision considering whether a civil forfeiture constitutes punishment under the Double Jeopardy Clause, we again affirmed the rule of *Various Items*. In United States v. One Assortment of 89 Firearms, 465 U.S. 354 (1984), the owner of the defendant weapons was acquitted of charges of dealing firearms without a license. The Government then brought a forfeiture action against the firearms under 18 U.S.C. §924(d), alleging that they were used or were intended to be used in violation of federal law.

In another unanimous decision, we held that the forfeiture was not barred by the prior criminal proceeding. We began our analysis by stating the rule for our decision:

Unless the forfeiture sanction was intended as punishment, so that the proceeding is essentially criminal in character, the Double Jeopardy Clause is not applicable. The question, then, is whether a §924(d) forfeiture proceeding is intended to be, or by its nature necessarily is, criminal and punitive, or civil and remedial. *89 Firearms*, supra, at 362 (citations omitted).

Our inquiry proceeded in two stages. In the first stage, we looked to Congress' intent, and concluded that "Congress designed forfeiture under §924(d) as a remedial civil sanction." 465 U.S., at 363. This conclusion was based upon several findings. First, noting that the forfeiture proceeding was in rem, we found it significant that "[a]ctions in rem have traditionally been viewed as civil proceedings, with jurisdiction dependent upon the seizure of a physical object." *89 Firearms*, id., at 363, citing Calero-Toledo v. Pearson Yacht Leasing Co., 416 U.S. [663,] 684 [(1974)]. Second, we found that the forfeiture provision, because it reached both weapons used in violation of federal law and those "intended to be used" in such a manner, reached a broader range of conduct than its criminal analogue. Third, we concluded that the civil forfeiture "further[ed] broad remedial aims," including both "discouraging unregulated commerce in firearms," and "removing from circulation firearms that have been used or intended for use outside regulated channels of commerce." *89 Firearms*, supra, at 364.

In the second stage of our analysis, we looked to "'whether the statutory scheme was so punitive either in purpose or effect as to negate' Congress' intention to establish a civil remedial mechanism," 465 U.S., at 365, quoting United States v. Ward, 448 U.S. 242, 248-249 (1980). Considering several factors that we had used previously in order to determine whether a civil proceeding was so punitive as to require application of the full panoply of constitutional protections required in a criminal trial, see id., at 248, we found only one of those factors to be present in the §924(d) forfeiture. By itself, however, the fact that the behavior proscribed by the forfeiture was already a crime proved insufficient to turn the forfeiture into a punishment subject to the Double Jeopardy Clause. Hence, we found that the petitioner had "failed to establish by the 'clearest proof' that Congress has provided a sanction so punitive as to 'transfor[m] what was clearly intended as a civil remedy into a criminal penalty.'" *89 Firearms*, supra, at 366, quoting Rex Trailer Co. v. United States, 350 U.S. 148, 154 (1956). We concluded our decision by restating that civil forfeiture is "not an additional penalty for the commission of a criminal act, but rather is a separate civil sanction, remedial in nature." *89 Firearms*, supra, at 366.

B

Our cases reviewing civil forfeitures under the Double Jeopardy Clause adhere to a remarkably consistent theme. Though the two-part analytical construct employed in *89 Firearms* was more refined, perhaps, than that we had used over 50 years earlier in *Various Items*, the conclusion was the same in each case: In rem civil forfeiture is a remedial civil sanction, distinct from potentially punitive in personam civil penalties such as fines, and does not constitute a punishment under the Double Jeopardy Clause. See Gore v. United States, 357 U.S. 386, 392 (1958) ("In applying a provision like that of double jeopardy, which is rooted in history and is not an evolving concept . . . a long course of adjudication in this Court carries impressive authority").

In the case that we currently review, the Court of Appeals for the Ninth Circuit recognized as much, concluding that after *89 Firearms*, "the law was clear that civil forfeitures did not constitute 'punishment' for double jeopardy purposes." 33 F.3d, at 1218. Nevertheless, that court read three of our decisions to have "abandoned" *89 Firearms* and the oft-affirmed rule of *Various Items*. According to the Court of Appeals for the Ninth Circuit, through our decisions in United States v. Halper, 490 U.S. 435 (1989), Austin v. United States, 509 U.S. 602 (1993), and Department of Revenue of Mont. v. Kurth Ranch, 511 U.S. 767 (1994), we "changed [our] collective mind," and "adopted a new test for determining whether a nominally civil sanction constitutes 'punishment' for double jeopardy purposes." 33 F.3d, at 1218-1219. The Court of Appeals for the Sixth Circuit shared the view of the Ninth Circuit, though it did not directly rely upon *Kurth Ranch*. We turn now to consider whether *Halper, Austin,* and *Kurth Ranch* accomplished the radical jurisprudential shift perceived by the Courts of Appeals. . . .

We think that the Court of Appeals for the Sixth Circuit and the Court of Appeals for the Ninth Circuit misread *Halper, Austin,* and *Kurth Ranch*. None of those decisions purported to overrule the well-established teaching of *Various Items, Emerald Cut Stones,* and *89 Firearms. Halper* involved not a civil *forfeiture,* but a civil penalty. That its rule was limited to the latter context is clear from the decision itself, from the historical distinction that we have drawn between civil forfeiture and civil penalties, and from the practical difficulty of applying *Halper* to a civil forfeiture. . . .

The narrow focus of *Halper* followed from the distinction that we have drawn historically between civil forfeiture and civil penalties. Since at least *Various Items,* we have distinguished civil penalties such as fines from civil forfeiture proceedings that are in rem. While a "civil action to recover . . . penaltie[s], is punitive in character," and much like a criminal prosecution in that "[i]t is the wrongdoer in person who is proceeded against . . . and punished," in an in rem forfeiture proceeding, "[i]t is the property which is proceeded against, and by resort to a legal fiction, held guilty and condemned." *Various Items,* 282 U.S., at 580-581. Thus, though for Double Jeopardy purposes we have never balanced the value of property forfeited in a particular case against the harm suffered by the Government in that case, we have balanced the size of a particular civil penalty against the Government's harm. See, e.g., Rex Trailer Co. v. United States, 350 U.S. 148, 154 (1956) (fines not "so unreasonable or excessive" as to transform a civil remedy into a criminal penalty); United States ex rel. Marcus v. Hess, 317 U.S. 537 (1943) (fine of $315,000 not so disproportionate to Government's harm of $101,500 as to transform the fine into punishment). Indeed, the rule set forth in *Halper* developed from the teaching of *Rex Trailer* and *Hess*. See *Halper,* supra, at 445-447.

It is difficult to see how the rule of *Halper* could be applied to a civil forfeiture. Civil penalties are designed as a rough form of "liquidated damages" for the harms suffered by the Government as a result of a defendant's conduct. See *Rex Trailer,* supra, at 153-154. The civil penalty involved in *Halper,* for example, provided for a fixed monetary penalty for each false claim count on which the defendant was convicted in the criminal proceeding. Whether a "fixed-penalty provision" that seeks to compensate the Government for harm it has suffered is "so extreme" and "so divorced" from the penalty's nonpunitive purpose of compensating the Government as to be a punishment may be determined by balancing the Government's harm against the size of the penalty. Civil forfeitures, in contrast to civil penalties, are designed to do more than simply compensate the Government. Forfeitures serve a variety of purposes, but are designed primarily to confiscate property used in violation of the law, and to require disgorgement of the fruits of illegal conduct. Though it may be possible to quantify the value of the property forfeited, it is virtually impossible to quantify, even approximately, the nonpunitive purposes served by a particular civil forfeiture. Hence, it is practically difficult to determine whether a particular forfeiture bears no rational relationship to the nonpunitive purposes of that forfeiture. Quite simply, the case-by-case balancing test set forth in *Halper*, in which a court must compare the harm suffered by the Government against the size of the penalty imposed, is inapplicable to civil forfeiture.

We recognized as much in *Kurth Ranch*. In that case, the Court expressly disclaimed reliance upon *Halper*, finding that its case-specific approach was impossible to apply outside the context of a fixed civil-penalty provision. . . . This is not to say that there is no occasion for analysis of the Government's harm. *89 Firearms* makes clear the relevance of an evaluation of the harms alleged. The point is simply that *Halper*'s case-specific approach is inapplicable to civil forfeitures.

In the cases that we review, the Courts of Appeals did not find *Halper* difficult to apply to civil forfeiture because they concluded that its case-by-case balancing approach had been supplanted in *Austin* by a categorical approach that found a civil sanction to be punitive if it could not "fairly be said solely to serve a remedial purpose." See *Austin*, 509 U.S., at 610; see also *Halper*, supra, at 448. But *Austin*, it must be remembered, did not involve the Double Jeopardy Clause at all. *Austin* was decided solely under the Excessive Fines Clause of the Eighth Amendment, a constitutional provision which we never have understood as parallel to, or even related to, the Double Jeopardy Clause of the Fifth Amendment. The only discussion of the Double Jeopardy Clause contained in *Austin* appears in a footnote that acknowledges our decisions holding that "[t]he Double Jeopardy Clause has been held not to apply in civil forfeiture proceedings . . . where the forfeiture could properly be characterized as remedial." *Austin*, supra, at 608, n. 4. And in *Austin* we expressly recognized and approved our decisions in *Emerald Cut Stones* and *89 Firearms*.

We acknowledged in *Austin* that our categorical approach under the Excessive Fines Clause was wholly distinct from the case-by-case approach of *Halper*, and we explained that the difference in approach was based in a significant difference between the purposes of our analysis under each constitutional provision. See *Austin*, supra, at 622, n. 14. It is unnecessary in a case under the Excessive Fines Clause to inquire at a preliminary stage whether the civil sanction imposed in that particular case is totally inconsistent with any remedial goal. Because the second stage of inquiry under the Excessive Fines Clause asks whether the particular sanction in question is so large as to be "excessive," see *Austin*, 509 U.S., at 622-623 (declining to establish criteria for excessiveness), a preliminary-stage inquiry that focused on the disproportionality of a particular sanction would be duplicative of the excessiveness analysis that would follow. See id., at 622, n. 14 ("[I]t appears to make little practical difference whether the Excessive Fines Clause applies to all forfeitures . . . or only to those that cannot be characterized as purely remedial," because the Excessive Fines Clause "prohibits only the imposition of 'excessive' fines, and a fine that serves purely remedial purposes cannot be considered 'excessive' in any event"). Forfeitures effected under 21 U.S.C. §§881(a)(4) and (a)(7) are subject to review for excessiveness under the Eighth Amendment after *Austin*; this does not mean, however, that those forfeitures are so punitive as to constitute punishment for the purposes of double jeopardy. The holding of *Austin* was limited to the Excessive Fines Clause of the Eighth Amendment, and we decline to import the analysis of *Austin* into our double jeopardy jurisprudence.

In sum, nothing in *Halper*, *Kurth Ranch*, or *Austin*, purported to replace our traditional understanding that civil forfeiture does not constitute punishment for the purpose of the Double Jeopardy Clause. Congress long has authorized the Government to bring parallel criminal proceedings and civil forfeiture proceedings, and this Court consistently has found civil forfeitures not to constitute punishment under the Double Jeopardy Clause. It would have been quite remarkable for this Court both to have held unconstitutional a well-established practice, and to have overruled a long line of precedent, without having even suggested that it was doing so. *Halper* dealt with in personam civil penalties under the Double Jeopardy Clause; *Kurth Ranch* with a tax proceeding under the Double Jeopardy Clause; and *Austin* with civil forfeitures under the Excessive Fines Clause. None of those cases dealt with the subject of this case: in rem civil forfeitures for purposes of the Double Jeopardy Clause.

C

We turn now to consider the forfeitures in these cases under the teaching of *Various Items*, *Emerald Cut Stones*, and *89 Firearms*. Because it provides a useful analytical tool, we conduct our inquiry within the framework of the two-part test used in *89 Firearms*. First, we ask whether Congress intended proceedings under 21 U.S.C. §881 and 18 U.S.C. §981 to be criminal or civil. Second, we turn to consider whether the proceedings are so punitive in fact as to "persuade us that the forfeiture proceeding[s] may not legitimately be viewed as civil in nature," despite Congress' intent. *89 Firearms*, 465 U.S., at 366.

There is little doubt that Congress intended these forfeitures to be civil proceedings. As was the case in *89 Firearms*, "Congress' intent in this regard is most clearly demonstrated by the procedural mechanisms it established for enforcing forfeitures under the statute[s]." 465 U.S., at 363. Both 21 U.S.C. §881 and 18 U.S.C. §981, which is entitled "Civil forfeiture," provide that the laws "relating to the seizure, summary and judicial forfeiture, and condemnation of property for violation of the customs laws . . . shall apply to seizures and forfeitures incurred" under §§881 and 981. See 21 U.S.C. §881(d); 18 U.S.C. §981(d). Because forfeiture proceedings under the customs laws are in rem, see 19 U.S.C. §1602 et seq., it is clear that Congress intended that a forfeiture under §881 or §981, like the forfeiture reviewed in *89 Firearms*, would be a proceeding in rem. Congress specifically structured these forfeitures to be impersonal by targeting the property itself. "In contrast to the in personam nature of criminal actions, actions in rem have traditionally been viewed as civil proceedings, with jurisdiction dependent upon seizure of a physical object." *89 Firearms*, 465 U.S., at 363, citing *Calero-Toledo*, 416 U.S., at 684. Other procedural mechanisms governing forfeitures under §§981 and 881 also indicate that Congress intended such proceedings to be civil. Forfeitures under either statute are governed by 19 U.S.C. §1607, which provides that actual notice of the impending forfeiture is unnecessary when the Government cannot identify any party with an interest in the seized article, and by §1609, which provides that seized property is subject to forfeiture through a summary administrative procedure if no party files a claim to the property. And 19 U.S.C. §1615, which governs the burden of proof in forfeiture proceedings under §881 and §981, provides that once the Government has shown probable cause that the property is subject to forfeiture, then "the burden of proof shall lie upon [the] claimant." In sum, "[b]y creating such distinctly civil procedures for forfeitures under [§§881 and 981], Congress has 'indicate[d] clearly that it intended a civil, not a criminal sanction.'" *89 Firearms*, supra, at 363, quoting Helvering v. Mitchell, 303 U.S., at 402.

Moving to the second stage of our analysis, we find that there is little evidence, much less the "clearest proof" that we require, see *89 Firearms*, supra, at 365, quoting *Ward*, 448 U.S., at 249, suggesting that forfeiture proceedings under 21 U.S.C. §§881(a)(6) and (a)(7), and 18 U.S.C. §981(a)(1)(A), are so punitive in form and effect as to render them criminal despite Congress' intent to the contrary. The statutes involved in this case are, in most significant respects, indistinguishable from those reviewed, and held not to be punitive, in *Various Items, Emerald Cut Stones*, and *89 Firearms*.

Most significant is that §981(a)(1)(A), and §§881(a)(6) and (a)(7), while perhaps having certain punitive aspects, serve important nonpunitive goals. Title 21 U.S.C. §881(a)(7), under which Ursery's property was forfeited, provides for the forfeiture of "all real property . . . which is used or intended to be used, in any manner or part, to commit, or to facilitate the commission of" a federal drug felony. Requiring the forfeiture of property used to commit federal narcotics violations encourages property owners to take care in managing their property and ensures that they will not permit that property to be used for illegal purposes. See Bennis v. Michigan, 516 U.S. 442, 452 (1996) ("Forfeiture of property prevents illegal uses . . . by imposing an economic penalty, thereby rendering illegal behavior unprofitable"); *89 Firearms*, supra, at 364 (forfeiture "discourages unregulated commerce in firearms"); *Calero-Toledo*, supra, at 687-688. In many circumstances, the forfeiture may abate a nuisance. See, e.g., United States v. 141st Street Corp., 911 F.2d 870 (CA2 1990) (forfeiting apartment building used to sell crack cocaine); see also *Bennis*, supra, at 452 (affirming application of Michigan statute abating car as a nuisance; forfeiture "prevent[s] further illicit use of" property). . . .

The forfeiture of the property claimed by Arlt and Wren took place pursuant to 18 U.S.C. §981(a)(1)(A), and 21 U.S.C. §881(a)(6). Section 981(a)(1)(A) provides for the forfeiture of "[a]ny property" involved in illegal money-laundering transactions. Section 881(a)(6) provides for the forfeiture of "[a]ll . . . things of value furnished or intended to be furnished by any person in exchange for" illegal drugs; "all proceeds traceable to such an exchange"; and "all moneys, negotiable instruments, and securities used or intended to be used to facilitate" a federal drug felony. The same remedial purposes served by §881(a)(7) are served by §§881(a)(6) and 981(a)(1)(A). Only one point merits separate discussion. To the extent that §881(a)(6) applies to "proceeds" of illegal drug activity, it serves the additional nonpunitive goal of ensuring that persons do not profit from their illegal acts.

Other considerations that we have found relevant to the question whether a proceeding is criminal also tend to support a conclusion that §981(a)(1)(A) and §§881(a)(6) and (a)(7) are civil proceedings. See *Ward*, supra, at 247-248, n. 7, 249 (listing relevant factors and noting that they are neither exhaustive nor dispositive). First, in light of our decisions in *Various Items, Emerald Cut Stones*, and *89 Firearms*, and the long tradition of federal statutes providing for a forfeiture proceeding following a criminal prosecution, it is absolutely clear that in rem civil forfeiture has not historically been regarded as punishment, as we have understood that term under the Double Jeopardy Clause. Second, there is no requirement in the statutes that we currently review that the Government demonstrate scienter in order to establish that the property is subject to forfeiture; indeed, the property may be subject to forfeiture even if no party files a claim to it and the Government never shows any connection between the property and a particular person. See 19 U.S.C. §1609. Though both §§881(a) and 981(a) contain an "innocent owner" exception, we do not think that such a provision, without more indication of an intent to punish, is relevant to the question whether a statute is punitive under the Double Jeopardy Clause. Third, though both statutes may fairly be said to serve the purpose of deterrence, we long have held that this purpose may serve civil as well as criminal goals. See, e.g., *89 Firearms,* supra, at 364; *Calero-Toledo,* supra, at 677-678. We recently reaffirmed this conclusion in Bennis v. Michigan, supra, at 452, where we held that "forfeiture . . . serves a deterrent purpose distinct from any punitive purpose." Finally, though both statutes are tied to criminal activity, as was the case in *89 Firearms,* this fact is insufficient to render the statutes punitive. See *89 Firearms,* 465 U.S., at 365-366. It is well settled that "Congress may impose both a criminal and a civil sanction in respect to the same act or omission," *Helvering,* 303 U.S., at 399. By itself, the fact that a forfeiture statute has some connection to a criminal violation is far from the "clearest proof" necessary to show that a proceeding is criminal.

We hold that these in rem civil forfeitures are neither "punishment" nor criminal for purposes of the Double Jeopardy Clause. The judgments of the Court of Appeals for the Sixth Circuit, in No. 95-345, and of the Court of Appeals for the Ninth Circuit, in No. 95-346, are accordingly reversed.

[The concurring opinion of Justice Kennedy is omitted.]

JUSTICE SCALIA, with whom JUSTICE THOMAS joins, concurring in the judgment.

In my view, the Double Jeopardy Clause prohibits successive prosecution, not successive punishment. See Department of Revenue of Mont. v. Kurth Ranch, 511 U.S. 767, 798 (1994) (Scalia, J., dissenting). Civil forfeiture proceedings of the sort at issue here are not criminal prosecutions, even under the standard of Kennedy v. Mendoza-Martinez, 372 U.S. 144, 164 (1963), and United States v. Ward, 448 U.S. 242, 248-251 (1980).

JUSTICE STEVENS, concurring in the judgment in part and dissenting in part.

The question the Court poses is whether civil forfeitures constitute "punishment" for purposes of the Double Jeopardy Clause. Because the numerous federal statutes authorizing forfeitures cover such a wide variety of situations, it is quite wrong to assume that there is only one answer to that question. For purposes of analysis it is useful to identify three different categories of property that are subject to seizure: proceeds, contraband, and property that has played a part in the commission of a crime. The facts of these two cases illustrate the point.

In No. 95-346 the Government has forfeited $405,089.23 in currency. Those funds are the proceeds of unlawful activity. They are not property that respondents have any right to retain. The forfeiture of such proceeds, like the confiscation of money stolen from a bank, does not punish respondents because it exacts no price in liberty or lawfully derived property from them. I agree that the forfeiture of such proceeds is not punitive and therefore I concur in the Court's disposition of No. 95-346.

None of the property seized in No. 95-345 constituted proceeds of illegal activity. Indeed, the facts of that case reveal a dramatically different situation. Respondent

Ursery cultivated marijuana in a heavily wooded area not far from his home in Shiawassee County, Michigan. The illegal substance was consumed by members of his family, but there is no evidence, and no contention by the Government, that he sold any of it to third parties. Acting on the basis of the incorrect assumption that the marijuana plants were on respondent's property, Michigan police officers executed a warrant to search the premises. In his house they found marijuana seeds, stems, stalks, and a growlight. I presume those items were seized, and I have no difficulty concluding that such a seizure does not constitute punishment because respondent had no right to possess contraband. Accordingly, I agree with the Court's opinion insofar as it explains why the forfeiture of contraband does not constitute punishment for double jeopardy purposes.

The critical question presented in No. 95-345 arose, not out of the seizure of contraband by the Michigan police, but rather out of the decision by the United States Attorney to take respondent's home. There is no evidence that the house had been purchased with the proceeds of unlawful activity and the house itself was surely not contraband. Nonetheless, 21 U.S.C. §881(a)(7) authorized the Government to seek forfeiture of respondent's residence because it had been used to facilitate the manufacture and distribution of marijuana. Respondent was then himself prosecuted for and convicted of manufacturing marijuana. In my opinion none of the reasons supporting the forfeiture of proceeds or contraband provides a sufficient basis for concluding that the confiscation of respondent's home was not punitive. . . .

Remarkably, the Court today stands *Austin* on its head—a decision rendered only three years ago, with unanimity on the pertinent points—and concludes that §881(a)(7) is remedial rather than punitive in character. Every reason *Austin* gave for treating §881(a)(7) as punitive—the Court rejects or ignores. Every reason the Court provides for treating §881(a)(7) as remedial—*Austin* rebuffed. The Court claims that its conclusion is consistent with decisions reviewing statutes "indistinguishable" "in most significant respects" from §881(a)(7), . . . but ignores the fact that *Austin* reached the opposite conclusion as to the *identical* statute under review here. . . .

Even if the point had not been settled by prior decisions, common sense would dictate the result in this case. There is simply no rational basis for characterizing the seizure of this respondent's home as anything other than punishment for his crime. The house was neither proceeds nor contraband and its value had no relation to the Government's authority to seize it. Under the controlling statute an essential predicate for the forfeiture was proof that respondent had used the property in connection with the commission of a crime. The forfeiture of this property was unquestionably "a penalty that had absolutely no correlation to any damages sustained by society or to the cost of enforcing the law." United States v. Ward, 448 U.S., at 254. As we unanimously recognized in *Halper*, formalistic distinctions that obscure the obvious practical consequences of governmental action disserve the "'humane interests'" protected by the Double Jeopardy Clause. 490 U.S., at 447, quoting United States ex rel. Marcus v. Hess, 317 U.S. 537, 554 (1943) (Frankfurter, J., concurring). Fidelity to both reason and precedent dictates the conclusion that *this forfeiture* was "punishment" for purposes of the Double Jeopardy Clause. . . .

One final example may illustrate the depth of my concern that the Court's treatment of our cases has cut deeply into a guarantee deemed fundamental by the Founders. The Court relies heavily on a few early decisions that involved the forfeiture of vessels whose entire mission was unlawful and on the Prohibition-era precedent sustaining the forfeiture of a distillery—a property that served no purpose other than the manufacture of illegal spirits. Notably none of those early cases involved the forfeiture of a home as a form of punishment for misconduct that occurred therein. Consider how drastic the remedy would have been if Congress in 1931 had authorized the forfeiture of every home in which alcoholic beverages were consumed. Under the Court's reasoning, I fear that the label "civil," or perhaps "in rem," would have been sufficient to avoid characterizing such forfeitures as "punitive" for purposes of the Double Jeopardy Clause. Our recent decisions in *Halper*, *Austin*, and *Kurth Ranch*, dictate a far different conclusion. I remain persuaded that those cases were correctly decided and should be followed today.

Accordingly, I respectfully dissent from the judgment in No. 95-345.

NOTES AND QUESTIONS

1. What is the right result in cases like *Ursery*? Should congressional intent control? If it does, why would Congress ever label such penalties "criminal" or "punitive"? But if the size of the penalty or forfeiture determines the outcome, a host of civil proceedings will have to comply with the many rules of constitutional criminal procedure. Would that be a bad thing?

2. To the extent that *Ursery* began to undermine the doctrinal foundations of *Halper* and *Kurth Ranch*, the Court completed the demolition job in Hudson v. United States, 522 U.S. 93 (1997). In *Hudson*, the three defendants—officers and directors of two small Oklahoma banks—were assessed civil penalties of $100,000, $50,000, and $50,000, respectively, pursuant to 12 U.S.C. §§84(a)(1) and 375b, for causing illegal loans to be made by their banks. The notice of violation, sent by the Office of the Comptroller of the Currency (OCC), made no mention of any specific harm to the government as a result of the defendants' actions. The defendants ultimately paid $16,500, $15,000, and $12,500, respectively, to settle the claims against them, and also agreed not to become involved with any banks in the future unless authorized by the OCC. Three years later, however, the defendants were indicted on charges of conspiracy, misapplication of bank funds, and making false bank entries, based on the same loans that had been involved in the earlier civil proceedings; they sought dismissal of the indictments, complaining that the subsequent criminal proceedings violated the Double Jeopardy Clause under *Halper*.

Chief Justice Rehnquist, writing for a five-member Court majority, rejected the defendants' double jeopardy claims, and in the process discarded the *Halper* test for determining whether a particular punishment is criminal or civil:

> Whether a particular punishment is criminal or civil is, at least initially, a matter of statutory construction. *Helvering*, supra, at 399. A court must first ask whether the legislature, "in establishing the penalizing mechanism, indicated either expressly or impliedly a preference for one label or the other." *Ward*, 448 U.S., at 248. Even in those cases where the legislature "has indicated an intention to establish a civil penalty, we have inquired further whether the statutory scheme was so punitive either in purpose or effect," id., at 248-249, as to "transfor[m] what was clearly intended as a civil remedy into a criminal penalty," Rex Trailer Co. v. United States, 350 U.S. 148, 154 (1956).
>
> In making this latter determination, the factors listed in Kennedy v. Mendoza-Martinez, 372 U.S. 144, 168-169 (1963), provide useful guideposts, including: (1) "[w]hether the sanction involves an affirmative disability or restraint"; (2) "whether it

has historically been regarded as a punishment"; (3) "whether it comes into play only on a finding of *scienter*"; (4) "whether its operation will promote the traditional aims of punishment—retribution and deterrence"; (5) "whether the behavior to which it applies is already a crime"; (6) "whether an alternative purpose to which it may rationally be connected is assignable for it"; and (7) "whether it appears excessive in relation to the alternative purpose assigned." It is important to note, however, that "these factors must be considered in relation to the statute on its face," id., at 169, and "only the clearest proof" will suffice to override legislative intent and transform what has been denominated a civil remedy into a criminal penalty, *Ward*, supra, at 249 (internal quotation marks omitted). . . .

We believe that *Halper*'s deviation from long-standing double jeopardy principles was ill considered. As subsequent cases have demonstrated, *Halper*'s test for determining whether a particular sanction is "punitive," and thus subject to the strictures of the Double Jeopardy Clause, has proved unworkable. We have since recognized that all civil penalties have some deterrent effect. See Department of Revenue of Montana v. Kurth Ranch, 511 U.S. 767, 777, n. 14 (1994); United States v. Ursery, 518 U.S. 267, 284-285, n. 2 (1996).[6] If a sanction must be "solely" remedial (i.e., entirely non-deterrent) to avoid implicating the Double Jeopardy Clause, then no civil penalties are beyond the scope of the Clause. Under *Halper*'s method of analysis, a court must also look at the "sanction actually imposed" to determine whether the Double Jeopardy Clause is implicated. Thus, it will not be possible to determine whether the Double Jeopardy Clause is violated until a defendant has proceeded through a trial to judgment. But in those cases where the civil proceeding follows the criminal proceeding, this approach flies in the face of the notion that the Double Jeopardy Clause forbids the government from even "*attempting* a second time to punish criminally." *Helvering*, 303 U.S., at 399 (emphasis added).

Finally, it should be noted that some of the ills at which *Halper* was directed are addressed by other constitutional provisions. The Due Process and Equal Protection Clauses already protect individuals from sanctions which are downright irrational. Williamson v. Lee Optical of Okla., Inc., 348 U.S. 483 (1955). The Eighth Amendment protects against excessive civil fines, including forfeitures. Alexander v. United States, 509 U.S. 544 (1993); Austin v. United States, 509 U.S. 602 (1993). The additional protection afforded by extending double jeopardy protections to proceedings heretofore thought to be civil is more than offset by the confusion created by attempting to distinguish between "punitive" and "nonpunitive" penalties.

522 U.S., at 99-100, 101-103.

3. After *Ursery* and *Hudson*, what is left of the Court's decision in *Halper*? Or *Kurth Ranch*? Clearly, the so-called "*Halper* test" is no longer useful as a means for determining whether a civil sanction is "punitive" enough to trigger the protection of the double jeopardy clause; henceforth, the *Hudson* Court has declared, the list of factors first identified in Kennedy v. Mendoza-Martinez, 372 U.S. 144, 168-169 (1963), will govern that question. But does the *result* in *Halper* survive? What about *Kurth Ranch*? Are there any cases in which the sheer size of the disparity between the civil sanction and the damage that is allegedly being compensated will make the civil sanction punitive?

6. In *Kurth Ranch*, we held that the presence of a deterrent purpose or effect is not dispositive of the double jeopardy question. 511 U.S., at 781. Rather, we applied a *Kennedy*-like test, see 511 U.S., at 780-783, before concluding that Montana's dangerous drug tax was "the functional equivalent of a successive criminal prosecution." Similarly, in *Ursery*, we rejected the notion that civil in rem forfeitures violate the Double Jeopardy Clause. 518 U.S., at 270-271. We upheld such forfeitures, relying on the historical support for the notion that such forfeitures are civil and thus do not implicate double jeopardy. Id., at 292.

4. Halper was assessed a civil penalty of $130,000 for Medicare fraud, after a prison sentence for the same conduct. The Kurths pled guilty to conspiracy to possess marijuana with intent to distribute and were sentenced for that crime, after which they were charged a "tax" of $900,000 on the marijuana they possessed. Police found drugs in Ursery's house, leading to a government civil forfeiture proceeding against the house. Ursery was later convicted of a drug offense, for which he was sentenced to more than five years in prison. Federal bank regulators imposed civil fines of $200,000 on Hudson and his codefendants. Later, a federal grand jury indicted those same defendants for crimes based on the same conduct that had given rise to the civil fines.

In all of these cases, the government sought to incarcerate the defendants for their crimes, and also sought to impose some financial penalty for the same conduct. The question in each case was whether the financial penalty was, in essence, another criminal punishment. The Supreme Court has struggled mightily with this question. But is it really so difficult? People are regularly sued and assessed huge damages bills, including punitive damages, and no one thinks those damages bills preclude criminal prosecution. Nor does criminal prosecution preclude a private tort claim: Remember O.J. Simpson, who famously won his criminal trial for murder, and equally famously lost his subsequent civil trial for wrongful death. Why should civil claims by the government be handled differently? Perhaps they shouldn't, as long as the government's civil penalty can be reduced to dollars.

5. But the reasoning in *Ursery* and *Hudson* extends beyond financial penalties. Kansas v. Hendricks, 521 U.S. 346 (1997), involved a state statute that authorized the civil commitment of persons who, due to a "mental abnormality" or "personality disorder," have a tendency to commit "predatory acts of sexual violence." Hendricks was convicted of child molestation; after serving ten years in prison, he was about to be released to a halfway house, when the state charged him under the civil commitment statute. Hendricks claimed this "civil" proceeding violated both double jeopardy and the ban on ex post facto laws. The Court disagreed, noting that civil commitment proceedings are, after all, civil—and using the same analysis as in *Ursery* and *Hudson*. The Kansas statute passed muster because the legislature's expressed goal was "to create a civil proceeding," and because the statute's characteristics were not so similar to those of a typical criminal statute as to establish "the clearest proof" of punitive purpose or effect. Absent such proof, the legislature's "manifest intent" that the statute be treated as civil rather than criminal was dispositive. 521 U.S., at 361-369.

Hendricks meant that laws like the Kansas sexual predator statute were not facially invalid. The defendant in Seling v. Young, 531 U.S. 250 (2001), challenged Washington's similar statute as applied to his case. Young claimed that the state failed to provide the mental-health treatment that was mandated by the statute, and generally treated those confined as if they were convicted criminals serving a prison sentence, not sick patients in need of treatment. All of which, Young argued, meant that the allegedly civil commitment was actually criminal for purposes of double jeopardy law; Young also made an ex post facto claim on the same grounds. The Court rejected both claims:

> Since deciding *Hendricks*, this Court has reaffirmed the principle that determining the civil or punitive nature of an Act must begin with reference to its text and legislative history. Hudson v. United States, 522 U.S. 93 (1997). In *Hudson*, . . . this Court

expressly disapproved of evaluating the civil nature of an Act by reference to the effect that Act has on a single individual. Instead, courts must evaluate the question by reference to a variety of factors "considered in relation to the statute on its face." . . . Id., at 100 (quoting Kennedy v. Mendoza-Martinez, 372 U.S. 144, 169 (1963)). . . .

We hold that respondent cannot obtain release through an "as-applied" challenge to the Washington Act on double jeopardy and ex post facto grounds. We agree with petitioner that an "as-applied" analysis would prove unworkable. Such an analysis would never conclusively resolve whether a particular scheme is punitive and would thereby prevent a final determination of the scheme's validity under the Double Jeopardy and Ex Post Facto Clauses. . . . Unlike a fine, confinement is not a fixed event. As petitioner notes, it extends over time under conditions that are subject to change. The particular features of confinement may affect how a confinement scheme is evaluated to determine whether it is civil rather than punitive, but it remains no less true that the query must be answered definitively. The civil nature of a confinement scheme cannot be altered based merely on vagaries in the implementation of the authorizing statute.

531 U.S., at 262-263.

Are you persuaded? Should the government be able to incarcerate its citizens twice for the same conduct? Isn't that what the laws at issue in *Hendricks* and *Seling* authorize? Given the breadth of the civil commitment power, what is to stop the government from transferring a large portion of the criminal code to the civil side of the legal ledger? Can the law of constitutional criminal procedure be evaded so easily?

Chapter 17

Appellate and Collateral Review

A. Appellate Review

1. The Defendant's Right to Appeal

In every state and the federal system, a defendant who has been convicted of a crime at trial has a right to appeal that conviction.[1] It might surprise you to learn that this right is not grounded in the United States Constitution; for more than 100 years, the Supreme Court has consistently maintained that the defendant's right to appeal in a criminal case is purely a creature of statute, not a component of due process, and thus presumably can be eliminated if the legislature chooses to do so. See, e.g., Jones v. Barnes, 463 U.S. 745 (1983); McKane v. Durston, 153 U.S. 684 (1894). Today, however, it seems unthinkable that a convicted defendant would be denied the right to appeal. Why might the Court refuse to recognize a constitutional right to appeal, despite the fact that such a right is seemingly taken for granted in every American jurisdiction? Is the Court worried about some further consequence — e.g., concerning the right to the effective assistance of counsel on appeal—that might follow from the recognition of such a constitutional right to appeal?

Most states and the federal government provide for a statutory "right" to appeal only to the level of the intermediate appellate court (where one exists); further appellate review by the highest court in the jurisdiction is available only if that court agrees to accept the case. The right to appeal is generally viewed as waivable; many (if not most) plea bargains include an explicit agreement by the defendant not to appeal his conviction. See Note, An Unjust Bargain: Plea Bargains and Waiver of the Right to Appeal, 51 B.C. L. Rev. 871 (2010). For further discussion of the effect of plea bargains on the right to appeal, see Chapter 13, at page 1285.

2. The Prosecution's Right to Appeal

Like defense appeals, the prosecution's right to appeal in a criminal case is also purely a creature of statute. But the prosecution's right to appeal is necessarily far more limited than that of the defendant. This is primarily because of the double jeopardy clause, which absolutely bars prosecution appeals from verdicts

---

1. The right to appeal a criminal conviction that is based on a guilty plea may be more limited. See, e.g., Michigan Constitution, Art. 1, §20 (providing that "an appeal by an accused who pleads guilty or nolo contendere shall be by leave of the court.").

of acquittal by the factfinder (or their functional equivalent, see Chapter 16). Thus, statutes granting the prosecution the right to appeal in criminal cases apply mostly in three special contexts: (1) interlocutory appeals from certain pretrial orders, such as suppression orders or orders dismissing an indictment; (2) appeals from post-trial rulings that set aside a guilty verdict rendered by the factfinder (in such situations, reinstatement of the guilty verdict, on appeal, does not violate double jeopardy); and (3) sentencing appeals, which were virtually nonexistent under traditional discretionary sentencing systems but have become commonplace under determinate or guideline sentencing systems. See, e.g., 18 U.S.C. §3731, authorizing prosecution appeals, in federal criminal cases, from all final orders except when the appeal would be barred by double jeopardy, as well as from certain kinds of suppression orders (even though not final); 18 U.S.C. §3742(b), authorizing prosecution appeals of sentences in federal criminal cases, to the extent those sentences were imposed "in violation of law" or in contravention of the Federal Sentencing Guidelines. In short, the right to appeal in criminal cases is far from symmetrical. See Kate Stith, The Risk of Legal Error in Criminal Cases: Some Consequences of the Asymmetry in the Right to Appeal, 57 U. Chi. L. Rev. 1 (1990).

In determinate sentencing jurisdictions, sentencing appeals — filed by both sides — have become a dominant feature of appellate litigation. For example, during the year ending September 30, 2012, the U.S. Courts of Appeals resolved 9,083 appeals in criminal cases that were subject to the Federal Sentencing Guidelines. Of those, more than 85.7 percent involved at least one sentencing issue. See Mark Motivans, Federal Justice Statistics, 2012 (NCJ 248470, January 2015), published by the U.S. Department of Justice, Bureau of Justice Statistics, and available online at http://bjs.ojp.usdoj.gov/.

3. Interlocutory Appeals

In Flanagan v. United States, 465 U.S. 259 (1984), the Supreme Court held that, under 28 U.S.C. §1291, the federal statute that generally governs appeals from final orders of federal district courts, a pretrial order disqualifying defense counsel in a criminal case is not a "final collateral order" subject to interlocutory appeal by the defendant. The Court explained that three conditions must be met for the so-called "collateral order" doctrine to apply: (1) the order "must conclusively determine the disputed question"; (2) the order must "resolve an important issue completely separate from the merits of the action"; and (3) the order must "be effectively unreviewable on appeal from a final judgment." The Court noted that these conditions have been interpreted "with the utmost strictness in criminal cases"; indeed, the only kinds of orders previously found to satisfy the test were those (1) denying a motion to reduce bail, (2) denying a motion to dismiss an indictment on double jeopardy grounds, and (3) denying a motion to dismiss an indictment for violation of the speech or debate clause. An order disqualifying counsel, according to the Court, "lacks the critical characteristics that make [such orders] immediately appealable. Unlike a request for bail reduction, a constitutional objection to counsel's disqualification is in no danger of becoming moot upon conviction and sentence. Moreover, it cannot be said that the right petitioners assert . . . is a right not to be tried. Double jeopardy and Speech or Debate rights are sui generis in this regard."

See also Midland Asphalt Corp. v. United States, 489 U.S. 794 (1989), holding that an order denying a claim of violation of Fed. R. Crim. P. 6(e), in connection with a grand jury proceeding, is not subject to interlocutory appeal by the defendant because the issues involved in the claim are "enmeshed in the merits of the dispute." The rub here is that such orders are *also* not generally reviewable *after* conviction, because the conviction itself establishes conclusively that the alleged defect in the indictment was "harmless error." Cf. United States v. Mechanik, 475 U.S. 66 (1986) (involving alleged Rule 6(d) violation). In many jurisdictions, prosecutors are granted somewhat greater leeway than defendants to file interlocutory appeals from pretrial orders, largely because of the aforementioned asymmetry that prevents the prosecutor from appealing most adverse trial verdicts. See, e.g., 18 U.S.C. §3731, authorizing interlocutory appeals by the prosecution, in federal criminal cases, from certain kinds of suppression orders.

4. What Law Applies?

In general, of course, an appellate court must review the decision of the court below on the basis of all of the relevant state and/or federal law. But what if the relevant law has changed since the time when the court below rendered its decision? Under what circumstances should a new legal rule apply "retroactively," to require the reversal of a decision that might have been proper under the law that was applicable at the time?

For more than two decades, beginning with the decision in Linkletter v. Walker, 381 U.S. 618 (1965), the Supreme Court held that the retroactivity of new constitutional rules was to be determined separately for each new rule, based on an analysis of three factors: "(a) the purpose to be served by the new standards, (b) the extent of the reliance by law enforcement authorities on the old standards, and (c) the effect on the administration of justice of a retroactive application of the new standards." See Stovall v. Denno, 388 U.S. 293, 297 (1967).

In Griffith v. Kentucky, 479 U.S. 314 (1987), however, the Court discarded the *Linkletter* approach, holding instead that, henceforth, all new constitutional rules must be applied retroactively to all cases still pending on direct appeal:

> [F]ailure to apply a newly declared constitutional rule to criminal cases pending on direct review violates basic norms of constitutional adjudication. . . . [I]t is a settled principle that this Court adjudicates only "cases" and "controversies." See U.S. Const., Art. III, §2. Unlike a legislature, we do not promulgate new rules of constitutional criminal procedure on a broad basis. Rather, the nature of judicial review requires that we adjudicate specific cases, and each case usually becomes the vehicle for announcement of a new rule. But after we have decided a new rule in the case selected, the integrity of judicial review requires that we apply that rule to all similar cases pending on direct review.

Id., at 322-323. The Court further held that no exception would be recognized for new constitutional rules that make a "clear break" with past precedent—even in such situations, the new rule would be applied retroactively, for two reasons:

First, the principle that this Court does not disregard current law, when it adjudicates a case pending before it on direct review, applies regardless of the specific characteristics of the particular new rule announced. . . .

Second, the use of a "clear break" exception creates the same problem of not treating similarly situated defendants the same. . . .

Id., at 326-327.

On the related issue of retroactivity in the context of collateral review, see Teague v. Lane, 489 U.S. 288 (1989), discussed at page 1634, infra.

5. Prejudice and Harmless Error

When a defendant seeks to overturn a criminal conviction on appeal, it is not always enough to persuade the appellate court that a legal (or even a constitutional) error occurred during the trial. Most of the time, the court also must decide whether any prejudice, or harm, resulted from the error. Depending on the particular kind of error involved, and on the procedural posture of the particular case, different rules with respect to prejudice will apply.

First, some relatively rare (except in capital cases) kinds of errors—including ineffective assistance of counsel under Strickland v. Washington, or prosecutorial failure to disclose material exculpatory evidence under Brady v. Maryland—contain a prejudice requirement as an inherent part of the definition of what constitutes error in the first place. For such kinds of errors, the appellate court cannot find error at all without first finding prejudice. Second, other relatively rare kinds of errors—such as denial of counsel under Gideon v. Wainwright, or denial of the right to self-representation under Faretta v. California—always lead to reversal (assuming they are preserved at trial and presented on appeal in the proper manner), even if the defendant cannot show any prejudice. This is either because such errors are presumed to be prejudicial, or because they are so fundamental that no prejudice is required. Third, for most kinds of errors, reversal on appeal is automatic (again, assuming proper preservation at trial and presentation on appeal), unless the *government* can prove that the error was "harmless." Finally, if an error is not preserved properly at trial (such as by failing to make a contemporaneous objection), then reversal on appeal depends on whether the defendant can persuade the appellate court that the error constituted "plain error," which—at least in the federal courts—requires a showing that it "affect[ed] substantial rights."

The following case and notes explore various aspects of these different prejudice rules.

CHAPMAN v. CALIFORNIA

Certiorari to the Supreme Court of California
386 U.S. 18 (1967)

JUSTICE BLACK delivered the opinion of the Court.

Petitioners, Ruth Elizabeth Chapman and Thomas LeRoy Teale, were convicted in a California state court upon a charge that they robbed, kidnaped, and murdered a bartender. She was sentenced to life imprisonment and he to death. At the time of the trial, Art. I, §13, of the State's Constitution provided that "in any criminal case, whether the defendant testifies or not, his failure to explain or to deny by his testimony any evidence or facts in the case against him may be commented upon by the court and by counsel, and may be considered by the court or the jury." Both petitioners in this case chose not to testify at their trial, and the State's attorney prosecuting them took full advantage of his right under the State Constitution to comment upon their failure to testify, filling his argument to the jury from beginning to end with numerous references to their silence and inferences of their guilt resulting therefrom. The trial court also charged the jury that it could draw adverse inferences from petitioners' failure to testify. Shortly after the trial, but before petitioners' cases had been considered on appeal by the California Supreme Court, this Court decided Griffin v. California, 380 U.S. 609 [(1965)], in which we held California's constitutional provision and practice invalid on the ground that they put a penalty on the exercise of a person's right not to be compelled to be a witness against himself, guaranteed by the Fifth Amendment to the United States Constitution and made applicable to California and the other States by the Fourteenth Amendment. . . . On appeal, the State Supreme Court, . . . admitting that petitioners had been denied a federal constitutional right by the comments on their silence, nevertheless affirmed, applying the State Constitution's harmless-error provision, which forbids reversal unless "the court shall be of the opinion that the error complained of has resulted in a miscarriage of justice." . . .

I

Before deciding the two questions here—whether there can ever be harmless constitutional error and whether the error here was harmless—we must first decide whether state or federal law governs. The application of a state harmless-error rule is, of course, a state question where it involves only errors of state procedure or state law. But the error from which these petitioners suffered was a denial of rights guaranteed against invasion by the Fifth and Fourteenth Amendments. . . . We have no hesitation in saying that the right of these petitioners not to be punished for exercising their Fifth and Fourteenth Amendment right to be silent—expressly created by the Federal Constitution itself—is a federal right which, in the absence of appropriate congressional action, it is our responsibility to protect by fashioning the necessary rule.

II

We are urged by petitioners to hold that all federal constitutional errors, regardless of the facts and circumstances, must always be deemed harmful. Such a holding, as petitioners correctly point out, would require an automatic reversal of their convictions and make further discussion unnecessary. We decline to adopt any such rule. All 50 states have harmless-error statutes or rules, and the United States long ago through its Congress established for its courts the rule that judgments shall not be reversed for "errors or defects which do not affect the substantial rights of the parties." 28 U.S.C. §2111. None of these rules on its face distinguishes between federal constitutional errors and errors of state law or federal statutes and rules. All of these rules, state or federal, serve a very useful purpose insofar as they block setting aside convictions for small errors or defects that have little, if any, likelihood of having changed the result of the trial. We conclude that there may be some constitutional errors which in the setting of a particular case are so unimportant and insignificant that they may, consistent with the Federal Constitution, be deemed harmless, not requiring the automatic reversal of the conviction.

III

In fashioning a harmless-constitutional-error rule, we must recognize that harmless-error rules can work very unfair and mischievous results when, for example, highly important and persuasive evidence, or argument, though legally forbidden, finds its way into a trial in which the question of guilt or innocence is a close one. What harmless-error rules all aim at is a rule that will save the good in harmless-error practices while avoiding the bad, so far as possible.

. . . We prefer the approach of this Court in deciding what was harmless error in our recent case of Fahy v. Connecticut, 375 U.S. 85 [(1963)]. There we said: "The question is whether there is a reasonable possibility that the evidence complained of might have contributed to the conviction." . . . Although our prior cases have indicated that there are some constitutional rights so basic to a fair trial that their infraction can never be treated as harmless error,[8] this statement in *Fahy* itself belies any belief that all trial errors which violate the Constitution automatically call for reversal. At the same time, however, like the federal harmless-error statute, it emphasizes an intention not to treat as harmless those constitutional errors that "affect substantial rights" of a party. An error in admitting plainly relevant evidence which possibly influenced the jury adversely to a litigant cannot, under *Fahy*, be conceived of as harmless. Certainly error, constitutional error, in illegally admitting highly prejudicial evidence or comments, casts on someone other than the person prejudiced by it a burden to show that it was harmless. It is for that reason that the original common-law harmless-error rule put the burden on the beneficiary of the error either to prove that there was no injury or to suffer a reversal of his erroneously obtained judgment. There is little, if any, difference between our statement in Fahy v. Connecticut about "whether there is a reasonable possibility that the evidence complained of might have contributed to the conviction" and requiring the beneficiary of a constitutional error to prove beyond a reasonable doubt that the error complained of did not contribute to the verdict obtained. We, therefore, do no more than adhere to the meaning of our *Fahy* case when we hold, as we now do, that before a federal constitutional error can be held harmless, the court must be able to declare a belief that it was harmless beyond a reasonable doubt. While appellate courts do not ordinarily have the original task of applying such a test, it is a familiar standard to all courts, and we believe its adoption will provide a more workable standard, although achieving the same result as that aimed at in our *Fahy* case.

IV

Applying the foregoing standard, we have no doubt that the error in these cases was not harmless to petitioners. . . .

---

8. See, e.g., Payne v. Arkansas, 356 U.S. 560 [(1958)] (coerced confession); Gideon v. Wainwright, 372 U.S. 335 [(1963)] (right to counsel); Tumey v. Ohio, 273 U.S. 510 [(1927)] (impartial judge).

. . . [T]he state prosecutor's argument and the trial judge's instruction to the jury continuously and repeatedly impressed the jury that from the failure of petitioners to testify, to all intents and purposes, the inferences from the facts in evidence had to be drawn in favor of the State—in short, that by their silence petitioners had served as irrefutable witnesses against themselves. And though the case in which this occurred presented a reasonably strong "circumstantial web of evidence" against petitioners . . . , it was also a case in which, absent the constitutionally forbidden comments, honest, fair-minded jurors might very well have brought in not-guilty verdicts. Under these circumstances, it is completely impossible for us to say that the State has demonstrated, beyond a reasonable doubt, that the prosecutor's comments and the trial judge's instruction did not contribute to petitioners' convictions. Such a machine-gun repetition of a denial of constitutional rights, designed and calculated to make petitioners' version of the evidence worthless, can no more be considered harmless than the introduction against a defendant of a coerced confession. See, e.g., Payne v. Arkansas, 356 U.S. 560 [(1958)]. Petitioners are entitled to a trial free from the pressure of unconstitutional inferences. . . .

JUSTICE STEWART, concurring in the result. . . .

. . . [C]onstitutional rights are not fungible goods. The differing values which they represent and protect may make a harmless-error rule appropriate for one type of constitutional error and not for another. I would not foreclose the possibility that a harmless-error rule might appropriately be applied to some constitutional violations.[2] Indeed, one source of my disagreement with the Court's opinion is its implicit assumption that the same harmless-error rule should apply indiscriminately to all constitutional violations.

. . . The adoption of any harmless-error rule . . . commits this Court to a case-by-case examination to determine the extent to which we think unconstitutional comment on a defendant's failure to testify influenced the outcome of a particular trial. This burdensome obligation is one that we here are hardly qualified to discharge. . . .

For these reasons I believe it inappropriate to inquire whether the violation of Griffin v. California that occurred in this case was harmless by any standard, and accordingly I concur in the reversal of the judgment.

[The dissenting opinion of Justice Harlan is omitted.]

NOTES AND QUESTIONS

1. What is the source of the Court's authority to develop a harmless-error rule for constitutional errors in *Chapman*? Is this an example of "constitutional common law"? See Daniel Meltzer, Harmless Error and Constitutional Remedies, 61 U. Chi. L. Rev. 1 (1994).

Does the existence of a harmless-error rule subvert the normal relationship between trial and appellate courts? What about the special role of the jury in our

2. For example, quite different considerations are involved when evidence is introduced which was obtained in violation of the Fourth and Fourteenth Amendments. The exclusionary rule in that context balances the desirability of deterring objectionable police conduct against the undesirability of excluding relevant and reliable evidence. The resolution of these values with interests of judicial economy might well dictate a harmless-error rule for such violations. . . .

criminal justice system? How is it possible for an appellate court to determine that a particular constitutional error was harmless, without intruding on the domain of the jury?

The Court in *Chapman* pointed out that harmless-error rules exist everywhere, for all kinds of errors. Why, then, was the Court so cautious in the articulation of its new harmless-error rule for federal constitutional violations? What kinds of problems might the Court have been trying to anticipate—and avoid? If enough instances of a particular constitutional error are found to be harmless, what are the consequences for the viability of the underlying constitutional rule? In such a situation, is it not likely that the wisdom of the rule itself might someday be revisited? See Steven Goldberg, Harmless Error: Constitutional Sneak Thief, 71 J. Crim. L. & Criminology 421 (1980).

2. In *Chapman*, the Court referred to Payne v. Arkansas, 356 U.S. 560 (1958), involving the introduction of a coerced confession, as an example of a case *not* subject to harmless-error review. See footnote 8, supra. In Arizona v. Fulminante, 499 U.S. 279 (1991), however, Chief Justice Rehnquist, writing for a majority on the issue, reached the opposite conclusion—and, in the process, developed a new approach for determining whether particular constitutional errors are subject to *Chapman* analysis:

> Since this Court's landmark decision in Chapman v. California, 386 U.S. 18 (1967), in which we adopted the general rule that a constitutional error does not automatically require reversal of a conviction, the Court has applied harmless-error analysis to a wide range of errors and has recognized that most constitutional errors can be harmless. See, e.g., Clemons v. Mississippi, 494 U.S. 738, 752-754 (1990) (unconstitutionally overbroad jury instructions at the sentencing stage of a capital case); Satterwhite v. Texas, 486 U.S. 249 (1988) (admission of evidence at the sentencing stage of a capital case in violation of the Sixth Amendment Counsel Clause); Carella v. California, 491 U.S. 263, 266 (1989) (jury instruction containing an erroneous conclusive presumption); Pope v. Illinois, 481 U.S. 497, 501-504 (1987) (jury instruction misstating an element of the offense); Rose v. Clark, 478 U.S. 570 (1986) (jury instruction containing an erroneous rebuttable presumption); Crane v. Kentucky, 476 U.S. 683, 691 (1986) (erroneous exclusion of defendant's testimony regarding the circumstances of his confession); Delaware v. Van Arsdall, 475 U.S. 673 (1986) (restriction on a defendant's right to cross-examine a witness for bias in violation of the Sixth Amendment Confrontation Clause); Rushen v. Spain, 464 U.S. 114, 117-118, and n. 2 (1983) (denial of a defendant's right to be present at trial); United States v. Hasting, 461 U.S. 499 (1983) (improper comment on defendant's silence at trial, in violation of the Fifth Amendment Self-Incrimination Clause); Hopper v. Evans, 456 U.S. 605 (1982) (statute improperly forbidding trial court's giving a jury instruction on a lesser included offense in a capital case in violation of the Due Process Clause); Kentucky v. Whorton, 441 U.S. 786 (1979) (failure to instruct the jury on the presumption of innocence); Moore v. Illinois, 434 U.S. 220, 232 (1977) (admission of identification evidence in violation of the Sixth Amendment Confrontation Clause); Brown v. United States, 411 U.S. 223, 231-232 (1973) (admission of the out-of-court statement of a nontestifying codefendant in violation of the Sixth Amendment Confrontation Clause); Milton v. Wainwright, 407 U.S. 371 (1972) (confession obtained in violation of Massiah v. United States, 377 U.S. 201 (1964)); Chambers v. Maroney, 399 U.S. 42, 52-53 (1970) (admission of evidence obtained in violation of the Fourth Amendment); Coleman v. Alabama, 399 U.S. 1, 10-11 (1970) (denial of counsel at a preliminary hearing in violation of the Sixth Amendment Counsel Clause).

The common thread connecting these cases is that each involved "trial error"—error which occurred during the presentation of the case to the jury, and which may therefore be quantitatively assessed in the context of other evidence presented in order to determine whether its admission was harmless beyond a reasonable doubt. In applying harmless-error analysis to these many different constitutional violations, the Court has been faithful to the belief that the harmless-error doctrine is essential to preserve the "principle that the central purpose of a criminal trial is to decide the factual question of the defendant's guilt or innocence, and promotes public respect for the criminal process by focusing on the underlying fairness of the trial rather than on the virtually inevitable presence of immaterial error." . . .

The admission of an involuntary confession—a classic "trial error"—is markedly different from the other two constitutional violations referred to in the *Chapman* footnote as not being subject to harmless-error analysis. One of those violations, involved in Gideon v. Wainwright, 372 U.S. 335 (1963), was the total deprivation of the right to counsel at trial. The other violation, involved in Tumey v. Ohio, 273 U.S. 510 (1927), was a judge who was not impartial. These are structural defects in the constitution of the trial mechanism, which defy analysis by "harmless-error" standards. The entire conduct of the trial from beginning to end is obviously affected by the absence of counsel for a criminal defendant, just as it is by the presence on the bench of a judge who is not impartial. Since our decision in *Chapman*, other cases have added to the category of constitutional errors which are not subject to harmless error the following: unlawful exclusion of members of the defendant's race from a grand jury, Vasquez v. Hillery, 474 U.S. 254 (1986); the right to self-representation at trial, McKaskle v. Wiggins, 465 U.S. 168, 177-178, n. 8 (1984); and the right to public trial, Waller v. Georgia, 467 U.S. 39, 49, n. 9 (1984). Each of these constitutional deprivations is a similar structural defect affecting the framework within which the trial proceeds, rather than simply an error in the trial process itself. "Without these basic protections, a criminal trial cannot reliably serve its function as a vehicle for determination of guilt or innocence, and no criminal punishment may be regarded as fundamentally fair." . . .

It is evident from a comparison of the constitutional violations which we have held subject to harmless error, and those which we have held not, that involuntary statements or confessions belong in the former category. The admission of an involuntary confession is a "trial error," similar in both degree and kind to the erroneous admission of other types of evidence. . . . When reviewing the erroneous admission of an involuntary confession, the appellate court, as it does with the admission of other forms of improperly admitted evidence, simply reviews the remainder of the evidence against the defendant to determine whether the admission of the confession was harmless beyond a reasonable doubt.

Nor can it be said that the admission of an involuntary confession is the type of error which "transcends the criminal process." This Court has applied harmless-error analysis to the violation of other constitutional rights similar in magnitude and importance and involving the same level of police misconduct. . . .

Of course an involuntary confession may have a more dramatic effect on the course of a trial than do other trial errors—in particular cases it may be devastating to a defendant—but this simply means that a reviewing court will conclude in such a case that its admission was not harmless error; it is not a reason for eschewing the harmless-error test entirely. . . .

Id., at 306-312.

Justice White, in dissent on the same issue in *Fulminante*, argued that "a coerced confession is fundamentally different from other types of erroneously admitted evidence to which the [*Chapman*] rule has been applied. . . . The inability to assess its effect on a conviction causes the admission at trial of a coerced confession to 'defy analysis by "harmless-error" standards,' just as certainly as do deprivation of counsel and trial before a biased judge." Id., at 289-290. On the separate issue of the application of the *Chapman* standard to the facts of the case, however, Justice White carried a majority, concluding that the erroneous introduction of the coerced confession was not harmless. See id., at 295-302.

3. Are you confident that you can recognize the distinction between "trial errors" and "structural errors"? What about errors in the jury instructions concerning the prosecution's burden of proof at trial? How do such errors fit into the *Fulminante* scheme? The Court has addressed this subject in several cases.

In Rose v. Clark, 478 U.S. 570 (1986), the Court—pre-*Fulminante*—held that a jury instruction that created an unconstitutional presumption about an element of the crime was subject to *Chapman* harmless-error analysis. Reviewing numerous harmless-error cases, the Court concluded that "harmless-error analysis . . . presupposes a trial, at which the defendant, represented by counsel, may present evidence and argument before an impartial judge and jury." Because the presumption instruction neither denied the defendant such a trial, nor operated as the equivalent of a directed verdict for the prosecution, the Court held *Chapman* applicable. The case was remanded to allow the lower court to decide, in the first instance, whether the error was harmless under *Chapman*.

Yates v. Evatt, 500 U.S. 391 (1991), involved a similar challenge—post-*Fulminante*—to an unconstitutional presumption instruction. This time, however, the lower court had previously tried, and failed, to apply the *Chapman* harmless-error standard properly. The Court, in a majority opinion by Justice Souter, thus felt compelled to provide the lower court with more guidance than it had in Rose v. Clark:

> To say that an error did not contribute to the verdict is, rather, to find that error unimportant in relation to everything else the jury considered on the issue in question, as revealed in the record. Thus, to say that an instruction to apply an unconstitutional presumption did not contribute to the verdict is to make a judgment about the significance of the presumption to reasonable jurors, when measured against the other evidence considered by those jurors independently of the presumption.
>
> Before reaching such a judgment, a court must take two quite distinct steps. First, it must ask what evidence the jury actually considered in reaching its verdict. If, for example, the fact presumed is necessary to support the verdict, a reviewing court must ask what evidence the jury considered as tending to prove or disprove that fact. Did the jury look at only the predicate facts, or did it consider other evidence bearing on the fact subject to the presumption? In answering this question, a court does not conduct a subjective enquiry into the jurors' minds. The answer must come, instead, from analysis of the instructions given to the jurors and from application of that customary presumption that jurors follow instructions and, specifically, that they consider relevant evidence on a point in issue when they are told that they may do so.
>
> Once a court has made the first enquiry into the evidence considered by the jury, it must then weigh the probative force of that evidence as against the probative force of the presumption standing alone. To satisfy *Chapman*'s reasonable-doubt standard, it will not be enough that the jury considered evidence from which it could have come to the verdict without reliance on the presumption. Rather, the issue under *Chapman* is whether the jury actually rested its verdict on evidence establishing the presumed fact beyond a reasonable doubt, independently of the presumption. Since that enquiry cannot be a subjective one into the jurors' minds, a court must approach it by asking whether the force of the evidence presumably considered by the jury in accordance

with the instructions is so overwhelming as to leave it beyond a reasonable doubt that the verdict resting on that evidence would have been the same in the absence of the presumption. It is only when the effect of the presumption is comparatively minimal to this degree that it can be said, in *Chapman*'s words, that the presumption did not contribute to the verdict rendered.

Id., at 403-405.

Finally, in Sullivan v. Louisiana, 508 U.S. 275 (1993), the Court, in a majority opinion by Justice Scalia, held that a constitutionally deficient "reasonable doubt" instruction cannot be harmless error. The Court explained that "[t]he inquiry . . . is not whether, in a trial that occurred without the error, a guilty verdict would surely have been rendered, but whether the guilty verdict actually rendered in *this* trial was surely unattributable to the error. That must be so, because to hypothesize a guilty verdict that was never in fact rendered—no matter how inescapable the findings to support that verdict might be—would violate the jury-trial guarantee." Id., at 279. Because the deficient instruction wholly deprived the defendant of a jury verdict of "guilty-beyond-a-reasonable-doubt," "[t]here is no *object*, so to speak, upon which the harmless-error scrutiny can operate. . . . The Sixth Amendment requires more than appellate speculation about a hypothetical jury's action, or else directed verdicts for the State would be sustainable on appeal; it requires an actual jury finding of guilty." Id., at 280.

The *Sullivan* Court distinguished the defective "reasonable doubt" instruction from an unconstitutional presumption: "A reviewing court may . . . be able to conclude that the presumption played no significant role in the finding of guilt beyond a reasonable doubt. *Yates*, supra, at 402-406. But the essential connection to a 'beyond a reasonable doubt' factual finding cannot be made where the instructional error consists of a misdescription of the burden of proof, which vitiates *all* the jury's findings. A reviewing court can only engage in pure speculation—its view of what a reasonable jury would have done. And when it does that, 'the wrong entity judge[s] the defendant guilty.'" Id., at 281.

Do you agree that there is a significant difference between Rose v. Clark and Yates v. Evatt on the one hand, and *Sullivan* on the other? Didn't all three cases involve similar failures by the prosecution to satisfy the constitutionally mandated burden of proof?

4. Six years after Sullivan, the Court further complicated the matter. In Neder v. United States, 527 U.S. 1 (1999), the defendant was prosecuted for tax fraud. The trial judge determined that the defendant's false statements were "material." This was error, because under United States v. Gaudin, 515 U.S. 506 (1995), materiality is an element of the crime of tax fraud, and thus should have been submitted to the jury for determination. On appeal, the defendant claimed, inter alia, that the error could not be harmless, because—under the rationale of *Sullivan*—there was no jury verdict on the issue of materiality to which harmless-error analysis could be applied.

The Court, in a majority opinion by Chief Justice Rehnquist, disagreed: "Unlike such defects as the complete deprivation of counsel or trial before a biased judge, an instruction that omits an element of the offense does not necessarily render a criminal trial fundamentally unfair or an unreliable vehicle for determining guilt or innocence." *Neder*, 527 U.S., at 9. The Court explained that, contrary to the "reasonable doubt" instruction error in *Sullivan*, the error in *Neder* did not "vitiate[] *all* the jury's findings"; instead, only one particular finding (materiality) was affected. Id., at 11. Moreover, according to the Court, many past harmless-error cases, such as Yates v. Evatt and Rose v. Clark, likewise involved defective jury instructions on one or more of the elements of the crime charged. The Court frankly conceded that "[i]t would not be illogical to extend the reasoning of *Sullivan* from a defective 'reasonable doubt' instruction to a failure to instruct on an element of the crime," but ultimately concluded that the sheer weight of precedent (such as Yates v. Evatt and Rose v. Clark), coupled with the fact that the defendant in *Neder* never seriously contested the materiality of his false statements, militated in favor of applying the *Chapman* harmless-error standard. Id., at 15. Under that standard, the Court held the error to be harmless beyond a reasonable doubt, and affirmed the tax fraud conviction.

Justice Scalia, joined by Justices Souter and Ginsburg in dissent on the harmless-error issue, responded: "A court cannot, no matter how clear the defendant's culpability, direct a guilty verdict. . . . The question that this raises is why, if denying the right to conviction by jury is structural error, taking one of the elements of the crime away from the jury should be treated differently from taking all of them away—since failure to prove one, no less than failure to prove all, utterly prevents conviction." Id., at 32-33.

Justice Stevens, in concurrence, also disagreed with the majority's harmless-error analysis but found that the jury had implicitly and necessarily decided the materiality issue and hence the error was, indeed, harmless "under any test of harmlessness." Id., at 26.

Can *Neder* be squared with *Sullivan?* Why was the defendant's failure to contest the issue of materiality relevant to the threshold question whether *Chapman* harmless-error analysis applies? What is the constitutional difference, if any, between directing a verdict for the prosecution in general, and doing so with respect to one element of the crime charged?

In Washington v. Recuenco, 548 U.S. 212 (2006), the Court relied on *Neder* to hold that *Blakely/Booker* errors (involving the failure to submit to a jury, under a "beyond reasonable doubt" standard, the existence of certain sentencing factors that operate functionally as elements of a new, enhanced crime—see Chapter 15, at page 1526) are subject to "harmless error" review.

5. In Kotteakos v. United States, 328 U.S. 750 (1946), the Court discussed the proper application of the federal harmless-error statute, which applies to most federal criminal cases involving nonconstitutional error: "[T]he question is, not were [the jurors] right in their judgment, regardless of the error or its effect upon the verdict. It is rather what effect the error had or reasonably may be taken to have had upon the jury's decision. . . . If, when all is said and done, the conviction is sure that the error did not influence the jury, or had but very slight effect, the verdict and the judgment should stand, except perhaps where the departure is from a constitutional norm or a specific command of Congress. But if one cannot say, after pondering all that happened without stripping the erroneous action from the whole, that the judgment was not substantially swayed by the error, it is impossible to conclude that substantial rights were not affected." *Kotteakos* returned to prominence when the Court relied upon it in Brecht v. Abrahamson, 507 U.S. 619 (1993), to define the appropriate harmless-error standard for federal habeas review of state convictions. See page 1668, infra.

6. As previously mentioned, an error that is not properly preserved at trial generally will not lead to reversal on appeal, unless the error is held to be "plain error." The Federal Rules of Criminal Procedure provide:

Rule 52. Harmless and Plain Error

(a) Harmless Error. Any error, defect, irregularity, or variance that does not affect substantial rights must be disregarded.

(b) Plain Error. A plain error that affects substantial rights may be considered even though it was not brought to the court's attention.

In United States v. Olano, 507 U.S. 725 (1993), the Court elaborated on the meaning of "plain error," and its relationship with "harmless error," under Rule 52. The case involved a violation of Rule 24(c), which at the time provided that alternate jurors must be dismissed after the jury has retired for deliberation. (Rule 24 was amended in 1999, and now permits alternate jurors to be retained during jury deliberation, so long as they do not discuss the case with anyone.) The defendant, however, did not object to the error. The Court, in an opinion by Justice O'Connor, explained:

> The first limitation on appellate authority under Rule 52(b) is that there indeed be an "error." . . . If a legal rule was violated during the district court proceedings, and if the defendant did not waive the rule, then there has been an "error" within the meaning of Rule 52(b) despite the absence of a timely objection.
>
> The second limitation on appellate authority under Rule 52(b) is that the error be "plain." "Plain" is synonymous with "clear" or, equivalently, "obvious." See [United States v. Young, 470 U.S. 1, 17, n. 14 (1985)]. . . . We need not consider the special case where the error was unclear at the time of trial but becomes clear on appeal because the applicable law has been clarified. At a minimum, a court of appeals cannot correct an error pursuant to Rule 52(b) unless the error is clear under current law.
>
> The third and final limitation on appellate authority under Rule 52(b) is that the plain error "affec[t] substantial rights." This is the same language employed in Rule 52(a), and in most cases it means that the error must have been prejudicial: It must have affected the outcome of the district court proceedings. See, e.g., . . . Kotteakos v. United States, 328 U.S. 750, 758-765 (1946). When the defendant has made a timely objection to an error and Rule 52(a) applies, a court of appeals normally engages in a specific analysis of the district court record—a so-called "harmless error" inquiry—to determine whether the error was prejudicial. Rule 52(b) normally requires the same kind of inquiry, with one important difference: It is the defendant rather than the Government who bears the burden of persuasion with respect to prejudice. In most cases, a court of appeals cannot correct the forfeited error unless the defendant shows that the error was prejudicial. See Young, supra, at 17, n. 14 ("Federal courts have consistently interpreted the plain-error doctrine as requiring an appellate court to find that the claimed error . . . had [a] prejudicial impact on the jury's deliberations"). This burden shifting is dictated by a subtle but important difference in language between the two parts of Rule 52: While Rule 52(a) precludes error correction only if the error "does *not* affect substantial rights" (emphasis added), Rule 52(b) authorizes no remedy unless the error *does* "affec[t] substantial rights." . . .
>
> We need not decide whether the phrase "affect[ing] substantial rights" is always synonymous with "prejudicial." See generally Arizona v. Fulminante, 499 U.S. 279, 310 (1991) (constitutional error may not be found harmless if error deprives defendant of the "basic protections [without which] a criminal trial cannot reliably serve its function as a vehicle for determination of guilt or innocence, and no criminal punishment may be regarded as fundamentally fair") (quoting Rose v. Clark, 478

U.S. 570, 577-578 (1986)). There may be a special category of forfeited errors that can be corrected regardless of their effect on the outcome, but this issue need not be addressed. Nor need we address those errors that should be presumed prejudicial if the defendant cannot make a specific showing of prejudice. Normally, although perhaps not in every case, the defendant must make a specific showing of prejudice to satisfy the "affect[ing] substantial rights" prong of Rule 52(b).

Rule 52(b) is permissive, not mandatory. If the forfeited error is "plain" and "affects substantial rights," the court of appeals has authority to order correction, but is not required to do so. . . .

We previously have explained that the discretion conferred by Rule 52(b) should be employed "in those circumstances in which a miscarriage of justice would other-wise result." *Young*, 470 U.S., at 15. . . . In our collateral-review jurisprudence, the term "miscarriage of justice" means that the defendant is actually innocent. . . . The court of appeals should no doubt correct a plain forfeited error that causes the conviction or sentencing of an actually innocent defendant, . . . but we have never held that a Rule 52(b) remedy is *only* warranted in cases of actual innocence.

Rather, the standard that should guide the exercise of remedial discretion under Rule 52(b) was articulated in United States v. Atkinson, 297 U.S. 157 (1936). The court of appeals should correct a plain forfeited error affecting substantial rights if the error "seriously affect[s] the fairness, integrity or public reputation of judicial proceedings[," id., at 160, which may be] independent of the defendant's innocence. Conversely, a plain error affecting substantial rights does not, without more, satisfy the *Atkinson* standard, for otherwise the discretion afforded by Rule 52(b) would be illusory.

With these basic principles in mind, we turn to the instant case. . . . The presence of alternate jurors during jury deliberations is not the kind of error that "affects sub-stantial rights" independent of its prejudicial impact. Nor have respondents made a specific showing of prejudice. Finally, we see no reason to presume prejudice here. . . .

. . . In sum, respondents have not met their burden of showing prejudice under Rule 52(b). Whether the Government could have met its burden of showing the absence of prejudice, under Rule 52(a), if respondents had not forfeited their claim of error, is not at issue here. This is a plain-error case, and it is respondents who must persuade the appellate court that the deviation from Rule 24(c) was prejudicial.

Because the conceded error in this case did not "affec[t] substantial rights," the Court of Appeals had no authority to correct it. We need not consider whether the error, if prejudicial, would have warranted correction under the *Atkinson* standard as "seriously affecting the fairness, integrity or public reputation of judicial proceed-ings." The judgment of the Court of Appeals is reversed. . . .

Id., at 732-737, 741. Justice Stevens, joined by Justices White and Blackmun, dis-sented on the ground that (1) Rule 24(c) errors implicate "substantial rights" even without a case-specific showing of prejudice, because they "undermin[e] the struc-tural integrity of the criminal tribunal itself," and (2) the appellate court—which retained the discretion to reverse, or not to reverse, under Rule 52(b)—did not abuse its discretion.

7. In Johnson v. United States, 520 U.S. 461 (1997), the trial judge, in a perjury case, decided the issue of the "materiality" of the defendant's alleged false state-ment. This was error, because materiality was an element of the crime of perjury and thus should have been submitted to the jury for determination. Compare Neder v. United States, 527 U.S. 1 (1999) (involving a similar error with respect to the issue of materiality in a tax fraud prosecution), page 1625, supra. In *Johnson*, however, the defendant failed to object. Reviewing the defendant's conviction under the *Olano*

"plain error" standard, the Court concluded that the error did not require reversal because the evidence of materiality was "overwhelming" and "uncontroverted." The Court emphasized that, under *Olano*, the determination whether an error "seriously affect[s] the fairness, integrity or public reputation of judicial proceedings" must be made on a case-by-case basis.

8. What is the standard for determining whether an error, to which the defendant did not contemporaneously object, "affect[ed] substantial rights"? The Court declined to answer that question with precision in *Olano*, but returned to it in United States v. Dominguez Benitez, 542 U.S. 74 (2004). *Dominguez Benitez* involved a failure by the trial court to warn the defendant, before he entered a guilty plea, that he could not withdraw the plea if the trial court did not accept the prosecutor's sentencing stipulations and recommendations. The failure to so warn the defendant violated Federal Rule of Criminal Procedure 11(c)(3)(B). For obvious reasons (specifically, because he was unaware of the Rule's requirements), the defendant did not object to the trial court's mistake at the time of the plea. Nevertheless, according to the Court's previous decision in United States v. Vonn, 535 U.S. 55 (2002), the defendant's failure to object meant that he could obtain relief on appeal only if he could show that the violation constituted "plain error" under Rule 52(b).

The *Dominguez Benitez* Court, in an opinion by Justice Souter, held as follows: "[A] defendant who seeks reversal of his conviction after a guilty plea, on the ground that the district court committed plain error under Rule 11, must show a reasonable probability that, but for the error, he would not have entered the plea. A defendant must thus satisfy the judgment of the reviewing court, informed by the entire record, that the probability of a different result is 'sufficient to undermine confidence in the outcome' of the proceeding." 542 U.S., at 83.

9. Does it make sense for the issue of prejudice, or harm, to be handled in so many different ways, depending on the particular legal issue involved and the procedural context of the particular case? Do you think that appellate courts are capable of making meaningful distinctions between the several different applicable legal standards?

Justice Scalia, for one, does not think so. In *Dominguez Benitez*, he wrote the following provocative opinion, concurring in the judgment:

> . . . By my count, this Court has adopted no fewer than four assertedly different standards of probability relating to the assessment of whether the outcome of trial would have been different if error had not occurred, or if omitted evidence had been included. See Chapman v. California, 386 U.S. 18, 24 (1967) (adopting "harmless beyond a reasonable doubt" standard for preserving, on direct review, conviction obtained in a trial where constitutional error occurred); Brecht v. Abrahamson, 507 U.S. 619, 637 (1993) (rejecting *Chapman* in favor of the less defendant-friendly "substantial and injurious effect or influence" standard of Kotteakos v. United States, 328 U.S. 750 (1946), for overturning conviction on collateral review); United States v. Agurs, 427 U.S. 97, 111-113 (1976) (rejecting *Kotteakos* for overturning conviction on the basis of *Brady* violations, in favor of an even less defendant-friendly standard later described in Strickland v. Washington, 466 U.S. 668, 694 (1984), as a "reasonable probability"); id., 466 U.S., at 693-694 (distinguishing the "reasonable probability" standard from the *still yet* less defendant-friendly "more likely than not" standard applicable to claims of newly discovered evidence). Such ineffable gradations of probability seem to me quite beyond the ability of the judicial mind (or any mind) to grasp, and thus harmful rather than helpful to the consistency and rationality of

judicial decisionmaking. That is especially so when they are applied to the hypothesiz-
ing of events that never in fact occurred. Such an enterprise is not factfinding, but
closer to divination.

For purposes of estimating what *would* have happened, it seems to me that the
only serviceable standards are the traditional "beyond a reasonable doubt" and "more
likely than not." We should not pretend to a higher degree of precision. I would not,
therefore, extend our "reasonable probability" standard to the plain-error context.
I would hold that, where a defendant has failed to object at trial, and thus has the
burden of proving that a mistake he failed to prevent had an effect on his substantial
rights, he must show that effect to be probable, that is, more likely than not.

542 U.S., at 86-87. Do you agree with Justice Scalia that the Court's four different
prejudice standards should be simplified? Does his opinion in *Dominguez Benitez*
presage a new period of instability in the law relating to appellate review?

B.   *Collateral Review*

A defendant's conviction becomes final when it has been affirmed on appeal (or
certiorari review has been declined) by the highest court available to review the
case (including the United States Supreme Court), or when the defendant has
failed to file an appeal (or a certiorari petition) from an adverse decision below
within the allotted time. Even after the conviction has become final, however, that
is not necessarily the end of the story. Today, in every American jurisdiction, there
exists at least one opportunity for a convicted defendant to seek so-called "collateral review" of his conviction.

There are three different kinds of collateral review: (1) state-court collateral
review for defendants who were convicted in state court (usually called a state postconviction or state habeas corpus proceeding); (2) federal-court collateral review
for defendants who were convicted in federal court (usually called a "Section 2255
proceeding," after the federal statute authorizing such review, 28 U.S.C. §2255);
and (3) federal-court collateral review for defendants who were convicted in state
court (usually called a federal habeas corpus proceeding). All three kinds of collateral review should be distinguished from the so-called "Great Writ" of habeas
corpus, which (as explained below) serves a different purpose altogether.

State postconviction review, or state habeas, was created by the states largely in
response to the expanded scope of federal habeas review of state convictions during
the second half of the twentieth century. It was believed that making such review
available in the state courts might help to minimize the need for habeas review
in the federal courts—either by resolving any constitutional issues that might be
present in the case, or at least by defining the factual contours of those issues more
clearly before the start of federal habeas review. As a practical matter, state habeas
today serves primarily as a procedure for post-trial litigation, especially of certain
kinds of fact-based claims that are not easily litigated on direct appeal, such as ineffective assistance, *Brady,* and newly discovered evidence claims.

Section 2255 review, for persons convicted in federal court, serves many of the
same functions as state and federal habeas do for those convicted in state court.
The federal statute, 28 U.S.C. §2255, provides that a person convicted in federal
court who claims "the right to be released upon the ground that the sentence was
imposed in violation of the Constitution or laws of the United States, or that the

court was without jurisdiction to impose such sentence, or that the sentence was in excess of the maximum authorized by law, or is otherwise subject to collateral attack," may file a petition in federal district court for collateral review. The Court has held that "an error of law does not provide a basis for habeas relief under 28 U.S.C. §2255 unless it constitutes 'a fundamental defect which inherently results in a complete miscarriage of justice.'" See Brecht v. Abrahamson, 507 U.S. 619, 634, n. 8 (1993) (quoting United States v. Timmreck, 441 U.S. 780, 783 (1979), and Hill v. United States, 368 U.S. 424, 428 (1962)).

Because the rules governing state postconviction review vary widely from state to state, and because the rules governing §2255 proceedings for federal prisoners often tend to mirror those governing federal habeas for state prisoners, we will focus our attention for the remainder of this section exclusively on the third kind of collateral review: federal habeas corpus review of state convictions.

1. The "Great Writ" of Habeas Corpus

The writ of habeas corpus, often called the "Great Writ," traces its roots back to Magna Carta in 1215. "Executive imprisonment has been considered oppressive and lawless since John, at Runnymede, pledged that no free man should be imprisoned, dispossessed, outlawed, or exiled save by the judgment of his peers or by the law of the land. The judges of England developed the writ of habeas corpus largely to preserve these immunities from executive restraint." Shaughnessy v. United States ex rel. Mezei, 345 U.S. 206, 218-219 (Jackson, J., dissenting). "Habeas corpus," which means literally "you may have the body," is a writ addressed to the person who has custody of a prisoner, requiring the production of the prisoner so that the judge may inquire into the fundamental justice of the detention. Throughout its long and storied history, habeas corpus has preserved individual liberty, protected the governmental balance of powers, and vindicated the rule of law.[2]

The Framers placed great stock in the "Great Writ." In Federalist No. 84, Hamilton cited it as a crucial protection against "the practice of arbitrary imprisonments . . . in all ages, [among] the favourite and most formidable instruments of tyranny." The writ was included in the first congressional statute granting jurisdiction to the federal courts, the Judiciary Act of 1789, and is codified today at 28 U.S.C. §2241, which authorizes a federal court to issue a writ of habeas corpus on behalf of a prisoner "in custody under or by color of the authority of the United States . . . ," or "in custody in violation of the Constitution or laws or treaties of the United States." The "Great Writ" also is enshrined in the American Constitution, which prohibits suspension of "the Privilege of the Writ of Habeas Corpus . . . unless when in Cases of Rebellion or Invasion the public Safety may require it." Art. I, §9, cl. 2.

An excellent example of the "Great Writ," as the traditional judicial remedy for allegedly unjust executive detention, can be seen in the terrorism cases of Hamdi v. Rumsfeld, 542 U.S. 507 (2004), and Rasul v. Bush, 542 U.S. 466 (2004). In *Hamdi*, the Court ruled that a U.S. citizen who had been detained for more than two years without criminal charges (initially in Afghanistan and later at the Naval

---

2. For the definitive history of the Great Writ in England and America, see Paul D. Halliday, Habeas Corpus: From England to Empire (2010).

Brigs in Norfolk, Virginia, and Charleston, South Carolina) was entitled under due process to some kind of independent review of his alleged status as an "enemy combatant" in the war against "forces hostile to the United States or coalition partners" in Afghanistan. Under the Court's ruling, if the military did not provide such independent review, then Hamdi could obtain such review in a federal court by means of a writ of habeas corpus.[3] In *Rasul*, the Court held that the statutory habeas jurisdiction of the federal courts extended to the review of the detention of non-U.S. citizens held (again, without criminal charges) at Guantanamo Bay, Cuba, in connection with the ongoing "war on terrorism."[4] In both cases, the Court squarely rejected the argument that judicial review by means of the "Great Writ" would be incompatible with the needs of the government in general, and of the military in particular. For more on *Hamdi*, see Chapter 2, at page 95.

Despite the historical importance of the "Great Writ," and its protection in the text of the American Constitution, this traditional version of habeas corpus offered no prospect of collateral review or relief to persons who had been convicted of crimes. This is because a facially valid criminal conviction, demonstrating that the prisoner was held in confinement as the result of judicial proceedings, traditionally served as a complete defense to a petition for a writ of habeas corpus. To provide for collateral review of criminal convictions, Congress needed to pass new legislation extending the writ of habeas corpus beyond its common-law origins. We next turn our attention to the statutory version of federal habeas corpus that was enacted by Congress, after the Civil War, to authorize federal collateral review of state criminal convictions.

2. The Nature and Purposes of Federal Habeas

Federal habeas for state prisoners has been available in one form or another since 1867, when the post–Civil War Congress enacted the Habeas Corpus Act. The original purpose of the Act was to extend the writ of habeas corpus in order to provide a federal forum for individuals—often either newly freed slaves or federal Reconstruction officials—who were wrongly convicted of crimes in state courts

---

3. There was no majority opinion in *Hamdi*, but Justice O'Connor's plurality opinion—which took a position between the two extremes expressed by Justice Thomas (no judicial review required) and Justice Scalia (the government must either suspend habeas corpus, file criminal charges, or release the prisoner)—effectively established the legal basis for the Court's decision.

4. As a general matter, habeas cases must be filed in the federal district court in which the habeas petitioner is being held in custody. See, e.g., Rumsfeld v. Padilla, 542 U.S. 426 (2004) (Padilla's habeas petition, which challenges his current confinement, must name as defendant the person with immediate custody over him, and must be filed in the district court in which he is confined (and which, by definition, also has jurisdiction over his immediate custodian)). Note that this is slightly different from the jurisdictional rule under the federal habeas statute authorizing collateral review of state criminal convictions, which—for states comprising more than one federal district—allows such a habeas petition to be filed either in the district of confinement or in the district where the criminal conviction was obtained. See 28 U.S.C. §2241(d).

According to the *Rasul* Court, in a habeas case involving persons held outside the sovereign territory of the United States, jurisdiction lies in any federal district court that has jurisdiction over the person or persons with custody of the habeas petitioner. Given that Rasul's effective custodians included the President of the United States, in his role as Commander-in-Chief of the Armed Forces, as well as the Secretary of Defense, the District Court for the District of Columbia (together with many other district courts as well) had jurisdiction over Rasul's habeas petition.

in violation of their federal constitutional rights. However, the nature of federal habeas, as well as its primary purposes, have changed substantially over the years.[5]

For almost 100 years after the Act's adoption, the scope of federal habeas review of state convictions was relatively narrow, primarily because the scope of federal constitutional rights applicable to state criminal cases was also relatively narrow. Hence, the statements by the Court in two prominent early twentieth-century federal habeas cases, Frank v. Mangum, 237 U.S. 309, 327 (1915), and Moore v. Dempsey, 261 U.S. 86, 91-92 (1923), that "the writ of habeas corpus [is available] . . . only in case the judgment under which the prisoner is detained is shown to be absolutely void."

In the second half of the twentieth century, however, federal habeas became much more important, for two related reasons. First, beginning in the 1950s, and accelerating rapidly in the 1960s, the scope of federal constitutional rights applicable to state criminal cases increased dramatically, as a result of due process incorporation and the Warren Court's criminal procedure revolution. Second, at about the same time, federal habeas jurisdiction was also significantly expanded, by the Court itself, as a means to empower the lower federal courts (which, unlike the Court, were unable to review state criminal cases directly) to assist the Court in the enforcement of these newly created federal constitutional rights. The defining purpose of federal habeas, during this period, was to provide an unrestricted federal forum for the litigation of federal constitutional claims.

The two leading cases in this expansion were Brown v. Allen, 344 U.S. 443 (1953), and Fay v. Noia, 372 U.S. 391 (1963). In Brown v. Allen, the Court rejected the view that prior determinations, in state court, of legal or mixed law-and-fact issues relating to federal constitutional claims should be given res judicata effect by federal habeas courts. "Although there is no need for the federal judge, if he could, to shut his eyes to the State consideration of such issues, no binding weight is to be attached to the State determination. . . . The State court cannot have the last say when it, though on fair consideration . . . , may have misconceived a federal constitutional right." 344 U.S., at 508 (opinion of Justice Frankfurter for the Court). In Fay v. Noia, one of several key federal habeas decisions authored by Justice Brennan, the Court held that a state prisoner's failure to present his federal constitutional claims properly in state court did not bar subsequent federal habeas review of the merits of his claims, unless he "deliberately by-passed" the state forum. "[T]he doctrine under which state procedural defaults are held to constitute an adequate and independent state law ground barring direct Supreme Court review is not to be extended to limit the power granted the federal courts under the federal habeas statute." 372 U.S., at 399.

Starting in the 1970s, as the criminal procedure revolution began to wane, a new Court majority—led by Justices Rehnquist, Powell, and O'Connor—began to impose new restrictions on the availability of federal habeas. In a series of decisions, the Court gradually made it much more difficult for state prisoners to obtain federal habeas review of the merits of their federal constitutional claims. One important rationale behind these decisions was that federal habeas—an equitable remedy designed to serve the "ends of justice"—should be used primarily to protect innocent defendants. See, e.g., Henry J. Friendly, Is Innocence Irrelevant? Collateral

---

5. For an excellent account of the history and significance of habeas in America, see Eric M. Freedman, Habeas Corpus: Rethinking the Great Writ of Liberty (2003); see also Nancy J. King & Joseph L. Hoffmann, Habeas for the Twenty-First Century (2011).

Attack on Criminal Judgments, 38 U. Chi. L. Rev. 142 (1970). Another was that Justice Brennan's view of federal habeas was insufficiently respectful of state courts, who, like their federal judicial counterparts, are sworn to obey and defend the federal constitution. The Court's changing views about federal habeas prompted numerous scholars to search for a new theory that might explain what habeas was all about. See, e.g., Joseph L. Hoffmann & William J. Stuntz, Habeas after the Revolution, [1993] Sup. Ct. Rev. 65 (1994); Evan Tsen Lee, The Theories of Federal Habeas Corpus, 72 Wash. U. L.Q. 151 (1994); Daniel J. Meltzer, Habeas Corpus Jurisdiction: The Limits of Models, 66 S. Cal. L. Rev. 2507 (1993); Jordan Steiker, Innocence and Federal Habeas, 41 UCLA L. Rev. 303 (1993); Ann Woolhandler, Demodeling Habeas, 45 Stan. L. Rev. 575 (1993); James S. Liebman, Apocalypse Next Time?: The Anachronistic Attack on Habeas Corpus/Direct Review Parity, 92 Colum. L. Rev. 1997 (1992); Larry W. Yackle, Form and Function in the Administration of Justice: The Bill of Rights and Federal Habeas Corpus, 23 U. Mich. J.L. Reform 685 (1990); Barry Friedman, A Tale of Two Habeas, 73 Minn. L. Rev. 247 (1988).

At the end of the 1980s, the Court handed down a decision—relatively little-noticed when it was first issued—that eventually turned out to be crucial to the development of a new understanding about the nature and purposes of federal habeas. In Teague v. Lane, 489 U.S. 288 (1989), one of the issues before the Court was whether a habeas petitioner should be entitled to claim the benefit of a "new rule" of constitutional criminal procedure that was declared after his state criminal conviction became "final" on direct appeal. Recall that in Griffith v. Kentucky, 479 U.S. 314 (1987), the Court had held that all such "new rules" should apply retroactively to all cases pending on direct appeal at the time the "new rule" was declared. See supra, at page 1617. In *Teague*, Justice O'Connor, writing for a plurality of the Court,[6] decided that, as a general matter, "new rules"—defined as any rule that "breaks new ground or imposes a new obligation on the States or the Federal Government," or in which "the result was not *dictated* by precedent existing at the time the defendant's conviction became final"—should not apply retroactively to habeas cases. The plurality acknowledged only two narrow exceptions in which a new rule should apply retroactively in habeas: (1) "if it places 'certain kinds of primary, private individual conduct beyond the power of the criminal law-making authority to proscribe'" and (2) "if it requires the observance of 'those procedures that . . . are "implicit in the concept of ordered liberty,"'" and "without which the likelihood of an accurate conviction is seriously diminished." With respect to this second exception, the plurality found it "unlikely that many such components of basic due process have yet to emerge."

The *Teague* plurality based its new habeas non-retroactivity rule on the following restatement of the goals of habeas:

> With regard to the nature of habeas corpus, Justice Harlan wrote:
>
>> Habeas corpus always has been a collateral remedy, providing an avenue for upsetting judgments that have become otherwise final. It is not designed as a substitute for direct review. The interest in leaving concluded litigation in a state of repose, that is, reducing the controversy to a final judgment not subject to further judicial revision, may quite

6. The plurality's view in *Teague* was later adopted by a majority of the Court in Penry v. Lynaugh, 492 U.S. 302 (1989), and Saffle v. Parks, 494 U.S. 484 (1990). The 1996 AEDPA amendments to the federal habeas corpus statute slightly modified, but did not substantially affect, the holding in *Teague*. See Terry Williams v. Taylor, infra, at page 1637.

legitimately be found by those responsible for defining the scope of the writ to outweigh in some, many, or most instances the competing interest in readjudicating convictions according to all legal standards in effect when a habeas petition is filed. . . .

[As Justice Harlan explained,] "the threat of habeas serves as a necessary additional incentive for trial and appellate courts throughout the land to conduct their proceedings in a manner consistent with established constitutional standards. In order to perform this deterrence function, . . . the habeas court need only apply the constitutional standards that prevailed at the time the original proceedings took place." . . . See also [Solem v.] Stumes, 465 U.S. [638], 653 [(1984)] (Powell, J., concurring in judgment) ("Review on habeas to determine that the conviction rests upon correct application of the law in effect at the time of the conviction is all that is required to 'forc[e] trial and appellate courts . . . to toe the constitutional mark' ") [quoting Mackey v. United States, 401 U.S. 667, 687 (1971) (Harlan, J., concurring in judgments in part and dissenting in part)]. . . .

We agree with Justice Harlan's description of the function of habeas corpus. "[T]he Court never has defined the scope of the writ simply by reference to a perceived need to assure that an individual accused of crime is afforded a trial free of constitutional error." . . . Rather, we have recognized that interests of comity and finality must also be considered in determining the proper scope of habeas review. . . .

. . . Application of constitutional rules not in existence at the time a conviction became final seriously undermines the principle of finality which is essential to the operation of our criminal justice system. Without finality, the criminal law is deprived of much of its deterrent effect. The fact that life and liberty are at stake in criminal prosecutions "shows only that 'conventional notions of finality' should not have *as much* place in criminal as in civil litigation, not that they should have *none*." Friendly, Is Innocence Irrelevant? Collateral Attacks on Criminal Judgments, 38 U. Chi. L. Rev. 142, 150 (1970). "[I]f a criminal judgment is ever to be final, the notion of legality must at some point include the assignment of final competence to determine legality." Bator, Finality in Criminal Law and Federal Habeas Corpus for State Prisoners, 76 Harv. L. Rev. 441, 450-451 (1963) (emphasis omitted). . . .

489 U.S., at 306-309. The plurality also agreed with Justice Harlan that a second purpose of habeas was "to assure that no man has been incarcerated under a procedure which creates an impermissibly large risk that the innocent will be convicted."

On a theoretical level, *Teague* represented a clear shift from the earlier view (expressed most forcefully by Justice Brennan) that federal habeas exists to provide a remedy to individuals for violations of their federal constitutional rights, to the view (expressed most forcefully by Justice Harlan, and ultimately adopted in *Teague* and its progeny) that federal habeas exists primarily to deter state courts from committing federal constitutional errors. This shift was important, because it set the stage for the conclusion that federal habeas review is not needed unless the state courts have behaved badly. See Joseph L. Hoffmann, The Supreme Court's New Vision of Federal Habeas Corpus for State Prisoners, [1989] Sup. Ct. Rev. 165 (1990); Robert Weisberg, A Great Writ While It Lasted, 81 J. Crim. L. & Criminology 9 (1990).

Another hidden dimension of *Teague* was its impact on the development of federal constitutional law. *Teague* certainly did not deprive the Supreme Court of the opportunity to declare new federal constitutional rights in state criminal cases, because the Court can always do so on direct certiorari review. But *Teague* did effectively take the lower federal courts out of the business of declaring new federal constitutional rights in state criminal cases—after *Teague*, such courts can only apply "old law" to such cases. In other words, the ongoing judicial dialogue about the proper scope of federal constitutional law in state criminal cases, post-*Teague*, was limited to the Supreme Court and the state courts, and no longer included the lower federal courts. Cf. Robert Cover & Alexander Aleinikoff, Dialectical Federalism: Habeas Corpus and the Court, 86 Yale L.J. 1035 (1977) (describing judicial dialogue between state courts and lower federal courts sitting in habeas).

What is a "new rule" under *Teague*? That is a tricky question. You must try to keep in mind that, under *Teague*, the broader the definition of "new law," or a "new rule," the more difficult it is to obtain federal habeas relief (because "new rules" cannot be applied to habeas cases). Thus, when Butler v. McKellar, 494 U.S. 407 (1990), explained that "[t]he 'new rule' principle . . . validates reasonable, good-faith interpretations of existing precedents made by state courts even though they are shown to be contrary to later decisions," and described the *Teague* "new rule" inquiry as asking whether the rule sought by the petitioner "was susceptible to debate among reasonable minds," such formulations—which narrowed the definition of "old law," and thus expanded the scope of "new law"—represented bad news for habeas petitioners. See also Lambrix v. Singletary, 520 U.S. 518 (1997), holding that a rule is "old law" only if it "was dictated by precedent" (i.e., "no other interpretation was reasonable").

Long before *Teague*, the federal habeas statute already provided that factual determinations made by state courts, in connection with the litigation of federal constitutional claims, must be presumed correct by federal habeas courts. See former 28 U.S.C. §2254(d) (providing for presumption of correctness, and defining narrow circumstances in which state-court factual findings may be revisited by federal habeas courts). And, as a direct result of *Teague* and its progeny, legal determinations (on federal constitutional issues) made by state courts cannot be overturned by federal habeas courts unless they were contrary to clearly established federal law at the time of the state-court decision. What, then, should be the proper habeas standard of review for mixed fact-and-law determinations (involving the application of federal law to the particular facts of a case) made by state courts—such as whether the defendant's counsel was constitutionally ineffective? After *Teague*, many observers thought that federal habeas review of such mixed issues would be governed by a similarly deferential standard.

But in Wright v. West, 505 U.S. 277 (1992), a majority of the Supreme Court—without a majority opinion—declined to decide this issue, preserving (at least temporarily) the tradition of de novo review of such mixed issues in federal habeas. In *West*, the U.S. Court of Appeals for the Fourth Circuit had ruled that the evidence against the defendant at trial was legally insufficient under the rule of Jackson v. Virginia, 443 U.S. 307 (1979) ("whether, after viewing the evidence in the light most favorable to the prosecution, any rational trier of fact could have found the essential elements of the crime beyond a reasonable doubt"). All nine justices agreed that the conviction should not have been overturned by the Fourth Circuit, but only the opinion of Justice Thomas (writing for three justices) suggested that federal habeas courts perhaps should defer to state court applications of federal law to the facts of a particular case. Justice O'Connor (also writing for three justices) flatly rejected the idea of deferring to such state court decisions.

The Antiterrorism and Effective Death Penalty Act of 1996 (AEDPA), enacted in a wave of anticrime sentiment following the 1995 terrorist bombing of the Murrah Federal Building in Oklahoma City, dramatically altered many of the statutory provisions governing federal habeas. One of the most important changes was in the habeas standard of review, as set forth in 28 U.S.C. §2254(d)(1). In AEDPA, Congress weighed in heavily on the same subject that had split the Court in Wright v. West. The next case represents the Court's first look at the new standard.

Please note that, with respect to the habeas standard of review under 28 U.S.C. §2254(d)(1), it was Part II of Justice O'Connor's opinion—and *not* Part II of Justice Stevens's opinion—that expressed the view of a majority of the Supreme Court.

TERRY WILLIAMS v. TAYLOR

Certiorari to the United States Court of Appeals for the Fourth Circuit
529 U.S. 362 (2000)

JUSTICE STEVENS announced the judgment of the Court and delivered the opinion of the Court with respect to Parts I, III, and IV, and an opinion with respect to Parts II and V.*

The questions presented are whether Terry Williams' constitutional right to the effective assistance of counsel as defined in Strickland v. Washington, 466 U.S. 668 (1984), was violated, and whether the judgment of the Virginia Supreme Court refusing to set aside his death sentence "was contrary to, or involved an unreasonable application of, clearly established Federal law, as determined by the Supreme Court of the United States," within the meaning of 28 U.S.C. §2254(d)(1). . . .

I

[The underlying facts of the case are as follows: Terry Williams was convicted of robbery and murder in connection with the death of Harris Stone. At the hearing to decide whether Williams should be sentenced to death, the prosecution introduced Williams's prior convictions for armed robbery, burglary, and grand larceny, and also told the jury about two auto thefts and two violent assaults committed by Williams after the Stone murder. One of these assaults, to which Williams had confessed, left an elderly woman in a "vegetative state" from which she was not expected to recover. Two expert witnesses testified that there was a "high probability" that Williams would be dangerous in the future. The only mitigating evidence presented on Williams's behalf came from his mother and two neighbors, all of whom briefly described Williams as a "nice boy" who was not violent, and from a psychiatrist who reported that Williams had removed the bullets from a gun prior to a robbery so that he would not injure anyone. In closing argument, Williams's defense lawyer talked about how difficult it was to find a reason to spare Williams's life. The jury sentenced Williams to death.—EDS.]

STATE HABEAS CORPUS PROCEEDINGS

In 1988 Williams filed for state collateral relief. . . . [T]he same judge who had presided over Williams' trial and sentencing . . . held an evidentiary hearing on

---

* Justice Souter, Justice Ginsburg, and Justice Breyer join this opinion in its entirety. Justice O'Connor and Justice Kennedy join Parts I, III, and IV of this opinion.

Williams' claim that trial counsel had been ineffective. Based on the evidence adduced after two days of hearings, Judge Ingram found that Williams' conviction was valid, but that his trial attorneys had been ineffective during sentencing. Among the evidence reviewed that had not been presented at trial were documents prepared in connection with Williams' commitment when he was 11 years old that dramatically described mistreatment, abuse, and neglect during his early childhood, as well as testimony that he was "borderline mentally retarded," had suffered repeated head injuries, and might have mental impairments organic in origin. . . . The habeas hearing also revealed that the same experts who had testified on the State's behalf at trial believed that Williams, if kept in a "structured environment," would not pose a future danger to society. . . .

Counsel's failure to discover and present this and other significant mitigating evidence was "below the range expected of reasonable, professional competent assistance of counsel." . . . Counsel's performance thus "did not measure up to the standard required under the holding of Strickland v. Washington . . . , and [if it had,] there is a reasonable probability that the result of the sentencing phase would have been different." . . . Judge Ingram therefore recommended that Williams be granted a rehearing on the sentencing phase of his trial.

The Virginia Supreme Court did not accept that recommendation. . . . Although it assumed, without deciding, that trial counsel had been ineffective, . . . it disagreed with the trial judge's conclusion that Williams had suffered sufficient prejudice to warrant relief. Treating the prejudice inquiry as a mixed question of law and fact, the Virginia Supreme Court accepted the factual determination that available evidence in mitigation had not been presented at the trial, but held that the trial judge had misapplied the law in two respects. First, relying on our decision in Lockhart v. Fretwell, 506 U.S. 364 (1993), the court held that it was wrong for the trial judge to rely "on mere outcome determination" when assessing prejudice. . . . Second, it construed the trial judge's opinion as having "adopted a per se approach" that would establish prejudice whenever any mitigating evidence was omitted. . . .

The court then reviewed the prosecution evidence. . . . [I]t found that the excluded mitigating evidence—which it characterized as merely indicating "that numerous people, mostly relatives, thought that defendant was nonviolent and could cope very well in a structured environment," . . . —"barely would have altered the profile of this defendant that was presented to the jury." . . . On this basis, the court concluded that there was no reasonable possibility that the omitted evidence would have affected the jury's sentencing recommendation, and that Williams had failed to demonstrate that his sentencing proceeding was fundamentally unfair.

FEDERAL HABEAS CORPUS PROCEEDINGS

Having exhausted his state remedies, Williams sought a federal writ of habeas corpus pursuant to 28 U.S.C. §2254. . . . After reviewing the state habeas hearing transcript and the state courts' findings of fact and conclusions of law, the federal trial judge agreed with the Virginia trial judge: The death sentence was constitutionally infirm.

After noting that the Virginia Supreme Court had not addressed the question whether trial counsel's performance at the sentencing hearing fell below the range of competence demanded of lawyers in criminal cases, the judge began by addressing that issue in detail. He identified five categories of mitigating evidence that counsel had failed to introduce,[4] and he rejected the argument that counsel's failure to conduct an adequate investigation had been a strategic decision. . . .

Turning to the prejudice issue, the judge determined that there was "'a reasonable probability that, but for counsel's unprofessional errors, the result of the proceeding would have been different.' *Strickland*. . . ." . . . He found that the Virginia Supreme Court had erroneously assumed that *Lockhart* had modified the *Strickland* standard for determining prejudice, and that it had made an important error of fact in discussing its finding of no prejudice.[5] . . . [T]he judge concluded that those errors established that the Virginia Supreme Court's decision "was contrary to, or involved an unreasonable application of, clearly established Federal law" within the meaning of §2254(d)(1).

The Federal Court of Appeals reversed. . . .

We granted certiorari, . . . and now reverse.

II

In 1867, Congress enacted a statute providing that federal courts "shall have power to grant writs of habeas corpus in all cases where any person may be restrained of his or her liberty in violation of the constitution, or of any treaty or law of the United States. . . ." . . . It is, of course, well settled that the fact that constitutional error occurred in the proceedings that led to a state-court conviction may not alone be sufficient reason for concluding that a prisoner is entitled to the remedy of habeas. See, e.g., Stone v. Powell, 428 U.S. 465 (1976); Brecht v. Abrahamson, 507 U.S. 619 (1993). On the other hand, errors that undermine confidence in the fundamental fairness of the state adjudication certainly justify the issuance of the federal writ. See, e.g., Teague v. Lane, 489 U.S. 288, 311-314 (1989). . . . The deprivation of the right to the effective assistance of counsel recognized in *Strickland* is such an error. . . .

The warden here contends that federal habeas corpus relief is prohibited by the amendment to 28 U.S.C. §2254 . . . , enacted as a part of the Antiterrorism and Effective Death Penalty Act of 1996 (AEDPA). The relevant portion of that amendment provides:

> (d) An application for a writ of habeas corpus on behalf of a person in custody pursuant to the judgment of a State court shall not be granted with respect to any claim that was adjudicated on the merits in State court proceedings unless the adjudication of the claim—

---

4. "(i) Counsel did not introduce evidence of the Petitioner's background. . . . (ii) Counsel did not introduce evidence that Petitioner was abused by his father. (iii) Counsel did not introduce testimony from correctional officers who were willing to testify that defendant would not pose a danger while incarcerated. Nor did counsel offer prison commendations awarded to Williams for his help in breaking up a prison drug ring and for returning a guard's wallet. (iv) Several character witnesses were not called to testify. . . . The testimony of Elliott, a respected CPA in the community, could have been quite important to the jury. . . . (v) Finally, counsel did not introduce evidence that Petitioner was borderline mentally retarded, though he was found competent to stand trial." . . .

5. ". . . The Virginia Supreme Court ignored or overlooked the evidence of Williams' difficult childhood and abuse and his limited mental capacity. It is also unreasonable to characterize the additional evidence as coming from 'mostly relatives.' . . . Bruce Elliott, a respected professional in the community, and several correctional officers offered to testify on Williams' behalf." . . .

(1) resulted in a decision that was contrary to, or involved an unreasonable application of, clearly established Federal law, as determined by the Supreme Court of the United States; . . .

In this case, the Court of Appeals applied the construction of the amendment that it had adopted in its earlier opinion in Green v. French, 143 F.3d 865 (CA4 1998). It read the amendment as prohibiting federal courts from issuing the writ unless:

(a) the state court decision is in "square conflict" with Supreme Court precedent that is controlling as to law and fact or (b) if no such controlling decision exists, "the state court's resolution of a question of pure law rests upon an objectively unreasonable derivation of legal principles from the relevant [S]upreme [C]ourt precedents, or if its decision rests upon an objectively unreasonable application of established principles to new facts." . . .

Accordingly, it held that a federal court may issue habeas relief only if "the state courts have decided the question by interpreting or applying the relevant precedent in a manner that reasonable jurists would all agree is unreasonable." . . .

We are convinced that that interpretation of the amendment is incorrect. It would impose a test for determining when a legal rule is clearly established that simply cannot be squared with the real practice of decisional law. It would apply a standard for determining the "reasonableness" of state-court decisions that is not contained in the statute itself, and that Congress surely did not intend. And it would wrongly require the federal courts, including this Court, to defer to state judges' interpretations of federal law. . . .

The inquiry mandated by the amendment relates to the way in which a federal habeas court exercises its duty to decide constitutional questions; the amendment does not alter the underlying grant of jurisdiction in §2254(a). . . . When federal judges exercise their federal-question jurisdiction under the "judicial Power" of Article III of the Constitution, it is "emphatically the province and duty" of those judges to "say what the law is." Marbury v. Madison, 5 U.S. 137, 1 Cranch 137, 177 (1803). At the core of this power is the federal courts' independent responsibility—independent from its coequal branches in the Federal Government, and independent from the separate authority of the several States—to interpret federal law. A construction of AEDPA that would require the federal courts to cede this authority to the courts of the States would be inconsistent with the practice that federal judges have traditionally followed in discharging their duties under Article III of the Constitution. If Congress had intended to require such an important change in the exercise of our jurisdiction, we believe it would have spoken with much greater clarity than is found in the text of AEDPA.

This basic premise informs our interpretation of both parts of §2254(d)(1): first, the requirement that the determinations of state courts be tested only against "clearly established Federal law, as determined by the Supreme Court of the United States," and second, the prohibition on the issuance of the writ unless the state court's decision is "contrary to, or involved an unreasonable application of," that clearly established law. We address each part in turn.

THE "CLEARLY ESTABLISHED LAW" REQUIREMENT

In Teague v. Lane, 489 U.S. 288 (1989), we held that the petitioner was not entitled to federal habeas relief because he was relying on a rule of federal law that had not been announced until after his state conviction became final. The anti-retroactivity rule recognized in *Teague*, which prohibits reliance on "new rules," is the functional equivalent of a statutory provision commanding exclusive reliance on "clearly established law." . . . It is perfectly clear that AEDPA codifies *Teague* to the extent that *Teague* requires federal habeas courts to deny relief that is contingent upon a rule of law not clearly established at the time the state conviction became final.

Teague's core principles are therefore relevant to our construction of this requirement. . . . *Teague* established some guidance for making this determination, explaining that a federal habeas court operates within the bounds of comity and finality if it applies a rule "dictated by precedent existing at the time the defendant's conviction became final." . . . A rule that "breaks new ground or imposes a new obligation on the States or the Federal Government," . . . falls outside this universe of federal law.

To this, AEDPA has added, immediately following the "clearly established law" requirement, a clause limiting the area of relevant law to that "determined by the Supreme Court of the United States." 28 U.S.C. §2254(d)(1). . . . If this Court has not broken sufficient legal ground to establish an asked-for constitutional principle, the lower federal courts cannot themselves establish such a principle with clarity sufficient to satisfy the AEDPA bar. . . . In this respect, . . . this clause "extends the principle of *Teague* by limiting the source of doctrine on which a federal court may rely in addressing the application for a writ." . . .

It has been urged, in contrast, that we should read *Teague* and its progeny to encompass a broader principle of deference requiring federal courts to "validat[e] 'reasonable, good-faith interpretations' of the law" by state courts. . . . This presumption of deference was in essence the position taken by three Members of this Court in Wright [v. West], 505 U.S. [277,] 290-291 [(1992)] (opinion of Thomas, J.) ("[A] federal habeas court 'must defer to the state court's decision rejecting the claim unless that decision is patently unreasonable' "). . . .

Teague, however, does not extend this far. The often repeated language that *Teague* endorses "reasonable, good-faith interpretations" by state courts is an explanation of policy, not a statement of law. The *Teague* cases reflect this Court's view that habeas corpus is not to be used as a second criminal trial, and federal courts are not to run roughshod over the considered findings and judgments of the state courts that conducted the original trial and heard the initial appeals. On the contrary, we have long insisted that federal habeas courts attend closely to those considered decisions, and give them full effect when their findings and judgments are consistent with federal law. . . . But as Justice O'Connor explained in *Wright*:

> [T]he duty of the federal court in evaluating whether a rule is "new" is not the same as deference; . . . *Teague* does not direct federal courts to spend less time or effort scrutinizing the existing federal law, on the ground that they can assume the state courts interpreted it properly.
>
> [T]he maxim that federal courts should "give great weight to the considered conclusions of a coequal state judiciary" . . . does not mean that we have held in the past that federal courts must presume the correctness of a state court's legal conclusions on habeas, or that a state court's incorrect legal determination has ever been allowed

to stand because it was reasonable. We have always held that federal courts, even on habeas, have an independent obligation to say what the law is.

505 U.S., at 305.

We are convinced that in the phrase, "clearly established law," Congress did not intend to modify that independent obligation.

THE "CONTRARY TO, OR AN UNREASONABLE APPLICATION OF," REQUIREMENT

The message that Congress intended to convey by using the phrases, "contrary to" and "unreasonable application of" is not entirely clear. The prevailing view in the Circuits is that the former phrase requires de novo review of "pure" questions of law and the latter requires some sort of "reasonability" review of so-called mixed questions of law and fact. . . .

We are not persuaded that the phrases define two mutually exclusive categories of questions. Most constitutional questions that arise in habeas corpus proceedings—and therefore most "decisions" to be made—require the federal judge to apply a rule of law to a set of facts, some of which may be disputed and some undisputed. . . . In constitutional adjudication, as in the common law, rules of law often develop incrementally as earlier decisions are applied to new factual situations. . . . But rules that depend upon such elaboration are hardly less lawlike than those that establish a bright-line test.

Indeed, our pre-AEDPA efforts to distinguish questions of fact, questions of law, and "mixed questions," and to create an appropriate standard of habeas review for each, generated some not insubstantial differences of opinion as to which issues of law fell into which category of question, and as to which standard of review applied to each. . . .

Even though we cannot conclude that the phrases establish "a body of rigid rules," they do express a "mood" that the federal judiciary must respect. . . . In this respect, it seems clear that Congress intended federal judges to attend with the utmost care to state-court decisions, including all of the reasons supporting their decisions, before concluding that those proceedings were infected by constitutional error sufficiently serious to warrant the issuance of the writ. . . . AEDPA plainly sought to ensure a level of "deference to the determinations of state courts," provided those determinations did not conflict with federal law or apply federal law in an unreasonable way. . . . Congress wished to curb delays, to prevent "retrials" on federal habeas, and to give effect to state convictions to the extent possible under law. When federal courts are able to fulfill these goals within the bounds of the law, AEDPA instructs them to do so.

On the other hand, it is significant that the word "deference" does not appear in the text of the statute itself. Neither the legislative history, nor the statutory text, suggests any difference in the so-called "deference" depending on which of the two phrases is implicated.[13] Whatever "deference" Congress had in mind with respect

---

13. As Judge Easterbrook has noted, the statute surely does not require the kind of "deference" appropriate in other contexts: "It does not tell us to 'defer' to state decisions, as if the Constitution means one thing in Wisconsin and another in Indiana. Nor does it tell us to treat state courts the way we treat federal administrative agencies. Deference [to agencies] depends on delegation. . . . Congress did not delegate interpretive or executive power to the state courts. They exercise powers under their domestic law, constrained by the Constitution of the United States. 'Deference' to the jurisdictions bound by those constraints is not sensible." Lindh v. Murphy, 96 F.3d 856, 868 (CA7 1996) (en banc), *rev'd on other grounds*, 521 U.S. 320 (1997).

to both phrases, it surely is not a requirement that federal courts actually defer to a state-court application of the federal law that is, in the independent judgment of the federal court, in error. . . .

Our disagreement with Justice O'Connor about the precise meaning of the phrase "contrary to," and the word "unreasonable," is, of course, important, but should affect only a narrow category of cases. The simplest and first definition of "contrary to" as a phrase is "in conflict with." Webster's Ninth New Collegiate Dictionary 285 (1983). In this sense, we think the phrase surely capacious enough to include a finding that the state-court "decision" is simply "erroneous" or wrong. . . . And there is nothing in the phrase "contrary to" . . . that implies anything less than independent review by the federal courts.

Moreover, state-court decisions that do not "conflict" with federal law will rarely be "unreasonable" under either her reading of the statute or ours. We all agree that state-court judgments must be upheld unless, after the closest examination of the state-court judgment, a federal court is firmly convinced that a federal constitutional right has been violated. Our difference is as to the cases in which, at first-blush, a state-court judgment seems entirely reasonable, but thorough analysis by a federal court produces a firm conviction that that judgment is infected by constitutional error. In our view, such an erroneous judgment is "unreasonable" within the meaning of the act even though that conclusion was not immediately apparent.

In sum, the statute directs federal courts to attend to every state-court judgment with utmost care, but it does not require them to defer to the opinion of every reasonable state-court judge on the content of federal law. If, after carefully weighing all the reasons for accepting a state court's judgment, a federal court is convinced that a prisoner's custody—or, as in this case, his sentence of death—violates the Constitution, that independent judgment should prevail. Otherwise the federal "law as determined by the Supreme Court of the United States" might be applied by the federal courts one way in Virginia and another way in California. In light of the well-recognized interest in ensuring that federal courts interpret federal law in a uniform way, we are convinced that Congress did not intend the statute to produce such a result.

III

In this case, Williams contends that he was denied his constitutionally guaranteed right to the effective assistance of counsel when his trial lawyers failed to investigate and to present substantial mitigating evidence to the sentencing jury. The threshold question under AEDPA is whether Williams seeks to apply a rule of law that was clearly established at the time his state-court conviction became final. That question is easily answered because the merits of his claim are squarely governed by our holding in Strickland v. Washington. . . .

It is past question that the rule set forth in *Strickland* qualifies as "clearly established Federal law, as determined by the Supreme Court of the United States." That the *Strickland* test "of necessity requires a case-by-case examination of the evidence," . . . obviates neither the clarity of the rule nor the extent to which the rule must be seen as "established" by this Court. This Court's precedent "dictated" that the Virginia Supreme Court apply the *Strickland* test at the time that court entertained Williams' ineffective-assistance claim. . . . Williams is therefore entitled to relief if the Virginia Supreme Court's decision rejecting his ineffective-assistance claim was either "contrary to, or involved an unreasonable application of," that established law. It was both.

IV

The Virginia Supreme Court erred in holding that our decision in Lockhart v. Fretwell, 506 U.S. 364 (1993), modified or in some way supplanted the rule set down in *Strickland*. It is true that while the *Strickland* test provides sufficient guidance for resolving virtually all ineffective-assistance-of-counsel claims, there are situations in which the overriding focus on fundamental fairness may affect the analysis. Thus, on the one hand, as *Strickland* itself explained, there are a few situations in which prejudice may be presumed. . . . And, on the other hand, there are also situations in which it would be unjust to characterize the likelihood of a different outcome as legitimate "prejudice." Even if a defendant's false testimony might have persuaded the jury to acquit him, it is not fundamentally unfair to conclude that he was not prejudiced by counsel's interference with his intended perjury. Nix v. Whiteside, 475 U.S. 157, 175-176 (1986).

Similarly, in *Lockhart*, we concluded that, given the overriding interest in fundamental fairness, the likelihood of a different outcome attributable to an incorrect interpretation of the law should be regarded as a potential "windfall" to the defendant rather than the legitimate "prejudice" contemplated by our opinion in *Strickland*. . . .

Cases such as Nix v. Whiteside . . . and Lockhart v. Fretwell . . . do not justify a departure from a straightforward application of *Strickland* when the ineffectiveness of counsel *does* deprive the defendant of a substantive or procedural right to which the law entitles him. In the instant case, it is undisputed that Williams had a right—indeed, a constitutionally protected right—to provide the jury with the mitigating evidence that his trial counsel either failed to discover or failed to offer.

Nevertheless, the Virginia Supreme Court read our decision in *Lockhart* to require a separate inquiry into fundamental fairness even when Williams is able to show that his lawyer was ineffective and that his ineffectiveness probably affected the outcome of the proceeding. . . .

Unlike the Virginia Supreme Court, the state trial judge omitted any reference to *Lockhart* and simply relied on our opinion in *Strickland* as stating the correct standard for judging ineffective-assistance claims. . . . The trial judge analyzed the ineffective-assistance claim under the correct standard; the Virginia Supreme Court did not.

We are likewise persuaded that the Virginia trial judge correctly applied both components of that standard to Williams' ineffectiveness claim. Although he concluded that counsel competently handled the guilt phase of the trial, he found that their representation during the sentencing phase fell short of professional standards—a judgment barely disputed by the State in its brief to this Court. . . .

[A]s the Federal District Court correctly observed, the failure to introduce the comparatively voluminous amount of evidence that did speak in Williams' favor was not justified by a tactical decision to focus on Williams' voluntary confession. Whether or not those omissions were sufficiently prejudicial to have affected the outcome of sentencing, they clearly demonstrate that trial counsel did not fulfill their obligation to conduct a thorough investigation of the defendant's background. . . .

We are also persuaded, unlike the Virginia Supreme Court, that counsel's unprofessional service prejudiced Williams within the meaning of Strickland. After hearing the additional evidence developed in the postconviction proceedings, the very judge who presided at Williams' trial and who once determined that the death penalty was "just" and "appropriate," concluded that there existed "a reasonable probability that the result of the sentencing phase would have been different" if the jury had heard that evidence. . . .

The Virginia Supreme Court's own analysis of prejudice reaching the contrary conclusion was thus unreasonable in at least two respects. First, as we have already explained, the State Supreme Court mischaracterized at best the appropriate rule, made clear by this Court in *Strickland*, for determining whether counsel's assistance was effective within the meaning of the Constitution. . . .

Second, the State Supreme Court's prejudice determination was unreasonable insofar as it failed to evaluate the totality of the available mitigation evidence—both that adduced at trial, and the evidence adduced in the habeas proceeding—in reweighing it against the evidence in aggravation. . . .

V

In our judgment, the state trial judge was correct both in his recognition of the established legal standard for determining counsel's effectiveness, and in his conclusion that the entire postconviction record, viewed as a whole and cumulative of mitigation evidence presented originally, raised "a reasonable probability that the result of the sentencing proceeding would have been different" if competent counsel had presented and explained the significance of all the available evidence. It follows that the Virginia Supreme Court rendered a "decision that was contrary to, or involved an unreasonable application of, clearly established Federal law." Williams' constitutional right to the effective assistance of counsel as defined in Strickland v. Washington was violated.

Accordingly, the judgment of the Court of Appeals is reversed, and the case is remanded for further proceedings consistent with this opinion. . . .

JUSTICE O'CONNOR delivered the opinion of the Court with respect to Part II (except as to the footnote), concurred in part, and concurred in the judgment.*

. . . The Court holds today that the Virginia Supreme Court's adjudication of Terry Williams' application for state habeas corpus relief resulted in just such a decision. I agree with that determination and join Parts I, III, and IV of the Court's opinion. Because I disagree, however, with the interpretation of §2254(d)(1) set forth in Part II of Justice Stevens' opinion, I write separately to explain my views.

I

Before 1996, this Court held that a federal court entertaining a state prisoner's application for habeas relief must exercise its independent judgment when deciding both questions of constitutional law and mixed constitutional questions (i.e., application of constitutional law to fact). . . . In other words, a federal habeas court

---

* Justice Kennedy joins this opinion in its entirety. Chief Justice Rehnquist and Justice Thomas join this opinion with respect to Part II. Justice Scalia joins this opinion with respect to Part II, except as to the footnote. . . .

owed no deference to a state court's resolution of such questions of law or mixed questions. . . . [I]n the case of Wright v. West, [505 U.S. 277 (1992)], we revisited our prior holdings by asking the parties to address the following question in their briefs:

> In determining whether to grant a petition for writ of habeas corpus by a person in custody pursuant to the judgment of a state court, should a federal court give deference to the state court's application of law to the specific facts of the petitioner's case or should it review the state court's determination de novo? . . .

Although our ultimate decision did not turn on the answer to that question, our several opinions did join issue on it. . . .

Justice Thomas, announcing the judgment of the Court, acknowledged that our precedents had "treated as settled the rule that mixed constitutional questions are 'subject to plenary federal review' on habeas." . . . He contended, nevertheless, that those decisions did not foreclose the Court from applying a rule of deferential review for reasonableness in future cases. . . . Justice Thomas suggested that the time to revisit our decisions may have been at hand, given that our more recent habeas jurisprudence in the nonretroactivity context, see, e.g., Teague v. Lane, 489 U.S. 288 (1989), had called into question the then-settled rule of independent review of mixed constitutional questions. . . .

I wrote separately in *Wright* because I believed Justice Thomas had "understate[d] the certainty with which Brown v. Allen rejected a deferential standard of review of issues of law." . . . I also explained that we had considered the standard of review applicable to mixed constitutional questions on numerous occasions and each time we concluded that federal habeas courts had a duty to evaluate such questions independently. . . . With respect to Justice Thomas' suggestion that *Teague* and its progeny called into question the vitality of the independent-review rule, I noted that "*Teague* did not establish a 'deferential' standard of review" because "[i]t did not establish a standard of review at all." . . . While *Teague* did hold that state prisoners could not receive "the retroactive benefit of new rules of law," it "did *not* create any deferential standard of review with regard to old rules." . . . (emphasis in original).

Finally, and perhaps most importantly for purposes of today's case, I stated my disagreement with Justice Thomas' suggestion that de novo review is incompatible with the maxim that federal habeas courts should "give great weight to the considered conclusions of a coequal state judiciary." . . . Our statement . . . signified only that a state-court decision is due the same respect as any other "persuasive, well-reasoned authority." . . . "But this does not mean that we have held in the past that federal courts must presume the correctness of a state court's legal conclusions on habeas, or that a state court's incorrect legal determination has ever been allowed to stand because it was reasonable. We have always held that federal courts, even on habeas, have an independent obligation to say what the law is." . . . Under the federal habeas statute as it stood in 1992, then, our precedents dictated that a federal court should grant a state prisoner's petition for habeas relief if that court were to conclude in its independent judgment that the relevant state court had erred on a question of constitutional law or on a mixed constitutional question.

If today's case were governed by the federal habeas statute prior to Congress' enactment of AEDPA in 1996, I would agree with Justice Stevens that Williams' petition for habeas relief must be granted if we, in our independent judgment, were to conclude that his Sixth Amendment right to effective assistance of counsel was violated. . . .

II

A

Williams' case is *not* governed by the pre-1996 version of the habeas statute. Because he filed his petition in December 1997, Williams' case is governed by the statute as amended by AEDPA. Section 2254 now provides:

> (d) An application for a writ of habeas corpus on behalf of a person in custody pursuant to the judgment of a State court shall not be granted with respect to any claim that was adjudicated on the merits in State court proceedings unless the adjudication of the claim—
>> (1) resulted in a decision that was contrary to, or involved an unreasonable application of, clearly established Federal law, as determined by the Supreme Court of the United States.

Accordingly, for Williams to obtain federal habeas relief, he must first demonstrate that his case satisfies the condition set by §2254(d)(1). That provision modifies the role of federal habeas courts in reviewing petitions filed by state prisoners.

Justice Stevens' opinion in Part II essentially contends that §2254(d)(1) does not alter the previously settled rule of independent review. Indeed, the opinion concludes its statutory inquiry with the somewhat empty finding that §2254(d)(1) does no more than express a "'mood' that the federal judiciary must respect." . . .

That Justice Stevens would find the new §2254(d)(1) to have no effect on the prior law of habeas corpus is remarkable given his apparent acknowledgment that Congress wished to bring change to the field. . . . That acknowledgment is correct and significant to this case. It cannot be disputed that Congress viewed §2254(d)(1) as an important means by which its goals for habeas reform would be achieved.

Justice Stevens arrives at his erroneous interpretation by means of one critical misstep. He fails to give independent meaning to both the "contrary to" and "unreasonable application" clauses of the statute. . . . By reading §2254(d)(1) as one general restriction on the power of the federal habeas court, Justice Stevens manages to avoid confronting the specific meaning of the statute's "unreasonable application" clause and its ramifications for the independent-review rule. It is, however, a cardinal principle of statutory construction that we must "give effect, if possible, to every clause and word of a statute." . . .

The Court of Appeals for the Fourth Circuit properly accorded both the "contrary to" and "unreasonable application" clauses independent meaning. The Fourth Circuit's interpretation of §2254(d)(1) in Williams' case relied, in turn, on that court's previous decision in Green v. French, 143 F.3d 865 (CA4 1998). . . . With respect to the first of the two statutory clauses, the Fourth Circuit held in *Green* that a state-court decision can be "contrary to" this Court's clearly established precedent in two ways. First, a state-court decision is contrary to this Court's precedent if the state court arrives at a conclusion opposite to that reached by this Court on a question of law. Second, a state-court decision is also contrary to this Court's precedent if the state court confronts facts that are materially indistinguishable from a relevant Supreme Court precedent and arrives at a result opposite to ours. . . .

The word "contrary" is commonly understood to mean "diametrically different," "opposite in character or nature," or "mutually opposed." Webster's Third New International Dictionary 495 (1976). The text of §2254(d)(1) therefore suggests that the state court's decision must be substantially different from the relevant precedent of this Court. The Fourth Circuit's interpretation of the "contrary to" clause accurately reflects this textual meaning. A state-court decision will certainly be contrary to our clearly established precedent if the state court applies a rule that contradicts the governing law set forth in our cases. Take, for example, our decision in Strickland v. Washington. . . . If a state court were to reject a prisoner's claim of ineffective assistance of counsel on the grounds that the prisoner had not established by a preponderance of the evidence that the result of his criminal proceeding would have been different, that decision would be "diametrically different," "opposite in character or nature," and "mutually opposed" to our clearly established precedent because we held in *Strickland* that the prisoner need only demonstrate a "reasonable probability that . . . the result of the proceeding would have been different." . . . A state-court decision will also be contrary to this Court's clearly established precedent if the state court confronts a set of facts that are materially indistinguishable from a decision of this Court and nevertheless arrives at a result different from our precedent. Accordingly, in either of these two scenarios, a federal court will be unconstrained by §2254(d)(1) because the state-court decision falls within that provision's "contrary to" clause.

On the other hand, a run-of-the-mill state-court decision applying the correct legal rule from our cases to the facts of a prisoner's case would not fit comfortably within §2254(d)(1)'s "contrary to" clause. Assume, for example, that a state-court decision on a prisoner's ineffective-assistance claim correctly identifies *Strickland* as the controlling legal authority and, applying that framework, rejects the prisoner's claim. Quite clearly, the state-court decision would be in accord with our decision in *Strickland* as to the legal prerequisites for establishing an ineffective-assistance claim, even assuming the federal court considering the prisoner's habeas application might reach a different result applying the *Strickland* framework itself. It is difficult, however, to describe such a run-of-the-mill state-court decision as "diametrically different" from, "opposite in character or nature" from, or "mutually opposed" to *Strickland*, our clearly established precedent. Although the state-court decision may be contrary to the federal court's conception of how *Strickland* ought to be applied in that particular case, the decision is not "mutually opposed" to *Strickland* itself.

Justice Stevens would instead construe §2254(d)(1)'s "contrary to" clause to encompass such a routine state-court decision. That construction, however, saps the "unreasonable application" clause of any meaning. If a federal habeas court can, under the "contrary to" clause, issue the writ whenever it concludes that the state court's *application* of clearly established federal law was incorrect, the "unreasonable application" clause becomes a nullity. . . .

The Fourth Circuit's interpretation of the "unreasonable application" clause of §2254(d)(1) is generally correct. That court held in *Green* that a state-court decision can involve an "unreasonable application" of this Court's clearly established precedent in two ways. First, a state-court decision involves an unreasonable application of this Court's precedent if the state court identifies the correct governing legal rule from this Court's cases but unreasonably applies it to the facts of the particular state prisoner's case. Second, a state-court decision also involves an unreasonable application of this Court's precedent if the state court either unreasonably extends a legal principle from our precedent to a new context where it should not apply or unreasonably refuses to extend that principle to a new context where it should apply. . . .

A state-court decision that correctly identifies the governing legal rule but applies it unreasonably to the facts of a particular prisoner's case certainly would qualify as a decision "involving an unreasonable application of . . . clearly established Federal law." . . .*

The Fourth Circuit also held in *Green* that state-court decisions that unreasonably extend a legal principle from our precedent to a new context where it should not apply (or unreasonably refuse to extend a legal principle to a new context where it should apply) should be analyzed under §2254(d)(1)'s "unreasonable application" clause. . . . Although that holding may perhaps be correct, the classification does have some problems of precision. Just as it is sometimes difficult to distinguish a mixed question of law and fact from a question of fact, it will often be difficult to identify separately those state-court decisions that involve an unreasonable application of a legal principle (or an unreasonable failure to apply a legal principle) to a new context. Indeed, on the one hand, in some cases it will be hard to distinguish a decision involving an unreasonable extension of a legal principle from a decision involving an unreasonable application of law to facts. On the other hand, in many of the same cases it will also be difficult to distinguish a decision involving an unreasonable extension of a legal principle from a decision that "arrives at a conclusion opposite to that reached by this Court on a question of law." . . . Today's case does not require us to decide how such "extension of legal principle" cases should be treated under §2254(d)(1). For now it is sufficient to hold that when a state-court decision unreasonably applies the law of this Court to the facts of a prisoner's case, a federal court applying §2254(d)(1) may conclude that the state-court decision falls within that provision's "unreasonable application" clause.

B

There remains the task of defining what exactly qualifies as an "unreasonable application" of law under §2254(d)(1). The Fourth Circuit held in *Green* that a state-court decision involves an "unreasonable application of . . . clearly established Federal law" only if the state court has applied federal law "in a manner that reasonable jurists would all agree is unreasonable." . . . The placement of this additional overlay on the "unreasonable application" clause was erroneous. It is difficult to fault the Fourth Circuit for using this language given the fact that we have employed nearly identical terminology to describe the related inquiry undertaken by federal courts in applying the nonretroactivity rule of *Teague*. . . .

Defining an "unreasonable application" by reference to a "reasonable jurist," however, is of little assistance to the courts that must apply §2254(d)(1) and, in fact, may be misleading. Stated simply, a federal habeas court making the "unreasonable application" inquiry should ask whether the state court's application of clearly

---

* The legislative history of §2254(d)(1) also supports this interpretation. See, e.g., 142 Cong. Rec. 7799 (1996) (remarks of Sen. Specter) ("[U]nder the bill deference will be owed to State courts' decisions on the application of Federal law to the facts. Unless it is unreasonable, a State court's decision applying the law to the facts will be upheld"); 141 Cong. Rec. 14666 (1995) (remarks of Sen. Hatch) ("[W]e allow a Federal court to overturn a State court decision only if it is contrary to clearly established Federal law or if it involves an 'unreasonable application' of clearly established Federal law to the facts").

established federal law was objectively unreasonable. The federal habeas court should not transform the inquiry into a subjective one by resting its determination instead on the simple fact that at least one of the Nation's jurists has applied the relevant federal law in the same manner the state court did in the habeas petitioner's case. The "all reasonable jurists" standard would tend to mislead federal habeas courts by focusing their attention on a subjective inquiry rather than on an objective one. . . .

The term "unreasonable" is no doubt difficult to define. That said, it is a common term in the legal world and, accordingly, federal judges are familiar with its meaning. For purposes of today's opinion, the most important point is that an *unreasonable* application of federal law is different from an *incorrect* application of federal law. Our opinions in *Wright*, for example, make that difference clear. . . . In §2254(d)(1), Congress specifically used the word "unreasonable," and not a term like "erroneous" or "incorrect." Under §2254(d)(1)'s "unreasonable application" clause, then, a federal habeas court may not issue the writ simply because that court concludes in its independent judgment that the relevant state-court decision applied clearly established federal law erroneously or incorrectly. Rather, that application must also be unreasonable.

Justice Stevens turns a blind eye to the debate in *Wright* because he finds no indication in §2254(d)(1) itself that Congress was "directly influenced" by Justice Thomas' opinion in *Wright*. . . . As Justice Stevens himself apparently recognizes, however, Congress need not mention a prior decision of this Court by name in a statute's text in order to adopt either a rule or a meaning given a certain term in that decision. . . . In any event, whether Congress intended to codify the standard of review suggested by Justice Thomas in *Wright* is beside the point. *Wright* is important for the light it sheds on §2254(d)(1)'s requirement that a federal habeas court inquire into the reasonableness of a state court's application of clearly established federal law. The separate opinions in *Wright* concerned the very issue addressed by §2254(d)(1)'s "unreasonable application" clause—whether, in reviewing a state-court decision on a state prisoner's claims under federal law, a federal habeas court should ask whether the state-court decision was correct or simply whether it was reasonable. . . . The *Wright* opinions confirm what §2254(d)(1)'s language already makes clear—that an *unreasonable* application of federal law is different from an *incorrect* or *erroneous* application of federal law.

Throughout this discussion the meaning of the phrase "clearly established Federal law, as determined by the Supreme Court of the United States" has been put to the side. That statutory phrase refers to the holdings, as opposed to the dicta, of this Court's decisions as of the time of the relevant state-court decision. In this respect, the "clearly established Federal law" phrase bears only a slight connection to our *Teague* jurisprudence. With one caveat, whatever would qualify as an old rule under our *Teague* jurisprudence will constitute "clearly established Federal law, as determined by the Supreme Court of the United States" under §2254(d)(1). . . . The one caveat, as the statutory language makes clear, is that §2254(d)(1) restricts the source of clearly established law to this Court's jurisprudence.

In sum, §2254(d)(1) places a new constraint on the power of a federal habeas court to grant a state prisoner's application for a writ of habeas corpus with respect to claims adjudicated on the merits in state court. Under §2254(d)(1), the writ may issue only if one of the following two conditions is satisfied—the state-court adjudication resulted in a decision that (1) "was contrary to . . . clearly established Federal law, as determined by the Supreme Court of the United States," or (2) "involved an unreasonable application of . . . clearly established Federal law, as determined by the Supreme Court of the United States." Under the "contrary to" clause, a federal habeas court may grant the writ if the state court arrives at a conclusion opposite to that reached by this Court on a question of law or if the state court decides a case differently than this Court has on a set of materially indistinguishable facts. Under the "unreasonable application" clause, a federal habeas court may grant the writ if the state court identifies the correct governing legal principle from this Court's decisions but unreasonably applies that principle to the facts of the prisoner's case.

III

Although I disagree with Justice Stevens concerning the standard we must apply under §2254(d)(1) in evaluating Terry Williams' claims on habeas, I agree with the Court that the Virginia Supreme Court's adjudication of Williams' claim of ineffective assistance of counsel resulted in a decision that was both contrary to and involved an unreasonable application of this Court's clearly established precedent. . . .

Accordingly, although I disagree with the interpretation of §2254(d)(1) set forth in Part II of Justice Stevens' opinion, I join Parts I, III, and IV of the Court's opinion and concur in the judgment of reversal.

CHIEF JUSTICE REHNQUIST, with whom JUSTICE SCALIA and JUSTICE THOMAS join, concurring in part and dissenting in part.

I agree with the Court's interpretation of 28 U.S.C. §2254(d)(1) . . . , but disagree with its decision to grant habeas relief in this case. . . .

I, like the Virginia Supreme Court and the Federal Court of Appeals below, will assume without deciding that counsel's performance fell below an objective standard of reasonableness. As to the prejudice inquiry, I agree with the Court of Appeals that evidence showing that petitioner presented a future danger to society was overwhelming. As that court stated:

> The murder of Mr. Stone was just one act in a crime spree that lasted most of Williams's life. Indeed, the jury heard evidence that, in the months following the murder of Mr. Stone, Williams savagely beat an elderly woman, stole two cars, set fire to a home, stabbed a man during a robbery, set fire to the city jail, and confessed to having strong urges to choke other inmates and to break a fellow prisoner's jaw. . . .

In *Strickland*, . . . we said that both the performance and prejudice components of the ineffectiveness inquiry are mixed questions of law and fact. . . . It is with this kind of a question that the "unreasonable application of" clause takes on meaning. While the determination of "prejudice" in the legal sense may be a question of law, the subsidiary inquiries are heavily factbound.

Here, there was strong evidence that petitioner would continue to be a danger to society, both in and out of prison. It was not, therefore, unreasonable for the Virginia Supreme Court to decide that a jury would not have been swayed by evidence demonstrating that petitioner had a terrible childhood and a low IQ. . . . The potential mitigating evidence that may have countered the finding that petitioner was a future danger was testimony that petitioner was not dangerous while in detention. . . . But, again, it is not unreasonable to assume that the jury would have viewed this mitigation as unconvincing upon hearing that petitioner set fire to his cell while awaiting trial for the murder at hand and has repeated visions of harming other inmates.

Accordingly, I would hold that habeas relief is barred by 28 U.S.C. §2254(d). . . .

NOTES AND QUESTIONS

1. In *Terry Williams*, Justice O'Connor (writing for the majority on this issue) interpreted AEDPA's new standard of review to mean that "a federal habeas court may not issue the writ simply because that court concludes in its independent judgment that the relevant state-court decision applied clearly established federal law erroneously or incorrectly. Rather, that application must also be unreasonable." What does this mean in practice? If you were a federal habeas judge, how would you decide whether a challenged state-court decision was not merely "erroneous" or "incorrect," but also "unreasonable"? Note that even the Supreme Court itself is limited by AEDPA's new standard of review. Is this result compatible with the Supremacy Clause and the proper constitutional role of the federal courts?

2. As mentioned in both Justice Stevens's and Justice O'Connor's opinions, AEDPA's new standard of review provides that federal habeas courts may reverse the decisions of state courts *only* if those decisions are contrary to, or involve an unreasonable application of, existing *Supreme Court* precedent. This was a change from the *Teague* standard, which allowed federal habeas courts to reverse the decisions of state courts on the basis of existing federal law as established in the decisions of the federal circuit and district courts. Why do you think that Congress enacted such a change? Are state courts and lower federal courts in the same federal circuit or district now free to disagree, for extended periods of time (i.e., unless and until the Supreme Court decides to resolve the dispute), over the proper interpretation of federal constitutional provisions? If so, is this a good thing?

3. What do you think Justice O'Connor meant when she wrote that AEDPA's "'clearly established federal law' phrase bears only a slight connection to our *Teague* jurisprudence"? Did she mean that the scope of "clearly established federal law" is somehow broader than the scope of "old law" under *Teague*? For an interesting argument that she may have meant exactly this, see Larry W. Yackle, Habeas: The Figure in the Carpet, 78 Tex. L. Rev. 1731 (2000).

4. To what extent do significant changes to the federal habeas statute (such as AEDPA) potentially implicate the Suspension Clause?

In Boumediene v. Bush, 553 U.S. 723 (2008), the Supreme Court, in a hotly contested 5-4 decision, ruled that aliens held as "enemy combatants" at Guantanamo Bay have the constitutional right, protected by the Suspension Clause, to file a habeas corpus petition in federal court challenging their status as an "enemy combatant" and thus their continued detention. The Court also held that the procedures set forth by Congress, in the Detainee Treatment Act of 2005 (DTA), for reviewing such challenges to alleged "enemy combatant" status before so-called Combatant Status Review Tribunals (CSRTs) are not an "adequate substitute" for a traditional habeas corpus action, and thus cannot suffice to satisfy the Suspension Clause.

Although the situation of aliens held in executive detention at Guantanamo Bay is not entirely analogous to that of prisoners convicted of crimes in judicial proceedings, and although Lakhdar Boumediene did not rely on the same statutory version of federal habeas that applies to state criminal cases, the *Boumediene* case is nonetheless of some significance in the context of a criminal procedure course. For one thing, *Boumediene* extensively reviews the historical role and significance of the writ of habeas corpus—a habeas primer well worth reading. For another, *Boumediene* represents the latest word on the meaning and scope of the Suspension Clause—although, in the end, that word turns out not to be very illuminating:

> The Court has been careful not to foreclose the possibility that the protections of the Suspension Clause have expanded along with post-1789 developments that define the present scope of the writ. See INS v. St. Cyr, 533 U.S. 289, 300-301 (2001). But the analysis may begin with precedents as of 1789, for the Court has said that "at the absolute minimum" the Clause protects the writ as it existed when the Constitution was drafted and ratified. Id., at 301.

553 U.S., at 746. In other words, *Boumediene* leaves unresolved the question whether the Suspension Clause protects the statutory version of federal habeas, originally enacted in 1867, that applies to state criminal cases and that is the primary focus of this chapter.

On the related question of what qualifies as an "adequate substitute" for habeas, although the Court did not purport to set forth a comprehensive guide, it did note that, at a minimum:

> [T]he privilege of habeas corpus entitles the prisoner to a meaningful opportunity to demonstrate that he is being held pursuant to "the erroneous application or interpretation" of relevant law. *St. Cyr*, 533 U.S. [289], at 302 [(2001)]. And the habeas court must have the power to order the conditional release of an individual unlawfully detained—though release need not be the exclusive remedy and is not the appropriate one in every case in which the writ is granted.

553 U.S., at 779. Because the CSRTs, as provided under the DTA, could not meet these minimum requirements, the Court concluded that the denial of access to habeas corpus would violate the Suspension Clause.

3. Procedural Issues in Federal Habeas

a. Timing

AEDPA, for the first time, sets a time limit for the filing of a federal habeas petition. In 28 U.S.C. §2244(d), the Act provides:

> (d)(1) A 1-year period of limitation shall apply to an application for a writ of habeas corpus by a person in custody pursuant to the judgment of a State court. The limitation period shall run from the latest of—
> (A) the date on which the judgment became final by the conclusion of direct review or the expiration of the time for seeking such review;
> (B) the date on which the impediment to filing an application created by State action in violation of the Constitution or laws of the United States is removed, if the applicant was prevented from filing by such State action;

(C) the date on which the constitutional right asserted was initially recognized by the Supreme Court, if the right has been newly recognized by the
Supreme Court and made retroactively applicable to cases on collateral review; or

(D) the date on which the factual predicate of the claim or claims presented
could have been discovered through the exercise of due diligence.

(d)(2) The time during which a properly filed application for State post-conviction or other collateral review with respect to the pertinent judgment or claim is
pending shall not be counted toward any period of limitation under this subsection.

b. Exhaustion

AEDPA changes the rules with respect to the long-standing requirement that
a petitioner must exhaust available state remedies before seeking federal habeas
relief. See Rose v. Lundy, 455 U.S. 509 (1982) (interpreting exhaustion requirement
under pre-AEDPA federal habeas law). In 28 U.S.C. §2254(b), the Act provides:

(b)(1) An application for a writ of habeas corpus on behalf of a person in custody pursuant to the judgment of a State court shall not be granted unless it appears
that—

(A) the applicant has exhausted the remedies available in the courts of the
State, or

(B)(i) there is an absence of available State corrective process; or

(B)(ii) circumstances exist that render such process ineffective to protect
the rights of the applicant.

(b)(2) An application for a writ of habeas corpus may be denied on the merits,
notwithstanding the failure of the applicant to exhaust the remedies available in the
courts of the State.

(b)(3) A State shall not be deemed to have waived the exhaustion requirement
or be estopped from reliance upon the requirement unless the State, through counsel, expressly waives the requirement.

In O'Sullivan v. Boerckel, 526 U.S. 838 (1999), the Court held that a habeas
petitioner, in order to meet the exhaustion requirement, must file a petition for
discretionary review in the state's highest appellate court, so long as such review is
part of the state's "established, normal appellate review procedure." Id., at 845. In
Slack v. McDaniel, 529 U.S. 473 (2000), the Court held inter alia that AEDPA's general prohibition on "second or successive" habeas petitions does not apply when the
initial petition was dismissed without an adjudication on the merits because of the
petitioner's failure, under 28 U.S.C. §2254(b), to exhaust state remedies.

c. Procedural Default

It is axiomatic that the federal courts "will not review judgments of state courts
that rest on adequate and independent state grounds." Michigan v. Long, 463 U.S.
1032, 1041 (1982). The "adequate and independent state ground" doctrine has
given rise to a special—and controversial—procedural rule that often bars federal
habeas courts from reaching the merits of a habeas petitioner's federal constitutional claims.

WAINWRIGHT v. SYKES, 433 U.S. 72 (1977):   We granted certiorari to consider the availability of federal habeas corpus to review a state convict's claim that testimony was admitted at his trial in violation of his rights under Miranda v. Arizona, 384 U.S. 436 (1966), a claim which the Florida courts have previously refused to consider on the merits because of noncompliance with a state contemporaneous-objection rule. . . .

[I]t is a well-established principle of federalism that a state decision resting on an adequate foundation of state substantive law is immune from review in the federal courts. . . . The application of this principle in the context of a federal habeas proceeding has therefore excluded from consideration any questions of state *substantive* law, and thus effectively barred federal habeas review where questions of that sort are either the only ones raised by a petitioner or are in themselves dispositive of his case. The area of controversy which has developed has concerned the reviewability of federal claims which the state court has declined to pass on because not presented in the manner prescribed by its *procedural* rules. . . .

The contemporaneous-objection rule itself is by no means peculiar to Florida, and deserves greater respect than [Fay v. Noia, 372 U.S. 391 (1963),[7]] gives it, both for the fact that it is employed by a coordinate jurisdiction within the federal system and for the many interests which it serves in its own right. A contemporaneous objection enables the record to be made with respect to the constitutional claim when the recollections of witnesses are freshest, not years later in a federal habeas proceeding. It enables the judge who observed the demeanor of those witnesses to make the factual determinations necessary for properly deciding the federal constitutional question. While . . . §2254 requires deference to be given to such determinations made by state courts, the determinations themselves are less apt to be made in the first instance if there is no contemporaneous objection to the admission of the evidence on federal constitutional grounds.

A contemporaneous-objection rule may lead to the exclusion of the evidence objected to, thereby making a major contribution to finality in criminal litigation. Without the evidence claimed to be vulnerable on federal constitutional grounds, the jury may acquit the defendant, and that will be the end of the case; or it may nonetheless convict the defendant, and he will have one less federal constitutional claim to assert in his federal habeas petition. If the state trial judge admits the evidence in question after a full hearing, the federal habeas court pursuant to . . . §2254 will gain significant guidance from the state ruling in this regard. Subtler considerations as well militate in favor of honoring a state contemporaneous-objection rule. An objection on the spot may force the prosecution to take a hard look at its hole card, and even if the prosecutor thinks that the state trial judge will admit the evidence he must contemplate the possibility of reversal by the state appellate courts or the ultimate issuance of a federal writ of habeas corpus based on the impropriety of the state court's rejection of the federal constitutional claim.

We think that the rule of Fay v. Noia, broadly stated, may encourage "sandbagging" on the part of defense lawyers, who may take their chances on a verdict of not guilty in a state trial court with the intent to raise their constitutional claims in a federal habeas court if their initial gamble does not pay off. The refusal of federal habeas courts to honor contemporaneous-objection rules may also make state

---

7. Fay v. Noia is discussed supra, at page 1633. — EDS.

courts themselves less stringent in their enforcement. Under the rule of Fay v. Noia, state appellate courts know that a federal constitutional issue raised for the first time in the proceeding before them may well be decided in any event by a federal habeas tribunal. Thus, their choice is between addressing the issue notwithstanding the petitioner's failure to timely object, or else face the prospect that the federal habeas court will decide the question without the benefit of their views.

The failure of the federal habeas courts generally to require compliance with a contemporaneous-objection rule tends to detract from the perception of the trial of a criminal case in state court as a decisive and portentous event. A defendant has been accused of a serious crime, and this is the time and place set for him to be tried by a jury of his peers and found either guilty or not guilty by that jury. . . . Any procedural rule which encourages the result that those proceedings be as free of error as possible is thoroughly desirable, and the contemporaneous-objection rule surely falls within this classification.

. . . The "cause"-and-"prejudice" exception . . . will afford an adequate guarantee, we think, that the rule will not prevent a federal habeas court from adjudicating for the first time the federal constitutional claim of a defendant who in the absence of such an adjudication will be the victim of a miscarriage of justice. Whatever precise content may be given those terms by later cases, we feel confident in holding without further elaboration that they do not exist here. . . .

NOTES AND QUESTIONS

1. Under Wainwright v. Sykes, a federal habeas petitioner is generally held responsible for the errors and omissions of his defense lawyer that lead to the procedural default of his claims—errors that, in a capital case, could potentially cost the defendant his life. Does this seem fair? This is another area in which the shift in the theoretical focus of federal habeas, from providing an individual remedy to deterring state-court misconduct, turns out to be quite important. Under the deterrence theory, if the state court was never given a chance to resolve the federal constitutional claim, then no misconduct occurred, and federal habeas relief is unwarranted.

Note, by the way, that the prevailing standard for ineffective assistance of counsel under Strickland v. Washington makes it extremely unlikely that a petitioner whose federal habeas claim is lost by a single isolated episode of procedural default will be able to convert that claim into one of ineffective assistance. See generally John C. Jeffries & William J. Stuntz, Ineffective Assistance and Procedural Default in Federal Habeas Corpus, 57 U. Chi. L. Rev. 679 (1990); Daniel J. Meltzer, State Court Forfeiture of Federal Rights, 99 Harv. L. Rev. 1128 (1986).

2. The doctrine of procedural default in Wainwright v. Sykes was a creation of the Court, not Congress. AEDPA contains no statutory provisions addressing procedural default, thus presumably leaving Wainwright v. Sykes unaffected. In Edwards v. Carpenter, 529 U.S. 446, (2000), a post-AEDPA decision, the Court applied Wainwright v. Sykes to hold that a procedural default may be excused by ineffective assistance of counsel—but only if the ineffective assistance claim itself was not procedurally defaulted, or if such procedural default was, in turn, excused by its own showing of "cause" and "prejudice." (At this point, you may find yourself consoled by Justice Breyer's frank admission, in a concurring opinion, that "few lawyers, let alone unrepresented state prisoners, will readily understand" the Court's decision in Edwards v. Carpenter.)

3. In Wainwright v. Sykes, the Court declined to overrule Fay v. Noia on its own facts (i.e., where the particular procedural default involved was the defense lawyer's failure to file the documents necessary to preserve an appeal). In Coleman v. Thompson, 501 U.S. 722 (1991), the Court completed the dismantling of Fay v. Noia, holding that the Wainwright v. Sykes "cause" and "prejudice" standard applied to defense counsel's failure to file a notice of appeal within the state's 30-day jurisdictional time limit. (This was a capital case, and the mistake was made by a lawyer from a respected Washington law firm. Coleman was subsequently executed. See Peter Applebome, Execution Stirs Up Troubling Questions, N.Y. Times, p. A14 (May 22, 1992).)

4. On the definition of "cause" for failing to pursue a claim in state court, compare Murray v. Carrier, 477 U.S. 478 (1986) (ignorance or inadvertence of defense lawyer is not "cause," unless it satisfies Strickland v. Washington standard for ineffective assistance of counsel) with Amadeo v. Zant, 486 U.S. 214 (1988) (state concealment of memorandum documenting discrimination in jury selection is "cause"); Reed v. Ross, 468 U.S. 1 (1984) (novelty of legal claim, so that it was not "reasonably available" to defense lawyer, is "cause").

In Martinez v. Ryan, 132 S. Ct. 1309 (2012), the Court addressed the issue of failure to pursue a claim in state collateral proceedings and its impact on federal habeas review. The habeas petitioner, Martinez, was convicted in Arizona, where—as in many states—claims of ineffective assistance of counsel at trial must be raised in a collateral proceeding, so that (if necessary) additional facts relevant to the claim can be developed at an evidentiary hearing. Although defendants have a constitutional right to counsel on their first direct appeal as of right, see Douglas v. California, 372 U.S. 353 (1963), they do not enjoy such a constitutional right in federal or state collateral proceedings, see Ross v. Moffitt, 417 U.S. 600 (1974) (see Chapter 3, at page 151). After Martinez's conviction was affirmed on direct appeal, his appellate counsel filed a "notice of post-conviction relief" on his behalf, but did not include a claim of ineffectiveness of trial counsel, and then essentially declined to continue representing Martinez. Later, in a second state collateral proceeding, Martinez (now represented by new counsel) tried to raise the trial ineffectiveness claim, but it was denied on grounds of procedural default because it had not been raised in the first state collateral proceeding. The Supreme Court ultimately held that Martinez should be allowed to raise his ineffectiveness claim in federal habeas—notwithstanding the state procedural default—because the lack of effective assistance of counsel in the first state collateral proceeding constituted "cause" for Martinez's failure to raise the trial ineffectiveness claim in that proceeding. The Court stressed (confusingly!) that it was *not* holding that there is a constitutional right to counsel in state collateral proceedings—only that a lack of effective counsel in such a proceeding may, under certain circumstances (such as where, as in *Martinez*, a particular claim *must* be raised in such a proceeding), excuse a procedural default and allow a federal habeas court to reach the merits of the claim.

5. On the definition of "prejudice," see United States v. Frady, 456 U.S. 152 (1982) (no "prejudice" where there was "no substantial likelihood" that petitioner would have prevailed absent the constitutional error that was procedurally defaulted).

6. The Wainwright v. Sykes procedural default doctrine applies even to cases involving a guilty plea. This is highly significant because, in almost all such cases, the defendant fails to contest his plea on direct appeal (because he believes he is getting a good deal), thereby procedurally defaulting any possible subsequent

constitutional challenges to the plea. In Bousley v. United States, 523 U.S. 614 (1998), the Court applied Wainwright v. Sykes to such a case, but ultimately held that the defendant (who was challenging his plea on a §2255 motion, based on the Court's later reinterpretation of the federal criminal statute under which he pleaded guilty) would be entitled to relief if he could make a sufficient showing of "actual innocence" to satisfy the "fundamental miscarriage of justice" exception to the procedural default bar.

d. Successive Petitions and Abuse of the Writ

Under AEDPA, 28 U.S.C. §2244(b):

> (b)(1) A claim presented in a second or successive habeas corpus application under section 2254 that was presented in a prior application shall be dismissed.
> (b)(2) A claim presented in a second or successive habeas corpus application under section 2254 that was not presented in a prior application shall be dismissed unless—
>> (A) the applicant shows that the claim relies on a new rule of constitutional law, made retroactive to cases on collateral review by the Supreme Court, that was previously unavailable; or
>> (B)(i) the factual predicate for the claim could not have been discovered previously through the exercise of due diligence; and
>> (B)(ii) the facts underlying the claim, if proven and viewed in light of the evidence as a whole, would be sufficient to establish by clear and convincing evidence that, but for the constitutional error, no reasonable factfinder would have found the applicant guilty of the underlying offense.

AEDPA also requires petitioners who seek to file a second or successive petition to obtain permission from the court of appeals before filing with the district court, see 28 U.S.C. §2244(b)(3), and requires the district court to dismiss any claims in such a petition unless the petitioner can show that the claim satisfies the statutory requirements, see 28 U.S.C. §2244(b)(4).

With respect to claims that were contained in a prior habeas petition (usually called a "successive petition"), AEDPA forecloses any realistic possibility of relief. But cf. Calderon v. Thompson, 523 U.S. 538 (1998) (Court allows lower court to recall mandate with respect to first habeas petition, in order to avoid AEDPA's ban on "successive petitions"); compare Kuhlmann v. Wilson, 477 U.S. 436 (1986) (treatment of "successive petitions" under pre-AEDPA law).

With respect to claims that were not contained in a prior habeas petition (usually called an "abuse of the writ"), AEDPA's new requirements, while not completely foreclosing habeas relief, are certainly much tougher than the requirements under pre-AEDPA law; compare McCleskey v. Zant, 499 U.S. 467 (1991) (treatment of "abuse of the writ" under pre-AEDPA law).

e. The "Fundamental Miscarriage of Justice" Exception

Prior to AEDPA, most procedural bars to federal habeas relief contained an exception for cases representing a "fundamental miscarriage of justice." See, e.g., Schlup v. Delo, 513 U.S. 298 (1995) (finding "fundamental miscarriage of justice" sufficient to avoid "abuse of the writ" procedural bar). Under AEDPA, the only exceptions to the "successive petition" and "abuse of the writ" bars are those expressed in the statute, see page 1658. The "fundamental miscarriage of justice" exception remains available, however, in procedural default cases under Wainwright v. Sykes.

f. Evidentiary Hearings

AEDPA also changes the rules with respect to the requirements for obtaining an evidentiary hearing in connection with a federal habeas petition. See Keeney v. Tamayo-Reyes, 504 U.S. 1 (1992) (interpreting requirements for evidentiary hearing under pre-AEDPA federal habeas law). In 28 U.S.C. §2254(e), the Act provides:

> (e)(1) In a proceeding instituted by an application for a writ of habeas corpus by a person in custody pursuant to a judgment of a State court, a determination of a factual issue made by a State court shall be presumed to be correct. The applicant shall have the burden of rebutting the presumption of correctness by clear and convincing evidence.
>
> (e)(2) If the applicant has failed to develop the factual basis of a claim in State court proceedings, the court shall not hold an evidentiary hearing on the claim unless the applicant shows that—
>> (A) the claim relied on—
>>> (i) a new rule of constitutional law, made retroactive to cases on collateral review by the Supreme Court, that was previously unavailable; or
>>> (ii) a factual predicate that could not have been previously discovered through the exercise of due diligence; and
>> (B) the facts underlying the claim would be sufficient to establish by clear and convincing evidence that but for constitutional error, no reasonable factfinder would have found the applicant guilty of the underlying offense.

See Michael Williams v. Taylor, 529 U.S. 420 (2000) (under AEDPA, petitioner did not "fail to develop the factual basis of a claim in State court" unless petitioner or his counsel exhibited a lack of diligence or some greater degree of fault).

In Cullen v. Pinholster, 131 S. Ct. 1388 (2011), the Court—in a majority opinion by Justice Thomas that was joined, in this particular aspect, by a total of seven Justices—held that federal habeas courts are generally required to apply the §2254(d)(1) review standard on the basis of the record as it existed at the time that the relevant state court made its decision on the merits. According to the *Pinholster* Court, any other interpretation would be incompatible with AEDPA's view that the purpose of habeas review is to ensure that state courts comply with federal law; if the state court made a decision that was "reasonable" in light of the record available to it at the time, then there is no lack of compliance for the habeas court to deter. Even though §2254(e)(2) clearly contemplates that the habeas court may hold an evidentiary hearing under certain circumstances, that provision—as construed by Michael Williams v. Taylor—is limited to situations where the state court did *not* make a decision on the merits.

4. What Law Applies?

We have already seen that under AEDPA the federal habeas courts, as a general matter, can apply only federal constitutional law that was clearly established, by decisions of the U.S. Supreme Court, as of the time of the state court's final decision. New rules of constitutional law do not apply, unless they fall within one of the two narrow exceptions created by Teague v. Lane (and reaffirmed by the Court under AEDPA). See supra, at page 1634. But this is not the only limitation on the law that applies to a federal habeas case.

STONE v. POWELL

Certiorari to the United States Court of Appeals for the Eighth Circuit
428 U.S. 465 (1976)

JUSTICE POWELL delivered the opinion of the Court.

Respondents in these cases were convicted of criminal offenses in state courts, and their convictions were affirmed on appeal. The prosecution in each case relied upon evidence obtained by searches and seizures alleged by respondents to have been unlawful. Each respondent subsequently sought relief in a Federal District Court by filing a petition for a writ of federal habeas corpus under 28 U.S.C. §2254. The question presented is whether a federal court should consider, in ruling on a petition for habeas corpus relief filed by a state prisoner, a claim that evidence obtained by an unconstitutional search or seizure was introduced at his trial, when he has previously been afforded an opportunity for full and fair litigation of his claim in the state courts. The issue is of considerable importance to the administration of criminal justice.

I

[This section summarized the facts and procedural history of each case. In each case, the petitioner moved to suppress certain evidence, claiming a violation of the Fourth Amendment, but the state court rejected the claim. In each case, the petitioner was convicted, subsequently renewed the Fourth Amendment claim in a federal habeas corpus petition, and ultimately obtained relief from the habeas court.—EDS.]

II

[This section began with a review of the history of federal habeas corpus review of state convictions, up to and including the expansions of federal habeas jurisdiction in Brown v. Allen, 344 U.S. 443 (1953), and Fay v. Noia, 372 U.S. 391 (1963).—EDS.]

During the period in which the substantive scope of the writ was expanded, the Court did not consider whether exceptions to full review might exist with respect to particular categories of constitutional claims. Prior to the Court's decision in Kaufman v. United States, 394 U.S. 217 (1969), however, a substantial majority of the Federal Courts of Appeals had concluded that collateral review of search-and-seizure claims was inappropriate on motions filed by federal prisoners under 28

U.S.C. §2255, the modern postconviction procedure available to federal prisoners in lieu of habeas corpus. The primary rationale advanced in support of those decisions was that Fourth Amendment violations are different in kind from denials of Fifth or Sixth Amendment rights in that claims of illegal search and seizure do not "impugn the integrity of the fact-finding process or challenge evidence as inherently unreliable; rather, the exclusion of illegally seized evidence is simply a prophylactic device intended generally to deter Fourth Amendment violations by law enforcement officers." . . .

Kaufman rejected this rationale and held that search-and-seizure claims are cognizable in §2255 proceedings. The Court noted that "the federal habeas remedy extends to state prisoners alleging that unconstitutionally obtained evidence was admitted against them at trial," . . . and concluded, as a matter of statutory construction, that there was no basis for restricting "access by federal prisoners with illegal search-and-seizure claims to federal collateral remedies, while placing no similar restriction on access by state prisoners." . . . Although in recent years the view has been expressed that the Court should re-examine the substantive scope of federal habeas jurisdiction and limit collateral review of search-and-seizure claims "solely to the question of whether the petitioner was provided a fair opportunity to raise and have adjudicated the question in state courts," . . . the Court, without discussion or consideration of the issue, has continued to accept jurisdiction in cases raising such claims . . .

The discussion in *Kaufman* of the scope of federal habeas corpus rests on the view that the effectuation of the Fourth Amendment, as applied to the States through the Fourteenth Amendment, requires the granting of habeas corpus relief when a prisoner has been convicted in state court on the basis of evidence obtained in an illegal search or seizure since those Amendments were held in Mapp v. Ohio, 367 U.S. 643 (1961), to require exclusion of such evidence at trial and reversal of conviction upon direct review. Until these cases we have not had occasion fully to consider the validity of this view. . . . Upon examination, we conclude, in light of the nature and purpose of the Fourth Amendment exclusionary rule, that this view is unjustified. We hold, therefore, that where the State has provided an opportunity for full and fair litigation of a Fourth Amendment claim, the Constitution does not require that a state prisoner be granted federal habeas corpus relief on the ground that evidence obtained in an unconstitutional search or seizure was introduced at his trial.

III

The Fourth Amendment assures the "right of the people to be secure in their persons, houses, papers, and effects, against unreasonable searches and seizures." The Amendment was primarily a reaction to the evils associated with the use of the general warrant in England and the writs of assistance in the Colonies, . . . and was intended to protect the "sanctity of a man's home and the privacies of life," Boyd v. United States, 116 U.S. 616, 630 (1886), from searches under unchecked general authority. . . .

The exclusionary rule was a judicially created means of effectuating the rights secured by the Fourth Amendment. Prior to the Court's decisions in Weeks v. United States, 232 U.S. 383 (1914), and Gouled v. United States, 255 U.S. 298 (1921), there existed no barrier to the introduction in criminal trials of evidence obtained in violation of the Amendment. . . . Thirty-five years after *Weeks* the Court held in Wolf v.

Colorado, 338 U.S. 25 (1949), that the right to be free from arbitrary intrusion by the police that is protected by the Fourth Amendment is . . . enforceable against the States. . . . The Court concluded, however, that the *Weeks* exclusionary rule would not be imposed upon the States. . . . The full force of *Wolf* was eroded in subsequent decisions, . . . and a little more than a decade later the exclusionary rule was held applicable to the States in Mapp v. Ohio, 367 U.S. 643 (1961).

. . . The *Mapp* majority justified the application of the rule to the States on several grounds, but relied principally upon the belief that exclusion would deter future unlawful police conduct. . . .

Although our decisions often have alluded to the "imperative of judicial integrity," . . . they demonstrate the limited role of this justification in the determination whether to apply the rule in a particular context. . . . While courts, of course, must ever be concerned with preserving the integrity of the judicial process, this concern has limited force as a justification for the exclusion of highly probative evidence. The force of this justification becomes minimal where federal habeas corpus relief is sought by a prisoner who previously has been afforded the opportunity for full and fair consideration of his search-and-seizure claim at trial and on direct review.

The primary justification for the exclusionary rule then is the deterrence of police conduct that violates Fourth Amendment rights. Post-*Mapp* decisions have established that the rule is not a personal constitutional right. It is not calculated to redress the injury to the privacy of the victim of the search or seizure, for any "[r]eparation comes too late." . . . Instead, "the rule is a judicially created remedy designed to safeguard Fourth Amendment rights generally through its deterrent effect. . . ."

Mapp involved the enforcement of the exclusionary rule at state trials and on direct review. The decision in *Kaufman*, as noted above, is premised on the view that implementation of the Fourth Amendment also requires the consideration of search-and-seizure claims upon collateral review of state convictions. But despite the broad deterrent purpose of the exclusionary rule, it has never been interpreted to proscribe the introduction of illegally seized evidence in all proceedings or against all persons. As in the case of any remedial device, "the application of the rule has been restricted to those areas where its remedial objectives are thought most efficaciously served." . . . [Here, Justice Powell noted that the exclusionary rule does not apply to grand jury proceedings, nor does it prohibit the use of illegally seized evidence to impeach a defendant who testifies at trial. — EDS.]

The balancing process at work in these cases also finds expression in the standing requirement. Standing to invoke the exclusionary rule has been found to exist only when the Government attempts to use illegally obtained evidence to incriminate the victim of the illegal search. . . . The standing requirement is premised on the view that the "additional benefits of extending the . . . rule" to defendants other than the victim of the search or seizure are outweighed by the "further encroachment upon the public interest in prosecuting those accused of crime and having them acquitted or convicted on the basis of all the evidence which exposes the truth." . . .

IV

We turn now to the specific question presented by these cases. Respondents allege violations of Fourth Amendment rights guaranteed them through the

Fourteenth Amendment. The question is whether state prisoners—who have been afforded the opportunity for full and fair consideration of their reliance upon the exclusionary rule with respect to seized evidence by the state courts at trial and on direct review—may invoke their claim again on federal habeas corpus review. The answer is to be found by weighing the utility of the exclusionary rule against the costs of extending it to collateral review of Fourth Amendment claims.

The costs of applying the exclusionary rule even at trial and on direct review are well known: The focus of the trial, and the attention of the participants therein, are diverted from the ultimate question of guilt or innocence that should be the central concern in a criminal proceeding. Moreover, the physical evidence sought to be excluded is typically reliable and often the most probative information bearing on the guilt or innocence of the defendant. . . . Application of the rule thus deflects the truth-finding process and often frees the guilty. The disparity in particular cases between the error committed by the police officer and the windfall afforded a guilty defendant by application of the rule is contrary to the idea of proportionality that is essential to the concept of justice. Thus, although the rule is thought to deter unlawful police activity in part through the nurturing of respect for Fourth Amendment values, if applied indiscriminately it may well have the opposite effect of generating disrespect for the law and administration of justice. These long-recognized costs of the rule persist when a criminal conviction is sought to be overturned on collateral review on the ground that a search-and-seizure claim was erroneously rejected by two or more tiers of state courts.

Evidence obtained by police officers in violation of the Fourth Amendment is excluded at trial in the hope that the frequency of future violations will decrease. Despite the absence of supportive empirical evidence, we have assumed that the immediate effect of exclusion will be to discourage law enforcement officials from violating the Fourth Amendment by removing the incentive to disregard it. More importantly, over the long term, this demonstration that our society attaches serious consequences to violation of constitutional rights is thought to encourage those who formulate law enforcement policies, and the officers who implement them, to incorporate Fourth Amendment ideals into their value system.

We adhere to the view that these considerations support the implementation of the exclusionary rule at trial and its enforcement on direct appeal of state-court convictions. But the additional contribution, if any, of the consideration of search-and-seizure claims of state prisoners on collateral review is small in relation to the costs. To be sure, each case in which such claim is considered may add marginally to an awareness of the values protected by the Fourth Amendment. There is no reason to believe, however, that the overall educative effect of the exclusionary rule would be appreciably diminished if search-and-seizure claims could not be raised in federal habeas corpus review of state convictions. Nor is there reason to assume that any specific disincentive already created by the risk of exclusion of evidence at trial or the reversal of convictions on direct review would be enhanced if there were the further risk that a conviction obtained in state court and affirmed on direct review might be overturned in collateral proceedings often occurring years after the incarceration of the defendant. The view that the deterrence of Fourth Amendment violations would be furthered rests on the dubious assumption that law enforcement authorities would fear that federal habeas review might reveal flaws in a search or seizure that went undetected at trial and on appeal.[35] Even if one rationally could assume that some additional incremental deterrent effect would be present in isolated cases, the resulting advance of the legitimate goal of furthering Fourth Amendment rights would be outweighed by the acknowledged costs to other values vital to a rational system of criminal justice.

In sum, we conclude that where the State has provided an opportunity for full and fair litigation of a Fourth Amendment claim, a state prisoner may not be granted federal habeas corpus relief on the ground that evidence obtained in an unconstitutional search or seizure was introduced at his trial.[37] In this context the contribution of the exclusionary rule, if any, to the effectuation of the Fourth Amendment is minimal and the substantial societal costs of application of the rule persist with special force.

Accordingly, the judgments of the Courts of Appeals are reversed.

[The concurring opinion of Chief Justice Burger is omitted.]

JUSTICE BRENNAN, with whom JUSTICE MARSHALL concurs, dissenting.

The Court today holds "that where the State has provided an opportunity for full and fair litigation of a Fourth Amendment claim, a state prisoner may not be granted federal habeas corpus relief on the ground that evidence obtained in an unconstitutional search or seizure was introduced at his trial." . . . To be sure, my Brethren are hostile to the continued vitality of the exclusionary rule as part and parcel of the Fourth Amendment's prohibition of unreasonable searches and seizures. . . . But these cases, despite the veil of Fourth Amendment terminology employed by the Court, plainly do not involve any question of the right of a defendant to have evidence excluded from use against him in his criminal trial when that evidence was seized in contravention of rights ostensibly secured by the Fourth and Fourteenth Amendments. Rather, they involve the question of the availability of a federal forum for vindicating those federally guaranteed rights. Today's holding portends substantial evisceration of federal habeas corpus jurisdiction, and I dissent. . . .

I

. . . The Court, assuming without deciding that respondents were convicted on the basis of unconstitutionally obtained evidence erroneously admitted against them

---

35. The policy arguments that respondents marshal in support of the view that federal habeas corpus review is necessary to effectuate the Fourth Amendment stem from a basic mistrust of the state courts as fair and competent forums for the adjudication of federal constitutional rights. . . . Despite differences in institutional environment and the unsympathetic attitude to federal constitutional claims of some state judges in years past, we are unwilling to assume that there now exists a general lack of appropriate sensitivity to constitutional rights in the trial and appellate courts of the several States. State courts, like federal courts, have a constitutional obligation to safeguard personal liberties and to uphold federal law. . . . Moreover, the argument that federal judges are more expert in applying federal constitutional law is especially unpersuasive in the context of search-and-seizure claims, since they are dealt with on a daily basis by trial level judges in both systems. In sum, there is "no intrinsic reason why the fact that a man is a federal judge should make him more competent, or conscientious, or learned with respect to the [consideration of Fourth Amendment claims] than his neighbor in the state courthouse." [Paul Bator, Finality in Criminal Law and Federal Habeas Corpus for State Prisoners, 76 Harv. L. Rev. 441, 509 (1963).]

37. . . . With all respect, the hyperbole of the dissenting opinion is misdirected. Our decision today is *not* concerned with the scope of the habeas corpus statute as authority for litigating constitutional claims generally. . . . [W]e hold only that a federal court need not apply the exclusionary rule on habeas review of a Fourth Amendment claim absent a showing that the state prisoner was denied an opportunity for a full and fair litigation of that claim at trial and on direct review. Our decision does not mean that the federal court lacks jurisdiction over such a claim, but only that the application of the rule is limited to cases in which there has been both such a showing and a Fourth Amendment violation.

by the state trial courts, acknowledges that respondents had the right to obtain a reversal of their convictions on appeal in the state courts or on certiorari to this Court. . . . It is simply inconceivable that that constitutional deprivation suddenly vanishes after the appellate process has been exhausted. And as between this Court on certiorari, and federal district courts on habeas, it is for *Congress* to decide what the most efficacious method is for enforcing *federal* constitutional rights and asserting the primacy of federal law. . . . The Court, however, simply ignores the settled principle that for purposes of adjudicating constitutional claims Congress, which has the power to do so under Art. III of the Constitution, has effectively cast the district courts sitting in habeas in the role of surrogate Supreme Courts.[10]

. . . [B]y conceding that today's "decision does not mean that the federal [district] court lacks jurisdiction over [respondents'] claim[s]," . . . the Court admits that respondents have sufficiently alleged that they are "in custody in violation of the Constitution" within the meaning of §2254 and that there is no "constitutional" rationale for today's holding. Rather, the constitutional "interest balancing" approach to this case is untenable, and I can only view the constitutional garb in which the Court dresses its result as a disguise for rejection of the longstanding principle that there are no "second class" constitutional rights for purposes of federal habeas jurisdiction; it is nothing less than an attempt to provide a veneer of respectability for an obvious usurpation of Congress' Art. III power to delineate the jurisdiction of the federal courts.

II

Therefore, the real ground of today's decision—a ground that is particularly troubling in light of its portent for habeas jurisdiction generally—is the Court's novel reinterpretation of the habeas statutes. . . . Much in the Court's opinion suggests that a construction of the habeas statutes to deny relief for non-"guilt-related" constitutional violations, based on this Court's vague notions of comity and federalism, . . . is the actual premise for today's decision, and although the Court attempts to bury its underlying premises in footnotes, those premises mark this case as a harbinger of future eviscerations of the habeas statutes that plainly does violence to congressional power to frame the statutory contours of habeas jurisdiction. . . . [T]he groundwork is being laid today for a drastic withdrawal of federal habeas jurisdiction, if not for all grounds of alleged unconstitutional detention, then at least for claims—for example, of double jeopardy, entrapment, self-incrimination, *Miranda* violations, and use of invalid identification procedures—that this Court later decides are not "guilt related." . . .

Federal habeas corpus review of Fourth Amendment claims of state prisoners was merely one manifestation of the principle that "conventional notions of finality

---

10. The failure to confront this fact forthrightly is obviously a core defect in the Court's analysis. For to the extent Congress has accorded the federal district courts a role in our constitutional scheme functionally equivalent to that of the Supreme Court with respect to review of state-court resolutions of federal constitutional claims, it is evident that the Court's direct/collateral review distinction for constitutional purposes simply collapses. . . .

The Court's arguments respecting the cost/benefit analysis of applying the exclusionary rule on collateral attack also have no merit. For all of the "costs" of applying the exclusionary rule on habeas *should already have been incurred* at the trial or on direct review if the state court had not misapplied federal constitutional principles. As such, these "costs" were evaluated and deemed to be outweighed when the exclusionary rule was fashioned. . . .

in criminal litigation cannot be permitted to defeat the manifest federal policy that federal constitutional rights of personal liberty shall not be denied without the fullest opportunity for plenary federal judicial review." Fay v. Noia, 372 U.S. 391, 424 (1963). . . . In effect, habeas jurisdiction is a deterrent to unconstitutional actions by trial and appellate judges, and a safeguard to ensure that rights secured under the Constitution and federal laws are not merely honored in the breach. . . .

At least since Brown v. Allen, detention emanating from judicial proceedings in which constitutional rights were denied has been deemed "contrary to fundamental law," and all constitutional claims have thus been cognizable on federal habeas corpus. There is no foundation in the language or history of the habeas statutes for discriminating between types of constitutional transgressions. . . . Today's opinion, however, marks the triumph of those who have sought to establish a hierarchy of constitutional rights, and to deny for all practical purposes a federal forum for review of those rights that this Court deems less worthy or important. . . .

I would address the Court's concerns for effective utilization of scarce judicial resources, finality principles, federal-state friction, and notions of "federalism" only long enough to note that such concerns carry no more force with respect to non-"guilt-related" constitutional claims than they do with respect to claims that affect the accuracy of the fact-finding process. Congressional conferral of federal habeas jurisdiction for the purpose of entertaining petitions from state prisoners necessarily manifested a conclusion that such concerns could not be controlling, and any argument for discriminating among constitutional rights must therefore depend on the nature of the constitutional right involved.

The Court, focusing on Fourth Amendment rights as it must to justify such discrimination, thus argues that habeas relief for non-"guilt-related" constitutional claims is not mandated because such claims do not affect the "basic justice" of a defendant's detention . . . ; this is presumably because the "ultimate goal" of the criminal justice system is "truth and justice." . . . Even if punishment of the "guilty" were society's highest value—and procedural safeguards denigrated to this end—in a constitution that a majority of the Members of this Court would prefer, that is not the ordering of priorities under the Constitution forged by the Framers, and this Court's sworn duty is to uphold that Constitution and not to frame its own. The procedural safeguards mandated in the Framers' Constitution are not admonitions to be tolerated only to the extent they serve functional purposes that ensure that the "guilty" are punished and the "innocent" freed; rather, every guarantee enshrined in the Constitution, our basic charter and the guarantor of our most precious liberties, is by it endowed with an independent vitality and value, and this Court is not free to curtail those constitutional guarantees even to punish the most obviously guilty. . . . To sanction disrespect and disregard for the Constitution in the name of protecting society from lawbreakers is to make the government itself lawless and to subvert those values upon which our ultimate freedom and liberty depend. . . . Enforcement of *federal* constitutional rights that redress constitutional violations directed against the "guilty" is a particular function of *federal* habeas review, lest judges trying the "morally unworthy" be tempted not to execute the supreme law of the land. State judges popularly elected may have difficulty resisting popular pressures not experienced by federal judges given lifetime tenure designed to immunize them from such influences, and the federal habeas statutes reflect the congressional judgment that such detached federal review is a salutary safeguard against *any* detention of an individual "in violation of the Constitution or laws . . . of the United States." . . .

. . . It is one thing to assert that state courts, as a general matter, accurately decide federal constitutional claims; it is quite another to generalize from that limited proposition to the conclusion that, despite congressional intent that federal courts sitting in habeas must stand ready to rectify any constitutional errors that are nevertheless committed, federal courts are to be judicially precluded from ever considering the merits of whole categories of rights that are to be accorded less procedural protection merely because the Court proclaims that they do not affect the accuracy or fairness of the fact-finding process. . . . To the extent state trial and appellate judges faithfully, accurately, and assiduously apply federal law and the constitutional principles enunciated by the federal courts, such determinations will be vindicated on the merits when collaterally attacked. But to the extent federal law is erroneously applied by the state courts, there is no authority in this Court to deny defendants the right to have those errors rectified by way of federal habeas; indeed, the Court's reluctance to accept Congress' desires along these lines can only be a manifestation of this Court's mistrust for federal judges. Furthermore, some might be expected to dispute the academic's dictum seemingly accepted by the Court that a federal judge is not necessarily more skilled than a state judge in applying federal law. . . . For the Supremacy Clause of the Constitution proceeds on a different premise, and Congress, as it was constitutionally empowered to do, made federal judges (and initially federal district court judges) "the *primary* and powerful reliances for vindicating every right given by the Constitution, the laws, and treaties of the United States." . . .

. . . Employing the transparent tactic that today's is a decision construing the Constitution, the Court usurps the authority—vested by the Constitution in the Congress—to reassign federal judicial responsibility for reviewing state prisoners' claims of failure of state courts to redress violations of their Fourth Amendment rights. Our jurisdiction is eminently unsuited for that task, and as a practical matter the only result of today's holding will be that denials by the state courts of claims by state prisoners of violations of their Fourth Amendment rights will go unreviewed by a federal tribunal. I fear that the same treatment ultimately will be accorded state prisoners' claims of violations of other constitutional rights; thus the potential ramifications of this case for federal habeas jurisdiction generally are ominous. The Court, no longer content just to restrict forthrightly the constitutional rights of the citizenry, has embarked on a campaign to water down even such constitutional rights as it purports to acknowledge by the device of foreclosing resort to the federal habeas remedy for their redress.

I would affirm the judgments of the Courts of Appeals.

[The dissenting opinion of Justice White is omitted.]

NOTES AND QUESTIONS

1. Despite Justice Brennan's fears, Stone v. Powell has not turned out to be the vanguard for wholesale substantive restrictions of federal habeas corpus jurisdiction. Indeed, the Court has rejected several calls to extend Stone v. Powell to other categories of claims. See, e.g., Jackson v. Virginia, 443 U.S. 307 (1979) (Fourteenth Amendment claim of insufficient evidence to support a conviction); Rose v. Mitchell, 443 U.S. 545 (1979) (Fourteenth Amendment claim of racial discrimination in selection of grand-jury foreman); Kimmelman v. Morrison, 477 U.S. 365 (1986)

(Sixth Amendment ineffective-assistance-of-counsel claim, based on counsel's failure to pursue Fourth Amendment search-and-seizure claim); Withrow v. Williams, 507 U.S. 680 (1993) (Fifth Amendment *Miranda* claim).

2. Can a federal habeas petitioner challenge his sentence on the ground that it was enhanced on the basis of a prior conviction that was allegedly unconstitutionally obtained? In Lackawanna County District Attorney v. Coss, 532 U.S. 394 (2001), the Court answered this question squarely in the negative, unless (1) the challenge to the prior conviction was based on a failure to appoint counsel for the defendant in violation of the Sixth Amendment, see Custis v. United States, 511 U.S. 485, 496-497 (1994); or (2) the defendant, through no fault of his own, never had a fair opportunity to challenge the prior conviction, so that the new petition represents "the first and only forum available for review of the prior conviction." See also Daniels v. United States, 532 U.S. 374 (2001), applying the same general rule and exceptions to a federal prisoner seeking collateral review under 28 U.S.C. §2255.

5.   Prejudice and Harmless Error

BRECHT v. ABRAHAMSON

Certiorari to the United States Court of Appeals for the Seventh Circuit
507 U.S. 619 (1993)

CHIEF JUSTICE REHNQUIST delivered the opinion of the Court.

In this case we must decide whether the *Chapman* harmless-error standard applies in determining whether the prosecution's use for impeachment purposes of petitioner's post-*Miranda* silence, in violation of due process under Doyle v. Ohio, 426 U.S. 610 (1976), entitles petitioner to habeas corpus relief. We hold that it does not. Instead, the standard for determining whether habeas relief must be granted is whether the *Doyle* error "had substantial and injurious effect or influence in determining the jury's verdict." Kotteakos v. United States, 328 U.S. 750, 776 (1946). The *Kotteakos* harmless-error standard is better tailored to the nature and purpose of collateral review than the *Chapman* standard, and application of a less onerous harmless-error standard on habeas promotes the considerations underlying our habeas jurisprudence. Applying this standard, we conclude that petitioner is not entitled to habeas relief.

[Petitioner Brecht fatally shot his brother-in-law in Alma, Wisconsin. Attempting to flee in his sister's car, he drove the car into a ditch. A police officer (unaware of the shooting) offered assistance, but petitioner refused. He hitchhiked to Winona, Minnesota, where he was stopped by the police. After initially concealing his identity, he later identified himself and was arrested. He was returned to Wisconsin, and was given *Miranda* warnings at his arraignment. At petitioner's trial for first-degree murder, he admitted the shooting, but claimed it was an accident. Over defense objections, petitioner was cross-examined about whether he had ever told anyone, at any time before trial, that the shooting was an accident, and he replied, "no." At closing argument, the prosecutor made several references to the fact that petitioner had never mentioned, prior to trial, that the shooting was an accident. Petitioner was convicted and sentenced to life imprisonment. —EDS.]

. . . The Wisconsin Court of Appeals set the conviction aside on the ground that the State's references to petitioner's post-*Miranda* silence . . . violated due process under Doyle v. Ohio . . . and that this error was sufficiently "prejudicial" to require reversal. The Wisconsin Supreme Court reinstated the conviction. Although it agreed that the State's use of petitioner's post-*Miranda* silence was impermissible, the court determined that this error "'was harmless beyond a reasonable doubt.'" . . . (quoting *Chapman* . . .). In finding the *Doyle* violation harmless, the court noted that the State's "improper references to Brecht's silence were infrequent," in that they "comprised less than two pages of a 900 page transcript, or a few minutes in a four day trial in which twenty-five witnesses testified," and that the State's evidence of guilt was compelling.

Petitioner then sought a writ of habeas corpus under 28 U.S.C. §2254, reasserting his *Doyle* claim. The District court agreed that the State's use of petitioner's post-*Miranda* silence violated *Doyle*, but disagreed with the Wisconsin Supreme Court that this error was harmless beyond a reasonable doubt, and set aside the conviction. . . .

The Court of Appeals held that the *Chapman* harmless-error standard does not apply in reviewing *Doyle* error on federal habeas. Instead, . . . the Court of Appeals held that the standard for determining whether petitioner was entitled to habeas relief was whether the *Doyle* violation "'had substantial and injurious effect or influence in determining the jury's verdict,'" . . . (quoting *Kotteakos* . . .). Applying this standard, the Court of Appeals concluded that petitioner was not entitled to relief. . . .

We granted certiorari . . . and now affirm. . . .

In Doyle v. Ohio, . . . we held that "the use for impeachment purposes of [a defendant's] silence, at the time of arrest and after receiving *Miranda* warnings, violate[s] the Due Process Clause of the Fourteenth Amendment." This rule "rests on 'the fundamental unfairness of implicitly assuring a suspect that his silence will not be used against him and then using his silence to impeach an explanation subsequently offered at trial.'" . . .

The Court of Appeals characterized *Doyle* as "a prophylactic rule." . . . It reasoned that, since the need for Doyle stems from the implicit assurance that flows from *Miranda* warnings, and "the warnings required by *Miranda* are not themselves part of the Constitution," "*Doyle* is . . . a prophylactic rule designed to protect another prophylactic rule from erosion or misuse." . . . But *Doyle* was not simply a further extension of the *Miranda* prophylactic rule. Rather, . . . it is rooted in fundamental fairness and due process concerns. However real these concerns, Doyle does not "overprotec[t]" them . . . Under the rationale of *Doyle*, due process is violated whenever the prosecution uses for impeachment purposes a defendant's post-*Miranda* silence. *Doyle* thus does not bear the hallmarks of a prophylactic rule.

Instead, we think *Doyle* error fits squarely into the category of constitutional violations which we have characterized as "trial error." See Arizona v. Fulminante, 499 U.S. 279, 307 (1991). Trial error "occur[s] during the presentation of the case to the jury," and is amenable to harmless-error analysis because it "may . . . be quantitatively assessed in the context of other evidence presented in order to determine [the effect it had on the trial]." . . . At the other end of the spectrum of constitutional errors lie "structural defects in the constitution of the trial mechanism, which defy analysis by 'harmless-error' standards." . . . The existence of such defects — deprivation of the right to counsel, for example — requires automatic reversal of the conviction because they infect the entire trial process. . . . Since our landmark decision in Chapman v. California, 386 U.S. 18 (1967), we have applied the harmless-beyond-a-reasonable-doubt standard in reviewing claims of constitutional error of the trial type.

. . . *Chapman* reached this Court on direct review, as have most of the cases in which we have applied its harmless-error standard. Although we have applied the *Chapman* standard in a handful of federal habeas cases, see, e.g., Yates v. Evatt, 500 U.S. 391 (1991); Rose v. Clark, 478 U.S. 570 (1986) . . . , we have yet squarely to address its applicability on collateral review. . . .

The federal habeas corpus statute is silent on this point. It permits federal courts to entertain a habeas petition on behalf of a state prisoner "only on the ground that he is in custody in violation of the Constitution or laws or treaties of the United States," 28 U.S.C. §2254(a), and directs simply that the court "dispose of the matter as law and justice require," §2243. The statute says nothing about the standard for harmless-error review in habeas cases. Respondent urges us to fill this gap with the *Kotteakos* standard, under which an error requires reversal only if it "had substantial and injurious effect or influence in determining the jury's verdict." . . . This standard is grounded in the federal harmless-error statute. 28 U.S.C. §2111 ("On the hearing of any appeal or writ of certiorari in any case, the court shall give judgment after an examination of the record without regard to errors or defects which do not affect the substantial rights of the parties"). On its face §2111 might seem to address the situation at hand, but to date we have limited its application to claims of non-constitutional error in federal criminal cases. . . .

. . . In the absence of any express statutory guidance from Congress, it remains for this Court to determine what harmless-error standard applies on collateral review of petitioner's *Doyle* claim. We have filled the gaps of the habeas corpus statute with respect to other matters, . . . and find it necessary to do so here. As always, in defining the scope of the writ, we look first to the considerations underlying our habeas jurisprudence, and then determine whether the proposed rule would advance or inhibit these considerations by weighing the marginal costs and benefits of its application on collateral review.

The principle that collateral review is different from direct review resounds throughout our habeas jurisprudence. . . . Direct review is the principal avenue for challenging a conviction. "When the process of direct review—which, if a federal question is involved, includes the right to petition this Court for a writ of certiorari—comes to an end, a presumption of finality and legality attaches to the conviction and sentence. The role of federal habeas proceedings, while important in assuring that constitutional rights are observed, is secondary and limited. Federal courts are not forums in which to relitigate state trials." . . .

In keeping with this distinction, the writ of habeas corpus has historically been regarded as an extraordinary remedy, "a bulwark against convictions that violate 'fundamental fairness.'" . . . "Those few who are ultimately successful [in obtaining habeas relief] are persons whom society has grievously wronged and for whom belated liberation is little enough compensation." Fay v. Noia, 372 U.S. 391, 440-441 (1963). . . . Accordingly, it hardly bears repeating that "'an error that may justify reversal on direct appeal will not necessarily support a collateral attack on a final judgment.'" . . .

The reason most frequently advanced in our cases for distinguishing between direct and collateral review is the State's interest in the finality of convictions that have survived direct review within the state court system. . . . We have also spoken of comity and federalism. . . . Finally, we have recognized that "[l]iberal allowance of the writ . . . degrades the prominence of the trial itself," . . . and at the same time encourages habeas petitioners to relitigate their claims on collateral review. . . .

In light of these considerations, we must decide whether the same harmless-error standard that the state courts applied on direct review of petitioner's *Doyle* claim also applies in this habeas proceeding. We are the sixth court to pass on the question whether the State's use for impeachment purposes of petitioner's post-*Miranda* silence in this case requires reversal of his conviction. Each court that has reviewed the record has disagreed with the court before it as to whether the State's *Doyle* error was "harmless." State courts are fully qualified to identify constitutional error and evaluate its prejudicial effect on the trial process under *Chapman,* and state courts often occupy a superior vantage point from which to evaluate the effect of trial error. . . . For these reasons, it scarcely seems logical to require federal habeas courts to engage in the identical approach to harmless-error review that *Chapman* requires state courts to engage in on direct review.

Petitioner argues that application of the *Chapman* harmless-error standard on collateral review is necessary to deter state courts from relaxing their own guard in reviewing constitutional error and to discourage prosecutors from committing error in the first place. Absent affirmative evidence that state-court judges are ignoring their oath, we discount petitioner's argument that courts will respond to our ruling by violating their Article VI duty to uphold the Constitution. . . . Federalism, comity, and the constitutional obligation of state and federal courts all counsel against any presumption that a decision of this Court will "deter" lower federal or state courts from fully performing their sworn duty. . . . In any event, we think the costs of applying the *Chapman* standard on federal habeas outweigh the additional deterrent effect, if any, that would be derived from its application on collateral review.

Overturning final and presumptively correct convictions on collateral review because the State cannot prove that an error is harmless under *Chapman* undermines the States' interest in finality and infringes upon their sovereignty over criminal matters. Moreover, granting habeas relief merely because there is a "reasonable possibility" that trial error contributed to the verdict, see Chapman v. California, 386 U.S., at 24 . . . , is at odds with the historic meaning of habeas corpus — to afford relief to those whom society has "grievously wronged." Retrying defendants whose convictions are set aside also imposes significant "social costs," including the expenditure of additional time and resources for all the parties involved, the "erosion of memory" and "dispersion of witnesses" that accompany the passage of time and make obtaining convictions on retrial more difficult, and the frustration of "society's interest in the prompt administration of justice." . . . And since there is no statute of limitations governing federal habeas,[8] and the only laches recognized is that which affects the State's ability to defend against the claims raised on habeas, retrials following the grant of habeas relief ordinarily take place much later than do retrials following reversal on direct review.

The imbalance of the costs and benefits of applying the *Chapman* harmless-error standard on collateral review counsels in favor of applying a less onerous standard on habeas review of constitutional error. The *Kotteakos* standard, we believe, fills the bill. The test under *Kotteakos* is whether the error "had substantial and injurious effect or influence in determining the jury's verdict." 328 U.S., at 776. Under this standard, habeas petitioners may obtain plenary review of their constitutional claims, but they are not entitled to habeas relief based on trial error unless they

---

8. This has changed, of course, since the enactment of AEDPA. See page 1653, supra. — EDS.

can establish that it resulted in "actual prejudice." . . . The *Kotteakos* standard is thus better tailored to the nature and purpose of collateral review and more likely to promote the considerations underlying our recent habeas cases. Moreover, because the *Kotteakos* standard is grounded in the federal harmless-error rule, 28 U.S.C. §2111, federal courts may turn to an existing body of case law in applying it. Therefore, contrary to the assertion of petitioner, application of the *Kotteakos* standard on collateral review is unlikely to confuse matters for habeas courts.

For the foregoing reasons, then, we hold that the *Kotteakos* harmless-error standard applies in determining whether habeas relief must be granted because of constitutional error of the trial type.[9] All that remains to be decided is whether petitioner is entitled to relief under this standard based on the State's Doyle error. Because the Court of Appeals applied the *Kotteakos* standard below, we proceed to this question ourselves rather than remand the case for a new harmless-error determination. . . . At trial, petitioner admitted shooting Hartman, but claimed it was an accident. The principal question before the jury, therefore, was whether the State met its burden in proving beyond a reasonable doubt that the shooting was intentional. Our inquiry here is whether, in light of the record as a whole, the State's improper use for impeachment purposes of petitioner's post-*Miranda* silence . . . "had substantial and injurious effect or influence in determining the jury's verdict." We think it clear that it did not.

The State's references to petitioner's post-*Miranda* silence were infrequent, comprising less than two pages of the 900-page trial transcript in this case. And in view of the State's extensive and permissible references to petitioner's pre-*Miranda* silence—i.e., his failure to mention anything about the shooting being an accident to the officer who found him in the ditch, the man who gave him a ride to Winona, or the officers who eventually arrested him—its references to petitioner's post-*Miranda* silence were, in effect, cumulative. Moreover, the State's evidence of guilt was, if not overwhelming, certainly weighty. The path of the bullet through Mr. Hartman's body was inconsistent with petitioner's testimony that the rifle had discharged as he was falling. The police officers who searched the Hartmans' home found nothing in the downstairs hallway that could have caused petitioner to trip. The rifle was found outside the house (where Hartman was shot), not inside where petitioner claimed it had accidently fired, and there was a live round rammed in the gun's chamber, suggesting that petitioner had tried to fire a second shot. Finally, other circumstantial evidence, including the motive proffered by the State, also pointed to petitioner's guilt.

In light of the foregoing, we conclude that the *Doyle* error that occurred at petitioner's trial did not "substantial[ly] . . . influence" the jury's verdict. Petitioner is therefore not entitled to habeas relief. . . .

JUSTICE STEVENS, concurring. . . .

To apply the *Kotteakos* standard properly, the reviewing court must . . . make a de novo examination of the trial record. The Court faithfully engages in such de novo review today. . . .

---

9. Our holding does not foreclose the possibility that in an unusual case, a deliberate and especially egregious error of the trial type, or one that is combined with a pattern of prosecutorial misconduct, might so infect the integrity of the proceeding as to warrant the grant of habeas relief, even if it did not substantially influence the jury's verdict. . . . We, of course, are not presented with such a situation here.

The purpose of reviewing the entire record is, of course, to consider all the ways that error can infect the course of a trial. . . . [W]e would misread *Kotteakos* itself if we endorsed only a single-minded focus on how the error may (or may not) have affected the jury's verdict. The habeas court cannot ask only whether it thinks the petitioner would have been convicted even if the constitutional error had not taken place. *Kotteakos* is full of warnings to avoid that result. It requires a reviewing court to decide that "the error did not influence the jury," . . . and that "the judgment was not substantially swayed by the error." . . .

The *Kotteakos* standard that will now apply on collateral review is less stringent than the Chapman v. California, 386 U.S. 18 (1967), standard applied on direct review. Given the critical importance of the faculty of judgment in administering either standard, however, that difference is less significant than it might seem. . . . In the end, the way we phrase the governing standard is far less important than the quality of the judgment with which it is applied.

Although our adoption of *Kotteakos* does impose a new standard in this context, it is a standard that will always require "the discrimination . . . of judgment transcending confinement by formula or precise rule. . . . " In my own judgment, for the reasons explained by the Chief Justice, the *Doyle* error that took place in petitioner's trial did not have a substantial and injurious effect or influence in determining the jury's verdict. . . .

JUSTICE WHITE, with whom JUSTICE BLACKMUN joins, and with whom JUSTICE SOUTER joins in part, dissenting.

Assuming that petitioner's conviction was in fact tainted by a constitutional violation that, while not harmless beyond a reasonable doubt, did not have "substantial and injurious effect or influence in determining the jury's verdict," Kotteakos v. United States, 328 U.S. 750, 776 (1946), it is undisputed that he would be entitled to reversal in the state courts on appeal or in this Court on certiorari review. If, however, the state courts erroneously concluded that no violation had occurred or (as is the case here) that it was harmless beyond a reasonable doubt, and supposing further that certiorari was either not sought or not granted, the majority would foreclose relief on federal habeas review. As a result of today's decision, in short, the fate of one in state custody turns on whether the state courts properly applied the Federal Constitution as then interpreted by decisions of this Court, and on whether we choose to review his claim on certiorari. Because neither the federal habeas corpus statute nor our own precedents can support such illogically disparate treatment, I dissent.

I

A

Chapman v. California, 386 U.S. 18 (1967), established the federal nature of the harmless-error standard to be applied when constitutional rights are at stake. . . . Under *Chapman*, federal law requires reversal of a state conviction involving a constitutional violation that is not harmless beyond a reasonable doubt. A defendant whose conviction has been upheld despite the occurrence of such a violation certainly is "in custody in violation of the Constitution or laws . . . of the United States," 28 U.S.C. §2254(a), and therefore is entitled to habeas relief. Although we have never explicitly held that this was the case, our practice before this day plainly supports this view, as the majority itself acknowledges. . . .

II

The majority's decision . . . is far from inconsequential. Under *Chapman*, the State must prove beyond a reasonable doubt that the constitutional error "did not contribute to the verdict obtained." . . . In contrast, the Court now invokes Kotteakos v. United States, 328 U.S. 750 (1946) —a case involving a non-constitutional error of trial procedure—to impose on the defendant the burden of establishing that the error "resulted in 'actual prejudice.'" . . . Moreover, . . . the Court extends its holding to all "constitutional error[s] of the trial type." . . . Given that all such "trial errors" are now subject to harmless-error analysis, see Arizona v. Fulminante, 499 U.S. 279, 307-308 (1991), and that "most constitutional errors" are of this variety, . . . the Court effectively has ousted *Chapman* from habeas review of state convictions. In other words, a state court determination that a constitutional error—even one as fundamental as the admission of a coerced confession, see *Fulminante* . . .—is harmless beyond a reasonable doubt has in effect become unreviewable by lower federal courts by way of habeas corpus.

I believe this result to be at odds with the role Congress has ascribed to habeas review, which is, at least in part, to deter both prosecutors and courts from disregarding their constitutional responsibilities. "[T]he threat of habeas serves as a necessary additional incentive for trial and appellate courts throughout the land to conduct their proceedings in a manner consistent with established constitutional standards." . . . Either state courts are faithful to federal law, in which case there is no cost in applying the *Chapman* as opposed to the *Kotteakos* standard on collateral review; or they are not, and it is precisely the role of habeas corpus to rectify that situation.

Ultimately, the central question is whether States may detain someone whose conviction was tarnished by a constitutional violation that is not harmless beyond a reasonable doubt. *Chapman* dictates that they may not; the majority suggests that, so long as direct review has not corrected this error in time, they may. If state courts remain obliged to apply *Chapman*, and in light of the infrequency with which we grant certiorari, I fail to see how this decision can be reconciled with Congress' intent.

III

Our habeas jurisprudence is taking on the appearance of a confused patchwork in which different constitutional rights are treated according to their status, and in which the same constitutional right is treated differently depending on whether its vindication is sought on direct or collateral review. I believe this picture bears scant resemblance either to Congress' design or to our own precedents. . . .

JUSTICE O'CONNOR, dissenting.

I have no dispute with the Court's observation that "collateral review is different from direct review." . . . But decisions concerning the Great Writ "warrant restraint," . . . for we ought not take lightly alteration of that fundamental safeguard against unlawful custody. . . .

In my view, restraint should control our decision today. . . . [W]e are asked to alter a standard that not only finds application in virtually every case of error but that also may be critical to our faith in the reliability of the criminal process. Because I am not convinced that the principles governing the exercise of our habeas powers—federalism, finality, and fairness—counsel against applying *Chapman*'s harmless-error standard on collateral review, I would adhere to our former practice of applying it to cases on habeas and direct review alike. . . .

A repudiation of the application of *Chapman* to *all* trial errors asserted on habeas should be justified, if at all, based on the nature of the *Chapman* rule itself. Yet, . . . one searches the majority opinion in vain for a discussion of the basis for *Chapman*'s harmless-error standard. We are left to speculate whether *Chapman* is the product of constitutional command or a judicial construct that may overprotect constitutional rights. More important, the majority entirely fails to discuss the effect of the *Chapman* rule. If there is a unifying theme to this Court's habeas jurisprudence, it is that the ultimate equity on the prisoner's side—the possibility that an error may have caused the conviction of an actually innocent person—is sufficient by itself to permit plenary review of the prisoner's federal claim. . . . Whatever the source of the *Chapman* standard, the equities may favor its application on habeas if it substantially promotes the central goal of the criminal justice system—accurate determinations of guilt and innocence. . . .

In my view, the harmless-error standard often will be inextricably intertwined with the interest of reliability. By now it goes without saying that harmless-error review is of almost universal application; there are few errors that may not be forgiven as harmless. . . . When such an error is detected, the harmless-error standard is crucial to our faith in the accuracy of the outcome: The absence of full adversary testing, for example, cannot help but erode our confidence in a verdict; a jury easily may be misled by such an omission. Proof of harmlessness beyond a reasonable doubt, however, sufficiently restores confidence in the verdict's reliability that the conviction may stand despite the potentially accuracy impairing error. Such proof demonstrates that, even though the error had the *potential* to induce the jury to err, in fact there is no reasonable possibility that it did. Rather, we are confident beyond a reasonable doubt that the error had no influence on the jury's judgment at all. . . .

At least where errors bearing on accuracy are at issue, I am not persuaded that the *Kotteakos* standard offers an adequate assurance of reliability. Under the Court's holding today, federal courts on habeas are barred from offering relief unless the error "had substantial and injurious effect or influence in determining the jury's verdict." . . . By tolerating a greater probability that an error with the potential to undermine verdict accuracy was harmful, the Court increases the likelihood that a conviction will be preserved despite an error that actually affected the reliability of the trial. . . .

. . . The Court does offer a glimmer of hope by reserving in a footnote the possibility of an exception: *Chapman* may remain applicable, it suggests, in some "unusual" cases. But the Court's description of those cases suggests that its potential exception would be both exceedingly narrow and unrelated to reliability concerns. . . .

. . . [T]he Court's decision buys the federal courts a lot of trouble. From here on out, prisoners undoubtedly will litigate—and judges will be forced to decide—whether each error somehow might be wedged into the narrow potential exception the Court mentions in a footnote today. Moreover, since the Court only mentions the *possibility* of an exception, all concerned must also address whether the exception exists at all. I see little justification for imposing these novel and potentially difficult questions on our already overburdened justice system.

Nor does the majority demonstrate that the *Kotteakos* standard will ease the burden of conducting harmless-error review in those cases to which it does apply.

Indeed, . . . *Kotteakos* is unlikely to lighten the load of the federal judiciary at all. The courts still must review the entire record in search of conceivable ways the error may have influenced the jury; they still must conduct their review de novo; and they still must decide whether they have sufficient confidence that the verdict would have remained unchanged even if the error had not occurred. . . . The only thing the Court alters today is the degree of confidence that suffices. But *Kotteakos*'s threshold is no more precise than *Chapman*'s; each requires an exercise of judicial judgment that cannot be captured by the naked words of verbal formulae. *Kotteakos*, it is true, is somewhat more lenient; it will permit more errors to pass uncorrected. But that simply reduces the number of cases in which relief will be granted. It does not decrease the burden of identifying those cases that warrant relief.

. . . [I]t seems to me that the Court's decision cuts too broadly and deeply to comport with the equitable and remedial nature of the habeas writ. . . .

[The dissenting opinions of Justices Blackmun and Souter are omitted.]

NOTES AND QUESTIONS

1. Will the shift, from the *Chapman* standard to the *Kotteakos* standard, make much of a difference in the way that federal habeas courts analyze questions of harmless error? Or is the decision in *Brecht* more about tone setting than about the actual legal standard to be used?

2. In O'Neal v. McAninch, 513 U.S. 432 (1995), in a majority opinion by Justice Breyer, the Court placed an important gloss on the holding in *Brecht*:

> This case asks us to decide whether a federal habeas court should consider a trial error harmless when the court (1) reviews a state-court judgment from a criminal trial, (2) finds a constitutional error, and (3) is in *grave doubt* about whether or not that error is harmless. We recognize that this last mentioned circumstance, "grave doubt," is unusual. Normally a record review will permit a judge to make up his or her mind about the matter. And indeed a judge has an obligation to do so. But we consider here the legal rule that governs the special circumstance in which record review leaves the conscientious judge in grave doubt about the likely effect of an error on the jury's verdict. (By "grave doubt" we mean that, in the judge's mind, the matter is so evenly balanced that he feels himself in virtual equipoise as to the harmlessness of the error.) We conclude that the uncertain judge should treat the error, not as if it were harmless, but as if it affected the verdict (i.e., as if it had a "substantial and injurious effect or influence in determining the jury's verdict"). . . . We repeat our conclusion: When a federal judge in a habeas proceeding is in grave doubt about whether a trial error of federal law had "substantial and injurious effect or influence in determining the jury's verdict," that error is not harmless. And, the petitioner must win.

Id., at 434-435, 436. In short, *O'Neal* makes clear that the harmless-error rule of *Kotteakos/Brecht*, like the harmless-error rule of *Chapman*, places the ultimate burden of persuasion on the prosecutor to establish "harmlessness."

6.   Innocence and the Future of Federal Habeas

In the 1960s, Justice Brennan expanded the scope of federal habeas as a way to ensure that individual state criminal defendants would have their federal constitutional rights vindicated. In the 1970s, Judge Friendly argued that federal habeas should be more concerned with protecting innocent defendants. In the 1980s, Justices Rehnquist, Powell, and O'Connor took the position that federal habeas is less about correcting errors on a case-by-case basis, and more about deterring misconduct by state courts. In the 1990s, Congress significantly amended the federal habeas statute in the hopes of making it more efficient and less of a burdensome intrusion into the criminal justice systems of the states.

But what do we know about how federal habeas review of state criminal cases actually works today? A recent empirical study led by Professor Nancy J. King—the first major study of its kind since AEDPA—found that, with the exception of capital cases (where federal habeas review is generally quite vigorous and many defendants obtain relief, at least from their death sentences), habeas is a complete waste of time that benefits almost no one:

> It is taking longer for habeas petitioners to reach federal court. The average period from conviction to habeas filing before AEDPA was about five years. The same average for prisoners in the [study] was 6.3 years—an increase of over a year. . . .
>
> It is also taking more time for federal courts to resolve the habeas petitions that are filed. Of the noncapital habeas cases filed in 2003 and 2004, almost one in ten were still pending as of October 2006. Disposition time for cases that courts managed to terminate increased from a median of six months in the early 1990s to a median of 7.1 months for cases filed in 2003 and 2004. On average, the slowest 25% of cases dragged on for more than 412 days. When one includes cases filed in 2003 or 2004 and still pending as of December 1, 2006, habeas cases are averaging at least 11.5 months to complete.
>
> The prolonged time required to satisfy the prerequisites for filing a habeas petition, and then to obtain a decision on that petition from a habeas court, dramatically skews the distribution of habeas cases among the overall population of state prison inmates. The [study] found that almost 30% of all noncapital habeas petitions were filed by inmates serving life sentences, even though only 1% of all prison sentences are for life. On the other hand, only 12% of all noncapital habeas petitions were filed by those serving sentences of five years or less, even though that group represents the majority of all those who are sent to prison. Because most federal habeas cases will not be resolved until years after the original conviction and sentencing, only inmates who receive life or other very long prison sentences will be in custody long enough even to file. For the vast majority of the more than two million people now incarcerated in America, the Great Writ is a pipe dream.
>
> Moreover, except in capital cases, those inmates who do manage to obtain federal habeas review can expect to lose. Although federal judges are taking longer to resolve petitions, they ultimately reject almost all of them. The chances that a petitioner will obtain any relief are even more miniscule now than they were before AEDPA. The grant rate for noncapital cases has dropped from 1% in the early 1990s to only 0.34% today. Only eight of the 2384 noncapital habeas filings the study examined resulted in a grant of habeas relief, and one of those eight grants was later reversed on appeal. At this rate, we estimate that fewer than sixty-five of the more than 18,000 petitions filed each year by noncapital petitioners will eventually be granted by district courts. Efforts to improve the efficiency of habeas litigation only appear to have exacerbated this trend.
>
> Today, the necessary prelude in the state courts to a first federal habeas filing is so lengthy, the habeas review process itself so prolonged, and habeas relief so unlikely that post-AEDPA federal habeas in noncapital cases is approaching a lottery for lifers.

Joseph L. Hoffmann & Nancy J. King, Rethinking the Federal Role in State Criminal Justice, 84 N.Y.U. L. Rev. 791, 806-810 (2009).

Does it make sense to continue to perpetuate a costly and time-consuming system of duplicative federal collateral review of state criminal cases when only 0.34 percent of all noncapital habeas petitioners—only 65 out of 18,000 per year—will ever obtain relief? Whatever Congress may have believed when it enacted AEDPA, the legislative effort to streamline and improve federal habeas clearly has failed. Given that failure, and assuming that the federal government still wants to try to improve the quality of state criminal justice and protect federal constitutional rights, is there a better way?

Hoffmann and King argue that there is:

We should redirect the resources that are currently spent on ineffective federal habeas litigation to where they will have a chance to make a bigger difference—to the beginning, not the end, of the criminal justice process. Our primary goal should be to avoid problems before they arise, not to try to find and correct them afterwards. The resources now wasted on reviewing and rejecting claims of constitutional error in habeas litigation should be redeployed to help prevent constitutional violations from occurring in the first place: They should be invested in the reform of state systems of defense representation.

. . . We propose first that Congress amend the federal habeas statute so that . . . an application for a writ of habeas corpus on behalf of a person in custody pursuant to a judgment of conviction entered by a state court shall not be granted unless the court finds that: (1) the petitioner is in custody in violation of the Constitution or laws or treaties of the United States and has established by clear and convincing new evidence, not previously discoverable through the exercise of due diligence, that no reasonable factfinder would have found him guilty of the underlying offense in light of the evidence as a whole; (2) the petitioner is in custody in violation of a new rule of constitutional law, made retroactive to cases on collateral review by the Supreme Court; or (3) the petitioner is under a sentence of death, and either (a) his death sentence was imposed in violation of the Constitution or laws or treaties of the United States or (b) he is legally ineligible to be executed.

. . . Whatever can be saved by cutting back on habeas review—and additional funds—should be devoted to a new federal initiative aimed at helping the states prevent and correct constitutional violations in their own courts.

. . . Congress [should] authorize a new federal initiative to help states provide competent defense representation . . . . In 1979, the House of Delegates of the American Bar Association (ABA) adopted a resolution from the Standing Committee on Legal and Indigent Defendants calling for "the establishment of an independent federally funded Center for Defense Services for the purpose of assisting and strengthening state and local governments in carrying out their constitutional obligations to provide effective assistance of counsel for the defense of poor persons in state and local criminal proceedings."

. . . We believe that the time has come for Congress to acknowledge not only that effective criminal defense at the trial and appellate levels is a far better means of guaranteeing constitutional rights in criminal cases than post hoc habeas litigation but also that state criminal defense systems are in crisis and require federal support. Our adversarial system relies on defense counsel to protect individual rights in criminal cases. Yet case-by-case litigation under Strickland v. Washington has failed, and will continue to fail, as a means of ensuring the right to counsel in noncapital cases. Systematic underfunding of criminal defense representation in the state courts persists, resulting in repeated and widespread breakdowns in defense representation in many states. As a chorus of commentators has observed, the scant postconviction reversals under *Strickland* have had little or no impact on the pervasive pressures on state and county legislative bodies to limit funding for defense services. This is a systemic problem that habeas is woefully inadequate to address.

Hoffmann & King, supra, at 818-827; see also Nancy J. King & Joseph L. Hoffmann, Habeas for the Twenty-First Century (2011).

The proposal offered by Hoffmann and King would limit federal habeas review to the three special categories of (1) strong claims of actual innocence based on new evidence, (2) new federal constitutional rules held retroactive, and (3) capital cases. The general issue of actual innocence as a possible ground for either appellate or habeas relief has long been controversial. See generally Brandon L. Garrett, Judging Innocence, 108 Colum. L. Rev. 55 (2008) (reporting and analyzing the results of an empirical study of DNA exonerations and how those cases were previously handled in the appellate and habeas courts).

In Herrera v. Collins, 506 U.S. 390 (1993), the Court addressed—but did not resolve—the novel claim that a habeas petitioner, despite having been convicted at a concededly fair trial, was nevertheless entitled to federal habeas review based on the allegation that he was factually innocent of the capital crime of which he had been convicted. The Court, in a majority opinion written by Chief Justice Rehnquist, noted:

> [P]etitioner does not come before this Court as an innocent man, but rather as one who has been convicted by due process of law of two capital murders. The question before us, then, is not whether due process prohibits the execution of an innocent person, but rather whether it entitles petitioner to judicial review of his "actual innocence" claim.

Id., at 408, n. 6. Treating the claim as arising under procedural (rather than substantive) due process, the Court concluded:

> [W]e cannot say that Texas' refusal to entertain petitioner's newly discovered evidence eight years after his conviction transgresses a principle of fundamental fairness "rooted in the traditions and conscience of our people." . . . This is not to say, however, that petitioner is left without a forum to raise his actual innocence claim. For under Texas law, petitioner may file a request for executive clemency. . . . Clemency is deeply rooted in our Anglo-American tradition of law, and is the historic remedy for preventing miscarriages of justice where judicial process has been exhausted.

Id., at 411-412. Finally, the Court acknowledged:

> We may assume, for the sake of argument in deciding this case, that in a capital case a truly persuasive demonstration of "actual innocence" made after trial would render the execution of a defendant unconstitutional, and warrant federal habeas relief if there were no state avenue open to process such a claim. But because of the very disruptive effect that entertaining claims of actual innocence would have on the need for finality in capital cases, and the enormous burden that having to retry cases based on often stale evidence would place on the States, the threshold showing for such an assumed right would necessarily be extraordinarily high. The showing made by petitioner in this case falls far short of any such threshold.

Id., at 417. Herrera was executed shortly after the Court handed down its decision in his case. See generally Joseph L. Hoffmann, Is Innocence Sufficient? An Essay on the U.S. Supreme Court's Continuing Problems with Federal Habeas Corpus and the Death Penalty, 68 Ind. L.J. 817 (1993).

Herrera may have been the first so-called "naked innocence" habeas case to reach the Court, but it was not the last. In 1985, Paul Gregory House was convicted of murdering a neighbor's wife and was sentenced to death. For more than two decades, House doggedly proclaimed his innocence. After unsuccessfully pursuing his state remedies, House filed a federal habeas petition arguing that his trial lawyer failed to conduct a proper factual investigation in violation of Strickland v. Washington, and that the prosecutor hid exculpatory evidence in violation of Brady v. Maryland. The claims were initially held to be procedurally defaulted under Wainwright v. Sykes, due to a different defense lawyer's strategic decision not to raise them in the state appellate courts. In February 1999, a federal district judge nevertheless decided to grant House an evidentiary hearing. At the hearing, House introduced persuasive new evidence of his innocence, eventually leading six judges of the U.S. Court of Appeals for the Sixth Circuit to conclude that it was "highly probable that [House] is completely innocent of any wrongdoing whatever." See House v. Bell, 386 F.3d 668, 708 (6th Cir. 2004) (en banc). The New York Times, the National Law Journal, and 60 Minutes reported extensively on the case, noting the strong likelihood that the victim's abusive husband, and not House, was the real killer.

On June 12, 2006, the Supreme Court held that, notwithstanding the prior procedural default, House should no longer be barred from litigating the merits of his *Strickland* and *Brady* claims. See House v. Bell, 547 U.S. 518 (2006). The Court reviewed House's new evidence in detail and concluded that—"had the jury heard all the conflicting testimony—it is more likely than not that no reasonable juror viewing the record as a whole would lack reasonable doubt [about House's guilt]." See Schlup v. Delo, 513 U.S. 298 (1995) (establishing "fundamental miscarriage of justice" exception to Wainwright v. Sykes procedural default), discussed supra, at page 1659. The Court held that House's new evidence so undermined the strength of the prosecution's case against him that he should be entitled to habeas review of his procedural claims. But the Court also ruled that House failed to meet the (still-undefined) Herrera v. Collins "actual innocence" standard, and therefore could not obtain immediate habeas relief on that basis. Instead, the case was remanded to the lower courts for further consideration of the *Strickland* and *Brady* claims. House, who had contracted multiple sclerosis in prison and was confined to a wheelchair, remained on Death Row for two additional years before the federal district court finally found his trial lawyer to have been constitutionally ineffective and he gained his release.

As one commentator has noted:

Compelling post-trial claims of innocence, like House's, pose the most excruciating dilemmas. Such claims have the potential to destroy our faith in a legal system that often represents our best hope for achieving a better society. They strike at the heart of the jury system, the foundation of American democracy. They force appellate judges into fact-finding roles with which they may be intensely uncomfortable, and produce conflicts between state and federal courts. They unsettle our notions of finality, creating cognitive dissonance by challenging what we have already accepted as true. The very thought of such an enormous injustice may be so intolerable that almost everyone associated with the legal system—including judges, jurors, prosecutors, police, and even defense attorneys—may prove vulnerable to cognitive biases that prevent them from concluding that a wrongful conviction actually has occurred.

All of this may explain why it is so hard for the courts to remedy an erroneous conviction, but the problem is one that simply must be solved. The case of Paul Gregory House is the kind that gives law, lawyers, and the death penalty a bad name. As one of House's Death Row guards, in late 2007, asked . . . a minister visiting the prison: "The Supreme Court has said any reasonable juror would find this man innocent, right? Then why is he still here?"

Joseph L. Hoffmann, House v. Bell and the Death of Innocence, in Death Penalty Stories 449-451, John H. Blume & Jordan M. Steiker eds. 2009).

Are federal habeas courts the best forum for addressing postconviction claims of actual innocence? The prolonged legal saga of Paul Gregory House illustrates that one big problem with federal habeas is that the same procedural barriers that have been developed in an effort to prevent abuses and frivolous habeas claims also serve to block access even for those very few defendants who might actually deserve substantive relief based on actual innocence. The Supreme Court may finally be starting to acknowledge this problem, and to recognize the special status of innocence claims in federal habeas and the corresponding need for special procedural rules to deal with such claims. In McQuiggin v. Perkins, 133 S. Ct. 1924 (2013), the Court held (by 5-4 per Justice Ginsburg, joined by Justices Kennedy, Breyer, Sotomayor, and Kagan in the majority) that "actual innocence, if proved, serves as a gateway through which a petitioner may pass whether the impediment is a procedural bar, as it was in *Schlup* and *House*, or, as in this case, expiration of the statute of limitations." The Court described this rule as an "equitable exception" to the normal one-year statute of limitations for federal habeas petitions, and held that even a petitioner's failure to engage in "due diligence" to find evidence of his innocence would not preclude him from claiming the exception (although it might undermine the reliability of any "new evidence" offered in support of his innocence claim).

Even if the Court continues to break down the procedural barriers that stand in the way of those who want to raise claims of actual innocence in habeas, however, that does not mean that actual innocence *itself* will become a basis for granting habeas relief. Recall that Herrera v. Collins declined to recognize the cognizability of such a "naked innocence" claim in habeas; the Court has not chosen to revisit the issue since.

At least a few state and local jurisdictions have devised their own means of handling such claims. In 2006, North Carolina created an Innocence Inquiry Commission for the purpose of reviewing claims of factual innocence in individual criminal cases. The Commission can hold hearings and refer a case of likely innocence to a special three-judge court, which holds the ultimate power to set aside the conviction. On February 17, 2010, Gregory F. Taylor, who had served 16 years in prison for the murder of a prostitute in 1991, became the first person to be freed by the three-judge court, which found "clear and convincing evidence" that Taylor was innocent of the crime. Taylor's case was only the third to gain a hearing before the Commission, and only the second to be referred to the three-judge court. See Robbie Brown, Judges Free Inmate on Recommendation of Special Innocence Panel, N.Y. Times, Feb. 17, 2010, available online at http://www.nytimes.com/2010/02/18/us/18innocent.html.

As the track record of the North Carolina Innocence Inquiry Commission suggests, the number of criminal cases in which factually innocent defendants are convicted is undoubtedly minuscule in comparison to the total number of criminal convictions. See also www.innocenceproject.org/ (reporting that, as of early 2016, "there have been 334 people exonerated by DNA evidence in the United States"). But such cases *do* occur—and our legal system seems not yet to have discovered the best way to respond.

United States Constitution (Selected Provisions)

ARTICLE I

Section 9. . . . . The Privilege of the Writ of Habeas Corpus shall not be suspended, unless when in Cases of Rebellion or Invasion the public Safety may require it.

No Bill of Attainder or ex post facto Law shall be passed. . . .

ARTICLE III

Section 1. The judicial Power of the United States, shall be vested in one supreme Court, and in such inferior Courts as the Congress may from time to time ordain and establish. . . .

Section 2. The judicial Power shall extend to all Cases, in Law and Equity, arising under this Constitution, the Laws of the United States, and Treaties made, or which shall be made, under their Authority; — to all Cases affecting Ambassadors, other public Ministers and Consuls; — to all Cases of admiralty and maritime Jurisdiction; — to Controversies to which the United States shall be a Party; — to Controversies between two or more States; — between a State and Citizens of another State; — between Citizens of different States; — between Citizens of the same State claiming Lands under Grants of different States, and between a State, or the Citizens thereof, and foreign States, Citizens or Subjects.

In all Cases affecting Ambassadors, other public Ministers and Consuls, and those in which a State shall be Party, the supreme Court shall have original Jurisdiction. In all the other Cases before mentioned, the supreme Court shall have appellate Jurisdiction, both as to Law and Fact, with such Exceptions, and under such Regulations as the Congress shall make.

The Trial of all Crimes, except in Cases of Impeachment, shall be by Jury; and such Trial shall be held in the State where the said Crimes shall have been committed; but when not committed within any State, the Trial shall be at such Place or Places as the Congress may by Law have directed. . . .

ARTICLE IV

Section 2. The Citizens of each State shall be entitled to all Privileges and Immunities of Citizens in the several States.

A Person charged in any State with Treason, Felony, or other Crime, who shall flee from Justice, and be found in another State, shall on Demand of the executive Authority of the State from which he fled, be delivered up, to be removed to the State having Jurisdiction of the Crime. . . .

ARTICLE VI

. . . This Constitution, and the Laws of the United States which shall be made in Pursuance thereof; and all Treaties made, or which shall be made, under the Authority of the United States, shall be the supreme Law of the Land; and the Judges in every State shall be bound thereby, any Thing in the Constitution or Laws of any State to the Contrary notwithstanding. . . .

AMENDMENT I

Congress shall make no law respecting an establishment of religion, or prohibiting the free exercise thereof; or abridging the freedom of speech, or of the press; or the right of the people peaceably to assemble, and to petition the Government for a redress of grievances.

AMENDMENT II

A well regulated Militia, being necessary to the security of a free State, the right of the people to keep and bear Arms, shall not be infringed.

AMENDMENT III

No Soldier shall, in time of peace be quartered in any house, without the consent of the Owner, nor in time of war, but in a manner to be prescribed by law.

AMENDMENT IV

The right of the people to be secure in their persons, houses, papers, and effects, against unreasonable searches and seizures, shall not be violated, and no Warrants shall issue, but upon probable cause, supported by Oath or affirmation, and particularly describing the place to be searched, and the persons or things to be seized.

AMENDMENT V

No person shall be held to answer for a capital, or otherwise infamous crime, unless on a presentment or indictment of a Grand Jury, except in cases arising in the land or naval forces, or in the Militia, when in actual service in time of War or public danger; nor shall any person be subject for the same offence to be twice put in jeopardy of life or limb; nor shall be compelled in any criminal case to be a witness against himself, nor be deprived of life, liberty, or property, without due process of law; nor shall private property be taken for public use, without just compensation.

AMENDMENT VI

In all criminal prosecutions, the accused shall enjoy the right to a speedy and public trial, by an impartial jury of the State and district wherein the crime shall have been committed, which district shall have been previously ascertained by law, and to be informed of the nature and cause of the accusation; to be confronted with the witnesses against him; to have compulsory process for obtaining witnesses in his favor, and to have the Assistance of Counsel for his defence.

AMENDMENT VII

In Suits at common law, where the value in controversy shall exceed twenty dollars, the right of trial by jury shall be preserved, and no fact tried by a jury, shall be otherwise re-examined in any Court of the United States, than according to the rules of the common law.

AMENDMENT VIII

Excessive bail shall not be required, nor excessive fines imposed, nor cruel and unusual punishments inflicted.

AMENDMENT IX

The enumeration in the Constitution, of certain rights, shall not be construed to deny or disparage others retained by the people.

AMENDMENT X

The powers not delegated to the United States by the Constitution, nor prohibited by it to the States, are reserved to the States respectively, or to the people.

AMENDMENT XIII

Section 1. Neither slavery nor involuntary servitude, except as a punishment for crime whereof the party shall have been duly convicted, shall exist within the United States, or any place subject to their jurisdiction.

Section 2. Congress shall have power to enforce this article by appropriate legislation.

AMENDMENT XIV

Section 1. All persons born or naturalized in the United States, and subject to the jurisdiction thereof, are citizens of the United States and of the State wherein they reside. No State shall make or enforce any law which shall abridge the privileges or immunities of citizens of the United States; nor shall any State deprive any person of life, liberty, or property, without due process of law; nor deny to any person within its jurisdiction the equal protection of the laws. . . .

Section 5. The Congress shall have power to enforce, by appropriate legislation, the provisions of this article.

Table of Cases

Principal cases are indicated by italics. Alphabetization is letter-by-letter (e.g., "Martinez" precedes "Martin Linen Supply Co.").

Table of Authorities

Carrington, Paul D., Daniel J. Meador, & Maurice Rosenberg, Justice on Appeal (1976), 254

Carroll, David, Commentary: Gideon's Despair (The Marshall Project Jan. 2, 2015), 154

Carroll, Leo, Race, Ethnicity and the Social Order of the Prison, in The Pains of Imprisonment (Robert Johnson & Hans Toch eds., 1982), 1033

Carter, Dan T., Scottsboro: A Tragedy of the American South (rev. ed. 1979), 75, 76

Cary, Robert M., et al., Federal Criminal Discovery (ABA 2011), 1221

Cassell, Paul G., The Rodney King Trials and the Double Jeopardy Clause: Some Observations on Original Meaning and the ACLU's Schizophrenic Views of the Dual Sovereignty Doctrine, 41 UCLA L. Rev. 693 (1994), 1597

Cassidy, R. Michael, Silencing Grand Jury Witnesses, 91 Ind. L. Rev. No. 4 (2015) (forthcoming), 1062

Chacon, Jennifer M., Overcriminalizing Immigration, 102 J. Crim. L. & Criminology 613 (2012), 34

Churchill, Winston, History of the English-Speaking People (1956), 1315

Clark, J., J. Austin, & D. Henry, "Three Strikes and You're Out": A Review of State Legislation (Nat'l Inst. of Justice, Sept. 1997), 1471

Clark, Steven E., & Ryan D. Godfrey, Eyewitness Identification Evidence and Innocence Risk, 16 Psychonomic Bull. & Rev. 22 (2009), 149

Colbert, Douglas L., Thirty-Five Years After *Gideon*: The Illusory Right to Counsel at Bail Proceedings, [1998] U. Ill. L. Rev. 1, 1002

Colbert, Douglas L., Ray Paternoster, & Shawn Bushway, Do Attorneys Really Matter? The Empirical and Legal Case for the Right to Counsel at Bail, 23 Cardozo L. Rev. 1719 (2002), 1002

Cooley, T., General Principles of Constitutional Law (1880), 104

Corbin, A., Contracts (1951), 1304

Cortner, Richard C., A Mob Intent on Death: The NAACP and the Arkansas Riot Cases (1988), 75, 76

————, A "Scottsboro" Case in Mississippi: The Supreme Court and *Brown v. Mississippi* (1986), 75, 76

Cover, Robert, & Alexander Aleinikoff, Dialectical Federalism: Habeas Corpus and the Court, 86 Yale L.J. 1035 (1977), 1636

Covey, Russell, Signaling and Plea Bargaining's Innocence Problem, 66 Wash. & Lee L. Rev. 73 (2009), 1246-1247

Crosskey, William Winslow, & Charles Fairman, "Legislative History," and the Constitutional Limitations on State Authority, 22 U. Chi. L. Rev. 1 (1954), 73

Davies, Thomas Y., Not "The Framers' Design": How the Framing-Era Ban Against Hearsay Evidence Refutes the *Crawford-Davis* "Testimonial" Formulation of the Scope of the Original Confrontation Clause, 15 J.L. & Pol'y 349 (2007), 1429

————, Recovering the Original Fourth Amendment, 98 Mich. L. Rev. 547 (1999), 419, 614

Dawson, Robert O., Joint Trials of Defendants in Criminal Cases: An Analysis of Efficiencies and Prejudices, 77 Mich. L. Rev. 1379 (1979), 1182, 1183

Decker, John F., The Sixth Amendment Right to Shoot Oneself in the Foot: An Assessment of the Guarantee of Self-Representation Twenty Years after *Faretta*, 6 Seton Hall Const. L.J. 483 (1996), 255

Demleitner, Nora V., Witness Protection in Criminal Cases: Anonymity, Disguise or Other Options?, 46 Am. J. Comp. L. 641 (1998), 1190

DeVito, Pasqual, An Experiment in the Use of Court Statistics, Judicature 56 (Aug./Sept. 1972), 43

Diamond, A Jury Experiment Reanalyzed, 7 U. Mich. J.L. Reform 520 (1974), 1323

Drake, The Art of Litigating: Deselecting Jurors Like the Pros, 34 Md. Bar J. 18 (Mar.-Apr. 2001), 1368

Dressler, Joshua, Understanding Criminal Procedure: Adjudication (2006), 1526

Duke, Steven, The Right to Appointed Counsel: *Argersinger* and Beyond, 12 Am. Crim. L. Rev. 601 (1975), 127

Dwyer, Jim, Peter Neufeld, & Barry Scheck, Actual Innocence: Five Days to Execution and Other Dispatches from the Wrongly Convicted (2000), 147, 1192

Elliott, Rogers, Expert Testimony About Eyewitness Identification, 17 L. & Hum. Behav. 423 (1993), 147

Emerson, Deborah Day, & Nancy L. Ames, The Role of the Grand Jury and the Preliminary Hearing in Pretrial Screening (1984), 1098

Erikson, E., Identity: Youth and Crisis (1968), 1486

Fagan, Jeffrey A., & Amanda Geller, Following the Script: Narratives of Suspicion in *Terry* Stops and Street Policing, 82 U. Chi. L. Rev. 51 (2015), 33

Fagan, Jeffrey, & Martin Guggenheim, Preventive Detention and the Judicial Prediction of Dangerousness for Juveniles: A Natural Experiment, 86 J. Crim. L. & Criminology 415 (1996), 1016-1017

Table of Statutes and Rules

Index